Enemies and Friends of the State

Enemies and Friends of the State

Ancient Prophecy in Context

edited by

CHRISTOPHER A. ROLLSTON

EISENBRAUNS
University Park, Pennsylvania

Library of Congress Cataloging-in-Publication Data

Names: Rollston, Chris A., editor.
Title: Enemies and friends of the state : ancient prophecy in context / edited by
    Christopher A. Rollston.
Description: University Park, Pennsylvania : Eisenbrauns, [2017] | Includes
    bibliographical references and index.
Identifiers: LCCN 2017042340 (print) | ISBN 9781575067643 (cloth : alk. paper)
Subjects: LCSH: Bible. Old Testament—Criticism, interpretation, etc. | Prophecy—
    Political aspects. | Prophecy—Biblical teaching. | Prophets—Middle East—History.
Classification: LCC BS1198 .E54 2017 (print)
LC record available at https://lccn.loc.gov/2017042340

Eisenbrauns is an imprint of The Pennsylvania State University Press.

The Pennsylvania State University Press is a member of the
Association of University Presses.

It is the policy of The Pennsylvania State University Press to use acid-free paper.
Publications on uncoated stock satisfy the minimum requirements of the National
Standard for Information Sciences—Permanence of Paper for Printed Library
Material, ANSI Z39.48—1992.

Contents

Part 1: Setting the Stage

Part 2:
The Ancient Near East

Part 3:
Prophets in the Deuteronomistic History
and the Chronicler

Part 4:
Prophets in the Prophetic Books of the First Temple and Exilic Periods

Part 5:
Prophets and Patriots of the Second Temple Period and Early Postbiblical Period

Preface

This volume is intended to focus heavily on the nexus of relationships between prophetic figures and the powers that be. Naturally, some prophets and prophetesses were critics of the political and religious power-brokers of their day and some were apologists for the political and religious establishment. Furthermore, it is often the case that prophets and prophetesses were on a continuum, somewhere in between those two poles. Moreover, at different times, and in different contexts, the very same prophet or prophetesses might be aligning himself or herself with the political and religious elite at a particular time regarding certain issues, and then at different times, the very same prophet might be an avowed critic, attempting to speak truth to power in a different context. Ultimately, within this volume, the distinguished authors discuss these sorts of salient, problematic, and fascinating aspects of prophecy. Readers will also be pleased to see the volume begin (i.e., the first two chapters) with some theoretical constructs that contribute substantially to the discussion and readers will also be pleased to see some articles that focus on the broader ancient Near East. I believe that such breadth is most useful for a volume of this sort. In sum, I firmly believe that the time has come for a volume such as this, and I am so very grateful to all of the authors who have contributed to this volume. Because of them, I consider this volume to be a sterling contribution to the field of Biblical Studies.

This volume has been a long time in coming. For me, this volume has been a learning experience. Not long after the invitations for this volume were sent, I wrote an article for the *Huffington Post* on the predominance of patriarchy in the Bible. The content of the article was the sort of thing often noted in biblical scholarship, but those in positions of power at my (former) institution in Tennessee were irate about the article's content, and so within a few short months, I was forced to resign my tenured professorship there. This was painful, but it also meant that I was without an academic home. The field rescued me, with wonderful visitation professorships at George Washington University and Tel Aviv University, and a marvelous NEH at the Albright in Jerusalem, but this left little time to work on this volume, causing delays. I was in survival mode. This is my fault. Moreover, Having served as the editor of *Maarav* for a number of years, and now as the co-editor of *BASOR*, I have done a fair amount of editorial work. But, putting together a volume such as this proved to be quite different, I learned. With a journal, one can simply go to press when the volume is full. There is no long waiting for this or that article to arrive. With a volume such as this, however, in which every article is absolutely essential, it is necessary to stay the course. Fortunately, many of the authors were able to complete their articles early, but in a few cases, the articles came in much later. We needed all the articles, and so we waited. And fortunately, almost all of the articles came in. In addition to the articles in this volume, I had commissioned articles on Deborah (of Judges) and on Wen-Amun: those articles did not arrive. But I am so pleased to say that all of the truly essential articles arrived and are included here. Also important for me to mention: there might be times when a reader might wish that an author in this volume might have included some particularly recent publication, rest assured that the reason for this is probably that the contributor to this volume submitted his or her article early (and so an article or book that came out within the past couple of years might not be present). But this will be the exception rather than the rule. Ultimately, I believe that the totality of the content of this volume is so very impressive, current, and cogent, and I am so grateful to all the wonderful contributors for all of their research and writing. The end result is certainly that the coverage of the Hebrew Bible is very thorough, and we have even included articles that span into not only Late Second Temple Judaism but also into Early Christianity. So the scope of this volume is broad indeed.

It is my distinct pleasure to emphasize my deep gratitude to George Washington University and to the Academic Dean of George Washington University's Columbian College of Arts and Sciences, namely, Dr. Benjamin Vinson, for his encouragement of scholarship and for his generous financial support of my research. Indeed, it was with funds from GW that I was able to hire a most gifted young scholar to assist me in producing a very clean manuscript, Nathaniel Greene. Without Nathaniel's work, this volume would have taken even longer. I shall always be grateful to him, and to George Washington, for all of the support and encouragement. In addition, I wish to offer a word of since thanks to Jim Eisenbraun. Jim is someone to whom I believe our field owes so very much, because of the high quality of the volumes his team publishes. Furthermore, he has been a particularly good friend for a number of years now. I owe him a debt of gratitude that would be very difficult to repay.

Finally, in terms of a dedication, I should like to close with this. Just as this volume was going to press, my mother, having fought stage-four cancer for four years, passed away peacefully at home. I wish that she could have seen this volume in print, but she knew about it and believed in its importance, and for this I am very grateful. Thus, with a fair amount of deep heartfelt sentiment, this volume is dedicated to my father and to the memory of my mother.

CHRISTOPHER ROLLSTON
George Washington University
Washington, DC

Abbreviations

The abbreviations used in this volume are primarily those of *The SBL Handbook of Style*, 2nd edition (Atlanta: Society of Biblical Literature, 2014). The following additional abbreviations also occur in the volume:

ATAT	Arbeiten zu Text und Sprache im Alten Testament
CBOT	Coniectanea biblica, Old Testament series
CBR	*Currents in Biblical Research*
CSMSJ	*Canadian Society for Mesopotamian Studies Journal*
ERC	Edition Recherche sur les civilisations
HÄB	Hildesheimer ägyptologische Beiträge
IFAO	Institut Français d'Archéologie Orientale (Cairo)
IBAES	Internet: Beiträge zur Ägyptologie und Sudanarchäologie (Studies from the Internet on Egyptology and Sudanarchaeology)
SAK	Studien zur Altägyptischen Kultur
SBLSS	Society of Biblical Literature Symposium Series
SEPOA	Société pour l'Étude du Proche-Orient Ancien
SHCANE	Studies in the History and Culture of the Ancient Near East
TBT	*The Bible Today*
ZAR/ZABR	*Zeitschrift für Altorientalische und Biblische Rechtsgeschichte*

Setting the Stage

Defining the State

ALEXANDER H. JOFFE
New York

Introduction

"States" have existed for more than 5000 years in the Old World. States exist today and provide a sense of familiarity that we extend, rightly and wrongly, into the past. Whether scaled down to individual city-states, particularized or "ethnicized" as nation-states, or scaled up to territorial states and empires, the idea of the state has proven both durable and elastic.

This sense of familiarity, and the very malleability of the idea of the state, has been a boon and bane to archaeologists. One result has been decades of archaeological quests to find states in the past. These explorations have focused on the sites most typically associated with states—cities—to the relative neglect of towns and villages and more ephemeral settlements belonging to tribes, nomads, and the like. The historical variability of states has also spawned elaborate evolutionary speculation and typologies as archaeologists have stretched and molded both theory and data to discover or invent ancient states.

Another result is that archaeological literature on the state is immense and unwieldy and yet another review would serve little purpose.[1] Instead, this paper will focus on ideas from both inside and outside archaeology that expand our understanding of states and that challenge thinking about the primary subject of this volume, prophecy.

What Is the "State"?

A "state" is an organized political entity with a territory. This much seems clear. But inside this bland assertion are many difficult-to-answer questions. Archaeology has had two primary problems with the idea of the state: how to distinguish states from other entities, and how to connect states with other entities in an

---

1. See generally V. Lull and R. Micó, *Archaeology of the Origin of the State: The Theories* (New York: Oxford University Press, 2011), 131–215.

evolutionary explanation. This latter problem includes understanding the origins of states.

In general, archaeologists have used a variety of criteria to identify states in the past—notably, evidence for specialized bureaucracy, hierarchical organization of settlements around a center, and unique symbols of power.[2] Obviously the task of identifying states is made easier with textual data that presents both evidence of the state's organization and operation, and its self-conception.

Archaeologists have also posited, not unreasonably, that more evolved political entities evolved from less evolved predecessors. Evidence for this has been sought, and not surprisingly, found, in the ethnographic record of the past few centuries. Chiefdoms, big men, and other forms—which have not evolved into states in the ethnographic present—were seen as ancestors of states in the past.[3] The overall pattern was presumed to be evolution from egalitarian to ranked society and then hierarchical and stratified society.[4] These evolutionary arguments have been the subject of considerable debate and criticism. Since the political forms recorded by ethnography are themselves the result of social evolution, they are not transitional forms to states but products of unique trajectories.[5]

Since destiny cannot be invoked, how states become states remains problematic. In general, archaeologists have posited that war and competition over critical resources, settlement growth and administrative necessity, exchange and colonialism were among the key mechanisms that spurred the growth of cities, political elites, and their bureaucratic and military specialists.[6] Others have proposed that multiple factors, including climate change affecting circumscribed environments such as southern Mesopotamia, produced states. [7]

The state formation process itself is suggested to have been uneven, with some scholars positing "cycling" between episodes characterized by competition and conflict and relative peace, and "experimentation" or "tinkering" with vari-

2. See generally G. Stein, "Understanding Ancient State Societies in the Old World," in *Archaeology at the Millennium: A Sourcebook* (ed. T. D. Price and G. M. Feinman; New York: Kluwer, 2001), 353–79.

3. E. R. Service, *The Origins of Civilizations and the State* (New York: Norton, 1975).

4. M. H. Fried, *The Evolution of Political Society* (New York: Random House, 1967).

5. N. Yoffee, *Myths of the Archaic State: Evolution of the Earliest Cities, States and Civilizations* (New York: Cambridge University Press, 2005).

6. R. L. Carneiro, "A Theory of the Origin of the State," *Science* 169 (1970) 733–738; K. A. Wittfogel, *Oriental Despotism* (New Haven, CT: Yale University Press, 1957); H. T. Wright, and G. A. Johnson, "Population, Exchange, and Early State Formation in Southwestern Iran," *American Anthropologist* 77 (1975) 267–89; G. Algaze, "The Prehistory of Imperialism: The Case of Uruk Period Mesopotamia," in *Uruk Mesopotamia and Its Neighbors* (ed. M. S. Rothman; Santa Fe, NM: School of American Research Press, 2001), 27–84.

7. D. J. Kennett and J. P. Kennett, "Early State Formation in Southern Mesopotamia: Sea Levels, Shorelines, and Climate Change," *The Journal of Island and Coastal Archaeology* 1 (2006) 67–99.

ous methods.[8] Other approaches suggest that "primary" states appeared first in a limited number of areas, such as Mesopotamia and Egypt, as a result of the unique concatenation of environmental and social conditions, which catalyzed the emergence of "secondary" states around the world.[9]

Rather than recapitulate these and similar arguments, we may move instead toward a series of preliminary definitions to preface the more substantive discussion below. States are physical entities, with patterns of power—both symbolic and "real"—that are tangible in the moment. But states are also ideas with both abstract and concrete aspects. How can we approach these broad dimensions?

Certain distinctions are necessary to locate the state. For one thing, a state is not a society, an abstract whole encompassing public and private institutions and their network of interrelations, given shape by ideas, traditions, and embedded in culture.[10] Nor is it a civilization, a cultural tradition writ large that perpetuates itself over world-historical time.[11] When we speak of states, we refer primarily to political organization manifest first in government and leadership—specifically, the (semi)-autonomous entities and networks involved in making and carrying out policy, rules, and decisions. These are necessarily derived from and woven into or superimposed above the political, economic, social, and physical worlds. But as one political scientist characterized it, the state often appears as "an amorphous complex of agencies with ill-defined boundaries, performing a great variety of not very distinctive functions."[12] This is especially the case when examining states in antiquity and archaeologically.

In an ideal sense, we may suggest that states have internal hierarchies, politics, borders, neighbors, as well as styles, discernible modes or patterns of behavior, and belief. States may be sovereign or hegemonic, autarkic or expansionary, depending on their circumstances and ideology. A state may operate in its own name or that of "the people," and in the interest of society as whole, specific sectors or elites, or simply its own. This immense variability, and the resulting categorical and semantic problems, has led some scholars to abandon the term *state* for "polity" or "complex polity."[13] Some scholars have also emphasized studying configurations of power, divisible into social, political, and economic dimensions, as the

---

8. H. T. Wright, "Recent Research on the Origin of the State," *Annual Review of Anthropology* 6 (1977) 379–97.

9. H. T. Wright, "Early State Dynamics as Political Experiment," *Journal of Anthropological Research* 62 (2006) 305–19.

10. T. Mitchell, "The Limits of the State: Beyond Statist Approaches and Their Critics," *American Political Science Review* 85 (1991) 77–96.

11. Cf. B. G. Trigger, *Understanding Early Civilizations: A Comparative Study* (New York: Cambridge University Press, 2003), 44–5.

12. P. Schmitter, "Neo Corporatism and the State," in *The Political Economy of Corporatism* (ed. W. Grant; New York: St. Martin's, 1985), 33.

13. E.g., A. T. Smith, *The Political Landscape: Constellations of Authority in Early Complex Polities* (Berkeley, CA: University of California Press, 2003), 94–102.

primary focus rather than states per se.[14] Recent work on political sovereignty as an avenue for archaeological investigation follows in this vein. [15]

States are often defined in terms of "government"—that is, a dedicated cadre of political, military, economic, and social specialists who are supported in part or in whole by surpluses extracted from other levels of society. States must also be territorial in some sense, although the meaning of territory necessarily varies. City-states are based in a single settlement, dominate a local territory, and may compete with one another for sources such as land, water, and labor, often in the form of villages or captives. They stand at the center of a small network of political, economic, social, and political relations, which may be perceived through hierarchies of settlement or flows of goods.[16]

Territorial states stand at the apex of larger hierarchies of subordinate settlements, and they dominate larger areas, as well as other states, or former states. They are not necessarily different in organization than city-states but by virtue of the need to integrate and dominate larger and more varied assortments of people they must employ different techniques. At the very least, more administration and larger ideas are required. These include abstract as well as legal and juridical concepts such as territory, property, and trespass.[17] Nation-states, on the other hand, are characterized by an integrative idea of a "nation," a unifying concept of ancestry, language, and belief that is rooted in a specific territory. [18]

Empires are also territorial, but they are far-flung and may be more difficult to reconstruct and represent.[19] They are states in the largest possible sense, integrating regions, states, tribes, and more. Their economic and symbolic universes are also far larger than city-states or territorial states. They have complex internal politics and economics, which may be brutal or benign, and they may be polyglot or domineering in terms of culture. They may have rigid and exploitative economic structures or be more loose and free-flowing. Their ideologies may be similarly variable, singular in their emphasis on core ideas or characterized by syncretism or hybridity. Obviously in all these concepts the local balances between sover-

14. M. Mann, *The Sources of Social Power, Volume I: A History of Power from the Beginning to AD 1760* (Cambridge: Cambridge University Press, 1986).

15. A. T. Smith, "Archaeologies of Sovereignty," *Annual Review of Anthropology* 40 (2011) 415–32.

16. D. L. Nichols and T. H. Charlton, "The City-State Concept; Development and Application," in *The Archaeology of City-States: Cross-Cultural Approaches* (ed. D. L. Nichols and T. H. Charlton; Washington, D.C.: Smithsonian Institution Press, 1997), 1–14.

17. S. S. Grosby, "Territoriality: The Transcendental, Primordial Feature of Modern Societies," *Nations and Nationalism* 1 (1995) 143–62.

18. S. S. Grosby, *Nationalism: A Very Short Introduction* (Oxford: Oxford University Press, 2005).

19. M. L. Smith, "Networks, Territories, and the Cartography of Ancient States," *Annals of the Association of American Geographers* 95 (2005) 832–49; C. M. Sinopoli, "The Archaeology of Empires," *Annual Review of Anthropology* 23 (1994) 159–80.

eignty and hegemony necessarily shift across time; in each, the state expresses its power on settlements and landscapes across its realm.[20]

Mentalities and Legitimacy

States have another dimension; for a state to exist there must be the idea of a "state." The participants must conceive the notion of a governed entity that is distinct from other forms of organization and from functionally equivalent rivals. It must be a recognized concept as well as a tangible reality. A political "state" is just that—a present condition, a concept and mindset that is both descriptive and prescriptive of reality.

Whether as an elite concept or a democratic ideal, the idea of a state need not be shared by all. Indeed, unanimity regarding the desirability, legitimacy, or sometimes even the existence of a state is unlikely to have ever existed. But the idea must be shared by or impressed upon *enough* people in order for the idea to come into being as a political unit, to gain legitimacy, and to be supported through willing participation or coercion. The idea of the state is the foundation for its ideology and for its effect on those it encompasses.

The state affects individual cognition, belief, and behavior. Alexis de Tocqueville's 1835 classic *Democracy in America* is not usually cited in archaeological literature, but it has considerable relevance here. As is well-known, after a two-year visit to the new United States, originally to examine the prison system, Tocqueville distilled his observations on American society and democracy, if distilled is the word, into two immense and perspicacious volumes. Tocqueville frankly "adored" liberty, and his observations were shaped by that core liberal belief.

Tocqueville's writings are chockablock with insights about political life; but, for our purposes, we may point to one of the book's most famous passages from volume II, chapter VI, entitled "What Type of Despotism Democratic Nations Have to Fear:"

> Above those men arises an immense and tutelary power that alone takes charge of assuring their enjoyment and of looking after their fate. It is absolute, detailed, regular, far-sighted and mild. It would resemble paternal power if, like it, it had as a goal to prepare men for manhood; but on the contrary it seeks only to fix them irrevocably in childhood; it likes the citizens to enjoy themselves, provided that they think only about enjoying themselves. It works willingly for their happiness; but it wants to be the unique agent for it and the sole arbiter; it attends to their security, provides for their needs, facilitates their pleasures, conducts their principal affairs, directs their industry, settles their estates, divides their inheritances;

---

20. See A. T. Smith, *The Political Landscape: Constellations of Authority in Early Complex Polities* (Berkeley, CA: University of California Press, 2003).

how can it not remove entirely from them the trouble to think and the difficulty of living?

. . .

After having thus taken each individual one by one into its powerful hands, and having molded him as it pleases, the sovereign power extends its arms over the entire society; it covers the surface of society with a network of small, complicated, minute, and uniform rules, which the most original minds and the most vigorous souls cannot break through to go beyond the crowd; it does not break wills, but it softens them, bends them and directs them; it rarely forces action, but it constantly opposes your acting; it does not destroy, it prevents birth; it does not tyrannize, it hinders, it represses, it enervates, it extinguishes, it stupifies, and finally it reduces each nation to being nothing more than a flock of timid and industrious animals, of which the government is the shepherd.[21]

Tocqueville was speaking of the descent of democracy into despotism, and he believed that tyrannies of the past had not possessed the powers he described. Furthermore, the despotic state he described was the outgrowth of an equality that lulled individuals into ignoring the changes around them. The "a very inquisitorial, very extensive, very centralized, very powerful executive power" that he foresaw would derive its power from democratic mechanisms but is the very antithesis of democracy, producing "servitude, regulated, mild and peaceful." Tocqueville's dystopian vision is wholly applicable to the condition of democracy today; but, what interests us here is his description of the mental process of subjugation, both coerced and embraced, to the state.

Michel Foucault explored this from a different angle with his concept of "governmentality." He noted that until the 18th century, "government" referred not only to the state but had a more general meaning that encompassed self-control, as well as management and guidance of families and households.[22] Government is thus the interrelatedness of governing the self and others, and the creation of mentalities that reflect these power relationships. Throughout his work, Foucault focused on the modern development of technologies of control, including institutions such as schools and prisons, social codes, and behaviors, and the shaping of discourse and knowledge itself. To Foucault and his followers, the very notions of freedom and choice in liberal societies are synthetic and forced by systems of domination that putatively create or ensure such conditions.

The question of domination goes further still. Studies have shown that nationalisms were frequently accompanied by the establishment of official dialects and

---

21. A. de Tocqueville, *Democracy in America: Historical-Critical Edition of De la démocratie en Amérique* (ed. Eduardo Nolla; trans. J. T. Schleifer. Indianapolis, IN: Liberty Fund, 2010), 4:1250–51.

22. M. Foucault, "The Subject and the Power," in *Michel Foucault: Beyond Structuralism and Hermeneutics* (ed. H. Dreyfus and P. Rabinow; Brighton: Harvester, 1982), 208–26.

languages disseminated through print culture.[23] This raises the question whether similar processes accompanied the rise of ancient states—that is, the domination of particular languages and their systems of communication and cognition over others. Such questions of language and category certainly played a role in the development of writing and bureaucracy, as well as history—what was to be remembered and what forgotten.[24] We may suggest that states in antiquity produced similar effects on mentality, behavior, and discourse, albeit lesser in extent and intensity. The earliest states were indeed "presumptive"[25]—slow, clumsy, ignorant, boisterous, aspirational, and often more notional than real—but they learned quickly.

The idea of the state is thus multifaceted. It pertains to leadership, governance, and organization, to the hierarchical ordering of social, economic, and political relations, and to beliefs and behaviors of those it encompasses. The idea of the state also pertains to social identities that may be "real," invented, derived, blended, and so on. States create "citizens," "leaders," "helots," and so on. The state itself also has an identity, not simply a name but a character based on its style of operation, an identity to give it form and color, and which is vital to maintaining social and economic relations. For the Bronze and Iron Ages, however, variability is often subsumed under the all-purpose description of "kingship," divine or otherwise.

The details of political styles are also extremely difficult to ascertain archaeologically. These may be perceptible through art, architecture, and texts, the material remains of standardization or massacres, or not at all. Without texts, for example, would it be possible to distinguish the identity of Athens from Sparta or Syracuse from Carthage, purely on an archaeological basis? Would democracy and oligarchy, tyranny and republic even be points of reference for these examples without texts? Absent obvious evidence, such as brutality in art or deed, this is questionable. But the problem is not merely analytical or classificatory. Even when there is ample evidence for animal and human sacrifice[26] and copious evidence of brutality in warfare,[27] scholars have been reluctant to judge the political style of

---

23. B. Anderson, *Imagined Communities, Reflections on the Origin and Spread of Nationalism* (London: Verso, 1991).

24. P. Michalowski, "Charisma and Control: On Continuity and Change in Early Mesopotamian Bureaucratic Systems," in *The Organization of Power: Aspects of Bureaucracy in the Ancient Near East* (ed. M. Gibson and R. D. Biggs; Chicago, IL: The Oriental Institute, 1988), 49–51. J. S. Cooper, "'I Have Forgotten My Burden of Former Days!' Forgetting the Sumerians in Ancient Iraq," *Journal of the American Oriental Society* 130 (2010) 327–35.

25. S. Richardson, "Early Mesopotamia: The Presumptive State," *Past and Present* 215 (2012) 3–49.

26. See the essays in A. M. Porter and G. M. Schwartz, eds., *Sacred Killing: The Archaeology of Sacrifice in the Ancient Near East* (Winona Lake, IN: Eisenbrauns, 2012).

27. E.g., A. McMahon, A. Sołtysiak, and J. Weber, "Late Chalcolithic Mass Graves at Tell Brak, Syria, and Violent Conflict during the Growth of Early City-states," *Journal of Field Archaeology* 36 (2011) 201–20.

the perpetrator negatively or even apply labels that, at least in the Classical period, were commonplace. In general, scholars of antiquity have been deeply reluctant to express anything smacking of moral judgment regarding the remote past.[28] This reluctance, in effect the unwillingness to confront what appears to be ancient states' deep addiction to violence and brutality, has impeded their study.[29]

Ancient states, however, were not shy about expressing their love of violence. If ancient art is to be taken seriously, violence against humans and nature was a common foundation for ruling ideology.[30] The legitimation of elite power and violence was thus a problem for states, to be played out on earth and in heaven. Baines and Yoffee have opened a new discussion regarding ancient states, focusing on what they call "order, legitimacy and wealth."[31] Their framework stresses that states were high-culture concepts that at once required the legitimation of rulers through cosmic associations, the propagation of supporting symbolism, and the circulation of wealth to subordinate elites and craft workers.

The terms of high-culture concepts were disseminated through society through art and architecture, tying elites not simply to symbols but to relations of production and relations of exchange, such as specialized or sumptuary materials obtained at a distance. Craft production and trade relations thus acquired cosmological significance. Wealth and symbols were circulated to assert elite superiority, to incorporate, subordinate, and negotiate the local, and to monopolize meaning. The advantage of their framework is that it is both explicitly materialist and ideological, and that it is adaptable to many examples.[32]

In such a scenario, prophets and prophecy would be among the key mediators of elite ideology. As dependents of elites—namely, kings and temples—their job would have entailed squaring both elite and cosmological requirements, attempting to satisfy both. But as self-serving elites in their own right, they would have had to ensure their own prerogatives and roles. Interference with the system and its priorities and its circulation of materials and rewards would have been unwelcome and possibly unwise.

---

28. This is not exclusive to antiquity. It is still possible today for some to valorize fascist architecture on the basis of its technique, planning, and aesthetics. E.g., L. Krier, "Krier on Speer," *The Architectural Review* 1032 (1983) 33–38.

29. On the question "at what point does the very desire not to appear barbaric, admirable as it is, become indifference to, or indeed approval of, barbarity" see L. Kolakowski, "Looking for the Barbarians," in *Modernity on Endless Trial* (Chicago, IL: University of Chicago Press, 1990), 14–31.

30. See generally Z. Bahrani, *Rituals of War: The Body and Violence in Mesopotamia* (Brooklyn, NY: Zone Books, 2008).

31. J. Baines and N. Yoffee, "Order, Legitimacy and Wealth in Ancient Egypt and Mesopotamia," in *Archaic States* (ed. G. M. Feinman and J. Marcus; Santa Fe, NM: School of American Research Press, 1998), 199–260.

32. See the essays in J. Richards and M. van Buren, eds., *Order, Legitimacy, and Wealth in Ancient States* (New York: Cambridge University Press, 2001).

At a larger scale of legitimacy are documents that express a pan-regional or "civilizational" ideal for Mesopotamian city-states. The Sumerian King List famously presents an idealized vision of Mesopotamian kingship in a sequential order, linking individual city-states to the gods. This informs us of at least two things: that manufacturing divine legitimation was important to Mesopotamian city-state politics, especially dynastic claims to legitimacy, and that individual city-states such as Kish had specific histories or traditions with which others found it useful to associate.[33]

Egyptian king lists, genealogies, and myths similarly linked the present political world to the divine order, although they did not privilege cities, only the king and by extension the national state—that is, the royal establishment. All this is to say that legitimation efforts were common and necessary in the ancient world; the idea that the gods favored particular states, leaders, and lineages was sufficiently powerful as a means to manufacture consent locally and challenge rivals that it was invoked again and again, ultimately across the canvas of "history" itself.

Such supra-ideologies, however, are likely to have meant one thing to kings, priests, and scribes and something else entirely to the person in the street. But they speak to the idea of the state as a high culture concept that was extended across a society as a whole.

A Word about Prophets

States are political entities that are governed, territorial systems with boundaries and internal hierarchies of politics, economics, religion, and so on. Prophets are individuals who assert election by the transcendent or by access to it. Receiving messages, interpreting dreams, omens, and auguries, and engaging in apocalyptic predictions are among the types of prophecy attested in the ancient world. Prophetic activity may be centered in a temple—that is, an institution specializing in religion—with a physical and social infrastructure requiring economic support, or it may be located in a cult or movement. Prophets may also be individuals in service (or in opposition) to a state, ruler, or cult.[34] Attachment to and dependence on, or opposition to and independence from, the state and its institutions and the sociopolitical situation of prophets and prophecy within a larger society are among the key questions to be discussed in other chapters in this book. Understanding prophets and prophecy, however, also requires understanding the nature of the particular state in which they functioned.

---

33. P. Michalowski, "History as Charter: Some Observations on the Sumerian King List," *Journal of the American Oriental Society* 103 (1984) 237–48; P. Steinkeller, "An Ur III Manuscript of the Sumerian King List," in *Literatur, Politik und Recht in Mesopotamien: Festschrift für Claus Wilcke* (ed. W. Sallaberger et al.; Wiesbaden: Harrassowitz, 2003), 267–92.

34. See the essays in A. Annus, ed., *Divination and Interpretation in the Ancient World* (Chicago, IL: The Oriental Institute, 2010).

Rationality and Anarchy

Archaeological thought regarding states is largely derivative of other disciplines. In that spirit of sharing, a variety of ideas not usually discussed by archaeologists are reviewed below. The line between political philosophy and anthropological studies of the state is thin, perhaps just a question of the latter's relative emphases on case studies as opposed to ideal types. Philosophical discussions regarding the nature of the state and government go back to the Greeks, such as Plato and his five types of government, or Aristotle's *Politics*, which classified types of *polis* in search of the best form of government. In the medieval period other thinkers speculated on large-scale patterns related to states. The foremost example is perhaps Ibn Khaldun's cyclical theory of history wherein nomads create states and empires that become decadent and weaken and are overthrown in a similar pattern by newcomers from the margins. Niccolo Machiavelli's 16th-century masterpiece *The Prince* is properly described as didactic rather than philosophical but is nevertheless a rich source for understanding how autocratic states actually work.

In the modern period, there has been a veritable explosion of scholarship on the state, prompted by its ubiquity. Among the most interesting approaches have been those broadly characterized as Marxist. In *The Origins of the Family, Private Property and the State*, Friedrich Engels built on the ideas of Lewis Henry Morgan and Karl Marx and proposed that the state arose as a device to protect private property. This was classic 19th-century evolutionism that combined evidence from both the historical past and the ethnographic present into a linear scheme. In it, the emergence, character, and institutions of the state were subordinate to the more fundamental issues of the division of labor, gender inequality, and the development of class structures and exploitation. More recently, along with class and ethnicity, gender relations in states have become important avenues for research.[35] Engel's line of reasoning reached its pinnacle with Vladimir Lenin's *The State and Revolution*, where states were understood as a tool of class oppression. In Lenin's view, it was only through revolution, the dictatorship of the proletariat, and the suppression of the bourgeoisie that the "withering away of the state" would occur.

As a thinker viewing the end of the absolutist state and the beginning of the liberal state, Thomas Hobbes stands out for his perspicacity on the state—or, as he called it, *Leviathan*. For Hobbes, Leviathan was constituted by a social contract between the people and the sovereign. A key factor making Leviathan necessary was as a defense against the chaos inevitably unleashed by the selfishness and ego-

---

35. C. L. Costin, "Exploring the Relationship among Craft Production, Gender, and Complex Societies: Methodological and Theoretical Issues of Gender Attribution," in *Gender and Archaeology* (ed. R. P. Wright; Philadelphia, PA: University of Pennsylvania Press, 1996), 111–42; G. Emberling, "Ethnicity in Complex Societies: Archaeological Perspectives," *Journal of Archaeological Research* 5 (1997) 295–344.

ism of human nature. Enlightened individuals perceive the limitations of human nature and voluntarily give up rights "to this man, or to this assembly of men"[36] in a covenantal relationship, although Hobbes also admitted that states could be created through conquest. Surrendering rights to the state is the only way in which humans can be protected from one another, and in what must be described as a liberal twist or innovation, for the public and private spheres to exist. Within the covenant, the sovereign has prescribed rights, duties, and protections but ultimately derives legitimacy from the consent of the governed. To Plato's five types of government, Hobbes proposed three: monarchy, aristocracy, and democracy.

The idea that complex human communities demand rational, bureaucratic management, wherein an elite offered both coercions and benefits for compliance, has underpinned much archaeological speculation regarding the origins of states. Fear of the anarchy inevitably unleashed by unchecked human nature is also a keynote theme for Hobbes, who held that the natural state of humankind was misery, and that competition, diffidence, and glory were the primary causes of conflict. His notion of anarchy finds particular resonance in the ancient world, for example in the Egyptian concept of *ma'at*, world order or balance. Personified as a goddess, *ma'at* was the primary responsibility of the Egyptian king who, as the "performer of *ma'at*" held off the chaos and restored balance, and who, as the executor of justice, honesty, and fairness, bound the universe together. So closely tied were *ma'at*, the king and the state, that one scholar has quipped "l'état, c'est Ma'at." [37]

Significantly, commensurate with his position on the cusp of a liberal age, Hobbes also explored the nature of Christian commonwealth, and the role of Scripture and revelation, in order to assert the subordinate position of religion to civil authority. In the "kingdom of darkness," Scripture is misinterpreted, primarily by the church, as a means of undermining civil authority. Fearful of ecclesiastical threats to power, he commented that "To maintain doctrines contrary to the religion established in the commonwealth is a greater fault in an authorized preacher than in a private person."[38] But Hobbes implied that the threat was broader still: "Fear of power invisible, feigned by the mind, or imagined from tales publicly allowed, religion; not allowed, superstition. And when the power imagined is truly such as we imagine, true religion."[39]

For our purposes, we may ask where prophets fit in the perpetual Hobbesian (and Egyptian) struggle of anarchy and the state, between the sovereign and his claims to embody balance, his covenantal relationship with those who consent to his rule, and finally, the destabilizing role of religious doctrine. For Hobbes, the

---

36. T. Hobbes, *Leviathan: Or the Matter, Form and Power of a Commonwealth, Ecclesiastical and Civil* (London: George Routledge, 1889), 84.

37. E. Teeter, *The Presentation of Maat: Ritual and Legitimacy in Ancient Egypt* (Chicago, IL: The Oriental Institute, 1977), 2.

38. T. Hobbes, *Leviathan*, 141.

39. Ibid., 34.

state was a rational response to the irrational passions of humans. This assumption is shared by many archaeologists. But the rationality of the state and its subjects may be exaggerated.

Bureaucracy, the "Iron Cage," and Their Agonistes

Max Weber shaped archaeological thought regarding the state, although largely without attribution. Weber's contributions to sociology, philosophy, religion, and economics were uniquely wide-ranging. It was Weber, in his famous 1918 lecture "Politics as a Vocation," who noted, "Today, however, we have to say that a state is a human community that (successfully) claims the *monopoly of the legitimate use of physical force* within a given territory."[40] This notion of the "monopoly of violence" is fundamental to most scholarship on the state.

But Weber's work on the state had many other facets that concern us here. For one thing, Weber saw legitimacy as the ultimate foundation for state violence, but he posited a variety of types or sources, as well as uses. For the unelected leader, for example, the personal qualities or charisma of the leader provides the legitimacy for violence, but only in certain situations such as treason or cowardice.[41] The development of permanent state structures, including what Weber called "the vocation of war," transformed charisma into an official coercive mechanism directed both inside and outside the state. Political communities (in effect, state structures) also took the lead in suppressing blood feuds and looting (which may have previously served the interest of a charismatic leader). The state thereby acquired for itself the role of arbiter of rights and justice and enhanced its own legitimacy.

High culture requires mechanisms for management. Thus, we turn to Weber's views on bureaucracy. Understanding bureaucracy has been a key element of studying ancient states—from the invention of writing to the administrators of states and empires, to the scribes who shaped the Great Traditions of ancient civilizations.[42] Weber approached bureaucracy from the point of view of modern capitalist society, where individuals no longer responded to labor as a "calling" but were instead coerced into vocations by "technical and economic conditions at the foundation of mechanical and machine production."[43] This trapped individuals

---

40. M. Weber, "Politics as a Vocation," in *From Max Weber: Essays in Sociology* (ed. H. H. Gerth, C. W. Mills, and B. S. Turner; Abingdon: Routledge, 1991), 78.

41. M. Weber, *Economy and Society* (Berkeley, CA: University of California Press, 1978), 906

42. See generally J. S. Cooper "Babylonian Beginnings: The Origin of the Cuneiform Writing System in Comparative Perspective," in *The First Writing* (ed. S. D. Houston; Cambridge: Cambridge University Press, 2004), 71–99. See also M. G. Morony, "'In a City without Watchdogs the Fox Is the Overseer:' Issues and Problems in the Study of Bureaucracy," in *The Organization of Power: Aspects of Bureaucracy in the Ancient Near East* (ed. M. Gibson and R. D. Biggs; Chicago, IL: The Oriental Institute, 1987) 7–18.

43. M. Weber, *The Protestant Ethic and the Spirit of Capitalism* (New York: Scribners, 1958), 123

in a "steel-hard casing"—the famous "iron cage"—a condition facilitated by bureaucracy. In general, Weber held that bureaucratization and specialization lead to rationalization and routinization of authority and decision-making. In turn, bureaucracy leads to centralization, impersonality, efficiency, self-promotion, and self-perpetuation. Weber described the result of untrammeled bureaucracy this way:

> An inanimate machine is mind objectified. Only this provides it with the power to force men into its service and to dominate their everyday working life as completely as is actually the case in the factory. Objectified intelligence is also that animated machine, the bureaucratic organization, with its specialization of trained skills, its division of jurisdiction, its rules and hierarchical relations of authority. Together with the inanimate machine it is busy fabricating a shell of bondage which men will perhaps be forced to inhabit some day, as powerless as the fellahs of ancient Egypt. This might happen *if* a technically superior administration *were to be the ultimate and sole value* in the ordering of their affairs, and that means: a rational bureaucratic administration with the corresponding welfare benefits, for this bureaucracy can accomplish much better that any other structure of domination.[44]

It is important to emphasize that Weber was describing a possible fate for modern capitalist society, but one that he likened to antiquity. Modern bureaucracies are hardly as efficient, much less rational, as Weber supposed, although there can be no doubt of their self-serving nature. Ancient bureaucracies were far less efficient but there is ample evidence showing the enterprise of bureaucrats using the prerogatives of office for their own advantage.[45] Institutional movement from stability to flux, and from official rectitude to freewheeling exploitation, is likely to have constituted a sort of ancient "bronze cage" for state subjects. On the one hand, some prophets would be called to defend this system of economic and social domination; on the other, some would stand against it.

Others have taken the idea of the rational, efficient state and turned it upside down. In *The Social Production of Indifference*, anthropologist Michael Herzfeld discusses the origins of what might be called the Western bureaucratic conundrum.[46] Bureaucrats, whether in totalitarian states or petty tyrannies, within what he characterized as rational, legally constituted systems, invariably behave with

---

44. M. Weber, *Economy and Society* (2 vols.; Berkeley, CA: University of California Press, 1978), 2:1402.

45. For the migration of economic prerogatives away from the royal court, see R. M. Adams, "Old Babylonian Networks of Urban Notables," *Cuneiform Digital Library Journal* 7 (2009), n.p. Online: http://cdli.ucla.edu/pubs/cdlj/2009/cdlj2009_007.html. See generally Norman Yoffee, "Political Economy in Early Mesopotamian States," *Annual Review of Anthropology* 24 (1995) 281–311.

46. M. Herzfeld, *The Social Reproduction of Indifference: Exploring the Symbolic Roots of Western Bureaucracy* (New York: Berg, 1992).

degrees of indifference. Power creates social distance between bureaucrats and "regular people," despite the ideals of accountability that participants see as explicit in the concept of bureaucracy itself. But these ideals are routinely violated by bureaucrats and, in turn, regular people expect to be violated by bureaucrats. Herzfeld explores the variations of these expectations and behaviors in modern European and Mediterranean national societies.

Herzfeld interprets bureaucracy and its victims as participants in a secular theodicy, a quasi-ritualized series of expectations and disappointments that acts as a means of coping with "failure." As a whole, this comprises a nonreligious experience of evil that generates a need for "transcendence." What Herzfeld calls "popular reactions to bureaucracy," including words and symbols, are key. Ultimately for Herzfeld—though his goal is to collapse the contrasts between the West and the non-West, the primitive and the modern—the common thread is inequality, which breeds various responses that are differentiated by their scale but not their character. The frustration of coping with expected bureaucratic and—by extension—state inefficiency and the need for transcendence has obvious relevance for the question of prophets and prophecy.[47]

But overall state success cannot be taken for granted any more than bureaucratic efficiency. In fact, there is little evidence of either in the modern world and much evidence to the contrary. In *Seeing Like a State*, James Scott surveyed in devastating detail the ways in which modern states have failed catastrophically at reorganizing agriculture and society.[48] Many more could be added to his examples of Soviet collectivization and Tanzanian forced villagization, as well as the planned city and the "scientific forest." What Scott called "high modernist ideology" combined an excess of scientific and technological self-consciousness, modern administrative techniques, authoritarianism, and weak civil society to produce carefully engineered disasters.

One common thread was hubris. As Latour put it (speaking specifically of the French), "the "common good," the "public good" was not supposed to be produced by experimental and carefully accountable procedures of inquiries. The "public," the "common," the "disinterested" is supposed to be *by nature and once for all* radically different from the "private," the "commercial," the "selfish," the "interested."[49] Another is the pattern of states and associated elites stepping in to

---

47. Herzfeld's view is similar to that of Meyer and Rowan, who held that institutionalized myths co-evolve with formal organizations. As complexity increases, greater efforts are made to preserve the formal structure through ceremonies, avoidance of oversight and reporting, and saving face, all of which "decouples" it from reality and transfers it into the mythical and ritual realms. J. W. Meyer and B. Rowan, "Institutionalized Organizations: Formal Structure as Myth and Ceremony," *American Journal of Sociology* 83 (1977) 340–63.

48. J. C. Scott, *Seeing like a State: How Certain Schemes to Improve the Human Condition Have Failed* (New Haven, CT: Yale University Press, 1998).

49. B. Latour, "How to Think like a State," in *The Thinking State* (ed. W. van de Donk; The Hague: Scientific Council for Government Policy, 2007), 4.

solve problems that they themselves caused. Scott concludes by contrasting local knowledge gained by practical experience with "state simplifications and utopian schemes."[50]

Reshaping space, mastering nature and controlling both human behavior and thought were, of course, among the characteristics of the very first cities and polities. At the same time, Scott himself has detailed the lengths to which peoples and regions on the margins have gone to avoid becoming part of states.[51] And despite copious evidence of malfeasance by Mesopotamian ruling elites, who then righteously proclaimed in "law codes" that they had reestablished "justice,"[52] a vast area of legal activity—perhaps most—went on without royal involvement.[53] The same might be said for the bulk of economic activity. If royal claims to establish law were propaganda, then the penetration of elites into daily life was accordingly limited, even in the urban core. Bureaucracy, a high-culture creation, shaped many conditions and mentalities but not all outcomes. Such unevenness is a caution against overstating the impact of states, as well as for understanding the nature of state "failure" or social "collapse" in the past.

There are corresponding gaps in our understanding of state control and failure. As noted earlier, states commonly remade cities and landscapes as expressions of elite ideologies and need. But on the whole, gauging the impacts of self-inflicted ecological collapse, economic catastrophe, or decisions regarding war and peace are difficult in the shortest term (as opposed to the longer term). The consequences of bad policy and failed political decisions may be perceived archaeologically; but our perceptions of successes and failures are more often strongly conditioned by available texts, written from the perspective of specific participants. Who protested Mesopotamian agricultural policies that led to salinization? Since institutions controlled writing and history, we cannot say. Were there Assyrian religious dissidents? Perhaps, although this seems less likely. The relationship between prophecy and failure seems especially challenging.

Finally, any discussion of bureaucracy and government leads inevitably to the question of corruption. In Western states governed by laws, contracts, and property, behaviors that violate rules and undermine trust in the system are deemed criminal. But anthropologist Lawrence Rosen has pointed out that even today this is culturally specific and conceptually limited.

In a series of books and articles, Rosen argues that the modern Arab world is not constituted in terms of individuals with rights, as in the West. Rather, "a

---

50. Scott, *Seeing like a State*, 318.

51. J. C. Scott, *The Art of Not Being Governed: An Anarchist History of Upland Southeast Asia* (New Haven, CT: Yale University Press, 2009).

52. J. J. Finkelstein, "Ammisaduqa's Edict and the Babylonian 'Law Codes'," *JCS* 15 (1961) 91–104.

53. S. van Wyk Claassens, "The So-Called "Mesopotamian Law Codes:" What Is in a Name?" *Journal for Semitics* 19 (2010) 481–98.

person is primarily identified in terms of his or her network of obligations." "Interpersonnal negotiation" with the community of Muslim believers is done "to fabricate a network of associations [is] to connect one's own actions with a world whose universal vision of humankind and its proper organizations appear both true and natural."[54]

In an ideal society with ideal relationships, such as Rosen conceives, relationships are dynamic rather than fixed, and property is merely one element that circulates in order for individuals to accrue real social capital—namely, honor (that is, reputations and reciprocal obligations). Thus, as Rosen has pointed out, in such a system, "corruption" is not so much a violation of law or an act of theft but a failure to share wealth and to energize networks of relationships. That which restricts an individual's ability to maneuver in pursuit of advantage—which, in the Western view, includes law—violates the sense of justice and legitimacy.

The inability of individuals to separate themselves and serve as "politicians," "law-makers," or "judges" or other roles presumably free of self-interest means that institutions cannot be autonomous repositories of trust or disappointment. Similarly, "corruption" is not a violation of "law" but rather a failure to use and move property to individual and reciprocal advantage. "Theft" is an entirely appropriate and expected appropriation of resources; what is unfair or unjust is failure to share in ways that bolster networks of relationships and obligation. Legitimacy is formed through sharing, but *fitna* (sedition or chaos) is created when sharing does not occur.

This system is wholly counterintuitive to Western philosophers' and anthropologists' thinking about states, not to mention that of diplomats and other interlocutors. It implies that the role of the state may not be to provide a "level playing field," create "equality under law," or even to "provide for the common defense." It may instead be the main player in a never-ending series of resource extractions and movements, thefts and payoffs, in which the state is both the largest player and the guarantor of the system.

Lest this sound too much like an uneasy equilibrium of criminal gangs, even Western anthropologists have posited that the emergence of the early state was precisely out of such "gangs"—only construed as tribes, ethnic, or other local groups in deadly competition with one another.[55] The difference is that the ideology of the classic Old World state gradually elevated gangsters to kings, theft to taxation, and payoffs to charity. There may be a certain honesty in calling things for what they are or simply not judging motives but rather measuring behaviors.

---

54. L. Rosen, "Expecting the Unexpected: Cultural Components of Arab Governance," *Annals of the American Academy of Political and Social Science* 603 (2006) 164.

55. C. Tilly, "War Making and State Making as Organized Crime," in *Bringing the State Back In* (ed. D. R. P. Evans and T. Skocpol; Cambridge, MA: Cambridge University Press, 1985), 169–91.

Regardless, prophecy in such a system has a radically different standpoint. What is normal and what is deviance? To what ideals would prophets aspire? And what does dependence or autonomy confer on prophets?

Prophets are classic examples of what philosopher Karl Jaspers deemed "axial age thinkers."[56] These are autonomous intellectuals including scholars and religious figures who emerged across the Old World from around 800 to 200 BCE. They included such widely varied sources such as traveling scholars who presaged Taoism and Confucianism in China, to Zoroaster, Socrates, Isaiah, and Jeremiah. Axial Age thinkers helped bring in a new era of philosophical inquiry to religious thought characterized by emerging emphasis on the individual and meaning, human dignity, liberty, and the division of religious, political, and economics into different spheres. Whether or not this was indeed a turning point in human consciousness, in historical terms it marked the emergence of elites that were independent of the existing power structures.

Little may be said directly on the basis of archaeology regarding how states contended with these competitors. If we regard Scriptural evidence as reliably historical, then various kings and priests from Zedekiah and Hilkiah to Caiphas and Pontius Pilate were displeased by prophetic competition. It should be noted, however, that Judaism and Christianity took these outsider perspectives and put them at the center of new religions.

Other Possibilities

Many other archaeological and social concepts could be discussed here. The problem of the city is critical to understanding states and, in turn, prophecy. This question deserves sustained examination.[57] Juxtaposed against this, however, are the many other roles of the city: as a locus of power and focal point for networks of relationships, and as a center for memory in landscapes inscribed with meanings, constituted by building and constructions, rituals and ceremonies, and negotiated identities.[58] The relationship of the state to the "urban mind" and the "normalcy" of urban life for ancient peoples—in presumed opposition to nature and ruralism—might also be explored.[59] Prophets were also only one element in complex

---

56. See generally, S. Eisenstadt, ed., *The Origins and Diversity of Axial Age Civilizations* (Albany, NY: State University of New York Press, 1986).

57. L. L. Grabbe and R. D. Haak, eds., *'Every City Shall Be Forsaken': Urbanism and Prophecy in Ancient Israel and the Near East* (Sheffield: Sheffield Academic Press, 2001).

58. Ö. Harmanşah, *Cities and the Shaping of Memory in the Ancient Near East* (New York: Cambridge University Press, 2013).

59. S. Fischer and F. Herschend, "The Urban Mind Is the Normalcy of Urbanity," in *The Urban Mind, Cultural and Environmental Dynamics* (ed. G. N. Paul et al.; Uppsala: African and Comparative Archaeology, Department of Archaeology and Ancient History, Uppsala University, 2010), 195–219.

symbolic environments. And since most state action took place orally, the performative aspects of states and prophets should also be taken into consideration. [60]

Finally, although the discussion here has focused on liberal thinkers, it may be useful as well to consider their antitheses—namely, the thought of fascist philosophers such as Carl Schmitt and Robert Michels. Schmitt extolled the "sovereign dictatorship" and the permanent state of crisis, famously declaring that "sovereign is he who decides on the exception." [61] He also theorized the realm of the political was potentially unlimited and that state power was ultimately founded on the distinction between friend and enemy.

Michels, a foremost student of Weber, moved from socialism to fascism and promulgated what became known as the "iron law of oligarchy;" "he who says organization, says oligarchy." [62] This states that all organizations, by virtue of their complexity and hierarchy are inevitably transformed into oligarchies to serve the few. Though it is important not to overstress the power, much less the efficiency, of ancient states, there can be little doubt that many aspired to what today would be called fascism and totalitarianism. In that sense, much more may be learned from the study of contemporary political religions. [63]

Conclusion

This review has aimed to examine states from unconventional angles. States are complex and dynamic entities, and archaeological thinking has tended to emphasize their material and ideological aspects. It is hoped that the above has shown that there is more to be done in order to incorporate social theory into archaeological thinking. Prophets, avatars of the imagination, require nothing less.

---

60. D. B. Redford, "Scribe and Speaker," in *Writings and Speech in Israelite and Ancient Near Eastern Prophecy* (ed. E. Ben Zvi and M. H. Flood; Atlanta, GA: SBL, 2000), 145–218.

61. C. Schmitt, *Political Theology: Four Chapters on the Concept of Sovereignty* (Cambridge, MA: MIT Press, 1985), 5.

62. R. Michels, *Political Parties: A Sociological Study of the Oligarchical Tendencies of Modern Democracy* (New York: Collier Books, 1962 [orig. 1911]).

63. See generally, E. Gentile, "Political Religion: A Concept and Its Critics–a Critical Survey," *Totalitarian Movements and Political Religions* 6 (2005) 19–32.

Bibliography

Adams, R. M. "Old Babylonian Networks of Urban Notables. *Cuneiform Digital Library Journal* 7, 2009.

Algaze, G. "The Prehistory of Imperialism: The Case of Uruk Period Mesopotamia." Pp. 27–84 in *Uruk Mesopotamia and Its Neighbors*. Ed. M. S. Rothman. Santa Fe, NM: School of American Research Press, 2001.

Anderson, B. *Imagined Communities, Reflections on the Origin and Spread of Nationalism*. London: Verso, 1991.

Annus, A., ed. *Divination and Interpretation in the Ancient World*. Chicago, IL: The Oriental Institute, 2010.

Bahrani, Z. *Rituals of War: The Body and Violence in Mesopotamia*. Brooklyn, NY: Zone Books, 2008.

Baines, J., and N. Yoffee. "Order, Legitimacy and Wealth in Ancient Egypt and Mesopotamia." Pp. 199–260 in *Archaic States*. Ed. G. M. Feinman and J. Marcus. Santa Fe, NM: School of American Research Press,1998.

Carneiro, R. L. "A Theory of the Origin of the State." *Science* 169 (1970) 733–38.

Cooper, J. S. "Babylonian Beginnings: The Origin of the Cuneiform Writing System in Comparative Perspective." Pp. 71–99 in *The First Writing*. Ed. S. D. Houston. Cambridge: Cambridge University Press, 2004.

_____. " 'I have forgotten my burden of former days!' Forgetting the Sumerians in Ancient Iraq." *Journal of the American Oriental Society* 130 (2010) 327–35.

Costin, C. L. "Exploring the Relationship among Craft Production, Gender, and Complex Societies: Methodological and Theoretical Issues of Gender Attribution." Pp. 111–42 in *Gender and Archaeology*. Ed. R. P. Wright. Philadelphia, PA: University of Pennsylvania Press, 1996.

Eisenstadt, S. N. *The Origins and Diversity of Axial Age Civilizations*. Albany, NY: State University of New York Press, 1986.

Emberling, G. "Ethnicity in Complex Societies: Archaeological Perspectives." *Journal of Archaeological Research* 5 (1997) 295–344.

Finkelstein, J. J. "Ammisaduqa's Edict and the Babylonian 'Law Codes.' " *JCS* 15 (1961) 91–104.

Fischer, S. and F. Herschend. "The Urban Mind is the Normalcy of Urbanity." Pp. 195–219 in *The Urban Mind, Cultural and Environmental Dynamics*. Ed. G. N. Paul et al. African and Comparative Archaeology, Department of Archaeology and Ancient History, Uppsala University, 2010.

Foucault, M. "The Subject and the Power." Pp. 208–26 in *Michel Foucault: Beyond Structuralism and Hermeneutics*. Ed. H. Dreyfus and P. Rabinow. Brighton: Harvester, 1982.

Fried, M. H. *The Evolution of Political Society*. New York: Random House, 1967.

Gentile, E. "Political Religion: A Concept and its Critics–A Critical Survey." *Totalitarian Movements and Political Religions* 6 (2005) 19–32.

Grabbe, L. L., and R. D. Haak ed. *"Every City shall be Forsaken:" Urbanism and Prophecy in Ancient Israel and the Near East*. Sheffield: Sheffield Academic, 2001.

Grosby, S. "Territoriality: The Transcendental, Primordial Feature of Modern Societies." *Nations and Nationalism* 1 (1995) 143–62.

_____. *Nationalism: A Very Short Introduction*. Oxford; New York: Oxford University Press, 2005.

Harmanşah, Ö. *Cities and the Shaping of Memory in the Ancient Near East*. New York: Cambridge University Press, 2013.

Herzfeld, M. *The Social Reproduction of Indifference: Exploring the Symbolic Roots of Western Bureaucracy*. New York: Berg, 1992.

Hobbes, T. *Leviathan, or the Matter, Form and Power of a Commonwealth, Ecclesiastical and Civil,* London: Routledge, 1889.

Kennett, D. J.; and Kennett, J. P. "Early State Formation in Southern Mesopotamia: Sea Levels, Shorelines, and Climate Change." *The Journal of Island and Coastal Archaeology* 1 (2006) 67–99.

Kolakowski, L. "Looking for the Barbarians." Pp. 14–31 in *Modernity on Endless Trial.* Chicago, IL: University of Chicago Press, 1990.

Krier, L. "Krier on Speer." *The Architectural Review* 1032 (1983) 33–8.

Latour, B. "How to Think like a State." Pp. 19–32 in *The Thinking State.* Ed. W. van de Donk. The Hague: Scientific Council for Government Policy, 2007.

Lull, V., and R. Micó. *Archaeology of the Origin of the State: The Theories.* New York: Oxford University Press, 2011.

Mann, M. *The Sources of Social Power, Volume I, A History of Power from the Beginning to AD 1760.* Cambridge: Cambridge University Press, 1986.

McMahon, A., Arkadiusz Sołtysiak and Jill Weber. "Late Chalcolithic Mass Graves at Tell Brak, Syria, and Violent Conflict during the Growth of Early City-states." *Journal of Field Archaeology* 36 (2011) 201–20.

Meyer, J. W., and Brian Rowan. "Institutionalized Organizations: Formal Structure as Myth and Ceremony." *American Journal of Sociology* 83 (1977) 340–63.

Michalowski, P. "History as Charter: Some Observations on the Sumerian King List." *Journal of the American Oriental Society* 103 (1984) 237–48.

_____. "Charisma and Control: On Continuity and Change in Early Mesopotamian Bureaucratic Systems." Pp. 55–68 in *The Organization of Power, Aspects of Bureaucracy in the Ancient Near East.* Ed. M. Gibson and R. D. Biggs. Chicago, IL: The Oriental Institute, 1988.

Michels, R. *Political Parties: A Sociological Study of the Oligarchical Tendencies of Modern Democracy.* New York: Free, 1962.

Mitchell, T. "The Limits of the State: Beyond Statist Approaches and Their Critics." *American Political Science Review* 85 (1991) 77–96.

Morony, M. G. "'In a City Without Watchdogs the Fox is the Overseer:' Issues and Problems in the Study of Bureaucracy." Pp. 7–18 in *The Organization of Power, Aspects of Bureaucracy in the Ancient Near East.* Ed. M. Gibson and R. D. Biggs. Chicago, IL: The Oriental Institute, 1987.

Nichols, D. L. and Charlton, T. H. "The City-State Concept; Development and Application." Pp. 1–14 in *The Archaeology of City-States, Cross-Cultural Approaches.* Ed. D. L. Nichols and T. H. Charlton. Washington, D.C.: Smithsonian Institution, 1997.

Porter, A. M. and G. Schwartz, ed. *Sacred Killing, The Archaeology of Sacrifice in the Ancient Near East.* Winona Lake, IN: Eisenbrauns, 2012.

Richards, J. and van Buren, M. ed. *Order, Legitimacy, and Wealth in Ancient States.* New York: Cambridge University Press, 2001.

Richardson, S. "Early Mesopotamia: The Presumptive State." *Past and Present* 215 (2012) 3–49.

Rosen, L. "Expecting the Unexpected: Cultural Components of Arab Governance." *Annals of the American Academy of Political and Social Science* 603 (2006) 163–78.

Schmitt, C. *Political Theology: Four Chapters on the Concept of Sovereignty.* Cambridge, MA: MIT Press, 1985.

Schmitter, P. "Neo Corporatism and the State." Pp. 32–62 in *The Political Economy of Corporatism.* Ed. W. Grant. New York: St. Martin's, 1985.

Scott, J. C. *Seeing like a State: How Certain Schemes to Improve the Human Condition have Failed.* New Haven, CT: Yale University Press, 1998.

———. *The Art of Not Being Governed: An Anarchist History of Upland Southeast Asia.* New Haven, CT: Yale University Press, 2009.

Service, E. R. *The Origins of Civilizations and the State.* New York: Norton, 1975.

Sinopoli, C. M. "The Archaeology of Empires." *Annual Review of Anthropology* 23 (1994) 159–80.

Smith, A. T. *The Political Landscape: Constellations of Authority in Early Complex Polities.* Berkeley, CA: University of California Press, 2003.

Smith, M. L. "Networks, Territories, and the Cartography of Ancient States." *Annals of the Association of American Geographers* 95 (2005) 832–49.

Stein, G. "Understanding Ancient State Societies in the Old World." Pp. 353–79 in *Archaeology at the Millennium: A Sourcebook.* Ed. T. D. Price and G. M. Feinman. New York: Kluwer, 2001.

Steinkeller, P. "An Ur III Manuscript of the Sumerian King List." Pp. 267–92 in *Literatur, Politik und Recht in Mesopotamien: Festschrift für Claus Wilcke.* Ed. Claus Wilcke et al. Wiesbaden: Harrassowitz, 2003.

Teeter, E. *The Presentation of Maat: Ritual and Legitimacy in Ancient Egypt.* Chicago, IL: The Oriental Institute, 1997.

Tilly, C. "War Making and State Making as Organized Crime." Pp. 169–91 in *Bringing the State Back In.* Ed. D. R. P. Evans and T. Skocpol. Cambridge: Cambridge University Press, 1985.

Tocqueville, A. de. *Democracy in America: Historical-Critical Edition of De la démocratie en Amérique.* Ed. Eduardo Nolla; trans. J. T. Schleifer. Indianapolis, IN: Liberty Fund, 2010.

Trigger, B. G. *Understanding Early Civilizations, A Comparative Study.* New York: Cambridge University Press, 2003.

Weber, M. *The Protestant Ethic and the Spirit of Capitalism* New York: Scribners, 1958.

———. *Economy and Society: An Outline of Interpretive Sociology.* Berkeley: University of California Press, 1978.

———. "Politics as a Vocation." Pp. 77–128 in *From Max Weber: Essays in Sociology.* Ed. H. H. Gerth and C. W. Mills. Abingdon: Routledge, 1991.

van Wyk Claassens, S. "The So-called 'Mesopotamian Law Codes:' What is in a Name?" *Journal for Semitics* 19 (2010) 481–98.

Wittfogel, K. A. *Oriental Despotism.* New Haven, CT: Yale University Press, 1957.

Wright, H. T. "Recent Research on the Origin of the State." *Annual Review of Anthropology* 6 (1977) 379–97.

———. "Early State Dynamics as Political Experiment. *Journal of Anthropological Research* 62 (2006) 305–19.

Wright, H. T. and G. A. Johnson. "Population, Exchange, and Early State Formation in Southwestern Iran." *American Anthropologist* 77 (1975) 267–89.

Yoffee, N. "Political Economy in Early Mesopotamian States." *Annual Review of Anthropology* 24 (1995) 281–311.

———. *Myths of the Archaic State: Evolution of the Earliest Cities, States and Civilizations.* New York: Cambridge University Press, 2005.

The Politics of Voice:
Reflections on Prophetic Speech as Voices from the Margins

MIRIAM Y. PERKINS

Emmanuel Christian Seminary at Milligan

I am profoundly interested in how speaking and coming to voice occur in environments where types of marginality with respect to power limit one's ability to inspire change. Biblical prophets often raised their voices to challenge reigning ways of thinking in volatile political situations. To shed light on how biblical interpreters might identify interpersonal dynamics of power informing prophetic dialogue and to identify strategies prophets utilized to gain public voice in confronting political overseers, I employ concepts from communication theory perhaps unfamiliar to biblical readers and interpreters: standpoint theory, strategic interaction, facework, and co-cultural communication from scholars Julia Wood, Sandra Harding, Erving Goffman, Stella Ting-Toomey, and Mark Orbe. Unlike broader conceptual treatments of communication and power, these theories consider on-the-ground strategies of human communication when social marginality is a contributing factor. I pair the confrontation between (1) Ahaz and Isaiah in Isaiah 7 with standpoint theory, (2) Amos and Amaziah in Amos 7 with strategic interaction and facework, and (3) Hananiah and Jeremiah in Jeremiah 28 with co-cultural communication. The interdisciplinary integration of communication theory with biblical interpretation in these three examples enables readers to see how a prophet's strategies of communication become more focused, self-assertive, and sharp-witted as their message and status become more marginal. I propose new diagrams to illustrate connections between increasing marginality and strategies of prophetic voice, specifically advancing from (1) the courage of standpoint, to (2) the courage of strategic interaction, to (3) the courage of cultural resistance.

Author's note: For their constructive insights and suggestions, I extend warm thanks to colleagues Dr. Jason Bembry, Dr. Theodore Hiebert, Dr. Christopher A. Rollston, Dr. Melinda McGarrah Sharp, and research assistant, Kelli Allen. Additional thanks to the Wabash Center for Teaching and Learning Summer Fellowship 2012.

I conclude with a summative chart of interpretive questions aimed at exploring the relationships between power, communication strategies, and prophetic voices of moral courage across contexts.

I want the reader to feel the ways in which social marginality for the prophets called for moral courage expressed as strategies of self-assertion and cultural engagement in situations where their voices were prone to be dismissed. Attention to how power shapes self-assertion and cultural engagement is vital to understanding the strength of the prophetic voice both then and now. To a certain degree, the prophets embody voice maturing into a type of moral courage needed in the contemporary world.[1] My hope is that attention to the power relationships in which prophetic communication is situated and naming advancing strategies of voice will show the complexities involved in coming into our own kinds of prophetic speech. It is important to recognize the often latent marginality of the prophetic voice and the way that power structures bore down upon and yet invigorated a prophet's capacity to critique and reimagine their social contexts. This invites the reader to consider their own complex relationships to power and status, ability or inability to hear marginal voices, and courage or lack of courage in resisting dominant cultural paradigms. Such interpretive practices can inspire us to cultivate brave habits of communication in equally complex contemporary situations of political, theological, and social conflict bearing on human life.

This chapter investigates three short dialogues from the books of Isaiah, Amos, and Jeremiah as case studies in communication from places of social marginality. What is the relationship between prophetic speech and access to power and influence? What strategies did prophets use to speak in the context of relationships marked by power difference? Even though the intersection between communication and power has been at the heart of a rich philosophical (Arendt, de Certeau, Foucault), theological (Keller, Reiger, Russell), and biblical (Ackerman, Schüssler Fiorenza) discussion, dynamics of power and voice are too often overlooked and unexamined in the process of biblical interpretation.[2] In the case

---

1. See B. Hinze, *Prophetic Obedience: Ecclesiology for a Dialogical Church* (Maryknoll, NY: Orbis, 2016); J. F. Darsey, *The Prophetic Tradition and Radical Rhetoric in America* (New York: New York University Press, 1997); C. Kaveny, *Prophecy Without Contempt: Religious Discourse in the Public Square* (Cambridge: Harvard University Press, 2016); G. C. Ellison II, *Fearless Dialogues: A New Movement for Justice* (Louisville: Westminster John Knox, 2017).

2. See S. Ackerman, *Warrior, Dancer, Seductress, Queen: Women in Judges and Biblical Israel* (New York: Doubleday, 1998); H. Arendt, *The Human Condition* (Chicago, IL: University of Chicago Press, 1998); M. de Certeau, *The Practice of Everyday Life* (Berkeley, CA: University of California Press, 1984); M. Foucault, *Power* (ed. J. D. Faubion; New York: New Press, 2001); C. Keller, *God and Power: Counter-Apocalyptic Journeys* (Minneapolis, MN: Fortress, 2005); J. Rieger, *Christ & Empire: From Paul to Postcolonial Times* (Minneapolis, MN: Fortress, 2007); L. M. Russell, *Human Liberation in a Feminist Perspective: A Theology* (Philadelphia, PA: Westminster, 1974); E. Schüssler Fiorenza, *In Memory of Her: A Feminist Theological Reconstruction of Christian Origins* (New York: Crossroad, 1983).

of the major prophets of the Hebrew canon, the resonance and strength of their voices as prominent textual witnesses mask the complex social dynamics of power that influenced their strategies for gaining a hearing and challenging dominant cultural frameworks. I believe that attending to the prophets' communicative strategies from within contexts shaped by distance from power opens up important interpretive questions relevant not only for thinking critically about the prophets, but also for thinking critically about the multiple vantage points that shape biblical scholarship as well as written and oral communication more generally.

Prophetic Speech as Voices from the Margins

The interdisciplinary approach of this chapter, which connects biblical scholarship and contemporary communication theory, rests on a premise that the biblical prophets often spoke from locations of social marginality. This premise needs careful explication: in what ways, and to what extent, were prophetic voices marginal? In contemporary contexts, social marginality can be the result of attributes such as race, gender, age, or sexual orientation that hinder social status in relation to more valued cultural traits. In the patriarchal contexts of the ancient Near East, biblical prophets were not marginal voices in this sense; they were predominately men speaking in contexts of shared racial descent. Though there were Hebrew prophets who were women, their exceptional nature and rare mention largely proves the rule.[3] Marginality, however, can also be defined by one's relative access to positions of influence and one's cultural worldview vis-à-vis those who are socially privileged. In these two senses, prophetic voice can be described as marginal, though even here further nuance is needed.

Social marginality often has to do with one's social status and standing relative to positions that offer power to those who hold them. Power can be defined in a number of different ways. In relation to prophetic speech, I define power as the ability to directly effect political change and/or access to forces of political influence. Figure 1 (p. 28) outlines a spectrum of relations to political influence for the three narratives considered in this piece: Isaiah 7, proximal distance to social power; Amos 7, intermediate distance to social power; and Jeremiah 28, peripheral distance to social power. In each narrative, the prophet's communication strategies respond to increasing distance from political influence. The prophetic passages and respective prophets considered here therefore offer case studies in communication in relation to increasing marginal social status.

The power to influence political realities reflects the general role of prophets in both Hebrew and broader ancient Near East contexts in which prophets

---

3. Exceptions include Miriam (Exod 15:20), Deborah (Judg 4:4), Huldah (2 Kgs 22:14; 2 Chr 34:22), the wife of Isaiah (Isa 8:3), Noadiah (Neh 6:14), Anna (Luke 2:36), daughters of Philip (Acts 21:9), and the women of Corinth (1 Cor 11:5).

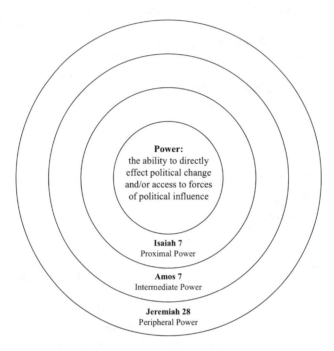

Figure 1. The prophetic vocations of Isaiah, Amos, and Jeremiah are pictured here along a spectrum that visualizes a prophet's power in relation to his interlocutors: Isaiah was a trusted prophet of King Ahaz in a position of proximal power; Amos was without official status in the court of King Jeroboam II in a position of intermediate power; and Jeremiah was repudiated and persecuted in a positon of peripheral power.

were most often called upon to seek or provide counsel and direction in times of political instability and war.[4] Even when other theological or moral themes are in the foreground, their prophetic exigency was often related to political survival and divine protection. Relative to the wider population, prophets were educated men of influence who spoke with intelligence, eloquence, and diplomatic skill. However, power is rarely an all or nothing phenomenon, and in many cases, the actual capacity of prophets to effect political change was indirect at best and entirely dependent upon their persuasive abilities with men of higher political positions. In this sense, the Hebrew prophets to whom canonical books are attributed

---

4. J. Blenkinsopp, *A History of Prophecy in Israel* (Philadelphia, PA: Westminster, 1983), 40–48.

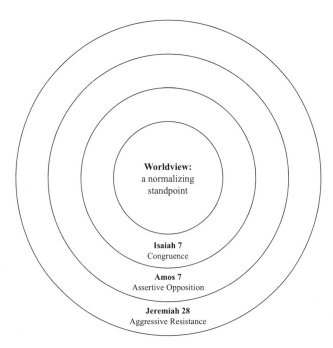

Figure 2. The political and religious perspectives of Isaiah, Amos, and Jeremiah are here pictured along a spectrum that relates a prophet's message to its distance from more dominant and normalizing worldviews: Isaiah, congruence with prevailing worldviews; Amos, assertive opposition to prevailing worldviews; Jeremiah, aggressive resistance to prevailing worldviews.

had marginal social standing relative to officials who could effect political change, and they operated along a spectrum of access to power.

The marginal nature of prophetic voice was also a consequence of the theological, ethical, and political standpoints prophets proposed and defended. In any given cultural context, positions of social status and standing are often linked to the capacity to normalize a particular worldview. People who hold the majority position are typically aligned with the cultural status quo and therefore often inclined to disregard, criticize, or suppress voices that challenge the more dominant view. The most well-attested prophetic voices in the Hebrew canon were voices of social challenge; they most often spoke messages aimed at undermining assumptions about religious privilege, justice, and the righteous life. As I consider below, Isaiah 7, Amos 7, and Jeremiah 28 showcase prophets with critical social declarations. The critical focus of the classical prophets of the Hebrew scriptures suffered status on this account; as biblical scholar Joseph Blenkinsopp describes, "all indications are that they were low on the economic and social scale and, in the eyes of some of their contemporaries, eccentric to the point of insanity."[5] Like the category of power, however, the marginality of prophetic standpoints was also not an all or nothing phenomenon and can be positioned along a continuum relative to the prevailing status quo.

Figure 2 points to the spectrum of relations between a prophet's message and a prevailing worldview for the passages under consideration in this chapter: Isaiah 7, congruence with dominant and normalizing worldviews; Amos 7, assertive opposition in relation to dominant and normalizing worldviews; and Jeremiah 28, aggressive resistance to dominant and normalizing worldviews. In each narrative, the prophet's strategies of self-assertion increase as the prophetic standpoint moves further from dominant cultural views. Rather than represent a strict typology, these three texts point to variances in cultural challenge present in prophetic messages. When taken together, they yield important insights and questions for considering how speech is related to cultural frameworks both then and now.

I selected prophets and narratives from Isaiah 7, Amos 7, and Jeremiah 28 to provide fruitful and suggestive intersections between marginality with respect to both power and message. Toward that end, narratives that contain back-and-forth dialogue between prophets and officials of higher social standing foreground the relationship between communication strategies and power. Any representative selection necessarily limits the range of reflection, in part because prophetic speech in the biblical record is generally not presented as real-time conversation. However, the more abundant sections in prophetic books of confessional and poetic denouncements and reassurances were spoken in equally contentious and complex situations of power and marginality, even if the marks of these tensions are no longer explicitly visible in the preserved record. In addition, it is impossible to know to what degree the selected passages from Isaiah, Amos, and Jeremiah represent artifacts of communication that happened in real historical time as recorded. And yet the dynamics of voice and power are certainly artifacts of the historical record as presented and were no doubt a guiding force in whatever narrative hand secured their legacy.

Comparing Isaiah 7, Amos 7, and Jeremiah 28 affords the opportunity to consider the interactions between strategies of voice and positions of marginality with respect to status and message. Considering these narratives in relation to the sociological study of communication across a spectrum of power afforded by locale, position, or role reveals suggestive and important patterns. Prophetic voice in these texts becomes more focused, shrewd, and confrontational as marginality increases. The figures throughout this article relate this movement to the prophetic

---

5. Ibid., 33.

voice of moral courage in which room to speak requires maturing strategies of communication attuned to marginality and power.

Isaiah 7: Proximal Power
and the Voice of Congruence

In his dialogue with Ahaz in ch. 7, Isaiah crafted a message attractive to the king and in opposition to supporters of a growing alliance against Assyria. In 734 B.C.E., Jerusalem was under immediate threat from a coalition between the King of Aram (Syria) and King Pekah of Israel, who together determined to resist Assyrian aggression led by Tiglath-pileser III.[6] They sought Judah's support in this effort, planned to attack Jerusalem, and replace Ahaz if he proved unfavorably disposed. Ahaz was caught between two aggressors: his near neighbors and the resurging empire of Assyria. He had hitherto been committed to neutrality, but a powerful alliance against encroaching Assyria appeared politically opportune to many in Jerusalem. As a prophet, Isaiah was also caught between two political persuasions: those in favor and those opposed to Assyrian alliance.[7] The narrative exchange between Ahaz and Isaiah is of interest to me because of the way in which Isaiah initiated the repartee, having both distance from and access to political power. The theoretical category of standpoint and its relation to complex social locations of power and status open a unique frame for reflecting on the interaction between the prophet Isaiah and the Judean king Ahaz in an intense time of political instability. Communication theorist Julia T. Wood describes the intersection between self-expression and social context in communication as a "standpoint," and her theory helps locate the intersections between the identity and social status of the prophet Isaiah and his message. His message cohered with the standpoints of his prophetic context and proximal position to those in power (see figs. 1 and 2).

Standpoint theory is a way of describing the vantage points or perspectives through which people engage in conversation. For a feminist writer such as Wood, standpoint theory acknowledges the unique perspective of women, collectively and individually, based on their experience as marginalized people in society.[8] Standpoint theory proposes that cultural and social contexts, particularly the social groups to which one belongs, shape what people know and understand about the world. One's place in society, and especially locations of belonging, foreground

---

6. See J. Blenkinsopp, *Isaiah 1–39: A New Translation with Introduction and Commentary* (New York: Doubleday, 2000), 99–105; 229–34.

7. Ibid., 240.

8. J. T. Wood, "Gender and Moral Voice: Moving from Woman's Nature to Standpoint Epistemology," *Women's Studies in Communication* 15 (1992): 1–24. Also see eadem, *Communication Theories in Action: An Introduction* (Belmont, CA: Wadsworth, 2004). For a comprehensive introduction to standpoint theory, see M. P. Orbe, *Constructing Co-cultural Theory: An Explication of Culture, Power, and Communication* (Thousand Oaks, CA: Sage, 1998), 19–34.

certain perspectives while other viewpoints are outside one's range of view. Since social locations shape standpoints, Wood suggests that the status, power, and privilege of social groups are a determinative component of one's standpoint. And while there are a range of perspectives among feminist theorists, Sandra Harding believes that those whose standpoint is shaped by marginal social status often perceive the world more clearly than those in social groups of power and privilege. A woman's standpoint, in her view, is more comprehensive and objective because she understands the world shaped by patriarchy while personally experiencing its consequences and limitations for women.[9] Patricia Hill Collins describes this in-between position of marginalized groups as the vantage point of an "outsider-within."[10] The intention is not to sanction marginalization and its causes, but rather express how those located at a distance from dominant social frameworks have a uniquely powerful vantage point for discerning social realities and opening up alternative perspectives.[11] According to Harding, this privileged vantage point is still partial, limited, and must be cultivated and learned through experience.[12] A communicator must advance his or her standpoint as a unique construction of personal experience and as a reflection of shared social distance from power in a culture.

Feminist standpoint theory has been careful to clarify a presumption that locations of social belonging are easily defined and demarcated for certain groups within a culture, when cultural belonging in actuality is multi-layered.[13] A human standpoint is shaped by a nexus of identity markers, primary and secondary, that are unique to each communicator with attributes that intersect with multiple communities of belonging.[14] In a modern contemporary context, this means that social location includes categories such as age, race, religion, nationality, language, sexual orientation, economic status, education, physical ability, as well as gender. Each of these contexts for understanding identity has unique markers of status and privilege that may or may not transfer to other situations of belonging. Communicators are never speaking from clear categories of power or marginalization but rather from a nexus of locations that can flex and move one's social status and power relative to particular situations and relationships. Thus, one's standpoint with respect to power and social standing will be unique to specific human en-

---

9. S. G. Harding, *Whose Science? Whose Knowledge? Thinking from Women's Lives* (Ithaca, NY: Cornell University Press, 1991), 269–70.

10. P. H. Collins, "Learning from the Outsider Within: The Sociological Significance of Black Feminist Thought," *Social Problems* 33, no. 6 (1986): S14-S23.

11. See eadem, *Black Feminist Thought: Knowledge, Consciousness, and the Politics of Empowerment* (New York: Routledge, 2000).

12. Harding, *Whose Science*, 159.

13. Wood, "Gender and Moral Voice," 15.

14. P. H. Collins and S. Bilge, *Intersectionality* (Cambridge, MA: Polity, 2016).

counters and relative to the power differentials at play whenever people with varying standpoints communicate.

Feminist standpoint theory launches important interpretive questions with respect to any prophetic communication: What are the identity markers that name a prophet's social location? How is what a prophet communicates in a given episode a crafting and coming to expression of a unique standpoint? What is the relationship between a prophet's standpoint and the standpoint of those to whom a message is directed? How do a prophet's words and actions heed, navigate, and nuance differences in social standing and standpoint? The cultural contexts and social environments of the ancient Near East make locating identity markers for prophets in the ancient Near East fraught with historical and textual complexity. However, contemporary biblical scholars know enough to suggest what kinds of identity markers would have influenced a prophet's status and access to political power:

- Gender: the ancient Near East was patriarchal and privileged male voices.[15]
- Race: the prophets were generally spokespersons "from within" the Israelite tribal groups in which they were active.
- Regional setting: during the tumultuous 8th and 9th centuries, a prophet's location in northern Israel or southern Judah—and its corresponding centers of political power and cult (e.g., Bethel or Jerusalem)—exercised determinative force on a prophet's orientation.
- Titles and designations: prophets in Hebrew could be named נביא 'one called', רֹאֶה 'seer', or חֹזֶה 'visionary' (among others). These terms referred to prophetic activities more than titles or positions but refer to an important social role.[16]
- Prophetic heritage or school of thought: initiation into prophetic work was likely connected to family heritage or bands of prophets associated with cultic or urban centers.[17]
- Education and literacy: though there is substantial debate about schooling or expressed literacy, prophetic functions signal that prophets were politically informed, engaged, and able to communicate with sophistication and poetic resonance.[18]
- Patronage and vocation: as political counsel in times of social turmoil and war, a prophet's political loyalties, official or cultic position, or independence had bearing on the orientation of a prophet's message.

---

15. For a treatment of woman as an exceptional case, see W. Gafney, *Daughters of Miriam: Women Prophets in Ancient Israel* (Minneapolis, MN: Fortress, 2008).

16. For an overview of terminology, see Blenkinsopp, *A History of Prophecy in Israel*, 26–30.

17. On social location, see ibid., 30–39.

18. See C. A. Rollston, "Scribal Education in Ancient Israel: The Old Hebrew Epigraphic Evidence," *BASOR* 344 (2006): 47–74; I. M. Young, "Israelite Literacy: Interpreting the Evidence," *VT* 48/2–3 (1998): 239–53; 408–22.

- Epistemology and theology: prophets often anchored their messages in unconventional types of logic arising from visions, revelations, reason, or direct encounter with a god, and they spoke from theological perspectives on Israel and Judah's history and future.
- Representation: prophetic communication was typically emissary in nature; who a prophet represented and spoke for signaled his credibility/discredibility.

The above list offers touchpoints and categories for finding the nexus of identity markers that potentially shaped a prophet's standpoint. In any given case, the historical and literary record inevitably presents a tenuous web of knowns and unknowns.

For the prophet Isaiah, the identity markers included the setting of his ministry in Jerusalem during the reigns of Uzziah, Jotham, Ahaz, and Hezekiah, from about 750 to 700 B.C.E. (Isa 1:1), when the aggression of Assyria threatened the survival of Israel and Judah. Isaiah was the son of Amoz, married to a woman perhaps also a prophet, with at least two sons (Isaiah 7–8). Each son was named symbolically to align with Isaiah's prophetic message, and his first son accompanied him on his mission to Ahaz in Isaiah 7. At this time, Isaiah had access to political leaders and the court, though Blenkinsopp surmises that his marginality increased as his protest against an anti-Assyrian alliance intensified.[19] His prophetic sayings suggest that his understanding of the political context was informed, his opinions strong, and his poetic skill compelling. Isaiah incorporated some of the theological and ethical themes of Amos, as well as metaphors that appear in Hosea; he was therefore familiar with a prophetic school of thought that preceded him in the northern regions of Israel. Blenkinsopp suggests that Isaiah was involved in political life for more than thirty years, accompanied by a small band of followers (see Isa 8:16). In his view, Isaiah spoke with political realism and ethical vision but grounded the credibility of his message in direct words from YHWH shaped by a powerful visionary encounter (Isaiah 6).[20] As an emissary of YHWH, Isaiah considered himself empowered to speak publicly from a privileged standpoint, often in the personified first-person voice of YHWH. How Isaiah made his living and his official status with respect to the Jerusalem court is entirely unknown. He appears to have been active both in times of political favor and disfavor, and his theological and political outlook was often not a majority perspective (8:11–12). These intersecting identity markers place Isaiah within circles of social respectability and political decision-making; he had to weigh potentially unpopular prophetic perspectives against the cost of gaining or losing access to his primary audiences.

The written record in ch. 7 suggests that Isaiah's communication with Ahaz was marked by an interesting attention to the status differential between himself and the king. Isaiah approached Ahaz "on the highway to the Fuller's Field" where

---

19. Blenkinsopp, *A History of Prophecy in Israel*, 106–7.
20. Ibid., 106.

he was surveying water supplies some distance from Jerusalem; Isaiah made the first move by approaching Ahaz at a neutral location of his own choosing, avoiding the more politically rife courts of Jerusalem. Yet, his choice implies that he may not have had the necessary credibility or status to appear before Ahaz in his political residence. In addition, Isaiah's son Še'ar-yašub ('a remnant will return') accompanied him on this mission and was presumably present during the interchange with Ahaz; perhaps this was an intentional signal to Ahaz—Isaiah approached him as a father confident in the survival of the next generation rather than as a prophet seeking political favor (Isa 7:3). Isaiah made clear to Ahaz that he had credible information on the developing threat from the Syrian-Israelite alliance and even knew that the name of the intended replacement king was the son of Tabeel. Together, these characteristics of Isaiah's approach toward Ahaz indicate his insider-outsider status.

In the context of a proximal relationship to power, Isaiah expressed a self-assertive standpoint of political and theological challenge presented as a direct word of counsel from Yhwh to Ahaz: Isaiah believed the protection of Yhwh would eventually prevail, but Assyrian aggression could not be avoided. Isaiah verbally pictured the ensuing plot against Ahaz as nothing of political consequence, Syria and Israel no more than "smoldering stumps" (Isa 7:4). He strongly advised Ahaz to avoid an alliance against Assyria and to have faith that Yhwh would preserve Judah and its royal line, even if Assyria reduced Judah to a land of nothing more than "briers and thorns" (Isa 7:23–25). Isaiah's message was presented as aligning with Ahaz's preference for political neutrality.[21] However, Ahaz's refusal to ask for a sign "as deep as Sheol or high as heaven" was less a pious redirection than the assertion of his independence. It signaled to Isaiah that Ahaz's standpoint would not be bound to a theological position or to the prophet's counsel. Though Ahaz heeded Isaiah's advice with respect to not aligning himself with Syria and Israel, Ahaz appealed directly to Assyria for assistance in resisting the alliance instead of expressing confidence in Yhwh; he feared Syria and Israel were more than "smoldering stumps." Ahaz navigated a shrewd path toward political self-preservation but also one that resulted in Judah becoming a vassal state of Assyria until it fell in the late 7th century. It is likely that Ahaz's decision cast Isaiah into political disfavor, even in his attempt to bring a message in support of the king's reluctance to align himself against Assyria.[22]

This interchange between Isaiah and Ahaz demonstrates that the prophetic standpoint is a communication expressed from a nexus of identity markers that place a prophet in a particular position of social standing vis-à-vis an interlocutor. Much like communication in our own circles of influence, Isaiah's very identity, social position, and experience as a prophet are what potentially enable him to

---

21. On Isaiah's message of political neutrality see S. A. Irvine, *Isaiah, Ahaz, and the Syro-Ephraimitic Crisis* (Atlanta, GA: Scholars, 1990).

22. Ibid.

influence Ahaz. His vocalized message and word to Ahaz laid claim to a specific theological and political vision that called to Ahaz for response. In conversation, their standpoints intersect based on their respective vocational commitments and perspectives, with consequences for Judah's next steps as a struggling territory. The biblical dialogue between Ahaz and Isaiah as driven by the nuances of standpoint further invites conversation on the multiple standpoints bearing on the textual record of this interchange. Irvine, for example, surmises that the dialogue in the first part of ch. 7 and the warnings of Assyrian invasion later in the chapter are likely a seaming together of two formerly independent scenes.[23] Both scenes are framed by opening editorial comments (Isa 7:1–2), later edited with Deuteronomistic themes counter to other competing perspectives (cf. 2 Kgs 16; 2 Chr 28), and shaped as a biblical book incorporating later post-exilic prophecies not attributable to Isaiah. In other words, Isaiah 7 is the artifact of a layering of standpoints situated within standpoints upon standpoints.

The connection between identity, standpoint, and communication helps name the differences in power and perspective between Ahaz and Isaiah. Isaiah's standpoint was expressed in relationship to the persuasive effect he hoped to have on Ahaz. This required an exercise of prophetic voice with attention to Ahaz's situation and political status as king. It also required the courage to craft a message of both coherence and appropriately nuanced challenge at the risk of being dismissed and regarded as an illegitimate standpoint.

Amos 7:
Intermediate Power and Assertive Opposition

Standpoint theory is a way of understanding acts of communication by considering how identity markers and experience shape points of view well before a word is spoken. A standpoint is something a person inhabits and brings into expression through communication with others, often across differences of power and influence, as described in the case of Isaiah and King Ahaz of Judah. Amos 7 provides an attractive opportunity to extend the theoretical lenses on prophetic communication to probe further into the dynamics of conversation as it unfolds, in this case in relation to a prophet with less status and access to political decision-makers than Isaiah. In addition to communicating from a specific point of view, people engage in conversation having to decide in real time how to respond to another human being who is attempting to do the same. The 20th-century sociologist Erving Goffman described this kind of real-time decision-making in communication as "strategic interaction" in which a person presents and protects a certain image of self.[24] Human identity in conversation was for Goffman not only

---

23. Ibid., 134–35.
24. Erving Goffman, *The Presentation of Self in Everyday Life* (Garden City, NY: Doubleday, 1959), 1–16.

expressed in a standpoint, but also constructed by constant strategic positioning of oneself in dialogue with others. Goffman's additional category of "facework," and its more contemporary cross-cultural theory developed by Stella Ting-Toomey described below, will help nuance situations like the one in Amos 7 in which a person's identity and dignity are challenged.[25]

Goffman was fond of conceptualizing human interaction as theatrics: that is, when a person interacts with other people, he or she self-presents to others much like an actor to an audience. How a person acts in the human drama of communication according to Goffman involves a continuous process of assessing situations and determining how best to respond. Though Goffman believed that any focused interaction between two people is organized (or in his words, "framed") by cultural and social categories and expectations, he nevertheless saw that people have considerable choices to make in human interaction. What guides communication choices is the intuitive sense, self-conscious or not, that a person is "staging" before other people who make assessments of this performance. Human communication therefore, according to Goffman, is best understood as "impression management" rather than simply the conveying of information. In every interaction, an observer is acquiring information about a subject based on all the expressive elements of the subject's performance. The subject can influence what the observer sees by controlling and managing the information they reveal or conceal.[26] A person's decisions about how and what to disclose or withhold, based on how he or she imagines another person will perceive and respond, prompted Goffman to describe human interaction as "strategic." When two people are engaged in focused interaction, they strategically negotiate dramas of self-presentation as impression management.

The strategic elements of communication often appeared to Goffman as game-like. He termed communicative choices that alter a situation in concrete ways as "moves," and strategic interaction as an "exchange of moves made on the basis of orientation to self and others."[27] Strategic interaction takes place when "two or more parties . . . find themselves in a well-structured situation of mutual impingement where each party must make a move and where every possible move carries fateful implications for all of the parties."[28] What Goffman hoped to convey was the power a communicator has in shaping not only another's impressions, but also how a situation is defined and understood. Goffman considered, for example, how

25. S. Ting-Toomey, "Intercultural Conflict Styles: Face Negotiation Theory," in *Theories in Intercultural Communication* (eds. Y. Y. Kim and W. B. Gudykunst; Newbury Park, CA: Sage, 1988), 213–38; S. Ting-Toomey and A. Kurogi, "Facework Competence in Intercultural Conflict: An Updated Face-Negotiation Theory," *International Journal of Intercultural Relations* 22 (1988): 187–225.

26. E. Goffman, *Strategic Interaction* (Philadelphia, PA: University of Pennsylvania Press, 1969), 10.

27. Ibid., 101.

28. Ibid., 100–101.

a first move of communication sets the parameters for how situations unfold in subsequent moves. In one of his reflections, he noted the deft skill and "subtle aggressiveness" people of lower social status need in order to set the parameters of their own interactions.[29] To illustrate, he drew upon the example of how a wait-ress or waiter, from a position of lower service status, must remain in control of a table even while simultaneously appearing deferential to the customer (as in a waiter immediately taking the lead by asking "What can I bring you to drink?"). As Goffman noted, such moves "exert a moral demand," because a person asserts their own expectation for how they wish to be considered and treated as a human being.[30] This assertion has inherent risk according to Goffman; any move to be heard or respected may be ignored, rebuffed, or attacked.[31] Strategic interaction is therefore a very high stakes game in which people seek recognition and influence even in the very ordinary interchanges and conversations of everyday life.

Because people interact with one another in ways that make their personal identities vulnerable and place them under scrutiny, Goffman noted that strategic interactions often require "face-work." Goffman described face-work as the ef-forts we make to present ourselves in line with traits that have social value and the efforts needed to redress any perceived challenges to those values. The sociolo-gist Stella Ting-Toomey has further developed the terms "face" and "facework" to describe how people deal with conflict and make attempts to resolve it across cultures. Ting-Toomey defines face as "a claimed sense of favorable social self-worth that a person wants others to have of her or him. It is a vulnerable identity-based resource because it can be enhanced or threatened in any uncertain social situation."[32] Facework is "a set of communicative behaviors people use to regulate their social dignity and to support or challenge the other's social dignity."[33] Ting-Toomey's research has shown that approaches to facework are culturally embed-ded and influenced by: whether a culture stresses individuality or community; whether a person within that culture is "I"-centered or "other/we"-centered; and whether the power distance in a culture is high (inequalities normative) or low (aimed at equality). In modern western contexts with lower power distances, the individuality and independence of the "I" perspective is stressed and valued. How-ever, in communal cultures with high power distance, low status communicators tend to avoid face threatening encounters, respond to threats with self-effacing strategies rather than confrontational strategies, and act with deference and con-cern for the face of the other.[34] These types of facework shed light on the interac-tions that transpire in Amos 7.

---

29. Goffman, *The Presentation of Self in Everyday Life*, 11.
30. Ibid., 13.
31. E. Goffman, *Interaction Ritual: Essays on Face-to-Face Behavior* (Garden City, NY: Doubleday, 1967), 37.
32. Ting-Toomey and Kurogi, "Facework Competence," 187.
33. Ibid., 188.
34. Ibid., 191–96.

Already alerted to the importance of standpoint, several identity markers distinguish Amos from Isaiah even within their shared vocation. Amos was a shepherd of cattle and sheep and fig tree orchardist originally from the region of Tekoa, in the eastern desert lands of Judah (Amos 1:1; 7:15). Rather than signal simplemindedness, which his sophisticated literary and rhetorically skilled pronouncements belie, the description signals that he made his living on the land and that he had no official standing or office as prophet.[35] Nonetheless, his prophecies suggest that he was familiar with and educated in the themes of Israelite history that predated him. However, he located the credibility of his prophecies to a direct calling of Yhwh: "the Lord took me from following the flock" (Amos 7:14). Most of his prophecy was attributed to visions and reported as direct words of Yhwh. Preceding Isaiah and the politically contentious times of Assyrian aggression by just a few decades, the opening lines of Amos place him during the reign of Jeroboam II (786–746), while Uzziah ruled Judah (783–742). Although from Judah, Amos prophesied in the northern territory of Israel. Unlike the later political instability Isaiah addressed, during the time of Amos, Israel had expanded her territories and grown in wealth. The increasing indulgence and ethical disregard for the poor that followed was at the heart of Amos's condemnation of Israel, including the "lavish cult" and "elaborate rites" of the flourishing northern shrines.[36]

The identity markers and central message of Amos indicate that he had a more distant outsider status when compared to Isaiah. In the only firsthand biographical account in the book, Amos had a charged dispute with the priest Amaziah (Amos 7:10–17). The interchange here between them was of a more charged nature because the power differential between them was not as wide as that between Isaiah and Ahaz. Amaziah, as further gleaned from the scene described below, had direct access to the King of Israel much like Isaiah, and Amos presumably did not. In addition, Amaziah was an official priest of the central and most important cultic temple center of Israel in Bethel. In the northern kingdom in particular, priests served at the king's discretion; Amaziah's alliance with the throne meant that under his watch, prophesy against the king in "the king's sanctuary" was out of the question (Amos 7:13; cf. 2 Chr 10:6–15).

The categories of strategic interaction and facework from Goffman and Ting-Toomey expose the passionate repartee between these two prophets and their attention to impression management. Unlike Isaiah, who initiated the exchange with Ahaz, the conflict between Amos and Amaziah was initiated by Amaziah. The narrator describes his first move: he went to Jeroboam directly and accused Amos of conspiracy against him from the center of his own seat of power (Amos 7:10). Though Jeroboam was not named in any of Amos's reported sayings, Amaziah supposedly quoted a prediction that Jeroboam would die by the sword and

---

35. Blenkinsopp, *A History of Prophecy in Israel*, 79.

36. S. M. Paul, *Amos: A Commentary on the Book of Amos* (Hermeneia; Minneapolis, MN: Fortress, 1991), 2.

Israel would be sent into exile (Amos 7:11). Based on Amos's lack of allegiance
to the king, Amaziah attacked his character as a prophet behind his back. Having done so, he presumably felt authorized to seek out Amos on his terms and
with political backing. Amaziah made a second move: he instructed Amos to leave
Israel while subtly but directly making face-affronting jabs. Amaziah addressed
Amos as a חֹזֶה 'seer/visionary', accenting his own superior standing as an official
who earned his living as a priest of Bethel.[37] He asserted his control over prophecy
under his jurisdiction by instructing Amos to "flee" back to his home territory
of Judah, earn his keep there, and "never again" prophesy at Bethel. Amaziah's
first moves allowed him to take the lead as the one who had power to define the
situation, and his words shored up and protected his own face while simultaneously attacking the face of Amos.

Amos must have assessed the difficulty of his predicament as a prophet without any official status being commanded to return home to Judah. And yet Amos
reproved Amaziah in a manner equally as subtle and cutting as Amaziah's previous
face attacks. Amos's countermove first appears to read as a common face-restoring
measure of acquiescence and deference in a high power-distance encounter: he
told Amaziah he was neither a prophet נָבִיא nor a prophet's son (Amos 7:14). And
he described his work as nothing more than herding and tree-tending. Yet, while
appearing to concede, Amos asserted his own self-status. From his standpoint,
disassociation from the term נָבִיא simply amplified his independence as one who
was not earning his keep at the king's bidding.[38] Amos's facework additionally
included appealing to an authority higher than either an official prophet or king;
he told Amaziah that he was a prophet at the direct call of YHWH, sent specifically
to Israel. To further claim his authority to prophesy irrespective of official position
or title, Amos set forth a devastating "word of YHWH" in denouncement of Amaziah. As in the preceding interchange, Amos took the directives aimed at him and
pointed them back at Amaziah. Amaziah would be the one to flee, and not to the
friendly neighbor Judah but to an unclean land of exile (Amos 7:17). Every marker
of his status would be taken away: wife, sons, land.

Amos's countermove was a strategically negotiated response to a threat to
his face, and his facework had the mark of the deft skill of one of lower status
able to redirect and reframe a situation as an assertion of his own claim to voice
and dignity. There is no record that he was deported from Israel, and his sayings

---

37. Whether חֹזֶה is meant here in a derogatory way is disputed; however, in context and in
light of Amaziah's injunction that Amos earn his living elsewhere (i.e., back in his home area of
Tekoa in Judah), Amaziah clearly means to accent Amos's negligible and unofficial status relative to himself. See ibid., 240–42. For comparison, see H. W. Wolff, *Joel and Amos* (Hermeneia;
Philadelphia, PA: Fortress, 1977), 311.

38. Though Amos's disavowal can be understood in a number of ways, I follow Paul in
understanding it to assert political/prophetic independence: Paul, *Amos: a Commentary on the
Book of Amos*, 245–49.

stood as a testimony of moral and religious indictment against Israel. On the other hand, there is strikingly no indication that Amos's prophecy against Amaziah was fulfilled. Additionally, a denouncement of Jeroboam is everywhere implied in his critiques of Israel, even if not stated explicitly, yet Jeroboam's reign came to a natural end without the predicted devastation of a day of judgment. This highlights the astute observation by Goffman that the strategic negotiation of impression management is often less about having a corner on truth than the skill necessary to gain the upper hand:

> In aggressive interchanges the winner not only succeeds in introducing information favorable to himself and unfavorable to the others, but also demonstrates that as interactant he can handle himself better than his adversaries. Evidence of this capacity is often more important than all the other information the person conveys in the interchange, so that the introduction of a "crack" in verbal interaction tends to imply that the initiator is better at footwork than those who must suffer his remarks.[39]

The drama of self-presentation between Amos and Amaziah was told as a triumph of the prophetic footwork/facework by Amos.

The story of Amaziah and Amos's confrontation is a drama of competing self-impressions; it is the tale of two people who each believed they had an authoritative voice and the right to be heard. Each of these men strongly signaled how he wanted the other person to perceive his identity, and in so doing, each made a claim on how his authority should be acknowledged and granted credibility. Amaziah claimed authority by right of the king and the Bethel temple to control who was allowed to prophecy in his district and to restrict messages against the throne; Amos claimed authority by right of YHWH to judge moral standing at every level of society. Their duel transpired as moves in a game of facework: an attempt to strengthen their own prophetic voice and identity while obfuscating that of the other. When interpreted as facework, one of the surprising dimensions of this exchange is how much it appears to follow Ting-Toomey's broad facework patterns for individualistic cultures, since neither Amos nor Amaziah seemed concerned to save the face of the other. In light of the strong communal nature of ancient Near East cultures, it is helpful to remember that both Amaziah and Amos were, to borrow Goffman's terms, "players" representing "parties." Their exchange was more "we"-centered than "I"-centered with respect to different loyalties: Amaziah to the king and upper class, Amos to YHWH and the poor. Additionally, the posturing between them was less a competition of individualistic identity than it was a dispute among the prophets over what marks an authentic prophetic identity. For Amos, the courage of the prophetic voice was grounded in allegiances that demanded human dignity and recognition for himself, his God, and the poor.

---

39. Goffman, *Interaction Ritual*, 25.

Jeremiah 28:
Peripheral Power and Aggressive Resistance

Both Goffman and Ting-Toomey's theories of facework accentuate the range of culturally embedded ways communicators assert their self-identity in order to make good impressions, work cooperatively with others, and resolve inevitable conflicts. Ting-Toomey, more than Goffman, was particularly attentive to the nature of power (high or low) and I/we tensions within a culture and their implications for communication across cultural divides. In this final section I consider Mark Orbe's co-cultural communication theory as a way of further nuancing communication from marginal social standpoints. The strategies of co-cultural communicators resonate in important ways with the two prophets already considered and provide a new critical lens for interpreting the posture and action of Jeremiah in ch. 28 as a prophetic voice from the margins.

Rather than thinking about communication across cultures, like Ting-Toomey, Mark Orbe's co-cultural theory focuses directly on sociological research on communication strategies from the standpoint (borrowing from feminist standpoint theory) of social marginality primarily within sub-cultures of the United States. He is interested specifically in the frameworks that help describe the communication patterns of those who do not belong to the "dominant" cultural categories of identity and standpoint as they attempt to interact and engage socially across the co-cultural divisions within a society. Significantly, Orbe opts for the term "co-cultural" because he feels it avoids the negative assumptions often made about those in the "minority" or a "subculture."[40] In particular, this choice is guided by a conviction that those who negotiate their voice in the context of a more prevalent cultural standpoint are not powerless. They creatively utilize a wide range of communication strategies for gaining a hearing. Co-cultural theory rests on the premise of standpoint theory: within any given culture, those who have social status control the prevailing worldview and the linguistic communication patterns that govern social interaction.[41] It follows that those in the dominant social group have a "muting" effect on co-cultural voices; these voices cannot necessarily be silenced, but they can be marginalized and made to appear nonexistent. Orbe is specifically interested therefore in both the strategies dominant cultures use to mute non-dominant voices and the strategies that counteract this muting.

Orbe's findings revealed that co-cultural communicators are more self-consciously aware that they are always creating or staging an impression performance for those of dominant social status in a way that resonates with Goffman's theatrical metaphor. In addition, Orbe discovered that, like all communicators, co-cultural communicators make strategic choices about self-presentation. Yet, because they must make their way and survive in a more dominant culture, co-

---

40. Orbe, *Constructing Co-cultural Theory*, 1–4.
41. Ibid., 20–23.

cultural communicators are more self-aware that they must constantly monitor and self-assess their communication choices as a "response" to dominant group members. As Orbe describes, "The selection of different communicative practices is the result of ongoing, constantly changing series of implementations, evaluations, and revisions."[42] Every choice must be carefully weighed in light of several independent factors bearing on a situation. Orbe's study found that, although reasoning and selection vary widely within co-cultures, six intersecting factors tend to inform the communication strategies of non-dominant voices: preferred outcome, field of experience, abilities, situational context, perceived costs and rewards, and communication approach.[43] In other words, a co-cultural communicator is constantly assessing a situation to determine how he or she should act and what he or she should say based on his or her experience interacting with dominant group members in constantly shifting situations of perceived risk and desired outcomes.

Two of these factors, orientation and preferred outcome, proved especially useful to Orbe in identifying patterns of communication prevalent among persons society considers nondominant communicators when relating to persons society considers dominant communicators. He classified communication orientations as nonaggressive, assertive, or aggressive.[44] Co-cultural communicators selected among these orientations on a case-by-case basis, depending upon other relevant factors listed above. He stressed that nonaggressive, assertive, and aggressive classifications describe how communication strategies appear to dominant group members and not necessarily how they, in fact, are or intend to be understood by the co-communicator. Following Orbe's continuum, Isaiah's self-assertive interaction with Ahaz would be considered nonaggressive: Isaiah sought out Ahaz without aggression or ill-will toward him. Amos, on the other hand, took an assertive communication approach with Amaziah: his message was decidedly confrontational.

Orbe further classified preferred outcome as aimed toward assimilation, accommodation, or separation. Co-cultural communicators seeking assimilation attempt to blend in and accept dominant frames of reference. Those who seek accommodation want their voices and cultural perspectives to be heard and respected, but ultimately negotiate this working within the dominant framework; both Isaiah and Amos followed this strategy. Other co-communicators are not optimistic that respectful coexistence is possible, and they seek separation; as will become clear, Jeremiah modeled an aggressive quest for separation. These six categories enabled Orbe to cluster strategic practices of self-assertion into nine pairs: nonaggressive assimilation, accommodation, or separation; assertive assimilation, accommodation, or separation; and aggressive assimilation, accommodation, or

---

42. Ibid., 87.
43. Ibid., 89–104.
44. Ibid., 108–20.

separation. According to Orbe, co-cultural communicators are intensely aware of the inherent benefits and costs of each of these postures, and they weigh these costs and benefits in the communication process as it unfolds in their own experience over time.

Jeremiah 28 describes a scene in Jerusalem in which Jeremiah interacted with another prophet, Hananiah, in a dramatic public scene in the temple court. Jeremiah (ca. 627 B.C.E.) was active in Judah later than both Amos and Isaiah and began prophesying sometime during the reign of King Josiah, possibly living through the king's religious reforms at a young age. Both Jeremiah and Hananiah were sons of prominent families, each from village communities only a few kilometers north of Jerusalem; Jeremiah was a son of the priest Hilkiah of Anathoth, who may have been active at the older shrine at Shiloh. [45] The book of Jeremiah, which includes more biographic narrative than most other prophetic books, suggests two important streams of identity markers frame Jeremiah's message. The first stream points to the strength of Jeremiah's prophetic identity and vocation: he was publicly outspoken; he had a scribe, Baruch, who recorded and often read his pronouncements; he had visions and dreams; he knew and borrowed themes from the full breadth of the Hebrew literary tradition, including Amos, Hosea, and Micah among others. [46] These resonances suggest that Jeremiah understood himself to be speaking from within a powerful prophetic heritage, and his status as prophet enabled him to address other priests and prophets openly in central cultic locations such as the temple in Jerusalem. Even against considerable opposition, he remained a proactive and self-assertive prophetic voice throughout his lifetime.

The second stream is the countervailing alienation and repudiation of Jeremiah by those who held equal or greater positions of influence. After his temple sermon in Jer 7, delivered shortly after Jehoiakim became king, Jeremiah was publicly tried by the reigning priests and prophets for speaking against Jerusalem and its temple. Jehoiakim had his scroll burned, and sometime later he was barred from entering the temple (Jer 26; 36). Jeremiah vehemently called out other prophets by name and openly spoke against the entire class of prophets of his time. As a consequence, Jeremiah was considered an embarrassment to his fellow prophets and a thorn in their political side. His message directly opposed theirs. Apparently even as far away as Babylon, Jeremiah was considered "a mad man who plays the prophet" at the expense of an official prophetic class unable to keep him under control (Jer 29:24–28).

Jeremiah's interchange with Hanaiah in ch. 28 typifies the antagonistic relationship between Jeremiah and the priests and prophets of Jerusalem more broadly. Drawing on the descriptive categories provided by Orbe, Jeremiah could

---

45. W. L. Holladay, *Jeremiah II: A Commentary on the Book of the Prophet Jeremiah, Chapters 26–52* (Hermeneia; Minneapolis, MN: Fortress, 1989), 26.

46. Ibid., 44–52.

notes

be considered a co-cultural communicator in a co-cultural community in dispute about the appropriate strategies for negotiating the dominant cultural standpoint. By co-cultural, I refer to the way in which prophets represented a unique subset of society and occupied a middle position of tension between those in political power and the people more broadly as well as those in political power and the perceived judgment of God. As presented in Jeremiah, many of the prophets who served the king were by and large opting for what Orbe would describe as taking a communication posture of "nonassertive assimilation," which advocated working within the system, maintaining positive face, avoiding controversy, and self-censoring.[47] Jeremiah, on the other hand, took a position of "aggressive separation." The communicative aim of separation when paired with an aggressive communication approach means that a co-cultural communicator practices strong public self-assertion while simultaneously distancing himself from the dominant group through direct attack and sabotage.[48]

Jeremiah 28 is a narrative about a violent clash of two co-cultural approaches to speaking on behalf of Yhwh.[49] In the preceding chapter, Jeremiah, at the instruction of Yhwh, made a wooden yoke for himself and political emissaries who had come to Jerusalem from the territories west of Judah. Though Judah was already under the control of Nebuchadnezzar of Babylon, who exiled many, King Zedekiah called a regional counsel to consider resistance. Jeremiah's yoke was a prophetic symbolic performance of his opposition: all the nations must "put their necks" under the rule of Babylon (Jer 27:8). Throughout ch. 27, Jeremiah aggressively asserted this message again and again to every level of political official, including the king himself, in a direct audience. In ch. 28, the prophet Hananiah, son of Azzur from Gibeon, took on Jeremiah in the temple in the presence of priests, prophets, and the broader public. Leslie Allen has described the interchange as disputation: thesis, dispute, and counterthesis.[50]

Consonant with his position and status, Hananiah made the first strategic move, speaking at the apparent behest of Yhwh, and confronted Jeremiah's symbolic metaphor of the yoke and his prediction in ch. 27 that the vessels of the temple would remain in Babylon for some time. Hananiah proclaimed that Yhwh had already broken the yoke of Babylon and that within two years Nebuchadnezzar would return temple vessels and the exiled son of the former King Jehoiakim (Jer 28:2–4). His message strongly privileged the power of Zedekiah over the threat of Nebuchadnezzar. Jeremiah's response was equally public and aggressive; he reasoned that Hananiah's prophesy could hypothetically come to pass, but then responded with his own counter-claim. Jeremiah appealed to the history of the

---

47. Orbe, *Constructing Co-cultural Theory*, 110.

48. Ibid.

49. Holladay, *Jeremiah II*, 130.

50. L. C. Allen, *Jeremiah: A Commentary* (Louisville, KY: Westminster John Knox, 2008), 314–15.

prophets as those who dared to preach a message of destruction rather than peace. By aligning Hananiah with false prophets who preach peace, Jeremiah attacked the face, intelligence, and credibility of Hananiah. His move provoked a counterattack from Hananiah, who reasserted his own standpoint on Babylon's fall by breaking the yoke of Jeremiah in front of the crowd, as he imagined God would break Nebuchadnezzar. In this scene of facework sparring, Hananiah appeared to have the upper hand as Jeremiah was silenced and dismissed (Jer 28:11).

Sometime later, Jeremiah returned to Hananiah. Like a skilled co-cultural communicator, he reviewed and assessed the situation and planned a well-crafted countermove of face attack. Jeremiah needed to revive his metaphor of the yoke in a way that sabotaged the meaning intended by Hananiah. His plan was executed with piercing effect. He came before Hananiah again, declaring that, by breaking the wooden yoke, Hananiah enabled YHWH to replace it with a yoke of unbreakable iron rods. His message was clear: the prophecy of Hananiah and the temple entourage were deepening Judah's peril. Jeremiah followed through in the spirit of aggressive separation. He accused Hananiah of being a false prophet, neither called nor sent by God, and a liar. Then he predicted his death within the year (one year less than Hananiah's prophetic timetable). According to the narrator, Hananiah's death followed just two months later, vindicating Jeremiah's credibility as a true prophet even if one entirely alienated from his own social class.

Though he did not physically harm Hananiah, Jeremiah cursed him to death publicly. According to Mark Orbe, co-cultural communication when aggressive is rarely aimed at intentionally hurting another person. Orbe discovered that most co-cultural communication perceived to be aggressive by dominant cultural voices is directed first and foremost at gaining respect and being heard. This insight is relevant to the interchange between Jeremiah and Hananiah. Having been dismissed and silenced by Hananiah, Jeremiah strategically found a way to reassert himself and his prophetic voice courageously. In that situation, confrontational verbal aggression and attack proved the most viable, and perhaps only, option. And yet the interchange was not principally a contest of aggression. For Jeremiah, this was a crisis of prophetic voice: it was vital that he be heard, even from a place of social scorn, and able to speak courageously words from YHWH that called the dominant worldview into question.

Courage and the Prophetic Voice

This chapter began with an orientation to prophetic speech as voices from the margins. The prophets, especially those central to the history narrated in the Hebrew scriptures, were marginal voices with respect to then-prevailing cultural and moral standpoints with marginal access to direct powers of political influence. Narratives from the careers of Isaiah, Amos, and Jeremiah illustrated how the prophetic vocation situated prophets within a tension between politically influential leaders and the discerned wisdom of YHWH for the collective community. I outlined this tension in fig. 1 (p. 28) as concentric circles of advancing distance from political influence: Isaiah's proximal relationship to power, Amos's intermediate relationship to power, and Jeremiah's peripheral relationship to power. I also pictured the relationship between a prophet's message and the prevailing political perspective with a similar series of concentric circles in fig. 2 (p. 29) that show advancing distance from a dominant worldview: Isaiah's message as one of congruence, Amos's message as one of assertive opposition, and Jeremiah's message as one of aggressive resistance. When these two forces of marginality intersect in the narratives surveyed above, they reveal an alliance between levels of marginality and a prophet's communicative strategies. As marginality increases, so does the degree of self-assertion and communicative skill. In other words, greater marginality demanded more assertive and sophisticated strategies of communication. Advancement in these strategies might be termed the courage of a maturing moral voice.

Courage requires that a person find the wherewithal to overcome personal and social limitations. Prophetic voice is the capacity to speak with moral conviction from a nondominant standpoint. Each of the prophets considered here speak with a type of moral courage. As a prophet of status and influence, Isaiah's moral courage was expressed in ch. 7 as a standpoint at odds with the political currents in Jerusalem, if also congruent with that of King Ahaz. His communication strategy was to anchor his message in his theological conviction that YHWH would ensure the survival of a remnant. Amos's interaction with the priest Amaziah in ch. 7 required a stronger kind of moral voice. As a prophet with no official status or standing, Amos's power was intermediate and indirect. His courage involved strategic interaction with the aim of securing his own credibility and face and discounting the credibility and face of Amaziah. His courage was not the courage of standpoint alone but the courage of self-assertion for the sake of his convictions and alliances with the poor. Jeremiah was a prophet not only repudiated by his compatriots but also persecuted and anathematized. To bring his own standpoint forward in ch. 28, Jeremiah exercised the moral courage of speaking prophetically as aggressive countercultural resistance in the face of the prophet Hananiah. His strategies therefore moved beyond strategic interaction and facework toward confrontation and aggressive denunciation. In each very unique situation and interchange, the sophistication of communicative skill increased in relation to social marginalization.

The moral courage of speaking prophetically as illustrated by the three narrative episodes from Isaiah, Amos, and Jeremiah reveals context-specific strategies for gaining voice from places of marginalization in the expression of standpoint, the utilization of strategic interaction and facework, and techniques of co-cultural resistance (see fig. 3). They also suggest overarching themes that pertain to nurturing the moral courage of speaking prophetically. Across the range of relations

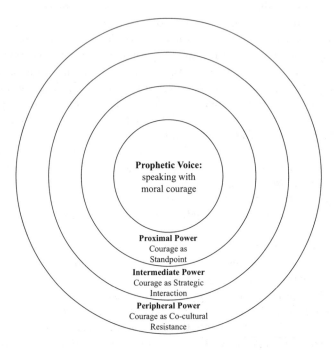

Figure 3. Prophetic voice is pictured here along a spectrum in which increasing distance from power demands more assertive communication: in situations of proximal power, prophetic voice calls for the courage of standpoint; in positions of intermediate power, the courage of strategic interaction; in positions of peripheral power, the courage of co-cultural resistance.

to power and dominant worldview, the prophetic vocation depended upon verbal self-assertion; the prophets would not have been heard or recorded apart from their concerted and self-conscious efforts to find creative opportunities and contexts for expressing their convictions. They creatively used what power and access they had in order to forge room for alternative vantage points that redirected the limitations of their liabilities and marginality. This effort often involved willingness to think outside the reigning ideological perspectives in order to draw upon ways of reasoning and sources of knowledge and experience less conventional. To some degree, this freedom was dependent upon distance from institutional structures. Isaiah, Amos, and Jeremiah also evince a comfort with risking conflict and confrontation even in situations where they did not have the upper hand and where stakes were high. Their courage to do so can be linked to marginality.

Marginality not only required more sophisticated communication skill but also created contexts in which moral courage and theological vision became possible. Contrary to how the prophetic voice on the page often reads, this kind of moral courage was less often the expression of a lone voice in the wilderness than the voice of one who cultivated solidarity both with the divine and persons of low repute.

I hope I have made it clear that recognizing the prophetic voice of moral courage and identifying the strategies that embody it are connected to the ability to identify, name, and reflect upon dynamics of power in communication. Strategies of voice are only useful if they meet specific contexts with attention to how power has already situated the relationship between parties. This realization is vital to understanding the prophets as marginal voices whose spoken word was an expression of moral and theological courage. In addition, attending to power and communication opens up interpretive questions not only for thinking critically about biblical texts but also about the standpoints upon standpoints that shape scholarly writing and the contours of any act of communication across time and contexts. As a summation of these interpretive themes, I have outlined questions that pertain to identifying strategies of voice in relation to power as a chart entitled "Communication and Power of Voice" at the end of this essay (see p. 54).

It can be challenging to orient interpretation toward sensitivity to power and authorial voice. In the accompanying chart, I picture interpretation as an opportunity to ask specific questions about the standpoints and strategies of voice that interrelate in communication. As in a "triptych" in which three panels speak to a central theme, each panel of the chart addresses a different "scene" or element of communication (standpoint, strategic interaction and facework, and co-cultural resistance), yet all are integrally related as a "landscape" of power in relation to communication. Each of the three key elements of communication surveyed in this chapter provide panel headings that summarize important questions for interpretation: What identity markers and experiences shape the person speaking or writing? What are the on-the-ground, here-and-now dynamics of the communication? How does this communication challenge assumed cultural norms? I have organized many of the communication strategies surveyed in this chapter under these headings to assist in naming strategies that are both present and absent in communication. Each of the three elements, and their accompanying strategies, are further aligned with relationships to power along the base of the triptych: proximal, intermediate, and peripheral. Each relationship to power calls forth opportunities, whether embraced or neglected, for the courage of moral voice. This voice becomes more focused and direct as one moves from proximal to peripheral relationships to power. The triptych of interrelated interpretive questions summarizes my own analysis of prophetic speech, and I offer it as an illuminative framework that can and should be modified and expanded as readers encounter and respond to different kinds of texts and communications.

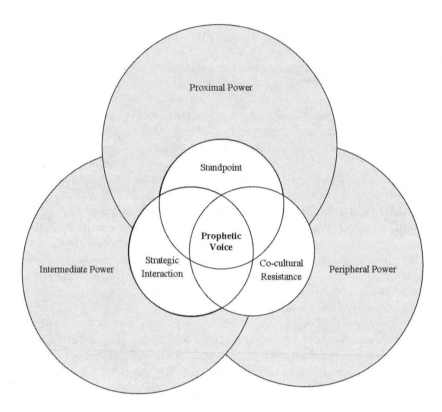

*Figure 4. Prophetic voice is pictured here as dynamic interactions that combine ele-
ments of proximal, intermediate, and peripheral power; these shifts in power call for
courage exercised as overlapping strategies of standpoint, strategic interaction, and
co-cultural resistance to gain a hearing and advance an objective.*

Though the triptych of interpretive questions can organize and guide the in-
vestigative process of naming strategies of voice in relationship to power, the chart
is not intended to represent a static typology for categorizing all communication.
Clearly defined categories belie the messy complexities of communication in relationship to power. The intersections between types of proximity to power and
the creative mix of determining factors and freedoms accompanying strategies of
voice are always unique to a given situation or act of communication. Rather than
clear concentric circles or columns in a table, strategies of communication from
the margins involve more dynamic interactions that combine elements of proximal, intermediate, and peripheral distance and overlapping strategies of standpoint, strategic interaction, and co-cultural resistance in order to gain a hearing

and advance an objective. In the case of the prophets, situation and strategy vary widely from one narrative context to another as a unique nexus of intersecting factors. Figure 4 captures the potential configurations of overlapping relationships to power and strategies of voice. Every act of communication, every author, every speech, every text must be treated as its own unfolding organic matrix of access to power and capacities of voice. This matrix includes the often ambiguous nature of marginality with respect to power. Distance from power and institutional loyalties may cultivate the gift of alternative standpoints but is often simultaneously the result of cultural dynamics that silence, incapacitate, and oppress segments of a community. Prophetic voice is always situated within the ambiguous tensions between how social-power dynamics suppress and inspire voice and create room for and complicate expressions of moral courage. To some degree, every scholar, pastor, social advocate, and impassioned moral voice experiences the ambiguous tensions of access to power and complications of speaking courageously in potentially costly contexts with respect to varying degrees and types of marginalization.

To address the configurations of overlapping relationships to power and the negotiation of voice is to invite reflection on the power relationships and standpoints that situate our own understanding and communication. It is appropriate at this juncture, therefore, to draw upon the summary triptych and fig. 4 to look back at this very chapter as an exercise marked by the dynamics of communication and power. For example, I have yet to disclose identity markers and standpoints that shape my own writing: that I am a white woman writer employed as a faculty member of a Christian theological school in the United States. The inclusion of this chapter in this volume speaks to my access to scholarly influence both in terms of educational background and the collegial relationships that made a contribution to this volume possible. At the same time, the content of this chapter—an interdisciplinary approach, an attention to prophetic voice, an interest in empowering readers to attend to power and marginality—provides textual clues about the shape of my own standpoint. As a scholar of theology and religion and culture, my standpoint in this volume is outside the more dominant interpretive frames governing biblical scholarship. My choice to lead with theoretical concepts rather than personal experience unmasks my own "facework" and "impression management" as a contributor to this volume from outside the prevailing field and its methods. As a female co-cultural voice with "intermediate" relationships to power, this piece stretched my own courage of communication, especially in presenting the prophets as in some ways models of the prophetic voice I think is necessary for living a fulfilling and faithful life. At the same time, my communication approach was strategically nonaggressive and accommodating as a way of insuring the opportunity to be heard. This choice of approach reveals that I have more work yet to do in living into the co-cultural voice of moral courage by stretching my own capacities to hear, attend, encourage, and speak to the inclusion of other co-cultural voices.

Beyond the strategic interactions related to academic writing, it can be tempting to imagine ourselves at considerable distance from the types of political interchange and exercise of prophetic voice illustrated by Isaiah, Amos, and Jeremiah. Though they represent types of marginal voices relative to dominant worldviews of their day, they were wrangling over pressing foreign policy matters with the most powerful political players of their time: kings, priests, and other prophets. In our own equally volatile political climate, with U.S. foreign policy shaping military conflicts and economic well-being across the globe, political opinions and commitments can seem innocuous and of little consequence by comparison. And yet my daily life in the seminary classroom is profoundly shaped by significant global political factors that too easily go unrecognized and unchallenged.

In a social ethics course, for example, I assigned Paul Farmer's *Pathologies of Power*, which explores the social forces that keep people sick and in poverty in places such as Haiti. Among the students in this class was a Haitian graduate student. On the day we were to discuss the chapters on Haiti he was visibly disturbed and distressed. Both he and I faced the challenge of power dynamics and courage of moral voice: would he risk sharing his experience when it might alienate and upset his more privileged seminary peers from the United States? As a professor, would I create room for him to speak even if it meant taking the discussion in unexpected and likely unsettling directions? After inviting him before class began to contribute to the discussion, the student poured out the painful experiences of his life and how U.S. policy had shaped his experiences of poverty as a child and his low sense of worth and pride in being Haitian. He expressed outrage and anger that citizens of the U.S. are so terribly misinformed through the media about the impact of U.S. policy on a neighboring country, and how long the U.S. withheld recognition of the Haitian state. As a resident of the U.S., he continues to feel the demeaning effects through complex fees and paperwork required to remain in this country. His testimony nearly filled the 90-minute class session.

Though there was palpable discomfort in the room, this student exercised a profound sense of propehtic voice as standpoint, strategic interaction, and co-cultural resistance in community with his peers and professor on U.S. foreign policy. In spite of the intricate and impossible-to-resolve discomfort it raised for us as a class, I have not regretted surrendering the class time. Though there were no political policy-makers in the room, the student's moral courage radically altered our perceptions about both Haitians and ourselves. My hunch is that this change of perception will embolden us to challenge dominant misunderstandings about Haiti and the often degrading effects of U.S. policy in solidarity with Haitians living within and close to our borders. Attention to the intersections of power and moral voice, whether when close to or distant from political policy-makers, unmasks perceptions that dominate our cultural frameworks in ways that open the door to more honest friendships and more tangible forms of solidarity. Such practices evoke the spirit of the biblical prophets and extend their moral courage into the politically significant interactions of everyday conversation.

The dynamics of prophetic voice unfold within a matrix of shifting marginality and power that can be hard to see without practice. Yet, the exercise of prophetic voice as the moral courage of standpoints, strategic interaction, and co-cultural resistance, whether we speak as close political insiders or seemingly distant outsiders, can alter the perceptions that govern how we make friendships, vote, and pursue vocations such as teaching and writing. Reflecting on my own access to and distance from power as a participant in institutions of higher education in the U.S. reveals ambiguous tensions in the contemporary exercise of prophetic voice. Connecting contemporary practices of moral courage with the prophetic voice evidenced in Isa 7, Amos 7, and Jer 28, illuminates a creative and constructive framing of the contemporary relevance of prophetic voice. As depicted in the figures throughout this essay, my reflections are decidedly shaped by an interest in the suppression and exertion of voice in relationship to access to power. Human perspectives and shifting opportunities to speak shape every act of communication for every one of us. While complicating easy claims to objectivity or expertise, standpoints upon standpoints make communication a dramatic unfolding of human understanding.

Conclusion

There is a strong need for prophetic voices of moral courage in the contemporary world, and yet many of us are reticent to speak up when our own standpoints run counter to accepted patterns of thought and behavior. From both a local and global perspective, we are surrounded by neighbors who suffer the consequences of poverty, hunger, and preventable death without partnering voices of solidarity. Though the affirmation of human dignity is central to many faith traditions, in the United States, the politics of identity make affirming the dignity of others across lines of economic status, race, class, sexual orientation, and religious belonging challenging. Our convictions can be either blinding preconceptions or vital sources for love of neighbor. In this chapter, I have explored the communication practices that develop the voice of moral courage. Becoming people of good will involves entering the messy dynamics of situational power and relative voice. When and how we exercise the voices of moral courage, whether as an expression of our own dignity or in recognition of the dignity of others, whether aligned with or against reigning social paradigms and persons embedded within them, involves awakening to our own shifting social status, access to channels of influences, powers of persuasion, and opportunities and obstacles to speaking and being heard. When marginality is a governing force, prophetic voice involves a maturing attention to and practice of standpoint, strategic interaction, facework, and co-cultural

Communication and the Politics of Voice
Miriam Y. Perkins

A Triptych of Interpretive Questions

Standpoint	Strategic Interaction and Facework	Co-cultural Resistance
What identity markers and experiences shape the person speaking or writing?	What are the on-the-ground here-and-now dynamics of the communication?	How does this communication challenge assumed cultural norms?
What textual clues provide evidence about a communicator's:	Where or how does the communication involve:	Where or how does the communication reveal:
* Age * Gender * Location * Race and nationality * Education and literacy * Socioeconomic status * Vocation or professional standing * Alliances of representation * Religious or moral commitments * Access to power or influence	* A drama of self-presentation * An interchange of "moves" * A choice of location/setting * An initiator of the interchange * Control over how the interchange unfolds * Information revealed/information concealed * Facework: positive face, negative face * Facework: face threats, face saving * "I" centered or "we" centered communication * High or low power distances	* Dominant cultural assumptions or viewpoints * Non-dominant or co-cultural perspectives * "Muting" of co-cultural voice * Creation of space for the co-cultural voice * Co-cultural self-assertion of voice * On-going risk assessment of cost and rewards * Preferred outcomes: assimilation, accommodation, separation * Communication approaches: non-aggressive, assertive, aggressive
What markers of identity and experience are not disclosed and what does this silence suggest?	What elements of strategic interaction and facework are absent and what does this absence suggest?	What elements of co-cultural voice are missing and what does this suggest about dominant standpoints?

Prophetic Voice as Progressing Moral Courage

Proximal Power	Intermediate Power	Peripheral Power
In what way does the communication express the courage of standpoint?	In what way does the communication express the courage of strategic interaction?	In what way does the communication express the courage of co-cultural resistance?

© M. Y. Perkins. Use of the chart "Communication & the Politics of Voice" for educational purposes granted. For theories of standpoint, strategic interaction, facework, and co-cultural theory see Goffman, *Strategic Interaction*; Harding, *Whose Science, Whose Science*; Orbe, *Constructing Co-cultural Theory*; Ting-Toomey, S. and A. Kurogi. "Facework Competence in Intercultural Conflict"; Wood, J. T. "Gender and Moral Voice."

negotiation. And it includes nimble interpretive skills attuned to these strategies of communication in historical texts as well as contemporary scholarship and dialogue.

The Hebrew prophetic traditions provide surprisingly appropriate and timely textual resources for becoming aware of dynamics of voice from locations of social marginality. The interchanges between Isaiah, Amos, and Jeremiah with reigning kings and more powerful prophets provide valuable resources for attending to the complex relationships between communication and power. There are resonant strategies of standpoint in Isa 7 shaped by proximal distance from power, strategic interaction and facework in Amos 7 shaped by intermediate distance from power, and co-cultural resistance in Jer 28 shaped by peripheral distance from power. These narratives help unveil the otherwise hard to recognize social arenas of power in which Isaiah, Amos, and Jeremiah came into the prophetic voice of moral courage exemplified in these texts. Naming the complexities of speaking truthfully, persuasively, and passionately against more dominant worldviews and in the presence of more powerful individuals exemplifies the prophetic voice many of us need to become people of good will in the contemporary world. The voices of moral courage in Isa 7, Amos 7, and Jer 28 are therefore an important legacy both for communities that honor these texts and those beyond who struggle to give voice to moral conviction from places of social marginality.

Bibliography

Ackerman, S. *Warrior, Dancer, Seductress, Queen: Women in Judges and Biblical Israel*. New York: Doubleday, 1998.

Allen, L. C. *Jeremiah: A Commentary*. Louisville, KY: Westminster John Knox, 2008.

Arendt, H. *The Human Condition*. Chicago, IL: University of Chicago Press, 1998.

Blenkinsopp, J. *A History of Prophecy in Israel*. Philadelphia, PA: Westminster Press, 1983.

————. *Isaiah 1–39: A New Translation with Introduction and Commentary*. New York: Doubleday, 2000.

Certeau, M. de. *The Practice of Everyday Life*. Berkeley, CA: University of California Press, 1984.

Collins, P. H. *Black Feminist Thought: Knowledge, Consciousness, and the Politics of Empowerment*. New York: Routledge, 2000.

————. "Learning from the Outsider Within: The Sociological Significance of Black Feminist Thought." *Social Problems* 33, no. 6 (1986): S14-S23.

Collins, P. H., and S. Bilge. *Intersectionality*. Cambridge, MA: Polity, 2016.

Darsey, J. F. *The Prophetic Tradition and Radical Rhetoric in America*. New York: New York University Press, 1997.

Ellison II, G. C. *Fearless Dialogues: A New Movement for Justice*. Louisville: Westminster John Knox, 2017.

Foucault, M. *Power*. Ed. J. D. Faubion. New York: New Press, 2001.

Gafney, W. *Daughters of Miriam: Women Prophets in Ancient Israel*. Minneapolis, MN: Fortress, 2008.

Goffman, E. *Interaction Ritual: Essays on Face-to-Face Behavior.* Garden City, NY: Doubleday, 1967.

————. *The Presentation of Self in Everyday Life.* Garden City, NY: Doubleday, 1959.

————. *Strategic Interaction.* Philadelphia, PA: University of Pennsylvania Press, 1969.

Harding, S. G. *Whose Science? Whose Knowledge?: Thinking from Women's Lives.* Ithaca, NY: Cornell University Press, 1991.

Hinze, B. *Prophetic Obedience: Ecclesiology for a Dialogical Church.* Maryknoll, NY: Orbis, 2016.

Holladay, W. L. *Jeremiah II: A Commentary on the Book of the Prophet Jeremiah, Chapters 26–52.* Hermeneia. Minneapolis, MN: Fortress, 1989.

Irvine, S. A. *Isaiah, Ahaz, and the Syro-Ephraimitic Crisis.* Atlanta, GA: Scholars, 1990.

Kaveny, C. *Prophecy Without Contempt: Religious Discourse in the Public Square.* Cambridge, MA: Harvard University Press, 2016.

Keller, C. *God and Power: Counter-Apocalyptic Journeys.* Minneapolis, MN: Fortress, 2005.

Orbe, M. P. *Constructing Co-cultural Theory: An Explication of Culture, Power, and Communication.* Thousand Oaks, CA: Sage, 1998.

Paul, S. M. *Amos: A Commentary on the Book of Amos.* Hermeneia. Minneapolis, MN: Fortress, 1991.

Rieger, J. *Christ & Empire: From Paul to Postcolonial Times.* Minneapolis, MN: Fortress, 2007.

Rollston, C. A. "Scribal Education in Ancient Israel: The Old Hebrew Epigraphic Evidence." *BASOR* 344 (2006): 47–74.

Russell, L. M. *Human Liberation in a Feminist Perspective: A Theology.* Philadelphia, PA: Westminster, 1974.

Schüssler Fiorenza, E. *In Memory of Her: A Feminist Theological Reconstruction of Christian Origins.* New York: Crossroad, 1983.

Ting-Toomey, S. "Intercultural Conflict Styles: Face Negotiation Theory." Pp. 213–38 in *Theories in Intercultural Communication.* Eds. Y. Y. Kim and W. B. Gudykunst. Newbury Park, CA: Sage, 1988.

Ting-Toomey, S., and A. Kurogi. "Facework Competence in Intercultural Conflict: An Updated Face-Negotiation Theory." *International Journal of Intercultural Relations* 22 (1988): 187–225.

Wolff, H. W. *Joel and Amos.* Philadelphia, PA: Fortress, 1977.

Wood, J. T. *Communication Theories in Action: An Introduction.* Belmont, CA: Wadsworth, 2004.

————. "Gender and Moral Voice: Moving from Woman's Nature to Standpoint Epistemology." *Women's Studies in Communication* 15 (1992): 1–24.

Young, I. M. "Israelite Literacy: Interpreting the Evidence." *VT* 48/2–3 (1998): 239–53; 408–22.

Part 2

The Ancient Near East

A Land without Prophets?

Examining the Presumed Lack of Prophecy in Ancient Egypt

THOMAS SCHNEIDER

University of British Columbia

---

1. Introductory Remarks

In his recent study of Ancient Near Eastern prophecy, Jonathan Stökl concludes that "the one exception to the general trend that prophecy existed in most cultures in the ancient Near East seems to be Egypt.... In sum, the scholarly consensus is correct that prophecy, in the form as defined above, did not exist in Egypt."[1] Likewise, Bernd Schipper has held that the so-called Egyptian prophecies are entirely different from Biblical and Near Eastern prophecy, stating that the very concept of a prophet as a deliverer of divine revelations is not attested in Egypt[2] and that the texts adduced for the phenomenon are of a totally different structure.[3]

Author's note: I would like to thank Christopher Rollston for inviting me to contribute to this volume. The manuscript of this contribution was submitted to the editor in early 2013. Literature after 2012 could not be included.

1. J. Stökl, *Prophecy in the Ancient Near East: A Philological and Sociological Comparison* (Culture and History of the Ancient Near East, 56; Leiden: Brill, 2012), 14, 16.

2. It is important to stress here that "ancient Egypt" must not be limited to pre-Hellenistic Egypt and that this contribution will explore prophetic phenomena attested from Graeco-Roman Egypt. Recent Egyptological scholarship, fuelled by the florescence of Demotic and Late Period studies, no longer perceives the political distinction between pre-Hellenistic and Graeco-Roman Egypt as a clear cultural divide (for a discussion of conventional periodization in Egyptology, see Thomas Schneider, "Periodizing Egyptian History: Manetho, Convention, and Beyond," in K.-P. Adam (ed.), *Historiographie in der Antike* [Zeitschrift für die alttestamentliche Wissenschaft Beiheft 373; Berlin: de Gruyter, 2008], 183–97; and for the outdated "separatist" approach of Egyptology vs. Classical Studies, Ian S. Moyer, *Egypt and the Limits of Hellenism* [Cambridge: Cambridge University Press, 2011], 28–30).

3. B. U. Schipper, "'Apokalyptik,' 'Messianismus,' 'Prophetie'—eine Begriffsbestimmung," in *Apokalyptik und Ägypten: Eine kritische Analyse der relevanten Texte aus dem griechisch-römischen Ägypten* (ed. B. U. Schipper and A. Blasius; OLA 107; Leuven: Peeters, 2002) 38. For

Those "prophecies" (such as the "Prophecy of Neferti") are texts of official political ideology.[4] As a matter of fact, it was this apparent lack of an Egyptian variety of Near Eastern prophecy that led Günter Lanczkowski to postulate the "Eloquent Peasant" as an unrecognized prophet in his monograph on Egyptian prophecy,[5] an attempt that has justly been regarded as failed.[6]

While this volume wishes to use actual evidence for prophecy in order to understand the phenomenon more precisely, with specific attention to the varied relationship between prophets and the state, the contention of this article is that understanding why there is a current consensus regarding the lack of prophecy and, if this is the case, why a culture does not exhibit prophecy, can indeed be as enlightening as case studies of the actual phenomenon. As a framework for the debate, it is useful to reproduce here Stökl's diagram (see top of p. 61) and definition according to which

> the term 'prophet' refers only to individuals who receive a divine message, the words of which are understandable without further analysis with a special skill

---

J. W. Hilber's attempt to classify divine speeches in Egyptian inscriptions as a testimony to prophecy, see pp. 67–68 below.

4. J. Goff, *Prophetie und Politik in Israel und im alten Ägypten* (Beiträge zur Ägyptologie 7; Veröffentlichungen der Institute für Afrikanistik und Ägyptologie der Universität Wien 41; Vienna, 1986); N. Shupak, "Egyptian 'Prophecy' and Biblical Prophecy: Did the Phenomenon of Prophecy, in the Biblical Sense, Exist in Ancient Egypt?" in *JEOL* 31 (1989–90) 5–40; R. Gundlach, "'Ich sage etwas, was noch geschehen wird.' Propheten im Staat der Pharaonen," in *Zur Erschließung von Zukunft in den Religionen. Zukunftshoffnung und Gegenwartsbewältigung in der Religionsgeschichte* (ed. H. Wißmann; Würzburg: Königshausen & Neumann, 1991) 11–25; E. Bresciani: "'Il pleut sur la pierre:' Prophéties politiques dans la littérature démotique," in *Literatur und Politik im pharaonischen und ptolemäischen Ägypten: Vorträge der Tagung zum Gedenken an Georges Posener, 5.-10. September 1996 in Leipzig* (ed. J. Assmann and E. Blumenthal; Bibliothèque d'étude 127; Cairo: IFAO, 1996), 279–84; different contributions in *Apokalyptik und Ägypten: Eine kritische Analyse der relevanten Texte aus dem griechisch-römischen Ägypten* (ed. B. U. Schipper and A. Blasius; OLA 107; Leuven: Peeters, 2002); N. Shupak: "The Egyptian 'Prophecy:' A Reconsideration," in *"Von reichlich ägyptischem Verstande": Festschrift für Waltraud Guglielmi zum 65. Geburtstag* (ed. K. Zibelius-Chen and H.-W. Fischer-Elfert; Philippika. Marburger altertumskundliche Abhandlungen 11; Wiesbaden: Harrassowitz, 2006), 133–44.

For the "Prophecy of Neferti," see: A. M. Gnirs, "Das Motiv des Bürgerkriegs in Merikare und Neferti—Zur Literatur der 18. Dynastie," in *jn.t dr.w: Festschrift für Friedrich Junge* (ed. G. Moers et al.; Göttingen: Seminar für Ägyptologie und Koptologie, 2006), 207–65.

Schipper has labeled these texts "wisdom prophecies" (Schipper, "Apokalyptik," 39), Koenen "prophetic king's novels" (L. Koenen, "Die Apologie des Töpfers," in *Apokalyptik und Ägypten: Eine kritische Analyse der relevanten Texte aus dem griechisch-römischen Ägypten* [ed. B. U. Schipper and A. Blasius; OLA 107; Leuven: Peeters, 2002], 172–79).

5. G. Lanczkowski, *Altägyptischer Prophetismus* (Ägyptologische Abhandlungen 4; Wiesbaden: Harrassowitz, 1960).

6. G. Burkard and H. J. Thissen, *Einführung in die altägyptische Literaturgeschichte I: Altes und Mittleres Reich* (Einführungen und Quellentexte zur Ägyptologie 1; Münster: LIT, 2003), 181. Lanczkowski's study is missing from Stökl, *Prophecy*.

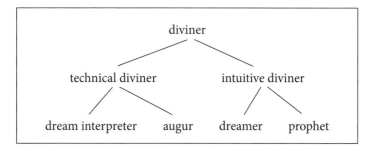

(such as reading livers); the message also cannot be intended for them but for some other individual or group, be that the king or the entire people. Prophets should be understood as belonging to the category 'diviner', and within this category, to the subcategory 'intuitive diviner.'[7]

This diagram (in which the category "augur" should be augmented by the related professions of haruspices, astrologers, etc., as Stökl clarifies) invites a number of observations. The terminology differs in other authors, such as Martti Nissinen, who labels the two categories "inductive" and "non-inductive" divination.[8] All areas of divination specified here except for prophecy pertain to the interpretation of divine signs conveyed through specific media. In those cases, the deities do not communicate directly; rather, the human observer uncovers and decodes implicit traces of the divine will in elements or phenomena of nature. When the dreamer receives explicit messages from a deity that do not need interpretation, it is comparable to prophecy in terms of the explicitness of the message. What is different is the status of the recipient of the divine message: the dreamer is both the recipient and beneficiary of the divine message, whereas the prophet only conveys the message to the true recipient. As such, a dream involves only one act of communication. In terms of the status of conveyor and recipient, prophecy is instead comparable to the interpretation of divinatory media, where the technical interpreter conveys a message not destined for himself to a third party. It should also be noted that the symbolic acts performed by the prophets and the use of specific speech forms could be seen as comparable to divinatory signs, with the prophet as

---

7. Stökl, *Prophecy*, 10.

8. Martti Nissinen, "What Is Prophecy? An Ancient Near Eastern Perspective," in *Inspired Speech: Prophecy in the Ancient Near East: Essays in Honor of Herbert B. Huffmon* (ed. J. Kaltner and L. Stulman; London: T. & T. Clark International, 2004), 21–22; idem, "Prophecy and Omen Divination: Two Sides of the Same Coin," in *Divination and Interpretation of Signs in the Ancient World* (ed. Amar Annus; Oriental Institute Seminars 6; Chicago: Oriental Institute, 2010), 341–42; idem, *Prophets and Prophecy in the Ancient Near East* (Writings from the Ancient World; Atlanta: Society of Biblical Literature, 2003), 1.

their medium.[9] The prophet's message is either explicit or is made explicit by the interpretation that the prophet himself provides. Even more complex is the case of Egyptian oracles where a query is submitted to a deity through the intermediary of priests, and the divine answer is again communicated from the deity through the priests to the questioner. If we add the case of oracles, the result is a quadrinomial situation, as exemplified in the following table, where the number of communication acts and their complexity decreases from left to right. "H" stands for the active human diviner, "h" the passive human receiver of a divine message, "G" for the active god or goddess sending messages and "g" for the passive divine will as inferable from omens:

I	II	III	IV
Explicit message	Implicit message	Explicit message	Explicit message
external addressee	external addressee	external addressee	internal addressee
$h \to H \to G \to H \to h$	$H \to g \to H \to h$	$G \to H \to h$	$G \to h$
4 communication acts	3 communication acts	2 communication acts	1 communication act
Oracles	Divination	Prophecy	Dreaming

In an oracle situation (I), an external inquirer submits a query to the oracle priest, who in turn addresses the deity, receives the divine response, and passes it on to the inquirer. In divination (II), the diviner (who may be propelled by a human query, which would liken the sequence of communication acts to [I])[10] does not inquire directly with the deity but deciphers the deity's intention from the form or behavior of natural elements and phenomena, in a strictly regulated procedure. In prophecy (III), the deity selects a human individual through whom it communicates its will to a human audience that did not normally request to hear that will. In dreams (IV), the deity speaks to humans directly (either unexpectedly or in humans seeking a dream revelation) and explicitly (wherever the dream needs interpretation, the pattern would need to be amended to $G \to h \to H \to h$). I and II share the fact that humans actively inquire of the divine will, whereas III

---

9. For symbolic acts, see T. Krüger, *Geschichtskonzepte im Ezechielbuch* (BZAW 180; Berlin: de Gruyter, 1989), 115–20. For prophetic speech forms in the Hebrew Bible, see the standard work of C. Westermann, *Grundformen prophetischer Rede* (Beiträge zur Evangelischen Theologie 31; Munich: Kaiser, 1978); for the message formula, A. Wagner, *Prophetie als Theologie: Die so spricht Jahwe-Formeln und das Grundverständnis alttestamentlicher Prophetie* (Göttingen: Vandenhoeck & Ruprecht, 2009), with a comparison of similar formulas in the ancient Near East.

10. A. von Lieven ("Divination in Ägypten," *AoF* 26 [1999] 78) sees divination as a procedure where the gods take the initiative. See also the classification of divinatory techniques and communication models given by F. Naether, *Die Sortes Astrampsychi: Problemlösungsstrategien durch Orakel im römischen Ägypten* (Orientalische Religionen in der Antike 3; Tübingen: Mohr Siebeck, 2010) 15–17.

and IV have the deity communicate directly to humans of their own volition.[11] Within the present evidence from ancient Egypt, category III/prophecy has been claimed to be unattested, a purported absence that I will examine in greater detail in two explanatory scenarios. I will first consider the view that the parameters of Egypt's religion did not allow for the existence of prophets. Modern case studies have indeed demonstrated that certain civilizations develop only some forms of access to the divine—for example, a society may have only technical but no intuitive divination.[12] A second scenario suggests that the purported absence of prophecy from Egypt is a misperception owing to the very visible limitations of our evidence in the fields of divination, personal religion, and religious practices. Special attention will be given to two examples of prophecy from Hellenistic Egypt that also are of pivotal significance for the question of prophecy in pre-Hellenistic Egypt. In consequence, the second possibility—lack of evidence, not absence of the phenomenon—might at present be the preferable scenario.

2. The Lack of Prophecy: A Religious Lacuna?

If the absence of prophecy is not a mere coincidence of preserved evidence or a result of selective display (decorum, see pp. 73, 75), genuine reasons for it must be sought that lie in the nature of prophecy and its possible incompatibility with Egyptian religion and ideology: in this scenario, prophecy would not belong to the culturally specific semantic universe of "divine presence" in Egypt, as claimed by Jan Assmann.

> By "divine presence" I understand a culturally formed and specifically determined area of experience in which specific spheres and roles are ascribed to deities and humans so that they can encounter and communicate with one another—roles such as priest, prophet, shaman, pilgrim, eremite, mystic, magician, oneiromancer, interpreter of omens, sage, and so forth, and spheres such as cult, nature, cosmos, history, myth, state, and the like, as well as forms of the otherworldly (transcendence) and supernatural (miracles). Of all these possibilities, only certain ones were realized in Egypt and others were excluded. By selection

---

11. In practice, the distinction is not always clear. For example, Hor (see p. 69 below) asks Isis and Thoth to send him dreams which he then receives.

12. As in the case of the Mambila: David Zeitlyn, "Professor Garfinkel Visits the Soothsayers: Ethnomethodology and Mambila Divination," *Man* N.S. 25/4 (1990) 654–66: "Natural, or emotive divination (sometimes also glossed as 'aleatory') depends on the recognition of a direct relationship between the operator and some occult force or spirit, such that truth is achieved through contact with spirits or by exercise of the 'intuition'. It typically involves some sort of 'possession' . . . By contrast, artificial divination aims to reveal truth through the performance of a variety of technical operations, all of which are mechanical in nature. The divination practices used by Mambila are exclusively of this kind, and are the subject of my discussion here." (http://www.era.anthropology.ac.uk/Divination/Garf/index.html, http://lucy.ukc.ac.uk/era/divination/garf/ accessed December 1, 2012).

and negation, the area we call "divine presence" receives its culturally specific form and structure as a semantic universe. Action and experience are possible only through the selection and negation of defined frameworks and within the bounded dimensions of a "semantic universe."[13]

On prophecy (at least prophecy including ecstasy), Assmann elaborates more specifically:

> Reading the works of Mircea Eliade, one could arrive at the impression that shamanism is a universal phenomenon. In Egypt, however, one searches in vain for the relevant phenomena. The facts are easily obscured, for the Greeks rendered the Egyptian priestly title ḥm-nṯr, "servant of the god," as *prophetes*, and this rendering has also become established in modern treatments of Egyptian religion. The Greek rendering is connected with the nature of oracles in the later periods of Egyptian history, and with the role of priests as interpreters of indications of divine will. As already indicated, deities expressed themselves through a language of movement. Priests were obliged to explain the oracle and evidently also to record it, and they were admonished to do so with the utmost conscientiousness. This has nothing at all to do with prophecy. There is no indication that access to "another reality" was gained with the aid of any form of ecstatic technique. The concept of another reality was definitely present, and we have associated it with the Egyptian concept *akh*, "radiant power," in the context of the verbal dimension of divine presence. There are many indications that knowledge of this *akh*-sphere was connected with special forms of induction or initiation. The authorized speaker was able to actualize this sphere with his words. But there was nothing of trances or ecstasy in this connection. In Wenamun's report of his travels in the eleventh century B.C.E., the appearance of a Syrian ecstatic is described with all the trappings of the exotic. It is only in the Graeco-Roman era that divination spells furnish positive indications with their mention of qualified mediums (especially boys); but here, it is no longer a matter of Egyptian religion in the sense of the cultural identity discussed earlier.[14]

Since we will see on pp. 73–78 below that this latter claim currently is undergoing a fundamental revision, I will not focus here on the aspect of the prophet's access to the divine realm by means of possession, trance, or ecstacy, but, rather, on the chain of communication and the prophetic message. Alternative explanations for the presumed absence of prophecy from Egypt would then be that (a) the pattern of communication whereby deities use a human "mouthpiece" to convey their messages to a third party is incongruent with divine-human communication as known from Ancient Egypt, and (b) that the divine expression of political support or critique used different media, creating no necessity for the use

---

13. J. Assmann, *In Search for God in Ancient Egypt* (Ithaca, NY: Cornell University Press, 2001), 6–7.

14. Assmann, *In Search for God*, 153–54.

of prophets. I concede that the reasoning in either case is again based on existing evidence and thus an argument by probability that can be inconclusive or false.[15]

In the table provided earlier (p. 62), prophecy occupies place III: deities select a human individual through whom they communicate their will to a human audience that has not normally requested to hear or has not inquired about that message. The message can be linguistic or metalinguistic (a symbolic act). The god or goddess is the active sender of the message, and the prophet is used as an instrument of communication:

> The term "prophecy" means that specific form of divine-human communication in which a person named "prophet," of male or female gender, has a cognitive experience (audition, vision, dream, or similar) through which it receives a revelation from one or several deities. According to the divine order, it passes this message on to a third instance, the actual addressee of the message.[16]

With the exception of texts from Greco-Roman times that will be discussed in the next paragraph, this form of divine–human communication is not at present attested in pre-Hellenistic Egyptian sources. Overall, it is conspicuous to note that the forms of divine–human interaction in ancient Egypt were very limited and regulated.[17] Egyptian deities either revealed their will directly to humans, in a dream or a miraculous event[18] or their will could be inferred indirectly through omens or asked for through oracles. Miracles as indicators of divine will are frequently attested in royal inscriptions: for example, the Gazelle and Well miracles under Mentuhotep IV or the miracle at Gebel Barkal under Thutmose III, when the rock pinnacle of the Barkal mountain in which Amun was believed to reside came to life one night as the king's fire-spitting uraeus snake and destroyed attacking enemies.[19] Examples of gods revealing themselves to believers in dreams and speaking to them ("message dreams") are only rarely attested—for three kings

---

15. Compare here the salient remarks by J. Gee, "Egyptologists' Fallacies: Fallacies Arising from Limited Evidence," *Journal of Egyptian History* 3 (2010) 137–58.

16. E. Frahm, "Prophetie," *RlA* 11 (2006–2008) 7–8.

17. See J. Assmann, *Ägyptische Hymnen und Gebete* (OBO; Fribourg: Universitätsverlag / Göttingen: Vandenhoeck & Ruprecht, 1999), 12, where the king is portrayed as the only earthly individual entitled to interact with the gods (and other individuals only insofar as they are delegated or empowered by the king); C. Traunecker, *The Gods of Egypt* (Ithaca, NY: Cornell University Press, 2001), 92–94.

18. G. Pinch, *Egyptian Mythology: A Guide to the Gods, Goddesses, and Traditions of Ancient Egypt* (Oxford: Oxford University Press, 2004), 85–86.

19. For the texts, see I. Shirun-Grumach, *Offenbarung, Orakel und Konigsnovelle* (ÄAT 24; Wiesbaden: Harrassowitz, 1993); for the Gebel Barkal miracle, also see T. Kendall, "Napatan Temples: A Case Study from Gebel Barkal. The Mythological Origin of Egyptian Kingship and the Formation of the Napatan State" (http://wysinger.homestead.com/kendall.doc, accessed December 1, 2012); T. Kendall, "The Monument of Taharqa on Gebel Barkal," in *Neueste Feldforschungen im Sudan und in Eritrea* (Akten des Symposiums vom 13. bis 14. Oktober 1999 in Berlin; Meroitica 21; Wiesbaden: Harrassowitz, 2004), 1–45; G. N. Gestoso, M. C. Bargués Criado, and

of the New Kingdom (Amenophis II, Thutmose IV, and Merneptah[20]) and two New Kingdom private individuals (Ipuy and Djehutiemhab[21]). "Symbolic message dreams" that needed interpretation so far occur only in the 1st millennium (Tanutamani[22]). Kings could also converse directly with gods: Thutmose IV conferred with Amun in the holy of holies at Karnak; Hatshepsut heard a direct order of Amun while in her father's sanctuary.[23] A singular earlier example of direct divine communication with a nonroyal human is the tale of the Herdsman from the early Middle Kingdom,[24] where the herdsman has a frightening encounter with a female goddess at night and pledges not to do "what she said."[25] It is striking to note that such a conversation could also be enforced by kings, at least in exceptional circumstances: during the catastrophic tempest under Ahmose I, perceived as a display of power of the enemies' patron god Seth-Baal much superior to that of the sun god Re and the Theban god Amun, the king confronted Amun with the situation and demanded accountability of his power.[26] In all these cases, the human addressee is the direct recipient of the divine message, not its mediator to a third party, as in the case of prophecy. If such direct communication was possible, a prophet would have been viewed as extraneous, which could then be an explanation for the absence of prophecy.

Particular consideration needs to be given to the relationship of priests to prophets. Could Egyptian priests be seen as assuming the role of prophets as in other Near Eastern cultures where cult prophets at least are attested side-by-side with priests serving in the temple cult? I prefer to keep the two roles distinct from

---

M. J. Feldman, *La estela de Gebel Barkal de Tuthmosis III* (Buenos Aires: Programa de Estudios de Egiptología, Consejo Nacional de Investigaciones Científicas y Técnicas, 1996).

20. K. Szpakowska, *Behind Closed Eyes: Dreams and Nightmares in Ancient Egypt* (Swansea: Classical Press of Wales, 2003), 47–57.

21. Szpakowska, *Behind Closed Eyes,* 135–42.

22. Ibid., 47–55; F. Breyer, *Tanutamani. Die Traumstele und ihr Umfeld* (ÄAT 57; Wiesbaden: Harrassowitz, 2003).

23. Traunecker, *Gods of Egypt,* 94–95. One might also add here Akhenaten's claim in the hymn to the Aten: "You are in my heart, there is no other who knows you, only your son, Neferkheprure, Sole-one-of-Re, whom you have taught your ways and your might." It is unknown how this instruction of Akhenaten by Aten occurred.

24. T. Schneider, "Contextualizing the Tale of the Herdsman," *Egyptian Stories: A British Egyptological Tribute in Honour of Alan B. Lloyd on the Occasion of His Retirement* (ed. T. Schneider and K. Szpakowska; AOAT 347; Münster: Ugarit-Verlag, 2007), 187–96; J. C. Darnell, "A Midsummer Night's Succubus: The Herdsman's Encounters in P. Berlin 3024, the Pleasures of Fishing and Fowling, the Songs of the Drinking Place, and the Ancient Egyptian Love Poetry," in *Opening the Tablet Box: Near Eastern Studies in Honor of Benjamin R. Foster* (ed. S. C. Melville and A. L. Slotsky; CHANE 42; Leiden: Brill, 2010), 99–140.

25. Normally taken as a real encounter and not a dream (although the beginning of the tale where this could have been clarified is lost).

26. Thomas Schneider, "A Theophany of Seth–Baal in the Tempest Stele," in *Egypt & the Levant* 20 (2010), 405–9.

each other and, by way of illustration, I will present two cases where an overlap may be seen or has been suggested (for the additional case of political prophecies, see below, §4): that of oracles and that of the communication of divine speech in the context of rituals (as will be essential in discussing John Hilber's approach below). In oracles, responses are actively requested by questioners, to whom the deity expresses its will. In the selection of Egyptian kings, the statue carried by priests answered directly to the gathered audience by movements expressing its decision; in the case of Thutmose III, the barque of Amun veered from its usual route and came to a halt before the future king.[27] Priests also served as oracular media so that private individuals would obtain divine judgments, as we know from inscribed ostraca found in the Theban workmen's village of Deir el-Medina: petitioners submitted their queries in the form of yes/no questions and the priests would pronounce the verdicts.[28] How their consultation with the gods was carried out escapes us, but the overall communicative situation with external questioners and addressees is different (slot I in the table on p. 66).

John W. Hilber[29] has recently postulated that there is evidence for Egyptian prophecy in a category of texts that have hitherto been overlooked: Egyptian royal and temple inscriptions in which divine speeches or pronouncements, which were originally recited by a priest, are rendered.[30] From a textual perspective, divine pronouncements inscribed in Egypt by priests and divine pronouncements of prophets written down by scribes in Israel and the Near East would thus be comparable. Hilber refers specifically to the case of Hatshepsut's endowment as king, when priests "pronounced her royal names, for the god caused that it should be in their hearts to make her names according to the form with which he had made them before."[31] As the "best example of royal cultic prophecy" he regards divine speeches in which the god reaffirms the king in his superiority over enemies (triumphal hymns, the conferral of the sword from the god to the king, or scenes of smiting the prisoners). He concludes, "Thus, some Egyptian reliefs citing divine speeches to the king *could have been construed by the original audience as 'prophetic,'* whether delivered through oral prophetic performance or *simply read aloud by a priest in the cult in the manner of a divine letter.* The simplest

---

27. Traunecker, *Gods of Egypt*, 94–95.

28. A. G. MacDowell, *Jurisdiction in the Workmen's Community of Deir el-Medina* (Leiden: Nederlands Instituut voor het Nabije Oosten, 1990), 107–41.

29. Hilber has reemphasized that the so-called Egyptian prophecies are a subspecies of wisdom literature. See also n. 4 above (end).

30. J. W. Hilber, "Prophetic Speech in the Egyptian Royal Cult," in *On Stone and Scroll: Essays in Honour of Graham Ivor Davies* (ed. J. K. Aitken, K. J. Dell, and B. A. Mastin; Berlin: de Gruyter, 2011), 47–53; J. W. Hilber, "The Culture of Prophecy and Writing in the Ancient Near East," in *Do Historical Matters Matter to Faith? A Critical Appraisal of Modern and Postmodern Approaches to Scripture* (ed. J. K. Hoffmeier and D. R. Magary; Wheaton, IL: Crossway, 2012), 237.

31. Hilber, "Culture of Prophecy," 237.

solution is that these were prophetic speeches, *composed in advance for liturgical performance*."[32] More succinctly even, he holds, "It is reasonable to suppose that royal and divine speeches recorded on these reliefs *were actually performed, which would constitute prophecy*,"[33] and concludes, "Therefore, it seems likely that priests functioned prophetically in the royal cult of Egypt."[34] In order to assess this claim, it seems important to determine the Sitz im Leben of these Egyptian texts. While on a textual level we are faced here with a record of (purportedly) divine statements comparable to a record of prophetic texts, the equation of such texts with prophecy is mistaken. By stating that these texts could merely have been "construed" by the audience to be prophetic, that they could have been "simply read out in the manner of a divine letter," perhaps even "composed in advance for liturgical performance," or that the simple performance of divine and royal speeches makes them prophetic, Hilbert dismisses several mandatory elements for prophecy to be prophecy: the divine revelation or cognitive experience of the prophet, the authenticity and inevitability of the event for the prophets themselves, and the communicative situation. More importantly still, the purpose and audience of these allegedly "prophetic" texts are opposed to those of prophecy sui generis. The divine speeches adduced by Hilber are part of a ritual affirming the king's present and future status, put on monumental display and part of a long ideological tradition, as is the creation of Hatshepsut's royal protocol.[35] We are not dealing here with momentary revelations in support of the state, nor can the king or the priests been seen as prophets speaking to a public that would be the intended recipients of the divine message. While it is true that some temple inscriptions may have been read aloud for the purpose of reference and dissemination,[36] the gods are in most cases their prime audience.[37] In a more general perspective, the Egyptian cult was a reenactment of divine constellations, and the priests speak on behalf of the gods

---

32. Ibid., 238–39; idem, Hilber, "Prophetic Speech," 53. Emphasis mine.

33. Ibid., 51–52; emphasis mine.

34. Hilber, "Culture of Prophecy," 238.

35. See, for the general background, D. O'Connor and D. P. Silverman, eds., *Ancient Egyptian Kingship* (Probleme der Ägyptologie 9; Leiden: Brill, 1994), and, as an example, "Amenophis III: A. Klug, "Machtübertragung und Herrschaft. Zur göttlichen Legitimation Amenophis' III.," in *Das ägyptische Königtum im Spannungsfeld zwischen Innen- und Außenpolitik im 2. Jahrtausend v. Chr.* (ed. R. Gundlach and A. Klug; Königtum; 2 vols.; Staat und Gesellschaft Fruher Hochkulturen; Wiesbaden: Harrassowitz, 2004), 221–75.

36. D. B. Redford, "Scribe and Speaker," in *Writings and Speech in Israelite and Ancient Near Eastern Prophecy* (ed. E. B. Zvi and M. H. Floyd; SBL Symposium Series 10; Atlanta, GA: SBL, 2000), 159–63; J. F. Quack, "Pharao und Hofstaat, Palast und Tempel: Entscheidungsfindung, Öffentlichkeit und Entscheidungsveröffentlichung im Alten Ägypten," in *Politische Kommunikation und öffentliche Meinung in der antiken Welt* (ed. C. Kuhn; Stuttgart: Franz Steiner, 2012) 290.

37. J. F. Quack, "Political Rituals: Sense and Nonsense of a Term and Its Application to Ancient Egypt," in *Ritual Dynamics and the Science of Ritual, Volume III: State, Power, and Violence* (ed. A. Michaels; Wiesbaden 2010) 218–19, 223.

or the divine king ("theurgic speech" of priests[38]). We are dealing, then, with an eternal display of the cultic and political order of the world for a divine audience rather than a divine revelation of an ephemeral event for a human audience.

In pursuance of Jan Assmann's view of a semantic universe that did not permit specific forms of cultural expression, it could therefore be postulated that divine communication to humans through selected individuals was not a legitimate form of conveying a deity's will in ancient Egypt. Assmann clearly delimited pre-Hellenistic Egypt from Hellenistic Egypt; examples of prophecy are indeed attested in the latter. It will be essential to assess whether the evidence for prophecy in Hellenistic Egypt points to a prehistory of the phenomenon in earlier times or whether the claim of two distinct semantic universes with a rigid temporal demarcation can indeed be upheld.

3. No Lack of Prophecy? Prophets of Salvation and Doom in Hellenistic Egypt

In the 2nd century B.C.E., there is unmistakeable evidence for a prophecy of salvation in the revelations and messages of Hor, whose personal notes have been preserved in Greek and Demotic ostraca found near the Serapeum of Memphis and published by John D. Ray in 1976.[39] Initially a *pastophoros* and scribe of the Isis temple of Temenesi (Isios Polis) in the Nile Delta near Sebennytos, Hor became attached to the cult of Thoth at the Serapeum around 170 B.C.E., where he was involved in the operation of the ibis cult. In his dreams, he received promises of salvation for his own life and afterlife, but also for the Egyptian king. In the context of the Sixth Syrian War (169/8 B.C.E.), ostraca 1–7 relate to a prophecy predicting the safety of Alexandria, the withdrawal from Egypt of Antiochos, the salvation of the reigning king, the guaranteed dynastic succession, and the birth of a male child by the queen. Ostracon 2 notes that "The dream that was told me

---

38. J. Assmann, *Ägyptische Geheimnisse* (Munich: Wilhelm Fink, 2004) 157–77; idem, *Death and Salvation in Ancient Egypt* (Ithaca, NY: Cornell University Press, 2005) 245–46.

39. The *editio princeps* is J. D. Ray, *The Archive of Hor* (Texts from Excavations Memoir 2; London: Egypt Exploration Society, 1976). See, more recently, T. M. Dousa, "Imagining Isis: On Some Continuities and Discontinuities in the Image of Isis in Greek Isis Hymns and Demotic Texts," in *Acts of the Seventh International Conference of Demotic Studies, Copenhagen, 23–27 August 1999* (ed. K. Ryholt; C. Niebuhr Institute Publications 27; Copenhagen: Museum Tusculanum, 2002) 158–59; F. Hoffmann, "Ägypten. Kultur und Lebenswelt," in *Griechisch-römischer Zeit. Eine Darstellung nach den demotischen Quellen* (Berlin: Akademie, 2000) 187–94; B. Legras, "Les experts égyptiens à la cour des Ptolémées," in *Revue historique* 624 (2002) 986–87; J. F. Quack, *Einführung in die altägyptische Literaturgeschichte III. Die demotische und gräko-ägyptische Literatur* (Einführungen und Quellentexte zur Ägyptologie 3; Münster: LIT, 2005) 91–92; H. Kockelmann, *Praising the Goddess: A Comparative and Annotated Re-Edition of Six Demotic Hymns and Praises Addressed to Isis* (Archiv für Papyrusforschung Beiheft 15; Berlin: de Gruyter, 2008) 11–18 (new edition of ostracon 10); C. Manassa, "Isis, Mistress of the Field: A New Reading of an Epithet in the Hor Ostraca," *Enchoria* 32 (2010–11) 54–61.

about the salvation of Alexandria [[. . .]] and the journeys of Antiochos (IV)" and that "He (Antiochos) will leave, he will leave, sail off from Egypt by year 2, second month of the summer, last day." Ostracon 3, containing a eulogy of Isis, predicts a fortunate year, military success, and that "Isis brings the crown to your son in the temple of Memphis, and his children after him for a very, very long time."[40] Hor conveyed the prophecies to the Greek commander Irenaios who wrote a letter in his presence, and the next month, delivered the letter "to the pharaohs" (Ptolemy VI, VIII and Cleopatra II) at the Serapeum in Alexandria.[41]

As much as Hor is a clear Egyptian prophet of salvation of the first half of the 2nd century B.C.E.,[42] an obvious example of a prophet of doom (and salvation in the long term)—"the parallels to the Old Testament are surprising"[43]—is the protagonist of the Potter's Apology.[44] The text's earliest manuscript from the last third of the 2nd century B.C.E. is around half a century later than the salvation prophecies of Hor. According to the prologue of the text, a potter operates a potter's kiln on an island formerly called the "Island of Helios (Re)," where there was a temple of Isis and Osiris. This activity was objected to by the local people or priests, who believed that the potter carried on his activities to spite the divine. The potter said in his defense that he had been sent to the island by the order of Hermes (Thoth). Some people then started to empty the kiln of the vessels; the potter is said to be "out of his mind" and "possessed by Hermes." Summoned before king Amenophis, the potter defends his action and predicts the future; the clearance of the kiln is here compared to the coming depopulation of Alexandria, the city of the belt-bearers—a symbolic act foreshadowing the future.[45] After the end of the Typhonians and many catastrophes, Egypt will be reestablished to a golden age. After

---

40. J. F. Quack, "Perspektiven zur Theologie im alten Ägypten: Antwort auf Jan Assmann," in *Theologie in Israel und in den Nachbarkulturen* (ed. M. Oeming, K. Schmid, and A. Schüle; Münster: LIT, 2004), 63–74, at 172–74 (with a new translation of ostracon 3).

41. J. F. Quack, "Zu einer angeblich apokalyptischen Passage in den Ostraka des Hor," in *Apokalyptik und Ägypten: Eine kritische Analyse der relevanten Texte aus dem griechisch-römischen Ägypten* (ed. B. U. Schipper and A. Blasius; OLA 107; Leuven: Peeters, 2002) 246–47; P. F. Mittag, *Antiochos IV. Epiphanes: Eine politische Biographie* (Berlin: Akademie, 2006) 173 n. 76. As Quack points out, apart from being a prophet of salvation, Hor is also a precursor of Hermetic literature (the ostraca are the ealiest evidence of Thoth [Hermes] "thrice great").

42. Quack, "Zu einer angeblich apokalyptischen Passage," 252.

43. W. Huß, *Der makedonische König und die ägyptischen Priester: Studien zur Geschichte des ptolemäischen Ägypten* (Historia Einzelschriften 85; Stuttgart: Franz Steiner, 1994) 167 n. 629 (quoting a similar assessment by L. Koenen).

44. For a comprehensive treatment of the text, see L. Koenen, "Die Apologie des Töpfers."

45. I see the potter here as symbolizing the creator god: Khnum creates mankind on his potter's wheel; withdrawing the vessels from the kiln before they could be burned would then mean that the life of these people is aborted. Jeremiah 19 is *not* comparable (the breaking of a pot, as Koenen suggests; he also compares the Egyptian enemy ritual of breaking the red pots ["Die Apologie des Töpfers," 175]) but Jeremiah 18 is (Jeremiah at the potter's house; Yahweh as the creator-god who can shape vessels = people into other forms as he wishes).

pronouncing his prediction, the potter dies, thereby embodying his apocalyptic message and generating another symbolic act (also encountered in the "Prophecy of the Lamb" and "Amenophis's desire to see the gods"[46]). The presence of crucial elements makes it possible to reclassify the Apology as a prophetic text: the revelation of the future by Thoth to a man "possessed" by the god, the symbolic act of producing pottery (and seeing the pottery removed), the communication of the message to the king as the true addressee, and the political references to Ptolemaios VIII and Harsiese.[47]

While the present text is a piece of literature, the situation it portrays must include phenomena that were familiar to the audience and could therefore render credibility to the account given.[48] Werner Huß connects features of the text with Hermopolis, the center of Thoth theology and political opposition to the Ptolemies.[49] I would like to suggest as a more feasible parallel an actual island: the island of Biggeh on Egypt's southern border, an island that adjoins the island of Philae, which demonstrates that an audience could easily situate the narrated events in their own world.[50] As early as the 12th dynasty, Khnum(–Re), the creator-god who created man on a potter's wheel, is attested as the "lord of Biggeh," "the Great God at the top of Biggeh."[51] The objections to the potter operating a kiln can be best explained by the restrictions that applied to access and perusal of sacred places. At the Khnum temple of Esna, "possessed ones," people wearing

---

46. See H. J. Thissen, "Das Lamm des Bokchoris," in *Apokalyptik und Ägypten: Eine kritische Analyse der relevanten Texte aus dem griechisch-römischen Ägypten* (ed. B. U. Schipper and A. Blasius; OLA 107; Leuven: Peeters, 2002), 113–38; for Amenophis' desire to see the gods, see T. Schneider, *Ausländer in Ägypten während des Mittleren Reiches und der Hyksoszeit, Teil 1: Die ausländischen Könige* (Ägypten und Altes Testament 42; Wiesbaden: Harrassowitz, 1998), 76–98; and J. Dillery, "The First Egyptian Narrative History: Manetho and Greek Historiography," ZPE 127 (1999) 93–116; most recently, J. Assmann, *The Price of Monotheism* (Stanford: Stanford University Press, 2010), 57–64.

47. Koenen, "Die Apologie des Töpfers," 179; Huß, *Der makedonische König*, 166–79.

48. It is not necessarily a "mythical place," as Koenen argues (see "Die Apologie des Töpfers," 174 n. 50, where he also refers to a proposed attempt to connect the island with Philae).

49. Huß, *Der makedonische König*, 178–79; on Thoth and Hermopolis (but without a reference to the Potter's Apology), see M. A. Stadler, *Weiser und Wesir: Studien zu Vorkommen, Rolle und Wesen des Gottes Thot im ägyptischen Totenbuch* (Orientalische Religionen in der Antike1; Tübingen: Mohr Siebeck, 2009), 66–115.

50. J. Locher, *Topographie und Geschichte der Region am ersten Nilkatarakt in griechisch-römischer Zeit* (Archiv für Papyrusforschung Beischrift 5; Stuttgart/Leipzig: Teubner, 1999) (with a discussion of the diverging ancient topography); H. Kockelmann, "L'abaton: Tombe et lieu de culte d'Osiris sur la première cataracte," *L'Égypte, Afrique & Orient* 60 (2010–2011) 31–44. (I thank Holger Kockelmann for sending me a copy of his paper.)

51. S. Sandri, *Har-pa-chered (Harpokrates): Die Genese eine ägyptischen Götterkindes* (OLA 151; Leuven: Peeters, 2006), 141; L. Török, *Between Two Worlds: The Frontier Region Between Ancient Nubia and Egypt, 3700 BC–500 AD* (Probleme der Ägyptologie 29; Leiden: Brill, 2009), 265 f.; M. Seidel, *Die königlichen Statuengruppen, Band 1: Die. Denkmäler vom Alten Reich bis zum Ende der 18. Dynastie* (HÄB 42; Hildesheim: Gerstenberg, 1996), 129 (Urk. IV, 458).

a ram's skin (Khnum's sacred animal was a ram), and craftsmen were prohibited from visiting the temple on the feast day of 19 Epiphi.[52] Access to the island of Biggeh was prohibited even much more rigidly. The site was famous for the Abaton, the "inaccessible" tomb of (the left leg of) Osiris and was also an important cultic place for Isis, who visited Osiris from her neighboring temple at Philae every ten days.[53] The divine decree for the Abaton was said to have been drafted by Thoth, who was the "great and splendid god in Biggeh," and was signed by Re, Shu, and Geb.[54] As much as getting access to the island by a potter (as if imitating Khnum) and operating a kiln would have been considered a sacrilege, the potter could have easily referred to the fact that it was the decree's divine author, Thoth, who commissioned him to do so, if we take Biggeh as a possible model. In the context of the island's Osiris worship, a prediction of the annihilation of the Typhonians (the followers of Seth) would be particularly appropriate.

What is of particular significance here is the fact that the phenomenon of a man possessed by a god and predicting a future seems anything but strange to the Egyptians and king Amenophis, implying the actual existence of such individuals. If this work is indeed translated from the Egyptian,[55] there may be Egyptian antecedents where individuals who are "possessed" pronounce prophecies on behalf of a god. Beyond the literary fiction of those texts, this would mean that the overall idea of an individual being used by god in order to (linguistically or metalinguistically) announce the future was known in Ancient Egypt.

Literary evidence for individuals predicting the future is extant in two "political prophecies" of the Middle or New Kingdom, pieces of political propaganda fictitiously set in the fourth dynasty but composed after the predicted events. In the *Tales of Wonder* from the Court of Kheops, the magician Djedji predicts the miraculous birth of the kings of the fifth dynasty.[56] In the "Prophecy of Neferti," a sage by the name of Neferti announces to Snofru, the predecessor of Kheops,

---

52. R. Müller-Wollermann, *Vergehen und Strafen: Zur Sanktionierung abweichenden Verhaltens im alten Ägypten* (Probleme der Ägyptologie 21; Leiden: Brill, 2004) 38.

53. Kockelmann, "L'abaton."

54. H. Junker, *Das Götterdekret über das Abaton* (Denkschriften der Österreichischen Akademie der Wissenschaften; Philosophisch-Historische Klasse, 56; Vienna: Hölder, 1913); C. Leitz, *Quellentexte zur ägyptischen Religion, Bd I: Die Tempelinschriften der griechisch-römischen Zeit* (Einführungen und Quellentexte zur Ägyptologie 2.1; Münster: LIT, 2004), 45; P. Boylan, *Thoth, the Hermes of Egypt: A Study of Some Aspects of Theological Thought in Ancient Egypt* (Oxford: Oxford University Press, 1922), 168–69.

55. This is what the text itself pretends. For an assessment, see Koenen, "Die Apologie des Töpfers," 180–83.

56. Verena M. Lepper, *Untersuchungen zu pWestcar: Eine philologische und literaturwissenschaftliche (Neu-)Analyse* (Ägyptologische Abhandlungen 70; Wiesbaden: Harrassowitz, 2008); for a composition of the text in the 12th dynasty, see Hanna Jenni, "Der Papyrus Westcar," in *Studien zur altägyptischen Kultur* 25 (1998) 113–41; Harold M. Hays, "The Historicity of Papyrus Westcar," in *Zeitschrift für ägyptische Sprache und Altertumskunde* 129 (2002) 20–30.

the advent of a messianic king "Ameny" and his dynasty—either the 12th Dynasty established by Amenemhet I or the 18th Dynasty founded by Amenophis I (both names could be abbreviated in Egyptian as "Ameny").[57] The literary existence of these figures points to the likelihood that such predictions by individuals occurred. However, and while both Djedji and Neferti clearly are from the priestly ranks, neither text mentions a divine revelation or cognitive experience as the source for their prophecies.

4. The Lack of Prophecy: Lack of Evidence?

The main reason for our deficient knowledge about any area of Egyptian culture is absence of evidence. Such absence can be caused by physical loss of evidence, the social lack of ability for people or groups to produce and leave evidence, and cultural norms that prevent documentation.[58] John Baines has warned against misleading interpretations of Egyptian culture due to a fallacious reliance on the preserved evidence. With reference to views on artistic expression he has stated that, "if interpretation sticks closely to the preserved record, insufficient allowance may be made for the context and for the improbability that evidence for other relevant contexts would survive."[59] Regarding the lack of mythical narratives from before the New Kingdom, he also concedes that there were deliberate filters of display, stating that the "reasons for lack of evidence lie in genre and rules of decorum governing the inscription of texts."[60]

Egyptian religion and religious practices are only very partially known and documented. The sources are very unevenly spread—chronologically, geographically, and with regard to specific areas of religion and religious activity. Singular religious texts such as the Memphite Theology[61] or the mythical manual from

---

57. A. M. Gnirs, "Das Motiv des Bürgerkriegs in Merikare und Neferti: Zur Literatur der 18. Dynastie," in *jn.t ḏr.w – Festschrift für Friedrich Junge* (ed. Gerald Moers, Heike Behlmer, Katja Demuß, and Kai Widmaier; Göttingen: Seminar für Ägyptologie und Koptologie, 2006) 207–65.

58. For a general approach to this problem, see the classic article by A. Esch, "Überlieferungs-Chance und Überlieferungs-Zufall als methodisches Problem des Historikers," in *Historische Zeitschrift* 240 (1985) 529–70, reprinted in A. Esch, *Zeitalter und Menschenalter: Der Historiker und die Erfahrung vergangener Zeiten* (Munich: Beck, 1994), 39–69. For Egyptological examples, see K. Jansen-Winkeln, "Die Rolle des Unbekannten in der ägyptischen Geschichte," in *Das Ereignis: Geschichtsschreibung zwischen Vorfall und Befund* (ed. M. Fitzenreiter; London: IBAES, 2009), 155–61; Gee, "Egyptologists' Fallacies."

59. J. Baines, *Visual & Written Culture in Ancient Egypt* (Oxford: Oxford University Press, 2007) 308–9 (commenting on a view expressed by Rosemarie Drenkhahn).

60. Baines, *Visual & Written Culture*, 191.

61. Most recently, A. E. Hawary has put forth an important new hypothesis on the provenance and later use of the monument, which was crucial for its preservation. See A. E. Hawary, *Wortschöpfung: Die Memphitische Theologie und die Siegesstele des Pije—zwei Zeugen kulturel-*

the Nile Delta in the recently published Pap. Brooklyn 47.218.84[62] contrast with compositions that are overrepresented from an epistemological viewpoint, such as the Book of the Dead. Official religious practice is richly attested and studied, in contrast to personal religious experience; an instructive example is the recent debate on personal piety in Egypt and its extent prior to the New Kingdom.[63] Finds such as the Salakhana trove at Asyut documenting a local worship of Anubis show that there existed very specific regional expressions of personal religious practice, most of which are unknown.[64]

The fragility of our assessments has become obvious in the wider area of divinity itself (under which Stöckl subsumes prophecy), where the past years have seen an unprecedented increase in evidence.[65] Under the impression of this shift in knowledge, Alexandra von Lieven has objected to an assessment by Jan Assmann according to which

> Unlike Mesopotamia, Egypt was not a fundamentally divinatory culture. Only in the New Kingdom do various forms of divination develop. And not until the Ramesside period do we find references to interpretation of dreams, birds' flight, or winds and stars. The oldest, most widespread, and classical form of divining a god's will was to consult oracles, yet there are no traces of oracular consultation in Egypt prior to the New Kingdom. This is less surprising than it may seem, for

---

ler Repräsentation in der 25. Dynastie (OBO 243; Fribourg: Academic Press / and Göttingen: Vandenhoeck & Ruprecht, 2010), 74–79.

62. D. Meeks, *Mythes et légendes du Delta d'après le papyrus Brooklyn 47.218.84* (Cairo: Institut français d'archéologie orientale, 2006); see also the review by J. F. Quack in *Or* 77 (2008) 106–11.

63. M. Luiselli, "Personal Piety," in *UCLA Encyclopedia of Egyptology* (ed. J. Dieleman and W. Wendrich; Los Angeles, CA, 2008) (http://digital2.library.ucla.edu/viewItem.do?ark=21198/zz000s3mss; accessed December 1, 2012); M. Luiselli, *Die Suche nach Gottesnähe: Untersuchungen zur persönlichen Frömmigkeit in Ägypten von der Ersten Zwischenzeit bis zum Ende des Neuen Reiches* (ÄAT 73; Wiesbaden: Harrassowitz, 2011).

64. T. DuQuesne, *Anubis, Upwawet, and Other Deities: Personal Worship and Official Religion in Ancient Egypt* (Cairo: Egyptian Museum, 2007); idem, *The Salakhana Trove: Votive Stelae and Other Objects from Asyut* (London: Darengo, 2009).

65. Lieven, "Divination"; J. Quaegebeur: "L'appel au divin: le bonheur des hommes mis dans la main des dieux," in *Oracles et prophéties dans l'antiquité: Actes du Colloque de Strasbourg, 15–17 juin 1995* (ed. J. G. Heintz; Travaux du Centre de Recherche sur le Proche Orient et la Grèce antiques 15; Strasbourg: De Boccard, 1997), 15–34; J. F. Quack, "A Black Cat from the Right, and a Scarab on Your Head: New Sources for Ancient Egyptian Divination," in *Through a Glass Darkly: Magic, Dreams & Prophecy in Ancient Egypt* (ed. K. Szpakowska; Swansea: Classical Press of Wales, 2006), 175–87; idem, "Präzision in der Prognose, oder: Divination als Wissenschaft," in *Writings of Early Scholars in the Ancient Near East, Egypt, Rome, and Greece* (ed. A. Imhausen and T. Pommerening; BzA 286; Berlin: de Gruyter, 2010), 69–91. For a selection of relevant texts, see idem, "Demotische magische und divinatorische Texte," in *Texte aus der Umwelt des Alten Testaments, Neue Folge Band 4: Omina, Orakel, Rituale und Beschwörungen* (ed. B. Janowski and G. Wilhelm; Gütersloh: Gütersloher Verlagshaus Mohn, 2008), 331–85.

oracular pronouncements are features of a theology of will that only established itself in the New Kingdom.[66]

It is anything but certain if this is true. A divergent view on the scarcity of evidence for earlier periods holds that this is by no means proof of absence of divination but that both evidence has not been preserved, and decorum did not allow for the display of divination in the preserved sources.[67] Even so, evidence from periods earlier than previously attested has emerged in the last years for lecanomancy and necromancy.[68] The field has also benefitted from increased scholarly interest and scrutiny, in particular regarding dream interpretation.[69] The scholarly reassessment of the importance of divination in Egypt is a direct consequence of the fact that more evidence has come forth, and the existence of evidence is owed to the fact that we are dealing with technical divination. Divination techniques required physical equipment (such as bowls, lamps, or oracular questions) and interpretive devices (such as hemerologies, dream manuals) that form the evidentiary basis for our current knowledge. These factors need to be accounted for when it comes to prophecy. The more covert nature of divine communication that we would expect there—as intuitive or natural diviners, prophets did not make use of technical devices—removes indirect indicators of the existence of prophecy. Prophecy does not lend itself to leaving evidence unless there is the need for and the possibility

66. J. Assmann, *The Mind of Egypt: History and Meaning in the Time of the Pharaohs* (Cambridge: Harvard University Press, 2003), 301.

67. Lieven, "Divination," 116–17; J. Baines, "Society, Morality, and Personal Practice," in *Religion in Ancient Egypt: Gods, Myths, and Personal Practice* (ed. B. E. Shafer; Ithaca: Cornell University Press, 1991), 149.

68. S. Demichelis, "La divination par l'huile à l'époque ramesside," in *La magie en Égypte: à la recherche d'une définition: Actes du colloque organisé par le musée du Louvre les 29 et 30 septembre 2000* (ed. Y. Koenig; Paris: Documentation française, 2002), 149–65; R. K. Ritner, "Des preuves de l'existence d'une nécromancie dans l'Égypte ancienne," in *La magie en Égypte: à la recherche d'une définition: Actes du colloque organisé par le musée du Louvre les 29 et 30 septembre 2000* (ed. Y. Koenig; Paris: Documentation française, 2002), 285–304; idem, "Necromancy in Ancient Egypt," in *Magic and Divination in the Ancient World* (ed. L. Ciraolo and J. Seidel; Ancient Magic and Divination 2; Leiden: Brill, 2002), 89–96.

69. Szpakowska, *Behind Closed Eyes*; E. Bresciani, *La porta dei sogni: Interpreti e sognatori nell'Egitto antico* (Turin: Einaudi, 2005); idem, *L'Égypte du rêve: rêves, rêveurs et interprètes au temps des pharaons* (Paris: Payot & Rivages, 2006); S. Noegel and K. Szpakowska, "'Word Play' in the Ramesside Dream Manual," in *SAK* 35 (2006) 193–212; *Through a Glass Darkly: Magic, Dreams & Prophecy in Ancient Egypt* (ed. K. Szpakowska; Swansea: Classical Press of Wales, 2006); S. Noegel, *Nocturnal Ciphers: The Allusive Language of Dreams in the Ancient Near East* (AOS, 89; New Haven: American Oriental Society, 2007); J. F. Quack, "Aus zwei spätzeitlichen Traumbüchern (Pap. Berlin P. 29009 und 23058)," in *Honi soit qui mal y pense: Studien zum pharaonischen, griechisch-römischen und spätantiken Ägypten zu Ehren von Heinz-Josef Thissen* (ed. H. Knuf, C. Leitz, and D. von Recklinghausen; OLA 194; Leuven: Peeters, 2010), 99–110; idem, "Remarks on Egyptian Rituals of Dream-Sending," in *Ancient Egyptian Demonology: Studies on the Boundaries between the Divine and the Demonic in Egyptian Magic* (ed. P. Kousoulis; OLA 172; Leuven: Peeters, 2011), 129–50.

of reporting, collecting, or writing down prophetic words and activities. An example is the case of Hor discussed above; he has left us notes about his prophecies,
whereas the more elaborate final version on papyrus (as submitted to Ptolemy
VI, VIII, and Cleopatra II) has not been preserved or found. And even his notes
are an unparalleled source. With specific reference to the fragmentary situation of
prophetic evidence from Mesopotamis, Eckard Frahm has emphasized that this is
due to the primarily oral character of prophetic communication.[70]

Not only is the prophetic word elusive, the prophets' techniques of interacting
with the divine have few chances of manifesting themselves in a direct way. Fran-
çoise Dunand and Christiane Zivie-Coche have remarked, "Contemplation, meditation, ecstasy, mystical experience: these are terms that scarcely appear in studies
on Egyptian religion, which is usually qualified as ritualistic and formalistic. But
by their very nature, these are experiences that are difficult to convey in discourse,
for they have no outward, tangible manifestations."[71] At the same time, Philippe
Derchain has reminded us that there has also been a modern scholarly bias toward
phenomena such as ecstasy, trance, or exorcism—"les oubliés de l'Egyptologie."[72]
Sabine Neureiter had little earlier pointed to the same bias with particular regard
to shamanism.[73] A fierce debate has been waged over the famous scenes nine and
ten of the ritual for manufacturing statues (a part of the ritual of Opening the
Mouth) and whether the main ritualist, the Sem priest, is here in a state of actual
trance or just experiencing a vision.[74] It can no longer be ruled out that such practices were common but that they are barely documented in our sources.

A last possible strategy in the search for Egyptian prophecy would be not
to find prophetic sayings, or attestations of prophetic practices, but to scrutinize
the attested religious professions and their professional portfolios. As I outlined
earlier, there is a natural affinity between prophecy and other divinatory practices that were carried out by professional religious personnel. Hor was a temple
employee who developed his prophetic abilities as a corollary to his professional

---

70. Frahm, "Prophetie," 11; cf. also Nissinen, *Prophets and Prophecy*, 4–5: "The relatively
small number of documents and their haphazard state of preservation for posterity indicate that
writing was only exceptionally part of the prophetic process of communication, and that when it
was, the written document was not necessarily filed in the archives, at any rate not for long-term
preservation."

71. F. Dunand and C. Zivie-Coche, *Gods and Men in Egypt: 3000 BCE to 395 CE* (Ithaca,
NY: Cornell University Press, 2004), 143; E. F. Wente, "Mysticism in Ancient Egypt?" in *JNES* 41
(1982) 161–79.

72. P. J. Derchain, "Possession, Transe et Exorcisme: Les Oubliés de l'Egyptologie," in *Göttinger Miszellen* 219 (2008) 9–18.

73. S. Neureiter, "Schamanismus im Alten Ägypten," in *SAK* 33 (2005) 283 and 284–85.

74. Ibid., against H. W. Fischer-Elfert, *Die Vision von der Statue im Stein. Studien zum altägyptischen Mundöffnungsritual: Mit einem zoologischen Beitrag von F. Hoffmann* (Schriften der
Philosophisch-Historischen Klasse der Heidelberger Akademie der Wissenschaften 5; Heidelberg: Winter, 1998).

activities. Ancient Near Eastern and biblical prophets could be employees of the state. The Egyptian Sem priest mentioned in the previous paragraph has more directly been linked to practices that might be relevant to the question of prophecy. Unfortunately, we often have no clear information on the precise duties of most religious office-holders; it is only the Demotic "Book of the Temple" that preserves descriptions of the professional responsibilities of temple personnel.[75] Even so, we do not normally know how specific duties were carried out. Some areas of interaction with the divine—such as the initiation of priests into the "mysteries" of individual gods—have only recently received more attention.[76] But as the case of Hor shows, individuals may well have kept their official religious responsibilities and their private revelations apart.[77] Yet another factor affecting preservation is the fulfillment of the prophecies: the Hebrew Bible hints at the writing down and dissemination, or else the disposal, of prophetic sayings, depending on whether the course of history revealed prophets to be true or false prophets.[78] Hor was eager to emphasize, when the written version of his prophecies was finally delivered to the pharaohs at Alexandria, that they had been received before the fact and reported to the governor, and that by this token he was a credible prophet.[79]

In this respect, it needs to be emphasized that the modern perusal of the terms "prophecy" and "prophet" veils a more complex ancient situation. The Old Babylonian, Hebrew, and Neo-Assyrian documents not only attest different designations for individuals that are all today categorized as "prophets." Modern scholars

---

75. J. F. Quack, "Das Buch vom Tempel und verwandte Texte: Ein Vorbericht," in *Archiv für Religionsgeschichte* 2 (2000) 10–17; idem, "Die Dienstanweisung des Oberlehrers aus dem Buch vom Tempel," in *5. Ägyptologische Tempeltagung: Würzburg, 23.–26. September 1999* (ed. H. Beinlich; ÄAT 33; Wiesbaden: Harrassowitz 2002), 159–71; idem, "Le manuel du temple: Une nouvelle source sur la vie des prêtres égyptiens," in *Egypte: Afrique & Orient* 29 (2003) 15–17; idem, "Organiser le culte idéal: Le manuel du temple," *Bulletin de la Société Française d'Égyptologie* 160 (2004) 20–24.

76. E. Hornung, "Altägyptische Wurzeln der Isismysterien," in *Études isiaques: Hommages à Jean Leclant* (ed. C. Berger, G. Clerc, and N. Grimal; 4 vols.; Bibliothèque d'étude 106; Cairo: IFAO, 1994), 3:287–93; T. du Quesne, "Anubis Master of Secrets (*ḥry-sštȝ*) and the Egyptian Conception of Mysteries," *Discussions in Egyptology* 36 (1996) 25–38, reprinted in *Schleier und Schwelle: Archäologie der literarischen Kommunikation 5, Band 2: Geheimnis und Offenbarung* (ed. J. Assmann and A. Assmann; Munich: Fink, 1998), 105–21; *Ägyptische Mysterien?* (ed. Jan Assmann and Martin Bommas; Munich: Beck, 2002); J. Assmann, *Ägyptische Geheimnisse*, 203–20; idem, *Les Mystères de l'Égypte: L'Égypte ancienne, entre mémoire et science: Cinq conférences données par Jan Assmann à Paris, Auditorium du Musée du Louvre, les 4, 7, 11, 14 et 18 mai 2009* (Paris: Hayan, 2009), 83–144.

77. D. Frankfurter notes that private revelations became more important for priests in Hellenistic Egypt. See "Ritual Expertise in Roman Egypt and the Problem of the Category 'Magician'," in *Envisioning Magic: A Princeton Seminar & Symposium* (ed. P. Schäfer and H. G. Kippenberg; Leiden: Brill, 1997), 122.

78. H. D. Preuß, *Old Testament Theology* (2 vols.; Louisville: Westminster John Knox, 1996), 2:83–86.

79. Hoffmann, *Ägypten*, 189.

have also extended the term "prophet" to cover individuals that did not receive any such title in contemporary texts. Compare here Stökl's statement:

> I distinguish between people who are given a professional prophetic title and those who happen to prophesy. In recent studies on Hebrew prophecy, the existence of so-called "lay-prophecy" has been questioned. However, the texts show evidence of prophets, such as Amos, who may well not have been perceived by their contemporaries as prophets in the professional sense, but who prophesied. It is for those people that I will use the term "lay-prophet."[80]

Given that the evidence from ancient Israel and the ancient Near East is itself fragmentary, it is evident that the modern term is a simplification of the state of affairs. There were different types of intuitive diviners (examples, from ancient Israel, include: court prophets, temple prophets, wandering prophets, etc.) just as there were different kinds of technical diviners, and there was prophecy as a practice rather than a formalized profession.[81] Additional evidence and further study of the field of divination in Ancient Egypt will have to determine if prophecy in the form of texts, practices, and religious functions can be ascertained, or if the lack of evidence can indeed be explained by a phenomenological lacuna.

5. Outlook

The observations made in the previous paragraphs have tried to stake out the feasibility of prophecy as a religious phenomenon. While a lacuna in the religious system of Ancient Egypt—the nonexistence of prophecy—cannot be ruled out, serious consideration needs to be given to the possibility that prophecy existed but is not at present documented before the Hellenistic age. The religious system does not preclude the possibility that prophecy existed as a mode of communication in which the prophet received revelations (for example, in dreams) and then conveyed them to a third party. The increasingly rich evidence on all types of divination from pre-Hellenistic Egypt does not permit the conclusion that examples such as the prophecies of Hor or the potter are Hellenistic innovations. There is no reason to believe that the societal or political context for prophecies was more propitious in Hellenistic than in pre-Hellenistic Egypt. What could have been those contexts? Traditional Egyptian state ideology maintained a clear distinction between the righteous king, who was the guarantor of *Maat*, and the lawless and chaotic forces opposing the divinely legitimized rule—the "enemies" outside Egypt and the "rebels" within.[82] "Political" literature in the widest sense supported

---

80. Stökl, *Prophecy*, 156.

81. See chapter 1 of Stökl, *Prophecy* (pp. 1–26).

82. Müller-Wollermann, *Vergehen und Strafen*, 51–69; J. F. Quack, "Demagogen, Aufrührer und Rebellen: Zum Spektrum politischer Feinde in Lebenslehren des Mittleren Reiches," in *Feinde und Aufrührer: Konzepte von Gegnerschaft in ägyptischen Texten besonders des Mittleren*

and legitimized that ideology, as did the apparatus of state and religious officials.[83] A prophecy of salvation could have contributed to that system of political stability and could have, by the same token, opposed foreign rule.[84] It is more difficult to assess whether there was a setting for prophecies implying critique of the state. The preponderance of our sources that were issued by the state makes it difficult to evaluate the dimension of opposition and critique within Egypt. Civil wars in Egypt, rival dynasties, tensions between state administration and the military, and competing religious centers certainly created significant cause for dissent. Whereas high treason aiming at the removal of the king was punished by death, a stela of the Third Intermediate Period attests to the banishment of political opponents ("arguing subjects") to the great oasis (Dakhla and Kharga).[85] Early historiography as a form of assessment of past and present political achievements, which inevitably implies assessment, criticism, and dissent, seems to have emerged in Mesopotamia and Egypt not in the state sector but in the priesthood and the military as state-related but discrete institutions.[86] This means that a search for prophets in Egypt who would be either "Enemies and Friends of the State" (to evoke the title of this volume) will also have to reflect on the societal and political contexts of religion and how those contexts nurtured religious practice as a response to the present.

Reiches (ed. H. Felber; Abhandlungen der Sächsischen Akademie der Wissenschaften zu Leipzig. Philologisch-historische Klasse 78/5; Leipzig: Sächsische Akademie der Wissenschaften, 2005), 74–85.

83. For example, see the various contributions to *Literatur und Politik im pharaonischen und ptolemäischen Ägypten* (n. 4); T. Schneider, "Mythos und Zeitgeschichte in der 30. Dynastie: Eine politische Lektüre des *Mythos von den Götterkönigen*," *Ein ägyptisches Glasperlenspiel: Ägyptologische Beiträge für Erik Hornung aus seinem Schülerkreis* (ed. A. Brodbeck; Berlin, 1998), 207–45; H. Felber, "Die Demotische Chronik," *Apokalyptik und Ägypten: Eine kritische Analyse der relevanten Texte aus dem griechisch-römischen Ägypten* (ed. B. U. Schipper and A. Blasius; OLA 107; Leuven: Peeters, 2002); W. Wettengel, *Die Erzählung von den beiden Brüdern: Der Papyrus d'Orbiney und die Königsideologie der Ramessiden* (OBO 195; Fribourg: Universitätsverlag / Göttingen: Vandenhoeck & Ruprecht, 2003); T. Schneider, "Innovation in Literature on Behalf of Politics: The Tale of the Two Brothers, Ugarit, and 19th dynasty history," *Egypt & the Levant* 18 (2008) 315–26.

84. An important topic of Greco-Roman messianic texts is dealt with in B. U. Schipper and A. Blasius, eds., *Apokalyptik und Ägypten*. For the Persian period, compare also G. Burkard, *Das Klagelied des Papyrus Berlin P. 23040 a–c: ein Dokument des priesterlichen Widerstandes gegen Fremdherrschaft* (Wiesbaden: Harrassowitz, 2003).

85. Müller-Wollermann, *Vergehen und Strafen*, 63–218; S. Lippert, *Einführung in die altägyptische Rechtsgeschichte* (Münster: LIT, 2008), 68–69.

86. T. Schneider, "A Reassessment of the Use of the Past and the Place of Historiography in Ancient Egyptian Thought," in *Thinking, Recording, and Writing History in the Ancient World* (ed. K. Raaflaub; The Ancient World: Comparative Histories; Malden, MA: Wiley-Blackwell, 2014), 117–43.

Bibliography

Assmann, J. Ägyptische Hymnen und Gebete. OBO Sonderband. Fribourg: Universitätsverlag / Göttingen: Vandenhoeck & Ruprecht, 1999.

_____. In Search for God in Ancient Egypt. Ithaca, NY: Cornell University Press, 2001.

_____. The Mind of Egypt. History and Meaning in the Time of the Pharaohs. Cam-
bridge: Harvard University Press, 2003.

_____. Ägyptische Geheimnisse. Munich: Wilhelm Fink, 2004.

_____. Death and Salvation in Ancient Egypt. Ithaca, NY: Cornell University Press,
2005.

_____. "Les Mystères égyptiens Initiation, rituel et souvenir dans La Flûte Enchantée
de Mozart." Pp. 83–144 in Les Mystères de l'Égypte: L'Égypte ancienne, entre mémoire
et science. Cinq conférences données par Jan Assmann à Paris, Auditorium du Musée
du Louvre, les 4, 7, 11, 14 et 18 mai 2009. Paris: Hayan, 2009.

_____. The Price of Monotheism. Trans. by R. Savage. Stanford: Stanford University
Press, 2010.

Assmann, J., and M. Bommas, eds. Ägyptische Mysterien? Munich: Beck, 2002.

Baines, J. "Society, Morality, and Personal Practice." Pp. 123–99 in Religion in Ancient
Egypt: Gods, Myths, and Personal Practice. Ed. B. E. Shafer. Ithaca: Cornell University
Press, 1991.

_____. Visual & Written Culture in Ancient Egypt. Oxford: Oxford University Press,
2007.

Boylan, P. Thoth, the Hermes of Egypt: A Study of Some Aspects of Theological Thought in
Ancient Egypt. Oxford: Oxford University Press, 1922.

Bresciani, E. "'Il pleut sur la pierre': Prophéties politiques dans la littérature démotique."
Pp. 279–84 in Literatur und Politik im pharaonischen und ptolemäischen Ägypten.
Vorträge der Tagung zum Gedenken an Georges Posener; 5.–10. September 1996 in
Leipzig. Bibliothèque d'étude 127. Cairo: IFAO, 1996.

_____. La porta dei sogni: Interpreti e sognatori nell'Egitto antico. Turin: Giulio Ein-
audi, 2005.

_____. L'Égypte du rêve: rêves, rêveurs et interprètes au temps des pharaons. Paris: Payot
& Rivages, 2006.

Breyer, F. Tanutamani: Die Traumstele und ihr Umfeld. ÄAT 57. Wiesbaden: Harrassowitz,
2003.

Burkard, G. Das Klagelied des Papyrus Berlin P. 23040 a–c: ein Dokument des priesterlichen
Widerstandes gegen Fremdherrschaft. Wiesbaden: Harrassowitz, 2003.

Burkard, G. and H.-J. Thissen. Einführung in die altägyptische Literaturgeschichte I: Altes
und Mittleres Reich. Einführungen und Quellentexte zur Ägyptologie 1. Münster:
LIT, 2003.

Darnell, J. C. "A Midsummer Night's Succubus: The Herdsman's Encounters in P. Berlin
3024, the Pleasures of Fishing and Fowling, the Songs of the Drinking Place, and the
Ancient Egyptian Love Poetry." Pp. 99–140 in Opening the Tablet Box: Near Eastern
Studies in Honor of Benjamin R. Foster. Ed. S. C. Melville and A. L. Slotsky. CHANE
42. Leiden: Brill, 2010.

Demichelis, S. "La divination par l'huile à l'époque ramesside." Pp. 149–65 in La magie
en Égypte: à la recherche d'une définition: Actes du colloque organisé par le musée du

Louvre les 29 et 30 septembre 2000. Ed. Y. Koenig. Paris: Documentation française, 2002.

Derchain, P. J. "Possession, Transe et Exorcisme: Les Oubliés de l'Egyptologie." *Göttinger Miszellen* 219 (2008) 9–18.

Dillery, J. "The First Egyptian Narrative History: Manetho and Greek Historiography." *ZPE* 127 (1999) 93–116.

Dousa, T. M. "Imagining Isis: On Some Continuities and Discontinuities in the Image of Isis in Greek Isis Hymns and Demotic Texts." Pp. 149–84 in *Acts of the Seventh International Conference of Demotic Studies, Copenhagen, 23–27 August 1999.* Ed. K. Ryholt. Carsten Niebuhr Institute Publications 27. Copenhagen: Museum Tusculanum Press, 2002.

Dunand, F., and C. Zivie-Coche. *Gods and Men in Egypt: 3000 BCE to 395 CE.* Ithaca, NY: Cornell University Press, 2004.

Esch, A. "Überlieferungs-Chance und Überlieferungs-Zufall als methodisches Problem des Historikers." *Historische Zeitschrift* 240 (1985) 529–70.

_____. *Zeitalter und Menschenalter: Der Historiker und die Erfahrung vergangener Zeiten.* Munich: Beck, 1994.

Fischer-Elfert, H.-W. *Die Vision von der Statue im Stein. Studien zum altägyptischen Mundöffnungsritual: Mit einem zoologischen Beitrag von F. Hoffmann.* Schriften der Philosophisch-Historischen Klasse der Heidelberger Akademie der Wissenschaften, 5. Heidelberg: Winter, 1998.

Frahm, E. "Prophetie." *RlA* 11 (2006–2008) 7–11.

Frankfurter, D. "Ritual Expertise in Roman Egypt and the Problem of the Category 'Magician.'" Pp. 115–36 in *Envisioning Magic: A Princeton Seminar & Symposium.* Ed. P. Schäfer and H. G. Kippenberg. Leiden: Brill, 1997.

Gee, J. "Egyptologists' Fallacies: Fallacies Arising from Limited Evidence." *Journal of Egyptian History* 3 (2010) 137–58.

Gestoso, G. N., M. C. Bargués Criado, and M. J. Feldman. *La estela de Gebel Barkal de Tuthmosis III.* Buenos Aires: Programa de Estudios de Egiptología, Consejo Nacional de Investigaciones Científicas y Técnicas, 1996.

Gnirs, A. M. "Das Motiv des Bürgerkriegs in Merikare und Neferti—Zur Literatur der 18. Dynastie." Pp. 207–65 in *jn.t d̠r.w: Festschrift für Friedrich Junge.* Ed. G. Moers, et al. Göttingen: Seminar für Ägyptologie und Koptologie, 2006.

Goff, J. *Prophetie und Politik in Israel und im alten Ägypten.* Beiträge zur Ägyptologie 7. Veröffentlichungen der Institute für Afrikanistik und Ägyptologie der Universität Wien 41: Vienna: AFRO-PUB, 1986.

Gundlach, R. "'Ich sage etwas, was noch geschehen wird.' Propheten im Staat der Pharaonen." Pp. 11–25 in *Zur Erschließung von Zukunft in den Religionen: Zukunftshoffnung und Gegenwartsbewältigung in der Religionsgeschichte.* Ed. H. Wißmann. Würzburg: Königshausen & Neumann, 1991.

Hawary, A. E. *Wortschöpfung: Die Memphitische Theologie und die Siegesstele des Pije: zwei Zeugen kultureller Repräsentation in der 25. Dynastie.* OBO 243. Fribourg: Academic Press / Göttingen: Vandenhoeck & Ruprecht, 2010.

Hays, Harold M. "The Historicity of Papyrus Westcar." *Zeitschrift für ägyptische Sprache und Altertumskunde* 129 (2002) 20–30.

Hilber, J. W. "Prophetic Speech in the Egyptian Royal Cult." Pp. 47–53 in *On Stone and Scroll: Essays in Honour of Graham Ivor Davies*. Ed. J. K. Aitken, K. J. Dell, and B. A. Mastin. Berlin: de Gruyter, 2011.

_____. "The Culture of Prophecy and Writing in the Ancient Near East." Pp. 219–42 in *Do Historical Matters Matter to Faith? A Critical Appraisal of Modern and Postmodern Approaches to Scripture*. Ed. J. K. Hoffmeier and D. R. Magary. Wheaton, IL: Crossway, 2012.

Hoffmann, F. *Ägypten. Kultur und Lebenswelt in griechisch-römischer Zeit: Eine Darstellung nach den demotischen Quellen*. Berlin: Akademie Verlag. 2000.

Hornung, E. "Altägyptische Wurzeln der Isismysterien." Pp. 287–93 in *Études isiaques: Hommages à Jean Leclant*, vol. 3. Ed. C. Berger, G. Clerc, and N. Grimal. Bibliothèque d'étude 106. Cairo: IFAO, 1994.

Huß, W. *Der makedonische König und die ägyptischen Priester: Studien zur Geschichte des ptolemaiischen Ägypten*. Historia Einzelschriften 85. Stuttgart: Franz Steiner, 1994.

Jansen-Winkeln, K. "Die Rolle des Unbekannten in der ägyptischen Geschichte." Pp. 155–61 in *Das Ereignis: Geschichtsschreibung zwischen Vorfall und Befund*. Ed. M. Fitzenreiter. London: IBAES, 2009.

Jenni, Hanna. "Der Papyrus Westcar." *Studien zur altägyptischen Kultur* 25 (1998) 113–41.

Junker, H. *Das Götterdekret über das Abaton: Denkschriften der Österreichischen Akademie der Wissenschaften*. Philosophisch-Historische Klasse, 56. Vienna: Hölder, 1913.

Kendall, T. "Napatan Temples: A Case Study from Gebel Barkal." *The Mythological Origin of Egyptian Kingship and the Formation of the Napatan State*" (http://wysinger .homestead.com/kendall.doc)

_____. "The Monument of Taharqa on Gebel Barkal." Pp. 1–45 in *Neueste Feldforschungen im Sudan und in Eritrea: Akten des Symposiums vom 13. bis 14. Oktober 1999 in Berlin*. Meroitica 21. Wiesbaden: Harrassowitz, 2004.

Klug, A. "Machtübertragung und Herrschaft: Zur göttlichen Legitimation Amenophis' III." Pp. 221–75 in *Das ägyptische Königtum im Spannungsfeld zwischen Innen–und Außenpolitik im 2. Jahrtausend v. Chr.* Ed. R. Gundlach and A. Klug. Königtum, Staat und Gesellschaft Fruher Hochkulturen, vol. 1. Wiesbaden: Harrassowitz, 2004.

Kockelmann, H. *Praising the Goddess: A Comparative and Annotated Re-Edition of Six Demotic Hymns and Praises Addressed to Isis*. Archiv für Papyrusforschung Beiheft 15. Berlin: de Gruyter, 2008.

_____. "L'abaton: Tombe et lieu de culte d'Osiris sur la première cataracte." *L'Égypte, Afrique & Orient* 60 (2010–2011) 31–44.

Koenen, L. "Die Apologie des Töpfers an König Amenophis oder das Töpferorakel." Pp. 139–87 in *Apokalyptik und Ägypten: Eine kritische Analyse der relevanten Texte aus dem griechisch-römischen Ägypten*. Ed. B. U. Schipper and A. Blasius. OLA 107. Leuven: Peeters, 2002.

Krüger, T. *Geschichtskonzepte im Ezechielbuch*. BZAW 180. Berlin: de Gruyter, 1989.

Lanczkowski, G. *Altägyptischer Prophetismus*. Ägyptologische Abhandlungen 4. Wiesbaden: Harrassowitz, 1960.

Legras, B. "Les experts égyptiens à la cour des Ptolémées." *Revue historique* 624 (2002) 963–991.

Leitz, C. *Quellentexte zur ägyptischen Religion, Bd. I: Die Tempelinschriften der griechisch-römischen Zeit.* Einführungen und Quellentexte zur Ägyptologie. Bd 2.1; Münster: LIT, 2004.

Lepper, Verena M. *Untersuchungen zu pWestcar: Eine philologische und literaturwissenschaftliche (Neu-)Analyse.* Ägyptologische Abhandlungen 70. Wiesbaden: Harrassowitz, 2008.

Lieven, A. von. "Divination in Ägypten." *AoF* 26 (1999) 77–126.

Lippert, S. *Einführung in die altägyptische Rechtsgeschichte.* Münster: LIT, 2008.

Locher, J. *Topographie und Geschichte der Region am ersten Nilkatarakt in griechisch-römischer Zeit.* Archiv für Papyrusforschung, Beischrift 5. Stuttgart/Leipzig: Teubner, 1999.

Luiselli, M. "Personal Piety." *UCLA Encyclopedia of Egyptology.* Ed. J. Dieleman and W. Wendrich. Los Angeles, CA, 2008. http://digital2.library.ucla.edu/viewItem.do?ark=21198/zz000s3mss;

————. *Die Suche nach Gottesnähe: Untersuchungen zur persönlichen Frömmigkeit in Ägypten von der Ersten Zwischenzeit bis zum Ende des Neuen Reiches.* ÄAT 73. Wiesbaden: Harrassowitz, 2011.

MacDowell, A. G. *Jurisdiction in the Workmen's Community of Deir el-Medîna.* Leiden: Nederlands Instituut voor het Nabije Oosten, 1990.

Manassa, C. "Isis, Mistress of the Field: A New Reading of an Epithet in the Hor Ostraca." *Enchoria* 32 (2010–11) 54–61.

Meeks, D. *Mythes et légendes du Delta d'après le papyrus Brooklyn 47.218.84.* Cairo: Institut français d'archéologie orientale, 2006.

Mittag, P. F. *Antiochos IV. Epiphanes: Eine politische Biographie.* Berlin: Akademie-Verlag, 2006.

Müller-Wollermann, R. *Vergehen und Strafen: Zur Sanktionierung abweichenden Verhaltens im alten Ägypten.* Probleme der Ägyptologie 21. Leiden: Brill, 2004.

Naether, F. *Die Sortes Astrampsychi: Problemlösungsstrategien durch Orakel im römischen Ägypten.* Orientalische Religionen in der Antike 3. Tübingen: Mohr Siebeck, 2010.

Neureiter, S. "Schamanismus im Alten Ägypten." *SAK* 33 (2005) 281–330.

Nissinen, Martti. "What Is Prophecy? An Ancient Near Eastern Perspective." Pp. in 17–37 in *Inspired Speech: Prophecy in the Ancient Near East: Essays in Honor of Herbert B. Huffmon.* Edited by J. Kaltner and L. Stulman. London: T. & T. Clark, 2004.

————. "Prophecy and Omen Divination: Two Sides of the Same Coin." Pp. 341–51 in *Divination and Interpretation of Signs in the Ancient World.* Edited by Amar Annus. Oriental Institute Seminars 6. Chicago: Oriental Institute, 2010.

————. *Prophets and Prophecy in the Ancient Near East.* Writings from the Ancient World. Atlanta: Society of Biblical Literature, 2003.

Noegel, S. *Nocturnal Ciphers: The Allusive Language of Dreams in the Ancient Near East.* American Oriental Series 89. New Haven, CT: American Oriental Society, 2007.

————, and K. Szpakowska. "'Word Play' in the Ramesside Dream Manual." *SAK* 35 (2006) 193–212.

O'Connor, D., and D. P. Silverman, eds. *Ancient Egyptian Kingship.* Probleme der Ägyptologie 9. Leiden: Brill, 1994.

Pinch, G. *Egyptian Mythology: A Guide to the Gods, Goddesses, and Traditions of Ancient Egypt.* Oxford: Oxford University Press, 2004.

Preuß, H. D. *Old Testament Theology.* Louisville, KY: Westminster John Knox, 1996.

Quack, J. F. "Das Buch vom Tempel und verwandte Texte. Ein Vorbericht." *Archiv für Religionsgeschichte* 2 (2000) 1–20.

_____. "Die Dienstanweisung des Oberlehrers aus dem Buch vom Tempel." Pp. 159–71 in *5. Ägyptologische Tempeltagung: Würzburg, 23.–26. September 1999.* Ed. H. Beinlich. ÄAT 33. Wiesbaden: Harrassowitz, 2002.

_____. "Zu einer angeblich apokalyptischen Passage in den Ostraka des Hor." Pp. 243–52 in *Apokalyptik und Ägypten. Eine kritische Analyse der relevanten Texte aus dem griechisch-römischen Ägypten.* Eds. B. U. Schipper and A. Blasius. OLA 107. Leuven: Peeters, 2002.

_____. "Le manuel du temple: Une nouvelle source sur la vie des prêtres égyptiens." *Egypte: Afrique & Orient* 29 (2003) 11–18.

_____. "Organiser le culte idéal: Le Manuel du temple." *Bulletin de la Société Française d'Égyptologie* 160 (2004) 9–25.

_____. "Perspektiven zur Theologie im alten Ägypten: Antwort auf Jan Assmann." Pp. 63–74 in *Theologie in Israel und in den Nachbarkulturen.* Ed. M. Oeming, K. Schmid, and A. Schüle. Münster: LIT, 2004.

_____. *Einführung in die altägyptische Literaturgeschichte III: Die demotische und gräko-ägyptische Literatur.* Einführungen und Quellentexte zur Ägyptologie 3. Münster: Lit, 2005.

_____. Review of Meeks, *Mythes et legends.* Or 77 (2008) 106–11.

_____. "A Black Cat from the Right, and a Scarab on Your Head: New Sources for Ancient Egyptian Divination." Pp. 175–87 in *Through a Glass Darkly: Magic, Dreams & Prophecy in Ancient Egypt.* Ed. K. Szpakowska. Swansea: Classical Press of Wales, 2006.

_____. "Demotische magische und divinatorische Texte." Pp. 331–85 in *Texte aus der Umwelt des Alten Testaments: Neue Folge. Band 4: Omina, Orakel, Rituale und Beschwörungen.* Ed. B. Janowski and G. Wilhelm. Gütersloh: Gütersloher Verlagshaus Mohn, 2008.

_____. "Political Rituals: Sense and Nonsense of a Term and its Application to Ancient Egypt." Pp. 215–30 in *Ritual Dynamics and the Science of Ritual, Volume III: State, Power, and Violence.* Ed. A. Michaels. Wiesbaden, 2010.

_____. "Präzision in der Prognose, oder: Divination als Wissenschaft." Pp. 69–91 in *Writings of Early Scholars in the Ancient Near East, Egypt, Rome, and Greece.* Ed. A. Imhausen and T. Pommerening. BzA 286. Berlin: de Gruyter, 2010.

_____. "Aus zwei spätzeitlichen Traumbüchern (Pap. Berlin P. 29009 und 23058)." Pp. 99–110 in *Honi soit qui mal y pense: Studien zum pharaonischen, griechisch-römischen und spätantiken Ägypten zu Ehren von Heinz-Josef Thissen.* Ed. H. Knuf, C. Leitz, and D. von Recklinghausen. OLA 194. Leuven: Peeters, 2010.

_____. "Remarks on Egyptian Rituals of Dream-Sending." Pp. 129–50 in *Ancient Egyptian Demonology: Studies on the Boundaries between the Divine and the Demonic in Egyptian Magic.* Ed. P. Kousoulis. OLA 172. Leuven: Peeters, 2011.

_____. "Pharao und Hofstaat, Palast und Tempel: Entscheidungsfindung, Öffentlichkeit und Entscheidungsveröffentlichung im Alten Ägypten." Pp. 277–95 in *Politische Kommunikation und öffentliche Meinung in der antiken Welt*. Ed. C. Kuhn. Stuttgart: Franz Steiner, 2012.

Quaegebeur, J. "L'appel au divin: le bonheur des hommes mis dans la main des dieux." Pp. 15–34 in *Oracles et prophéties dans l'antiquité: Actes du Colloque de Strasbourg; 15–17 juin 1995*. Ed. J. G. Heintz. Travaux du Centre de Recherche sur le Proche Orient et la Grèce antiques 15. Strasbourg: De Boccard, 1997.

Quesne, T. du. "Anubis Master of Secrets (ḥry-sšt3) and the Egyptian Conception of Mysteries." *Discussions in Egyptology* 36 (1996) 25–38. Reprinted, pp. 105–21 in *Schleier und Schwelle: Archäologie der literarischen Kommunikation, 5. Band 2: Geheimnis und Offenbarung*. Ed. J. Assmann and A. Assmann. Munich: Fink, 1998.

_____. *Anubis, Upwawet, and Other Deities: Personal Worship and Official Religion in Ancient Egypt*. Cairo: The Egyptian Museum, 2007.

_____. *The Salakhana Trove: Votive Stelae and other Objects from Asyut*. London: Darengo, 2009.

Ray, J. D. *The Archive of Hor: Texts from Excavations Memoir 2*. London: Egypt Exploration Society, 1976.

Redford, D. B. "Scribe and Speaker." Pp. 145–218 in *Writings and Speech in Israelite and Ancient Near Eastern Prophecy*. Ed. E. Ben Zvi and M. H. Floyd. SBL Symposium Series 10. Atlanta, GA: SBL, 2000.

Ritner, R. K. "Des preuves de l'existence d'une nécromancie dans l'Égypte ancienne." Pp. 285–304 in *La magie en Égypte: à la recherche d'une définition. Actes du colloque organisé par le musée du Louvre les 29 et 30 septembre 2000*. Ed. Y. Koenig. Paris: Documentation française, 2002.

_____. "Necromancy in Ancient Egypt." Pp. 89–96 in *Magic and Divination in the Ancient World*. Ed. L. Ciraolo and J. Seidel. Ancient Magic and Divination 2. Leiden: Brill, 2002.

Schipper, B. U., and A. Blasius. *Apokalyptik und Ägypten: Eine kritische Analyse der relevanten Texte aus dem griechisch-römischen Ägypten*. OLA 107. Leuven: Peeters, 2002.

_____. "'Apokalyptik,' 'Messianismus,' 'Prophetie'—eine Begriffsbestimmung." Pp. 21–40 in *Apokalyptik und Ägypten: Eine kritische Analyse der relevanten Texte aus dem griechisch-römischen Ägypten*. Ed. B. U. Schipper and A. Blasius. OLA 107. Leuven: Peeters, 2002.

Sandri, S. *Har-pa-chered (Harpokrates). Die Genese eine ägyptischen Götterkindes*. OLA 151. Leuven: Peeters, 2006.

Schneider, T. *Ausländer in Ägypten während des Mittleren Reiches und der Hyksoszeit, Teil 1: Die ausländischen Könige*. Ägypten und Altes Testament 42. Wiesbaden: Harrassowitz, 1998.

_____. "Contextualizing the Tale of the Herdsman." Pp. 187–96 in *Egyptian Stories: A British Egyptological Tribute in Honour of Alan B. Lloyd on the Occasion of His Retirement*. Ed. T. Schneider and K. Szpakowska. AOAT 347. Münster: Ugarit Verlag, 2007.

_____. "History as Festival? A Reassessment of the Use of the Past and the Place of Historiography in Ancient Egyptian Thought." Pp. 117–43 in *Thinking, Recording, and Writing History in the Ancient World.* Ed. K. Raaflaub. The Ancient World: Comparative Histories. Malden, MA: Wiley-Blackwell, 2014.

_____. "A Theophany of Seth–Baal in the Tempest Stele." *Egypt & the Levant* 20 (2010) 405–9.

Seidel, M. *Die königlichen Statuengruppen. Band 1: Die Denkmäler vom Alten Reich bis zum Ende der 18. Dynastie.* HÄB 42. Hildesheim, 1996.

Shirun-Grumach, I. *Offenbarung, Orakel und Konigsnovelle.* ÄAT 24. Wiesbaden: Harrassowitz, 1993.

Shupak, N. "Egyptian 'Prophecy' and Biblical Prophecy: Did the Phenomenon of Prophecy, in the Biblical Sense, Exist in Ancient Egypt?" *JEOL* 31 (1989–90) 5–40.

_____. "The Egyptian 'Prophecy:' A Reconsideration." Pp. 133–44 in *"Von reichlich ägyptischem Verstande": Festschrift für Waltraud Guglielmi zum 65. Geburtstag.* Ed. K. Zibelius-Chen and H. W. Fischer-Elfert. Philippika. Marburger altertumskundliche Abhandlungen 11. Wiesbaden: Harrassowitz, 2006.

Stadler, M. A. *Weiser und Wesir: Studien zu Vorkommen, Rolle und Wesen des Gottes Thot im ägyptischen Totenbuch.* Orientalische Religionen in der Antike 1. Tübingen: Mohr Siebeck, 2009.

Stökl, J. *Prophecy in the Ancient Near East: A Philological and Sociological Comparison.* Culture and History of the Ancient Near East 56. Leiden: Brill, 2012.

Szpakowska, K. *Behind Closed Eyes: Dreams and Nightmares in Ancient Egypt.* Swansea: Classical Press of Wales, 2003.

_____, ed. *Through a Glass Darkly: Magic, Dreams & Prophecy in Ancient Egypt.* Swansea: Classical Press of Wales, 2006.

Thissen, H.-J. "Das Lamm des Bokchoris." Pp. 113–38 in *Apokalyptik und Ägypten: Eine kritische Analyse der relevanten Texte aus dem griechisch-römischen Ägypten.* Ed. B. U. Schipper and A. Blasius. OLA 107. Leuven: Peeters, 2002.

Török, L. *Between Two Worlds: The Frontier Region Between Ancient Nubia and Egypt, 3700 BC–500 AD.* Probleme der Ägyptologie 29. Leiden: Brill, 2009.

Traunecker, C. *The Gods of Egypt.* Ithaca, NY: Cornell University Press, 2001.

Wente, E. F. "Mysticism in Ancient Egypt?" *JNES* 41 (1982) 161–79.

Westermann, C. *Grundformen prophetischer Rede.* Beiträge zur Evangelischen Theologie 31. Munich: Kaiser, [5]1978.

Zeitlyn, D. "Professor Garfinkel Visits the Soothsayers: Ethnomethodology and Mambila Divination." *Man* N.S. 25/4 (1990) 654–66 (http://www.era.anthropology.ac.uk/Divination/Garf/index.html, http://lucy.ukc.ac.uk/era/divination/ garf/)

A Royal Advisory Service:
Prophecy and the State in Mesopotamia

Jonathan Stökl

Kings College, London

1. Introduction

Like the other studies in this book, this contribution sets out to study the re-lationship between prophets and the state. As its title suggests, it is concerned not with the biblical text but with the evidence for prophetic activity in Mesopotamia. When studying the relationship between prophets and the state in the ancient Near East, some clarity about terms and concepts is important. What do we mean by prophecy? What is its function, and how is it related to other forms of divina-tion? What is the nature of our sources? It is important to keep these questions in mind as we progress through the evidence.

With these aims in mind, I will provide a preliminary definition of prophecy as it is applicable to the ancient Near East.[1] Prophets transmitted divine messages to to their human addressees. There is good reason to assume that the same defi-nition also applies to historical Israel and Judah, but the nature of the available evidence—the Hebrew Bible—makes it difficult to verify this assertion. There is general agreement among scholars working on prophecy in the ancient Near East that it is best understood as a form of divination. As we will see below, the function of prophets in the ancient Near East was identical to that of other divin-ers—namely, to provide the king (and, potentially, other decision makers) with

---

1. See, for example, J. Stökl, "Ancient Near Eastern Prophecy," in *Dictionary of the Old Testament: Prophets* (ed. J. G. McConville and M. J. Boda; Downer Grove, IL: InterVarsity, 2012), 16–24; idem, *Prophecy in the Ancient Near East: A Philological and Sociological Comparison* (CHANE 56; Leiden: Brill, 2012), 7–11; M. Nissinen, "What is Prophecy? An Ancient Near Eastern Perspective," in *Inspired Speech: Prophecy in the Ancient Near East: Essays in Honour of Herbert B. Huffmon* (ed. J. Kaltner and L. Stulman; JSOTSup 378; London: T. & T. Clark, 2004), 17–37; idem, "Prophecy and Omen Divination: Two Sides of the Same Coin," in *Divination and Interpretation of Signs in the Ancient World* (ed. A. Annus; OIS 6; Chicago: The Oriental Institute, 2010), 341–51.

information in order to help them in their decision-making process. Unlike other advisers who provided intelligence gathered by ambassadors and intelligence officers, diviners provided information about the will of the gods.[2] Their position was comparable to that of specialist advisers to modern governments in areas such as science and economy. The ancient diviners based their predictions on the observation of natural phenomena, in the case of technical diviners, and their ability to receive messages from the divine, in the case of intuitive diviners.[3]

Having preliminarily defined the common function of technical and intuitive diviners, we can move on to the differences between them. The distinction between intuitive and technical divination can already be found in Plato's *Phaedrus*.[4] While Plato's terminology is, in my view, helpful, the distinction they are making does not hold up to scrutiny. As has been pointed out by Lester Grabbe, many cultures know of learnable skills that help an intuitive diviner reach an altered state of consciousness in which they can receive divine messages.[5] Thus, the distinction between technical diviners and intuitive diviners does not lie in the different ways in which they acquire divine messages; instead, it lies in their interpretation. A technical diviner's message requires a learnable skill: a haruspex needs to learn and consult reference works in their interpretation of the physical shape of the liver, which is considered to be the "tablet" on which the consulted deity wrote their message.[6] The technical diviner, thus, needed a skill to be able to read the divine message.

---

2. On the intelligence service in the Neo-Assyrian empire, see P. Dubovský, *Hezekiah and the Assyrian Spies: Reconstruction of the Neo-Assyrian Intelligence Services and its Significance for 2 Kings 18–19* (BibOr 49; Rome: Pontifical Biblical Institute, 2006). On the importance of access to secret information and state-craft, see A. Lenzi, *Secrecy and the Gods: Secret Knowledge in Ancient Mesopotamia and Biblical Israel* (SAAS 19; Helsinki: Neo-Assyrian Text Corpus Project, 2008) and, for divination and statecraft, B. Pongratz-Leisten, *Herrschaftswissen in Mesopotamien: Formen der Kommunikation zwischen Gott und König im 2. und 1. Jahrtausend v. Chr* (SAAS 10; Helsinki: The Neo-Assyrian Text Corpus Project, 1999).

3. Omen lists, however, are not based on observations only but, as A. Winitzer, *Early Mesopotamian Divination Literature: Its Organizational Frameworks and Generative and Paradigmatic Characteristics* (AMD 12; Leiden: Brill, 2017), demonstrates, are largely scholarly constructs already in the Old Babylonian period.

4. See Stökl, *Prophecy in the Ancient Near East*, 8–10.

5. See, for example, L. L. Grabbe, *Priests, Prophets, Diviners, Sages: A Socio-Historical Study of Religious Specialists in Ancient Israel* (Valley Forge, PA: Trinity Press International, 1995), 150–51; see also M. Nissinen, "Prophecy and Omen Divination: Two Sides of the Same Coin," in *Divination and Interpretation of Signs in the Ancient World* (ed. A. Annus; OIS 6; Chicago: The Oriental Institute of the University of Chicago, 2010), 341–51

6. On the practical aspects of technical divination, see, e.g., S. M. Maul, "Aleuromantie: Von der Altorientalischen Kunst, mit Hilfe von Opfermehl das Maß göttlichen Wohlwollens zu ermitteln," in *Von Göttern und Menschen: Beiträge zu Literatur und Geschichte des Alten Orients: Festschrift für Brigitte Groneberg* (ed. D. Shehata, F. Weiershäuser, and K. V. Zand; CM 41; Leiden: Brill, 2010), 115–30; idem, "Die Wissenschaft von der Zukunft: Überlegungen zur Bedeutung der Divination im Alten Orient," in *Babylon: Wissenskultur in Orient und Okzident* (ed. E. Cancik-

In contrast, intuitive diviners, such as prophets and dreamers, pronounced the divine messages, however they received them, in human language, without another intermediary to turn these messages into human language (this does not apply to the *meaning* of the message). This distinction can be most clearly seen in the case of dreams. There are three different kind of dreams: the first kind is a nonsignificant dream; the second kind is a significant dream that needed to be interpreted by a dream-interpreter who could consult dream-books containing the interpretive tradition; the third and final kind are "message" dreams, which contain a clear divine message that does not need to be decoded with the help of a dream-book.[7] The distinction between the first and second kind of dream would be made using technical divination. When someone came and reported their dream to an official, they could use the divinatory resources at their disposal to find out whether a dream was significant or not. According to Annette Zgoll, the fact that a dream had been reported was transmitted upward in the hierarchy, together with the results of the inquiry. If the dream was insignificant, the diviner's report would include the words *ūl naṭlat* ('the dream was not seen'), meaning that this dream did not contain a divine message, while the expression *šuttam naṭālum* signifies that the dream was significant.[8] As Zgoll states, these reports do not question whether the person who had the dream is speaking the truth but whether the dream is significant.[9]

Most readers who start their exploration of the ancient Near East begin with biblical material, which holds prophets in very high esteem, while technical divination is often regarded negatively. Indeed, according to Deut 13 and 18, technical

---

Kirschbaum, M. van Ess, and J. Mahrzahn; Topoi: Berlin Studies of the Ancient World; Berlin: de Gruyter, 2011), 135–51; idem, *Die Wahrsagekunst im Alten Orient: Zeichen des Himmels und der Erde* (Munich: Beck, 2013); F. Rochberg, "Heaven and Earth: Divine-Human Relations in Mesopotamian Celestial Divination," in *Prayer, Magic, and the Stars in the Ancient and Late Antique World* (ed. S. B. Noegel, J. T. Walker, and B. M. Wheeler; Magic in History; University Park, PA: Pennsylvania State University Press, 2003), 169–85.

7. While A. L. Oppenheim is still the classic study of this topic ("The Interpretation of Dreams in the Ancient Near East: With a Translation of an Assyrian Dream-Book," *Transactions of the American Philosophical Society* 46 [1956] 179–373), there has been significant progress on dreams in recent years. See A. Zgoll, *Traum und Welterleben im antiken Mesopotamien: Traumtheorie und Traumpraxis im 3.–1. Jahrtausend v. Chr. als Horizont einer Kulturgeschichte des Träumens* (AOAT 333; Münster: Ugarit-Verlag, 2006); idem, "Die Welt im Schlaf sehen: Inkubation von Träumen im alten Mesopotamien," *WO* 32 (2002) 74–101; S. A. L. Butler, *Mesopotamian Conceptions of Dreams and Dream Rituals* (AOAT 258; Münster: Ugarit-Verlag, 1998). See also E. J. Hamori and J. Stökl (eds.), *Dream Divination in the Hebrew Bible and the Ancient Near East* (ANEM; Atlanta: SBL, 2018).

8. Zgoll, *Traum und Welterleben*, 355–58.

9. It is probable that the "hair and hem" mentioned in several letters from Mari that contain either prophetic messages or reports of message dreams served as base material for a similar test. For a summary of the current state of debate, see Stökl, *Prophecy in the Ancient Near East*, 81–86; E. J. Hamori, "Verification of Prophecy at Mari," *WO* 42 (2012) 1–22.

divination was not permitted in ancient Israel and Judah. However, it is clear that other biblical traditions view technical divination positively: the High Priest's Umim and Thumim appear to be a form of a yes-no oracle. Another such case is the (s)election of several important biblical characters by lot, a form of technical divination.[10]

Throughout most of the ancient Near East—and perhaps also in pre-exilic Israel and Judah—technical diviners had a higher status. Technical diviners could reliably produce divine guidance where intuitive diviners had to wait until the deity chose to communicate with humans.

Another preliminary consideration centers on the nature of the available sources for prophecy in the ancient Near East. The vast majority of our data is pre-Persian. Apart from copies of lexical texts, I am aware of only one text reporting on prophetic activity that dates from the Seleucid period.[11] All of the evidence prior to the single Neo-Babylonian report comes from royal archives. The vast majority of the Old Babylonian evidence comes from the royal archives of Mari, while we know of only a handful of texts from Ešnunna, Uruk, and Kiš.[12] It is possible that the absence of later prophetic texts is related to the nonexistence of royal cuneiform archives after the fall of Babylon to the Persians—even though cuneiform culture was alive and well and continued for another 700 years into the first or even second century CE.[13] It is logical, and beneficial for our current enterprise, to conclude that royal archives contain texts that are relevant for the royal administration. There is comparatively little evidence for the interaction between diviners and private individuals, even though we know that private persons took advantage of divination.[14] Conversely, we are relatively well informed about the

---

10. On the issue see F. Cryer, *Divination in Ancient Israel and Its Near Eastern Environment: A Socio-Historical Investigation* (JSOTSup 142; Sheffield: JSOT Press, 1994).

11. M. Nissinen, "A Prophetic Riot in Seleucid Babylonia," in *"Wer darf hinaufsteigen zum Berg JHWHs?" Beiträge zu Prophetie und Poesie des Alten Testaments: Festschrift für Sigurður Örn Steingrímsson zum 70. Geburtstag* (ed. H. Irsigler; ATAT 72; St. Ottilien: EOS, 2002), 64–74.

12. On the nature and origin of the prophetic texts, see Stökl, "Ancient Near Eastern Prophecy;" idem, *Prophecy in the Ancient Near East*, 29–34, 103–9. For the actual texts, see M. Nissinen, *Prophets and Prophecy in the Ancient Near East: With Contributions by C. L. Seow and Robert K. Ritner* (SBLWAW 12; Atlanta: SBL, 2003); a new edition of this volume with additional texts is forthcoming. In my work on the interplay between prophecy and the state I am much indebted to D. Charpin, "Prophètes et rois dans le Proche-Orient amorrite: Nouvelles données, nouvelles perspectives," in *Florilegium Marianum VI: Recueil d'études à la mémoire d'André Parrot* (ed. D. Charpin and J.-M. Durand; Mémoires de N.A.B.U. 7; Paris: SEPOA, 2002), 7–38.

13. On cuneiform documents from Hellenistic Mesopotamia, see now T. Boiy, *Late Achaemenid and Hellenistic Babylon* (OLA 136; Leuven: Peeters, 2004).

14. Large amounts of omen reports for private clients are known from the Late Old Babylonian period onward; see, for example, the *tamītu*-texts: W. G. Lambert, *Babylonian Oracle Questions* (Mesopotamian Civilizations 13; Winona Lake, IN: Eisenbrauns, 2007). The most obvious form of divination addressed to private individuals may be horoscopes: F. Rochberg, "Babylonian Horoscopes," *TAPA* 88 (1998) 1–164.

interaction of technical divination and prophecy with the royal administration in Old Babylonian Mari and the Neo-Assyrian empire in the early seventh century, when it was at the height of its power. Another consequence of the nature of the archives is that we should not expect to find much material that is critical of the king and the royal administration; it was simply not in the interest of the royal administration to preserve such material.

A related consideration is that prophecy is essentially an oral phenomenon, and because it is, we never have access to the *ipsissima verba* or prophets themselves but always rely on a written version, transmitted by an official to the king. Prophetic messages pronounced in the presence of the king would, in all likelihood, not have been written down, as the king had already heard it, unless they were being preserved as reference copies and/or for reuse in other texts.[15] As we will see below, we find this process of secondary use in collections in the Neo-Assyrian empire.[16] After these preliminary remarks, we can now look at the texts and from them deduce how prophets in the Old Babylonian and Neo-Assyrian periods interacted with the state and vice versa.

2. Old Babylonian Prophecy

In 1933, a then entirely unknown political entity was discovered in Syria on the bank of the Euphrates, on the border with Iraq: ancient Mari (modern Tell Ḥariri). The site is close to modern day Dēr ez-Zōr. A great palace was discovered, together with a large cuneiform archive allowing modern scholars to reconstruct much of the history of ancient Mari in the 18th century B.C.E.[17] Under

---

15. K. van der Toorn, "Old Babylonian Prophecy between the Oral and the Written," *JNSL* 24 (1998) 55–70; idem, "From the Oral to the Written: The Case of Old Babylonian Prophecy," in *Writings and Speech in Israelite and Ancient Near Eastern Prophecy* (ed. E. Ben Zvi and M. H. Floyd; SBLSymS 10; Atlanta: SBL, 2000), 219–34; idem, "From the Mouth of the Prophet: The Literary Fixation of Jeremiah's Prophecies in the Context of the Ancient Near East," in *Inspired Speech: Prophecy in the Ancient Near East: Essays in Honour of Herbert B. Huffmon* (ed. J. Kaltner and L. Stulman; JSOTSup 378; London: T. & T. Clark, 2004), 191–202.

16. See the discussion below and M. J. de Jong, *Isaiah among the Ancient Near Eastern Prophets: A Comparative Study of the Earliest Stages of the Isaiah Tradition and the Neo-Assyrian Prophecies* (VTSup 117; Leiden: Brill, 2007); on the related issue of the use of previously known material in Neo-Assyrian prophetic texts, see the classic M. Weippert, "'Das Frühere, siehe, ist eingetroffen.' Über Selbstzitate im altorientalischen Prophetenspruch," in *Oracles et prophéties dans l'Antiquité: Actes du colloque de Strasbourg, 15–17, juin 1995* (ed. J. G. Heintz; Travaux du Centre de recherche sur le Proche-Orient et la Grèce antiques 15; Paris: de Boccard, 1997), 147–69; and, more recently, de Jong, *Isaiah Among the Ancient Near Eastern Prophets*, 395–47; Stökl, *Prophecy in the Ancient Near East*, 131–41; C. Halton, "Allusions to the Stream of Tradition in Neo-Assyrian Oracles," *ANES* 56 (2009) 50–61.

17. On the archaeology of Mari, see J.-C. Margueron, *Mari, métropole de l'Euphrate au III ͤ et au début du II ͤ millénaire avant J-C* (Paris: Picard, 2004). On the history of Mari and Amorite Mesopotamia, see D. Charpin, "Histoire politique du Proche-Orient Amorrite (2002–1595),"

King Yaḫdun-Lim, the city had been the capital of an independent state in the beginning of the 18th century B.C.E., with good relationships in particular with Yamḫad, a kingdom with its capital at Ḥalab (Aleppo). But Šamši-Addu, the ruler of the kingdom of Upper Mesopotamia, conquered Mari and installed his younger son Yasmaḫ-Addu on the throne there; his older son, Išme-Dagan inherited the overall control of the kingdom of Upper Mesopotamia. Yarim-Lim, the king of Yamḫad, supported Zimri-Lim, the "descendant" of Yaḫdun-Lim in his successful campaign to oust Yasmaḫ-Addu and to install himself on the "throne of the house of his fathers."[18]

There are about 80 texts from Mari with references to prophets, prophecy, and people elsewhere identified as prophesying in the royal archive.[19] There are also a few texts from other sites: two tablets from Iščali contain oracles in support of the

---

in *Mesopotamien: Die altbabylonische Zeit* (ed. P. Attinger, W. Sallaberger, and M. Wäfler; OBO 160/4; Fribourg: Academic Press / Göttingen: Vandenhoeck & Ruprecht, 2004), 25–480. On the Mari archive, see idem, "La fin des archives dans le palais de Mari," *RA* 89 (1995) 29–40; idem, "The Historian and the Old Babylonian Archives," in *Too Much Data? Generalizations and Model-Building in Ancient Economic History on the Basis of Large Corpora of Documentary Evidence: Proceedings of the Second START Conference in Vienna (17–19th July 2008)* (ed. H. D. Baker and M. Jursa; Oxford: Oxbow, 2014), 24–58). Mari had been an important player also in the later phases of the Early Bronze age; it appears that the massive palace was originally built in the 24th century B.C.E. when Mari was Ebla's main rival in the Upper Euphrates region.

18. FM 7 39: 16–17; see J.-M. Durand, *Florilegium marianum VII: Le culte d'Addu d'Alep et l'affaire d'Alahtum* (Mémoires de N.A.B.U. 8; Paris: SEPOA, 2002), 137–40. This is part of the self-introduction of Adad of Kallassu in this prophetic oracle: [14]*ul anāku* [15]*Addu bēl Kallassu ša ina birīt* [16]*paḫalliya urabbûšuma ana kussi bīt abīšu* [17]*uterrûšu* . . . ('Am I not Adad, the sovereign of Kallassu who I have raised him between my thighs; I returned him onto the throne of the house of his fathers.') On Adad/Addu, see D. Schwemer, *Die Wettergottgestalten Mesopotamiens und Nordsyriens im Zeitalter der Keilschriftkulturen: Materialien und Studien nach den schriftlichen Quellen* (Wiesbaden: Harrassowitz, 2001).

19. For a recent list of the texts see Stökl, *Prophecy in the Ancient Near East*, 29–34. The texts themselves were edited by the French *Equipe de Mari* first under the aegis of Jean-Marie Durand and more recently Dominique Charpin. Most of the material with references to prophecy can be found in J.-M. Durand and D. Charpin, *Archives épistolaires de Mari* (ARM 26; Paris: ERC, 1988). Further information on all Mari texts can now be accessed through the excellent portal www.archibab.fr. English translations can be found in Nissinen, *Prophets and Prophecy*; J. J. M. Roberts, "The Mari Prophetic Texts in Transliteration and English Translation," in *The Bible and the Ancient Near East: Collected Essays* (ed. J. J. M. Roberts; Winona Lake, IN: Eisenbrauns, 2002), 157–253; W. Heimpel, *Letters to the King of Mari: A New Translation, With Historical Introduction, Notes, and Commentary* (Mesopotamian Civilizations 12; Winona Lake, IN: Eisenbrauns, 2003). An Italian translation can be found in L. Cagni, *Le profezie di Mari* (Brescia: Paideia, 1995). Some of the letters are translated into German in M. Dietrich, "Prophetenbriefe aus Mari," in *Religiöse Texte: Deutungen der Zukunft in Briefen, Orakeln und Omina* (ed. M. Dietrich et al.; TUAT II/1; Gütersloh: Mohn, 1986), 83–93; R. Pientka-Hinz, "I. Texte aus Mesopotamien: Akkadische Texte des 2. und 1. Jt. v. Chr., 1. Omina und Prophetien," in *Omina, Orakel, Rituale und Beschwörungen* (ed. I. T. Abusch, et al.; TUAT.NF 4; Gütersloh: Gütersloher Verlagshaus, 2008), 16–60.

king;[20] there is a tablet from Uruk containing an oracle in support of Sin-kašid;[21] and, according to Stephanie Dalley, the bilingual inscription C of Samsu-Iluna of Kiš contains an oracle in support of that king.[22]

Most of these texts are letters from local governors and court officials to the king of Mari, Zimri-Lim. They often contain reports of prophetic oracles and, in the same letter, reports about other events in the province where the official was stationed. A good example of this practice is ARM 26 215:

> [1]To my lord [2]speak, [3]thus (says) Lanasûm, [4]your servant:
> [5]My lord wrote to me like this; [6]thus (said) my lord: "[6]Herewith [7]I cause [6]a sacrifice [7]to be conducted for Dagan. [8][Bri]ng one bull and six sheep!" [9]Now, the sacrifice of my lord [10]arrived safely in the city [11]and it was sacrificed before Dagan. [12]The land dined [13]and the entire city [14]rejoiced [g]reatly [13]because of the sacrifice of my lord.
> [15]An ecstatic (*muḫḫûm*) [16][r]ose [15]before Dagan and spoke, [17]he (said) t[h]us: "[18]Until when [19]will I not drink [18]clean water? [20]Write to your lord [21]so that I may drink clean water!" [22]Now, herewith [25]I send [23]a curl of his head [24]and his hem to my lord. [25]May my lord perform a purification-ritual.
> [26]Second, regarding the tax for my lord—[28]let [27]a reliable man from among the servants of my lord [28]come to me [30]so that he [m]ay take [28]the tax [29]for my lord from the inhabitants of the city. [31]And the inhabitants of the city [33]tore out [32]two(?) doors for Dagan [31]without my permission.

Zimri-Lim had evidently given an order to Lanasûm, who was stationed in Tuttul, to provide resources for a festival to the temple of Adad (lines 5–8). The Adad

---

20. M. deJong Ellis, "The Goddess Kititum Speaks to King Ibalpiel: Oracle Texts from Ishchali," *Mari* 5 (1987) 235–66; idem, "The Archive of the Old Babylonian Kititum Temple and Other Texts from Ishchali," *JAOS* 106 (1987) 757–86. Texts no. 66–67 in Nissinen, *Prophets and Prophecy.*

21. See J. G. Westenholz, "The True Shepherd of Uruk," in *Studies Presented to Robert D. Biggs, June 4, 2004* (ed. M. T. Roth et al.; AS 27; Chicago: Oriental Institute of the University of Chicago, 2007), 305–24. For a drawing, see J. van Dijk, "Die Tontafeln aus dem Palast des Sînkāšid," in *XVIII. vorläufiger Bericht über die von dem Deutschen Archäologischen Institut und der Deutschen Orient-Gesellschaft aus Mitteln der Deutschen Forschungsgemeinschaft unternommenen Ausgrabungen in Uruk-Warka: Winter 1959/60* (ed. H. Lenzen; ADOG 7; Berlin: Mann, 1962). 61–62, Taf. 20, 28. See also R. D. Biggs, "Akkadian Oracles and Prophecies," in *Ancient Near Eastern Texts Relating to the Old Testament* (ed. J. B. Pritchard; Princeton, NJ: Princeton University Press, 1969), 604–7; S. Dalley, "Old Babylonian Prophecies at Uruk and Kish," in *Opening the Tablet Box: Near Eastern Studies in Honor of Benjamin R. Foster* (ed. S. C. Melville and A. L. Slotsky; CHANE 42; Leiden: Brill, 2010), 86–92; and A. Lenzi, "Revisiting Biblical Prophecy: Revealed Knowledge Pertaining to Ritual, and Secrecy in Light of Ancient Mesopotamian Prophetic Texts," in *Divination, Politics and Ancient Near Eastern Empires* (ed. A. Lenzi and J. Stökl; ANEM; Atlanta: SBL, 2014), 65–86.

22. Dalley, "Old Babylonian Prophecies at Uruk and Kish," 92–94. For the text, see D. Frayne, *Old Babylonian Period (2003–1595 BC)* (RIME 4; Toronto: University of Toronto Press, 1990), 386 (RIME 4.3.7.7: 63–79).

temple of Tuttul was an important regional sanctuary and, therefore, the gift is not insignificant: a bull and six sheep. As is clear from the text, as it was a festival rather than one of the normal everyday sacrifices, the food was handed out to the wider population and not only the priesthood, and we get the impression of a public BBQ sponsored by the king, with religious overtones (lines 9–14).[23] It is interesting to see that the ecstatic (*muḫḫûm*) pronounces an oracle containing a request for clean water to be supplied to the temple (lines 15–21).[24] Lanasûm sends the "hair and hem" of the ecstatic along so that the oracle can be verified by Zimri-Lim's technical diviners (lines 22–25). In the remainder of the letter, Lanasûm writes about the need for a reliable tax collector and informs the king that the inhabitants of the city destroyed two gates. This change in topic is introduced by the particle *šanītam* so frequent in Old Babylonian administrative texts and used in letters to indicate a sudden shift of topic.[25]

In this letter, we see, therefore, how important it was to transmit prophetic messages to the king but also that they are part of the normal process of transmission of information from the kingdom to wherever the king happened to be.[26] Another text that indicates the importance of transmitting divine messages to the king is FM 7 39, a letter from Nūr-Sîn, Zimri-Lim's man in Aleppo.[27] As this long text touches on many pertinent issues, I will cite it in full here.

[1]To my lord speak: [2]Thus (says) Nūr-Sîn, your servant:

---

23. On aspects of the Old Babylonian priesthood, see D. Cocquerillat, "Les prébendes patrimoniales dans les temples à l'époque de la Ire dynastie de Babylone," *Revue internationale des droits de l'antiquité* 3 (1955) 39–106.

24. There are two Akkadian words that are often regarded as technical terms for 'prophet' in Old Babylonian Akkadian: *muḫḫûm/muḫḫūtum* ('ecstatic') and *āpilum/āpiltum* ('spokesperson'). I regard the *āpilum* as a technical term for a professional prophet and *muḫḫûm* as the term for an ecstatic cult-official/priest who occasionally prophesies; see Stökl, *Prophecy in the Ancient Near East*, 37–69; and for a summary, idem, "Ancient Near Eastern Prophecy," 19. For the translation of the *āpilum* as 'spokesperson' and not 'answerer', see the discussion in idem, *Prophecy in the Ancient Near East*, 41–43. The translation ultimately goes back to a suggestion by P. Fronzaroli, "Gli equivalenti di EME-BAL nelle liste lessicali Eblaite," *Studi Eblaiti* 2 (1980) 95.

25. Indeed, there is no real difference in the way that this letter works when compared to a number of letters that report that royal servants had inquired of technical diviners. Thus, for example, ARM 26 181 reports to the king that Ila . . . (the latter part of the sender's name has not been preserved) had had extispicies performed to see whether there was any danger to Mari in his absence. Apparently, there was no danger. In the second half of the letter, Ila-. . . goes on to report that there is a food shortage in the palace and the houses of the commoners and that immediate resupply was necessary. For the text, see J.-M. Durand, *Archives épistolaires de Mari I*, 364–65; and, for an English translation, see Heimpel, *Letters*, 245.

26. For an interpretation of the location of the senders of the letters with prophetic messages, see J. M. Sasson, "The Posting of Letters with Divine Messages," in *Florilegium marianum II: Recueil d'études à la mémoire de Maurice Birot* (ed. D. Charpin and J.-M. Durand; Mémoires de N.A.B.U. 3; Supplément à N.A.B.U. 1994 no. 2; Paris: SEPOA, 1994), 299–316.

27. This text is text no. 1 in Nissinen, *Prophets and Prophecy*.

[3]Once, twice, even five times [5]I wrote to my lord [3]regarding the givi[ng] of the *zukrum*-sacrifice[28] to Adad [4]and [regarding] the inheritance[29] which Adad of Kallassu [5]demands [from u]s.

[6][Regard]ing the [g]iving of the Zukrum t[o Adad], [7]in the presence of Zuḫadnim, Abi-šad[i and Zu]ḫān [6]Alpān [8]spoke to me thus: [9]"Give the [8]*zukr*[*um* which is his desire?] [9]and the cows!" [9]In the presence of [. . .] my lord [10]told me to give the *zukrum* thus: [11]"In future he shall not change his mind! [12]I appointed witnesses for him." [12]May my lord know (this).

[13]In oracles, Adad of Kallassu [14][stan]ds (saying) thus: [14]"Am I not [15]Adad of Kallassu who between my [16]thighs have raised him? [17]I returned him to the [16]throne of the house of his fathers. [17]After [18]I returned him to the throne of the house of his fathers, I again [19]gave him [18]a residence. [19]Now, as [20]I returned him [19]to the throne of the house of his fathers, [20]I will take the inheritance from his house, [21]if he will not give (it to me). [22]I am the [21]lord of throne, [22]lands and city! What I gave [23]I can take away. If not so (and if) [24]he fulfills my desires, [26]I will give him [24]throne upon throne, [25]house upon house, lands upon lands, [26]city upon city. [27]And the land from the sunrise [28]to the sunset I will give to him." [29]The *āpilum*s said this, and he [=Adad] [30]stands [29]in oracle.

[30]Now, moreover, [31]an *āpilum* of Adad of Kallassu [33]will curse [32]the *maškanum* of Alaḫtum, (which is) intended as the inheritance. [33]May my lord know this.

[34]Previously, when I lived in Māri, [36]I transmitted [35]whatever an *āpilum* or an *āpiltum* [36]said to me to my lord. [37]Now that I live in a foreign country, [39]should I not write [38]what I hear and what they say to me [39]to my lord? [40]If in future some offence were to happen, [41]will not my lord speak, (saying) thus: [43]"why [44]did you not write to me [42]the word which the *āpilum* spoke to you (i.e: [43]'and he will curse your *maškanum*'). [44]Herewith [45]I write [44]to my lord. [45]May my lord know this.

[46][Secon]dly, an *āpilum* of Adad of Aleppo [47]came to me, [together with Abu]-ḫalim (and) [48]thus [47]he spoke to me: [48]"write to your lord [49]thus: 'Am I not Adad of Aleppo [50]who raise[d] you under the crooks of my arms, [51]returned you to the throne of the house of your fathers? [52]I deman[d] [n]othing from you. [53]When a wronged man or a wronged wo[man] [54]cry to you stand there! Judge their cas[e] s! [55]This is what demand from you. [56]Hear this what I wrote to you. [57]Respect my words and [59]I will give you [58]the land from the s[unris]e to the sunset [59]and the land of XXX.'" [60][T]his is what the *ā*[*pilum* of] Adad of Aleppo [61]spoke to me in the presence of A[b]u-ḫalim. [62]May my lord know this.

As becomes clear, Nūr-Sîn in this letter writes that he has witnessed prophetic oracles that demand a certain bit of real-estate belonging to Zimri-Lim to be

---

28. In Late Bronze Emar, the *zukrum* is a memorial-ritual for dead kings (see D. E. Fleming, *Time at Emar: The Cultic Calendar and the Rituals from the Diviner's Archive* [Mesopotamian Civilizations 11; Winona Lake, IN: Eisenbrauns, 2000]), as the name of the ritual ('remembrance') suggests. It presumably performed a similar function also in Mariote society, but we do not have a ritual liturgy for a Mari *zukrum*, so this question cannot be answered with absolute certainty.

29. On the so-called affair of Alaḫtum, see Durand, *Culte d'Addu*, which also contains the rc-cdition of this text.

transferred to the ownership of Adad of Kallassu. Indeed, he says that he has informed his king several times already, and he adds that when he lived in Mari he
also informed Zimri-Lim of all prophetic activity. Presumably, Nūr-Sîn is covering
his bases so thoroughly because he assumes that his message is not going to be met
with approval by the royal court; not only does he say that he has transmitted the
initial message several times (lines 3–5), but he also writes that curious paragraph
in lines 34–43 in which he insists that he transmits the message because he feels
obliged to do so.

The way he expresses himself suggests that this obligation may have applied more widely and may not be restricted to him.[30] There are similarities with
the "oath of the diviner" (ARM 26 1), which may have been a normal oath that
(technical) diviners had to swear in order to oblige these specialists to keep royal
divination secret within the royal court but also to make all possibly dangerous
information from private requests for divination available to the king.[31]

FM 7 39 is interesting also because this text is one of the few texts in which a
prophet addresses a king of another country.[32] Adad of Kallassu's claim that "[15]be-
tween [his] [16]thighs [he] raised him [=Zimri-Lim]?" is very similar to some of
the Neo-Assyrian prophecies in support of Assurbanipal.[33] Indeed, virtually all
Mesopotamian prophetic texts that we have access to are addressed to the king
and address matters of interior politics, be they religious or regarding the royal
succession. As we have already mentioned, they are all found either in royal archives or royal inscriptions, and thus a royal focus is not surprising.

---

30. We will see a similar stipulation in the section on Neo-Assyrian prophecy (below); one
of the stipulations of the VTE is that vassals and/or bodyguards should transmit any potentially
dangerous rumors, including divinatory reports, to the king; see SAA 2 6: 108–22; S. Parpola
and K. Watanabe, *Neo-Assyrian Treaties and Loyalty Oaths* (SAA 2; Helsinki: Helsinki University
Press, 1988), 33; text no. 102 in Nissinen, *Prophets and Prophecy*.

31. Durand, *ARM 26/I*, 13–15. See also Heimpel, *Letters*, 174–75.

32. See J. Stökl, "(Intuitive) Divination, (Ethical) Demands and Diplomacy in the Ancient
Near East," in *Mediating Between Heaven and Earth: Communication with the Divine in the An-
cient Near East* (ed. C. L. Crouch, J. Stökl, and A. E. Zernecke; LHBOTS 566; London: T. & T.
Clark, 2012), 82–92; idem, "Divination as Warefare: The Use of Divination across Borders," in
Divination, Politics and Ancient Near Eastern Empires (ed. A. Lenzi and J. Stökl; ANEM; Atlanta:
SBL, 2014), 49–63 for an interpretation of this and other texts as indicating that Yamḫad may
have regarded Mari not as a completely foreign nation but as part of the area ultimately under the
control of the king of Yamḫad and therefore also under the control of Adad of Aleppo and Adad
of Kallassu. See also the famous text A. 482: 20–27 (G. Dossin, "Les archives épistolaires du palais
de Mari," *Syria* 19 [1938] 117–18; for an English translation see W. L. Moran, "Akkadian Letters,"
in *Ancient Near Eastern Texts Relating to the Old Testament*[3] [ed. J. B. Pritchard; Princeton, NJ:
Princeton University Press, 1969], 628). The overlord's deity addresses the vassal-king as if he
were part of the local political scene. Oracles to Yarim-Lim would presumably have sounded very
similar—but no archive has yet been found in Aleppo. The current political and humanitarian
situation in Aleppo does not make it likely that this will change in the near future.

33. See the discussion of SAA 9 2.5 below; see also the important study on prophecy and
royal accession by Dalley, "Old Babylonian Prophecies at Uruk and Kish."

If we take into account Old Babylonian prophetic texts written and found in kingdoms other than Mari, we can see that there is a focus not only on kings in general but on royal succession. Deities were thought to lend their support to the kings, and this was expressed in prophetic oracles.[34] This support is often expressed either in the promise of social and economic welfare and by stressing the pedagogical qualities of a state-deity with regard to the king. Adad of Kallassu's claim that he raised Zimri-Lim between his thighs presumably expresses the religious and military support afforded to Zimri-Lim by the establishment of Yamḫad in the years between Šamši-Addu's take-over of Mari and Zimri-Lim's installation on the "throne of the house of his fathers."

Unlike in the supportive texts from elsewhere in the Old Babylonian world, the first oracle in FM 7 39 has an edge to it: Adad's support is not unconditional. If Zimri-Lim does not give him the piece of real estate that he desires, Adad can just as well take away what he has given (lines 22–23).[35] In the other oracle contained in this text, another aspect is added: Zimri-Lim does not only have to provide Adad of Kallassu with a certain piece of real estate. Adad of Aleppo—apparently a different deity—demands nothing (material) of him; he demands justice for people who have been wronged (lines 52–55).[36] This demand for the fulfillment of the royal image as guarantor of justice is rare in the cuneiform prophetic material but is common in other cuneiform texts.[37]

As pointed out by Martti Nissinen, the preserved material does not contain fundamental criticism of kingship. Only limited criticism can be found, such as the preceding example of a general demand for justice and requests to support temples with their cultic duties; additionally, there is some advice on foreign politics contained in the famous oracles containing a warning against concluding an alliance with Ešnunna. Two of these oracles, ARM 26 197 and 199, contain the

---

34. See W19.900 (Uruk), FLP 1674, and 2064 (Ešnunna) as well as Samsu-Iluna's bilingual inscription C, RIME 4.3.7.7 (Kiš). For the literature, see ibid. and nn. 18–20 here.

35. Similarities to Job 1:21 are striking, but the ideology behind Job and FM 7 39 is the opposite: Adad threatens punishment in case Zimri-Lim does not fulfill Adad's "request"; Job states that YHWH has punished him, but without Job's transgressing any commandments. Indeed, Job's friends insist that the punishment must be just, while Job insists that it is not.

36. While there is a definite connection between providing justice for the wronged and kingship, this oracle also provides some example of ethical demands by diviners in general and prophets in particular. For a discussion of this issue, see M. Nissinen, "Das kritische Potential in der altorientalischen Prophetie," in *Propheten in Mari, Assyrien und Israel* (ed. M. Köckert and M. Nissinen; FRLANT 201; Göttingen: Vandenhoeck & Ruprecht, 2003), 1–33. See also Stökl, "(Intuitive) Divination."

37. On this, see, for example, P. Machinist, "Kingship and Divinity in Imperial Assyria," in *Text, Artifact, and Image: Revealing Ancient Israelite Religion* (ed. G. M. Beckman and T. J. Lewis; BJS 346; Providence, RI: Brown Judaic Studies, 2006), 152–88; J. N. Postgate, "Royal Exercise of Justice under the Assyrian Empire," in *Le palais et la royauté (archéologie et civilisation): Compte rendu du XIXᵉ Rencontre Assyriologique Internationale organisée par le groupe François Thureau-Dangin, Paris, 29 juin—2 juillet 1971* (ed. P. Garelli; Paris: Geuthner, 1974), 417–26.

same expression, *šapal tibnim mê illakū* ('under straw, water flows').[38] I agree with Jack Sasson, that this expression is presumably an idiom to indicate treachery. It is possible that Zimri-Lim disregarded this prophetic warning when concluding an alliance with Ibal-pî-El of Ešnunna, but it is also possible that the oracles were pronounced when the war between Ešnunna and Mari was still ongoing.[39]

An interesting case of direct prophetic criticism of political decisions can be found in ARM 26 371. Like FM 7 39, this text is a report sent by one of Zimri-Lim's ambassadors to a foreign court. Yarim-Addu, Zimri-Lim's man at the court of Hammurapi the Great at Babylon reports that an *āpilum* of Marduk had spoken in the assembly, openly criticizing Išme-Dagan for having made a peace treaty with Elam and implicitly also with Hammurapi for granting Išme-Dagan asylum in Babylon. The criticism that is leveled at Išme-Dagan is that he used the temple treasury to pay off the Elamites.[40]

In the past, the majority of interpreters have seen the position of prophets in the Old Babylonian period in the temple, based on the fact that the majority of oracles is situated in temples by the authors of the reports.[41] Not a single tablet is extant authorizing a payment from a temple to any person with either a prophetic title or who pronounces a prophecy. It is tempting to see the fact that there are a number of such tablets authorizing payment from the royal dispensaries as evidence that prophecy was regarded as connected to the royal court rather than the temple. But we need to remember that our information comes from royal, not temple, archives.[42] Having said this, there appears to be a difference between

---

38. The same expression is also used in an unrelated prophecy, ARM 26 202. For a discussion of the imagery, see J. M. Sasson, "Water Beneath Straw: Adventures of a Prophetic Phrase in the Mari Archives," in *Solving Riddles and Untying Knots: Biblical, Epigraphic, and Semitic Studies in Honor of Jonas C. Greenfield* (ed. Z. Zevit, S. Gitin, and M. Sokoloff; Winona Lake, IN: Eisenbrauns, 1995), 599–608; W. Heimpel, "Euristic Dog Behaviour," *NABU* 1996 (1996) §45. For a discussion of the prophecies, see D. Charpin, "Le contexte historique et géographique de prophéties dans les textes retrouvés à Mari," *BCSMS* 23 (1992) 22–25; Sasson, "Posting," 305–6.

39. While it is true that, initially, Zimri-Lim did not make a treaty with Ešnunna on account of the fact that his benefactor and (unofficial) overlord Yarim-Lim of Aleppo did not want him to do so, in the end, Ibal-pî-El and Zimri-Lim did have a treaty. See D. Charpin, "Un traité entre Zimri-Lim de Mari et Ibâl-pî-El II d'Ešnunna," in *Marchands, diplomates et empereurs: Études sur la civilisation mésopotamienne offertes à Paul Garelli* (ed. D. Charpin and F. Joannès; Paris: ERC, 1991), 139–66. On the general relationship between Mari and Ešnunna, see Heimpel, *Letters*, 43–45, and with considerably more detail, Charpin, "Histoire politique," 196–210.

40. For the historical context, see ibid., 220–22.

41. For example, van der Toorn, "Old Babylonian Prophecy;" D. E. Fleming, "Prophets and Temple Personnel in the Mari Archives," in *The Priests in the Prophets: The Portrayal of Priests, Prophets, and Other Religious Specialists in the Latter Prophets* (ed. L. L. Grabbe and A. O. Bellis; JSOTSup 408; London: T. & T. Clark, 2004), 44–64.

42. On temple-court relations in the Neo-Babylonian period, see K. Kleber, *Tempel und Palast: Die Beziehungen zwischen dem König und dem Eanna-Tempel im spätbabylonischen Uruk* (AOAT 358; Münster: Ugarit-Verlag, 2008); C. Waerzeggers, "The Pious King: Royal Patronage of Temples in the Neo-Babylonian Period," in *The Oxford Handbook of Cuneiform Culture* (ed.

some of the specialists involved in prophecy: the *āpilum* ('spokesperson') appears to have been closely linked to the court and received direct orders to visit shrines in other cities, while the *muḥḥûm* appears mostly in texts directly linking them to a specific temple.[43]

This portrayal of the relationship between Old Babylonian prophecy and the state has shown a number of things: prophecy was integrated into the state apparatus and, like other forms of divination, was meant to support it. It is important to realize that the relative absence of critical prophetic oracles cannot be entirely attributed to the character of the Mari archive as royal, and the presence of a handful of critical texts attest to an important function of divination in general and prophecy in particular: warning the king of the potentially negative outcome of an enterprise. These messages are to be understood not as unconditional announcements of doom but as warnings that something has to be done about a looming catastrophe, be it a ritual to appease the gods, the rectification of a juridical or cultic wrong, or a military campaign.[44] Thus, "prophecies of doom" can, in this context, be understood not as announcing a catastrophe but warning the king that "doom" would come if nothing was done about it. Another function of Old Babylonian prophecy can be seen from the texts from Uruk, Ešnunna, the bilingual inscription C by Samsu-Iluna, and FM 7 39: prophecy (or prophetic-like texts) was used as a means of legitimating new rulers. This legitimizing function of prophecy is particularly present in ancient Near Eastern prophecy, as we shall see in a moment.

3. Neo-Assyrian Prophecy

The Neo-Assyrian kings Esarhaddon (reigned 680–669 B.C.E.) and Ashurbanipal (reigned 668 through ca. 630 B.C.E.) are well known for their respect for astrology and prophecy.[45] The available cuneiform evidence for prophecy in the

---

E. Robson and K. Radner; Oxford: Oxford University Press, 2011), 725–51; M. Jursa, "Cuneiform Writing in Neo-Babylonian Temple Communities," in *The Oxford Handbook of Cuneiform Culture* (ed. E. Robson and K. Radner; Oxford: Oxford University Press, 2011), 184–204. Their thoughts are structurally comparable to previous periods.

43. There is a possible exception to this general divide in a Neo-Assyrian text recently discovered in Ziyaret Tepe, ZTT 25 see S. Parpola, "Cuneiform Texts from Ziyaret Tepe (Tušḫān), 2002–2003 (Plates I–XXV)," *SAAB* 17 (2008) 98–99.

44. A good example of this model of prophecy can be seen in the narrative of Jonah, which almost explicitly posits a model of prophecy diametrically opposed to that of Deuteronomy 18. On this question in biblical prophecy see W. H. Schmidt, "Einsicht als Ziel prophetischer Verkündigung," in *Ich bewirke das Heil und erschaffe das Unheil (Jesaja 45,7): Studien zur Botschaft der Propheten: Festschrift für Lothar Ruppert zum 65. Geburtstag* (ed. F. Diedrich and B. Willmes; FB 88; Würzburg: Echter Verlag, 1998), 377–96; L.-S. Tiemeyer, "Prophecy as a Way of Cancelling Prophecy—the Strategic Uses of Foreknowledge," *ZAW* 117 (2005) 329–50; de Jong, *Isaiah Among the Ancient Near Eastern Prophets*, 308–13 and most recently idem, "The Fallacy of True and False in Prophecy Illustrated by Jer 28:8–9," *JHebS* 12 (2012) Article 10.

45. For text editions of the prophetic texts see S. Parpola, *Assyrian Prophecies* (SAA 9; Helsinki: Helsinki University Press, 1997); M. Nissinen, *References to Prophecy in Neo-Assyrian*

Neo-Assyrian period comes from the Neo-Assyrian state archives.[46] This means that, as for the Old Babylonian period, the available evidence comes from royal archives, which has an effect on the way that prophets are portrayed and on the messages they proclaim. As in the Old Babylonian period, we find two kinds of specialists who are regularly mentioned in the context of prophecy. The Old Babylonian *āpilum* is replaced by the Neo-Assyrian *raggimu* and the *muḫḫûm* by the *maḫḫû*.[47]

Unlike the Old Babylonian corpus, where the majority of texts are reports of oracles in letters that add some context to the oracles, the majority of Neo-Assyrian prophetic texts contain only the oracles. Some of them are on individual tablets, while many of them are collected on three tablets usually referred to by their German label, *Sammeltafeln* ('collective tablets').[48] Although the Old Babylonian tablets also do not allow access to the *ipsissima verba* of the prophet, the Neo-Assyrian texts are one further step removed from the prophetic performance.[49] Many scholars think that the function of the *Sammeltafeln* was to provide a textual trove that could be used for royal inscriptions. While this interpretation is emi-

---

Sources (SAAS 7; Helsinki: Neo-Assyrian Corpus Project, 1998). For English translations, as with other ancient Near Eastern prophetic texts, see Nissinen, *Prophets and Prophecy*, 97–177.

46. For a summary discussion of the three Transjordanian royal inscriptions from the first millennium containing references to prophecy, see Stökl, *Prophecy in the Ancient Near East*, 19–23. For further treatment, see M. Weippert, "Aspekte israelitischer Prophetie im Lichte verwandter Erscheinungen des Alten Orients," in *Ad bene et fideliter seminandum: Festgabe für Karlheinz Deller zum 21. Februar 1987* (ed. U. Magen and G. Mauer; AOAT 220; Kevelaer: Butzon & Bercker; Neukirchen-Vluyn: Neukirchener Verlag, 1988), 287–319; A. Lemaire, "Oracles, politique et littérature dans les royaumes Araméens et Transjordaniens (IXᵉ–VIIIᵉ s.av. n.è.)," in *Oracles et prophéties dans l'Antiquité: Actes du colloque de Strasbourg, 15–17, juin 1995* (ed. J. G. Heintz; Travaux du Centre de recherche sur le Proche-Orient et la Grèce antiques 15; Paris: de Boccard, 1997), 171–93; B. Margalit, "Ninth-Centruy Israelite Prophecy in the Light of Contemporary NWSemitic Epigraphs," in *"Und Mose schrieb dieses Lied auf": Studien zum Alten Testament und zum Alten Orient: Festschrift für Oswald Loretz zur Vollendung seines 70. Lebensjahres mit Beiträgen von Freunden, Schülern und Kollegen* (ed. M. Dietrich and I. Kottsieper; AOAT 250; Münster: Ugarit-Verlag, 1998), 515–32; E. Blum, "Israels Prophetie im altorientalischen Kontext: Anmerkungen zu neueren religionsgeschichtlichen Thesen," in *"From Ebla to Stellenbosch": Syro-Palestinian Religions and the Hebrew Bible* (ed. I. Cornelius and L. Jonker; ADPV 37; Wiesbaden: Harrassowitz in Kommission, 2008), 81–115 (Tafel I).

47. On the *raggimu* and the *maḫḫû*, see Stökl, *Prophecy in the Ancient Near East*, 111–21; de Jong, *Isaiah Among the Ancient Near Eastern Prophets*, 287–92.

48. Eight texts (SAA 9 4–11) contain individual oracles, while the three *Sammeltafeln* contain a total of 21 oracles. The first one, SAA 9 1, contains ten; SAA 9 2 six; and SAA 9 3 five oracles. On the nature of these tablets and the related shapes, see K. Radner, "The Relation Between Format and Content of Neo-Assyrian Texts," in *Nineveh, 612 BC: The Glory and Fall of the Assyrian Empire. Catalogue of the 10th Anniversary Exhibition of the Neo-Assyrian Text Corpus Project* (ed. R. Mattila; Helsinki: Helsinki University Press, 1995), 63–78, and the discussion in de Jong, *Isaiah Among the Ancient Near Eastern Prophets*, 171–72; Stökl, *Prophecy in the Ancient Near East*, 129–31.

49. On the Old Babylonian prophetic texts as edited texts, see van der Toorn, "Old Babylonian Prophecy;" Stökl, *Prophecy in the Ancient Near East*, 131–41.

nently plausible, none of the extant royal inscriptions mentioning oracles explicitly cite one of the preserved prophetic oracles.[50]

The character of the oracles quoted and alluded to in the royal inscriptions and in the preserved oracles in the *Sammeltafeln* and individual inscriptions all are very supportive of the king. This particular aspect is clearer in the oracles, but one of Aššurbanipal's inscriptions contains the following lines: "Ištar heard my desperate sighs and said to me: 'Fear not!' She made my heart confident: 'Because of the hand-lifting prayer you said (and) your eyes being filled with tears, I have mercy (with you).'"[51] Indeed, SAA 9 1.6, an oracle by Ištar of Arbela, exemplifies support for the royal house:[52]

iii 7'-8'I am Issār[53] of [Arbela], oh Esarhaddon, king of the land of A[ššur].

9'-15'I will grant lon[g] days (and) etern[al] years in the Inner City[54], Niniv[eh], Kalaḫ (and) Arbe[la][55] to Esarhaddon, my king.

16'-22'I am yo[ur] great midwife, I am [your] good wet-nurse who has established your throne (for) long days (and) eternal years under the great heavens.

23'-29'I keep watch in a golden chamber in the middle of the heavens. I let an amber light shine before Esarhaddon king of the land of Aššur. I will guard him like the crown of my head.[56]

30'-iv 4Fear not, O king! I have spoken to you, I did not slander y[ou]! I inspire[d you], I did not make [you] ashamed. I will bring you across the river in good order.[57]

---

50. For the references to prophetic texts, see Nissinen, *References*; idem, *Prophets and Prophecy*, 133–51.

51. Prism B v 46–49. An English translation of this text can be found in Nissinen, *References*, 44, and idem, *Prophets and Prophecy*, 146–50. See also R. Borger, *Beiträge zum Inschriftenwerk Assurbanipals: Die Prismenklassen A, B, C = K, D, E, F, G, H, J und T sowie andere Inschriften* (Wiesbaden: Harrassowitz, 1996).

52. Other examples could easily be given; see, for example, SAA 9 1.8, 2.5, 2.6, 3.2, 3.3 and 3.5.

53. This is the Neo-Assyrian form of Ištar's name.

54. That is, the city of Aššur.

55. These four cities are elsewhere referred to as the "four doorjambs of Assyria"; see SAA 9 3.5:19.

56. For this passage, see J. Stökl, "'I Have Rained Stones and Fiery Glow on Their Heads!' Celestial and Meteorological Prophecy in the Neo-Assyrian Empire," in *"Thus Speaks Ishtar of Arbela": Prophecy in Israel, Assyria and Egypt in the Neo-Assyrian Period* (ed. R. P. Gordon and H. M. Barstad; Winona Lake, IN: Eisenbrauns, 2013), 239–51. For amber in ancient Near Eastern sources, see M. Heltzer, "On the Origin of the Near Eastern Archaeological Amber," in *Languages and Cultures in Contact: At the Crossroads of Civilizations in the Syro-Mesopotamian Realm; Proceedings of the 42nd RAI* (ed. K. van Lerberghe and G. Voet; OLA 96; Leuven: Peeters, 1999), 169–76, and refer to D. Bodi, *The Book of Ezekiel and the Poem of Erra* (OBO 104; Fribourg: Universitätsverlag / Göttingen: Vandenhoeck & Ruprecht, 1991), 82–94, for the connections between Akkadian *elmēšu* and Hebrew חשמל.

57. According to E. J. Banks, "Eight Oracular Responses to Esarhaddon," *AJSL* 14 (1898) 273; Nissinen, *Prophets and Prophecy*, 107–8 note c, the reference to a river might be more than mythological; it also might refer to the river Tigris, which Esarhaddon had to cross before

[5-13]Esarhaddon, legitimate heir, son of Mullissu, with a sharp[?] dagger[?][58] in my hands will destroy your enemies. Esarhaddon, the king of the land of Aššur, (is) a cup filled with lye, a double-axe[?][59]!

[14-19]Esarhaddon, I will give yo[u] long days (and) eternal years in the Inner City. Esarhaddon, I am your good shield in Arbe[la].

[20-35]Esarhaddon, le[gitimate] heir, son of Mul[lissu], [I] keep thinking of [you]. I have (always) loved [you] dee[ply]. I hold you by [your] locks in the great heavens. I will cause smoke to smoke in your right. I will [. . .] fire on your left. [. . .] the kingship upon [. . .]

This support for the Neo-Assyrian royal house is expressed both through maternal protective as well as martial language. The majority of the maternal references are attributed to Mullissu, and Ištar of Arbela shows her war-like character.[60] Bēl-ušezib appears to quote from an oracle of Bēl (Marduk): "May Esarhaddon,

entering the city at the end of the civil war. A reference to the crossing of the river can be found in Nin A i 84–86, R. Borger, *Die Inschriften Asarhaddons, Königs von Assyrien* (Archiv für Orientforschung Beihefte 9; Graz: Selbstverlag, 1956), 44–45; Nissinen, *Prophets and Prophecy*, 140.

58. The translation of these lines is somewhat tentative. Following Nissinen, *Prophets and Prophecy*, 107–8, I translate *ḫangaru akku* as 'sharp dagger'. Parpola (*Assyrian Prophecies*, 8), basing his translation on W. von Soden ("Aramäische Wörter in neuassyrischen und neu- und spätbabylonischen Texten: Ein Vorbericht III," *Or* 46 [1977] 18) connects *ḫangaru* to Aramaic *ḫangrā*. However, M. Weippert ("'König, fürchte dich nicht!' Assyrische Prophetie im 7. Jahrhundert v. Chr," *Or* 71 [2002] 41) points out that it is only attested in Syriac and later languages. Having said this, there are a number of Neo-Assyrian words that are only attested in Syriac. The second word of the expression is no easier. Nissinen, *Prophets and Prophecy*, 107–8 note d, links it to the verbal root *akāku/ekēku* ('scratch'). Whatever the etymology, the general meaning is clear.

59. With S. Langdon, *Tammuz and Ishtar: A Monograph Upon Babylonian Religion and Theology: Extensive Extracts from the Tammuz Liturgies and all of the Arbela Oracles* (Oxford: Clarendon, 1914), 231; M. Weippert, "Die Bildsprache der neuassyrischen Prophetie," in *Beiträge zur prophetischen Bildsprache in Israel und Assyrien* (ed. H. Weippert, K. Seybold, and M. Weippert; OBO 64; Fribourg: Universitätsverlag / Göttingen: Vandenhoeck & Ruprecht, 1985), 59 n. 10; idem, "Assyrische Prophetie," 41–42—Weippert reads GÍN at the end of line 13 as *pāšu* 'axe, axe-head'. Parpola, *Assyrian Prophecies*, 8 writes that Deller's suggestions to Weippert originated with him but also that this suggestion is unlikely, because in Neo-Assyrian Akkadian the reading of GÍN as *pāšu* is restricted to lexical texts. While Parpola's argument regarding the equation being limited to lexical lists is strong, the alternative—namely, to read *šiqlu* 'sheqel'—presents us with two unsatisfactory options: (1) either the axe is very light (2 sheqels are roughly 32 grams; thus Nissinen, *Prophets and Prophecy*, 107–8 n. 3; (2) or it refers to the cost (so Parpola, *Assyrian Prophecies*, 8). That Ištar would compare Esarhaddon to a cup of lye, thereby calling him a destroyer, makes sense in this context; why, however, she should compare him to either a relatively modestly priced or a very light axe appears less meaningful. Jointly, a cup of lye and a double-bladed battle-axe could stand for various forms of ancient warfare, but the interpretation must remain provisional.

60. On the archaeology of the Ištar cult in Assur, see W. Meinhold, *Ištar in Aššur: Untersuchung eines Lokalkultes von ca. 2500 bis 614 v. Chr* (AOAT 367; Münster: Ugarit-Verlag, 2009). See also G. J. Selz, "Five Divine Ladies: Thoughts on Inana(k), Ištar, In(n)in(a), Annunītum, and Anat, and the Origin of the Title 'Queen of Heaven,'" *Nin* 1 (2000) 29–62.

king of the land of Assyria sit on his throne like Marduk-šāpik-zēri,[61] and I will deliver all the countries into his hands." That a Babylonian astrologer would write these words to Esarhaddon, likening him to a Babylonian king of the 11th century, is at the same time clever, flattering rhetoric and using the well-known theme of divine support for the king in order to cajole him into having a more positive relationship with Bēl-ušezib's home, Babylonia.

Divine support in war is the focus of a passage in one of Esarhaddon's inscriptions (Nin A i 59–62). In this passage, Aššur, Sîn, Šamaš, Bēl, Nabû, Nergal, Ištar of Nineveh, and Ištar of Arbela are all said to answer Esarhaddon's prayers, to provide clear answers—presumably through forms of technical divination—and to keep sending an oracle of encouragement.[62] The following text looks like a direct quotation and presumably is the text of the content: "Advance! Do not hold back! We constantly go at your side! We annihilate your enemies."[63] The examples of support in conflict and war could easily be multiplied; they are one of the most important aspects of Neo-Assyrian prophetic texts that have been preserved.[64] This is not surprising, because warfare was one of the most important aspects of Neo-Assyrian rulership and many forms of divination played a role in helping the kings decide their actions. Divine assistance would have been judged as vital for success in any military action, as well as in general.[65]

In addition to waging war, another important aspect of ancient Near Eastern kingship was support for temple religion, be it through constructing or refurbishing the buildings or by supporting the ongoing cult. As shown by Hurowitz, the building of temples required divine authorization, and it is, therefore, not surprising to find that temple building is mentioned in a number of oracles.[66] Thus, in

---

61. The mention of a Babylonian king is significant because of the uneasy relationship between Babylon and the Neo-Assyrian kings. Marduk-šāpik-zēri (ca. 1082–1069 B.C.E.) probably was allied to Assyria and was known as a builder in Babylonia; see the *Synchronistic Chronicle* ii 25'–37' (text no. 10, pp. 176–83, in Glassner) and the Chronicle of the Kings of Babylon from the Second Isin Dynasty to the Assyrian Conquest 2'–5' (text no. 47, pp. 284–89, in Glassner); for texts of the chronicles, see now, conveniently, J.-J. Glassner, *Mesopotamian Chronicles* (SBLWAW 19; Atlanta: SBL, 2004).

62. Borger, *Inschriften*, 43–45; Nissinen, *Prophets and Prophecy*, 139.

63. Lines 61–62: [61]*šir takilti ištapparūnimma alik lā kalâta* [62]*idāka nittallakma ninâra gārēka*.

64. See, e.g., SAA 9 1.1, 1.2, 1.6, 1.7, 2.2, 3.3, 3.5, 5, and 8.

65. For more general support, especially in accession, see SAA 9 1.4, 1.9, 1.10, 2.1, 2.2, 2.3, 2.4, 3.5, 4, 6, 7, and 9. One of these texts, SAA 9 1.4, spoken by the famous Baiā, contains the words 'Do not trust in humans' (*ina muḫḫi amēlūti lā tatakkil*), which are reminiscent of Ps 146:3 and similar expressions in the biblical text. On Baiā, see M. Nissinen and M. C. Perroudon, "Bāia," in *PNA* 1/II: 253; J. Stökl, "Gender Ambiguity in Ancient Near Eastern Prophecy? A Re-Assessment of the Data Behind a Popular Theory," in *Prophets Male and Female: Gender and Prophecy in the Hebrew Bible, the Eastern Mediterranean and the Ancient Near East* (ed. J. Stökl and C. L. Carvalho; AIL 15; Atlanta: SBL, 2013), 59–79.

66. V. A. Hurowitz, *I Have Built You an Exalted House: Temple Building in the Bible in Light of Mesopotamian and North-West Semitic Writings* (JSOTSup 115; ASOR Monograph Series 5;

Prism C i 71–98 (= T ii 29—iii 14) Aššurbanipal claims that, in the distant past, Sîn had ordained that Aššurbanipal would rebuild the Eḫulḫul: "Aššurbanipal will (re)build that temple and will install me [= Sîn] in an eternal sanctuary."[67] Bēl-ušezib, the already mentioned Babylonian astrologer, quotes a similar oracle, but to Aššurbanipal's father, Essarhaddon, that "Esarhaddon will rebuild Babylon and restore Esagil."[68]

As is well known, there is little ancient Near Eastern prophecy that can be considered critical of the king and none that is critical of kingship as such. Since the function of prophecy and other forms of divination was to assist the king and his advisers in ruling the country, this is hardly surprising.[69] As de Jong and Nissinen point out, there are some cases where a prophetic oracle goes against the current king, such as the oracle in favor of Sasî in SAA 16 59:

> It is the word of Nusku: "The Kingship is for Sasî. I will destroy the name and seed of Sennacherib!"[70]

These words are undoubtedly critical of Sennacherib. But the prophecy was presumably addressed to Sasî and therefore praised Sasî. In other words, what may be perceived as a prophecy critical of Sennacherib was spoken in a different social circle that regarded Sennacherib as its enemy; this oracle is essentially like an oracle against a "foreign" enemy that is threatened with divine wrath and destruction.

As in the Old Babylonian prophetic texts, cultic concerns are also voiced by at least one Neo-Assyrian prophet:

Sheffield: JSOT Press, 1992), 64. For an overview of temple building in the Ancient Near East, see the contributions in M. J. Boda and J. R. Novotny, ed., *From the Foundations to the Crenellations: Essays on Temple Building in the Ancient Near East and Hebrew Bible* (AOAT 366; Münster: Ugarit-Verlag, 2010).

67. The word used for sanctuary here, *parakku*, often refers to a small chapel within a larger temple but can also refer to the throne-room of a deity; compare CAD P 145. For the text, see Borger, *Inschriftenwerk*, 141–42, with German translation on p. 207.

68. SAA 10 109:14–15. The fact that Bēl-ušezib says that he told the king about this oracle (*ittu* 'sign') indicates that this oracle was arrived at through astrology. Prophecy is an inherent part of divination, and its social function was identical to that of other forms of divination; see Nissinen, "Omen Divination"; Stökl, *Prophecy in the Ancient Near East*, 9–13.

69. For a summary of the situation, see de Jong, "The Fallacy of True and False in Prophecy Illustrated by Jer 28:8–9," 1–4. For a discussion of critical prophecy in Neo-Assyrian sources see M. Nissinen, "Prophecy against the King in Neo-Assyrian Sources," in *"Lasset uns Brücken bauen": Collected Communications to the XVth Congress of the IOSOT, Cambridge 1995* (ed. K.-D. Schunck and M. Augustin; Frankfurt a.M.: Lang, 1998), 157–70; idem, "Das kritische Potential."

70. M. Luukko and G. van Buylaere, *The Political Correspondence of Esarhaddon* (SAA 16; Helsinki: Helsinki University Press, 2002), 53. See also SAA 16 60 and 61. For a discussion of the Sasî affair, see now E. Frahm, "Hochverrat in Assur," in *Assur-Forschungen: Arbeiten aus der Forschungsstelle "Edition literarischer Keilschrifttexte aus Assur" der Heidelberger Akademie der Wissenschaften* (ed. S. M. Maul and N. P. Heeßel; Wiesbaden: Harrassowitz, 2010), 89–137.

"Why did you give the [. . . l-wood, the grove, and the . . . to the Egyptians? Say in the king's presence that they should be given back to me. I will (then) give total abundance [to] his [. . . l."[71]

The similarity to Old Babylonian prophecy also extends to the fact that the deity promises "total abundance"—presumably in return for the property that Nabû-rēšī-išši is demanding from the king.[72] A similar tone can also be found in SAA 9 3.5, a text in which Ištar bitterly complains to Esarhaddon about missing provisions in her temple. If SAA 9 3 is indeed written for Esarhaddon's coronation, it is unlikely that the complaint describes a real situation; after all, Ištar would hardly criticize the king this openly in that setting. Rather, we may have to envisage a ritualized complaint as part of the coronation ceremony.

Interestingly, there are no Neo-Assyrian oracles reminding the king of his ethical duties to his subjects. On the surface, this is a difference between Old Babylonian and biblical prophecy on the one hand and Neo-Assyrian prophecy on the other. Nissinen's argument that social justice was an intrinsic part of ancient Near Eastern concepts of a good king and that this concept applied just as much to Old Babylonian, Israelite, and Judean rulers as to Neo-Assyrian kings is convincing. But it does not follow that Neo-Assyrian prophecy actually did cite ethical concerns.

In summary, we can say that, like their Old Babylonian counterparts, Neo-Assyrian prophets were part of the royal intelligence service. Like other diviners, they provided the king with information that he and his advisers relied on when ruling the vast empire. They are servants of the state and, therefore, a particular interest can be detected in their messages. Legitimacy of kingship especially seems to have stood at the center of their (and their deities') attention: questions of the right succession, of temple-building, and defense of order against chaos, as represented by conflict against foreign enemies. The fact that we have one case (in three texts) of a non-state prophet who criticizes the (current) king strengthens this portrait further: instead of working for Esarhaddon's state, the female servant referred to in SAA 13 59–61 is presumably part of Sasî's retinue.[73] The difference between her and state-prophets is simply that her "employers" represented a different "state." Her function within her group mirrored that of state prophets in the wider Neo-Assyrian empire.

---

71. SAA 13 144: rev. 7—s. 1.

72. Nissinen's ("Das kritische Potential," 6) suggestion that the deity in question is Ištar seems very likely, if it has been correctly identified as belonging to the Arbela corpus; M. C. Perroudon, "Nabû-rēšī-išši," *PNA* 2/II: 864 (6); S. W. Cole and P. Machinist, *Letters from Priests to the Kings Esarhaddon and Assurbanipal* (SAA 13; Helsinki: Helsinki University Press, 1998), 116–17. Nissinen rightly points out that Nabû-rēšī-išši probably cites this oracle because it gives his requests divine backing.

73. This holds true, irrespective of whether the whole rebellion was the result of a sting operation or whether Sasi was actually a rebel.

But just as with Old Babylonian prophets, we also have to add the caveat here that our data about Neo-Assyrian prophets comes from the state archives of the Assyrian empire. It is possible—indeed, not unlikely—that oral prophecy would have included messages that were less concerned with kingship and the correct running of the cult than the messages that we have at our disposal today. It is also likely that the vast majority of these messages would never have been written down.[74]

4. Conclusions

Ancient Near Eastern prophecy existed in monarchic states and is closely connected to the individual rulers in whose archives references to prophecy can be found. It is clear that within these archives there is a clear preference for prophecies regarding matters of state and religion, because the king was involved in the upkeep and running of temples. Royal concerns are focussed on a relatively small number of subjects. Of prime importance for our purposes here is the matter of royal succession. Divine support for the claim to kingship seems to have been useful to the kings in our texts to such an extent that they maintained the memory of this support on inscriptions and in archival copies of texts that were preserved for their successors.[75] Being the "correct" successor, whether as the son of the previous king, as in the case of the Neo-Assyrian kings, or as a usurper to the crown (as in the case of Zimri-Lim), was the precondition of becoming an ancient Near Eastern king.

In addition, the upkeep of social and cultic norms was an important aspect of prophetic messages from the Old Babylonian period. In the Neo-Assyrian period, the king is reminded of cultic norms. Upkeep of the cult and support for social justice are important aspects of being an ancient Near Eastern king. The fact that Neo-Assyrian prophecy does not mention social justice is, in this context, peculiar but may be the result of the accident of preservation. In the evidence from Mari, we find an insistence on social norms.[76] When cultic and social norms are maintained, various deities promise to provide the king with larger kingdoms, the succession of the king's sons to the throne, or other rewards. The final major topic of ancient Near Eastern prophecy is conflict. Not surprisingly, it corresponds to another important aspect of ancient Near Eastern kingship: the defense of the established, "orderly" world against the chaos represented by foreign and home-

---

74. Nissinen, "What is Prophecy?" idem, "How Prophecy Became Literature," *SJOT* 19 (2005) 153–72.

75. Dalley, "Old Babylonian Prophecies at Uruk and Kish."

76. Most of these are stated in a fairly generalized language. On the debate about granting asylum between Zimri-Lim and his overlord Yarim-Lim, see now Stökl, "(Intuitive) Divination;" idem, "Divination as Warfare."

grown enemies.[77] Indeed, these enemies threatened the king, who had so carefully been raised by the deities and put on the throne by them.

Ancient Near Eastern prophecy as it appears in the sources available to us, all of which are from royal archives, is dependent on the monarchy. Potential criticism is not geared toward the establishment of a new form of government or essentially critical of the king in power. Instead, its ultimate aim, just as all other forms of the cult and state, was to enable the king to establish and maintain ideal kingship. If the king manages to do so by following divine commands, the king will be rewarded. This relationship is best expressed in FM 7 39:19–28, where Adad of Kallassu says:

> Now, like I restored him to the throne of the house of his fathers, I can take the inheritance from his house, if he should not give (the estate to me).[78] I am the lord of throne, lands, and city! What I gave I can take away. If on the contrary,[79] he fulfils my desires, I will give him throne upon throne, house upon house, lands upon lands, city upon city. And the land from the sunrise to the sunset I will give to him.

Ancient Near Eastern prophecy can therefore be characterized as deeply involved in the establishment and maintenance of just kingship by the "correct" king, with the promise of a good outcome if this just kingship is established and maintained correctly. This image is, of course, dependent on the available sources. The oral prophecy phenomenon may well have shown interest in other aspects of ancient Near Eastern life. However, only prophecy that is intimately connected to the monarchy survives in the documents available to us today.[80]

---

77. On the justification for war in the Neo-Assyrian empire, see C. L. Crouch, *War and Ethics in the Ancient Near East: Military Violence in Light of Cosmology and History* (BZAW 407; Berlin: de Gruyter, 2009), 15–28, 35–64.

78. This refers to the "Alaḫtum Affair"; see Durand, *Culte d'Addu*.

79. This rather elegant translation goes back to Nissinen, *Prophets and Prophecy*, 19. Literally, the text reads "If not so, he fulfills my desires."

80. It is likely that ancient Israelite and Judean prophecy was to some extent similar in historical reality, but the literature now preserved in the Hebrew Bible paints a more complex picture: Stökl, *Prophecy in the Ancient Near East*; de Jong, *Isaiah Among the Ancient Near Eastern Prophets*; Nissinen, "What is Prophecy"; idem, "How Prophecy Became Literature"; idem, "Das Problem der Prophetenschüler," in *Houses Full of All Good Things: Essays in Memory of Timo Veijola* (ed. J. Pakkala and M. Nissinen; Publications of the Finnish Exegetical Society 95; Helsinki: The Finnish Exegetical Society / Göttingen: Vandenhoeck & Ruprecht, 2008), 337–53. On the way that the prophetic literature in individual biblical books interact with empire and kingship, see the other essays in this volume and the contributions to A. Lenzi and J. Stökl, eds., *Divination, Politics and Ancient Near Eastern Empires* (ANEM; Atlanta: SBL, 2014).

Bibliography

Banks, E. J. "Eight Oracular Responses to Esarhaddon." *AJSL* 14 (1898) 267–77.

Biggs, R. D. "Akkadian Oracles and Prophecies." Pp. 604–7 in *Ancient Near Eastern Texts Relating to the Old Testament*. 3rd edition. Edited by J. B. Pritchard. Princeton: Princeton University Press, 1969.

Blum, E. "Israels Prophetie im altorientalischen Kontext: Anmerkungen zu neueren religionsgeschichtlichen Thesen." Pp. 81–115 (Tafel I) in *"From Ebla to Stellenbosch:" Syro-Palestinian Religions and the Hebrew Bible*. Edited by I. Cornelius and L. Jonker. ADPV 37. Wiesbaden: Harrassowitz, 2008.

Boda, M. J., and J. R. Novotny, eds. *From the Foundations to the Crenellations: Essays on Temple Building in the Ancient Near East and Hebrew Bible*. AOAT 366. Münster: Ugarit-Verlag, 2010.

Bodi, D. *The Book of Ezekiel and the Poem of Erra*. OBO 104. Fribourg: Universitätsverlag; Göttingen: Vandenhoeck & Ruprecht, 1991.

Boiy, T. *Late Achaemenid and Hellenistic Babylon*. OLA 136. Leuven: Peeters, 2004.

Borger, R. *Die Inschriften Asarhaddons, Königs von Assyrien*. Archiv für Orientforschung Beihefte 9. Graz: Selbstverlag, 1956.

_____. *Beiträge zum Inschriftenwerk Assurbanipals: Die Prismenklassen A, B, C = K, D, E, F, G, H, J und T sowie andere Inschriften*. Wiesbaden: Harrassowitz, 1996.

Butler, S. A. L. *Mesopotamian Conceptions of Dreams and Dream Rituals*. AOAT 258. Münster: Ugarit-Verlag, 1998.

Cagni, L. Le profezie di Mari. Brescia: Paideia, 1995.

Charpin, D. "The Historian and the Old Babylonian Archives." Pp. 24–58 in *Too Much Data? Generalizations and Model-Building in Ancient Economic History on the Basis of Large Corpora of Documentary Evidence: Proceedings of the Second START Conference in Vienna (17–19th July 2008)*. Edited by H. D. Baker and M. Jursa. Oxford: Oxbow, 2014.

_____. "Histoire politique du Proche-Orient Amorrite (2002–1595)." Pp. 25–480 in *Mesopotamien: Die altbabylonische Zeit*. Edited by P. Attinger, W. Sallaberger, and M. Wäfler. OBO 160/4. Fribourg: Academic Press; Göttingen: Vandenhoeck & Ruprecht, 2004.

_____. "La fin des archives dans le palais de Mari." *RA* 89 (1995) 29–40.

_____. "Le contexte historique et géographique de prophéties dans les textes retrouvés à Mari." *BCSMS* 23 (1992) 21–31.

_____. "Prophètes et rois dans le Proche-Orient amorrite: Nouvelles données, nouvelles perspectives." Pp. 7–38 in *Florilegium marianum VI: Recueil d'études à la mémoire d'André Parrot*. Edited by D. Charpin and J.-M. Durand. Mémoires de N.A.B.U. 7. Paris: SEPOA, 2002.

_____. "Un traité entre Zimri-Lim de Mari et Ibâl-pî-El II d'Ešnunna." Pp. 139–66 in *Marchands, diplomates et empereurs: Études sur la civilisation mésopotamienne offertes à Paul Garelli*. Edited by D. Charpin and F. Joannès. Paris: ERC, 1991.

Cocquerillat, D. "Les prébendes patrimoniales dans les temples à l'époque de la Ire dynastie de Babylone." *Revue Internationale des Droits de l'antiquite* 3 (1955) 39–106.

Cole, S. W., and P. Machinist. *Letters from Priests to the Kings Esarhaddon and Assurbanipal*. SAA 13. Helsinki: Helsinki University Press, 1998.

Crouch, C. L. *War and Ethics in the Ancient Near East: Military Violence in Light of Cosmology and History.* BZAW 407. Berlin: de Gruyter, 2009.

Dalley, S. "Old Babylonian Prophecies at Uruk and Kish." Pp. 85–97 in *Opening the Tablet Box: Near Eastern Studies in Honor of Benjamin R. Foster.* Edited by S. C. Melville and A. L. Slotsky. CHANE 42. Boston, MA: Brill, 2010.

de Jong, M. J. *Isaiah Among the Ancient Near Eastern Prophets: A Comparative Study of the Earliest Stages of the Isaiah Tradition and the Neo-Assyrian Prophecies.* VTSup 117. Leiden: Brill, 2007.

_____. "The Fallacy of True and False in Prophecy Illustrated by Jer 28:8–9." *JHS* 12 (2012) Article 10.

Dietrich, M. "Prophetenbriefe aus Mari." Pp. 83–93 in *Religiöse Texte: Deutungen der Zukunft in Briefen, Orakeln und Omina.* Edited by M. Dietrich et al. TUAT II/1. Gütersloh: Mohn, 1986.

Dossin, G. "Les archives épistolaires du palais de Mari." *Syria* 19 (1938) 105–26.

Dubovský, P. *Hezekiah and the Assyrian Spies: Reconstruction of the Neo-Assyrian Intelligence Services and its Significance for 2 Kings 18–19.* BibOr 49. Rome: Pontifical Biblical Institute, 2006.

Durand, J.-M. *Archives épistolaires de Mari I.* ARM 26/1. Paris: ERC, 1988.

_____. *Florilegium marianum VII: Le culte d'Addu d'Alep et l'affaire d'Alahtum.* Mémoires de N.A.B.U. 8. Paris: SEPOA, 2002.

Durand, J.-M. and D. Charpin. *Archives épistolaires de Mari.* ARM 26. Paris: ERC, 1988.

Ellis, M. deJong "The Archive of the Old Babylonian Kititum Temple and Other Texts from Ishchali." *JAOS* 106 (1987) 757–86.

_____. "The Goddess Kititum Speaks to King Ibalpiel: Oracle Texts from Ishchali." *MARI* 5 (1987) 235–66.

Fleming, D. E. "Prophets and Temple Personnel in the Mari Archives." Pp. 44–64 in *The Priests in the Prophets: The Portrayal of Priests, Prophets, and Other Religious Specialists in the Latter Prophets.* Edited by L. L. Grabbe and A. O. Bellis. JSOTSup 408. London: T. & T. Clark, 2004.

_____. *Time at Emar: The Cultic Calendar and the Rituals from the Diviner's Archive.* MesCiv 11. Winona Lake, IN: Eisenbrauns, 2000.

Frahm, E. "Hochverrat in Assur." Pp. 89–137 in *Assur-Forschungen: Arbeiten aus der Forschungsstelle "Edition literarischer Keilschrifttexte aus Assur" der Heidelberger Akademie der Wissenschaften.* Edited by S. M. Maul and N. P. Heeßel. Wiesbaden: Harrassowitz, 2010.

Frayne, D. *Old Babylonian Period (2003–1595 BC).* RIME 4. Toronto: University of Toronto Press, 1990.

Fronzaroli, P. "Gli equivalenti di EME-BAL nelle liste lessicali Eblaite." *Studi Eblaiti* 2 (1980) 91–95.

Glassner, J.-J. *Mesopotamian Chronicles.* SBLWAW 19. Atlanta: SBL, 2004.

Grabbe, L. L. *Priests, Prophets, Diviners, Sages: A Socio-Historical Study of Religious Specialists in Ancient Israel.* Valley Forge, PA: Trinity Press International, 1995.

Halton, C. "Allusions to the Stream of Tradition in Neo-Assyrian Oracles." *ANES* 56 (2009) 50–61.

Hamori, E. J. "Verification of Prophecy at Mari." *WO* 42 (2012) 1–22.

_____. and J. Stökl, eds., *Dream Divination in the Hebrew Bible and the Ancient Near East*. ANEM. Atlanta: SBL, 2018.

Heimpel, W. "Euristic Dog Behaviour." *NABU* 1996 (1996) §45.

_____. *Letters to the King of Mari: A New Translation, With Historical Introduction, Notes, and Commentary*. MesCiv 12. Winona Lake, IN: Eisenbrauns, 2003.

Heltzer, M. "On the Origin of the Near Eastern Archaeological Amber." Pp. 169–76 in *Languages and Cultures in Contact: At the Crossroads of Civilizations in the Syro-Mesopotamian Realm; Proceedings of the 42nd RAI*. Edited by K. van Lerberghe and G. Voet. OLA 96. Leuven: Peeters, 1999.

Hurowitz, V. A. *I Have Built you an Exalted House: Temple Building in the Bible in Light of Mesopotamian and North-West Semitic Writings*. JSOTSup 115; ASOR Monograph Series 5. Sheffield: JSOT Press, 1992.

Jursa, M. "Cuneiform Writing in Neo-Babylonian Temple Communities." Pp. 184–204 in *The Oxford Handbook of Cuneiform Culture*. Edited by E. Robson and K. Radner. Oxford: Oxford University Press, 2011.

Kleber, K. *Tempel und Palast: Die Beziehungen zwischen dem König und dem Eanna-Tempel im spätbabylonischen Uruk*. AOAT 358. Münster: Ugarit-Verlag, 2008.

Lambert, W. G. *Babylonian Oracle Questions*. MesCiv 13. Winona Lake, IN: Eisenbrauns, 2007.

Langdon, S. *Tammuz and Ishtar: A Monograph upon Babylonian Religion and Theology: Extensive Extracts from the Tammuz Liturgies and all of the Arbela Oracles*. Oxford: Clarendon, 1914.

Lemaire, A. "Oracles, politique et littérature dans les royaumes Araméens et Transjordaniens (IXe–VIIIe s.av. n.è.)." Pp. 171–93 in *Oracles et prophéties dans l'Antiquité: Actes du colloque de Strasbourg, 15–17, Juin 1995*. Edited by J. G. Heintz. Travaux du Centre de recherche sur le Proche-Orient et la Grèce antiques 15. Paris: de Boccard, 1997.

Lenzi, A. *Secrecy and the Gods: Secret Knowledge in Ancient Mesopotamia and Biblical Israel*. SAAS 19. Helsinki, Finland: Neo-Assyrian Text Corpus Project, 2008.

_____. "Revisiting Biblical Prophecy, Revealed Knowledge Pertaining to Ritual, and Secrecy in Light of Ancient Mesopotamian Prophetic Texts." Pp. 65–86 in *Divination, Politics and Ancient Near Eastern Empires*. Edited by A. Lenzi and J. Stökl. ANEM 7. Atlanta: SBL, 2014.

_____, and J. Stökl, eds. *Divination, Politics and Ancient Near Eastern Empires*. ANEM. Atlanta: SBL, 2014.

Luukko, M. and G. v. Buylaere. *The Political Correspondence of Esarhaddon*. SAA 16. Helsinki: Helsinki University Press, 2002.

Machinist, P. "Kingship and Divinity in Imperial Assyria." Pp. 152–88 in *Text, Artifact, and Image: Revealing Ancient Israelite Religion*. Edited by G. M. Beckman and T. J. Lewis. BJS 346. Providence, RI: Brown Judaic Studies, 2006.

Margalit, B. "Ninth-Centruy Israelite Prophecy in the Light of Contemporary NWSemitic Epigraphs." Pp. 515–32 in *"Und Mose schrieb dieses Lied auf": Studien zum Alten Testament und zum Alten Orient: Festschrift für Oswald Loretz zur Vollendung seines 70. Lebensjahres mit Beiträgen von Freunden, Schülern und Kollegen*. Edited by M. Dietrich and I. Kottsieper. AOAT 250. Münster: Ugarit-Verlag, 1998.

Margueron, J.-C. *Mari, métropole de l'Euphrate au IIIe et au début du IIe millénaire avant J-C*. Paris: Picard, 2004.

Maul, S. M. "Aleuromantie: Von der Altorientalischen Kunst, mit Hilfe von Opfermehl das Maß göttlichen Wohlwollens zu ermitteln." Pp. 115–30 in *Von Göttern und Menschen: Beiträge zu Literatur und Geschichte des Alten Orients: Festschrift für Brigitte Groneberg*. Edited by D. Shehata, F. Weiershäuser, and K. V. Zand. CM 41. Leiden: Brill, 2010.

_____. "Die Wissenschaft von der Zukunft—Überlegungen zur Bedeutung der Divination im Alten Orient." Pp. 135–51 in *Babylon: Wissenskultur in Orient und Okzident*. Edited by E. Cancik-Kirschbaum, M. van Ess, and J. Mahrzahn. Topoi. Berlin Studies of the Ancient World. Berlin: de Gruyter, 2011.

Meinhold, W. *Ištar in Aššur: Untersuchung eines Lokalkultes von ca. 2500 bis 614 v. Chr.* AOAT 367. Münster: Ugarit-Verlag, 2009.

Moran, W. L. "Akkadian Letters." Pp. 623–32 in *Ancient Near Eastern Texts Relating to the Old Testament*. 3rd edition. Edited by J. B. Pritchard. Princeton, NJ: Princeton University Press, 1969.

Nissinen, M. "A Prophetic Riot in Seleucid Babylonia." Pp. 64–74 in *"Wer darf hinaufsteigen zum Berg JHWhs?" Beiträge zu Prophetie und Poesie des Alten Testaments: Festschrift für Sigurður Örn Steingrímsson zum 70. Geburtstag*. Edited by H. Irsigler. ATAT 72. St. Ottilien: EOS, 2002.

_____. "Das kritische Potential in der altorientalischen Prophetie." Pp. 1–33 in *Propheten in Mari, Assyrien und Israel*. Edited by M. Köckert and M. Nissinen. FRLANT 201. Göttingen: Vandenhoeck & Ruprecht, 2003.

_____. "Das Problem der Prophetenschüler." Pp. 337–53 in *Houses Full of All Good Things: Essays in Memory of Timo Veijola*. Edited by J. Pakkala and M. Nissinen. Publications of the Finnish Exegetical Society 95. Helsinki: The Finnish Exegetical Society; Göttingen: Vandenhoeck & Ruprecht, 2008.

_____. "How Prophecy Became Literature." *SJOT* 19 (2005) 153–72.

_____. "Prophecy against the King in Neo-Assyrian Sources." Pp. 157–70 in *"Lasset uns Brücken bauen:" Collected Communications to the XVth Congress of the IOSOT, Cambridge 1995*. Edited by K.-D. Schunck and M. Augustin. Frankfurt a.M.: Lang, 1998.

_____. "Prophecy and Omen Divination: Two Sides of the Same Coin." Pp. 341–51 in *Divination and Interpretation of Signs in the Ancient World*. Edited by A. Annus. OIS 6. Chicago, IL: Chicago University Press, 2010.

_____. *Prophets and Prophecy in the Ancient Near East: With Contributions by C. L. Seow and Robert K. Ritner*. SBLWAW 12. Atlanta: SBL, 2003.

_____. *References to Prophecy in Neo-Assyrian Sources*. SAAS 7. Helsinki: Neo-Assyrian Corpus Project, 1998.

_____. "What is Prophecy? An Ancient Near Eastern Perspective." Pp. 17–37 in *Inspired Speech: Prophecy in the Ancient Near East: Essays in Honour of Herbert B. Huffmon*. Edited by J. Kaltner and L. Stulman. JSOTSup 378. London: T. & T. Clark, 2004.

Oppenheim, A. L. "The Interpretation of Dreams in the Ancient Near East: With a Translation of an Assyrian Dream-Book." *TAPS* 46 (1956) 179–373.

Parpola, S. *Assyrian Prophecies*. SAA 9. Helsinki: Helsinki University Press, 1997.

_____. "Cuneiform Texts from Ziyaret Tepe (Tušḫān), 2002–2003 (Plates I–XXV)." *SAAB* 17 (2008) 1–115.

_____, K. Radner, and H. D. Baker. *The Prosopography of the Neo-Assyrian Empire*. 3 volumes in 6 parts. Helsinki: Neo-Assyrian Text Corpus Project, 1998–2012.

_____, and K. Watanabe. *Neo-Assyrian Treaties and Loyalty Oaths*. SAA 2. Helsinki: Helsinki University Press, 1988.

Pientka-Hinz, R. "I. Texte aus Mesopotamien: Akkadische Texte des 2. und 1. Jt. v. Chr.; 1. Omina und Prophetien." Pp. 16–60 in *Omina, Orakel, Rituale und Beschwörungen*. Edited by I. T. Abusch et al. TUAT.NF 4. Gütersloh: Gütersloher Verlagshaus, 2008.

Pongratz-Leisten, B. *Herrschaftswissen in Mesopotamien: Formen der Kommunikation zwischen Gott und König im 2. und 1. Jahrtausend v. Chr.* SAAS 10. Helsinki: The Neo-Assyrian Text Corpus Project, 1999.

Postgate, J. N. "Royal Exercise of Justice under the Assyrian Empire." Pp. 417–26 in *Le palais et la royauté (archéologie et civilisation). Compte rendu du XIXe Rencontre Assyriologique Internationale organisée par le groupe François Thureau-Dangin, Paris, 29 juin—2 juillet 1971*. Edited by P. Garelli. Paris: Geuthner, 1974.

Radner, K. "The Relation Between Format and Content of Neo-Assyrian Texts." Pp. 63–78 in *Nineveh, 612 BC: The Glory and Fall of the Assyrian Empire. Catalogue of the 10th Anniversary Exhibition of the Neo-Assyrian Text Corpus Project*. Edited by R. Mattila. Helsinki: Helsinki University Press, 1995.

Roberts, J. J. M. "The Mari Prophetic Texts in Transliteration and English Translation." Pp. 157–253 in *The Bible and the Ancient Near East: Collected Essays*. Edited by J. J. M. Roberts. Winona Lake, IN: Eisenbrauns, 2002.

Rochberg, F. "Babylonian Horoscopes." *TAPS* 88 (1998) 1–164.

_____. "Heaven and Earth: Divine-Human Relations in Mesopotamian Celestial Divination." Pp. 169–85 in *Prayer, Magic, and the Stars in the Ancient and Late Antique World*. Edited by S. B. Noegel, J. T. Walker, and B. M. Wheeler. University Park, PA: Pennsylvania State University Press, 2003.

Sasson, J. M. "The Posting of Letters with Divine Messages." Pp. 299–316 in *Florilegium marianum II: Recueil d'études à la mémoire de Maurice Birot*. Edited by D. Charpin and J.-M. Durand. Mémoires de N.A.B.U. 3. Supplément à N.A.B.U. 1994 no. 2. Paris: SEPOA, 1994.

_____. "Water Beneath Straw: Adventures of a Prophetic Phrase in the Mari Archives." Pp. 599–608 in *Solving Riddles and Untying Knots: Biblical, Epigraphic, and Semitic Studies in Honor of Jonas C. Greenfield*. Edited by Z. Zevit, S. Gitin, and M. Sokoloff. Winona Lake, IN: Eisenbrauns, 1995.

Schmidt, W. H. "Einsicht als Ziel prophetischer Verkündigung." Pp. 377–96 in *Ich bewirke das Heil und erschaffe das Unheil (Jesaja 45,7): Studien zur Botschaft der Propheten: Festschrift für Lothar Ruppert zum 65. Geburtstag*. Edited by F. Diedrich and B. Willmes. FB 88. Würzburg: Echter Verlag, 1998.

Schwemer, D. *Die Wettergottgestalten Mesopotamiens und Nordsyriens im Zeitalter der Keilschriftkulturen: Materialien und Studien nach den schriftlichen Quellen*. Wiesbaden: Harrassowitz, 2001.

Selz, G. J. "Five Divine Ladies: Thoughts on Inana(k), Ištar, In(n)in(a), Annunītum, and Anat, and the Origin of the Title 'Queen of Heaven.'" *Nin* 1 (2000) 29–62.

Soden, W. von. "Aramäische Wörter in neuassyrischen und neu- und spätbabylonischen Texten: Ein Vorbericht III." *Or* 46 (1977) 183–97.

Stökl, J. "Ancient Near Eastern Prophecy." Pp. 16–24 in *Dictionary of the Old Testament: Prophets*. Edited by J. G. McConville and M. J. Boda. Downers Grove, IL: Inter-Varsity, 2012.

————. "Divination as Warfare: The Use of Divination across Borders." Pp. 49–63 in *Divination, Politics and Ancient Near Eastern Empires*. Edited by A. Lenzi and J. Stökl. ANEM 7. Atlanta: SBL, 2014.

————. "Gender Ambiguity in Ancient Near Eastern Prophecy? A Re-Assessment of the Data Behind a Popular Theory." Pp. 59–79 in *Prophets Male and Female: Gender and Prophecy in the Hebrew Bible, the Eastern Mediterranean and the Ancient Near East*. Edited by J. Stökl and C. L. Carvalho. AIL 15. Atlanta: SBL, 2013.

————. "'I Have Rained Stones and Fiery Glow on Their Heads!' Celestial and Meteorological Prophecy in the Neo-Assyrian Empire." Pp. 239–251 in *"Thus Speaks Ishtar of Arbela:" Prophecy in Israel, Assyria and Egypt in the Neo-Assyrian Period*. Edited by R. P. Gordon and H. M. Barstad. Winona Lake, IN: Eisenbrauns, 2013.

————. "(Intuitive) Divination, (Ethical) Demands and Diplomacy in the Ancient Near East." Pp. 82–92 in *Mediating Between Heaven and Earth: Communication with the Divine in the Ancient Near East*. Edited by C. L. Crouch, J. Stökl, and A. E. Zernecke. LHBOTS 566. London: T & T Clark, 2012.

————. *Prophecy in the Ancient Near East: A Philological and Sociological Comparison*. CHANE 56. Leiden: Brill, 2012.

Tiemeyer, L.-S. "Prophecy as a Way of Cancelling Prophecy: the Strategic Uses of Foreknowledge." *ZAW* 117 (2005) 329–50.

Toorn, K. van der. "From the Mouth of the Prophet: The Literary Fixation of Jeremiah's Prophecies in the Context of the Ancient Near East." Pp. 191–202 in *Inspired Speech: Prophecy in the Ancient Near East: Essays in Honour of Herbert B. Huffmon*. Edited by J. Kaltner and L. Stulman. JSOTSup 378. London: T. & T. Clark, 2004.

————. "From the Oral to the Written: The Case of Old Babylonian Prophecy." Pp. 219–34 in *Writings and Speech in Israelite and Ancient Near Eastern Prophecy*. Edited by E. Ben Zvi and M. H. Floyd. SBLSymS 10. Atlanta: SBL, 2000.

————. "Old Babylonian Prophecy between the Oral and the Written." *JNSL* 24 (1998) 55–70.

Van Dijk, J. "Die Tontafeln aus dem Palast des Sînkāšid." Pp. 61–62, Taf. 20, 28 in *XVIII. vorläufiger Bericht über die von dem Deutschen Archäologischen Institut und der Deutschen Orient-Gesellschaft aus Mitteln der Deutschen Forschungsgemeinschaft unternommenen Ausgrabungen in Uruk-Warka: Winter 1959/60*. Edited by H. Lenzen. ADOG 7. Berlin: Mann, 1962.

Waerzeggers, C. "The Pious King: Royal Patronage of Temples in the Neo-Babylonian Period." Pp. 725–51 in *The Oxford Handbook of Cuneiform Culture*. Edited by E. Robson and K. Radner. Oxford: Oxford University Press, 2011.

Weippert, M. "'König, fürchte dich nicht!' Assyrische Prophetie im 7. Jahrhundert v. Chr." *Or* 71 (2002) 1–54.

————. "'Das Frühere, siehe, ist eingetroffen': Über Selbstzitate im altorientalischen Prophetenspruch." Pp. 147–69 in *Oracles et prophéties dans l'Antiquité: Actes du colloque de Strasbourg, 15–17, juin 1995*. Edited by J. G. Heintz. Travaux du Centre de recherche sur le Proche-Orient et la Grèce antiques 15. Paris: de Boccard, 1997.

_____. "Aspekte israelitischer Prophetie im Lichte verwandter Erscheinungen des Alten Orients." Pp. 287–319 in *Ad bene et fideliter seminandum: Festgabe für Karlheinz Deller zum 21. Februar 1987*. Edited by U. Magen and G. Mauer. AOAT 220. Kevelaer: Butzon & Bercker; Neukirchen-Vluyn: Neukirchener Verlag, 1988.

_____. "Die Bildsprache der neuassyrischen Prophetie." Pp. 55–93 in *Beiträge zur prophetischen Bildsprache in Israel und Assyrien*. Edited by H. Weippert, K. Seybold, and M. Weippert. OBO 64. Fribourg: Universitätsverlag; Göttingen: Vandenhoeck & Ruprecht, 1985.

Zgoll, A. "Die Welt im Schlaf sehen—Inkubation von Träumen im alten Mesopotamien." *WO* 32 (2002) 74–101.

_____. *Traum und Welterleben im antiken Mesopotamien: Traumtheorie und Traumpraxis im 3.–1. Jahrtausend v. Chr. als Horizont einer Kulturgeschichte des Träumens*. AOAT 333. Münster: Ugarit-Verlag, 2006.

Prophecy in Syria:
Zakkur of Hamath and Lu ͨash

HÉLÈNE SADER

American University of Beirut

It is a very difficult, if not impossible, task to investigate a topic as complex as ancient prophecy in the absence of a substantial number of written documents. This is unfortunately the case for ancient Northwest and South Syria, where no Bronze or Iron Age texts relating to prophetic activity are extant.[1] The only direct evidence for the existence of prophecy in this area[2] is a short passage in the inscription of the stele of Zakkur of Hamath and Lu ͨash, which reads as follows:

> Now I lifted my hands to Baalshamayn and Baalshamay[n] answered me, [and] Baalshamayn [spoke] to me [thr]ough seers and through visionaries,[3] [and] Baalshamayn [said] "F[e]ar not, for I have made [you] king, [and I who will st] and with [you], and I will deliver you from all [these kings who] have forced a siege against you . . .[4]

---

1. For a review of all ancient Near Eastern written sources relating to prophecy, see J. Stökl, *Prophecy in the Ancient Near East: A Philological and Sociological Comparison* (Culture and History of the Ancient Near East 56; Leiden: Brill, 2012); for original texts in transliteration and translation relating to ancient Near Eastern prophecy, see M. Nissinen, *Prophets and Prophecy in the Ancient Near East* (Writings from the Ancient World 12; Atlanta: SBL, 2003).

2. There is another reference to what seems to be prophetic activity in the trilingual inscription of Incirli (S. A. Kaufman, "The Phoenician Inscription of the Incirli Trilingual: A Tentative Reconstruction and Translation," *Maarav* 14.2 [2007] 7–26). The inscribed monument, which was erected by Awarikku, king of Que, mentions in its Phoenician version a 'wise man' (חכם, a word attested in Imperial Aramaic only as חכים) who 'gave advice' (ועץ) (Front, line 13) to Matiʾilu, the Aramean king of Arpad. However, the fact that the text speaks of a 'wise man' instead of a "seer," or "diviner," or "messenger," one who 'gives advice' and not one who repeats the words of the divinity or utters words on its behalf, speaks against the prophetic nature of the event. On the other hand, there are three prophetic texts written in Aramaic but found outside Syria. These are the Deir ͨAllah inscription, the Amman Citadel inscription, and the Deir Rifa inscription (Stökl, *Prophecy*, 19–22).

3. For the meaning of עדדן, see pp. 125–26 below.

4. C. L. Seow, "Zakkur Stela," in Nissinen, *Prophets and Prophecy,* 206.

Prophecy is the "human transmission of allegedly divine messages."[5] It also contains a clear prophetic process of transmission that "consists of the divine sender of the message, the message itself, the human transmitter of the message, and the recipient(s) of the message."[6] Based on this definition, the Zakkur inscription clearly contains all the elements of a prophecy. The divine sender of the message is the god Baalshamayn, the divine message is clearly uttered by human transmitters, 'seer's (חזין) and 'messengers' (עדדן), and the recipient is, of course, Zakkur himself. In order to gain a better understanding of the Syrian prophetic tradition expressed in the Zakkur inscription, this paper will first describe the historical and archaeological context of the text; it will then try to place the above passage relating to prophecy in its ancient Near Eastern context and to establish the interconnections between the various ancient Near Eastern prophetic traditions that may have helped shape Syrian prophecy.

The Inscription[7]

The stele of Zakkur, King of Hamath and Lu'ash, also known as the Afis Stele, was discovered in a secondary context in 1903 by Pognon,[8] who did not disclose the name of the site where he found it, although it was later known to be Tell Afis.[9] The stele is today in the Louvre Museum. It presents a figure standing on a pedestal decorated with metopes containing an oblique cross-shaped motif, known as a St. Andrew cross, alternating with triglyphs. Only the feet of the statue and the lower part of the garment are preserved. Below the decorated pedestal, the badly damaged stone is inscribed on its front (A) and lateral (B and C) sides with an Old Aramaic text that records a victory of Zakkur over a coalition of Syro-Hittite kings, a victory that the Aramean ruler owed to the divine intervention of the god Baalshamayn, the "Lord of Heaven." The overwhelming majority of scholars are of the opinion that Zakkur was in fact saved by the intervention of the Assyrian army, most probably in 796 B.C.E., the date of the campaign of Adad-nērārī III against Mansuate.[10] Fuchs differs from this general consensus, pointing out that the Afis inscription itself does not hint at such an event and that Zakkur could

5. Nissinen, *Prophets and Prophecy*, 1.

6. Ibid., 2.

7. For a study and translation of this inscription, see H. Donner and W. Röllig, *Kanaanäische und aramäische Inschriften* (3 vols.; Wiesbaden: Harrassowitz, 1973) 2:47–48; J. C. L. Gibson, *Textbook of Syrian Semitic Inscriptions, II: Aramaic Inscriptions, Including Inscriptions in the Dialect of Zenjirli* (Oxford: Clarendon, 1975) 6–17; A. R. Millard, "The Inscription of Zakkur King of Hamath," in *The Context of Scripture: Monumental Inscriptions from the Biblical World* (3 vols.; ed. W. H. and K. L. Younger Jr.; Leiden: Brill, 2000) 2:155; Seow, "Zakkur," with bibliography.

8. Henri Pognon, *Inscriptions sémitiques de la Syrie, de la Mésopotamie et de la région de Mossoul* (Paris: Imprimerie Nationale, 1907) 156.

9. René Dussaud, "La stèle araméenne de Zakir au Musée du Louvre," *Syria* 3 (1922) 176.

10. A. Jepsen, "Israel und Damaskus," *Archiv für Orientforschung* 14 (1941–44) 170; P.-E. Dion, *Les Araméens à l'âge du Fer: Histoire politique et structures sociales* (Études Bibliques Nou-

have successfully resisted the coalition without Assyrian help.[11] The inscription is generally dated to the end of the 9th or the early years of the 8th century B.C.E.

The Historical Context

In order to better understand the historical circumstances and the cultural background of the prophecy recorded in the Zakkur inscription, it is useful to recall the main phases of the history of the Aramean kingdom of Hamath and Lu'ash and the circumstances of Zakkur's accession to the throne. As his royal title indicates, Zakkur joined two distinct geographical districts under his rule, the kingdom of Hamath and the land of Lu'ash, and called himself king of Hamath and Lu'ash. In the Antakya stele dated between 786–783 B.C.E., however, Zakkur is called "Zakkur of the land of Hamath," without the mention of Lu'ash.[12]

The Kingdom of Hamath

After the collapse of the Hittite empire and the local Late Bronze Age kingdoms of Syria at the end of the second millennium B.C.E., polities such as Carchemish, Masuwari, and Malatya emerged in the 11th century B.C.E. as independent political entities ruled by Luwian dynasties, probably splinter groups of the fallen Hittite royal family.[13] The inscriptions from Tell Tayinat and Aleppo have recently proved the existence of yet another kingdom in North Syria in the 11th century B.C.E.: Palistin/Walistin.[14] This polity had extended its dominion under the rule of King Taita from the Amuq Plain to Aleppo. Taita, king of Palistin/Walistin, is also mentioned in the Meharde and Sheizar inscriptions.[15] This evidence immediately

---

velle Série 34; Paris: Gabalda, 1997) 153; E. Lipiński, *The Aramaeans: Their Ancient History, Culture, Religion* (Orientalia Lovaniensia Analecta 100; Leuven: Peeters, 2000) 310.

11. A. Fuchs, "Der Turtān Šamšī-ilu und die große Zeit der assyrischen Großen (830–746)," *Die Welt des Orients* 38 (2008) 73 n. 42.

12. This may be a simple omission or it may bear historical implications. If we opt for the second hypothesis, the evidence of the Antakya stele may lead to the assumption that Lu'ash was annexed either later by Zakkur—and this would lower the date of the Afis stele to after 783 B.C.E.—or that the annexation of Lu'ash took place before 786 B.C.E. but was then cut off from Zakkur's territory by the Assyrian king's decision to fix the borders between Hamath and Bit Agusi in favor of the latter. Regarding the stele, see A. K. Grayson, *Assyrian Rulers of the Early First Millennium BC II (858–745 BC)* (3 vols.; The Royal Inscriptions of Mesopotamia, Assyrian Periods; Toronto: University of Toronto Press, 1996) 3: A. O. 104.2, 4. For the date, see Fuchs, "Der Turtān Šamšī-ilu," 79.

13. Tim Harrison, "Neo-Hittites in the 'Land of Palestin': Renewed Investigations at Tell Ta'yinat on the Plain of Antioch," *Near Eastern Archaeology* 74.4 (2009) 187.

14. J. D. Hawkins, "Cilicia, the Amuq, and Aleppo: New Light on a Dark Age," *Near Eastern Archaeology* 72.4 (2009) 164–73; idem, "The Inscriptions of the Aleppo Temple," *Anatolian Studies* 61 (2011) 35–54.

15. Idem, *Corpus of Hieroglyphic Luwian Inscriptions*, vol. 1: *Inscriptions of the Iron Age* (Studies in Indo-European Language and Culture New Series 8.1; Berlin: de Gruyter, 2000) 1:415–16.

led to the assumption that the rule of this 11th century B.C.E. king extended as far south as Hamath.[16] However, based on the development of the Hieroglyphic Luwian sign L.386, Hawkins came to the conclusion that the Meharde and Sheizar inscriptions were later than the Aleppo texts and that, consequently, there were two Taitas, "Taita I King of Palistin and Taita II King of Walistin,"[17] Taita II probably being the grandson of Taita I. This new evidence led Hawkins to suggest the existence of a "kingdom of perhaps three generations, 11th to early 10th centuries BC, ruled from the Amuq by Taita I controlling Aleppo and Karkamiš(?); and by Taita II controlling (additionally?) as far south as Meharde-Sheizar"—that is, the territory of Hamath.[18] This new epigraphic evidence seems to answer the reservations of Sass, who suggested a lower date for Taita I's rule in the mid-10th century B.C.E.[19]

Dated also to the 10th century B.C.E. is the rule of two kings of Hamath mentioned in the Old Testament (2 Sam 8:9–10 and 1 Chr 18:9–10): To'i or To'u and his son Joram or Hadoram, who were contemporaries of David and Hadadezer of Sobah.[20] Neither are known from extrabiblical sources. The first question is in regard to their historicity and the second is about the date of their reign. There is no way to prove that these two kings actually existed. Steitler has argued that the biblical name To'i is the same as Luwian Taita and Hurrian *Taḫḫe*, an identification adopted by Janeway; both Steitler and Janeway identified him with the Taita of the Aleppo inscription.[21] Collins also suggested, with a question mark, the identification of To'i with the Taita of the Aleppo inscription.[22] If the equation To'i = Taita is accepted, then the biblical king should be equated with Taita II of the Hieroglyphic Hittite inscriptions of Meharde-Sheizar rather than Taita I. The former's rule, based on palaeographic analysis, is also placed in the 10th century B.C.E. and would correspond to the biblical dating. If, on the other hand, the equation To'i = Taita is rejected, there remains the possibility of biblical To'i, Hurrian *Taḫ'e*, being yet another 10th-century B.C.E. king of Hamath, a predecessor to or successor of Taita II.

---

16. Hawkins, *Corpus of Hieroglyphic Luwian Inscriptions*, 1:51.

17. Ibid.

18. Ibid. It is perhaps in the light of this sweeping conquest of parts of Hatti and Syria by Taita I, king of Palastin, that one should understand Ramses III's inscription in Medinet Habu.

19. B. Sass, "Taita, King of Palistin: ca. 950–900 BCE?" n.p. [accessed October 2010]. Online: http://www.bu.edu/asor/pubs/nea/digit-al-nea-html.

20. According to B. J. Collins, *The Hittites and Their World* (Archaeology and Biblical Studies 7; Leiden: Brill, 2007) 198 n. 4, To'i is "of Hurrian origin and is attested in the thirteenth century at Meskene-Emar in its Hurrian form Tah'e" (see Hawkins, *Corpus of Hieroglyphic Luwian Inscriptions*, 1:400 with n.30).

21. C. Steitler, "The Biblical King Toi of Hamath and the Late Hittite State 'P/Walas(a)tin,'" *Biblische Notizen* 146 (2010) 81–99; B. Janeway, "Old Testament King discovered?" n.p. [accessed 2011]. Online: http://www.biblearchaeology.org/post/2011/02/11/Old-Testament-King-Discovered.aspx.

22. Collins, *The Hittites*, 198 n. 2.

As for Joram/Hadoram, nothing can be said about the circumstances or the historicity of his rule. However, it seems odd that a ruler bearing a Semitic name should find a place in a long, almost continuous sequence of dynasts with non-Semitic names who used Hieroglyphic Hittite in their royal inscriptions and who ruled through the 10th and 9th centuries B.C.E. The possibility that the mention of Hadoram as a son of Toʿi may be an error on the part of the biblical writer cannot be ruled out. One possible explanation for this confusion, which cannot be verified, is that the biblical writer knew of Adrame son of Gusi, ruler of Arpad, and mistakenly confused him as the ruler of the kingdom of Hamath.

Whether Taita I's dynasty continued to rule throughout the 10th and 9th centuries or whether a new branch of the Luwian royal family seized the throne and founded an independent kingdom of Hamath sometime around 900 B.C.E. remains an open question. In favor of the second option is the fact that the three kings who ruled in the course of the 9th century, after the reign of Taita II, called themselves, and were called by others, "King of Hamath," not "King of Walistin." Hieroglyphic Hittite royal inscriptions, which were found in the vicinity of the modern city of Hama, in fact mention the name of the kingdom and the names of three of its rulers: Parita, Urḫilinas, and Uratami.[23] The date of their rule can be roughly estimated based on, first, the mention of Urḫilinas, son of Parita and father of Uratami, in the annals of Shalmaneser III as the head of an anti-Assyrian coalition from 853 B.C.E. until 845 B.C.E.; and, second, on the fact that Uratami (840–820 B.C.E.) was a contemporary of Marduk-Apla-Uṣur, a ruler of Suḫu who paid tribute to Shalmaneser III, most probably in 838 B.C.E.[24] Thus, the rule of Parita, Urḫilinas, and Uratami may have occupied most of the 9th century B.C.E. The above evidence clearly indicates that Hamath was within the neo-Hittite cultural sphere until the end of the 9th century B.C.E.

It is toward the end of the 9th century, after the reign of Uratami, that Zakkur must have seized the throne of Hamath and put an end to the rule of the Hittite dynasty.[25] The details of this event remain totally in the dark, and the usurpation of the throne can be assumed first, from the fact that Zakkur does not give a royal genealogy and, second, from his inscription, where he clearly says that he owes his throne to the divine favor of the god Baalshamayn (line 3: ‏והמלכני בעלשמין‎). Lemaire notes in this context that the rule of kings who are not part of the lineage of the ruling dynasty is always justified by an oracle and a prophetic intervention in

23. Hawkins, *Corpus of Hieroglyphic Luwian Inscriptions*, 402.

24. Grayson, *Assyrian Rulers*, 102.2, 10, 23; Hawkins, *Corpus of Hieroglyphic Luwian Inscriptions*, 402; Simo Parpola, "A letter from Marduk-apla-usur of Anah to Rudamu/Uratamis, King of Hamath," in J.-P. Riis and M.-L. Buhl, *Hama: Fouilles et recherches 1931–1938: Les objets de la période dite syro-hittite (âge du Fer)* (2 vols.; Copenhagen: Nationalmuseet, 1990), 2:261.

25. The succession Uratami → Zakkur was suggested also by E. Fugmann, *Hama: Fouilles et recherches 1931–1938: L'architecture des périodes pré-hellénistiques* (Copenhagen: Nationalmuseet, 1958), 171.

the Old Testament.[26] Moreover, it has been noted that the verb מלך in the Hiphil, as it appears in the Zakkur inscription, is often used in the Old Testament to refer to irregular accession to the throne, such as the foundation of a new dynasty.[27] Finally, Zakkur, as well as all the kings who ruled after him on the throne of Hamath, bear Aramaic, not Hittite/Hurrian, names. Zakkur is also the first king of Hamath who left an inscription written in Aramaic and not in Hieroglyphic Hittite, as did all his predecessors on the throne. The building of a "fortress" by Uratami, who dedicated a stele to commemorate the event, seems to hint at a troubled situation in the kingdom of Hamath during his reign, which may have led eventually to the overthrow of the ruling dynasty.[28] The rise of Zakkur to power represents a clear break and a turning point in the history of the kingdom—namely, the regression of Hittite political predominance and the rise to power of rulers of Aramean stock.

The kingdom of Hamath occupied the territory stretching from the modern city of Hama to Labwe in the northern Lebanese Biqāʿ, as well as the area extending west of this north–south line, from the Orontes to the Mediterranean. The eastern extension of the kingdom cannot be fixed with certainty, but Hamath may also have controlled the trade route linking the Euphrates and North Syria through Palmyra.[29]

The Kingdom of Luʿash

The second territory over which Zakkur was able to extend his rule is Luʿash. Luʿash has been unanimously identified with the Late Bronze Age kingdom of Nuhašše and with the land of Luḫuti of the Assyrian inscriptions.[30] Its territory extended north of the land of Hamath, east of the Orontes, between Aleppo and Maʿarret en-Noʿmān,[31] more especially the Jazr area.[32] Its capital was Ḫatarrika, the חזרך of the Zakkur inscription and the Hadrach of the Old Testament. This city has been identified with Tell Afis, 45 km southwest of Aleppo, where the Zakkur stele was found.[33] The occurrence of both place names, חזרך and אפש, in Zakkur's

---

26. A. Lemaire, "Oracles, politique et littérature dans les royaumes araméens et jordaniens (IXᵉ–VIIIᵉ s. av. n.è.)," in Oracles et Prophéties dans l'Antiquité, Actes du Colloque de Strasbourg 15–17 juin 1995 (ed. J.-G. Heintz; Paris: de Boccard, 1997), 172, 184.

27. I. Jaruzelska, "Les prophètes face aux usurpations dans le royaume du Nord," Vetus Testamentum 54.2 (2004) 169.

28. Hawkins, Corpus of Hieroglyphic Luwian Inscriptions, 1:413.

29. Ibid., 399; Lipiński, Aramaeans, 278.

30. A. Bagg, Die Orts- und Gewässernamen der neuassyrischen Zeit, Teil I: Die Levante (Répertoire Géographique des Textes Cunéiformes 7/1; Wiesbaden: Reichert, 2007), 159; Lipiński, Aramaeans, 257.

31. Ibid., 93–9.

32. S. Mazzoni, "Tell Afis and the Luash in the Aramaean Period," in The World of the Aramaeans II: Studies in History and Archaeology in Honour of Paul-Eugène Dion (ed. M. Daviau, J. W. Wevers, and M. Weigl; Journal for the Study of the Old Testament Supplement Series 324–326; Sheffield, England: Sheffield Academic Press, 2001), 110–112.

33. Bagg, Orts- und Gewässernamen, 93–94.

inscription, led Mazzoni and Lipiński to suggest that the former, חזרך/Ḫatarrika, refers to the city itself and the latter, אפש, to the acropolis where temples and palaces were located.[34] Other scholars reject the identification of חזרך/Ḫatarrika with Tell Afis because of the mention of the place-name אפש in the inscription. They suggest that the latter should be identified with the modern site of Tell Afis, while Hatarikka should be looked for elsewhere.[35]

The land of *Luḫuti* belonged in the 11th century B.C.E. to the kingdom of Palistin, the Patina/Unqi of the Assyrian annals, since the rule of Taita I extended at least as far as Aleppo. This area was coveted by the rising Aramean state of Bit Agusi, which had established itself north of and around Aleppo at the beginning of the 9th century B.C.E. during the rule of Arame, son of Gusi, the founder of the dynasty. The capital, Arnê, modern Erin or Tell ʿAran, was located near Aleppo and was later replaced by Arpad, modern Tell Rifaat, north of Aleppo.[36] Gusi and his successors may have taken advantage of the growing weakness of Palistin/Patina, which was caused by the repeated incursions of the Assyrian army west of the Euphrates intent on claiming part of its former territory. It seems that the kingdom of Palistin was progressively forced to withdraw from its eastern provinces, which came under the control of the new Aramean politiy of Bit Agusi.

The circumstances of Zakkur's rise to power are unknown, but what is certain is that, by the end of the 9th century B.C.E., he was able to extend his dominion over the territory of Hamath as well as the area extending between Hamath and Aleppo, where Bit Agusi had been trying to progressively extend its hegemony. The competition over part or the entirety of the territory of *Luḫuti* may have been the cause of the border dispute between Zakkur of Hamath and Atаršumki of Arpad, a dispute that was settled by Adad-nērārī III at the beginning of the 8th century B.C.E.[37]

The aggressive territorial expansion of Zakkur may have led to the extension of his dominion over the larger part of Luʿash. There is no evidence to help clarify whether this territory was conquered before or after the conquest of Hamath. It is impossible to determine the succession of events, but it is not far-fetched to suggest that the homeland of Zakkur was probably in Luʿash, since it is there that he chose to found his new capital, not in the territory of Hamath. Like many usurpers before and after him, he founded a new capital for his kingdom in an area loyal to him, most likely his homeland. Some scholars have suggested a Ḫanaean origin for Zakkur and interpreted the expression אש ענה אנה as referring to the city of ʿĀna on the Euphrates.[38] It seems highly unlikely to assume that Zakkur was a

---

34. Mazzoni, "Tell Afis," 100; Lipiński, *Aramaeans*, 256.

35. Lipiński, *Aramaeans*, 256.

36. Bagg, *Orts- und Gewässernamen*, 23–25.

37. Grayson, *Assyrian Rulers*, A.O. 104.2.

38. A. R. Millard, "The Homeland of Zakkur," *Semitica* 39 (1990) 47–52; Lipiński, *Aramaeans*, 299 n. 326; identification rejected by Jonas Greenfield, "The Zakir Inscription and the Danklied," in *Proceedings of the Fifth World Congress of Jewish Studies, I* (Jerusalem, 1972) 178.

total stranger without any connection to the area because no foreigner could have usurped the throne without strong internal support, especially that of the religious establishment. Since there is no implicit or explicit evidence for external support or imposition by an external power, as assumed by Ross, it is more plausible to think that Zakkur was himself a local figure, not a total stranger.[39]

It is thus not far-fetched to assume that Zakkur's rise to power started in the area of Luʿash, which was only loosely controlled by the kingdom of Patina toward the end of the 9th century B.C.E. and which may have upset the Arameans of Bit Agusi. The conquest of Hamath may have occurred later, when Zakkur had tightened his grip on Luʿash and had secured for himself a fortified capital. The aggression against Hamath, a traditional ally of Damascus against the Assyrians since Urḫilina's reign, may have triggered an immediate and violent reaction of the king of Damascus, who led a vast coalition of Syro-Hittite kings against him. It is thus not surprising to see that only the kings of Aram-Damascus and Bit Agusi are mentioned by name in the inscription. It is on this occasion that the prophecy was uttered.

Prophecy in the Zakkur inscription

Since the discovery of the Afis stele, the prophetic passage in Zakkur's inscription has been studied in depth by several scholars.[40] The etymology and interpretation of its prophetic terminology have been discussed, and attempts at establishing the origins and cultural connections of this tradition have been made.

The passage of the inscription quoted above is the only clear evidence for prophecy from Bronze and Iron Age North and South Syria; it is therefore extremely difficult to draw conclusions about Syrian prophecy from this one example. The only factual information is that this passage clearly attests the existence of prophetic activity in Syrian religion in the first millennium B.C.E. A close look at all the stakeholders involved in the prophecy will help clarify some of its aspects and characteristic features.

The God of the Prophecy

The votive stele erected by Zakkur to commemorate his victory over the enemy coalition was erected before the god Iluwer, as mentioned in the first line

---

39. J. F. Ross, "Prophecy in Hamath, Israel, and Mari," *Harvard Theological Review* 63 (1970) 27, but doubted by Greenfield, "The Zakir Inscription," 178–79.

40. Donner and Röllig, *KAI*, 2:204–11; Ross, "Prophecy in Hamath"; H.-J. Zobel, "Das Gebet um Abwendung der Not und seine Erhörung in den Klageliedern des Alten Testaments und in der Inschrift des Königs Zakir von Hamath," *Vetus Testamentum* 21 (1971) 91–99; Greenfield, "The Zakir Inscription"; Lemaire, "Oracles," 171–93; Herbert Niehr, *Baʿalšamem: Studien zu Herkunft, Geschichte und Rezeptionsgeschichte eines phönizischen Gottes* (Orientalia Lovaniensia Analecta 123; Studia Phoenicia 17; Leuven: Peeters, 2003) 89–96.

of side A of the inscription: ‫נ.[צבא . זי . שם . זכר . מלך] . ח[מ]ת[ן] . ולעש . לאלור]‬
However, the king's prayer and request for help were addressed to another god,
Baalshamayn, "Lord of Heaven." It is the latter who answered him by sending his
message through prophets. The first question that comes to mind is: why is the
stele dedicated to Iluwer when Baalshamayn is the god who rescued Zakkur from
his enemies? In order to explain the occurrence of both divine names in the same
inscription, Parker, followed by Niehr, convincingly argued that the Afis Stele is
a votive inscription dedicated to the god Iluwer, which incorporates an earlier
inscription commemorating the rescue of Zakkur by Baalshamayn from the enemy
coalition: "I would argue that the best explanation for these features is that our
inscription contains a copy of an earlier memorial inscription."[41] The combined
inscription was completed and set up in the temple after the building of the temple
of Iluwer.

Regarding the nature and function of the two gods mentioned in the inscription, it is interesting to note that the god Ilu-wer or Ilu-mer is a Mesopotamian
deity known from the AN=*Anum* list, where he is identified with the storm-god
Adad.[42] Lambert believes that he was the patron deity of Mari and the original
storm-god of Northern Mesopotamia and Syria.[43] The presence of this god in Afis
and his worship by the Aramean Zakkur are explained by the widely accepted
assumption that Zakkur was a Hanaean whose homeland was on the Middle Euphrates, a territory that was in the cultural orbit of Mari. Niehr, who shares this
opinion, points out, however, that even though Iluwer was very popular on the
Middle Euphrates in the third millennium and the first half of the second millennium B.C.E., there is no evidence for his cult there in the first millennium B.C.E.[44]
It is therefore without support to claim that Zakkur introduced the cult of Iluwer
to North Syria from the Euphrates area and to imply that the cult of this god was
not known in North Syria. It is plausible to assume that the cult of Iluwer may have
survived in North Syria, particularly in the land of Luʿash.

Baalshamayn, the "Lord of Heaven," is identified by some scholars with Adad,
the storm-god. According to Lipiński, the theonym "Baal of Heaven" alludes to the
storm-god Adad "manifesting himself in the skies by means of his thunder and
lightning."[45] According to Niehr, who dedicated a comprehensive study to this
deity, Baalshamayn is a Phoenician god who was adopted by the people of North
Syria at the beginning of the first millennium B.C.E.[46] Niehr does not reject the

---

41. S. B. Parker, "The Composition and Sources of Some Northwest Semitic Royal Inscriptions," *Studi Epigrafici e Linguistici* 16 (1999) 54; Niehr, *Baʿalšamem*, 92.

42. Lipiński, *Aramaeans*, 616 n. 133; Ross, "Prophecy in Hamath," 22.

43. W. G. Lambert, "The Pantheon of Mari," *Mari, Annales de recherches interdisciplinaires*
4 (1985) 533.

44. Niehr, *Baʿalšamem*, 95 n. 36.

45. Lipiński, *Aramaeans*, 630.

46. Niehr, *Baʿalšamem*, 89–93.

possibility that Baalshamayn and Adad may have shared the same nature, because they were both identified later with Zeus and because they are both storm-gods, but he refuses to see them as identical. Adad, according to him, was a regional storm-god, always associated with a specific city, while Baalshamayn was a "trans-regional" one.[47]

Several scholars are of the opinion that Iluwer and Baalshamayn are one and the same divine being and that Baalshamayn is the Aramean counterpart of Iluwer.[48] Niehr, following Parker, rejects the identification of Iluwer with Baalshamayn because both are mentioned side by side on face B, lines 23–24, of the Afis inscription.[49] Parker states that "while [Iluwer and Baalshamayn] may be equivalent in terms of divine types, there is clearly a consistent distinction between the king's patron [that is, Baalshamayn], on the one hand, and the local god of Apish [that is, Iluwer], on the other."[50] Other scholars claim that Baalshamayn was the god of the city and Iluwer the personal god of Zakkur.[51] The fact that Zakkur turns to Baalshamayn to save the besieged city of Hazrak adds further support to the latter assumption.

To sum up, it appears from the Zakkur inscription that, in cases of national threat, prophecy in Syria was solicited from the protective, highest divinity of the land, in this case Baalshamayn, who was the head of the Luʿash pantheon.[52] He made Zakkur king and gave him legitimacy and he was therefore responsible for safeguarding his kingdom.

Were prophecies in Syria always solicited from one specific deity, the highest god of the city or land, or were they solicited indifferently from any god? The evidence from Mari and Assyria seems to point to the first option. In Mari, "prophecy as it was found in royal archives in the Old Babylonian period originated from the highest echelon of the pantheon," which corresponds to the evidence from the Zakkur inscription.[53] The same seems to apply to Assyria, where Ishtar, the highest female goddess, is the only deity attested in the prophetic texts.[54]

The Syrian Prophets

Nissinen correctly points out that "there is no single word for a prophet in . . . Akkadian, Egyptian, Hebrew, and other West Semitic."[55] According to him, the

---

47. Ibid., 96.

48. Namely Ross, "Prophecy in Hamath"; Greenfield, "The Zakkur Inscription"; S. C. Layton, "Literary Sources for the History of Syria Palestine: Old Aramaic Inscriptions," *The Biblical Archaeologist* 51 (1988) 178; S. Noegel, "Zakkur Inscription," in *The Ancient Near East: Historical Sources in Translation* (ed. M. Chavalas; Malden, MA: Wiley-Blackwell, 2006) 308.

49. Niehr, *Baʿalšamem*, 95; Parker, "Composition and Sources," 54 n. 11.

50. Parker, "Composition and Sources," note 11.

51. Niehr, *Baʿalšamem*, 91 n. 6.

52. Ibid. 91.

53. Stökl, *Prophecy*, 87.

54. Ibid., 221; Nissinen, *Prophets and Prophecy*, 98.

55. Ibid., 5.

term prophet is given to the category of professional who "transmits divine words that allegedly derive from direct communication with a deity."[56] The two categories of professionals, who transmitted the message of Baalshamayn to Zakkur, and hence deserve to be called prophets are the חזין and the עדדן. In the current state of the evidence, it is difficult to determine the duties of each group and their exact prerogatives. The חזין have been unanimously understood as 'seers' since the word derives from the common Semitic root חזה = 'to see'. This term is also known from the Old Testament, where it is clearly connected with prophecy.[57] The etymology of עדדן, on the other hand, has raised (and is still raising) controversy. Barstad has recently discussed this term and has critically evaluated all the suggested etymologies.[58] He acknowledged the fact that most scholars opted for the Ugaritic etymology ערר 'to send' and translated the term 'messenger' but he concluded that עדדן "is still imperfectly understood."[59] Nissinen's proposal, to ascribe the origin of the term עדדן to Egyptian *'dd'?* 'great seer', attested in the Wenamon text, can be added to the long list compiled by Barstad.[60]

When comparing the terminology used for prophets in the Zakkur inscription with that of other ancient Near Eastern texts, it appears that, with the exception of biblical חזה, which is equivalent to Aramaic חזין, there is no terminology identical to that of the Zakkur inscription. The Mari texts use different terms to refer to prophets.[61] The terms most commonly used are *muhhû/mahhû/mahhûtu* and *āpilu/āpiltu*. *Muhhû/mahhû* is derived from the root *mahû* 'to go into frenzy', while *āpilum* comes from the root *apālum* 'to answer, interpret'.[62] The Assyrian texts use the word *raggimu/raggintu* from the root *ragāmu* 'to proclaim, prophecy'.[63] The Old Testament refers to prophetic agents by three different terms: נביא, חזה, and ראה, of which only חזה is found in the Zakkur inscription. However, and in spite of the different terminology, Ross was the first to note that, "the role of the *āpilum*-respondent seems to be quite similar to that of the עדד-messenger."[64]

The question whether these two terms, חזין and עדדן, refer to two different classes of prophets was discussed by Barstad.[65] The first to raise this issue was Zobel, who seems to suggest that the two terms, though different, refer to one

---

56. Ibid., 5.

57. Ross, "Prophecy in Hamath," 4; Stökl, *Prophecy*, 192.

58. H. M. Barstad, "The Prophet Oded and the Zakkur Inscription: A Case of Obscuriore Obscurum?" in *Reading from Right to Left: Essays on the Hebrew Bible in Honour of David J. A. Clines* (ed. J. C. Exum and H. G. M., Williamson; JSOTSup 373; London: Sheffield Academic Press, 2003) 26–30.

59. Ibid., 33.

60. Nissinen, *Prophets and Prophecy*, 8.

61. Ibid., 6–7; Stökl, *Prophecy*, 37–38.

62. For an exhaustive discussion of these terms, see Stökl, *Prophecy*, 38–43, who opts for the meaning 'spokesperson' for this category.

63. For an exhaustive discussion of the term, see ibid., 111–18,.

64. Ross, "Prophecy in Hamath," 14.

65. Barstad, "The Prophet Oded," 32–33.

and the same activity and to the same professional category.[66] Jeffers asks whether the seer is the one who has the vision and the עדד is the one who tells the news.[67] While he abstains from taking a stand, Lipiński answers the question positively.[68] Noegel also sees a difference between these two professionals. In his opinion, the seer is "a non-professional, who randomly receives divine messages depending on the deity's will, whereas the diviner represents an expert who solicits oracles from the divine" and he concludes that "Baal-shamayin communicated his intention to Zakkur through every possible means," by using different categories of oracle priests.[69]

The prophetic agents in the Zakkur inscription, based on the etymology of their names, seem to have enjoyed two characteristics: seeing (the future?) and speaking/conveying (the god's message). These two features also characterize the Hebrew prophets: "Ces deux termes, renvoyant à la vision ou à la parole comme caractéristique de chacun des groupes qui transmettent les oracles de Baalshama-yin, sont parallèles à deux aspects de la vision et de la parole qui caractérisent aussi les prophètes hébreux."[70]

It cannot be inferred from the Zakkur inscription that there were female prophets in Syria. Female prophets are known from Mari, Assyria, and the Hebrew Bible, and the possibility of their existence in Syria during this period cannot be ruled out.[71] The Afis Stele clearly suggests that the prophets played a major political role in the life of the Syrian city-states. Indeed, it seems that the national god was solicited every time an important decision had to be made.[72] One aspect of the political role played by the prophets in Syria is that they legitimized the usurpation of the throne by claiming that it was the expression of a divine will. It is highly probable, though not explicitly stated, that when Baalshamayn made Zakkur king he also spoke through prophets. Divine support was clearly needed in order to accede to power and this indicates the large influence religion, and more specifically the prophets, had on the rulers. Legitimacy of the usurpation of power through prophets is also attested in the Old Testament.[73] Since the prophets were the transmitters of the divine message, it is not far-fetched to assume that they could eventually manipulate it according to what they perceived as the state's interest. In Mari, prophecy was closely linked to the king, but the latter did not always follow the advice of the god. It seems that the Mari rulers were aware of the

---

66. Zobel, "Das Gebet," 98.

67. Ann Jeffers, *Magic and Divination in Ancient Palestine and Syria* (Studies in the History and Culture of the Ancient Near East 8; Leiden: Brill, 1996) 37.

68. Lipiński, *Aramaeans*, 509.

69. Noegel, "Zakkur Inscription," 311.

70. Jaruzelska, "Les prophètes,"173.

71. Stökl, *Prophecy*, 67, 121, 186.

72. Lemaire, "Oracles," 186.

73. Jaruzelska, "Les prophètes," 186.

manipulative tendency of the prophets and often took decisions in contradiction to the divine message, as was the case of the alliance with Eshnunna, which was opposed by the gods but concluded by the king.[74]

Prophetic Transmission and Structure

The process of prophetic transmission is clearly described in the Zakkur inscription: it is solicited by the king, who addresses a request to the deity, and the answer is given to him through prophetic agents. In all the known examples from the West Semitic world, the occasions on which prophecies were uttered as an answer to the king's prayer were usually cases of serious threat to the integrity and survival of the state. In Mari, too, the outstanding theme of the prophecies is the well-being and the warfare of the king.[75] It is on one such occasion that Zakkur's request is addressed to the national god, Baalshamayn. It is safe to assume that the request was presented in the temple, most likely in front of the deity's image. The answer was also received by the prophets, most probably again in front of the divine statue.

Based on the evidence from the Afis Stele, as well as from texts from Mari and Assyria, the temple seems to have been the place where prophetic activity was exercised, at least in some major instances involving royal duties. According to Zobel, the inscription emphasizes the temple in such a way that it would be very difficult to imagine that the hand-lifting ceremony and the god's answer could have taken place outside the temple.[76] This assumption finds additional support in the Mari tradition, where "prophets were primarily servants of the gods whose words they proclaimed . . . This indicates the attachment of the prophets to particular deities and temples. In many cases, the prophecy is said to have been uttered . . . in the temple of a god or a goddess."[77] In Assyria too, prophets were closely bound to the temple.[78]

Another feature of Syrian prophecy, which is also attested in the Old Testament and in ancient Jordan, is that prophecies uttered on major occasions and verified by the events were written down and eventually served royal propaganda and official historiography.[79] According to Parker, the prophetic event involving the rescue of Zakkur was recorded twice: once when it took place and a second time when it was incorporated in the votive stele that Zakkur dedicated to Iluwer. Assyrian examples of recording prophecies and placing them in the temple before the divine statue are also attested. In one of these oracles, for example, it is clearly stated that the prophecy was written down on a tablet and placed before the god:

---

74. Nissinen, *Prophets and Prophecy*, 17.

75. Ibid., 16.

76. Zobel, "Das Gebet," 97.

77. Nissinen, *Prophets and Prophecy*, 160.

78. Ibid, 98.

79. Lemaire, "Oracles," 187.

"This is the oracle of peace placed before the statue. This covenant tablet of Aššur enters the king's presence on a cushion. . . ."[80]

Regarding the terminology used to describe the prophetic activity and the structure of the prophetic passage, Ross, Lemaire, Greenfield, and Zobel identified the expressions used in the Afis Stele[81] and found "notable similarities between the words used by Baʿal-Shamayn and Yahweh when speaking through prophets."[82] From these comparative studies, it appears that the form of Zakkur's appeal to the god "And I lifted my hands," the way the god answers him "by the hand of" agents, the title of these agents, and formulas such as "do not fear," "I have made you king," "I will stand by you," "I will rescue you" place Syrian prophecy in the tradition of contemporary West Semitic and Israelite prophecies.

These scholars have identified elements common to the Zakkur prophecy and the psalms. Greenfield has identified in the Zakkur inscription the three elements of the *Danklied*: Declaration, narrative, and acknowledgment.[83] The prophetic process in Zakkur's inscription starts indeed with the erection of the stele to thank the god for having rescued the king. The description of a situation of fear and anxiety (the siege of Hazrak by an enemy coalition) follows. This situation triggered a prayer to the god, a lament (*Klagelied*), to request divine intervention. The prayer is expressed in the hand-lifting formula, "And I lifted my hands," and the answer of the god is acknowledged by the formula "and Baalshamayn answered me." The answer of the god is transmitted to the prophets, who utter a salvation oracle (*Heilsorakel*): "Fear not," "I will stand by you," "I will rescue you." Zobel has raised the possibility that the king may have made a vow, such as the promise to erect a stele and/or to build a temple in order to thank the god for having answered his request.[84] This assumption is supported by the fact that a commemorative stele was indeed erected and placed in the newly built temple.

Syrian Prophecy in Its Near Eastern Context

In recent years, the scholarly world renewed its interest in ancient Near Eastern prophecy after the publication of text corpora from Mari and Assyria containing prophetic passages. The collection and publication of all texts relating to Near Eastern prophecy by Nissinen has allowed a better understanding of this phenomenon and has provided the necessary ground for comparative studies.[85]

---

80. Nissinen, *Prophets and Prophecy*, 120.
81. Ross, "Prophecy in Hamath"; Lemaire, "Oracles"; Greenfield, "The Zakur Inscription"; Zobel, "Das Gebet."
82. Ross, "Prophecy in Hamath," 11.
83. Greenfield, "The Zakur Inscription," 180.
84. Zobel, "Das Gebet," 96.
85. Nissinen, *Prophets and Prophecy*; Stökl, *Prophecy*, is the most recent comparative study. Stökl focused, however, only on the large text corpora of the Bible and the Old Babylonian and Assyrian periods.

The prophetic phenomenon found in the Zakkur inscription is not an isolated case and is part of an ancient Near Eastern tradition that is deeply rooted and attested since the second millennium B.C.E. Similarities to Israelite prophecy have been intensively studied and need not be repeated here. The issue whether prophetic traditions were transmitted from Syria to the Israelite kingdoms or vice versa cannot be answered at this stage. The fact that the prophetic corpus in the Old Testament is substantial while the Syrian corpus is restricted thus far to the Zakkur prophecy may have biased the discussion on the origin of West Semitic prophecy. Greenfield, for example, tried to explain the similarities between the Zakkur and the biblical prophecies by assuming either a dependence of early Aramaic prophecy on Canaanite-Hebrew tradition or an unsuspected richness of Early Aramaic that has not yet come to light. His conclusion, "What is clear is that the Arameans by this period were familiar with the *Danklied* and the *Heilsorakel* and were able to put them to excellent use to shape a royal inscription," seems clearly to favor the first option.[86]

As it appeared from the historical context of the inscription, the kingdom of Hamath and Luʿash was under the influence of two cultural spheres: the Hittite-Luwian and the West Semitic Aramean. Hutter believes that the kingdom of Hamath was the place where Syrian and Luwian culture interacted and the source from which these traditions were transmitted to the Israelite kingdoms.[87] Many scholars have indeed underlined the cultural and religious interaction between Syria and Anatolia.[88] This reality is also the reason that has led Greenfield to look at Hittite influence in the Zakkur prophecy: "It is in the Zakir inscription that we find an aspect of the symbiosis between these two cultures."[89] He was able to trace the earliest occurrences of the expression "Fear not" to Hittite material.[90] However, apart from this feature, little can be said about Hittite influence on Syrian prophecy because of the lack of substantial evidence for prophecy in Hittite texts.[91] As pointed out by Collins:

---

86. Greenfield, "The Zakur Inscription," 191.

87. M. Hutter, "Wiederspiegelungen religiöser Vorstellungen der Luwier im Alten Testament," in *Die Auswirkung des Späthethitischen kulturraumes: Güteraustausch-Kulturkontakte-Kulturtransfer* (ed. M. Novák, F. Prayon, and A.-M. Wittke; Alter Orient und Altes Testament 323; Münster: Ugarit, 2004) 429–32.

88. For example, H. Niehr, "Religiöse Wechselbeziehungen zwischen Syrien und Anatolien im 1. Jahrtausend v. Chr.," in *Brückenland Anatolien? Ursachen, Extensität und Modi des Kulturaustausches zwischen Anatolien und seinen Nachbarn* (ed. H. Blum et al; Tübingen: Attempto, 2002) 339–62; M. Novák, "Akkulturation von Aramäern und Luwiern und der Austausch von Ikonographischen Konzepten in der späthethitischen Kunst," in *Brückenland Anatolien? Ursachen, Extensität und Modi des Kulturaustausches zwischen Anatolien und seinen Nachbarn* (ed. H. Blum et al; Tübingen: Attempto, 2002) 147–72.

89. Greenfield, "The Zakur Inscription," 187.

90. Ibid., 185–86.

91. For a discussion of prophecy in Hittite materials, see Stökl, *Prophecy*, 16–17.

While the Hittites shared an interest in dreams, they did not rely heavily on prophecy as a means of communication with the divine. Mursili's prayer . . . refers to a 'man of god' (*siyuniant*) who might "(come and) declare" the cause of suffering, while in another prayer the priest Kantuzili refers to consulting the will of the deity by means of a seeress (ENSI). Clearly, then, prophets were active in parts of Anatolia in the Late Bronze Age, but we know nothing about who they were and where they might have functioned.[92]

Another culture that might have influenced Syrian prophecy is Hurrian culture because of the widely attested presence of Hurrians in North Syria in the Late Bronze Age. It is important to note in this context that, at that time, a Hurrian dynasty and a Hurrian-speaking population was living not far from Hamath, in Tell el-Mishrife, ancient Qatna, as revealed by the recent discoveries on that site.[93] Unfortunately, nothing is known so far about Hurrian prophecy.

Regarding the influence of Mari, Ross was the first to suggest a common origin for both Syrian and biblical prophecy in the Mari prophetic texts.[94] He claims that the Mari prophetic tradition reached North Syria through Zakkur because he assumes that the latter was of Ḥanaean origin and hence familiar with the culture of the kingdom of Mari. Greenfield disagreed with Ross's assumption that Zakir was a Hanaean and an "Assyrian henchman or vassal" and found the historical reconstruction drawn by Ross to support his view to be very tenuous.[95] While admitting that Mari prophecy belongs to the same West Semitic tradition, Greenfield rightly denies any direct similarity between the Mari prophecies, on the one hand, and Syrian and biblical prophecies, on the other, because the Mari prophecies do not share the same vocabulary, idioms, and structure.[96]

While Syrian prophecy may have been influenced in one way or another by Hittite, Hurrian, or Mariote religion, it may have influenced, in turn, Assyrian prophecy. It is important to remember in this context, first, that almost all Assyrian prophetic texts date to the rule of 8th and 7th century B.C.E. kings, mainly Esarhaddon and Ashurbanipal; second, in the Neo-Assyrian period, military invasions west of the Euphrates brought the Assyrians into contact with the Arameans of Syria as early as the 9th century B.C.E. There has been growing evidence for the "aramaïzation" of Assyrian culture and the spread of Aramaic language and culture to the heartland of Assyria.[97] As already pointed out by Greenfield, many

92. Collins, *The Hittites*, 169.

93. T. Richter, "Akkadisch und hurritisch-Die verschiedensprachige Bevölkerung," in *Schätze des Alten Syriens: Die Entdeckung des Königreichs Qatna* (Stuttgart: Württemburgisches Landesmuseum, 2009) 142–45.

94. Ross, "Prophecy in Hamath," 11–20.

95. Greenfield, "The Zakur Inscription," 179.

96. Ibid., 185.

97. S. Görke, "Aramäischer Einfluss in Assyrien," in *Die Auswirkung des späthethitischen Kulturraumes: Güteraustausch-Kulturkontakte-Kulturtransfer* (ed. M. Novák, F. Prayon, and A.-M. Wittke; Alter Orient und Altes Testament 323; Münster: Ugarit-Verlag, 2004); W. Röllig,

queens in the Neo-Assyrian court were of Aramean origin and may have brought with them some Aramean religious traditions.[98] He was the first to recognize Aramean influence on Neo-Assyrian prophecy. Indeed, a quick look at the Assyrian corpus of prophecies clearly reveals strong similarities to the Zakkur prophecy. The first striking parallel is in the use of the formula "fear not" addressed to the king in almost every oracle. Another borrowed idiom is the hand-lifting in supplication and prayer, as attested in an oracle to Assurbanipal, for example: "Ištar heard my desperate sighs and said to me: 'Fear not!' She made my heart confident, saying: 'Because of the prayer you said with your hands lifted up, your eyes being filled with tears, I have compassion for you.'"[99] Expressions promising protection by the deity "I will stand guard for you," legitimization of kingship "I will establish your crown," salvation from enemies "your enemies, whatever they are I will defeat . . ." are also found in most of them. The prophecy reaches the king "by or from the mouth of" a prophetess, a parallel to the expression "by the hand of" the prophets used in the Zakkur inscription.[100] Perhaps the most striking parallel to the Zakkur prophecy is the prophecy of Ishtar to Assurbanipal. The similarity here is not only in the use of the same idioms but also in the structure of the prophecy. The text starts by describing the dire situation in which Assurbanipal finds himself because of the threat of the Elamite king, Teumman. He cries out to Ishtar for help and Ishtar hears him and answers him: "Fear not! . . . because of the prayer you said with your hands lifted up, you eyes filled with tears, I have compassion for you." The text ends with the defeat of the Elamite king and the salvation of Assurbanipal.[101] All these examples seem to suggest a transmission of prophetic expressions and traditions from West to East via the Arameans of North Syria.

It is difficult in the present state of the evidence to decide where prophecy originated. There is, however, a consensus among scholars that it was not native to Mesopotamia but had a western origin—meaning Mari and the area west of the Euphrates. Charpin tried to slightly nuance this assertion in the light of the evidence from Eshnunna by saying that, while not native to the area, prophecy spread in Mesopotamia under Amorite influence: "Il est très clair dès lors qu'on ne peut plus dire que le prophétisme est propre à l'ouest. Je ne nie pas que le phénomène prophétique soit *d'origine* occidentale: je pense simplement qu'on a sous-estimé l'amorritisation' de la Mésopotamie."[102] If prophecy originated in the West, then

---

"Assyrer und Aramäer: Die Schriftzeugnisse bis zum Ende des Assyrerreiches," in *Essays on Syria in the Iron Age* (Ancient Near Eastern Studies Supplement 7; ed. G. Bunnens; Leuven: Peeters, 2000) 177–86.

98. Greenfield, "The Zakur Inscription," 187–8.

99. Nissinen, *Prophets and Prophecy*, 134.

100. Ibid., 107, 112–13.

101. Ibid., 146–49.

102. D. Charpin, "Le contexte historique et géographique des prophéties dans les textes retrouvés à Mari," in *The Origin of Prophecy: Seers, Soothsayers, and Prophets in the Cradle of Civilization,* The Canadian Society for Mesopotamian Studies Bulletin 23 (1992) 30.

Syrian prophecy must have played an instrumental role in shaping this religious tradition. Additional evidence is needed, however, in order to assess the role of Syrian prophecy in creating and shaping western prophetic traditions.

Bibliography

Bagg, A. *Die Orts- und Gewässernamen der neuassyrischen Zeit, Teil I: Die Levante.* Répertoire Géographique des Textes Cunéiformes 7/1. Wiesbaden: Reichert, 2007.

Barstad, H. "The Prophet Oded and the Zakkur Inscription: A Case of Obscuriore Obscurum?" Pp. 25–37 in *Reading from Right to Left: Essays on the Hebrew Bible in Honour of David J. A. Clines,* ed. J. C. Exum and, H. G. M. Williamson. JSOTS 373. London: Sheffield Academic Press, 2003.

Charpin, D. "Le contexte historique et géographique des prophéties dans les textes retrouvés à Mari." Pp. 21–31 in *The Origin of Prophecy: Seers, Soothsayers, and Prophets in the Cradle of Civilization = The Canadian Society for Mesopotamian Studies Bulletin* 23, 1992.

Collins, B. J. *The Hittites and Their World.* Archaeology and Biblical Studies 7. Leiden: Brill, 2007.

Dion, P.-E. *Les Araméens à l'âge du Fer: Histoire politique et structures sociales.* Études Bibliques Nouvelles Série 34. Paris: Gabalda, 1997.

Donner, H., and W. Röllig. *Kanaanäische und aramäische Inschriften.* 3 volumes. Wiesbaden: Harrassowitz, 1973.

Dussaud, R. "La stèle araméenne de Zakir au Musée du Louvre." *Syria* 3 (1922) 175–76.

Fuchs, A. "Der Turtān Šamšī-ilu und die große Zeit der assyrischen Großen (830–746)." *Die Welt des Orients* 38 (2008) 61–145.

Fugmann, E. *Hama. Fouilles et recherches 1931–1938. L'architecture des périodes pré-hellénistiques.* Copenhagen: Nationalmuseet, 1958.

Gibson, J. C. L. *Textbook of Syrian Semitic Inscriptions, vol. 2: Aramaic inscriptions, including inscriptions in the dialect of Zenjirli.* Oxford: Clarendon, 1975.

Görke, S. "Aramäischer Einfluss in Assyrien." Pp. 325–33 in *Die Auswirkung des Späthethitischen kulturraumes: Güteraustausch-Kulturkontakte-Kulturtransfer.* Ed. M. Novák, F. Prayon, and A.-M. Wittke. Alter Orient und Altes Testament 323. Münster: Ugarit-Verlag, 2004.

Grayson, A. K. *Assyrian Rulers of the Early First Millennium BC II (858–745 BC).* The Royal Inscriptions of Mesopotamia Assyrian Periods, Volume 3. Toronto: University of Toronto Press, 1996.

Greenfield, J. C. "The Zakir Inscription and the Danklied." Pp. 174–91 in *Proceedings of the Fifth World Congress of Jewish Studies, I.* Jerusalem: Magnes, 1972.

Harrison, T. "Neo-Hittites in the "Land of Palistin:" Renewed Investigations at Tell Taʿyinat on the Plain of Antioch." *Near Eastern Archaeology* 74.4 (2009) 174–89.

Hawkins, J. D. *Corpus of Hieroglyphic Luwian Inscriptions, Volume I: Inscriptions of the Iron Age.* Studies in Indo-European Language and Culture New Series 8.1. Berlin: de Gruyter, 2000.

_____. "Cilicia, the Amuq, and Aleppo: New Light on a Dark Age." *Near Eastern Archaeology* 72.4 (2009) 164–73.

_____. "The Inscriptions of the Aleppo Temple." *Anatolian Studies* 61 (2011) 35–54.

Hutter, M. "Wiederspiegelungen religiöser Vorstellungen der Luwier im Alten Testament." Pp. 425–442 in *Die Auswirkung des Späthethitischen kulturraumes: Güteraustausch-Kulturkontakte-Kulturtransfer.* Ed. M. Novák, F. Prayon, and A.-M. Wittke. Alter Orient und Altes Testament 323. Münster: Ugarit-Verlag, 2004.

Janeway, B. "Old Testament King Discovered?" Online: http://www.biblearchaeology.org/post/2011/02/11/Old-Testament-King-Discovered.aspx (accessed 2011).

Jaruzelska, I. "Les prophètes face aux usurpations dans le royaume du Nord." *Vetus Testamentum* 54.2 (2004) 165–87.

Jeffers, A. *Magic and Divination in Ancient Palestine and Syria.* Studies in the History and Culture of the Ancient Near East 8. Leiden: Brill, 1996.

Jepsen, A. "Israel und Damaskus." *Archiv für Orientforschung* 14 (1941–44) 153–72.

Kaufman, S. A. "The Phoenician Inscription of the Incirli Trilingual: A Tentative Reconstruction and Translation." *Maarav* 14.2 (2007) 7–26.

Lambert, W. G. "The Pantheon of Mari." *Mari, Annales de recherches interdisciplinaires* 4 (1985) 525–39.

Layton, S. C. "Literary Sources for the History of Syria Palestine: Old Aramaic Inscriptions." *The Biblical Archaeologist* 51 (1988) 172–89.

Lemaire, A. "Oracles, politique et littérature dans les royaumes araméens et jordaniens (IXe–VIIIe s. av. n.è.)." Pp. 171–93 in *Oracles et Prophéties dans l'Antiquité, Actes du Colloque de Strasbourg 15–17 juin 1995.* Ed. J.-G. Heintz. Paris: de Boccard, 1997.

Lipiński, E. *The Aramaeans: Their Ancient History, Culture, Religion.* Orientalia Lovaniensia Analecta 100. Leuven: Peeters, 2000.

Mazzoni, S. "Tell Afis and the Luash in the Aramaean Period." Pp. 99–114 in *The World of the Aramaeans II: Studies in History and Archaeology in Honour of Paul-Eugène Dion.* Journal for the Study of the Old Testament Supplement 324–326. Ed. M. Daviau, W. Wevers, and M. Weigl. Sheffield: Sheffield Academic Press, 2001.

Millard, A. R. "The Homeland of Zakkur." *Semitica* 39 (1990) 47–52.

_____. "The Inscription of Zakkur King of Hamath." Pp. 155 in *The Context of Scripture* vol. 2.35: *Monumental Inscriptions from the Biblical World.* Ed. W. Hallo and K. L. Younger Jr. Leiden: Brill, 2000.

Niehr, H. "Religiöse Wechselbeziehungen zwischen Syrien und Anatolien im 1. Jahrtausend v. Chr." Pp. 339–362 in *Brückenland Anatolien? Ursachen, Extensität und Modi des Kulturaustausches zwischen Anatolien und seinen Nachbarn.* Ed. H. Blum et al. Tübingen: Attempto, 2002.

_____. *Ba'alšamem: Studien zu Herkunft, Geschichte und Rezeptionsgeschichte eines phönizischen Gottes.* Orientalia Lovaniensia Analecta 123. Studia Phoenicia 17. Leuven: Peeters, 2003.

Nissinen, M. *Prophets and Prophecy in the Ancient Near East.* Writings from the Ancient World 12. Atlanta: Society of Biblical Literature, 2003.

Noegel, S. "Zakkur Inscription." Pp. 307–11 in *The Ancient Near East: Historical Sources in Translation.* Ed. M. Chavalas. Malden, MA: Wiley-Blackwell, 2006.

Novák, M. "Akkulturation von Aramäern und Luwiern und der Austausch von Ikonographischen Konzepten in der späthethitischen Kunst." Pp. 147–72 in *Brückenland Anatolien? Ursachen, Extensität und Modi des Kulturaustausches zwischen Anatolien und seinen Nachbarn.* Ed. H. Blum et al. Tübingen: Attempto, 2002.

Parker, S. B. "The Composition and Sources of Some Northwest Semitic Royal Inscriptions." *Studi Epigrafici e Linguistici* 16 (1999) 49–62.

Parpola, S. "A Letter from Marduk-apla-uṣur of Anah to Rudamu/Uratamis, King of Hamath." Pp. 257–65 in *Hama: Fouilles et recherches 1931–1938, volume II: Les objets de la période dite syro-hittite (âge du Fer)*. Ed. P. J. Riis and M.-L. Buhl. Copenhagen: Nationalmuseet, 1990.

Pognon, H. *Inscriptions sémitiques de la Syrie, de la Mésopotamie et de la région de Mossoul.* Paris: Imprimerie Nationale, 1907.

Richter, T. "Akkadisch und hurritisch-Die verschiedensprachige Bevölkerung." Pp. 142–45 in *Schätze des Alten Syriens: Die Entdeckung des Königreichs Qatna.* Stuttgart: Württembergisches Landesmuseum, 2009.

Röllig, W. "Assyrer und Aramäer. Die Schriftzeugnisse bis zum Ende des Assyrerreiches. " Pp. 177–186 in *Essays on Syria in the Iron Age.* Ancient Near Eastern Studies Supplement 7. Ed. G. Bunnens. Leuven: Peeters, 2000.

Ross, J. F. "Prophecy in Hamath, Israel, and Mari." *Harvard Theological Review* 63 (1970) 1–28.

Sass, B. "Taita, King of Palistin: ca. 950–900 BCE?" Online: http://www.bu.edu/asor/pubs/nea/digit-al-nea-html. Accessed 2010.

Seow, C. L. "Zakkur Stela." Pp. 203–7 in M. Nissinen, *Prophets and Prophecy in the Ancient Near East.* Writings from the Ancient World 12. Atlanta: Society of Biblical Literature, 2003.

Steitler, C. "The Biblical King Toi of Hamath and the Late Hittite State 'P/Walas(a)tin.'" *Biblische Notizen* 146 (2010) 81–99.

Stökl, J. *Prophecy in the Ancient Near East: A Philological and Sociological Comparison.* Culture and History of the Ancient Near East 56. Leiden: Brill, 2012.

Zobel, H.-J. "Das Gebet um Abwendung der Not und seine Erhörung in den Klageliedern des Alten testaments und in der Inschrift des Königs Zakir von Hamath." *Vetus Testamentum* 21 (1971) 91–99.

Prophecy in Transjordan: Balaam Son of Beor

JOEL S. BURNETT

Baylor University

The mantic persona "Balaam son of Beor" emerges as the central figure in texts from the Hebrew Bible (especially Numbers 22–24) and in the plaster inscriptions from Dayr ʿAlla in the eastern Jordan Valley, a rare instance of epigraphic evidence for prophecy in the Iron Age Levant.[1] The Dayr ʿAlla Plaster Texts (henceforth DAPT),[2] like the biblical Balaam texts, offer a literary portrayal of a renowned

---

Authors' note: Thanks to Deirdre N. Fulton and James D. Nogalski for reading earlier drafts or portions of this piece and offering helpful feedback.

1. See C. L. Seow, "West Semitic Sources," in *Prophets and Prophecy in the Ancient Near East* (ed. M. Nissinen and P. Machinist; SBLWAW 12; Atlanta: SBL, 2003), 201–18; compare J. Stökl, *Prophecy in the Ancient Near East: A Philological and Sociological Comparison* (CHANE 56; Leiden: Brill, 2012), 19–23. The other Balaam texts from the Hebrew Bible are Num 31:8, 16; Deut 23:5–6 [4–5]; Josh 13:22; 24:9–10; Mic 6:5; Neh 13:2. In further instances where verse numbering for English-language editions of the Bible differs from the Hebrew text, I will refer only to the Hebrew numbering.

2. For the Dayr ʿAlla Plaster Texts (DAPT), see the brilliant collation and reading of the fragments in the *editio princeps* by J. Hoftijzer and G. van der Kooij (*Aramaic Texts from Deir ʿAlla* [DMOA 19; Leiden: Brill, 1976]), the adjusted placement of fragments by A. Caquot and A. Lemaire ("Les textes araméens de Deir ʿAlla," *Syria* 54 [1977] 189–208), and further improved readings by P. K. McCarter Jr. ("The Balaam Texts from Deir ʿAllā: The First Combination," *BASOR* 239 [1980] 46–60) and by J. A. Hackett (*The Balaam Text from Deir ʿAlla* [HSM 31; Chico, CA: Scholars Press, 1984], 21–85). The latter work forms the basis for the text as presented in *KAI* 312. See also Puech's placement of some fragments near the beginning of the inscription (É. Puech, "Le texte 'ammonite' de Deir ʿAlla: Les admonitions de Balaam [première partie]," in *La vie de la parole, de l'Ancien au Nouveau Testament: Études d'exégèse et d'herméneutique biblique offertes à Pierre Grelot* [ed. P. Grelot; Paris: Desclee, 1987], 13–30, especially 15–17), and the studies by H. Weippert and M. Weippert ("Die 'Bileam'-Inschrift von Tell Dēr ʿAllā," *ZDPV* 98 [1982]: 77–103). Building on this foundational work on the text, three important studies by E. Blum offer some new readings and additional placement of fragments: "Die Kombination I der Wandinschrift vom Tell Deir ʿAlla: Vorschläge zur Rekonstruktion mit historisch-kritischen Anmerkungen," in *Berührungspunkte: Studien zur Sozial- und Religionsgeschichte Israels und seiner Umwelt: Festschrift für Rainer Albertz zu seinem 65. Geburtstag* (ed. I. Kottsieper et al.; AOAT 350; Münster: Ugarit-Verlag, 2008), 573–601; "'Verstehst du dich nicht auf die Schreibkunst. . . ?' Ein weisheitlicher Dialog über Vergänglichkeit und Verantwortung: Kombination II der

prophetic figure from the past. All of these texts present Balaam as a foreigner, and they all associate Balaam with Transjordan.

Accordingly, the following discussion considers the various textual portrayals of Balaam as a prophet interacting with peoples and kingdoms in ancient Transjordan. After examining the DAPT within in their own cultural, historical, and archaeological contexts, attention turns to the Balaam traditions in the Hebrew Bible. As this discussion shows, these texts present distinct literary interactions with the Balaam tradition from varying historical and ideological circumstances— nonetheless, as texts that can be understood in relationship to one another.

This examination of the whole West Semitic Balaam corpus will show that these texts point to a broader, common tradition of Balaam as an archetypal doomsayer beholden to no single kingdom, a spokesman for the divine at an international level. Balaam thus poses a potential threat to any and all of the highland kingdoms surrounding the east Jordan Valley. The main distinction to be observed among the texts is not so much between favorable or unfavorable attitudes toward Balaam but rather between the biblical texts' shared preference for Israel and the lack of any such preference or affinity for a specific people or kingdom in the DAPT. The biblical and epigraphic Balaam texts thus reflect two different ways in which the communities behind those texts related to kingdoms and national identities. Balaam's persistent associations with west-central Transjordan warrant some attention first to the nature of this territory as a perpetually contested area throughout Iron Age II.

I. Rival Kingdoms and Their Gods:
West-Central Transjordan during Iron Age II

The surviving Balaam traditions encompass a geographic area extending ca. 30 miles / 48 km from the Mt. Peor-Nebo area of the Plateau's western edge to

---

Wandinschrift vom Tell Deir ʿAlla," in *Was ist der Mensch, dass du seiner gedankst? (Psalm 8,5): Festschrift für Bernd Janowski zum 65. Geburtstag.* (ed. M. Bauks et al.; Neukirchen-Vluyn: Neukirchener Verlag, 2008), 33–53; "Die altaramäischen Wandinschriften vom Tell Deir ʿAlla und ihr institutioneller Kontext," in *Metatexte: Erzählungen von Schrifttragenden Artefakten in der alttestamentlichen und mittelalterlichen Literatur* (Materiale Textkulturen 15; ed. F.-E. Focken and M. R. Ott; Berlin: de Gruyter, 2016), 21–52.

See also the readings and discussion offered by E. Lipiński, "The Plaster Inscription from Deir ʿAllā," in *Studies in Aramaic Inscriptions and Onomastics II* (OLA 57; Leuven: Peeters, 1994), 103–70; M. Dijkstra, "Is Balaam Also among the Prophets?" *JBL* 114 (1995) 43–64; and the readings and English translations by B. A. Levine, *Numbers 21–36: A New Translation with Introduction and Commentary* (AB 4A; New Haven, CT: Yale University Press, 2000), 241–47; and Seow, "West Semitic Sources," 207–12. Rather than follow any one scholar's distinct readings of the text or offering a new one requiring its own defense, the scope and aims of the present discussion call for working within the broad area of agreement among these numerous publications on the DAPT.

Dayr ʿAlla in the central Jordan Valley.[3] Although biblical traditions consistently advance Israelite claims to this territory, both texts and archaeology show that during Iron Age II it frequently changed hands among bordering rivals and that populations living in this vicinity regularly found themselves caught in the middle of the surrounding kingdoms and their competing territorial claims.[4]

Accordingly, the Mesha Stele Inscription (ca. 840 B.C.E.) discusses the town of Nebo and contiguous areas to the south in the context of the larger "[lan]d of Madeba" (modern Madaba), which in the previous generation Omri the king of Israel (ca. 883–872 B.C.E.) "had taken into possession" (*yrš*), but according to Mesha, "Chemosh [the god of Moab] returned it in my days" (lines 7–9).[5] The Mesha Inscription thus projects the ideological viewpoint of the Moabite "state," which assumes a clear-cut differentiation of identity in which territories, populations, and leading gods align in comparable but mutually exclusive relationships: Israel- YHWH versus Moab-Chemosh.[6] As Mesha reports, these irreconcilable oppositions are resolved not merely through territorial conquest but also through the ritual execution (*ḥrm*) of populations and the spoliation of cult images, all measures of organized violence sanctioned and carried out by the "state" (lines 16–18).[7] Viewed through this polarizing lens of Moab's national ideology, populations of Transjordan associated with Israel are unequivocally identified with the god YHWH by the mid-9th century B.C.E. (line 17).

Both this ideological viewpoint of mutually exclusive gods, people, and territory and Israelite claims to territories and populations among Transjordan's

---

3. Biblical Balaam texts locate his activity at Peor (Num 23:28; Num 31:16), which is described as a mountain along the western Transjordanian Plateau overlooking the plains of Moab (in the Dead Sea–Jordan Valley to the west and northwest) and standing near Mt. Nebo (Deut 34:1–6; Jebel en-Neba, including its western extension Ras eS-Siyaġa. See R. W. Younker, "Peor," *EDB*, 1028. Tell Dayr ʿAlla lies ca. 30 miles (48 km) to the northwest, in the east Jordan Valley. See S. Mittmann and G. Schmitt, eds., *Tübinger Bibelatlas* (Stuttgart: Deutsche Bibelgesellschaft, 2001), map B IV 6.

4. See B. MacDonald, *"East of the Jordan:" Territories and Sites of the Hebrew Scriptures* (ASOR Books 6; Boston: ASOR, 2000), 101–56; T. D. Petter, *The Land between the Two Rivers: Early Israelite Identities in Central Transjordan* (Winona Lake, IN: Eisenbrauns, 2014), 35–55.

5. See K. P. Jackson and J. A. Dearman, "The Text of the Meshaʿ Inscription," and K. P. Jackson, "The Language of the Meshaʿ Inscription," both in *Studies in the Mesha Inscription and Moab* (Atlanta: Scholars Press, 1989), 93–130, here 94, 97. See also, conveniently, the English translation and notes by K. A. D. Smelik in *COS* 2.23:137–38.

6. B. Routledge, "The Politics of Mesha: Segmented Identities and State Formation in Iron Age Moab," *JESHO* 43 (2000) 221–56, especially 237–38.

7. On the practice of *ḥerem* (as noun and verb *ḥrm*, traditionally translated "(put to) the ban," "(devote to) destruction," etc.), which is described in biblical texts as a measure of ritual warfare followed by Israelites (e.g., Deut 7:2; 20:16–18; Josh 6:17–19; 7:1, 11–15; 8:2), see R. de Vaux, *Ancient Israel: Its Life and Institutions* (trans. J. McHugh; reprinted, Grand Rapids, MI: Eerdmans, 1997 [1961]), 260–61.

shifting political boundaries are also well known from the Hebrew Bible.[8] The ritual execution (*ḥrm*) of enemies encroaching on the deity's land, as described by Mesha, is also enshrined in the 7th-century B.C.E. Deuteronomic law collection (Deuteronomy 12–26; see specifically Deut 13:15; 20:16–17)[9] and figures prominently in the biblical narrative traditions of the Israelite conquest (Josh 6:17–21; 7:10–26; 8:26; etc.) and early monarchy (1 Sam 15:1–33). As we will see, the literary legacy of this polarizing state ideology eventually results in Balaam's literary death in Transjordan, as a perpetual foreigner who claims to speak for the divine.

Mesha's recognition of "the men of Gad" as an Israel-affiliated group having inhabited west-central Transjordan 'forever' (*mʿlm*, line 10) is consistent with tribal lists in biblical poems likely composed during Iron II monarchic times— namely, Genesis 49 ("the blessing of Jacob") and Deuteronomy 33 ("the blessing of Moses").[10] In both poems, Gad stands out for its violent character, matching its surrounding circumstances: "Gad—a raiding band may attack him, but he will attack at their heels" (Gen 49:19); "Gad lives like a lion; he tears at arm and scalp" (Deut 33:20). In an earlier tribal list preserved in Judges 5 ("the Song of Deborah"), Gilead appears instead of Gad as a population dwelling "beyond the Jordan" as part of a larger "people of Yhwh" (*ʿam yhwh*, Judg 5:13) obligated to join in battle against a Canaanite enemy (Judg 5:19–20).[11] The poem ascribes this same obligation to Reuben (Judg 5:15b–16), which other biblical texts locate in Transjordan

---

8. In addition to the biblical texts discussed here, see also the reflection on the contested nature of west-central Transjordan reflected in the Song of Heshbon (Num 21: 27–30). See the discussion by Petter, *The Land between the Two Rivers*, 39–55.

9. The 7th-century B.C.E. dating of Deuteronomy based on its correspondences with Assyrian vassal treaties/loyalty oaths has received decisive support in the 2009 discovery of a copy of Esarhaddon's Succession Treaty displayed in the inner sanctum of a temple at Tell Tayinat in Syria, in striking congruence to Deut 31:26 and to other details of Deuteronomy 12–26. See J. Lauinger, "Esarhaddon's Succession Treaty at Tell Tayinat: Text and Commentary," *JCS* 64 (2012) 87–123; B. M. Levinson, "Die neuassyrischen Ursprünge der Kanonformel in Deuteronomium 13,1," in *Viele Wege zu dem Einen: Historische Bibelkritik: die Vitalität der Glaubensüberlieferung in der Moderne* (ed. S. Beyerle et al.; Biblisch-theologische Studien 121; Neukirchen-Vluyn: Neukirchener Verlag, 2012), 61–82; B. M. Levinson and J. Stackert, "The Limitations of 'Resonance:' A Response to Joshua Berman on Historical and Comparative Method," *Journal of Ancient Judaism* 4.3 (2013) 123–40; H. U. Steymans, "Deuteronomy 28 and Tell Tayinat," *Verbum et Ecclesia* 34:2 (2013) 1–13.

10. For a concise review of scholarship and bibliography, see M. S. Smith, *Poetic Heroes: Literary Commemorations of Warriors and Warrior Culture in the Early Biblical World* (Grand Rapids, MI: Eerdmans, 2014), 211–12, 496–99 nn. 1–23. On Gen 49, see also D. E. Fleming, *The Legacy of Israel in Judah's Bible: History, Politics, and the Reinscribing of Tradition* (Cambridge: Cambridge University Press, 2012), 72–90.

11. The poem in Judges 5 appears to be an early Iron II (10th or 9th century B.C.E.) composition incorporating traditions from Iron I times. See Smith, *Poetic Heroes*, 211–66, especially 247. As scholars have noted, although the list of groups may well derive from a premonarchic context, the designation of this coalition as "the people of Yhwh" seems to belong to subsequent development of the poem during monarchic times, perhaps during the tenth or early 9th century

as an Israelite tribe (Num 32; Deut 3:12–16; 29:7–8; Josh 13:15–23; 22:1, etc.) and to Machir (Judg 5:14b), which other texts locate in Transjordan (Num 32:39–40; Deut 3:15) and regard not as a tribe but rather as a clan of Manasseh (Num 26:29; 27:1). In other biblical texts, Gilead has become generalized to include the entire western half of Transjordan from the Arnon north, as a territorial designation overlapping with the idealized tribal territories of Gad, Reuben, and eastern Manasseh.[12]

Also consistent with Mesha's portrayal of conflicting territorial interests between Israel and Moab is the persistent claim among biblical settlement traditions to the Arnon as Israel's rightful southern boundary in Transjordan (Num 21:24; Deut 2:36–37; 3:8–17; 4:47–49; Josh 12:1; 13:9, 16; Judg 11:18–26; 2 Kgs 10:32–33; 1 Chr 5:3–8; cf. Isa 16:2b; Jer 48:18–20). At the same time, considerable variance among biblical traditions regarding the precise locations of tribal affiliations and boundaries of Israelite territories in Transjordan suggests fluid boundaries and shifting allegiances behind these idealized literary depictions, the prevailing circumstance reflected in the Mesha Inscription.[13] The pervasive view among biblical texts that Transjordanian territories and populations were integral to the makeup of earliest Israel is consistent with the Mesha Inscription's depiction of Israelite affiliation by populations of west-central Transjordan long prior to the mid-9th century B.C.E.—in the case of Gad, 'forever' (*m'lm*, line 10). On the basis of the textual evidence, scholars rightly speak of a distinctly Transjordanian segment of Israelite population and identity.[14]

Nonetheless, even the biblical evidence makes clear that Israelite control of Transjordan territories was not constant throughout the Iron Age. According to 2 Kgs 10:32–33, the full extent of Israelite territory in Transjordan was conquered by Hazael of Aram-Damascus and thus fell under that kingdom's hegemony

---

B.C.E. See Smith, *Poetic Heroes*, 245–51; Fleming, *The Legacy of Israel in Judah's Bible*, 64–66, 68–69 n. 20.

12. See MacDonald, *"East of the Jordan,"* 195–208.

13. Ibid., 149–51, 195–208, and for conclusions with attention to theoretical issues concerning sociopolitical formation and the relevant written sources, Petter, *The Land between the Two Rivers*, 12–14, 35–55.

14. See B. A. Levine, "The Balaam Inscription from Deir 'Alla: Historical Aspects," in *Biblical Archaeology Today: Proceedings of the International Congress on Biblical Archaeology, Jerusalem, April 1984* (Jerusalem: Israel Exploration Society, 1985), 326–39; J. A. Hackett, "Religious Traditions in Israelite Transjordan," in *Ancient Israelite Religion: Essays in Honor of Frank Moore Cross* (ed. P. D. Miller Jr. et al.; Philadelphia: Fortress, 1987), 125–36; R. G. Boling, *The Early Biblical Community in Transjordan* (Sheffield: Sheffield Academic Press, 1988), especially 37–63; F. M. Cross, *From Epic to Canon: History and Literature in Ancient Israel* (Baltimore: The Johns Hopkins University Press, 1998), 53–70; S. C. Russell, *Images of Egypt in Early Biblical Literature: Cisjordan-Israelite, Transjordan-Israelite, and Judahite Portrayals* (BZAW 403; Berlin: de Gruyter, 2009); J. M. Hutton, "Southern, Northern and Transjordanian Perspectives," in *Religious Diversity in Ancient Israel and Judah* (ed. F. Stavrakopoulou and J. Barton; New York: T. & T. Clark, 2010), 149–74; Petter, *The Land between the Two Rivers*, 56–74.

during the decades following ca. 841 B.C.E. By this time, Mesha's conquests and supposedly irredentist recovery of territory from Israel—described in the Hebrew Bible as Mesha's "rebellion" from vassalage to Israel after Ahab's death (2 Kgs 3:5)—would have already taken place beginning ca. 850 B.C.E. Israel's loss of its Transjordanian territories to Hazael, if not a direct factor in events described in the Mesha Inscription, would have certainly solidified Mesha's northward territorial expansion into formerly Israelite areas.

Israel's subsequent recovery of towns and cities in Transjordan through military victories by Joash of Israel (ca. 802–787 B.C.E.) over Hazael's son and successor Ben Hadad (2 Kgs 13:25) was expanded under Jeroboam II (ca. 787–748 B.C.E.), who reportedly "restored the border of Israel" from the Dead Sea to the north beyond Damascus (2 Kgs 14:25, 28).[15] The resulting economic prosperity for Israel during the first half of the 8th century B.C.E. is reflected in the book of Amos (Amos 3:15; 6:1–8), as are the brutalities of war involved in pursuing that prosperity in regional conflicts in Transjordan involving Damascus, Ammon, and Moab during the half-century following Hazael's conquests (Amos 1:3, 13; 2:1).[16] But, by the late 8th century, Israelite hegemony in Transjordan had receded considerably, to the benefit of Damascus, as reflected in Tiglath-Pileser III's textual references to "the city of Gilead" as part of "the land of the House of Hazael" in connection with Assyria's conquest of Damascus and annexation of Gilead (ca. 733–732 B.C.E.; 2 Kgs 15:29; 16:9; 1 Chr 5:6, 26).[17]

---

15. According to 2 Kgs 14:25, all the way to Lebo-Hamath, a likely exaggeration that nonetheless might reflect the extent of military and trade agreements advantageous to Israel under Assyrian hegemony. See B. Halpern, "The Taking of Nothing: 2 Kings 14.25, Amos 6.14 and the Geography of the Deuteronomistic History," in *The World of the Aramaeans I: Biblical Studies in Honour of Paul-Eugène Dion* (ed. P. M. M. Daviau et al.; JSOTSup 324; Sheffield: Sheffield Academic, 2001), 186–204, especially 191–93.

16. Amos 1:13 alleges Ammonite brutalities against Israelites "in order to enlarge their territory." Presumably such territorial disputes would have been a perennial circumstance during the 9th and 8th centuries B.C.E., and it seems reasonable to assume that the Ammonite kingdom would have sought to advance its influence, if not control, farther west along the Wadi Zarqa's (biblical Jabbok's) descent into the Jordan Valley (thus, L. G. Herr, "The Iron Age II Period: Emerging Nations," *BA* 60:3 [1997] 114–83, here 146, 148). But the archaeological and epigraphic record provides no evidence for a regular Ammonite presence beyond a 9-mile (15 km) radius on the plateau surrounding the Ammonite capital Rabbath Ammon (modern Amman) until the late 8th century at the earliest (at Tell Dayr 'Alla) and more evidently during the 7th century B.C.E. and later (see pp. 188–90 below).

17. "The city of Gilead" (cf. Hos 6:8) is usually understood to be Mizpeh-Gilead (Gen 31:43–55; Judg 11:29), the location of which is unknown, or Ramoth-Gilead (identified with ar-Ramtha on the modern Jordan–Syria border; with Tell Ramith, just south of there, Rainey and Notley, *The Sacred Bridge*, 231–32); or with Tell Husn southeast of Irbid, MacDonald, *"East of the Jordan,"* 201–2). For the references by Tiglath Pileser III, see H. Tadmor, *The Inscriptions of Tiglath-Pileser III King of Assyria: Critical Edition, with Introductions, Translations and Commentary* (Jersusalem: The Israel Academy of Sciences and Humanities), 138–39, 186–87 n. 3, 192, 280

Map of west-central Jordan.

In short, during Iron Age IIb (ca. 850–730 B.C.E.), the area of west-central Transjordan encompassed by the Balaam traditions perpetually fell under conflicting claims among Israelite, Moabite, Ammonite, and Aramean (Damascene) kingdoms before it came under the imperial hegemony of Assyria during the late 8th century B.C.E. It was this setting of perpetually disputed territory at the intersection of rival kingdoms and their gods that formed the broader geographic and historical backdrop for the literary Balaam traditions. Bound up with Balaam's portrayal in these various literary traditions is the contested nature of west-central Transjordan as a zone of shifting and intersecting national-religious identities and loyalties.

II. The Balaam Inscription from Dayr ʿAlla

The DAPT were recovered through the archaeological excavation of plaster fragments around a collapsed wall at Tell Dayr ʿAlla.[18] Although the surviving fragments allow for only partial reconstruction, the inscription clearly invokes the authority of "Balaam son of Beor" and presents his dire message of warnings from "the gods" (DAPT I.1, 5). The fragmentary state of the inscription and the elusive nature of much of its contents calls for a disciplined approach of interpretation focusing on what is actually extant in the text in relationship to its own geographic, archaeological, cultural, and historical contexts. These matters thus provide the starting point for this discussion of the inscriptions.

A. The DAPT in Their Setting

Geographic, Archaeological, and Historical Context

Tell Dayr ʿAlla lies in the east Jordan Valley near the Wadi Zarqa's (biblical Jabbok's) descent from the Transjordanian Plateau. The mound of Dayr ʿAlla rises prominently from the surrounding valley floor, attesting to the site's ongoing importance in regional trade during the second millennium B.C.E., as evident in the remains of a Middle Bronze Age town wall and a Late Bronze Age sanctuary yielding abundant prestige items typical of the period.[19] Occupational remains from

---

n. 4, 281 n. 10, 282. For a convenient English translation, see K. L. Younger Jr., trans., Summary Inscriptions 4:3–7 in *COS* 2.117C: 287–89 and 9–10:3–4 in *COS* 2.117F: 291–92.

18. See H. J. Franken, "Archaeological Evidence Relating to the Interpretation of the Text," 3–22, here 8–10, and G. van der Kooij, "The Plaster and Other Materials Used," 22–28, both in *Aramaic Texts from Deir ʿAlla* (ed. J. Hoftijzer and G. van der Kooij; Leiden: Brill, 1976); G. van der Kooij and M. M. Ibrahim, *Picking up the Threads . . . A Continuing Review of Excavations at Deir Alla, Jordan* (Leiden: Univ. of Leiden Archaeological Centre, 1989), 63–65, figs. 79–81; G. van der Kooij, "Book and Script at Deir ʿAlla," in *The Balaam Text from Deir ʿAlla Re-Evaluated: Proceedings of the International Symposium held in Leiden 21–24 August 1989* (ed. J. Hoftijzer and G. van der Kooij; Leiden: Brill, 1991), 239–62, here 239–41, fig. 1.

19. Those items include luxury goods from the Mycenean world, Egypt, and northern Syria. See van der Kooij and Ibrahim, *Picking up the Threads*, 76–80, 91–92 and, with more detail,

Iron I and IIA attest to repeated violent destructions and disruptions of settlement by earthquake as the environmental legacy of Dayr ʿAlla, leading up to the Phase IX context of the DAPT.[20] The site's location made it a perennial regional hub for ancient travel and trade passing from central Transjordan both westward through the Damiyyah crossing and northward along the east Jordan Valley corridor to Pella and points beyond.

The Phase IX occupational context of the DAPT was destroyed by an earthquake and fire and is dated by radiocarbon testing to ca. 800 B.C.E.[21] The pottery and other aspects of the material culture of Phase IX fit generally within a 9th–8th century B.C.E. date range, with no trace of Assyrian cultural influence and no connections to Ammonite ceramic assemblages, such as would appear later, beginning in Phase VI (late 8th and 7th centuries B.C.E.). The use of the contemporary formal Aramaic script and language in the other, briefer inscriptions from this occupational phase reflect the cultural and administrative impact of Damascene hegemony in the region beginning under Hazael ca. 841 B.C.E.

Thus, the DAPT can be dated within the century following Hazael's conquests (ca. 841 B.C.E.; 2 Kgs 10:32–33) and preceding the Assyrian annexation of Gilead, presumably including Dayr ʿAlla, by Tiglath-Pileser III in 733–732 B.C.E. (2 Kgs 15:29; 1 Chr 5:6, 25–26).[22] The archaeological evidence from Tell Dayr ʿAlla indicates that the DAPT come from a time when Dayr ʿAlla was effectively under the political hegemony of Aram-Damascus (even if remaining far from culturally assimilated), or perhaps soon afterward, when cities and territories of Gilead had reportedly been recovered by the northern Israelite kingdom under Joash (ca.

H. J. Franken, *Excavations at Tell Deir ʿAlla: The Late Bronze Age Sanctuary* (Louvain: Peeters, 1992). Most of the site's Late Bronze pottery, like that from the Iron Age level of the DAPT (Phase IX), was made of clays from the immediate vicinity in the Jordan Valley and from basalt areas of the central and northern Transjordanian Plateau. See Franken, *Excavations at Tell Deir ʿAlla*, 105–14; M. M. Ibrahim and G. van der Kooij, "The Archaeology of Deir ʿAlla Phase IX," 16–29, here 22–27. On the distinct social implications of Mycenean pottery in Transjordan, see G. J. van Wijngaarden, "Dots Close Together on a Map: Mycenaean Pottery in the Jordan Valley," in *Sacred and Sweet: Studies on the Material Culture of Tell Deir ʿAlla and Tell Abu Sarbut* (ed. M. L. Steiner and E. J. van der Steen; ANES 24; Leuven: Peeters, 2008), 53–67.

20. See H. J. Franken, "Deir ʿAlla, Tell. Archaeology," *ABD* 2:128. In the original labeling system of the excavations at Tell Dayr ʿAlla, the archaeological stratum of the DAPT, now called Phase IX, was designated Phase M. See E. J. van der Steen, "Introduction: Tell Deir ʿAlla in the Late Bronze and Iron Ages," in *Sacred and Sweet: Studies on the Material Culture of Tell Deir ʿAlla and Tell Abu Sarbut* (ed. M. L. Steiner and E. J. van der Steen; ANES 24; Leuven: Peeters, 2008), 17–24, here 17–18.

21. For the information in this paragraph, see Ibrahim and van der Kooij, "The Archaeology of Deir ʿAlla Phase IX," 26–28.

22. See B. Oded, "Observations on Methods of Assyrian Rule in Transjordania after the Palestinian Campaign of Tiglath-Pileser III," *JNES* 29 (1970) 177–86, especially 177–80; Tadmor, *The Inscriptions of Tiglath-Pileser III*, 138–39, 186–87 n. 3, 192, 281 n. 10, 282; Rainey and Notley, *The Sacred Bridge*, 230–33.

802–787 B.C.E.; 2 Kgs 13:24–25) and consolidated under Jeroboam II (ca. 787–748 B.C.E.; 2 Kgs 14:25, 28).[23]

Language and Script at Dayr ʿAlla Phase IX

Consistent with Dayr ʿAlla's geographic setting and material culture, the language of the DAPT has defied simple classification, exhibiting features of Aramaic but in other respects resembling Hebrew and other attested "Canaanite" languages.[24] It thus falls on a point along the continuum of Northwest Semitic corresponding to the site's location between Aramaic and Canaanite areas of dialect geography.[25]

In similar fashion, the text's paleography represents a regional development of the Aramaic script tradition that during the 8th century B.C.E. would come to

---

23. See the similar conclusion reached by E. Blum, citing Wenning and Zenger: "Die altaramäischen Wandinschriften vom Tell Deir ʿAlla, 23–24 and n. 12; A. Wenning and E. Zenger, "Heiligtum ohne Stadt — Stadt ohne Heiligtum? Anmerkungen zum archäologischen Befund des Tell Dēr ʿAllā," *ZAH* 4 (1991): 186.

24. Compare the varying assessments by P. K. McCarter, "The Dialect of the Deir ʿAlla Texts," 87–99; D. Pardee, "The Linguistic Classification of the Deir ʿAlla Text Written on Plaster," 100–105; J. C. Greenfield, "Philological Observations on the Deir ʿAlla Inscription," 109–20; and J. Huehnergard, "Remarks on the Classification of the Northwest Semitic Languages," 282–93; all in *The Balaam Text from Deir ʿAlla Re-Evaluated: Proceedings of the International Symposium held at Leiden 21–24 August 1989* (Leiden: Brill, 1991). Prior to this, Hackett had argued for DAPT's linguistic classification as Canaanite, and in recent years, other scholars have added support for their initial designation as Aramaic by Hoftijzer and van der Kooij in the *editio princeps* (e.g., J. Tropper, "Dialektvielfalt und Sprachwandel im frühen Aramäischen: Soziolinguistische Überlegungen," in *The World of the Arameans III: Studies in Language and Literature in Honour of Paul-Eugene Dion* [JSOTSup 326; ed. P. M. M. Daviau, J. W. Wevers, and M. Weigl; Sheffield: Sheffield Academic, 2001] 214–15). Blum's intimation that the DAPT and Tel Dan Inscription might represent the same Damascene dialect of Old Aramaic because of a supposed "exact correspondence" in verbal system overstates the importance of *wyqtl* verbs in each (which are now commonly recognized as occurring both in Canaanite and Old Aramaic in the Zakkur Stele Inscription) and must be rejected in view of differences between the two: the direct object marker *yt* in line 10 of Tel Dan never occurs in the DAPT; the verb *hwk* 'to go' in Tel Dan (*yhk*, lines 3, 5) vs. *hlk* in DAPT (*lkw*, I.5; *hlk*, II.7); and *br* 'son' in Tel Dan (lines 7, 8) and in Balaam's patronymic in DAPT (I.2, 4, in keeping with his Aramean identity) but *bn* 'son, offspring' in DAPT (*bny*, I.8). The DAPT and Tel Dan Stele inscriptions do not represent the same language dialect.

25. See W. R. Garr, *Dialect Geography of Syria-Palestine, 1000–586 B.C.E.* (Philadelphia: University of Pennsylvania Press, 1985; repr., Winona Lake, IN: Eisenbrauns, 2004), 229–31 and, similarly but with emphasis on the literary character of the dialect, McCarter, "The Dialect of the Deir ʿAlla Texts," 96–98; and B. Halpern, "Dialect Distribution in Canaan and the Deir ʿAlla Inscriptions," in *"Working With No Data": Semitic and Egyptian Studies Presented to Thomas O. Lambdin* (ed. D. M. Golomb; Winona Lake, IN: Eisenbrauns, 1987), 119–39, especially 133–38, with Halpern ultimately classifying the DAPT as a local dialect of "Canaanite" but in an elevated, perhaps archaizing, literary style intelligible and accessible (in written form) to speakers of regional dialects of both Canaanite and Aramaic comprising the text's audience of pilgrims, merchants, and regional (in Halpern's view, mostly Israelite) inhabitants.

be employed as the national script of the Ammonite kingdom.[26] This national association for this script tradition is borne out by the concentration of provenanced name seals and inscriptions in the Ammonite language on the Transjordanian plateau, within a 9-mile (15-km) radius of the Ammonite capital Rabbat Ammon (modern Amman).[27] Yet, in Dayr ʿAlla Phase IX, this script occurs unambiguously only in the DAPT. Other, briefer inscriptions from this occupational level are consistent with a standard Aramaic script and Aramaic language, both distinct from those of the DAPT, indicating that the everyday or administrative language in use at the site during this time was likely Aramaic.[28] None of the Phase IX inscriptions are in the Ammonite language.[29] This absence of the Ammonite language, the lack of any mention of Ammon or Ammonites among any of the preserved inscriptions (see below), and the absence of Ammonite material culture or its predecessors at the site or anywhere in the surrounding Jordan Valley preclude an ascription of Ammonite political affiliation or identity to Phase IX Dayr ʿAlla.[30]

---

26. For a general overview of the development of the Northwest Semitic national alphabetic scripts, see C. A. Rollston, *Writing and Literacy in the World of Ancient Israel: Epigraphic Evidence from the Iron Age* (Atlanta: SBL, 2010), 42–46. On the identification of a distinct Ammonite national script and its development from the parent Aramaic script tradition, see F. M. Cross, "Notes on the Ammonite Inscription from Tell Sīrān," in *Leaves from an Epigrapher's Notebook: Collected Papers in Hebrew and West Semitic Palaeography and Epigraphy* (Winona Lake, IN: Eisenbrauns, 2003), 100–102 (repr. of *BASOR* 212 [Dec, 1973] 12–15); and W. E. Aufrecht, "Prolegomenon to the Study of Old Aramaic and Ammonite Lapidary Inscriptions," in *"An Eye for Form:" Epigraphic Essays in Honor of Frank Moore Cross* (ed. J. A. Hackett et al.; Winona Lake, IN: Eisenbrauns, 2014), 100–106. For the interpretive nuance by which the DAPT may be understood in terms of a more broadly regional script, see McCarter: "In view of the fact that there is nothing else Ammonite about the Deir ʿAllā texts, perhaps we should now speak of this script tradition as regional or ephichoric, rather than national, and call it not 'Ammonite' but 'Transjordanian' or better (to distinguish it from Moabite) 'Gileadite'" (McCarter, "The Balaam Texts from Deir ʿAllā," 50).

27. W. E. Aufrecht, "Ammonite Texts and Language," in *Ancient Ammon* (ed. B. MacDonald and R. W. Younker; SHCANE 17; Leiden: Brill, 1999), 163–88, here 164–67, 170–71; L. G. Herr, "Aramaic and Ammonite Seal Scripts," in *"An Eye for Form": Epigraphic Essays in Honor of Frank Moore Cross* (ed. J. A. Hackett and W. E. Aufrecht; Winona Lake, IN: Eisenbrauns, 2014), 175–78, 182–86.

28. The Phase IX Aramaic inscriptions would consist of a jar and a stone inscribed, *zy šrʿ*, 'belonging to *šrʿ*/the gate', and *ʾbn šrʿ*, 'the stone of *šrʿ*/the gate', respectively. See also from Phase IX an abecedary inscription incised on a bowl rim (G. G. van der Kooij and M. M. Ibrahim, *Picking Up the Threads . . . A Continuing Review of Excavations at Deir Alla, Jordan* (Leiden: University of Leiden Archaeological Centre, 1989), 69–70 and fig. 87, 97 cat. 63. See Hofijzer and van der Kooij, *Aramaic Texts from Deir ʿAlla*, pls. 19–22 and, in the same volume, J. Hoftijzer, "General Remarks on the Plaster Texts," 268–82, here 274–75.

29. For Ammonite inscriptions dated to the 7th and 6th centuries b.c.e. at Dayr ʿAlla, see van der Kooij and Ibrahim, *Picking Up the Threads*, 69–70.

30. Archaeological and epigraphic evidence indicates the general spread of Ammonite cultural and political presence beyond Amman's 9-mile (15-km) radius to the western edge of the plateau at Tell Hisban and into the Jordan Valley occurred only during the 7th and 6th centuries b.c.e. See Herr, "The Iron Age II Period," 165, 168–72; cf. 146, 148. The interpretation of the

The DAPT thus represents this script's early development at the hands of local scribes trained in the scribal system of Aram-Damascus and supported under
Damascene authority,[31] as a regional variant of the Aramaic script appropriate for
representing indigenous literary-religious traditions of Gilead, like this one about
Balaam. The overt differences in technique and style from the Hebrew script tradition associated with the central political authorities of Cisjordan meant that, with
the northern Israelite kingdom's recovery of Gilead territories, these scribes and
their writing tradition found employment not in the service of the Israelite state's
reclaiming of Gilead but rather in the Ammonite kingdom, which embraced this
distinct Gilead script as its own, as a cultural resource reinforcing its expansion-
ist claims to territory in Gilead during the first half of the 8th century (Amos
1:13–15). Thus, the script of the DAPT favors the earlier period of Damascene
hegemony in central Transjordan for the date of its execution as a display inscription (ca. 840–800 b.c.e.).[32]

---

archaeological evidence from Tell Hisban has been pivotal for this determination. See J. A. Saur,
"The Pottery at Hesban and Its Relationship to the History of Jordan: An Interim Hesban Pottery
Report, 1993," in *Hesban after 25 Years* (ed. D. Merling and L. T. Geraty; Berrien Springs, MI: The
Institute of Archaeology/Siegried H. Horn Archaeological Museum, 1994), 225–81, here 241–47.
According to the final report on Hisban, the pottery from ca. 925–700 b.c.e. has its closest paral-
lels in contemporary Moabite sites such as Dibon and Arair and, in relationship with historical
information from relevant textual sources, indicates the site's Moabite identity throughout this
time. The following archaeological phase (ca. 700–500 b.c.e.) shows a dramatically different
settlement plan, Ammonite inscriptions, and ceramics with parallels at Umayri, Amman, and
Jawa (south). See P. J. Ray Jr., *Tell Hesban and Vicinity in the Iron Age* (Hesban 6; Berrien Springs,
MI: Andrews University Press, 2001), 53–61, 121–26.

As for biblical evidence, Heshbon (usually identified with Tell Hisban) is considered a
Moabite city during the late 8th century b.c.e. (Isa 15:4; 16:8–9) but during the late 7th century is
no longer considered Moabite (Jer 48:1–2, 45) but instead is regarded explicitly as an Ammonite
city (Jer 49:3 cf. Herr, "The Iron Age II Period," 169).

Ammonite pottery and inscriptions dating to the 7th and 6th centuries b.c.e. have been
found at Hisban and in the Jordan Valley at Dayr ʿAlla and just 2 miles (3 km) to the northwest
at Tell al-Mazar. See Herr, "The Iron Age II Period," 170; Ray, *Tell Hesban*, 57–61, 137–47; F. M.
Cross Jr. and L. T. Geraty, "The Ammonite Ostraca from Tell Hesban," in *Hesban after 25 Years*
(ed. D. Merling and L. T. Geraty; Berrien Springs, MI: The Institute of Archaeology/Siegried H.
Horn Archaeological Museum, 1994), 169–75; van der Kooij and M. Ibrahim, *Picking Up the
Threads*, 69–70; K. Yassine and J. Teixidor, "Aramaic and Ammonite Inscriptions from Tell el-
Mazār in Jordan," *BASOR* 264 (1986) 45–50. At Tell es-Saʿidiyye in the east Jordan Valley just
5 mile (9 km) northwest of Dayr ʿAlla, pottery forms and assemblages dated ca. 820–600 b.c.e.
show very little connection with pottery from the area of Amman and the plateau as a whole. See
J. B. Pritchard, *Tell es-Saʿidiyeh: Excavations on the Tell, 1964–1966* (University Museum Monographs 60; Philadelphia: The University Museum, University of Pennsylvania, 1985), 44–56, especially 51–52.

31. Van der Kooij has argued that the ductus of the DAPT letter-forms indicate a writing technique found in Aramaic scribal tradition that differed from that employed in Hebrew
and other Northwest Semitic scribal traditions. See van der Kooij and Ibrahim, *Picking Up the
Threads*, 65–67; van der Kooij, "Book and Script at Deir ʿAllā," 253–55.

32. An even earlier date of composition is possible for the text itself or for any source from
which it may have been taken. See the discussion of the text on pp. 151–53.

Like the material culture from Phase IX, the epigraphic evidence from this occupational phase shows that Dayr ʿAlla occupied an intermediate cultural area between the political centers of the surrounding highland kingdoms. This situation stands in marked contrast to the well-defined national identities signaled primarily by language dialect (and secondarily by script) associated with the regional political centers of Damascus and of the highland kingdoms both east and west of the Jordan, as represented by royal monumental inscriptions of the late 9th century B.C.E., roughly contemporary with the DAPT: the Amman Citadel Inscription (Ammonite language, Aramaic script), the Mesha Stele Inscription at Dhiban (Moabite language, Hebrew script), and the Tel Dan Stela Inscription (Aramaic language and script).[33] The formulation of the DAPT in a local dialect falling in between these "national" language dialects of the royal inscriptions not only reflects Dayr ʿAlla's perennial role as a place at the boundaries of these surrounding political centers but also signals the articulation of a religious tradition set apart from the polarized national theologies of those kingdoms, one centering not on Israelite, Ammonite, Moabite, or Damascene national gods and royal authority but rather on prophetic authority in relationship to "the gods" more broadly considered, as discussed more fully below. This inclusive formulation of the divine world in the DAPT was commensurate not only with Dayr ʿAlla's geographically liminal character but also with the international reach of Hazael's dominion, and initially that of his son Ben/Bar Hadad, from Philistia to the Upper Euphrates during the late 9th century B.C.E.[34] Even if under Damascene hegemony, it was at the intersecting peripheries of the surrounding regional kingdoms and cultures that Balaam was invoked at Dayr ʿAlla.

The DAPT's Architectural Context and Function

The function of the small room (measuring ca. 3×4 m, in somewhat rhomboid shape) where the Phase IX plaster wall inscription was displayed remains a matter of debate.[35] It was part of an architectural complex of about 40 small rooms

---

33. For an overview of these and other Northwest Semitic monumental and royal inscriptions in stone, see Rollston, *Writing and Literacy*, 47–60. For the Amman Citadel and Tel Dan Stele inscriptions as representing a distinctly Aramaic script diverging from its parent Phoenician script already by the 9th century B.C.E., see F. M. Cross, "Palaeography and the Date of the Tell Faḫariyeh Bilingual Inscription," in *Leaves from an Epigrapher's Notebook: Collected Papers in Hebrew and West Semitic Palaeography and Epigraphy* (Winona Lake, IN: Eisenbrauns, 2003), 51–60 (revised reprint of the same essay in *Solving Riddles and Untying Knots* [Jonas Greenfield festschrift], [Winona Lake, IN: Eisenbrauns, 1995), 393–409; Aufrecht, "Prolegomenon to the Study of Old Aramaic and Ammonite," 100.

34. See P.-E. Dion, "Syro-Palestinian Resistance to Shalmaneser III in the Light of New Documents," *ZAW* 107 (1995) 482–89.

35. See M. M. Ibrahim and G. van der Kooij, "The Archaeology of Deir ʿAlla Phase IX," *The Balaam Text from Deir ʿAlla Re-Evaluated: Proceedings of the International Symposium held at Leiden 21–24 August 1989* (ed. J. Hoftijzer and G. van der Kooij; Leiden: Brill, 1991), 19 fig. 1, 20–21; in the same volume, G. van der Kooij, "Book and Script at Deir ʿAllā," 241 fig. 1. For a review of scholarship regarding the room's religious function, see J. H. Boertien, "Unravelling

serving mostly as facilities for storage, work, and food preparation around adjoining courtyards.[36] Numerous groups of loom weights show that intensive textile production was a significant activity at the site during this time.[37] The lack of ornamental vessels or other cultic artifacts within the room displaying the DAPT militates against its interpretation as a sanctuary.[38]

Yet, the room's plaster walls and benches are consistent with a religious function, and a religious focus is clearly at work in the inscription's display on one of the walls, where it is inscribed in black and red ink and accompanied by the iconography of a sphinx or cherub figure guarding the boundary drawn to separate the inscription from the surrounding wall space.[39] A religious function associated with the Iron II complex might have fittingly resumed the role once filled by the Late Bronze sanctuary, even if on a much smaller scale.[40] Among other things, the Dayr ʿAlla complex would have served an interregional and international trade community's needs for the sanctioning of oaths sealing commercial agreements and for invoking the aid of various deities to ensure safety during travel and success in the risk-laden endeavors of commerce.[41] In any case, the display of an in-

---

the Threads: Textiles and Shrines in the Iron Age," in *Sacred and Sweet: Studies on the Material Culture of Tell Deir ʿAlla and Tell Abu Sarbut* (ed. M. L. Steiner and E. J. van der Steen; ANES 24; Leuven: Peeters, 2008), 135–51, here 139–40. For recent arguments for the room as a location for scribal training, see Blum, "Die altaramäischen Wandinscrhiften fom Tell Deir ʿAlla," 35–41.

36. Ibrahim and van der Kooij, "The Archaeology of Deir ʿAlla Phase IX," 18–23.

37. J. Boertien, "Iron Age Loom Weights from Tell Dayr ʿAlla in Jordan," *ADAJ* 48 (2004) 305–32; idem, *Unravelling the Fabric: Textile Production in Iron Age Transjordan* (Ph.D. diss., Rijksuniversiteit Groningen, 2013).

38. Ibrahim and van der Kooij, "The Archaeology of Deir ʿAlla Phase IX," 20–21. Some have ascribed a religious meaning and function to artifacts excavated near, but not within, the room where the DAPT was displayed—namely, a few figurine fragments, the ceramic jug with the incised inscription *zy šrᵒ*, 'belonging to *šrᵒ*' and the stone inscribed *ʾbn šrᵒ*, 'the stone of *šrᵒ*' (the meaning of *šrᵒ* remains elusive), and a chalice vessel. See van der Kooij and Ibrahim, eds., *Picking up the Threads*, 70, 87, 94 cat. 32, 101 cat. 97, and, comments also on H. J. Franken, "Deir ʿAlla and its Religion," in *Sacred and Sweet: Studies on the Material Culture of Tell Deir ʿAlla and Tell Abu Sarbut* (ed. M. L. Steiner and E. J. van der Steen; ANES 24; Leuven: Peeters, 2008), 25–52, here 44–48.

39. See Hoftijzer and van der Kooij, *Aramaic Texts from Deir ʿAlla*, pl. 15. See also Boertien's arguments favoring the Dayr ʿAlla room's religious function based on criteria for identifying archaeological spaces as sacred or cultic put forth by C. Renfrew and P. Bahn and by M. Coogan (Boertien, "Unravelling the Threads, 141–44).

40. Compare the shift in architectural plan, scale, and orientation between the LB direct-access pillared temple (12 × 18 m) and the early Iron II bent-axis sanctuary (only 8 × 12 m) 18 miles (29 km) to the north in the east Jordan Valley at Pella (Ṭabaqāt Faḥil). See S. Bourke, "The Six Canaanite Temples of Ṭabaqāt Faḥil: Excavating Pella's 'Fortress' Temple (1994–2009)," in *Temple Building and Temple Cult: Architecture and Cultic Paraphernalia of Temples in the Levant (2.–1. Mill. B.C.E.)* (ed. Jens Kamlah; ADPV 41; Wiesbaden: Harrassowitz, 2012), 159–201 and pls. 31–43, here 161, 171, 184, and pls. 36–38.

41. Compare Franken's suggestion that the Late Bronze sanctuary served to sanction international trade involving tribal and clan groups of the region. See Franken, *The Late Bronze*

scription centering on the mantic figure Balaam and relating a message from "the gods," generally speaking (DAPT I.1, 5), substantiates some form of religious focus at this site located at the geographic and political boundaries of surrounding rival kingdoms.

This appeal to common ground within the divine realm, as opposed to the polarizing royal theologies of specific kingdom deities (e.g., in the Mesha and Tel Dan Inscriptions; see above), would have served the needs and interests of Dayr ʿAllaʾs continuing role during the Iron Age as a regional hub of exchange in the geographically liminal and politically volatile context of shifting kingdom boundaries in west-central Transjordan.

Summary: The International Political and Religious Framework of the DAPT

Even while falling under the political hegemony of a distant Damascus, Iron IIb Dayr ʿAllaʾs paramount value to that far-reaching Iron Age kingdom centered on the continuing flow of trade through this regional hub of exchange. Both Dayr ʿAllaʾs character in this regard and the international scale of Damascus's own hegemonic interests under Hazael and then Bar Hadad (see the Zakkur Stele Inscription A.4–9) would have favored a religious vision that successfully negotiated intersecting national identities on a broader, common basis. Consistent with this geopolitical framework of Syria–Palestine, the DAPT's reference to "the gods," broadly speaking, in its opening lines (DAPT I.1–2) represents an appeal to higher powers of the divine realm, mediated not by a king but rather by a prophet of reputed international standing.

B. Balaam in the DAPT

The DAPT have been reconstructed from two major clusters of inscribed plaster fragments recovered around the collapsed wall. Combination I quite fortuitously preserves the beginning of the inscription, as indicated by a horizontal line drawn above a first line of text and a vertical line at the left margin. [42] These features, along with the use of red and black ink for different portions of the text, allow for a fairly confident reconstruction of the inscription's first ten lines with relatively few gaps due to missing fragments. A formal heading opens the inscription, designating it "the admonition of the book of Balaam, son of Beor," and then the text proper begins with a narrative introduction describing how Balaam

---

Sanctuary, 166, 175–76; also van der Kooij and Ibrahim, *Picking up the Threads*, 79–80.

42. For this point and those that follow in this and the next paragraph, see, for example, Lipiński, "The Plaster Inscription," 104–10, 113–59. In his most recent publications, Blum has opted for the alternative designations "Kombination A" and "Kombination B" ("Die altaramäischen Wandinscrhiften fom Tell Deir ʿAlla," 24 n. 17). For the present discussion, I retain the conventional terminology.

in great distress disclosed to his community a divine revelation he had received in the night (lines 1–5). From there, the text presents Balaam's report of the divine disclosure, an elaborate vision of upheaval on earth that becomes the focus of Combination I and that continues through the remainder of its surviving text (lines 5–16), which becomes increasingly fragmented and eventually gives way to a section of text forever lost in the ancient destruction of the Phase IX site.

Combination II is a less well preserved and more poorly understood section, mostly fragments, with less agreement among scholars regarding its reconstruction and interpretation and even whether it represents a continuation of the same text found in Combination I or is a different text. The repeated occurrence of the root *mlk* both as a verb and a noun (DAPT II.9 [2×], 13, 15, and 18) [43] and of *nqr*, 'sprout' (lines 5, 12, and 14), possibly meaning (royal) 'scion', [44] conveys no apparent reference to a specific named ruler or national identity and might be said only to refer to kingship and perhaps royal succession, generally speaking, as perennial factors in the world's order from an ancient perspective. [45] The mention of 'death' (*mwt*, line 13) and the rendering of a 'judgment' (*špṭ*) and a 'verdict' or 'punishment' (*lqḥ*, line 17) are close at hand, with many interpreters understanding line 18 to read 'I have punished/will punish the king/kings' (*w'nšty.lmlk*[. . .], II.18). [46] The notion of punishment for a ruler fits with the pattern of reversals of expected

---

43. In keeping with the preceding parallel clause employing the root *y'ṣ* / *'wṣ* 'advise' (*hl'šh. bk. lyt'ṣ*, line 9), the two instances of *mlk* in line 9 (*'w lmlkh. lytmlk. yšb-*[. . .]) relate to advising and giving counsel, as translated by Hoftijzer ("As to counsel one will not ask you for it, and as to advice one will not ask (you) for it . . ." Hoftijzer, "Interpretation and Grammar," 180, 228; similarly, Levine, "Deir 'Alla," 144 n. 4; as an interrogative, Caquot and Lemaire, "Les textes araméens," 204; Hackett, *The Balaam Text*, 30; Blum, "'Verstehst du dich nicht auf die Schreibkunst. . . ?'," 37; as a past-tense interrogative, Seow, "West Semitic Sources," 212). Compare Lipiński's translation: "To rebel against you, will he not plot or, to reign himself, will he not take over?" (Lipiński, "The Plaster Inscription," 142).

44. Compare BH *nēṣer*, Isa 11:1. See Caquot and Lemaire, "Les textes araméens," 202–3; McCarter, "The Balaam Texts," 51; Hackett, *The Balaam Text*, 57, 77–78; compare Blum, "'Verstehst du dich nicht auf die Schreibkunst. . . ?'," 36–38, 41–43, 46.

45. Hackett's interpretation of Combination II as relating to a ritual of child sacrifice, despite its compelling points, does not fully account for the occurrences of *mlk* in lines 13, 15, 18, only allowing that it might denote "a king, perhaps a sacrificial term, but perhaps a divine epithet." See Hackett, *The Balaam Text*, 30, 77–85; "Religious Traditions in Israelite Transjordan," 126, 128, 131–34, quoting here from p. 128.

46. These elements of Combination II represent basic points of scholarly agreement among various nuances of precise interpretation of the text as a whole. See Caquot and Lemaire, "Les textes araméens," 202–3; Hackett, *The Balaam Text*, 73–74; McCarter, cited in Hackett, *The Balaam Text*, 74; Lipiński, "The Plaster Inscription," 142–59; Seow, "West Semitic Sources," 208, 210–12; Levine, *Numbers 21–36*, 255–62. Compare, though with less agreement, Dijkstra, "Is Balaam also among the Prophets?" 49–51, 55–60. Compare also Blum, who reconstructs from the fragments additional line fragments for Combination II. See "'Verstehst du dich nicht auf die Schreibkunst. . . ?'," 38; "Die altaramäischen Wandinscrhiften fom Tell Deir 'Alla," 31–32, 46–48, and fig. 2.

norms that prevails throughout Balaam's vision of earthly and cosmic upheaval in Combination I (cf. Prov 17:26; see below).

By contrast, from its opening lines, Combination I is clearly focused on prophetic authority, specifically that of Balaam son of Beor, with no apparent mention of any king. Where the word "king(s)" is mentioned in Combination II, the surrounding context (fragmented though it may be) indicates that royal authority is not so much promoted as objectified, perhaps even minimized or criticized. Whether representing one continuous or two separate texts, the publicly displayed juxtaposition of Combinations I and II at Dayr ʿAlla plays down royal authority in deference to prophetic authority. In keeping with Dayr ʿAlla's context at the boundaries of regional kingdoms during the late 9th century B.C.E., the DAPT appeals to the prophetic figure Balaam as one who mediates the authority of higher, cosmic powers in his role as spokesman for "the gods" (DAPT I.1, 5). Balaam thus ranks as one seeing beyond the claims of the surrounding kingdoms and so stands as a potential friend or enemy of the state. In connection with Balaam's authority, one further aspect of the literary character of the DAPT bears attention.

The Book of Balaam

Combination I begins with a heading written in red ink that introduces the text as

ysr[.][47] *spr [.blʿm . br bʿ]r . ʾš . ḥzh . ʾlhn*
The admonition of the Book of Balaam, son of Beor, the man (who was) a seer of the gods. (I.1)[48]

---

47. Although it is not clear that all the fragments adduced by Puech fit together at the beginning of line 1 to render the plural form *ysry*, fragment IIIf does supply the word *ysr*, and Puech may well be correct in relating this expression to the often misunderstood wording *yswry bʾrṣ yktbw* ('my [i.e., the prophet's] chastisement(s) against the land are written') in Jer 17:13 (MT *Kethiv*). See Puech, "Le texte 'ammonite' de Deir ʿAlla," 15–17 and, more recently, Émile Puech, "Balaam and Deir ʿAlla," in *The Prestige of the Pagan Prophet Balaam in Judaism, Early Christianity and Islam* (ed. G. H. van Kooten and J. van Ruiten; Themes in Biblical Narrative: Jewish and Christian Traditions 11; Leiden: Brill, 2008), 32–33.

48. Balaam's full name with patronymic is partially restored in this line from its occurrences in DAPT I.2, 4. This reading of *ʾš* as the common noun 'man' in the clause designating Balaam a 'seer of the gods' (*ʾš . ḥzh*) receives strong support from numerous instances of *ʾyš* 'man' immediately preceding a functional title in Biblical Hebrew and older Aramaic (Exod 2:14; Lev 21:9; Judg 6:8; Aḥiqar 125; etc.; see Hoftijzer, "Interpretation and Grammar," 184) and is the reading also by Caquot and Lemaire, "Les textes araméens," 194; McCarter, "The Balaam Texts," 51; Weippert and Weippert, "Die 'Bileam'-Inschrift," 84; Puech, "Balaam and Deir ʿAlla," 31. Alternatively, *ʾš* can be understood as a relative pronoun, with the word following *ʾlhn*, the word *hʾ*, serving as a copula or resumptive (3 m.s.) independent personal pronoun completing the relative clause. See J. A. Fitzmyer, review of J. Hoftijzer and G. van der Kooij, *Aramaic Texts from Deir ʿAlla. CBQ* 40 (1978): 94–95; Hackett, *The Balaam Text*, 30–32. Somewhat problematic for this view are both the resulting word order and the disagreement between the proposed syntax and the pattern of ink color in the text, which shifts from red to black beginning with *hʾ*

A heading of this kind signals the "literary" nature of the inscription, either in citing a known text as the inscription's source—"the Book of Balaam" (*spr [.bl'm*), perhaps a specific "warning, chastisement, admonition" (*ysr*) section[49]—or alternatively, in introducing the 'account' (*spr*) of Balaam, which includes Balaam's vision report (DAPT I.5–18) within the context of dialogue contained in a third-person narrative (DAPT I.1–5). The central focus of this literary text is clearly Balaam and his words, as a 'seer of the gods' (*ḥzh . ʾlhn*, DAPT I.1).

The authoritative status of this literary text is clear from its form of presentation. The horizontal (top) and marginal boundary lines setting the text off from the rest of the wall space are accompanied by the drawing of a sphinx or cherub figure, indicating the sacred status of the words thus demarcated.[50] Within the inscription, a further degree of sacredness might be indicated by the use of red ink both for the inscription heading and for the initial divine words conveyed by Balaam within the narrative, setting these portions of the text apart from the rest of Combination I (DAPT I.1, 2).[51] These textual rubrics highlight Balaam's status

---

(cf. DAPT I.2, II.17, where red ink is used again and where color and syntax align). Compare Hackett, *The Balaam Text*, 30–32. Alternatively, and in line with the former view (i.e., *ʾš* as 'man'), *hʾ* can be read in relationship to the following clause (*hʾ. wyʾtw .ʾlwh .ʾlhn*, DAPT I.1) as the 3 m.s. independent personal pronoun functioning anaphorically or as *casus pendens*, followed by a *waw apodosis*," thus translated, "As for him, the gods came to him at night." See Hoftijzer, "Interpretation and Grammar," 179, 184–85; Puech, "Balaʿam and Deir ʿAlla," 31, 33. A variation on this solution is that *hʾ* is an interjection 'behold' followed by *wayyiqtol* (Puech, "Balaʿam and Deir ʿAlla," 33; see also Caquot and Lemaire, "Les textes araméens," 194; McCarter, "The Balaam Texts," 52; Hackett, *The Balaam Text*, 30–32. Compare, further, Lipiński, who argues that the *wayyiqtol* (*wyʾtw*) "has to be preceded by another sentence, either verbal or nominal" and thus regards *hʾ* as a pronoun belonging to the previous clause, translating, "He was a man seeing the gods, and the gods came to him . . ." (Lipiński, "The Plaster Inscription," 116–18). Aside from the conflict with the ink-color schema, Lipiński's objection is countered by occurrences in Biblical Hebrew of *wayyiqtol* preceded by a nominal or adverbial element (that is, *waw apodosis*). See P. Joüon and T. Muraoka, *A Grammar of Biblical Hebrew* (Subsidia Biblica 14/1; Rome: Pontifical Biblical Institute, 1993), 588 §156.l, 646–47 §176.b.

49. See, for example, Puech, "Balaʿam and Deir ʿAlla," 32–33 n. 19.

50. See van der Kooij, "Book and Script at Deir ʿAllā," 242–44, fig. 2. As Blum points out, the sphinx appeared above the thick, red horizontal line above the beginning of Combination I, likely over the line's extension to the left of the vertical border line of the DAPT and thus above an area apparently prepared for an additional column of writing that was never completed. See Blum, "Die altaramäischen Wandinschriften vom Tell Deir ʿAlla," 36 and fig. 3.

51. Also written in red ink is the sequence of words dealing with judgment in Combination II (DAPT II.17). If the recognition of *nun* instead of *mem* in these word-forms is correct, along with their understanding as 1 c.s. verb-forms, then these words, like the words in red in DAPT I.2, seem to convey divine speech: 'to know [i.e., "make known"] the account that he spoke to his people orally, come let us judge and give verdict' (*ldʿt . spr . dbr . lʿmh . ʾl . lšn . lk . nšpṭ . wnlqh*, DAPT II.17), as read and translated by Seow, "West Semitic Sources," 210, 212; see also Caquot and Lemaire, "Les textes araméens," 207–8; cf. Hackett, *The Balaam Text*, 28, 30, 73–74. Again, the red ink indicates the citation both of the prophet's authoritative (written) 'book' (*spr*, DAPT I.1) or (spoken) 'account' (*spr dbr . . . ʾl lšn*, DAPT II.17), and of the divine words at the basis

in relationship to "the gods" and thus the ultimately divine origin of his words as the basis for the text's sacred and authoritative character.

With the broader scope of the DAPT now in view, one may consider in more detail Balaam's identity, roles, and relationship to the divine in the DAPT.

A *"Seer of the Gods" and "His People"*

In keeping with the DAPT's "intermediate" place among the national dialects of the region—somewhere between Aramaic and the Canaanite "national" dialects of epigraphic Hebrew, Ammonite, and Moabite—the inscription is conspicuously vague regarding Balaam's homeland and his national identity. Balaam's patronymic with the Aramaic word for 'son', *br bʿr* (preserved fully in DAPT I.4), stands out against the use of the Canaanite equivalent *bn*, later in the text (DAPT I.8, 15).[52] This formulation of Balaam's identity suggests his Aramean heritage, consistent with biblical and other textual evidence for the origin of his name (discussed below), but the text avoids any reference to a specific place or identity for Balaam, referring only generically to 'his people' (*ʿmh* DAPT I.4; II.17).[53] Balaam is thus presented to the text's audience as a proverbial outsider, from somewhere else.

Nonetheless, within the textual setting, Balaam performs his prophetic role among 'his people'. In the text's portrayal, Balaam did not seek out the divine disclosure granted to him. Instead, it came to him unsolicited. The narrative introduction reports that 'the gods came to him in the night, and he saw a vision' (*wyʾtw. ʾlwh ʾlhn. blylh. wyḥz. mḥzh* DAPT I.1), in keeping with the textual heading that refers to Balaam as a 'seer of the gods' (*ḥzh.ʾlhn*, DAPT I.1).[54] The 'vision' included words that the gods spoke to Balaam (*wyʾmrw. l[blʿ]m. br bʿr*, DAPT I.2), and, the next day, he reluctantly reported the message to his community. Beyond this, the DAPT provide little information regarding the phenomenology of

---

of the prophet's authority (as in DAPT I.1, 2). Compare Lipiński's rendering of *spr* as 'scribe' in DAPT II.17 (Lipiński, "The Plaster Inscription," 142–43, 154–55). On the function of the red ink portions of the DAPT as textual rubrics, see McCarter, "The Balaam Texts," 49, 59 n. 1. On the use of red ink for textual rubrics in Egyptian scribal tradition, see Puech, "Balaʿam and Deir ʿAlla," 28–29. Compare Blum's view that the selection of words written in red is arbitrary as to their contents and is guided rather by a symmetry marking the first half of the first line and the second half of second line in this fashion; see "Die aramäischen Wandinschriften vom Tell Deir ʿAlla," 26–27, 29 n. 33.

52. In reference to the 'young' of the NḤṢ-bird (*bny . nḥṣ*, DAPT I.8) and of another animal, the name of which is lost to a break in the text (*bn* [   ], I.15).

53. For discussion of the frequent use of *ʿm* 'people' in place of a specific group name, in connection with Balaam in Num 22–24, see pp. 168–69.

54. Similar language is used for Balaam's activity in the poetic portions of Num 22–24, while the prose portions describe Balaam's efforts to solicit oracles through ritual and divination. See p. **000** for discussion of this language in these and other texts.

prophetic activity or aspects of prophecy that might be considered peculiar to a given region or people.[55]

The prophetic mode of seeing visions and delivering verbal messages described for Balaam in DAPT resonates with the vocabulary and portrayals of prophetic activity in biblical texts and in the roughly contemporary Zakkur Stele Inscription.[56] The DAPT can thus be recognized as reflecting a broader, common tradition of prophecy across Iron II Syria–Palestine, one generally fitting either for the royal court (as in the Zakkur inscription's royal commemoration) or for the prophet's community ("people") more broadly considered (as in the DAPT's legendary narrative).[57] The DAPT describes in general terms what would have been a widely recognized mode of prophecy that might have been at home among "his people" in most any location in Syria–Palestine. The main purpose within the context of the DAPT's literary portrayal is to substantiate the divine origin of Balaam's message and thus of the text extensively recording it. In short, for the DAPT, prophetic authority translates to textual authority.

Further examination of the text shows how the ongoing narrative conspicuously plays down distinct national associations both for this liminal figure Balaam and for the deities on whose behalf he speaks.

---

55. Levine's identification of vocabulary and roles of divination ascribed to Balaam in the DAPT is based on unconvincing interpretations of certain terms within the vision section of Combination I, which are best accounted for by the pattern of reversals first recognized in the passage by McCarter ("The Balaam Text," 51–52, 58–59): ḥkm 'wise (one)' (line 11) as 'skilled diviner;' ʿnyh 'the poor woman' (line 11) as 'oracle'; ḥšb 'to esteem/one who esteems' (line 12) as 'augurer'; ḥršn 'the deaf' (line 13) as 'incantations'. See Levine, Numbers 21–36, 246, 252–53.

56. For Biblical Hebrew ḥōzeh (plural ḥōzîm) in reference to prophets as seers of visions, see 2 Kgs 17:13; Isa 28:15; Amos 7:12; etc. Prophets can be said to see (BH ḥzh) a 'vision' (maḥăze(h) Num 24:4, 16; Ezek 13:7; ḥāzôn Isa 1:1; Ezek 12:27; etc.) but also a 'word' or 'message' (dābār Isa 2:1; Mic 1:1; etc.; dibrê Amos 1:1) or an 'oracle' (maśśāʾ Isa 13:1; Hab 1:1; etc.).

In the Zakkur Stele Inscription, the King of Hamath recalls how, in seeking deliverance while under siege by a coalition of rival kingdoms, he received in verbal form a divine message of affirmation and deliverance via prophetic specialists, with no direct mention of solicitation by divinatory means: "I lifted my hands to Baalshamayn, and Baalshamay[n] answered me. / Baalshamayn [spoke] to me [thr]ough seers and through oracle specialists ([b]yd . ḥzyn . wbyd . ʿddn), / [and] Baalshamayn [said], 'F[e]ar not, for I have made [you] king' . . ." (Zakkur Stele Inscription A lines 11–13). In contrast to the DAPT, the Zakkur Inscription portrays prophetic activity in service to the royal court. See Seow, "West Semitic Sources," 203–7; Stökl, Prophecy in the Ancient Near East, 21–22; R. Schmitt, Mantik im Alten Testament (AOAT 411; Münster: Ugarit-Verlag, 2014), 25–26.

57. And perhaps even more broadly in connection with prophecy throughout the Semitic-speaking ancient Near East, as represented by Mari and Neo-Assyrian prophetic texts. See H. B. Huffmon, "A Company of Prophets: Mari, Assyria, Israel," in Prophecy in Its Ancient Near Eastern Context: Mesopotamian, Biblical, and Arabian Perspectives (ed. M. Nissinen; SBLSS 13; Atlanta: SBL, 2000), 48.

Balaam and "the Gods"

Consistent with the avoidance of Balaam's nationality in the DAPT, the text speaks of the divine in relationship to Balaam in the most general of terms, as 'the gods' (*'lhn*) in the inscription heading (DAPT I.1) and in the onset of the text's narrative introduction, which relates that "the gods came to him in the night" (DAPT I.2). The term *'lhn*, the dialectic counterpart to Biblical Hebrew (plural) *(hā)'ĕlōhîm* ('[the] gods') serves as the primary designation for the divine in the DAPT, occurring as the first and most frequent divine designation in the preserved text (DAPT I.1 [2×], 5 [2×]).[58] The narrative introduction goes on to relate that the Ilahin delivered a divine communication to Balaam 'according to the pro[nounce]ment of El' (*km[ś]'* . *'l* , I.2).[59] The god El figures as the traditional head of the pantheon in West Semitic texts from the Bronze Age (especially at Ugarit) and continues to be invoked in this role in Iron Age international contexts, as reflected in biblical prophetic oracles against other nations and their kings (Isa 14:13–14; Ezek 28:2).

In an oracle against the king of Babylon, Isa 14 draws on an ancient Canaanite myth of rebellion among the gods, with the accusation, "You said in your heart, 'I will ascend to heaven; I will raise my throne above the stars of El; I will sit on the mount of assembly on the heights of Zaphon . . . I will make myself like the Most High (*'elyôn*)'" (Isa 14:13–14).[60] The imagery of the divine court also figures in an accusation of hubris against the leader of Tyre in the oracle in Ezekiel 28: ". . . your heart is proud and you have said, 'I am El; I sit on the seat of the gods (*môšab 'ĕlōhîm*)'" (Ezek 28:2). These oracles against foreign kings employ traditional language and imagery of the divine assembly as "the gods" (manifest in the stars of the night sky in Isa 14), under the authority of El. From its opening lines, DAPT Combination I focuses on Balaam's relationship to the divine, whom it depicts in

---

58. For BH *(hā)'ĕlōhîm* and its various extrabiblical counterparts, see J. S. Burnett, *A Reassessment of Biblical Elohim* (SBLDS 183; Atlanta: SBL, 2001), 7–78. No identifiable definite article appears in the DAPT. See Hackett, *The Balaasm Text*, 113–14.

59. As a regular term for prophetic oracles in BH (Isa 13:1; Hab 1:1; Ezek 12:10; etc.), *maśśā'* suggests a translation 'pronouncement' or the like, based on the idiom of 'raising' a locution 'to one's mouth' to speak or recite (*nāśā' 'al-pe(h)*, Ps 16:4; 50:16; cf. Job 13:14); cf. *HALOT*, 639. See also the prose introduction of all four oracles of Balaam in Num 23–24 with, 'And he took up his oration, saying' (*wayyiśśā' měśālô wayyō'mar*, Num 23:7, 18; 24:3, 15). 2 Kings 9:25 speaks of Yhwh having 'raised an oracle against' Ahab (*wyhwh nāśā' 'ālā(y)w 'et-hammaśśā' hazze(h)*).

60. Levine contends for parallels of theme and diction between Isa 14 and DAPT Combination II, based on precise readings of Combination II that exceed the limits of broad scholarly agreement that provide the basis for the present discussion. See Levine, *Numbers 21–36*, 267–68. Levine suggests that these texts belonged to a Transjordanian Israelite archive or repertoire of El literature from the late 8th century and earlier that is now manifest in biblical and epigraphic Balaam texts, Isa 14, and other biblical texts, an intriguing hypothesis that is well beyond the scope and space limits of this discussion. See Levine, *Numbers 21–36*, 208–9 and "The Balaam Inscription," 326–39.

these traditional terms with international implications as "the gods" under the authority of El.

El's vital importance to the religious heritage of ancient Israel is evident in the occurrence of *ʾl* in reference to its god in biblical texts (especially, in various titles found among the ancestral traditions, e.g., *ʾēl ʿelyon*, Gen 14:18; *ʾēl ʿōlām*, Gen 21:33; *ʾēl ʾĕlōhê yiśrāʾēl*, Gen 33:20; *hāʾēl ʾĕlōhê ʾābîkā*, Gen 46:3) and in Israel's very name (*yiśrā-ʾēl*, as opposed to **yiśrā-yāh*).[61] The various biblical and epigraphic documents indicate that, early on, Israel worshiped the deity El and eventually came to equate El with the distinctly Israelite national deity YHWH.[62]

In Ammonite personal names, *ʾl* ('god' or 'El') remains the most frequent divine element throughout Iron II times, even though Milcom is consistently identified as the Ammonite national god in biblical texts (e.g., 1 Kgs 11:5, 53; cf. Judg 11:24) and in the Amman Citadel Inscription (*KAI* 307:1) already in the late 9th century B.C.E.[63] El's consistent but somewhat muted appearance in royal inscriptions from Iron II Syria may express a continuing, tacit recognition of El as the head of the greater pantheon, ultimately sanctioning royal authority among various kingdoms but somewhat in the background of more active junior gods credited with directly promoting and ensuring the rule of their kings.[64]

---

61. For this point and for discussion of the equation of El and YHWH in Israelite religion, see Smith, *The Origins of Biblical Monotheism*, 142–43. The invocation of El in connection with the exodus in Balaam's poetic oracles in Num 23:22 and 24:8 will receive attention in the examination of these texts in light of the DAPT later in this discussion.

62. See, for example, M. S. Smith, *The Early History of God: Yahweh and the Other Deities in Ancient Israel* (Grand Rapids, MI: Eerdmans, 2002), 32–43; John Day, *Yahweh and the Gods and Goddesses of Canaan* (JSOTSup 265; Sheffield: Sheffield Academic, 2000), 13–17, and secondary literature cited there; cf. F. M. Cross, *Canaanite Myth and Hebrew Epic* (Cambridge, MA: Harvard University Press, 1973), 44–75.

63. On Ammonite personal names, see W. E. Aufrecht, "The Religion of the Ammonites," in *Ancient Ammon* (ed. B. MacDonald and R. W. Younker; SHCANE 17; Leiden: Brill, 1999), 156–58 n. 25; J. S. Burnett, "Iron Age Deities in Word, Image, and Name: Correlating Epigraphic, Iconographic, and Onomastic Evidence for the Ammonite God," *SHAJ* 10 (2009) 153–64. For the Amman Citadel Inscription, see W. E. Aufrecht, *A Corpus of Ammonite Inscriptions* (Lewiston, NY: Edwin Mellen, 1989), 154–63:59 and the convenient English translation by Aufrecht in *COS* 2.24:139.

64. El's role as head of the pantheon is clearly portrayed among the abundant texts from Late Bronze Ugarit, and his widespread presence among Iron Age texts indicates his continuing status in this role. See M. S. Smith, *The Origins of Biblical Monotheism: Israel's Polytheistic Background and the Ugaritic Texts* (Oxford: Oxford University Press, 2001), 135–39. As Smith's review of scholarship illustrates, the evidence for the active worship of El during the Iron Age is in many cases ambiguous, and so El's status during the Iron Age remains debated among scholars. The evidence in question suggests the ongoing widespread worship of El throughout Syria–Palestine during the Iron Age, even while most surviving inscriptions (which are produced under the strong influence of political kingdoms of the period) tend to focus on the warrior deities identified with those kingdoms even though these deities rank within the cosmic pantheon as subordinate to El. On this working concept of a common "world theology," see M. S.

In sum, El belongs to the common religious heritage of ancient Syria–Palestine as the traditional head of the broader pantheon. The deities by whom the Iron Age kingdoms differentiated themselves over against one another, though tacitly acknowledged to be under El's authority, figure more visibly than El in the West Semitic royal inscriptions of the period. This is precisely because of their common, defining role as national gods identifying with rival territorial states, analogous and comparable to one another at a level of parity across Syria–Palestine.

This pattern of comparable and differentiating national deities was already in place among the Iron Age kingdoms surrounding Dayr ʿAlla by the time of the DAPT, as is well documented in royal inscriptions from the second half of the 9th century B.C.E.—namely, Ammonite Milcom (Amman Citadel Inscription), Damascene Hadad (Tel Dan Stele Inscription), and Israelite Yhwh and Moabite Chemosh (Mesha Stele Inscription).[65] El is invoked at Dayr ʿAlla not as the national god of the Israelites, Ammonites, or any other kingdom but rather in his traditional role as the head of "the gods" as a whole, a notion of pantheon commonly acknowledged throughout ancient Syria–Palestine and thus providing a broader, potentially international framework for considering the divine.

This is the conception of the divine presented in the DAPT, which speak not in terms of a distinct national divine persona of one kingdom over against others. Rather, the focus is the traditional West Semitic pantheon of "the gods" generally speaking, headed by El, the one deity commonly acknowledged on both sides of the Jordan and throughout Syria–Palestine. The focus on the divine at Dayr ʿAlla is not at the level of competing national gods of Iron Age kingdoms but rather that of the divine assembly of "the gods" as a whole, headed by El.

Smith, *God in Translation: Deities in Cross-Cultural Discourse in the Biblical World* (Grand Rapids, MI: Eerdmans, 2008), 119 n. 106. In keeping with this common view of a broader pantheon, El appears frequently, even if somewhat in the background, among royal inscriptions as the head of the pantheon, the god who ultimately sanctions the authority of the national or royal deity in question. The name element ʾl dominates in Aramaic, Ammonite, and South Arabian personal names, and ʾl occurs clearly in reference to the deity El in the international context of the Sefire treaty inscription (*KAI* 222A: 11) and regularly along with Hadad, Rakib-ʾEl ('the Charioteer of El'), the sun-god Shamash, and sometimes Resheph in royal inscriptions from Iron Age Samʾal (Zinjirli) (*KAI* 214:1, 2, 11, 18; 215: 14, 22), and in the divine title ʾl qnʾrṣ, 'El, Creator of the earth' in the 8th-century B.C.E. Karatepe inscription in Phoenician (*KAI* 26 A III:18) and in a 2nd-century B.C.E. Neo-Punic inscription (*KAI* 129:1). See W. Herrmann, "El," in *DDD*[2]: 274–80.

65. The Mesha Inscription honors Chemosh as the god of Moab, granting military victories, territorial expansion, and general success to the King Mesha, and refers to Yhwh as the Israelite counterpart. See Mesha Inscription, lines 14–18. See B. Routledge, *Moab in the Iron Age: Hegemony, Polity, Archaeology* (Philadelphia: University of Pennsylvania Press, 2004), 133–41; idem, "The Politics of Mesha," 237–38. Similarly, the Tel Dan Stela honors Hadad with the achievements and conquests of the king of Damascus it represents and, in connection with his conquest of Israel, mentions a defeated king with a Yhwh name. See A. Biran and J. Naveh, "The Tel Dan Inscription: A New Fragment," *IEJ* 45:1–18 and the convenient English translation, notes, and bibliography by A. Millard in *COS* 2.39:161–62.

The Shaddayin

Less frequently, the DAPT employ a second term in connection with the assembled deities and always in parallelism with Ilahin, namely, Shaddayin (*šdyn*, DAPT I.5, 6). As explained in the previous section, the term Ilahin is employed first and most frequently as the primary designation for the assembled deities (DAPT I. 1 [2×], 5 [2×]). The term Shaddayin is then introduced within the pattern of verbal parallelism that becomes evident starting in line 3 and that prevails throughout the rest of Combination I. After introducing Balaam as a "seer of the Ilahin," the text relates that the Ilahin came to him at night, under the authority of El ('according to the pro[nounce]ment of El', *km*[*š*]' '*l*, DAPT I.2), and presented divine revelations. Balaam relates the message of the gods to his community by saying,

> I will tell you what the Shadda[yin have done] (*mh . šd*[*yn . p*ʿ*lw*].)
> Come, see the deeds of the Ilahin (*p*ʿ*lt . 'lhn*)!
> The Ilahin have gathered (*'lh*[*y*]*n . 'tyḥdw*),
> and the Shaddayin have set up an assembly (*wnṣbw . šdyn . mw*ʿ*d*)"
>   (DAPT 1.5–6)

The pairing of Shaddayin and Ilahin with comparable terms for divine action and the inverted ordering of *šdyn* // *'lhn* :: *'lhn* // *šdyn* within this sequence indicates that the two plural designations for the divine likewise function interchangeably, if not synonymously.[66] That is to say, Shaddayin and Ilahin may be different terms for the same group of deities, or the Shaddayin may have been an important group among the Ilahin, "the gods" more generally, at Dayr ʿAlla.[67] In either case, the

---

66. As current scholarship commonly recognizes, synonymous elements in verbal parallelism (like any other two words) are never exact equivalents in meaning. See W. G. E. Watson, *Classical Hebrew Poetry: A Guide to Its Techniques* (corrected edition; London: T. & T. Clark, 2007) and various essays found in A. Wagner, ed. *Parallelismus membrorum* (OBO 224; Göttingen: Vandenhoeck & Ruprecht, 2007).

67. McCarter, "The Balaam Texts," 57. For Levine, the Ilahin sent by El to speak to Balaam are separate from the Ilahin who team up with the Shaddayin, the latter two together forming an inimical council of deities (Levine, "The Deir ʿAlla Plaster Inscriptions," 196, 202; idem, "The Plaster Inscriptions," 66–67; idem, *COS* 2.27:141; idem, *Numbers 21–36*, 274; somewhat like Levine, Victor Sasson similarly sees the Ilahin and Shaddayin as completely separate groups of good and evil gods, respectively: "The Book of Oracular Visions of Balaam from Deir ʿAlla," *UF* 17 (1986) 285, 288 n. 13, 294, 295, 298, 306–9). Neither the division of the Ilahin into favorable and unfavorable groups nor, more generally, the indication of conflict among the gods finds any explicit basis in the text of the DAPT, and both ideas even run counter to the implications of the patterns of verbal parallelism in the relevant sections of Combination I (lines 5–6). Rather, Levine's interpretation imposes onto the DAPT the "divine council conflict" narrative type so well known from Mesopotamian sources (but also reflected in biblical literature, for example, in Psalm 82), in support of his perception that the divine council are punishing the goddess they address in the text (DAPT I.6–7; Sasson follows Levine on this point as well; see discussion

scenario is not one of conflict among the gods but rather the more expected circumstance of unified deliberations within the divine assembly.

The sense of Shaddayin either as a synonym for Ilahin or as a term for a special ruling council among the gods fits the etymology of Shaddayin that associates these gods with a "mountain," the cosmic mountain being the place of assembly and deliberation among the gods.[68] Accordingly, the singular form Shadday often appears in the Hebrew Bible as an epithet for Israel's god, at least twice in association with mountains.[69] In one of these instances, a rare occurrence of Shadday in the book of Psalms (Ps 68:15) appears in connection primarily with Mt. Zalmon and, by extension, with Mt. Bashan and Mt. Sinai, along with the accompanying divine names Yнwн, Adonay, and Elohim (Ps 68:15–17). The blessing for Joseph in Gen 49 (Gen 49:22–27) employs various divine epithets, including Shadday followed shortly by mention of "the blessings of the eternal mountains,[70] the bounties of the everlasting hills" (Gen 49:25–26).

In other instances in the Hebrew Bible, Shadday appears in close connection with the divine title El, including the biblical Balaam text in Num 22–24, to be examined in more detail later in this discussion (Num 24:4, 16). To cite this text briefly, Balaam is described as

---

below). This latter notion also finds no support within the Dayr ʿAlla text itself but rather is imported into the DAPT from the Mesopotamian" Descent of Ishtar" mythic narrative (see further discussion, below).

Contrary to the view of the Shaddayin in the DAPT as inherently inimical deities, in BH Shadday occurs in connection both with divine disaster (Isa 13:6b; Joel 1:15; Ps 68:15; Ruth 1:20–21) and blessing (Gen 49:25; Ps 91:1), as a regular title for God in Job (5:17–40:2), and in the frequent divine title El Shadday in P (Gen 17:1; etc.), regularly in explicit connection with divine mercy (Gen 43:14) or blessing (Gen 28:3; 35:11). The appearance of *šdy* as a divine element in Hebrew (*šdyʾwr*, 'Shadday is light', Num 1:5; etc.), Ugaritic, Phoenician, and Thamudic PNN (which tend to convey trust, praise, and thanksgiving for one's own deity) weighs against the notion that the plural form in the DAPT designates an inimical deity. For other specific examples of these PNN, see E. A. Knauf, "Shadday," *DDD* 749–53, here 750.

68. McCarter, "The Balaam Texts," 57; Cross, *Canaanite Myth and Hebrew Epic*, 52–60.

69. For other biblical texts with Shadday standing alone and usually in parallel with Yнwн, see Isa 13:6; Joel 1:15; Ruth 1:20–21; etc.; in parallel with Elyon in Ps 91:1; and with various divine epithets in Job 5:17–40:2. The appearance of *šdy* as a singular in West Semitic PNN (E. A. Knauf, "Shadday," 750) is not surprising, given the fact that such names typically do not include plural theophoric elements.

In light of these correspondences between DAPT *šdyn* and BH *šadday*, a plural *šaddayîn seems conspicuously absent from the Hebrew Bible. This fact, along with the occurrence of *šēdîm*, 'demons' (Deut 32:17; Ps 106:37; cf. Akk. *šēdu*, pl. *šēdū*, 'protective spirit') only as a plural, suggests that this Akkadian loanword may have been employed in these instances as a substitute for Shaddayin, which was otherwise avoided and secondarily equated with this class of foreign "protective spirits" as a way to collectively disparage and demote regional deities deemed foreign to Israel's proper worship of its God, as indicated in Deut 32:17; Ps 106:37.

70. Reading with the LXX (*oreōn monimōn*), which reflects *hárărê ʿad. See the *BHS* critical apparatus.

One who hears the words of El,
who sees a vision of Shadday
(*šōmē(a)ʿ ʾimrê ʾēl maḥăzē(h) šadday yeḥĕze(h)* Num 24:4, 16).[71]

The pairing of *šadday* and *ʾēl* in verbal parallelism in this repeated couplet shows the two to be compatible terms for the divine, as is the case for their plural counterparts in the DAPT (*šdyn* // *ʾlhn*, I.5–6; see above). The two terms are most closely paired in biblical usage in the title El Shadday, mostly in P texts of the Pentateuch (Gen 17:1; 28:3; 35:11; 43:14; 48:3; Exod 6:3; also Ezek 10:5; but cf. non-P Gen 49:25).[72] As an epithet designating a leading deity by association with "the (cosmic) mountain" of the celestial abode, Shadday figures in the Hebrew Bible as a fitting honorific for Israel's God.

Accordingly, in the DAPT the plural form *šdyn* designates a special class or general council of high deities exercising jurisdiction over various peoples and territories and, within the verbal parallelism of the DAPT, serves as an alternative to *ʾlhn* as a designation for the divine assembly. Just as singular *šadday* functions as a compatible, and sometimes complementing, alternative to *ʾēl* in the Hebrew Bible, so does the plural form *šdyn* alternate with plural *ʾlhn* in designating the pantheon ruled by the deity El at Dayr ʿAlla. Whether Shaddayin is, more strictly speaking, a synonym of Ilahin or a subset of the gods, Balaam clearly speaks for the Ilahin and Shaddayin, thus for all the gods in general and not just one specific deity or group of deities over against others.[73]

---

71. Levine understands El and Shadday in these lines originally to refer to different deities, here reflecting a form of Israelite religion in which distinct divine beings are not yet "fully synthesized" (Levine, *Numbers 21–36*, 217–34).

72. In preference to MT *wʾt šdy* in Gen 49:25, some interpreters follow certain Hebrew manuscripts, the Septuagint, the Samaritan Pentateuch, and the Peshiṭta, to read *wʾl šdy*. See the BHS critical apparatus and HALOT 1420–21.

73. Though being typically identified with a specific deity (for example, Dagan, Adad, Shamash, or Ishtar of Ninet), prophets in the Mari texts often interact with various deities and perhaps with a broader council of the gods, whereas, those in Neo-Assyrian texts are more concentrated in divine focus, especially on Ishtar of Arbela and sometimes Assur, but also include various deities from throughout the empire (K. van der Toorn, "Mesopotamian Prophecy between Immanence and Transcendence: A Comparison of Old Babylonian and Neo-Assyrian Prophecy," in *Prophecy in Its Ancient Near Eastern Context: Mesopotamian, Biblical, and Arabian Perspectives* [ed. M. Nissinen; SBLSS 13; Atlanta: SBL, 2000] 78–79; H. B. Huffmon, "The One and the Many: Prophets and Deities in the Ancient Near East," in *Propheten in Mari, Assyrien und Israel* [ed. M. Köckert and M. Nissinen; FRLANT 201; Göttingen: Vandenhoeck & Ruprecht, 2003] 116–31; Stökl, *Prophecy in the Ancient Near East*, 146–47). In any case, in keeping with the royal context of the texts, the prophets they represent tend to speak on behalf of deities representing "the highest echelon of the pantheon" (Stökl, *Prophecy in the Ancient Near East*, 87; use of this expression in the context of Old Babylonian Mari applies equally, even with some differences, to Neo-Assyrian prophecy, as Stökl discusses on pp. 146–48). See also Huffmon, "A Company of Prophets," 55–60; A. Malamat, "The Secret Council and Prophetic Involvement in Mari and Israel," in *Prophetie und geschichtliche Wirklichkeit im alten Israel: Festschrift für*

In keeping with the DAPT's avoidance of naming Balaam's specific homeland or nationality, its portrayal of the divine in a broad and generic sense serves to portray Balaam as a prophet who speaks for the whole of the pantheon, El and the gods, with international implications. In addition to El as head of the pantheon, the DAPT names at least one other deity, a goddess, in a special role with implications for Balaam's authority and role as spokesman for the divine at Dayr 'Alla.

The Goddess as Agent of Divinely Ordained Doom

The focus of the DAPT's portrayal of the divine assembly is the dire verdict of the Ilahin, by which a goddess is charged to bring absolute darkness over the skies, thus causing a cataclysmic disruption of life on earth (DAPT I.6–7).[74] Damage to the text obscures the goddess's identity with only the initial letter *shin* remaining from her name (lines 6–7).[75]

Following the commission to the goddess, the rest of Combination I describes a lengthy series of reversals of the cosmic order, as first pointed out by Kyle Mc-Carter and followed by commentators since:

> There let there be darkness and no (7) perpetual shining and n[o] radiance! For you will put a sea[l upon the thick] cloud of darkness and you will not remove it forever! For the swift has (8) reproached the eagle, and the voice of vultures resounds. The st[ork has] the young of the NHṢ-bird and ripped up the chicks of the heron. The swallow has belittled(9) the dove, and the sparrow [ ]and [ ] the staff. Instead of ewes the stick is driven along. Hares have eaten (10)

Siegfried Herrmann zum 65. Geburtstag (ed. R. Liwak and S. Wagner; Stuttgart: Kohlhammer, 1991), 231–36.

74. A sequence of feminine singular verb forms in lines 6–7 indicates the commissioning of a goddess with this task. See Hackett, *The Balaam Text*, 41–46. Levine's contention that the goddess here comes under punishment from the divine council is ill-supported in the text of the DAPT and seems to be read into the text from a similar motif in the Mesopotamian "Descent of Ishtar." See Levine, "The Deir 'Alla Plaster Inscriptions," 204; *Numbers 21–36*, 243, 246. The one detail of the DAPT Levine adduces in support of his view is his reading of one part of the speech to goddess: *w'l* [.] *thgy . 'd . 'lm* (DAPT I.7), which Levine translates 'Never raise your voice again!' (cf. BH *hgh* 'mutter, utter a sound') but is better rendered 'May it never be removed!' (cf. BH *hgh* 'remove'; following the placement of the "seal" over the heavens' light; McCarter, "The Balaam Texts," 54) or "May you never again be aglow!" (cf. Arab. *wahaja*; citing R. Hazim and O. Ghul, Lipiński "The Plaster Inscription," 130 and n. 132) in keeping with the surrounding context of light-darkness imagery. In any case, the gods' decree is not against the goddess, as Levine contends, but rather against the earth, which is thrown into turmoil as a result of the indefinite darkening of the skies.

75. No clear solution has prevailed regarding the goddess's identity, but scholars have put forward several possibilities, including a feminine form of the solar deity Shamash (comparable to feminine Shapshu at Ugarit), Sheol as a divine personification of death's realm, and a fertility goddess Shagar. The expression *šgr w'štr* appears later in the text (DAPT I.14), and scholars have suggested that this word pair refers to a goddess of fertility perhaps sublimated in the biblical expression *šĕgar-'ălāpêkā wĕ'aštĕrōt ṣō'nekā* ('the *offspring* of your cattle and the issue of your flock', Deut 7:13; 28:4, 18, 51). See Hackett, *The Balaam Text*, 41–42; Puech, "Balaam and Deir 'Alla," 35–36; Levine, *Numbers 21–36*, 249–50.

[   ]. Freemen[   ]have drunk wine, and hyenas have listened to instruction. The whelps of the (11) flox] laughs at wise men, and the poor woman has mixed myrrh, and the priestess (12) [   ] to the one who wears a girdle of threads. The esteemed esteems and the esteemer is es[teemed. (DAPT I.6–13) [76]

This series of reversals elaborates an inversion of norms spanning the realms of nature and society, one so thoroughgoing as to merit divine reprisal. [77]

These various reversals all center on basic dynamics of relative power and status. They represent the natural, social, and moral ramifications of a larger, unifying cosmic order established and overseen by the gods, in keeping with a common ancient Near Eastern view of the world. [78] It is this larger cosmic order that subsumes the political realms of kings and kingdoms. The enumeration of various concrete examples of reversal provides a vivid and multifaceted illustration of how thoroughly misaligned life on earth has become from the divinely established order undergirding nature and society. In response, the gods issue their cataclysmic decree, the unnatural darkening of the sky likewise running counter to the usual order of life on earth.

These motifs of celestial darkness and reversal on the terrestrial plane in the DAPT also occur regularly in biblical prophetic literature. A brief example including both motifs is Isa 13:10–13:

> For the stars of the sky and their constellations
> will not give their light;
> the sun will be dark at its rising,
> and the moon will not shed its light.
> I [YHWH] will punish the world for its evil,
> The wicked for their guilt.
> I will put an end to the pride of the arrogant;
> I will bring low the haughtiness of the ruthless. (Isa 13:10–13) [79]

---

76. Here citing McCarter's translation (McCarter, "The Balaam Texts, pp. 51–52).

77. While some interpreters have suggested that these lines indicate the consequences of the divine verdict, others understand the syntax of the text to indicate the reasons for the gods' verdict (Hackett, *The Balaam Text*, 46–56). Favoring the latter understanding of these lines are two interrelated factors that Blum points out—namely, that this elaborate and extensive section of the text is fitting as a proportional justification for the threat of cosmic catastrophe by the gods and that it thus accounts for what would otherwise be a missing portion of the story (Blum, "Die Kombination I," 593).

78. The common ancient Near Eastern enterprise of observation and speculation regarding natural, social, and moral ramifications of the unifying cosmic order is most commonly recognized in association with "wisdom" literature and thought. See, for example, L. G. Perdue, "Cosmology and the Social Order in the Wisdom Tradition," in *The Sage in Israel and the Ancient Near East* (ed. J. G. Gammie and L. G. Perdue; Winona Lake, IN, 1990) 457–78.

79. Other biblical examples of the darkening of heavenly luminaries include Ezek 32:7–8; Joel 2:10; 3:3–4; 4:15; Zeph 1:14–17. These and other biblical parallels were first pointed out by Hoftijzer (in Hoftijzer and van der Kooij, *Aramaic Texts from Deir ʿAlla*, 183–267, here 197).

In Isa 29:13–21, the motif of reversal characterizes both divine intervention and its causes in abuses of power by those occupying cultic (Isa 29:13), judicial (v. 21), and political (v. 20) leadership roles—human positions of authority, all rightly understood to mediate divine oversight within the world as part of a larger cosmic order.[80] Other texts from the Hebrew Bible and the broader ancient Near East frequently employ the motif of reversal to characterize either divine action or human actions in violation of divine oversight, such as treaty violations or unfavorable rule, or both.[81] As these comparative examples show, the reversals and celestial portents in the DAPT represent an undoing of the natural and social order from which kings derive their power and over which they claim to rule.

The role of a leading goddess in association with prophets and in relating divine messages to the king—even mediating messages from other, male deities—occurs frequently and even characteristically in prophetic texts from Mari and Assyria.[82] The historical and geographic span of these texts suggests broader, long-standing Mesopotamian tradition in which goddesses characteristically play a mediating role as the divine liaison between the pantheon and the human king, communicating the messages of the divine council to kings via prophets. The possible relevance of this Mesopotamian background for the common heritage of ancient Near Eastern prophecy more broadly may lie behind the goddess's role in the DAPT. Accordingly, the task of darkening the skies, with which the other gods have commissioned her, could represent a rupture, perhaps an irreversible one, in divine support for any king or kings that might come into consideration.

---

80. Isaiah 29:13–21 both casts the offenses of the people and their "wise" leaders in terms of a reversal of norms ("You turn things upside down!" v. 16) and anticipates outcomes of divine response in terms of reversal ("The wisdom of their wise shall perish, and the discernment of the discerning shall be hidden. . . . The deaf shall hear the words of a scroll, and out of their gloom and darkness the eyes of the blind shall see," vv. 14, 18). For discussion of the reversal motif in biblical and ancient Near Eastern prophetic literature, see P. A. Kruger, "A World Turned on its Head in ancient Near Eastern Prophetic Literature: A Powerful Strategy to Depict Chaotic Scenarios," *VT* 62 (2012) 58–76. See also J. S. Burnett, "'Come and See What God Has Done!' Divine Presence and the Reversal of Reproach in the Elohistic Psalter and in Iron Age West Semitic Inscriptions," in *Divine Presence and Absence in Exilic and Post-Exilic Judaism: Studies of the Sofja Kovalevskaja Research Group on Early Jewish Monotheism, Vol. II* (ed. N. MacDonald and I. J. de Hulster; FAT II/61; Tübingen: Mohr Siebeck, 2013), 213–54.

81. Numerous biblical and comparative ancient Near Eastern examples of reversal are collected in B. Becking, *Between Fear and Freedom: Essays on the Interpretation of Jeremiah 30–31* (Outestamentische Studiën 51; Leiden: Brill, 2004), 138, 141–49.

82. Martti Nissinen, "The Socioreligious Role of the Neo-Assyrian Prophets," in *Prophecy in Its Ancient Near Eastern Context: Mesopotamian, Biblical, and Arabian Perspectives* (ed. M. Nissinen; SBL Symposium Series 13; Atlanta: SBL, 2000) 89–114, here 95–102, 104–5, 110–11; Beate Pongratz-Leisten, "When the Gods are Speaking: Toward Defining the Interface between Polytheism and Monotheism," in *Propheten in Mari, Assyrien und Israel* (ed. M. Köckert and M. Nissinen; FRLANT 201; Göttingen: Vandenhoeck & Ruprecht, 2003), 132–68, especially 141–62; Stökl, *Prophecy in the Ancient Near East*, 68–69, 146–49.

However, as in the narrative leading up to Balaam's account of the divine council (DAPT I.1–5), any direct mention of kings is conspicuously absent from the divine deliberations and earthly upheavals Balaam describes (DAPT I.5–18). As discussed, even the mention of a "king" or "kings" in Combination II is not specific but rather appears abstract or proverbial in nature. This suggestion of judgment on kings with possible implications for succession ('scion', *nqr*, DAPT II.5, 14) is ominous enough, but all the more so are the implications for the broader cosmic order elaborated in Combination I. The DAPT as a whole, whether constituting one continuous inscription or two juxtaposed texts, consistently signal a focus not on a specific king or kingdom but rather on the order of human society and nature more generally, with kings being a perennial part of that order.

The DAPT thus communicates a standing, latent threat of divine judgment against any unspecified "king" and kings in general. Though not stated as an explicit polemic against a particular kingdom, the message of divinely ordained doom decreed by a cosmic, politically neutral pantheon presented at Dayr ʿAlla stood as a theoretical challenge to all surrounding kings and kingdoms as powers perennially subject to rise and fall.

Conclusion:
Balaam as a Potential Enemy of the State in the DAPT

The DAPT's full contents and the function of the room within which it was displayed remain only partially understood. What is clear is that Balaam, although cast as a prophet of doom, is portrayed sympathetically and favorably as an authority who speaks for "the gods" in general. The text represents the divine at a supranational level, the greater pantheon headed by El, the high god of Syria–Palestine long before the rise of Iron Age kingdoms and still understood as the deity transcending those kingdoms. This inclusive vision of the divine matched Dayr ʿAlla's role as an interregional and international hub of exchange at the contested boundaries of Iron Age kingdoms. While this politically neutral view of the divine held the potential for inclusivity, it also highlighted the limits of national ideologies and claims and thus stood in possible tension with them.

The DAPT portrays the same general kind of prophetic activity also invoked in support of Levantine states (for example, in the Zakkur Inscription)—that is, the mediation of verbal messages from the gods based on visions and other direct communications from the divine without reference to divinatory or cultic solicitation. But, as a non-royal inscription, it represents a different institutional context. During the time of the DAPT, the site of Dayr ʿAlla lay within territory conquered by Aram-Damascus (ca. 840–800 B.C.E.) or, less likely, reclaimed by the northern Israelite kingdom (ca. 800–750 B.C.E.). In any case, the inscription indicates no clear affiliation with a specific kingdom or people identity. Its appeal to the higher pantheon of "the gods" reflects an interest in divine oversight over the earth and its ruling authorities, more generally.

In contrast to the royal court setting and the explicit support for the monarchy represented by the cuneiform archives from Mari and Assyria, the viewpoint of the DAPT is consistent with its setting as a regional trade hub with perhaps shifting national affiliation. Ancient Dayr ʿAlla served a pivotal function in coordinating and facilitating the movement of interregional trade and enjoyed a longstanding reputation as a regional sanctuary site from Bronze Age times. Thus, this unwalled Iron Age site would warrant different treatment by the surrounding Iron Age kingdoms than that often endured by towns and populations along shifting political boundaries, under the polarizing national ideology of *herem* between competing deities as well known from the Mesha Stele Inscription and biblical texts (Deut 7:2; 20:16–18; Josh 6:17–19; etc.). By contrast, Dayr ʿAlla held a special status and value as a liminal node of economic, political, and religious mediation and accordingly gave focus to the higher pantheon of El and "the gods" and with the standing threat of divine judgment against kings and earthly powers, as articulated in the DAPT.

Within that religious framework, Balaam in the DAPT can be considered to embody the legacy of prophets later recalled in the biblical books of Micah (3:5–12; 6:9–16) and Jeremiah, those appointed "over peoples and kingdoms" (Jer 1:10) to prophesy disaster "against many countries and great kingdoms" (Jer 28:8; see also 26:18, discussed below).[83] Nonetheless, like the biblical Jeremiah, Balaam in the DAPT is a reluctant prophet who suffers under the weight of the message of doom he must present to his own people. In the DAPT, the prophet Balaam speaks not to the concerns of a particular king or people but rather to human accountability to the divine, more broadly, with implications for the whole earth. The persona of Balaam as a politically neutral prophet of doom takes a different trajectory among texts in the Hebrew Bible.

III. Balaam in Texts of the Hebrew Bible

Balaam appears in the Hebrew Bible as the central figure in Numbers 22–24 and, with different emphases, in a variety of briefer literary units. All of these biblical texts locate Balaam's activity in Transjordan, and they all portray Balaam as a renowned intermediary to the divine whose acts of speech posed a potential threat to Israel. A basic distinguishing factor among the biblical texts is a divergence between relatively positive (Num 22–24 [minus 22:22–35]; Micah 6:5) and negative (Num 22:22–35; 31:8, 16; Deut 23:5–6; Josh 13:22; 24:9–10; Neh 13:2) portrayals of Balaam. This difference rests on the perception of Balaam's prophetic activity as either favoring or opposing Israel. It thus provides an appropriate point of departure for considering each text in relationship to the DAPT and to each other as

---

83. As suggested by H. O. Thompson, "Balaam in the Bible and at Deir ʿAllā," sidebar to J. A. Hackett, "Some Observations on the Balaam Tradition at Deir ʿAllā," *BA* 49.4 (Dec 1986), 218–19.

reflections on prophecy vis-à-vis states in Iron Age Transjordan, beginning with the most extensive example, Num 22–24.

A. Numbers 22–24

Apart mainly from the secondary addition of the donkey story (Num 22:22–35), the "Balaam Pericope" of Num 22–24 represents a literary unity of prose and poetic material that was created prior to its placement within its present literary context in Numbers.[84] Like the DAPT, Num 22–24 offers a relatively favorable portrayal of Balaam as a religious authority who speaks for the divine. Uniting these chapters is a prose narrative in which King Balak of Moab summons Balaam from his homeland to pronounce a curse on Israel as his feared enemy.

Balaam's place of residence is identified as "Pethor, which is on the River"—that is, the Euphrates (Num 22:5).[85] Pethor is identified with the ancient city Pitru located on the west bank of the upper Euphrates, near its convergence with River Sajur. Ancient Pitru enjoyed some degree of international prominence: it is mentioned during the mid-9th century by Shalmaneser III (860–825 B.C.E.) as a city that was conquered ca. 1000 B.C.E. by a "king of Aram" and, much earlier, in topographic lists of Thutmose III (1450–1425 B.C.E.).[86] The specific mention of Pethor/Pitru in Num 22:5 agrees with the more general designation of Balaam's homeland in poetic parallelism in the first poetic oracle, in Num 23:7, as "Aram . . . the eastern mountains (harĕrê-qedem)," referring to the earliest known Aramean homeland of northeast Syria, including the Jebel Bishri region.[87] As discussed fur-

---

84. See Levine, *Numbers 21–36*, 135–275; J. Milgrom, *Numbers* (The JPS Torah Commentary; Philadelphia: Jewish Publication Society, 1990), 185, 319 nm. 1–2, 467–69; and the careful analysis recently by J. M. Robker, "The Balaam Narrative in the Pentateuch/Hexateuch/Enneateuch," in *Torah and the Book of Numbers* (FAT II/62; ed. C. Frevel et al.; Tübingen: Mohr Siebeck, 2013), 334–66, especially, 334–51, 362–64. Efforts to divide Num 22–24 into separate Yahwist (J) and Elohist (E) Pentateuchal sources have faltered mainly on the lack of clear patterns in divine names that could be connected with other indications of changing prose sources within these texts. See Levine, *Numbers 21–36*, 137–39, 207, 237; Robker, "The Balaam Narrative," 342–43.

85. For "the River" as the usual biblical expression to refer to the Euphrates, see Exod 23:31; Josh 24:2, 3, 14. The understanding of the final *h* in the place name *ptwrh* as a locative in the MT is preferred; the alternative explanation, that it is a vestigial determinative ending on an Aramaic title for Balaam as 'the interpreter' (cf. Syriac *pšwr'* in the Peshiṭta; see, for example, M. Delcor, "Balaam *Patôrah*: Interprete de songes au pays d'Ammon, d'apres Num 22:5," *Semeia* 32 [1982] 89–91), in addition to being a "blatantly Midrashic explanation" (Levine, *Numbers 21–36*, 148), presents two major problems: the use of an Aramaic title would be inconsistent with Balaam's immediately preceding patronymic using Hebrew *bn*, 'son', rather than Aramaic *br*, and the resulting relative clause accounting for Balaam's location would read somewhat awkwardly, with no verb for "living/dwelling" (*'šr 'al-hannāhār*, 'who *was* on the River', Num 22:5).

86. P.-E. Dion, "Les araméens du Moyen-Euphrate au VIIIe siècle à la lumière des inscriptions des maîtres de Suhu et Mari," in *Congress Volume, Paris 1992* (ed. J. Emerton; VTSup 61; Leiden: Brill, 1995), 69. For a convenient English transition of the Shalmaneser III text, see the "Kurkh Monolith" Inscription, ii 36–38, translated by K. L. Younger Jr. (*COS* 2.113A:263).

87. The Jebel Bishri region was the territorial base from which Aramean peoples seem to have emerged from the north Syrian desert and spread along areas of the middle and upper

ther below, Deut 23:5 agrees in identifying Balaam's home as "Pethor, in Aram-Naharaim." Consistent with the intimation of Balaam's Aramean heritage in the DAPT (*blʿm br bʿr*, DAPT I.1, 2, 4; cf. *bn* in lines 8, 15), biblical texts clearly locate Balaam's homeland far away from central Transjordan, in northeast Syria near the Euphrates. In fact, the name Balaam appears as the patronymic of an Aramean chief located in the middle Euphrates region in a cuneiform text of the 8th century B.C.E. (written ¹*Ba-la-am-mu* and ¹*Ba-li-am-mu*).[88]

Euphrates during the late second millennium B.C.E., as attested in their earliest appearances in textual sources. Tiglath-Pileser I (ca. 1100 B.C.E.) described a significant presence of Arameans extending from Jebel Bishri throughout the upper Euphrates region, as far north as Carchemish, a situation documented already in Mesopotamian sources by the 13th century B.C.E. See A. K. Grayson, "History and Culture of Assyria," *ABD* 4:732–55; A. F. Rainey and R. S. Notley, *The Sacred Bridge: Carta's Atlas of the Biblical World* (Jerusalem: Carta, 2006), 106–7. The more specific location Pethor/Pitru on the River (Euphrates) mentioned in Num 22:5, even if stemming from the later prose framework of Num 22–24, would lie within the expanse of a broader Aramean homeland indicated by "Aram . . . the eastern mountains," a poetic parallelism accounting for both rural and urban, desert and flood land, components of Aramean territory and identity. As Dion emphasizes, the pass at Jebel Bishri was the key route between the middle Euphrates and southern Syria in association with Aramean peoples during the early first millennium B.C.E. and previously. See P.-E. Dion, *Les Araméens à l'âge du fer: histoire politique et structures sociales* (Études bibliques NS 34; Paris: Gabalda, 1997), 17, 27, 59, 85, 148, 175.

Levine affirms that the expression "mountains of the east" (Num 23:7) places Balaam's homeland near the mountains of northeast Syria but also (following Mowinckel) argues that a second tradition was incorporated into Num 22–24, one that regarded Transjordan as Balaam's homeland. See Levine, *Numbers 21–36*, 145–46, 168, 208, 239; S. Mowinckel, "Die Ursprung der Bileamsage," *ZAW* 48 (1930) 233–71. Accordingly, for Levine, "the eastern mountains" might be understood secondarily to refer to the Transjordanian Plateau as viewed from west of the Jordan. Not only does this suggestion disregard the vantage point of Num 23:7 being on the Plateau itself (see also v. 9), but the supposed alternate tradition of Balaam's origins requiring this suggestion proves illusory in view of other factors.

One of these involves the MT's identification of the figure "Bela son of Beor" (Gen 36:32) as a "king of Edom" before the time of the Israelite monarchy. As various scholars have pointed out, Bela (*belaʿ*) is a variant of Balaam's name (*bilʿām*) and may derive from a variant Balaam tradition; but see the following note on the derivation and etymology of Balaam's name. The clear Aramean associations for Balaam support the view that this "Bela son of Beor," and the Edomite king list in Gen 36:31–39 more generally, involves a textual confusion for an original king of "Aram," specifically, one resulting from a list of kings of Aram, involving a confusion of the letter *r* for *d*. See A. Lemaire, "Les premiers rois araméens dans la tradition biblique," in *The World of the Aramaeans I: Biblical Studies in Honour of Paul-Eugène Dion* (ed. P. M. M. Daviau et al.; JSOTSup 324; Sheffield: Sheffield Academic Press, 2001), 113–43, here 116–17. See Paul-Eugène Dion, "Les Araméens du Moyen-Euphrate au VIIIe siècle à la lumière des inscriptions des maîtres de Suhu et Mari," in *Congress Volume, Paris 1992* (ed. J. Emerton; VTSup 61; Leiden: Brill, 1995), 53–74, here 68–69. Other arguments for an alternative tradition connecting Balaam's home to Transjordan, specifically Ammon, will also prove ill-founded in the course of this discussion.

88. See Dion, "Les Araméens du Moyen-Euphrate," 68–69 n. 106. In keeping both with Balaam's Aramean identity in the DAPT and his explicit geographic associations with the upper Euphrates in biblical texts, the cuneiform spelling favors the derivation of Balaam's name from an original form *Bēl-Amma*, '(the god) Bel is a kinsman (*ʿamm-)'. Compelling alternatives invoke the BH verbal root *blʿ* I 'to swallow' (cf. Arb. *baliʿa*) or II 'to announce' (Piel, Prov 19:28; cf. Arab.

As in the DAPT, once Num 22–24 has established Balaam's foreignness (Num 22:5; 23:7), it speaks only vaguely of Balaam's home community referring simply to Balaam's return to his "place" (Num 24:11, 25).[89] In keeping with the DAPT's seeming avoidance of national identities in referring generically to Balaam's 'people' (*'mh*, DAPT I.4; II.17), the frequent use of *'am*, 'people', in place of specific national names in Num 22–24 is striking: the reference to Jacob/Israel as "a people" in the first and second poetic oracles (Num 23:9; 23:24) and regularly within the prose narrative either as "a people" (Num 22:5, 11) or "this/the people" (Num 22:3, 6, 12, 17, 41; 24:14; cf. 23:7, 10); Balaam's reference to the Moabites in his speech to Balak as "your people" (Num 24:14); and Balaam's reference to his imminent return home: "I am going to my people" (Num 24:14).[90] The heaping of the last three of these instances of the term in a single verse is especially noteworthy: "Now, I am going to my *people*. So let me inform you what this *people* will do to your *people* in the days to come" (Num 24:14). This intensified, even exaggerated, use of *'am* in lieu of a particular people or national designation explains the unusual phrasing that elaborates the initial mention of Balaam's home in Pethor: 'the land of the sons of his people' (*'ereṣ bĕnê 'ammô* Num 22:5).[91] This generic reference to Balaam's ancestral homeland matches both the DAPT's reference to Balaam's community simply as 'his people' (*'mh*) and the elaborated usage of *'am*

---

baluǧa 'to be eloquent') or the noun form *belaʿ* 'slander' (Ps 55:10; cf. Arb. *balāǧ* 'report to the police'), in any case with the nominal affirmative *-ām* and meaning, alternatively, 'the swallower/ destroyer', 'the eloquent', or 'slanderer'. Thus, a variant form of the personal name *bilʿām* is *belaʿ*, which is associated with individuals from Benjamin (Gen 46:21; etc.) and Reuben (1 Chr 5:8), and in one case as a "king of Edom," *belaʿ ben-bĕʿôr*, Gen 36:32. Both *belaʿ* (Gen 14:2, 8) and *bilʿām* (Judg 8:3) also occur as toponyms, as does *yiblĕʿām* (Josh 17:11; etc.), the last suggesting a derivation from *ybl* + *'am* with a possible meaning 'watercourse of the kinsman/people', or perhaps from *bûl / yĕbül* + *'am*, 'harvest of the kinsman'. In either case, an alternation between *yiblĕʿām* (Judg 1:27) with *bilʿām* (1 Chr 6:55) occurs for the same place. It is possible that, early in the Balaam tradition, the name *Bēl-Amma* became reanalyzed in terms of these more familiar proper names, especially given the location of *yiblĕʿām* (Judg 1:27) / *bilʿām* (1 Chr 6:55) in Transjordanian Manasseh and *belaʿ* (Gen 14:2, 8) at the south end of the Dead Sea. For more discussion of these and other suggestions, and the related philological data, see Levine, *Numbers 21–36*, 146–47; *HALOT*, 115, 134–35, 382, 383.

89. The word *māqôm* here means 'home' or 'place' of origins, as in Gen 30:26. Favoring this meaning and militating against the word's suggested meaning in Num 24:11, 25 as 'sanctuary' or 'cult place' are both the narrative's lack of any mention of such in connection with Balaam's point of origin at the beginning of the narrative and Balaam's reference to his imminent return trip with the words, "I am going to my people" (Num 24:14).

90. The parallel between "to my people" in Num 24:14 and "his people" in DAPT I.4 is underscored by McCarter, "The Balaam Texts," 57. The variant reading "to my place" (*māqôm*) reflected in the Septuagint and Syriac likely stems from the reference to Balaam's homeland by this term in the surrounding context, specifically in Num 24:11, 25.

91. This unusual phrasing nonetheless has a partial analog (also with *he* directive) in '(to) the land of the sons of the East' (*'arṣā(h) bĕnê-qedem*, Gen 29:1), which happens to refer to the same Upper Euphrates region later related to Balaam, the difference being the intentionally vague reference to Balaam's tribal affiliation as *bĕnê 'ammô*.

throughout Num 22–24, in both playing down national identities and underscoring Balaam's foreignness among the peoples of Transjordan.[92]

---

92. In mostly exilic or later biblical texts, the phrase 'sons of my/your/the people' (*bĕnê ʿamm-/hāʿam*) refers to members of one's community, typically in a partitive sense of some, any, or certain members of one's community, especially from the viewpoint of an outsider (e.g., Lev 19:18; 20:17; Judg 14:16, 17; Ezek 3:11; 33:2, 12, 17, 30; 37:18; Dan 12:1; but cf. 'the grave(s) of sons of the people', *qeber/qibrê bĕnê hāʿam*, in the sense of "common graves," 2 Kgs 23:6; 2 Chr 35:5, 7, 12; Jer 26:23). Thus, alternatively, the precise indication in Num 22:5 might be that *a portion* of Balaam's people, the Arameans, live in the Upper Euphrates region around Pethor/Pitru, but the other texts using the expression in this way seem to originate considerably later than Num 22:5, as established in the course of this discussion.

The alternative reading of this phrase as referring to a proper place-name, "the land of the sons of Ammaw," to the extent that this place can be identified with the region of similar name mentioned in the 14th century B.C.E. statue inscription of Idrimi in Akkadian (but written differently, "land of Amaʾe" *ma-at / a-ma-e*[KI], lines 22–23), faces a few obstacles: (1) the difference between a primarily territorial designation in the inscription and a primarily people-based designation in this reading of the biblical text (cf. *bĕnê qedem* Gen 29:1); (2) changes in sociopolitical circumstances that would have developed over the intervening centuries (not so problematic with regard to specific city names, which tend to endure over time and through changes in political structure, for example, Pethor/Pitru, discussed above); and (3) the notable differences between the names Amaʾe and Ammaw (cf. also 'the land of Ammiya' ([URU]*am-mi-ia*[KI]) in 'Canaan' (*ki-in-a-nim*[KI]) in the preceding lines in the Idrimi text (lines 19–20). See Sidney Smith, *The Statue of Idri-mi* (London: British Institute of Archaeology in Ankara, 1949) 14–15.

The third possibility, suggested already in 1922 by Gray and followed by Levine, is that the final nun fell away from the original reading *bĕnê ʿammôn* (reflected in the Samaritan Pentateuch, Vulgate, and Peshitta, the text thus preserving two variant traditions of Balaam's origins (as Aramean and, alternatively, Ammonite; for Gray belonging to E and J, respectively). See G. Buchanan Gray, *A Critical and Exegetical Commentary on Numbers* (ICC 4; Edinburgh, T. & T. Clark, 1903) 312, 315, 326–27; Levine, *Numbers 21–36*, 141, 145–49. This solution suffers from some fundamental problems: first, the lack of an apparent mechanism by which this textual error would have occurred, one that would have been especially difficult for scribes to overlook given Balaam's persistent associations (even as an outsider) with Transjordan (reinforced in modern times with the discovery of the DAPT). Another problem is that this explanation leaves "the river" to refer not in its usual sense to the Euphrates (*hannāhār* = the Euphrates, Gen 31:21; etc.) but rather to the Jordan or the Zarqa/Jabbok, which never happens in BH without the setting of the Jordan or Jabbok already being established (see, e.g., *hayyardēn hazze(h)* = the Jordan, Gen 32:11; cf. *yabbōq* then *hannāḥal* = the Jabbok, Gen. 32:23–24; also Exod 23:31, where even in the context of Canaan, *hannāhār* without antecedent clearly refers to the Euphrates).

More likely, the reading of the Samaritan Pentateuch, Peshitta, and the Vulgate reflects the addition of a final nun to read "Ammon" (*ʿammôn; cf. *ʿammô* 'his people' in the MT and reflected in the LXX), resulting from confusion prompted by several converging factors: the unusual, but genuine, phrasing *ʾereṣ bĕnê ʿammô* (discussed above); the setting of Num 22–24 in Transjordan; Deuteronomy's naming of the Ammonites along with the Moabites in connection with Balaam (Deut 23:5, followed by Neh 13:2; discussed below); and, most decisively, the addition of the donkey story in Num 22:22–35 either as part of the Priestly editing of Num 22–24 or sometime following in its wake (see below).

The insertion of the donkey story into the Num 22 narrative, by specifying this mode of travel for Balaam and for Balak's messengers, further underscored the long period of time needed for two embassies from Moab to Pitru and back (estimated to be as much as 80 days round trip

Balaam's geographic origins in the Upper Euphrates, once identified, are not as important as is the fact that he is from another place, a proverbial foreigner who crosses boundaries and holds no direct stake in the national claims of Israel, Moab, or any other kingdoms of Iron Age Transjordan. Rather, Balaam comes from somewhere else, as intimated in the DAPT and as made explicit in the biblical Balaam Pericope (Num 22–24). Balaam's character as a politically and geographically liminal figure is in keeping with his role as an intermediary between the divine and human realms, a role for which Balak seeks him out.

Numbers 22–24 gives explicit attention to Balak's request and to Balaam's qualifications both in the prose narrative and in the poetic oracles, which represent a distinct, cohesive compositional horizon in their own right and one likely earlier than that of the prose.[93] As discussed, the DAPT designate Balaam a 'seer of the gods' (*ḥzh . ʾlhn* DAPT I.1) and describes how he 'saw a vision' (*wyḥz . mḥzh*, I.1) and how the gods communicated a verbal message to Balaam ('according to

---

by camel, not donkey, each time; see H. O. Thompson, "Amaw," *ABD* 1:183). In sum, the closer location necessitated by the added donkey story, along with the general setting in Transjordan and mention of the Ammonites in Deut 23:5 (and Neh 13:2), influenced the alteration of *běnê ʿammô* to *běnê ʿammôn* in Num 22:5.

A further change necessitated by this one and, most likely, accompanying it is where the Syriac and Vulgate in Num 22:5 reflect a rereading of *ptwrh* (as found in the MT), the place-name (with -*h* directive) given as Balaam's home-town following his name (thus "[Balak] sent messengers to Balaam son of Beor at/to Pethor [*pětôrâ*]" in the Masoretic pointing of MT) to mean instead "the interpreter," as in Post-Biblical Hebrew *pātôrāʾ* (see M. Jastrow, *A Dictionary of the Targumim, the Talmud Babli and Yerushalmi, and the Midrashic Literature* [repr., New York: Judaica, 1992] 1250b; cf. what in BH would be **happôtēr*), hence Syriac *pšwr* in the Peshiṭta of Num 22:5 (also reflected in the Vulgate), even though an Aramaic title for Balaam as "interpreter" would be out of step with the Hebrew form of his patronymic (*bn bʿwr* and not *br bʿwr* as attested in the DAPT I.1, 4, 5). The Samaritan Pentateuch, in turn, "corrects" the mention in Deut 23:5 of Balaam as being "from Pethor" (*mptr, mippětôr*, MT) to read *ptrh*.

To summarize, lexical, text-critical, literary-critical, and basic content considerations indicate that the variant reading 'Ammon' (*ʿmwn*) for the earlier reading 'his people' (*ʿmw*) in Num 22:5 is a development generated mainly by scribal confusion and then perpetuated among the Syriac, Vulgate, and Samaritan versions.

93. See Levine, *Numbers 21–36*, 135–275. As Levine explains, in comparison with the poetry, the prose reflects a more fully "synthesized" view of the divine in favor of YHWH as Israel's god (see further discussion on pp. 175–77). Compare the argument for the priority of the prose narrative and the poetry's dependence on the prose by Milgrom, *Numbers*, 467–68. The various details of the narrative progression paralleled in both the prose and poetry cited by Milgrom just as readily indicate the priority of the poems, which (contra Milgrom) would have been comprehensible within an existing Israelite Balaam tradition and need not assume the exact prose instantiation we now have in the present text. The prose narrative is crafted not only to provide a literary context for the oracles (which may have known an earlier narrative context) but also an adjusted theological context for interpreting the oracles, most importantly in simplifying their view of the divine to give even greater prominence to YHWH. There is no comparable rationale supporting the case for the poetry's composition to complement an already existing prose narrative.

an oracle of El', *km*[*š*]' *'ēl*, DAPT I.2) which he reported to other human beings (DAPT I.1–2, 5–16). With similar emphasis on both visual and verbal aspects of divine communication, the third and fourth poetic oracles in Num 22–24 include an introduction as

> the utterance (*nĕ'um*) of Balaam son of Beor,
> the utterance of the man of opened eye (*ne'um haggeber šĕtum hā'āyin*),
> the utterance of the one who hears the words of El (*'imrê-'ēl*),[94]
> who sees (*ḥzw/y*) the vision (*maḥăzē(h)*) of Shadday,
> falling (asleep; *nōpēl*), but with eyes uncovered (*ûgĕlûy 'ēnāyim*).[95]
>
> (Num 24:3b–4, 15b–16)

In keeping with Balaam's ability to receive divine visions, whether asleep or awake (Num 24:4b, 16b), the surrounding prose narrative situating all four oracles portrays Balaam in a fully conscious state while receiving the relevant divine communications and earlier portrays divine visitations to Balaam during his nighttime repose (Num 22:7–21).[96]

The latter includes night-vision reports with striking verbal parallels to the DAPT's introductory narrative:

1. *wy'tw 'lhn 'lwh blylh . . .*
   wy'mrw lbl'm br b'r
   'Gods came to him in the night . . .
   and they said to Balaam son of Beor . . .'
   (DAPT I.1, 2)

1. *wyb' 'lhym 'l bl'm wy'mr,* '
   God came to Balaam and said . . .'
   (Num 22:9)
   wyb' 'lhym 'l bl'm lylh wy'mr lw,
   'God came to Balaam at night and said to him . . .''
   (Num 22:20)

2. *wyqm bl'm mn mḥr*
   'And Balaam rose in the morning . . .'
   (DAPT 1.3).

2. *wyqm bl'm bbqr,*
   'And Balaam rose in the morning . . .'
   (Num 22:13, 21)[96]

---

94. Compare *m*[*š*]' *'ēl*, 'a pronouncement of El', (DAPT I.2). The Old Greek and the Samaritan Pentateuch do not include the clause *nĕ'um šōmē(a)' 'imrê-'ēl* in Num 24:3b–4. Its occurrence in Num 24:16 is followed by *wĕyōdē(a)' da'at 'elyôn*, 'and (who) knows the knowledge of the Elyon'.

95. For this translation, see Levine, *Numbers 21–36*, 188–89, 194. As Levine explains, the verb *npl* (with "sleep" as the subject) occurs at the onset of nocturnal dream visions in Gen 15:12 and Job 33:15.

96. In each instance of the latter, the description of the nocturnal divine communication is followed by the statement that Balaam 'got up [*qwm*] in the morning' (*wayyāqom bil'ām babbōqer*, Num 22:13, 21), perhaps with some relevance for *npl* 'fall' in Num 24:4b, 16b.

97. As discussed in McCarter, "The Balaam Texts," 57. Another extensive verbal parallel is DAPT I.5 // Ps 46:9; 66:5. See Burnett, *A Reassessment of Biblical Elohim*, 37, and, for more discussion, Burnett, "Come and See What God Has Done," 231–36. For a summary of numerous parallels of language and vocabulary between the DAPT and biblical texts, see Puech, "Bala'am and Deir 'Alla," 41–43.

Both the prose and poetry of Num 22–24 show close affinities of diction and religious viewpoint with the DAPT, reflecting a familiarity with the Balaam tradition as represented in the DAPT.[98] In each case, Balaam's primary prophetic role involves speaking verbal messages based on visionary and verbal divine communications, the same basic *modus operandi* described for prophetic figures in service to the king in the Zakkur Stele Inscription (see above).

While kings and kingdoms are noticeably deemphasized in the DAPT (*mlk* DAPT II. 13, 15, 18; see above), the entire narrative of Num 22–24 is driven by the insistence of a king, Balak of Moab, who is present throughout most of the Balaam Pericope. Balak sends national emissaries ('messenger' *malʾākîm*, Num 22:5 = 'the elders of Moab', *ziqnê môʾāb*, v. 7 = 'the officials of Moab', *śārê môʾāb*, v. 14 = 'the officials of Balak', *śārê bālāq*, v. 13) and even higher-level officials (*śārîm rabbîm wĕnikbādîm mēʾēlle(h)*, Num 22:15 = 'the servants of Balak', *ʿabdê bālāq*, v. 18 = 'the officials of Moab', *śārê môʾāb*, v. 21 = 'the officials of Balak', *śārê bālāq*, v. 35), and hires Balaam to curse Israel as Moab's enemy (Num 22:6–7, etc.).[99] Balaam's disclaimer that he can only speak what Yнwн/Elohim permits (Num 22:18, 38; 23:12, 26; 24:12–13) may not be a negotiating tactic, but neither is it a refusal of payment, as implied by Balak's angry words of dismissal to Balaam near the end of the story (Num 24:11).[100] Notwithstanding his disclaimer of divine constraint on his activities (presumably a given for any genuine prophet), once Balaam agrees to answer Balak's summons, he enters into the employ of a king. Even within an ironic literary narrative, the Balaam Pericope portrays prophecy in the service of a king within the context of an international dispute.[101]

Key to the story's denouement is that Balaam acts against expectations, both those of Balak and the audience. In keeping with the DAPT's portrayal of Balaam, the working assumption in Num 22–24 (which, as noted, reflects an intimate familiarity with the same tradition) is that Balaam is a prophet of doom, a figure associated primarily with words of disaster. As the Zakkur Stele Inscription illustrates (A.12–17), prophecy concerning royal fortunes, as a matter of course, is stated in terms of success or failure,[102] and thus in its essence lies close at hand

---

98. Making this point in connection with the prose portions of Num 22–24, McCarter, "The Balaam Texts," 57.

99. The traditional rendering of *qsmym* in Num 22:7 as '*fees* for divination' remains debatable (see Levine, *Numbers 21–36*, 150–51; Robker, "The Balaam Narrative," 339–40 and nn. 18–19), but the expectation of substantial payment for Balaam's services is clearly at work in the narrative (Num 22:18; 24:11).

100. Compare E. Noort, "Balaam the Villain: The History of Reception of the Balaam Narrative in the Pentateuch and the Former Prophets," in *The Prestige of the Pagan Prophet Balaam in Judaism, Early Christianity and Islam* (ed. G. H. van Kooten and J. van Ruiten; Themes in Biblical Narrative: Jewish and Christian Traditions 11; Leiden: Brill, 2008) 3–23, here 12.

101. For discussion of the relationship between prophets and kings in Mari and Neo-Assyrian texts, see Nissinen, "The Socioreligious Role of the Neo-Assyrian Prophets," 102–7.

102. See Seow, "West Semitic Sources," 204, 206; COS 2.35:155. This general point also applies to more abundantly attested prophecy among Mari texts and Neo-Assyrian sources, both representing royal archives. See Huffmon, "A Company of Prophets," 55–56, 60–61.

to ideas of blessing or curse. The rhetoric of Balak's summons notwithstanding ("whomever you bless is blessed, and whomever you curse is cursed," Num 22:6), it is telling for Balaam's reputation as a prophet of doom that he is hired not to bless Moab but rather to curse its enemy.

At Balak's behest, Balaam proceeds to three different locations along the heights overlooking the Israelite encampment. At each place, Balak constructs altars and offers *ʿōlâ* ('whole burnt offering') sacrifices for the purpose of invoking a divine response favorable to the pronouncement of the desired curse.[103] Ritual performance thus precedes Balaam's solicitation of divine communications delivered verbally in the form of poetic oracles Balaam pronounces at each location (the final instance involving two poems, appearing as the third and fourth in the series poetic oracles; Num 23:7b–10; 18b–24; 24:3b–9; 15b–19).[104] Throughout Num 22–24, two BH terms for curse are used interchangeably (*ʾrr*, Num 22:6, 12; 23:7; *qbb* 22:11, 17; 23:8, 11, 13, 25, 27; 24:10).[105] This ritual inducement of divine presence leading to prophetic speech also involves Balaam's instruction to Balak to

---

103. As Levine explains, curses and magic more generally in the ancient Near East were understood to be fully under the control of the gods, hence the rationale for a ritual invocation of the deity's favorable presence (the purpose of the *ʿōlâ*; see Lev 1) and for a prophetic spokesman of Balaam's stature to ensure the effectiveness of the curse desired by Balak. The first set of sacrifices is offered by Balak and Balaam together (Num 23:1–2, 4), in keeping with the fact that Balaam is in Balak's employ. See Levine, *Numbers 21–36*, 161–63. For a thorough exposition of the understanding of divine control over curse in the broader ancient Near East, see A. M. Kitz, *Cursed Are You! The Phenomenology of Cursing in Cuneiform and Hebrew* Texts (Winona Lake, IN: Eisenbrauns, 2014) 9–196, and specifically for Balaam in Num 22–24 as a case in point, pp. 161–62.

Texts from Mari and Neo-Assyrian sources strongly associate prophecy with the institution, if not the cult, of the temple (Stökl, *Prophecy in the Ancient Near East*, 51–62, 143–46, 209–11) and regularly mention prophecy in connection with extispicy and other modes of technical divination, sometimes portraying the work of prophets in coordination with the activities of the *bāru* or other specialists. See Huffmon, "A Company of Prophets," 49–53; Nissinen, "The Socio-Religious Role of the Neo-Assyrian Prophets," 107–11. In connection with ritual performed by Balaam in Num 22–24, Kitz compares Balaam to cultic functionaries in Mesopotamian texts (e.g., the 'exorcist', Akk. *āšipu* or 'diviner', *bārû*) who might serve as professional curse practitioners; see Kitz, *Cursed Are You!* 372–73 n. 6, 397–99. If the Mesopotamian settings are relevant, one may infer from Kitz's comparisons that Balaam's role as a prophet sets him apart from other cultic specialists who might be hired to invoke a formal curse. Whereas the usual procedure involves pronouncing a curse, which the relevant divine powers may or may not enforce (see Kitz, *Cursed Are You!* 9–196), Balaam's role as prophet is to speak *for* the divine, and his capacity as one 'seeing' (*ḥzw/y*) the divine realm (Num 24:4, 16) would inform him that Yhwh is the deity with jurisdiction over this territorial dispute between Moab and Israel (see discussion below).

104. The fourth oracle in Num 24:14–19 is followed by a series of secondarily appended brief oracles in vv. 20–24. See Levine, *Numbers 21–36*, 204, 237–38. Against the suggestion that Num 24:14–19 might also be a secondary addition, Levine points out its connections of theme and diction to the preceding three oracles. See Levine, *Numbers 21–36*, 204, 211–12; cf. Robker, "The Balaam Narrative," 341–42.

105. Also paralleling each of the other two terms in the first poetic oracle is *zʿm* 'denounce', (Num 23:7b–8a), and Num 23:23 adds the nouns *naḥaš* 'enchantment', and *qesem* 'divination', in parallel to one another.

'stand' (*hityaṣēb*) with his burnt offerings while Balaam walks away from the area of the altar so that the deity might 'meet' (Niphal of *qrw/y*) Balaam and impart a verbal message to him (Num 23:3, 15).[106]

As a result, in the first two instances, YHWH "put a word in his mouth" and told Balaam, "this is what you shall say" (Num 23:5, 16). In the third instance, though, Balaam declines to go as at other times, 'to invoke omens' (*liqra't nĕḥāšîm*, Num 24:1), and the third oracle is attributed more ambiguously to 'the spirit of God/a god' (*rû(a)ḥ 'ĕlōhîm*, Num 24:3). Commentators tend to lay this change of procedure to Balaam's resignation to YHWH's will to bless Israel; thus, seeing no need to consult YHWH any further, Balaam presumably proceeds on his own initiative and by his own means with the intent to speak further messages favoring Israel.[107]

This generous assumption regarding Balaam's motives notwithstanding, Balaam's decision not to seek YHWH's guidance in this third attempt to fulfill Balak's request stands out against YHWH's command to Balaam from the start, "Do only what I tell you to do" (Num 22:20) and Balaam's determination not to go against the 'command of YHWH' (*pî yhwh*, Num 22:18). Thus, Num 24:1–2 might also be understood to indicate that Balaam avoids YHWH's "command" to pronounce a certain oracle (no doubt, one favoring Israel) in this third instance, so as to circumvent YHWH's direction of his speech ("YHWH's command (*pe(h)*)," Num 22:18; "whatever YHWH puts into my mouth," 23:12; "whatever YHWH says," 23:26; 24:13; cf. "the word that *'ĕlōhîm* puts into my mouth," 22:38) and thereby give one last chance for possibly pronouncing the curse Balak has brought him there to declare.

This third instance thus lends itself to both positive and negative interpretations regarding Balaam's intentions and their bearing on Israel. When all is said and done, the outcome of even more explicitly favorable predictions for Israel in the third and fourth oracles (Num 24:3–9, 15–19) inclines readers and commentators to a favorable view of Balaam.[108] Yet the ambiguous indications regarding Balaam's motives in Num 24:1–2 will have implications for our discussion of Balaam's appearance in Deut 23:5–6 (below). For now, it suffices to note that in this literary depiction of prophecy in royal service in Num 23–24, mantic activity is coordinated with ritual practice in a way that is absent in the setting at Balaam's home earlier in the narrative (Num 22) and in the DAPT's parallel depiction of

---

106. For the possible ritual implications of both of these verbs, see Levine, *Numbers 21–36*, 166.

107. Thus Levine, *Numbers 21–36*, 190–91; Milgrom, *Numbers*, 201. This interpretation follows from the understanding that Num 22 portrays Balaam as a prophet of YHWH, especially as suggested by the MT of Num 22:18, which has Balaam refer to 'my god, YHWH' (*yhwh 'ĕlōhāy*), but compare the reading reflected in the Old Greek tradition, which instead indicates 'YHWH Elohim' (*yhwh (h)'lhym*), 'YHWH, the god', i.e., 'the god YHWH'. See further discussion on p. 177.

108. See, e.g., the discussion of Noort, "Balaam the Villain," 3, 10–11.

nocturnal divine communications to Balaam (DAPT I.1–5).[109] The presentation in Num 22–24 provides one indication that, in the Iron Age Levant, the same prophet who receives divine communications unsolicited or informally might nonetheless also be expected to employ ritual invocations of divine presence when seeking divine communication at the behest of a king.

The appropriate procedure requested by Balak also involved a visual element, requiring Balaam to look at the Israelites as the intended object of curse. Balak chooses all three locations for their line of sight to the Israelite camp, with different vantage points potentially affecting the prophet's efforts or the deity's involvement (Num 22:41; 23:13, 27). The visual dimensions of curse/blessing and prophecy are another factor showing the two activities to be potentially interrelated (especially, *ḥzw/y*).[110] The prophet's special abilities of "seeing" (as elaborated in Num 24:3–4, 15–16) relate to both elements of the intended curse, both the specific target (here, Israel) and the divinely ordained outcome.

Before turning to the oracles and to the narrative's progression around them, the matter of the specific deity or deities consulted by Balaam bears special consideration. The poetic oracles stand out from the surrounding prose framework by their references to Yнwн, El, Elyon, and Shadday: *yhwh* (Num 23:8, 21; 24:6), *'ēl* (Num 23:8, 19, 22, 23; 24:4, 8, 16, 23), *šadday* (Num 24:4, 16), and *'elyôn* (Num 24:16). The repeated use of these terms for the divine admits to their construal as synonymous titles in reference to Israel's God, especially in instances of poetic parallelism: *'ēl // yhwh*, Num 23:8, 21–22; *'ēl // šadday*, Num 24:4; *'ēl // 'elyôn // šadday*, Num 24:16. Yet, as Levine points out, the pairing of *yhwh* and *'ēl* in parallelism is surprisingly unusual in Biblical Hebrew, and this repeated variety of

---

109. Perhaps as a function of genre, explicit reference to ritual in connection with prophecy is also lacking from the royal setting of the Zakkur Stele Inscription and, as Levine points out, in biblical prophetic literature; see Levine, *Genesis 21–36*, 162. See also the narrative depiction of prophecy in a royal context in 1 Kgs 22, and compare the implied ritual setting of the prophetic call scene in Isaiah 6.

110. This, in spite of the fact that diviners and other ritual specialists appear as professional cursers in Mesopotamian texts, hence the form of Balaam's "blessings/curses" as predictions rather than invocations as found in other texts (see Kitz, *Cursed Are You!* 372–73 n. 6, 397–99). Terms for 'seer' in BH include both *ḥōze(h)* (2 Sam 24:11; 2 Kgs 17:13; Isa 29:10; 30:10; Amos 7:12; Mic 3:7; etc.; cf. *ḥzyn*, Zakkur Inscription, *KAI* 202 A l.12) and *rō'e(h)* 1 Sam 9:9, 11; Isa 30:10; etc.). When confronted by the "little boys" jeering him on the road from Jericho to Bethel, the prophet Elisha 'looks at' (*r'w/y*) them and 'curses' (*qll*) them in the name of Yнwн, causing two female bears to emerge from the woods and kill 42 of them (2 Kgs 2:24). Forty-two is also the total number of *'ôlâ* offerings Balak offers in his efforts to secure a curse against Israel in Num 22–24 (seven altars with two animals each, at three locations). In these narratives and in the broader ancient Near East, 42 serves as a symbolic number demonstrating divine enforcement of blessing or curse. For more discussion, see J. S. Burnett, "'Going Down' to Bethel: Elijah and Elisha in the Theological Geography of the Deuteronomistic History," *JBL* 129 (2010) 281–97, here 295–96. See Kitz (*Cursed Are You!* 398) for other suggested means of forming a connection between the cursing specialist and intended victim.

divine names reflects a system of separate deities not yet "fully synthesized" as the theological framework from which the texts first emerged, a framework essentially corresponding with the depiction of El's pantheon of *'lhn* // *šdyn* in the DAPT, though with the introduction of YHWH into the pantheon of the biblical poetic oracles.[111]

By comparison, the prose narrative of Num 22–24 represents a further consolidation of this pantheon in favor of YHWH as Israel's god, with *yhwh* and *(hā) 'ĕlōhîm* occurring as the only two terms for the divine. The literal parallels to the DAPT involving (sg.) *'ĕlōhîm* (Num 22:9, 20) // (pl.) *'lhn* (DAPT I.1, 2) show that a pantheon of "the gods" still lies close beneath the surface of the prose narrative of Num 22–24. Yet, here, *yhwh* and *(hā)'ĕlōhîm* function interchangeably (see, e.g., Num 23:3–5, 26–27; 24:1–2), with *yhwh* being the preferred and more frequent divine term.[112] The poetic oracles explicitly identify YHWH as Israel's god (Num 23:21b) and connect Balaam directly to El, Shadday, and Elyon but not to YHWH (Num 24:3b–4, 15b–16, quoted above). By contrast, the prose has the non-Israelite Balaam refer not only to Elohim (Num 22:38) but primarily to YHWH (Num 22:8, 13, 18, 19; 23:3, 12; 24:13) in connection with his prophetic activities.[113]

Balaam's deference to YHWH in the prose narrative is also in keeping with the political ramifications of a larger pantheon, as reflected in the literary background

---

111. See Levine, *Number 21–36*, 218–24. Compare the designation of the pantheon as 'the council of El' (*'ădat-'ēl*) in Ps 82:1 and the use of the epithet Elyon for the head of the gods in Deut 32:8–9. For Levine, Num 23:8 is the only instance in BH of a true parallelism between YHWH and El (cf. Ps 10:12), and Num 23:21b–22 is to be excluded because it involves an intervening refrain. See Levine, *Number 21–36*, 184–85, 218, 222–23.

112. *Yhwh*: Num 22:8, 18, 19; 23:3, 5, 12, 16, 17; 24:1, 11, 13 [2x]; *(hā)'ĕlōhîm*: Num 22:9, 10, 12, 20, 38; 23:4, 27; 24:2.

113. Where the MT has Balaam refer to 'my god, YHWH' (*yhwh 'ĕlōhāy*, Num 22:18 MT), the Old Greek tradition instead indicates the reading 'YHWH Elohim' (*yhwh (h)'lhym*), either as the combination of both divine terms otherwise used separately within the prose or with the meaning 'the god YHWH', in keeping with the context portrayed of a conversation between non-Israelites. See the proposed analogies for *yhwh (h)'lhym* in this sense from Mesopotamian cuneiform and Palmyrene Aramaic texts suggested by Speiser and Hillers, respectively: E. A. Speiser, *Genesis: Introduction, Translation, and Notes* (AB 1; Garden City, NY: Doubleday, 1964), 15–16; D. R. Hillers, "Palmyrene Aramaic Inscriptions and the Bible," *ZAH* 11 (1998) 32–49, here 32–36. In either case, the sequence *yhwh (hā)'ĕlōhîm* occurs only selectively and exceptionally in BH, appearing twenty times in Gen 2:4b–3:24, twelve times in Chronicles, and only nine times elsewhere (Exod 9:30; 1 Sam 6:20; Ezra 9:7; Neh 8:6; etc.; see S. Japhet, *The Ideology of the Book of Chronicles and Its Place in Biblical Thought* [trans. A. Barber; Winona Lake, IN: Eisenbrauns, 2009] 37–41), thus making it the *lectio difficilior* and the preferred reading in this instance. Accordingly, the MT reading might have been influenced by locutions more familiar in various contexts throughout BH, namely, *yhwh 'ĕlōhā(y)w* nearby in the poetry of Num 23:21 (also Exod 32:11; Lev 4:11; Deut 17:19; etc.) and the corresponding form for first-person speech *yhwh 'ĕlōhāy* (Deut 4:5; 18:16; etc.). The variant reading, simply *yhwh*, reflected in the Old Latin tradition, one Greek miniscule, and the Ethiopic would thus represent a simplification of the somewhat unusual *yhwh 'ĕlōhā(y)w* in line with Balaam's previous words to the first group of messengers (Num 22:8, 13). See the *BHS* critical apparatus.

of the prose and its language for the divine (sg.*'ĕlōhîm*, Num 22:9, 20 // pl. *'lhn*, DAPT I.1, 2) and more expressly indicated in the poetic oracles. [114] The oracles, in describing Balaam as a spokesman for El, Shadday, and Elyon (Num 24:3b–4, 15b–16), tout the prophet's rapport with the highest level of the pantheon on an international scale. The exclusion of YHWH in this regard indicates that the poetic parallel of *'ēl* // *yhwh* (Num 23:8) refers to two different deities, YHWH as "[Israel's] god" (*yhwh 'ĕlōhā(y)w*, Num 23:21) and El as the head of the pantheon who ultimately sanctions YHWH's authority in the land and who acts for Israel on a broader international stage: "El, who brings him out of Egypt, is like the horns of a wild ox for him" (Num 23:22; 24:8).

The prose narrative reflects a conceptual collapsing of the pantheon headed by El simply into singular *(hā)'ĕlōhîm*, a term that does not occur in the poetry but, as observed, parallels plural *'lhn*, 'the gods', in the DAPT (*'ĕlōhîm*, Num 22:9, 20 // *'lhn*, DAPT I.1, 2; see above). Thus, the notion of an international pantheon of "the gods" still lies close beneath the surface of the use of *(hā)'ĕlōhîm*'s as a singular in the prose of Num 22–24. The interchange between *yhwh* and *'ĕlōhîm* in the prose accordingly builds on the recognition of a broader pantheon (*(hā)'ĕlōhîm* as "the gods") sanctioning YHWH's activity amid the international tensions between Israel and Moab, the same basic conceptual framework reflected in the poetic oracles: "Balak . . . the king of Moab [says]: 'Come, curse Jacob for me; come, denounce Israel.' How can I curse whom *El* has not cursed, how can I denounce whom YHWH has not denounced?" (Num 23:7–8). The poetic oracles of Num 23–24 thus suggest that YHWH, as Israel's god, is the appropriate deity for Balaam to address, along with El as the head of the pantheon.

The geopolitical circumstance portrayed in the prose narrative is Israelite territorial control bordering Moab. As Balak initially relates to Balaam, "A people has come out of Egypt; they have spread over the face of the land, and they have settled next to me" (Num 22:5). Balaam's invocation of YHWH, as opposed to the Moabite god Chemosh, in this context is in keeping with the implications of divine jurisdiction borne out in the broader narrative context of Num 22–24. In Num 21, the Israelites have defeated King Sihon and the Amorites and have taken possession of their former territory stretching "from the Arnon to the Jabbok," which in turn had formerly belonged to the Moabites (Num 21:21–31). Regardless of Moab's prior claims, dominion over this territory, now having been won in battle over an intervening third party (the Amorites of Heshbon), rightfully belongs (from the perspective of the larger narrative) to Israel and its god, a political fact on the ground within the purview of this internationally famous seer. [115]

---

114. By contrast, most interpreters assume that in the narrative Balaam simply shares an Israelite viewpoint in which YHWH is recognized as supreme over the whole earth. See Milgrom, *Numbers*, 469–70; Levine, *Numbers 21–36*, 217–18; Noort, "Balaam the Villain," 3.

115. Here, the biblical text of Numbers, even though portraying premonarchic times, aligns with the "polarizing" national theology observed in 9th-century royal inscriptions, over

This explanation of how west-central Transjordan came to be Israel's rightful territory that we find in Num 21 is consistent with related assumptions regarding Israel's and YHWH's territory expressed within Num 22–24. As scholars have long recognized, the note in Num 22:2, that Balak "saw all that Israel had done to the Amorites" (Num 22:2), was likely not part of the original literary unit of Num 22–24 but rather emerged as a secondary editorial device added to connect it with the episode of Israel's defeat of Sihon and the Amorites at Heshbon in Num 21:21–32, as part of an extended, non-Priestly narrative sequence.[116] Even so, the earlier form of the Balaam Pericope now found in Num 22–24 includes Balak's initial message to Balaam in Num 22:5, including Balak's stated aim to defeat the Israelites in battle and "drive them from the land" (Num 22:5–6). In other words, similar concerns over conflicting territories, nations, and their deities implied by the broader literary context into which Num 22–24 came to be placed were integral to this literary unit from its earliest form.

Also integral to this early form of the Balaam Pericope were similar assumptions regarding national boundaries. The locations in Num 22–24 of both of the promontories from which Balaam views the Israelites in his efforts to curse them (especially, "the top of Pisgah," 23:14 and "the top of Peor," 23:28) and the Israelites' settlement in the "wasteland" and "wilderness" below (Num 23:28; 24:1) lie within territory of west-central Transjordan north of the Arnon (modern Wadi Mujib),[117] territory that biblical narrative traditions are virtually unanimous in regarding as rightfully belonging to Israel and its God.[118] Furthermore, Num 22:36 explicitly describes the Arnon as Moab's northern border, and, as mentioned, Balak complains about Israel's settlement "next to" him (Num 22:5). These details integral to the internal literary unity of Num 22–24 together indicate that the Israelites on Moab's boundary are settled to its north—that is, north of the Arnon—and that this territory is recognized as Israelite territory, including the specific setting of Balaam's attempted cursing of Israel. The god exercising jurisdiction over that land would thus be YHWH.[119]

---

against the harmonizing international theology reflected in the DAPT. See pp. 136–42 (I. Rival Kingdoms and Their Gods: Iron Age II in West-Central Transjordan).

116. See Levine, "Numbers 21–36," 143; Robker, "The Balaam Narrative," 335–38, 344, 363. For the purposes of this discussion, I use the term Priestly to refer both to a Pentateuchal documentary source P and to any subsequent redactional contributions following its influence and characterized by similar vocabulary and concerns.

117. Although the first location, Bamot-Baal (Num 22:41), has not been securely identified, Pisgah is identified with Râs es-Siyaghah just north of Jebel en-Nebâ (Mt. Nebo; cf. Num 21:20; Deut 3:17; etc.), and in any case, the heights described are widely recognized as lying along the Abarim hills overlooking the northeast Dead Sea and Jordan Rift Valley. See F. Ninow, "Pisgah," EDB, 1060; R. W. Younker, "Peor," EDB, 1028.

118. For the ideal of the Arnon as Israel's southern boundary in Transjordan, see Num 21:13, 24; Deut 2:36–37; 3:8–17; 4:47–49; Josh 12:1; 13:9, 16; Judg 11:18–26; 2 Kgs 10:32–33; 1 Chr 5:3–8; cf. Isa 16:2b; Jer 48:18–20. See also MacDonald, "East of the Jordan," 101–55, 171–74.

119. Compare Mesha's statement that in former times the Moabite god Chemosh "was angry with his land" (Mesha Inscription, line 5), resulting in Israel's control of that land, the same

Balak's words to Balaam (Num 23:17, 24:11) and his participation with Balaam in ritual directed to Yʜwʜ (Num 23:3, 6, 15) signal even the Moabite king's acknowledgment that cursing Israel would require the assent of Yʜwʜ as the deity exerting control over the territory it inhabits. Thus Balaam, a foreign prophet with no stake in this regional conflict but nonetheless accountable to the higher divine powers overseeing it, issues his repeated disclaimer that he can only speak what Yʜwʜ/Elohim allows him to say (Num 22:18, 38; 23:12, 26; 24:13; see also Num 23:7–8, 18b–23).

A closer look at the poetic oracles and accompanying narrative shows these concerns to be stated in terms of clashing kingdoms, the perennial status quo for Iron II west-central Transjordan, as known from textual and archaeological sources (see p. 136–42 above). Both the prose narrative and the first two poetic oracles progress with Balaam's pronouncement not of the anticipated curses but rather of blessings for Israel and predictions of its assured success and flourishing (see Num 23:7b–10, 18b–24).[120] Balaam's third and fourth poetic oracles (Num 24:3–9, 15–19) focus on predictions of the emergence and expansion of an Israelite monarchy (Num 24:7, 17; cf. Gen 49:10) at the expense of its surrounding neighbors, most notably its exaltation over "Agag" (Num 24:7; cf. v. 20; 1 Sam 15:8), incursions against "the borderlands of Moab" (Num 24:17), and the taking of Edom as a "possession" (Num 24:18). These details resonate with biblical traditions of the early monarchy, whose full historicity lies beyond our reach due to a scarcity of contemporary sources.[121] But the general depiction of the oracles is consistent with Israel's longstanding dominance in Transjordan leading up to the mid-9th

broader territory in view in Num 22–24. See pp. 136–42 (I. Rival Kingdoms and Their Gods: Iron Age II in West-Central Transjordan).

120. As Kitz observes, Balaam's pronouncements are, strictly speaking, neither curses nor blessings, in the form typically found in biblical and cuneiform texts but rather predictions of Israel's prosperity and, as a consequence, Moab's misfortune; see Kitz, *Cursed Are You!* 397–98.

121. But note the lack of any reference to Saul, David, or language directly linking Balaam's oracles to the Samuel account of the early monarchy, and the separation of Agag (Num 24:7) from Amalek (Num 24:30) between the third oracle and later additions to the fourth oracle (cf. Robker's statement that "Agag, the king of the Amalekites" appears "in the Balaam story," "The Balaam Narrative," 356). Compare Robker's assumption that the third Balaam oracle (Num 24:3–9, particularly "Agag" in v. 7) refers specifically to the "Saul" tradition and that the fourth oracle shifts focus to David and is dependent on (or is otherwise brought into literary connection with) the Samuel account as part of "an early incarnation of the Enneateuch" (Robker, "The Balaam Narrative," 356–58, 360, 361–63; cf. Levine, *Numbers 21–36*, 188, 197, 211). Since the Israelite monarchy (and, presumably, Agag) had a historical existence independent of the texts of Samuel and since the traditions known to the biblical writers were not confined to those we now find in the Hebrew Bible, the assumption that these references have a direct literary relationship with those texts is ill-founded. Even so, Robker's contention of a northern Israelite origin for the Num 22–24 Balaam narrative (Robker, "The Balaam Narrative," 363–64) is best borne out by all four oracles' preference for the national designation "Jacob" (Num 23:7b, 10a, 21a, 23; 24:5, 17a, 19; cf. 18b; Levine, *Numbers 21–36*, 211) and by the text's many connections with the DAPT as discussed here, including the relevance of Dayr ʿAlla and broader west-central Transjordan to the history of the northern Israelite kingdom during the 9th century and earlier (see, for example,

century B.C.E., as substantiated by the Mesha Inscription (see above) and by the prominence accorded to Israel in the Assyrian records of Shalmaneser III ca. 853 B.C.E.[122] These political circumstances favor an understanding of Balaam's blessings of Israel in the Num 23–24 oracles as *ex eventu* predictions formulated some time prior to Israelite losses of Transjordanian territory due to Hazael's conquests (beginning ca. 840 B.C.E.; see 2 Kgs 10:32–33) and Moabite northern expansion under Mesha ca. 850 B.C.E. or perhaps after Israel's recovery and consolidation of territorial control in Transjordan under Joash (802–787 B.C.E.) and Jeroboam II (786–746 B.C.E.), as discussed above.

To summarize, Num 22–24 provides literary reflection on the disputed nature of west-central Transjordan during Iron Age II. Both its impressive correspondences of theme and wording to the DAPT and the political circumstances celebrated in the third and fourth poetic oracles (Num 24:3–9, 15–19) indicate a time of composition prior to the northern Israelite kingdom's loss of its Transjordanian territories in the Assyrian conquests beginning in 734 B.C.E. Although reflecting historical circumstances roughly contemporary with the DAPT (ca. 800 B.C.E.), Num 22–24 advances a very different perspective and a different application of the same Balaam tradition. Whereas the DAPT avoids reference to specific national identities and portrays Balaam as a prophet of doom potentially for all of humankind, Num 22–24 culminates in oracles predicting Israel's military and political dominance over its Transjordanian neighbors. Although Balaam's renown as the quintessential prophet of doom first sets the narrative in motion, his repeated pronouncement of triumphalist blessings favoring Israel, or for that matter any kingdom, would have come as a surprise not only to Balak but likely to the ancient audience as well.

As Levine has emphasized, Balaam's disclaimer that he can say only what YHWH permits him to say (Num 22:18, 38; 23:12, 26; 24:12–13) is not so much a matter of Balaam's obedient choice as it is an acknowledgment of divine constraint upon his words.[123] The overall positive portrayal of Balaam in Num 22–24 concerns his authenticity as a reliable spokesman for the divine rather than as a true friend of Israel or its God. As noted, ambiguity regarding Balaam's intentions permits one to conclude that Balaam may well have sought to pronounce a curse against Israel, had YHWH only allowed it.

---

the Mesha Stele Inscription) as reviewed here (see also Levine, *Numbers 21–36*, 208–9, 211–12, 241–75).

122. On this general point, see Levine, *Numbers 21–36*, 208, 210–12. For Israel's prominence in inscriptions of Shalmaneser III, see, for example, the Kurkh Monolith Inscription (*COS* 2.113A: 260–64) and the Black Obelisk, which includes a relief panel and inscription portraying Israel's king *Ia-ú-a* (apparently, Jehu) offering tribute and obeisance to the Assyrian king (*COS* 2.113F: 269–70), both translated by K. L. Younger Jr.

123. Levine, *Numbers 21–36*, 215–17.

Thus, read against the background of the DAPT, Israel's endorsement by Balaam rings truly ironic, as if to say Israel's national fortunes were so assured that even a figure most infamous for pronouncing doom could only speak of Israel's success. In short, Balaam in Num 22–24 is not so much a celebrated figure as he is a known literary persona coopted in favor of Israel.

Numbers 22–24 invokes the authority of Balaam, the legendary foreign prophet so well known in Gilead (see the DAPT) as an apt, even if ironic, validation of Israel's hegemony over west-central Transjordan—a political reality that existed only prior to the Assyrian conquest of the region beginning 734 B.C.E.—as having been divinely ordained and foretold in much earlier times. This clarification of what is involved in the positive portrayal of Balaam in Num 22–24 proves helpful in turning to the other biblical texts about Balaam.

B. Briefer Balaam Texts in the Hebrew Bible

Micah 6:5

The only other relatively favorable portrayal of Balaam in the Hebrew Bible occurs in a prophetic text,, the book of Micah (6:5), which is set during the late 8th century B.C.E. (Mic 1:1). [124] Like Balaam, the persona of Micah figures primarily as a prophet of doom, both in the threats, laments, and accusations against Samaria, Jerusalem, and all "Israel" that make up most of the book (Mic 1–3; 6:1–7:7) [125] and in the prophetic legend in Jer 26, which quotes an oracle found in the book of Micah threatening Jerusalem's destruction (Mic 3:12; Jer 26:18–19). It thus seems

---

124. Most commentators understand only material in Micah 1–3 to derive from late-8th-century times. See, e.g., F. I. Andersen and D. N. Freedman, *Micah: A New Translation with Introduction and Commentary* (AB 24E; New York: Doubleday, 2000) 6–10; J. Jeremias, *Die Propheten Joel, Obadja, Jona, Micha* (Das Alte Testament Deutsch 24,3; Göttingen: Vandenhoeck & Ruprecht, 2007) 114–21; J. D. Nogalski, *The Book of the Twelve: Micah–Malachi* (Smyth & Helwys Bible Commentary; Macon, GA: Smyth & Helwys, 2011) 511–14; cf. D. R. Hillers, *Micah: A Commentary on the Book of the Prophet Micah* (Hermeneia; Philadelphia: Fortress, 1984) 1–9. Mic 6:1–7:7 is often dated to late exilic (see Nogalski, *The Book of the Twelve*, 512–13) or even postexilic (Jeremias, *Die Propheten Joel, Obadja, Jona, Micha*, 120 n. 15) times. However, the contents of this portion of the book are most relevant to late-8th/early-7th century B.C.E. Jerusalem, especially, the warning of desolation for following "the statutes of Omri and all the works of the house of Ahab" (Mic 6:16) and the elaborate description of social chaos and disintegrating kin-based structures (Mic 7:1–6) as "the faithful have disappeared from the land" (v. 2), a circumstance already set in motion by the 722/21 B.C.E. fall of Samaria and accelerated by Sennacherib's 701 B.C.E. desolation of Judah. Sennacherib's claim of having deported more than 200,000 people, even if an exaggeration, represents a social disruption of dramatic proportions (as emphasized, for example, by M. S. Smith, *The Memoirs of God: History, Memory, and the Experience of the Divine in Ancient Israel* [Minneapolis, MN: Fortress, 2004] 38–39). This historical horizon matches that reflected in Mic 1–3 (see Nogalski, *The Book of the Twelve*, 512).

125. The eschatological character of most of chs. 4–5 suggests a Persian-period date for this material. Compare Nogalski, *The Book of the Twelve*, 513.

fitting that an oracle attributed to this 8th-century doom-saying prophet would include a reference to the archetypal prophet of doom, Balaam (Mic 6:5a). [126]

That reference occurs in Mic 6:1–8, in which YHWH presents a 'lawsuit' (rîb) against Israel, including the following admonition:

> O my people, remember now what Balak king of Moab devised (y'ṣ),
> what Balaam son of Beor answered ('nw/y) him,
> and what happened from Shittim to Gilgal,
> in order that you may know the just deeds of YHWH (ṣidqôt yhwh). (Mic 6:5)

Consistent with the broader literary context of Num 22–24, Mic 6 situates Israel's encounter with Balaam within a sequence of saving acts by Israel's God, following the exodus from Egypt (Mic 6:4; cf. Num 22:5, 11; 23:22; 24:8) and preceding the events "from Shittim to Gilgal," possibly an elliptical reference to the Baal Peor episode (Mic 6:5b; cf. Num 25:1–5) and the Israelites' crossing of the Jordan (cf. Num 25:1; Josh 2:1; 3:1; 4:19–20). [127] Micah's mention of Balaam within this

---

126. The literary complexity at work in the biblical prophetic books and in the narrative portrayal of prophets in the books of Samuel–Kings warrants caution against speaking too simply of prophets of doom or salvation, and the comparative ancient Near Eastern sources are instructive. As an enterprise and body of knowledge supporting the throne (in German, *Herrschaftswissen*, as elucidated by Pongratz-Leisten), prophecy at Mari and in Assyria included the potential for both affirmation and critique of royal policy, and unmitigated criticism was typically leveled only at foreign peoples and kingdoms. See M. Nissinen, "Das kritische Potential in der altorientalischen Prophetie," in *Propheten in Mari, Assyrien und Israel* (ed. M. Köckert and M. Nissinen; FRLANT 201; Göttingen: Vandenhoeck & Ruprecht, 2003) 1–32, especially 31–32; Beate Pongratz-Leisten, *Herrschaftswissen in Mesopotamien: Formen der Kommunikation zwischen Gott und König im 2. und 1. Jahrtausend v. Chr.* (SAAS 10; Helsinki: The Neo-Assyrian Text Corpus Project, 1999) 47–127. As Nissinen underscores, the exilic and Persian-period final editing and shaping of biblical prophetic and historical texts makes it difficult to determine the degree to which the experience of the exile colors the biblical portrayals of preexilic court prophets and nonroyal prophets. On the other hand, one might add, the nature of the Mari and Assyrian sources as royal texts leaves one wondering how prominent nonroyal prophecy may have been in those societies and whether it might have involved more typically critical and threatening messages against the throne and broader society that characterize the preexilic Israelite prophets in biblical portrayals.

127. The sequence of episodes from Israel's early history recounted elliptically in Mic 6:4–5 might reflect the formulation of the larger narrative found in the Deuteronomistic History in its connection already with the currently preceding biblical books as the Enneateuch (as suggested, for example, by Nogalski, *The Book of the Twelve*, 513 and 521 n. 4). Yet, the episodes cited represent a narrative span extending only to Israel's crossing of the Jordan and encampment at Gilgal, thus corresponding to the likely extent of the non-Priestly, pre-Deuteronomistic narrative into which an early version of the Num 22–24 Balaam narrative came to be placed (see Robker, "The Balaam Narrative," 344–51, 362–63, and discussion of Num 22–24, above).

The earliest form of the Balaam narrative in Num 22–24 (as discussed above) presupposes the exodus as a prior event (Num 22:5, 11; 23:22; 24:8) and early on (perhaps in two separate stages) was placed within an ongoing non-Priestly literary sequence, in which it thus came to follow the conquest of the Amorites under Sihon at Heshbon (Num 21:21–31; Robker, "The

sequence may refer to the same literary tradition found in Num 22–24 and, in any case, is consistent with its portrayal.[128] It was Balak who orchestrated matters out of malice for Israel and Balaam who, under Yʜᴡʜ's direction, decisively answered in Israel's favor.

Deuteronomy 23:5–6 and Joshua 24:9–10

By contrast, Deuteronomic and Deuteronomistic texts[129] looking back at Israel's encounter with Balaam place the prophet in a wholly negative light, shifting emphasis to Balaam's own intent as being at odds with Yʜᴡʜ's will:

Balaam Narrative," 362) and to precede Israelite worship of Baal of Peor at Shittim (Num 25:1–5; Levine, *Numbers 21–36*, 279–80, 282). The mention of Shittim already in Num 25:1 (as part of a non-Priestly, non-Deuteronomistic text, Num 25:1–5) has the Israelites in place to cross the Jordan to Gilgal in the ongoing narrative's continuation (see Josh 2:1; 3:1; 4:19, 20). Gilgal's location near the Jordan's major southern ford and its prominence as a sanctuary site during the 8th century ʙ.ᴄ.ᴇ. and earlier (1 Sam 7:16; 14:8–15; Hos 4:15; 9:15; 12:11; Amos 4:4; 5:5; and with royal associations 1 Sam 10:8; 11:14–15; 15:12, 26–28; 2 Sam 19:15) favors the likelihood that any pre-Deuteonomistic narrative complex connecting early Israel in Transjordan (Num 21:21–31; 22:3–25:5) with an Israelite crossing of the Jordan would have eventuated in Gilgal as the key site of that westward crossing. In short, Mic 6:4–5 may well reflect a non-Priestly narrative complex spanning the exodus to the Israelite crossing of the Jordan to Gilgal, a literary work that had not yet been combined and integrated with the Deuteronomistic History. (The mention of "Moses, Aaron, and Miriam" in Mic 6:4b would correspond with the non-Priestly material in Exod 15:20–21 and Num 12.)

128. The verbs *yʿṣ* 'advise/devise' and *ʿnw/y* 'answer' in the terse formulation of Mic 6:5a both occur in the prose of Num 22–24: *yʿṣ*, not with Balak as the subject but rather in Balaam's words to Balak, "I will advise you . . ." (Num 24:14) and *ʿnw/y*, where Balaam 'answered' both Balak's second embassy and Balak himself with the disclaimer that he can only proceed or speak in accordance with Yʜᴡʜ's will (Num 22:18; 23:12, 26).

129. The 7th-century ʙ.ᴄ.ᴇ. dating of Deuteronomy based on its numerous affinities with Assyrian vassal treaties/loyalty oaths from the period (see Moshe Weinfeld, *Deuteronomy 1–11: A New Translation with Introduction and Commentary* [AB 5; New York: Doubleday, 1991] 4–9, 17) has received decisive confirmation in the 2009 discovery of a copy of Esarhaddon's Succession Treaty displayed in the inner sanctum of a temple at Tell Tayinat in Syria, in striking correspondence to Deut 31:26. See Jacob Lauinger, "Esarhaddon's Succession Treaty at Tell Tayinat: Text and Commentary," *JCS* 64 (2012) 87–123; B. M. Levinson, "Die neuassyrischen Ursprünge der Kanonformel in Deuteronomium 13,1," in *Viele Wege zu dem Einen: Historische Bibelkritik— die Vitalität der Glaubensüberlieferung in der Moderne* (ed. S. Beyerle et al.; Biblisch-theologische Studien 121; Neukirchen-Vluyn: Neukirchener Verlag, 2012) 61–82; Levinson and Stackert, "The Limitations of 'Resonance,'" 123–40; H. U. Steymans, "Deuteronomy 28 and Tell Tayinat," *Verbum et Ecclesia* 34:2 (2013) 1–13.

Martin Noth's hypothesis of the Deuteronomistic History (DH) as a unified redactional work of the exile encompassing Deuteronomy–2 Kings was modified in two major developments: the two-stage theory of Cross, who argued that the principal edition of the DH was composed during the late 7th century ʙ.ᴄ.ᴇ., during the reign of Josiah, and was then completed during the exile; and the model of Smend, which posited multiple stages of exilic editing. A number of subsequent variations on the hypothesis follow either Cross or Smend in positing successive editions, with at least one occurring each during preexilic and exilic periods. Recent

Yhwh your God did not consent to heed Balaam (wĕlō'-'ābâ yhwh 'ĕlōhêkā lišmōă' 'el-ĕbil'ām); Yhwh your God turned the curse (haqqĕlālâ) into a blessing for you, because Yhwh your God loves you. (Deut 23:6) [130] Balak son of Sippor, king of Moab set out to fight against Israel. He sent and called for Balaam son of Beor to curse (qll) you. But I did not consent to heed Balaam (wĕlō' 'ābîtî lišmō(a)' lĕbil'ām), and so he blessed you; thus I delivered you from his hand. (Josh 24:9–10) [131]

These texts cast the matter in terms of Yhwh's refusal to 'heed' (šm') Balaam, implying Balaam's own intent or effort to curse Israel. It is possible that they derive from a different version of the story, one in which Balaam's opposition to Israel is more overt. On the other hand, the Numbers Balaam Pericope's (Num 22–24) close affinities with the DAPT and its apparent date well prior to the 7th-century B.C.E. date of Deuteronomy (as discussed above) warrant some consideration of

---

analysis has demonstrated editorial activity and sporadic additions continuing after the exile. See M. Noth, *The Deuteronomistic History* (JSOTSup 15; Sheffield: JSOT Press, 1981); Cross, *Canaanite Myth and Hebrew Epic*, 274–89; Rudolph Smend, "The Law and the Nations: A Contribution to Deuteronomistic Tradition History," in *Reconsidering Israel and Judah: Recent Studies on the Deuteronomistic History* (trans. P. T. Daniels; ed. G. N. Knoppers and J. G. McConville; Source for Biblical and Theological Study 8; Winona Lake, IN: Eisenbrauns, 2000), 95–110; German orig., 1971); Thomas Römer, *The So-Called Deuteronomistic History: A Sociological, Historical and Literary Introduction* (New York: T. & T. Clark, 2005; repr., 2007).

130. For a classic treatment on "love" as a key covenant theme in Deuteronomy, see W. L. Moran, "The Ancient Near Eastern Background of the Love of God in Deuteronomy," *CBQ* 25 (1963) 77–87. Whereas Num 22–24 always refers to 'curse' using verbal forms (of 'rr and qbb, see above), the verb qll employed in Deut 23:5 corresponds to the noun form qĕlālâ in expressing the notion of Yhwh's 'turning' (hpk) the curse into a blessing in Deut 23:6, and qĕlālâ is a term for 'curse' used elsewhere in Deuteronomy (Deut 21:23; 28:15; cf. the noun form mĕ'ērâ, from 'rr, Deut 28:20; Mal 2:2; etc.). Joshua 24:9–10, in turn, follows Deut 23:5.

131. Other relevant texts within the span of biblical books conventionally associated with the Deuteronomistic History are Josh 13:21–22 (discussed below) and Judg 11:25 from Jephthah's diplomatic exchange with the Ammonite king: "Now are you any better than Balak son of Zippor, king of Moab? Did he ever quarrel (ryb) with Israel, let alone go to war (lḥm) with them?" For this nuance of translation, see J. M. Sasson, *Judges 1–12: A New Translation with Introduction and Commentary* (AB 6D; New Haven, CT: Yale University Press, 2014), 417, 430, 528 n. 38. As Sasson observes, Jephthah's assertion stands somewhat in tension with matters as presented in Num 22–24, but this fact may owe to the diplomatic rhetoric employed by Jephthah (Sasson, *Judges 1–12*, 430–31). In any case, in Num 22–24, Balak never directly engages Israel in any dispute, verbal or otherwise, and only anticipates going to war against them (Num 22:6) without every doing so, once the attempted curse by Balaam fails. This matches the notice in Josh 24:9 that Balak 'set out to fight against Israel' (wayyāqom bālāq . . . wayyillāḥem bĕyiśrā'ēl) by calling on Balaam to curse Israel. In sum, the texts relevant to Balaam in Deuteronomy, Joshua, and Judges reviewed thus far are consistent with one another and with the basic portrayal of Num 22–24, their major difference from Num 22–24 being the shift to a negative view of Balaam. Compare Robker's assertion that Josh 24:9–10 "presupposes a violent clash between Israel and Moab that is unknown in Num, Deut, and the other traditions, and that directly contradicts Judg 11:19–25" (Robker, "The Balaam Narrative," 355).

whether Deut 23 and Josh 24 may be interacting with the same Balaam tradition reflected in Num 22–24. Before considering Balaam's mention in Deut 23:6 more thoroughly, the possible relevance of Num 22–24 and of the broader context of Deuteronomy for this decidedly negative turn in the view of Balaam merit consideration.

As noted, Balaam's primary associations with doom (as reflected in the DAPT) and curse make his blessing of Israel in Num 22–24 stand out as ironic and unexpected. As discussed, Balaam's potential willingness to curse Israel in Num 22–24—implicit in his hiring by Balaam and possibly inferred from his change of procedure with the third oracle—is bounded only by Yhwh's power and resolve to bless Israel instead. As articulated in the final instance of Balaam's repeated disclaimer to Balak, "I am not able to go beyond the word of Yhwh to do either good or harm by my own will (BH *millibbî*, literally, 'from my own heart'), what Yhwh says is what I must say" (Num 24:13). Although Balaam's own "will" ultimately proves inconsequential, it is nonetheless subject to interpretation. Deut 23 aligns with the more suspicious interpretation of Balaam's intentions described above in connection with Num 24:1–2. Deuteronomy's reluctance to grant Balaam the benefit of the doubt must be considered in light of its own stated criteria for evaluating prophets in Deut 13:1–5; 18:9–22.

Like Deut 23:6, these regulations on prophets occur within the legal corpus of Deuteronomy (chs. 12–26), which scholarship has long recognized as the core of the biblical book.[132] Deuteronomy 13:1–5 occurs within that legal core, within a section of admonitions ensuring exclusive loyalty to Yhwh (Deut 13:1–18). With potential application to Balaam, Deut 13 warns against any prophet (*nābîʾ*) or 'dreamer of a dream' (*ḥōlēm ḥǎlôm*) who advocates the worship of gods other than Yhwh, even if pronouncing signs (*ʾôt*) or portents (*môpēt*) that come about (Deut 13:2–6). Even if a prophet's prediction comes true, as would have been the perception of Balaam's oracles in Num 24, it is no guarantee that his message is authentic and not simply a test from Yhwh (Deut 13:4). Although Num 22 does not use the language of "dream," "sign," or "portent," it presents a congruent portrayal of nocturnal divine visitations to Balaam (Num 22:8–13; 19–21). As discussed, Balaam's decision not to seek Yhwh in oracles, as before, but otherwise to deliver an oracle by a 'spirit of God/divine spirit' (*rûʾaḥ ʾělōhîm*, Num 24:1–2), an oracle introduced in different language than the preceding ones, as 'the oracle of Balaam' (*nĕʾum bilʿām*, v. 3; also v. 15),[133] might be perceived as Balaam's own pursuit of other gods. Though Balaam is not an immediate target of Deut 13:1–5, these warnings against prophets and diviners as a possible threat to loyalty to Yhwh might place Balaam in a more suspicious light, as he is presented in Deut 23:5–6 (see below).

---

132. See, e.g., Weinfeld, *Deuteronomy 1–11*, 3, 10.

133. But compare the prose introduction of all four oracles with, "And he took up his oration, saying" (*wayyiśśāʾ mĕšālô wayyōʾmar*, Num 23:7, 18; 24:3, 15).

Deuteronomy deals with prophets more directly in 18:9–22. This passage presents a section of prohibitions against divinatory and other religious practices ascribed to other nations (Deut 18:9–14) and then offers an alternative channel of divine communication as normative for Israel—namely, the ideal Mosaic prophet, whom Yhwh will "raise up" from among the people of Israel and who will speak Yhwh's very words (Deut 18:15–19).[134] The law then adds two criteria for evaluating various prophets and for discerning between conflicting prophetic messages: "the prophet who speaks in the name of other gods, or presumes (BH *zyd*) to speak in my name a word that I have not commanded the prophet to speak—that prophet shall die" (Deut 18:20). A corollary to the second criterion follows: "If a prophet speaks in the name of Yhwh but the thing does not take place or prove true, it is a word that Yhwh has not spoken. The prophet has spoken it presumptuously (*bĕzādôn*); do not be frightened by it" (Deut 18:22).[135]

The prerequisite criterion of Israelite identity (Deut 18:15, 18) from the start rules out Balaam as a Mosaic prophet and perhaps as an acceptable prophet of any kind. In any case, the immediately preceding warnings against pagan 'enchanters' (*mĕnahēš*, Deut 18:10) and 'diviners' (*qōsēm qĕsāmîm, qōsĕmîm,* vv. 10, 14) would certainly incriminate Balaam as he is presented in Num 22–24. In one of his poetic oracles, Balaam declares, seemingly in spite of himself: "Surely, there is no omen (*naḥaš*) against Jacob, no divination (*qesem*) against Israel" (Num 23:23), and the narrator both notes that Balak's messengers approach Balaam with (*qĕsāmîm,* 22:7) and characterizes Balaam's cultic procedure as seeking 'omens' (*nĕḥāšîm,* Num 24:1).

Deuteronomy's negative view of Balaam may also have to do with both criteria offered in ch. 18, rejecting prophets who speak "in the name of other gods" or who 'presume' (BH *zyd*) to speak in Yhwh's name a message that is not actually from Yhwh (Deut 18:20). In view of this warning, the equivocal description of Balaam's change of procedure in his third oracle (Num 24:1–2, as discussed above) might suggest in view of Deut 18:20 that he had indeed "presumed" to speak a word that Yhwh had not commanded or even tried to speak in the name of another god.

In sum, from the perspective of Deuteronomy's laws on prophets, Balaam at best falls under suspicion as a foreign prophetic figure who practices divination (*qĕsāmîm,* 22:7; *qesem,* Num 23:23; cf. Deut 18:9–14), seeks 'omens' (*naḥaš,* 23:23; *nĕḥāšîm,* Num 24:1; cf. Deut 18:9–14), and apparently receives dream communi-

---

134. This law describing the Mosaic prophet (Deut 18:9–22) and its placement alongside laws for Israel's judges (Deut 16:18–17:13), kings (17:14–20), and priests (18:1–8) suggests to some scholars a normative prophetic office within the Deuteronomic vision of the ideal state, but compare the discussion by R. R. Wilson, *Prophecy and Society in Ancient Israel* (Philadelphia: Fortress, 1980) 157–66.

135. As commentators routinely note, this means for determining whether a prophet has spoken truly in Yhwh's name can only be applied after the fact and thus is virtually useless as a test for evaluating prophets' future predictions.

cations from the divine (Num 22:8–13; 19–21; cf. Deut 13:1–8). At worst, he might also be suspected of speaking in the name of other gods or "presuming" to speak in YHWH's name contrary to YHWH's will (Deut 18:19–20), offenses worthy of the death penalty (Deut 18:20; cf. 13:5). With relevance for Balaam's true predictions of Israel's success at the expense of its Transjordanian neighbors (Num 24:15–19), Deuteronomy allows that YHWH may permit foreign prophets to predict correctly in order to test Israel's commitment to YHWH (Deut 13:1–3). Neither Num 22–24 nor Deut 23 accuses Balaam of instructing Israelites to worship other gods (Deut 13:1–8), and neither portrays his death. But, as we will see, Deuteronomy seems to set the stage for other texts to do so. In any case, it marks the decisive turning point to an increasingly negative view of Balaam in biblical tradition.[136]

The fuller immediate context of Balaam's mention in Deuteronomy reveals further insights regarding literary reflection on prophets and states:

> No Ammonite or Moabite shall enter the assembly of YHWH. Even to the tenth generation, they shall not enter the assembly of YHWH forever. Because they did not meet you with bread and water on your journey out of Egypt, and they hired against you Balaam son of Beor, from Pethor in Aram-Naharaim, to curse you. But YHWH your God did not consent to heed Balaam (*wĕlōʾ- ʾābâ yhwh ʾĕlōhêkā lišmōăʿ ʾel-ĕbilʿām*); YHWH your God turned the curse (*haqqĕlālâ*) into a blessing for you, because YHWH your God loves you. You shall never promote their welfare or their prosperity all the days of your life, forever. (Deut 23:4–7)

Balaam's homeland in the northern Euphrates region, his Aramean identity, the hiring of Balaam to curse Israel, the result being blessing instead of curse, and the involvement of the Moabites are all elements consistent with the portrayal of Num 22–24. What stands out as different, besides the suggestion of Balaam's intent to curse, is the involvement of Ammon.

Deuteronomy's recollection of Balaam is situated within a sequence of instructions (Deut 23:2–9) regarding Israel's relationships to its Transjordanian neighbors and to Egypt (Deut 23:4–9) as groups whose possible inclusion in "the assembly of YHWH" stands in question. Singled out for exclusion are the Ammonites and Moabites, and their descendants "to the tenth generation . . . [even] forever": *lōʾ-yābōʾ ʿammōnî ûmôʾābî biqhal yhwh* (Deut 23:4–5, here quoting v. 4a). This pairing of Ammon and Moab following the exclusion of anyone 'born of an illicit union' (BH *mamzēr*, Deut 23:3) suggests an oblique reference to the polemical tradition of incestuous origins for these ancient rivals of Israel as related in Gen 19:30–38.[137]

---

136. Levine, *Numbers 21–36*, 154; cf. 240.

137. Compare the following inclusion of the Edomite, "for he is your brother," and even the Egyptian, "for you were a sojourner (BH *gēr*) in his land," with no mention of Israel's oppression in Egypt (Deut 23:8).

Nonetheless, the more explicit warrant for their exclusion offered in the following motive clause (Deut 23:5) invokes a twofold accusation. The first accusation is that both the Ammonites and Moabites denied hospitality to the Israelites when they journeyed through Transjordan from Egypt ("*They* did not meet you [*qiddĕmû*] with bread and water on the way when you came out of Egypt," Deut 23:5a).[138] Quite remarkably, the text proceeds to overlook traditions of Edomite hostility (including similar reported offenses, Num 20:14–21; cf. Deut 2:1–8) and Egypt's oppression of the Israelites (cf. Deut 4:20; 5:6, 15; 6:21), allowing both of these traditional enemies into "the assembly of Yhwh" (Deut 23:8–9)![139] Second, the motive clause adds the charge "and because *he* hired (3 m.s. *śākar*) against you Balaam son of Beor . . . to curse you (*lĕqalĕlekā*)." Although the singular verb form *śākar* ('*he* hired'; cf. plural *qiddĕmû* in the first accusation, Deut 23:5a) might imply the subject to be only "the Moabite," or, more specifically, Balak, the subject is not explicitly named as expected in such a case, and the formulation of these clauses therefore implicates both Moabites and Ammonites, even though the wilderness accounts indicate that the wandering Israelites never encountered the Ammonites (Num 21:24; Deut 2:19, 37).[140]

Deuteronomy's curious reframing of the Balaam tradition and of Moabite hostility against Israel in west-central Transjordan to include the Ammonites accords with the earliest evidence for an Ammonite presence in this area beginning in the 7th century B.C.E., as well attested in epigraphic and archaeological evidence from Tell Jalul, Tell Hisban, Tell Dayr ʿAlla, Tell al-Mazar, and Tell es-Saʾidiyya.[141] By

---

138. This accusation is somewhat at odds with the narrative summary of these events in the narrative introduction to Deuteronomy (Deut 1:1–4:43), which indicates no hostilities from Moab and suggests that the Israelite might have purchased food and water from Moab as they had from the Edomites (Deut 2:8b-13; cf. vv. 5–6, 28–29) and similarly indicates Israel's avoidance of any encounter with the Ammonites, whose border lay completely outside the area of the Israelites' migration and settlement (Deut 2:19, 37). In keeping with the confinement of Ammonite territory prior to the Assyrian conquests to the 9-mile (15-km) radius around Amman (see above), the non-Priestly text in Num 21:24 acknowledges the Ammonite border as a limit to Israel's territorial acquisitions in greater Gilead, "for the boundary of the Ammonites was strong (BH ʿaz 'fortified')." Similarly, Deut 2 describes Ammonite territory as consisting of "the whole upper region of the Wadi Jabbok" (modern Wadi Zarqa, Deut 2:37), but in contrast to Num 21:24 explains that the Ammonites' territory had been assigned by Yhwh (Deut 2:19). Deuteronomy's take on the long-standing and more limited extent of Ammonite territory suggests an indirect argument against Ammonite expansion into west-central Transjordan during the 7th century B.C.E., as evident in archaeological and epigraphic evidence. On the related archaeological and epigraphic evidence, see below. On the differences among the accounts of Israel's wilderness encounters of Edom, Moab, and Ammon among Deuteronomy, P, and non-Priestly Numbers, see Weinfeld, *Deuteronomy 1–11*, 165–67.

139. At least, after "the third generation" (Deut 23:9).

140. See J. H. Tigay, *Deuteronomy* (The JPS Torah Commentary; Philadelphia: Jewish Publication Society, 1996) 211, 386 n. 35, 422–29.

141. See Herr, "The Iron Age II Period," 165, 168–72. Although the correlation of ethnicity with archaeological evidence has posed a challenge to archaeology in general, the discovery at

this time, Assyria's declining control of the region had opened the way for Ammonite territorial expansion into the western Transjordanian Plateau and east Jordan Valley. Also, Egyptian hegemony over Palestine under Psammetichus I (664–610 B.C.E.), reflected in the inclusion of Egyptians into "the assembly of YHWH" (Deut 23:8–9), was confined mainly to coastal areas of Philistia.[142]

Belying Deut 23's revision concerning traditional hostilities against Edom (e.g., Num 20:18–21; 24:18) and Egypt (see the exodus tradition; cf. Deut 23:5) is the necessity of the commands not to 'abhor' (*tʿb*) members of either nation (Deut 23:8–9). The inclusion of both peoples' descendants ("after the third generation") into "the assembly of YHWH" would later be unthinkable following the irreparable betrayal of Israelite "brotherhood" with Edom in 586 B.C.E.[143] and most likely preceded Josiah's death at the hands of Psammetichus' successor, Necho II (610–595 B.C.E.; 2 Kgs 23:29–35; 2 Chr 35:20–24). These shifts in Israel's and Judah's relationships with Egypt and its Transjordanian neighbors are in agreement with the 7th-century date of Deuteronomy, a time of shifting circumstances, perhaps rendering Balaam's predictions of Israelite strength in Transjordan, and even the very survival of the northern kingdom of Israel, as failed predictions from the perspective of Deuteronomy (see especially Deut 18:22; cf. 13:2–3).

Although Deuteronomy does not explicitly condemn Balaam, it assumes his status as a foreign enemy overcome by YHWH's intent to bless Israel. This negative view of Balaam is in keeping with Deuteronomy's distinct instructions regarding foreign prophets and other mediators of divine communication as perennial threats to Israel's exclusive devotion to YHWH (Deut 13:1–8; 18:9–22). Deut 23:5–6 (and 23:3–9, more broadly), in keeping with its 7th-century date, reflects a shift in political circumstances from Israel-Judah's domination of Transjordanian neighbors and territories reflected in Num 22–24 (especially, Num 24:17–19) to those in which Ammon encroaches on formerly Israelite holdings in Transjordan and in which Edom is no longer a vanquished "possession" (Num 24:18) but rather a "brother" (Deut 23:8).

While differences of language and focus between Num 22–24 and Deut 23:5–6 render any notion of direct literary dependence between these texts indemonstrable,[144] they share the same basic elements in common: in a territorial dispute, Balaam, an Aramean prophet from the upper Euphrates region, is

---

these sites of material cultural assemblages matching those from Amman and its immediate surroundings indicates the expansion of a political system and its economic networks to the west-central plateau and east Jordan valley during the 7th and 6th centuries B.C.E. For more discussion of this evidence, see p. 145 nn. 28–29 above.

142. See G. Ahlström, *The History of Ancient Palestine* (Minneapolis: Fortress, 1994) 750–53, 758–59.

143. Biblical texts decidedly indicate Edomite betrayal of Judah in the Babylonian destruction of Jerusalem (Ps 137:7; Obadiah; Mal 1:2–5).

144. As thoroughly explicated by Robker, "Reception, Citation, and Balaam," 1–6.

hired by the Moabites to curse Israel, yet YHWH in his devotion to Israel ensures that Israel should instead be blessed. Balaam's intent to curse Israel is nonetheless already latent within Num 22–24 (especially 24:1–2) and accords with Deuteronomy's suspicion and rejection of foreign prophets and diviners (Deut 13:1–8; 18:9–22). Differences of language and style (e.g., terms for "curse" and YHWH's "love" for Israel)[145] can be accounted for by the literary and ideological context of Deuteronomy. The other differences of substance, the implication of the Ammonites along with the Moabites and friendship with Edom and Egypt, follow from Deuteronomy's polemic against the former two nations (Moab and Ammon) and its conciliation with the latter two (Edom and Egypt), within the larger context of Deut 23 (Deut 23:3–9), all in keeping with Deuteronomy's 7th-century setting, a time when international political circumstances for the kingdom of Judah had shifted from those reflected in Num 22–24.

In sum, Deut 23 marks a negative turn of attitude toward Balaam among biblical texts reviewed thus far (Num 22–24; Mic 6:5; and Deut 23:5–6). Like other differences among these texts, this one suggests not so much discrete Balaam traditions that had separate origins but rather developments of essentially the same Balaam tradition, with different emphases, in keeping with these texts surrounding literary and historical contexts. Other remaining Balaam texts from the Hebrew Bible (Num 31:8; Josh 13:22; Neh 13:1–2) continue along that trajectory, with an increasingly negative view of Balaam. Because of its distinct literary relationship to Deut 23:5–6, Neh 13:1–2 is the next Balaam text for discussion.

Nehemiah 13:1–2

Reflecting further shifting circumstances in Persian-Period Judea, the book of Nehemiah cites Deut 23:4–6:

> On that day, they read from the book of Moses in the hearing of the people; and in it was found written that no Ammonite or Moabite shall enter the assembly of YHWH forever. For they did not meet the Israelites with bread and water, and they hired against them Balaam to curse them. But our God turned the curse to blessing. (Neh 13:1–2)[146]

---

145. For the verb 'love' (*'hb*) as a term for devotion between YHWH and Israel, Deut 13:4; 23:6; cf. Num 23:19–23; 24:6. Compare terms for 'curse:' *qll*, *qĕlālâ*, Deut 21:23; 23:5, 6; 28:15; cf. Num 22–24: *'rr*, Num 22:6, 12; 23:7; *qbb* 22:11, 17; 23:8, 11, 13, 25, 27; 24:10. The noun form related to *'rr* (*mĕ'ērâ*, Deut 28:20) occurs within the distinct literary context of the "blessings and curses" section of Deut 28, where it may have a particular sense and, in any case, corresponds to the use of *'rr* as the verb repeated in the sequence of curses articulated in this passage (Deut 28:16–19; cf. *qĕlālôt*, verse 15). See Tigay, *Deuteronomy*, 261–62, 489–97.

146. Even though Neh 13:1–2 clearly cites Deut 23, there are minor differences in orthography, second-person pronouns in Deuteronomy vs. third-person pronouns in Nehemiah, conjunctive structures, and Nehemiah's omission of some phrases from Deuteronomy, all in keeping with the language style of Nehemiah and later historical setting portrayed in Nehemiah.

The context is the expulsion of Tobiah "the Ammonite" (Neh 2:10) and others regarded as foreigners from Jerusalem and the temple, as related in Neh 13:3–9, 23–30. In Nehemiah's citation of Deut 23 (cited as "the book of Moses," Neh 13:1), it is not so much prophetic authority as scriptural authority that is at work. Within the Persian-Period historical setting portrayed in the book of Nehemiah, Balaam is invoked not as a prophet interacting with states and peoples but rather as a fixed literary figure within an authoritative text receiving imperial sanction. Thanks to Deuteronomy, Balaam's identity as a villain has become well established, supporting the justification for anti-"Ammonite" and, more broadly, anti-"foreigner" sentiment in the portrayal of Nehemiah's reforms. The negative view of Balaam in Deut 23 has become the developing trend in Balaam's treatment by biblical authors.

Numbers 31:8–16

Balaam's treatment becomes even more negative in Num 31:8–16, which relates that, in the context of a war against the Midianites ordered by YHWH (Num 25:16–18 and again in 31:1–2), the Israelites eventually killed Balaam along with the five kings of Midian (Num 31:8), as part of a *ḥerem*-like extermination of all the Midianites except for female children (Num 31:1–18).[147] This account of Israel's vengeance against the Midianites blames Balaam along with the Midianites for the Israelites' unfaithfulness in "the matter of Peor" (Num 31:16). Numbers 31, in keeping with 25:16–18, thus conflates the two originally separate episodes brought together in Num 25: Israelite worship of a deity Baal of Peor resulting from cohabitation between Israelite men and Moabite women (Num 25:1–5) and the added Priestly account of Phinehas' "zeal" in executing an Israelite man with a Midianite woman *in flagrante* (Num 25:6–15). The conflation of these two stories is completed in the Priestly editorial conclusion that follows them (Num 25:16–18).[148] The virtual equation of Moabites and Midianites in this broader literary context is further facilitated by the Priestly insertion of "the elders of Midian" in reference to their consultation by Moab prior to sending for Balaam (Num 22:4) and then again to join Balak's messengers in v. 7, with Midian never to be mentioned again in Num 22–24.[149]

Balaam, having returned to his home in Num 24:25, is presumably nowhere near the events of Num 25 and receives no mention there, and other biblical texts reflect on the apostasy of Peor without any mention of Balaam (Deut 4:3; Josh 22:17; Hos 9:10; Ps 106:28). Yet, the place-name Peor has already appeared in the

---

147. Neither noun nor verb forms of *ḥrm* appear in Num 31. In the editorial conclusion to the story of Phinehas' "zeal" (Num 25:14–18), the Midianite woman is identified as Cozbi daughter of Zur, the head of a clan and ancestral house in Midian and ostensibly the same Zur who appears among the five Midianite rulers named in Num 31:8.

148. Levine, *Numbers 21–36*, 279–80.

149. Ibid., 144–45.

prose of Num 23–24 as the location of Balaam's third and fourth oracles (Num 23:28–24:3a). Here lies the slight basis on which Num 31 implicates Balaam in "the matter of Peor" and asserts that the Midianite women led the Israelites to apostasy 'by the word of Balaam' (běděbar bilʿām, Num 31:16). The purported 'word of Balaam' thus points back to the 'utterance of Balaam' (něʾum bilʿām, Num 24:3b) set at Peor, appearing as his third poetic oracle (Num 24:3b–9). Among other things, this oracle includes male fertility imagery amenable to secondary association with the episodes that come to follow Num 22–24 in its eventual attachment to Num 25:1–5 (and then later, 25:6–9): "Water flows from his [Israel's] buckets, and his seed (flows) with abundant water" (Num 24:7a). This imagery of unbounded male fertility secondarily resonates with Num 25's cumulative portrayal of the male Israelites' tragic propensity for pursuing sexual relations with Moabite women (vv. 1–5) / a Midianite woman (vv. 6–9, 18; cf. Midianite women in 31:16) as a recurring problem leading to religious apostasy and disaster. It is only Num 31:16 that makes this connection between Balaam's "word" in Num 23–24 and "the matter of Peor" in Num 25, including the Priestly addition of Num 25:6–18.

In reinterpreting Balaam's oracle at Peor (Num 23:28–24:9) in connection with "the matter of Peor" (Num 25), Num 31 recasts Balaam's blessing there as a curse calling forth Israel's disloyalty to its God and resulting disaster. Deuteronomy 23 (and perhaps Num 24:1–2) had intimated only Balaam's intention to curse Israel, though Yhwh decisively "turned the curse into a blessing" (Deut 23:6). Numbers 31 turns even that blessing into a curse, at least the portion pronounced in Balaam's third oracle (Num 24:7a).[150] In short, an earlier form of the Numbers Balaam Pericope had been connected with the Baal Peor episode (Num 22–24* + Num 25:1–5 on Moabite women) in a non-Priestly literary narrative sequence that came to be modified by the following Priestly texts reflecting an anti-Midianite polemic, one perhaps developing in stages that eventually also implicate Balaam: Num 22:4, 7 (interpolation of "elders of Midian"); Num 25:6–13; Num 25:14–18; and Num 31.[151]

---

150. Balaam's decision in this instance not to solicit a response from Yhwh (Num 24:1), which as discussed may have already aroused the suspicion reflected in Deut 23:5–6, might have further encouraged a connection between the oracle (especially Num 24:7a) and the apostasy and disaster that followed for Israel in Num 25.

151. Levine, Numbers 21–36, 445; Compare Robker, "The Balaam Narrative," 363. The donkey story (Num 22:22–35) being to disparage Balaam, it was added sometime following the trend beginning with Deut 23:5–6 to denigrate Balaam. This might have come about as part of this Priestly editing, but the donkey narrative lacks clear affinities with the other Priestly additions mentioned, and so it is difficult to discern when it might have been added.

In a compelling case for historical circumstances reflected in the Priestly polemic against Midian, Levine points to Aramaisms in Num 31, to E. A. Knauf's explanation of the names it gives to the five Midianite kings as toponyms on a trade itinerary between north Arabia and Transjordan, and to texts reflecting an association between Midian and Arab groups (especially

Balaam's death along with the five Midianite "kings" (Num 31:8) would seem to imply a regard for Balaam as a royal figure.[152] Indeed an alternative tradition of Balaam as a tribal ruler is reflected in the "Edomite king list" in Gen 36:31–39, which includes the figure 'Bela son of Beor' (*bela' ben-bě'ôr*, v. 32), Beor being the same patronymic always given to Balaam (DAPT I.1, 2, 4; Num 22:5; 31:8; Deut 23:5; Josh 13:22; 24:9; Mic 6:5) and *bela'* being a variant form of the name *bil'ām*. The appearance of the name Balaam in an 8th-century B.C.E. Assyrian text (written ¹*Ba-la-am-mu* and ¹*Ba-li-am-mu*), as the patronymic of an Aramean chief located in the middle Euphrates region, suggests the Aramean heritage both of the name Balaam and of the legendary figure "Balaam/Bela son of Beor."[153] In keeping with André Lemaire's discussion of Gen 36:31–39, at least some of the kings of "Edom" presented in fact derive from records of kings of "Aram" (see also "Hadad son of Bedad," vv. 35–36), these names becoming reinterpreted and reappropriated (along with Transjordanian place-names), and thus were incorporated into this list, based on the easy confusion between the letters *r* and *d*, and thus 'Aram' *'rm* and 'Edom' *'dm*, in West Semitic alphabetic writing of the first millennium B.C.E.[154] This likely alternative tradition of Balaam as tribal leader notwithstanding, any suggestion of its direct relevance to Num 31 proves illusory. Balaam is killed in the battle against the Midianites not for being one of their "kings" (Num 31:8) but rather because of his supposed complicity in the Midianite women's inducement of Israelites into apostasy "by the word of Balaam" (Num 31:16). Balaam is killed, along with the Midianites, not as an enemy king but rather as an enemy prophet.

With the depiction of Balaam's violent death as an enemy of Israel in Num 31, the negative turn regarding Balaam in biblical literature that began with Deuteronomy reaches its logical consequence. Balaam's death as a foreign prophetic figure who purportedly led the Israelites to worship gods other than Yʜwʜ is consistent with the larger concern and threatened punishment in the Deuteronomic prophetic legislation (Deut 13:1–8; 18:9–22). But Balaam is not executed as a prophet who exhorted the Israelites directly to worship other gods (Deut 13:2) or who made false predictions while speaking for Yʜwʜ (18:22) but rather is killed

---

Isa 60:6–7). These factors, along with Ezra–Nehemiah's presentation of "Geshem the Arab" (cf. King Gashmu of the Qedarite Arabs in a 5th-century B.C.E. Aramaic inscription) as a principal enemy of Jerusalem (Neh 2:19; 6:1–2, 6; see also Isa 21:16–17) suggest the Priestly polemic may represent a retrojection into the premonarchic past of Persian-Period concerns over the powerful Qedarite Arab kingdom as a hostile enemy. See Levine, *Numbers 21–36*, 57–58, 472–74.

152. As argued, also on the basis of Num 22–24, in J. T. Greene, *Balaam and His Interpreters: A Hermeneutical History of the Balaam Traditions* (Brown Judaic Studies 244; Atlanta: Scholars Press, 1992) 70. Greene's suggestion that Balak's dialogue with Balaam reflects a discourse between equals is not a persuasive argument for Balaam's royal status in this text or in the broader tradition of the prophetic figure Balaam.

153. Dion, "Les Araméens du Moyen-Euphrate," 68–69 n. 106.

154. Lemaire, Les premiers rois araméens," 116–17.

in battle under a divinely decreed annihilation of the Midianites (Num 31:7–18; cf. 25:16–18; 31:1–2), representing a Priestly appropriation of the *ḥerem* theology enshrined in Deuteronomy and in Deuteronomistic texts (Deut 7:2; 13:15; 20:16–17; Josh 6:17–21; 7:10–26; etc.).[155]

Joshua 13:22

The remaining Balaam text in the Hebrew Bible, Josh 13:22, occurs within an account of land distribution in the Israelite settlement (Josh 13–21). In describing the territory of Reuben, including Heshbon (Josh 13:17) and Beth Peor (v. 20), the text assumes Midianite habitation in this area, as portrayed in Num 25:6–18, and includes the same list of five Midianite rulers killed, along with Balaam, by the Israelites, mentioned in Num 31:8 (Josh 13:21).[156] Joshua 13 thus implies that the Midianite rulers were politically subordinate to Sihon of Heshbon or otherwise in league with him. Joshua 13, like Deut 3, has Israel taking Transjordan north of the Arnon (and excluding Ammonite territory) from "the two kings of the Amorites," Sihon and Og, but Deut 3 makes no mention of Midianites there. Thus, Josh 13 offers a telescoped account of Israelite settlement in Transjordan that follows both the narrative introduction to Deuteronomy (Deut 1:1–4:43) and the Priestly editing of Num 21–25 and 31 described above, including the Israelites' killing of Balaam along with Midianites. But Josh 13 adds something new in calling Balaam a *qōsēm*, 'diviner', perhaps as an added rationale for his killing in keeping with this text's Deuteronomistic literary and theological context, following Deuteronomy's explicit rejection of divination (*qsm*) as "an abhorrent practice of the nations" forbidden by Israel's devotion to Yʜwʜ (see Deut 18:9–14; cf. 2 Kgs 17:17). Josh 13:22 thus reflects a negative trajectory regarding Balaam as an enemy of Israel that began with Deuteronomy and that developed in Deuteronomistic and Priestly texts, thus reflecting both continuity and some remove in its theological outlook from the presentation of the Balaam's apparently nonproblematic association with "divination" in the Balaam Pericope (*qĕsāmîm*, Num 22:7; *qesem* 23:23).

This negative trajectory of Balaam's image among biblical texts beginning with Deuteronomy and arguably tracing its roots ultimately to Num 22–24 continues to dominate the view of Balaam in the New Testament (2 Pet 2:15–16; Jude 11; Rev 2:14) and in postbiblical Jewish texts (Philo: *1 Mos.* 285–86; Josephus: *Ant.* IV.119–22; VI.6–13; Tannaitic literature: *m. Avot* 5:19; *Sanh.* 105a–106b; Targums to Num 22–24), which consistently portray Balaam as a villain.[157] On the other

---

155. Levine, *Numbers 21–36*, 445, 456.

156. Joshua 13:21 refers to the five Midianite rulers as 'princes' (*nĕśî'ê* and *nĕswîkê*) rather than 'kings' (*malkê*, Num 31:8). Extending from Aroer on the Wadi Arnon northward to "the plateau to Madeba" (Josh 13:16), Reuben's territory as described here is roughly equivalent to the territory Mesha claims in the Mesha Inscription. See the English translation by K. A. D. Smelik in *COS* 2.23:137–38.

157. Milgrom, *Numbers*, 471; Greene, *Balaam and His Interpreters*, 142–54.

hand, the overall more positive view of Balaam reflected in Num 22–24 and in Mic 6:5 also reverberates in Pseudo-Philo, in midrashic literature, and in a tradition of Christian reception history linking the star of Matt 2:1–12 with Num 24:17 and thus Balaam as the forerunner of the magi.[158]

Conclusion: The Biblical Balaam Texts

Although reflecting various literary aims and shifting historical circumstances, the biblical Balaam traditions, like that of the DAPT, hark back to the same Balaam son of Beor, an authoritative prophetic figure known in the context of Iron II Transjordan, as a figure from earlier times. One can hardly speak of a "historical Balaam." Such a person may in fact lie behind our literary textual tradition, but Balaam is accessible to us more as a type-figure, appropriated in various ways in the literature of Iron II and later. The extensive parallels of wording and detail between the DAPT and Num 22–24 show that, even with their significant differences, the Balaam pericope was created with knowledge of the same formulation of the Balaam tradition found in the DAPT. In contrast with the DAPT's portrayal of Balaam as a foreign seer within a politically neutral divine and human landscape, Num 22–24 coopts Balaam in favor of the Israelite monarchy at the expense of its neighbors in Transjordan. This explicitly pro-Israelite viewpoint distinguishing Num 22–24 from the DAPT is assumed and even sharpened in the other biblical Balaam texts.

With the exception of Deut 23:5's citation in Neh 13:2, direct literary dependence or influence among the biblical Balaam texts is difficult to prove with certainty. But the texts nonetheless lend themselves to explanation according to various interactions with a common Balaam tradition if not according to a unilinear development among these texts. In any case, in view of the extensive similarities of basic content among these texts (in some ways, greater than those between the DAPT and Num 22–24), the differences among them and Balaam's increasingly negative character are best explained in relationship to their respective literary-theological and historical contexts. Those developments follow shifts in geopolitical circumstances for Israel, Judah, and Achaemenid Yehud and accompanying religious-historical developments. In short, the differences among the various biblical portrayals of Balaam are not simply disjointed "positive" and "negative" traditions, but rather they fit within a unified pattern in relationship to what we can establish regarding the history of ancient Transjordan and the development of texts in the Hebrew Bible.

---

158. See T. Nicklas, "Balaam and the Star of the Magi," in *The Prestige of the Pagan Prophet Balaam in Judaism, Early Christianity and Islam* (Themes in Biblical Narrative. Jewish and Christian Traditions 11; Leiden: Brill, 2008) 233–46; and in the same volume J. Leemans, "'To Bless with a Mount Bent on Cursing:' Patristic Interpretations of Balaam (Num 24:17)," 287–99.

Within this process, the pronounced negative turn for Balaam begins in the heightened nationalism of Deuteronomy and, in keeping with the nationalistic *ḥerem* theology known from earlier Iron II times in the Mesha Stele Inscription, its castigation of "foreign" religious practices and personages. In addition to the exclusion of "diviners" and non-Israelite prophets holding suspect motives (Deut 13:1–8; 18:9–22), it is the *ḥerem* theology that eventually carries through for Balaam to consequence of war-time slaughter at the hands of Priestly (Num 31) and later-Deuteronomistic tradents (Josh 13).

Summary

The DAPT and the poetic oracles of Num 22–24 represent a Transjordanian tradition of Balaam as an international "seer of the gods," privy to the higher, international level of the pantheon headed by El. As a spokesman for the whole of "the gods," who oversee the larger cosmic framework within which kings receive their power to rule their own realms, Balaam stands as a potential friend of the state but, for the same reason, as a latent threat. Balaam's consistent associations with divinely ordained disaster in these texts suggests that he was viewed ultimately as an enemy of kings and kingdoms, the archetype of the prophet known throughout biblical literature (see especially Mic 3:5–12; Jer 28:8; cf. the Zakkur Inscription).

The other biblical Balaam texts may be understood to derive from essentially the same Balaam tradition found in Num 22–24, in which Balaam encounters Israel subsequent to the exodus and in the course of settlement east of the Jordan. The biblical Balaam traditions are set apart from the DAPT and together reflect a trajectory of Israelite-Judean literary appropriation, and then rejection, of the renowned prophetic figure Balaam for nationalistic purposes. Israel and Judah's changing fortunes in relationship to neighboring kingdoms and imperial powers throughout Iron II times and later correlate with the biblical texts' shifting views of Balaam and cultic roles ascribed to him. The final loss of Israelite holdings in Transjordan (734 B.C.E.), the fall of the northern Israelite kingdom (721 B.C.E.), and Deuteronomy's reframing of Israel's legacy in terms of heightened nationalism under the kingdom of Judah form the historical-political background against which Balaam appeared increasingly to speak for divine powers at odds with Israel during the 7th century B.C.E. and later. It is this ideological and literary legacy of the state that eventually brought about the literary death of Balaam as one who presumes to advocate divine authority over peoples and kingdoms that transcends the purview of YHWH, Israel's God.

Bibliography

Ahlström, G. W. *The History of Ancient Palestine*. Minneapolis, MN: Fortress, 1994.

Andersen, F. I., and David Noel Freedman. *Micah: A New Translation with Introduction and Commentary*. AB 24E. New York: Doubleday, 2000.

Aufrecht, W. E. *A Corpus of Ammonite Inscriptions*. Ancient Near Eastern Texts and Studies 4. Lewiston, NY: Mellen, 1989.

_____. "Ammonite Texts and Language." Pp. 163–88 in *Ancient Ammon*. Edited by Burton MacDonald and Randall W. Younker. SHCANE 17. Leiden: Brill, 1999.

_____. "Prolegomenon to the Study of Old Aramaic and Ammonite Lapidary Inscriptions." Pp. 100–106 in *"An Eye for Form:" Epigraphic Essays in Honor of Frank Moore Cross*. Edited by J. A. Hackett, W. E. Aufrecht, and M. G. Amadasi. Winona Lake, IN: Eisenbrauns, 2014.

_____. "The Religion of the Ammonites." Pp. 152–62 in *Ancient Ammon*. Edited by B. MacDonald, R. W. Younker, and W. E. Aufrecht. SHCANE 17. Leiden: Brill, 1999.

Becking, B. *Between Fear and Freedom: Essays on the Interpretation of Jeremiah 30–31*. OtSt 51. Leiden: Brill, 2004.

_____. *Biblical Archaeology Today: Proceedings of the International Congress on Biblical Archaeology, Jerusalem, April 1984*. Jerusalem: Israel Exploration Society, 1985.

Biran, A., and J. Naveh. "The Tel Dan Inscription: A New Fragment." *IEJ* 45 (1995) 1–18.

Blum, E. "Die altaramäischen Wandinschriften vom Tell Deir ʿAlla und ihr institutioneller Kontext." Pp. 21–52 in *Metatexte: Erzählungen von Schrifttragenden Artefakten in der alttestamentlichen und mittelalterlichen Literatur*. Edited by F.-E. Focken and M. R. Ott. Materiale Textkulturen 15. Berlin: de Gruyter, 2016.

_____. "Die Kombination I der Wandinschrift vom Tell Deir ʿAlla: Vorschläge zur Rekonstruktion mit historisch-kritischen Anmerkungen." Pp. 573–601 in *Berührungspunkte: Studien zur Sozial- und Religionsgeschichte Israels und seiner Umwelt. Festschrift für Rainer Albertz zu seinem 65. Geburtstag*. Edited by I. Kottsieper et al. AOAT 350. Münster: Ugarit-Verlag, 2008.

_____. "ʿVerstehst du dich nicht auf die Schreibkunst. . . ?' Ein weisheitlicher Dialog über Vergänglichkeit und Verantwortung: Kombination II der Wandinschrift vom Tell Deir ʿAlla." Pp. 33–53 in *Was ist der Mensch, dass du seiner gedankst? (Psalm 8,5): Festschrift für Bernd Janowski zum 65. Geburtstag*. Edited by M. Bauks et al. Neukirchen-Vluyn: Neukirchener Verlag, 2008.

Boertien, J. "Iron Age Loom Weights from Tall Dayr ʿAlla in Jordan." *ADAJ* 48 (2004) 305–32.

_____. *Unravelling the Fabric Textile Production in Iron Age Transjordan*. PhD diss., Rijksuniversiteit Groningen, 2013.

_____. "Unravelling the Threads: Textiles and Shrines in the Iron Age." Pp. 135–51 in *Sacred and Sweet: Studies on the Material Culture of Tell Deir ʿAlla and Tell Abu Sarbut*. Edited by M. Steiner and E. J. van der Steen. ANESSup 24. Leuven: Peeters, 2008.

Bourke, S. "The Six Canaanite Temples of Ṭabaqāt Faḥil: Excavating Pellaʾs 'Fortress' Temple (1994–2009)." Pp. 159–201 in *Temple Building and Temple Cult: Architecture and Cultic Paraphernalia of Temples in the Levant (2.-1. Mill. B.C.E.)*. Edited by J. Kamlah. ADPV 41. Wiesbaden: Harrassowitz, 2012.

Boling, R. G. *The Early Biblical Community in Transjordan*. The Social World of Biblical Antiquity Series 6. Sheffield: Sheffield Academic, 1988.

Burnett, J. S. *A Reassessment of Biblical Elohim*. SBLDS 183. Atlanta: SBL, 2001.

_____. "'Come and See What God Has Done!' Divine Presence and the Reversal of Reproach in the Elohistic Psalter and in Iron Age West Semitic Inscriptions." Pp. 213–54 in *Divine Presence and Absence in Exilic and Post-Exilic Judaism: Studies of the Sofja Kovalevskaja Research Group on Early Jewish Monotheism, Vol. II*. Edited by N. MacDonald and I. J. de Hulster. FAT II/61. Tübingen: Mohr Siebeck, 2013.

_____. "'Going Down' to Bethel: Elijah and Elisha in the Theological Geography of the Deuteronomistic History." *JBL* 129 (2010) 281–97.

_____. "Iron Age Deities in Word, Image, and Name: Correlating Epigraphic, Iconographic, and Onomastic Evidence for the Ammonite God." *SHAJ* 10 (2009) 153–64.

Caquot, A., and A. Lemaire. "Les textes araméens de Deir 'Alla." *Syria* 54 (1977) 189–208.

Cross, F. M. *Canaanite Myth and Hebrew Epic*. Cambridge, MA: Harvard University Press, 1973.

_____. *From Epic to Canon: History and Literature in Ancient Israel*. Baltimore: Johns Hopkins University Press, 1998.

_____. *Leaves from an Epigrapher's Notebook: Collected Papers in Hebrew and West Semitic Palaeography and Epigraphy*. HSS 51. Winona Lake, IN: Eisenbrauns, 2003.

_____, and L. T. Geraty. "The Ammonite Ostraca from Tell Hesban." Pp. 169–75 in *Hesban after 25 Years*. Edited by D. Merling and L. T. Geraty. Berrien Springs, MI: The Institute of Archaeology/Siegried H. Horn Archaeological Museum, 1994.

Day, J. *Yahweh and the Gods and Goddesses of Canaan*. JSOTSup 265. Sheffield: Sheffield Academic, 2000.

Delcor, M. "Balaam pâtôrâh, interprète de songes au pays d'Ammon, d'après Num 22, 5. Les témoignages épigraphiques parallèles." *Sem* 32 (1982) 89–91.

Dijkstra, M. "Is Balaam Also among the Prophets?" *JBL* 114 (1995) 43–64.

Dion, P.-E. *Les Araméens à l'âge du fer: histoire politique et structures sociales*. Études bibliques, NS 34. Paris: Gabalda, 1997.

_____. "Les araméens du Moyen-Euphrate au VIIIᵉ siècle à la lumière des inscriptions des maîtres de Suhu et Mari." Pp. 53–74 in *Congress Volume, Paris 1992*. Edited by J. Emerton. VTSup 61. Leiden: Brill, 1995.

_____. "Syro-Palestinian Resistance to Shalmaneser III in the Light of New Documents." *ZAW* 107 (1995) 482–89.

Fitzmyer, J. A. Review of *Aramaic Texts from Deir 'Alla*, by J. Hoftijzer and G. van der Kooij. *CBQ* 40 (1978) 94–95.

Fleming, D. *The Legacy of Israel in Judah's Bible: History, Politics, and the Reinscribing of Tradition*. New York: Cambridge University Press, 2012.

Franken, H. J. "Deir 'Alla and Its Religion." Pp. 25–52 in *Sacred and Sweet: Studies on the Material Culture of Tell Deir 'Alla and Tell Abu Sarbut*. Edited by M. L. Steiner and E. J. van der Steen. ANESSup 24. Leuven: Peeters, 2008.

_____. "Archaeological Evidence Relating to the Interpretation of the Text." Pp. 3–22 in *Aramaic Texts from Deir 'Alla*. Edited by J. Hoftijzer and G. van der Kooij. DMOA 19. Leiden: Brill, 1976.

_____. *Excavations at Tell Deir 'Alla*. DMOA 16. Leiden: Brill, 1969.

Freedman, D. N., Edited by *Anchor Bible Dictionary*. 6 vols. New York: Doubleday, 1992.

_____, Edited by *Eerdmans Dictionary of the Bible*. Grand Rapids, MI: Eerdmans, 2000.

Garr, W. R. *Dialect Geography of Syria-Palestine, 1000–586 B.C.E.* Philadelphia: University of Pennsylvania Press, 1985. Repr., Winona Lake, IN: Eisenbrauns, 2004.

Gray, G. B. *A Critical and Exegetical Commentary on Numbers*. ICC 4. Edinburgh: T. & T. Clark, 1903.

Greene, J. T. *Balaam and His Interpreters: A Hermeneutical History of the Balaam Traditions*. BJS 244. Atlanta: Scholars Press, 1992.

Greenfield, J. C. "Philological Observations on the Deir ʿAlla Inscription." Pp. 109–20 in *The Balaam Text from Deir ʿAlla Re-Evaluated: Proceedings of the International Symposium Held at Leiden, 21–24 August 1989*. Edited by J. Hoftijzer and G. van der Kooij. Leiden: Brill, 1991.

Hackett, J. A. "Religious Traditions in Israelite Transjordan." Pp. 125–36 in *Ancient Israelite Religion: Essays in Honor of Frank Moore Cross*. Edited by P. D. Miller Jr., P. D. Hanson, and S. D. McBride. Philadelphia: Fortress, 1987.

_____. "Some Observations on the Balaam Tradition at Deir ʿAllā." *BA* 49:4 (1986) 216–22.

_____. *The Balaam Text from Deir ʿAlla*. HSM 31. Chico, CA: Scholars Press, 1984.

Hallo, W. W., ed. *Monumental Inscriptions from the Biblical World*. Vol. 2 of *The Context of Scripture*. Leiden: Brill, 1997.

Halpern, B. "Dialect Distribution in Canaan and the Deir ʿAlla Inscriptions." Pp. 119–39 in *"Working with No Data": Semitic and Egyptian Studies Presented to Thomas O. Lambdin*. Edited by D. M. Golomb and S. T. Hollis. Winona Lake, IN: Eisenbrauns, 1987.

_____. "The Taking of Nothing: 2 Kings 14.25, Amos 6.14 and the Geography of the Deuteronomistic History." Pp. 186–204 in *The World of the Aramaeans I: Biblical Studies in Honour of Paul-Eugène Dion*. Edited by P. M. M. Daviau et al. JSOTSup 324. Sheffield: Sheffield Academic, 2001.

Herr, L. G. "Aramaic and Ammonite Seal Scripts." Pp. 175–86 in *"An Eye for Form: Epigraphic Essays in Honor of Frank Moore Cross*. Edited by J. A. Hackett and W. F. Aufrecht. Winona Lake, IN: Eisenbrauns, 2014.

_____. "The Iron Age II Period: Emerging Nations." *BA* 60:3 (1997) 114–83.

Herrmann, W. "El." Pp. 274–80 in *Dictionary of Deities and Demons in the Bible*. 2nd rev. Edited by Edited by K. van der Toorn, B. Becking, and P. W. van der Horst. Grand Rapids, MI: Eerdmans, 1999.

Hillers, D. R. *Micah: A Commentary on the Book of the Prophet Micah*. Hermeneia. Philadelphia: Fortress, 1984.

_____. "Palmyrene Aramaic Inscriptions and the Bible." *ZAH* 11 (1998) 32–49.

Hoftijzer, J. "General Remarks on the Plaster Texts." Pp. 268–82 in *Aramaic Texts from Deir ʿAlla*. Edited by J. Hoftijzer and G. van der Kooij. DMOA 19. Leiden: Brill, 1976.

Hoftijzer, J., and G. van der Kooij. *Aramaic Texts from Deir ʿAlla*. DMOA 19. Leiden: Brill, 1976.

Huehnergard, J. "Remarks on the Classification of the Northwest Semitic Languages." Pp. 282–93 in *The Balaam Texts from Deir ʿAlla Re-evaluated: Proceedings of the International Symposium Held at Leiden, 21–24 August 1989*. Leiden: Brill, 1991.

Huffmon, H. B. "A Company of Prophets: Mari, Assyria, Israel." Pp. 47–70 in *Prophecy in Its Ancient Near Eastern Context: Mesopotamian, Biblical, and Arabian Perspectives*. Edited by M. Nissinen. SBLSS 13. Atlanta: SBL, 2000.

_____ . "The One and the Many: Prophets and Deities in the Ancient Near East." Pp. 116–31 in *Propheten in Mari, Assyrien und Israel*. Edited by M. Köckert and M. Nissinen. FRLANT 201. Göttingen: Vandenhoeck & Ruprecht, 2003.

Jackson, K. P. "The Language of the Mesha⁽ Inscription." Pp. 93–130 in *Studies in the Mesha Inscription and Moab*. Edited by J. A. Dearman. ABS 2. Atlanta: Scholars Press, 1989.

_____ , and J. A. Dearman. "The Text of the Mesha⁽ Inscription." Pp. 93–130 in *Studies in the Mesha Inscription and Moab*. Edited by J. A. Dearman. ABS 2. Atlanta: Scholars Press, 1989.

Japhet, S. *The Ideology of the Book of Chronicles and Its Place in Biblical Thought*. Translated by A. Barber. Winona Lake, IN: Eisenbrauns, 2009.

Jastrow, M. *A Dictionary of the Targumim, the Talmud Babli and Yerushalmi, and the Midrashic Literature*. New York: Judaica, 1992.

Jeremias, J. *Die Propheten Joel, Obadja, Jona, Micha*. ATD 24,3. Göttingen: Vandenhoeck & Ruprecht, 2007.

Joüon, P., and T. Muraoka. *A Grammar of Biblical Hebrew*. SubBi 14/1. Rome: Pontifical Biblical Institute, 1993.

Kitz, A. M. *Cursed Are You! The Phenomenology of Cursing in Cuneiform and Hebrew Texts*. Winona Lake, IN: Eisenbrauns, 2014.

Knauf, E. A. "Shadday." Pp. 749–53 in *Dictionary of Deities and Demons in the Bible*. Edited by K. van der Toorn, B. Becking, and P. W. van der Horst. Leiden: Brill, 1995.

Koehler, L, W. Baumgartner, and J. J. Stamm. *The Hebrew and Aramaic Lexicon of the Old Testament*. Trans. M. E. J. Richardson. Leiden: Brill, 1994.

Kooij, G. van der. "Book and Script at Deir ⁽Alla." Pp. 239–62 in *The Balaam Text from Deir ⁽alla Re-Evaluated: Proceedings of the International Symposium Held at Leiden, 21–24 August 1989*. Edited by J. Hoftijzer and G. van der Kooij. Leiden: Brill, 1991.

_____ . "The Plaster and Other Materials Used." Pp. 22–28 in *Aramaic Texts from Deir ⁽Alla*. Edited by J. Hoftijzer and G. van der Kooij. DMOA 19. Leiden: Brill, 1976.

_____ , and M. H. Ibrahim. *Picking up the Threads . . . A Continuing Review of Excavations at Deir Alla, Jordan*. Leiden: University of Leiden Archaeological Centre, 1989.

Kruger, P. A. "A World Turned on Its Head in Ancient Near Eastern Prophetic Literature: A Powerful Strategy to Depict Chaotic Scenarios." *VT* 62 (2012) 58–76.

Lauinger, J. "Esarhaddon's Succession Treaty at Tell Tayinat: Text and Commentary." *JCS* 64 (2012) 87–123.

Leemans, J. " 'To Bless with a Mount Bent on Cursing': Patristic Interpretations of Balaam (Num 24:17)." Pp. 287–99 in *The Prestige of the Pagan Prophet Balaam in Judaism, Early Christianity and Islam*. Edited by G. H. van Kooten and J. van Ruiten. TBN 11. Leiden: Brill, 2008.

Lemaire, A. "Les premiers rois araméens dans la tradition biblique." Pp. 113–43 in *The World of the Aramaeans I: Biblical Studies in Honour of Paul-Eugène Dion*. Edited by P. M. M. Daviau, J. W. Wevers, and M. Weigl. JSOTSup 324. Sheffield: Sheffield Academic, 2001.

Levine, B. A. *Numbers 21–36: A New Translation with Introduction and Commentary*. AB 4A. New Haven, CT: Yale University Press, 2000.

_____ . "The Balaam Inscription from Deir ⁽Alla: Historical Aspects." Pp. 326–39 in *Biblical Archaeology Today: Proceedings of the International Congress on Biblical Archaeology, Jerusalem, April 1984*. Jerusalem: Israel Exploration Society, 1985.

Levinson, B. M. "Die neuassyrischen Ursprünge der Kanonformel in Deuteronomium 13,1." Pp. 61–82 in *Viele Wege zu dem Einen: Historische Bibelkritik—die Vitalität der Glaubensüberlieferung in der Moderne*. Edited by Stefan Beyerle, Axel Graupner, Udo Rüterswörden, and Ferdinand Ahuis. Biblisch-theologische Studien 121. Neukirchen-Vluyn: Neukirchener Verlag, 2012.

————, and J. Stackert. "The Limitations of 'Resonance:' A Response to Joshua Berman on Historical and Comparative Method." *Journal of Ancient Judaism* 4 (2013) 310–33.

Lipiński, E. *Studies in Aramaic Inscriptions and Onomastics II*. OLA 57. Leuven: Peeters, 1994.

MacDonald, B. *"East of the Jordan:" Territories and Sites of the Hebrew Scriptures*. ASOR Books 6. Boston, MA: ASOR, 2000.

Malamat, A. "The Secret Council and Prophetic Involvement in Mari and Israel." Pp. 231–36 in *Prophetie und geschichtliche Wirklichkeit im alten Israel: Festschrift für Siegfried Herrmann zum 65. Geburtstag*. Edited by R. Liwak and S. Wagner. Stuttgart: Kohlhammer, 1991.

McCarter, P. K., Jr. "The Balaam Texts from Deir ʿAllā: The First Combination." *BASOR* 239 (1980) 49–60.

————. "The Dialect of the Deir ʿAlla Texts." Pp. 87–99 in *The Balaam Text from Deir ʿAlla Re-Evaluated: Proceedings of the International Symposium Held at Leiden, 21–24 August 1989*. Edited by J. Hoftijzer and G. van der Kooij. Leiden: Brill, 1991.

Milgrom, J. *Numbers*. The JPS Torah Commentary. Philadelphia: JPS, 1990.

Mittmann, S., and G. Schmitt. *Tübinger Bibelatlas*. Stuttgart: Deutsche Bibelgesellschaft, 2001.

Moran, W. L. "Ancient Near Eastern Background of the Love of God in Deuteronomy." *CBQ* 25 (1963) 77–87.

Mowinckel, S. "Die Ursprung Der Bileamsage." *ZAW* 48 (1930) 233–71.

Nicklas, T. "Balaam and the Star of the Magi." Pp. 233–46 in *The Prestige of the Pagan Prophet Balaam in Judaism, Early Christianity and Islam*. Edited by G. H. van Kooten and J. van Ruiten. TBN 11. Leiden: Brill, 2008.

Nissinen, M. "Das kritische Potential in der altorientalischen Prophetie." Pp. 1–32 in *Propheten in Mari, Assyrien und Israel*. Edited by M. Köckert and M. Nissinen. FRLANT 201. Göttingen: Vandenhoeck & Ruprecht, 2003.

————. "The Socioreligious Role of the Neo-Assyrian Prophets." Pp. 89–114 in *Prophecy in Its Ancient Near Eastern Context: Mesopotamian, Biblical, and Arabian Perspectives*. Edited by M. Nissinen. SBLSS 13. Atlanta: SBL, 2000.

Nogalski, J. D. *The Book of the Twelve: Micah–Malachi*. SHBC. Macon, GA: Smyth & Helwys, 2011.

Noort, E. "Balaam the Villain: The History of Reception of the Balaam Narrative in the Pentateuch and the Former Prophets." Pp. 3–23 in *The Prestige of the Pagan Prophet Balaam in Judaism, Early Christianity and Islam*. Edited by G. H. van Kooten and J. van Ruiten. TBN 11. Leiden: Brill, 2008.

Noth, M. *The Deuteronomistic History*. JSOTSup 15. Sheffield: JSOT Press, 1981.

Oded, B. "Observations on Methods of Assyrian Rule in Transjordania after the Palestinian Campaign of Tiglath-Pileser III." *JNES* 29 (1970) 177–86.

Pardee, D. "The Linguistic Classification of the Deir ʿAlla Text Written on Plaster." Pp. 100–105 in *The Balaam Text from Deir ʿAlla Re-Evaluated: Proceedings of the International*

Symposium Held at Leiden, 21–24 August 1989. Edited by J. Hoftijzer and G. van der Kooij. Leiden: Brill, 1991.

Perdue, L. G. "Cosmology and the Social Order in the Wisdom Tradition." Pp. 457–78 in *The Sage in Israel and the Ancient Near East*. Edited by J. G. Gammie and L. G. Perdue. Winona Lake, IN: Eisenbrauns, 1990.

Petter, T. D. *The Land between the Two Rivers: Early Israelite Identities in Central Transjordan*. Winona Lake, IN: Eisenbrauns, 2014.

Pongratz-Leisten, B. *Herrschaftswissen in Mesopotamien: Formen der Kommunikation zwischen Gott und Konig in 2. und 1. Jahrtausend v. Chr*. SAAS 10. Helsinki: Neo-Assyrian Text Corpus Project, 1999.

_____. "When the Gods are Speaking: Toward Defining the Interface between Polytheism and Monotheism." Pp. 132–68 in *Propheten in Mari, Assyrien und Israel*. Edited by M. Köckert and M. Nissinen. FRLANT 201. Göttingen: Vandenhoeck & Ruprecht, 2003.

Pritchard, J. B. *Tell Es-Sa'idiyeh: Excavations on the Tell, 1964–1966*. University Museum Monograph 60. Philadelphia: University Museum, University of Pennsylvania, 1985.

Puech, E. "Balaam and Deir ʿAlla." Pp. 25–47 in *The Prestige of the Pagan Prophet Balaam in Judaism, Early Christianity and Islam*. Edited by G. H. van Kooten and J. van Ruiten. TBN 11. Leiden: Brill, 2008.

_____. "Le texte 'ammonite' de Deir ʿAlla: Les admonitions de Balaam (première partie)." Pp. 13–30 in *La vie de la parole, de l'Ancien au Nouveau Testament: Études d'exégèse et d'herméneutique bibliques offertes à Pierre Grelot*. Edited by P. Grelot. Paris: Desclée, 1987.

Rainey, A. F., and R. S. Notley. *The Sacred Bridge: Carta's Atlas of the Biblical World*. Jerusalem: Carta, 2006.

Ray, P. J. *Tell Hesban and Vicinity in the Iron Age*. Hesban 6. Berrien Springs, MI: Andrews University Press, 2001.

Robker, J. M. "Reception, Citation, and Balaam: A Test-Case and Methodological Reflections." Paper presented at the annual meeting of the Society of Biblical Literature. San Diego, CA, November 23, 2014.

_____. "The Balaam Narrative in the Pentateuch/Hexateuch/Enneateuch." Pp. 334–66 in *Torah and the Book of Numbers*. Edited by C. Frevel, T. Pola, and A. Schart. FAT II/62. Tübingen: Mohr Siebeck, 2013.

Röllig, W., and H. Donner. *Kanaandische und aramäische Inschriften*. 2nd ed. Wiesbaden: Harrassowitz, 1966.

Rollston, C. A. *Writing and Literacy in the World of Ancient Israel: Epigraphic Evidence from the Iron Age*. ABS 11. Atlanta: SBL, 2010.

Römer, T. *The So-Called Deuteronomistic History: A Sociological, Historical and Literary Introduction*. New York: T. & T. Clark, 2005. Repr., 2007.

Routledge, B. *Moab in the Iron Age: Hegemony, Polity, Archaeology*. Philadelphia: University of Pennsylvania Press, 2004.

_____. "The Politics of Mesha: Segmented Identities and State Formation in Iron Age Moab." *JESHO* 43 (2000) 221–56.

Russell, S. C. *Images of Egypt in Early Biblical Literature: Cisjordan-Israelite, Transjordan-Israelite, and Judahite Portrayals*. BZAW 403. Berlin: de Gruyter, 2009.

Sasson, J. M. *Judges 1–12*: A New Translation with Introduction and Commentary. AB 6D. New Haven, CT: Yale University Press, 2014.

Sasson, V. "The Book of Oracular Visions of Balaam from Deir ʿAlla." *UF* 17 (1986) 283–309.

Sauer, J. A. "The Pottery at Hesban and Its Relationship to the History of Jordan: An Interim Hesban Pottery Report, 1993." Pp. 225–81 in *Hesban after 25 Years*. Edited by D. Merling and L. T. Geraty. Berrien Springs, MI: The Institute of Archaeology/ Siegried H. Horn Archaeological Museum, 1994.

Schmitt, R. *Mantik im Alten Testament*. AOAT 411. Münster: Ugarit-Verlag, 2014.

Seow, C. L. "West Semitic Sources." Pp. 201–218 in *Prophets and Prophecy in the Ancient Near East*, by M. Nissinen. Edited by Peter Machinist. WAW 12. Atlanta: SBL, 2003.

Smend, R. "The Law and the Nations: A Contribution to Deuteronomistic Tradition History." Pp. 95–110 in *Reconsidering Israel and Judah: Recent Studies on the Deuteronomistic History*. Edited by G. N. Knoppers and J. G. McConville. Sources for Biblical and Theological Study 8. Winona Lake, IN: Eisenbrauns, 2000.

Smith, M. S. *God in Translation: Deities in Cross-Cultural Discourse in the Biblical World*. FAT 57. Grand Rapids, MI: Eerdmans, 2010.

_____. *Poetic Heroes: Literary Commemorations of Warriors and Warrior Culture in the Early Biblical World*. Grand Rapids, MI: Eerdmans, 2014.

_____. *The Early History of God: Yahweh and the Other Deities in Ancient Israel*. 2nd Edited by The Biblical Resource Series. Grand Rapids, MI: Eerdmans, 2002.

_____. *The Memoirs of God: History, Memory, and the Experience of the Divine in Ancient Israel*. Minneapolis, MN: Fortress, 2004.

_____. *The Origins of Biblical Monotheism: Israel's Polytheistic Background and the Ugaritic Texts*. Oxford: Oxford University Press, 2001.

Smith, S. *The Statue of Idri-Mi*. London: British Institute of Archaeology in Ankara, 1949.

Speiser, E. A. *Genesis*. AB 1. Garden City, NY: Doubleday, 1964.

Stavrakopoulou, F., and J. Barton, Edited by *Religious Diversity in Ancient Israel and Judah*. New York: T. & T. Clark, 2010.

Steen, E. J. van der. "Introduction: Tell Deir ʿAlla in the Late Bronze and Iron Ages." Pp. 17–24 in *Sacred and Sweet: Studies on the Material Culture of Tell Deir ʿAlla and Tell Abu Sarbut*. Edited by M. L. Steiner and E. J. van der Steen. ANESSup 24. Leuven: Peeters, 2008.

Steymans, H. U. "Deuteronomy 28 and Tell Tayinat." *Verbum et Ecclesia* 34:2 (2013) 1–13.

Stökl, J. *Prophecy in the Ancient Near East: A Philological and Sociological Comparison*. CHANE 56. Leiden: Brill, 2012.

Tadmor, H. *The Inscriptions of Tiglath-Pileser III, King of Assyria: Critical Edition, with Introductions, Translations, and Commentary*. Jerusalem: Israel Academy of Sciences and Humanities, 1994.

Tigay, J. H. *Deuteronomy*. The JPS Torah Commentary. Philadelphia: JPS, 1996.

Thompson, H. O. "Balaam in the Bible and at Deir ʿAllā." Sidebar to "Some Observations on the Balaam Tradition at Deir ʿAllā," by J. A. Hackett. *BA* 49:4 (1986) 218–19.

Toorn, K. van der. "Mesopotamian Prophecy between Immanence and Transcendence: A Comparison of Old Babylonian and Neo-Assyrian Prophecy." Pp. 71–87 in *Prophecy in Its Ancient Near Eastern Context: Mesopotamian, Biblical, and Arabian Perspectives*. Edited by Martti Nissinen. SBLSS 13. Atlanta: SBL, 2000.

Tropper, J. "Dialektvielfalt und Sprachwandel im frühen Aramäischen: Sozioloinguistische Überlegungen." Pp. 213–22 in *The World of the Arameans III: Studies in Language and Literature in Honour of Paul-Eugene Dion.* Edited by P. M. M. Daviau, J. W. Wevers, and M. Weigl. JSOTSup 326. Sheffield: Sheffield Academic, 2001.

Vaux, R. de. *Ancient Israel: Its Life and Institutions.* Trans. J. McHugh. New York: McGraw-Hill, 1961. Repr., 1997.

Wagner, A. Edited by *Parallelismus membrorum.* OBO 224. Göttingen: Vandenhoeck & Ruprecht, 2007.

Watson, W. G. E. *Classical Hebrew Poetry: A Guide to Its Techniques.* Corrected edition. JSOTSup 26. London: T. & T. Clark, 1984.

Weinfeld, M. *Deuteronomy 1–11: A New Translation with Introduction and Commentary.* AB 5. New York: Doubleday, 1991.

Weippert, H., and M. Weippert. "Die „Bileam"-Inschrift von Tell Dēr ʾAllā." *ZDPV* 98 (1982) 77–103.

Wenning, Robert, and E. Zenger. "Heiligtum ohne Stadt—Stadt ohne Heiligtum? Anmerkungen zum archäologischen Befund des Tell Dēr ʿAllā." *ZAH* 4 (1991) 171–93.

Wijngaarden, G. J. van."Dots Close Together on a Map: Mycenaean Pottery in the Jordan Valley." Pp. 53–67 in *Sacred and Sweet: Studies on the Material Culture of Tell Deir ʿAlla and Tell Abu Sarbut.* Edited by M. L. Steiner and E. J. van der Steen. ANESSup 24. Leuven: Peeters, 2008.

Wilson, R. R. *Prophecy and Society in Ancient Israel.* Philadelphia: Fortress, 1980.

Yassine, K., and J. Teixidor. "Ammonite and Aramaic Inscriptions from Tell El-Mazār in Jordan." *BASOR* 264 (1986) 45–50.

Part 3

---

*Prophets in the Deuteronomistic
History and the Chronicler*

Prophets in the Early Monarchy

WILLIAM M. SCHNIEDEWIND

University of California, Los Angeles

The origins of biblical prophecy are difficult to ascertain, but the appearance of prophets in the biblical accounts is closely associated with the rise of the monarchy.[1] Unfortunately, there are few contemporary sources (apart from the Bible) to rely upon when analyzing prophets in the early monarchy. The biblical accounts themselves are unlikely to have been penned in the days of David and Solomon but rather represent later textualization of oral traditions as well as literary and theological renderings of Israel's early history. In light of this, the following analysis of the prophets in the court of David attempts to summarize and contextualize the biblical accounts of the early prophets.[2] According to later Jewish tradition, prophecy rose with the monarchy and disappeared with the last Judean king.[3] This is not far from the perspective of the biblical narratives. While the anthropological role of prophets might be much more complex, the biblical literary portrait of prophets and prophecy conforms to the later Jewish tradition. The role of prophets in ancient Israel is closely tied to the rise of the monarchy and to the court of David. Biblical prophets played a critical role in establishing the monarchy, counseling the kings, and overseeing the succession.

It is worth beginning with a short discussion of the relevant terms for *prophet*. These terms are most variable in the accounts of prophets of the early monarchy. The Hebrew title most commonly associated with biblical prophets is נביא. While the term נביא for the prophet has etymological parallels stretching back into at least the Middle Bronze Age at places such as Mari, it is unclear whether this would have been the term used in the early Iron Age. For example, we read among the accounts of Samuel's anointing of Saul the following:

---

1. Classically articulated by F. M. Cross, *Canaanite Myth and Hebrew Epic: Essays in the History of the Religion of Israel* (Cambridge, MA: Harvard University Press, 1973), 223–29.

2. Note, for example, a similar approach in the recent work by W. Oswald, *Nathan der Prophet: Eine Untersuchung zu 2 Samuel 7 und 12 und 1 Könige 1* (ATANT, 94; Zurich: Theologischer Verlag, 2008).

3. See L. S. Cook, *On the Question of the "Cessation of Prophecy" in Ancient Judaism* (Texts and Studies in Ancient Judaism 145; Tübingen: Mohr Siebeck, 2011).

The boy answered Saul again, "Here, I have with me a quarter shekel of silver;
I will give it to the man of God [איש האלהים], to tell us our way." (Formerly in
Israel, anyone who went to inquire of God would say, "Come, let us go to the seer
[הראה]"; for the one who is now called a prophet [נביא] was formerly called a
seer.) Saul said to the boy, "Good; come, let us go." So they went to the town where
the man of God was. As they went up the hill to the town, they met some girls
coming out to draw wate, and said to them, "Is the seer here?" (1 Sam 9:8–11).

This passage should give us pause about the usefulness of early parallels that have
been used to explain the meaning of נביא. The biblical understanding of this role is
probably rooted in the formative literary period of biblical literature, particularly
prophetic literature—namely, the late eighth and seventh centuries, when this
self-reflective scribal note was probably penned. Interestingly enough, the term
ראה itself is not the main word for "seer" in the Hebrew Bible. It is much more
common to use the term חזה, which also may be translated "seer." Both terms are
nevertheless derivations of words for "seeing," as opposed to the word נביא, which
seems to emphasize the calling of the prophet. This indicates that the most typical term for prophet in the Hebrew Bible, נביא, was coined later and then applied
(anachronistically) to earlier stories, and it probably reflects later developments
in the understanding of the function of the prophet. The term ראה is restricted
in biblical narratives to the early stories about prophets. It is particularly applied
to Samuel but also applied in Chronicles to Hanani (2 Chr 16:7, 10), who appears
in the account of King Asa, the grandson of Solomon. The term is not used for
prophets later in the narrative, which suggests an awareness of the anachronistic
nature of the term on the part of later writers, as is indicated by 1 Sam 9:9.

Narratives dealing with the early Israelite monarchy utilize a court 'seer' (חזה)
as a central adviser to the king. For example, we read in 2 Sam 24:1: "When David rose in the morning, the word of the LORD came to Gad, the prophet [נביא],
David's seer [חזה]." The royal stela of King Zakir of Hamath (ca. 800 B.C.E.) also
mentions 'seers' (חזין and עדדן) who are inspired by Baal-shamaym to prophesy
in the service of the court against the king's enemies (KAI 202A:13–15). In this
respect, these figures seem to function as court prophets who advise the king,
particularly in matters of warfare. The term 'seer' (חזה) is also known from the
Deir ʿAlla plaster text (ca. 800 B.C.E.), where it is applied to a certain Balaam, who
is also known in the Bible. Balaam is described in early biblical poetry as follows:
"The oracle of Balaam son of Beor, the oracle of the man whose eye is clear, the
oracle of one who hears the words of God, who *sees the vision* of the Almighty
[מחזה שדי יחזה], who falls down, but with eyes uncovered" (Num 24:3–4). The
other term in the Zakir inscription, עדדן 'seers/prophets', may be preserved in a
few personal names given to prophetic figures in the biblical accounts, particularly
Azariah, son of Oded (עדד), a prophet who counseled the Judean king Asa (late
tenth or early ninth century B.C.E.) according to Chronicles (2 Chr 15:8; cf. also
2 Chr 28:9). Chronicles also records that "Iddo, the seer" (עדו החזה) wrote down

the records for Solomon, Rehoboam, and Abijah (2 Chr 9:29; 12:15; 13:22). Both names, Iddo and Oded, are formed from the same root עדד known from the Zakir inscription, and it seems likely that Chronicles has created a personal name from an early title for a court prophet.

Before the appearance of the monarchy in the biblical narrative, prophets play no significant role. Most notably, prophets play almost no role in the patriarchal narratives nor do they play a significant role in the books of Joshua and Judges. The few applications of the title "prophet" in the Pentateuch serve later literary and theological purposes. For example, Aaron is a נביא 'prophet' for Moses (Exod 7:1), but the title is not carried on in the narrative. Elsewhere, the book of Deuteronomy promises that "a prophet like Moses" shall arise (Deut 18:15–18), although ironically Moses is never labeled a נביא elsewhere in the Pentateuch. A major literary figure in Judges is the prophetess Deborah, who appears in support of Barak, a local ruler from Kedesh (north of Lake Huleh). Barak was summoned by Deborah to fight against a Canaanite coalition of "kings" (Judg 5:19) headed by Sisera; the role of Deborah highlights the role that prophets seem to play in advising, particularly with regard to military decisions. There have been observations about possible parallels to the prophet in Near Eastern texts from Mari; however, these few parallels are chronologically remote, and they do not constitute evidence of a common social institution that ancient Israel could have been drawing upon centuries later.[4] To be sure, there are some interesting linguistic and functional correspondences, but these should not be overdrawn, given the limited number of parallels and the temporal and geographical distance between these and the much later Judean accounts of prophets and kings.

The role of the prophet rises and falls with the monarchy in biblical literature. We have already noted that the term is lightly used in premonarchial narratives, but it is also true that the term נביא 'prophet' begins to disappear in post-exilic narratives, where it is replaced by terms such as "messenger" and the role of the scribe.[5] It should be emphasized, however, that the disappearance of prophecy is more a literary and theological idea than an anthropological reality.[6] The particular role of the prophet in biblical narratives, however, is tied up with the king, which thereby explains its rise and fall. This may be nicely illustrated in biblical

---

4. The parallels with Mari are especially associated with the work of A. Malamat; see, for example, his *Mari and the Bible* (Studies in the History and Culture of Ancient Near East 12; Leiden: Brill, 1998). Compare B. Levine, review of *Mari and the Bible, IEJ* 50 (2000) 141–43.

5. See W. Schniedewind, *The Word of God in Transition: From Prophet to Exegete in the Second Temple Period* (JSOTSup 197; Sheffield: JSOT, 1995); J. E. Wright, "Baruch: His Evolution from Scribe to Apocalyptic Seer," in *Biblical Figures Outside the Bible* (ed. M. Stone and T. Bergren; Harrisburg, PA: Trinity Press International, 1998), 264–89.

6. See the classic works by R. Wilson, *Prophecy and Society in Ancient Israel* (Philadelphia: Fortress, 1980); T. Overholt, *Channels of Prophecy: The Social Dynamics of Prophetic Activity* (Minneapolis: Fortress, 1989); J. Blenkinsopp, *A History of Prophecy in Israel* (Louisville: Westminster John Knox, 1996), 194–212.

literature by a letter ascribed to Sanballat in the post-exilic book of Nehemiah: "Word has reached the nations, and Geshem too says that you and the Jews are planning to rebel — for which reason you are building the wall — and that you are to be their king. Such is the word. You have also set up prophets in Jerusalem to proclaim about you, 'There is a king in Judah!'" (Neh 6:6–7). From the biblical perspective, the role of the prophet was central to legitimating the king.

The role of the prophet in legitimating the king appears early in the biblical narrative, already in the stories of the prophet Samuel and King Saul. The rise of the prophet essentially comes in the transition from judges to kings as leaders in biblical literature. The figure of Samuel serves as a telling example of the transition from judges to kings and the appearance of the prophets. Samuel is both the last of the judges and the first of the prophets. According to 1 Sam 7:15, "Samuel judged Israel all the days of his life," and when he was old, "he made his sons judges over Israel" (8:1). Yet, Samuel is difficult to classify. He seemingly begins his life as a priest, serving as an apprentice to the priest Eli, and functions in that role when offering sacrifices (see 1 Sam 2:11; 3:1; 7:9; 9:13; 16:1–5). At the same time, the narratives never label Samuel as a priest. Rather, he is a "man of God" (1 Sam 9:7–10) who is known for his clairvoyance as a seer. The title ראה 'seer' is most typically used of Samuel (1 Sam 9:9, 11, 18, 19; 1 Chr 9:22; 26:28; 29:29). Samuel is also labeled a נביא 'prophet' (1 Sam 3:20; cp. 2 Chr 35:18; 1 Esdr 1:20; Sir 46:13–20), and he utilizes the messenger formula "thus says the LORD" that typifies the speech of the classical prophets (see 1 Sam 10:18; 15:2).

All of Samuel's roles—prophet, judge, and priest—are subservient to his literary function as the king designator. Two major narratives framing Samuel's life are his role in designating Saul as the first king of Israel (1 Sam 9:1–10:16) and David as his successor (1 Sam 16:1–13). Moreover, the transition from judges to kings is facilitated by the failure of Samuel's sons as judges (1 Sam 8:1–3). As a result, the elders of Israel turn to Samuel to demand a new type of leadership—kingship (8:4–22); and, this role of Samuel in facilitating the new figure of the king is reiterated by Samuel in the narrative (1 Sam 12:11–17). Even beyond the grave, Samuel is conjured up as an adviser to the king in the well-known story of the medium of En-Dor (1 Sam 28:7–25), in which Samuel gives his last prophecy, foreseeing the downfall of the Saulide dynasty.

Nathan is the first figure in the narrative history that exclusively receives the title נביא 'prophet'. Nathan is also especially tied to the prophetic roles of both legitimating and advising the king. He plays critical roles in the major episodes of David's life according to the biblical accounts: the dynastic oracle to David (2 Sam 7:1–16); his liaison with Bathsheba (2 Sam 12); and, the transfer of power from David to Solomon (1 Kgs 1). Nathan appears suddenly in the biblical narrative in 2 Sam 7 in the role of adviser to King David. David consults this prophet, who is given no pedigree or introduction, about his desire to build a temple. As the narrative constructs it, Nathan gives his own advice to David to go forward with building a temple (2 Sam 7:2–3), a desire that is then thwarted by a prophetic word and vision (חזון) that comes to Nathan, promising an enduring dynasty for the line of David (vv. 4–17). Later, when David commits his egregious sin by taking Bathsheba and having Uriah killed, Nathan confronts him quite cleverly with a story about a rich man who took a poor man's only ewe (2 Sam 12). After the son of the adulterous affair dies, Nathan is also mentioned as coming to support David at the birth of Solomon, presumably to recommend a throne name (Jedidiah) for the newborn (2 Sam 12:25). The critical role of Nathan for the dynastic succession culminates with the account of the transfer of power from David to Solomon, in which the prophet Nathan plots with others concerning the succession and then anoints the new king (1 Kgs 1:11–17, 45).

The prophet Gad also appears as an adviser and confidant of King David. He first appears in the narrative while David is still aspiring to the throne, being pursued by Saul. After David was anointed by Samuel to succeed Saul as king, but before he actually became king, Gad appeared and gave him a word of advice (not explicitly from God) about avoiding capture by Saul (1 Sam 22:5). This actually also fits well with the initial advice given by Nathan to David about the idea of building a temple. That is, the prophets seem to advise without any mention of having received a divine communication. The other story of Gad concerns David's census and is not woven into the narrative account of the DtrH, a situation remedied in the Chronicler's version of David's rise to power (compare 2 Sam 24 and 1 Chr 21). In this story, David is in the middle of an inexplicable crisis arising from his taking of a census (note Exod 30:11–16), and the prophet Gad comes to advise him after "the word of the LORD" comes to Gad. The prophet is still serving in an advisory capacity, but his initial words come directly from God: "Thus says the LORD" (vv. 11–12). Later, Gad seems to offer some of his own practical advice: go make an altar and offer sacrifices in the hope that this would mollify the anger of God (vv. 18–19). The prophet certainly serves as an adviser to the king, yet the prophet's advice is not invariably the words of God. To be sure, the prophet is portrayed as someone with whom God speaks, but he also appears as simply a wise and trusted adviser to the king.

Shortly after the division of the kingdom, a prophet (נביא) by the name of Azariah son of Oded appears in the Chronicler's narrative, offering a word of encouragement to King Asa (1 Chr 15:1–8). As mentioned above, the name Oded can be associated etymologically with the name Iddo, who is described as a 'seer' (חזה) and a scribe in the source citations of Solomon, Rehoboam, and Abijah (2 Chr 9:20, 12:15, and 13:22). Both names are formed from the root עדד, which means 'to declare, respond' and is used in Ugaritic and Old Aramaic for messengers or heralds[7]; it is important to note that this root is not used in Rabbinic Hebrew or later Aramaic. In other words, it was not a term widely used in the post-exilic

---

7. See G. del Olmo Lete and J. Sanmartín, *A Dictionary of the Ugaritic* Language (ed. and trans. W. G. E. Watson; Leiden: Brill, 2004), 1:149; J. Hoftijzer and K. Jongeling, *Dictionary of the North-West Semitic Inscriptions* (Leiden: Brill, 1995), 2:827–28.

period. Thus, it seems most likely the Chronicler found this lexeme in an older source pertaining to royal annals and interpreted it as a personal name. It is a fascinating bit of evidence and adds some tangential support for the correlation of the prophets and monarchy in the early monarchy.

The monarchy begins with Saul and Samuel but also with "a band of prophets" that figures prominently in the tales of Saul's ascension to the throne. While out looking for his uncle's asses, Saul happens upon Samuel, who takes a flask of oil and anoints him as king with the words "Surely, the LORD has anointed you as ruler over his inheritance" (1 Sam 10:1). On his way from this encounter, he meets a band of prophets (חבל נביאים), and he gets caught up in their prophetic ecstasy (v. 5). As a result, there arises a proverb, "Is Saul among the prophets?" (v. 11). The meaning of the proverbial saying is of some debate, but the centrality of the story for the rise of Saul is undeniable as is indicated not only by its place in the narrative but also the dissemination of a proverbial saying about it. There is a hint in the story that the purpose of the prophetic ecstasy is ultimately militaristic: Saul is on his way "to where the Philistine prefects reside" (v. 5). Yet, nothing is made of this reference in the story itself. Actually, the concept of the spirit coming upon people (as in ecstasy) in the Hebrew Bible is most closely associated with the judges, not with prophets.[8] So, for example, the "spirit of the LORD" rushed upon Samson, and he went down and fought in Ashkelon (Judg 14:19; compare Judg 3:10, 11:29, 14:6, 15:14). The position of the judge can be militaristic but also prophetic. The Saul proverb might suggest that Saul, like Samuel, was also functioning as a transitional figure between the judges, where apparently the prophetic and ruling roles are joined, and the era of the kings, when the prophet arises in a more symbiotic relationship with the king.

Another prophetic title that appears in the early monarchy is the "man of God." For example, the account in 1 Sam 9, which has the etiological aside about the term prophet, also calls Samuel "the man of God" (v. 7, 8, 10). It is a label that is also used for Moses in the preface to the "Blessing of Moses" (Deut 33:1) as well as in later texts, but it is not otherwise used in the Pentateuch. The use of the label in Deut 33:1 must therefore be understood as a later superscription. Shortly after the division of the Solomonic kingdom, two men of God appear in the biblical narrative. First, Shemaiah, "the man of God," appears to Rehoboam warning him not to start a civil war with Jeroboam (1 Kgs 12:21–24). Thereafter, an unnamed "man of God" appears before Jeroboam, prophesying the birth of Josiah, the Josianic reforms, and the downfall of the house of Jeroboam (1 Kgs 13:1–10).

The story of the unnamed man of God then turns to a clever "old prophet" from Bethel. This is a story quite reminiscent of some of the Elijah-Elisha tales. The old prophet tracks down this "man of God," deceives him into disobeying the

---

8. This was first pointed out by in a classic article by S. Mowinckel, "'The Spirit' and the 'Word' in the Pre-Exilic Reforming Prophets," *JBL* 53 (1934) 199–227.

"word of the LORD" incumbent upon him, and ultimately causes the death of the man of God—mauled by a lion! The old prophet then apparently feels some guilt and gives him an honorable burial. This latter half of the story is instructional inasmuch as it does not have anything to do with the monarchy. There is a tendency to associate the rise of prophets with the monarchy, but this may have more to do with the topic of our historical narrative than with the actual function of prophets in ancient Israel and Judah. To be sure, the prominence of prophets—particularly in the books of Samuel and Kings as opposed to the Pentateuch, Joshua, and Judges—underscores a special relationship between prophets and kings for the biblical authors. Nevertheless, there are enough counterexamples (e.g., the man of God, the Elisha tales) to demonstrate that prophets were not exclusively associated with the rise of kingship nor did they function exclusively in relationship to the king.

The most telling examples that relate kingship to prophets and prophecy are texts legitimating the institution of monarchy. This begins with the request by the elders to the prophet Samuel to establish a king (1 Sam 8). The prophet then plays a formative role in supporting the new institution, choosing its first two leaders and guiding them. Perhaps even more critical is the role that the prophet Nathan plays in the establishment of the monarchy. The monarchy gets an enduring stamp of approval through him. A particularly important tie between the prophets and kingship must be the dynastic oracle in 2 Sam 7, where Nathan receives "the word of the LORD" that promised the sons of David an enduring dynasty sanctioned by God. The importance of the dynastic oracle may be judged not just by its role in the Succession Narratives, but even more by the role it plays in shaping the entire Deuteronomistic history.[9] Later, Nathan plays a critical role in ensuring the proper transition from David to Solomon (1 Kgs 1).

Biblical literature uses the Near Eastern messenger formula as the classic form of prophetic speech.[10] The messenger formula, "thus says PN," is a formula adopted from letters throughout the ancient Near East.[11] The letter writer sends a messenger, with their exact words written for the messenger to speak, and the preface is a messenger formula. The formula is usually known from and associated with royal correspondence, but this reflects the scribal institutions that thrived

---

9. See, for example, L. Rost, *The Succession to the Throne of David* (Sheffield: Almond, 1982) 35–56; M. Noth, *The Deuteronomistic History* (trans. J. Doull; Sheffield: JSOT, 1991); and, W. Schniedewind, *Society and the Promise to David: A Reception History of 2 Samuel 7:1–17* (New York: Oxford University Press, 1999).

10. A classic discussion of this phenomenon is C. Westermann, *Basic Forms of Prophetic Speech* (trans. H. White; Louisville: Westminster John Knox, 1991), 98–128.

11. See J. Greene, *The Role of the Messenger and the Message in the Ancient Near East* (BJS 169; Atlanta: Scholars Press, 1989), J. Holladay, "Assyrian Statecraft and the Prophets of Israel," *HTR* 63 (1970) 29–51; and, M. Weinfeld, "Ancient Near Eastern Patterns in Prophetic Literature," *VT* 27 (1977) 178–95.

under institutional support. We can cite many examples even in the Bible, such as "thus says Pharaoh" (Exod 5:10), "thus says Balak" (Num 22:16), "thus says Jephthah" (Judg 11:15), "thus says Ben-Hadad" (1 Kgs 20:5), or "thus says Heze-kiah" (2 Kgs 19:3). In the Amarna Letters, for example, messenger formulas are embedded in the letters from local rulers. Fundamentally, the messenger formula is a scribal formula. The letter is one of the most essential forms in the scribal rep-ertoire. Indeed, there are wonderful examples of scribal exercises that involve the formulas of letter writing.[12] The prophetic use of this scribal formula suggests an association of the prophets with the scribal enterprise. In this respect, the later de-velopment of the "writing prophets" is not a surprising phenomenon. The proph-ets utilize a scribal formula already in the early monarchic narratives (e.g., 1 Sam 10:18; 15:2; 2 Sam 7:5, 8; 2 Sam 12:7, 11; 24:12; 1 Kgs 11:31). Whether this is the product of later scribes or arose in the formative period of the monarchy would be difficult to prove. Certainly, the messenger formula is found in narratives dealing with the very beginnings of prophecy and the monarchy.

The messenger formula also highlights the role of the prophet as a royal ad-viser. More generally, scribes were among the advisers to the king. We find scribes listed among the royal officials of David and Solomon. For example, a Masoretic list of David's officials includes the figure of "Jehoshaphat, son of Ahilud, the re-corder, and Sheva, scribe" יהושפט בן אהילוד המזכיר ושוא ספר (2 Sam 20:24–25), and a list of officials of King Solomon includes two court scribes: "Elihoreph and Ahijah, the sons of Shisha" (1 Kgs 4:3). On closer inspection, the two lists seem archaic and garbled. Note that the first list apparently has the name Sheva, but the name seems to be an appellative derived from the Egyptian title *sš šʿt* 'the writer of letters' rather than a proper noun.[13] Moreover, the term "recorder" is properly prefixed with a definite article, but not the title "scribe." This leads us to suspect that the title "scribe" here is a gloss explaining an obscure Egyptian loanword for a royal scribe. In the Solomonic list, the name Elihoreph is of Egyptian derivation from *ʾr-ḥp* 'Apis is my God',[14] and the name "Shisha" seems to be a straightforward

---

12. *KTU* 5:9, 5:10, 5:11; see J.-L. Cunchillos, "The Ugaritic Letters," in *Handbook of Ugaritic Studies* (ed. W. G. E. Watson and N. Wyatt; Leiden: Brill, 1999), 359–74; W. Schniedewind, "Un-derstanding Scribal Education in Ancient Israel: A View from Kuntillet ʿAjrud," *MAARAV* 21 (2014) 287–89.

13. As suggested by T. Mettinger, *Solomonic State Officials* (ConBOT 5; Lund, 1971), 29–30. Mettinger also argued that the name "Elihoreph" is a Hebraized Egyptian name, using *ḥp* to represent the god Apis (note that the Greek transliterations show no evidence of a *reš*). See also N. Fox, *In the Service of the King: Officialdom in Ancient Israel and Judah* (Cincinnati: Hebrew Union College Press, 2000), 106–10. The name "Sheva" is misunderstood, as reflected in the vari-ant readings of the Qere-Ketiv.

14. See R. de Vaux, "Titres et fonctionnaires égyptiens à la cour de David et Solomon," *RB* 48 (1939) 394–405. A wide variety of alternative suggestions have been offered, but none have the simplicity and elegance of the Egyptian explanation, especially when viewed in the context of other Egyptian loanwords, the use of hieratic numerals, and the history of Egyptian administra-tion in the region.

Hebraizing of the Egyptian word for royal scribe.[15] The name "Shisha" is likely a simple misinterpretation by a later Hebrew scribe of the Egyptian word *sš*, 'scribe', as a personal name. Since the Hebrew term בן 'son' often means 'guild' when combined with a profession, it is possible that the original meaning of the Hebrew expression בני שישא, which is usually translated 'sons of Shisha', may have been 'members of a scribal guild'. Prophets, however, are not listed among the royal officials, and there is no direct connection made between scribes and prophets in the Deuteronomistic History.

The Book of Chronicles does make a connection between scribes and prophets by listing the prophets among the recorders of the royal annals. For example, 1 Chr 29:29 suggests that "the acts (דברי) of King David, early and late, were written in the records (דברי) of Samuel the seer, the records of Nathan the prophet, and the records of Gad the seer." 2 Chr 9:29 records that "the rest of the acts of Solomon, from first to last, are they not written in the records of the prophet Nathan, and in the prophecy of Ahijah the Shilonite, and in the visions of the seer Iddo concerning Jeroboam son of Nebat?" And, 2 Chr 12:15 notes that "the acts of Rehoboam, from first to last, are they not written in the records of the prophet Shemaiah and of the seer Iddo, recorded by genealogy?" What are scholars to make of these (late) source citations in Chronicles? The tendency has been to dismiss them, since the Chronicler is a Persian author who is probably simply reflecting contemporary ideas of his own generation. Is it possible that the Chronicler has merely misread an old title עדו/עדד from one of his sources as a personal name and then used it to create a source citation? Or, it is more likely that the Chronicler simply invents these source citations out of thin air, so to speak? It seems more likely that the Chronicler was trying to make sense of received traditions (indeed, this is what the book of Chronicles as a whole is doing) rather than inventing wholesale traditions. From the viewpoint of historical criticism, it is difficult to know the source or date of the traditions and sources that the Chronicler used, and therefore it can have only limited value for reconstructing the early history of the prophets. On the other hand, it is valuable information for understanding the literary presentation of the prophets and the prophetic office in the biblical tradition. From the Chronicler's viewpoint, the early prophets were also scribes.

In general, there is little interest in presenting the prophets as scribes until the post-exilic period. Thus, the so-called writing prophets are not usually presented as writers or scribes even in their superscriptions. For example, the superscription for Isaiah, who seems to be a court prophet or seer of Hezekiah, reads, "The vision of Isaiah, son of Amoz, which he *saw* (חזה) concerning Judah and Jerusalem"

---

15. It has been suggested that Shisha is to be derived from the Hurrian name *Šawa-šarri*, but this derivation is quite fanciful and begins with the presumption that this figure was originally part of the old Hurrian/Jebusite administration (see M. Cogan, *1 Kings* [Anchor Bible 10; New York: Doubleday, 2001], 200–201). Also see A. Cody, "Le titre égyptien et le nom propre du scribe de David," *RB* 72 (1965) 381–93.

(Isa 1:1). There is a passage that suggests that Isaiah's testimony (תעודה, from the root עדד) was collected by his disciples, but there is no direct statement in the book itself that Isaiah himself was a writer. Of course, the later tradition in the book of Chronicles suggests that Isaiah himself was a scribal prophet and recorder of the royal annals: "the rest of the acts of Hezekiah, and his good deeds, are written in the vision of the prophet Isaiah son of Amoz in the Book of the Kings of Judah and Israel" (2 Chr 32:32). There is also a hint in the book of Samuel itself that Samuel also functioned as a scribe: "Samuel told the people the rules of the kingship; and he wrote them in the scroll and deposited it before the LORD" (1 Sam 10:25). In this case, the rules of kingship (משפט המלכה) are in some respects a treaty type of relationship that is written down and then deposited. The formal nature of the establishment of the royal institution in writing further legitimates it, and the prophet Samuel functions as the scribe who writes down the rules. Even so, the connection between the prophet and scribe is more inferred (e.g., through etymologies, textual criticism) than central to the literary presentation of the prophets in court narratives of the early monarchy. The mention of Samuel writing down the rules of kingship is parenthetical to the general presentation of Samuel in the Deuteronomistic History. To be sure, Chronicles will make Samuel a recorder for the reign of David, and the Talmud will even accord Samuel the status of author of the books.

In sum, early prophets in biblical literature are closely associated with the rise of kingship. In the literary narrative, Samuel functions as a transition figure from the judges to the king. He is the last judge of ancient Israel, but he is in some respects the first prophet. The deuteronomic narratives accord Samuel a variety of titles—"man of God," "prophet," and "judge"—although more typically he has no title at all. The prophet also serves a critical role in establishing the monarchy and overseeing its success. He even becomes a kingmaker. It is primarily in later tradition that the prophets become writers and scribes. There is some evidence to suggest that the role of the prophet became related to the scribal profession, but the development of this concept was especially tied to post-exilic concepts of textual authority, authorship, and canon. These were not issues of any particular importance in the deuteronomistic narratives about kings and prophets in the early monarchy.

Bibliography

Blenkinsopp, J. *A History of Prophecy in Israel.* Louisville: Westminister John Knox, 1996.

Cody, A. "Le titre égyptien et le nom propre du scribe de David." *RB* 72 (1965) 381–93.

Cogan, M. *1 Kings: A New Translation and Commentary.* AB 10. New York: Doubleday, 2001.

Cook, L. S. *On the Question of the "Cessation of Prophecy" in Ancient Judaism.* Texts and Studies in Ancient Judaism 145. Tübingen: Mohr Siebeck, 2011.

Cross, F. M. *Canaanite Myth and Hebrew Epic: Essays in the History of the Religion of Israel.* Cambridge, MA: Harvard University Press, 1973.

Cunchillos, J.-L. "The Ugaritic Letters." Pp. 359–74 in *Handbook of Ugaritic Studies.* Edited by W. G. E. Watson and N. Wyatt. Leiden: Brill, 1999.

Fox, N. *In the Service of the King: Officialdom in Ancient Israel and Judah.* Cincinnati: Hebrew Union College Press, 2000.

Greene, J. *The Role of the Messenger and the Message in the Ancient Near East.* BJS 169. Atlanta: Scholars Press, 1989.

Hoftijzer, J. and K. Jongeling, *Dictionary of the North-West Semitic Inscriptions.* 2 vols. Leiden: Brill, 1995.

Holladay, J. "Assyrian Statecraft and the Prophets of Israel." *HTR* 63 (1970) 29–51.

Levine, B. Review of *Mari and the Bible. IEJ* 50 (2000) 141–43.

Malamat, A. *Mari and the Bible.* Studies in the History and Culture of Ancient Near East 12. Leiden: Brill, 1998.

Mettinger, T. *Solomonic State Officials.* ConBOT 5. Lund, 1971.

Mowinckel, S. " 'The Spirit' and the 'Word' in the Pre-Exilic Reforming Prophets." *JBL* 53 (1934) 199–227.

Noth, M. *The Deuteronomistic History.* Trans. J. Doull. Sheffield: JSOT Press, 1991.

Olmo Lete, G. del, and J. Sanmartín. *A Dictionary of the Ugaritic Language.* 2 vols. Edited and translated by W. G. E. Watson. Leiden: Brill, 2004.

Oswald, W. *Nathan der Prophet: Eine Untersuchung zu 2 Samuel 7 und 12 und 1 Könige 1.* ATANT 94. Zurich: Theologischer Verlag, 2008.

Overholt, T. *Channels of Prophecy: The Social Dynamics of Prophetic Activity.* Minneapolis: Fortress, 1989.

Rost, L. *The Succession to the Throne of David.* Trans. M. D. Rutter and D. M. Gunn. Sheffield: Almond, 1982.

Schniedewind, W. *The Word of God in Transition: From Prophet to Exegete in the Second Temple Period.* JSOTSup 197. Sheffield: JSOT, 1995.

_____. *Society and the Promise to David: A Reception History of 2 Samuel 7:1–17.* Oxford: Oxford University Press, 1999.

Vaux, R. de. "Titres et fonctionnaires égyptiens à la cour de David et Solomon." *RB* 48 (1939) 394–405.

Weinfeld, M. "Ancient Near Eastern Patterns in Prophetic Literature." *VT* 27 (1977) 178–95.

Westermann, C. *Basic Forms of Prophetic Speech.* Trans. H. White. Louisville: Westminister John Knox, 1991.

Wilson, R. *Prophecy and Society in Ancient Israel.* Philadephia: Fortress, 1980.

Wright, J. E. "Baruch: His Evolution from Scribe to Apocalyptic Seer." Pp. 264–89 in *Biblical Figures Outside the Bible.* Edited by M. Stone and T. Bergren. Harrisburg, PA: Trinity Press International, 1998.

Friends or Foes?
Elijah and Other Prophets in the Deuteronomistic History

GARY N. KNOPPERS   and   ERIC L. WELCH
The University of Notre Dame   *The University of Kansas*

Introduction

Benjamin Franklin is credited with the aphorism, "Love your enemies, for they tell you your faults."[1] This sentiment finds a particular resonance in the fraught relationships depicted between monarchs and prophets in Samuel–Kings. Among the various responsibilities prophets exercise is telling monarchs in no uncertain terms what their faults are.[2] In the case of Samuel, he plays this prophetic role to the Israelite people, spelling out in great detail the problems with monarchic rule, before the monarchy has even arrived (1 Sam 8:1–18; 12:1–25). Indeed, one of the most typical roles played by prophets in Samuel–Kings, especially within the northern monarchy, is delivering judgment oracles against errant monarchs.[3] Despite the hope embodied within Franklin's adage, prophetic words of confrontation do not typically elicit kingly love but rather suspicion, resistance, and defiance.

---

1. B. Franklin, *Poor Richard's Almanack* (Waterloo, IA: U.S.C. Publishing, 1914), no. 338.

2. E.g., 1 Sam 13:10–14; 15:10–31; 28:18–19; 2 Sam 12:7–12; 1 Kgs 11:11–13; 14:1–18; 16:1–4; 21:19, 21–24; 2 Kgs 9:6–10.

3. W. Dietrich, *Prophetie und Geschichte* (FRLANT 108; Göttingen: Vandenhoeck & Ruprecht, 1972); idem, "Prophetie im deuteronomistischen Geschichtswerk," in *The Future of the Deuteronomistic History* (ed. T. C. Römer; BETL 147; Leuven: Peeters, 2000) 47–65; A. F. Campbell, *Of Prophets and Kings: A Late Ninth-Century Document (1 Samuel 1–2 Kings 10)* (CBQMS 17; Washington, DC: Catholic Biblical Association of America, 1986); idem and M. A. O'Brien, *Unfolding the Deuteronomistic History: Origins, Upgrades, Present Text* (Minneapolis: Augsburg Fortress, 2000); H. N. Wallace, "Oracles against the Israelite Dynasties in 1 and 2 Kings," *Bib 67* (1986) 21–40; S. L. McKenzie, *The Trouble with Kings: The Composition of the Book of Kings in the Deuteronomistic History* (VTSup 42; Leiden: Brill, 1991), 81–100; H. Barstad, "Some Remarks on Prophets and Prophecy in the 'Deuteronomistic History,'" in *Houses Full of All Good Things: Essays in Memory of Timo Veijola* (ed. J. Pakkala and M. Nissinen; Publications of the Finnish Exegetical Society 95; Göttingen: Vandenhoeck & Ruprecht, 2008), 300–315.

The subject of this volume is "ancient prophecy in context," but it must be acknowledged at the outset that placing the prophetic materials in Joshua–Kings squarely within an ancient Near Eastern political, historical, and religious context is difficult. Literary analysis of Samuel–Kings, including the Elijah-Elisha stories, suggests a long history of composition and editing, even if scholars cannot agree about the details, extent, and dates of this extensive process.[4] Careful examination of the major textual witnesses (MT, LXX, OL) indicates significant fluidity in the development of Samuel–Kings during the early Second Temple period.[5] If one wishes to track the compositional history of Kings, one is in effect chasing a moving target. The core analysis of this essay will focus on the contextualization and content of the prophetic narratives within Samuel–Kings, but we acknowledge at the outset that the components of this literary work have multiple *Sitzen im Leben*, not a single *Sitz im Leben*.

---

4. A number of features point to a long history of composition for this material, including additions and editing in postexilic times, A. Rofé, *The Prophetical Stories* (Jerusalem: Magnes, 1988); W. Thiel, "Deuteronomistische Redaktionsarbeit in den Elia-Erzählungen," in *Congress Volume: Leuven 1989* (ed. J. A. Emerton; VTSup 43; Leiden: Brill, 1991), 148–71; M. C. White, *The Elijah Legends and Jehu's Coup* (BJS 311; Atlanta: Scholars Press, 1997); E. Blum, "Die Nabotüberlieferungen und die Kompositionsgeschichte der Vorderen Propheten," in *Schriftauslegung in der Schrift: Festschrift für Odil Hannes Steck zu seinem 65. Geburtstag* (ed. R. G. Kratz, T. Krüger, and K. Schmid; BZAW 300; Berlin: de Gruyter, 2000), 111–28; J. Keinänen, *Traditions in Collision: A Literary and Redaction-Critical Study on the Elijah Narratives 1 Kings 17–19* (Schriften der Finnischen Exegetischen Gesellschaft 80; Göttingen: Vandenhoeck & Ruprecht, 2001); S. Otto, *Jehu, Elia und Elisa: Die Erzählung von der Jehu-Revolution und die Komposition der Elia-Elisa-Erzählungen* (BWANT 152; Stuttgart: Kohlhammer, 2001); P. T. Cronauer, *The Stories about Naboth the Jezreelite: A Source, Composition, and Redaction Investigation of 1 Kings 21 and Passages in 2 Kings 9* (LHB/OTS 424; London: T. & T. Clark, 2005); L. M. Wray Beal, *The Deuteronomist's Prophet: Narrative Control of Approval and Disapproval in the Story of Jehu (2 Kings 9 and 10)* (LHBOTS 478; London: T. & T. Clark International, 2007). It is not altogether surprising that source- and redaction-critical reconstructions of the relevant material differ to such a great degree, because even within the Elijah and Elisha legends there is significant literary variety. Thus, within the Elijah materials, each major pericope (1 Kgs 17:1–24; 18:1–46; 19:1–21; 21:1–29; 2 Kgs 1:1–18; 2:1–14) and sub-pericope (e.g., 1 Kgs 17:8–16, 17–24) within larger pericopes evinces its own particular character and individual traits.

5. J. C. Trebolle Barrera, *Jehú y Joás: texto y composición literaria de 2 Reyes 9–11* (Institución San Jerónimo 17; Valencia: Institución San Jerónimo, 1984); idem, *Centena in libros Samuelis et Regum. variantes textuales y composición literaria en los libros de Samuel y Reyes* (Textos y estudios "Cardinal Cisneros" 47; Madrid: Consejo Superior de Investigaciones Científicas Instituto de Filología, 1989); McKenzie, *The Trouble with Kings*, 81–100; E. Tov, *The Text-Critical Use of the Septuagint in Biblical Research* (2nd ed.; Jerusalem Biblical Studies 3; Simor, 1997); idem, *Textual Criticism of the Hebrew Bible* (3rd ed.; Minneapolis: Fortress, 2012); A. Schenker, *Septante et texte massorétique dans l'histoire la plus ancienne du texte de 1 Rois 2–14* (Cahiers de la Revue biblique 48; Paris: J. Gabalda, 2000); idem, *Älteste Textgeschichte der Königsbücher: die hebräische Vorlage der ursprünglichen Septuaginta als älteste Textform der Königsbücher* (OBO 199; Göttingen: Vandenhoeck & Ruprecht, 2004); P. Hugo, *Les deux visages d'Élie: Texte massorétique et Septante dans l'histoire la plus ancienne du texte de 1 Rois 17–18* (OBO 217; Fribourg: Academic, 2006).

This essay begins by making several observations about prophetic diversity within the Deuteronomistic historical writing.[6] The topics to be dealt with include the terms used for prophetic figures, the range of prophetic behaviors, the imbalance in the allocation of coverage devoted to mantics in the northern and southern realms, and the multiple roles played by some prophets. The second section of the essay will focus on several features of the prophetic narratives of Samuel–Kings in general and the Elijah-Elisha stories, in particular, that do not fit easily within an ancient Near Eastern prophetic framework.[7] Most of the cross-cultural comparisons will be made with the prophetic materials surviving from the Neo-Assyrian period, although the scattered epigraphic remains from the West Semitic world will also be considered.[8] Limited comparisons with another major biblical writing in which many prophetic figures appear—that is, Chronicles—will also prove useful.[9]

---

6. If one wished to expand the literature under review to that of a Deuteronomistic library, the diversity would only grow. On the possibilities, see T. C. Römer, "How Many Books (teuchs): Pentateuch, Hexateuch, Deuteronomistic History, or Enneateuch?" in *Pentateuch, Hexateuch, or Enneateuch: Identifying Literary Works in Genesis through Kings* (ed. T. B. Dozeman, T. C. Römer, K. Schmid; SBLAIL 8; Atlanta: SBL, 2011), 37–42.

7. Such cross-cultural comparisons have their limitations. Thus, for example, J. Schaper expresses reservations about the extent to which the scribal process of reworking selective prophetic texts (reports, references in letters, etc.) within an imperial setting might be similar to the types of scribal reworking of older prophecies found within the long literary tradition of biblical texts: "Prophecy in Israel and Assyria: Are We Comparing Apples and Pears? The Materiality of Writing and the Avoidance of Parallelomania," in *"Thus Speaks Ishtar of Arbela": Prophecy in Israel, Assyria, and Egypt in the Neo-Assyrian Period* (ed. R. P. Gordon and H. M. Barstad; Winona Lake, IN: Eisenbrauns, 2013), 225–38.

8. Most of the latter are conveniently discussed by C.-L. Seow, "West Semitic Sources," in *Prophets and Prophecy in the Ancient Near East* (ed. M. Nissinen; SBLWAW 12; Atlanta: SBL, 2003), 201–18; and by R. K. Ritner, "Report of Wenamon," *Prophets and Prophecy in the Ancient Near East*, 219–20. Similarly, for the Zakkur monumental royal inscription, A. Millard, "The Inscription of Zakkur, King of Hamath," in *The Context of Scripture* (3 vols.; ed. W. H. Hallo and K. Lawson Younger Jr.; Leiden: Brill, 2002), 2.35 (155–56).

9. Some scholars have boldly returned to the common-source hypothesis in which both Chronicles and Samuel–Kings represent literary developments in the same (postexilic) era of a much shorter shared *Vorlage*: A. G. Auld, "Salomo und die Deuteronomisten—eine Zukunftsvision?" *TZ* 48 (1992) 343–54; idem, *Kings Without Privilege: David and Moses in the Story of the Bible's Kings* (Edinburgh: T. & T. Clark, 1994); idem, "Synoptic David: The View from Chronicles," in *Raising Up a Faithful Exegete: Essays in Honor of Richard D. Nelson* (ed. K. L. Noll and B. Schramm; Winona Lake, IN: Eisenbrauns, 2010), 117–28. On the history of this idea in modern scholarship, see K. Peltonen, *History Debated: The Historical Reliability of Chronicles in Pre-Critical and Critical Research* (2 vols.; Publications of the Finnish Exegetical Society 64; Göttingen: Vandenhoeck & Ruprecht, 1996). While we do not find the common-*Vorlage* view to be compelling, we would acknowledge fluidity in the continuing development of Samuel–Kings in postexilic times (see n. 5, p. 220 above). This means that the text(s) of Samuel–Kings employed by the authors of Chronicles was not frozen in time but continued to experience some changes after the authors of Chronicles used it to prepare their own composition. In any event, we would wish to underscore the value of looking carefully at the unique material found within

Particular attention will be paid to not only the varied construction of pro-phetic messages and behaviors in relation to royalty but also the manner in which the biblical text promotes the pivotal status enjoyed by Elijah, over against the reigning northern monarch of his time, King Ahab, as safeguarding the historic legacy of ancient Israel.[10] The critical claim made for prophecy as the guardian of historic Israelite orthopraxis is linked, in turn, to the extraordinary claims made for Elijah's prophetic office as the critical nexus between the divine and human realms. In this schema, the prophet, rather than the king, occupies the crucial mediating position in the divine economy. In the highly-contested sphere of royal-prophetic power dynamics, the king proves to be operationally subordinate to the prophet.

The third part of our essay takes a different turn, exploring the extent to which the role of Elijah, as an opponent of the king, may be illumined against the backdrop of ancient Near Eastern prophecy. That the Elijah narratives valorize him as a complete outsider, an independent freelancer who does not conform to the typical prophetic profile of public servants supporting the king, reveals some understanding of the expectations that prophets were normally thought to fulfill within a larger monarchical polity. That is, the very critique that these stories level against the majority of prophets as royal sycophants paradoxically indicates that the authors possessed at least some rudimentary comprehension of how prophetic figures normally functioned within a centralizing monarchy dominated by state interests. The expectations that the figure of Ahab has of Elijah point in the same direction. Seen from this larger comparative perspective, the Elijah materials may be understood, among other things, as a literary and theological attempt to dis-tance Elijah from his prophetic contemporaries in monarchic Israel.

I. Chasing Chameleons?
Prophets in Joshua–Kings

Generalizations about prophecy in Joshua–Kings are difficult to make, much less establish, because prophecy within this vast, composite, and multi-layered

---

Samuel–Kings and its configuration within a larger literary work, which manifests at some levels Deuteronomistic editing. That is, assuming for the sake of argument, that the common-source hypothesis possibly explains how and why Chronicles differs from Samuel–Kings, it is neverthe-less important to analyze the significance of the *Sondergut* of Samuel–Kings within the literary context in which such material appears. For assessments of the common source hypothesis, see G. N. Knoppers, *I Chronicles 1–9* (AB 12; New York: Doubleday, 2004), 66–68; idem, "Projected Age Comparisons of the Levitical Townlists: Divergent Theories and Their Significance," *Text* 22 (2005) 21–63; idem, "Changing History: Nathan's Dynastic Oracle and the Structure of the Davidic Monarchy in Chronicles," in *Shai le-Sara Japhet: Studies in the Bible, Its Exegesis, and Its Language* (ed. M. Bar-Asher et al.; Jerusalem: Bialik Institute, 2007), 99*–123*.

10. On the narrative texts relating to prophecy as literary constructs, see M. Nissinen, "Prophecy as Construct: Ancient and Modern," in *"Thus Speaks Ishtar of Arbela,"* 11–35.

corpus takes so many different forms.[11] To begin with, there is a wide range of mantic figures who appear in the work, including the *nābî'*, 'prophet', the *nĕbî'â*, 'prophetess', the *rō'eh*, 'seer', the *ḥōzeh*, 'visionary', and the *'îš hā'ĕlōhîm*, 'man of God'.[12] In some cases, the terms used find parallels within a larger West Semitic context, but in other cases one has to search further afield.[13] Whether all of these figures should be considered as bona-fide prophets is matter of ongoing debate.[14]

Second, the range of divinatory practices found within Joshua–Kings is quite remarkable.[15] Among the divinatory techniques attested are necromancy (1 Sam 28:3–19), oneiromancy (Judg 7:13–15; 1 Kgs 3:4–14), binomial divination (1 Sam 14:40–42; 23:11–12), cleromancy or sortition (Josh 7:14–18; 1 Sam 10:20–24),[16] oracular inquiry (Judg 17:5; 18:11–20; 1 Sam 23:9–12; 2 Sam 5:23), clairvoyance

---

11. J. Kegler, "Prophetengestalten im deuteronomistischen Geschichtswerk und in den Chronikbüchern: Ein Beitrag zur Kompositions- und Redaktionsgeschichte der Chronikbücher," *ZAW* 105 (1993) 484–97.

12. M. J. de Jong provides a useful survey of the variety of titles found within the Deuteronomistic work and other relevant biblical writings: *Isaiah among the Ancient Near Eastern Prophets* (VTSup 117; Leiden: Brill, 2007), 318–44.

13. The Aramaic royal inscription relating to King Zakkur of Hamath and Lu'ash mentions both 'seers' (חזין) and 'messengers' (עדדן; *KAI* 202.11–12).The extrabiblical inscriptions from Deir 'Allā refer to Balaam as 'a seer of the gods' (חזה אלהן), to whom the gods came at night and spoke (I.1). The very fragmentary text of Combination II.16 may refer to a distant vision (חזן רחק). For reconstructions and discussions, see G. van der Kooij, "Palaeography," in *Aramaic Texts from Deir 'Alla* (ed. J. Hoftijzer and G. van der Kooij; Documenta et monumenta Orientis antiqui 19; Leiden: Brill, 1976), 133–34; J. Hoftijzer, "Interpretation and Grammar," in *Aramaic Texts from Deir 'Alla*, 174, 243; J. Hackett, *The Balaam Text from Deir 'Allā* (HSM 31; Chico, CA: Scholars Press, 1984), 25–74; C.-L. Seow, "West Semitic Sources," in *Prophets and Prophecy in the Ancient Near East* (ed. M. Nissinen; SBL Writings from the Ancient World 12; Atlanta: Society of Biblical Literature, 2003), 209–12; A. Lemaire, "Prophètes et rois dans les inscriptions oust-sémitiques (IXᵉ–VIᵉ siècle av. J.-C.)," in *Prophètes et rois: Bible et Proche-Orient* (LD; ed. A. Lemaire; Paris: Cerf, 2001), 96–101. There may be a reference to a vision (. . .]חזן) in one of the Lachish letters (21.B.3), but the context is quite fragmentary. J. Renz and W. Röllig prefer to read [. . .]חין: *Handbuch der althebräischen Epigraphik, 1: Die althebräischen Inschriften, Text und Kommentar* (Darmstadt: Wissenschaftliche Buchgesellschaft, 1995), 437. On the disputed origins and meanings of נבא, see J. Stökl, *Prophecy in the Ancient Near East: A Philological and Sociological Comparison* (CHANE 56; Leiden: Brill, 2012), 157–67, and the references cited there.

14. J. Blenkinsopp, *A History of Prophecy in Ancient Israel* (rev. ed.; Louisville: Westminster John Knox, 1996), 9–39.

15. M. Nissinen, "Prophètes et temples dans le Proche-Orient ancien et les textes bibliques," in *Les recueils prophétiques de la Bible: origines, milieux, et contexte proche-oriental* (ed. J.-D. Macchi, C. Nihan, T. C. Römer, and J. Rückl; Geneva: Labor et fides, 2012), 74–111; idem, "Prophets and Prophecy in Joshua–Kings: A Near Eastern Perspective," in *Israelite Prophecy and the Deuteronomistic History* (ed. M. R. Jacobs and R. F. Person Jr.; SBLAIL 14; Atlanta: SBL, 2013), 103–28; R. Thelle, "Reflections of Ancient Israelite Divination in the Former Prophets," in *Israelite Prophecy and the Deuteronomistic History*, 7–33.

16. The method is consistently employed in determining the tribal allotments in the Priestly-like section of Joshua (14:2; 15:1; 16:1; 17:1–2, 14, 17; 18:6, 8, 10, 11; 19:1, 10, 17, 24, 32, 40, 51; 20:9; 21:4–10).

(1 Kgs 18:41; 2 Kgs 6:8–12), belomancy (2 Kgs 13:14–19), and ecstatic prophecy (1 Sam 10:5–13; 19:19–24; cf. 2 Kgs 3:15).[17] One interesting aspect of this variety is that major figures (i.e., Saul, David, Solomon, Elisha), and not simply peripheral figures or lower level functionaries, exhibit such behaviors. Another interesting aspect of the variety is that, although these mantic behaviors are attested elsewhere in the ancient world, many contrast with what Israelite prophecy is supposed to consist of, according to the book of Deuteronomy (18:15–22).[18]

Third, within the larger Deuteronomistic corpus, traditionally called the Former Prophets, there is a fundamental issue of distribution and allocation of coverage. Prophets and prophecy hardly appear, if at all, in Joshua and Judges. The point has been often made, so it need not be belabored here.[19] Yet, less noticed is the fact that, even within the monarchy, prophecy has an uneven distribution. This imbalance constitutes an unusual feature of prophecy within Samuel–Kings. During the period of the United Kingdom, a number of prophets (Samuel, Gad, Nathan, Ahijah) come into play, yet the dual monarchies feature mostly northern prophets. The prophetic figures populating northern Israelite history include Ahijah (1 Kgs 11:31–39; 14:1–18), the anonymous old prophet from Bethel (1 Kgs 13:11–32), Jehu (1 Kgs 16:1–4), Elijah (1 Kgs 17:1–19:21; 21:17–29; 2 Kgs 2:1–11), the anonymous prophets and the man of God counseling the king of Israel (1 Kgs 20:13–14, 22, 28, 35–42), Micaiah (1 Kgs 22:8–28), the "sons of the prophets" (1 Kgs 20:25–32; 2 Kgs 2:2, 3, 7, 15; 4:1, 38; 5:22; 6:1–2; 9:1–3), Elisha (1 Kgs 19:15, 19–21; 2 Kgs 2:1–13:21), the young prophet appointed by Elisha to anoint and charge Jehu (2 Kgs 9:1–10), and Jonah (2 Kgs 14:25).[20] To this list may be added

---

17. On the range of types, see further R. Wilson, *Prophecy and Society in Ancient Israel* (Philadelphia: Fortress, 1980); J. Blenkinsopp, *Sage, Priest, Prophet: Religious and Intellectual Leadership in Ancient Israel* (Louisville: Westminster John Knox, 1995); idem, *History of Prophecy*; R. E. Clements, *Old Testament Prophecy: From Oracles to Canon* (Louisville: Westminster John Knox, 1996); L. L. Grabbe, *Priests, Prophets, Diviners, Sages: A Socio-Historical Study of Religious Specialists in Ancient Israel* (Philadelphia: Trinity Press International, 1996); M. Nissinen, "Biblical Prophecy from a Near Eastern Perspective: The Cases of Kingship and Divine Possession," in *Congress Volume: Ljubljana 2007* (ed. A. Lemaire; VTSup 133; Leiden: Brill, 2010), 441–68; idem, "Prophets and Prophecy," 104–9; idem, "Prophetic Madness: Prophecy and Ecstasy in the Ancient Near East and in Greece," in *Raising Up a Faithful Exegete: Essays in Honor of Richard D. Nelson* (ed. K. L. Noll and B. Schramm; Winona Lake, IN: Eisenbrauns, 2010), 3–29.

18. H. Barstad, "The Understanding of the Prophets in Deuteronomy," *SJOT* 8 (1994) 236–51; B. M. Levinson, *"The Right Chorale": Studies in Biblical Law and Interpretation* (FAT 54; Tübingen: Mohr Siebeck, 2008), 58–86; J. Stackert, *A Prophet Like Moses: Prophecy, Law and Israelite Religion* (New York: Oxford University Press, 2014), 126–67.

19. Recently, Barstad, "Some Remarks," 301–7; D. Edelman, "Court Prophets during the Monarchy and Literary Prophets in the So-called Deuteronomistic History," in *Israelite Prophecy and the Deuteronomistic History*, 51–73.

20. The prophets as a collective are cited in two of the Deuteronomistic comments on the fall of Israel (2 Kgs 17:13–14, 23), but the prophets have different functions within these two different literary contexts: calling the people to repentance (vv. 13–14) and predicting the future (v. 23), Dietrich, *Prophetie und Geschichte*, 41–42; E. Würthwein, *Die Bücher der Könige: 1 Kön. 17–2 Kön. 25* (ATD 11/2; Göttingen: Vandenhoeck & Ruprecht, 1984), 392–97.

the prophets of Baal (1 Kgs 18:19–40; 2 Kgs 10:19–28; cf. 1 Kgs 16:29–32) and the prophets of Asherah (1 Kgs 18:19; cf. 1 Kgs 16:33).

The stream of prophets in Israel contrasts markedly with the situation in Judah. Following the activity of Shemaiah in the time of Rehoboam (1 Kgs 12:21–24), southern prophets do not appear on the scene again until the late 8th century, when Isaiah answers Hezekiah's pleas during and following the Assyrian crisis (2 Kgs 19:2, 6–7, 20–34; 20:4–11) and the northern kingdom is no more.[21] During the reigns of Hezekiah's successors, an oracle stemming from anonymous prophets is cited in reference to Manasseh's reign (2 Kgs 21:10–15), and a prophetess (Huldah) is summoned during Josiah's reign (2 Kgs 22:12–20), but otherwise prophets are hard to come by in Judah.

The portrayal of so many mantics in Israel, even if most of those figures are not allied in any way to Elijah and Elisha, accentuates the disparity between the northern realm and the southern realm.[22] In the latter, there is a prophetic gap from the time of the early Judahite monarchy in the late 10th century (the time of Rehoboam) to the late 8th century (the time of Hezekiah). It is not the case that Judah has many errant prophets and a dearth of good ones but rather that Judah lacks prophets throughout some two centuries, or more, of its history.[23]

The prophetic discrepancy between the two realms constitutes an internal literary peculiarity with one biblical book.[24] As such, it does not assist directly in the larger task of comparing biblical with extrabiblical prophecy. Nevertheless, it may inform the quest to understand the distinctive role(s) the writers thought that prophecy may have played, if at all, in one ancient society over against the next. That is, it may be that the authors of Kings either believed that prophecy did not play a substantial role in Judahite society or had no compelling reasons (e.g., sources, traditions, theological reasons) to posit such a prophetic presence in Judahite society from the late tenth to the late eighth centuries BCE.[25] One is

---

21. A southern "man of God" appears in the early divided monarchy but does so in northern Israel during the early reign of Jeroboam (1 Kgs 13:1–32).

22. Accordingly, the attention devoted to Ephraimite prophecy (pp. 135–252) dwarfs that devoted to Judean prophecy (pp. 253–95) in Wilson, *Prophecy and Society*.

23. Perhaps this disparity may be explained by recourse to sources. The editors may have had at their disposal a good many prophetic legends and anecdotes relating to northern Israel, which they selected to shape and augment, but only a few late sources (relating to Isaiah and Huldah), dealing with Judahite history. We suspect, however, that there is more going on in the allocation and depiction of prophetic history than an explanation focusing only on available sources allows. In this respect, it is relevant to observe that the (perceived) disparity is remedied in the Chronistic work. There, a plenitude of prophetic figures—oracular mediators, pro-tem prophets, historical writers, Levitical singers, and so forth—populate Judahite history.

24. E. Ben Zvi suggests that what he terms the "biblical prophets collection" (Isaiah, Jeremiah, Ezekiel, and the Minor Prophets) was created, in part, to correct this imbalance, "Prophetic Memories in the Deuteronomistic Historical and the Prophetic Collections of Books," in *Israelite Prophecy and the Deuteronomistic History*, 75–102.

25. On the very different picture in Chronicles, see T. Willi, *Die Chronik als Auslegung: Untersuchungen zur literarischen Gestaltung der historischen Überlieferung Israels* (FRLANT

reminded of Gordon's comment that prophecy in the ancient Near East was "unevenly experienced and variously regarded."[26] That so many prophets populate northern history may not have been necessarily viewed by the editors of Kings as a positive mark of distinction for the northern kingdom. We wish to return to this matter below (III).

Fourth, prophets sometimes fulfill multiple roles in society. This is another unusual dimension of prophecy in the complex literary work that is the Former Prophets. Thus, Deborah appears as a prophetess (נביאה), judge, and mother in Israel (אם בישראל; Judg 4:4–5; 5:7).[27] For his part, Samuel appears as a chieftain (e.g., 1 Sam 4:18; 7:6, 15, 17; 8:2; 12:6–17), priest (e.g., 1 Sam 2:18; 7:9–10), seer (ראה; 1 Sam 9:9, 11, 18–19), and prophet (נביא; 1 Sam 3:20; cf. 1 Sam 28:6, 15).[28] That these different titles and roles are attributed to one figure is often explained as the conflation and (re)editing of several literary sources.[29] While this may be indeed a plausible explanation of the textual and literary evidence, it is surely remarkable that this process occurs at all. The aggregation of multiple societal roles to select prophets in the Deuteronomistic work reimagines, reshapes, and complicates the legacy of ancient Israelite leadership.

The figure of Elijah is a good example of how the process of augmenting, reworking, and editing older texts within a larger literary tradition turns a prophet

---

106; Göttingen: Vandenhoeck & Ruprecht, 1972), 216–44; I. L. Seeligmann, "Die Auffassung von der Prophetie in der deuteronomistischen und chronistischen Geschichtsschreibung," in *Congress Volume, Göttingen 1977* (ed. J. A. Emerton; VTSup 29; Leiden: Brill, 1978), 254–84; J. P. Weinberg, "Die 'ausserkanonischen Prophezeiungen' in der Chronikbüchern," *Acta Antiqua* 26 (1978) 387–404; R. Micheel, *Die Seher- und Prophetenüberlieferungen in der Chronik* (BBET 18; Frankfurt-am-Main: Lang, 1983), 57–67; C. T. Begg, "The Classical Prophets in the Chronistic History," *BZ* 32 (1988) 100–10; W. Schniedewind, *The Word of God in Transition: From Prophet to Exegete in the Second Temple Period* (JSOTSup 197; Sheffield: Sheffield Academic, 1995), 80–230; idem, "Prophets and Prophecy in the Book of Chronicles," in *The Chronicler as Historian* (ed. M. P. Graham, K. G. Hoglund, and S. L. McKenzie; JSOTSup 238; Sheffield: JSOT Press, 1997), 204–24; R. W. Klein, "Prophets and Prophecy in the Books of Chronicles," *TBT* 36 (1998) 227–32.

26. Gordon, "Prophecy," 38.

27. On the political and martial connotations of the last epithet, see S. Ackerman, *Warrior, Dancer, Seductress, Queen: Women in Judges and Biblical Israel* (New York: Doubleday, 1998), 35–44.

28. Chronicles explains his sacerdotal functions by asserting that he stemmed from the tribe of Levi (1 Chr 6:11–13). In Samuel, his family hails from Ephraim (1 Sam 1:19; 2:11; 7:17; 25:1): G. N. Knoppers, *I Chronicles 1–9*, 421. The roles that Samuel fulfills in Chronicles are those of seer, prophet, temple benefactor, and literary author (1 Chr 9:22; 26:28; 29:29; 2 Chr 35:18).

29. M. A. Sweeney offers an alternative suggestion, namely, that Samuel and other northern prophets (in distinction from southern prophets) had important priestly functions: "Prophets and Priests in the Deuteronomistic History: Elijah and Elisha," in *Israelite Prophecy and the Deuteronomistic History*, 35–49. But in Edelman's view, Israelite prophets should be generally thought of as sub-specialists of priests: "Court Prophets," 51–56. On Samuel's priestly functions in Samuel, see further M. Leuchter, "Samuel: A Prophet or Priest like Moses?" in *Israelite Prophecy and the Deuteronomistic History*, 147–68.

into a composite figure, a complex of different roles, actions, and responsibilities. In one text, he appears in a priestly role sacrificing a bull upon Mt. Carmel (1 Kgs 18:30–39), while in another he appears in a Moses-like role at the 'mountain of God' (הר האלהים), Mt. Horeb, awaiting a Horeb-like divine revelation (1 Kgs 19:8–12).[30] In one text, he attends to the dire needs of the widow of Zarephath and her son (1 Kgs 17:7–24), while in another he implements Deuteronomic law (13:2–6) against those seditiously agitating for the worship of other gods (1 Kgs 18:17–29), by slaughtering (וישחטם) the 450 prophets of Baal in the Wadi Qishon (1 Kgs 18:40).[31]

In short, the variations in terminology, the wide range of divinatory behaviors, the uneven distribution of prophetic figures, and the multiple roles played by certain figures complicates any attempt to articulate clearly who or what a prophet is in the Deuteronomistic work. Prophecy in the Former Prophets resists simple categorization.

II. Powerful Prophets: Unusual Features of Prophecy in Samuel–Kings

The prophetic materials within Samuel–Kings exhibit several quixotic features. A number of these characteristics—prophetic positions, actions, and messages—contrast not only with Neo-Assyrian prophecy but also with some other instances of prophecy within the limited corpus of ancient West Semitic inscriptions relating to prophecy. An inner-biblical comparison may also be helpful. Several features of prophecy in Samuel–Kings may be contrasted with those appearing in Chronicles.[32]

---

30. That both Elijah (1 Kgs 17:1; 18:15) and Elisha (2 Kgs 3:14; 5:16) repeatedly swear oaths with the declaration, "As Yʜwʜ (the God of Israel/Ṣebaoth) lives, before whom I stand," underscores their close relation to the deity. The location "stand before Yʜwʜ" often has cultic connotations (Num 5:16, 30; Deut 10:8; 18:7; 19:17; 29:10; Jer 15:1; Ezek 44:15; 2 Chr 29:11). At the "mountain of God" (Mt. Horeb), Elijah is told to "stand before Yʜwʜ" (1 Kgs 19:11).

31. It is this sort of zeal (קנא) for Yʜwʜ (1 Kgs 19:10, 14), among other factors, that led some early interpreters to view Elijah as Phineas (Num 5:14, 30) *redivivus*. See Pseudo Philo, *LAB* xlviii; *Pirqe R. El.* 29, 47; *Tg. Ps.-J.* Deut 33:11; (Pseudo-)Jerome, *Quaestiones Hebraicae in libros Regum et Paralipomenon* (PL 23, 1391–1470); R. Hayward, "Phinehas—The Same is Elijah: The Origins of a Rabbinic Tradition," *JJS* 29 (1978) 22–34. We thank Henri Vellançon for drawing our attention to this tradition of interpretation.

32. Another way of understanding the differences between Samuel–Kings and Chronicles is to regard each work as an incomplete or partial written realization of a much-broader shared oral tradition. See R. F. Person, *The Deuteronomic School: History, Social Setting, and Literature* (Atlanta: SBL, 2002); idem, *The Deuteronomic History and the Book of Chronicles: Scribal Works in an Oral World* (SBLAIL 6; Atlanta: SBL, 2010); idem, "Prophets in the Deuteronomic History and the Book of Chronicles: A Reassessment," in *Israelite Prophecy and the Deuteronomistic History*, 187–99. Seen from this perspective, the *Sondergut* of Chronicles and the *Sondergut* of Samuel–Kings represent written versions of earlier material preserved in common oral tradition. While we would agree that Judean tradition valued diversity and multiformity (otherwise, we

In Samuel–Kings, prophets often speak directly to kings, rather than sending messages to the king through subordinates.[33] Whether kings summon prophets (e.g., 1 Kgs 20:13–14; 22:5–6, 15–17; 2 Kgs 3:11–12) or whether prophets appear before kings on their own accord (e.g., 1 Kgs 18:2, 17–19; 21:17–24), the direct head-to-head contact is quite remarkable. Such a *modus operandi* may be contrasted not only with Neo-Assyrian prophetic customs but also with the behaviors of an unnamed prophet (הנבא) who is mentioned in one of the Lachish letters (3.rev.4).[34] In one scholarly reconstruction, this prophet sent a message saying (לאמר), 'be careful' (השמר), which was received by Šallûm son of Yaddûªᶜ and circulated by Ṭôbyāhû, a high-ranking servant of the king (3.rev.3–5).[35] This writing (ספר), in turn, was sent by Hôšaʿyāhû (the author of this particular letter), to his superior Yāʾûš (3.obv.1–2).[36] In this reading of the Lachish correspondence, the protocol followed comports broadly with that regularly employed in the Neo-Assyrian realm in that the prophetic message was sent to a relevant official, rather than communicated directly in person to the monarch.[37]

---

would not have separate writings consisting of Samuel–Kings and Chronicles), we would wish to stress that Samuel–Kings and Chronicles are literary works, reflecting deliberate composition and editing by a series of writers who participated in an ongoing, dynamic tradition. Each of these works has its own peculiar literary traits, even though the two share common material and draw upon both oral and written sources. To put matters differently, we are interested in the distinctive features of these works that allow scholars to speak of multiformity.

33. E.g., 1 Sam 13:10–13; 15:1–3; 2 Sam 7:1–16; 12:1–12; 1 Kgs 11:11–13; 12:22–24; 13:1–3; 14:1–18; 16:1–4; 22:10–25; 2 Kgs 22:15–20.

34. In the numbering system of D. Pardee, the material pertaining to the prophet appears in lines 19–21, "Lachish 3: Complaints and Information (3.42B)," in *The Context of Scripture* (3 vols.; ed. W. H. Hallo and K. Lawson Younger Jr.; Leiden: Brill, 2002), 3.79.

35. S. Aḥituv, *Echoes from the Past: Hebrew and Cognate Inscriptions from the Ancient Past* (Jerusalem: Carta, 2008), 62–69.

36. Either the prophet mentioned in this missive or another with a Yahwistic name ([y]hw hnbʾ) appears in an additional Lachish letter (16.obv.5). Some have attempted to reconstruct yet another reference to "the prophet(s)" in Lachish letter 6.5, but the text is highly fragmentary: h[ ]. Most reconstruct h[śrm], 'the officials'. See W. F. Albright, "'The Oldest Hebrew Letters: The Lachish Ostraca," *BASOR* 70 (1938) 11–17; R. de Vaux, "Les Ostraka de Lachis," *RB* 48 (1939) 189–201; A. Lemaire, *Inscriptions hébraïques* (LAPO 9; Paris: Cerf, 1977) 121–24.

37. M. Weippert, "Die Bildsprache der neuassyrischen prophetie," in *Beiträge zur prophetischen Bildsprache in Israel und Assyrien* (ed. H. Weippert, K. Seybold, and M. Weippert; OBO 64; Göttingen: Vandenhoeck & Ruprecht, 1985) 55–93; H. B. Huffmon, "Prophecy: Ancient Near Eastern Prophecy," in *The Anchor Bible Dictionary* (6 vols.; ed. D. N. Freedman; Garden City, NY: Doubleday, 1992), 5:477–82; S. Parpola, *Assyrian Prophecies* (SAA 9; Helsinki: University of Helsinki Press, 1997); S. W. Cole and P. Machinist, *Letters from Priests to Kings Esarhaddon and Assurbanipal* (SAA 13; Helsinki: University of Helsinki Press, 1998); M. Nissinen, *Letters from Assyrian and Babylonian Scholars* (SAA 10; Helsinki: University of Helsinki Press, 1993); idem, *References to Prophecy in Neo-Assyrian Sources* (SAA 7; Helsinki: Neo-Assyrian Text Corpus Project, 1998); idem, "How Prophecy became Literature," *SJOT* 19 (2005) 153–72; P. Villard, "Les prophètes à l'époque néo-assyrienne," in *Prophètes et rois: Bible et Proche-Orient* (ed. A. Lemaire; LD; Paris: Cerf, 2001), 55–84; Stökl, *Prophecy in the Ancient Near East*, 157–92.

Nevertheless, it is not altogether clear whether the second-person admonition, "be careful," ultimately stemmed from the prophet. In an alternative reconstruction, the missive was dispatched to him by a state functionary to warn him about the consequences of his prophetic activities.[38] In either scenario, the process of communication involved the transmission of messages rather than direct meetings. To be sure, in one case Elijah sends a written missive (מכתב), but he does so in Chronicles, not in Kings.[39] When Elijah wishes to send a message to Ahab in Kings, he deploys one of Ahab's aides (Obadiah) to communicate orally with the king (1 Kgs 18:8–16). The prophetic message directs Obadiah to inform the king that "Elijah is here" (1 Kgs 18:11, 15), the implication being that the prophet is available for a direct consultation.

It was not unusual for Neo-Assyrian prophets to contribute to domestic and foreign policy debates by pontificating about the prospects and timing of royal initiatives. Indeed, this was a regular and important part of their service to the crown.[40] Prophets and prophetesses speak words of encouragement in times of turmoil and war, whether to the king (SAA 9 1.4 ii 16′–40′; 9 2.1 i 1′–14′; 9 2.4 ii 29′–iii 18′; 9 2.5 iii 19′–36′; 9 3.2 i 27–ii 9; 9 7 1–11; 9 8 1–8), the crown prince (SAA 9 1.2 i 30′–31′; ii 1′–8′), or the Queen Mother (9 1.7 v 1–11; 9 5 1–6).[41]

A few oracles espouse a multi-generation perspective. Thus, for example, a prophetic utterance from Lā-dāgil-ili to Esarhaddon promises him not only security within his palace but also that both his son and his grandson will exercise kingship in the lap of Ninurta (SAA 9 1.10 vi.19–31).[42] Multi-generation oracles are well attested in Samuel–Kings (e.g., 2 Sam 7:7–16), but most are negative (e.g., 1 Sam 2:27–35; 13:10–14; 1 Kgs 13:1–3; 14:1–18; 16:34; 2 Kgs 22:15–20).[43] In spite of this overlap, there is something unusual about the literary portrayal of many prophecies, whether for weal or woe, in Samuel–Kings. Within the narrative world of the text, prophetic messages take on a life of their own. By means of their

---

38. Pardee, "Lachish 3," 79–80.

39. The letter is sent to a Judahite king: Micheel, *Die Seher- und Prophetenüberlieferungen*, 55–56; B. J. Diebner, "Überlegungen zum 'Brief des Elia' (*2 Chr* 21,12–15)," *Hen* 9 (1987) 199–227; S. Japhet, *I & II Chronicles* (OTL; Louisville: Westminster John Knox, 1993) 812–14; R. W. Klein, *2 Chronicles* (Hermeneia; Minneapolis: Fortress, 2012), 306–8.

40. Nissinen, *References to Prophecy*, 164–66.

41. Parpola, *Assyrian Prophecies*, 5–40; Nissinen, *References to Prophecy*, 103–29.

42. Cf. SAA 9 1.6 iii 7′–14′; iv 15–16; 9 2.3 ii 13′–14′. On these texts and the unusual prophetic name, "One who does not see God," see Parpola, *Assyrian Prophecies*, L–LI, 7–8, 10–11, 15–16; Nissinen, *References to Prophecy*, 29–30, 106–8, 113–14.

43. That 1 Kgs 16:34 is missing from LXX[L] (likely, in this case to be the oldest reading) suggests that the longer text in the MT and LXX[AB] represents a later Deuteronomistic-worded addition to the text, designed to impugn Ahab and signal the realization of the curse uttered by Joshua (6:26). See, e.g., E. Tov, *The Text-Critical Use of the Septuagint in Biblical Research* (Jerusalem Biblical Studies 3; Jerusalem: Simor, 1981), 259–60. This is one more indication of continuing development in the text of Kings in the postexilic era.

oracles, prophets shape history not only on an immediate or short-term basis but also more remarkably on a long-term basis.[44]

One royal response to offensive mantic speeches is to persecute the prophets who utter them (1 Kgs 18:17; 19:2, 10; 2 Kgs 1:9–16; 6:31), but such actions cannot ultimately defeat the prophetic word. In this literary construction, prophetic utterances become ultimately generative of history itself. To be sure, this contrast may be explained, partially at least, by recourse to the nature of sources at our disposal. The Neo-Assyrian sources comprise scattered letters, oracle reports, select literary paraphrases, and the like, whereas Samuel–Kings comprises a continuous, complicated literary narrative that selectively engages centuries of Israelite and Judahite political history.

The emphasis on the miraculous is another unusual feature of prophetic tales in Samuel–Kings, especially within the Elijah-Elisha stories. Prophets control the weather (1 Sam 12:17–18; 1 Kgs 17:1; 18:1, 42–45), perform (un)natural wonders (1 Kgs 19:19; 2 Kgs 1:10, 12; 2:14, 22; 4:38–44). In one case, a prophet even unleashes a divine judgment that results in wild animals mauling insolent children (2 Kgs 2:23–24). There is one case in the Deir ʿAllā plaster texts in which the seer Balaam fasts and weeps because of what the gods have revealed to him (Combination I.1.3–9.).[45] In this important, albeit fragmentary, text an unnamed goddess is instructed by the Šaddayīn to cause havoc in the earth, breaking the bolts of heaven and creating pitch darkness and chaos in the world of nature. What is unclear, among other things, is whether the catastrophe is imminent or possibly set to occur sometime in the near or distant future. To complicate matters, the discussion of the chaos is set within the divine council, whose executive decision could set limits to the devastation.[46] In the Samuel text (1 Sam 12:17–18) and in the Elijah-Elisha texts, there is an immediate cause- (prophetic utterance) and-effect (natural disorder) relationship.

In Kings, prophets sometimes display extraordinary medical powers, healing Israelites (2 Kgs 13:20–21; 20:1–11) and non-Israelites (1 Kgs 17:8–24; 2 Kgs 4:12–37; 5:1–19) alike. As a sign (אות) to an ailing Hezekiah of his imminent recov-

---

44. See G. von Rad, "The Deuteronomic Theology of History in I and II Kings," in his *The Problem of the Hexateuch and Other Essays* (New York: McGraw-Hill, 1966), 205–21; H. Weippert, "Geschichten und Geschichte: Verheißung und Erfüllung im deuteronomistischen Geschichtswerk," in *Congress Volume: Leuven, 1989* (ed. J. A. Emerton; VTSup 43; Leiden: Brill, 1991), 116–31 [trans. " 'Histories' and 'History:' Promise and Fulfillment in the Deuteronomistic History," in *Reconsidering Israel and Judah: The Deuteronomistic History in Recent Thought* (ed. G. N. Knoppers and J. G. McConville; SBTS 8; Winona Lake, IN: Eisenbrauns, 2000), 47–61], and the references listed in these works.

45. Hoftijzer, "Interpretation," 173–74, 188–200; Hackett, *Balaam Text*, 25–50; Seow, "Deir ʿAllā," 210–11; Lemaire, "Prophètes et rois," 97.

46. M. Weippert, "The Balaam Text from Deir ʿAllā and the Study of the Old Testament," in *The Balaam Text from Deir ʿAlla Re-evaluated* (ed. J. Hoftijzer and G. van der Kooij; Leiden: Brill, 1991), 169–74.

ery, Isaiah even turns back the sun's shadows (2 Kgs 20:8–11).[47] Such inexplicable events, in which prophetic intermediations result in prompt, direct divine interventions to heal severe human illnesses or to alter the course of natural affairs, are unattested in the available prophetic materials surviving from the Neo-Assyrian period. Yet, it is also important to point out that such prophetic behaviors are not attested either in other biblical historiographic writings, such as Chronicles and Ezra–Nehemiah.[48] In Chronicles, prophets occasionally predict medical disorders (e.g., 2 Chr 21:14–15) but do not perform miracles.

The miraculous elements in Samuel–Kings are sometimes explained simply on literary grounds as representing late legendary accretions. Yet, if the supposition is that such features were characteristic of late Hebrew literature in the post-exilic age, the supposition proves to be too simplistic.[49] This is not to deny that the Elijah-Elisha stories, in whole or in part, are likely later additions to the history of the northern monarchy in Kings. But, as we have seen, the preternatural appears elsewhere within prophetic contexts in Samuel–Kings and is not confined to these particular sets of tales. Given that literary works, such as Chronicles and Ezra–Nehemiah, lack prophetic miracles, one may recognize that the miraculous in historiographic literature is something specific to particular passages in the Former Prophets. An explanation should be sought within this literary context to illumine the appearance of miraculous elements.

It would be easy to dismiss idiosyncrasies within the prophetic stories—such as the fire from heaven, the astonishing healings, and the odd meteorological phenomena—as the stuff of prophetic legends, but to do so would be to miss the degree to which the miraculous contributes to a larger reimagination of the relationship between kings and prophets in ancient Israel. This is not to deny the hagiographic nature of many prophetic stories.[50] Rather, the point is to explore the integration of these disparate many tales into a larger narrative that is ostensibly dedicated to evaluating the activities of kings. In the Elijah-Elisha materials, prophets invade the mythic space monarchs normally arrogate to themselves in ancient Near Eastern royal ideology.

---

47. Compare also Joshua's effective speech to Yhwh in the context of the Israelite victories at Gibeon, Bet-ḥoron, Azeqah, and Maqqedah: "Sun stand still at Gibeon and Moon (stand still) in the Valley of Ayyalon" (Josh 10:12–13).

48. S. Japhet argues that this discrepancy is a critical clue to understanding the different historiographic assumptions underlying the works of Samuel–Kings and Chronicles: *The Ideology of the Book of Chronicles and Its Place in Biblical Thought* (2nd ed.; BEATAJ 9; Frankfurt am Main: Lang, 1997), 150–91.

49. Thus, the portrait of Hezekiah's reign in Chronicles obliquely refers to a sign (מופת) accorded to a deathly-ill Hezekiah by Yhwh and Hezekiah's surprising lack of gratitude (2 Chr 32:24–25), but Chronicles does not mention Isaiah in this context, nor the turning back of the sun's shadows.

50. Rofé, *Prophetical Stories*, 13–142.

In the traditional view, kingship is an institution that traverses the divine and human spheres and mediates between them.[51] The king represents the people to the divine and the divine to the people. To be sure, there is a place for prophetic personnel within such a hierarchical universe, inasmuch as prophets transmit messages from the divine, which in one form or another may prove useful as the king faces challenges and contemplates new initiatives in governing the state.[52] By sharing messages from the divine sphere, prophets assist the king in maintaining the equilibrium between heaven and earth. More than this, prophetic messages may be used for royal propaganda.[53] If recognized mouthpieces of the god(s) publicly back the king, their messages enhance royal authority. Yet, prophets represent only one category of personnel serving the crown. Because the monarch ostensibly represents the divine choice to govern the body politic, he is the human figure most critical to ensuring the health, prosperity, and success of the populace. Indeed, kingship is "an integral constituent of the cosmic order."[54] Traditional royal ideology emphasizes the benefits of such a socially-stratified dynastic polity: continuity, stability, military victory, prosperity, and justice.[55]

---

51. R. Labat, *Le caractère religieux de la royauté assyro-babylonienne* (Études d'assyriologie 2; Paris: Adrien-Maisonneuve, 1939); H. Frankfort, *Kingship and the Gods: A Study of Ancient Near Eastern Religion as the Integration of Society and Nature* (Chicago: University of Chicago Press, 1948); K.-H. Bernhardt, *Das Problem der altorientalischen Königsideologie im Alten Testament* (VTSup 8; Leiden: Brill, 1961), 67–90; J. Gray, "Sacral Kingship in Ugarit," *Ugaritica* 6 (1969) 289–302; S. N. Kramer, "Kingship in Sumer and Akkad: The Ideal King," in *Le palais et la royauté: archéologie et civilisation: compte rendu—Rencontre assyriologique internationale (19th: 1971)* (ed. P. Garelli; Paris: P. Geuthner, 1974), 163–76; M. T. Larsen, "The City and its King: On the Old Assyrian Notion of Kingship," in *Le palais et la royauté*, 285–300; G. W. Ahlström, *Royal Administration and National Religion in Ancient Palestine* (Studies in the History of the Ancient Near East 1; Leiden: Brill, 1982) 1–25; H. Cazelles, "Sacral Kingship," *ABD* 5:863–66; Parpola, *Assyrian Prophecies*, xxxvi–xliv; M. W. Hamilton, *The Body Royal: The Social Poetics of Kingship in Ancient Israel* (BI 78; Leiden: Brill, 2005); N. Wyatt, *There's such divinity doth hedge a king: Selected Essays of Nicolas Wyatt on Royal Ideology in Ugaritic and Old Testament Literature* (Aldershot: Ashgate, 2005); Nissinen, Prophecy as Construct," 18–24; Gordon, "Prophecy," 49–56.

52. M. Weippert, '"Das Frühere, siehe, ist eingetroffen. . . .:' Über Selbstzitate im altorientalischen Prophetenspruch," in *Oracles et prophéties dans l'Antiquité: Actes du colloque de Strasbourg, 15–17, juin 1995* (ed. J.-G. Heintz; Travaux du Centre de recherche sur le Proche-Orient et la Grèce antiques 15; Strasbourg: Publications de l'Université de Strasbourg, 1997), 147–69; M. Nissinen, "What Is Prophecy? An Ancient Near Eastern Perspective," in *Inspired Speech: Prophecy in the Ancient Near East: Essays in Honor of Herbert B. Huffmon* (ed. J. Kaltner and L. Stulman; JSOTSup 372; London: T. & T. Clark, 2004), 17–37.

53. B. Pongratz-Leisten, *Herrschaftswissen in Mesopotamien: Formen der Kommunikation zwischen Gott und Konig in 2. und 1. Jahrtausend v.Chr.* (SAA 10; Helsinki: Neo-Assyrian Text Corpus Project, 1999); idem, "Cassandra's Colleagues: Prophetesses in the Neo-Assyrian Empire," *CSMSJ* 1 (2006) 15–21.

54. B. Pongratz-Leisten, "The King at the Crossroads of between Divination and Cosmology," in *Divination, Politics, and Ancient Near Eastern Empires* (ed. A. Lenzi and J. Stökl; SBLANEM 7; Atlanta: SBL, 2014), 48.

55. For the purposes of this essay, it suffices to limit discussion to some broad features. There were, of course, distinct nuances of royal ideology in different societies and development

Insofar as the fate of Ahab's land and people are inextricably tied to his policies, Ahab plays this traditional mediatory role. Yet, insofar as he fulfills this function, he also fails it, because his rule brings drought, famine, injustice, and defeat to his land.[56] His rule represents an inversion of the royal ideal. Moreover, his dependence on the divine realm becomes effectively a dependence on a hostile prophet, who represents divinity to him. Ahab's only communication to or from the divine realm comes through Elijah (1 Kgs 17:1; 18:1–2, 18–19; 21:17–19, 20–24, 28–29) or through Micaiah (1 Kgs 22:14, 17, 19–23, 25, 28).[57] It is a prophet who first pronounces drought in the land (1 Kgs 17:1) and who later pronounces its end (1 Kgs 18:17). In the narrative, the king makes no firsthand attempt to communicate with any deity, much less the God of Israel.[58] In comparison, King Zakkur of Hamath and Luʿash recalls how after he raised his hands to Baʿlšamayn in the midst of an enemy attack and siege, Baʿlšamayn answered him "through seers (*ḥzyn*) and through messengers" (*ʿddn*).[59] Within Samuel–Kings, David (e.g., 2 Sam 7:17–29), Solomon (e.g., 1 Kgs 3:4–14; 8:22–61), and Hezekiah (1 Kgs 18:36–37; 19:14–37; 20:1–3) successfully practice intermediation, whether on behalf of the people or on behalf of themselves.[60]

While the consistent stress on Elijah's critical position in mediating between the divine sphere and Ahab's royal court is one of the distinctive traits of the Elijah

---

within royal ideology within various states. See, for example, P. Machinist, "Kingship and Divinity in Imperial Assyria," in *Text, Artifact, and Image: Revealing Ancient Israelite Religion* (ed. G. Beckman and T. J. Lewis; BJS 346; Providence: Brown Judaic Studies, 2006), 152–88.

56. Such a profound questioning of the tenets underlying royal ideology is by no means unique to biblical literature. See, for example, S. B. Parker, "The Historical Composition of KRT and the Cult of El," *ZAW* 89 (1977) 173; J. C. De Moor, "The Crisis of Polytheism in Late Bronze Age Ugarit," *OTS* 24 (1986) 12–14; G. N. Knoppers, "Dissonance and Disaster in the Legend of Kirta," *JAOS* 114 (1994) 572–82; N. Wyatt, *Myths of Power: A Study of Royal Myth and Ideology in Ugaritic and Biblical Tradition* (Ugaritisch-biblische Literatur 13; Münster: Ugarit-Verlag, 1996).

57. To complicate matters, the messages of the prophets competing with Micaiah are also divinely sent, inasmuch as Yᴀʜᴡʜ authorizes a lying spirit (רוח שקר) to speak via the mouth of all his prophets to deceive Ahab (1 Kgs 22:20–23).

58. In the narrative depicting an invasion by King Ben-hadad, an anonymous prophet (נביא) serendipitously appears before the Israelite king, announcing that Yᴀʜᴡʜ had delivered the "great throng" (ההמון הגדול) of invading forces into his control (1 Kgs 20:13–14). The prophetic intervention thus turns out to be a critical factor in rallying the Israelites in the face of a potential catastrophe. Subsequently, when Ben-hadad invades Israel once more (1 Kgs 20:22–27), an intervention by an unnamed "man of God" (איש האלהים; 1 Kgs 20:28) proves to be decisive in addressing the international crisis. The surprising triumph (1 Kgs 20:29–30) will inform Ahab, כי־אני יהוה, "that I am Yᴀʜᴡʜ" (1 Kgs 20:28). Insofar as the Israelite king follows prophetic counsel, he succeeds during these two military conflicts, yet in neither case does the Israelite monarch (identified with Ahab in vv. 13–15) consult a Yahwistic prophet. Rather, the prophet and the man of God come to him to offer unsolicited but timely advice.

59. Millard, "Inscription of Zakkur," A 9–17 (*KAI* 202.9–17).

60. Again, the situation differs in the much shorter account found in Chronicles. There, Isaiah and Hezekiah together petition the deity "and cry out to the heavens" in response to the crisis precipitated by Sennacherib's massive incursion into Judah (2 Chr 32:20).

narratives, the weight placed on prophetic authority is attested more broadly within Samuel–Kings. One might think that monarchs, as the most powerful and important political figures in the land, would enjoy primary authority over all other leaders, such as military officials, elders, and priests. The hierarchy of power favoring the king holds true with respect to virtually all office holders, but it does not hold true with respect to royal-prophetic relational dynamics with figures such as Samuel, Ahijah, Elijah, Elisha, and Isaiah.[61] This represents another way in which the power dynamics of certain prophetic-royal relations differ in Samuel–Kings from most of those known elsewhere in the surviving writings from the ancient Near East.[62] In portraying encounters between kings and the prophets the literary work upholds, kings are sometimes functionally subordinate to prophets, not vice versa.

Elijah and Elisha engage the potentates of their time with authority. They never address the monarchs of their times by a deferential title. Quite the contrary: when Elisha is asked for a prophecy in the joint campaign to retake Ramoth-Gilead, he declares dismissively to Ahab: "As Yhwh of hosts lives, before whom I stand, were it not out of respect for Jehoshaphat, the king of Judah, I would neither look at you nor take notice of you at all" (2 Kgs 3:14). Later, when King Joash of Israel visits a terminally-ill Elisha (2 Kgs 13:14), the weeping king addresses him, "My father, my father . . . the chariotry of Israel and its horsemen!" In this instance, the monarch demonstrates respect for the prophet and addresses him as his superior.[63]

The functional subordination of royalty to prophecy in the case of Elijah is evident in the manner in which Elijah's encounters with Ahab are depicted in the Mt. Carmel contest narrative. When the prophet meets King Ahab, he orders the king: "Now, send (word and) convoke to me (וְעַתָּה שְׁלַח קְבֹץ אֵלַי) all Israel at Mt. Carmel . . ." (1 Kgs 18:19). The narration of Ahab's response carefully signifies

---

61. An exception occurs when Josiah reads the "Book of the Covenant" and cuts a covenant before Yhwh (2 Kgs 23:1–3), because he does so in charge of a national gathering, consisting of "all the people of Judah and the inhabitants of Jerusalem (who were) with him, the priests and the prophets—all of the people from small to great" (2 Kgs 23:2). In this covenant ceremony, all of the community—laity and leaders alike—recommit to the authority of (Deuteronomic) law. Interestingly, instead of "and the prophets," 2 Chr 34:30 reads "and the Levites." On whether the Levites were, for all intents and purposes, viewed as prophetic figures by the Chronicler, see G. von Rad, *Das Geschichtsbild des chronistischen Werkes* (Stuttgart: Kohlhammer, 1930), 72, 114; D. L. Petersen, *Late Israelite Prophecy: Studies in Deutero-Prophetic Literature and in Chronicles* (SBLMS 23; Missoula, MT: Scholars Press, 1977) 85; L. C. Jonker, *1 & 2 Chronicles* (Grand Rapids, MI: Baker, 2013), 292. For a different view, see J. Wellhausen, *Prolegomena to the History of Ancient Israel* (trans. J. S. Black and A. Menzies; Edinburgh: Adams and Charles Black, 1885), 192; Schniedewind, *Word of God*, 185–87.

62. There may be one intriguing allusion in one of the Deir ʿAllā plaster texts (II.9–13) to a failure of "kings" or "our king" (.mlkn.) to seek counsel in the midst of divinely-induced turmoil, but the text is too fragmentary to determine the implications of this reference (Hoftijzer, "Interpretation," 228–41).

63. The address (2 Kgs 13:14) echoes that used by Elisha of his mentor, Elijah (2 Kgs 2:12).

his compliance with Elijah's imperatives: "And Ahab sent word (וישלח אחאב) throughout all Israel and gathered (ויקבץ) the prophets to Mt. Carmel" (1 Kgs 18:20).[64] When the contest is over, Elijah orders Ahab: "Go up, eat, and drink (עלה אכל ושתה), because there is a sound of heavy rain" (1 Kgs 18:41). Again, the text carefully notes royal compliance: "And Ahab went up, to eat, and to drink" (ויעלה אחאב לאכל ולשתות; 1 Kgs 18:42). The verbal and lexical correspondences are too consistent to be coincidental. The king is operationally subservient to the prophet.

A comparison to this portrayal may be drawn with prophetic–royal relations in Neo-Assyrian times. There, prophetic figures form part of the institutional state apparatus: "Prophets belonged to the machinery of imperial propaganda, the purpose of which was to substantiate the necessity of the existence and growth of the imperium."[65] Nevertheless, it would be simplistic to speak of stark opposites. Neo-Assyrian mantics could and did register mild criticisms of monarchs. The prophetic demands Neo-Assyrian prophets and prophetesses brought to the king, usually couched in the form of questions, include increased veneration of the goddess (SAA 9 1.10 vi 13–18) and due recognition through burnt offerings of the gods of the Esaggil, who "languish in an evil, chaotic wilderness'" (SAA 9 2.3 ii 24′–27′).[66] In one case, Ishtar of Arbela raises a series of pointed questions to Esarhaddon, perhaps via Lā-dāgil-ili, because the king had failed to show proper gratitude to the goddess for defeating the king's enemies: "As if I did not do or give you anything! Did I not bend the four doorjambs of Assyria and did I not give them to you? Did I not vanquish your enemy? Did I not collect your haters and foes [like but]terflies?" (SAA 9 3.5 ii 18–24).[67] In return for these beneficent actions undertaken on behalf of Esarhaddon, the goddess expects commensurate offerings of food and drink (SAA 9 3.5 ii 26–36).[68] The carefully-worded questions raised by some prophets and prophetesses in Neo-Assyrian sources are important, because they demonstrate that prophetic figures did occasionally dispatch messages from the divine realm, requesting the king to change course and take actions on behalf of a deity.[69] Nevertheless, the concept of the human agent of divine revelation as

---

64. At the beginning of the verse, we read with the LXX* (*lectio brevior*). The MT expands to "throughout all of the children of Israel" (בכל־בני ישראל). Many Heb. MSS read גבול, instead of כל. Later in the verse, we read with the MT (*lectio brevior*). The LXX expands to παντας τους προφητας, "all of the prophets."

65. Nissinen, *References to Prophecy*, 164.

66. Following the translation of Nissinen, *Prophets and Prophecy*, 114; cf. Parpola, *Assyrian Prophecies*, lxvi–lxvii, 10, 15–16.

67. Parpola, *Assyrian Prophecies*, 25–26. The prophetic name is largely a restoration: [La-dagil-i]li.

68. Parpola, *Assyrian Prophecies*, 25–27; H. Marlow, "Ecology, Theology, Society: Physical, Religious, and Social Disjuncture in Biblical and Neo-Assyrian Texts," in *"Thus Speaks Ishtar of Arbela,"* 187–202.

69. See, further, J. W. Hilber, *Cultic Prophecy in the Psalms* (BZAW 352; Berlin: de Gruyter, 2005), 56–57; idem, "Royal Cultic Prophecy in Assyria, Judah, and Egypt," in *"Thus Speaks Ishtar*

not only the ethical compass but also the dominant figure in the prophetic-royal relationship is foreign to the Neo-Assyrian corpus of prophetic texts.

There is yet another means by which Elijah and Elisha appear as independent figures who are not employed by, of functionally lesser rank than, or controlled by the monarchs of their time.[70] Unlike prophets such as Nathan and Isaiah, who are associated in one way or another with the royal court or state-sponsored cultic establishment, Elijah and Elisha do not bear any relation to or reveal any dependency on the royal court. Although self-identifying as prophets of YHWH, Elijah and Elisha curiously do not bear any stated affiliation with or dependence on known Yahwistic sanctuaries, such as the state-sponsored temples situated at Bethel and Dan.[71]

To be sure, the mention of the timing of Elijah's sacrifice on Mt. Carmel as coinciding with the lifting up of the meal offering (בעלות המנחה; 1 Kgs 18:39) is sometimes construed as a reference to the daily regimen of sacrifices at the Jerusalem temple. In this interpretation, the cult Elijah identifies with is implicitly construed as the cultic establishment. Nevertheless, Elijah neither mentions Jerusalem nor its temple. When the prophet himself seeks a divine revelation, following Jezebel's death threat (1 Kgs 19:1–2), he journeys not from Beersheba to Jerusalem but rather from Beersheba to Mt. Horeb (1 Kgs 19:3–8). While there, Elijah repeatedly complains to YHWH that the Israelites "have torn down your altars" (1 Kgs 19:10, 14) but he does not identify where these altars were located. In the Mt. Carmel contest, Elijah repairs and rebuilds the altar of YHWH that had been torn down (1 Kgs 18:30).[72] Elijah regards these altars as legitimate Yahwistic sacrificial installations; otherwise, he would not lament the demise of these altars and rebuild one himself. The reference in 1 Kgs 18:39 may be best considered, therefore, as openly allusive.[73] In short, Elijah appears as a Yahwistic prophet, who

---

of Arbela," 161–86. For a somewhat different view, see R. P. Gordon, "Prophecy in the Mari and Nineveh Archives," in "Thus Speaks Ishtar of Arbela": Prophecy in Israel, Assyria, and Egypt in the Neo-Assyrian Period (ed. R. P. Gordon and H. M. Barstad; Winona Lake, IN: Eisenbrauns, 2013), 47–49.

70. By lesser rank, we mean within the larger world of theopolitics. Politically, Ahab's grip on power in his own lifetime goes largely uncontested.

71. The Deuteronomistically-formulated judgment of Ahab (1 Kgs 16:33) faults him for, among other things, following in the sins of Jeroboam the son of Nebat (בחטאות בן־נבט), but the topic of the Bethel and Dan sanctuaries never comes up in the Elijah-Elisha narratives.

72. Reading with the MT (lectio difficilior). The shorter and more ambiguous lemma of LXX 1 Kgs 18:32, και ιασατο το θυσιαστηριον το κατεσκαμμενον, "and he repaired the altar that had been thrown down," avoids the implication that a Yahwistic altar previously stood on Mt. Carmel.

73. There is also an interpretive issue in the reference to the Baal prophets, who "continued to prophesy (ויתנבאו) from noon until the lifting up of the meal offering" (עד לעלות המנחה; 1 Kgs 18:29). Does this notice allude to the ritual schedule of the Baal temple (1 Kgs 16:31–32), one of the Yahwistic shrines in the northern kingdom, or the Jerusalem temple? The text does not say.

has (or had) an attachment to various Yahwistic altars in the northern Israel but is not affiliated with any one particular Yahwistic temple.

The unusual situation in the Elijah-Elisha materials may be also compared with that obtaining in another major biblical narrative work—Chronicles. There, prophets do not generally enjoy such independent standing and power.[74] In fact, most prophetic figures in Chronicles support the temple or are themselves supported by the temple (e.g., 1 Chr 25:1–9).[75] One caveat must be added, however, to this discussion of prophecy in Kings. Prophets generally do not displace kings as the primary literary interest of the writers. The case of Elijah and Elisha is largely exceptional.[76] The tenures of monarchs consistently comprise the central organizing compositional principle in arranging the flow of history in the work. The past is measured according to a regnal principle.[77] Within this foundational regnal framework, the editors sometimes include materials—such as prophetic narratives, legends, and oracles—that they deem suitable for evaluating the larger era under review. One may debate whether a good deal of this prophetic material represents later additions to a shorter, more narrowly-focused, and more tightly-organized Deuteronomistic composition, but the concern of this essay lies with the effect that the integration of such prophetic material has on redirecting and reframing readers' understandings of the past.

The revision that amounts to more than a literary diversion or a delay in the action requires comment. In the Elijah and Elisha stories, prophets displace monarchs as the major topic of discussion. Elijah appears on the scene during Ahab's tenure (1 Kgs 17:1), soon after the reign of Ahab has been introduced and found to be wanting (1 Kgs 16:29–33). Thereafter, Elijah, other prophets (1 Kgs 20:13–43;

---

74. P. Beentjes, "Prophets in the Book of Chronicles," in *The Elusive Prophet: The Prophet as a Historical Person, Literary Character and Anonymous Artist* (ed. J. C. de Moor; OtSt 45; Leiden: Brill, 2001), 45–53; Y. Amit, "The Role of Prophecy and Prophets in the Chronicler's World," in *Prophets, Prophecy and Prophetic Texts in Second Temple Judaism* (ed. M. H. Floyd and R. L. Haak; LHBOTS 427; London: T. & T. Clark, 2006), 94–99; G. N. Knoppers, "Democratizing Revelation? Prophets, Seers, and Visionaries in Chronicles," in *Prophecy and the Prophets in Ancient Israel: Proceedings of the Oxford Old Testament Seminar* (ed. J. Day; LHBOTS 531; London: T. & T. Clark Continuum, 2010), 391–409; idem, '"To Him You must Listen:' The Prophetic Legislation in Deuteronomy and the Reformation of Classical Tradition in Chronicles," in *Chronicling the Chronicler: The Book of Chronicles and Early Second Temple Historiography* (ed. P. S. Evans and T. F. Williams; Winona Lake, IN: Eisenbrauns, 2013), 161–94.

75. G. N. Knoppers, *I Chronicles 10–29* (AB 12A; New York: Doubleday/New Haven: Yale University Press, 2004), 843–60.

76. In the portrayal of the reign of Hezekiah of Judah, the allocation of coverage privileges the intermediation and oracles of Isaiah (2 Kgs 19:6–7, 20–34; 20:1, 4–7, 9, 11, 14, 15–18), yet as important a figure as Isaiah is during Hezekiah's tenure, he does not dominate the stage as much as prophets do during Ahab's reign.

77. So, for example, when writing about the Israelite and Judahite monarchies, the Deuteronomistic work proceeds, as is well-known, by switching back and forth synchronistically between the histories of the northern and southern kingdoms.

22:1–38), and Elisha receive the bulk of coverage until the end of the Omride dynasty. Perhaps not coincidentally, this period marks the introduction and end of Baal worship in the Israelite monarchy (1 Kgs 16:29–33; 2 Kgs 10:18–28; cf. 2 Kgs 17:16). The reign of King Ahab (1 Kgs 16:29–22:40), one of Israel's most accomplished northern monarchs, is thus dominated by prophetic activities and prophetic interactions, some of which have nothing to do with the royals themselves (e.g., 1 Kgs 17:2–6, 7–16, 17–24).

A corollary to the great interest shown in creating a formative role for prophets is a relative lack of interest shown in royal accomplishments. The writers of Kings mention the transfer of the Israelite capital from Tirzah to Samaria (1 Kgs 16:23–24) but otherwise spend precious little time examining the expansion of the Israelite state under Omride monarchs and do not discuss, much less mention, Ahab's impressive contributions to the allied coalition arrayed against the forces of Shalmaneser III in the pivotal battle at Qarqar.[78] In the concluding comments to Ahab's reign, the writers refer to Ahab's major public works, including an ivory house (בית השן) and an assortment of unnamed towns that he had built (1 Kgs 22:39).[79] For details on these royal deeds, readers are referred to the "annals of the kings of Israel" (1 Kgs 22:39).

To summarize: discussions of the projection of Omride geopolitical power are exceedingly rare. The larger presentation in Kings gives the impression that Ahab was a weak leader whose regime was vulnerable to social-religious conflicts from within and whose reign ended ignominiously with a catastrophic defeat by Aramean forces resulting in the loss of Ahab's life (1 Kgs 22:1–38).[80] From the vantage points of economy, societal stability, military expansion, and international diplomacy, the account masks rather than illuminates how the Omride dynasty was one of the most successful dynasties, if not the most successful dynasty, in northern Israelite history.[81] On a historical level and a literary level (allocation of coverage, themes, and plot), prophecy generates most of the action during the Omride era.

---

78. A. K. Grayson, *Assyrian Rulers of the Early First Millennium BC II (858–745 B.C.)* (RIMA 3; Toronto: University of Toronto Press, 1996), 23 (RIM. A.0.102.2.ii 89b-102). The inscription attributes to Ahab (*Aḫabbu*) the Israelite (*Sirʾalāia*) "2,000 chariots, 10,000 soldiers," but the number of chariots seems too high: N. Naʾaman, "Two Notes on the Monolith Inscription of Shalmaneser III from Kurkh," *TA* 3 (1976) 89–106; M. Cogan, *The Raging Torrent: Historical Inscriptions from Assyria and Babylonia relating to Ancient Israel* (Jerusalem: Carta, 2008), 12–22.

79. Even if one were to excise all of the prophetic materials as late additions, the lack of interest shown in royal investments in public infrastructure remains.

80. D. Jobling, "The Syrians in the Book of the Divided Kingdoms: A Literary/Theological Approach," *BibInt* 11 (2003) 531–42.

81. S. Timm, *Die Dynastie Omri: Quellen und Untersuchungen zur Geschichte Israels im 9. Jahrhundert vor Christus* (FRLANT 124; Göttingen: Vandenhoeck & Ruprecht, 1982); G. W. Ahlström, *The History of Ancient Palestine from the Paleolithic Period to Alexander's Conquest* (JSOTSup 146; Sheffield: Sheffield Academic Press, 1993), 569–606; D. Ussishkin, "Jezreel, Samaria and Megiddo: Royal Cities of Omri and Ahab," in *Congress Volume: Cambridge 1995* (VTSup 66; Leiden: Brill, 1997), 351–64; J. M. Miller and J. Hayes, *A History of Ancient Israel and Judah* (2nd ed.; Louisville: Westminster John Knox, 2006), 284–326.

The displacement of royalty in mythic space by prophecy in divine-human relations is complemented, therefore, by a displacement of royalty by prophecy in literary space. In the Elijah-Elisha stories, we witness the extension of the definition of "prophet" to that of a pivotal public figure, actively dispensing divine weal and woe to the monarch and people of his time.

We have been discussing a number of the ways in which the portrayal of prophecy in Samuel–Kings, but especially within the Elijah-Elisha narratives, may be considered unusual within a larger ancient Near Eastern setting. The direct head-to-head meetings with kings, the open hostility shown toward monarchs, the functional subordination of monarchs to prophets in prophetic-royal encounters, the prophetic control exercised over meteorological and medical matters, and the large allocation of coverage devoted to human agents of divine revelation are all important features of the prophetic legacy. One might be tempted to generalize that prophets serve as the loyal opposition, holding kings to account as an important check on royal power, but such a generalization, while certainly true, would not do justice to the pivotal function certain prophets come to play in Israelite life. Rather than kings occupying a critical position in political, economic, and religious affairs, mediating divine weal or woe to the populace as one finds among the traditions of ancient Near Eastern royal ideology, Elijah and Elisha occupy this pivotal institutional role within the history of the Omride dynasty.

III. The Theopolitics of Prophecy: False Prophets in Assyria and in Israel

Having pointed out several largely distinctive elements in the Elijah-Elisha narratives, we consider it helpful to explore how the prophet-monarch social dynamics in the Elijah stories may be illumined by two points of comparison. The first involves a comparative analysis of the limited epigraphic remains relating to false prophecy in the Neo-Assyrian realm. We shall argue that Ahab's hostile responses to Elijah's declarations and actions presuppose a certain set of beliefs about normal prophetic behavior. In other words, prophetic-royal relations may be clarified by gaining a better understanding of the social, cultic, and political functions prophets might have been expected to play within the service of a large state apparatus.

The second exercise involves pursuing an internal comparison within the literary world of Kings—namely, to explore how the work positions Elijah, Micaiah, and Elisha in relation to the other prophets of their times. What does the valorization of select individuals, such as Elijah and Elisha, over against the majority of other prophets reveal about what the writers thought about prophecy in monarchic Israel? This comparative analysis will shed light on the degree to which the prophets whose deeds the work promotes actually deviate from the norm the work concedes prevailed in monarchic times.

The first comparison explores the degree to which Elijah's antagonism toward the Omride state conforms to an ancient Near Eastern analogue—the false or rogue prophet. Analyses of Neo-Assyrian prophetic texts have pointed to the extent to which the messages referred to or embedded within texts are made in support of the king or, at the very least, are not rendered in antagonism to the king. To speak of "false prophets" presupposes an ancient dichotomy between those prophets who were "true" and those who were "false."[82] Embodying a representational view of truth, the traditional dichotomy supposes that somehow authentic prophets were delivering accurate prophecy, while their counterparts, inauthentic prophets, were delivering inaccurate prophecy. The former could be considered as reliable, while the latter could be considered as unreliable or as intentionally deceptive. This binary definition fails to recognize the occasional nature of prophecy, the many variables in the relationship between the state and cult, and the sociopolitical contexts in which prophecies were delivered and transcribed. It also makes the veracity of the product—prophecy itself—the metric for defining what is a true or false prophet. In reality, the Neo-Assyrian portrait of what defines a false prophet is much more relational.

Because "false prophecy" was unlikely to be preserved in the Neo-Assyrian system of archiving, there are limits to the extent to which we might define a Neo-Assyrian model for what constitutes a false prophet.[83] Yet, the available information, even in its very limited state, provides some useful insights. Many prophetic figures in the Neo-Assyrian realm were attached to the state via state-supported cults, with no small number of prophecies taking place in the context of temple precincts. A proper prophet was normally an officially recognized figure who functioned as a part of a state-sponsored divinatory apparatus responsible for supporting the empire. Whether such individuals were regular prophets or *pro tem* prophets, these figures mediated messages from the divine realm to the world of human affairs.[84] To move toward a definition of false or unacceptable prophecy, we might look for prophetic messages and actions that did not conform to the standard paradigm; specifically, we might look for situations in which a prophet or one claiming to deliver prophetic messages was neither attached to the official cult nor functioned in a way that upheld the stability of the kingdom. From these

---

82. The issue of what constitutes true and false prophecy looms large in Jeremiah. See C. J. Sharp, *Prophecy and Ideology in Jeremiah* (OTS; London: T. & T. Clark, 2003) and the essays in *Prophecy in the Book of Jeremiah* (ed. H. M. Barstad and R. G. Kratz; BZAW 388; Berlin: de Gruyter, 2009). For a brief exploration of fundamental problems in defining false prophecy in the Hebrew scriptures, see D. N. Freedman and R. Frey, "False Prophecy is True," in *Inspired Speech: Prophecy in the Ancient Near East—Essays in Honor of Herbert B. Huffmon* (JSOTSup 372; London: T. & T. Clark, 2004), 82–87.

83. The important element of selection comes into play. It is doubtful, as Nissinen points out, that most officials serving in palaces and temples would self-consciously inscribe, keep, and archive treasonous prophetic messages, *References to Neo-Assyrian Prophecy*, 166.

84. Stökl, *Prophecy in the Ancient Near East*, 7–10.

broad categories, two possible candidates for instances of false prophecy emerge in preserved Neo-Assyrian texts. The first is illustrated in the Succession Treaty of Esarhaddon (SAA 2 6 § 10), which outlines a scenario in which prophets might prove disloyal to the state.[85]

> If you hear any evil, improper, ugly word, which is neither seemly nor good to Assurbanipal, the great crown prince designate, son of Esarhaddon, king of Assyria, our lord, either from the mouth of his enemy or from the mouth of his ally ... or from the mouth of a prophet, an ecstatic, an inquirer of oracles, or from the mouth of any human being at all, you shall not conceal it, but come and report it to Assurbanipal, the great crown prince designate, son of Esarhaddon, king of Assyria. (SAA 2 6 § 10.108–12, 116–122)[86]

Like many ancient Near Eastern diplomatic treaties, this legal arrangement includes an injunction to the client(s) to report immediately those who bring a false word concerning the treaty. These lists typically include members of the royal family or court but could apply theoretically to anyone. In the case of the Succession Treaty of Esarhaddon, an important difference is to be noted in that the treaty warns against false words emanating from the *raggimu, maḫḫû*, and *šā'ilu amat ili* (prophet, ecstatic, and inquirer of divine words). Whether the *raggimu, maḫḫû*, and *šā'ilu* represent separate classes or a group of synonymous professions, they are undoubtedly specialists in divinatory methods.[87] To be sure, the prophetic figures mentioned in the Succession Treaty of Esarhaddon are only a few of the many "mandatory reporters" who are obligated to inform the crown about any party they hear of who engages in seditious agitation or who opposes the terms of the succession.[88]

That treasonous words might emanate from the mouths of prophets is surprising in light of the fact that almost no messages of this sort have survived. Inasmuch as they touch on political matters, virtually every attested prophecy was written in favor of the king and was used to support his regime.[89] Prophets and the monarch normally enjoyed a "close and confidential" relationship.[90] The inclusion of the clause pertaining specifically to the *raggimu, maḫḫû*, and *šā'ilu* suggests that

---

85. S. Parpola and K. Watanabe, *Neo-Assyrian Treaties and Loyalty Oaths* (SAA 2; Helsinki: Helsinki University Press, 1988), 28–59.

86. Thus, the translation of Nissinen, *Prophets and Prophecy*, 150–51.

87. M. Nissinen, *References to Neo-Assyrian Prophecy*, 161. For the theory that the *maḫḫû* was a lay prophet, see Stökl, *Prophecy in the Ancient Near East*, 118–21.

88. H. B. Huffmon, "The Exclusivity of Divine Communication in Ancient Israel: False Prophecy in the Hebrew Bible and the Ancient Near East," in *Mediating between Heaven and Earth: Communication with the Divine in the Ancient Near East* (ed. C. L. Crouch, J. Stökl, and A. E. Zernecke; London: T. & T. Clark, 2012), 69.

89. Nissinen, *References to Neo-Assyrian Prophecy*, 161.

90. Ibid.

false prophecy—that is, prophecy perceived to be disloyal to the king or to his designated successor—was more of a threat than the surviving epigraphic evidence otherwise suggests. Moreover, the very fact that the treaty lists different kinds of mantics and obligates its clients to keep the oath indicates that not all prophetic figures were firmly under royal control.

In sum, false prophecy may be understood as "prophecy . . . not transmitted in due order but fabricated for political purposes using the proclaimer of the message . . . as a decoy."[91] Words spoken against the king or crown prince were considered to be of dubious divine origin.[92] That the list in the Succession Treaty of Esarhaddon includes a wide variety of figures implies that the central issue is not cultic or divinatory but political.[93] A "prophecy against the ruling king is false, no matter who the proclaimer is and what powers he or she claims to be vested with."[94]

Although the Succession Treaty of Esarhaddon provides one indication that false prophecy was possible, the Nusku Oracle quoted in ABL 1217 r.2–5 "proves undisputedly that words presented as divine messages could be used against the king."[95] In this oracle, a slave girl speaks against Sennacherib, indicating that the god Nusku has spoken and declared that Sasî will be king.

> A slave girl of Bēl-aḫu-uṣur [. . .] upon [. . .] on the outskirts of Ḫ[arrān]; since Sivan (III) she is enraptured and speaks a good word about him: "This is the word of Nusku: The kingship is for Sāsî! I shall destroy the name and seed of Sennacherib!"[96]

The texts involved (ABL 1217+CT 53 118, CT 53 17+107, and CT 53 938) are a series of letters from an otherwise unknown Nabû-rēḫtu-uṣur in the midst of what appears to be a conspiracy originating from the "outskirts of Ḫarrān," far from the heart of the kingdom centered in Nineveh. The identity of the would-be future king, Sāsî, is obscure. The prophecy speaks against Sennacherib, predict-

---

91. Ibid., 166–67. In this sense, it is a seemingly authentic revelation devised to mislead the intended audience.

92. Huffmon, "Exclusivity," 68–69; Stökl, *Prophecy in the Ancient Near East*, 117–18.

93. Huffmon sees the matter slightly differently, "A Company of Prophets: Mari, Assyria, Israel," in *Prophecy in Its Ancient Near Eastern Context: Mesopotamian, Biblical, and Arabian Perspectives* (ed. M. Nissinen; SBLSymS 13; Atlanta: SBL, 2000), 62. For him, the central issue is not really whether a prophecy is "true" or "false" but whether it is favorable to the king. The metric is loyalty or disloyalty to the crown that may be discerned from the message. Yet, insofar as Huffmon stresses that the Succession Treaty of Esarhaddon leaves no room for the possibility that the gods could oppose the king, his views may be considered to be not far from those of Nissinen.

94. Nissinen, *References to Prophecy*, 167.

95. Ibid., 166; S. W. Holloway, *Aššur is King! Aššur is King! Religion in the Exercise of Power in the Neo-Assyrian Empire* (CHANE 10; Leiden: Brill, 2002), 410–14.

96. ABL 1217, rev. 2–5; Nissinen, *References to Prophecy*, 110–11.

ing the ruin of Sennacherib's reputation and posterity, while promoting the rule of another. Intriguingly, the text states that the prophecy came from a slave girl (GEMÉ) and that the message stems not from Ishtar but from Nusku, a subordinate deity within the larger pantheon. That the report refers to a "slave girl," rather than to a prophetess, may indicate reluctance on the part of the reporter to state that the prophecy bore a clear imprint of divine authority.[97]

The Nusku oracle and the Succession Treaty of Esarhaddon demonstrate that it was conceivable for someone in the prophetic classes to issue a message contrary to the interests of the throne. Indeed, because the Nusku oracle speaks of the destruction of the present king, the end of his seed, and the bestowal of kingship on another candidate, it may be liable to the charge of inciting mutiny against the ruling royal house. Accordingly, the author of the letters, Nabû-rēḫtu-uṣur, urges that a number of steps be taken, including the interrogation of the household of Bēl-aḫu-uṣur under the gate of the temple of Nabû, the transport of the slave girl, the performance of a(n extispicy) ritual on her (account), and the transport of Bēl-aḫu-uṣur from Ḫarrān.[98] Given the content of the oracle, it is no wonder that Nabû-rēḫtu-uṣur expresses his wish both that the name and seed of Sāsî, Bēl-aḫu-uṣur, and their confreres perish and that "Bēl and Nabû establish the name and seed of the king, my lord, until far-off days."[99]

Discussion of the Succession Treaty of Esarhaddon and the slave girl's prophecy complicates simple definitions of true and false prophecy. Understanding the political resonances that prophecy held within a given social location suggests the operation of a relational definition of false prophecy. The words issued by a prophetess were not false because a deity issued a false revelation—that is, a prediction that was not about to come true. From a royal vantage point, a representational view of truth is disallowed from the outset. Instead, the false proclamation has a very human aspect. Even a prophecy issued from a marginalized individual spoken in the name of a minor god might threaten to weaken or subvert royal power, casting doubt on the perdurability of royal house, and promoting the aspirations of another claimant to the throne. When would-be prophetic figures employ their voices to issue oracles against the king in a Neo-Assyrian context, they are considered to be pseudo-prophets.[100] While these examples are limited, perhaps too lim-

---

97. Nissinen, *References to Prophecy*, 167. Alternatively, only a critical prophecy stemming from someone of such low rank could be admitted for consideration, Pongratz-Leisten, "Cassandra's Colleagues," 19.

98. ABL 1217, rev. 6–8; Nissinen, *References to Prophecy*, 110–11.

99. ABL 1217, rev. 9–11; Nissinen, *References to Prophecy*, 110–11.

100. For Huffmon ("Exclusivity," 70), the central issue in the oracle from Nusku is not whether the revelation was received correctly by the slave girl but that the message represented an interest contradictory to Esarhaddon's throne. Huffmon does not think the Nusku Oracle, while treasonous, falls in the same spectrum as the treason outlined in the Succession Treaty of Esarhaddon. It may be that each of the types of individuals articulated in the Succession Treaty of Esarhaddon would have their own particular means of committing offenses against the crown.

ited to build any sort of comprehensive model of false prophecy, they offer helpful analogues to demonstrate that not only was false prophecy possible but it had the potential to delegitimize and destabilize the ruling royal house.

Working from this expanded definition of what might have been considered "false prophecy," it may be helpful to reexamine the reactions of King Ahab to the initiatives undertaken by Elijah. The royal expectations of the prophet, as portrayed in the text, provide insight into how the writers understood the regular course of king-prophet power dynamics. Like the prophetess residing in the outskirts of Harran, Elijah stems from a relatively marginal area—in this case, the northern Transjordan, far from Samaria, the new capital Ahab established for the Israelite kingdom (1 Kgs 16:29; 17:1). The first act of the prophet could only be perceived as hostile to the ruling elite: he dispatched a message to Ahab proclaiming a drought in the land (1 Kgs 17:1). Rather than function within or in concert with a state apparatus, Elijah works to undermine it. Royal-prophetic relations are defined within a binary framework.

Inasmuch as ancient Near Eastern monarchs were responsible for safeguarding, if not improving, their state economies, a long-term drought would threaten the exercise of Ahab's sovereignty over his own territory. Within antiquity, drought was an enormous challenge even to the best prepared of societies. While short-term survival is possible under drought conditions, a sustained absence of rain and dew results in the exhaustion of food stores and the desiccation of established water sources, such as wells and seasonal springs (1 Kgs 17:1; 18:2, 5, 42–44).[101] Within the narrative world imagined by the text, the officials in Israel's capital, Samaria, were under extreme pressure to find ways to sustain the very viability of the kingdom.

In the wake of successive years of dry weather, it is quite revealing that Ahab identified the offending prophet as the "troubler of Israel" (עכר ישראל; 1 Kgs 18:17).[102] The royal comment represents a stinging indictment of Elijah. The epithet "troubler of Israel," ע(ו)כר ישראל, appears elsewhere only once when, in the Judahite genealogies of Chronicles, Carmi's son is referred to as "Achar (עכר), the troubler of Israel (עוכר ישראל), who violated the ban" (1 Chr 2:7).[103] The Chronistic pun is, in turn, indebted to the play on words occurring in Josh 7:24–26, involving the death sentence imposed upon "Achan" (MT עכן) or "Achar" (LXX* Αχαρ; Josephus, Ant. 5.43–44 Αχαρος) and his family in the "Valley of Achor" (עמק עכור). Joshua asks the offender: "What trouble have you caused us (מה עכרתנו)? May YHWH bring trouble (יעכרך) upon you today" (Josh 7:25). In Kings, the offender is, however, not one who transgressed the ban, endangering the future of his people, but the prophet, who brought about a devastating drought against his own people.

---

101. Given the lack of rain, even the refugee Elijah is sent away from the land (1 Kgs 17:2).
102. R. Hess, "Achan and Achor: Names and Wordplay in Joshua 7," *HAR* 14 (1994) 89–98.
103. Knoppers, *I Chronicles 1–9*, 304.

This brings us to another example of how Ahab's reactions to Elijah illumine the world of royal expectations of prophets. In ancient Near Eastern monarchies, participants in the state hierarchy are expected to support the cultic initiatives undertaken by or on behalf of the king. Temple refurbishments, benefactions, offerings, endowments, and the construction of new sanctuaries are some of the significant ways in which monarchs could demonstrate their gratitude to the gods and their cultic establishments. In this context, the reign of Ahab is especially important, because he inaugurates a new cultic initiative in Samaria. He constructs an altar and a temple for Baal (1 Kgs 16:33). According to the evaluation of Ahab's reign, Ahab "went and served Baal (וילך ויעבד את־הבעל) and worshiped him" (וישתחו לו; 1 Kgs 16:29–32). The veneration of Baal (or of the Baals) does not appear in the history of the northern kingdom until the reign of Ahab (1 Kgs 16:31–32).[104] Indeed, the deity Baal is not mentioned in Samuel–Kings until the time of Ahab.[105] Baal worship becomes, however, a prominent and sustained theme in the tenure of Ahab and his dynastic successors (1 Kgs 18:18, 19, 21, 22, 25, 26, 40; 19:18; 22:54) until Jehu's reforms (are said to) extirpate Baal from Samaria (2 Kgs 10:19–28).[106]

Yet, there is a second and rather unusual dimension to Ahab's cultic initiatives. In addition to promoting the cult(s) of Baal and Asherah in Israel, his Sidonian wife Jezebel actively persecutes the prophets of Yʜwʜ and executes them (1 Kgs 18:4, 13; 19:2, 10), leading Elijah to lament repeatedly that he alone remains as a prophet to Yʜwʜ (1 Kgs 18:22; 19:10, 14).[107] The promotion of the cult of Baal and that of Asherah has, therefore, a negative corollary in the oppression of the Yahwistic cult in the northern kingdom.[108] The accusation is not simply that Ahab introduced Baal worship into the northern kingdom but also that he effectively abandoned Israel's patron deity. The reforms of Ahab represent, therefore, a negative mirror image of the types of reforms implemented by Judah's best kings, Hezekiah and Josiah. Rather than campaign for the Yahwistic cult and against foreign cults, Ahab and Jezebel do the opposite. The literary depiction may have little to

---

104. H.-D. Hoffmann, *Reform und Reformen: Untersuchungen zu einem Grundthema der deuteronomistischen Geschichtsschreibung* (ATANT 66; Zürich: Theologischer Verlag, 1980).

105. In his farewell speech, Samuel mentions Israel serving the Baals (1 Sam 12:10), but that worship relates to the era of the chieftains (e.g., Judg 2:13; 6:25, 28, 30, 31, 32; 3:7; 8:33; 10:6, 10).

106. See J. M. Robker, *The Jehu Revolution: A Royal Tradition of the Northern Kingdom and Its Ramifications* (BZAW 435; Berlin: de Gruyter, 2012), and the references cited there.

107. A claim that Yʜwʜ qualifies (1 Kgs 19:18).

108. Although Baal worship and Yʜwʜ worship are portrayed as mutually exclusive alternatives (e.g., 1 Kgs 18:17–39), certain details within the prophetic narratives suggest a more complex picture of life within northern Israel. For instance, in the Ramoth-gilead narrative, Micaiah and the other prophets all speak in the name of Yʜwʜ. Clearly, the writers are not sympathetic to Ahab's favored prophets, but none of these prophets explicitly claims to speak on behalf of any god other than Adonai (MT 1 Kgs 22:6; *Tg. J.* and many Heb. MSS: Yʜwʜ) or Yʜwʜ (1 Kgs 22:11, 12, 15, 17, 19–23, 24, 28). *Tg. J.* labels the prophets in vv. 6, 10, 12, 13 as "prophets of falsehood" (נביי שקרא).

do with what is actually known about the tolerance practiced in Canaanite cultic centers, but it comports inversely with Deuteronomistic ideals.[109]

Elijah, for his part, is hardly a passive bystander. The prophet appears as an active participant in his state's social and political affairs. In the aftermath of the showdown between Elijah and the Baal prophets on Mt. Carmel (1 Kgs 18:17–39), Elijah oversees the systematic roundup of the 450 prophets of Baal, and Elijah subsequently slaughters them (וישׁחטם) in the Wadi Qishon (1 Kgs 18:40).[110] While Elijah's actions resonate with certain features of Deuteronomic law, they collide with the interests of the highest military, cultic, and political office in the land.[111] Rather than serving as a supportive figure with a larger state apparatus, Elijah is enmeshed within an inner-Israelite struggle against the kingdom's highest elite. His actions would be viewed by the king as traitorous, because he was openly opposing an official cultic establishment created and sanctioned by his government. It is no wonder, then, that the next time the two meet Ahab exclaims, "Have you found me, my enemy (אִיְבִי; 1 Kgs 21:20)?" Even though prophets take on adversarial functions elsewhere in Samuel–Kings, Elijah is the only prophet to be identified by a ruler as both a national troubler (עכר) and a personal enemy (איב).

To summarize: inasmuch as Elijah's behaviors correlate to behaviors of prophetic figures in the Neo-Assyrian realm, they correlate much better with those of Neo-Assyrian false prophets than they do with those of state prophets. Elijah's place as a political adversary who resides in a far-off region and belongs to a marginalized cult is consistent with the type of rogue prophecy set against the leadership of a centralized dynastic regime. In this case, the metric of the veracity of the prophecy is not based in its possible factuality but in its congruence with the aims of the state. Because Elijah's prophecies do not uphold royal interests but undermine them, he conforms, in some respects, to the image of a false prophet.[112] Elijah is not a team player but rather an enemy of the state.

We have been discussing royal-prophetic confrontations during the reign of Ahab as indicative of a civil conflict in which the monarch regards his "enemy"

---

109. "The portrayal of Jezebel as a zealot of Baal who undertook to exterminate the prophets of Yhwh is a caricature, with little to recommend it. The intolerance that it implies is inconsistent with pagan thought" (M. Cogan, *I Kings* [AB 10; New York: Doubleday, 2001], 447).

110. Four hundred prophets of Asherah are mentioned once (1 Kgs 18:19), but they do not appear along with the Baal prophets executed by Elijah.

111. On this remarkable passage (Deut 13:2–6), see the incisive discussion of Levinson, *Deuteronomy*, 102–35. A helpful overview of recent discussions may be found in U. Rüterswörden, "Dtn 13 in der neueren Deuteronomiumforschung," in *Congress Volume, Basel 2001* (ed. A. Lemaire; VTSup 92; Leiden: Brill, 2002), 185–203.

112. The only case in which Ahab heeds, in any way, Elijah's prophetic utterances is when Elijah proclaims doom on Ahab, Jezebel, and his royal house (1 Kgs 21:27). On Ahab's curious repentance and its possible literary indebtedness to the story of David's repentance following the murder of Uriah, see P. Buis, *Le livre des Rois* (Sources bibliques; Paris: Gabalda, 1997), 169; White, *Elijah Legends*, 17–24; Cronauer, *Stories about Naboth*, 107–9, 191–93.

as a rogue prophet. The portrayal of Elijah as a marginal voice, who nonetheless manages to command great power over against the king, raises a larger question about how the authors of Samuel–Kings contextualize Elijah, Micaiah, and Elisha within the larger cohort of prophets inhabiting the northern realm, and this is our next topic. What did the writers wish to convey to readers about the course of prophetic history during the northern monarchy? In depicting Ahab's reign, the text sometimes refers to great numbers of competing prophets in northern Israel, who were loyal to, if not employed by, the state (e.g., 1 Kgs 18:4, 19–20, 25–29, 40; 19:1, 10; 22:6, 11–12, 24). These comments are quite telling, because the writers acknowledge that prophets such as Elijah and Elisha, along with their supporters, "the sons of the prophets" (בני־הנביאים) were aberrations.[113]

Although Elijah, Micaiah, and Elisha are presented as exemplary prophets, this does not hold true for most other northern prophets. The vast majority are depicted as being attached to the palace and serving the crown or as being implicitly associated with cultic centers supported by the crown.[114] Although lampooned as royal sycophants (e.g., 1 Kgs 18:18–19; 22:6, 11–12, 24; 2 Kgs 3:13), these figures conform more closely to types of prophetic figures appearing in many Neo-Assyrian and West Semitic texts than do Elijah, Micaiah, and Elisha. If one were to attempt to reconstruct some semblance of what the authors thought (or wished readers to think) that northern prophecy consisted of, one would have to steer away, paradoxically enough, from the very figures the authors promote in their writing and concentrate on the figures they caricature. The number of quasi-independent religious specialists, such as Elijah, Micaiah, and Elisha, pales in comparison to the number of such specialists supported by or allied to the crown.[115] The relational power dynamics in the Elijah-Micaiah-Elisha stories concern, therefore, not simply king against prophet but also prophet against prophet.

---

113. 1 Kgs 20:25–32; 2 Kgs 2:2, 3, 7, 15; 4:1, 38; 5:22; 6:1–2; 9:1–3; cf. Amos 7:14. Note also the phenomenon of the "band of prophets" (חבל נביאים; 1 Sam 10:5, 10; 19:20) who become associated for a time with Saul. On the latter, see the essay by Bembry in this volume.

114. Elisha sometimes appears, however, to be more of a friend to the state than its enemy (2 Kgs 3:11–19; 6:9–23; 6:24–7:20; 9:1–13; 13:14–19). In these episodes, Elisha provides timely counsel both to the Israelite king and to certain individuals about how they might survive stark challenges and succeed in war. In this respect, a contrast may be drawn with Elijah, who consistently appears as an opponent of the Omride state.

115. The case of Micaiah is complicated because there is no clear indication that he is grouped with the "sons of the prophets" associated with Elijah and Elisha. Rather, when Jehoshaphat insists on asking whether there is a prophet of Yhwh present (1 Kgs 22:7), in addition to the 400 the king of Israel consults, the king concedes that there is such a prophet (Micaiah son of Imlah), but he hates him, because "he does not prophesy good, but rather evil" (1 Kgs 22:8). The implication seems to be that Micaiah is part of the larger retinue of prophets available to and supported by the state but that he is not a team player.

Conclusions

In seeking to set human agents of divine revelation, such as Elijah and Elisha, apart from their northern peers, the writers of Kings show some familiarity with the behaviors, roles, and institutional affiliations of prophets in ancient Near Eastern monarchies. The very promotion of Elijah as an enemy of the Omride state and of many other prophets of his time as friends of the state demonstrates at least some knowledge on the part of the authors that many human agents of divine revelation were supportive of and supported by the royal regimes that held sway in their societies. Such prophetic figures receive only scattered, disparaging, and limited attention from the biblical writers, but the writers concede that the prophets who wear "hairy garments and leather belts" (2 Kgs 1:8) were the exception and not the norm.

For the writers, the contributions of Elijah and Elisha to life within northern Israel and the inner-Israelite struggle waged both against northern kings and against other prophets, whether Yahwistic or non-Yahwistic, were crucial to defining major religious issues for their readers. But, if one were to generalize based on numbers and other hints within the prophetic narratives, the broader situation might well be something similar to that obtaining in the Neo-Assyrian realm, albeit on a smaller scale and with certain regional and cultural differences. Most prophets in one way or another supported the major initiatives of the state, were loyal to the crown, and provided oracles of encouragement and direction for royal initiatives.

Bibliography

Ackerman, S. *Warrior, Dancer, Seductress, Queen: Women in Judges and Biblical Israel.* New York: Doubleday, 1998.

Aḥituv, S. *Echoes from the Past: Hebrew and Cognate Inscriptions from the Ancient Past.* Jerusalem: Carta, 2008.

Ahlström, G. W. *Royal Administration and National Religion in Ancient Palestine.* Studies in the History of the Ancient Near East 1. Leiden: Brill, 1982.

_____. *The History of Ancient Palestine from the Paleolithic Period to Alexander's Conquest.* Journal for the Study of the Old Testament Supplement 146. Sheffield: Sheffield Academic, 1993.

Albright, W. F. " 'The Oldest Hebrew Letters: The Lachish Ostraca," *BASOR* 70 (1938) 11–17.

Amit, Y. "The Role of Prophecy and Prophets in the Chronicler's World." Pp. 80–101 in *Prophets, Prophecy and Prophetic Texts in Second Temple Judaism.* Ed. M. H. Floyd and R. L. Haak. The Library of Hebrew Bible/Old Testament Studies 427. London: T. & T. Clark, 2006.

Auld, A. G. "Salomo und die Deuteronomisten—eine Zukunftsvision?" *Theologische Zeitschrift* 48 (1992) 343–54.

_____. "Synoptic David: The View from Chronicles." Pp. 117–28 in *Raising Up a Faithful Exegete: Essays in Honor of Richard D. Nelson.* Ed. K. L. Noll and B. Schramm. Winona Lake, IN: Eisenbrauns, 2010.

_____. *Kings Without Privilege: David and Moses in the Story of the Bible's Kings.* Edinburgh: T. & T. Clark, 1994.

Barstad, H. "Some Remarks on Prophets and Prophecy in the 'Deuteronomistic History'," Pp. 300–315 in *Houses Full of All Good Things: Essays in Memory of Timo Veijola.* Ed. J. Pakkala and M. Nissinen. Publications of the Finnish Exegetical Society 95. Göttingen: Vandenhoeck & Ruprecht, 2008.

_____. "The Understanding of the Prophets in Deuteronomy." *SJOT* 8 (1994) 236–51.

Beentjes, P. "Prophets in the Book of Chronicles." Pp. 45–53 in *The Elusive Prophet: The Prophet as a Historical Person, Literary Character and Anonymous Artist.* Ed. J. C. de Moor. Oudtestamentische Studiën 45. Leiden: Brill, 2001.

Begg, C. T. "The Classical Prophets in the Chronistic History." *Biblische Zeitschrift* 32 (1988) 100–10.

Ben Zvi, E. "Prophetic Memories in the Deuteronomistic Historical and the Prophetic Collections of Books." Pp. 75–102 in *Israelite Prophecy and the Deuteronomistic History.* Ed. M. R. Jacobs and R. F. Person Jr. SBL Ancient Israel and Its Literature 14. Atlanta: Society of Biblical Literature, 2013.

Bernhardt, K.-H. *Das Problem der altorientalischen Königsideologie im Alten Testament.* Vetus Testamentum Supplement 8. Leiden: Brill, 1961.

Blenkinsopp, J. *A History of Prophecy in Ancient Israel.* Louisville: Westminster John Knox, 1996.

_____. *Sage, Priest, Prophet: Religious and Intellectual Leadership in Ancient Israel.* Louisville: Westminster John Knox, 1995.

Blum, E. "Die Nabotüberlieferungen und die Kompositionsgeschichte der Vorderen Propheten," Pp. 111–28 in *Schriftauslegung in der Schrift: Festschrift für Odil Hannes Steck zu seinem 65. Geburtstag.* Ed. R. G. Kratz, T. Krüger, and K. Schmid. Beiheft zur Zeitschrift für die alttestamentliche Wissenschaft 300. Berlin: de Gruyter, 2000.

Buis, P. *Le livre des Rois.* Sources bibliques. Paris: Gabalda, 1997.

Campbell, A. F., and M. A. O'Brien. *Unfolding the Deuteronomistic History: Origins, Upgrades, Present Text.* Minneapolis: Augsburg Fortress, 2000.

_____. *Of Prophets and Kings: A Late Ninth-Century Document (1 Samuel 1–2 Kings 10).* Catholic Biblical Quarterly Monograph 17. Washington, DC: The Catholic Biblical Association of America, 1986.

Cazelles, H. "Sacral Kingship." Pp. 863–66 in vol. 5 of *The Anchor Bible Dictionary.* Ed. D. N. Freedman. 6 vols. New York: Doubleday, 1992.

Clements, R. E. *Old Testament Prophecy: From Oracles to Canon.* Louisville: Westminster John Knox, 1996.

Cogan, M. *I Kings.* Anchor Bible 10. New York: Doubleday, 2001.

_____. *The Raging Torrent: Historical Inscriptions from Assyria and Babylonia relating to Ancient Israel.* Jerusalem: Carta, 2008.

Cole, S. W., and P. Machinist, *Letters from Priests to Kings Esarhaddon and Assurbanipal.* SAA 13. Helsinki: University of Helsinki Press, 1998.

Cronauer, P. T. *The Stories about Naboth the Jezreelite: A Source, Composition, and Redaction Investigation of 1 Kings 21 and Passages in 2 Kings 9.* The Library of Hebrew Bible/Old Testament Studies 424. London: T. & T. Clark, 2005.

De Jong, M. J. *Isaiah among the Ancient Near Eastern Prophets.* Vetus Testamentum Supplement 117. Leiden: Brill, 2007.

De Moor, J. C. "The Crisis of Polytheism in Late Bronze Age Ugarit." *Old Testament Studies* 24 (1986) 12–14.

Diebner, B. J. "Überlegungen zum 'Brief des Elia' (*2 Chr* 21,12–15)." *Henoch* 9 (1987) 199–227.

Dietrich, W. "Prophetie im deuteronomistischen Geschichtswerk." Pp. 47–65 in *The Future of the Deuteronomistic History*. Ed. T. C. Römer. Bibliotheca ephemeridum theologicarum lovaniensium 147. Leuven: Peeters, 2000.

————. *Prophetie und Geschichte*. Forschungen zur Religion und Literatur des Alten und Neuen Testaments 108. Göttingen: Vandenhoeck & Ruprecht, 1972.

Edelman, D. "Court Prophets during the Monarchy and Literary Prophets in the So-called Deuteronomistic History." Pp. 51–73 in *Israelite Prophecy and the Deuteronomistic History*. Ed. M. R. Jacobs and R. F. Person Jr. SBL Ancient Israel and Its Literature 14. Atlanta: SBL, 2013.

Frankfort, H. *Kingship and the Gods: A Study of Ancient Near Eastern Religion as the Integration of Society and Nature*. Chicago: University of Chicago Press, 1948.

Franklin, B. *Poor Richard's Almanack*. Waterloo, IA: U.S.C. Publishing, 1914.

Freedman, D. N. and R. Frey, "False Prophecy is True." Pp. 82–87 in *Inspired Speech: Prophecy in the Ancient Near East—Essays in Honor of Herbert B. Huffmon*. Journal for the Study of the Old Testament Supplement 372. London: T & T Clark, 2004.

Gordon, R. P. "Prophecy in the Mari and Nineveh Archives." Pp. 37–57 in *"Thus Speaks Ishtar of Arbela": Prophecy in Israel, Assyria, and Egypt in the Neo-Assyrian Period*. Ed. R. P. Gordon and H. M. Barstad. Winona Lake, IN: Eisenbrauns, 2013.

Grabbe, L. L. *Priests, Prophets, Diviners, Sages: A Socio-Historical Study of Religious Specialists in Ancient Israel*. Philadelphia: Trinity Press International, 1996.

Gray, J. "Sacral Kingship in Ugarit." *Ugaritica* 6 (1969) 289–302.

Grayson, A. K. *Assyrian Rulers of the Early First Millennium BC II (858–745 B.C.)*. Royal Inscriptions of Mesopotamia and Assyria 3. Toronto: University of Toronto Press, 1996.

Hackett, J. *The Balaam Text from Deir 'Allā*. Harvard Semitic Monograph 31. Chico, CA: Scholars, 1984.

Hamilton, M. W. *The Body Royal: The Social Poetics of Kingship in Ancient Israel*. Biblical Interpretation 78. Leiden: Brill, 2005.

Hayward, R. "Phinehas—The Same is Elijah: The Origins of a Rabbinic Tradition." *Journal of Jewish Studies* 29 (1978) 22–34.

Hess, R. "Achan and Achor: Names and Wordplay in Joshua 7." *Hebrew Annual Review* 14 (1994) 89–98.

Hilber, J. W. "Royal Cultic Prophecy in Assyria, Judah, and Egypt." Pp. 161–86 in *"Thus Speaks Ishtar of Arbela": Prophecy in Israel, Assyria, and Egypt in the Neo-Assyrian Period*. Ed. R. P. Gordon and H. M. Barstad. Winona Lake, IN: Eisenbrauns, 2013.

————. *Cultic Prophecy in the Psalms*. Beiheft zur Zeitschrift für die alttestamentliche Wissenschaft 352. Berlin: de Gruyter, 2005.

Hoffmann, H-D. *Reform und Reformen: Untersuchungen zu einem Grundthema der deuteronomistischen Geschichtsschreibung*. Abhandlungen zur Theologie des Alten und Neuen Testaments 66. Zürich: Theologischer Verlag, 1980.

Holloway, S. W. *Aššur is King! Aššur is King! Religion in the Exercise of Power in the Neo-Assyrian Empire.* Culture and History of the Ancient Near East 10. Leiden: Brill, 2002.

Huffmon, H. B. "A Company of Prophets: Mari, Assyria, Israel." Pp. 47–70 in *Prophecy in Its Ancient Near Eastern Context: Mesopotamian, Biblical, and Arabian Perspectives.* Ed. M. Nissinen. SBL Symposium Series 13. Atlanta: SBL, 2000.

_____. "Prophecy: Ancient Near Eastern Prophecy." Pp. 477–82 in vol. 5 of *The Anchor Bible Dictionary.* Ed. D. N. Freedman. 6 vols. New York: Doubleday, 1992.

_____. "The Exclusivity of Divine Communication in Ancient Israel: False Prophecy in the Hebrew Bible and the Ancient Near East." Pp. 67–81 in *Mediating between Heaven and Earth: Communication with the Divine in the Ancient Near East.* Ed. C. L. Crouch, J. Stökl, and A. E. Zernecke. London: T. & T. Clark, 2012.

Hugo, P. *Les deux visages d'Élie: Texte massorétique et Septante dans l'histoire la plus ancienne du texte de 1 Rois 17–18.* Orbis biblicus et orientalis 217. Fribourg: Academic Press, 2006.

Japhet, S. *I & II Chronicles.* Old Testament Library. Louisville: Westminster John Knox, 1993.

_____. *The Ideology of the Book of Chronicles and its Place in Biblical Thought.* 2nd edition. Beiträge zur Erforschung des Alten Testaments und des antiken Judentum 9. Frankfurt am Main: Lang, 1997.

Jobling, D. "The Syrians in the Book of the Divided Kingdoms: A Literary/Theological Approach," *Biblical Interpretation* 11 (2003) 531–42.

Jonker, L. C. *1 & 2 Chronicles.* Grand Rapids, MI: Baker, 2013.

Kegler, J. "Prophetengestalten im deuteronomistischen Geschichtswerk und in den Chronikbüchern: Ein Beitrag zur Kompositions- und Redaktionsgeschichte der Chronikbücher." *Zeitschrift für die alttestamentliche Wissenschaft* 105 (1993) 484–97.

Keinänen, J. *Traditions in Collision: A Literary and Redaction-Critical Study on the Elijah Narratives 1 Kings 17–19.* Schriften der Finnischen Exegetischen Gesellschaft 80. Göttingen: Vandenhoeck & Ruprecht, 2001.

Klein, R. W. "Prophets and Prophecy in the Books of Chronicles," *TBT* 36 (1998) 227–32.

_____. *2 Chronicles.* Hermeneia. Minneapolis: Fortress, 2012.

Knoppers, G. N. "'To Him You Must Listen': The Prophetic Legislation in Deuteronomy and the Reformation of Classical Tradition in Chronicles." Pp. 161–94 in *Chronicling the Chronicler: The Book of Chronicles and Early Second Temple Historiography.* Ed. P. S. Evans and T. F. Williams. Winona Lake, IN: Eisenbrauns, 2013.

_____. "Changing History: Nathan's Dynastic Oracle and the Structure of the Davidic Monarchy in Chronicles." Pp. 99*–123* in *Shai le-Sara Japhet: Studies in the Bible, Its Exegesis, and Its Language.* Ed. M. Bar-Asher et al. Jerusalem: Bialik Institute, 2007.

_____. "Democratizing Revelation? Prophets, Seers, and Visionaries in Chronicles." Pp. 391–409 in *Prophecy and the Prophets in Ancient Israel: Proceedings of the Oxford Old Testament Seminar.* Ed. J. Day. The Library of Hebrew Bible/Old Testament Studies 531. London: T. & T. Clark, 2010.

_____. "Dissonance and Disaster in the Legend of Kirta." *JAOS* 114 (1994) 572–82.

_____. "Projected Age Comparisons of the Levitical Townlists: Divergent Theories and Their Significance." *Text* 22 (2005) 21–63.

_____. *I Chronicles 1–9*. Anchor Bible 12. New York: Doubleday/New Haven: Yale University Press, 2004.

_____. *I Chronicles 10–29*. Anchor Bible 12A. New York: Doubleday/New Haven Yale University Press, 2004.

Kramer, S. N. "Kingship in Sumer and Akkad: The Ideal King." Pp. 163–76 in *Le palais et la royauté, archéologie et civilisation: Compte rendu de la Rencontre assyriologique internationale (19th: 1971)*. Ed. P. Garelli. Paris: Geuthner, 1974.

Labat, R. *Le caractère religieux de la royauté assyro-babylonienne*. Études d'assyriologie 2. Paris: Adrien-Maisonneuve, 1939.

Larsen, M. T. "The City and its King: On the Old Assyrian Notion of Kingship." Pp. 285–300 in *Le palais et la royauté, archéologie et civilisation: Compte rendu de la Rencontre assyriologique internationale (19th: 1971)*. Ed. P. Garelli. Paris: Geuthner, 1974.

Lemaire, A. "Prophètes et rois dans les inscriptions ouest-sémitiques (IXe–VIe siècle av. J.-C.)." Pp. 96–101 in *Prophètes et rois: Bible et Proche-Orient*. Ed. A. Lemaire. Paris: Cerf, 2001.

_____. *Inscriptions hébraïques*. Littératures anciennes du Proche-Orient 9. Paris: Cerf, 1977.

Leuchter, M. "Samuel: A Prophet or Priest like Moses?" Pp. 147–68 in *Israelite Prophecy and the Deuteronomistic History*. Ed. M. R. Jacobs and R. F. Person Jr. SBL Ancient Israel and Its Literature 14. Atlanta: SBL, 2013.

Levinson, B. M. *"The Right Chorale": Studies in Biblical Law and Interpretation*. Forschungen zum Alten Testament 54. Tübingen: Mohr Siebeck, 2008.

Machinist, P. "Kingship and Divinity in Imperial Assyria," Pp. 152–88 in *Text, Artifact, and Image: Revealing Ancient Israelite Religion*. Ed. G. Beckman and T. J. Lewis. Brown Judaic Studies 346. Providence, RI: Brown Judaic Studies, 2006.

Marlow, H. "Ecology, Theology, Society: Physical, Religious, and Social Disjuncture in Biblical and Neo-Assyrian Texts." Pp. 187–202 in *"Thus Speaks Ishtar of Arbela": Prophecy in Israel, Assyria, and Egypt in the Neo-Assyrian Period*. Ed. R. P. Gordon and H. M. Barstad. Winona Lake, IN: Eisenbrauns, 2013.

McKenzie, S. L. *The Trouble with Kings: The Composition of the Book of Kings in the Deuteronomistic History*. Vetus Testamentum Supplement 42. Leiden: Brill, 1991.

Micheel, R. *Die Seher- und Prophetenüberlieferungen in der Chronik*. Beiträge zur biblischen Exegese und Theologie 18. Frankfurt-am-Main: Lang, 1983.

Millard, A. "The Inscription of Zakkur, King of Hamath." Pp. 155–56 in volume 2 of *The Context of Scripture*. Ed. W. H. Hallo and K. Lawson Younger Jr. Leiden: Brill, 2002.

Miller, J. M. and J. Hayes, *A History of Ancient Israel and Judah*. 2nd edition. Louisville: Westminster John Knox, 2006.

Na'aman, N. "Two Notes on the Monolith Inscription of Shalmaneser III from Kurkh." *Tel Aviv* 3 (1976) 89–106.

Nissinen, M. "Biblical Prophecy from a Near Eastern Perspective: The Cases of Kingship and Divine Possession." Pp. 441–68 in *Congress Volume Ljubljana 2007*. Ed. A. Lemaire. Vetus Testamentum Supplement 133. Leiden: Brill, 2010.

_____. "How Prophecy became Literature." *Scandinavian Journal of the Old Testament* 19 (2005) 153–72.

_____. "Prophecy as Construct: Ancient and Modern." Pp. 11–35 in *"Thus Speaks Ishtar of Arbela": Prophecy in Israel, Assyria, and Egypt in the Neo-Assyrian Period.* Ed. R. P. Gordon and H. M. Barstad. Winona Lake, IN: Eisenbrauns, 2013.

_____. "Prophètes et temples dans le Proche-Orient ancien et les textes bibliques." Pp. 74–111 in *Les recueils prophétiques de la Bible: Origines, milieux, et contexte proche-oriental.* Ed. J.-D. Macchi et al. Geneva: Labor et fides, 2012.

_____. "Prophetic Madness: Prophecy and Ecstasy in the Ancient Near East and in Greece." Pp. 3–29 in *Raising Up a Faithful Exegete: Essays in Honor of Richard D. Nelson.* Ed. K. L. Noll and B. Schramm. Winona Lake, IN: Eisenbrauns, 2010.

_____. "Prophets and Prophecy in Joshua–Kings: A Near Eastern Perspective." Pp. 103–28 in *Israelite Prophecy and the Deuteronomistic History.* Ed. M. R. Jacobs and R. F. Person Jr. SBL Ancient Israel and Its Literature 14. Atlanta: SBL, 2013.

_____. "What is Prophecy? An Ancient Near Eastern Perspective." Pp. 17–37 in *Inspired Speech: Prophecy in the Ancient Near East—Essays in Honor of Herbert B. Huffmon.* Ed. J. Kaltner and L. Stulman. Journal for the Study of the Old Testament Supplement 372. London: T. & T. Clark, 2004.

_____. *Letters from Assyrian and Babylonian Scholars.* SAA 10. Helsinki: University of Helsinki Press, 1993.

_____. *References to Prophecy in Neo-Assyrian Sources.* SAA 7. Helsinki: Neo-Assyrian Text Corpus Project, 1998.

Otto, S. *Jehu, Elia und Elisa: Die Erzählung von der Jehu-Revolution und die Komposition der Elia-Elisa-Erzählungen.* Beiträge zur Wissenschaft vom Alten (und Neuen) Testament 152. Stuttgart: Kohlhammer, 2001.

Pardee, D. "Lachish 3: Complaints and Information (3.42B)." Pp. 79 in volume 3 of *The Context of Scripture.* Ed. W. H. Hallo and K. Lawson Younger Jr. Leiden: Brill, 2002.

Parker, S. B. "The Historical Composition of KRT and the Cult of El." *Zeitschrift für die Alttestamentliche Wissenschaft* 89 (1977) 173.

Parpola, S., and K. Watanabe. *Neo-Assyrian Treaties and Loyalty Oaths.* SAA 2. Helsinki: Helsinki University Press, 1988.

_____. *Assyrian Prophecies.* SAA 9. Helsinki: University of Helsinki Press, 1997.

Peltonen, K. *History Debated: The Historical Reliability of Chronicles in Pre-Critical and Critical Research.* 2 volumes. Publications of the Finnish Exegetical Society 64. Göttingen: Vandenhoeck & Ruprecht, 1996.

Person, R. F. "Prophets in the Deuteronomic History and the Book of Chronicles: A Reassessment." Pp. 187–99 in *Israelite Prophecy and the Deuteronomistic History.* Ed. M. R. Jacobs and R. F. Person Jr. SBL Ancient Israel and Its Literature 14. Atlanta: SBL, 2013.

_____. *The Deuteronomic History and the Book of Chronicles: Scribal Works in an Oral World.* SBL Ancient Israel and Its Literature 6. Atlanta: SBL, 2010.

_____. *The Deuteronomic School: History, Social Setting, and Literature.* Atlanta: SBL, 2002.

Petersen, D. L. *Late Israelite Prophecy: Studies in Deutero-Prophetic Literature and in Chronicles.* SBL Monograph 23. Missoula, MT: Scholars, 1977.

Pongratz-Leisten, B. "Cassandra's Colleagues: Prophetesses in the Neo-Assyrian Empire." *CSMSJ* 1 (2006) 15–21.

_____. "The King at the Crossroads of between Divination and Cosmology." Pp. 33–48 in *Divination, Politics, and Ancient Near Eastern Empires*. Ed. A. Lenzi and J. Stökl. SBL Ancient Near Eastern Monograph 7. Atlanta: SBL, 2014.

_____. *Herrschaftswissen in Mesopotamien: Formen der Kommunikation zwischen Gott und Konig in 2. und 1. Jahrtausend v.Chr.* SAA 10. Helsinki: Neo-Assyrian Text Corpus Project, 1999.

Rad, G. von. "The Deuteronomic Theology of History in I and II Kings." Pp. 205–21 in *The Problem of the Hexateuch and Other Essays*. Ed. G. von Rad. New York: McGraw-Hill, 1966.

_____. *Das Geschichtsbild des chronistischen Werkes*. Stuttgart: Kohlhammer, 1930.

Renz, J. and W. Röllig. *Handbuch der althebräischen Epigraphik, 1: Die althebräischen Inschriften, Text und Kommentar*. Darmstadt: Wissenschaftliche Buchgesellschaft, 1995.

Ritner, R. K. "Report of Wenamon." Pp. 219–20 in *Prophets and Prophecy in the Ancient Near East*. Ed. M. Nissinen. SBLWAW 12. Atlanta: SBL, 2003.

Robker, J. M. *The Jehu Revolution: A Royal Tradition of the Northern Kingdom and Its Ramifications*. Beiheft zur Zeitschrift für die alttestamentliche Wissenschaft 435. Berlin: de Gruyter, 2012.

Rofé, A. *The Prophetical Stories*. Jerusalem: Magnes, 1988.

Römer, T. C. "How Many Books (teuchs): Pentateuch, Hexateuch, Deuteronomistic History, or Enneateuch?" Pp. 37–42 in *Pentateuch, Hexateuch, or Enneateuch: Identifying Literary Works in Genesis through Kings*. Ed. T. B. Dozeman, T. C. Römer, and K. Schmid. SBL Ancient Israel and its Literature 8. Atlanta: SBL, 2011.

Rüterswörden, U. "Dtn 13 in der neueren Deuteronomiumforschung." Pp. 185–203 in *Congress Volume, Basel 2001*. Ed. A. Lemaire. Vetus Testamentum Supplement 92. Leiden: Brill, 2002.

Schaper, J. "Prophecy in Israel and Assyria: Are We Comparing Apples and Pears? The Materiality of Writing and the Avoidance of Parallelomania." Pp. 225–38 in *"Thus Speaks Ishtar of Arbela": Prophecy in Israel, Assyria, and Egypt in the Neo-Assyrian Period*. Ed. R. P. Gordon and H. M. Barstad. Winona Lake, IN: Eisenbrauns, 2013.

Schenker, A. *Älteste Textgeschichte der Königsbücher: die hebräische Vorlage der ursprünglichen Septuaginta als älteste Textform der Königsbücher*. Orbis biblicus et orientalis 199. Göttingen: Vandenhoeck & Ruprecht, 2004.

_____. *Septante et texte massorétique dans l'histoire la plus ancienne du texte de 1 Rois 2-14*. Cahiers de la Revue biblique 48. Paris: Gabalda, 2000.

Schniedewind, W. "Prophets and Prophecy in the Book of Chronicles." Pp. 204–24 in *The Chronicler as Historian*. Ed. M. P. Graham, K. G. Hoglund, and S. L. McKenzie. Journal for the Study of the Old Testament Supplement 238. Sheffield: JSOT Press, 1997.

_____. *The Word of God in Transition: From Prophet to Exegete in the Second Temple Period*. Journal for the Study of the Old Testament Supplement 197. Sheffield: Sheffield Academic Press, 1995.

Seeligmann, I. L. "Die Auffassung von der Prophetie in der deuteronomistischen und chronistischen Geschichtsschreibung." Pp. 254–84 in *Congress Volume, Göttingen 1977*. Ed. J. A. Emerton. Vetus Testamentum Supplement 29. Leiden: Brill, 1978.

Seow, C.-L. "West Semitic Sources." Pags 201–18 in M. Nissinen, ed., *Prophets and Prophecy in the Ancient Near East*. SBL Writings from the Ancient World. Atlanta: Society of Biblical Literature, 2003.

_____. "West Semitic Sources." Pp. 201–18 in *Prophets and Prophecy in the Ancient Near East*. Ed. M. Nissinen. SBL Writings from the Ancient World 12. Atlanta: SBL, 2003.

Sharp, C. J. *Prophecy and Ideology in Jeremiah*. Old Testament Studies. London: T. & T. Clark, 2003.

_____. *Prophecy in the Book of Jeremiah*. Ed. H. M. Barstad and R. G. Kratz. Beiheft zur Zeitschrift für die alttestamentliche Wissenschaft 388. Berlin: de Gruyter, 2009.

Stackert, J. *A Prophet Like Moses: Prophecy, Law and Israelite Religion*. Oxford: Oxford University Press, 2014.

Stökl, J. *Prophecy in the Ancient Near East: A Philological and Sociological Comparison*. Culture and History of the Ancient Near East 56. Leiden: Brill, 2012.

Sweeney, M. A. "Prophets and Priests in the Deuteronomistic History: Elijah and Elisha." Pp. 35–49 in *Israelite Prophecy and the Deuteronomistic History*. Ed. M. R. Jacobs and R. F. Person Jr. SBL Ancient Israel and Its Literature 14. Atlanta: SBL, 2013.

Thelle, R. "Reflections of Ancient Israelite Divination in the Former Prophets." Pp. 7–33 in *Israelite Prophecy and the Deuteronomistic History*. Ed. M. R. Jacobs and R. F. Person Jr. SBL Ancient Israel and Its Literature 14. Atlanta: SBL, 2013.

Thiel, W. "Deuteronomistische Redaktionsarbeit in den Elia-Erzählungen." 148–71 in *Congress Volume: Leuven 1989*. Ed. J. A. Emerton. Vetus Testamentum Supplement 43. Leiden: Brill, 1991.

Timm, S. *Die Dynastie Omri: Quellen und Untersuchungen zur Geschichte Israels im 9. Jahrhundert vor Christus*. Forschungen zur Religion und Literatur des Alten und Neuen Testaments 124. Göttingen: Vandenhoeck & Ruprecht, 1982.

Tov, E. *The Text-Critical Use of the Septuagint in Biblical Research*. 2nd edition. Jerusalem Biblical Studies 3. Jerusalem: Simor, 1997.

_____. *Textual Criticism of the Hebrew Bible*. 3rd ed. Minneapolis: Fortress, 2012.

Trebolle Barrera, J. C. *Centena in libros Samuelis et Regum. variantes textuales y composición literaria en los libros de Samuel y Reyes*. Textos y estudios "Cardinal Cisneros" 47. Madrid: Consejo Superior de Investigaciones Científicas Instituto de Filología, 1989.

_____. *Jehú y Joás: texto y composición literaria de 2 Reyes 9–11*. Institución San Jerónimo 17. Valencia: Institución San Jerónimo, 1984.

Ussishkin, D. "Jezreel, Samaria and Megiddo: Royal Cities of Omri and Ahab." Pp. 351–64 in *Congress Volume: Cambridge 1995*. Vetus Testamentum Supplement 66. Leiden: Brill, 1997.

van der Kooij, G. "Palaeography." Pp. 133–34 in *Aramaic Texts from Deir ʿAlla*. Ed. J. Hoftijzer and G. van der Kooij. Documenta et monumenta Orientis antiqui 19. Leiden: Brill, 1976.

Vaux, R. de. "Les Ostraka de Lachis." *Revue Biblique* 48 (1939) 189–201.

Villard, P. "Les prophètes à l'époque néo-assyrienne." Pp. 55–84 in *Prophètes et rois: Bible et Proche-Orient*. Ed. A. Lemaire. Paris: Cerf, 2001.

Wallace, H. N. "Oracles against the Israelite Dynasties in 1 and 2 Kings." *Biblica* 67 (1986) 21–40.

Weinberg, J. P. "Die 'ausserkanonischen Prophezeiungen' in der Chronikbüchern." *Acta Antiqua* 26 (1978) 387–404.

Weippert, H. "'Histories' and 'History:' Promise and Fulfillment in the Deuteronomistic History." Pp. 47–61 in *Reconsidering Israel and Judah: The Deuteronomistic History in Recent Thought*. Edited by G. N. Knoppers and J. G. McConville. Sources for Biblical and Theological Study 8. Winona Lake, IN: Eisenbrauns, 2000.

_____. "Geschichten und Geschichte: Verheiβung und Erfüllung im deuteronomistischen Geschichtswerk." Pp. 116–31 in *Congress Volume: Leuven, 1989*. Ed. J. A. Emerton. Vetus Testamentum Supplement 43. Leiden: Brill, 1991.

Weippert, M. '"Das Frühere, siehe, ist eingetroffen...:' Über Selbstzitate im altorientalischen Prophetenspruch." Pp. 147–69 in *Oracles et prophéties dans l'Antiquité: Actes du colloque de Strasbourg, 15–17, Juin 1995*. Edited by J.-G. Heintz. Travaux du Centre de recherche sur le Proche-Orient et la Grèce antiques 15. Strasbourg: Publications de l'Université de Strasbourg, 1997.

_____. "Die Bildsprache der neuassyrischen prophetie." Pp. 55–93 in *Beiträge zur prophetischen Bildsprache in Israel und Assyrien*. Ed. H. Weippert, K. Seybold, and M. Weippert. Orbis biblicus et orientalis 64. Göttingen: Vandenhoeck & Ruprecht, 1985.

_____. "The Balaam Text from Deir ʿAllā and the Study of the Old Testament." Pp. 169–74 in *The Balaam Text from Deir ʿAlla Re-evaluated*. Edited by J. Hoftijzer and G. van der Kooij. Leiden: Brill, 1991.

Wellhausen, J. *Prolegomena to the History of Ancient Israel*. Edinburgh: Adams and Charles Black, 1885.

White, M. C. *The Elijah Legends and Jehu's Coup*. Brown Judaic Studies 311. Atlanta: Scholars Press, 1997.

Willi, T. *Die Chronik als Auslegung: Untersuchungen zur literarischen Gestaltung der historischen Überlieferung Israels*. Forschungen zur Religion und Literatur des Alten und Neuen Testaments 106. Göttingen: Vandenhoeck & Ruprecht, 1972.

Wilson, R. *Prophecy and Society in Ancient Israel*. Philadelphia: Fortress, 1980.

Wray Beal, L. M. *The Deuteronomist's Prophet: Narrative Control of Approval and Disapproval in the Story of Jehu (2 Kings 9 and 10)*. The Library of Hebrew Bible/Old Testament Studies 478. London: T. & T. Clark, 2007.

Würthwein, E. *Die Bücher der Könige: 1 Kön. 17–2 Kön. 25*. Das Alte Testament Deutsch 11/2. Göttingen: Vandenhoeck & Ruprecht, 1984.

Wyatt, N. *Myths of Power: A Study of Royal Myth and Ideology in Ugaritic and Biblical Tradition*. Ugaritisch-biblische Literatur 13. Münster: Ugarit-Verlag, 1996.

_____. *There's such divinity doth hedge a king: Selected Essays of Nicolas Wyatt on Royal Ideology in Ugaritic and Old Testament Literature*. Aldershot: Ashgate, 2005.

Unnamed Prophets in the
Deuteronomistic History

JASON BEMBRY

Emmanuel Christian Seminary

A number of unnamed people appear in the Hebrew Bible and some play prominent roles within the stories in which they appear. It is not uncommon for commentators to interpret namelessness in negative terms. E. J. Revell, for example, concludes that "an individual who was not named was not sufficiently prominent in the [biblical] narrative, or in the history of the community, to warrant specific identification." Mieke Bal has suggested that namelessness in a story is a kind of narrative violence against the anonymous character.[1] While Bal's assessment might be true in some biblical stories, namelessness is not always negative. Consider, for example, a few instances of anonymous characters in the Deuteronomistic History (hereafter "DH").[2] Samson's mother (Judges 13), though unnamed, is the only one to whom the divine messenger speaks. Her husband, whose name is given as Manoaḥ, is nowhere addressed by the messenger of Yahweh. The Queen of Šeba (1 Kgs 10) and the young Israelite woman who directs Naʿaman to Elisha (2 Kgs 5)

Author's note: I would like to thank my colleague Gene McGarry, who has been an excellent interlocutor during my research into this subject. He also provided skillful editorial suggestions regarding wording and content throughout. Thanks also to my research assistants, Mr. Jack Weinbender, Ms. Serena McMillan, and Mr. Patrick Harvey, who have assisted me with proofreading. Any mistakes that remain are mine, of course.

1. M. Bal, *Death and Dissymmetry: The Politics of Coherence in the Book of Judges* (Chicago: University of Chicago Press, 1988), 43.

2. In this paper, I have elected to limit this literary block along Nothian lines. Because none of the unnamed prophets appear in Joshua, one need not necessarily side with Noth to appreciate the observations I make in this essay (see M. Noth, *Überlieferungsgeschichtliche Studien* [Tübingen: Max Niemeyer, 1967]). For more discussion regarding the division, or lack thereof, between the DH and Pentateuch, see K. Schmid, "The Emergence and Disappearance of the Separation between the Pentateuch and the Deuteronomistic History in Biblical Studies," in *Pentateuch, Hexateuch, or Enneateuch? Identifying Literary Works in Genesis through Kings* (ed. T. B. Dozeman, T. Römer, and K. Schmid; Atlanta: SBL, 2011), 11–24. See also T. C. Römer, *The So-Called Deuteronomistic History* (London: T. & T. Clark, 2005), 29–43.

are unnamed. There are entire stories in the DH in which all of the characters are nameless. Judges 19 features a Levite, his concubine, his father-in-law, and his servant, along with an elderly Ephraimite sojourner—all of whom remain nameless. Yet they are all important characters in the story that leads to the tragic ending of the book of Judges. For the DH, it is clear that namelessness does not indicate marginality or require the suppression of voice.[3] In her examination of anonymous characters throughout the Hebrew Bible, Adele Reinhartz likewise suggests that anonymity does not necessarily suppress personal identity; rather, it can highlight the role the unnamed person plays and the consistency (or inconsistency) of their behavior within that role.[4]

Reinhartz's work sheds a helpful light on anonymity and its purpose in the Hebrew Bible. I would like to proceed along a similar path regarding the significance of the nameless figures in five episodes in the DH where an anonymous prophet appears. I will argue that it is likely that these unnamed prophets have been inserted to illustrate points important to the Deuteronomistic tradents through the prominent roles they play in the narratives. Whether these stories are invented or simply part of old traditions in which details such as names are simply forgotten is impossible to know with certainty.[5] Even so, when we look at the similarities among these episodes, interesting patterns emerge.

---

3. E. J. Revell, *The Designation of the Individual: Expressive Usage in Biblical Narrative* (Kampen, Netherlands: Kok Pharos, 1996), 51.

4. A. Reinhartz, *"Why Ask My Name?" Anonymity and Identity in Biblical Narrative* (Oxford: Oxford University Press, 1998), 9.

5. Pancratius Beentjes has argued that invented episodes and characters in the Chronicler's work are likely designed to make theological points to the audience (P. Beentjes, "Prophets in the Book of Chronicles," in *The Elusive Prophet: The Prophet as a Historical Person, Literary Character and Anonymous Artist* [ed. J. C. De Moor; Leiden: Brill, 2001], 48–49). If true, we might suggest the same possibility for the DH tradents. See, for example, 2 Chr 25:5–10, where the Chronicler records a nameless man of God who comes to the Judahite king Amaziah and warns him against an alliance with Israel. Later in the story (vv. 14–16), the Chronicler states that Yahweh again sent an unnamed prophet to Amaziah to chastise him for worshiping the gods of the Edomites, a people the Judahite king had just subdued in battle. These are the only two unnamed prophets in the Chronicler's work. That neither account is attested in the DH might suggest that these brief interchanges are added to the story to explain some of the details seen in the DH. McKenzie suggests that the two prophetic oracles are probably inventions of the Chronicler (S. McKenzie, *The Chronicler's Use of the Deuteronomistic History* [HSM 33; Winona Lake, IN: Eisenbrauns, 2006], 92). Sara Japhet suggests that the Chronicler was motivated to explain the incongruity of Amaziah doing what was right in the eyes of Yahweh (2 Kgs 14:3) and then facing a military defeat (vv. 12–14) and a violent assassination (vv. 19–20) (S. Japhet, *I & II Chronicles* [Louisville: Westminster/John Knox, 1993], 858). Yet, it is curious that the Chronicler uses not one but two unnamed prophets to convey this point. The two are described in language seen elsewhere (although not in adjacent texts) in the DH: one is called "man of God" and the other simply "prophet." In the first case (v. 7), the opening expression is אִישׁ אֱלֹהִים בָּא 'a man of God came'—the same phrase seen in 1 Kgs 13:1. The second introductory expression is similar to the one found in Judg 6:8, where Yahweh is said to send a prophet to someone.

In what follows, I examine the five episodes within the DH in which an anonymous prophet appears. I will address each episode in the order in which it appears in Joshua–Kings. I should note that I have not treated unnamed prophets who appear in a group, such as the "messengers of Saul who prophesy" (1 Sam 19:20), "sons of the prophets" (2 Kgs 2:3, 5, 7, 15; 4:1, 38; 6:1), "prophets" (1 Kgs 22:6, 10; 2 Kgs 23:2), "his prophets" (2 Kgs 17:23; 21:10), or "seers/every seer" (2 Kgs 17:13) but examine only the individual unnamed prophets in the DH.[6] By isolating these episodes, my goal is to establish their redactional origins by demonstrating their thematic connectivity and its significance within the message of the DH.

Texts

Prophets with no name appear throughout the DH as mouthpieces for the God of Israel. These individuals speak to a king on two occasions, to a future king on one occasion, to a priest on one occasion, to another unnamed prophet who, in turn, speaks a word back to the unnamed prophet on one occasion, and finally to the people of Israel in still another (see references below). These anonymous prophets are referred to in Hebrew as נביא 'prophet', הנביא 'the prophet', איש נביא 'a prophet man', איש האלהים 'man of God,' and איש אחד מבני הנביאים 'a certain man from the sons of the prophets.' In the episodes where an unnamed prophet appears, the familiar Deuteronomistic theme of disobedience and punishment is present.[7] In most of these stories, either a leader or a group is rebuked for faithlessness or a new leader is commissioned as a rebuke to the current leadership. In these episodes, either a rebuke is given to a prophet, a king and the tribes as a whole, or the end of a priestly house or a royal house is proclaimed. We will see that thematic consistency of rebuke and condemnation, as well as overlaps in content among the stories, will help locate the sources for these episodes.

Judges 6

The first occurrence of an unnamed prophet in the DH is found in Judg 6:7–10, where the people of Israel are said to have cried out to Yahweh because of the Midianites. Yahweh responds by sending a prophet who comes to the people and reminds them of the deliverance from Egyptian bondage. The prophet says:

> Thus says Yahweh, the God of Israel: I led you up from Egypt and brought you out of the house of slavery and I delivered you from the hand of the Egyptians and

---

6. Ehud Ben Zvi has written about "the prophets" (plural) where they appear anonymously in the DH (E. Ben Zvi, " 'The Prophets': References to Generic Prophets and Their Role in the Construction of the Image of the 'Prophets of Old' with in the Postmonarchic Readership(s) of the Books of Kings," in *The Books of Kings: Sources, Composition, Historiography and Reception* [ed. A. Lemaire and B. Halpern; Leiden: Brill, 2010], 387–99).

7. F. M. Cross, *Canaanite Myth and Hebrew Epic* (Cambridge: Harvard University Press, 1973), 284.

from the hand of all who oppressed you and drove them out before you and gave you their land. I said to you, "I am Yahweh your God, you shall not pay homage to the gods of the Amorites in whose land you dwell." But you have not listened to my voice. (Judg 6:8b–10)

The term rendered "prophet" in v. 8 is actually איש נביא 'a prophet man'.[8] His role is threefold: to recount Yahweh's acts of deliverance and the subsequent settlement in the land, to warn the Israelites against worshiping the Amorites' gods, and to chastise the people for not heeding the divine command.

The text of this episode involving the איש נביא is in question. 4QJudg[a] omits Judg 6:7–10, connecting the cry of the Israelites to Yahweh (v. 6) with the arrival of the messenger of Yahweh (v. 11). This Qumran fragment represents a wholly independent text tradition unattested elsewhere.[9] That the MT's 6:7–10 is not attested in 4QJudg[a] suggests that the MT's fuller text represents a later redaction.[10] Within the context of this section of Judges, this episode appears intrusive, lacking any real connection to what precedes or follows.[11] The MT has two phrases that are remarkably similar in immediate succession so that vv. 6b–7a reads, "The Israelites cried out to Yahweh. And when the Israelites cried out to Yahweh, . . ." This repetition has the palpable feel of a redactional seam. Additionally, there are no text-critical triggers that would precipitate a scribal parablepsis and thereby explain the Qumran text. When these verses are removed, a smooth reading from 6:6 to 6:11 is achieved: "The Israelites cried out to Yahweh and a messenger of Yahweh came and sat under the oak which is in Ophrah." So all indications in this example appear to suggest that this unnamed-prophet episode is a later addition.

Judges 13:2–20

The second example is an anomaly among the stories of unnamed prophets because the person assumed to be a "man of God" is actually a "messenger of

---

8. In Judg 4:4, Deborah is called אשה נביאה 'a woman prophetess'. Some have seen this interesting juxtaposition as a literary connection between the two stories. See L. R. Klein, *The Triumph of Irony in the Book of Judges* (Sheffield: Almond, 1988), 50 and D. Edelman, "Court Prophets During the Monarchy and Literary Prophets in the So-Called Deuteronomistic History," in *Israelite Prophecy and the Deuteronomistic History: Portrait, Reality, and the Formation of a History* (ed. M. R. Jacobs and R. F. Person Jr.; Atlanta: SBL, 2013), 63.

9. J. Trebolle Barrera, "Textual Variants in 4QJudg[a] and the Textual and Editorial History of the Book of Judges," *Revue de Qumran* 54 (1989) 237. While one cannot draw firm conclusions about omissions in Josephus, it is interesting to note that he also omits this episode (and many more) from the Gideon story. See *Ant.* V, 212–13.

10. R. Wilson, *Prophecy and Society in Ancient Israel* (Philadelphia: Fortress, 1980), 168. Emanuel Tov also notes this possibility (E. Tov, *Textual Criticism of the Hebrew Bible* [Minneapolis: Fortress, 1992], 344).

11. The intrusive nature of this pericope has been noted by a number of commentators long before the publication of 4QJudg[a]. See, for example, G. F. Moore, *Judges* (ICC; Edinburgh, T. & T. Clark, 1895), 181 and J. A. Soggin, *Judges* (Philadelphia: Westminster, 1981), 112.

Yahweh" or "messenger of God." It is clear in the context of the story that this messenger is a superhuman being and, therefore, not like the other human prophetic
figures discussed in this essay. I include this episode because the human characters
in this story assume the figure to be a "man of God," and they explicitly note that
they are not told the figure's name.

In Judg 13:2–20, the wife of Manoah is described as barren but is visited by
a messenger of Yahweh who informs her that she will have a son who is to be
raised as a Nazirite. When she reports the encounter to her husband, Manoah's
wife assumes that the messenger was a "man of God"—he had a countenance like
that of a messenger of God. Note the change from "messenger of Yahweh" in the
narrator's voice in v. 3 to "man of God" in v. 6. In v. 8, Manoah adopts his wife's
assumption and refers to the visitor as "the man of God." This is the last time the
visitor is referred to by this term by the other characters; he is referred to simply
as "the man" in direct speech from this point on. Nonetheless, in the narrator's
language, the terminology for the messenger returns to the title "the messenger of
God" in v. 9 rather than "messenger of Yahweh" (in v. 3). This variation between
vv. 6 and 9 on the one hand and vv. 3, 13, 15, 16 [2×], 17, 18, and 20 on the other is
also reflected in the LXX.[12] The audience is made aware of the status of this visitor
in v. 20, where the messenger is said to ascend skyward along with the flames of
the altar on which Manoah had offered a goat and a cereal offering. While I have
included this story here in order to examine exactly how the DH tradents treat all
characters labeled "man of God" (without a name), I have elected to exclude this
pericope from my analysis overall since it is clear that the author/editor(s) see this
figure as someone distinct from human prophets.

1 Sam 2:27–36

The third story comes from 1 Sam 2:27–36, where the priest Eli encounters
a man of God who pronounces judgment on Eli's house and foretells the coming
deaths of both his sons, Hophni and Phinehas. Within this condemnation, the
man of God recounts the past events that have led up to Eli's status as priest. The
man of God reports that Yahweh says (vv. 27–36):

> I revealed myself to the house of your father when they were in Egypt, subject
> to the house of Pharaoh. And I chose him out of all the tribes of Israel to be my
> priest, to ascend to my altar, to burn incense, to wear an ephod before me and I
> gave to the house of your father all my offerings by fire from the people of Israel.
> Why do you look upon my sacrifice and my offering with a selfish eye[13]—and

---

12. Josephus refers to this person as a φαντασμα . . . αγγελος του θεου "a specter, an angel
of God" (*Ant.* V 277), and throughout the narrative the being is referred to as an "angel." See, for
example, *Ant.* V 279, 280, 284.

13. This translation follows P. Kyle McCarter's reconstruction and translation (P. K. Mc-
Carter, *1 Samuel* [AB 8; New York: Doubleday, 1980] 86). The MT has the nonsensical "Why do
you kick against my sacrifice and my offering which I commanded a dwelling."

honor your sons more than me in order to make yourselves fat from the best of all the offerings of Israel for my people? Therefore—oracle of Yahweh, God of Israel—indeed I have said, "Your house and the house of your father will serve me forever" but now—oracle of Yahweh—"Far be it from me, for the ones who honor me I will honor, but the ones who despise me will be cursed." Now the days are approaching when I sever your descendants and the descendants of the house of your father from becoming old in your house. You will see but a narrow dwelling in all that goes well for Israel. There will not be an old man in your house all the days. A man I will not cut off for you from my altar in order to destroy your eyes and to grieve your soul, but most of your house will die by men. This will be a sign for you—that will come to your two sons, to Ḥophni and Phineḥas—on a single day the two of them will die. I will establish for myself a true priest; he will do just as I have in my mind. I will build a true house for him and will serve before my anointed one all the days. All who are left in your house will come to bow before him for a piece of silver or a loaf of bread and they will say, "Put me among one of the priestly divisions so that I can eat a piece of bread."

The specific nature of the condemnation concerns the practice of taking the choicest parts of the offerings, of which Ḥophni and Phineḥas were guilty (v. 29). Yahweh promises to raise up a faithful priest and condemns Eli's descendants to poverty.

The unnamed spokesman is called אִישׁ אֱלֹהִים 'man of God'. The theme of Israel's exodus from Egypt is shared with the first unnamed-prophet episode (Judg 6:8).[14] The specific mention of slavery in Egypt is an additional shared element (Judg 6:8), if we emend the MT by adding the word, עֲבָדִים 'slaves' in v. 27, which is attested in 4QSamᵃ and supported in the LXX (so that it reads "when you were *slaves* in Egypt").[15][16]

1 Kings 13

The fourth story involving an unnamed prophet appears in 1 Kgs 13 and features two prophetic figures whose names are not given. The first is a man of God from Judah who has been instructed to journey to Bethel to condemn the altar

---

14. Recollection of the exodus appears 32 times in Joshua–2 Kings. See J. E. Harvey, *Retelling the Torah; The Deuteronomistic Historian's Use of the Tetrateuchal Narratives* (London: T. & T. Clark, 2004), 11–12.

15. McCarter, *1 Samuel*, 87. Josephus conflates elements of this tradition involving the MT's unnamed man of God in 1 Sam 2:27–36 with the tradition about the young boy Samuel in 1 Sam 3:2–14. For Josephus, there is no mention of a man of God—only the prophecy of the boy Samuel. Yet, components of 1 Sam 2:27–36 are transferred to the message Samuel delivers to Eli in 1 Samuel 3. Mention of Eli's sons dying on the same day, in 1 Sam 2:34, is said to be uttered by Samuel (*Ant.* V 350). Josephus also has Samuel mention the house of Eleazar specifically, a detail unspoken in either 1 Samuel 2 or 3. In addition, Josephus goes to great lengths to establish the young Samuel as a prophet even though nowhere in the MT or LXX of 1 Samuel 2–3 is the boy specifically named as a prophet. For the references that speak of Samuel as a prophet or as prophesying, see *Ant.* V 347, 348, 351 [2x].

there. He goes to Bethel and proclaims that a Davidic son named Josiah will be born and will sacrifice the priests of the high places on this same altar. Jeroboam, the king of Israel, was present and gave orders that this man of God be seized.[16] At that moment, the king's arm was paralyzed or shriveled and he begged the man of God to heal his arm. The man of God entreated Yahweh on the king's behalf and the arm was restored. The king then invited the man to receive a gift but the invitation was refused. The man of God had been instructed by Yahweh to eat no bread nor drink water in Bethel. Additionally, he was told to return to Judah by a route different from the one by which he entered.

The second unnamed prophet appears in the story at this point—an old prophet who lived in Bethel.[17] Upon hearing about the actions of the man of God, this old prophet sought to find him in order to invite the Judahite visitor to stay with him. The old prophet reached the man of God, and upon inviting him into his home, the man of God repeated the command from Yahweh that he refrain from eating and drinking in that place. At this point, the prophet told him that an angel of Yahweh had given orders to bring the man of God back to the old prophet's house. But we are told that this was a lie. The man of God then accepted the invitation to dine at the prophet's table. During the meal, the prophet proclaimed the word of Yahweh, condemning the man of God for disobeying Yahweh's instruction. As punishment, the prophet proclaimed that the man of God's body would not be buried in the tomb of his fathers. The man of God is referred to as a prophet in v. 23 as he begins his journey back to Judah. On the way, a lion killed him, but his body was left in the road, while the donkey upon which the man rode was unharmed. When the old prophet heard the report, he went to retrieve the body and he had it buried in his own grave. He instructed his sons to bury him beside the man of God when he died.

The narration is a bit inconsistent, in that the punishment declared against the man of God by the mouth of the old prophet has nothing to do with a lion. So, one might suggest that the lion episode is an addition to the original story.

Among commentators, it is common to assume that the references to Josiah are *ex eventu* predictions and that vv. 33–34 are the work of a late Deuteronomistic hand.[18] While I am convinced of this understanding as well, it is curious that our late redactor has refrained from explicit condemnation of the calves Jeroboam made for the sanctuaries at Dan and Bethel—especially in light of other places where Jeroboam's heterodoxy is exploited. In 2 Kgs 10:29 the calves are explicitly

---

16. The name of the Israelite king might be a secondary addition in 13:1, and the name is not attested in the LXX of v. 4. See S. L. McKenzie, *The Trouble with Kings* (SVT 42; Leiden: Brill, 1991), 55.

17. Curiously, this prophet is said to be from Samaria in the later account that connects this story in 1 Kgs 13 with Josiah's day. See 2 Kgs 23:18.

18. See, for example, M. Cogan, *1 Kings* (AB 10; New York: Doubleday, 2000), 375 and already Cross, *Canaanite Myth and Hebrew Epic,* 279–80.

condemned and are connected to Bethel and Dan. The calves are one of the reasons for the northern kingdom's capture, according to 2 Kgs 17:16. The calves are even mentioned just before this story in 1 Kgs 12:28 and again in v. 30, where they are said to be a "matter which became a sin." In 1 Kgs 12:32, mention is made of the sacrifices being offered to the calves that Jeroboam made. It is indeed curious that in such proximity the story in 1 Kgs 13 centers around the altar, with no mention of the calves and no explicit condemnation of them from the prophetic figures in the chapter.

This apparent omission has been taken by some to indicate that portions of 1 Kgs 13 derive from tradents who did not consider the calf at the shrine in Bethel to be heterodox idolatry.[19] In fact, no polemic against the calves survives in the Elijah-Elisha narratives or in Amos, when those prophets visited Bethel. It might be that the calves were understood by these tradents to be attribute-animals of Yahweh, not rival cultic figures.[20] I conclude that this story's omission of any reference to the calves suggests that the story's original form is probably quite old.[21] So the silence regarding the calves can be attributed to an earlier author who, for whatever reason, saw no need to condemn the calves explicitly. Yet, the connection this story makes with 2 Kgs 23:15–20 bears the unmistakable marks of editorial work in Josiah's day.[22]

---

19. Cross, *Canaanite Myth and Hebrew Epic*, 75. Others suggest that the story is late and therefore no longer concerned about the calves as forbidden cult objects. Rofé, on linguistic grounds, concludes that this story dates from the 5th century B.C.E. (A. Rofé, "Classes in the Prophetical Stories: Didactic Legenda and Parable," in *Studies on Prophecy* [Vetus Testamentum Supplement 26; Leiden: Brill, 1974] 163). I would simply say that this story has been retouched by a later hand who employed later idioms; but the core components of the story are much older.

20. See J. Blenkinsopp, *A History of Prophecy in Israel* (Philadelphia: Westminster John Knox, 1996), 58. This suggestion is consistent with Othmar Keel and Christoph Uehlinger's thesis that over time these "attribute animals" (like the calf) became the symbol of a particular deity, coinciding with the tendency in Iron Age I Israel to avoid anthropomorphic depictions of deities (O. Keel and C. Uehlinger, *Gods, Goddesses, and Images of God in Ancient Israel* [Minneapolis: Fortress, 1998], 141).

21. It has been suggested that the story of 1 Kgs 13 is based on the prophet Amos, who also spoke against the sanctuary at Bethel (Amos 3:13–15; 4:5). There are definite points of contact between the two traditions. Both Amos and the man of God are southern prophets speaking against the practices at Bethel, and the altar is the metonymic target of rebuke in both texts. Yet, too many differences between the two episodes probably preclude any organic connection. Amos seems to be more interested in pointing out the inconsistency of ethical actions in relation to offering sacrifices at a sanctuary, rather than issuing a blanket condemnation (J. Gray, *I & II Kings*; 2nd ed.; Philadelphia: Westminster, 1970), 319.

22. Josephus refers to both prophetic figures of this story with the label "prophet." Yet, he calls the old prophet a *false* prophet who deliberately misled the Judahite man in order to undermine his credibility before Jeroboam. Josephus names the southern prophet Ιαδων, probably connecting him with Iddo, the prophet mentioned in 2 Chr 9:29. See *Ant.* VIII 230–45. Rabbinic tradition (*Sifre Devarim*, 177) makes this connection as well. See R. N. Sandberg, *Development and Discontinuity in Jewish Law* (Lanham, MD: University Press of America, 2001), 22.

1 Kings 20

1 Kgs 20 has three scenes involving interactions between unnamed spokes-men for God and the Israelite king. In 1 Kgs 20:13–22, an unnamed prophet comes to Ahab, the king of Israel, and promises him success in the coming battle with the Syrian, Ben Hadad. The relevant text reads:

> And now a prophet drew near to Ahab, the king of Israel and he said, "Thus Yahweh has said, 'Do you see this great multitude? I am about to give it into your hand today and you will hereby know that I am Yahweh.'" Ahab said, "By whom?" And he said, "Thus has Yahweh said, 'by the young men of the leaders of the regions.'" And he said, "Who will run the battle?" and he said, "you will." (1 Kgs 20:13–14)

After the victory, the prophet comes back to Ahab a second time:

> The prophet drew near to the king of Israel and he said to him, "Go, strengthen yourself. Know and see what you must do, because by the time of the spring of the year the king of Aram will ascend against you." (1 Kgs 20:22)

The king of Aram does indeed do as the prophet foretells, and when the army of Israel was gathered to confront the invading army at Aphek, an unnamed man of God comes to Ahab. The change in terminology from "prophet" in the earlier scene to "man of God" in this scene might suggest a different person, but this is uncertain.[23] In v. 28, we read:

> The man of God drew near and he said to the king of Israel, "Thus Yahweh has said, 'Because Aram said that Yahweh is a god of the mountains and he is not a god of the valleys, I have given all this great multitude into your hands and you will hereby know that I am Yahweh.'"

As before, the words of the prophet come to fruition with the Israelite victory over Aram and Ben Hadad in vv. 29–30. In all three references to this prophetic figure, note that the verb "draw near" is used each time, and each interaction with the king brings a kind of divine assurance to Ahab.

The last scene in 1 Kgs 20 appears in vv. 35–43. In v. 35, the protagonist is introduced as a certain man from the sons of the prophets, a locution we will see again in the Jehu story (2 Kgs 9). By the word of Yahweh, this man instructs one of his associates to strike him. When the man refuses his request, the man from the sons of the prophets pronounces judgment on him, which quickly comes to pass: the man is killed by a lion. The man from the sons of the prophets asks another man to strike him. His request is granted, and then the reader sees the reason behind this strange request: it is part of a ruse he is planning to use against

---

23. Josephus retains the title "the prophet" throughout. See *Ant.* VIII 382.

the king. In v. 38, the man is referred to as "the prophet" as he approaches[24] the king to present him with a contrived story designed to trick the king into passing judgment on himself. The prophet tells the king that he was asked by a soldier to guard a captive, and the soldier demanded he pay for his life or a talent of silver if the prisoner escaped under his care. With the wound and bandage as part of the ruse, the prophet convinces the king of the story's veracity. When he begs the king to help him in his cause, the king simply says, "your own judgment you have declared." At this point, the prophet removes the bandage and the king recognizes him as one of the prophets. In v. 42, the prophet then pronounces judgment on the king for not killing the man Yahweh had devoted to destruction, saying, "your life for his life, your people for his people." The theme of judgment directed toward the king in this encounter departs from the earlier two episodes involving Ahab and the unnamed prophet/man of God.

It is impossible to know with certainty if "a prophet" (20:13), "the prophet" (20:22), and "a certain man from the sons of the prophets" (20:35) who is later called "the prophet" (20:38) all refer to the same person. In the final episode, the king recognizes the prophetic figure as "one of the prophets" in v. 41, suggesting some familiarity with this man. Even so, the various terms here might suggest a number of sources being brought together.[25] The depiction of the prophetic figure drawing near (Hebrew נגשׁ) to the king (vv. 13, 22, and 28) coincides with the theme of divine assurance given to the king in each story. The tone changes in the final episode, vv. 35–43, where the king of Israel is the target of the divine rebuke. It is almost as if there are two distinct outlooks on this king in these brief stories centered on unnamed prophets.[26]

2 Kings 9

The final unnamed prophet in the DH is found in the story of Jehu's coup, 2 Kgs 9:1–10. In this account, Elisha has chosen one of the "sons of the prophets" to find Jehu, Jehoram's field commander, on the battlefield at Ramoth Gilead, with instructions to anoint him king over Israel. This story is unique among the anonymous prophets stories in that the nameless prophet is acting on behalf of another prophet. In v. 4, the person who is sent is called הנער הנביא—literally, "the youth, the youth the prophet." The LXX inverts the MT's wording with "the prophet, the youth," probably to smooth out the slightly awkward phrasing in the

---

24. The verbs used to describe the encounter are "the prophet went [וילך] and stood [ויעמד]," departing from the previous three episodes use of "drew near" (ויגשׁ).

25. Marvin A. Sweeney, I & II Kings (Old Testament Library; Louisville: Westminster/John Knox, 2007) 240.

26. While it is also possible that the phrases identifying an anonymous prophet refer to one person, commentators are divided on the question. Mordechai Cogan thinks all these phrases refer to one person; see Cogan, I Kings, 467. Sweeney, however, asserts that "these prophets can hardly be the same man"; see Sweeney, I & II Kings, 238.

MT. Once anointed, Jehu foments rebellion and overthrows Jehoram by political assassination. There is an earlier allusion to this act in the Elijah stories. In 1 Kgs 19:16, Elijah is commanded by Yahweh to anoint Jehu, in addition to his other assignments. Jehu is the only northern king to be anointed as a way of marking his ascension to the throne.[27] In v. 7, the divine word is continued as a punishment upon the house of Ahab and vengeance for "my servants the prophets."

A number of commentators see the account of Jehu's revolt as an early narrative that was brought into the DH at a later stage.[28] The consensus suggests that, within this episode, recounting the prophetic announcement given to Jehu on the battlefield, 2 Kgs 9:1–6 is the original story to which many verses following it (7–10a; 14–15a; 25–26 etc.) were added.[29] While the prophet reports verbatim the instructions given by Elisha to the prophetic messenger in v. 3, for example, he says nothing about the speech in vv. 7–10a. This distinction between vv. 1–6 and vv. 7–10a suggests that these latter set of verses are a later addition to the older core narrative.[30]

Analysis of DH Texts

I turn now to a more detailed discussion of the thematic connections these biblical episodes share, their likely redactional shaping, and the significance this has for the message the DH tradents seek to convey. As I mentioned in the analysis above, the "man of God" aspect of the Samson story (Judg 13:2–20) is only operative from the human characters' point of view. The one assumed to be a "man of God" is actually a divine messenger, as the story makes clear at the end (v. 20). So I will omit this story from the analysis that follows.

I am convinced that the DH represents two levels of redactional activity, as argued by Cross: one from Josiah's day (Dtr 1) and a second one during the Exile (Dtr 2).[31] This is the nomenclature and relative dating I will use in the following analysis. It is tempting to accept the so-called Göttingen School approach, which

---

27. The threefold mention of anointing in this short episode is interesting. Saul (1 Sam 10:1), David (1 Sam 16:13; 2 Sam 2:4–7; 5:3, 17; 12:7; 1 Chr 11:3; 14:8), and Solomon (1 Kgs 1:34, 39, 45; 5:15; 1 Chr 29:22) are anointed, along with the Davidids Joash (2 Kgs 11:12) and Jehoahaz (2 Kgs 23:30). The pretender Absalom was said to be anointed, too (2 Sam 19:11). Jehu is the only non-Davidid (besides Saul, of course) to be anointed as king. Of further interest is the fact that there are only 4 places in the Hebrew Bible where Yahweh is reported to have said, "I have anointed you," and three of them appear here in this episode in reference to Jehu.

28. Marvin A. Sweeney, *I & II Kings*, 331. See also James A. Montgomery, *A Critical and Exegetical Commentary on the Books of Kings* (Edinburgh: T. & T. Clark, 1951) 400. John Gray sees two sources coming together here, too; see Gray, *I & II Kings*, 538.

29. M. L. Barré, *The Rhetoric of Political Persuasion* (CBQMS 20; Washington, D.C.: Catholic Biblical Association, 1988), 9.

30. McKenzie, *The Trouble with Kings*, 70–1.

31. See Cross, *Canaanite Myth and Hebrew Epic*, 274–89.

posits a prophetic layer of redaction within the DH, labeled DtrP. Particularly interesting is Timo Veijola's suggestion that DtrP tempered the positive attitude toward the monarchy seen in the base text (DtrG) by inserting prophetic stories within the tradition.[32] The most substantive disagreement I have with this approach is the late date they posit for these redactions—all post 586 B.C.E. I find that reconstruction unpersuasive in general and less able to address the early appearance of these stories of unnamed prophets in particular.

Turning again to the remaining five episodes, the theme of judgment paints a consistent thread linking almost all of these texts. Judg 6:7–10 contains a word of judgment against the people for not listening to Yahweh. The phrase that conveys this sentiment, שמע + ב + קול, in v. 10 is also seen in 1 Kgs 20:36, where the unnamed prophet condemns a man for not listening to Yahweh in Ahab's day. This phrase is used a number of times scattered throughout the DH, but the last time it is used is 2 Kgs 18:12, where the phrase is employed to explain the reason behind the Assyrian exile for the northern kingdom—very likely a Dtr 1 text. So the phrase "you have not listened to my voice" suggests that this text might be at home in a Josianic context (Dtr 1) rather than an exilic one (Dtr 2).[33] Yet other indicators that buttress this suggestion are lacking, and the text-critical evidence surrounding the omission of Judg 6:7–10 in 4QJudgª argues for a later provenance. 1 Sam 2:27–36 is a judgment against the house of Eli for the sins of his sons. 1 Kgs 13 is a judgment against the heterodox practices of the northern kingdom and the disobedience of the southern prophet. In this sense, the identities of the two prophetic figures in 1 Kgs 13 merge in their anonymity and convey a note of judgment to the prophetic voices of both north and south.[34] In 1 Kgs 20, the first two scenes in the episode relating to Ahab are positive directives toward his military campaigns. Yet, the third scene, the only one in which the prophet does not "draw near" to the king, contains divine judgment against Ahab for disobedience. While the Jehu story is a judgment against the line of Omri and Ahab as it now stands within the greater context of 2 Kgs 9, the original oracle in v. 3 says nothing about the condemnation of Ahab's house that is mentioned in v. 7. The explicit connection made with a condemnation of Ahab may stem from a later hand, as I noted earlier.[35] Yet the divine anointing of Jehu is a de facto rejection of the status quo and as such carries the connotation of judgment.

---

32. See T. Veijola, *Die ewige Dynastie: David und die Entstehung seiner Dynastie nach der deuteronomistischen Darstellung* (Helsinki: Suomalainen Tiedeakatemia, 1975).

33. It is interesting that the phrase appears nowhere in the account of Jerusalem's destruction, an event apposite for the expression of such sentiments.

34. See further Reinhartz, *"Why Ask My Name?"* 150–51. Although Reinhartz nowhere cites him, her analysis is rather reminiscent of Karl Barth's theological reading of 1 Kgs 13. See K. Barth, *Church Dogmatics* (trans. G. W. Bromiley et al.; vol II/2; Edinburgh: T. & T. Clark, 1957), 393–409.

35. See Barré, *The Rhetoric of Political Persuasion*, 9. See also E. Würthwein, *Die Bücher de Könige: 1 Kön. 17– 2 Kön. 25* (Göttingen: Vandenhoeck & Ruprecht, 1984), 329–30.

Out of all of these stories depicting anonymous prophets, the only two that do not express a clear theme of judgment are centered on Ahab and the divine assurance he is given in regard to his conflict with the Arameans in 1 Kgs 20:13–28. It is possible that the difference in tone here, one of positive assurance and then one of judgment later in the chapter, can be explained by suggesting that these stories once referred to different kings.[36] While Ahab's name does appear in some of the verses in the MT—vv. 13 and 14, for example—the king is usually referred to as "the king of Israel" in vv. 21, 22, 28, 32, and 40. Furthermore, a number of LXX traditions omit Ahab's name in v. 13.[37] This leaves only v. 14 as a firm textual indicator of the specific royal referent in these episodes in 1 Kgs 20. Cogan suggests on historical grounds that Ahab is most likely to be the original referent in the story.[38] There are, however, a number of scholars who suggest that these stories are out of place and do not conform to the historical picture of Aramean-Israelite cooperation during Ahab's reign.[39] In any case, there are unique aspects to these two episodes over against the other unnamed prophets. The use of the verb נגשׁ 'to draw near' (vv. 13, 22, 28) to convey the action of the prophet correlates with these episodes of positive assurance given to the king. Nowhere else in the anonymous prophets stories is this verb employed. So it seems rather likely that these two scenes recounted in 1 Kgs 20:13–28 do not have the same origin as the other stories of unnamed prophets in the DH.

Another aspect shared by most of these stories is a clear northern connection. Eli, Ḥophni, and Phineḥas were connected to Shiloh. Although the unnamed man of God is from Judah, he has journeyed to the northern city of Bethel to confront Jeroboam, the king of Israel. The man of God's downfall is linked to the prophet from Bethel. Ahab and Jehu are northern kings. The unnamed prophet in Judg 6:7–10, however, has no explicit connection to the north, although he does appear just before the Gideon stories, which have a northern backdrop. The pattern of explicit negative evaluation of the north seen in four of the five pericopes is in keeping with the themes of Dtr 1's oration in the wake of the fall of Samaria in 2 Kgs 17.

In addition, all of these stories are set within accounts that predate the close of the 9th century. Although one cannot make too much of this fact for the purposes of dating this level of redaction, it seems that editorial additions can more easily be inserted in older stories than late ones. It is perhaps significant that there are no

---

36. Sweeney, *I & II Kings*, 239. Historical issues attend the questions concerning how 1 Kgs 20 relates to 1 Kgs 22, especially regarding the conflicts between Aram and Israel and the chronology of these events. See McKenzie, *The Trouble with Kings*, 88.

37. The traditions that omit the name are attested in the Vaticanus and Lucianic texts of the LXX.

38. Cogan, *I Kings*, 472.

39. This suggestion extends back to A. Jepsen, "Israel und Damaskus," *Archiv für Orientforschung* 14 (1942) 153–72. See also see J. M. Miller, "The Elisha Cycle and the Accounts of the Omride Wars," *JBL* 85 (1966) 441–54, and McKenzie, *The Trouble with Kings*, 88–93.

anonymous prophets placed within the narratives of the DH from the 8th or 7th century down to the exile in the 6th century.

The theme of prophetic decree and fulfillment is seen often in Dtr 1.[40] This theme is present in all of these texts except Judg 6:7–10 and perhaps the oldest layer of the Jehu story in 2 Kgs 9. In 1 Sam 2:27–36, the prophetic decree is fulfilled in the death of Eli's sons in 1 Sam 4:11 and Solomon's expulsion of Abiathar in 1 Kgs 2:27. In 1 Kgs 13, the prophetic decree is explicitly connected to 2 Kgs 23:17–19 in Josiah's day. In the stories from 1 Kgs 20, decree and fulfillment occur within each scene. In 1 Kgs 20:13–14, the divine promise of victory is given to the king, and it is said to be carried out in vv. 16–21. Likewise, the second divine assurance in this chapter comes in 1 Kgs 20:28 and is fulfilled in vv. 29–30. The third scene in 1 Kgs 20 involves a prophetic decree of punishment against the man who refused to strike the man from the sons of the prophets. The anonymous prophet decrees death by lion, and it is carried out in the same verse (v. 36). The same prophetic figure pronounces death for the king in v. 42, and this ostensibly is carried out when Ahab dies at Ramoth Gilead in 1 Kgs 22:37, although no explicit connection is made with this earlier proclamation. The episode involving Jehu probably had no prophetic decree and fulfillment theme in its original layer. I noted earlier that 2 Kgs 9:1–6 is probably the oldest strata of this story and that v. 7's explicit reference to striking the house of Ahab was a later addition. The words of v. 7 could be seen along the lines of decree and fulfillment, since Jehu ruthlessly carries out these orders in the ensuing bloodbath. Thus, as this story currently stands, it follows the same pattern attested in most of the other anonymous prophet episodes.

There also seems to be a special connection between 1 Kgs 20:35–43 and 1 Kgs 13, suggesting that the compositions are related.[41] First of all, judgment is pronounced by unnamed prophets on the Israelite kings in both stories. Second, the phrase, "at the word of Yahweh" is employed in both stories as well.[42] This phrase is not a common idiom within the DH. While employed seven times in 1 Kgs 13 (vv. 1, 2, 5, 9, 17, 18, 32), these words appear only once in 1 Kgs 20:35. The relative uniqueness of this phrase within the DH suggests a stronger connection between these two texts.[43] The third similarity worthy of note is judgment in the form of a lion (אריה) mauling a person for not obeying the word of Yahweh. In 1 Kgs 13:21–22, the old prophet from Bethel pronounced judgment on the man of God from Judah for not obeying the word of God, and in 1 Kgs 20:36, the man of the sons of the prophets pronounced judgment on the man who refused to strike

40. Cross, *Canaanite Myth and Hebrew Epic*, 281.

41. McKenzie, *The Trouble with Kings*, 55.

42. W. E. Lemke, "The Way of Obedience: I Kings 13 and the Structure of the Deuteronomistic History," in *Magnalia Dei, The Mighty Acts of God: Essays on the Bible and Archaeology in Memory of G. Ernest Wright* (ed. F. M. Cross, W. E. Lemke, and P. D. Miller Jr.; Garden City, NY: Doubleday, 1976), 314.

43. Lemke, "The Way of Obedience," 314.

him. In 1 Kgs 13:21–22, however, the pronounced judgment is simply that the
man of God from Judah would not be buried in the tomb of his fathers. The man
is later killed by a lion on the way back to Judah. In 1 Kgs 20:36, the judgment
pronounced is death by lion. Outside the DH, too, Yahweh is said to use a lion for
divine punishment. In Jer 5:6, a lion is used to punish the people of Judah, and in
Isa 15:9, the threat of a lion is directed at Moab. Within the DH, lions are used by
Yahweh to punish the foreign settlers brought in by the Assyrians to the cities of
Samaria after the Israelites had been exiled. After the lions had killed some of the
settlers, the Assyrians sent an Israelite priest to instruct the people to fear Yahweh,
in 2 Kgs 17:25–26.[44] The connections the texts of 1 Kgs 13 and 1 Kgs 20:35–43
have with 2 Kgs 17:25–26 regarding the use of the lions suggests that all of these
texts are from the same editorial hand.[45]

I would like to turn now to suggesting a tentative chronology for the redactional activity that placed the anonymous prophets stories within the DH. I am
convinced that the story in 1 Kgs 13 originates from a time before Dtr 1 but was
brought into the DH in Josiah's day, bearing the markers of the *ex eventu* prophecy
centered on Josiah's actions. The Eli episode in 1 Sam 2:27–36 also attests the editorial work of Josiah's day (Dtr 1)—the prophecy-fulfillment theme concerns the
words of indictment given to Eli and the way priests were treated in the wake of
the Josianic reforms in 2 Kgs 23:9.[46] The use of the lion for divine judgment suggests a connection between the episodes in 1 Kgs 20:35–43 and 1 Kgs 13, which, as
I noted above, is most at home in Josiah's day. This connection is further strengthened by a similar use of lions for Yahweh's judgment in 2 Kgs 17, after the fall of
Samaria in 721 B.C.E. In addition, the phrase "cities of Samaria" appears in only
four verses in the Hebrew Bible—1 Kgs 13:32; 2 Kgs 17:24, 26—the two stories that
share the lion-as-judgment motif—and 2 Kgs 23:19, the verse just after the reference to the Josianic fulfillment of the prophecy of the man of God in 1 Kgs 13.[47]
The Jehu story in 2 Kgs 9:1–6 shares the phrase "from the sons of the prophets"
with 1 Kgs 20:35, and it is very likely an early text as well, at least as old as the days

---

44. The use of lions as divine punishment by Yahweh in these texts finds parallels in comparative evidence in the broader ancient Near Eastern context. See B. Strawn, *What is Stronger
Than a Lion? Leonine Image and Metaphor in the Hebrew Bible and the Ancient Near East* (OBO
212; Fribourg: University Press / Göttingen: Vandenhoeck & Ruprecht, 2005), 250.

45. See Würthwein, *Die Bücher de Könige*, 243.

46. McCarter points out what he calls "the devices and cliches of the Josianic historian" in
this text, noting the similarities it shares with 1 Kgs 13 (McCarter, *1 Samuel*, 92). Patrick Miller
and J. J. M. Roberts note this possibility as well. But they also suggest that this oracle might have
been written by the author of the ark narrative, who was working much earlier (see P. D. Miller Jr.
and J. J. M. Roberts, *The Hand of the Lord: A Reassessment of the "Ark Narrative" of 1 Samuel*
[Baltimore: Johns Hopkins University Press, 1977], 41). Miller and Roberts do not address the
thematic connections this story has with the texts I am addressing in this essay.

47. Lemke, "The Way of Obedience," 307.

of Josiah.[48] It is likely that 9:1–6 were the oldest strata of this story, antedating Dtr 1's day, and that Dtr 1 brought these verses in and added the explicit theme of judgment against the house of Ahab and the theme of decree and fulfillment by connecting this episode with the eventual death of Ahab in 1 Kgs 22:37.

As I have suggested above, the episodes that depict an unnamed prophet that do not share the clear markers of the work of Dtr 1 are Judg 6:7–10 and the two scenes attested in 1 Kgs 20:13–28. First of all, it is important to note that of our 5 episodes, Judg 6:7–10 is the shortest. We have, therefore, the least amount of textual data with which to work when analyzing this story. Even so, on the one hand, it shares two themes with 1 Sam 2:27–36: the reference to slavery in Egypt and the notion of warning against disobedience. Also, Judg 6:7–10 shares the notion of not listening to the voice of Yahweh with 1 Kgs 20:36. As noted earlier, this idiom is not used after 2 Kgs 18:12, where it is used to explain the Assyrian exile of the Northern Kingdom, and this suggests that Judg 6:7–10 may be a Dtr 1 text. Yet, on the other hand, Judg 6:7–10 lacks the prophecy-fulfillment theme and other markers that would connect it firmly to the earlier redactional level of the DH. Further, if my assumption about the textual history of Judg 6:7–10 in light of the Qumran text is correct, positing a later date for its insertion is more likely. That these verses do not appear in 4QJudgᵃ, coupled with their intrusive feel within the greater context of Judges 6, suggests that they constitute a late Deuteronomistic scribal expansion within the MT's tradition.

The two scenes attested in 1 Kgs 20:13–28 seem to me to be in their own category. First of all, they both depict the prophetic figure as "drawing near" to the king to make his pronouncement. No other anonymous prophet is said to "draw near." Second, they both constitute divine assurance given to a northern king, another unique feature of this prophet. These data suggest to me that these stories antedate Dtr 1's work. While it is possible that they are later additions that were inserted in a much later layer of the redaction of the DH, it seems to me passing strange that anyone in the postexilic period would want to insert stories of divine assurance given to a northern king. Conversely, it is easier to see a Deuteronomistic redactor including these old stories of an assured northern king and associating them with Ahab just before the prophetic condemnation of the Israelite king. Although the two older stories lack a prophetic rebuke, given their current placement, their assurances are eclipsed by the condemnation in v. 42.

In conclusion, of the five episodes of unnamed prophetic figures that remain (when Judges 13 is excluded), 1 Sam 2:27–36, 1 Kgs 13, 1 Kgs 20:35–43, and 2 Kgs 9:1–6 stem from Josiah's day. The two episodes in 1 Kgs 20:13–22 and 26–28 seem to come from an earlier source that, to my mind, seems to antedate Dtr 1. Judg

---

48. Sweeney argues that this story goes back to the days of Hezekiah, and he suggests that this narrative points to Israel's inability to govern itself without constant revolt and violence. See Sweeney, *I & II Kings*, 331. For a similar perspective on this text's date, see Blenkinsopp, *A History of Prophecy in Israel*, 32.

6:7–10 is most likely a rather late Deuteronomistic insertion, but in keeping with the spirit of the other unnamed prophets. So, of our tales of anonymous prophets, Judg 6:7–10 is later than the others on textual grounds, and the two scenes in 1 Kgs 20:13–28 do not belong on thematic grounds—providing assurance to a northern king and lacking other clear features of Dtr 1.

Despite their possible chronological diversity, these stories of anonymous prophets address a rebuke to the people (Judg 6:7–10), to a priest (1 Sam 2:27–36), to a king and two prophets (1 Kgs 13), and a king again (1 Kgs 20:35–43). Perhaps the Jehu story in 2 Kgs 9 was meant to convey a rebuke to Jehoram and the entire line of Ahab, as the context now makes clear (vv. 7–10). While an explicit condemnation is lacking in the original oracle, the story in 2 Kgs 9:1–6 does convey Yahweh's anointing of another king, an implicit rejection of the *status quo ante*. This particular grouping suggests that these unnamed prophetic stories are programmatic for the redactor(s), addressing both leaders and people within Israel to emphasize God's concern for these people to be obedient. When we combine the observations set forth in this essay, we see a constellation of evidence that suggests that these episodes centered on unnamed prophets are voices of Deuteronomistic ideology directed toward the northern tribes and their leaders—priestly, prophetic, and kingly.

Bibliography

Bal, M. *Death and Dissymmetry: The Politics of Coherence in the Book of Judges.* Chicago: University of Chicago Press, 1988.

Barré, L. M. *The Rhetoric of Political Persuasion.* Catholic Biblical Quarterly Manuscript Series 20; Washington, D.C.: Catholic Biblical Association, 1988.

Barrera, J. T. "Textual Variants in 4QJudg^a and the Textual and Editorial History of the Book of Judges." *Revue de Qumran* 54 (1989) 229–45.

Barth, K. *Church Dogmatics.* Vol II/2. Translated by G. W. Bromiley et al. Edinburgh: T. & T. Clark, 1957.

Beentjes, P. "Prophets in the Book of Chronicles." Pp. 45–53 in *The Elusive Prophet: The Prophet as a Historical Person, Literary Character and Anonymous Artist.* Edited by Johannes C. De Moor. Leiden: Brill, 2001.

Ben Zvi, E. " 'The Prophets': References to Generic Prophets and Their Role in the Construction of the Image of the 'Prophets of Old' with in the Postmonarchic Readership(s) of the Books of Kings." Pp. 387–99 in *The Books of Kings; Sources, Composition, Historiography and Reception.* Ed. André Lemaire and Baruch Halpern. Leiden: Brill, 2010.

Blenkinsopp, J. *A History of Prophecy in Israel.* Louisville: Westminster John Knox, 1996.

Cogan, M. *1 Kings.* Anchor Bible 10. New York: Doubleday, 2000.

Cross, F. M. *Canaanite Myth and Hebrew Epic.* Cambridge: Harvard University Press, 1973.

Edelman, D. "Court Prophets during the Monarchy and Literary Prophets in the So-Called Deuteronomistic History." Pp. 51–74 in *Israelite Prophecy and the Deuteronomistic History: Portrait, Reality, and the Formation of a History.* Edited by Mignon R. Jacobs and Raymond F. Person Jr. Atlanta: SBL, 2013.

Gray, J. *I & II Kings.* 2nd ed. Philadelphia: Westminster, 1970.

Harvey, J. E. *Retelling the Torah: The Deuteronomistic Historian's Use of the Tetrateuchal Narratives.* London: T. & T. Clark, 2004.

Japhet, S. *I & II Chronicles.* Louisville: Westminster/John Knox, 1993.

Jepsen, A. "Israel und Damaskus." *Archiv für Orientforschung* 14 (1942) 153–72.

Keel, O., and C. Uehlinger. *Gods, Goddesses, and Images of God in Ancient Israel.* Minneapolis: Fortress, 1998.

Klein, L. R. *The Triumph of Irony in the Book of Judges.* Sheffield: Almond Press, 1988.

Lemke, W. E. "The Way of Obedience: I Kings 13 and the Structure of the Deuteronomistic History." Pp. 301–26 in *Magnalia Dei: The Mighty Acts of God: Essays on the Bible and Archaeology in Memory of G. Ernest Wright.* Edited by F. M. Cross, W. E. Lemke, and P. D. Miller Jr. Garden City, NY: Doubleday, 1976.

McCarter, P. K. *1 Samuel.* Anchor Bible 8. New York: Doubleday, 1980.

McKenzie, S. L. *The Trouble with Kings.* Vetus Testamentum Supplement 42. Leiden: Brill, 1991.

_____. *The Chronicler's Use of the Deuteronomistic History.* Harvard Semitic Monograph 33. Winona Lake, IN: Eisenbrauns, 2006.

Miller, J. M. "The Elisha Cycle and the Accounts of the Omride Wars." *Journal of Biblical Literature* 85 (1966) 441–54

Miller, P. D., and J. J. M. Roberts. *The Hand of the Lord: A Reassessment of the "Ark Narrative" of 1 Samuel.* Baltimore: Johns Hopkins University Press, 1977.

Montgomery, J. A. *A Critical and Exegetical Commentary on the Books of Kings.* Edinburgh: T. & T. Clark, 1951.

Moore, G. F. *Judges.* International Critical Commentary: Edinburgh: T. & T. Clark, 1895.

Noth, M. *Überlieferungsgeschichtliche Studien.* Tübingen: Max Niemeyer, 1967.

Reinhartz, A. *"Why Ask My Name?" Anonymity and Identity in Biblical Narrative.* Oxford: Oxford University Press, 1998.

Revell, E. J. *The Designation of the Individual: Expressive Usage in Biblical Narrative.* Kampen, Netherlands: Kok Pharos, 1996.

Rofé, A. "Classes in the Prophetical Stories: Didactic Legenda and Parable." Pp. 143–64 in *Studies on Prophecy.* Vetus Testamentum Supplement 26. Leiden: Brill, 1974.

Römer, T. C. *The So-Called Deuteronomistic History.* London: T. & T. Clark, 2005.

Sandberg, R. N. *Development and Discontinuity in Jewish Law.* Lanham, MD: University Press of America, 2001.

Schmid, K. "The Emergence and Disappearance of the Separation between the Pentateuch and the Deuteronomistic History in Biblical Studies." Pp. 11–24 in *Pentateuch, Hexateuch, or Enneateuch? Identifying Literary Works in Genesis through Kings.* Edited by T. B. Dozeman, Thomas Römer, and Konrad Schmid. Atlanta: SBL, 2011.

Soggin, A. *Judges.* Old Testament Library. Philadelphia: Westminster, 1981.

Strawn, B. *What is Stronger Than a Lion? Leonine Image and Metaphor in the Hebrew Bible and the Ancient Near East.* Orbis Biblicus et Orientalis 212. Fribourg: University Press / Göttingen: Vandenhoeck & Ruprecht, 2005.

Sweeney, M. A. *I & II Kings.* Old Testament Library. Louisville: Westminster/John Knox, 2007.

Tov, E. *Textual Criticism of the Hebrew Bible.* Minneapolis: Fortress, 1992.

Veijola, T. *Die ewige Dynastie: David und die Entstehung seiner Dynastie nach der deuterono-mistischen Darstellung*. Helsinki: Suomalainen Tiedeakatemia, 1975.

Wilson, R. *Prophecy and Society in Ancient Israel*. Philadelphia: Fortress, 1980.

Würthwein, E. *Die Bücher de Könige: 1 Kön. 17– 2 Kön. 25*. Göttingen: Vandenhoeck & Ruprecht, 1984.

The Prophet Huldah and the Stuff of State

Francesca Stavrakopoulou

University of Exeter

For a number of scholars, Huldah is a hero: she is celebrated as the Bible's first canonizer; the catalyst for radical religious reform; a "spiritual leader" — and even a "role model."[1] Her positive appraisal within scholarship is but one iteration within a longer and somewhat mixed reception history of the prophet, throughout which her religious authority, status, and influence in post-biblical Judaisms and Christianities has long been considered.[2] This interest in Huldah is likely prompted in part by her significant and yet surprisingly limited portrayal in the Hebrew Bible; for a figure who appears to perform a pivotal role in one of the key dramas in the biblical portrayal of the past, she is merely a bit-player.

Huldah appears only in the well-known narratives dealing with the discovery of the so-called Book of the Law during the reign of Josiah and his subsequent cult purge (2 Kgs 22–23; 2 Chr 34–35). While these narratives differ in their

---

1. On Huldah as first canonizer: P. Trible, "Huldah's Holy Writ: On Women and Biblical Authority," *Touchstone* 3 (Jan 1985) 6–13; C. V. Camp, "Female Voice, Written Word: Women and Authority in Hebrew Scripture," in *Embodied Love: Sensuality and Relationship as Feminist Values* (ed. P. M. Cooey, S. A. Farmer, and M. E. Ross; San Francisco: Harper & Row, 1987), 100–101; J. E. McKinlay, "Filling the Gaps and Putting Huldah to Use," in *The One Who Reads May Run: Essays in Honour of Edgar W. Conrad* (ed. R. Boer, M. Carden, and J. Kelso; London: T. & T. Clark, 2012), 10–27; E. J. Hamori, "The Prophet and the Necromancer: Women's Divination in Kings," *JBL* 132 (2013), 827–43 (at p. 838). Adrian Janis Bledstein's proposal that Huldah is the author of the Deuteronomistic History has not won much support; see A. J. Bledstein, "Is Judges a Woman's Satire of Men Who Play God?" in *A Feminist Companion to Judges* (ed. A. Brenner; Sheffield: JSOT Press, 1993), 54. On Huldah as catalyst: J. E. McKinlay, "Gazing at Huldah," *Bible & Critical Theory* 1/3 (2005), 1–11 (cited 5 May 2015; online: http://novaojs.newcastle.edu.au/ojsbct/index.php/bct/article/view/40/26). On Huldah as spiritual leader: D. G. Kent, "2 Chronicles," in *The IVP Women's Commentary* (ed. C. C. Kroeger and M. J. Evans; Downers Grove, IL: InterVarsity, 2002), 243; see, too, A. O. Bellis, *Helpmates, Harlots, and Heroes: Women's Stories in the Hebrew Bible* (2nd ed.; Louisville: Westminster John Knox, 2007), 209. On Huldah as role model: R. J. Weems, "Huldah, the Prophet: Reading a (Deuteronomistic) Woman's Identity," in *A God So Near: Essays on Old Testament Theology in Honor of P. D. Miller* (ed. B. A. Strawn and N. R. Bowen; Winona Lake, IN: Eisenbrauns, 2003), 321.

2. See further L. K. Handy, "Reading Huldah as Being a Woman," *Biblical Research* 55 (2010) 5–44.

sequencing of key events in the story of Josiah's activities, they offer, in essence, the same presentation of her role: she endorses both the newly-discovered scroll and Josiah's anguished interpretation of its words by delivering an oracle from YHWH warning of an impending disaster that the king himself will not witness in his lifetime (2 Kgs 22:15–20; 2 Chr 34:23–28). Her credentials are also given: she is designated a prophet (נביאה) located in the Mishneh district of Jerusalem and is said to be the wife of a certain Shallum ben Tikvah, a man whose title or occupation is 'keeper of the garments' (שׁמר הבגדים) and whose ancestry is briefly noted (2 Kgs 22:14; cf. 2 Chr 34:22).[3] And yet, in spite of these details, Huldah herself remains a "blank character."[4] Following her oracle, she disappears from the story of Judah just as suddenly as she had appeared. Nothing more is said of her in the biblical literature.[5]

Discerning anything about Huldah's assumed or imagined interaction with the state has tended to rely both upon scholarly reconstructions of 7th-century Judahite history and theories about the extent to which (if at all) the narratives in 2 Kgs 22–23 and 2 Chr 34–35 can be taken as historically reliable.[6] Despite the best efforts of certain defenders of the Books of Chronicles (or their hypothetical sources), most privilege the closing chapters of the Books of Kings as a collection of texts more likely to have been composed or compiled at a period closer in

---

3. The names in Shallum's ancestry in 2 Chr 34:22 differ from those in 2 Kgs 22:14; this might be indicative of an unstable geneaology within the tradition (so A. Brenner, *I Am . . . Biblical Women Tell Their Own Stories* [Minneapolis: Augsburg Fortress, 2005], 159).

4. R. L. Cohn, "Characterization in Kings," in *The Books of Kings: Sources, Composition, Historiography and Reception* (ed. B. Halpern, A. Lemaire, and M. J. Adams; VTSup 129; Leiden: Brill, 2010), 94. On the possibility that Huldah's name is suggestive of a folk-tale origin or association, see Hamori, "The Prophet and the Necromancer," 841 n. 28; T. Römer, "From Prophet to Scribe: Jeremiah, Huldah and the Invention of the Book," in *Writing the Bible: Scribes, Scribalism and Script* (ed. P. R. Davies and T. Römer; London: Acumen, 2013), 86–96; B. Scheuer, "Huldah: A Cunning Career Woman?" in *Prophecy and Prophets in Stories: Papers Read at the Fifth Meeting of the Edinburgh Prophecy Network, Utrecht, October 2013* (ed. B. Becking and H. Barstad; Leiden: Brill, 2015), 104–23.

5. Many scholars express frustration that she does not reappear in the story of the kingdom of Judah, that she goes unmentioned in other biblical texts, that no biblical collection of prophetic literature bears her name. To a certain degree, this scholarly frustration reflects the loaded assumption that any prophetic figure related to Josiah and his supposed reforms must have been a prominent figure or of great historical and theological significance. Indeed, as Marvin Sweeney comments, 2 Kgs 22–23 is "a pivotal text in scholarly discussion and has shaped the entire discipline of Hebrew Bible studies" (M. Sweeney, *King Josiah of Judah: The Lost Messiah of Israel* [Oxford: Oxford University Press, 2001], 5). See also the discussion in G. J. Venema, *Reading Scripture in the Old Testament: Deuteronomy 9–10; 31; 2 Kings 22–23; Jeremiah 36; Nehemiah 8* (Leiden: Brill, 2004), 54–61.

6. As Niels Peter Lemche points out, the presence in Chronicles of a portrayal of Josiah's reign alternative to that in Kings "warns us against presuming that the deuteronomistic version represents historical fact" (N. P. Lemche, "Did a Reform Like Josiah's Happen?" in *The Historian and the Bible: Essays in Honour of Lester L. Grabbe* [ed. P. R. Davies and D. V. Edelman; London: T. & T. Clark, 2010], 18).

time to the events they seek to describe and on which the Chronicler likely drew.[7] Within this context, the frequent correlation of the newly-discovered "Book of the Law" with an assumed 7th-century form of the biblical book of Deuteronomy— and by implication, Huldah's endorsement of its ideologies—has led many to assume she was a historical figure associated with a local religiopolitical faction, perhaps originating in the former Northern Kingdom of Israel, pressing for the "monotheistic" reform of the Jerusalem cult and—by extension—a remodeling of the religious role of the king, related to the paradigm set out in Deut 17:14–20.[8] But problems abound with this model, not the least of which is the dual assumption that a form of (at least parts of) Deuteronomy preceded or emerged alongside the narrative in 2 Kgs 22–23, and that Josiah did indeed carry out a purge of Judah's religious centers.[9]

---

7. For a more positive appraisal of the historical priority of 2 Chr 34–35, see D. A. Glatt-Gilead, "The Role of Huldah's Prophecy in the Chronicler's Portrayal of Josiah's Reform," *Biblica* 77 (1996) 16–31. On the relationship between 2 Kgs 22 and Chronicles, see especially L. C. Jonker's analyses in *Reflections of King Josiah in Chronicles: Late Stages of the Josiah Reception in 2 Chr 34 f.* (Gütersloh: Gütersloher Verlaghaus, 2003) and "Huldah's Oracle: The Origin of the Chronicler's Typical Style?" *Verbum et Ecclesia* 33.1 (2012) article 7 (cited 13 June 2015; online http://www.ve.org.za/index.php/VE/article/viewFile/714/1042. On the theory that the books of Kings and Chronicles share a source, see the classic study by A. G. Auld, *Kings Without Privilege: David and Moses in the Story of the Bible's Kings* (Edinburgh: T. & T. Clark, 1994).

8. On the identification of the so-called "Book of the Law" in 2 Kgs 22:8–13 with Deuteronomy, see W. M. L. de Wette, *Beiträge zur Einleitung in das Alten Testament* (2 vols.; Halle: Schimmelpfennig, 1806–7), 1:168–79, plus (among others) E. Reuter, *Kultzentralisation: Entstehung und Theologie von Dtn 12* (BBB 87; Frankfurt: Anton Hain, 1993), 213–62. For the proposal that a form of the Holiness Code, rather than Deuteronomy, is to be identified with the book discovered in the Jerusalem temple, see G. R. Berry, "The Code Found in the Temple," *JBL* 39 (1920) 44–51; cf. L. A. S. Monroe, *Josiah's Reform and the Dynamics of Defilement: Israelite Rites of Violence and the Making of a Biblical Text* (Oxford: Oxford University Press, 2011). On the assumed association of Huldah with political and regional factions, see R. R. Wilson, *Prophecy and Society in Ancient Israel* (Philadelphia: Fortress, 1980), 219–23, 298; D. L. Christensen, "Huldah and the Men of Anathoth: Women in Leadership in the Deuteronomistic History," in *Society of Biblical Literature 1984 Seminar Papers* (ed. K. H. Richards; Chico: Scholars Press, 1984), 399–404; M. Leuchter, *Josiah's Reform and Jeremiah's Scroll: Historical Calamity and Prophetic Response* (Sheffield: Sheffield Phoenix Press, 2006).

9. The amount of scholarly literature debating these issues is vast; I offer here only a highly selective bibliography.

On the dating of Deuteronomy to a period later than 2 Kgs 22–23, see E. Würthwein, "Die josianische Reform und das Deuteronomium," *ZTK* 73 (1976) 395–423; J. R. Linville, *Israel in the Book of Kings: The Past as a Project of Social Identity* (JSOTSup 272; Sheffield: Sheffield Academic, 1998); R. F. Person, *The Deuteronomic School: History, Social Setting, and Literature* (Atlanta: SBL, 2002); E. Ben Zvi, "Imagining Josiah's Book and the Implications of Imagining It in Early Persian Yehud," in *Berührungspunkte: Studien zur Sozial- und Religionsgeschichte Israels und seiner Umwelt: Festschrift für Rainer Albertz zu seinem 65* (ed. I. Kottsieper, R. Schmitt, and J. Wöhrle; AOAT 350; Münster: Ugarit-Verlag, 2008), 193–212. For the relationship of the Books of Kings to the composition of a "preexilic" Deuteronomistic History, see B. Halpern and D. S. Vanderhooft, "The Editions of Kings in the 7th–6th Centuries BCE," *HUCA* 62 (1991) 179–244; E. Eynikel, *The*

Given these uncertainties, it is perhaps more constructive to approach the character of Huldah and the narrative in which she appears by engaging directly with the precise socioreligious dynamics in the story offered in the Books of Kings—that is, by looking afresh at the three indexes of statehood the Josiah narratives themselves highlight—temple, scribalism, kingship—within the context of the discursive world created within and by the texts, set against the broader ancient Near Eastern cultural backdrop from which the biblical literature emerged.[10] As such, the religious practices and activities associated with temple, kingship, and scribalism are to be taken not only as localized, literary reflections or instruments of statehood but as material manifestations of perceived cosmic realities. In the discursive world of the biblical texts, these activities engage the materiality—the very "stuff"—of both religion and state.[11] It is within this world that the protagonists of the story perform—and within which Huldah's portrayed interaction with the state is best understood.

Reform of King Josiah and the Composition of the Deuteronomistic History (OtSt 33; Leiden: Brill, 1996). For recent surveys of the composition and redaction of Kings, engaging various models of composition and compilation, see M. Avioz, "The Book of Kings in Recent Research (Part I)," *CBR* 4 (2005) 11–44; M. Avioz, "The Book of Kings in Recent Research (Part II)," *CBR* 5 (2006) 11–57; G. N. Knoppers, "Theories of the Redaction(s) of Kings," in *The Books of Kings: Sources, Composition, Historiography and Reception* (ed. B. Halpern, A. Lemaire and M. J. Adams; VTSup 129; Leiden: Brill, 2010), 69–88.

For arguments against a Josianic reform, see (for example) L. K. Handy, "Historical Probability and the Narrative of Josiah's Reform in 2 Kings," in *The Pitcher is Broken: Memorial Essays for Gösta W. Ahlström* (ed. S. W. Holladay and L. K. Handy; JSOTSup 190; Sheffield: Sheffield Academic, 1995), 252–75; H. Niehr, "Die Reform des Joschija: methodische, historische und religionsgeschichtliche Aspekte," in *Jeremia und die 'deuteronomistiche Bewegung'* (ed. W. Groß; BBB 98; Weinheim: Beltz Athenäum, 1995), 33–55; L. S. Fried, "The High Places (*Bâmôt*) and the Reforms of Hezekiah and Josiah: An Archaeological Interpretation," *JAOS* 122 (2002) 437–65; P. R. Davies, "Josiah and the Law Book" in *Good Kings and Bad Kings: The Kingdom of Judah in the Seventh Century BCE* (ed. L. L. Grabbe; LHBOTS 393; London: T. & T. Clark, 2005), 65–77; N. P. Lemche, "Did a Reform Like Josiah's Happen?" J. Pakkala, "Why the Cult Reforms in Judah Probably Did Not Happen," in *One God — One Cult — One Nation: Archaeological and Biblical Perspectives* (ed. R. G. Kratz and H. Spieckermann; Berlin: de Gruyter, 2010), 201–35. For arguments in favor of Josiah's reform, see (for example) R. Albertz, "Why a Reform like Josiah's Must Have Happened," in *Good Kings and Bad Kings: The Kingdom of Judah in the Seventh Century BCE* (ed. L. L. Grabbe; LHBOTS 393; London: T. & T. Clark, 2005), 27–46; N. Na'aman, "The 'Discovered Book' and the Legitimation of Josiah's Reform," *JBL* 130 (2011) 47–62.

10. Ehud Ben Zvi makes a similar point about the "imagined worlds" created in the prophetic books of the Hebrew Bible: "The Yehudite Collection of Prophetic Books and Imperial Contexts: Some Observations," in *Divination, Politics and Ancient Near Eastern Empires* (ed. A. Lenzi and J. Stökl; Atlanta: SBL, 2014), 145–69.

11. The "stuff" in view here concerns what Daniel Miller describes as the "specificity of material domains and the way form itself is employed to become the fabric of cultural worlds" (D. Miller, "Why Some Things Matter," pp. 3–21 in *Material Cultures: Why Some Things Matter* [ed. D. Miller; London: UCL Press, 1998], 6); see further, D. Morgan (ed.), *Religion and Material Culture: The Matter of Belief* (Abingdon, U.K.: Routledge, 2010).

Huldah, Temple, and Scroll in 2 Kings 22

Unlike other prophets (both named and anonymous) in the Books of Kings, Huldah does not appear to engage those issues of statehood that some scholars imagine might preoccupy a vassal kingdom caught up in the power-play of regional and imperial politics. Indeed, in a number of instances, kings of both Israel and Judah are presented as requesting or ignoring prophetic oracles concerning specific interactions with foreign or rival powers, while several prophets are presented more explicitly as ritual advisers to the state on matters of policy and polity.[12] But Huldah is different. Following the discovery of the scroll, and in response to Josiah's request for (seemingly further) divine information from Yhwh (22:12–13), the first part of Huldah's oracle contains nothing of explicit political or imperial relevance:

> Thus says Yhwh, the God of Israel: Tell the man who sent you to me, "Thus says Yhwh, Behold, I am bringing evil on this place and on its inhabitants—all the words of the scroll that the king of Judah has read. Because they have abandoned me and have burnt incense to other gods, so that they have provoked me to anger with all the work of their hands, therefore my wrath will be kindled against this place, and it will not be quenched." (2 Kgs 22:15–17)

While the oracle offers very little information about the precise nature of the coming disaster, the trigger for divine displeasure is clearly articulated: the cult of Yhwh has been abandoned, for his worshipers offer incense (קטר) to other deities.[13] The crime of cultic malpractice suggests the target of punishment will be the cult place itself: the phrase המקום הזה 'this place', employed elsewhere to index sacred space or a locus of divine encounter, is pointedly repeated both here (22:16, 17) and in the second half of the oracle, in which Yhwh speaks about Josiah's death

---

12. See, for example, the explicit political contexts of the encounters between Nathan and Solomon (1 Kgs 1); Ahijah and Jeroboam ben Nebat (1 Kgs 11; 14); Shemaiah and Rehoboam (12:22–23); Elijah, Ahab, and Jehu (1 Kgs 18–19); Elisha and Jehoshaphat (1 Kgs 22); Jonah ben Amittai and Jeroboam II (2 Kgs 14); Isaiah and Hezekiah (2 Kgs 19–20), plus the anonymous prophetic figures and groups warning of political and or state defeat in (for example) 1 Kgs 20:13–32; 2 Kgs 9:4–10; 17:13, 23; 21:10; 24:2. Note also the emphatic portrayal of Jeremiah throughout the book bearing his name as a prophet embroiled in the domestic and international politics of state during the reigns of Josiah, Jehoahaz, Jehoiakim, Jehoiachin, and Zedekiah. On the political function of prophecy, see recently M. Nissinen, "Prophecy in Joshua–Kings: Ancient Near Eastern Perspectives," in *Israelite Prophecy and the Deuteronomistic History: Portrait, Reality and the Formation of a History* (ed. M. R. Jacobs and R. F. Person; Atlanta: SBL, 2013), 103–28; and A.-M. Wetter, "The Prophet and the King: Is There Such a Thing as Free Prophetic Speech?" in *Prophecy and Prophets in Stories: Papers Read at the Fifth Meeting of the Edinburgh Prophecy Network, Utrecht, October 2013* (ed. B. Becking and H. Barstad; Leiden: Brill, 2015), 29–44.

13. Indeed, the fiery imagery is a common biblical trope associated elsewhere with divine anger and punishment. On burning incense, see D. V. Edelman, "The Meaning of *qiṭṭēr*," *VT* 35 (1985) 395–404.

(22:19, 20).[14] This makes good sense within the wider narrative, for the entire account of Josiah's reign in 2 Kgs 22–23 is preoccupied with the places and practices of cult.

Indeed, following the standard regnal prologue (22:1) and the evaluation of the king's religious behavior (22:2), the Josiah narrative opens with the claim that in the eighteenth year of his reign, he commanded the "repair" of breaches or fissures in the temple of Yhwh (22:3–7, 9). While this part of the narrative (likely intentionally) shares something in common with the story of King Jehoash's attempts to repair the Jerusalem temple (12:4–16),[15] it nonetheless implies that the temple itself requires material renewal. Within the context of ancient Near Eastern ritual ideologies, the perceived deterioration of sacred space might manifest cosmic and theological danger.[16] As such, and in concert with their divine counterparts, kings were entrusted with the construction, alteration, and maintenance of divine dwelling places by means of safeguarding temple space. Josiah's concern with the fabric of the temple is not simply an act of personal piety or governmental curation[17] but an aspect of ritual performance bound up with kingship.[18]

It is for this reason that Josiah and his temple staff are also portrayed as being so precise in their dealings with the cult place: each member of the Jerusalem temple's sacred community is credited with trusted and specialist authority for the tasks for which they have particular responsibility: the 'keepers of the threshold' (שֹׁמְרֵי הַסַּף) interface between the worshippers and the sanctuary by collecting donations of silver to the temple, while the high priest Hilkiah handles this sacred silver and allocates it to the various temple craftsmen so that they can purchase stone and timber (22:4–7, 9). The temple is thus a material space created and managed

---

14. See further *TDOT* 8, 532–44, especially 543; for further discussion of the term, see D. F. Murray, "MQWM and the Future of Israel," *VT* 40 (1990) 298–320.

15. See further O. Lipschits, "On Cash-Boxes and Finding or Not Finding Books: Jehoash's and Josiah's Decisions to Repair the Temple," in *Essays on Ancient Israel in Its Near Eastern Context: A Tribute to Nadav Na'aman* (ed. Y. Amit, E. Ben Zvi, I. Finkelstein, and O. Lipschits; Winona Lake, IN: Eisenbrauns, 2006), 239–54; N. Na'aman, "Notes on the Temple 'Restorations' of Jehoash and Josiah," *VT* 63 (2013) 640–51.

16. See further N. Wyatt, *Space and Time in the Religious Life of the Near East* (Biblical Seminar 85; Sheffield: Sheffield Academic Press, 2001).

17. Alongside Solomon, Jeroboam ben Nebat, Jehoash, Hezekiah, and Josiah, a number of other Israelite and Judahite monarchs are also presented as materially establishing, repairing, enriching, or altering temple cults in the Books of Kings, including Asa, Jehu, Ahab, Jehoshaphat, Jehoiada, Jehoahaz, Ahaz, and Manasseh.

18. See further E. Bloch-Smith, "Solomon's Temple: The Politics of Ritual Space," in *Sacred Time, Sacred Place: Archaeology and the Religion of Israel* (ed. B. M. Gittlen; Winona Lake, IN: Eisenbrauns, 2002), 83–94; N. Wyatt, "Royal Religion in Ancient Judah," in *Religious Diversity in Ancient Israel and Judah* (ed. F. Stavrakopoulou and J. Barton; London: T. & T. Clark, 2010), 61–81. On the rhetorical ramifications, see D. Launderville, *Piety and Politics: The Dynamics of Royal Authority in Homeric Greece, Biblical Israel, and Old Babylonian Mesopotamia* (Grand Rapids, MI: Eerdmans, 2003).

by the careful delineation and orchestration of participants, objects, and actions.[19] Significantly, however, it is Shaphan the scribe who is tasked with coordinating this ritual performance, so that even the high priest Hilkiah must report to him (22:3, 8–10).

The prominence of Shaphan, coupled with this concentrated focus on the materiality of the Jerusalem temple, necessarily elevates the ritual status of the discovered scroll as a sacred object, demanding careful handling. Although it is Hilkiah who finds and initially holds the scroll, he gives it to Shaphan, who reads it twice: first for himself and then aloud to the king (22:8, 20). That this act of reading is to be understood as a material, cultic performance is evident not only within the broader biblical context, in which the writing, reading, copying, exhibition, and enactment of the divine word of Yhwh is privileged above all else,[20] but in the ritual responses it sparks. The first is the king's rending of his garments (22:11)—an action a number of commentators frequently gloss over, assuming it is merely a standardized sign of petition;[21] the second is the king's ritual request for an oracle about the scroll, as indicated in the use of the technical term דרשׁ (22:13), and the third is the utterance of the oracle itself (22:15–20). In 2 Kgs 22, the scroll is thus clearly presented as a powerful cultic object for which the scribe and the king, rather than the high priest, have authoritative responsibility.[22] Within this context, the oracle Huldah delivers in response to the king's request may be devoid of political precision, but it is wholly bound up with the materiality of the state.

Indeed, Huldah's role is not to offer a political commentary but to endorse the status of the scroll as a cult object and as a material source of divine information—hence her pointed reference to "all the words of the scroll" in the first half of her oracle (22:16). This is entirely in keeping with the royal concern to maintain the fabric of the cosmos by means of temple-cult construction, repair, or restoration. As is well known, a number of ancient Near Eastern monarchs (including

---

19. This cultic precision is also attested in the narrative detailing the purging of the Jerusalem temple and Judah's other cult places (2 Kgs 23:4–14). On the dynamic interrelation of the material aspects of ritual (objects, bodies, actions, and space), see F. Stavrakopoulou, "Religion at Home: The Materiality of Practice," in *The Wiley-Blackwell Companion to Ancient Israel* (ed. S. Niditch; Chichester: Wiley & Sons, 2016), 347–65 and the works cited therein.

20. See further F. Stavrakopoulou, "Materialism, Materiality, and Biblical Cults of Writing," in *Biblical Interpretation and Method: Essays in Honour of John Barton* (ed. K. J. Dell and P. M. Joyce; Oxford: Oxford University Press, 2013), 223–42; cf. J. Schaper, "A Theology of Writing: The Oral and the Written, God as Scribe, and the Book of Deuteronomy," in *Anthropology and Biblical Studies: Avenues of Approach* (ed. L. J. Lawrence and M. I. Aguilar; Leiden: Deo, 2004), 97–119.

21. See further on pp. 288–88 below.

22. Note that in 2 Kgs 23:2–3, this ritual authority is subsequently transferred in the cult place solely to the king. On the portrayed role of "officials" of the state, see I. Eph'al-Jaruzelska, "Officialdom and Society in the Book of Kings: The Social Relevance of the State," in *The Books of Kings: Sources, Composition, Historiography and Reception* (ed. B. Halpern, A. Lemaire, and M. J. Adams; VTSup 129; Leiden: Brill, 2010), 467–500.

Sennacherib, Esarhaddon, and Nabonidus), are similarly credited with seeking oracular or other forms of divinatory verification for these activities,[23] particularly in circumstances in which a foundation inscription or sacred text is (supposedly) discovered, prompting materially transformative action in the temple or its city.[24] In 2 Kgs 22, the scroll found in the Jerusalem temple is similarly implied to be an ancient material manifestation of divine will concerning the cult.

Debate surrounds the extent to which this particular biblical tradition is to be taken primarily as a calculated literary strategy (as is similarly attested elsewhere), drawing upon the broader cultural realities of temple and cult modification in order to elevate the status of scroll-religion in Judahite or Yehudite religious practice.[25] However, it maps closely onto the torah ideologies of the Hebrew Bible, in which the cultic authority of scribalism, and the divine agency of material texts, is presented as eclipsing other forms of obedient religiosity—an ideology modeled by the state's immediate adoption and promotion of the scroll in the narratives in 2 Kgs 22–23.[26]

It might be assumed, however, that this state-sponsored scribal authority is undermined in the text by the figure of Huldah herself. While she is labeled without further qualification as a נביאה 'prophet',[27] a number of scholars find themselves preoccupied by her gender. And yet ritual specialists of all genders[28]—

---

23. There is no distinction to be drawn between prophetic, oracular, and divinatory rituals. All these activities form a part of a broad spectrum of religious techniques designed to discern or verify the will of the gods. In a number of Mesopotamian texts, oracular endorsement of alteration to temples is often accompanied by other forms of divination. Most of these forms are also attested in the Hebrew Bible, with the possible exception of extispicy (although note, for example, the imagery and language of Jer 31:33). Accordingly, "priestly" and "prophetic" functions are more difficult to distinguish than some biblical texts (and scholars) might suggest.

24. See further L. K. Handy, "The Role of Huldah in Josiah's Cult Reform," *ZAW* 106 (1994) 40–53; J. Ben Dov, "Writing as Oracle and as Law: New Contexts for the Book-Find of King Josiah," *JBL* 127 (2008) 223–39.

25. See further T. Römer, "Transformations in Deuteronomistic and Biblical Historiography: On 'Book-Finding' and Other Literary Strategies," *ZAW* 109 (1997) 1–11; K. Stott, "Finding the Lost Book of the Law: Re-reading the Story of the 'Book of the Law' (Deuteronomy–2 Kings) in Light of Classical Literature," *JSOT* 30 (2005) 145–69; cf. A. J. Droge, "'The Lying Pen of the Scribes:' Of Holy Books and Pious Fraudes," *Method and Theory in the Study of Religion* 15 (2003) 117–47; D. Henige, "Found But Not Lost: A Skeptical Note on the Document Discovered in the Temple Under Josiah," *JHS* 7 (2007) article 1, 2–17 (cited 7 August 2015; online: http://www .jhsonline.org/Articles/article_62.pdf); Römer, "From Prophet to Scribe," 86–96.

26. Cf. 2 Kgs 23:1–4, 21, 24. See further P. R. Davies, *Scribes and Schools: The Canonization of the Hebrew Scriptures* (Louisville: Westminster John Knox, 1998); K. van der Toorn, *Scribal Culture and the Making of the Hebrew Bible* (Cambridge: Harvard University Press, 2007); and the works cited in n. 20 (p. 283 above).

27. This is one among a number of terms employed of diviners in the Hebrew Bible; see further J. Stökl, *Prophecy in the Ancient Near East: A Philological and Sociological Comparison* (CHANE 56; Leiden: Brill, 2012), 155–202.

28. Notions of "gender" are modern social constructs—and hence inherently problematic for those attempting to use gender as a tool with which to interrogate ancient literature, ico-

including prophets—are attested throughout ancient Near Eastern religious liter-ature; thus, Huldah's gender is not in itself an anomaly.[29] It is, however, relatively unusual within the portrayal of prophecy in the Hebrew Bible,[30] leading some commentators to problematize it and to suppose her role in the story of Josiah's reform is either a historical peculiarity,[31] a reflection of an anxious concern to ensure discretion,[32] or a literary strategy of surprise, intended to shock the reader into recognizing the inevitable nature of the catastrophe that "even a woman" could see coming.[33] But as Lowell Handy observes, Huldah's gender is of far more interest to subsequent readers and receivers of the tradition than it appears to have been to the biblical writers.[34]

Rather, it is Huldah's location in the Mishneh district of Jerusalem (2 Kgs 22:14) that potentially destabilizes her endorsement of state-sponsored scribal religion. Many commentators assume her designation as נביאה, her marriage to the "keeper of the garments," and her technical use of the language of the temple cult are indicative of her position as an "official" cult prophet of the Jerusalem temple.[35] Yet, for some, this raises questions as to why she prophesies beyond the

---

nography, and artifacts. There has long been a tendency (whether intentional or not) among Western biblical scholars to project the conventionally binary model of gender pervading their own Euro-American cultures onto the ancient societies from which the biblical texts emerged. However, it would appear that "gender" categories were much more fluid in ancient Near Eastern societies than has been assumed. See further the entries by I. Zsolnay ("Gender and Sexuality: Ancient Near East," 273–87) and D. Guest ("Gender Transgression: Hebrew Bible," 287–93) in *The Oxford Encyclopedia of the Bible and Gender Studies* (ed. J. M. O'Brien; Oxford: Oxford University Press, 2014).

29. See further, the collection of essays in J. Stökl and C. L. Carvalho (eds.), *Gender and Prophecy in the Hebrew Bible, the Eastern Mediterranean, and the Ancient Near East* (Atlanta: SBL, 2013).

30. Alongside Huldah, Miriam (Exod 15:20), Deborah (Judg 4:4), Noadiah (Neh 6:14), and the unnamed woman of Isa 8:3 are designated "prophet." Many other female characters, how-ever, are portrayed as diviners or religious specialists, including the women at En-Dor (1 Sam 28:3–25), Tekoa (2 Sam 14:1–20), and Abel (2 Sam 20:16–22); see further E. J. Hamori, *Women's Divination in Biblical Literature: Prophecy, Necromancy, and Other Arts of Knowledge* (New Ha-ven: Yale University Press, 2015).

31. Some follow ancient commentators in claiming that Jeremiah was unavailable for con-sultation when Josiah needed him; note, however, M. D. Terblanche, "No Need for a Prophet Like Jeremiah: The Absence of the Prophet Jeremiah in Kings," in *Past, Present, Future: The Deuteronomistic History and the Prophets* (ed. J. C. de Moor and H. F. van Rooy; OTS 44; Leiden: Brill, 2000), 306–14.

32. E.g., J. Gray, *I & II Kings: A Commentary* (3rd ed.; OTL; London: SCM, 1977), 726.

33. Weems, "Huldah, the Prophet," 323; cf. McKinlay, "Gazing at Huldah," 3.

34. Handy, "Reading Huldah," 7.

35. J. Priest, "Huldah's Oracle," *VT* 30 (1980) 366–68; M. Cogan and H. Tadmor, *II Kings: A New Translation with Introduction and Commentary* (AB 11; New York: Doubleday, 1988), 283 n. 14; S. Ackerman, "Why is Miriam also among the Prophets? (And is Zipporah among the Priests?)," *JBL* 121 (2002) 49; Ben Dov, "Writing as Oracle and as Law," 235; Hamori, "The Prophet and the Necromancer," 837.

biblical boundaries of the temple's sacred landscape, in the absence of the king. The Mishneh (מִשְׁנֶה), or "Second (Quarter)" of the city (2 Kgs 22:14; 2 Chr 34:22; Zeph 1:10–11), is widely identified as an area of urban (and primarily residential) expansion onto Jerusalem's western hill, established in the Iron IIC.[36] It is here that Huldah is located. But spatially and ideologically, it renders her distanced from the temple. To a certain extent, this might complement the content of her oracle, in which the cult itself is damned by YHWH (22:15–17). And yet it also marginalizes Huldah by setting her apart both from the temple and the elite locus of the state.[37]

Although the biblical narrator does not explicitly claim that the scroll is presented to Huldah (as it was Josiah) by those sent to consult her (2 Kgs 22:14), it nonetheless triggers her prophecy, suggesting its function as a mantic cult object (cf. Ezek 2:9–3:4; Lam 2:9) and attesting to the ritual efficacy of scribal Yahwism beyond the bounds of the Jerusalem temple, as attested elsewhere in the biblical literature (for example, Deut 6:6–9; 11:18–21; Neh 8:1–8). But Huldah's oracle also offers an interpretive commentary on the words of the scroll (as is made explicit in 2 Kgs 22:16), rendering her in some ways paradigmatic of the interpretive function of the *Nebi'im* collection in relation to *Torah* within canonical Judaism,[38] and encouraging rabbinic tradition to locate her not in the Mishneh, but in a house of *mishnah* ('instruction').[39] While initially the biblical writer might thus appear to be at pains to constrict Huldah's role, the mechanics and literary textures of the narrative itself suggest she is thoroughly caught up in the powerful materiality of a state-sponsored religious scribalism.

Huldah and the King's Body in 2 Kings 22

If the first half of Huldah's oracle indexes issues concerning the interrelation of divination, scribalism, and the state, the second focuses on the king himself. Following her warning of the approaching cultic calamity, Huldah declares:

> But as to the king of Judah, who sends you to inquire of YHWH, thus you shall say to him: "Thus says YHWH, the God of Israel: Concerning the words which you have heard, because your heart was softened and you humbled yourself before YHWH when you heard what I said against this place and against its inhabitants, that it will become a desolation and a curse, and you tore your garments and wept before me, I have indeed heard"—oracle of YHWH. "Therefore, behold, I will gather you to your ancestors, and you shall be gathered to your grave in peace;

---

36. See the classic study by M. Broshi, "The Expansion of Jerusalem in the Reigns of Hezekiah and Manasseh," *IEJ* 24 (1974) 21–6.

37. Weems, "Huldah, the Prophet," 323. McKinlay ("Gazing at Huldah," 7) assumes that, as a woman, Huldah would defile the temple.

38. Römer, "From Prophet to Scribe," 94.

39. See further M. A. Sweeney, *I & II Kings: A Commentary* (OTL; Louisville: Westminster John Knox, 2007), 438 n. c–c.

your eyes shall not see all the evil which that I am bringing on this place." (2 Kgs 22:18–20b)

This oracle has prompted more dispute among scholars than perhaps any other in the Hebrew Bible, for many assume that the claim that Josiah will go to his grave "in peace" (בשלום) is directly contradicted by the fleeting story of Josiah's execution at the hands of Pharaoh Neco in 23:29–30 (cf. 2 Chr 35:20–24).[40] Not only might this be thought to weaken the coherence of the prophecy-fulfillment schema believed by many to structure the Books of Kings, but it might also be perceived to undermine Huldah's prophetic validation of the scroll in the first half of her oracle. For many scholars, the second part of Huldah's prophecy is rendered "false,"[41] for her declaration concerning Josiah is simply "wrong."[42] However, in the discursive world of the narrative, Huldah's prophetic voice speaks to a concern for the material manifestations of the state, and in this sense, the divine declaration about Josiah's death is wholly congruent with its context.

Throughout the Books of Kings, the perpetuation of Judahite kingship is emphasized by the seemingly formulaic dynastic notices framing the stories of each monarch's reign: the accession notice states the kin relationship of the new ruler to the previous king and pointedly includes his mother's name and ancestry, while the death notice briskly reports the king's demise and/or burial. These are not merely narrative-structuring devices; rather, they reflect a wider cultural emphasis and prioritization of the ongoing social interrelation of ancestors and descendants. Within the royal ancestral cult of Judah (as elsewhere among high-status communities in the ancient Near East), the continued post-mortem existence of kings—and by correlation, the ideological stability of the dynasty and its patrimony—was dependent upon the material well-being of their royal remains, both before and after burial, in a world in which corpse abuse and tomb desecration were powerful tools of political attack.[43]

---

40. It is often assumed that the alternative account of Josiah's death is deliberately crafted in response to the version in Kings so as to smooth the theological tension between Huldah's oracle and Josiah's assassination. See further Z. Talshir, "The Three Deaths of Josiah and the Strata of Biblical Historiography," *VT* 46 (1996) 213–36; S. Delamater, "The Death of Josiah in Scripture and Tradition: Wrestling with the Problem of Evil?" *VT* 54 (2004) 29–60.

41. Cogan and Tadmor, *II Kings*, 295; Scheuer, "Huldah: A Cunning Career Woman?" 106; cf. D. N. Freedman and R. Frey, "False Prophecy is True," in *Inspired Speech: Prophecy in the Ancient Near East in Honour of Herbert B. Huffmon* (ed. J. Kaltner and L. Stulman; London: T. & T. Clark, 2004), 82–7.

42. Hamori, "The Prophet and the Necromancer," 837.

43. See further, F. Stavrakopoulou, *Land of Our Fathers: The Roles of Ancestor Veneration in Biblical Land Claims* (LHBOTS 473; London: T. & T. Clark, 2010), esp. 103–20; M. J. Suriano, *The Politics of Dead Kings: Dynastic Ancestors in the Book of Kings and Ancient Israel* (FAT 2/48; Tübingen: Mohr Siebeck, 2010), esp. 89–90. On corpse abuse, see S. M. Olyan, "Some Neglected Aspects of Israelite Interment Ideology," *JBL* 124 (2005) 601–16; F. Stavrakopoulou, "Gog's Grave and the Use and Abuse of Corpses in Ezekiel 39:11–20," *JBL* 129 (2010) 67–84.

Huldah's claim in 22:20 both that Yhwh will 'gather' (אָסַף) Josiah to his ancestors and that the king will be "gathered" to his grave 'in peace' (בְשָׁלוֹם) reflects this cultural concern for the materiality of the royal dead and the perpetuation of the dynasty: in view is the ritual deposition of the king's corpse and the secondary burial of his bones within the tomb, alongside those of his ancestors.[44] The king's post-mortem body is cast as a high-status ritual object that Yhwh himself will handle (note the participle in MT 22:20a), much as in other biblical texts the deity buries Moses' corpse (MT Deut. 34:5–6) and disinters the bones of his dead exiles to return them to the homeland (Ezek 37:11–14).[45]

It is for this reason that the biblical narrator is careful to assert that Josiah's corpse was brought back from Megiddo to Jerusalem for burial in its rightful place (2 Kgs 23:30; cf. 9:27–28; 14:19–20). Indeed, that Josiah himself is portrayed as recognizing the religious, material, and territorial value of an undisturbed burial is evident in the story of his actions at Bethel: after disinterring and burning the bones of the cult center's ancestral dead, he insists that the tomb of the Judahite Man of God is left undisturbed (23:16–18).[46] Thus, far from implying a natural or nonviolent death, as some have argued,[47] the language employed in 2 Kgs 22:20 of Josiah's own burial is indicative instead of the material well-being of the corpse of the king.[48] In being gathered to his grave in corporeal 'peace', Yhwh gifts Josiah שָׁלוֹם in the "fullest sense."[49]

Huldah's oracle about Josiah's death is thus shaped by the cultural and social contours of a narrative landscape of state materiality, in which the king's body (both pre- and post-mortem) is a significant feature. This is an aspect of prophecy attested elsewhere in the biblical literature, including 2 Kgs 1:2–6, in which Ahaziah sends a delegation to request a healing oracle from the deity Baal-Zebub, rather than Yhwh (much to Elijah's disapproval), and 20:1–11 (cf. Isa 38), in which Isaiah heals Hezekiah following a divine curse. These examples comple-

---

44. Note that some scholars assume that the language of this verse refers only to "proper" primary burial, rather than also an ongoing concern for the material condition of the remains; see, for example, D. Edelman, "Huldah the Prophet—of Yahweh or Asherah?" in *A Feminist Companion to Samuel and Kings* (ed. A. Brenner; Sheffield: Sheffield Academic, 1994), 240–41; P. S. F. van Keulen, "The Meaning of the Phrase *wn'spt 'l-qbrtyk bšlwm* in 2 Kings XXII 20," *VT* 46 (1996) 256–60; M. Pietsch, "Prophetess of Doom: Hermeneutical Reflections on the Huldah Oracle (2 Kings 22)," in *Soundings in Kings: Perspectives and Methods in Contemporary Scholarship* (ed. M. Leuchter and K.-P. Adam; Minneapolis: Fortress, 2010), 71–80.

45. Stavrakopoulou, *Land of Our Fathers*, 56–57, 126–27.

46. Ibid., 81–91.

47. E.g., Halpern, "Why Manasseh is Blamed," 500–503, followed by Hamori, *Women's Divination*, 154.

48. A number of other biblical characters, including Saul and his sons (2 Sam 21:13) and Ahaziah (2 Kgs 9:27–28) are similarly "gathered" or buried in their own graves, despite suffering a violent death.

49. J. Blenkinsopp, "Remembering Josiah," in *Remembering Biblical Figures in the Late Persian and Early Hellenistic Periods* (ed. D. V. Edelman and E. Ben Zvi; Oxford: Oxford University Press, 2013), 241.

ment evidence elsewhere to suggest that diviners and temple-based ritual specialists traditionally played a role in dealing with the body (cf., 1 Kgs 17:17–24; 2 Kgs 4:18–37; 5:8–14; 8:7–10).[50]

In the story of Hezekiah's healing in the Books of Kings, Hezekiah performs בכה 'ritual weeping' (20:3), prompting Yhwh's material reversal of the curse, as declared in an oracle (20:4–7). Weeping of this nature is not simply an emotional petition to the deity but one among a series of ritual actions associated with mortuary-cult practices in which performers use their bodies to mimic or enact the transformation and fragmentation of the body.[51] While in some contexts this likens or manifests a mourner's identification with a buried and decomposing corpse, it also appears to function as an apotropaic rite, in which the danger of harm to the body (whether living or a corpse) is diminished or averted by its controlled representation. As such, Josiah's fear of bodily harm may well be signaled in his actions following the discovery of the scroll in the Jerusalem temple: he tears his garments and weeps (22:11, 19), a ritual performance of which Yhwh approves and which prompts the oracular promise that Yhwh will "gather" the king to his grave "in peace" (22:19–20). By ritually enacting the mortuary fragmentation of his body, Josiah thus ensures the ongoing material integrity of his body—both in life and in death.

It is perhaps no coincidence that, as the prophet who delivers this oracle of bodily salvation to the king, Huldah is associated by proximity with what appears to be the ritual garments of the state cult. Her husband is designated שמר הבגדים 'the keeper of the garments' (22:14), a role widely understood to refer to the cultic curation of temple vestments used in religious performance and commonly likened to the official who is 'over the wardrobe' (על המלתחה) at Baal's temple in Samaria (10:22).[52] Ritual clothing and other religious textiles frequently feature in the Hebrew Bible. While some of these may have dressed the sanctuaries and their cult statues,[53] others were worn and used as magical devices by ritual performers, as is similarly attested in other ancient Near Eastern texts and iconography.[54] Alongside other functions, these garments appear to have functioned

---

50. Hector Avalos has written extensively on these themes in *Illness and Health Care in the Ancient Near East: The Role of the Temple in Greece, Mesopotamia, and Israel* (HSM 54; Atlanta: Scholars Press, 1995); and idem, *Health Care and the Rise of Christianity* (Peabody, MA: Hendrickson, 1999).

51. Other ritual actions within this group include the rending of garments, body-modification (shaving and cutting), throwing dirt or ashes upon oneself or at others, sitting on the ground, and fasting. See further S. M. Olyan, *Biblical Mourning: Ritual and Social Dimensions* (Oxford: Oxford University Press, 2004).

52. Although a *hapax legomenon*, commentators are broadly agreed the context suggests this is a suitable rendering of the term; see (for example) T. R. Hobbs, *2 Kings* (WBC 13; Waco, TX: Word, 1985), 130; Cogan and Tadmor, *II Kings*, 115.

53. For example, Exod 26:1–14, 31, 36; 2 Kgs 23:7; Jer 10:9; Ezek 16:18; cf. Isa 6:1.

54. E.g., 1 Sam 15:27; 28:3–25; 2 Sam 6:14; 1 Kgs 11:29–30; 22:10; 1 Chr 15:27; Ezra 3:10; Neh 7:70; Ezek 9:2–4; 13:17–18; 42:14–19; Zeph 1:8. See further M.-L. Nosch, H. Koefoed and

apotropaically, to guard against the dangerous gaze of the deity, thereby protecting the wearer from harm.[55] But they also functioned as a corporeal, material extension of the body itself—much like other materials (such as amulets, make-up, and hair styles) employed to manifest and modify the body in ritual contexts.[56]

Set against this backdrop, Josiah's rending of his garments is to be taken as an act of extreme ritual power and explains why it affects YHWH with such force that he promises to protect the king from any bodily and sensory distress bound up with the coming destruction: "you will be gathered to your grave in peace and your eyes shall not see all the evil I am bringing on this place" (22:20). The authority of Huldah's oracle is thus strengthened by the narrator's explicit reference to her close relationship with the "keeper of the garments."[57] In this way, it is not only Josiah who might be persuaded of the stability and surety of her oracle but the reader, too—in spite of the the king's execution at Megiddo.

Conclusions:
Reinstating Huldah

It might be assumed that Huldah's biblical status as a prophet is necessarily compromised or marginalized by her presentation as a woman whose activity is located only at a distance from the Jerusalem temple. Yet this assumption is challenged by a close reading of the narrative dynamics and broader contexts of the story in 2 Kgs 22. Although she is not portrayed as a prophet with a distinctively political voice—unlike, for example, Elisha or Isaiah—her interaction with the state is best traced along the contours of a wider cultural landscape in which the materiality of religion, in all its varied forms, textures the very fabric of the ancient societies from which the biblical texts emerged.

Accordingly, Huldah is characterized as a prophet bound up with the specifics of the stuff of state—the tangible material forms, whether places, objects, or bodies, dominating the biblical narrator's construction of the past. Thus, the Jerusalem temple, the discovered scroll, and the body of the king himself are foregrounded

---

E. Andersson Strand (eds.), *Textile Production and Consumption in the Ancient Near East: Archaeology, Epigraphy, Iconography* (Oxford: Oxbow, 2013).

55. See further J. Schipper and J. Stackert, "Blemishes, Camouflage, and Sanctuary Service: The Priestly Deity and His Attendants," *HBAI* 2 (2013) 458–78. In 2 Kgs 10:18–26, the biblical writer plays on the power of ritual garments: in the story of Jehu's destruction of the Baal temple in Samaria, the temple's "keeper of the wardrobe" is commanded to remove the worshipers' vestments from the sanctuary, enabling Jehu (acting on behalf of YHWH) to kill them inside the cult place.

56. F. Stavrakopoulou, "Making Bodies: On Body Modification and Religious Materiality in the Hebrew Bible," *HBAI* 2 (2013) 532–53.

57. Perhaps a similar pairing of ritual experts is evident in the partnership of Isaiah and the unnamed female prophet of Isa 8:1–4, who appear to collaborate in the verification of a written oracle by birthing a son together. On this text, see further E. J. Hamori, "Heavenly Bodies: Pregnancy and Birth Omens in Israel," *HBAI* 4 (2013) 479–99.

in the text as the tangible subjects of her oracular engagement. Each of these materialities is colored with the biblical narrative's explicitly ideological hue and is employed within the story as a means of indexing Yhwh's relationship with the state and (more precisely) Judah's ruling dynasty. In some ways, Huldah's spatial distance from the temple successfully removes her from a cult place that is not only in need of architectural repair and—by extension—mytho-ritual renewal (22:3–7, 9) but destined for divine destruction (22:16–17), so that she appears to share more in common with those prophetic groups and figures elsewhere in Kings further removed from, or hostile to, the state. In other ways, however, she is firmly embedded within the world of statehood, a conceptual location in which her expertise and authority as a diviner is inextricably linked to the material objects, ritual actions, and very bodiliness of the Jerusalem temple cult itself.

To this end, her characterization underscores the value not of the theological dynamics often thought to dominate the Books of Kings or an assumed Deuteronomistic History but of the religious materialities with which the narrator of 2 Kgs 22–23 is so concerned. Hence, her prophecy prompts the cultic installation and exhibition of the newly discovered scroll as the new material presence in the temple (23:1–3), which displaces the cult statues, ritual objects, priests, and functionaries of other deities (23:4–14) and confirms the continued and palpable stability and material integrity of both the royal ancestral grave and its inhabitants—including Josiah (22:20; 23:30).

Within the biblical portrayal of the past—and subsequently, within scholarship—Huldah's role is heavily overshadowed by the idealization of the written word of Yhwh and the assumed legacy of King Josiah. But despite her momentary appearance in the texts, the figure of Huldah serves as a reminder of the place of the material in the imagined world of the divine.

Bibliography

Ackerman, S. "Why is Miriam also among the Prophets? (And is Zipporah among the Priests?)." *JBL* 121 (2002) 47–80.

Auld, A. G. *Kings Without Privilege: David and Moses in the Story of the Bible's Kings.* Edinburgh: T. & T. Clark, 1994.

Avalos, H. *Illness and Health Care in the Ancient Near East: The Role of the Temple in Greece, Mesopotamia, and Israel.* HSM 54. Atlanta Scholars, 1995.

_____. *Health Care and the Rise of Christianity* (Peabody: Hendrickson, 1999).

Avioz, M. "The Book of Kings in Recent Research (Part I)." *CBR* 4 (2005) 11–44.

_____. "The Book of Kings in Recent Research (Part II)." *CBR* 5 (2006) 11–57.

Ben Dov, J. "Writing as Oracle and as Law: New Contexts for the Book-Find of King Josiah." *JBL* 127 (2008) 223–39.

Ben Zvi, E. "Imagining Josiah's Book and the Implications of Imagining It in Early Persian Yehud." Pp. 193–212 in *Berührungspunkte: Studien zur Sozial- und Religionsgeschichte Israels und seiner Umwelt: Festschrift für Rainer Albertz zu seinem 65.* Edited by I. Kottsieper, R. Schmitt and J. Wöhrle. AOAT 350. Münster: Ugarit-Verlag, 2008.

_____. "The Yehudite Collection of Prophetic Books and Imperial Contexts: Some Observations." Pp. 145–69 in *Divination, Politics and Ancient Near Eastern Empires*. Edited by A. Lenzi and J. Stökl. Atlanta: SBL, 2014.

Bellis, A. O. *Helpmates, Harlots, and Heroes: Women's Stories in the Hebrew Bible*. 2nd ed. Louisville: Westminster John Knox, 2007.

Berry, G. R. "The Code Found in the Temple." *JBL* 39 (1920) 44–51.

Bledstein, A. J. "Is Judges a Woman's Satire of Men Who Play God?" Pp. 34–54 in *A Feminist Companion to Judges*. Edited by A. Brenner. Sheffield: JSOT Press, 1993.

Blenkinsopp, J. "Remembering Josiah." Pp. 236–56 in *Remembering Biblical Figures in the Late Persian and Early Hellenistic Periods*. Edited by D. V. Edelman and E. Ben Zvi. Oxford: Oxford University Press, 2013.

Bloch-Smith, E. "Solomon's Temple: The Politics of Ritual Space." Pp. 83–94 in *Sacred Time, Sacred Place: Archaeology and the Religion of Israel*. Edited by B. M. Gittlen. Winona Lake, IN: Eisenbrauns, 2002.

Brenner, A. *I Am . . . Biblical Women Tell Their Own Stories*. Minneapolis: Augsburg Fortress, 2005.

Bronner, L. L. *Stories of Biblical Mothers: Maternal Power in the Hebrew Bible*. Lanham, MD: University Press of America, 2004.

Broshi, M. "The Expansion of Jerusalem in the Reigns of Hezekiah and Manasseh." *IEJ* 24 (1974) 21–26.

Camp, C. V. "Female Voice, Written Word: Women and Authority in Hebrew Scripture." Pp. 97–113 in *Embodied Love: Sensuality and Relationship as Feminist Values*. Edited by P. M. Cooey, S. A. Farmer, and M. E. Ross. San Francisco: Harper & Row, 1987.

Christensen, D. L. "Huldah and the Men of Anathoth: Women in Leadership in the Deuteronomistic History." Pp. 399–404 in *Society of Biblical Literature 1984 Seminar Papers*. Edited by K. H. Richards. Chico, CA: Scholars Press, 1984.

Cogan, M., and H. Tadmor. *II Kings: A New Translation with Introduction and Commentary*. AB 11. New York: Doubleday, 1988.

Cohn, R. L. "Characterization in Kings." Pp. 89–105 in *The Books of Kings: Sources, Composition, Historiography and Reception*. Edited by B. Halpern, A. Lemaire, and M. J. Adams. VTSup 129. Leiden: Brill, 2010.

Davies, P. R. *Scribes and Schools: The Canonization of the Hebrew Scriptures*. Louisville: Westminster John Knox, 1998.

_____. "Josiah and the Law Book." Pp. 65–77 in *Good Kings and Bad Kings: The Kingdom of Judah in the Seventh Century BCE*. Edited by L. L. Grabbe. LHBOTS 393. London: T. & T. Clark, 2005.

Delamater, S. "The Death of Josiah in Scripture and Tradition: Wrestling with the Problem of Evil?" *VT* 54 (2004) 29–60.

Droge, A. J. "'The Lying Pen of the Scribes:' Of Holy Books and Pious Fraudes." *Method and Theory in the Study of Religion* 15 (2003) 117–47.

Edelman, D. V. "The Meaning of *qiṭṭēr*." *VT* 35 (1985) 395–404.

_____. "Huldah the Prophet—of Yahweh or Asherah?" Pp. 231–50 in *A Feminist Companion to Samuel and Kings*. Edited by A. Brenner. Sheffield: Sheffield Academic, 1994.

Eph'al-Jaruzelska, I. "Officialdom and Society in the Book of Kings: The Social relevance of the State." Pp. 467–500 in *The Books of Kings: Sources, Composition, Historiography and Reception*. Edited by B. Halpern, A. Lemaire, and M. J. Adams. VTSup 129. Leiden: Brill, 2010.

Freedman, D. N., and R. Frey. "False Prophecy is True." Pp. 82–87 in *Inspired Speech: Prophecy in the Ancient Near East in Honour of Herbert B. Huffmon*. Edited by J. Kaltner and L. Stulman. London: T. & T. Clark, 2004.

Fried, L. S. "The High Places (*Bâmôt*) and the Reforms of Hezekiah and Josiah: An Archaeological Interpretation." *JAOS* 122 (2002) 437–65.

Glatt-Gilad, D. A. "The Role of Huldah's Prophecy in the Chronicler's Portrayal of Josiah's Reform." *Biblica* 77 (1996) 16–31.

Gray, J. *I & II Kings: A Commentary*. 3rd ed. OTL. London: SCM, 1977.

Guest, D. "Gender Transgression: Hebrew Bible." Pp. 287–93 in *The Oxford Encyclopedia of the Bible and Gender Studies*. Edited by J. M. O'Brien. Oxford: Oxford University Press, 2014.

Halpern, B. "Why Manasseh is Blamed for the Babylonian Exile: The Evolution of a Biblical Tradition." *VT* 48 (1998) 473–514.

Hamori, E. J. "Heavenly Bodies: Pregnancy and Birth Omens in Israel." *HBAI* 4 (2013) 479–99.

————. "The Prophet and the Necromancer: Women's Divination in Kings." *JBL* 132 (2013) 827–43.

————. *Women's Divination in Biblical Literature: Prophecy, Necromancy, and Other Arts of Knowledge*. New Haven: Yale University Press, 2015.

Handy, L. K. "The Role of Huldah in Josiah's Cult Reform." *ZAW* 106 (1994) 40–53.

————. "Reading Huldah as Being a Woman." *Biblical Research* 55 (2010) 5–44.

Henige, D. "Found But Not Lost: A Skeptical Note on the Document Discovered in the Temple Under Josiah." *JHS* 7 (2007) article 1, 2–27. Cited 7 August 2015. Online: http://www.jhsonline.org/Articles/article_62.pdf.

Hobbs, T. R. *2 Kings*. WBC 13. Waco, TX: Word, 1985.

Jonker, L. C. *Reflections of King Josiah in Chronicles: Late Stages of the Josiah Reception in 2 Chr 34 f*. Gütersloh: Gütersloher Verlaghaus, 2003.

————. "Huldah's Oracle: The Origin of the Chronicler's Typical Style?" *Verbum et Ecclesia* 33.1 (2012) article 7. Cited 13 June 2015. Online http://www.ve.org.za/index.php/VE/article/viewFile/714/1042.

Kent, D. G. "2 Chronicles." Pp. 235–46 in *The IVP Women's Commentary*. Edited by C. C. Kroeger and M. J. Evans. Downers Grove, IL: InterVarsity, 2002.

Keulen, P. S. F. van. "The Meaning of the Phrase *wn'spt 'l-qbrtyk bšlwm* in 2 Kings XXII 20." *VT* 46 (1996) 256–60.

Knoppers, G. N. "Theories of the Redaction(s) of Kings." Pp. 69–88 in *The Books of Kings: Sources, Composition, Historiography and Reception*. Edited by B. Halpern, A. Lemaire, and M. J. Adams. VTSup 129. Leiden: Brill, 2010.

Launderville, D. *Piety and Politics: The Dynamics of Royal Authority in Homeric Greece, Biblical Israel, and Old Babylonian Mesopotamia*. Grand Rapids, MI: Eerdmans, 2003.

Lemche, N. P. "Did a Reform Like Josiah's Happen?" Pp. 11–19 in *The Historian and the Bible: Essays in Honour of Lester L. Grabbe.* Edited by P. R. Davies and D. V. Edelman. New York: T. & T. Clark, 2010.

Leuchter, M. *Josiah's Reform and Jeremiah's Scroll: Historical Calamity and Prophetic Response.* Sheffield: Sheffield Phoenix Press, 2006.

Linville, J. R. *Israel in the Book of Kings: The Past as a Project of Social Identity.* JSOTSup 272. Sheffield: Sheffield Academic, 1998.

Lipschits, O. "On Cash-Boxes and Finding or Not Finding Books: Jehoash's and Josiah's Decisions to Repair the Temple." Pp. 239–54 in *Essays on Ancient Israel in Its Near Eastern Context: A Tribute to Nadav Na'aman.* Edited by Y. Amit et al. Winona Lake, IN: Eisenbrauns, 2006.

McKinlay, J. E. "Gazing at Huldah." *Bible & Critical Theory* 1/3 (2005) 1–11. Cited 5 May 2015. Online: http://novaojs.newcastle.edu.au/ojsbct/index.php/bct/article/view/40/26.

———. "Filling the Gaps and Putting Huldah to Use." Pp. 10–27 in *The One Who Reads May Run: Essays in Honour of Edgar W. Conrad.* Edited by R. Boer, M. Carden, and J. Kelso. London: T. & T. Clark, 2012.

Miller, D. "Why Some Things Matter." Pp. 3–21 in *Material Cultures: Why Some Things Matter.* Edited by D. Miller. London: UCL Press, 1998.

Monroe, L. A. S. *Josiah's Reform and the Dynamics of Defilement: Israelite Rites of Violence and the Making of a Biblical Text.* Oxford: Oxford University Press, 2011.

Morgan, D., ed. *Religion and Material Culture: The Matter of Belief.* Abingdon, U.K.: Routledge, 2010.

Murray, D. F. "MQWM and the Future of Israel." *VT* 40 (1990) 298–320.

Na'aman, N. "The 'Discovered Book' and the Legitimation of Josiah's Reform." *JBL* 130 (2011) 47–62.

———. "Notes on the Temple 'Restorations' of Jehoash and Josiah." *VT* 63 (2013) 640–51.

Niehr, H. "Die Reform des Joschija: methodische, historische und religionsgeschichtliche Aspekte." Pp. 33–55 in *Jeremia und die 'deuteronomistiche Bewegung.'* Edited by W. Groß. BBB 98. Weinheim: Beltz Athenäum, 1995.

Nissinen, M. "Prophecy in Joshua-Kings: Ancient Near Eastern Perspectives." Pp. 103–28 in *Israelite Prophecy and the Deuteronomistic History: Portrait, Reality and the Formation of a History.* Edited by M. R. Jacobs and R. F Person. Atlanta: SBL, 2013.

Nosch, M.-L., H. Koefoed, and E. A. Strand, eds. *Textile Production and Consumption in the Ancient Near East: Archaeology, Epigraphy, Iconography.* Oxford: Oxbow, 2013.

Olyan, S. M. *Biblical Mourning: Ritual and Social Dimensions.* Oxford: Oxford University Press, 2004.

———. "Some Neglected Aspects of Israelite Interment Ideology." *JBL* 124 (2005) 601–16.

Pakkala, J., "Why the Cult Reforms in Judah Probably Did Not Happen." Pp. 201–35 in *One God — One Cult — One Nation: Archaeological and Biblical Perspectives.* Edited by R. G. Kratz and H. Spieckermann. Berlin: de Gruyter, 2010.

Person, R. F., *The Deuteronomic School: History, Social Setting, and Literature.* Atlanta: Society of Biblical Literature, 2002.

Pietsch, M., "Prophetess of Doom: Hermeneutical Reflections on the Huldah Oracle (2 Kings 22)." Pp. 71–80 in *Soundings in Kings: Perspectives and Methods in Contem-*

porary Scholarship. Edited by M. Leuchter and K.-P. Adam. Minneapolis: Fortress, 2010.

Priest, J. "Huldah's Oracle." *VT* 30 (1980) 366–68.

Römer, T. "Transformations in Deuteronomistic and Biblical Historiography: On 'Book-Finding' and Other Literary Strategies." *ZAW* 109 (1997) 1–11.

_____. "From Prophet to Scribe: Jeremiah, Huldah and the Invention of the Book." Pp. 86–96 in *Writing the Bible: Scribes, Scribalism and Script*. Edited by P. R. Davies and T. Römer. London: Acumen, 2013.

Schaper, J. "A Theology of Writing: The Oral and the Written, God as Scribe, and the Book of Deuteronomy." Pp. 97–119 in *Anthropology and Biblical Studies: Avenues of Approach*. Edited by L. J. Lawrence and M. I. Aguilar. Leiden: Deo, 2004.

Scheuer, B. "Huldah: A Cunning Career Woman?" Pp. 104–23 in *Prophecy and Prophets in Stories: Papers Read at the Fifth Meeting of the Edinburgh Prophecy Network. Utrecht, October 2013*. Edited by B. Becking and H. Barstad. Leiden: Brill, 2015.

Schipper, J., and J. Stackert. "Blemishes, Camouflage, and Sanctuary Service: The Priestly Deity and His Attendants." *HBAI* 2 (2013) 458–78.

Stavrakopoulou, F. *Land of Our Fathers: The Roles of Ancestor Veneration in Biblical Land Claims*. LHBOTS 473. London: T. & T. Clark, 2010.

_____. "Gog's Grave and the Use and Abuse of Corpses in Ezekiel 39:11–20." *JBL* 129 (2010) 67–84.

_____. "Making Bodies: On Body Modification and Religious Materiality in the Hebrew Bible." *HBAI* 2 (2013) 532–53.

_____. "Materialism, Materiality, and Biblical Cults of Writing." Pp. 223–42 in *Biblical Interpretation and Method: Essays in Honour of John Barton*. Edited by K. J. Dell and P. M. Joyce. Oxford: Oxford University Press, 2013.

_____. "Religion at Home: The Materiality of Practice." Pp. 347–65 in *The Wiley-Blackwell Companion to Ancient Israel*. Edited by S. Niditch. Chichester: Wiley & Sons, 2016).

Stökl, J. *Prophecy in the Ancient Near East: A Philological and Sociological Comparison* CHANE 56. Leiden: Brill, 2012.

_____, and C. L. Carvalho (eds.). *Gender and Prophecy in the Hebrew Bible, the Eastern Mediterranean, and the Ancient Near East*. Atlanta: Society of Biblical Literature, 2013.

Stott, K. "Finding the Lost Book of the Law: Re-reading the Story of the 'Book of the Law' (Deuteronomy–2 Kings) in Light of Classical Literature." *JSOT* 30 (2005) 145–69.

Suriano, M. J. *The Politics of Dead Kings: Dynastic Ancestors in the Book of Kings and Ancient Israel*. FAT 2/48. Tübingen: Mohr Siebeck, 2010.

Sweeney, M. A., *King Josiah of Judah: The Lost Messiah of Israel*. Oxford: Oxford University Press, 2001.

_____. *I & II Kings: A Commentary*. OTL. Louisville: Westminster John Knox, 2007.

Talshir, Z. "The Three Deaths of Josiah and the Strata of Biblical Historiography." *VT* 46 (1996) 213–36.

Terblanche, M. D. "No Need for a Prophet Like Jeremiah: The Absence of the Prophet Jeremiah in Kings." Pp. 306–14 in *Past, Present, Future: The Deuteronomistic History and the Prophets*. Edited by J. C. de Moor and H. F. van Rooy. OtSt 44. Leiden: Brill, 2000.

Toorn, K. van der. *Scribal Culture and the Making of the Hebrew Bible.* Cambridge: Harvard University Press, 2007.

Trible, P. "Huldah's Holy Writ: On Women and Biblical Authority." *Touchstone* 3 (January 1985) 6–13.

Venema, G. J. *Reading Scripture in the Old Testament: Deuteronomy 9–10; 31; 2 Kings 22–23; Jeremiah 36; Nehemiah 8.* Leiden: Brill, 2004.

Weems, R. J. "Huldah, the Prophet: Reading a (Deuteronomistic) Woman's Identity." Pp. 321–99 in *A God So Near: Essays on Old Testament Theology in Honor of P. D. Miller.* Edited by B. A. Strawn and N. R. Bowen. Winona Lake, IN: Eisenbrauns, 2003.

Wetter, A.-M. "The Prophet and the King: Is There Such a Thing as Free Prophetic Speech?" Pp. 29–44 in *Prophecy and Prophets in Stories: Papers Read at the Fifth Meeting of the Edinburgh Prophecy Network. Utrecht, October 2013.* Edited by B. Becking and H. Barstad. Leiden: Brill, 2015.

Wilson, R. R. *Prophecy and Society in Ancient Israel.* Philadelphia: Fortress, 1980.

Wyatt, N. *Space and Time in the Religious Life of the Near East.* Biblical Seminar 85. Sheffield: Sheffield Academic Press, 2001.

_____. "Royal Religion in Ancient Judah." Pp. 61–81 in *Religious Diversity in Ancient Israel and Judah.* Edited by F. Stavrakopoulou and J. Barton. London: T. & T. Clark, 2010.

Zsolnay, I. "Gender and Sexuality: Ancient Near East." Pp. 273–87 in *The Oxford Encyclopedia of the Bible and Gender Studies.* Edited by J. M. O'Brien. Oxford: Oxford University Press, 2014.

Prophets in the Chronicler:
The Books of 1 and 2 Chronicles
and Ezra–Nehemiah

LESTER L. GRABBE

University of Hull, England

This study considers the references to prophets in the four books 1 Chronicles, 2 Chronicles, Ezra, and Nehemiah. They are treated together for convenience, without assuming that the same picture of prophets emerges in each of the books. All of the references to prophetic-type figures are surveyed and analyzed before any conclusions are drawn. Although 1 and 2 Chronicles are parallel to books such as 2 Samuel and 1–2 Kings, the question of whether the latter served as the sources of Chronicles is considered as a part of the study and not assumed before investigation of the individual passages.

We shall proceed by looking at each individual passage mentioning a prophet-like figure in the Texts section, after which a more holistic approach is taken in the Discussion section to see whether more general conclusions about connections between individual passages can be drawn. Finally, the Conclusion summarizes the results of the earlier study and analysis.

The Texts

The passages in 1 and 2 Chronicles are not of equal value in providing perspective on the prophets. A number of passages only mention prophets in passing, while others indicate prophets as the authors of writings. Therefore, the main texts are discussed in the first section, with the passing references in the second section, and then the passages listing prophetic writings. After this, the passages in Ezra–Nehemiah are considered.

1 and 2 Chronicles: Main Texts

1 Chronicles 9:22 (no parallel): here a seer (ראה) named Samuel helps David to establish the temple gatekeepers in their office. Samuel is also said to have dedicated certain things to God (1 Chr 26:28). Finally, he is the supposed author of a writing (דברי שמואל הראה) that includes the acts of David.

1 Chronicles 17 (//2 Samuel 7): David's desire to build a temple to Yhwh. He discusses the idea with Nathan the prophet (17:1: נביא); however, Yhwh sends a message back to David: God will build a "house" (dynasty) for David, but it will be his son who will build the temple, not himself. Nathan spoke according to all these words and all this 'prophecy' (17:15: חזון). This mostly agrees word-for-word with 2 Sam 7.

1 Chronicles 21 (//2 Samuel 24): a rare negative event in the life of David in the Chronicler (since 1 Chronicles omits the incident of David's sin with Bathsheba). In both 1 Chr 21 and the parallel passage 2 Sam 24, David sins by taking a census of the young men capable of military service. It is Gad who brings the message of God's displeasure. Gad is referred to in 1 Chr 21:9 as "Gad, David's seer (חזה)," but he is "Gad the prophet (נביא), David's seer (חזה)" in 2 Sam 24:11. On the whole, the two parallel accounts agree verbatim.[1]

1 Chronicles 25 (no parallel): listing of the various orders of Levites who sang and played instruments in the temple service. It is noted that some of these 'prophesied' (הנבאים) to the accompaniment of musical instruments (25:1–3). Some of these were sons of Heman, the seer (חזה) of the king who pronounced "words of God" (25:5). Elsewhere Heman is a called a 'singer' (משורר: 1 Chr 6:18; 15:19; 2 Chr 5:12).

2 Chronicles 10–12 (//1 Kings 12, 14): reign of Rehoboam. Rehoboam plans to make war on Israel, but Shemaiah 'the man of God' (איש־האלהים) brings a message from Yhwh not to do so (11:2–4). Later, the invasion of Pharaoh Shishak is described (12:2–12). As Shishak advances toward Jerusalem, Shemaiah the prophet (נביא) comes to Rehoboam with a message of warning that the Egyptians would have a free hand (12:5). Because the king and his officers humble themselves (12:6), Yhwh sends a further message that he would not destroy them at this time, but they would serve Shishak (12:7–8). The latter subsequently confiscates the treasures of the temple and palace, including the golden shields of the temple (for which Rehoboam had bronze shields made as a substitute). The prophet Shemaiah and also Iddo the seer (חזה) are said to have recorded the deeds of Rehoboam (12:15). The invasion of Shishak is also described (rather more briefly) in 1 Kgs 14:25–28, but nothing is said about a prophet.

2 Chronicles 14–16 (//1 Kings 15:9–24): the reign of King Asa of Judah. It is clear that he is considered a "good king" for much of his reign, though there are some negative incidents. He was attacked by Zerah the Cushite and an army of one million men, but Yhwh defeated the army of Zerah, and the Judahites took much spoil (14:8–14). After this incident, the spirit of Yhwh came upon Azariah

---

1. There are some slight differences between the wording of the accounts, the main one being the identity of the one who instigates David's decision: according to 2 Sam 24:1, it was Yhwh who was angry with Israel and incited David to take the census, whereas 1 Chr 21:1 states that this was done by "Satan" (whether this means "the Adversary" who is a part of Yhwh's court, as in Job, or refers to a demonic figure is a debatable point).

ben Oded to give a message from YHWH to Asa (15:1–7). Although Azariah is not called a prophet, his message is referred to as the 'prophecy' [נבואה] of Oded the 'prophet' [נביא] (15:8); the change from "Azariah son of Oded" to "Oded" is not explained. Asa had already begun to remove various non-YHWH altars (14:1–6), but now he took courage and removed the abominable things (15:8–18, including a statue of Asherah put up by the Queen Mother [15:16]). Although Asa didn't remove the high places (15:17; yet, 14:2 says that he *did* remove the high places!), he restored proper worship in the temple.

2 Chronicles 16 (//1 Kings 15:17–24): an incident during the reign of Asa— opposition between him and Baasha king of Israel. When Baasha seized Ramah with the aim of making it a roadblock to movement within Asa's kingdom, Asa paid Ben Hadad king of Damascus to attack Israel (16:1–6). This had the necessary effect, and Baasha withdrew from Ramah, leaving it to Asa. Hanani the seer (ראה) warned Asa that YHWH had defeated the Cushites and had been capable of assisting him out of the problem with Israel; now, because of his foolish alliance with the Arameans, Asa would suffer wars (16:7–10). Instead of repenting Asa incarcerated Hanani. The account of Asa's reign in 1 Kgs 15:9–24 does not mention any prophets.

2 Chronicles 18 (//1 Kings 22): the alliance of Ahab and Jehoshaphat. There are 400 court prophets of YHWH who tell the kings that they can go up to battle, for God will deliver the enemy into their hands. At Jehoshaphat's instigation, a further prophet of YHWH is consulted—Micaiah, who warns of a defeat. Although the account in Chronicles is from Jehoshaphat's perspective, much of the narrative is word-for-word the same as 1 Kgs 22:5–23. Here we have a classic account of prophetic conflict, except that the prophets are not "true" versus "false" prophets, but all are prophets of YHWH.

As in 2 Kgs 22, I find the situation described here somewhat unrealistic. Although kings did not like human opposition, they certainly did not want divine opposition. It was customary in seeking divine guidance through divination to test the results. One method would be to put the question first in such a way as to expect a positive answer; after that it would be put in such a way as to seek a negative response.[2] If the two oracles matched, the result was considered conclusive, but if they gave opposite results, the action was not undertaken. It seems unlikely that a king would refuse to look for counter-indications for an action. One should note the declaration by Esarhaddon with regard to the crown prince Ashurbanipal:

---

2. A good example of this is the famous poison oracle practiced among the Azande, in which a poison is administered to a young chicken, with the request that, if one should do something, let the chicken live. Once an answer is obtained, it is repeated in the opposite mode (with another chicken, of course): if one should do something, let the chicken die. Only if the two oracles agree will the person embark on the proposed action. See E. E. Evans-Pritchard, *Witchcraft, Oracles and Magic among the Azande* (Oxford: Clarendon, 1937), 120–63.

If you hear any evil, improper, ugly word which is not seemly nor good to Assurbanipal, . . . from the mouth of a prophet (^{LÚ}ra-gi-me), an ecstatic (^{LÚ}maḫ-ḫe-e),
an inquirer of oracles (^{DUMU}šá-ʾi-li a-mat DINGIR), or from the mouth of any human being at all, you shall not conceal it but come and report it to Assurbanipal,
the great crown prince designate, son of Esarhaddon, king of Assyria.[3]

This command suggests that negative oracles were not uncommon. In this case,
Esarhaddon was concerned about seditious oracles, but official oracles contrary to
the king's intent were also well known.[4]

2 Chronicles 19 (no parallel): although Ahab died, Jehoshaphat returned safely
to Jerusalem (19:1). At this point, 2 Chr 19:1–3 gives a further incident that has no
parallel elsewhere in the Bible: he was met by Jehu son of Hanani the seer (חזה),
who states that Yнwн is not happy with Jehoshaphat's actions (presumably his
excursion with Ahab), but there is some good in the king because he has removed
the symbols of Asherah from the land and worships Yнwн (19:2–3). The text goes
on to show Jehoshaphat leading Judah back to worship of Yнwн and appointing
judges who would make their judgments according to the laws of Yнwн, including priests and Levites among their number (19:4–11). Although no parallel to this
passage is found in 1 Kings, a Jehu son Hanani is said to have prophesied against
Baasha, king of Israel (1 Kgs 16:1–4); this Jehu was called a 'prophet' (נביא: 16:7).
From a historical point of view, this individual is in the same chronological period
as the one in 2 Chr 19; they could be identical. On the other hand, it is possible
that the figure in 2 Chr 19 is a literary construction based on 1 Kgs 16.

2 Chronicles 20 (no parallel): an episode in which Judah was threatened by a
coalition of Moabites and Ammonites, including the inhabitants of Mt. Seir (20:1,
10, 22–23). When Jehoshaphat addressed a congregation of Jews, calling on Yнwн
to protect them (20:3–13), Jahaziel (son of Zechariah son of Benaiah son of Jeiel
son of Mattaniah the Levite, belonging to the sons of Asaph) responded with a
message when the spirit of Yнwн came on him: they were not to fear but let Yнwн
fight the battle (20:14–19). The next day the soldiers of the opposing army fought
among themselves, killing each other and leaving nothing but corpses and vast
spoil for the Judahites to take (20:20–28). It is not stated that Jahaziel is a prophet,
but his position among the sons of Asaph suggests that he functions as a prophet
at least in this instance (compare 1 Chr 25:1, where the sons of Asaph "prophesy").

2 Chronicles 20:35–37 (//1 Kings 22:48–49): a final act of Jehoshaphat. In
this case, Jephoshaphat allies with King Ahaziah of Israel for a sea expedition to
Tarshish. Eliezer son of Dodavahu of Maresha prophesies against Jehoshaphat,

---

3. Translation from S. Parpola and K. Watanabe, *Neo-Assyrian Treaties and Loyalty Oaths*
(SAA 2; Helsinki: Helsinki University, 1988), 33 (no. 6, lines 108–22).

4. For a further discussion, see my article, "Ancient Near Eastern Prophecy from an Anthropological Perspective," in *Prophecy in Its Ancient Near Eastern Context: Mesopotamia, Biblical, and Arabian Perspectives* (ed. M. Nissinen; SBLSS 13; Atlanta: SBL, 2000), 13–32.

and the ships are wrecked. Again, Eliezer is not called a prophet, but the verb 'prophesy' (התנבא) is used of his statement, suggesting that he acts as a prophet in this case. (The parallel in 1 Kgs 22:48–49 does not mention the prophecy against Jehoshaphat.)

2 Chronicles 21:12–15 (no parallel): a letter from Elijah the prophet to the son of Jehoshaphat, Jehoram king of Judah. The letter admonishes Jehoram for following the kings of Israel rather than his father Jehoshaphat and his grandfather Asa and portends a divine blow on the people and also personally on the king. There is no parallel to this incident, or to this letter of Elijah, in 2 Kings.

2 Chronicles 24:17–27 (no parallel): Yʜwʜ sent prophets to bring Israel back to him when Joash abandoned the true path after the death of Jehoiada the high priest, but he failed to heed them. Finally, Zechariah, son of Jehoiada the high priest, rebuked the people for forsaking Yʜwʜ, but they stoned him to death. As a result, Joash was attacked by the Arameans, wounded in the battle, and his courtiers assassinated him. (None of this episode occurs in 2 Kings except for a reference to Joash's assassination in 2 Kgs 12:19–21.)

2 Chronicles 25 (//2 Kings 14): the reign of Amaziah, son of Joash. He assembled an army from Judah and Benjamin but also hired mercenaries from the kingdom of Israel. A 'man of God' (איש האלהים) warned him about employing mercenaries (promising that God could provide compensation for the 100 silver talents that he had paid for the Ephraimite mercenaries), and he reluctantly sent them home (25:7–10). (Angry at this treatment, the mercenaries made raids against Judah, slaughtering citizens and taking booty.) But the Judahite army defeated the Edomites of Seir; however, in spite of this defeat, Amaziah adopted the deities of Mt Seir (25:11–14). For this he was admonished by an anonymous prophet (נביא: 25:15–16). When Amaziah warned him not to interfere, the prophet declared that ignoring God's instructions would lead to his destruction. True enough, Amaziah was defeated when he attacked Israel; subsequently, he was assassinated in a conspiracy. 2 Kings 14:1–20 also tells the story of Amaziah but says nothing about a prophet or man of God.

2 Chronicles 28 (2 Kings 16): the story of king Ahaz of Judah. He is described as taking actions displeasing to Yʜwʜ, including false worship. As a result, he was defeated by the Arameans and by Pekah, the king of Israel, who took many Judahites and their families captive. Oded a prophet (נביא) of Yʜwʜ met the victorious Israelite army as it returned to Samaria and warned the Israelites to return the captives to their home (28:9–11). Coincidentally, some leading Ephraimites also warned the Israelite army about bringing Judahite captives to Samaria. They then clothed and fed the captives and provided donkeys for transport, bringing them to Jericho to turn them over to Judah. In the account of Ahaz's reign in 2 Kgs 16, there are many differences: much of the detail about Judah's defeat and suffering is not only absent but does not seem to be envisaged by the situation described; neither is any prophet mentioned in the account.

2 Chronicles 32:1–23 (//2 Kings 18:13–19:37//Isaiah 36–37): the story of Hezekiah and Sennacherib's invasion. This is a complicated narrative, taking up several parallel passages in the Bible. The version in 2 Chronicles is rather shorter than the parallels. On the surface, the differences can be most easily explained by postulating that the fuller, more original account is found in 2 Kings and Isaiah, while 2 Chronicles contains a summary of the other account. Whereas Isaiah has a very active part in the account in 2 Kings and Isaiah, the only reference to a prophet in 2 Chronicles is 32:20, in which Hezekiah and the prophet Isaiah pray because of threats from the Assyrians. (God answers by sending an angel to annihilate the Assyrian army.)

2 Chronicles 34–35 (2 Kings 22–23): the story of Josiah. After Josiah ordered the repair of the temple, a copy of the law was found (34:8–28). Josiah commanded Hilkiah the priest to inquire of YHWH (34:21). Hilkiah and his entourage approached the prophetess Huldah, and she responded with a message from YHWH to Hilkiah and the others to report back to the king (34:22–28). Chapter 35 describes the Passover kept by Josiah (mostly absent in 2 Kgs 23); reference is made to the "singers of the sons of Asaph" who had been established in their posts by David, Asaph, Heman, and Jeduthun the king's seer (חוזה). The parallel in 2 Kgs 22–23 has a lot in common but also differs from 2 Chr 34–35 (but no reference is made to Jeduthun the king's seer).

1 and 2 Chronicles: Passing References

1 Chronicles 16:22 (//Psa 105:1–15): do not harm my prophets

1 Chronicles 25:1 (no parallel): David had the sons of Asaph set apart, who were prophesying (הנבאים) with harps and other musical instruments.

2 Chronicles 29:25 (no parallel): at the time of Hezekiah, reference is made to the establishment of Levites as players of musical instruments by David, Gad the seer, and Nathan the prophet.

2 Chronicles 35:18 (//2 Kgs 23:22): no Passover kept like this since the time of the prophet Samuel.

2 Chronicles 36:12 (//2 Kgs 24:19): Zedekiah did what displeased YHWH and did not humble himself before the prophet Jeremiah.

2 Chronicles 36:14–16 (no parallel): wickedness of the leaders and all the people, including mocking the messengers of God, disdaining his words, and taunting his prophets (36:16).

1 and 2 Chronicles: Statements of Authorship

1 Chronicles 29:29 (no parallel): David's acts written in the 'words' (דברי) of Samuel the seer, Nathan the prophet, and Gad the seer.

2 Chronicles 9:29 (//1 Kgs 11:41): deeds of Solomon in the 'words' (דברי) of prophet Nathan, the 'prophecy' (נבואת) of Ahijah, and the 'visions' (חזות) of Jedo the seer.

2 Chronicles 12:15 (//1 Kgs 14:29 but no parallel to mention of a prophet): Rehoboam's deeds recorded in the 'words' (דברי) of the prophet Shemaiah and Iddo the seer.

2 Chronicles 13:22 (//1 Kgs 15:7): written in the story (מדרש; 1 Kgs 15:7 has 'book of days' [ספר דברי ימים]) of the prophet Iddo.

2 Chronicles 26:22 (//2 Kgs 15:6): prophet Isaiah recorded (כתב) events of Uzziah's reign.

2 Chronicles 32:32 (no parallel): the deeds of Hezekiah were recorded in the vison (חזון) of Isaiah the prophet.

Ezra–Nehemiah

Ezra 5:1–2: the prophets Haggai and Zechariah son of Iddo and their support of Zerubbabel and Joshua in rebuilding the temple. The chances are that this information is simply taken from the books of Haggai and Zechariah rather than being independent memory.[5]

Ezra 6:14: the prophecy of Haggai the prophet and Zechariah son of Iddo encourages the progress of building the temple. The statement is not taken from the extant books of Haggai and Zechariah (since it mentions the completion of the temple) but is an easy inference from them. Also, the proleptic reference to Artaxerxes long before that king reigned indicates that this passage is a literary construction rather than being a survival from an early source.

Ezra 9:11: this is only a passing reference: in giving a speech about Israel's past, the scribe Ezra refers to God's "servants the prophets."

Nehemiah 6:7: this is a statement of Sanballat, claiming that Nehemiah had established prophets to proclaim him king. Whether this is true or not, we do not know, but it is likely that Nehemiah had his prophetic supporters. If they made such a statement about Nehemiah's becoming king, this might well be considered treasonous by the Persians if such things were reported to them. This suggests, though, that there were pro-Nehemiah prophets in Jerusalem, even if they did not make such blatant predictions as claimed here.

Nehemiah 6:10–13: Nehemiah asserts that the prophet Shemaiah ben Delaiah ben Mehetabel has tried to intimidate him by prophesying that "they" are coming to kill him. He states that this was not a revelation from God, but Tobiah and Sanballat had hired him. This is of course only Nehemiah's supposition, but it is a natural one to make for someone like Nehemiah who is convinced that anyone not for him is against him. We have to accept, though, that Shemaiah may have been sincere in his revelation, may have had nothing to do with Sanballat and Tobiah, and may indeed not have been anti-Nehemiah as such.

Nehemiah 6:14: an important statement about a prophet who not only opposes Nehemiah but is female; even her name is given as Noadiah. Or at least Nehemiah claims she opposes him: we do not have enough information to be sure

---

5. Cf. H. G. M. Williamson, "The Composition of Ezra i–vi," *JTS* 34 (1983) 1–30.

whether this was actually the case, but Nehemiah took her pronouncements—whatever they were—as evidence of opposition. It is also noted that there are other prophets who oppose him—again, according to Nehemiah's perception.

Nehemiah 9:26, 30, 32: passing references to prophets: 9:26 mentions those prophets in the past who were killed for admonishing the people; 9:30 refers to the prophets who admonished the people but were ignored; while 9:32 includes the prophets among those who suffered, beginning with the time of the Assyrian kings.

Discussion

1–2 Chronicles

For convenience, the various data from 1–2 Chronicles will be discussed under five points, as follows:

1. The first point to note is the extent of parallels between the passages in 1–2 Chronicles and those elsewhere in the Hebrew Bible, primarily 2 Samuel and 1–2 Kings. This can be tabulated as shown in Table 1 (p. 305).

2. Some of these parallels represent much the same narrative in two separate sections of the Bible, with mostly verbal agreement between the accounts, primarily the following:

- David's desire to build a temple and the prophet Nathan
- David's census of fighting men and the seer Gad
- Alliance of Ahab and Jehoshaphat, and the 400 prophets of YHWH plus Micaiah
- The finding of the law under Josiah and the consultation of Huldah

3. In spite of some parallel passages with large agreement, there are many instances of prophets or prophetic-like figures that are mentioned only in 1–2 Chronicles:

- Samuel the seer
- Heman, the king's seer (and other Levites who play musical instruments and prophesy)
- Shemaiah, both man of God and prophet
- Azariah ben Oded (or Oded the prophet?)
- Hanani the seer
- Jehu ben Hanani the seer (but cf. 1 Kgs 16:1–4)
- Jahaziel, of the sons of Asaph
- Eliezer ben Dodavahu ("prophesies")
- Elijah the prophet writes a letter
- Zechariah ben Jehoiada (a priest but not designated a prophet)
- "Man of God"
- Anonymous prophet
- Oded the prophet

Table 1

Chronicles	Parallel Accounts	Relationship of Accounts
1 Chronicles	**2 Samuel**	
9:22; 26:28: Samuel the seer	No parallel	No parallel
17: Nathan the prophet	7: Nathan the prophet	Very similar
21: Gad the seer	24: Gad the prophet, David's seer	Very similar
25: Levites prophesy, including sons of Heman seer of the king	No parallel	No parallel
2 Chronicles	**1 Kings**	
11–12: Shemaiah, "man of God" and prophet	14:25–28: no prophet	Different
15:1–7: Azariah ben Oded (not designated but "prophesies")	15:9–24: no prophet	Different
15:8: Oded the prophet (same as Azariah?)	ditto: no prophet	Different
16:7–10: Hanani the seer	ditto: no prophet	Different
18:4–27: 400 prophets of Yhwh and Micaiah	22:5–28: 400 prophets of Yhwh and Micaiah	Very similar
19:1–3: Jehu ben Hanani the seer	No parallel [but cf. 1 Kgs 16:1–4]	No parallel
20:14–19: Jahaziel, of sons of Asaph	No parallel	No parallel
20:35–37: Eliezer ben Dodavahu (not designated)	22:48–49: no prophet	Different
21:12–15: letter of Elijah	No parallel	No parallel
	2 Kings	
24:17–27: Zechariah ben Jehoiada (priest)	(12:19–21: no prophet or priest)	No parallel
25:7–10: "man of God"	14:1–20: no man of God or prophet	Different
25:15–16: anonymous prophet		Different
28:9–11: Oded the prophet	16: no prophet	Different
32:1–23: Sennacherib's invasion; brief reference to Isaiah (v 20)	18:13–19:37//Isaiah 36–37: Isaiah prominent in the account	Different
34:8–28: Huldah the prophetess	22: Huldah	Very similar

The view of the Chronicler seems to be that a message from a prophet-like individual is important. Many episodes in Samuel and Kings have no prophet pronouncing on them, whereas more such figures appear to occur in Chronicles. A number of prominent prophets occur in Samuel and Kings, often covering a fairly lengthy section of text, such as the Samuel, Elijah, Elisha, and Isaiah cycles; these receive much less space in Chronicles. Nonetheless, minor prophetic figures seem to be more frequent in Chronicles.

4. A variety of terms are used for the prophetic figures: 'prophet' (נביא), 'seer' (חזה), 'seer' (ראה), and 'man of God' (איש האלהים). These are terms familiar from a number of passages outside Chronicles, but this does not exhaust the figures found in some further passages. We have Jahaziel among the sons of Asaph—that is, a Levite. Yet, in the eyes of the Chronicler, certain groups of Levites "prophesied" as a part of their duties. This seems to have been mainly in the temple cult, but there are examples of prophesying in others contexts, such as 2 Chr 20:14–19. Another figure is Zechariah ben Jehoiada, son of a high priest. Although the terms "prophet" or "prophesy" are not used of him, his message is similar to that of the various figures called "prophet" or "seer." Some might object to labeling these figures as prophets, but what they do is sometimes called "prophesying," and even when it is not, their pronouncements do not look different from prophetic statements. What seems to be clear is that the author of Chronicles does not make particular distinctions between these figures, however they are designated. For example, Shamaiah is called both "man of God" and "prophet."

5. When we start to analyze the messages pronounced by the various prophetic figures, we first have to eliminate those prophets who do not actually deliver a prophecy in 1–2 Chronicles: Samuel, a seer who helps David to establish the temple gatekeepers in their office; Hamen, the king's seer, and his sons and other Levites who prophesy to musical instruments (because no specific prophecy is given); Isaiah who only prays to God (along with Hezekiah) about Sennacherib's threat. The relevant prophecies are the following:

- Nathan: his message first supports David in his intent to build a temple; however, this seems to be made without consulting YHWH. YHWH's message is that the temple will be built by David's son, and David is promised a dynasty. Positive.
- Gad: choice of punishment because of David's census. Later Gad gives the message that David is to sacrifice on the threshing floor of Ornan. Mainly negative, though a means to mitigate the problem is revealed.
- Shemaiah: his first message is to tell Rehoboam not to wage war on Judah. Then at the time of Shishak's invasion, he warns Rehoboam that Shishak will have a free hand, though when the Israelite leadership humble themselves, he tells them that Shishak will not destroy them, though they will serve him. Negative, though there are some positive elements.
- Azariah ben Oded (or is it Oded the prophet?): both warns and encourages Asa in his religious reform. Positive.
- Hanani: admonishes Asa for trusting in the Arameans to help against Israel. Negative.
- 400 prophets of YHWH: support Ahab's plans with Jehoshaphat. Positive.
- Micaiah: warns Ahab and Jehoshaphat that they will lose their battle. Negative.
- Jehu ben Hanani: admonishes Jehoshaphat (apparently for his alliance with Ahab) but recognizes some good in him. Mainly negative.
- Jahaziel: YHWH promises to deliver the invading army into Jehoshaphat's hands. Positive.

- Eliezer ben Dodavahu: warns Jehoshaphat that partnership with Israel is wrong and the endeavor will not suceed. Negative.
- Elijah: letter to Jehoram, warning that both he personally and his people will suffer for his actions. Negative.
- Zechariah ben Jehoiada: admonishes the people and king Joash. Negative.
- "Man of God": warns Judahites against using Israelite mercenaries; Amaziah heeds. Negative but positive response.
- Anonymous prophet: warns Amaziah about adopting Edomite gods. Negative.
- Oded: warns Israelites about taking Judahites captive. Negative but a positive response.
- Huldah: warns of disaster on Judah and Jerusalem but because Josiah had humbled himself, it would not happen in his lifetime. Mainly positive.

Most of the prophecies are warnings or admonitions. This means that most of them are negative, though in a few cases the admonition is heeded and the outcome is positive. Generally, the prophecies to "good" kings are positive and to "bad" kings negative, but there are exceptions: (a) when "good" kings do bad things, and (b) when "bad" kings repent or heed the prophecy by responding in an appropriate way.

What about the content of the messages—the prophecies? They are overwhelmingly religious. That is, the prophets support certain actions as approved by God and other actions as opposed by God. Some of these actions may be "political" from the point of view of a modern person, but the prophet almost always interprets these in religious terms. Thus, David is criticized for his census, not because it is an unwise political move: from a political or military point of view, the census probably made a lot of sense, since it would allow him to know the military strength of the country. Yet the prophetic view is that by doing this, he is not trusting YHWH, because victory lay not in military numbers but in God's help. Similarly, a number of kings (including "good" kings such as Asa and Jehoshaphat) are condemned for making alliances with other powers. What they did might have been examples of political wisdom, but the prophecy gives a simple religious message of trust in YHWH. Prophets are not political commentators or political scientists, and their pronouncements should not be taken as models of political conduct for a later age.

Ezra–Nehemiah

Basically, the passages in Ezra–Nehemiah fall into two groups. The first group contains the two passages in Ezra (5:1–2; 6:14) that relate to the prophets Haggai and Zechariah, who encourage and support the rebuilding of the temple. The context is rather different from that presupposed in Samuel, Kings, and Chronicles since there is no longer a king, and the Jewish leadership is somewhat different.

Indeed, in Ezra 6:14, the prophets support the 'elders of Judah' (שָׂבֵי יְהוּדָיֵא). The rebuilding of the temple is not so much a project of the leadership, however, as of the whole community. (These passages were probably created from the books of Haggai and Zechariah rather than containing independent references, but a number of references to prophets elsewhere could be considered literary creations rather than genuine memory.)

The second group are the passages in Nehemiah. Nehemiah claims that he was accused of setting up prophets to proclaim him king. Whether he was actually accused of such, it seems unlikely that any prophets actually proclaimed Nehemiah king of Judah. It would not have helped Nehemiah, and any such prophetic pronouncement might have been seen as an act of treason by the Persians. But all we have is Nehemiah's interpretation of the situation, which may have been exaggerated. He goes on to accuse two named prophets, along with several unnamed ones, of opposing him. This is unusual in highlighting prophetic opposition to a "good" leader.

The passages on prophets in Ezra–Nehemiah do not seem to be a continuum with those in 1 and 2 Chronicles. Although all such passages have certain elements in common, the ones in Ezra–Nehemiah have a different ethos from those in Chronicles. First, the prophets Haggai and Zechariah support the leadership of the Jewish community at the beginning of the temple rebuilding, but there are some differences: (a) the leadership does not contain a king in the first instance (Ezra 5:1–2), and the leadership is only "the elders" of the Jews in the second passage (Ezra 6:14), and (b) the prophecies specifically support a building project, perhaps the nearest parallel being David and Nathan (1 Chr 17). Next, the passages in Nehemiah also relate to a governor, not a king. The main focus, however, is on those who oppose the "good" leader, which is very unusual in biblical prophetic stories.

Conclusions

For convenience, the present study has considered references to prophets in both 1–2 Chronicles and Ezra–Nehemiah but without presuming that the two sets of writings had anything to do with each other. In the end, no evidence was found that the treatment of prophets in Chronicles was related to Ezra–Nehemiah. Therefore, in summing up, the two sets of writings will be considered separately:

1–2 Chronicles

Several conclusions have emerged from the study of passages on prophets in these books. They can be summarized as follows:

- No assumptions were made as to whether 1–2 Chronicles were dependent on any of the parallels. A few passages in 1–2 Chronicles have almost verbatim parallels in Samuel or Kings, but there are many unique references to prophets in 1–2 Chronicles not found elsewhere in the Hebrew Bible.

- A variety of terminology is used to refer to prophet-like figures, but the writer does not seem to distinguish them: thus, no distinction seems to be made between "prophet" and "seer." What is not clear, however, is how the author regards the undesignated individuals (at least one of whom is a priest). There is one innovation in Chronicles that does not appear clearly elsewhere: some Levitical singers "prophesy" in the cultic service. Unfortunately, we are not given any concrete examples of this prophesying. One of the singers, Heman, however, is also referred to as the king's seer. What needs to be recognized is that in Chronicles the concept of prophet seems wider than in some other passages—certainly wider than some scholars want to allow.

- With regard to message, prophetic figures generally support "good" kings and oppose "bad" kings, but there are exceptions. Ahab, who is a "bad" king, is supported by 400 prophets of YHWH. In some cases, there is a positive response to a negative pronouncement, which is often followed by a more positive reaction from the prophet. The message is always religious, even if it relates to political decisions and actions—that is, the action is always judged on religious grounds, not whether it was an astute political maneuver. What the king or other figure did might have been an example of political wisdom, but the prophecy gives a simple religious message of trust in YHWH. Prophets are not political commentators or political scientists, and their pronouncements should not be taken as models of political conduct for a later age.

Ezra–Nehemiah

Nothing especially appears to connect the allusions to prophets in 1–2 Chronicles with those in Ezra–Nehemiah. The points that arise from references to prophets in Ezra and Nehemiah are the following:

- The passages fall into two groups. The first group (Ezra 5:1–2; 6:14) relates to the prophets Haggai and Zechariah, who encourage the rebuilding of the temple. In the first passage, they relate primarily to Zerubbabel and Joshua, but in the second it is the "elders of Judah" who are supported by the prophets in completing the rebuilding. The references in these verses were probably derived from the books of Haggai and Zechariah rather than being independent traditions.

- The second group contains the prophetic encounters in Nehemiah. What we have are his melodramatic interpretation of his interaction, though to what extent we can take his statements literally is a major question. But there appear to have been pro-Nehemiah prophets (since Nehemiah claims that he was accused of setting up prophets to proclaim him king). He follows this statement with an accusation against two named prophets, along with several unnamed ones, that they opposed him. What is especially unusual—unique—is that the text depicts prophetic opposition to the positive deeds of a "good" leader. Elsewhere, negative prophecies against a "good" king are for wrong actions that he has taken.

Bibliography

Evans-Pritchard, E. E. *Witchcraft, Oracles and Magic among the Azande.* Oxford: Clarendon, 1937.

Grabbe, L. L. "Ancient Near Eastern Prophecy from an Anthropological Perspective." Pp. 13–32 in *Prophecy in its Ancient Near Eastern Context: Mesopotamia, Biblical, and Arabian Perspectives.* Edited by M. Nissinen. SBLSS 13. Atlanta: SBL, 2000.

Parpola, S., and K. Watanabe. *Neo-Assyrian Treaties and Loyalty Oaths.* SAA 2. Helsinki: Helsinki University Press, 1988.

Williamson, H. G. M. "The Composition of Ezra i–vi." *JTS* 34 (1983) 1–30.

Part 4

*Prophets in the Prophetic Books
of the First Temple
and Exilic Periods*

Prophecy and the State in 8th-Century Israel:
Amos and Hosea

ROBERT R. WILSON

Yale University

Scholars often treat the books of Amos and Hosea together for obvious reasons. Both books address audiences in the Northern Kingdom (Israel), and, if their superscriptions are to be believed, both of the prophets involved were active during the reign of Jeroboam II (788–748 B.C.E.).[1] For this reason, these two books have usually been taken to be reliable sources for reconstructing the nature of prophetic activity in 8th-century Israel.

However, in recent years, scholars have come to recognize that this sort of reconstruction is more complicated than it seems. The two prophets whose words are recorded in the books are otherwise unknown, and outside of a brief biographical narrative about Amos (Amos 7:10–17), there is no indication of where they carried out their activities. The oracles that the books contain are presented without historical or social contexts and sometimes seem to be randomly arranged. Where groupings of oracles do exist, the collections appear to be based on literary form rather than content. In Amos 1–3, for example, the unit begins with a rigidly structured collection of oracles against foreign nations before turning to oracles against Judah and Israel. However, although the Judah and Israel oracles seem to continue the already established literary pattern, their focus and contents are quite different. Elsewhere in Amos, oracles are grouped together because they begin with the same word: "hear" (Amos 3:13; 4:1; 5:1) or "alas" (5:18; 6:1, 4). Hosea begins with two biographical narratives involving the prophet's marriages, and these narratives then become the basis for further theological reflection and additional oracles (Hosea 1–3). These chapters have often been taken to grow out of the prophet's personal experiences, but current scholarship tends to understand

---

1. Throughout this paper, the word "Israel" refers to the Northern Kingdom. The dates used in the paper are taken from M. Miller and J. H. Hayes, *A History of Ancient Israel and Judah*, 2nd ed. (Louisville: Westminster John Knox, 2006).

them as elaborate symbolic actions rather than as genuine biography. All of these literary characteristics suggest a great deal of post-prophetic scribal activity.

Along the same lines, an additional complication is raised by the fact that both books sometimes seem to refer to events that occurred after the historical period indicated by the superscriptions. These references are minimal in Amos but are more prominent in Hosea. Until the modern period, such chronological issues were explained by taking them to represent genuine prophecies dealing with the future. However, contemporary scholars have usually responded in other ways. Some have questioned the accuracy of the dates in the superscriptions and have redated the books to a later historical period, usually to the Exile or Persian Period. As an alternative, interpreters have instead appealed to the idea that the original collection of prophetic words was reworked by later editors or scribes, who reshaped the books and at the same time introduced new interpretations and theological themes. Most recently, there has been a scholarly tendency to extend this scribal activity into the postexilic period and to suggest that both Amos and Hosea were reshaped in order to integrate them into the prophetic collection now known as the Book of the Twelve Prophets.[2]

In short, the literary characteristics of Amos and Hosea, as well as the chronological problems raised by the books' contents, raise serious questions about the use of these books as windows into the actual words of the prophets involved. Increasingly scholars recognize the role of scribes in shaping biblical books, and there is a growing tendency to understand such activity as part of the books' early interpretive tradition. However, understanding the books of Amos and Hosea in this way does not necessarily involve accepting the conclusion that scribal operations on the books completely obscured or modified the prophets' original message. It may well be that the scribes understood their work as an act of interpretation of the prophets' oracles, and if so, a connection still remains between the prophets and the literature in its present form. To be sure, understanding the books' development in this way does involve giving up the quest for original prophetic words, and it is for this reason that the scholarly consensus has largely given up the quest for the historical Amos and Hosea and in some cases also given up trying to track the editorial history of the books. In the light of this consensus, the discussion that follows will concentrate on the books as they now appear and will not attempt to reconstruct earlier stages of the text or recover the prophets' original words.[3]

---

2. For a discussion of this recent tendency, see M. H. Floyd, "New Form Criticism and Beyond: The Historicity of Prophetic Literature Revisited," in *The Book of the Twelve & the New Form Criticism* (ed. M. J. Boda, M. H. Floyd, and C. M. Toffelmire; Atlanta: SBL Press, 2015), 17–36.

3. For a discussion of this type of approach to Amos and Hosea, see the methodological reflections of P. Machinist, "Hosea and the Ambiguity of Kingship in Ancient Israel," in *Consti-

However, the chronological issues raised by the contents of Amos and Hosea must still be resolved. If the text of these two books was finally shaped in the 8th century or shortly thereafter, then it is reasonable to use this material to analyze prophetic views of the state in that period. If editorial work on the books is understood to have taken place in a much later period, then the books reflect the views of that later period. This issue is much more critical in the case of Hosea than it is in the case of Amos. Most scholars see very little scribal editing in Amos after the 8th century. Hosea is another matter, although the scholarly consensus remains that Hosea, too, is best understood against the background of the 8th century.[4] These questions will be discussed in greater detail below.

Just as the idea of reading Amos and Hosea as 8th-century literature raises the sorts of methodological issues mentioned above, so also an investigation of Amos's and Hosea's views on the state is not without its difficulties. In the first place, neither prophetic book has a great deal to say about the state specifically, although both books are sharply critical of the society of which the state is a part. This situation is somewhat puzzling, given recent scholarly claims that the scribes who collected and shaped the prophets' words were themselves state employees who worked in the state's best interests.[5] No matter how this situation is to be explained, it is important to examine both Amos and Hosea in detail to try to interpret their views on the state, although at the beginning it must be recognized that this interpretation involves a good bit of reconstruction.

A second difficulty associated with reconstructing prophetic views of the state in 8th-century Israel arises from the recognition that more than one state is involved. These prophetic texts reflect attitudes about the Israelite monarchy and the bureaucracy associated with it, but both Amos and Hosea also contain opinions about the state of Judah as well as the states immediately surrounding Israel. In particular, the texts deal by necessity with the Assyrians, who were the imperial presence engaged with Israel for much of the period covered by the books. Views of all of these states probably merged and interacted in the minds of the scribal authors, but for the sake of analytical clarity, opinions about the various states will be analyzed separately in the discussion that follows. Similarly, an attempt will be made to determine whether Amos and Hosea hold distinctive views on the state in general or simply on individual kings and officials.

---

tuting the Community: Studies on the Polity of Ancient Israel in Honor of S. Dean McBride Jr. (ed. J. T. Strong and S. S. Tuell; Winona Lake, IN: Eisenbrauns, 2005), 157–58.

4. In support of the traditional dating of Hosea, see J. Day, "Hosea and the Baal Cult," in *Prophecy and Prophets in Ancient Israel* (ed. J. Day; LHBOTS 531; London: T. & T. Clark, 2010), 202–03; Machinist, "Hosea," 155.

5. For a strong argument in support of the idea that scribes in the preexilic period worked in the context of the royal court, see W. M. Schniedewind, *How the Bible Became a Book* (Cambridge: Cambridge University Press, 2004).

The Northern Kingdom in the 8th Century:
Historical and Social Background

In order to better understand the nature of the political and social situation in Israel during the reign of Jeroboam II (788–748 B.C.E.), it would be useful to consider briefly the events that led up to it. According to the archaeological evidence, the first settlements in what would become Israel and Judah were in the highlands of Canaan, where around 1200 B.C.E. small unfortified villages began to appear. The people in these villages practiced subsistence agriculture and lived in small three- or four-room houses large enough to accommodate four to six people. These dwellings represent nuclear families, which lived independently. In sociological terms, these family groups constituted small lineages, a form of social organization based on the model of the family. Lineages are minimally hierarchical but are perceived by outsiders as cohesive and independent units. As the family lineages grow and expand, larger lineage units of genuine or fictive kin can be formed, and if the lineages band together, they can form a maximal lineage, sometimes called a tribe. Lineages of this size are based on fictive kinship, and are often characterized as being egalitarian, although that term is somewhat misleading. Because even small lineages are minimally hierarchical, social and political power within the lineage is not equally shared by all of its members. At the same time, those exercising power can do so only with the cooperation of other lineage members. This means that the use of power has to be negotiated within the lineage. In larger groupings of lineages, the negotiations involve the heads of the constituent lineages. These lineage heads or elders in theory are equal, but in fact some elders have more power than others. In the early Israelite settlements, there is little evidence of trade or interaction between large lineage groupings or with surrounding groups.

Lineages that grow to incorporate more than about five hundred people tend to lose their ability to function efficiently, and when this happens they often fragment to form new lineage groupings. Because of this limitation in size, lineage systems are not very good at dealing with certain kinds of crises that require large numbers of people to act together. The best example of such a crisis is a military threat, where large coordinated groups are required to mount a successful response. When such a response is needed, lineages may temporarily modify their structure and delegate power to a single individual or "chief," who has the task of unifying the lineages and forcing them to act together to achieve a common goal. When the crisis has been met, the lineages usually resume their normal functions, but under certain conditions, the temporary chief can become a permanent one, and when this occurs, the society is on its way to becoming a centralized monarchical state.[6]

---

6. For a more detailed description of lineages, see R. R. Wilson, *Genealogy and History in the Biblical World* (New Haven: Yale University Press, 1977), 18–37. For a description of early Israelite and Judean settlement patterns, see the fundamental work of L. E. Stager, "The Archae-

In Israel and Judah, the archaeological evidence for centralized polities begins to appear about the mid-10th century B.C.E. Some of the earlier small settlements are replaced by larger ones, and fortification walls, gateways, larger houses, palaces, and evidence of local and international trade begin to appear. As is the case with all hierarchical polities, there is also evidence of social stratification based on wealth. In contrast to the small highland villages, the new, larger cities provide evidence of variable housing size, imported goods, government buildings, and variations in burial practices. The newly enlarged political centers imply an increase in population, which by the 8th century in Israel eventually spread to the highlands and probably put pressure on the previously isolated lineage villages. The population shifts increased pressure on outlying land and likely led to boundary disputes and concerns with group identity. Disputes over boundaries also eventually came to involve the neighboring non-Israelite peoples occupying the same geographical area. As a result, tensions broke out with the Philistines and Phoenicians on the coast, the Arameans to the north, and the Ammonites, Moabites, and Edomites to the east, and Judah to the south. However, as centralized rule began to spread, the older lineage-based system remained in place. The lineages continued to interact with the centralized governments, although that interaction was often tense.[7]

In Israel, there seem to have been several short-lived efforts to bring centralized rule to the northern lineages or tribes, but the archaeological data suggest that the whole area did not become a unified polity until the reign of Omri (879–869 B.C.E.) and his dynastic successor Ahab (868–854 B.C.E.). Omri seems to have been able to subdue the Philistines and annex the northern part of Moab. Ahab joined forces with the Arameans of Damascus to form a coalition against the Assyrians. Relations with the Phoenicians were cemented when Ahab married Jezebel, a Tyrian princess, who brought with her to Israel the worship of Baal of Tyre. Edom and Judah also became vassal states under Ahab. With the growing political power of the state, there were also economic consequences. The kings controlled domestic and foreign trade and had the power to tax, as well as to reward the officials who were part of the royal bureaucracy. Thus, early in the Omri dynasty, both political and economic inequality increased, particularly in the cities. However, after the death of Ahab, the power of the dynasty began to decline. The surrounding polities began to drift away from Israel's control, and there were renewed tensions with the Arameans, Moabites, Phoenicians, and Judahites. In the east, a brief period of

---

ology of the Family in Ancient Israel," *BASOR* 260 (1985) 1–35; J. S. Holladay Jr., "The Kingdoms of Israel and Judah: Political and Economic Centralization in the Iron IIA–B (ca. 1000–750 BCE," in *The Archaeology of Society in the Holy Land* (ed. T. E. Levy; London: Leicester University Press, 1995), 368–98; and A. Faust, *The Archaeology of Israelite Society in Iron Age II* (Winona Lake, IN: Eisenbrauns, 2012).

   7. For a discussion of the social dimensions of political centralization in Israel, see T. M. Lemos, "Kinship, Community, and Society," in *The Wiley Blackwell Companion to Ancient Israel* (Ed. S. Niditch; Chichester: Wiley Blackwell, 2016), 386–88.

Assyrian decline allowed the Arameans to become a regional power again. When Jehu (839–748 B.C.E.) overthrew the last king of the House of Omri, the power of the central state continued its decline until the last of Jehu's line, Jeroboam II (788–748 B.C.E.), once again subdued the Arameans and much of Transjordan. However, his grip on the area began to loosen toward the end of his reign, and Israel again became an unstable polity. Not long after Jeroboam's death, the Assyrian king Tiglath-pileser III (745–727 B.C.E.) campaigned in the west, and Israel and Judah both became Assyrian vassals. The Israelite kings of the period continued to vacillate in their foreign policy, and the Assyrians responded by trying to destabilize the Northern Kingdom, cutting off parts of the state and bringing them directly under Assyrian control. This policy was followed by Shalmaneser V and Sargon II from 727–720 B.C.E., with the result that the Israelite capital, Samaria, was finally destroyed, and Israel became an Assyrian province.[8]

This brief account of the Israelite state during its zenith and decline highlights several interesting general features that are worth noting. They are most clearly seen when they are contrasted with the Davidic state in Judah. First, as Israel over the course of its history underwent the process of state formation, it had several royal capitals (Gibeah, Shechem, Tirzah, Samaria), while in Judah, according to the biblical texts, there was only one: Jerusalem. Furthermore, the northern capitals were not Israel's traditional cult centers (Dan, Gilgal, Mizpah, Mount Carmel), so politics and religion did not necessarily mix. By contrast, in Judah, the biblical texts suggest that by the reign of David the single capital was also the only legitimate place of worship. Politics and religion were thus intimately related throughout the history of the Southern Kingdom. Second, in Israel, the biblical texts suggest that rulers could be easily deposed, a fact that led to multiple changes of dynasty and considerable instability in the northern state. In Judah, on the other hand, the texts claim that the royal Davidic line continued unbroken until the Babylonians finally put an end to it. Finally, in Israel, the stories about the kings suggest that they held their position as head of state because of the support of their lineages. This fact suggests the continuing vitality of the old lineage system and also provides a possible explanation for the turmoil that seems to have characterized the Northern Kingdom. The texts also indicate that there were more major lineages in the north than in the south, and this too probably led to political

---

8. For an account of Israelite political history during the Omri and Jehu dynasties, see Hayes and Miller, *History*, 305–54. For Assyria's interactions with Israel through the fall of Samaria, see Machinist, "Hosea," 155–56. For a discussion of Israelite interactions with the Transjordanian states in this period, see E. Bloch-Smith, "A Stratified Account of Jephthah's Negotiations and Battle: Judges 11:12–33 from an Archaeological Perspective," *JBL* 134 (2015) 291–311. For a discussion of the economic implications of the Israelite political situation, see D. N. Premnath, *Eighth Century Prophets: A Social Analysis* (St. Louis: Chalice, 2003), 46–50. For a more extensive account of Israel's history in this period, see Antoon Schoors, *The Kingdoms of Israel and Judah in the Eighth and Seventh Centuries* B.C.E. (trans. M. Lesley; Atlanta: SBL, 2013).

conflict. In contrast, for practical purposes, there was only one important lineage in the south: the tribe of Judah. This fact suggests that lineages played a less prominent political role in the south than they did in the north.[9]

Attitudes toward the State in Amos

Little is known about the prophet Amos or the specific details of his activities. The superscription to the book bearing his name identifies him as a *nōqēd* from the Judean town of Tekoa, just south of Bethlehem. The title given to him is usually understood to refer to a shepherd of some sort. The only other occurrence of the title is in 2 Kgs 3:4, where it is applied to the King of Moab, who is said to have paid Ahab of Israel a tribute of 100,000 lambs and the wool of 100,000 rams. The association of the title with sheep-keeping is reinforced by Akkadian cognates and by the rare term *bōqēr*, herder, which Amos applies to himself in Amos 7:14. In Ugaritic, the word *nqd* appears in a colophon as one of several political and religious titles held by the scribe (*KTU* 1.6 vi 53–57), and the word occurs in other texts linked to various sorts of officials (*KTU* 4.68 71; 4.103 44). All of these references have suggested to interpreters that the prophet was no simple sheepherder but may have held some position in Judah's state or temple bureaucracy, although there is still no agreement on this point.[10]

The superscription also identifies the time during which the prophet was active. His revelatory visions occurred during the reigns of Uzziah of Judah (785–760? B.C.E.) and Jeroboam II of Israel (768–748 B.C.E.), and, more specifically, two years before the earthquake, an event not elsewhere recorded. Given the book's references to political instability (Amos 1–2) and economic stratification (Amos 3–6), it is likely that Amos was active during the latter years of Jeroboam's reign, when his earlier political successes had begun to disintegrate. Most scholars are content to assign the majority of the book's oracles to this period, although there is some evidence of later editing that has caused a few interpreters to opt for a longer period of prophetic activity. For example, some scholars have detected signs of Deuteronomistic language and theology, particularly in Amos 9:11–15, which describes a restoration of the Davidic empire, a rebuilding of Jerusalem, and the return of people to the land.[11] This passage clearly reflects knowledge of

---

9. For an analysis of the differences between the Israelite and Judean states, see D. E. Fleming, *The Legacy of Israel in Judah's Bible: History, Politics, and the Reinscribing of Tradition* (Cambridge: Cambridge University Press, 2012), 24–27.

10. For a recent thorough discussion of the problem, see R. C. Steiner, *Stockmen from Tekoa, Sycamores from Sheba: A Study of Amos' Occupations*, CBQMS 36 (Washington, D.C.: Catholic Biblical Association, 2003). For a more conservative view, see F. I. Andersen and D. N. Freedman, *Amos* (AB 24A; New York: Doubleday, 1989), 187–88; and S. M. Paul, *Amos: A Commentary on the Book of Amos*, Hermeneia (Minneapolis: Fortress, 1991), 34–35.

11. W. H. Schmidt, "Die deuteronomistische Redaktion des Amosbuches," *ZAW* 77 (1965) 168–93.

the Babylonian exile and must be a later addition. The notion of the exile of the Northern Kingdom also appears in 5:27 and in the oracles against Jeroboam and Amaziah in 7:11, 17. These references have suggested to some scholars that Amos was active after the fall of Samaria, although later scribal interpretation could be invoked as an alternative explanation.[12]

A summary of Amos's message appears at the very beginning of the book: "Yahweh roars from Zion and utters his voice from Jerusalem; the pastures of the shepherds wither, and the top of Carmel dries up" (1:2). The southern prophet thus receives a divine message from Yahweh who dwells in the temple in Jerusalem, but the message is aimed at the people and sanctuaries of Israel. The oracles of Amos are addressed to various audiences. Sometimes the people as a whole are condemned (4:4–12; 5:1–7; 5:10–24), and sometimes the oracles are directed against the northern sanctuaries, particularly the sanctuary at Bethel (3:14; 4:4–5; 5:6). However, the more normal addressees are the elites who have benefited from the centralized government originally set up by Omri and continued by his successors. These elites are never identified by name or title but are addressed only as the ones who have perpetuated the oppression brought about by the stratified society that the monarchy created. They sell the righteous, trample the poor, push aside the afflicted, appropriate the money they have taken from the poor, and defile their own sanctuaries (2:6–8). In general, the complaints are against those at the top of the hierarchical social and economic system, whose position should also have given them certain obligations to maintain the welfare of those below them in the hierarchy. Yet the elites pervert justice, oppress the poor, and in general engage in behavior that dramatizes their superiority. They have multiple houses and houses made of hewn stone (3:10, 15; 5:11; 6:8). They indulge in lavish feasts (4:1; 5:11; 6:4, 6), use choice oils, recline on beds inlaid with ivory, and drink to excess (6:1–7).

It is not clear who these elites are. They are certainly people who have benefited from centralized government and the economic stratification that this form of political organization has created. They are certainly land-owners and very likely run businesses. They might also be lineage elders with judicial and political responsibilities. However, their relationship to the monarchy is unclear, and they are never condemned for being part of the royal court. Furthermore, in only one place does the text actually condemn the king or a high official, and that is in 7:11, 16–17. In this passage, Amaziah, the priest at the Bethel sanctuary, informs Jeroboam that Amos has delivered a judgment oracle against him, although the quoted oracle does not actually appear elsewhere in the book. Amos in turn delivers a judgment against Amaziah, not because of his abuse of his position but because

---

12. For an argument favoring a longer period of activity for Amos, see M. Haran, "The Historical Background of the Prophecies of Amos," in *Birkat Shalom: Studies in the Bible, Ancient Near Eastern Literature, and Postbiblical Judaism Presented to Shalom M. Paul on the Occasion of His Seventieth Birthday* (ed. C. Cohen et al.; Winona Lake, IN: Eisenbrauns, 2008), 1:251–59.

he has tried to prevent Amos from speaking. Other than this passage, which some scholars consider to be secondary, the book contains no specific oracles against an individual king, and it does not appear to reflect any negative opinions about Israelite kingship in general.

This fact has greatly disturbed some scholars, who read the book as if it were an oblique condemnation of the state, if not an explicit one. For this reason, there have been recent efforts to argue that all of the elites mentioned in the book were members of the royal court. This argument proceeds by giving evidence that Israel did indeed have an elaborate bureaucracy, complete with royal titles, but none of these titles can actually be found in Amos.[13] In the end, then, Amos seems to be worried about the social and economic abuses created by the existence of the state, but the book does not argue for a return to an alternative lineage form of governance.

Just as the Book of Amos does not try to mount a case against Israelite kingship, it also does not make a sustained case in support of the Davidic monarchy in Judah. Only in one passage is there a suggestion that the prophet understands the Judean monarchy to be superior to the one in the north. In Amos 9:8, there is a threat to destroy the "evil kingdom" and to blot it out completely. However, the verse then immediately promises not to completely destroy the "house of Jacob." By itself, this remark could be interpreted as a promise of a remnant in Israel. If that was the book's original intent, it has been thwarted by the long promise oracle that follows in 9:11–15, which talks about the restoration of the "booth of David" (perhaps the temple or the city of Jerusalem?) and looks forward to reestablishing the exiled people in their land. This is clearly an exilic or postexilic passage that is aware of the Babylonian captivity, and the phrasing of the promise suggests that the identity of the Northern Kingdom of Israel has now been absorbed into the reality of a restored Judah.[14]

Some scholars have also tried to see a pro-Judean perspective in the oracles against the nations in Amos 1:3–2:16. The argument in support of this position points out that when 2:4–5, an oracle against Judah, is set aside as a later addition, the remaining oracles against Damascus, Gaza, Tyre, Edom, Ammon, Moab, and Israel all deal with treaty violations involving states that were once part of the old Davidic empire. These nations would have had treaty relations with David and therefore obligations toward one another. As far as Amos is concerned, those treaties are still in effect, but they have been violated by the actions of the nations. All of the activities condemned in the oracles, including those of Israel, will be punished by the God who dwells in Jerusalem, and a new era of harmony can

---

13. For a detailed presentation of the argument, see I. Jaruzelska, *Amos and the Officialdom in the Kingdom of Israel: The Socio-economic Position of the Officials in the Light of the Biblical, the Epigraphic and Archaeological Evidence* (Poznan: Wydawnietwo Naukowe Uniwersytetu, 1998).

14. For this argument, see G. Goswell, "David in the Prophecy of Amos," *VT* 61 (2011) 243–57.

be possible with the restoration of David's old empire.[15] However, the difficulty with this argument is that although the biblical text claims that David had friendly relations with the nations mentioned in Amos 1–2, the archaeological data pertaining to the Northern Kingdom of Israel suggest that treaty relations with the Philistines, Phoenicians, Arameans, and the Transjordanian states fit better into the period of Omri and his successors than they do into the Davidic period. If this is true, then Amos's oracles against the nations remain something of a puzzle. It would seem to be the case that the prophet is arguing that Jerusalem's God is endorsing judgment against the breakup of Omri's expanded state. The utility of pressing such a position is not clear, although it may be that these oracles are from the same editorial layer that added the Pro-Davidic material in Amos 9:11–15. In this case, the oracles against the nations might be intended as a prelude to a Judean takeover of the Northern Kingdom in its expanded form, after the fall of Samaria. Such an idea, however, is purely speculative.[16]

Finally, it is somewhat ironic that Assyria, the state that will eventually destroy Israel, plays no explicit role in Amos's oracles. The texts do mention exile as a punishment (5:5, 27; 6:7; 7:11; 9:4), and exile was a standard Assyrian political tool, but there is no reference to the Assyrians as God's agent for punishing Israel.[17] Rather Amos seems to imply that God acts directly in various ways to chastise the people of the northern state, and the Assyrians are only one means of implementing God's plans.

Attitudes Toward the State in Hosea

Almost nothing is known about the prophet Hosea as an individual. The superscription to the book (Hos 1:1) identifies him only as the son of Beeri, who is otherwise unknown. The text itself never portrays him delivering oracles in a particular geographical location, but the contents of the book seem to focus primarily on the Northern Kingdom, and this fact has led scholars to assume that he was an Israelite prophet. This traditional understanding is reinforced by the fact that most of the places referred to in his oracles are located in the north: Samaria (Hos 7:1; 8:5–6; 10:5, 7; 14:1); Bethel (Hos 4:15; 5:8; 10:5; 12:5); Gilgal (Hos 4:15; 9:15; 12:12); the Valley of Achor (Hos 2:17); Adam (Hos 6:7); Ramah, Gibeah (Hos 5:8); and Gilead (Hos 6:8; 12:12).

---

15. For various arguments in favor of this position, see G. E. Wright, "The Nations in Hebrew Prophecy," *Encounter* 26 (1965) 236; J. Mauchline, "Implicit Signs of a Persistent Belief in the Davidic Empire," *VT* 20 (1970) 287–303; and M. E. Polley, *Amos and the Davidic Empire: A Socio-Historical Approach* (Oxford: Oxford University Press, 1989), 55–82.

16. See Goswell, "David," 243–57.

17. In Amos 3:6, the LXX does replace the reference to Ashdod with a reference to Assyria, thus making both Assyria and Egypt witnesses to the turmoil in Samaria and possibly the agents of its punishment. However, rather than being a recovery of Amos's original text, this shift in the LXX could also be attributed to later scribal reinterpretation.

The superscription also dates the prophet's activities to the reign of the Israelite king Jeroboam II (788–748 B.C.E.), as is also the case with Amos. However, in addition, Hosea is said to have worked during the reigns of the Judean kings Uzziah (785–760? B.C.E.), Jotham (759–744 B.C.E.), Ahaz (735–715 B.C.E.), and Hezekiah (715–687/86 B.C.E.). This chronology, if it is accurate, suggests that Hosea's activities continued well past the fall of Samaria in 722 B.C.E., or at least work on Hosea's book continued for that length of time. The superscription also raises the question of why the northern kings who reigned between Jeroboam's death in 748 B.C.E. and the fall of Samaria in 722 B.C.E. are not mentioned. Scholars have tended to approach this problem in two ways. The first is to treat the list of Judean kings as an expansion of an earlier version of the superscription that mentioned only Uzziah. The second is to suggest that the omission of the Israelite kings following Jeroboam II is an indication that the scribes who wrote the superscription did not accept the legitimacy of the last kings of Israel. If the latter explanation is accepted, then the kings who ruled at the end of Israel's national life may be the ones condemned in Hosea.[18]

No matter how the problem of the superscription is resolved, most scholars accept the claim that the original prophet worked in Israel, in the 8th century, probably toward the end of Jeroboam's reign.[19] Interpreters also agree, however, that the original collection of prophecies was later edited and reinterpreted by scribes, who may or may not have been part of the "school" of Hosea that preserved the book. This later shaping of Hosea is indicated by the book's contents, which suggest knowledge of events after the time of Jeroboam II. Hosea 10:3, for example, refers to a time when Israel had no king, and this reference may suggest that the writer knew of the fall of Samaria. Similarly, Hos 1:7 speaks of God personally saving Judah by nonmilitary means, a possible reference to the miraculous deliverance of Jerusalem during Hezekiah's reign, when the Assyrian king Sennacherib threatened the city in 701 B.C.E. It has recently been suggested that other references to Sennacherib also appear in the book, and if this should turn out to be true, then it would indicate scribal activity on Hosea at least as late as the 7th century.[20] Scholars have even suggested that scribal shaping continued well into the Persian Period, although major revision of the book in that late period seems unlikely.[21] It is important to remember, though, that any literary revisions that

---

18. For a discussion of this issue, see H. W. Wolff, *Hosea: A Commentary on the Book of the Prophet Hosea*, Hermeneia (trans. G. Stansell; Philadelphia: Fortress, 1974), 2–4; A. A. Macintosh, *A Critical and Exegetical Commentary on Hosea*, ICC (Edinburgh: T. & T. Clark, 1997), 1–4; and Machinist, "Hosea," 156.

19. See, for example, J. L. Mays, *Hosea*, OTL (Philadelphia: Westminster, 1969), 3–5; Francis I. Andersen and David Noel Freedman, *Hosea*, AB 24 (Garden City, NY: Doubleday, 1980), 31–39; Wolff, *Hosea*, xxi; and Machinist, "Hosea," 155.

20. For a discussion of possible references to Sennacherib, see H. D. Dewrell, "Yareb, Shalman, and the Date of the Book of Hosea," *CBQ* 78 (2016) 413–29.

21. For a discussion of the lengthy literary history of Hosea, see S. Rudnig-Zelt, *Hoseastudien: Redaktionskritische Untersuchungen zur Genese des Hoseabuches*, FRLANT 213 (Göttingen:

occurred after 722 B.C.E. would likely have taken place in Judah rather than in an Israel that was part of the Assyrian empire.

Another feature of Hosea that needs to be noted is the fact that it seems to be strongly associated with the language and thought of the Deuteronomic movement. This feature of the book has often been analyzed and has been used in arguments about the northern origins of Deuteronomism. It has sometimes been suggested that Hosea was in fact the creator of Deuteronomic thought, although it is probably more accurate to consider Hosea to be a reflection of Deuteronomistic ideas and language that were already in circulation, ideas that later influenced other literary works. The most commonly accepted theory about the spread of Deuteronomism assumes that it developed in the north and then moved south to the Jerusalem area after Israel became part of the Asyrian empire following the destruction of Samaria. In Judah, the Deuteronomistic traditions crystalized in the Book of Deuteronomy, an early version of which was "discovered" in the Jerusalem Temple in Josiah's time, and the traditions were also reflected in the so-called Deuteronomistic History. If this understanding of the matter is accurate, then scribes working on Hosea, who themselves may have been influenced by Deuteronomism, probably carried out their work in Judah, and this fact may well have influenced their treatment of the Southern Kingdom in the book.[22]

Interpreters usually consider Hosea to be concerned primarily with opposing Israel's worship of the god Baal, whose presence became more prominent in Israel during the Omride dynasty. Along with tirades against Baal worship, the prophet encourages the traditional worship of Yahweh and urges a return to the covenant with Yahweh that Israel had broken. Along with theological reflections on the perversion of the relationship between God and Israel, which is the primary focus of the elaborate symbolic actions in Hosea 1–3, the prophet also condemns inappropriate worship at Israel's traditional cult centers, particularly the veneration of the bull images at Bethel (Hos 4:15; 5:8; 10:5; 12:5). The prophet also speaks out against worship at the high places (Hos 4:13; cf. Deut 12:2) and describes the folly of worshiping idols (Hos 8:6; 13:2; 14:4; cf. Deut 4:28; 28:36, 64; 31:29; 2 Kgs 19:18).

However, in contrast to Amos, Hosea has a great deal to say about the Israelite kings and the officials in the royal bureaucracy. Most of what he says about them is negative. The book actually begins with the condemnation of a specific king, Jehu,

---

Vandenhoeck & Ruprecht, 2006). A Persian period date for the entire book has been suggested by J. M. Bos, *Reconsidering the Date and Provenance of the Book of Hosea: The Case for Persian-Period Yehud*, LHBOTS 580 (London: Bloomsbury, 2013).

22. For a discussion of the northern origins of Deuteronomism and its relationship to Hosea, see M. Weinfeld, *Deuteronomy and the Deuteronomic School* (Oxford: Oxford University Press, 1972; repr., Winona Lake, IN: Eisenbrauns, 1992), 364–70; H. L. Ginsberg, *The Israelian Heritage of Judaism* (New York: Jewish Theological Seminary of America, 1982), 1, 19–22; Machinist, "Hosea," 173; and Bos, *Date and Provenance*, 16–21.

because of the blood that he shed overthrowing the last of the dynasty of Omri, and establishing a new dynasty, of which Jeroboam II was a part (Hos 1:4; cf. 2 Kgs 9–10). Recalling this event at the beginning of the book suggests that the typical actions that kings take to acquire political power and to retain that power lead to evil and corrupt all levels of the hierarchical political structure. What begins as the sin of one king will later be seen as a flaw in the whole institution of kingship.

The negative evaluation of Israelite kingship appears throughout the book. In Hos 5:1–2, the priests, the house of the king, and all the people of Israel are called to hear God's decree of judgment against them, because the king and priests have lead the people to sin by worshiping Baal at Mizpah, Tabor, and Shittim. In an obscure oracle in Hos 6:11–7:7, people and king seem to engage in mutually destructive acts, with the result that all of the kings fall, and none of them call on Yahweh. The same theme is repeated in Hos 7:16, which talks about the officials falling because they turn away from the God who is waiting to redeem them. In Hos 9:15, God threatens not to love Israel because their officials are rebellious. Because of rebellion, the king in Samaria is also being cut off, and the high places and sinful Israel will be destroyed (Hos 10:7–8). Eventually the situation becomes so serious that the institution of kingship itself is questioned. God complains that the people insisted on installing kings and officials without consulting the deity and getting divine approval, and for this reason neither the kings nor the officials are legitimate (Hos 8:4; cf. the divine election of the king in Deut 17:15). God has also destroyed kings because they trusted in their military power rather than seeking divine help (Hos 10:13–15; cf. Deut 20). Once the king is gone, the people complain that the king was useless anyway (Hos 10:1–4). Finally, Israel recognizes that God is the true king of Israel, and God admits that when the people asked for a king, God gave them one in anger and then took him away in wrath (Hos 13:9–11). Many of these passages have a resonance with the stories about the rise of kingship in Israel that are now preserved in the Deuteronomistic History (1 Sam 8–12). In these texts, too, the Israelites are said to have been ambivalent about kingship, recognizing both its strengths and weaknesses.

In only two passages in Hosea is the Israelite king viewed positively, and in both cases kingship is viewed positively because Israel and Judah again join together. Both of the passages refer to a return from exile. In Hos 1:11 (Heb. 2:2), the people of Judah and the people of Israel will in the future join together under one head. A similar theme is found in Hos 3:4–5, which speaks of the people of Israel dwelling for a long time without kings, officials, or the means of worship. After this exile, Israel will again seek Yahweh and David their king.

When thinking about the Northern Kingdom, then, Hosea views the state negatively, and kingship itself is considered an institution that causes trouble. It is tempting to think that Hosea has this attitude because of the traditional lineage structure of the north, which would favor decentralized government. However, Hosea does not suggest that the lineage is the ideal form of political organization.

Rather, the prophet finally longs for a future in which Israel and Judah are reunited under a restored Davidic ruler. This shift from a negative to a positive view of kingship may be the result of the northern Deuteronomistic traditions coming south after the fall of Samaria and perhaps being influenced by the royal theology of Jerusalem. In this connection, it is interesting to note that the Deuteronomistic History displays a similar tension in its attitudes toward decentralized and centralized government. In Deut 17:14–20, the king in the Deuteronomic state has no power and is subservient to the Torah. In general, local governance prevails throughout the Deuteronomic polity. In the Book of Kings, all of the northern kings and some of the southern ones are evaluated negatively. Yet, the History also accepts the Judean claim that God has elected the Davidic house in perpetuity (2 Sam 7).

It comes as no surprise, then, to discover that Hosea has a more positive view of the state in Judah than in the north. To be sure, there are some northern judgment oracles that are secondarily applied to Judah, as in Hos 6:11, where the writer suggests that the preceding oracle against Israel also applies to Judah, although no elaboration of this remark appears in the text. A similar situation may exist in Hos 12:2 (Heb. 12:3), which begins as an oracle against Judah but then continues in a way that appears to be a theological reflection on the history of the Northern Kingdom. Only in Hos 5:8–14 are Israel and Judah paired in a mutual prophecy of judgment. However, Hosea's usual stance toward Judah is a positive one. In Hos 11:12 (Heb. 12:1), sinful Israel is contrasted with faithful Judah, which is still in the right relationship with God. The same contrast is found in Hos 1:6–7, where God refuses to have pity on Israel but will have pity on Judah and personally save it through divine action. A similar idea lies behind Hos 4:15, which is a plea that Judah not become like faithless Israel. Finally, as noted above, Hosea looks forward to Israel's repentance and return to God and to "David their king" (Hos 3:1–5).

In contrast to Amos, Hosea does not seem to be too concerned with the particular states that immediately surround Israel. In general, the notion of mixing with the nations is evaluated negatively and seen as a form of punishment (Hos 7:8). However, Hosea does share with the Deuteronomists a fear of alliances with the great powers for political purposes (Hos 5:13; 7:11; 8:8–10; cf. 2 Kgs 15:19–20; 17:3). Not surprisingly, given the book's original setting, the prophet holds particularly harsh views of the Assyrians, who are thought to be unreliable political partners with whom Israel should not try to negotiate (Hos 5:8–6:6), and the prophet looks forward to the time when Israel will recognize that Assyria cannot replace God as Israel's savior (Hos 14:3). However, the book also knows that Assyria will eventually be Israel's king (Hos 11:5), and the prophet views the Assyrians as the means by which God will punish Israel (Hos 10:6).

In conclusion, then, it is clear that these two 8th-century prophets did not hold a single consistent view of the state. Rather, their views varied considerably, depending on whether the state in question was Israel, Judah, one of the surrounding nations, or one of the great powers. It is probably impossible to understand the reasons for this variety of opinions with any certainty. It is always possible that Amos and Hosea were not consistent in the contents of their prophecies and that they simply reported their revelations as they occurred. However, it is more likely that the prophets and their later interpreters developed different understandings of the state in response to the changing circumstances within which the divine words were heard and reheard. Prophecy, after all, reflects an effort at communication between the divine and human worlds. In that process, the divine word is not exhausted by a single human understanding. Rather, human understanding is an ongoing process, and even the now-fixed biblical texts are a testimony to that process.

Bibliography

Andersen, F. and D. N. Freedman. *Hosea*. AB 24. Garden City, NY: Doubleday, 1980.

_____. *Amos*. AB 24A. New York: Doubleday, 1989.

Bloch-Smith, E. "A Stratified Account of Jephthah's Negotiations and Battle: Judges 11:12–33 from an Archaeological Perspective." *JBL* 134 (2015) 291–311.

Day, J. "Hosea and the Baal Cult." Pp. 202–24 in *Prophecy and Prophets in Ancient Israel*. Edited by J. Day. LHBOTS 531. London: T. & T. Clark, 2010.

Faust, A. *The Archaeology of Israelite Society in Iron Age II*. Winona Lake, IN: Eisenbrauns, 2012.

Fleming, D. E. *The Legacy of Israel in Judah's Bible: History, Politics, and the Reinscribing of Tradition*. Cambridge: Cambridge University Press, 2012.

Floyd, M. H. "New Form Criticism and Beyond: The Historicity of Prophetic Literature Revisited." Pp. 17–36 in *The Book of the Twelve & the New Form Criticism*. Edited by M. J. Boda, M. H. Floyd, and C. M. Toffelmire. Atlanta: SBL Press, 2015.

Goswell, G. "David in the Prophecy of Amos." *VT* 61 (2011) 243–257.

Haran, M. "The Historical Background of the Prophecies of Amos." Pages 251–259 in vol. 1 of *Birkat Shalom: Studies in the Bible, Ancient Near Eastern Literature, and Postbiblical Judaism Presented to Shalom M. Paul on the Occasion of His Seventieth Birthday*. Edited by Chaim Cohen et al. Winona Lake, IN: Eisenbrauns, 2008.

Holladay, J. S., Jr. "The Kingdoms of Israel and Judah: Political and Economic Centralization in the Iron IIA–B (ca. 1000–750 BCE." Pp. 368–98 in *The Archaeology of Society in the Holy Land*. Edited by Thomas E. Levy. London: Leicester University Press, 1995.

Lemos, T. M. "Kinship, Community, and Society." Pp. 379–95 in *The Wiley Blackwell Companion to Ancient Israel*. Edited by S. Niditch. Chichester: Wiley Blackwell, 2016.

Machinist, P. "Hosea and the Ambiguity of Kingship in Ancient Israel." Pp. 153–81 in *Constituting the Community: Studies on the Polity of Ancient Israel in Honor of S. Dean McBride Jr.* Edited by J. T. Strong and S. S. Tuell. Winona Lake, IN: Eisenbrauns, 2005.

Macintosh, A. A. *A Critical and Exegetical Commentary on Hosea*. ICC. Edinburgh: T. & T. Clark, 1997.

Mays, J. L. *Hosea*. Old Testament Library. Philadelphia: Westminster, 1969.

Miller, J. M. and J. H. Hayes. *A History of Ancient Israel and Judah*. 2nd ed. Louisville: Westminster John Knox, 2006.

Paul, S. M. *Amos: A Commentary on the Book of Amos*. Hermeneia. Minneapolis: Fortress, 1991.

Polley, M. E. *Amos and the Davidic Empire: A Socio-Historical Approach*. Oxford: Oxford University Press, 1989.

Schmidt, W. H. "Die deuteronomistische Redaktion des Amosbuches." *ZAW* 77 (1965) 168–93.

Schoors, A. *The Kingdoms of Israel and Judah in the Eighth and Seventh Centuries B.C.E.* Trans. M. Lesley. Atlanta: SBL, 2013.

Stager, L. E. "The Archaeology of the Family in Ancient Israel." *BASOR* 260 (1985) 1–35.

Wilson, R. R. *Genealogy and History in the Biblical World*. Yale Near Eastern Researches 7. New Haven, CT: Yale University Press, 1977.

Wolff, H. W. *Hosea: A Commentary on the Book of the Prophet Hosea*. Trans. G. Stansell. Hermeneia. Philadelphia: Fortress, 1974.

Enemies and Friends of the State:
First Isaiah and Micah

J. J. M. ROBERTS

Professor Emeritus, Princeton Theological Seminary

First Isaiah—or, more precisely, the 8th-century B.C.E. Isaiah of Jerusalem—and his contemporary, Micah of Moresheth, a city in the Judean Shephelah southwest of Jerusalem, were citizens of the Judean state. Shaped by the theological traditions that undergirded that state, they also remained friends of the Judean state despite their often severe criticism of their government's policies and their occasional bitter disagreements with and sometimes personal enmity toward many in the Judean governmental elite. In contrast, one must regard them as enemies of the northern state of Israel, though they were concerned for and regarded the Israelite citizens of the northern state as kinfolk and ideally fellow worshipers of YHWH. That Isaiah and Micah were critical of the governmental policies of both Israel and Judah should not be allowed to obscure the fact that their attitudes toward their own state, Judah, was more favorable than those toward the secessionist and idolatrous north.

In contrast to their 8th-century prophetic contemporaries, the northern prophet Hosea and the Judean prophet Amos, who prophesied in the north at Bethel, there is no reliable evidence that either Isaiah or Micah ever visited, much less actually gave a prophetic oracle in, the territory of the Northern Kingdom. Isaiah's ministry, as far as we know, was exercised in Jerusalem, and Micah's in all likelihood may have been, since the temple in Jerusalem would be a major draw for Judean prophets, particularly after Hezekiah's religious reforms shut down the sanctuaries in the countryside (2 Kgs 18:4–6; 2 Chr 30–31).[1] But the truth of the matter is that we do not know where Micah gave his oracles. The biblical text of Micah and other relatively early traditions about Micah preserved in Jeremiah (Jer 26:18–19) are basically silent on the subject, and we must be honest about the limitations of our knowledge.

---

1. A. G. Vaughn, *Theology, History, and Archaeology in the Chronicler's Account of Hezekiah* (Atlanta: Scholars, 1999).

On the other hand, both Micah and Isaiah apparently addressed oracles to the Northern Kingdom (Mic 1:2–7; 2:12–13; 5:7–15; 6:9–16; Isa 2:5–22; 9:7–20 and 5:26–30; 8:9–10; 17:1–14; 28:1–6). Many of the passages in Micah are questionable, however, since the book of Micah sometimes uses the language of Jacob and Israel in an inclusive sense, to refer to Judean authorities rather than just Israelite officials. Mic 3:9–10 is a case in point, since "the rulers of the house of Jacob and chiefs of the house of Israel . . . who build Zion with blood and Jerusalem with wrong" must be Judean rulers. Northern officials would not be building Zion at all.

Nonetheless, despite the slight evidence for Micah addressing oracles to the Northern Kingdom and the much clearer evidence for Isaiah doing so, the total lack of evidence that either actually spoke to a real northern audience suggests that we should consider that they addressed northern audiences as fictive audiences, as mere rhetorical devices. The real audience was a southern audience, and that has a significant bearing on whether such messages reveal the prophets as enemies or friends of the state. In the context of the Syro-Ephraimitic War of 735–732, for instance, a negative oracle of judgment against Israel would, at least on one level, be a positive oracle of salvation for Judah: so Isa 2; 8:9–10; 9; 17; and 28:1–6. But, of course, the issue is more complex than this. Most oracles of salvation, whether rhetorically addressed as a threat to an enemy nation or more straightforwardly addressed to the leadership of one's own nation as a promise, normally have an element of conditionality to them. The promise is usually conditional on the national leadership responding in an appropriate fashion to the foreign threat, and what the prophet and the prophet's God considers the appropriate response is often counterintuitive to the political and military calculations of the nation's ruling elite. This may be easily illustrated from a number of Isaiah's oracles.

In Isa 7:4–9, Isaiah and his small son Shear-jashub go out to meet Ahaz and his royal retinue, who are inspecting Jerusalem's water supply in panicked anticipation of an imminent attack by Rezin of Damascus and Pekah, the son of Remaliah, of Samaria. Isaiah reassures Ahaz that the plans of his Aramean and Ephraimite enemies will neither succeed nor come to pass. YHWH's promises to Jerusalem and the Davidic house will stand firm. But—and this is the conditional "but" mentioned above—if Ahaz and his court advisers (note the plural verb) do not believe and trust Isaiah's oracle, they (again the plural verb) will not stand firm (v. 9).[2] The promise is repeated in a second oracle involving a second child, Immanuel (7:10–17), and this time the promise is that the Aramean and Ephraimite threat will be neutralized before this child reaches the age of weaning, but the prophet's irritation with the king's reluctance to ask for a sign from YHWH confirming the promise (vv. 11–13) shows that Ahaz and his advisers were unwilling

---

2. See J. J. M. Roberts, "The Context, Text, and Logic of Isaiah 7.7–9," in *Inspired Speech: Prophecy in the Ancient Near East: Essays in Honour of Herbert B. Huffmon* (ed. J. Kaltner and L. Stulman; JSOTS 378; London: T. & T. Clark, 2004), 161–70.

to simply trust in the promises of YHWH's protection and were planning a different course of action.[3] The promise that the plans of these foreign enemies will be thwarted by YHWH is repeated a third time with yet a third child, Maher-shalal-hash-baz, involving an even shorter time limit (Isa 8:1–10), but the Judean court's refusal to trust leads Isaiah to threaten Judah with being flooded up to the neck with the same Assyrian enemy that will deluge Israel (vv. 5–8). The full narrative makes it clear that Isaiah was pushing Ahaz to trust in YHWH and not to ask Tiglath-pileser III, the Assyrian king, for help against his enemies. The reluctance of Ahaz and the court to ask for a sign was clearly perceived by Isaiah as an excuse, lamely disguised as piety, to avoid being constrained into accepting the prophet's advice, when the court had already decided on a different course of action. This conflict between Isaiah's insistence that the royal court trust in and rely on the promises of YHWH to Jerusalem and the Davidic house, versus the penchant of the royal court to opt for defensive alliances with strong military allies—whether Assyria, Nubian Egypt and their Philistine clients, or an independent Babylon and its Elamite backers—characterized the debate between the prophet and his opponents in the Judean court during the whole course of his ministry. His repeated promises of deliverance for Jerusalem hinged on the Judean royal court trusting in the divine promises, and when the court rejected those promises in reliance on their substitute human plans, Isaiah threatened that Jerusalem's deliverance would only come after a punitive near-death experience.[4]

Isaiah's attitude toward the northern state was more uniformly negative, as one might expect from a Judean immersed in the Zion Tradition. He regarded Israel's participation with the Arameans, and perhaps the Philistines, in the Syro-Ephraimitic attack on Jerusalem as an idolatrous Israelite betrayal of its own God and its own people (Isa 2:5–6; cf. 17:10),[5] and like the northern Hosea, he had little respect for the kings and political elite of Israel in that state's final years (Isa 28:1–6). The arrogance of the failed state's elite astounded him, even as he chronicled how the sectional rivalries within the Northern Kingdom devoured the nation in a cannibalistic orgy of self-destruction (Isa 9:7–20). Micah appears to have shared this basically negative view of the Northern Kingdom and its ruling elite, who provide a model of wickedness for him. He appears to castigate the Judean leadership for keeping "the statutes of Omri, and all the works of the house of Ahab, and for following their counsels" (Mic 6:16). It is probably this same linking of the behavior of the Judean elite with the abhorrent model of their corrupt northern

---

3. Idem, "Isaiah and His Children," in *Biblical and Related Studies Presented to Samuel Iwry* (ed. A. Kort and S. Morschauser; Winona Lake, IN: Eisenbrauns, 1985), 193–203.

4. See the broader discussion of this point in idem, "Isaiah, National Security, and the Politics of Fear," in *The Bible and the American Future* (ed. R. Jewett, W. L. Alloway Jr., and J. G. Lacey; Eugene, OR: Cascade Books [Wipf and Stock], 2009), 72–92; and idem, "Security and Justice in Isaiah," *Stone-Campbell Journal* 13 (2010) 71–9.

5. See idem, "Isaiah 2 and the Prophet's Message to the North," *JQR* 75 (1985) 290–308.

counterparts that led Micah to address the Judean elite who built Zion with blood as "the rulers of the house Jacob and chiefs of the house of Israel" (Mic 3:9–10). This is not an innocuous, generic inclusive use of Jacob and Israel to refer to all Israel, but a judgmental reference to the elite of Judah as just as wicked and judicially perverted as their northern models. Moreover, Micah, like Isaiah, regarded the Northern Kingdom as idolatrous, and Samaria's destruction was a just judgment on all her images and idols (Mic 1:7).

On the other hand, if both Micah and Isaiah could be regarded as enemies of the northern state of Israel, they both had a more hopeful view toward at least the remnant of the citizens of that state. According to the heading of the book, Micah's prophetic ministry took place during the reign of three Judean kings, Jotham, Ahaz, and Hezekiah (Mic 1:1)—or basically during the same period as Isaiah's ministry. This may suggest that some of Micah's oracles, originally given well before Sennacherib's campaign in 701 B.C.E., may have been revised and reused in a later context with an updated and slightly different meaning. The oracle in Mic 2:12–13, for instance, addressed to Jacob and the survivors of Israel, may have originally been addressed to the survivors of the Northern Kingdom after the disaster of 734–732 B.C.E. or the later disaster of 725–722 B.C.E. The promise to the remnant of Jacob in Mic 5:7–15 may likewise have originally been a promise to the remnant of the Northern Kingdom well before Sennacherib's devastation of Judah. In contrast, the promise of the return of the former dominion of Jerusalem and the return of exiles to Zion (Mic 4:6–13), the coming of the new Davidic king and the return of "the rest of his kindred (Mic 5:3)," and the return of exiles from Assyria and Egypt to resettle, not just in Judah, but in Bashan and Gilead, northern territories, as in the days of old (Mic 7:12–14), probably dates to the period during or, more likely, soon after Sennacherib devastation of Judah and deportation of a significant portion of the Judean population. The promise of return and renewal is not limited to the exiled Judeans but includes the former inhabitants of the Northern Kingdom as well. Note that the return is primarily from Assyria and Egypt (Mic 7:12), not from Babylon, and the enemy mentioned is Assyria (Mic 5:5–6), not the Babylonians. Babylon is mentioned as the place from which Zion will be rescued in Mic 4:10, but this is the only mention of Babylon in the book, and it is unclear whether Babylon was simply the location to which some Judean exiles were deported by the Assyrians, or whether this is just a later gloss to update the book in the time of the Babylonian exile.

Isaiah also had a word of hope for the remnant of the Northern Kingdom, even early on, when he was announcing Ephraim's destruction and the failure of its plans against Jerusalem. In Isa 10:20–23, he proclaimed that the remnant of Israel and the survivors of the house of Jacob would no longer rely on the one who had smitten them—that is, Rezin of Damascus, but upon Yhwh the Holy One of Israel, and a remnant would return (שְׁאָר יָשׁוּב, the name of Isaiah's first child, who was with him at his initial confrontation with Ahaz), a remnant of Jacob to the mighty God (אל גבור, one of the crown names of the ideal Davidic king in Isa 9:5), a motif that suggests Isaiah expected a remnant of the Northern Kingdom to return under the hegemony of the Davidic kings of Judah, a view also supported by his admonition to the house of Jacob in Isa 2:5–22. Even after Sennacherib's decimation of Judah in 701 B.C.E., Isaiah still expected a remnant of the outcasts of Israel as well as the dispersed of Judah to return to their land and, without their former hostility and jealousy toward one another, to be united in their conquest of their former enemies both east and west (Isa 11:11–16). This return of the exiles of Israel and Judah was to be from Assyria and Egypt, not Babylon, and there is no compelling reason to late-date this oracle to the period of the Babylonian exile. There are other fragments in Isaiah that probably were originally addressed to the remnants of the Northern Kingdom, such as Isa 31:6–7, but these are sufficient to prove that Isaiah envisioned a future with God of a remnant of the population of the Northern Kingdom. He was an enemy of the northern state but not of the Israelite people, whom he considered kinsmen and, ideally, worshipers of his Yhwh, the Holy One of Israel, not the aberrant Yhwh of Samaria.[6]

Both Isaiah and Micah were also bitter critics of the Judean royal bureaucracy and the civic and religious elite who oversaw or, by their power and wealth, influenced the day-to-day administration of justice in Judah on behalf of the king. Isaiah and Micah's criticism was trenchant and biting enough that both of them no doubt made the "enemies of the state" list for many of their bureaucratic and religious opponents, if not the Judean king's own "enemies' list." Micah (2:1–5, 8–9) and Isaiah (Isa 5:8–10) both complained about the ease with which the wealthy and powerful were "legally" able to expropriate the inherited fields, houses, and other property of the less influential. Isaiah spoke of the officials writing evil decrees and statutes so that they could deprive the poor, widow, and orphan of justice (Isa 10:1–2). Both prophets spoke in graphic terms of the ruling elite's perversion of justice and violent oppression of the people (Mic 3:1–2; Isa 3:14–15), and both complained about the rampant bribery that influenced the outcome of both civil and religious disputes (Mic 3:5, 11; Isa 1:23; 5:23). Isaiah makes fun of the political correctness of his day that tried to give an aura of respectability to the rampant corruption by renaming "evil" as "good," "darkness" as "light," and "bitter" as "sweet" (Isa 5:20; cf. 32:5–8). Lie glibly and repeatedly, and reframe the discussion by the choice of words, and perhaps the public will be distracted from the otherwise obvious problems in the recent royal administration of justice.

Isaiah occasionally became very personal in his rebuke of royal officials, as when he condemned Shebna and praised Eliakim (Isa 22:15–23), or when he later criticized Eliakim in an addendum to this oracle (Isa 22:24–25), though we are

---

6. For this distinctively local manifestation of Yhwh, see the inscriptions from Kuntillet ʿAjrud in F. W. Dobbs-Allsopp et al., eds., *Hebrew Inscriptions: Texts from the Biblical Period of the Monarchy with Concordance* (New Haven, CT: Yale University Press, 2005) 290, KAjr 18:2.

reduced to educated guessing as to what really lay behind the prophet's hostility to Shebna. Micah is more global and less specific in his criticism of Jerusalem's rulers, priests, and prophets (Mic 3:11), though it is clear from his own comments that his oracles provoked a very negative reaction from those whom he criticized, who apparently tried to silence Micah (Mic 2:6, 11; 3:5–8). It is worth noting, however, how seldom either prophet specifically mentions the king in their criticism of the royal administration. In Isaiah's confrontation with Ahaz at the beginning of the Syro-Ephraimitic War, Isaiah does express his disgust at Ahaz's feigned piety, but it is striking that he addresses his rebuke to this feigned piety in the plural to the whole "house of David" (7:13), probably implying that he saw the real problem behind this response as a reflection of the attitudes of the older royal counselors who were influencing the judgment of the young king. It is likely that Isaiah's dismissive attitude toward the young Ahaz is probably also reflected in his announcement of judgment, "I will make boys their officials, and the capricious/small children will rule over them (Isa 3:4)," and in his statement, "O my people—whose oppressor is a child, Over whom women rule—O my people, your leaders are misleaders; The course of your paths they have confused (Isa 3:12)." One may imagine how popular this made Isaiah to Ahaz and his court, even though he offered them repeated reassurance during the Syro-Ephraimitic War. After the repeated confrontations with Ahaz and his court during the initial stages of the Syro-Ephraimitic War, Isaiah seems to have withdrawn from active involvement with the court to await YHWH's resolution of the situation (Isa 8:16–17), and it is not clear how often his oracular advice was sought by the royal court during the rest of Ahaz's reign, though it seems clear that Isaiah remained sharply critical of the royal administration of justice during this period. In contrast to his at least originally negative view of Ahaz, Isaiah appears to have had a more positive initial expectation for Hezekiah. He probably composed Isa 8:23b–9:6 as a coronation oracle for Hezekiah,[7] and Isaiah's characterization of Hezekiah at the beginning of his reign, "in the year Ahaz died," as a "flying seraph" is totally positive (Isa 14:28–32).[8] Isaiah was worried that Hezekiah might give in to the promises of the Philistines and their Nubian supporters and join their anti-Assyrian coalition in the Ashdod crisis of 715–711 B.C.E., but he tirelessly demonstrated against this policy (Isa 14:28–32; 18:1–7; 20:1–6) and eventually dissuaded Hezekiah from joining this league.[9] His

---

7. See J. J. M. Roberts, "Whose Child Is This? Reflections on the Speaking Voice in Isaiah 9:5," *HTR* 90 (1997) 115–29.

8. See idem, "The Rod that Smote Philistia: Isaiah 14:28–32," in *Literature as Politics, Politics as Literature* (ed. D. Vanderhooft and A. Winitzer; Winona Lake, IN: Eisenbrauns, 2013) 381–95.

9. See idem, "Isaiah's Egyptian and Nubian Oracles," in *Israel's Prophets and Israel's Past: Essays on the Relationship of Prophetic Texts and Israelite History in Honor of John H. Hayes* (ed. B. E. Kelle and M. B. Moore; LHBOTS 446; London: T. & T. Clark, 2006), 311–36; and the earlier "Egypt, Assyria, Isaiah, and the Ashdod Affair: An Alternative Proposal," in *Jerusalm in Bible and*

success, however, apparently made him many enemies among Hezekiah's royal advisers. When Sargon II of Assyria was killed in 705 B.C.E., opening up another more promising opportunity for revolt against the hated Assyrians, these advisers apparently succeeded in blocking Isaiah's access to Hezekiah's most sensitive political discussions with his advisers. Isaiah complains bitterly about being shut out and about these advisers' attempt to hide their plans from YHWH.[10] He characterizes the Judean priests, prophets, and royal advisers who promoted the defensive alliance with Nubian Egypt as drunken fools (Isa 28:7–8), and his opponents responded with equally caustic scorn (Isa 8:9–10). Despite his vicious attacks on Hezekiah's royal advisers, however, Isaiah does not appear to have insulted the king directly, and thus he was apparently able to remain on reasonably good terms with Hezekiah. Hezekiah was willing to reveal the identity of the messengers of Merodach-baladan to Isaiah, though only after their visit had ended (Isa 39:1–8), and both when Hezekiah fell ill, and when Sennacherib's campaign of 701 B.C.E. revealed the folly of Hezekiah's other royal advisers, the king seems to have sought the prophet's advice on a number of occasions (Isa 37–38).

We have less information about Micah's direct interaction with any royal figure, though there is the tradition preserved in Jeremiah's day that Hezekiah did not retaliate against Micah for his negative prophecy about Jerusalem (Jer 26:18–19) but, rather, the king feared YHWH and besought his favor, so changing YHWH's mind about the disaster that God had threatened against Jerusalem. There is also the subtle judgment on the current ruling family in Jerusalem, when both Micah and Isaiah see the ideal Davidic king of the future coming from Bethlehem, not Jerusalem (Mic 5:2), from the stump or root of Jesse, not of David (Isa 11:1, 10). It is hard to say, assuming that these oracles are genuine 8th-century oracles as I do, whether they stem originally from the time of Ahaz or Hezekiah, thus implying a negative judgment on one or perhaps both of these kings as having failed the ancient ideal of Davidic kingship.

Nonetheless, despite both Micah and Isaiah's devastatingly negative criticism of the royal bureaucracy, both seem far more reticent in their explicit criticism of the king. This relative reticence on the part of both Micah and Isaiah to specifically name and explicitly condemn the Judean king in their criticism of his royal administration differs strikingly from Amos' explicit judgment on Jeroboam II and his house (Amos 7:9–11), Hosea's dismissal of all the Israelite kings of his time as reprobate (Hos 7:7), not chosen by God (Hos 8:4), and taken away in God's anger

---

Archaeology: The First Temple Period (ed. A. G. Vaughn and A. E. Killebrew; SBLSS 18; Atlanta: SBL, 2003), 265–83.

10. See idem, "Blindfolding the Prophet: Political Resistance to First Isaiah's Oracles in the Light of Ancient Near Eastern Attitudes toward Oracles," in *Oracles et prophéties dans l'Antiquité* (ed. J.-G. Heintz; Actes du Colloque de Strasbourg 15–17 juin 1995; Université des Sciences Humaines de Strasbourg, Travaux du Centre de Recherche sur le Proche-Orient et la Gréce Antiques, 15; Strasbourg: De Boccard, 1997), 135–46.

(Hos 13:10–11), and Jeremiah's later explicit judgments announced on Jehoahaz (Shallum, Jer 22:10–12), Jehoiakim (Jer 22:13–10), Jehoiachin (Jer 22:24–30), and later Zedekiah (Jer 38:17–23). This reticence may have something to do with the desire of the prophet to maintain a working relationship with the king despite very hard feelings between the prophet and particular royal counselors and advisers whose advice the prophet considered foolish at best, and corrupt, idolatrous, and/or oppressively evil at worst. This is not that unusual in a monarchical system, where the reassuring, even if fictional, belief is often maintained that if one could just get by the roadblock of the corrupt bureaucracy to the person of the just king himself, the idealized king would correct the injustice. Of course, it was and is to the advantage of the king, and in a more modern democratic society to the highest elected official, to maintain this useful fiction. No doubt, some royal officials did occasionally violate official royal policy, but most often one must assume they did precisely what the court had decided on with at least the consent, if not the eager urging of the king. If the policy failed, however, particularly if it was a disastrous failure, it was and is always helpful to have a bureaucratic, preferably low level, scapegoat. It surely could not be the official policy of the king, or the president, that produced such a disaster.

On the other hand, such a fiction, while maintained, could also be an advantage to the prophetic critics of royal policy. Criticism of royal policy, particularly when it took the form of an oracular judgment against the person of the king himself, could easily provoke the charge of conspiracy and rebellion against the king, a capital offense.[11] Without a very strong and influential support group, such a charge could easily lead to the royal execution of the prophet. That was the fate of Jeremiah's contemporary, Uriah son of Shemaiah from Kiriath-jearim, whom Jehoiakim extradited from Egypt, where he had fled, and summarily executed (Jer 26:20–23). Jeremiah, who had a far more influential support group (Jer 26:24), escaped that fate, but even Jeremiah could not escape being prohibited from appearing in the temple (Jer 36:5), from being struck and put in stocks (Jer 20:2), from being accused of desertion to the Babylonians (Jer 37:11–16), and from being imprisoned in horrible conditions, where he barely escaped death (Jer 37:17–38:13). Micah may have flirted with such a reaction from the royal court, according to the tradition preserved in Jer 26:16–19, but—perhaps because Micah had been more careful to avoid a direct attack on the person of the king, or perhaps because Hezekiah was a far more just king than those who followed Josiah—Hezekiah's court did not react in the violent way that Jehoiakim and the court of Zedekiah reacted in the time of Jeremiah. During Ahaz's reign, especially during the Syro-Ephraimitic War, people were throwing around the charge of "conspiracy" very

---

11. See idem, "Prophets and Kings: A New Look at the Royal Persecution of Prophets against Its Near Eastern Background," in *A God So Near: Essays on Old Testament Theology in Honor of Patrick D. Miller* (ed. B. A. Strawn and N. Bowen; Winona Lake, IN: Eisenbrauns, 2003), 341–54.

loosely (Isa 8:11–12), but Isaiah, perhaps because his oracles promised the deliverance of Jerusalem from the Aramean-Ephraimite threat, even while he critiqued the policy of Ahaz's court, would hardly qualify as someone who encouraged the enemy while undermining Judah's own military forces. Moreover, Isaiah appears to have come from an influential family and to have had a strong support group in Jerusalem. He was not an insignificant individual from the hinterland who could be executed with impunity. Even in the later period, at the beginning of Hezekiah's revolt against Assyria, when many of his court opponents wanted to limit his influence on the king, Isaiah's reputation and influence within Jerusalem and with at least portions of the Jerusalem elite, made it impossible for his opponents to arrest him or throw him in prison. Despite the bitter conflict between Isaiah and his opponents at court, these opponents could not successfully portray him as a "dangerous enemy of the state." They were reduced to more devious work-arounds, and when their policies failed disastrously, Isaiah remained a viable voice to encourage Hezekiah to adjust his policies in a different direction. In short, despite his sharp criticism of the Judean court, Isaiah was able to remain, even through several difficult times, a "friend of the Judean state."

Bibliography

Dobbs-Allsopp, F. W., et al., eds. *Hebrew Inscriptions: Texts from the Biblical Period of the Monarchy with Concordance.* New Haven, CT: Yale University Press, 2005.

Hillers, D. R. *Micah: A Commentary on the Book of the Prophet Micah.* Hermeneia. Philadelphia: Fortress, 1984.

Roberts, J. J. M. "Blindfolding the Prophet: Political Resistance to First Isaiah's Oracles in the Light of Ancient Near Eastern Attitudes toward Oracles." Pp. 135–46 in *Oracles et prophéties dans l'Antiquité.* Edited by J.-G. Heintz. Actes du Colloque de Strasbourg 15–17 juin 1995. Université des Sciences Humaines de Strasbourg, Travaux du Centre de Recherche sur le Proche-Orient et la Grèce Antiques 15. Srasbourg: De Boccard, 1997.

_____. "The Context, Text, and Logic of Isaiah 7.7–9." Pp. 161–70 in *Inspired Speech: Prophecy in the Ancient Near East: Essays in Honour of Herbert B. Huffmon.* Edited by J. Kaltner and L. Stulman. JSOTS 378. London: T. & T. Clark International, 2004.

_____. "Egypt, Assyria, Isaiah, and the Ashdod Affair: An Alternative Proposal." Pp. 265–83 in *Jerusalem in Bible and Archaeology: The First Temple Period.* Edited by A. G. Vaughn and A. E. Killebrew. SBLSS 18. Atlanta: SBL, 2003.

_____. *First Isaiah: A Commentary.* Hermeneia. Minneapolis: Fortress, 2015

_____. "Isaiah 2 and the Prophet's Message to the North." *JQR* 75 (1985) 290–308.

_____. "Isaiah and His Children." Pp. 193–203 in *Biblical and Related Studies Presented to Samuel Iwry.* Edited by A. Kort and S. Morschauser. Winona Lake, IN: Eisenbrauns, 1985.

_____. "Isaiah, National Security, and the Politics of Fear." Pp. 72–92 in *The Bible and the American Future.* Edited by R. Jewett, W. L. Alloway Jr., and J. G. Lacey. Eugene, OR: Cascade, 2009.

_____. "Isaiah's Egyptian and Nubian Oracles." Pp. 311–336 in *Israel's Prophets and Israel's Past: Essays on the Relationship of Prophetic Texts and Israelite History in Honor of John H. Hayes*. Edited by B. E. Kelle and M. B. Moore. LHBOTS 446. London: T. & T. Clark, 2006.

_____. "Prophets and Kings: A New Look at the Royal Persecution of Prophets against Its Near Eastern Background." Pp. 341–54 in *A God So Near: Essays on Old Testament Theology in Honor of Patrick D. Miller*. Edited by B. A. Strawn and N. Bowen. Winona Lake, IN: Eisenbrauns, 2003.

_____. "The Rod that Smote Philistia: Isaiah 14:28–32." Pp. 381–95 in *Literature as Politics, Politics as Literature: Essays on the Ancient Near East in Honor of Peter Machinist*. Edited by D. Vanderhooft and A. Winitzer. Winona Lake, IN: Eisenbrauns, 2013.

_____. "Security and Justice in Isaiah." *Stone-Campbell Journal* 13 (2010) 71–79.

_____. "Whose Child Is This? Reflections on the Speaking Voice in Isaiah 9:5." *HTR* 90 (1997) 115–29.

Vaughn, A. G. *Theology, History, and Archaeology in the Chronicler's Account of Hezekiah*. Atlanta: Scholars, 1999.

Jeremiah as State-Enemy of Judah:
Critical Moments in the Biblical Narratives about the "Weeping Prophet"

CHRISTOPHER A. ROLLSTON

George Washington University

Introduction

On the lips of Jeremiah. . . .

It was Yahweh who made it known to me and (so) I knew it. (And) at that time, you showed me their deeds. And I was like a pet lamb brought to slaughter. And I did not know that they devised schemes against me. "Let us destroy the tree with its produce, and let us cut him off from the land of the living so that his name is not mentioned again." But Yahweh Sabaoth judges righteously, with grace (he judges) the innermost heart. I wish to see your vengeance upon them because to you I have committed my case." (Jer 11:18–20)

On the lips of Jeremiah's enemies . . .

They said, "come and let us devise schemes against Jeremiah because instruction shall not perish from the priest, nor counsel from the wise man, not the word from the prophet. Come, let us smite him with a verbal charge, and let us not heed any of his words." (Jer 18:18)

On the lips of Yahweh . . .

Therefore, thus says Yahweh concerning the people of Anathoth who are seeking your life (and) saying "you must not prophesy in the name of Yahweh and or you will die by our hand." Therefore, thus says Yahweh Sabaoth, "I am about to bring a visitation upon them. The young men shall die by the sword, their sons and their daughters shall die by famine. And there shall be no remnant for them because I shall bring evil to the people of Anathoth, the year of their visitation." (Jer 11:21–23)

Author's note: I am grateful for the assistance of my research assistants, Nathaniel Greene and Danielle Weeks, in the preparation of this article. All translations are my own.

In many respects, these three pericopes from the book of Jeremiah encapsu
late the turbulent life of the prophet. Difficult though it was for him (see especially
Jer 11:18–20:18), Jeremiah uttered prophetic oracles from Yahweh just as he was
called to do (Jer 1:4–10). He encountered fierce resistance from much of the political and religious establishment (even though he himself was of priestly descent,
Jer 1:1). He continued to proclaim, however, that destruction would come at the
hands of the Babylonians because of the sinfulness and apostasy of the people (e.g.,
Jer 2, 5; 7:9; 8:1–3; 11; 23:13–14; cf. also the Idol Satire of Jer 10), the oppression
of the sojourner, the orphan, and the widow (Jer 7:5–7), stealing, murder, adultery, and perjury (Jer 7:5–6). There were certainly some calls for repentance and
hope on the lips of Jeremiah (e.g., Jer 3:1–4:4; 18:1–12; 22; 31:31–34), including
even restoration after exile (e.g., Jer 23:1–8; 33). But, in spite of this, it seems that
Jeremiah's core message was one of the impending destruction by the Babylonians
(Jer 4:5–31; 6:1–30; 8–9; 15; 19; 21; 25; cf. Jer 13 and the narrative of the worthless
loincloth). Among the most striking things is the reference to Nebuchadnezzar as
the 'servant' (עֶבֶד) of Yahweh who brings about this destruction (Jer 27:6), with
resistance to Babylon, therefore, being absolutely futile and contrary to the will
of Yahweh (Jer 27:8–14). Of course, this sort of understanding has strong parallels within the prophetic tradition—with Habakkuk, for example, embracing this
same basic belief about the impending Babylonian invasion (Hab 1:5).[1]

This article will begin with a description of the salient details of the historical
context of the late 7th and early 6th centuries B.C.E. This will be accompanied by a
discussion of many of the references in the book of Jeremiah to the Judean kings
Josiah, Jehoahaz, Jehoiakim, Jehoiachin, Zedekiah, and to the assassinated Judean
Governor Gedaliah. It is also useful for me to emphasize that my references to
deeds and words surrounding the life of Jeremiah do not actually presuppose the
historicity of these events.[2] Jeremiah was certainly a historical figure, and I think
that there is a core historicity to the overall thread of these oracles and narratives.
However, I am confident that reconstructing "the historical Jeremiah" is about as
difficult and problematic as reconstructing "the historical Jesus." Thus, this article
is based heavily on the oracles and narratives of Jeremiah (as presented in the book
of Jeremiah) and the details noted in those narratives and oracles, but my discussion of these materials should not be construed as evidence that I consider every
word or deed attributed to Jeremiah to be the *ipsissima verba* or *acti* of Jeremiah.
Furthermore, it should also be emphasized that although there is some substantial
agreement about the assignment of many pericopes to the A, B, or C material,

---

1. For the same basic sentiment, see also the book of Zephaniah. Also, although different
in result, a similar basic motif of a foreign ruler as an agent of Yahweh is contained in Second
Isaiah, with its reference to King Cyrus of Persia (r. ca. 550–530 B.C.E.) as Yahweh's Messiah
(Isa 45:1).

2. For a thorough analysis of the unique, literary nature of Israelite prophecy, please see
U. Becker, "Die Wiederentdeckung des Prophetenbuches," *Berliner Theologische Zeitschrift* 21
(2004) 30–60.

this article will not attempt to argue for the placement of the herein-referenced texts to a particular block of material. Nevertheless, it is useful to mention that in terms of conventional terminology, the Poetic Oracles are designated as "A Material" (heavily present in Jer 1–25); the Prose Biographical Material is designated as the "B Material" (heavily present in Jer 26–45); the Prose Oracles or Sermonic Material is designated as "C Material" (interspersed through the A and B Materials). Note that "Oracles against the Nations" are a common component of much of the prophetic literature (e.g., Amos 1–3 as a paradigmatic example), and those of Jeremiah (Jer 46–51) fall outside the designations A, B, and C (they constitute a stock motif in prophetic literature, rather than something distinctive to Jeremiah or the source-blocks of Jeremiah).

I. Judah and Geopolitics from King Ahaz to Governor Gedaliah: From Vassal to Vanquished

Jeremiah's Time

The superscription of the book of Jeremiah locates the prophet in the tumultuous final decades of First Temple Judah:

> The words of Jeremiah, son of Hilkiah, from the priests who are in Anathoth in the land of Benjamin, when the word of Yahweh came to him in the days of Josiah the son of Amon, king of Judah, in the thirteenth year of his reign. And so it continued in the days of Jehoiakim son of Josiah king of Judah, until the completion of the eleventh year of Zedekiah the son of Josiah, king of Judah, until the captivity of Jerusalem in the fifth month. (Jer 1:1–3)

The thirteenth regnal year of King Josiah of Judah (r. ca. 640–609 B.C.E.) was ca. 627 B.C.E., and the eleventh year of King Zedekiah of Judah (r. ca. 597–586 B.C.E.) was ca. 586 B.C.E. These are the basic chronological bookends for the prophetic activities of Jeremiah in Judah: 627–586 B.C.E., although, the presence of narratives within the book about the Judean rule of Gedaliah demonstrate that there was a strong tradition that Jeremiah remained in Judah until ca. 582 B.C.E., followed thereafter by his move to Egypt (Jer 41–43).[3]

---

3. The precise date for the assassination of Gedaliah is not specified in an unambiguous manner, but it is usually argued that 582 is a reasonable terminus. Also of import is the fact the (loan)word for governor (פחה) is not used of Gedaliah nor is the root for king or rule (מלך). Rather, the root פקד is used, a usage that is more general than specific in nature. On these things, see especially J. Blenkinsopp, *David Remembered: Kingship and National Identity in Ancient Israel* (Grand Rapids, MI: Eerdmans, 2013), 48–52. In this connection, it is worth emphasizing that פחה is an Akkadian loanword (Akk. *pīḥātu(m)*), one that is normally associated with officials of the Persian Period (and thus after the chronological horizon of the Babylonian Empire). On this, see P. V. Mankowski, *Akkadian Loanwords in Biblical Hebrew* (HSS 47; Winona Lake, IN: Eisenbrauns, 2000), 128–29. Note that this word is used in the book of Jeremiah once with regard to the Medes (51:28) and once with regard to the Babylonians (51:57; cf. 51:23).

Judean history during these years of Jeremiah's prophetic activity was marked by bloodshed and betrayal, coupled with, and aggravated by, bondage to the ebb and flow of the great powers of the ancient Near East. After all, King Josiah's father (Amon) had been assassinated, after a reign of some two years (r. ca. 642–640 B.C.E.), at the hands of his own high officials in a palace coup (2 Kgs 21:19–26; 2 Chr 33:21–25), an assassination that arguably occurred because Amon was a loyal vassal of the Neo-Assyrian Empire.[4] The Neo-Assyrian Empire had been powerful during the reign of Asshurbanipal (r. ca. 668–627 B.C.E.)[5] but began to crumble after his reign. The great Neo-Assyrian capital cities of Asshur and Nineveh fell in 614 B.C.E. and 612 B.C.E., and the Neo-Assyrian stump government in Haran fell in 609 B.C.E. Josiah himself died at Megiddo in a battle against Egyptian Pharaoh Neco II in 609 B.C.E., as he (Neco II) was en route to Haran in order to engage in battle against the Babylonians (2 Kgs 23:28–30; 2 Chr 35:20–24).[6] After Josiah's death, his son Jehoahaz (Shallum) began to reign in his place (in 609 B.C.E.), but Neco II (r. ca. 610–594 B.C.E.) removed Jehoahaz from the throne after a reign of just three months (2 Kgs 23:31–33).[7] Pharaoh Neco II placed Josiah's son Eliakim on the throne of Judah (r. ca. 609–598 B.C.E.) as an Egyptian vassal, and Neco is credited with giving him the throne-name Jehoiakim (2 Kgs 23:34). But, not long after this, Jehoiakim felt compelled to repudiate his Egyptian vassalage so as to become a vassal of King Nebuchadnezzar of Babylon (r. ca. 605–562 B.C.E.), a decision that was prompted by Nebuchadnezzar's defeat of Egypt at the Battle of Carchemish in 605 B.C.E. (Jer 46:2). However, after some three years, because of the seeming success of Neco II in battle against Nebuchadnezzar ca. 601 B.C.E. (and Nebuchadnezzar's corresponding decision to return to Babylon), Jehoiakim rebelled against Nebuchadnezzar (2 Kgs 24:1). Nebuchadnezzar soon fortified his army and set out again from Babylon on a punitive campaign. Jehoiakim died, just prior to the arrival of the brunt of Nebuchadnezzar's siege (2 Kgs 24:2–7). King Jehoiakim was succeeded on the throne by his eighteen-year-old son named Jehoiachin (r. late 598/early 597 B.C.E.), who surrendered to Nebuchadnezzar after a reign of just three months (2 Kgs 24:8–12). At that time (597 B.C.E.), Nebuchadnezzar plundered Jerusalem's Temple and Palace, deported many of Judah's military, Judah's artisans, and much of the royal family, and then placed Josiah's son Mattaniah (597–586 B.C.E.) on the throne of Judah (2 Kgs 24:17) as

---

4. That is, I find myself largely in agreement with Abraham Malamat's contention that Amon was a loyal vassal of Assyria (following in the footsteps of his father Manasseh) and that the assassins were high officials of Amon's who were anti-Assyrian. See A. Malamat, "The Historical Background of the Assassination of Amon, King of Judah," *IEJ* 3 (1953) 26–29.

5. It is rather interesting that the superscription places the beginning of Jeremiah's prophetic work in the very year that Asshurbanipal dies.

6. For a brief but useful discussion of this, see M. Liverani, *Israel's History and the History of Israel* (London: Equinox, 2005), 180–81.

7. Within Kings, this monarch is referred to as "Jehoahaz," but within Jeremiah he is referred to as Shallum (Jer 22:11).

a Babylonian vassal, with Nebuchadnezzar giving to Mattaniah the throne-name Zedekiah. King Zedekiah was a rather faithful vassal of Babylon for a number of years; but, he ultimately rebelled against Babylon, based in part because powerful figures in Judah believed that Egypt (under Pharaoh Hophra, r. ca. 589–570 B.C.E.) was strong enough to deter Babylon. An ostracon discovered at the Judean fortress city of Lachish and dating to ca. 587 or 586 B.C.E. refers to an army commander (שׂר הצבא) named Coniah son of Elnathan "heading down to enter into Egypt" (Lachish 3.14–16) within the broader context of acquiring supplies.[8] Naturally, in response to the rebellion, Nebuchadnezzar returned to make another punitive campaign. In the end, Zedekiah was captured and exiled in 586 B.C.E., as a rebellious vassal, having first been forced to witness the murder of his two sons by Babylonian soldiers, followed immediately by the gouging out of his own eyes. Jerusalem was then burned to the ground, including the First Temple and the Royal Palace (2 Kgs 25:1–10). Nebuchadnezzar subsequently appointed a certain Judean named Gedaliah the son of Ahikam the son of Shaphan as the governor (ca. 586–582 B.C.E.); but a high official, who was also a member of the Judean royal family, orchestrated the assassination of Gedaliah during a dinner party (2 Kgs 25:22–26; Jer 41:1–4).

Precursors: Ahaz and Hezekiah's Time

The period of Judean history from the reign of Josiah to the governorship of Gedaliah is not unique, in terms of the foreign hegemony and vassalage of Judah. For example, the Northern Kingdom of Israel and the Kingdom of Damascus in Syria were kingdoms that had been vassals of the Neo-Assyrian Kingdom during the years immediately prior to the Syro-Ephraimite War (a war dated to ca. 735–732 B.C.E.), the evidence for this vassalage being reference in the royal inscriptions of the Neo-Assyrian King Tiglath-pileser III (r. ca. 745–727 B.C.E.) to both Menahem of Israel (r. ca. 745–737 B.C.E.) and Rezin of Damascus (r. ca. 740–732 B.C.E.) as tributaries, a fact also mentioned (regarding Menahem) in the book of Kings as well (2 Kgs 15:17–22). Among the other tributaries were Hiram of Tyre, Shipiṭbaʻl of Byblos, Panammu of Samʼal.[9] Menahem seems to have died a natural death and Menahem's son and successor was Pekahiah (r. ca. 737–736 B.C.E.), who reigned just a brief year or two, and was then assassinated in a coup that was initiated by his own military captain, Pekah son of Remaliah (2 Kgs 15:23–26). After usurping the throne (via the assassination), King Pekah of Israel (r. ca. 736–732 B.C.E.), along with King Rezin of Damascus (r. ca. 740–732 B.C.E.) rebelled against Tiglath-pileser III, forming an anti-Assyrian alliance (cf. Isa 7). Of course, Pekah

---

8. H. Tur-Sinai (Torczyner), *Lachish I: The Lachish Letters* (Oxford: Oxford University Press, 1938).

9. See H. Tadmor and S. Yamada, *The Royal Inscriptions of Tiglath-pileser III (744–727 BC), and Shalmaneser V (726–722 BC), Kings of Assyria* (Royal Inscriptions of the Neo-Assyrian Period 1; Winona Lake, IN: Eisenbrauns, 2011), 38 (#11.4); 46 (#14.10); 70 (#27.2–7); 77 (#32.1); 86–87 (#35 iii.4).

and Rezin (and the rest of the coalition) knew that Tiglath pileser III would rapidly respond with a punitive campaign against their coalition, and they also knew that it was strategically important for Judah to be part of the anti-Assyrian coalition (cf. 2 Kgs 15:37, during the reign of Jotham of Judah). But King Ahaz of Judah did not wish to be part of that coalition, arguably because he believed that this alliance was not strong enough to resist the great might of Tiglath-pileser III. Therefore, Ahaz sent messengers to Tiglath-pileser III stating that he wished to be a vassal (2 Kgs 16:7) "I am your vassal and your son" (עבדך ובנך), "come and save me from the palm of the king of Aram and the palm of the king of Israel who have arisen against me," following this request with tribute of silver and gold from the First Temple and the Royal Palace (2 Kgs 16:1–9; Isa 7).[10] Rezin and Pekah besieged Ahaz in Jerusalem, with the hope of Killing Ahaz and (according to the book of Isaiah) placing a puppet king named "the son of Tabeel" on the throne of Judah (2 Kgs 16:5; Isa 7:6). The rationale for the siege is readily apparent: Rezin and Pekah needed Judah's participation in the anti-Assyrian coalition, because they did not wish to engage the military of Tiglath-pileser III in the north and simultaneously engage the Judean army (as a loyal vassal of Tiglath-pileser III) in the south.[11] But, Rezin and Pekah utterly failed. According to the royal inscriptions of Tiglath-pileser III, Damascus was vanquished and Rezin deposed in 732 B.C.E., and Damascus was annexed to Assyria.[12] As for Pekah of Israel, the book of Kings states that a northern Israelite named Hoshea son of Elah assassinated Pekah and usurped the throne (2 Kgs 15:29–31). Similarly, the royal inscriptions of Tiglath-pileser III state that Pekah was killed and that Tiglath-pileser III replaced Pekah with Hoshea.[13] Neo-Assyrian inscriptions list Jehoahaz of Judah (that is, Ahaz) among the tributaries of Tiglath-pileser III.[14] As for King Hoshea of Israel (r. ca. 732–724 B.C.E.), he was a loyal Neo-Assyrian vassal for the duration of the reign of Tiglath-pileser III, but he rebelled against Shalmaneser V (r. ca. 726–722 B.C.E.) and formed an alliance with Egypt (2 Kgs 17:3–6). The end result was the destruction of the Northern Kingdom of Israel, something that was begun during the reign of Shalmaneser V and completed during the first year of the reign of Sargon II (r. ca. 721–705 B.C.E.). From the perspective of the cold eye of the historian, the decision of Ahaz to become a vassal of Tiglath-pileser III had proved to be wise, at least in terms of Judah's avoidance of destruction during the second half of the 8th century B.C.E.

---

10. On the presentation of Neo-Assyria in First Isaiah (Isa 1–39), see the nuanced and detailed study of P. Machinist, "Assyria and Its Image in the First Isaiah," *JAOS* 103 (1983) 719–37.

11. It should be remembered that a standard demand in parity and vassal treaties was assistance in military engagements against enemies.

12. See Tadmor and Yamada, *The Royal Inscriptions of Tiglath-pileser III*, 58–59 (#20.1–17); 131 (# 49rev.3–4); 134 (#50.5).

13. See ibid., 106 (#42.17'); 112 (#44.18')

14. See ibid., 122 (#47, lines 6–9), with reference to "Jehoahaz of the land of Judah"—that is, Ahaz, in a list of tributaries.

The son and successor of King Ahaz of Judah was King Hezekiah (r. ca. 715–687 B.C.E.), a king given high praise in the Deuteronomistic History of Kings (2 Kgs 18:1–6).[15] At the beginning of his reign, he continued to be a vassal to Sennacherib (r. ca. 704–681 B.C.E.), the successor of Sargon II, but he decided to rebel against Assyrian hegemony (2 Kgs 18:7). Sennacherib, of course, soon came knocking on Judah's door, with a powerful and destructive punitive campaign in 701 B.C.E. The events of Sennacherib's campaign are among the best documented in all of Judean history, including literary, epigraphic, and archaeological evidence: namely, (a) detailed narratives in the Hebrew Bible (2 Kgs 18:13–19:37; Isa 36:1–37:38; 2 Chronicles 32);[16] (b) Sennacherib's account in Neo-Assyrian (Akkadian) of his siege of Judah, including the fact that he had Hezekiah "trapped in Jerusalem like a bird in a cage;"[17] (c) Sennacherib's "South West Palace Reliefs" in Nineveh, depicting the siege and destruction of Lachish;[18] (d) excavations at Lachish, in particular, replete with the military destruction of Stratum III dated to 701 B.C.E;[19] (e) Jerusalem's Siloam Tunnel Inscription, written in the Old Hebrew script and dating palaeographically to the chronological horizon of the late 8th century or early 7th century B.C.E. and connected in literary texts with the reign of Hezekiah (2 Kgs 20:20; 2 Chr 32:30; Sir 48:17–22).[20]

In sum, it is often noted that Israel and Judah could be understood as a land bridge between the great ancient Near Eastern powers of Mesopotamia and Egypt.[21] For this reason, strong kings in Egypt would attempt to campaign to the north—that is, through the Levant. And strong kings in Assyria and Babylonia would campaign from the north to the south, through the Levant (because of the difficulty of crossing the desert). For a century, Judean kings had navigated these

---

15. On Hezekiah's reforms and the archaeological record, see the classic synthetic article of O. Borowski, "Hezekiah's Reforms and the Revolt against Assyria," *NEA* 58 (1995) 148–55.

16. For the biblical, archaeological, and epigraphic material, see especially L. Grabbe, *Like a Bird in a Cage: The Invasion of Sennacherib in 701 B.C.E.* (London: Sheffield Academic, 2003).

17. A. K. Grayson and J. Novotny, *The Royal Inscriptions of Sennacherib, King of Assyria (704–681 BC), Part 1* (Royal Inscriptions of the Neo-Assyrian Period 3/1; Winona Lake, IN: Eisenbrauns, 2012), 64–66 [#4.42–58].

18. See, most conveniently, T. C. Mitchell, *The Bible in the British Museum: Interpreting the Evidence* (Mahwah, NJ: Paulist, 2004), 67–71.

19. See in particular D. Ussishkin, *The Conquest of Lachish by Sennacherib* (Tel Aviv: The Institute of Archaeology, Tel Aviv University, 1982).

20. The recent attempt of Ronny Reich and Eli Shukron ("The Date of the Siloam Tunnel Reconsidered," *Tel Aviv* 38 [2011] 147–57) to date the building of the Siloam Tunnel (and the chiseling of its inscription) to the late 9th or early 8th century is problematic. In essence, the paleographic data are such that a date so early is just not possible. Moreover, the archaeological data that Reich and Shukron have used have been contested by Israel Finkelstein (personal communication). In short, I am confident that the traditional dating of the inscription to the late 8th century B.C.E. will continue to be the most convincing and accepted.

21. With the title of one of the most authoritative atlases reflecting this, of course: A. F. Rainey and R. S. Notley, *The Sacred Bridge: Carta's Atlas of the Biblical World* (2nd ed.; Jerusalem: Carta, 2014).

turbulent international waters tolerably well, but it had obviously (as discussed above) not been without difficulties and it had not been without a high cost. Thus, the morass that Judah found itself in during the terminal period of Judean history was very deep, but it was not entirely unique.

II. Jeremiah's Prophetic Oracles and the Powers That Be: Speaking Truth to Power

The Minor Regnal Players in the Book of Jeremiah: Josiah, Jehoahaz, and Jehoiachin

Within the book of Jeremiah, Josiah (r. ca. 640–609 B.C.E.) is referred to in the superscription (Jer 1:2) and in the patronymics of his sons (i.e., "Jehoahaz (Shallum) son of Josiah" [Jer 22:11], "Jehoiakim son of Josiah" [e.g., Jer 25:1, 26:1], "Zedekiah son of Josiah" [Jer 27:1 37:1]), but there are very few additional references. Among the most important is this pericope:

> Yahweh said to me in the days of King Josiah, "Have you seen what faithless Israel has done? She has gone onto every high hill and every green tree and committed harlotry there." And I said, "After her doing all these things, she shall return to me," but she did not return. And her faithless sister Judah saw it. And she [reading with Q, LXX] saw that, for the very reason that faithless Israel had committed adultery, I had sent her away and I gave the certificate of her divorce to her, but her faithless sister Judah did not fear, and she herself went and she committed fornication also. She took her harlotry so lightly that she polluted the land and she committed adultery with stone and with tree. But even in all this, her faithless sister Judah did not return to me with her whole heart, except with a lie, says Yahweh (Jer 3:6–10).[22]

The actual date of this oracle could be debated and certainly has been,[23] but the fact remains that the precise language presupposes that the faithless worship "with stone and tree" was something that people were engaging in even during the reign of Josiah—perhaps before the Josianic reforms, perhaps during them, or perhaps after them—but during his reign nonetheless. A second substantive reference to Josiah is the command that there be no lamentation for the slain King Josiah. Here is the precise reading of this brief poetic oracle:

> You should not weep for the one who is dead. Do not grieve deeply for him. Rather, weep grievously for the one going (away), because he will not return again or see the land of his birth. (Jer 22:10)

---

22. With regard to the religious practices described here, see especially S. Ackerman, *Under Every Green Tree: Popular Religion in Sixth-Century Judah* (HSM 46; Atlanta: Scholars, 1992).

23. For some discussion of this, see J. R. Lundbom, *Jeremiah 1–20: A New Translation with Introduction and Commentary* (AB 21A; New York: Doubleday, 1999), 308–9.

The verse that follows this poetic oracle provides its interpretation:

> For thus says Yahweh concerning Shallum [Jehoahaz] son of King Josiah of Ju-
> dah, the successor of his father Josiah, who has gone forth from this place: he
> shall not return here again, because he will die in the place to which they have
> exiled him, and he will not see this land again. (Jer 22:11–12)

Jehoahaz was the fourth son of Josiah (1 Chr 3:15) and was placed on the throne
by "the people of the land" (2 Kgs 23:30), but (as noted above) after his brief reign
of three months (609 B.C.E.), he was deported to Egypt and died there (2 Kgs
23:31–34).[24] As for Jehoiachin, he is referred to five times in the book of Jeremiah,
three times using his given name (Jer 22:24, 28; 37:1) and twice using his throne
name (Jer 52:31, 33). He was the son of Jehoiakim and was placed on the throne
in the wake of his father's death. He reigned a mere three months (in 598 or early
597 B.C.E.) and then, according to the book of Kings (as noted above), he surrendered to Nebuchadnezzar II, along with his mother, his servants, his officers, and
his palace officials. Moreover, at that time, Nebuchadnezzar took all the treasures
of the Jerusalem Temple and the royal palace. In addition, he deported thousands
of warriors and artisans, leaving only the poorest of the land (2 Kgs 24:8–17).
Arguably, the most consequential material in Jeremiah regarding Jehoiachin are
two oracles, one prose (Jer 22:24–27) and one poetic (Jer 22:28–30). The point of
both of these oracles is to declare that Jehoiachin will not return to Jerusalem to
be restored to kingship in Judah but will die in exile. In addition, the poetic oracle
declares that he should be recorded as "childless": none of his offspring will be able
to sit upon the throne of David in Jerusalem. To be sure, the author of this oracle
knew that Jehoiachin had sons. Indeed, according to the tradition in Chronicles,
he had seven sons (1 Chr 3:17–18), so the author of the oracle seems to be saying, in essence, that for all practical purposes, he is without heir, without sons.
Particularly interesting and striking is the fact that the final verses of the book
of Jeremiah record the fact that Jehoiachin was ultimately brought out of prison
and was able to dine with the king on a regular basis and also received a daily allowance until the day of his death (Jer 52:31–34), something also corroborated by
Babylonian texts.[25]

The Major Regnal Players in the Book of Jeremiah:
Jehoiakim, Zedekiah

With King Jehoiakim (r. ca. 609–598), son of Josiah, there were a number of
dramatic, derisive, and decisive moments. Jehoiakim was a perennial nemesis of

---

24. It should be noted that the name of an uncle of Jeremiah was also Shallum (Jer 32:7) and
there is still another person named Shallum in the book of Jeremiah—the father of a threshold-
keeper (Jer 35:4).

25. M. Cogan, *Bound for Exile: Israelites and Judeans under Imperial Yoke: Documents from
Assyria and Babylonia* (Jerusalem: Carta, 2013), 140–43.

Jeremiah. He had ascended to the throne after the very brief reign of Jehoahaz, a reign that lasted a mere three months (2 Kgs 23:31–34). Jehoiakim's given name was Eliakim, but Pharaoh Neco II (r. ca. 610–594 B.C.E.) gave him the throne-name Jehoiakim. Neco II also placed a very heavy tribute on Jehoiakim (2 Kgs 23:34–35), as was customarily the case with vassals. However, after the Babylonian victory over the Egyptian forces at Carchemish (in 605 B.C.E.), Jehoiakim became a vassal of Nebuchadnezzar II. For this reason, Jehoakim became a vassal of Nebuchadnezzar for three years but then rebelled against him (2 Kgs 24:1). A poetic oracle reflects the disdain with which those loyal to Jeremiah viewed Jehoiakim:

> They will not sound a lament for him (saying) "Woe, my brother, woe, my sister."
> They will not sound a lament for him (saying) "Woe, O lord, Woe, O majesty."
> And with the burial of a donkey, he will be buried, dragged off and jettisoned
> from beyond the gates of Jerusalem. (Jer 22:18–19)

A number of events prefigured that lament.

There are arguably two version of Jeremiah's Temple Sermon, as has long been noted: Jeremiah 7 and Jeremiah 26.[26] In chap. 26, the Temple Sermon is set at the beginning of the reign of Jehoiakim. Jeremiah was commanded, the narrative suggests, to stand in the court of Yahweh's Temple and to speak to all the people of Judah coming to worship there. The purpose of the sermon was ostensibly to be the aversion of the disaster, brought about by a desire no longer to do evil. Conversely, within this version of Jeremiah's Temple Sermon, it is also declared that if the people do not listen, then Yahweh would make the Jerusalem Temple like Shiloh and the entire city of Jerusalem would be accursed (Jer 26:1–6). The religious establishment (i.e., the priests and prophets) all heard Jeremiah's words, as did the worshipers at the Temple. And after he finished speaking, the priests and prophets seized him and proclaimed that he must die (cf. also Jer 8:10; 23:10–11 on priest and prophet). They interrogated him about the reason for his oracles about the Temple and its impending doom. At this juncture, a quorum of officials came from the royal palace to the Temple and sat in the area of the entry of the "New Gate" of the Temple. The priests and prophets declared before the officials and the people: "This man deserves to die because he has uttered prophesies against this city" (Jer 26:7–10).

At that time, Jeremiah himself began to speak to all of the officials and the people, as a means of defending himself. He did not deny that he had uttered prophesies stating that Jerusalem would become like Shiloh—that is, utterly destroyed. Rather, he declared that he was uttering these prophesies in the name of

---

26. See, for example, W. L. Holladay, *Jeremiah 1: A Commentary on the Book of the Prophet Jeremiah Chapters 1–25* (Hermeneia; Philadelphia: Fortress, 1986), 235–74; W. L. Holladay, *Jeremiah 2: A Commentary on the Book of the Prophet Jeremiah Chapters 26–52* (Hermeneia; Philadelphia: Fortress, 1989), 99–110.

Yahweh himself, the national God of Judah. He then reiterated his call for peni-
tence, a turning from the sinfulness that was the causative factor in the impending destruction of Jerusalem. Striking is the fact that he also boldly said to his
listeners: "Behold, I am in your hands. Do with me as you consider good and
right." Then he proclaimed that, if they killed him, they would bring innocent
blood upon their own hands, as Yahweh himself had indeed sent him to utter
these oracles (Jer 26:12–15). After listening to Jeremiah's words, the decision of
the royal officials (with the seeming support of the worshipers who were listening)
was that Jeremiah had done nothing deserving death, for he had uttered these
oracles in the name of "Yahweh your God" (thus, not in the word of a forbidden,
foreign God, see Jer 26:12–15). In addition, some of the older men, elders of the
land (Hebrew: זקני הארץ) appealed to precedent—namely, that in the days of King
Hezekiah of Judah (715–687 B.C.E.), Micah of Moresheth made similar statements
about the destruction of Judah, and Hezekiah did not put him to death. In fact, the
elders emphasized that Hezekiah's decision was to pray to Yahweh for his favor so
that the disaster might be averted. The elders concluded that killing Jeremiah (and
ignoring his message) would, in essence, bring disaster (Jer 26:16–19).

Jeremiah was able to survive this attempt on his life in part, at least according to a narrator, because of the power of a friend in a high place—Ahikam son of
Shaphan (Jer 26:24).[27] Not all, of course, were so fortunate. Indeed, the narrative
notes that there was a prophet uttering oracles that were similar to Jeremiah's, a
man named Uriah the son of Shemaiah, from Kiriath-jearim. King Jehoiakim and
all his soldiers learned of Uriah's words and they sought to kill him, but Uriah
learned of this plot and fled to Egypt. Sadly for Uriah, Judah was in an alliance with
Egypt and (as per standard practice in ancient alliances) Jehoiakim dispatched a
certain Elnathan son of Achbor and a contingent of Judean soldiers; they traveled
to Egypt, captured him, and brought him before Jehoiakim in Jerusalem. Jehoiakim struck him down with the sword and had his corpse cast into the burial place
of the common people (Jer 26:20–23).

During the fourth year of Jehoiakim, the first year of Nebuchadnezzar of
Babylon (r. ca. 605–562), Jeremiah uttered a prophetic oracle in which he declared
that, since the thirteenth year of Josiah, he had been delivering prophetic oracles
to Judah, but to no avail. No one listened (Jer 25:3–4). Jeremiah indicates that he
had attempted to call Judah away from the worship of different Gods and wicked
ways, but to no effect. For this reason, declared Jeremiah, Yahweh would "send the
tribes of the North, to Nebuchadnezzar King of Babylon, my servant, against this
land (of Judah). . ." (Jer 25:9).

That same fourth year of King Jehoiakim, the following word of Yahweh came
to Jeremiah: "Take for yourself a scroll of the book and write upon it all the words

---

27. On Jeremiah's possible connections with Shaphan, see especially Blenkinsopp, *David
Remembered*, 42–45.

which I am speaking to you concerning Israel and concerning Judah and concerning all the people, from the day that I spoke to you during the days of Josiah until this day" (Jer 36:2). The goal of this written composition of Jeremiah's oracles was so that Judah might hear the words and turn away from their wicked ways, with the result that Yahweh might forgive them" (Jer 36:3). According to the narrative, Jeremiah then summoned Baruch the son of Neriah, the scribe, and he wrote the words that Jeremiah spoke to him. Jeremiah then told Baruch that he himself was constrained, not able to enter the Temple (Jer 36:5). The narrator states that Baruch did all that Jeremiah had commanded him. The precise timing of the actual reading would come, according to the narrative, in the fifth year of Jehoiakim, in the ninth month, at a time when Jerusalem was full of those observing a fast before Yahweh. Namely, in the hearing of all the people, Baruch read the words from the scroll, while he was in the temple, in the room of Gemariah the son of Shaphan the scribe (Jer 36:8–10).[28]

When Micaiah the son of Gemariah the son of Shaphan heard all the words of Yahweh from the scroll, he went down to the Royal Place.[29] According to the narrator, "all of the officials were sitting there": Elishama the scribe, Delaiah son of Shemaiah, Elnathan son of Achbor, Gemariah son of Shaphan, Zedekiah son of Hannaniah, and all (the rest of) the officials." Micaiah told them everything from Jeremiah that he had heard Baruch read (Jer 36:11–13). At that juncture, Jehudi was dispatched to bring Baruch to them, and they told Baruch to sit down and read it to them. He did so. After he finished, the officials were disturbed and told Baruch that they had to report all of this to King Jehoiakim. But before informing the king, they queried the precise origins of the content, and Baruch indicated that he recorded the words as Jeremiah uttered them. The officials told Baruch to go and hide, and for Jeremiah to do the same, letting no one know their whereabouts (Jer 36:14–19).

The officials then went to the royal court, leaving the scroll in Elishama's chamber. They reported the words of the scroll to King Jehoiakim, and then the king sent Jehudi to retrieve the scroll. Then Jehudi read it to the king and all the officials in his presence. The narrator notes that it was winter and that there was a fire burning in the king's brazier. As Jehudi read three or four columns, the king would cut them off with his pen-knife and throw them into the fire, until the entire scroll was burned up. The narrator notes that neither the king nor his servants were afraid and they did not tear their garments as a penitential act. This is, of

---

28. On the "Bullae of Baruch" from the antiquities market as a modern forgery, see C. A. Rollston, "The Bullae of Baruch ben Neriah the Scribe and the Seal of Maʿadanah Daughter of the King: Epigraphic Forgeries of the 20th Century," in *Eretz Israel 32: The Joseph Naveh Volume* (ed. J. Aviram et al.; Jerusalem: Israel Exploration Society, 2016), 79–90.

29. On the bullae of Gemaryahu and Shaphan, see L. J. Mykytiuk, *Identifying Biblical Persons in Northwest Semitic Inscriptions of 1200–539 B.C.E.* (SBL Academia Biblica 12; Atlanta: SBL, 2004), 139–47.

course, the narrator means as tacit condemnation of them. Striking is the fact that the narrator notes that Elnathan, Delaiah, and Gemariah had all urged Jehoiakim not to burn the scroll, but he had done so anyway. Moreover, Jehoiakim commands Jerahmeel (his own son) and Seraiah and Shelemiah to arrest Baruch and Jeremiah, but the narrator states that "God hid them" (Jer 36:20–26). Finally, the narrative of this incident concludes by stating that the word of Yahweh came to Jeremiah and instructed him to write all the words that had been in the scroll that had been burned. In addition, the fate of Jehoiakim is predicted:

> There shall not be to him anyone to sit upon the throne of David, and as for his corpse, someone shall cast it out to the heat by day and the frost by night. And I shall visit upon him and upon his seed and upon his servants, all their guilt, and I shall bring upon them and upon all the inhabitants of Jerusalem and to each person of Judah all the evil which I had said to them. But they would not listen. (Jer 36:27–31)

At this juncture, one of the most interesting editorial notations is provided: a new scroll was written, with all of the words of the first scroll, but with many similar words added to them (Jer 36:32).

Zedekiah, the son of Josiah, was placed on the throne of Judah by Nebuchadnezzar of Babylon as a successor to Jehoiachin the son of Jehoiakim (Jer 37:1). The year was ca. 597 B.C.E. The assumption of the narrator is that even at the beginning of Zedekiah's reign neither Zedekiah himself, nor the servants of Zedekiah, nor even the people of the land, listened to the prophetic words of Jeremiah (Jer 37:2). In light of the fact that it is stated at the beginning of this pericope that Zedekiah did not listen to Jeremiah's words, it is interesting (and revealing) that the narrator also indicates that Zedekiah sent Jehucal son of Shelemiah and the priest Zephaniah son of Maaseiah to Jeremiah with this message: "Please pray for us to Yahweh our God" (Jer 37:3). This suggests that Zedekiah was interested in Jeremiah's message. Also of particular importance is the parenthetical notation at this point in the narrative that Jeremiah had not yet been placed in prison (Jer 37:4). In any case, the fact that Zedekiah requested that Jeremiah pray to Yahweh regarding the situation is arguably important, because it reflects a broader pattern of some sympathy toward Jeremiah on the part of King Zedekiah, something that continues to be evident in the biographical narratives.

Naturally, Jeremiah's bold criticisms of "the prophets of falsehood" (e.g., Jer 14:13–18; Jer 23) galvanized these prophets to confront Jeremiah. Among the most fascinating cases is that of the showdown in the Jerusalem Temple between Jeremiah and Hananiah (both of whom understood themselves to be prophets of Yahweh). It is stated to have occurred in the fourth year and fifth month of Zedekiah's reign (i.e., ca. 593 B.C.E.). The prophet Hananiah was from Gibeon, not far from Jerusalem. He entered the Jerusalem Temple and declared to Jeremiah in the presence of the priests that the sacred vessels that had been removed to Babylon in 597 B.C.E. would be returned to Jerusalem and that exiled King Jeconiah (Je-hoiachin) would be returned to Jerusalem, all the Judeans whom Nebuchadnez-zar had exiled would return to Judah, as the yoke of Babylon would be broken within two years (Jer 28:1–4). With tongue firmly planted in cheek, Jeremiah said "Amen! May Yahweh do so!" (Jer 28:5). Jeremiah responded by noting that proph-ets normally prophesy war, famine, and pestilence against many countries, even great ones. In other words, prophecies of doom and gloom were the norm, so any prophet who prophesied peace should be scrutinized, and only if that prophet's predictions regarding peace and prosperity came true should that prophet be con-sidered a true prophet of Yahweh (Jer 28:6–9; cf. Deut 18:20–22). According to the narrative, after Jeremiah uttered those words, Hananiah the Prophet took the wooden yoke from Jeremiah and in a dramatic act he broke it and then said, "Thus says Yahweh, in this fashion, I will break the yoke of Nebuchadnezzar King of Babylon" (Jer 28:11). Jeremiah then left the Jerusalem Temple, but soon began to declare that Yahweh had replaced the wooden yoke with an iron one. At the con-clusion of this pericope, Jeremiah denied that Yahweh had sent Hananiah and he also predicted Hananiah's death. Then follow the poignant words: "Hananiah the Prophet died in that year, in the seventh month," (Jer 28:17), just two months after that fateful showdown in the Temple.

But the state's watchful eye was ever upon Jeremiah, and because Jeremiah was continuing to prophesy that Judah's surrender to Babylon was the only real means of avoiding destruction, some believed that he would soon depart from Jerusalem for the warm and welcome embrace of the Babylonian enemy. Thus, one day as he walked outside of Jerusalem in order to go to the land of Benjamin for the purposes of acquiring a piece of property, a sentinel named Irijah the son of Shelemiah son of Hananiah arrested Jeremiah, accusing him of deserting (נפל) to the Babylonians. Jeremiah denied that he was deserting, but to no avail. Jeremiah was brought before the Judean officials, and they beat him and imprisoned him in the house of the Jonathan the scribe, in a cistern. The narrator laconically states that he remained there "many days" (Jer 37:11–16). Zedekiah does not seem to have ordered Jeremiah's arrest, but he did not have him released at this time, ei-ther. Nevertheless, the narrator states that Zedekiah actually sent for Jeremiah at one point and questioned him in secret (בסתר) regarding whether or not there was an(other) "word from Yahweh." Jeremiah replied that there was, and the word from Yahweh was that Zedekiah would be handed over to Nebuchadnezzar. Ac-cording to the narrative, Jeremiah decided that he would also take the opportu-nity to remind Zedekiah that he (Jeremiah) had done nothing that justified his imprisonment and he also reminded the king that he himself (i.e., Jeremiah) had accurately prophesied that the Babylonians would come and besiege Jerusalem. He also reminded Zedekiah that the prophets who had prophesied that Babylon would not come were not around or not in prison. At that point, Jeremiah then made an ardent request of the king—namely, that he (Jeremiah) not be sent back to the house of Jonathan, as Jeremiah was confident that, if he were returned there, he would also die there. Zedekiah honored this request, and Jeremiah was placed in the "court of the guard" and was given daily rations of a loaf of bread until all the bread in the city was gone (Jer 37:17–21). Again, it is worth emphasizing that Zedekiah sought out the prophetic counsel of Jeremiah in this pericope, and it is also worth emphasizing that he honored Jeremiah's request not to be sent back to the house of Jonathan. Obviously, Zedekiah was not without concern for Jeremiah's safety, nor was he without respect for Jeremiah's prophetic oracles.

Probably during the fourth year of Zedekiah's reign,[30] diplomatic envoys from the countries of Edom, Moab, Ammon, Tyre, and Sidon had come to meet in Jerusalem (Jer 27:1–3).[31] The diplomatic envoys in attendance represented the countries of a coalition that had formed against Nebuchadnezzar. The message of Jeremiah for the entire delegation was dire: Yahweh had created the worlds and entrusted all within those worlds to those whom he pleased and he had decided to give Judah, Edom, Moab, Ammon, Tyre, and Sidon into the hand of Nebuchadnezzar (Jer 27:4–7).[32] Therefore, because of Yahweh's decision, all of these nations would 'serve' (עבד) Nebuchadnezzar (Jer 27:7). The nations that would not serve Nebuchadnezzar of Babylon would be punished by Yahweh, with "sword, famine, and pestilence" until, says Yahweh, "my destruction of them is complete" (Jer 27:8). Set on the lips of the prophet Jeremiah are also exhortations not to listen to "your prophets, your diviners, your dreamers, your soothsayers, or your sorcerers who are saying to you: 'Do not serve the king of Babylon'" (Jer 27:9). The reason for not listing to them is stated: "they are prophesying falsehood to you" (Jer 27:10). Conversely, according to the text, Jeremiah also stated that, if the nations submitted to the yoke of Babylon and served it (עבד), Yahweh would permit them to remain on their land and to work (עבד) it (Jer 27:11). Within this pericope, the text declares that Jeremiah delivered the very same message to Zedekiah himself (Jer 27:12–15). Naturally, the priests of the Jerusalem Temple continued to wish for the return of the sacred vessels that Nebuchadnezzar had deported

---

30. The fourth year, depending on precisely how one understands the language of Jer 28:1 ("in that year, at the beginning of the reign of King Zedekiah of Judah, in the fourth year the fifth month . . ."). That is, the language of Jer 28:1 could be understood as meaning that the events described in Jer 27 were events that also occurred in the fourth year of Zedekiah. Note that, while the Peshitta retains the phrase "at the beginning," the Septuagint does not. The plus in the MT (i.e., the words "at the beginning") can be reasonably regarded as a later addition.

31. Note that some Hebrew manuscripts, along with the Syriac, read "Zedekiah" in 27:1. However, most Masoretic manuscripts read "Jehoiakim." This verse is not present in the Septuagint. Emanuel Tov has reasonably argued that this verse was not present in the Hebrew text at an earlier stage (hence the minus in the Septuagint) but "was probably added in the forerunner of most textual witnesses at a larger stage in the development of the book, while the earlier stage, in which it was lacking, is represented by the Septuagint," with the trigger being the reference to Jehoiakim in 26:1. Tov also notes that the presence of the name "Zedekiah" in 27:3, 12; 28:1 demonstrates that this pericope is about Zedekiah, not Jehokakim (E. Tov, *Textual Criticism of the Hebrew Bible* [3rd ed.; Minneapolis: Fortress, 2012], 11, 369–71).

32. The MT has the word עבדי 'my servant' after the name Nebuchadnezzar (Jer 27:6), but the Septuagint has "to serve him"—that is, an infinitive and 3ms pronoun.

to Babylon in 597 B.C.E., but Jeremiah's message for them is that those who were prophesying that the vessels would soon be returned were prophesying falsehood. In fact, says Jeremiah, the sacred vessels that still remain in Jerusalem would soon be removed to Babylon as well (Jer 27:16–23).

Among the most interesting aspects of the prophetic and priestly polemics is the correspondence which is said to have been written between Judean priests and prophets in Jerusalem and Judean priests and prophets in Babylon (Jer 29). In terms of time-frame, it is reasonable to posit that this correspondence occurred at about the same time as the events narrated in the two preceding chapters of Jeremiah (i.e., ca. 593 B.C.E.).

Letter #1: According to the narrative, the first letter was sent by Jeremiah from Jerusalem to the Judean elders, priests, prophets, and people who had been brought into exile in Babylon ca. 598 B.C.E. This letter was hand-carried by Elash son of Shaphan and Gemariah son of Hilikiah, both of whom had been sent as an official delegation of King Zedekiah of Judah. The basic content of that letter is in keeping with Jeremiah's oracles to those in Jerusalem, but with some additional exhortations and details. To be precise, the letter commands the Judean exiles to build houses, plant crops, engage in marriage, and to pray to Yahweh for the welfare (שלום) of the city of Babylon. Moreover, the Judean exiles were commanded not to listen to the prophets, diviners, and dreamers among them who declared that the exile would be brief. Rather, prophesied Jeremiah, it would last seventy years, and then the restoration would occur (Jer 29:5–14). Two prophets among the exiles are singled out for condemnation as false prophets: Ahab son of Kolaiah and Zedekiah son of Maaseiah. In fact, Jeremiah even declares that these prophets would soon be delivered to Nebuchadnezzar and then be killed by being burned in a fire" (Jer 29:21–23).

Letter #2: According to this pericope, Shemaiah of Nehelam (who was in exile in Babylon) sent a letter in his own name from Babylon to the priest Zephaniah son of Maaseiah in Jerusalem. In this letter, Shemaiah said to Zephaniah:

> Yahweh has placed you as a priest in place of Jehoiada the priest to be the so that there may be inspectors (פקדים) in the Temple of Yahweh so that you may place any mad-man who prophesies in stocks and neck-iron. But now why is it that you have not rebuked Jeremiah of Anathoth who is prophesying to you? Because, after all, he has sent to us in Babylon saying "It will be a long time, (so) build houses and settle in, and plant gardens, and eat their produce." (Jer 29:28)

Ultimately, according to the narrative, "the priest Zephaniah, who had been sent this letter from Shemaiah, read that letter in the ears of Jeremiah the prophet."

Letter #3: Jeremiah is commanded to recount the words of Letter #2 to Shemaiah and then to "Send (a letter or message) to all the exiles, saying

> Thus says Yahweh about Shemaiah of Nehelam, because Shemaiah prophesied to you, though I did not send him, and he caused you to trust in falsehood, there-

fore, thus says Yahweh, "I am about to call Shemaiah of Nehelam and his seed to account (פקד). And there will be no one from him (i.e., from his seed) who will be dwelling in the midst of this people and no one shall see the good which I am doing for my people." Thus says Yahweh, because he spoke rebellion against Yahweh. (Jer 29:31–32)

Among other things, this pericope and the epistolary references within it reveal a fair amount about the resistance and criticism that Jeremiah was receiving and the ways in which the major Judean power-players were attempting to silence his voice.

During the tenth year of King Zedekiah (ca. 587 B.C.E.), Jeremiah is told that his kinsman Hanamel the son of Shallum was going to come to him in order to offer to Jeremiah the right of redemption for ancestral land in Anathoth (Jer 32:6–8). At this time, the army of Nebuchadnezzar was besieging Jerusalem and Jeremiah was still confined in the court of the guard (Jer 32:12). Naturally, King Zedekiah seems to have continued to have been quite frustrated with Jeremiah's prophetic oracles, and he was asking why Jeremiah continued to prophesy that Jerusalem would be given into the hand of Nebuchadnezzar and that Zedekiah himself would be captured, would meet face to face with Nebuchadnezzar, and would then be deported to Babylon (Jer 32:3–5). Indeed, Hanamel did indeed come to Jeremiah (demonstrating that Jeremiah could receive visitors at this point during his confinement) and Jeremiah bought the family land from Hanamel for seventeen shekels of silver (demonstrating that Jeremiah also had access to funds at this time). The deed of purchase was signed and sealed in the presence of witnesses and the silver was weighed on scales. Jeremiah then entrusted Baruch with the sealed copy and the open copy of the purchase contract and instructed him to bury it in an earthen jar for safe-keeping. Obviously, Jeremiah's assumption is that depositing this purchase contract in temple archives, palace archives, or the home archives of high officials would not be wise, because those buildings would soon be burned and all the documents therein would be destroyed. The purpose of this purchase is stated in the narrative not simply to be a property acquisition for Jeremiah but a symbolic demonstration that houses, fields, and vineyards will again be bought and sold in Judah (Jer 32:6–15). In short, this purchase was intended to reveal that Babylon's destruction of Judah would not be the final word; Judah would rise from the ashes of destruction to live again (Jer 32:36–44; 33:1–26).

Jeremiah's status as a pariah of the Judean officials continued. At one point, Pashhur the priest the son of Immer struck Jeremiah and put him in stocks in the upper Benjamin Gate of the Jerusalem Temple. After Jeremiah was released the next morning, he declared that Yahweh had renamed Pashhur as "Terror-All-Around" and he predicted that Pashhur himself and his family would die in Babylon and be buried there (Jer 20:1–6). Also, in a different incident, Shephatiah the son of Mattan, Gedaliah the son of Pashhur, Jucal the son of Shelemiah, and Pashhur the son of Malchiah heard the words that Jeremiah was uttering and became particularly enraged (cf. also Jer 21:1–10). In essence, Jeremiah was prophesying that those who might remain in the city of Jerusalem would die by pestilence and the sword but that those who would go out to the Babylonians would live. After all, said Jeremiah, the city and its king would soon be in the hands of the Babylonian king (Jer 38:1–3). The high officials considered these words treasonous and contended that Jeremiah should be put to death because his words were discouraging (reading the root רפה, not רפא) the remaining soldiers, as well as the people still residing in Jerusalem. And they argued that Jeremiah was not seeking the welfare of the people but, rather, evil (Jer. 38:4). Among the most striking and most telling statements in this pericope is Zedekiah's response to these officials: "Behold, he is in your (plural) hand, because as for the king, he has no power with you (plural) regarding this matter" (Jer 38:5). That is, according to this narrative, Zedekiah felt that his own power base had eroded so much that his high officials were holding the reins of power, not he himself. As a result, the high officials took Jeremiah and threw him into the cistern of Malchiah, the king's son, which was in the court of the guard. The narrator notes that there was no longer any water in the cistern, only deep mud, and into this mud Jeremiah sank (Jer 38:1–6). An official known in the narrative as 'Servant of the King' (Hebrew: עבד מלך), who was of Cushite origin and who served in the house of the king went to Zedekiah and told him that these high officials had placed Jeremiah in a waterless cistern and left him for dead.[33] Ebed-Melek condemns these officials, telling the king that these officials have acted in an evil fashion. The king then commands that Jeremiah be pulled from the cistern and he is then placed again in the court of the guard (Jer 38:7–13).

At this juncture, King Zedekiah sent for Jeremiah and met him, but not in the palace, nor in the king's house but rather in the Jerusalem Temple (Jer 38). The meeting was secret. Zedekiah swore an oath that he would not hand Jeremiah over to those who wished to have him killed. Jeremiah yet again warned Zedekiah that surrender to the Babylonians was the only means of national survival.[34] Zedekiah listened but indicated that he feared that, if he surrendered, he would be handed over to the Judeans who had already capitulated to Babylon and that they would abuse him. Jeremiah reassured him that this would not happen. As the conversation concluded, Zedekiah told Jeremiah to tell no one about this meeting lest he (Jeremiah) be killed. Moreover, Zedekiah told Jeremiah that, if the officials came to him (Jeremiah) in order to see what he and Zedekiah had talked about, Jeremiah was to state that he was only pleading with the king not to send him back to the house of Jonathan. Ultimately, the officials did come and ask Jeremiah about this meeting, and he answered just as Zedekiah had suggested. This pericope con-

---

33. On the term עבד המלך, see especially N. S. Fox, *In the Service of the King: Officialdom in Ancient Israel and Judah* (Monographs of the Hebrew Union College 23; Cincinnati, OH: Hebrew Union College Press, 2000), 53–63.

34. Rather similar content is also present in Jer 34:1–7, a narrative that refers in particular to the fact that, of the fortified cities of Judah, only Lachish and Azekah were still in Judean hands; the rest of the fortified cities of Judah had fallen.

cludes by noting that Jeremiah remained in the court of the guard until Jerusalem fell (Jer 38:28).

Arguably set during this time is the narrative about Zedekiah's covenant with all the people of Jerusalem that they should free their male and female Hebrew slaves (Jer 34:8–9). The high officials in Jerusalem and the citizenry in general all agree, and they all release their Hebrew slaves. Part of the rationale for this was the fact that the Babylonian army of Nebuchadnezzar was besieging Jerusalem. However, at some point after all of Jerusalem freed their slaves, the Babylonian army withdrew for a time from Jerusalem (Jer 34:21). Although the reason for the withdrawal is not mentioned here, it is reasonable to posit (based on Jer 37:5, for example) that it was because the Egyptian army (under Pharaoh Hophra, r. 589–570 B.C.E.; cf. Jer 44:30) had moved northward in order to do battle with the Babylonian army in Judah. Jeremiah's prophetic response (Jer 34:22; 37:5–10), however, is candidly and emphatically to declare that Egypt's army will depart and return to Egypt and Babylon's army will return to besiege and destroy Jerusalem. At the end of the day, Jeremiah's words about Zedekiah are arguably enshrined most ably in his parable of the baskets of good and bad figs, in which Zedekiah and those supporting him will be treated as a "basket of bad figs"—to be discarded and destroyed (Jer 24:1–10).

Ultimately, Jeremiah's words all came true, as it were, and Nebuchadnezzar destroyed Jerusalem, just as Jeremiah said would be the case (Jer 39). Jeremiah is shown substantial mercy: it seems that Nebuchadnezzar knew of his counsel about Babylon (Jer 39:11–40:6). After killing Zedekiah's sons before his own eyes and then blinding him (2 Kgs 25:7–8), Nebuchadnezzar appointed Gedaliah as governor, but he was soon assassinated (2 Kgs 25:22–26; Jer 39:11–14; 40:7–41:18). Jeremiah is brought, apparently under duress, to Egypt, and there he presumably died (Jer 43:1–7), still, according to the narrative delivering oracles (Jer 43:8–13). Among the most poignant words of the entire book are those in which Jeremiah curses the day of his birth, wishing that he had died in the womb (Jer 20:14–17).[35] Although he had some friends in high places, and even the Babylonians ultimately treated him with dignity, most of Jeremiah's life was one of marginalization and punishment at the hands of the powerful. Although his prophesies came true, he was, for this very reason, an enemy of the State.[36]

---

35. These words are reminiscent of those put on the lips of Job (Job 3:1–19).

36. For more details on some of the history and archaeology, see especially O. Lipschits and J. Blenkinsopp, eds., *Judah and the Judeans in the Neo-Babylonian Period* (Winona Lake, IN: Eisenbrauns, 2003).

Bibliography

Ackerman, S. *Under Every Green Tree: Popular Religion in Sixth-Century Judah*. HSM 46. Atlanta: Scholars, 1992.

Becker, U. "Die Wiederentdeckung des Prophetenbuches." *Berliner Theologische Zeitschrift* 21 (2004) 30–60.

Blenkinsopp, J. *David Remembered: Kingship and National Identity in Ancient Israel.* Grand Rapids, MI: Eerdmans, 2013.

Borowski, O. "Hezekiah's Reforms and the Revolt against Assyria." *NEA* 58 (1995) 148–55.

Cogan, M. *Bound for Exile: Israelites and Judeans under Imperial Yoke: Documents from Assyria and Babylonia.* Jerusalem: Carta, 2013.

Fox, N. S. *In the Service of the King: Officialdom in Ancient Israel and Judah.* Monographs of the Hebrew Union College 23. Cincinnati, OH: Hebrew Union College Press, 2000.

Grabbe, L. *Like a Bird in a Cage: The Invasion of Sennacherib in 701 B.C.E.* London: Sheffield Academic Press, 2003.

Grayson, A. K., and J. Novotny. *The Royal Inscriptions of Sennacherib, King of Assyria (704–681 BC), Part 1.* RINAP 3/1. Winona Lake, IN: Eisenbrauns, 2012.

Holladay, W. L. *Jeremiah 1: A Commentary on the Book of the Prophet Jeremiah Chapters 1–25.* Hermeneia. Philadelphia: Fortress, 1986.

_____. *Jeremiah 2: A Commentary on the Book of the Prophet Jeremiah Chapters 26–52.* Hermeneia. Philadelphia: Fortress, 1989.

Lipschits, O., and J. Blenkinsopp, eds. *Judah and the Judeans in the Neo-Babylonian Period.* Winona Lake, IN: Eisenbrauns, 2003.

Liverani, M. *Israel's History and the History of Israel.* London: Equinox, 2005.

Lundbom, J. R. *Jeremiah 1–20: A New Translation with Introduction and Commentary.* AB 21A. New York: Doubleday, 1999.

Machinist, P. "Assyria and Its Image in the First Isaiah." *JAOS* 103 (1983) 719–37.

Malamat, A. "The Historical Background of the Assassination of Amon, King of Judah." *IEJ* 3 (1953) 26–29.

Mankowski, P. V. *Akkadian Loanwords in Biblical Hebrew.* HSS 47. Winona Lake, IN: Eisenbrauns, 2000.

Mitchell, T. C. *The Bible in the British Museum: Interpreting the Evidence.* Mahwah, NJ: Paulist, 2004.

Mykytiuk, L. J. *Identifying Biblical Persons in Northwest Semitic Inscriptions of 1200–539 B.C.E.* SBL Academia Biblica 12. Atlanta: SBL, 2004.

Rainey, A. F. and R. S. Notley. *The Sacred Bridge: Carta's Atlas of the Biblical World.* 2nd ed. Jerusalem: Carta, 2014.

Reich, R. and E. Shukron. "The Date of the Siloam Tunnel Reconsidered." *Tel Aviv* 38 (2011) 147–57.

Rollston, C. A. "The Bullae of Baruch ben Neriah the Scribe and the Seal of Ma'adanah Daughter of the King: Epigraphic Forgeries of the 20th Century." Pp. 79–90 in *Eretz Israel 32: The Joseph Naveh Volume.* Edited by J. Aviram et al. Jerusalem: Israel Exploration Society, 2016.

Tadmor, H. and S. Yamada. *The Royal Inscriptions of Tiglath-pileser III (744–727 BC), and Shalmaneser V (726–722 BC), Kings of Assyria.* Winona Lake, IN: Eisenbrauns, 2011.

Tov, E. *Textual Criticism of the Hebrew Bible.* 3rd ed. Minneapolis: Fortress, 2012.

Tur-Sinai (Torczyner), H. *Lachish I: The Lachish Letters.* Oxford: Oxford University Press, 1938.

Ussishkin, D. *The Conquest of Lachish by Sennacherib.* Tel Aviv: The Institute of Archaeology, Tel Aviv University, 1982.

Nahum, Habakkuk, and Zephaniah

C. L. Crouch
University of Nottingham

Introduction

The prophetic books of Nahum, Habakkuk, and Zephaniah are traditionally dated, as their contents seem to indicate, to the late 7th and early 6th centuries B.C.E. Only Zephaniah has the usual heading allocated to books in the prophetic corpus of the Hebrew Bible, identifying it as originating in the reign of King Josiah, but Nahum is entirely focused on Nineveh, which ceased to exist in 612, and Habakkuk is focused on what it calls the Chaldeans, or the Babylonians, who succeeded the Assyrians as the chief Near Eastern power in the late 7th century.

All three form part of the Minor Prophets, also known as the Book of the Twelve. Due both to recent research on the interconnectedness of these books and to longer-standing discussions regarding their contents and origins, most parts of each of these books have been suggested, at some stage or another, to derive from later redactional work. Space precludes us from undertaking any comprehensive discussion of the redactional strata of these texts; some specific issues will be dealt with as they arise.

Regardless of the detailed redactional debates over specific elements of these books, their explicit statements and implicit sentiments regarding their prophets' and the people's relationships to the state are expressed against the background of the late 7th and early 6th centuries. In the case of Zephaniah, the state in question is Judah, apparently in the context of a dying Assyrian empire; Nahum and Habakkuk are concerned with the imperial states of Assyria and Babylonia. In the present context, it is worth remarking on the absence of prophetic texts between these prophets, active in probably the late 7th and early 6th centuries, and the late 8th-century prophets, Isaiah of Jerusalem and Micah. Although both the major and the minor prophets address a wide range of issues, from cultic matters to social justice and beyond, it seems that affairs of state may have the most persuasive claim for being the *raison d'être* of prophetic activity. In the relative political calm of the 7th century's *pax Assyriaca*, Judah's prophets are also quiet. As Assyria begins to collapse in the last third of the century, however, the need for powerful prophetic communication once more raises its head.

Context

The hegemony of Assyria's political grip over Mesopotamia and most of the Levant began to deteriorate about the time of the death of its last powerful king, Assurbanipal, in 627. Overextended and struggling to maintain control over the Egyptian and Babylonian reaches of the empire, Assyria retreated from the Levant, leaving it to an uncertain authority for much of the next two decades. The traditional interpretation has been that, in the absence of Assyria and prior to the arrival of the Babylonians, Judah and the other southern Levantine states enjoyed a period of independence. It is against this background that the apparent nationalism of Josianic expansion and reform—relevant particularly to the context of Zephaniah—has been generally understood. More recently, however, extra-biblical evidence has been interpreted to suggest a more-or-less peaceful transfer of power from Assyria to Egypt, as the Assyrian administrative and military presence withdrew from the region. The direct power and involvement of the Egyptians in inland Judah seems to have been relatively low, with the new imperial presence interested primarily in the commercial potential of the coastal port cities. Its power was sufficient, however, that upon the death of Josiah it could depose his chosen successor (Jehoahaz) and install its own puppet king (Jehoiachim) in Jerusalem.

The remaining years of Judah's existence were characterized by grave uncertainty over which rising power would ultimately come out victorious. The Egyptians and the Assyrians allied for some years in an attempt to fend off the rising Babylonian tide; even the fall of Nineveh in 612 does not appear to have decisively concluded the Assyrians' defeat, as three years later Egypt was still on campaign toward Mesopotamia. Ultimately, however, this alliance failed; Assyrian fell to Babylonia and Egypt was left in control of the Levant.

This respite did not last long: Egypt and Babylonia continued their contest for control of Assyria's former territories. In 605, Nebuchadnezzar defeated Neco at Carchemish, provoking a shift of southern Levantine—including Judahite—allegiances to Babylonia. On-going skirmishes between Babylonia and Egypt, however, continually raised the question of the permanency of this arrangement, and in 601, Jehoiachim rebelled against his Babylonian masters. This prompted the Babylonians' first invasion of Judah in 598/597, the first fall of Jerusalem, and the deportation of a first group of exiles to Babylonia. The following decade is equally turbulent, and a second ill-advised rebellion by the Babylonians' own puppet king, Zedekiah, culminated in the destruction of Jerusalem and a second round of deportations in 587/586.

These chaotic decades form the backdrop for the prophetic texts of Nahum, Habakkuk, and Zephaniah. Although parts of these books have almost certainly been edited and revised by later editors, the Assyrian, Egyptian, and Babylonian imperial ambitions of this period, including ongoing uncertainty over the likely success of these ambitions, comprise the background against which these texts' statements regarding state power and state responsibilities are cast.

Nahum

Current research on the book of Nahum is characterized by a near-complete lack of agreement on all aspects of the book.[1] Some argue for its three chapters as a unified or a nearly-unified whole, while others contend that they comprise a more-or-less random collection of orcales united only by their common interests in Assyria and Nineveh.[2] Scholars have argued for the text(s)'s origins in the 7th century—shortly after the fall of Thebes in 663, in connection with the supposed revolt of Manasseh reported in Chronicles, or around the fall of Nineveh in 612— in the exilic period, and in the Persian period.[3] Assertions of the text's hopelessly

---

1. For an introduction to the history of interpretation on Nahum, see D. L. Christensen, "The Book of Nahum: A History of Interpretation," in *Forming Prophetic Literature: Essays on Isaiah and the Twelve in Honor of John D. W. Watts* (ed. J. W. Watts and P. R. House; JSOTSup 235; Sheffield: Sheffield Academic, 1996), 187–94.

2. Confining these particular references to commentaries in favor of significant redaction are, among others, L. Perlitt, *Die Propheten Nahum, Habakuk, Zephanja* (ATD 25,1; Göttingen: Vandenhoeck & Ruprecht, 2004); K. Seybold, *Nahum Habakuk Zephanja* (ZBK 24,2; Zurich: Theologische Verlag, 1991); J. M. O'Brien, "Nahum," in *The Oxford Bible Commentary* (ed. J. Barton and J. Muddiman; Oxford: Oxford University Press, 2001); cf. A. C. Hagedorn, "Nahum— Ethnicity and Stereotypes: Anthropological Insights into Nahum's Literary History," in *Ancient Israel: The Old Testament in Its Social Context* (ed. P. F. Esler; London: SCM, 2005), 223–29. In favor of an essentially unified book, K. Spronk, *Nahum* (HCOT; Kampen: Kok Pharos, 1997); M. H. Floyd, *Minor Prophets: Part 2* (FOTL 22; Grand Rapids, MI: Eerdmans, 2000); D. L. Christensen, *Nahum: A New Translation with Introduction and Commentary* (AB 24F; New Haven, CT: Yale University Press, 2009).

3. Spronk (*Nahum*, 1) favors a date immediately after the defeat of Thebes; Floyd prefers the decade following the fall of Nineveh in 612, prior to the appearance of the Babylonians in the southern Levant, with this main text drawing on older prophetic material from around 701 (*Minor Prophets*, 19–20); Vuilleumier concludes that it is prior to 630 (C.-A. Keller and R. Vuilleumier, *Michée, Nahoum, Habacuc, Sophonie* [CAT; Paris: Delachaux & Niestlé, 1971] 103). Seybold has a main collection of oracles originating sometime between 663 and 612, with salvation for Judah added sometime after 612 (probably after 587) and ch. 1 much later, in the postexilic period (*Nahum*, 11–12), and Perlitt devises a similar schema (*Die Propheten*, 1–4). Christensen at one stage argued for a text originating around the time of Manasseh's supposed revolt (D. L. Christensen, "Acrostic of Nahum Reconsidered," *ZAW* 87 [1975] 27–29) but by the time of his 2009 commentary concluded that the historical prophet is entirely "lost" to the canonical redactor of the Book of the Twelve, effectively locating the text in the Persian period (*Nahum*, 54–57); O'Brien similarly shuns any attempt to identify a pre-redactional component of the text (J. M. O'Brien, *Nahum* [Readings; Sheffield: Sheffield Phoenix, 2009], 21–22; compare her application of film theory to contend that the vivacity of Nahum's language has little to do with its date, in J. M. O'Brien, "Violent Pictures, Violent Cultures? The 'Aesthetics of Violence' in Contemporary

corrupt state appear repeatedly, as do declarations that it is essentially well preserved.[4] Some insist on the impossibility of interpreting the book without complete reference to the Book of the Twelve of which it forms a part; others dismiss this wider context as largely irrelevant or ignore it altogether.[5]

A major point of issue in most of these diverging opinions is the state and status of the theophanic "hymn" in Nah 1. Aside from this opening paean to YHWH, the book of Nahum is essentially one long oracle against Nineveh and the king of Assyria. Unsurprisingly, the unity of Nah 1 and Nah 2–3 has been questioned regularly, with the broad and cosmic language of the opening poetry deemed incompatible or inconsistent with the more specific focus on the particular military woes in chs. 2–3. Contributing to this discussion has been the particular literary construction of ch. 1: ever since Delitzsch suggested an alphabetic influence on 1:3–7, the chapter's core (variably identified as 1:2–8 or 1:2–10) has attracted a significant proportion of Nahum scholarship.[6] Because the acrostic identified by Delitzsch was neither complete nor entirely consistent, much subsequent energy and creativity was expended attempting to reconstruct a full alphabetic acrostic, a redactional and emendational enterprise largely responsible for continuing negative evaluations of the text's relative degree of corruption.[7]

The major interpretive effect of the attention to 1:2–8 (etc.) as an acrostic or potentially acrostic poem has been the conclusion that, if all or part of this first chapter was indeed an acrostic, it is substantially unlike the rest of the book and ought therefore to be identified as a later addition. One of the earliest and most influential proponents of such a view was Gunkel, who, under the influence of the

---

Film and in Ancient Prophetic Texts," in *Aesthetics of Violence in the Prophets* [ed. C. Franke and J. M. O'Brien; LHBOTS 517; London: T. & T. Clark, 2010], 112–30). The Maccabean period, once favored by Haupt, went out of possibility upon the discovery of a Nahum *pesher* at Qumran (P. Haupt, "Eine alttestamentliche Festliturgie für den Nikanortag," *ZDMG* 61 [1907] 275–97). For an attempt at dating the book on an empirical basis, see R. E. Bee, "An Empirical Dating Procedure for Old Testament Prophecy," *JSOT* 11 (1979) 23–35, the critique by B. Becking ("Bees's Dating Formula and the Book of Nahum," *JSOT* 18 [1980] 100–104), and Bee's response ("Dating the Book of Nahum: A Response to the Article by Bob Becking," *JSOT* 18 [1980] 104).

4. O'Brien declares the text "notoriously difficult" ("Nahum," 599; note her response to this issue in *Nahum*, 25–26). Arguments in favor of an essentially uncorrupted text include those of Christensen, *Nahum*, 64–66 (on the basis of logoprosodic analysis) and Spronk, *Nahum*, 2–3, who traces the generally poor opinion of the book's text to the attempts to reconstruct an acrostic in ch. 1.

5. For the former, see Christensen, *Nahum*, 54–57; O'Brien, *Nahum*, 21–22 and J. M. O'Brien, "Nahum–Habakkuk–Zephaniah: Reading the 'Former Prophets' in the Persian Period," *Int* 61 (2007) 168–83; J. Nogalski, *Literary Precursors to the Book of the Twelve* (BZAW 217; Berlin: de Gruyter, 1993), 37–40 and Nogalski, *Redactional Processes in the Book of the Twelve* (BZAW 218; Berlin: de Gruyter, 1993), 93–128; in forceful contrast, see Perlitt, *Die Propheten*, xiv–xv.

6. F. Delitzsch, *Biblischer Commentar über die Psalmen* (Leipzig: Dörflin & Franke, 1867), 107.

7. For a recent history of research on this chapter see T. Renz, "A Perfectly Broken Acrostic in Nahum 1?" *JHS* 9 (2009) 4–9.

Urzeit-Endzeit cosmological-eschatological system, according to which he understood much of Israelite religion, theology, and practice, argued that the material in Nah 1 had been added to oracles against Nineveh in the postexilic period in order to cast Nineveh and its defeat in the context of a future eschatological end-time.[8] Many scholars subsequently followed his conclusion that the original Nahum, if such could be identified, was restricted to Nah 2–3. The assertion that the material in Nah 1 is a late addition to the book remains common.[9]

Current research on Nah 1 has drawn this into question. Most scholars have now abandoned earlier radical attempts to reconstruct a full acrostic, conceding that, if an acrostic did exist, it extended no further than *kaf* at the most; others have gone even further, denying that the text originally contained an acrostic at all.[10] More common are suggestions that the author of (this part, at least, of) Nahum was using a preexisting poetic text for his own purposes and/or was not concerned about preserving a perfectly acrostic aspect of the text.[11] Perhaps most significant, however, are arguments to the effect that these verses do not form some foreign appendage to the book of Nahum but are intimately linked to it. Two particular cases are of note. First is the suggestion by Renz that the acrostic elements of 1:3–7 are neither accidental nor adopted from some preexisting text but ignored in the current one, but rather that its brokenness is a deliberate means of articulating and emphasizing Yʜwʜ's role in the creation and destruction of order in the world.[12]

---

8. H. Gunkel, "Nahum 1," *ZAW* 11 (1893) 223–44, cf. H. Gunkel, *Creation and Chaos in the Primeval Era and the Eschaton: A Religio-Historical Study of Genesis 1 and Revelation 12* (trans. K. W. Whitney Jr.; Grand Rapids, MI: Eerdmans, 2006) 314–15 n. 244.

9. E.g., Seybold, *Nahum*, 11–12; Perlitt, *Die Propheten*, 1–4; B. Renaud, "La composition du livre de Nahum: une proposition," *ZAW* 99 (1987) 198–219; J. Nogalski, "The Redactional Shaping of Nahum 1 for the Book of the Twelve," in *Among the Prophets: Language, Image and Structure in the Prophetic Writings* (ed. P. R. Davies and D. J. A. Clines; JSOTSup 144; Sheffield: JSOT Press, 1993), 193–202; Nogalski, *Literary Precursors*, 37–40; Nogalski, *Redactional Processes*, 115–17, 127–28. With regard to the latter's arguments, see, however, B. M. Zapff, "Die Volkerperspektive des Michabuches als 'Systematisierung' der divergierenden Sicht der Volker in den Buchern Joel, Jona und Nahum: Uberlegungen zu einer buchubergreifenden Exegese im Dodekapropheton," *BN* 98 (1999) 86–99, and B. M. Zapff, "The Perspective of the Nations in the Book of Micah as a 'Systematization' of the Nations' Role in Joel, Jonah and Nahum: Reflections on a Context-Oriented Exegesis in the Book of the Twelve," *Society of Biblical Literature Seminar Papers* 38 (1999) 596–616.

10. M. H. Floyd, "The Chimerical Acrostic of Nahum 1:2–10," *JBL* 113 (1994) 421–37.

11. E.g., K. Seybold, "Vormasoretische Randnotizen in Nahum 1," *ZAW* 101 (1989) 71–85; compare with K. Spronk, "The Line-Acrostic in Nahum 1: New Evidence from Ancient Greek Manuscripts and from the Literary Analysis of the Hebrew Text," in *The Impact of Unit Delimitation on Exegesis* (ed. R. de Hoop, M. C. A. Korpel, and S. E. Porter; Leiden: Brill, 2009), 228–40; also Christensen, who prioritizes the poem's logoprosodic structure ("The Acrostic of Nahum Reconsidered"; and "The Acrostic of Nahum Once Again: A Prosodic Analysis of Nahum 1:1–10," *ZAW* 99 [1987] 409–415) and Nogalski, who attributes the disruption to the book's integration into the Book of the Twelve (*Literary Precursors*, 37–40; *Redactional Processes*, 115–17).

12. Renz, "Perfectly Broken."

Second, a few scholars have recently observed that the opening lines of the book form a short sentence acrostic of a type otherwise known only from Mesopotamia: the first letters of 1:2a, 2b, 3a form the word אני 'I', while the last letters of 1:1, 2a, 2b, 3a form the Tetragrammaton, יהוה.[13] Together, this acrostic-telestic forms the familiar divine self-declaration, אני יהוה 'I am Yhwh'. Significant from a redactional point of view is that these words link the poem of 1:2 and following to the heading in 1:1, which is normally marked off as being one of the usual headings added at a late stage to prophetic collections. Developing this observation into the book as a whole has been the identification of other short name-acrostics, references to Assyria (אשור) and Nineveh (נינוה), at 1:12 and 3:18, indicating deliberate structuring techniques "at the beginning, at the end and at the major break of the book."[14]

As these more recent developments suggest, the rationale for dividing the material in Nah 1 from the rest of the book on text-critical grounds has lost much of its former footing. Contributing further to this is a more-sophisticated understanding of the mythological language used by the poem to describe Yhwh, which Gunkel had taken to be gross eschatological imagery deriving only from the late postexilic period in which prophecy was transforming into apocalyptic. Contrary to Gunkel's claim that Yhwh's battle against chaotic forces was a particular characteristic of narratives about creation, appearing otherwise only with descriptions of a final, ultimate battle at the *Endzeit*, more recent research has demonstrated that Yhwh's battle against chaos was an ongoing historical process, involving both the divine and earthly realms.[15]

As mentioned tangentially by some commentators, Nah 1 is characterized by language associated with theophany, the revelation of the divine nature. Less often recognized is that the theophanic language in Nah 1 is part of a network of ideas surrounding the presentation of Yhwh in military guise and, in particular, as a deity who battles both earthly and cosmic enemies in the production of a universal order. Some elements of this are more to the fore in Nahum than others; certainly the idea that Yhwh's earthly counterpart in these military efforts is the king of

---

13. First A. S. van der Woude, "The Book of Nahum: A Letter Written in Exile," in *Instruction and Interpretation: Studies in Hebrew Language, Palestinian Archaeology and Biblical Exegesis: Papers Read at the Joint British-Dutch Old Testament Conference Held at Louvain, 1976* (ed. H. A. Brongers; OtSt 20; Leiden: Brill, 1977), 108–26, followed and elaborated by K. Spronk, "Acrostics in the Book of Nahum," *ZAW* 110 (1998) 209–22.

14. Spronk, "Acrostics," 222; cf. Spronk, "Line-Acrostics."

15. C. L. Crouch, *War and Ethics in the Ancient Near East: Military Violence in Light of Cosmology and History* (BZAW 417; Berlin: de Gruyter, 2009), 29–32, 65–80. On Nahum specifically, see Crouch, "On Floods and the Fall of Nineveh: A Note on the Origins of a Spurious Tradition," in *New Perspectives on Old Testament Prophecy and History: Essays in Honour of Hans M. Barstad* (ed. Rannfrid I. Thelle, Terje Stordalen, and Mervyn E. J. Richardson; VTSup 168; Leiden: Brill, 2015), 212–16.

Judah is in the background, if explicitly present at all.[16] Of particular import for the question of continuity between Nah 1 and Nah 2–3, however, is that the image of the deity who battles against the forces of cosmic chaos (typically personified as or described with reference to the sea or rivers, although the polytheistic aspects of this are heavily played down in most biblical renderings) is closely connected to the idea that both the deity and his human counterpart act together against earthly chaos.[17]

The point of this, as far as Nahum is concerned, is that there is no meaningful distinction between the earthly battles enacted against earthly enemies and the cosmological battles enacted by Yhwh against cosmological chaos. Such a theoretical distinction is not, therefore, a legitimate cause for separating Nah 1 from Nah 2–3 and, furthermore, not a reason to suggest that the material in Nah 1 represents a generalizing, later spin on the specific discussion of Nineveh that follows.[18]

In light of this more nuanced understanding of Yhwh's warrior persona, active on both the heavenly and earthly planes, there is much less cause for dividing Nah 1's theophanic description of Yhwh battling against those who challenge him from the more prosaic description in Nah 2–3 of Yhwh battling against earthly enemies—namely, Nineveh. Indeed, once the conceptual continuity between these sections is recognized, the artistic continuity and literary sophistication of these chapters may be more clearly acknowledged. Throughout Nah 1–3, the text is notable for its use of remarkably vivid imagery: "In its poetic form," writes Christensen, "the book of Nahum has no superior within the prophetic literature of the Tanakh."[19] In Nah 1, this is focused on Yhwh's tempestuous efforts toward marshalling the created order. When the text turns to Nineveh, there are vivid descriptions of soldiers sent to attack and to defend the city and descriptions of the

---

16. On the matter of the often-unspecified addressees in Nahum, see M. A. Sweeney, "Concerning the Structure and Generic Character of the Book of Nahum," *ZAW* 104 (1992) 364–66, with further references.

17. In the traditional form of this relationship the human counterpart is the king of Judah (see, for example, Pss 18 and 89). That the advent of world empires might demand a non-Judahite agent for Yhwh, however, is an idea seen quite clearly in the polemicizing of Ezekiel in particular (see C. A. Strine and C. L. Crouch, "Yahweh's Battle against Chaos in Ezekiel: The Transformation of a Traditional Motif for a New Situation," *JBL* 132 [2013] 883–903).

18. For a related discussion, see Sweeney, "Concerning the Structure," 369–71; also Floyd, *Minor Prophets*, 10–12, who, while disagreeing with Sweeney in his genre classification, agrees that 1:2–8 should not be described as eschatological. In somewhat more general terms, Floyd writes that the two-fold structure of the book (1:1–2:11, with a Judahite orientation, and 2:12–3:19, from an Assyrian perspective) effectively presents the fall of Nineveh "as an event to be vicariously relived again and again, and as an event that maintains its relevance for succeeding generations, because it is a concrete historical example of a recurring situation in which Yahweh typically acts the same way. As creator of the world he can influence comic forces in favor of those who cooperate with him in maintaining a just world order, and he can influence cosmic forces to the detriment of those who oppose him in this regard" (Floyd, *Minor Prophets*, 7).

19. Christensen, *Nahum*, 23.

former city in leonine terms, transformed into the shamed and publicly humiliated female. Though not generally recognized, cosmological language appears in these descriptions too.[20] Although the present text of the book is highly unlikely to be a facsimile of the original, there is no need to separate the opening poetry from what follows.

Though somewhat circuitously, this brings us at last to the matter of Nahum's relationship to the state. The relationships between YHWH, Nineveh (as *pars pro toto* for Assyria), and—although very much a secondary character—Judah in Nahum present clearly the conclusion that, however powerful in earthly perspective, the imperial power of the Assyrian state is no match for the ultimate power of YHWH.[21] In support of this point, one might cite nearly any passage in the book, from the opening description of YHWH's control over the universe, designed to emphasize his power and authority against any who might challenge it, to the final oracle against the king of Assyria, describing the disarray of his empire. This latter is particularly interesting, concluding as it does with the rhetorical question:

> There is no assuaging your hurt, your wound is mortal.
> All who hear the news about you clap their hands over you.
> For who has ever escaped your endless cruelty? (3:19)

In addition to suggesting a talionic principle of justice at work in YHWH's punishment of Assyria—note also the links between Assyria's economic exploitation (3:1–4) and the disappearance of its commercial agents (3:16), as well as the focus on the king's demise (3:18–19) after attention to the disgraceful behavior of the royal family (2:12–14)—the text effectively declares that the state is not a law unto itself: its cruelty is not unlimited but is accountable to the ultimate power of YHWH.[22]

The extended leonine metaphor in 2:12–14 makes a similar point, using intensely violent language to describe the activities of the Assyrian king demonstrating his power: "The lion has torn enough for his whelps and strangled prey for his lionesses; he has filled his caves with prey and his dens with torn flesh" (2:13 [ET 2:12]).[23] Yet even this king of beasts is subordinate to YHWH, and YHWH assures

---

20. Crouch, "On Floods and the Fall of Nineveh."

21. Note in particular Sweeney's suggestion that the frequent ambiguity of antecedent for pronouns in Nahum is not a result of editorial sloppiness but designed to force the audience to consider their own place in the schema that Nahum describes (for or against YHWH) (Sweeney, "Concerning the Structure," 364–65, 371–73). The message, in other words, is not specifically limited to a statement about the limited power of the Assyrian state but rather comprises a wider point with regard to the subordination of all power to YHWH. As the most powerful state yet known to the ancient world, Assyria serves as the extreme example: if even this sprawling empire is ultimately under the power of YHWH, how much more must this be true of the less powerful?

22. On talionic justice see Floyd, *Minor Prophets*, 6; compare with Crouch, *War and Ethics*, 169–72.

23. This is often supposed to be a particularly Assyrian image, but see M. Cogan, "The Lions of Nineveh (Nahum 2:12–14): A Check on Nahum's Familiarity with Assyria," in *Birkat*

his audience that such violence will see its just end.[24] Not even the most powerful agents of the state—its king and its ruling classes—are exempt from the consequences of their actions (3:10, 18–19).

Although Assyria's domination has/had its place, it is always and ever under the ultimate control of YHWH. Just as the success and power of Egypt were ultimately illusory, so too Assyria's reach is depicted as a limited and destructible phenomenon (3:7–11). Acquiescence to the imperial state is absent, if not rejected outright in the case of an empire extended beyond just bounds; allegiance is due always and only to the deity who pulls its strings.

Habakkuk

Whether or not the following book of Habakkuk approaches the remit of the imperial state with a similar attitude depends on identification of the book's antagonist. The sole named entity in the book, aside from Habakkuk and YHWH, is the "Chaldeans" (the Neo-Babylonians) specified in 1:6. The Babylonians are thus commonly considered to be the antagonists of the piece or of at least a significant part of it.[25] Complicating this association of Babylonia with that against which the prophet rails are the fact that the Babylonians appear explicitly as YHWH's own agents in 1:6 and the various references, throughout the book, to the "righteous"

Shalom: Studies in the Bible, Ancient Near Eastern Literature, and Postbiblical Judaism Presented to Shalom M. Paul on the Occasion of His Seventieth Birthday (2 vols.; ed. C. Cohen et al.; Winona Lake, IN: Eisenbrauns, 2008), 1:433–39; see also B. A. Strawn, *What Is Stronger than a Lion? Leonine Image and Metaphor in the Hebrew Bible and the Ancient Near East* (OBO 212; Göttingen: Vandenhoeck & Ruprecht, 2005). Various other elements of the book are often thought to reveal particular knowledge of Assyria and its history, including the reference to the defeat of Thebes in 3:8–10 (J. R. Huddlestun, "Nahum, Nineveh, and the Nile: The Description of Thebes in Nahum 3:8–9," *JNES* 62 [2003] 97–110), possible references to the goddess Ishtar in 2:8 (M. Delcor, "Allusions à la déesse Ištar en Nahum 2:8," *Bib* 58 [1977] 73–83; A. Pinker, "Descent of the Goddess Ishtar to the Netherworld and Nahum II 8," *VT* 55 [2005] 89–100), and the long-standing tradition that Nahum knew some of the particulars of the mechanics of Nineveh's destruction (see H. W. F. Saggs, "Nahum and the Fall of Nineveh," *JTS* 20 [1969] 220–25 and the various discussions by Pinker, of which "Nahum and the Greek Tradition on Nineveh's Fall," *JHS* 6 [2006] n.p., provides the most extensive references to the relevant literature).

24. As with all oracles against nations in the Hebrew Bible, it is unlikely in the extreme that the rhetorical "you," Assyria (or its representative), was ever expected to actually hear the words in question; the audience of these texts is the Yahwistic listener(s) who knows this imperial excess first hand. (Floyd draws an analogy to the narrative of Isaiah, Hezekiah, and the Assyrian delegation in 2 Kgs 19, concluding that "[l]ike the first speech addressed to the character of the Assyrian king (1:14), the speeches in 2:2–3:19 addressed to Nineveh and to him are never actually meant for their ears. They are rather meant to be overheard by the character playing the role of Judah's representative and are actually for Judah's benefit" [*Minor Prophets*, 17]).

25. Among others, Floyd, *Minor Prophets*, 82–86; D. E. Gowan, "Habakkuk," in *The Oxford Bible Commentary* (ed. J. Barton and J. Muddiman; Oxford: Oxford University Press, 2001), 601; M. A. Sweeney, "Structure, Genre, and Intent in the Book of Habakkuk," *VT* 41 (1991) 67–69, 73–78; M. D. Johnson, "The Paralysis of Torah in Habakkuk 1:4," *VT* 35 (1985) 257–66.

and the "wicked," sometimes taken as referring to divisions within the population of Judah or even to specific individuals, such as Jehoiachim or the prophet.[26] It is also striking that neither Judah nor Israel—nor, indeed, any specific individual—are explicitly mentioned at any stage in the book as the target of Habakkuk's condemnation.[27] Given that the prophetic books do not elsewhere have any compunction about naming Israel/Judah as the target of their condemnations if that is their intention, it therefore seems unlikely that the author(s) meant the text to be construed as, in whole or in part, against Israel/Judah.

This returns us to the matter of the Babylonians, whose mention constitutes the sole historical reference in the book. They are, indeed, introduced as the agents of YHWH—whose speech in 1:5–11 declares that "I am rousing the Chaldeans, that fierce and impetuous nation"—but an actual and highly negative experience of the Babylonian empire is probably the cause of the complaint which comprises the impetus for the book.[28]

The first chapter (sometimes continuing to include part or all of the second) is traditionally seen as a dialogue between YHWH and Habakkuk, in which they converse regarding the particularities of divine justice.[29] Habakkuk begins

---

26. Andersen identifies the righteous man as the prophet and the wicked as Jehoiachim, damned as an Egyptian puppet against the background of a rising Babylonian empire; he thereby accounts for the positive description of the Chaldeans in 1:6 by identifying them as on the side of the righteous (F. I. Andersen, *Habakkuk: A New Translation with Introduction and Commentary* [AB 25; New York: Doubleday, 2001], 24–25). Seybold is not dealing with a unified text that must make consistent sense, but in what he identifies as the original prophetic layer of the text he emphasizes a concern with (in)justice within Judah, to which the Babylonians are an essentially ancillary player, akin to the social justice critiques of Isaiah and Amos (*Nahum*, 46–47). Haak identifies both the wicked and the righteous as royal figures within Judah, with the deposed Jehoahaz as the righteous and Jehoiachim as his wicked replacement; even more than Andersen, he emphasizes the positive depiction of the Babylonians, going so far as to argue that the entirety of the book is pro-Babylonian (primarily by explaining the woe oracles as concerning Jehoiachim, rather than the Babylonians) (R. D. Haak, *Habakkuk* [VTSup 44; Leiden: Brill, 1992], 107–45). Sweeney separates the righteous Judah and the wicked Babylonians ("Structure," 73–78), while Holladay splits the difference by arguing that the woe oracles in ch. 2 were originally directed against Jehoiachim in 601 but that several were revised in 594 to be against Nebuchadnezzar (W. L. Holladay, "Plausible Circumstances for the Prophecy of Habakkuk," *JBL* 120 [2001] 123–30). Pinker suggests that *ṣdyq* 'righteous one' in 2:4 should be read as Zedekiah (A. Pinker, "Habakkuk 2.4: An Ethical Paradigm or a Political Observation?" *JSOT* 32 [2007] 91–112); Gunneweg traces the language to wisdom traditions (A. H. J. Gunneweg, "Habakuk und das Problem des leidenden צדיק," *ZAW* 98 [1986] 400–415).

27. The nearest the book gets is a reference to YHWH's people and YHWH's anointed, in 3:13.

28. M. H. Floyd, "Prophetic Complaints about the Fulfillment of Oracles in Habakkuk 1:2–17 and Jeremiah 15:10–18," *JBL* 110 (1991) 397–418. See also Johnson, "Paralysis of Torah," for an argument against the general assumption that Babylonians are positively presented in 1:5–11.

29. So, for example, Andersen, *Habakkuk*, 15; K. J. Cathcart, " 'Law is Paralysed' (Habakkuk 1.4): Habakkuk's Dialogue with God and the Language of Legal Disputation," in *Prophecy and the Prophets in Ancient Israel: Proceedings of the Oxford Old Testament Seminar* (ed. J. Day; LHBOTS 531; New York: T. & T. Clark, 2010), 339–53; Gowan, "Habakkuk," 602; Sweeney,

the dialogue with an expression of concern about abundant violence for which there seems to be no justice (1:2–4); this is addressed by an oracle from Yhwh which promises the arrival of the Babylonians, acting on a punitive mission from Yhwh (1:5–11). This is followed by Habakkuk's concerns about the excessive and violent nature of Yhwh's Babylonian agents and, in particular, the theological implications of this for Yhwh (1:12–17). This discussion may stop here or may continue into ch. 2; 2:1 appears to be a description of a prophetic solicitation of an oracle, which is then given in 2:2–20 as a series of "woe" oracles, although some would limit the oracular response to the material between 2:2 and either 2:5 or 2:6 (or part thereof) and classify the following woe oracles separately. However far Yhwh's response extends, the obvious point is Yhwh's assurance to Habakkuk that the wicked will surely be punished.[30]

More recently, however, there has been some suggestion that the oracle in 1:5–11 may be a quotation of an earlier oracle announcing the coming Babylonians, which is proving problematic at the point of the book's composition (and, indeed, prompting it) because of the excessive violence employed by the Babylonians. The preceding (1:2–4) and following (1:12–17) complaint passages, rather than being a linear development of the prophet's thinking, both articulate a single concern about the implications of the quoted text.[31] Habakkuk 2 is accordingly

---

"Structure," 74. Although text- and form-critical analyses of Habakkuk are slightly less diverse in their conclusions than those regarding Nahum, there is still considerable disagreement regarding the unity of the book and, accordingly, the respective dating of its constituent parts. Seybold, for example, divides the book into three types of texts: prophetic (parts of chs. 1 and 2), hymnic (parts of ch. 3) and parts belonging to a *Klage- und Dankpsalm* (interspersed throughout) (*Nahum*, 43–45). Perlitt follows a similar division between chs. 1–2 and ch. 3, but ultimately prioritizes the individual growth processes of each separate section/chapter (1:1–2:5; 2:6–20; 3:1–19), denying the type of overall redaction which Seybold understands has having produced the final form of the book (*Die Propheten*, 42–43). Andersen, by contrast, assumes an essentially unified text, albeit one comprised of three distinct genres: dialogue (1:1–2:6a), woe oracles (2:6b–20), and psalm (3:1–19) (*Habakkuk*, 14–15). Haak sees the entire book as a unified prophetic complaint (*Habakkuk*, 11–20). Floyd is more limited in this ascription, seeing 1:2–17 and 3:2–19a as prophetic complaints, the latter more particularly as a psalmodic representation of prophecy; 2:1–20 constitutes a report of oracular enquiry (*Minor Prophets*, 81–86). That the text is, despite its generic vagaries, thematically unified, he argues with particular attention to the theme of "unjust imperial domination [which] is common to all sections of the book" (*Minor Prophets*, 82). Although he appears ultimately agnostic with regard to whether the first person speaker which dominates all three chapters ought to be identified with Habakkuk himself or is a fictional "I," he sees no indications of a long redactional process (*Minor Prophets*, 87–88).

30. Sweeney, "Structure," 81: "The intent and setting center around an attempt to explain the rise of the oppressive Neo-Babylonian empire in the late-7th century b.c.e. as an act of YHWH which does not contradict divine righteousness and fidelity to Judah;" compare with, for example, Floyd, "Prophetic Complaints," 406.

31. Floyd, "Prophetic Complaints," which is presupposed by Floyd, *Minor Prophets*, 79–161; cf. Sweeney, "Structure," who draws on Johnson, "Paralysis of Torah," to argue that 1:5–11 is a heightened version of the complaint in 1:2–4 and the Babylonians are in fact not portrayed

understood as a description of the complainant seeking and receiving an oracular response to these concerns.

In fact, this understanding of Hab 1–2 makes much better sense out of the book as a whole; seen as a dialogue culminating in a series of woe oracles, it has often proved difficult for interpreters to understand what relationship chs. 1–2 have to ch. 3.[32] If ch. 1 is a statement of the prophet's complaint concerning the excesses of the Babylonians, however, chs. 2–3 constitute a twofold response to that complaint. Habakkuk 2, as reflected by the relative degree of scholarly comfort in its form and message, constitutes the more usual presentation of that response: a report of the solicitation and receipt of an oracle by a prophet. It is, in other words, Yhwh's own response to Habakkuk's complaint. Habakkuk 3, in turn, is Habakkuk's response and conclusion, developing Yhwh's assurance about Yhwh's actions and his pursuit of justice on behalf of his people through reference to broader mythological themes.[33] "The theme of unjust imperial domination is

---

positively. The classic *Forschungsgeschichte* of Habakkuk is P. Jöcken, *Das Buch Habakuk* (Cologne: Hanstein, 1977); for an update of the subsequent three decades, see G. T. M. Prinsloo, "Petuhot/setumot and the Structure of Habakkuk: Evaluating the Evidence," in *The Impact of Unit Delimitation on Exegesis* (ed. R. de Hoop, M. C. A. Korpel, and S. E. Porter; Pericope 7; Leiden: Brill, 2009), 198–203.

32. Indeed, while the majority of scholars (certainly among Anglophone scholarship, although this is less the case among Continental scholarship) continue to see Hab 3 as somehow forming a united whole with Hab 1–2, there is a vocal minority who reject Hab 3 as (often) a later addition to a "Habakkuk" originally comprising only chs. 1–2 (see above; and also Nogalski, *Redactional Processes*, 154–81). Indeed, the general isolation of Hab 3 in the scholarly mind is indicated by the number of studies focusing on it to the exclusion of the preceding two chapters; for example, S. Ahituv, "The Sinai Theophany in the Psalm of Habakkuk," in *Birkat Shalom: Studies in the Bible, Ancient Near Eastern Literature, and Postbiblical Judaism Presented to Shalom M. Paul on the Occasion of His Seventieth Birthday* (2 vols.; ed. C. Cohen et al.; Winona Lake, IN: Eisenbrauns, 2008), 1:225–32; J. E. Anderson, "Awaiting an Answered Prayer: The Development and Reinterpretation of Habakkuk 3 in Its Contexts," *ZAW* 123 (2011) 57–71; B. Margulis, "Psalm of Habakkuk: A Reconstruction and Interpretation," *ZAW* 82 (1970) 409–42; J. W. Watts, "Psalmody in Prophecy: Habakkuk 3 in Context," in *Forming Prophetic Literature: Essays on Isaiah and the Twelve in Honor of John D. W. Watts* (ed. J. W. Watts and P. R. House; JSOTSup 235; Sheffield: Sheffield Academic, 1996), 209–23. On the textual and versional evidence regarding the book's unity, see Haak, *Habakkuk*, 1–11.

33. Although the psalmic form of Hab 3, combined with its superscription (3:1) and use of liturgical instructions (3:19 and the repeated use of the term *selâ*), usually results in assumptions of an independent liturgical origin—its presence explained as either a late addition or rather clumsy contemporary insertion into the book—Watts makes a convincing case in favor of these elements' use as overt signals of what he calls "inset hymnody," akin to the use of psalms in narrative texts. In particular, he suggests that the curious combination of both lament and hymnic elements in the psalm reflects the particularly prophetic expectations that arise from the wider prophetic context ("Psalmody in Prophecy," 213–14, 219–20). For thoughts on the subject more generally, see E. S. Gerstenberger, "Psalms in the Book of the Twelve: How Misplaced Are They?" in *Thematic Threads in the Book of the Twelve* (ed. P. L. Redditt and A. Schart; BZAW 325; Berlin: de Gruyter, 2003), 72–89.

common to all sections of the book; but each treats this theme in a somewhat different way so as to indicate a progression in the way Yahweh is understood to be involved in the world situation."[34]

Throughout the complaint of ch. 1, the prophet's protest does not concern Yнwн's justice as such, insofar as there is no claim that those on the receiving end of the Babylonians' actions are without guilt; rather, the protestation concerns the appropriate extent of punishment, contending that the Babylonians have gone too far (1:8–11, 17). Given that they act in the name of Yнwн and Yнwн is indeed just (1:13), the prophet calls on Yнwн to rectify the injustice (1:2–4, 13). The ultimate issue for Habakkuk is not that Yнwн has seen fit to employ a foreign power but that the power in question has gone to such extreme as to abuse its commission, "destroying nations without mercy" (1:17).[35]

Yнwн's response is to assure Habakkuk that Yнwн's justice will prevail. Again, the repeated accusation against the Babylonian empire is criminal excess (2:6, 8, 12, 15, 17; probably also 2:4). The oracles reported in this chapter confirm Yнwн's awareness of this excess and affirm Habakkuk's expectation that such excess must in turn be subject to consequences, thereby regaining the cosmos's equilibrium.[36] "Yahweh affirms that the imperialists have lost all claims to legitimacy

---

34. Floyd, *Minor Prophets*, 82.

35. It is curious that the imagery used in 1:14–17 to describe Babylonian recklessness is of humanity caught in a net, especially given that the description of humanity as "fish of the sea" is clarified as akin to being like "creeping things among whom there is no ruler." Although there is no extant Hebrew version of Yнwн's battle against the chaotic sea, the net is one of Marduk's weapons in *Enuma elish*, and it appears (using two other words for net) in a related mythological context in Ezekiel (Strine and Crouch, "Yнwн's Battle"); the term used here for a hook appears also in this context in Job 40:25 (a similarity noted also by Sweeney, who articulates the issue thus: "Rather than acknowledging God as the source of their success, the Chaldeans look to their own power, worshipping their nets/weapons"; "Structure," 69). Cathcart has also suggested that the term *miqqedem* in 1:12 "is a comprehensive term that Habakkuk uses to remind Yahweh of his victories in ancient times" ("'Law is Paralysed'," 344–45). Although it is difficult to interpret the connotations here (and the associations may be entirely coincidental), one does wonder whether the author is using the language associated with Yнwн's battle against chaos (language that is used elsewhere to align the activities of Yнwн's human agent with those of Yнwн; see Crouch, *War and Ethics*, 29–32, 65–76) to suggest that Yнwн's agent has abused its divinely-granted power by working not for order (justice) but for chaos (evil, wickedness) and articulating the disrupted cosmological structure in these terms. Rather than Yнwн's agent bringing about order, complete with a divinely-appointed ruler, the Babylonians have upended the cosmos, employing weapons designed for use against chaos in order to create it.

36. Again, although neither overt (to the modern reader, at least) nor extensive, there are a few passing references that seem to allude to—and anticipate Hab 3's fuller exposition of—the basis of Yнwн's claim to power (including the ability to ensure justice and order) in his defeat of chaos. The slightly clearer of these is 2:14: "And the earth will be filled / to know the glory of Yнwн / as the waters cover over Sea." One of the difficulties in attempts to identify allusions to Yнwн's battles against chaos is that water may appear both as Yнwн's opponent and as Yнwн's weapon; Yнwн's status as storm deity, whose unconventional weaponry (as opposed to standard-issue bows, arrows, etc.) includes the storm itself, is the underlying source of the problem. In any

by greedily pursuing conquest for its own sake and that he has therefore destined them to fall."[37] As in Nahum, the text reiterates that all earthly powers are subject to Yнwн; those who go beyond their remit will be sharply curtailed.

That Hab 3 is a declaration of Yнwн's power and Yнwн's promise to enact justice is generally recognized; that this is a reiteration of Hab 2 somewhat less so. The passage's use of mythological themes to convey this point is generally acknowledged; the psalm is frequently called a theophany, and reference is usually made to the use of Yнwн's victory over the chaos waters as a means of articulating Yнwн's power to act.[38] These two elements are sometimes separated, thought to represent two separate traditions regarding Yнwн's character, but this is a false dichotomy; the language and imagery associated with Yнwн's specific battle against chaos are part of his more general character, often revealed in "theophanic" texts.[39] The first part of the passage, usually labeled the theophany, establishes Yнwн's fighting character, describing his strength in royal terms and as deriving from his power over the whole created order (3:3–4, 5–6); this is turned against the specific enemy, characterized as the chaotic waters of rivers and sea, using similar declarations of his military might and creative authority (3:9, 11–14; 3:9–11).[40]

Commonly overlooked in discussions of the chapter, however, and partially responsible for the uncertainty regarding the chapter's relationship to Hab 1–2, is that the description of Yнwн's battle against chaos in Hab 3 is not a description of a primordial battle but rather anticipates Yнwн's present action against an enemy that is characterized as the chaotic waters as a result of it having threatened Yнwн's created order.[41] Although verb forms in poetry are notoriously slippery, it is notable that throughout the description of Yнwн's action against the chaotic wa-

---

event, one does wonder whether the language here might be a description of Yнwн's defeat of chaos.

37. Floyd, *Minor Prophets*, 82.

38. On the use of liturgical markers in the chapter, see Watts, "Psalmody in Prophecy."

39. See Anderson, "Awaiting an Answered Prayer," especially 60–61, for one such argument; cf. Seybold, *Nahum*, 77–83; Perlitt, *Die Propheten*, 82–83. For brief specific counterargument to this type of division, see the *Postscript* in J. Day, "Echoes of Baal's Seven Thunders and Lightnings in Psalm 29 and Habakkuk 3:9 and the Identity of the Seraphim in Isaiah 6," *VT* 29 (1979) 151.

40. For further links between the "theophany" and Yнwн's battle against chaos, see M. L. Barré, "Habakkuk 3:2: Translation in Context," *CBQ* 50 (1988) 184–97, who argues that 3:2 ought to be understood as a reference to this battle; J. Day, "New Light on the Mythological Background of the Allusion to Resheph in Habakkuk 3:5," *VT* 29 (1979) 353–55, who suggests that the references to pestilence and plague in 3:5 should be understand against the same background; and B. Peckham, "The Vision of Habakkuk," *CBQ* 48 (1986) 633, who notes various similarities to *Enuma elish* and to Genesis 1 and Exodus 14.

41. Although note Floyd, who does pick up on this idea: "an imminent conclusive change . . . will be a re-creation of the world order that recapitulates the process through which Yahweh created the world to begin with. Just as he then did battle with the forces of evil and chaos in order to establish the possibility of a just existence for all creatures, so he will now do battle with the

ters (variously the rivers, the sea, and the deep; 3:8, 10) the verbs indicate ongoing action; this is a battle in the present, not the past. They only shift to completed action (a prophetic perfect) after the triumphant declaration of Yhwh's purpose in 3:13.[42] Habakkuk 3 is a description of Yhwh's action against a present enemy, the Babylonians, who have threatened his created order. It repeats and reiterates the promise of divine action made in prosaic terms in ch. 2 and develops the brief allusions to Yhwh's battles against chaos in chs. 1–2 into a full-blown rendering of the current threat to divine justice and order in these terms.

Compared to Nahum, Habakkuk is less concerned with Yhwh's power, as such, than it is with Yhwh's use of that power. There is never any real doubt that Yhwh has power and is the driving force behind the Babylonians; the question is whether Yhwh will use his power to ensure the justice and order on which his reputation are based. This question comprises the complaint of Hab 1; Hab 2–3 provide the answer. The Babylonian Empire, Habakkuk assures the reader, is merely an instrument of Yhwh, albeit one that has careened beyond its allotted role. No earthly agent, even if commissioned by Yhwh, has the authority to extend itself to the level of violence and excess that the Babylonians have exhibited. Those that do so upset the equilibrium of Yhwh's rule and will, in time, be eliminated for its restoration.

Zephaniah

Zephaniah's relationship to the state is much less clear than either Nahum's or Habakkuk's, in no small part a result of ambiguity regarding the state in question. On the one hand, its superscription locates it in the reign of Josiah (640–609), placing its message squarely in the last decades of Judah's monarchy. On the other hand, its canonical location undermines this historical location; whereas Nahum and Habakkuk (and indeed the minor prophetic books more generally) proceed in chronological sequence, from the Assyrian period to the Babylonian, Zephaniah is—in both the Masoretic and Septuagint orderings of the Twelve—placed after Habakkuk. Canonically, therefore, the book may demand a post-monarchic reading, perhaps as an explanation for the fall of Jerusalem to the aforementioned Babylonians or perhaps as an articulation of a post-monarchic society.[43] The

---

tyrannical oppressor to reestablish this possibility for all, and thus bring about the deliverance of his people" (*Minor Prophets*, 89).

42. That Yhwh acts not only on behalf of the people but also on behalf of his anointed (3:13) is also related to the present form of Yhwh's battle against chaos, in which the norm is for a Yahwistic king to serve as Yhwh's earthly agent; the statement appears to anticipate a return to this normal arrangement upon the defeat of the agent-turned-chaos, Babylon.

43. Although the book's canonical location is generally noted by commentators and its place in the Twelve widely acknowledged (see, for example, M. B. Shepherd, "Compositional Analysis of the Twelve," *ZAW* 120 [2008] 189–90), the extent of the effect of the wider context on the interpretation of Zephaniah itself is debated; note Hadjiev's argument that little of the book

combination of these makes for an ambiguous message, at the least: is the book to be understood against the background of the late 7th century and, if so, does it align itself with the royal house or against it? Or is the association with a monarchic prophet merely a claim to a certain type of prophetic authority, made to buttress an essentially post-monarchic message?

The book is conventionally divided into three parts, according to the three types of material found in prophetic books: oracles against Judah and Jerusalem (1:2–2:3), oracles against the nations (2:4–3:8), and oracles of salvation for Judah/Jerusalem and the nations (3:9–20).[44] According to this analysis, the book's logic follows a standard prophetic progression, beginning with judgment on YHWH's people, followed by judgment on their enemies, and culminating with an announcement of the salvation to come after judgment. Elsewhere, however, this supposedly standard progression is seen only in Ezekiel and in the LXX ordering of Jeremiah; it is also problematic within Zephaniah, and it is accordingly of little surprise that recent scholarship has begun to question the accuracy of this division.[45]

After the superscription, the book begins with a broad declaration of YHWH's intention to undo the work of his creation (1:2–3).[46] This serves as a prelude, setting the scene for the following, more specific judgment on Judah and Jerusalem (1:4–18). This judgment is said to be the consequence of a number of related actions on the part of the inhabitants of Jerusalem. First among these is the pursuit of non-Yahwistic worship practices, with particular reference made to the worship of Baal, to the kəmārîm priests, to the host of heaven, and, apparently, the wor-

---

can be attributed to efforts to integrate it into the Twelve, suggesting that this canonical reading is not inherent to the book itself (T. Hadjiev, "Zephaniah and the 'Book of the Twelve' Hypothesis," in *Prophecy and the Prophets in Ancient Israel: Proceedings of the Oxford Old Testament Seminar* [ed. J. Day; LHBOTS 531; London: T. & T. Clark, 2010], 325–38); contra Nogalski, *Literary Precursors*, 171–215. Compare Sweeney's observations regarding the LXX translation of 2:1–3, which does produce such an effect (M. A. Sweeney, *Zephaniah: A Commentary* [Hermeneia; Minneapolis: Fortress, 2003], 21–23).

44. So E. Ben Zvi, *A Historical-Critical Study of the Book of Zephaniah* (BZAW 198; Berlin: Walter de Gruyter, 1992), 325–46; Nogalski, *Literary Precursors*, 170–71; Perlitt, *Die Propheten*, 98; Seybold, *Nahum*, 85–86, 88; J. Vlaardingerbroek, *Zephaniah* (trans. J. Vriend; HCOT; Louvain: Peeters, 1999), 1–9. Berlin abdicates and relies on the divisions in the Leningrad Codex (A. Berlin, *Zephaniah: A New Translation with Introduction and Commentary* [AB 25A; New York: Doubleday, 1993], 17–20). For a brief history of research, see Floyd, *Minor Prophets*, 165–69.

45. See especially M. A. Sweeney, "A Form-Critical Reassessment of the Book of Zephaniah," *CBQ* 53 (1991) 388–408 and Sweeney, *Zephaniah*, 5–10; Sweeney's influence is seen in, for example, Floyd, *Minor Prophets*, 166–73.

46. M. de Roche, "Zephaniah 1:2–3: The 'Sweeping' of Creation," *VT* 30 (1980) 104–9; note that Sweeney argues that the specific terminology indicates that the background of these verses is not the present text of Genesis (which in extant form is certainly later than the 7th century) (*Zephaniah*, 16).

ship of the Ammonite god Milkom (1:4b-5a); this is explicated as a summary of non-Yahwistic worship among those who also worship Yнwн (but should do so exclusively), those who previously worshiped Yнwн (but have now forsaken him), and those who have never worshiped Yнwн (but presumably ought to) (1:5b-6).[47] Subsequent verses elaborate the nature of Yнwн's forthcoming punishment (1:7–18) and specify that the guilty culprits who will be on the receiving end of Yнwн's judgment are the elites of society ("the princes" and "the sons of the king"), connecting their aforementioned offense to the foreign associations of their actions (1:8–9a) and their disregard for justice (1:9b).[48] Commerce and wealth are recurring elements in this description of Yнwн's judgment on these elites (1:11, 13, 18).[49]

This declaration of judgment, however, is not irrevocable. Having terrified its audience in ch. 1, Zephaniah presents in 2:1–3 an opportunity to repent. Here the wealth and superior status of the lawless and fraudulent elite, accused in ch. 1, are contrasted with the humble and law-abiding repentant (2:1–3); the latter's discovery of shelter in Yнwн (2:3) is contrasted with the destruction of the homes of the wealthy (1:13).[50] Having heard the black announcement of judgment in ch. 1—the imminent destruction of the sinful—the subsequent verses present a

---

47. Those who locate Zephaniah under the reign of Josiah and consider (at least part of) the book to reflect his message with some accuracy tend to point to the general plausibility of its attacks on cult syncretism against the background of both Josiah's cult reforms and the growth of Yнwн-alone advocacy around the same time, as reflected in the Deuteronomic and Deuteronomistic literature. This debate, as well as subordinate discussions of whether the various references to Baal, Milkom, and the host of heaven reflect a period prior to the reform (which is never explicitly mentioned) or afterward are all further related to and dependent upon historiographical issues surrounding the reliability of the 2 Kings account of Josiah's reign and, in particular, whether (or to what extent and what type) any reform actually occurred. On the cult practices in question and their relationship (or otherwise) to such a reform, see Sweeney, *Zephaniah*, 16–17; Vlaardingerbroek, *Zephaniah*, 17–22; R. Mason, *Zephaniah, Habakkuk, Joel* (OTG; Sheffield: JSOT Press, 1994) 35–43; note that one potential counter-argument to analyses that emphasize the essentially post-monarchic nature of the book is the fact that while the syncretistic worship practices described in ch. 1 appear to have been relatively common in the preexilic period (and were becoming a point of contention in the late monarchic period), the exclusive worship of Yнwн was well-established by the postexilic period (Berlin, *Zephaniah*, 36). As O'Brien notes with regard to Nahum, of course, historical vivacity need not necessarily have any direct correlation to the actual date of a text's composition ("Violent Pictures, Violent Cultures?"); one may, however, wonder as to the point of such lengthy condemnation in a context where such practices are no longer a real issue. On the relationship between 1:4b–5a and 1:5b–6, see Sweeney, "Form-Critical Reassessment," 394–95; also K. Jeppesen, "Zephaniah 1:5b," *VT* 31 (1981) 372–73.

48. The possible association of the prophet with royalty in the superscription, combined with the book's particular focus on Jerusalem and Judah's elite, has produced a full spectrum of theories regarding Zephaniah's social location; see Vlaardingerbroek, *Zephaniah*, 12–13; Mason, *Zephaniah*, 26–33.

49. On the relationship between this and the preceding, see M. Rose, "«Atheismus» als Wohlstandserscheinung (Zephanja 1,12)," *TZ* 37 (1981) 193–208, especially 197–200.

50. On the possibility of a connection with the ʿănāwâ of the psalms, see Ben Zvi, *Historical-Critical Study*, 354.

positive argument for repentance: those nations that are or have been superior to the inhabitants of Jerusalem will be brought low by the powerful and trustworthy YHWH.[51] Zephaniah 2:4–7 describes the forthcoming fate of the Philistine city-states, articulating YHWH's power and control over these neighboring nations and culminating in the declaration that the territories dominated by Philistia will become the possession of Judah (2:6–7).[52] This theme is elaborated in the oracle concerning Moab and Ammon, in which YHWH's speech assures its audience that they need not despair but should trust in YHWH, who is aware of everything (2:8) and controls all (2:11). Again, the repentance to which the audience was summoned in 2:1–3 is here justified in positive terms, describing the rationale for repentance and return to YHWH in terms of YHWH's trustworthiness and power. These declarations of YHWH's power culminate in the announcement that even the most powerful states of the period will succumb to YHWH (2:12–15).[53]

The option of exhortative coaxing toward repentance having been exhausted (and perhaps having failed to succeed, 3:7), Zeph 3 reiterates the declaration of YHWH's justice (3:5) and power (3:6) in negative terms, despairing that this is not recognized (3:7). Those in authority are again the focus of attention ("her princes,"

---

51. Sweeney, "Form-Critical Reassessment," 397–99.

52. On the 7th-century context of the nations listed by these oracles, see D. L. Christensen, "Zephaniah 2:4–15: A Theological Basis for Josiah's Program of Political Expansion," *CBQ* 46 (1984) 669–82; more recently, Sweeney, *Zephaniah*, 14; Nogalski, *Literary Precursors*, 172–75. On the rhetorical mechanisms of the passage, see L. Zalcman, "Ambiguity and Assonance at Zephaniah 2:4," *VT* 36 (1986) 365–71, and R. Gordis, "A Rising Tide of Misery: A Note on a Note on Zephaniah 2:4," *VT* 37 (1987) 487–90. Worth note from a historical point of view is that the beginning of the 7th century had seen the Assyrian reassignment of much of Judah's territory in the Shephelah to the Philistine city of Ekron (S. Gitin, "Tel Miqne-Ekron: A Type Site for the Inner Coastal Plain in the Iron Age II Period," in *Recent Excavations in Israel: Studies in Iron Age Archaeology* [ed. S. Gitin and W. G. Dever; AASOR 49; Winona Lake, IN: Eisenbrauns, 1989], 43; cf. N. Naʾaman, "Two Notes on the History of Ashkelon and Ekron in the Late Eighth-Seventh Centuries B.C.E.," *TA* 25 (1998) 219–27; N. Naʾaman, "Population Changes in Palestine following Assyrian Deportations," in *Ancient Israel and Its Neighbors: Interaction and Counteraction* [vol. 1 of *Collected Essays*; Winona Lake, IN: Eisenbrauns, 2005], 209). Ashdod and Gaza are also said to have profited from Judah's punishment, as did Ashkelon (H. Tadmor, "Philistia under Assyrian Rule," *BA* 29 [1966] 97). This area had been Judah's primary agricultural region, and its reallocation to Philistia constituted a major blow to Judah as a viable regional power in the 7th century. Against the background of the Philistine domination of the area in the 7th century, the declaration that this territory will be returned to Judah (2:6–7) constitutes a statement of a major change in Philistia's status in the region.

53. There has traditionally been some difficulty in understanding the relevance of Egypt (Cush) to a late-7th-century context, but recent research suggests that Egypt took over the southern Levant more or less as the Assyrians withdrew from it, possibly in a deliberate arrangement between the two states (see B. U. Schipper, "Egypt and the Kingdom of Judah under Josiah and Jehoiakim," *TA* 37 [2010] 200–226; also N. Naʾaman, "The Kingdom of Judah under Josiah," *TA* 18 [1991] 3–71). Berlin notes that the absence of an oracle against Babylon may be thought odd if the book derives from very much later than the reign of Josiah (*Zephaniah*, 34–37; cf. Nogalski, *Literary Precursors*, 172–73).

"her judges," "her prophets," "her priests," 3:3–4). Yet all is apparently not lost; those of whom the message speaks will surely recognize YHWH when he acts in ultimate fury, in a judgment that returns to the creation traditions (cf. 1:2–3) to declare that YHWH will, unrelentingly, enforce his recognition, undoing the confusion of Babel (3:9) and reestablishing the universal worship of YHWH (3:9, cf. 2:11).[54] The language of humility and the eradication of the overweening pride of the accused reappear in this declaration (3:11–13), an emphasis on YHWH's glorification that is elaborated in the final passage (3:14–20).[55]

Whether this criticism of the elites of Judah and Jerusalem intends to reform the existing leadership structures of the state or to undermine them entirely is a matter for debate. The superscription not only associates the book with one of Judah's most revered kings but may trace the ancestry of the prophet to whom its words are attributed to king Hezekiah; if this is deliberate, it implies that what follows constitutes a critique from within, not a critique from the margins.[56] If the book is understood to derive from—or be intended to be read as reflecting—a monarchic context, it may also be taken as significant that it does not seem to be the elites' existence, or any particular aspect of their structural arrangement, that is offensive to the prophet's sensibilities.[57] Rather, it is the elites' actions which are

---

54. On 2:11, see D. Rudman, "A Note on Zephaniah," *Bib* 80 (1999) 109–12. One might also wonder whether the reference to the rivers of Cush and the presentation of offerings by *bat-pûṭay* might be some kind of allusion to the rivers of Eden, but this cannot be more than speculation. For a summary of allusions to the creation traditions, which appear in all three chapters, see Berlin, *Zephaniah*, 13–14.

55. How much of this latter is later elaboration(s) is variously analyzed; see, for example, M. Beck, "Das Tag YHWHs-Verständnis von Zephanja iii," *VT* 58 (2008) 159–77; H. Irsigler, *Zefanja* (HThKAT; Basel: Herder, 2002) 56; Nogalski, *Literary Precursors*, 176–78; Seybold, *Nahum*, 87–89; Vlaardingerbroek, *Zephaniah*, 9–10.

56. With four generations, Zephaniah's patronymic is the longest in the prophetic corpus. This peculiarity, combined with the final named ancestor being one "Hezekiah," has raised speculation that the superscription intends to claim royal descent for the prophet. Whether this is the case remains unclear (see Vlaardingerbroek, *Zephaniah*, 11–13 for a summary of the arguments).

57. Although most recent commentators are very cautious with regard to any critical technique's ability to identify older or more "original" parts of the book, it is still probably the majority of scholars who attribute at least some meaningful part of the book to a 7th-century prophet, although rarely with any great exuberance or confidence. Foremost among these is Sweeney, who "demonstrates no major redactional work in the book of Zephaniah" (*Zephaniah*, 14–18). Seybold dates parts of chs. 1–2 to a late-Josianic Zephaniah, attributing the more hopeful material of ch. 3 to a post-exilic redactor and various "apocalyptic/eschatological" material to yet another (*Nahum*, 87–89); Vlaardingerbroek attributes most of 1:2–3:8 to the prophet himself and limits most of the additions to 3:9–20 (*Zephaniah*, 9–10; cf. O'Brien, "Nahum–Habakkuk–Zephaniah," 178). Going against the trend of locating the original material primarily in ch. 1, Hagedorn sees the book's origins in the oracles against the nations in ch. 2, against a background of Josianic expansion (A. C. Hagedorn, "When Did Zephaniah Become a Supporter of Josiah's Reform?" *JTS* 62 [2011] 253–275). Floyd acknowledges the possibility of post-monarchic completion raised by Ben Zvi but circumvents the issue by concluding that, although the text should probably not be traced to a Josianic prophet in its entirety, the Josianic period is nonetheless the context

the problem: their entanglement with foreign practices, their failure to worship YHWH exclusively, and—the cause of both of these—their failure to trust in YHWH. If 2:1–3, in particular, is understood to be in any way integral to the overall message, these verses' exhortation to repentance suggests that the prophet's goal is not the total eradication of the government of which these elites form a(n errant) part but rather its reformation, in alignment with a recognition of YHWH as the ultimate power and source of justice in the world.

Complicating a reading of the book in its attributed monarchical context are both its aforementioned canonical location and the presence of elements within the book that may reflect a post-monarchic context for its final form and, depending on the extent of these elements' influence on and extricability from the rest of the book, demand a post-monarchic interpretation for its message.[58] Indeed, much of recent critical scholarship emphasizes a post-monarchic completion, context, and meaning for the book.[59] Taken to extreme, this produces a reading of Zephaniah that constructs its meaning in a late, non-monarchic context, in which the author's interest in the state is little more than as a contrast to a future (present) ideal society unsaddled with any political, monarchical elite—a society in which the only king is YHWH and the idealized community is a community of the pious and humble.[60]

Which of these interpretations is the more accurate reflection of the book's intent is difficult to say and, indeed, it is entirely possible that both reflect some of the revisions inherent to most prophetic texts, as each subsequent generation attempted to reinterpret prophetic words for changing social and political cir-

in which the book is designed to be read (he also argues that there is nothing in the text that requires an exilic or postexilic date and seems to imply that its production may well have been quite close to its self-described context in the Josianic period; *Minor Prophets*, 177–79).

58. Most extreme in this regard is Ben Zvi, who acknowledges the possibility, even likelihood, of earlier prophetic content in the book but denies the possibility that this content may now be recovered (*Historical-Critical Study*, 357–58). Contrast Sweeney, *Zephaniah*, 14; note also Hadjiev, "Zephaniah." Contrast especially Ben Zvi's deemphasis of the figure of the prophet in favor of the word of YHWH (*Historical-Critical Study*, 349) with Sweeney's subordination of the word of YHWH to its presentation in the context of prophetic exhortation ("Form-Critical Reassessment").

59. See especially Ben Zvi, *Historical-Critical Study*, the influence of which is prominent throughout subsequent scholarship: for example, Berlin, *Zephaniah*, 31–43; Floyd, *Minor Prophets*; and Sweeney, *Zephaniah*, although all to a lesser extent. Explicitly acknowledging Ben Zvi, but making a more determined attempt to identify what Ben Zvi refers to as the "pre-compositional material" (that is, the material that might—although need not necessarily—be attributed to a preexilic prophet), Perlitt identifies early material in the judgment on Judah and Jerusalem in ch. 1; he attributes the rest of the book—including the "apocalyptic" perspective of, for example, 1:2–3—to a long process of redaction culminating in the pre-Hellenistic period (*Die Propheten*, 98–99; compare with Seybold, *Nahum*, 86–86 and Irsigler, *Zefanja*, 55–65, although both are more inclined to consider the possibility that chs. 2–3 may also contain some material from a Josianic Zephaniah [or his immediate tradents, in the case of Irsigler]).

60. Ben Zvi, *Historical-Critical Study*, 353–56.

cumstances. Which interpretation takes priority depends on the reader's relative weighting of the book's self-identification as monarchic, its likely redactional completion in the postexilic period, and its canonical location between Habakkuk and Haggai.

Final Observations

Nahum, Habakkuk, and Zephaniah are agreed on one thing: Yhwh is the ultimate authority in all affairs of state. Though he may employ a variety of human agents—both foreign kings and home-grown leaders—to enact his will, Yhwh is the source and arbiter of all human claims to power. All who exercise such power on his behalf must answer to him as regards their use of it. In Nahum, the acknowledgement of this fact takes the form of a declaration that Yhwh will not allow the Assyrians untrammeled scope for the implementation of violent capacities; in Habakkuk the focus is on the implications of Yhwh's control over the Babylonians for understanding the justice of the divine nature. Zephaniah, whether understood in a monarchic or post-monarchic context, reiterates that even the leaders of Judah and Jerusalem must acquiesce to Yhwh's authority; if they do not, they cannot survive. No human power, however superlative, is independently founded; every state, great or small, derives its power from Yhwh and is accountable to him for its use of it.

Bibliography

Ahituv, S. "The Sinai theophany in the Psalm of Habakkuk." Pp. in 255–32 in vol. 1 of *Birkat Shalom: Studies in the Bible, Ancient Near Eastern Literature, and Postbiblical Judaism Presented to Shalom M. Paul on the Occasion of His Seventieth Birthday*. Edited by C. Cohen et al. 2 vols. Winona Lake, IN: Eisenbrauns, 2008.

Andersen, F. I. *Habakkuk: A New Translation with Introduction and Commentary*. AB 25. New York: Doubleday, 2001.

Anderson, J. E. "Awaiting an Answered Prayer: The Development and Reinterpretation of Habakkuk 3 in Its Contexts." *ZAW* 123 (2011) 57–71.

Barré, M. L. "Habakkuk 3:2: Translation in Context." *CBQ* 50 (1988) 184–97.

Beck, M. "Das Tag YHWHs-Verständnis von Zephanja iii." *VT* 58 (2008) 159–77.

Becking, B. "Bee's Dating Formula and the Book of Nahum." *JSOT* 18 (1980) 100–104.

Bee, R. E. "Dating the Book of Nahum: A Response to the Article by Bob Becking." *JSOT* 18 (1980) 104.

————. "An Empirical Dating Procedure for Old Testament Prophecy." *JSOT* 11 (1979) 23–35.

Ben Zvi, E. *A Historical-Critical Study of the Book of Zephaniah*. BZAW 198. Berlin: de Gruyter, 1992.

Berlin, A. *Zephaniah: A New Translation with Introduction and Commentary*. AB 25A. New York: Doubleday, 1993.

Cathcart, K. J. " 'Law is Paralysed' (Habakkuk 1.4): Habakkuk's Dialogue with God and the Language of Legal Disputation." Pp. 339–53 in *Prophecy and the Prophets in Ancient Israel: Proceedings of the Oxford Old Testament Seminar*. Edited by J. Day. LHBOTS 531. New York: T. & T. Clark, 2010.

Christensen, D. L. "The Acrostic of Nahum Reconsidered." *ZAW* 87 (1975) 17–30.

―――――. "The Acrostic of Nahum Once Again: A Prosodic Analysis of Nahum 1:1–10." *ZAW* 99 (1987) 409–15.

―――――. "The Book of Nahum: A History of Interpretation." Pp. 187–94 in *Forming Prophetic Literature: Essays on Isaiah and the Twelve in Honor of John D. W. Watts*. Edited by J. W. Watts and P. R. House. JSOTSup 235. Sheffield: Sheffield Academic, 1996.

―――――. *Nahum: A New Translation with Introduction and Commentary*. AB 24F. New Haven, CT: Yale University Press, 2009.

―――――. "Zephaniah 2:4–15: A Theological Basis for Josiah's Program of Political Expansion." *CBQ* 46 (1984) 669–82.

Cogan, M. "The Lions of Nineveh (Nahum 2:12–14): A Check on Nahum's Familiarity with Assyria." Pp. 433–39 in vol. 1 of *Birkat Shalom: Studies in the Bible, Ancient Near Eastern Literature, and Postbiblical Judaism Presented to Shalom M. Paul on the Occasion of His Seventieth Birthday*. 2 vols. Edited by C. Cohen et al. Winona Lake, IN: Eisenbrauns, 2008.

Crouch, C. L. "On Floods and the Fall of Nineveh: A Note on the Origins of a Spurious Tradition." Pp. 212–16 in *New Perspectives on Old Testament Prophecy and History: Essays in Honour of Hans M. Barstad*. Edited by Rannfrid I. Thelle, Terje Stordalen, and Mervyn E. J. Richardson. VTSup 168. Leiden: Brill, 2015.

―――――. *War and Ethics in the Ancient Near East: Military Violence in Light of Cosmology and History*. BZAW 417. Berlin: de Gruyter, 2009.

Day, J. "Echoes of Baal's Seven Thunders and Lightnings in Psalm 29 and Habakkuk 3:9 and the Identity of the Seraphim in Isaiah 6." *VT* 29 (1979) 143–51.

―――――. "New Light on the Mythological Background of the Allusion to Resheph in Habakkuk 3:5." *VT* 29 (1979) 353–55.

De Roche, M. "Zephaniah 1:2–3: The 'Sweeping' of Creation." *VT* 30 (1980) 104–9.

Delcor, M. "Allusions à la déesse Ištar en Nahum 2:8." *Bib* 58 (1977) 73–83.

Delitzsch, M. *Biblischer Commentar über die Psalmen*. Leipzig: Dörflin & Franke, 1867.

Floyd, M. H. "The Chimerical Acrostic of Nahum 1:2–10." *JBL* 113 (1994) 421–37.

―――――. *Minor Prophets: Part 2*. FOTL 22. Grand Rapids, MI: Eerdmans, 2000.

―――――. "Prophetic Complaints about the Fulfillment of Oracles in Habakkuk 1:2–17 and Jeremiah 15:10–18." *JBL* 110 (1991) 397–418.

Gerstenberger, E. S. "Psalms in the Book of the Twelve: How Misplaced Are They?" Pp. 72–89 in *Thematic Threads in the Book of the Twelve*. Edited by P. L. Redditt and A. Schart. BZAW 325. Berlin: de Gruyter, 2003.

Gitin, S. "Tel Miqne-Ekron: A Type Site for the Inner Coastal Plain in the Iron Age II Period." Pp. 23–58 in *Recent Excavations in Israel: Studies in Iron Age Archaeology*. Edited by S. Gitin and W. G. Dever. AASOR 49. Winona Lake, IN.: Eisenbrauns, 1989.

Gordis, R. "A Rising Tide of Misery: A Note on a Note on Zephaniah 2:4." *VT* 37 (1987) 487–90.

Gowan, D. E. "Habakkuk." Pp. 601–4 in *The Oxford Bible Commentary*. Edited by J. Barton and J. Muddiman. Oxford: Oxford University Press, 2001.

Gunkel, H. *Creation and Chaos in the Primeval Era and the Eschaton: A Religio-Historical Study of Genesis 1 and Revelation 12*. Trans. K. William Whitney Jr. Grand Rapids, MI: Eerdmans, 2006.

_____. "Nahum 1." *ZAW* 11 (1893) 223–44.

Gunneweg, A. H. J. "Habakuk und das Problem des leidenden קידצ." *ZAW* 98 (1986) 400–415.

Haak, R. D. *Habakkuk*. VTSup 44. Leiden: Brill, 1992.

Hadjiev, T. "Zephaniah and the 'Book of the Twelve' Hypothesis." Pp. 325–38 in *Prophecy and the Prophets in Ancient Israel: Proceedings of the Oxford Old Testament Seminar*. Edited by J. Day. LHBOTS 531. London: T. & T. Clark, 2010.

Hagedorn, A. C. "Nahum—Ethnicity and Stereotypes: Anthropological Insights into Nahum's Literary History." Pp. 223–39 in *Ancient Israel: The Old Testament in Its Social Context*. Edited by P. F. Esler. London: SCM, 2005.

_____. "When Did Zephaniah Become a Supporter of Josiah's Reform?" *JTS* 62 (2011) 253–75.

Haupt, P. R. "Eine alttestamentliche Festliturgie für den Nikanortag." ZDMG 61 (1907) 275–97.

Holladay, W. L. "Plausible Circumstances for the Prophecy of Habakkuk." *JBL* 120 (2001) 123–30.

Huddlestun, J. R. "Nahum, Nineveh, and the Nile: The Description of Thebes in Nahum 3:8–9." *JNES* 62 (2003) 97–110.

Irsigler, H. *Zefanja*. HThKAT. Basel: Herder, 2002.

Jeppesen, K. "Zephaniah 1:5b." *VT* 31 (1981) 372–73.

Jöcken, P. *Das Buch Habakuk*. Cologne: Hanstein, 1977.

Johnson, M. D. "The Paralysis of Torah in Habakkuk 1:4." *VT* 35 (1985) 257–66.

Keller, C.-A., and R. Vuilleumier. *Michée, Nahoum, Habacuc, Sophonie*. CAT. Paris: Delachaux & Niestlé, 1971.

Margulis, B. "Psalm of Habakkuk: A Reconstruction and Interpretation." *ZAW* 82 (1970) 409–42.

Mason, R. *Zephaniah, Habakkuk, Joel*. OTG. Sheffield: JSOT Press, 1994.

Naʾaman, N. "The Kingdom of Judah under Josiah." *TA* 18 (1991) 3–71.

_____. "Population Changes in Palestine following Assyrian Deportations." Pp. 200–219 in *Ancient Israel and Its Neighbors: Interaction and Counteraction*. Vol. 1 of *Collected Essays*. Winona Lake, IN: Eisenbrauns, 2005.

_____. "Two Notes on the History of Ashkelon and Ekron in the Late Eighth-Seventh Centuries B.C.E." *TA* 25 (1998) 219–27.

Nogalski, J. *Literary Precursors to the Book of the Twelve*. BZAW 217. Berlin: de Gruyter, 1993.

_____. *Redactional Processes in the Book of the Twelve*. BZAW 218. Berlin: de Gruyter, 1993.

_____. "The Redactional Shaping of Nahum 1 for the Book of the Twelve." Pp. 193–202 in *Among the Prophets: Language, Image and Structure in the Prophetic Writings*. Edited by P. R. Davies and D. J. A. Clines. JSOTSup 144. Sheffield: JSOT Press, 1993.

O'Brien, J. M. "Nahum." Pp. 599–601 in *The Oxford Bible Commentary*. Edited by J. Barton and J. Muddiman. Oxford: Oxford University Press, 2001.

_____. *Nahum*. Readings. 2nd ed. Sheffield: Sheffield Phoenix, 2009.

_____. "Nahum–Habakkuk–Zephaniah: Reading the 'Former Prophets' in the Persian Period." *Int* 61 (2007) 168–83.

_____. "Violent Pictures, Violent Cultures? The 'Aesthetics of Violence' in Contemporary Film and in Ancient Prophetic Texts." Pp. 112–30 in *Aesthetics of Violence in the Prophets*. Edited by C. Franke and J. M. O'Brien. LHBOTS 517. London: T. & T. Clark, 2010.

Peckham, B. "The Vision of Habakkuk." *CBQ* 48 (1986) 617–36.

Perlitt, L. *Die Propheten Nahum, Habakuk, Zephanja.* ATD 25,1. Gottingen: Vandenhoeck & Ruprecht, 2004.

Pinker, A. "Descent of the Goddess Ishtar to the Netherworld and Nahum II 8." *VT* 55 (2005) 89–100.

_____. "Habakkuk 2.4: An Ethical Paradigm or a Political Observation?" *JSOT* 32 (2007) 91–112.

_____. "Nahum and the Greek Tradition on Nineveh's Fall." *JHS* 6 (2006) n.p.

Prinsloo, G. T. M. "Petuhot/setumot and the Structure of Habakkuk: Evaluating the Evidence." Pp. 196–227 in *The Impact of Unit Delimitation on Exegesis*. Edited by R. de Hoop, M. C. A. Korpel and S. E. Porter. Pericope 7. Leiden: Brill, 2009.

Renaud, B. "La composition du livre de Nahum: une proposition." *ZAW* 99 (1987) 198–219.

Renz, T. "A Perfectly Broken Acrostic in Nahum 1?" *JHS* 9 (2009) n.p.

Rose, M. "«Atheismus» als Wohlstandserscheinung (Zephanja 1,12)." *TZ* 37 (1981) 193–208.

Rudman, D. "A Note on Zephaniah." *Bib* 80 (1999) 109–12.

Saggs, H. W. F. "Nahum and the Fall of Nineveh." *JTS* 20 (1969) 220–25.

Schipper, B. U. "Egypt and the Kingdom of Judah under Josiah and Jehoiakim." *TA* 37 (2010) 200–226.

Seybold, K. "*Nahum Habakuk Zephanja*. ZBK 24,2. Zurich: Theologische, 1991.

_____. Vormasoretische Randnotizen in Nahum 1." *ZAW* 101 (1989) 71–85.

Shepherd, M. B. "Compositional Analysis of the Twelve." *ZAW* 120 (2008) 184–93.

Spronk, K. "Acrostics in the Book of Nahum." *ZAW* 110 (1998) 209–22.

_____. "The Line-Acrostic in Nahum 1: New Evidence from Ancient Greek Manuscripts and from the Literary Analysis of the Hebrew text." Pp. 228–40 in *The Impact of Unit Delimitation on Exegesis*. Edited by R. de Hoop, M. C. A. Korpel, and S. E. Porter. Pericope 7. Leiden: Brill, 2009.

_____. *Nahum.* HCOT. Kampen: Kok Pharos, 1997.

Strine, C. A., and C. L. Crouch, C. L. "Yahweh's Battle against Chaos in Ezekiel: The Transformation of a Traditional Motif for a New Situation." *JBL* 132 (2013) 883–903.

Sweeney, M. A. "Concerning the Structure and Generic Character of the Book of Nahum." *ZAW* 104 (1992) 364–77.

_____. "A Form-Critical Reassessment of the Book of Zephaniah." *CBQ* 53 (1991) 388–408.

_____. "Structure, Genre, and Intent in the Book of Habakkuk." *VT* 41 (1991) 63–83.

_____. *Zephaniah: A Commentary.* Hermeneia. Minneapolis: Fortress, 2003.

Tadmor, H. "Philistia under Assyrian Rule." *BA* 29 (1966) 86–102.

Van der Woude, A. S. "The Book of Nahum: A Letter Written in Exile." Pp. 108–26 in *Instruction and Interpretation: Studies in Hebrew Language, Palestinian Archaeology and Biblical Exegesis: Papers Read at the Joint British-Dutch Old Testament Confer-ence Held at Louvain, 1976.* Edited by H. A. Brongers. OtSt 20. Leiden: Brill, 1977.

Vlaardingerbroek, J. *Zephaniah.* Trans. J. Vriend. HCOT. Louvain: Peeters, 1999.

Watts, J. W. "Psalmody in Prophecy: Habakkuk 3 in Context." Pp. 209–23 in *Forming Pro-phetic Literature: Essays on Isaiah and the Twelve in Honor of John D. W. Watts.* Edited by J. W. Watts and P. R. House. JSOTSup 235. Sheffield: Sheffield Academic, 1996.

Zalcman, L. "Ambiguity and Assonance at Zephaniah 2:4." *VT* 36 (1986) 365–71.

Zapff, B. M. "The Perspective of the Nations in the Book of Micah as a 'Systematization' of the Nations' Role in Joel, Jonah and Nahum: Reflections on a Context-Oriented Exegesis in the Book of the Twelve." *Society of Biblical Literature Seminar Papers* 38 (1999) 596–616.

_____. "Die Volkerperspektive des Michabuches als 'Systematisierung' der divergieren-den Sicht der Volker in den Buchern Joel, Jona und Nahum: Uberlegungen zu einer buchubergreifenden Exegese im Dodekapropheton." *BN* 98 (1999) 86–99.

Obadiah: Judah and Its Frenemy

ALEJANDRO F. BOTTA and MÓNICA I. REY

Boston University

"Los hermanos sean unidos
Porque esa es la ley primera—Tengan unión verdadera
En cualquier tiempo que sea—Porque si entre ellos pelean
Los devoran los de afuera."

José Hernández, *El Gaucho Martin Fierro*[1]

Introduction

The book of Obadiah is part of the collection named in Aramaic עשר תרי 'The Twelve', whose compositional history spans several centuries.[2] The order of the individual books within this collection varies in the LXX and the MT, reflecting different theological foci:[3] the order of the MT points to a main concern for the fate of Jerusalem, while the LXX order reflects a "concern with the anticipated judgment against the northern kingdom of Israel."[4] H. W. Wolff dated Obadiah

---

1. "Brothers should stand by each other, because this is the first law. Keep a true bond between them always, at every time—because if they fight among themselves they are devoured by outsiders" (José Hernández, *El Gaucho Martin Fierro* [Albany, NY: SUNY Press, 1967] 492).

2. For a recent survey of redactional theories, see M. A. Sweeney, *The Twelve Prophets*, vol. 1 of *Berit Olam: Studies in Hebrew Narrative & Poetry: The Twelve Prophets: Hosea–Jonah*, ed. D. W. Cotter, J. T. Walsh, and C. Franke (Collegeville, MN: Liturgical, 2000), 1:xv–xxix; J. Wöhrle, *Der Abschluss des Zwölfprophetenbuches: Buchübergreifende Redaktionsprozesse in der späten Sammlungen* (Berlin: de Gruyter, 2008), 2–14; Wöhrle proposes several stages in which a variety of oracles were integrated into a final composition; for a summary, see Wöhrle, *Der Abschluss*, 439–46.

3. The LXX arranges the books as follows: Amos, Micah, Joel, Obadiah, Jonah, Nahum, Habakkuk, Zephaniah, Haggai, Zachariah, and Malachi. The MT arranges the individual books in the following order: Hosea, Joel, Amos, Obadiah, Jonah, Micah, Nahum, Habakkuk, Zephaniah, Haggai, Zechariah, and Malachi.

4. M. A. Sweeney, "Synchronic and Diachronic Concerns in Reading the Book of the Twelve Prophets," in *Perspectives on the Formation of the Book of the Twelve: Methodological Foundations—Redactional Processes—Historical Insights* (ed. R. Albertz, J. D. Nogalski, and J. Wöhrle; Berlin: de Gruyter, 2012), 27.

a few years after 587 B.C.E., remarking, quite optimistically, "what Obadiah says is so independent and so specific that we can only conclude that it was directly based on happenings during those catastrophic days; he cannot have fabricated the material."[5] Several commentators, however, have accepted a date close to the destruction of Jerusalem, and 554/3 B.C.E. is the date proposed by J. Renkema in his recent commentary.[6] On the other hand, B. Dicou suggested a late exilic date and J. Wehrle proposed 587–400 B.C.E. as the period in which the text developed.[7] Despite the lack of consensus about its date, there is some agreement that Obadiah "represents an adaptation of source material that was originally composed for another purpose"[8] and the final redaction/additions to the book (cf. vv. 19–20) should be dated during the early postexilic period, when the returnees are struggling to recover their ancestral homeland from their encroaching neighbors.

Three source blocks have been proposed in the compositional development of the book: 1–9, 10–14+15b and 15a+16–21.[9] The events narrated in vv. 11–14 clearly point to the deportation of the Jerusalem elite and about ten thousand Judeans after the city was conquered by the Babylonians in 587 B.C.E. (2 Adar, March 16, cf. Ps 137:7; Ezek 25:12–14; 35:5ff.; Lam 4:21ff.).[10] J. Renkema has identified the following macrostructure in the final MT canonical form of the book: YHWH's initiative (Obad 1b-4), the collapse of Edom (Obad 5–7), YHWH's judgment concerning Esau's disposition (Obad 8–12), all the peoples and their deeds fall under YHWH's judgment (Obad 13–16), and Israel's restoration (Obad 17–19/21).[11] The very brief life of Obadiah in the late hagiographical *Vitae prophetarum* (9:1–4) states that he came from near Siquem, from the district of Beth-Haran, and was a disciple of Elijah and officer of Ochoziah before he began his own prophetic career.[12] Later Jewish tradition makes him a proselyte Edomite (cf. 1 Kgs 18:1–16; 2 Kgs 1:13–15).

---

5. H. W. Wolff, *Obadiah and Jonah: A Commentary* (Minneapolis: Augsburg, 1986), 18.

6. J. Renkema, *Obadiah* (Leuven: Peeters, 2003), 251–62, and the bibliography cited there.

7. B. Dicou, *Edom: Israel's Brother and Antagonist, the Role of Edom in Biblical Prophecy and Story* (Sheffield: Sheffield University Press, 1994), 87; J. Wehrle, *Prophetie und Textanalyse: Die Komposition Obadja 1–21 interpretiert auf der Basis textlinguistischer und semiotischer Konzeptionen* (St. Ottilien: EOS, 1987), 346.

8. J. D. Nogalski, "Not Just another Nation: Obadiah's Placement in the Book of the Twelve," in *Perspectives on the Formation of the Book of the Twelve* (ed. R. Albertz, J. D. Nogalski, and J. Wöhrle; Berlin: de Gruyter, 2012), 89.

9. Ibid., 97.

10. See O. Lipschits, *The Fall and Rise of Jerusalem* (Winona Lake, IN: Eisenbrauns, 2005), 68–97.

11. J. Renkema, "The Literary Structure of Obadiah," in *Delimitation Criticism: A New Tool in Biblical Scholarship* (eds. M. C. A. Korpel and J. M. Oesch; Assen: Van Gorcum, 2000), 269–70.

12. A. M. Schwemer, *Studien zu den frühjüdischen Prophetenlegende Vitae Prophetarum* (Tübingen: Mohr Siebeck, 1995), 2:43–47.

As a whole, the vision of Obadiah can be categorized among the oracles against foreign nations (German: *Fremdvolkelorakel, Fremdvölkerspruch*)[13] found in the prophetic corpus of the Hebrew Bible.[14] Such oracles address the transgressions of various foreign nations and God's punishment of these nations' actions.[15] Egypt is indicted for its arrogance and the destruction it caused (Jer 46:8; Ezek 29:3, 9b; 31:10; 32:2, 32), idolatry, false gods (Isa 19:1–3; Ezek 30:13a), and false wisdom (Isa 19:11–15). The Philistines (helpers of Tyre and Sidon? Jer 47:4) are condemned for their hostility and vengeance (Ezek 25:15) and slave trade (Amos 1:6).[16] Moab's arrogance, pride, and insolence in trusting in her treasures is also denounced (Jer 48:7; Isa 16:6), as well as the breaking of covenant (Ezek 25:8).[17] The Ammonites are accused of the dispossession of Gad (Jer 49:1) and rejoicing over the destruction of the Jerusalem and its Temple and the exile (Ezek 25:3); they are also charged with war crimes (Amos 1:13). Babylon is accused of arrogance (Jer 50:31–32; Isa 14:12, 14). Damascus is indicted for war crimes (Amos 1:3; Jer 49:23–27). The Phoenicians list of transgressions includes being powerful (Isa 23:9), violent (Ezek 26:17), arrogant (Ezek 28:2), and violent in trading practices (Ezek 28:16, 24). Edom, the focus of Obadiah, also appears in oracles of war and oracles against foreign nations in other prophets. Amos condemned Edom "Because he pursued his brother with the sword and repressed all pity, because his anger raged unceasing and his fury stormed unchecked" (1:11), and Ezekiel denounced Edom "Because Edom acted vengefully against the House of Judah and incurred guilt by wreaking revenge upon it" (24:12–14). Jeremiah, on the other hand, proclaimed Edom's arrogance: "Your arrogant heart has seduced you, you who dwell in clefts of the rock"; but no specific behavior is mentioned. In Lam 1, Jerusalem is described as a widow with no lovers. Edom was one of these former

---

13. Defined by Marvin Sweeney as "a prophetic speech form that announces punishment or disaster against a foreign nation" (M. Sweeney, *Isaiah 1–39* with an Introduction to Prophetic Literature [FOTL 16; Grand Rapids, MI: Eerdmans, 1996], 528).

14. Isa 13:1–14:23 (Babylon); 14:24–27 (Assyria); 14:28–32 (Philistines); 15:1–16:14 (Moab); 17:1–4 (Damascus); 18:1–7 (Ethiopians); 19:1–24 (Egypt); 21:1–10 (Babylon); 21:11–12 (Dumah); 21:13–17 (Arabia); 23:1–18 (Phoenicians); Jer 46:2–28 (Egypt); 47:1–7 (Gaza); 48:1–47 (Moab); 49:1–6 (Ammonites); 49:7–22 (Edom); 49:23–27 (Damascus); 49:28–33 (Kedar / Hazor); 49:34–39 (Elam); 50:1–51:58 (Babylon); Ezek 25:1–7 (Ammonites); 25:8–11 (Moab and Seir); 25:12–14 (Edom); 25:15–17 (Philistines); 26:1–28:19 (Tyre); 28:20–24 (Sidon); 29:1–32:32 (seven oracles against Egypt); Amos 1:3–5 (Damascus); 1:6–8 (Gaza); 1:9–10 (Tyre); 1:11–12 (Edom); 1:13–15 (Ammonites); 2:1–3 (Moab); Zeph 2:4–6 (Philistines); 2:8–11 (Moab and Ammon), 2:13–15 (Assyria).

15. See D. L. Christensen, *Transformations of the War Oracle in Old Testament Prophecy: Studies in the Oracles Against the Nations* (HDR 3; Missoula, MT: Scholars Press, 1975); Y. Hoffman, *Ha-Nevu'ot 'al ha-goyim ba-Miḳra* (Tel Aviv: Tel Aviv University Press, 1977).

16. See S. M. Paul, *Amos* (Hermeneia; Minneapolis: Fortress, 1991), 56–57.

17. Ibid., 72.

lovers, "bound with Judah in covenant to resist Babylonian hegemony."[18] As a result of Edom's role in the destruction of Jerusalem, which is the central focus of the book of Lamentations, Edom now stands alongside other nations in judgment for this violation.

Edom as Friend and Enemy of the State:
Not a Friend, Not an Enemy—a Frenemy[19]

"Et tu, Brute?"—Shakespeare's *Julius Caesar*

Obadiah condemns actions taken against the state (Judah) by the Edomites (portrayed as friends of the state who seem to have acted as enemies) during the destruction of the first temple in collusion with the Babylonians. Obadiah roots himself in the aforementioned prophetic traditions and also denounces Edom for its arrogance: "Your arrogant heart has seduced you, you who dwell in clefts of the rock, in your lofty abode. You think in your heart, 'Who can pull me down to earth?'" (Obad 3, JPS[20]). In denouncing Edom for its actions against Jacob, he states, "For the outrage to your brother Jacob" (Obad 10a), Obadiah 11 likens the Edomites to 'foreigners' (נכרים) and 'strangers' (זרים—the most despised, least invested group of foreigners)[21] and, in v. 12, highlights the non-brotherly behavior of Edom in light of Judah's tragedy:

Judah	Edom
his calamity (נכרו)	(you) gaze with glee (תרא)
their ruin (אבדם)	(you) rejoice (תשׂמח)
distress (צרה)	(you) boast (תגדל פיך)

Oracles of war and oracles against foreign nations are clear ideological expressions of nationalism. The biblical god is, after all, a national god (certainly with universal pretensions, though), and his pretended sovereignty over the rest of the nations of the world is both a manifestation and a consequence of Judah's nationalistic aspirations.

---

18. S. M. Olyan, "Honor, Shame and Covenant Relations in Ancient Israel and its Environment," in *Social Inequality in the World of the Text: The Significance of Ritual and Social Distinctions in the Hebrew Bible* (Göttingen: Vandenhoeck & Ruprecht, 2011), 32.

19. The term *frenemy* was first coined by Walter Winchell in 1953 in a statement he wrote describing the relationship the United States had with the Russians, suggesting the Russians be called "frienemies." As an oxymoron and portmanteau, frenemy is defined as an enemy pretending to be a friend. Alternatively, it can also be understood as a person who is a friend but also a competitor and rival. See Walter Winchell, "Howz about calling the Russians our Frienemies?" *Nevada State Journal* (1953).

20. All translations are taken from the JPS.

21. J. Mayshar, "Who was the Toshav?" *JBL* 133 (2014) 227.

But, unlike other prophets and prophetic works that at the same time both condemn foreign nations for their behavior and also engage in intrapolitical conflict and antagonism toward the state political and religious institutions and officials (e.g., Jeremiah), the book of Obadiah does not engage in political or socio-economic struggles. Obadiah fully focuses instead on the relationship between the Judean state and a neighbor's (i.e., Edom) state actions. Obadiah is unique as an oracle against the nations precisely because of Judah's particular historical and ancestral relationship with Edom.[22] What Obadiah and other texts make clear is that Edom and Judah definitely had a relationship that was different from other nations. The Hebrew Bible consistently refers to the relationship between these two peoples as a brotherhood (e.g., Gen 25:19, 27:40–41; Num 20:14; Deut 2:4, 23:8; Amos 1:9, 11; Obad 10, 12). In addition to the parallel passage about Edom in Jeremiah (49:8, 10), the Book of the Twelve is unique in the prophetic corpus in portraying Edom as Israel's brother (Amos 1:1; Mal 1:2–5).[23] Amos 1:9 describes the relationship between Edom and Judah as ברית אחי 'a covenant of kinship'.

In similar fashion, the expression אחיך 'your brother' is used twice in Obadiah. In v. 10, it is further qualified by stating that Jacob is the brother against whom the offense has been alleged. This kinship-motif is strengthened through the various appellations used to describe Edom. "Mount Esau" is used seven times throughout the book (vv. 6, 8, 9, 18, 19, 21), referring to the eponymous ancestor of the Edomites. Brotherhood takes on multiple meanings in this regard. First, as a literary device, the term brothers and references to Jacob and Esau are very specific figurative terminology that relate to the Jacob-Esau cycle in Genesis.

> Two nations are in your womb,
> two separate peoples shall issue from your body;
> one people shall be mightier than the other
> and the older shall serve the younger. (Gen 25:23)

The blessing given by Isaac in Gen 27:29 also solidifies Edom as subordinate:

> Let peoples serve you,
> and nations bow down to you;
> Be master over your brothers,
> and let your mother's sons bow down to you.
> Cursed be they who curses you,
> Blessed they who bless you.

---

22. See G. Langer, "Esau in der hebräischen Bible," in *Esau: Bruder und Feind* (ed. G. Langer; Göttingen: Vandenhoeck & Ruprecht, 2009), 17–30.

23. R. Scoralick, "The Case of Edom in the Book of the Twelve," in *Perspectives on the Formation of the Book of the Twelve: Methodological Foundations—Redactional Processes—Historical Insights* (ed. R. Albertz, J. D. Nogalski, and J. Wöhrle; Berlin: de Gruyter, 2012), 45; Dicou, *Edom*, 113–14.

This relationship is divinely sanctioned, and Edom stands to exist in perpetual servitude. Jacob will be lord over his brothers—here, most obviously, Esau. Certainly the Jacob-Esau brotherhood narrative and its national-political implications would have been common knowledge at this point.[24] As B. Dicou points out, "more than in the other narratives [of foreign nations], in the Jacob-Esau stories it is stressed that the two brothers represent nations."[25] This emphasis on their relationship as twin brothers/nations points to a special bond between the two that other nations did not share with Israel and Judah. This is significant, considering the consequences the Edomites would face as a result of their supposed betrayal.

At the same time, the Hebrew Bible also presents this "brotherhood" as characterized by continuous conflict and enmity. The biblical tradition portrays the Edomites as suffering defeats during the reign of Saul (1 Sam 14:47) and David (2 Sam 8:13–14; 1 Kgs 11:15–17), and they are described as "making trouble" (רעה) for Solomon (1 Kgs 11:21–25). Until the reign of Jehoshaphat, according to the Bible "there was no king (מלך) in Edom; a deputy (נצב) was king," which, together with 2 Kgs 3:8–9 suggests that Edom was a vassal of the Judean kings until their rebellion and independence during the reign of king Jehoram (son of Jehoshaphat) of Judah (2 Kgs 8:20–22, in the mid-9th century B.C.E.). A new defeat at the hands of the Judean king Amaziah (2 Kgs 14:7; 2 Chr 25:11–12)[26] and a later resurgence and independence gained during the reign of Ahaz (2 Kgs 16:6) are witnesses to the ongoing conflict relationships between these two "brothers" in the Judean stories. The several refortifications and destructions of the fortress of Arad, situated at the border of Judah and Edom are a witness to the conflictive relations between the two kingdoms, and Arad Ostraca 24 and 40 seem to indicate a situation of tension in the border between the two nations.[27] In this close rivalry, the brotherhood myth promotes Edom as the subordinate brother to Judah.

Therefore, the suggestion that Edomites were involved in the fall of Jerusalem and the consequences faced by the Edomites laid out in the book of Obadiah suggest that a grievous transgression has taken place. In light of the oracles and the narratives, it is clear that "Obadiah makes use of the patriarchal tradition equating

---

24. J. M. Tebes, "The Edomite Involvement in the Destruction of the First Temple: A Case of Stab-in-the- Back Tradition?" *JSOT* 36:2 (2011) 248.

25. Dicou, *Edom*, 134.

26. Whether Edom fell under the control of Judah or Amaziah's capture of Sela only represented a borderline conquest is a matter of dispute. See M. Haran, "Observations on the Historical Background of Amos 1:2–2:6," *BIES* 30 (1966) 56–59.

27. M. Aharoni, "Arad: The Israelite Citadels," in *The New Encyclopedia of Archaeological Excavations in the Holy Land* (Jerusalem: Carta, 1993), 1:82. For the Arad Ostraca, see the recent edition of Shmuel Aḥituv, *Echoes from the Past: Hebrew and Cognate Inscriptions from the Biblical Period* (Jerusalem: Carta, 2008), 92–153; for an alternative view, see P. Guillaume, "The Myth of the Edomite Threat: Arad Letters 24 and 40," *Kleine Untersuchungen zur Sprache des Alten Testaments und Seiner Umwelt* 15 (2013) 97–108.

Edom with Esau ... in order to emphasize the seriousness of the crime."[28] The severity of the transgressions committed by the Edomites can be seen in the consequences assigned to the Edomites. Unlike the other nations, which this oracle also addresses (v. 15), the Edomites stand to be cut off forever (vv. 9–10), with no survivors (v. 18). This is one of the severest punishments that can be allotted by YHWH to a foreign nation.

Several scholars, however, have raised the possibility that this hostility was unfounded, either due to the fact that the Edomites had not been really involved in the fall of the city or in the idea that the enmity did not originate in the behavior of the Edomites towards Judah before the fall of Jerusalem but came about due to the political situation and ideological challenges that the postexilic community faced during the restoration period.[29] After major national catastrophes, there is a propensity on the part of those who experienced trauma to believe in conspiracy theories. In fact, "a tendency to hold conspiracy beliefs has been linked to a victimhood-based identity."[30] As one social scientist suggests, "situations that evoke feelings of a lack of control increase illusory pattern perceptions, including a belief in conspiracies and superstitions."[31]

As Tebes notes, "the presence of Edomite population in lands of the now defunct kingdom of Judah did not go unnoticed by the Golah returnees. They may have seen it as an actual invasion of Judaean land."[32] Therefore, in order to answer how it is that the Edomites did not fall under Babylonian rule, and how it is that Edom maintained and even encroached upon land that was once held by the Judeans, the Judeans may have been inclined to answer by perpetuating the myth of the Edomites' involvement in the fall of Jerusalem. This conspiracy theory—that the Edomites were actually agents and co-conspirators with the Babylonians—answered these questions, questions that must have certainly plagued the trauma-stricken survivors (why was Edom not subjugated under Babylon? How were they able to encroach upon our Judean land?). In this way, the belief that the Edomites were involved leaves nothing to chance but instead attributes the current Judean situation to intentional action on the part of the Edomites: their tumultuous history and rivalry with the Judeans implied that the Edomites had deliberately conspired against the Judeans. This is one of the ways conspiracy theories function: "the appeal of some conspiracy theories, then, lies in the attribution of otherwise

---

28. D. E. Gowan, *Theology of the Prophetic Books: The Death and Resurrection of Israel* (1st ed.; Louisville: Westminster John Knox, 1998), 118.

29. See E. Assis, "Why Edom? On the Hostility Towards Jacobs' Brother in Prophetic Sources," *VT* 56 (2006) 1–20; Tebes, "The Edomite Involvement in the Destruction of the First Temple," the literature quoted there, and Guillaume, "The Myth of the Edomite Threat."

30. M. Bilewicz, A. Cichocka, and W. Soral, *The Psychology of Conspiracy* (London: Routledge, 2015), 44.

31. Ibid., ix.

32. Tebes, "The Edomite Involvement in the Destruction of the First Temple," 250.

inexplicable events to intentional action, and to an unwillingness to accept the possibility that significant adverse consequences may be a product of invisible hand mechanisms . . . or of simple chance, rather than of anyone's plans."[33] The actors/conspirators are typically believed to be "those who stand to benefit."[34] In the rivalry between Edom and Judah, it seems natural for a Judean to suggest that Edom stands to benefit from their demise, especially if this is the current situation they find themselves in (with Edomites having taken over portions of Judean land). The conspiracy theory of Edomite involvement helps answer for the Judeans the question of how it is that Edom appears to go untouched during their own demise. For the victim community, this question is a necessary one that needs explanation. For victims, often there is a need for a totalizing answer; this is why conspiracy theories flourish. Another function we see played out in Obadiah is the stressing of Judah's victimhood under the hands of the Edomites. Obadiah describes the fall as misfortune (נכר) (v. 12), destruction (אבד) (v. 12), distress (צרה) (vv. 12, 14), calamity (איד) (v. 13), (Judah's) disaster (רעה) (v. 13). All of these are described as taking place under the witness of and because of deliberate actions by the Edomites. In Obadiah, the primary perpetrators are not the Babylonians, who remained unnamed in Obadiah, but, instead, the Edomites.[35]

These series of victim and perpetrator descriptions (vv. 10–14) are useful in the establishment of a conspiracy theory involving the Edomites because, "stressing the importance of one's own in-group victimhood creates a paradoxical psychological situation: It might allow for fostering feelings of in-group power."[36] Therefore, the book of Obadiah has the ability to foster in-group power despite the survivor status of the Judeans, which affords them little or no felt control in their current situation.

Finally, promoting a conspiracy such as Edomite involvement does not need to be done as a conscious, deliberate lie on the part of the Judeans. In fact, promoters of conspiracy beliefs can be "entirely sincere"[37] in their estimations, despite the conspiracy itself being a falsehood. This is because conspiracy theorists are seeking to make sense of the devastating events that occurred and will offer up a variety of explanations as a means of mitigating pain, loss, and outrage in their current situation.[38]

---

33. C. R. Sunstein and A. Vermeule, "Conspiracy Theories: Causes and Cures," *The Journal of Political Philosophy* 17 (2009) 208.

34. Ibid.

35. The absence of explicit oracles condemning Egypt and Babylon in the postexilic period could be explained as serving the interests of the diaspora communities that had settled there. A. C. Hagedorn, *Die Anderen im Spiegel: Israels auseinandersetzung mit den Völkern in den Büchern Nahum, Zefanja, Obadja und Joel* (BZAW 414; Berlin: de Gruyter 2011), 299.

36. Bilewicz, Cichocka, and Soral, *The Psychology of Conspiracy*, 44.

37. Sunstein and Vermeule, "Conspiracy Theories," 212.

38. Ibid., 213.

An incident such as the fall of Jerusalem probably caused precisely this kind of psychological trauma: those who survived needed answers to any questions and uncertainties that may have lingered. If the Edomites were not involved but were merely bystanders, the sentiments presented by Obadiah and other prophetic works suggests the development of a conspiracy theory of their involvement after the destruction of the temple. Major national catastrophes invite conspiracy theories in part because of a need by survivors and later generations to make sense of their current situation, the trauma of the past, and the paranoia it produces about their future.

Bibliography

Achenbach, R., R. Albertz, and J. Wöhrle, eds. *The Foreigner and the Law: Perspectives from the Hebrew Bible and the Ancient Near East.* Wiesbaden: Harrassowitz, 2011.

Aharoni, M. "Arad: The Israelite Citadels." Pp. 82–87 in *NEAEHL* vol. 1. New York: Simon & Schuster, 1993.

Ahituv, S. *Echoes from the Past: Hebrew and Cognate Inscriptions from the Biblical Period.* Jerusalem: Carta, 2008.

Albertz, R., J. Nogalski, and J. Wöhrle, eds. *Perspectives on the Formation of the Book of the Twelve: Methodological Foundations, Redactional Processes, Historical Insights.* Berlin: de Gruyter, 2012.

Albertz, R., and J. Wöhrle. *Between Cooperation and Hostility: Multiple Identities in Ancient Judaism and the Interaction with Foreign Powers.* Göttingen: Vandenhoeck & Ruprecht, 2013.

Assis, E. "Why Edom? On the Hostility Towards Jacob's Brother in Prophetic Sources." *VT* 56 (2006) 1–20.

Bilewicz, M., A. Cichocka, and W. Soral, eds. *Psychology of Conspiracy.* London: Routledge, 2015.

Christensen, D. L. *Transformations of the War Oracle in Old Testament Prophecy: Studies in the Oracles Against the Nations.* Missoula, MT: Scholars, 1975.

Dicou, B. *Edom, Israel's Brother and Antagonist: The Role of Edom in Biblical Prophecy and Story.* England: Sheffield Academic, 1994.

Guillaume, P. "The Myth of the Edomite Threat: Arad Letters 24 and 40." *Kleine Untersuchungen zur Sprache des Alten Testaments und Seiner Umwelt* (2013) 97–108.

Hagedorn, A. C. *Die Anderen im Spiegel: Israels Auseinandersetzung mit den Völkern in den Büchern Nahum, Zefanja, Obadja und Joel.* Berlin: de Gruyter, 2011.

Haran, M. "Observations on the Historical Background of Amos 1:2–2:6." *IEJ* 18 (1968) 201–12.

Hoffman, Y. *Ha-Nevu'ot ʿal Ha-Goyim ba-Miḳra.* Tel Aviv: Tel Aviv University, 1977.

Langer, G. "Esau in Der Hebräischen Bibel." Pp. 17–30 in *Esau: Bruder und Feind.* Ed. G. Langer; Göttingen: Vandenhoeck & Ruprecht, 2009.

Lipschitz, O. *The Fall and Rise of Jerusalem: Judah Under Babylonian Rule.* Winona Lake, IN: Eisenbrauns, 2005.

Mayshar, J. "Who was the Toshav?" *JBL* 133 (2014) 225–46.

Olyan, S. M. "Honor, Shame, and Covenant Relations in Ancient Israel and its Environment." Pp. 17–35 in *Social Inequality in the World of the Text: The Significance of Ritual and Social Distinctions in the Hebrew Bible*. Göttingen: Vandenhoeck & Ruprecht, 2011.

Renkema, J. "Data Relevant to the Dating of the Prophecy of Obadiah." Pp. 251–62 in *Past, Present, Future: The Deuteronomistic History and the Prophets*. Ed. J. C. Moor and H. F. Rooy. Leiden: Brill, 2000.

_____. "The Literary Structure of Obadiah." Pp. 269–70 in *Delimitation Criticism: A New Tool in Biblical Scholarship*. Ed. M. Korpel and J. Oesch. Assen: Van Gorcum, 2000.

_____. *Obadiah*. Leuven, Belgium: Peeters, 2003.

Schwemer, A. M. *Studien zu den Frühjüdischen Prophetenlegenden Vitae Prophetarum*. Tübingen: Mohr Siebeck, 1995.

Sunstein, C. R., and A. Vermeule. "Symposium on Conspiracy Theories Conspiracy Theories: Causes and Cures." *The Journal of Political Philosophy* 17 (2009) 202–27.

Sweeney, M. A. *Isaiah 1–39: With an Introduction to Prophetic Literature*. Grand Rapids, MI: Eerdmans, 1996.

_____. *The Twelve Prophets: Hosea–Jonah*. Edited by D. W. Cotter, J. T. Walsh, and C. Franke. Collegeville, MN: Liturgical, 2000.

_____. "Synchronic and Diachronic Concerns in Reading the Book of the Twelve Prophets." Pp. 21–34 in *Perspectives on the Formation of the Book of the Twelve: Methodological Foundations—Redactional Processes—Historical Insights*. Edited by R. Albertz, J. D. Nogalski, and J. Wöhrle. Berlin: de Gruyter, 2012.

Tebes, J. M. "The Edomite Involvement in the Destruction of the First Temple: A Case of Stab-in-the-Back Tradition?" *JSOT* (2011): 219–255.

Wehrle, J. *Prophetie und Textanalyse: Die Komposition Obadja 1–21 Interpretiert auf der Basis Textlinguistischer und Semiotischer Konzeptionen*. St. Ottilien: EOS, 1987.

Wöhrle, J. *Der Abschluss des Zwölfprophetenbuches: Buchübergreifende Redaktionsprozesse in Den Späten Sammlungen*. Berlin: de Gruyter, 2008.

Wolff, H. W. *Obadiah and Jonah: A Commentary*. Minneapolis: Augsburg, 1986.

The Prophet Ezekiel:
State Priest, State Enemy

STEPHEN L. COOK

Virginia Theological Seminary

The 6th-century prophet Ezekiel occupies an intriguing position in Israelite history and society. The prophet and his followers hail from the circle of Judah's central priests. At the time of Babylonia's sieges and eventual destruction of Jerusalem (597 and 587 B.C.E.), they were among the Zadokite lineage of clerics in power at the temple.[1] Paradoxically, this conservative priest, bearer of a hierarchical theology, is single minded in his radical critique of the Judean state. Wearing the twin hats of state priest and state enemy, he bears a vision of the revolutionary overthrow of the entirety of Judean society.

The nature and sources of Ezekiel's hierarchical theology are becoming increasingly clear to scholars. The prophet and his circle took a specific set of priestly traditions with them into Babylonian exile in 597 B.C.E., a stream of tradition preserved in the Pentateuch known as the "Holiness School" (HS).[2] This theology,

---

1. The Zadokites, one of at least three major Israelite priestly lineages, controlled the preexilic chief-priesthood in Jerusalem. According to biblical tradition, King Solomon elevated Zadok as chief priest after banishing his Levite colleague Abiathar (2 Sam 20:25; 1 Kgs 1:7–8, 41–45; 2:26–27). Texts such as 1 Chr 6:50–53 and 24:31 trace Zadok's ancestry back to Eleazar, Aaron's son, and key studies by F. M. Cross and S. M. Olyan affirm an Aaronide pedigree as historical. In Num 25:10–13, the Zadokites claim that God granted a covenant of eternal priesthood to Eleazar's son, Phinehas. For discussion and bibliography, see Mark Leuchter, *The Polemics of Exile in Jeremiah 26–45* (New York: Cambridge University Press, 2008), 225 n. 12; F. M. Cross, *Canaanite Myth and Hebrew Epic* (Cambridge, MA: Harvard University Press, 1973), 213–15; S. M. Olyan, "Zadok's Origins and the Tribal Politics of David," *JBL* 101 (1982) 177–93; S. L. Cook, review of Alice Hunt, *Missing Priests: The Zadokites in Tradition and History*, *CBQ* 71 (2009) 372–73. On the unique Zadokite understandings of Ezekiel's book, see S. L. Cook and C. L. Patton [Carvalho], "Introduction: Hierarchical Thinking and Theology in Ezekiel's Book," in *Ezekiel's Hierarchical World: Wrestling with a Tiered Reality* (ed. S. Cook and C. Patton; SBLSS 31; Atlanta: SBL, 2004), 11–12.

2. Israel Knohl and Jacob Milgrom have identified a Priestly Torah (PT) document within the Pentateuch, which was later joined with Holiness School (HS) writings to form what has hitherto been considered a basically unified P document. See J. Milgrom, *Leviticus 1–16: A New Translation with Introduction and Commentary* (AB 3; New York: Doubleday, 1991), 1–2, 13–42,

which pervades the prophet's book, is extraordinarily authoritative, totalizing, and rigorous toward dissent.

Ezekiel's central priestly Zadokite identity is assured.[3] His book's superscription identifies him as a priest (1:3), and later texts of the book align overtly with a Zadokite priestly perspective (40:46; 43:19; 44:15–31; 48:11). His reference to the "thirtieth year" in 1:1 probably refers to his having reached the age for assuming duties at the temple (Num 4:3 HS).[4] He draws directly on the thinking and theology of the Holiness School (HS) throughout his prophetic career, a tradition thoroughly enmeshed in temple concerns. He possesses technical knowledge of temple architecture, forms, garments, and processes (e.g., 8:16; 10:2, 18–19; 28:13; 43:7–9).[5] He is intensely concerned with ritual purity (e.g., 4:14; 5:11; 18:6; 36:17; 44:25). Ezekiel never gives up his priestly role to become a prophet, as some have argued.[6] Even toward the end of the book, he is performing the priestly role of transmitting torah to Israel (43:12; cf. 44:23).

Ezekiel, the priestly power-holder, is simultaneously Ezekiel the radical revolutionary. His opposition to the Judean state of his time is unambiguous. He speaks definitively of "an end!" (7:6). By this, he understands that God is terminat-

---

48; I. Knohl, *The Sanctuary of Silence: The Priestly Torah and the Holiness School* (Minneapolis: Fortress, 1995); idem, *The Divine Symphony: The Bible's Many Voices* (Philadelphia: JPS, 2003). B. J. Schwartz advances this new understanding of P in "The Priestly Account of the Theophany and the Lawgiving at Sinai," in *Texts, Temples, and Traditions: A Tribute to Menahem Haran* (ed. M. V. Fox et al.; Winona Lake, IN: Eisenbrauns, 1996), 103–34; and idem, *The Holiness Legislation: Studies in the Priestly Code* (Jerusalem: Magnes, 1999), in Hebrew. All three scholars argue that HS is mostly later than PT and has its own emphases, but they disagree on the extent of its polemical disagreement with PT. Schwartz argues ably against Knohl that HS aims not so much to react against PT as to complement and supplement it. For additional recent discussion, see D. P. Wright, "Holiness in Leviticus and Beyond: Differing Perspectives," *Int* 53 (1999) 351–64; A. Ruwe, *"Heiligkeitsgesetz" und "Priesterschrift:" Literaturgeschichtliche und rechtssystematische Untersuchungen zu Leviticus 17,1–26,2* (FAT 26; Tübingen: Mohr Siebeck, 1999) 5–35; J. Stackert, *Rewriting the Torah: Literary Revision in Deuteronomy and the Holiness Legislation* (FAT 52; Tübingen: Mohr Siebeck, 2007), 194–95; Leuchter, *The Polemics*, 258 n. 48; M. S. Smith, *The Priestly Vision of Genesis 1* (Minneapolis: Augsburg Fortress, 2010), 172–73, 271 n. 41, 291 n. 62.

3. For sample discussion, see S. L. Cook, *Prophecy and Apocalypticism: The Postexilic Social Setting* (Minneapolis: Fortress, 1995), 97–98, 105–8, 215–16; Leuchter, *The Polemics*, 51, 156–59; 216 n. 52; M. A. Sweeney, *Form and Intertextuality in Prophetic and Apocalyptic Literature* (FAT 45; Tübingen: Mohr Siebeck, 2005), 124–43; C. L. Patton [Carvalho], "Priest, Prophet, and Exile: Ezekiel as a Literary Construct," in *Ezekiel's Hierarchical World*, 84–87; A. Mein, "Ezekiel as a Priest in Exile," in *The Elusive Prophet: The Prophet as a Historical Person, Literary Character, and Anonymous Artist* (OtSt 45; Leiden: Brill, 2001), 199–213; Knohl, *The Sanctuary of Silence*, 103, 200–203; R. R. Wilson, *Prophecy and Society in Ancient Israel* (Philadelphia: Fortress, 1980), 282.

4. Sweeney, *Form and Intertextuality*, 130–31; Patton, "Priest, Prophet, and Exile," 84–85; J. E. Miller, "The Thirtieth Year of Ezekiel 1:1," *RB* 99 (1992) 499–503.

5. For discussion, see L. Monloubou, "La signification du culte selon Ézéchiel," in *Ezekiel and His Book: Textual and Literary Criticism and Their Interrelation* (ed. J. Lust; BETL 74; Louvain: Louvain University Press/Peeters, 1986), 7–20.

6. See the arguments in Sweeney, *Form and Intertextuality*, 127–29.

ing an entire epoch. God is bringing the destruction of Jerusalem and the temple, the downfall of the nation, the banishment of the people. These prophecies are not warnings of what might happen. They are a foregone conclusion. This is the meaning of Ezekiel's speechlessness and the swallowed scroll (2:8–3:3; 3:22–27; 24:25–27; 33:21–22). His tongue is frozen, for there can be no new prophetic word reversing judgment. Judgment is inscribed and fixed. God's forcible interruption of Judah's political development is inevitable.[7]

What God particularly opposes, according to Ezekiel, is the people's Jerusalem-centered nationalism.[8] He exhorts the audience to drop their loyalty to the capital. Contrary to official claims, Jerusalem is no impenetrable "pot," where food (i.e., the populace) is safely stored (11:1–13). Rather, it is a dirty pot about to be cleaned by overheating (24:6–11). Or, to use another metaphor, Jerusalem is an adulterous wife, guilty of a capital offense (16:40; cf. Lev 20:10 HS). Ezekiel's audience takes none of these figures of speech seriously, appreciating his words, at most, solely on an aesthetic level. "Isn't he one for making metaphors?" they laugh (Ezek 20:49 CEB; cf. 33:32).

Even in the new age of redemption, Jerusalem will not regain its former status. In their blueprint for the future, the Ezekiel school relocates the temple north and away from "the city" (Ezek 45:6). Now the possession of "the whole house of Israel," not just of royal officials and nobles, "the city" will lie below Ezekiel's new holy district (48:9–15). No one will even call it "Jerusalem" anymore. At least, the book nowhere gives that name to the new city of Ezekiel's sacred reservation (see 48:35).

Ezekiel took on not just royal officials and nobles but even his fellow central priests at the Jerusalem temple. For the prophet and his circle, Israel's pervasive sin during the monarchic period extended to everybody. The temple priests were no exception, as is fully apparent from Ezek 7:26; 8; and 22:26. In his vision of abominations in Jerusalem's temple, Ezekiel sees the temple priests allowing veneration of Tammuz (also known as Dumuzi). It goes on right at the shrine's north gate (8:14–15). What is worse, the state's official priests permit solar worship (worship of the sun god Shamash?) in the temple's inner court at the building's very porch.[9]

---

7. Thomas Renz develops well Ezekiel's prospect of a complete annihilation, of a "fundamental discontinuity" between old Israel and an entirely new beginning. See his *The Rhetorical Function of the Book of Ezekiel* (VTSup 76; Leiden: Brill, 1999), 198–99. On Ezekiel's speechlessness, see S. L. Cook, "The Speechless Suppression of Grief in Ezekiel 24:15–27: The Death of Ezekiel's Wife and the Prophet's Abnormal Response," in *Thus Says the Lord: Essays on the Former and Latter Prophets in Honor of Robert R. Wilson* (ed. S. L. Cook and J. J. Ahn; LHBOTS 502; London: T. & T. Clark, 2009), 222–33.

8. Jon Levenson remarks on Ezekiel's opposition to the Davidic rulers of his time and their "chauvinistic Judean self-image" (*Theology of the Program of Restoration of Ezekiel 40–48* [HSM 10; Missoula, MT: Scholars, 1976], 93).

9. For an interesting discussion of Zadokite links with solar worship, see J. G. Taylor, *Yahweh and the Sun: Biblical and Archaeological Evidence for Sun Worship in Ancient Israel* (Sheffield:

How can Ezekiel so radically oppose his state, his society, and even his fellow central priests? At first blush, his position makes little social sense. The welfare of a strong central authority was crucial for all advanced agrarian states of his time in withstanding internal and external conditions of threat. How, in good conscience, can an official priest work to undermine it? The basic integration of Judah as a viable political and economic entity depended on the successful operations of state and capital.[10]

Ezekiel breaks with what social scientists describe as the normal alliance of political and religious leadership. As Gerhard Lenski puts it, across societies there is often "strong supernatural sanction for the existing system of power and privilege."[11] Society's priests enforce the sanction, thus buttressing the *status quo*. "When rebellious voices challenged the right of the governing class to control the economic surplus produced by the peasants, the clergy usually defended the elite, asserting that their power had been given them by God and any challenge to it was a challenge to His authority."[12]

Ezekiel's position as both state priest and state enemy, however, cannot be interpreted as completely anomalous. Social-scientific study allows that even society's official priests may raise their voices against what they come to see as an evil and corrupt system. As Lenski writes, "Though it is clear that the clergy usually fell considerably short of the ideals they professed, and furthermore that they contributed to the stability and perpetuation of systems of inequality by legitimizing the rule of the political elite, this is not the whole story. On many occasions, especially in the Judaic-Christian tradition, though not there alone, the priestly class opposed tyranny and injustice."[13]

JSOT, 1993), 134–36. That Ezekiel's group roundly condemned their fellow Zadokites of the Jerusalem temple is in no way contradicted by Ezek 44:15–16 (compare with 48:11). Contrary to a commonplace assumption, that text does not exonerate the monarchic-period activities of the Zadokite priests. The picture of Zadokite faithfulness in Ezek 44 does not fit the Ezekiel group's recollection of Israel's history in the land but a narrative of the Holiness School in Num 16–18 about Israel's wanderings in the wilderness. For full discussion, see S. L. Cook, "Innerbiblical Interpretation in Ezekiel 44 and the History of Israel's Priesthood," *JBL* 114 (1995) 193–208.

10. See G. Lenski, *Human Societies: A Macrolevel Introduction to Sociology* (New York: McGraw-Hill, 1970) 257. The social-scientific models and insights of Lenski (b. 1924) are powerfully illuminating of the social dynamics of ancient Israelite history.

11. G. Lenski, *Power and Privilege: A Theory of Social Stratification* (New York: McGraw-Hill, 1966), 39.

12. Lenski, *Human Societies,* 284. Lenski further states: "The political elite badly needed the blessing of the priestly class. Only the latter could establish the legitimacy of a regime which constantly used its power to separate the common people from the major part of what they produced. The significance of this power to confer legitimacy is difficult to exaggerate" (Lenski, *Power and Privilege,* 260).

13. Lenski, *Power and Privilege,* 263. Compare with Lenski's observation that within some religions, notably Judaism and Christianity, there arose a strong element of "ethical criticism of the existing order." An impulse to "encourage attacks on the *status quo*" is, in fact, attested

Lenski's model of the typical workings of an advanced agrarian state indicates that Ezekiel would likely have seen much to criticize in the society surrounding him. The governing class of such a state generally used political power for personal advantage and self-aggrandizement rather than for helping the common people. The buying and selling of justice and favor were rampant. Officials of the state often required bribes before acting; judicial decisions depended on who had money to offer.[14]

Neither an inborn ethical sensibility nor a spirit of humanism can account for Ezekiel's opposition to the state. Rather, inherited priestly traditions affected him at every turn, propelling him against his society (3:14). The pages of his book drip with evidence of a sophisticated education and temple training from childhood.[15] The traditions of the Holiness School particularly impressed themselves on his mind and conscience, even impelling him to argue with God over a command to defile himself (Ezek 4:14; see Lev 17:10–16 HS). Holiness School traditions especially directed Ezekiel's stress on social justice and care for the poor (e.g., Lev 19:9–15, 33–35; 23:22; 25:13–17 all HS).

Ezekiel spoke in good conscience of Judah's full "end"—its imminent termination as a state—because his traditions pointed him to envision that exact eventuality. The Holiness School understands God's people to be fully bound by a vassal treaty, a 'covenant' (ברית; Lev 26:9, 15, 25). As elsewhere in the ancient world, this sort of binding agreement includes serious, even devastating, sanctions for disobedience.[16]

According to HS, Israel cannot remain on God's land without maintaining their side of the treaty. In his allegory of the unfaithful wife (Ezek 16), the prophet rehearses the failed history of the covenant. God "entered into a covenant [ברית] with you" (Ezek 16:8), he rails, but Jerusalem has proved an adulterous wife, a wife whom the law requires to be stoned (Ezek 16:40; cf. Lev 20:10 HS). Jerusalem is doomed, because the people have "despised the oath, breaking the covenant [ברית]" (16:59; cf. 17:19).

(*Power and Privilege*, 39). Amos, whose example Lenski mentions (p. 262 n. 57), was another prophet like Ezekiel from within Jerusalem's orbit, a member of the Judean establishment, who challenged the powers that be (see Wilson, *Prophecy and Society*, 267–70). In cases where sacral and political forces collide, the state often wins the initial battle but the priestly position triumphs in the end. As Robert Bellah states, "Religious organizations have been more resilient than political ones and have survived the downfall of many political regimes, often overtly or covertly contributing to their downfall" (a personal communication cited in Lenski, *Power and Privilege*, 261 n. 54a).

14. See, for example, Lenski, *Human Societies*, 258; idem, *Power and Privilege*, 222–23.

15. Thus, one of Lenski's observations about Israelite religion certainly applies to Ezekiel: "It was the priestly class which was the basic transmitter of the Mosaic tradition and its concept of Yahweh's concern for justice and righteousness" (*Power and Privilege*, 264).

16. Like typical vassal treaties of the ancient Near East, HS lists blessings for obedience (Lev 26:3–13; cf. Ezek 34:25–31; 36:29–30) and curses for infidelity (Lev 26:14–39).

Without denying that God has made certain irrevocable promises to Israel (Lev 26:42; cf. Ezek 16:60), HS lays out the very real possibility that defilement, injustice, and covenantal infidelity can lead Israel down a path to catastrophe.[17] A breakdown in God's hierarchical structures of holiness in Israel can lead first to disasters in the land (Lev 26:16–32; cf. Ezek 4:4–5) and eventually to the people's expulsion into outer darkness (Lev 26:33–39; cf. Ezek 4:6).[18]

It is precisely as a central priest, trading in the theology of the Holiness School, that Ezekiel challenges the status quo. As an HS tradent, he blasts royal officials who fiercely defend the impregnability of Jerusalem, the impenetrable "pot." Given the conditionality of the HS ברית and the sensitivity of the land's structures of holiness, how can any Israelite nurture "proud glory" (Ezek 33:28–29 NJPS)? Such misplaced confidence is scorned in Lev 26:19 (HS), to which the prophet's idiom traces. Ezek 24:21 uses the selfsame terminology as well, specifically with reference to Zion and the sanctuary understood as inviolable (a widespread tradition, according to Lam 4:12).

So also, it is as a Zadokite priest bearing the traditions of HS that Ezekiel attacks the clerics in charge at the temple. As Jon Levenson argued more than 35 years ago, Ezekiel's circle of temple priests was hardly a "highly jealous and endocentric body, incapable of a theology which is more than a rationale for self-interest."[19] Social-scientific theory allows that protests against priestly behavior may arise from within the priestly class itself. Temple officials can mount an internal critique of their colleagues.[20] In Ezekiel's case, the critique turns on the traditional Zadokite value of holiness. Worship abominations have desecrated the temple precincts, necessitating its radical purgation in fire (Ezek 8:1–18; 10:2). Israel's assault on God's holiness has penetrated the sacred center of covenantal life, temporarily damning the entire covenantal matrix.[21]

---

17. Citing Lev 26:40–45, James W. Watts rightly notes that HS "explicitly excludes the ultimate threat of nullifying Israel's covenant" ("Rhetorical Strategy in the Composition of the Pentateuch," *JSOT* 68 [1995] 18).

18. Frequent verbal echoes of HS signal that the curses of their vassal treaty with God were coming into effect. Ezekiel warns of "pestilence," "famine," and "sword" (Ezek 5:10; cf. 6:11–12; 7:15; 12:16; 14:21), threats linked as modes of destruction in Lev 26:25–26. God's threat to "break the staff of bread" (Ezek 4:16; 5:16) comes straight out of Lev 26:26. So, as well, does the threat of destroying the "high places" (Ezek 6:3; Lev 26:30). On the land as a delicate lattice of holiness, see S. L. Cook, "Cosmos, *Kabod,* and Cherub: Ontological and Epistemological Hierarchy in Ezekiel," in *Ezekiel's Hierarchical World,* 187–90. As Knohl writes, "Holiness . . . emerges from the Priestly center, radiating out to all sectors of society and to all walks of life" (*The Sanctuary of Silence,* 198). Compare with J. F. Kutsko, *Between Heaven and Earth: Divine Presence and Absence in the Book of Ezekiel* (Biblical and Judaic Studies from the University of California, San Diego 7; Winona Lake, IN: Eisenbrauns, 2000), 126 n. 110.

19. Levenson, *Theology of the Program of Restoration,* 93.

20. Lenski finds that influential priests may protest against "the materialism, power grabbing, and self-seeking of so many religious leaders" (*Power and Privilege,* 262).

21. Sweeney aptly writes, "The vision [of chap. 8] depicts the violence that permeates the land at large as a result of the disruption of sanctity in the holy center. *From the perspective of a*

Ezek 22:26 illuminates holiness as the core value of Ezekiel and his forebears. Here, God damningly condemns the priesthood on the following terms:

> Its priests have done violence to my teaching and have profaned my holy things; they have made no distinction between the holy and the common, neither have they taught the difference between the unclean and the clean, and they have disregarded my sabbaths, so that I am profaned among them.

When he excoriates society's central priests for making "no distinction between the holy and the common . . . between the unclean and the clean," Ezekiel is simply carrying forward the theology of priesthood in his HS traditions. Lev 10:10–11 (HS) states clearly, "You are to distinguish between the holy and the common, and between the unclean and the clean."[22] Other cross-references confirm this as a persisting Zadokite emphasis: Lev 20:25 HS; Ezek 44:23; Hag 2:11–14.

Immediately, the prominence of priestly theology and Zadokite emphases in Ezekiel's book raises eyebrows. Despite Levenson's caution, noted above, critics accuse the book of being priestly propaganda, a self-interested polemic of Zadokite clerics. Despite the circle's apparent ability to critique its own members, critics argue that accruing power and privilege is the agenda at hand. Certainly, the book points to the triumph of the central cult upon return from Babylonian exile (Ezek 40–48). Thus, Mark Leuchter claims to see in Ezekiel's program an attempt to "place the Zadokites in charge both during the exile and, consequently, once the exile was to come to an end."[23]

Such a hermeneutic of suspicion seems rather cynical and theologically tone-deaf. It is also an unnecessary interpretation. Lenski's model understands self-interest to be but one among several key motivators of human conduct. Prime among other influential forces in group-behavior are respect for the power and will of the divine realm and a penchant for ethical criticism.[24] Such drives may dull the sharp edge of self-interest. "This humanizing role," Lenski writes, "can easily be exaggerated, but it can also be overlooked; in the social sciences the latter tendency has been the more common."[25]

Ezekiel's book contains sparse evidence of priestly propaganda in support of any Zadokite worldly interests.[26] The authors' program for a restored Israel emphasizes God's new temple, to be sure. There are little to no signs, however, of a

---

priest, such profanity requires purification in order to remove the impurity" (*Form and Intertextuality,* 135; emphasis mine).

22. J. Begrich, "Die priesterliche Tora," *Werden und Wesen des Alten Testaments* (ed. P. Volz, et al.; BZAW 66; Berlin: Töpelmann, 1936), 63–88; Sweeney, *Form and Intertextuality,* 150.

23. Leuchter, *The Polemics,* 161; cf. the examples in Renz, *The Rhetorical Function,* 243.

24. Thus, Rainer Albertz rightly asserts that the Zadokites were "driven by a higher power" (*A History of Israelite Religion in the Old Testament Period, Volume 2: From the Exile to the Maccabees* [Louisville: Westminster John Knox, 1994], 433).

25. Lenski, *Power and Privilege,* 39.

26. Cook and Patton, "Introduction," 15–17; Renz, *The Rhetorical Function,* 244.

priestly power grab. As Rainer Albertz writes, "The amazing thing about this new order is that the marked emphasis on the temple at the expense of the monarchy and the capital was not matched by any political claim to power on the part of the priesthood."[27]

The Ezekiel group was not interested in a hierocracy, a rule of priests. They envisioned a true theocracy, with God physically present, enthroned as king. The temple-building rhetoric of Ezek 40–48 represents the Lord's claim to be king over Israel's territory.[28] Ezek 34:11–31 anticipates no future Davidic royal "shepherd" but only the Lord taking possession of the flock. God states, "I, the LORD, will be their God, and my servant David shall be prince [נשיא] among them; I, the LORD, have spoken" (34:24).

In the ideal future, according to Ezek 34, Israel will have only the Lord as king. There is no mention of any political power for the Zadokite priests, although a Davidic נשיא will serve as God's under-shepherd. Moreover, in Ezek 40–48, neither prince nor priests have any clear administrative role. In a controversy, the Zadokites do act as judges (44:24), but they do not run a state or control social policy. Levenson writes, "In a theocracy, one need devote no attention to the mechanics of government."[29]

In contrast to all other Israelite groups, the Zadokites are barred from inheriting and possessing land in the vision of Ezek 40–48 (see 44:28–30; Num 18:20–24 HS). Instead, their sole privilege, which actually endangered their lives (cf. Lev 10:6–11 HS), is temple access.[30] Do not underestimate the restrictive import of this provision. In advanced agrarian societies, a chief enticement of political power was its potential to multiply income from land. On the heels of power came increased wealth, brought forth from the soil. As Lenski writes, "The leading office holders . . . were usually the chief land-holders as well, and in these societies land was the most important economic resource."[31]

It should now be apparent that self-interest was not the driving force behind Ezekiel's theology but God's word and the influence of theological tradition (especially the HS source).[32] In fact, the theology of HS directly opposes priestly nar-

---

27. Albertz, *A History of Israelite Religion*, 436.

28. K. R. Stevenson, *The Vision of Transformation: The Territorial Rhetoric of Ezekiel 40–48* (SBLDS 154; Atlanta: Scholars, 1996), 115–19.

29. Levenson, *Theology of the Program of Restoration*, 113, see also 99–100, 114–15, 119. See also D. L. Petersen, "Creation and Hierarchy in Ezekiel: Methodological Perspectives and Theological Prospects," in Cook and Patton, *Ezekiel's Hierarchical World*, 177; D. I. Block, *The Book of Ezekiel, vol. 2, Chapters 25–48* (NICOT; Grand Rapids, MI: Eerdmans, 1998), 746; I. M. Duguid, *Ezekiel and the Leaders of Israel* (VTSup 56; Leiden: Brill, 1994), 50–55.

30. Renz, *The Rhetorical Function*, 244; Stevenson, *The Vision*, 87–89.

31. Lenski, *Human Societies*, 263.

32. See Renz, *The Rhetorical Function*, 242–45. Lenski argues that the degree to which a priestly circle stands up for the peripheral members of society and against the accumulation of goods in private hands relates especially to the content of the theological traditions they bear.

cissism and power grabs. It aims instead to extend sanctity out from the center to Israel at large.[33]

In Lev 19:1–2, God demands, "Speak to *all the congregation* of the people of Israel and say to them: You shall be holy" (emphasis added). The people should constantly grow in personal and collective holiness through their interaction with the divine presence (Exod 31:13; Lev 11:44–45; 20:7; 21:15, 23; 22:32; Num 5:3; 35:34 all HS; Ezek 11:12; 20:12; 37:28). God's seeping holiness will reach even to those on the periphery, such as widows, orphans, and resident aliens.[34]

From the midst of Israel, God radiates the divine holiness out to the entire land and to every sector of society. No one will be left out of God's ongoing work to heal and sanctify every nook and cranny of Israel (Ezek 34:4, 16). The goal of sanctifying the entire community is why both HS and Ezekiel stress not only the glory's association with the temple but also its presence "in the midst" (בתוך) of the Israelite people (Exod 25:8; 29:45–46; Lev 15:31; 26:12; Num 5:3; 16:3; 35:34; Ezek 11:23; 37:26, 28; 39:7; 43:7, 9; 48:8, 10, 21).[35] God values the worth and holiness of all of God's people, the whole congregation of the children of Israel (Lev 19:2; cf. Ezek 20:12; 37:28; 43:9).[36]

Ezekiel's book orients itself on HS's vision of fulsome life effusing out of a sacred center through an ideal latticework of holiness. Center and periphery are linked in dynamic interconnectivity, empowering both smaller and larger aggregates of the populace. Life within every corner of the lattice is precious, to be uplifted. HS purity rules symbolize this value system and form Israel in its spirit.[37]

He writes, "The extent to which the priestly class performed this important function varied considerably . . . Of all the factors responsible for this variation, the most important seems to have been the actual content of a faith and the degree to which God was believed to be concerned with social justice" (*Power and Privilege*, 266).

33. In the perspective of HS, the Lord's divine intent is to *sanctify* the community of faith and the land on which they live. Speaking of God's people, Ezekiel's God proclaims, "I the Lord sanctify them" (Ezek 20:12). Just so, in Lev 21:8 (HS), God exclaims, "I the Lord, *I who sanctify you*, am holy" (emphasis mine; compare with Lev 20:8; 22:16, 32 all HS).

34. On the care for widows, orphans, the poor, and the alien, see Ezek 22:7, 29. Ezekiel's final chapters offer foreign sojourners within Israel's borders the unprecedented provision of a permanent allotment of family land alongside native Israelites (Ezek 47:22–23). In this, Ezekiel's book radically extends the theological norm of the HS strand for the treatment of resident aliens. It takes the force of Lev 19:34 to its logical conclusion: "You shall love the alien as yourself" (cf. Lev 24:22; Num 15:29 both HS).

35. Knohl, *The Sanctuary of Silence*, 109; T. N. D. Mettinger, *The Dethronement of Sabaoth: Studies in the Shem and Kabod Theologies* (trans. F. H. Cryer; ConBOT 18; Lund: Gleerup, 1982), 96 n. 64.

36. See Cook and Patton, "Introduction," in *Ezekiel's Hierarchical World*, 16.

37. See nn. 18 and 21 above, p. 400, and Milgrom, *Leviticus 1–16*, 43; Knohl, *The Sanctuary of Silence*, 185–86. In this theology, in HS thinking, God's land is a delicately organized lattice of holiness, an intricate system for delivering holiness to every sector of the land. Defiling any part of the land, God's holy territory, constitutes an assault of impurity on the sacred center, God's shrine (for example, Lev 15:31; 19:30; 26:2; Num 5:3; 19:13; Ezek 8:6; 9:9). The system is supple

The stress on holiness radiating from an indwelling God, powerfully present, circles us back to Ezekiel's commitment to a literal rule of God on earth. Theocracy must push aside all other political systems, including monarchy and hierocracy. From now on, the children of Israel are to be servants of God, not primarily of an earthly ruler (see Ezek 20:33, 40; 45:8; cf. Lev 25:55 HS).[38] Ezekiel takes God's promise in Lev 26:12 (HS) at face value: "I will walk among you, and will be your God, and you shall be my people."

Both HS and Ezekiel emphasize the ideal of the Lord's glory (כבוד יהוה) 'settling' (שכן) in the central temple, at the core of Israel (Exod 25:8; 29:45–46; 40:35; Lev 26:11, Num 35:34 all HS; Ezek 37:27–28; 43:7). The כבוד takes up corporeal residence in Israel's central shrine, calling it "my sanctuary" (Lev 19:30; 20:3; 26:2 all HS; Ezek 5:11; 8:6; 9:6; 23:39; 37:28).

As Benjamin Sommer has now shown, we should probably understand this glory as something akin to God's body. The כבוד יהוה is a physical incarnation of God on earth.[39] God is intensely, even patriotically devoted to the earthly home of the כבוד, God's land and its sacral center, the temple (Lev 25:23 HS; Ezek 7:22; 34:26; 35:10; 36:5). The Lord's glory is deeply attached to Israel's mountain heights (Ezek 9:3; 20:40; 37:26; 43:7). Israel is the center of the nations, the earth's navel, and God's fiery hearth (Ezek 5:5; 38:12; 43:15).

The phenomenon of human royalty does not sit easily within HS's and Ezekiel's ideal hierarchical structure of holiness and empowerment. Hierarchical systems of all sorts have a natural vulnerability to the incursion of competing nuclei of power. When an alternative new nucleus forms off center, it may throw off the delicately balanced system. Extending its reach like a cancer, the new center may collapse the sensitive web of interconnectivity linking its tiered strata. This is the threat posed by monarchy to the Zadokites' ideal world.

Respect and empowerment do not easily flow down to the outer layers of society in a centralized monarchic state. Monarchic systems tend to contradict the idea of an entirely *hallowed land*, where the humanity and value of every sector, even those at the periphery, is upheld. They tend instead to divest the land of its sacral character, focusing on militarizing state capitals and fortifying royal cities.[40]

Centralized monarchies in the ancient world were often guilty of depriving society's outer sectors of security and human dignity. The material independence

---

and sensitive like an uneasy stomach, ready to vomit those who defile it (Lev 18:24–28). Ezek 36:16–19 insists that just such regurgitation has happened in the present generation's experience. This must never happen again! Fixed gradations of holiness within the temple and land must safeguard the people's safety with God's burning glory sojourning among them (compare with, for example, Ezek 42:14; 44:19; 46:20).

38. See nn. 28–29 above, p. 402.

39. Sommer argues that the priestly authors of HS and of Ezekiel explicitly equate the כבוד and God's self. See B. D. Sommer, *The Bodies of God and the World of Ancient Israel* (Cambridge: Cambridge University Press, 2009), 70–72.

40. See S. L. Cook, *The Social Roots of Biblical Yahwism* (Studies in Biblical Literature 8; Atlanta: SBL, 2004), 51–52.

of the periphery often cannot withstand such monarchic policies as heavy taxation, corvée, marshal law, judicial manipulation, redistricting, and land grabbing. In Israel, monarchic power seems inevitably to have worked against the HS ideal of permanent land tenure for each family on its ancestral homestead (for example, Lev 19:35; 25:10, 23–24, 42 all HS).

Beyond supporting ancient land-tenure values, the Holiness School moves in other ways to promote theocracy, check monarchic power, and uphold old Israel's tribes. As noted above, HS claims the people of Israel are God's servants, not a king's servants (Lev 25:23, 55; 26:12). It transfers to the populace standard monarchic prerogatives such as proclaiming a release from slavery and debts.[41] It speaks of Israelite society using early Hebrew vocabulary, such as מטה 'tribe', associated with sociopolitical life before the rise of a monarchic state (Num 1:49; 2:5, etc.). It describes human wielders of political authority in lineage-based terms: they are נשיאים 'chieftains', heads of the *tribes* (Num 10:4 HS). The authority of such chieftains is strictly bounded. They are quickly incinerated when they assault God's latticework of holiness (Num 16:2, 35 HS).

In its ideal new blueprint for Israel, Ezekiel's book moves concretely to undo and prevent past abuses inflicted by monarchy. Displacing Jerusalem and royalty off center (Ezek 43:7, 9; 45:6–7), the book reactivates Israel's prestate, tribal era. This effort at turning back the societal clock is most obvious in Ezek 40–48. Albertz puts it well:

> We can only be amazed at how serious an attempt is made here, in the planning of the new beginning after the exile, to revise the erroneous social developments of the period of the state and again take up the ideals of freedom from the prestate period. Granted, the reformers did not deny the central institutions which had accrued to Israel during the monarchy. . . . But they did reflect on how they could so separate and reorder this religious and political conglomerate of power with the help of their priestly pattern of thought and their hierarchical sacred precincts that these institutions could be integrated without any damage into the tribal social structure.[42]

A gradual weakening of tribal and lineage-based power and custom generally accompanies the growth of centralized monarchy in a society.[43] Remnants of

---

41. Knohl sees an example of HS backing away from monarchy in its converting the Mesopotamian concept of *durarum* (release from debts), a royal prerogative, into the Hebrew concept of דרר (jubilee release), a function of the whole people. Note how Lev 25:10 (HS) addresses the entire community in the second-person plural. See Knohl, *The Sanctuary of Silence*, 217; idem, *The Divine Symphony*, 93.

42. Albertz, *A History of Israelite Religion*, 436.

43. Lenski, *Human Societies*, 242–43, 246, 285–86, 306; Cook, *The Social Roots*, 143–94; M. S. Smith, *The Origins of Biblical Monotheism: Israel's Polytheistic Background and the Ugaritic Texts* (Oxford: Oxford University Press, 2001), 164. Smith correctly documents a "diminished lineage system" in the Israelite society of Ezekiel's time. He rightly discerns a society "less embedded in traditional family patrimonies." Smith is mistaken, however, to associate the shift away

an older genealogical and tribal structure often continue to subsist as a societal substratum, however, as was the case in Israel through Ezekiel's era.[44] It is this decentralized tribal structure that Ezekiel's book seeks to rehabilitate and buttress. The goal is to realize "the ideals of freedom from the pre-state period" of which Albertz speaks.

In prestate tribal Israel, the guaranteed tenure of tribes, kin-groups, and extended families on ancestral lands effectively established local justice and fellowship. Specifically, the security of kin-plus-land units blocked any process of the rich getting richer and the poor getting poorer, with property continually concentrated in the hands of the few. It fostered other-centered life on the land, rather than selfish exploitation of people and nature. Lenski's social-scientific model allows for Ezekiel's working to preserve the ancient ethic of an older way of life, a bygone tribal model of society.[45]

Ezekiel is not interested in the political divisions of Israel's monarchic-era state. His book does not use the name "Israel" for the northern kingdom as distinguished from the southern kingdom of Judah. When the prophet wants to describe the separate history of the kingdoms, he refers to them by terms such as "Samaria," "Ohola," "Joseph," and "Ephraim." The latter two rubrics are significant, since they are tribal names. Indeed, for Ezekiel, the ideal "Israel" comprises the totality of the people's ancient tribes, including both Joseph and Judah (see 37:15–28).

---

from family ties with the origins of biblical monotheism. True, Ezekiel both stresses *individual* human accountability (see 18:4) and holds an *individual* deity, the Sovereign Lord, accountable for the cosmos (see, for example, 17:24). He never correlates the two themes as Mark Smith does, however. Nor do these twin ideas even originate in Ezekiel's era. God already holds individuals responsible for themselves in Ezekiel's source texts (see Num 16:22–24 HS). HS assumes that a God who owns "all lives" (Ezek 18:4), that is, "the spirits of all flesh" (Num 16:22 HS), will surely allow innocent individuals to separate themselves and avoid judgment (Num 16:24 HS). Individual accountability is here distinct from communal accountability. So too, HS knows well *God's* cosmic accountability. When Ezek 17:24 articulates this accountability, it can do so using the self-revelation formula of HS (cf. Exod 7:5; 10:2; 14:18). For both HS and Ezekiel, the formula "I am the LORD" is pregnant with assumptions about God's identity as sovereign over all emerging reality.

44. Ezekiel names the advice of tribal elders alongside the visions of prophets and the instruction of priests as key societal supports (7:26). He names the "people of the land" (rural gentry, cf. 2 Kgs 21:23–24; 23:30; 23:35) alongside "the king" and "the prince" as among those who will suffer in God's coming judgment (7:27). This group constitutes a premonarchic, tribal power base (see Cook, *The Social Roots*, 46–48, and the bibliography cited there). During Israel's late monarchic period, these remnants of tribal Israel's decentralized power structures asserted their traditional authority at junctures of political chaos and anarchy (see Lenski, *Power and Privilege*, 230).

45. Lenski, *Power and Privilge*, 266; compare with Stevenson, *The Vision*, 122. Ezekiel stands within those circles of priestly leaders that Lenski describes as sometimes playing a "unique role among the privileged classes in agrarian societies." Priests of his stripe could work to check the "massive flow of goods and services from the many to the few."

Ezek 37:22 bluntly states that God wills an undivided people, no longer separated into twin monarchies. Ezek 34:30–31 understands the redeemed House of Israel to be one flock, occupying a single pasture. Ezek 47:13–48:29 carefully allots the holy land as specifically tribal patrimonies. The text moves tribe-by-tribe, giving each one unique, permanent security and standing. It wipes away all memory of royal chauvinism, of the monarchic state's blurring of tribal divisions and powers. There is nothing here of the monarchy's system of administrative districts (1 Kgs 4:7–19).[46]

As already noted, Ezekiel's preferred term for Israel's national leader is *prince* (נשׂיא, for example, Ezek 34:24; 37:25; 44:3; 45:7–9), a term deriving from Israel's tribal past. We saw above how HS employed the term to designate tribal chieftains of Israel before the settlement of the land. They were of strictly bounded authority, constrained by God's latticework of graded holiness. Ezekiel's applying the rubric נשׂיא to a Davidic ruler is not completely idiosyncratic, as Duguid has shown. In 1 Chr 2:10, for example, the figure Nahshon is a נשׂיא with a proto-Davidic role.[47]

Ezekiel lands on the term נשׂיא as his designation for a constrained "tribal" Davidic monarch. In Ezek 40–48, the prince is carefully integrated into a new, tribally organized people of God. He is fully subordinate to the Lord. He possesses no sacral kingship, no divine sonship (46:2).[48] He acts as the people's representative (46:10), not their exploiter. As noted above, the book earlier sketched a similar picture of the prince. Ezek 34:23–24 used the term נשׂיא to restrict Israel's future rulers to the role of "under-shepherd." Humble before God, such a ruler is a sprig, a tender twig (Ezek 17:22). Or, as a later follower of Ezekiel will put it, he is lowly, riding only on a donkey (Zech 9:9). Levenson rightly observes, "The origins of that Davidid are not regal but humble; he is a . . . 'low tree' awaiting his exaltation."[49]

Exaltation of the prince/נשׂיא is not the agenda of Ezek 40–48; reversing the wrongs of the past and securing the future is. Thus, in the visionary landscape of these chapters, the prince no longer possesses the temple; it will never again be a state cult, a royal shrine.[50] The prince also loses his entrenched bureaucracy (see 46:16–17). And, most definitively, he loses all power to evict Israelites from their ancestral farms (Ezek 45:8–9; 46:18; cf. 22:27). Society's periphery becomes secure and strong.[51] Relying on the HS strand (e.g., Lev 25:10, 23–24, 41), Ezekiel's goal is

---

46. As Levenson writes, the new tribe-based allocation of the land is "a deliberate attempt to recreate the archaic period in Israel's history" (*Theology of the Program of Restoration*, 112). Compare with ibid., 118, 121–22. Zech 12:7 will later echo the theme that Jerusalem and David's dynasty must never again overshadow the countryside.

47. Duguid, *Ezekiel and the Leaders of Israel*, 14–16.

48. Albertz, *A History of Israelite Religion*, 434; Stevenson, *The Vision*, 112–14, 122.

49. Levenson, *Theology of the Program of Restoration*, 95; cf. pp. 67–68, 88.

50. Albertz, *A History of Israelite Religion*, 432; Stevenson, *The Vision*, 112–14.

51. Levenson, *Theology of the Program of Restoration*, 114; S. S. Tuell, *The Law of the Temple in Ezekiel 40–48* (HSM 49; Atlanta: Scholars, 1992), 110.

for all family lines to dwell in perpetuity on their own patrimonies, for the entire land to be valued as sacral.[52]

Wielding a hermeneutic of suspicion, some may reconstruct ulterior motives in Ezekiel's creative resurrection of old lineage and tribal norms. Skeptics will imagine Ezekiel twisting Israel's traditional genealogical values to his own group's ends. Is his repristinating program not an ideal justification for the Zadokites to assert their phratry's rights at the temple and for the exile group as a whole to assert rights to lands taken over by those who remained in Judah (cf. Ezek 11:15; 33:24; Ezra 2:59; Neh 7:61)?

Several pieces of evidence converge against a hypothesis of sectarian self-promotion in Ezekiel. Most notably, Ezek 47:13–48:29 envisions a new, equitable allotment of the promised land, not a reinstatement of old holdings. The territory of Judah moves north, above Benjamin, the temple, and the Levites. All Judean exiles must now receive new landed patrimonies. The aim is tribal balance and a dampening of sectionalism, not the privileging of one faction. Ezekiel does *not* prioritize the exiled "remnant" in the restoration; he proffers no mounting sectarianism.[53]

To sum up, in both HS and Ezekiel, the Zadokites propound a future vision of a united, holy community arrayed about a sacred center indwelt by God's glory. They long to see Israel's entire land become God's holy territory, every corner valued. They advocate for the humanity and economic independence of all society's members living on the land, on the mountains of Israel. This thinking and theology befits establishment priests employed at society's center. It simultaneously befits "state enemies," looking for God's new theocracy to overthrow what they understood to be a sorry history of monarchic and Judean hubris and excess.

---

52. Hence, Ezekiel's book refers to the holy land the "mountains of Israel" (6:2, 3; 19:9; 33:28), marking all God's territory, not just Zion, as God's holy mountain paradise.

53. Renz, *The Rhetorical Function*, 221, 227; Levenson, *Theology of the Program of Restoration*, 93, 118. Compare this with how Zechariah, whose theology closely follows that of Ezekiel, insists that what is left of the northern kingdom is still a part of God's saving plans (Zech 8:13; also see 1:19). He accepts without challenge an assumption of those who remained in the land that they are integral within God's people (Zech 7:5; 8:18–19).

Bibliography

Albertz, R. *A History of Israelite Religion in the Old Testament Period, Volume 2: From the Exile to the Macabees.* Louisville: Westminster John Knox, 1994.

Begrich, J. "Die priesterliche Tora." Pp. 63–88 in *Werden und Wesen des Alten Testaments.* Edited by P. Volz et al. BZAW 66. Berlin: Töpelmann, 1936.

Block, D. I. *The Book of Ezekiel, vol. 2, Chapters 25–48.* NICOT. Grand Rapids, MI: Eerdmans, 1998.

Cook, S. L. "Cosmos, Kabod, and Cherub: Ontological and Epistemological Hierarchy in Ezekiel." Pp. 179–97 in *Ezekiel's Hierarchical World: Wrestling with a Tiered Reality.* Edited by S. L. Cook and C. L. Patton. SBLSS 31. Atlanta: SBL, 2004.

_____. "Innerbiblical Interpretation in Ezekiel 44 and the History of Israel's Priesthood." *JBL* 114 (1995) 193–208.

_____. *Prophecy and Apocalypticism: The Postexilic Social Setting.* Minneapolis: Fortress, 1995.

_____. Review of Alice Hunt, *Missing Priests: The Zadokites in Tradition and History, CBQ* 71 (2009) 372–73.

_____. *The Social Roots of Biblical Yahwism.* SBL Studies in Biblical Literature 8. Atlanta: SBL, 2004.

_____. "The Speechless Suppression of Grief in Ezekiel 24:15–27: The Death of Ezekiel's Wife and the Prophet's Abnormal Response." Pp. 222–33 in *Thus Says the Lord: Essays on the Former and Latter Prophets in Honor of Robert R. Wilson.* Edited by S. L. Cook and J. J. Ahn. LHBOTS 502. London: T. & T. Clark, 2009.

Cook, S. L., and C. Patton, ed. *Ezekiel's Hierarchical World: Wrestling with a Tiered Reality.* SBLSS 31. Atlanta: SBL, 2004.

Cross, F. M. *Canaanite Myth and Hebrew Epic.* Cambridge, MA: Harvard University Press, 1973.

Duguid, I. M. *Ezekiel and the Leaders of Israel.* VTSup 56. Leiden: Brill, 1994.

Knohl, I. *The Divine Symphony: The Bible's Many Voices.* Philadelphia: Jewish Publication Society, 2003.

_____. *The Sanctuary of Silence: The Priestly Torah and the Holiness School.* Minneapolis: Fortress, 1995.

Kutsko, J. F. *Between Heaven and Earth: Divine Presence and Absence in the Book of Ezekiel.* Biblical and Judaic Studies from the University of California, San Diego 7. Winona Lake, IN: Eisenbrauns, 2000.

Lenski, Gerhard. *Human Societies: A Macrolevel Introduction to Sociology.* New York: McGraw-Hill, 1970.

_____. *Power and Privilege: A Theory of Social Stratification.* New York: McGraw-Hill, 1966.

Leuchter, Mark. *The Polemics of Exile in Jeremiah 26–45.* Cambridge: Cambridge University Press, 2008.

Levenson, J. D. *Theology of the Program of Restoration of Ezekiel 40–48.* HSM 10. Missoula, MT: Scholars, 1976.

Mein, A. "Ezekiel as a Priest in Exile." Pp. 199–213 in *The Elusive Prophet: The Prophet as a Historical Person, Literary Character, and Anonymous Artist.* Edited by J. C. de Moor. OtSt 45. Leiden: Brill, 2001.

Mettinger, T. N. D. *The Dethronement of Sabaoth: Studies in the Shem and Kabod Theologies.* Trans. F. H. Cryer. ConBOT 18. Lund: Gleerup, 1982.

Milgrom, J. *Leviticus 1–16: A New Translation with Introduction and Commentary.* AB 3. New York: Doubleday, 1991.

Miller, J. E. "The Thirtieth Year of Ezekiel 1:1." *RB* 99 (1992) 499–503.

Monloubou, L. "La signification du culte selon Ézéchiel." Pp. 7–20 in *Ezekiel and His Book: Textual and Literary Criticism and Their Interrelation.* Edited by J. Lust. BETL 74. Louvain: Louvain University Press/Peeters, 1986.

Olyan, S. M. "Zadok's Origins and the Tribal Politics of David." *JBL* 101 (1982) 177–93.

Renz, T. *The Rhetorical Function of the Book of Ezekiel*. VTSup 76. Leiden: Brill, 1999.

Ruwe, A. *"Heiligkeitsgesetz" und "Priesterschrift:" Literaturgeschichtliche und rechtssystematische Untersuchungen zu Leviticus 17,1–26,2*. FAT 26. Tübingen: Mohr Siebeck, 1999.

Schwartz, B. J. *The Holiness Legislation: Studies in the Priestly Code*. Jerusalem: Magnes, 1999. [In Hebrew]

————. "The Priestly Account of the Theophany and the Lawgiving at Sinai." Pp. 103–34 in *Texts, Temples, and Traditions: A Tribute to Menahem Haran*. Edited by M. V. Fox, et al. Winona Lake, IN: Eisenbrauns, 1996.

Smith, M. S. *The Origins of Biblical Monotheism: Israel's Polytheistic Background and the Ugaritic Texts*. Oxford: Oxford University Press, 2001.

————. *The Priestly Vision of Genesis 1*. Minneapolis: Augsburg Fortress, 2010.

Sommer, B. D. *The Bodies of God and the World of Ancient Israel*. New York: Cambridge University Press, 2009.

Stackert, J. *Rewriting the Torah: Literary Revision in Deuteronomy and the Holiness Legislation*. FAT 52. Tübingen: Mohr Siebeck, 2007.

Stevenson, K. R. *The Vision of Transformation: The Territorial Rhetoric of Ezekiel 40–48*. SBLDS 154. Atlanta: Scholars, 1996.

Sweeney, M. A. *Form and Intertextuality in Prophetic and Apocalyptic Literature*. FAT 45. Tübingen: Mohr Siebeck, 2005.

Taylor, J. Glen. *Yahweh and the Sun: Biblical and Archaeological Evidence for Sun Worship in Ancient Israel*. Sheffield: JSOT Press, 1993.

Tuell, S. S. *The Law of the Temple in Ezekiel 40–48*. HSM 49. Atlanta: Scholars, 1992.

Watts, J. W. "Rhetorical Strategy in the Composition of the Pentateuch." *JSOT* 68 (1995) 3–22.

Wilson, R. R. *Prophecy and Society in Ancient Israel*. Philadelphia: Fortress, 1980.

Wright, D. P. "Holiness in Leviticus and Beyond: Differing Perspectives." *Int* 53 (1999) 351–64.

Yhwh's Cosmic Estate:
Politics in Second Isaiah

Mark W. Hamilton

Abilene Christian University

Even a casual reading of Isa 40–55 reveals the interests of its creator(s) in the workings of states and the groups subject to them. The work's gorgeous poetry employs in turn a critique of the Marduk cult,[1] a paean to Cyrus, invitations to foreign kings to regard Israel, and an exalted call to nations to return home or go into exile, depending on Yhwh's will regarding them. At one level, then, a discussion of the politics of Second Isaiah seems straightforward. As Klaus Baltzer puts it, "DtIsa's program is to link city, country, and Diaspora. . . . If we look at the situation as a whole, we can reconstruct the picture of a differentiated society."[2]

Yet, on closer examination, this inquiry soon runs into serious methodological difficulties. To begin, what do we mean by politics? If the term refers, for example, to governmental administrative techniques, jockeying for power among stakeholders, or the creation, preservation, and ongoing legitimation of hierarchies, then Isa 40–55 offers little, in part because the text did not stem from a bureaucratic setting, but more significantly because Deutero-Isaiah and, to some extent, the rest of the creators of the book of Isaiah showed little interest in the practicalities of political life, an attitude that apparently originated with the 8th-century prophet whose name the book bears.[3] Moreover, how do we understand

---

1. On the more extended Israelite interaction with Babylonian high-status religion, see also M. Kessler, *Battle of the Gods: The God of Israel Versus Marduk of Babylon: A Literary/Theological Interpretation of Jeremiah 50–51* (SSN 42; Assen: Van Gorcum, 2003). However, J. Blenkinsopp (*Isaiah 40–55* [AB 19A; New York: Doubleday, 2000], 107) considerably overstates the case when he writes that "the central message of Isa 40–55 can be construed as a kind of mirror-image of the ideology expressed in the *akitu* liturgy and the *Enuma Elish* myth," not only because many elements of Isa 40–55 have ample precedents in earlier stages of the Isaiah tradition (though admittedly, even there influenced by contact with Mesopotamian theologies), but also because the creator of Second Isaiah worked out a series of ideas that went far beyond mere response to Babylonian stimuli. Moreover, most of the texts that Blenkinsopp cites appear in Isa 40–48.

2. K. Baltzer, *Isaiah 40–55* (Hermeneia; Minneapolis: Fortress, 2001), 32.

3. On the one hand, the texts by and about the First Isaiah show a high interest in the movements of world empires (see, for example, P. Machinist, "Assyria and Its Image in the First

the relationship between the intra- and extra-Israelite dimensions of the poems' ideas about power, both human and divine? Granted that the work knows of, and responds to, Babylonian theological ideas and perhaps even a specific religious contretemps, the conflict between the devotees of Sin and Marduk in the reign of Nabonidus;[4] still, the terms of the debate and the text's positions within it grow out of Israel's ongoing theological reflection. A sense of the breadth of the conversation thus becomes crucial.

Here I argue, then, that in constructing a politics of a renewed Israel, Second Isaiah, or its constituent parts,[5] drew on an apparently nonspecialist knowledge of ancient repertoires of rule, especially of practices of displaying royal might and virtue. Governmental techniques do not feature in detail, not merely because the creator(s) of the text did not write political science, nor because the impression-

---

Isaiah," *JAOS* 103 [1983] 719–37; J. J. M. Roberts, "Blindfolding the Prophet: Political Resistance to First Isaiah's Oracles in the Light of Ancient Near Eastern Attitudes Toward Oracles," in *Oracles et Prophéties dans l'Antiquité* [ed. J.-G. Heintz; Paris: Boccard, 1997], 135–46). On the other, however, the advice that Isaiah gives, notably to Ahaz in 7:1–17 seems remarkably utopian, since it allows for no meaningful political action by the state, assuming instead unmediated divine intervention of some sort. See, however, the strictures of O. Bäckersten, *Isaiah's Political Message* (FAT 2/29; Tübingen: Mohr Siebeck, 2008); and the theological implications of the Isaiah tradition as explored in the essays in R. Cohen and R. Westbrook, eds., *Isaiah's Vision of Peace in Biblical and Modern International Relations* (New York: Macmillan, 2008).

4. On which see M. Albani, *Der eine Gott und die himmlischen Heerscharen: Zur Begründung des Monotheismus bei Deuterojesaja im Horizont der Astralisierung des Gottesverständnisses im Alten Orient* (ABG 1; Leipzig: Evangelische Verlagsanstalt, 2000); idem, "Deuterojesajas Monotheismus und der babylonische Religionskonflikt unter Nabonid," in *Der eine Gott und die Götter: Polytheismus und Monotheismus im antiken Israel* (ed. M. Oeming and K. Schmid; ATANT 82; Zurich: TVZ, 2003), 171–201; P. Machinist, "Mesopotamian Imperialism and Israelite Religion: A Case Study from the Second Isaiah," in *Symbiosis, Symbolism, and the Power of the Past: Canaan, Ancient Israel, and Their Neighbors from the Late Bronze Age through Roman Palaestina* (ed. W. G. Dever and S. Gitin; Winona Lake, IN: Eisenbrauns, 2003), 237–64; S. Timm, "Jes 42,10 ff. und Nabonid," in *"Gott kommt von Teman . . .": Kleine Schriften zur Geschichte Israels und Syrien-Palästinas* (ed. C. Bender and M. Pietsch; AOAT 314; Münster: Ugarit-Verlag, 2004), 237–59; H. Schaudig, "'Bel Bows, Nabu Stoops!' The Prophecy of Isaiah xlvi 1–2 as a Reflection of Babylonian 'Processional Omens,'" *VT* 58 (2008): 557–72. As Machinist notes, however, the biblical material does not neatly fit the intra-Babylonian argument, meaning that Second Isaiah knew of the theological dispute at the imperial center but went his own way in the conversation. In general, dating Isa 40–55, even assuming that it was written all at the same period, is difficult. See the discussion in U. Berges, *Jesaja 40–48* (HTKAT; Vienna: Herder, 2008), 43–45; and the well-considered caution of P. R. Davies, "God of Cyrus, God of Israel: Some Religio-Historical Reflections on Isaiah 40–55," in *Words Remembered, Texts Renewed: Essays in Honour of John F. A. Sawyer* (ed. J. Davies, G. Harvey, and W. G. E. Watson; JSOTSS 195; Sheffield: Sheffield Academic, 1995), 207–25.

5. It is perhaps debatable whether one can reconstruct a coherent viewpoint for Isaiah 40–55 as a unitary work given the possibility of a redactional process for its creation. See the careful discussion in R. Albertz, *Israel in Exile: The History and Literature of the Sixth Century B.C.E.* (Atlanta: SBL, 2003), 376–99. However, enough unity in the work exists to see a coherent picture, as I hope to show.

istic, imagistic mode of the poetry made other requirements, but because the text claimed to see beyond the surface of phenomena to a deeper reality. In some sense, that is to say, the very other-worldliness of Second Isaiah's approach—its lack of specific policy proposals—mirrors its well-known emphasis on the oracle as window onto the world.[6] By creating a political myth counter to the Babylonian alternative but surprisingly congruent with at least parts of its emerging replacement, the Achaemenid royal ideology, Second Isaiah lays the groundwork for a new identity for Israel/Jacob, one in which the old stories of creation and exodus, of the remote ancestors and the returnees from the Golah (and not just from Babylonia!) converge to make possible not only a religious solution to the returnees' problems but a political one.[7] Since the true understanding of human history belongs only to Yhwh, whose 'thoughts are not your thoughts and ways are not your ways' (לֹא מַחְשְׁבוֹתַי מַחְשְׁבוֹתֵיכֶם וְלֹא דַרְכֵיכֶם דַּרְכָי; 55:8), for Isa 40–55, focusing on the cosmic inner mechanisms of politics takes on urgency, while the ways and means can take care of themselves.

---

6. The literature on oracles and their political uses is, of course enormous. See, for example, A. L. Oppenheim, "Divination and Clestial Observation in the Late Assyrian Empire," *Centaurus* 14 (1969) 97–135; M. deJ. Ellis, "Observations on Mesopotamian Oracles and Prophetic Texts: Literary and Historiographic Considerations," *JCS* 41 (1989) 127–86; I. Starr, *Queries to the Sungod: Divination and Politics in Sargonid Assyria* (SAAS 4; Helsinki: Neo-Assyrian Text Corpus Project, 1990); M. Nissinen, *References to Prophecy in Neo-Assyrian Sources* (SAAS 7; Helsinki: Neo-Assyrian Text Corpus Project, 1998), 163–72; H. Hunger and D. Pingree, *Astral Sciences in Mesopotamia* (HdO 1/44; Leiden: Brill, 1999); S. M. Maul, "Die Wissenschaft von der Zukunft: Überlegungen zur Bedeutung der Divination im Alten Orients," in *Babylon: Wissenskultur in Orient und Okzident* (ed. E. Cancik-Kirschbaum, M. van Ess, and J. Marzahn; Topoi: Berlin Studies of the Ancient World 1; Berlin: de Gruyter, 2011), 135–51. A full-blown study of divinatory language in Isa 40–55 lies beyond the scope of this study, but one should note the dominance of the vocabulary of knowledge (ידע) especially in chs. 40–48 (25 times in 40–48 versus 8 times in 49–55). Second Isaiah insists that true knowledge comes from Yhwh rather than the gods of Babylon, that such knowledge is available to Israel (by reading earlier prophetic texts) and now to Cyrus and the Persians, that it is unavailable to idolaters, and that the lack of knowledge greatly impairs the foes' ability to succeed. See Isa 40:13, 14, 21, 28; 41:20, 22, 23, 26; 42:16 (twice), 25; 43:10, 19; 44:8, 9, 18; 45:3, 4, 5, 6, 20; 47:8, 11, 13; 48:4, 6, 7, 8 (twice); 49:23, 26; 50:4, 7; 51:7; 52:6; 53:3; 55:5. The use of the often-parallel verb ראה 'to see' is more evenly distributed, however (Isa 40:5, 26; 41:5, 20, 23, 28; 42:18, 20; 44:9, 18; 47:3, 10; 49:7, 18; 52:8, 10, 15; 53:2, 11). It is not always clear whether ideas like the islands seeing (41:5) implies divination or merely messages sent by the Persian information system or simply merchants' gossip, though this very ambiguity as to the medium simply reinforces the impression that Isa 40–55 gives that the news of Israel's restoration and return will become universally known by whatever means available, all of which point in the same direction, toward a revelatory deity bent on redemption.

7. However, see the theoretical discussion in J. Assmann, "Memory, Narration, Identity: Exodus as a Political Myth," in *Literary Construction of Identity in the Ancient World* (ed. H. Liss and M. Oeming; Winona Lake, IN: Eisenbrauns, 2010), 3–18; F. Joannès, "L'écriture publique du pouvoir à Babylone sous Nabuchodonosor II," in *Babylon: Wissenskultur in Orient und Okzident* (ed. E. Cancik-Kirschbaum, M. van Ess, and J. Marzahn; Topoi: Berlin Studies of the Ancient World 1; Berlin: de Gruyter, 2011), 113–20.

The Politics of Display as Identity-Formation

To be sure, a Levantine intellectual of the 6th century B.C.E. would have known of several styles of political self-display, from rituals of tribute presentation (either real or captured in reliefs) to building projects of temples and palaces to the visible reminders of ruined cities that resisted the hegemon. [8] Moreover, since display requires the ideological construction of both an in-group and an out-group, entities who perceive the new politics from complementary yet opposite vantage points, as well as an attempt at describing, valorizing, and legitimating their relationship, such an author would have gained access to an elaborate set of ways of constructing such an identity for readers. Such construction could, for example, take the form of a monarch describing himself in a series of grand titles resting on universalizing religious warrants and casting his enemies as irrational, evil-minded rebels against the divine realm.[9] Or it could emphasize the system of tribute revolving around the imperial center.[10] The goal was 'to make myself seen before all my enemies' (וכי הראני בכל שנאי) as Mesha put it in the 9th century.[11]

In whatever form it takes, then, such display requires objects, performers, and audiences. It is thus a species of identity-formation, an admittedly highly contestable term in modern political discourse but still a useful one if one focuses on identity-making as a complex combination of group labeling or identification, cat-

---

8. For the basic Neo-Assyrian examples of tribute, see J. Bär, "Tributdarstellungen in der Kunst des Alten Orients," in *Geschenke und Steuern, Zölle und Tribute: Antike Abgabenformen in Anspruch und Wirklichkeit* (ed. H. Klinkott, S. Kubisch, and R. Müller-Wollermann; CHANE 29; Leiden: Brill, 2007), 231–61; on building, see, among others, S. Lackenbacher, *Le Roi Bâtisseur: Les récits de construction assyriens des origines à Teglathphalasar III* (Paris: ERC, 1982); J.-W. Meyer, "Tempel und Palastbauten im eisenzeitlichen Palästina und ihre bronzezeitlichen Vorbilder," in *Religionsgeschichtliche Beziehungen zwischen Kleinasien, Nordsyrien und dem Alten Testament* (ed. B. Janowski, K. Koch, and G. Wilhelm; OBO 129; Göttingen: Vandenhoeck & Ruprecht, 1993), 319–28.

9. W. R. Mayer, "Ein neues Königsritual gegen feindliche Bedröhung," *Or* 57 (1988) 145–65. This construction fits a larger program of casting foreign space as exotic, yet subject to the domination of the ruler who displays his prowess in reliefs; see the discussion of M. Marcus, "Geography as Visual Ideology: Landscape, Knowledge, and Power in Neo-Assyrian Art," in *Neo-Assyrian Geography* (ed. M. Liverani; Rome: CNR, 1995), 193–208; D. M. Bonacossi, "'Landscapes of Power': The political Organisation of Space in the Lower Ḥabur Valley in the Neo-Assyrian Period," *SAAB* 10 (1996) 15–49. On the influence of this larger tradition on biblical texts, see E. Otto, "Psalm 2 in neuassyrischer Zeit: Assyrische Motive in der judäischen Königsideologie," in *Textarbeit: Studien zu Texten und ihrer Rezeption aus dem Alten Testament und der Umwelt Israels* (ed. K. Kiesow and T. Meurer; Münster: Ugarit-Verlag, 2003), 335–49; J. W. Hilber, "Psalm CX in the Light of Assyrian Prophecies," *VT* 53 (2003) 353–77.

10. As in Ps 72, for example.

11. KAI 181, line 4. Often the C infinitive construct of ראה is translated as 'to prevail over' or some equivalent (citing Mic 7:10; Ps 118:7; see K. P. Jackson, "The Language of the Mesha Inscription," in *Studies in the Mesha Inscription and Moab* [ed. A. Dearman; Atlanta: Scholars, 1989], 106); however, such a paraphrase is unnecessary.

egorization, self-undestanding, and commonality. As Cooper and Brubaker have argued with regard to modern studies of colonialism, "identity" is best understood as "a dispositional term that designates what might be called situated subjectivity: one's sense of who one is, of one's social location, and of how (given the first two) one is prepared to act."[12] That is, identity has both an intra-psychic ("subjective") and extra-psychic ("objective") dimension understandable by others through the linking of actions and self-understandings. In creating an identity for revived Israel/Jacob, then, Second Isaiah constructs the politics of display in at least three ways: narration of a story of political change, concentration on the act of seeing and being seen, and a reconception of the implied audience's mental geography.

Narrative-making

In fashioning an appropriate narrative, Second Isaiah stages a group of characters who act and reflect upon their actions: Israel/Jacob (and Jerusalem/Zion), whom the text often exhorts to reimagine its future and whose redemption marks the true object of display of Yнwн's accomplishments; the nations who sometimes must experience defeat in order to free Israel but who usually appear simply as witnesses and tribute-bringers; and, most significantly, Yнwн the divine מלך (41:21; 43:15; 44:6). (I leave to the side the very complex question of the relationship of the Servant to Israel.) The intertwined "situated subjectivity" of these characters intersect to invite the implied audience of Isa 40–55 to reconsider its position and, accordingly, to act in ways befitting a new exodus (55:1). Thus the literary depictions of the three characters functions rhetorically as an argument from the nature of reality as if to say, "since the world really works as Yнwн says, then the exiles should have new confidence."

This narratival rhetorical strategy underwrites the prophet's views of political life. Accordingly, when he speaks of human kings, he refers not only to Cyrus's domination of מלכים (45:1)[13] but of their awed silence before Israel's tragic, then joyous, fate (49:7; 52:15). Isaiah 52:15, similarly, speaks of kings shutting their mouths (יקפצו מלכים פיהם) when confronted with the servant's restoration (in direct contrast with his earlier "shame" before "many" [רבבים[14] עליך שממו 52:14]), while 49:7 similarly anticipates the nation's reversal of fortune with an oracle:

---

12. F. Cooper, *Colonialism in Question: Theory, Knowledge, History* (with R. Brubaker, in Chapter 3; Berkeley: University of California Press, 2005), 73; compare with the narratival approach of Margaret Somers ("The Narrative Constitution of Identity: A Relational and Network Approach," *Theory and Society* 23 [1994] 605–49), which underlies some of my framing of Second Isaiah's approach.

13. Compare with 41:2, and see the discussion of Baltzer, *Deutero-Isaiah*, 88–89; J. Blenkinsopp, *Isaiah 40–55* (AB 19A; New York: Doubleday, 2002), 195–96; A. Laato, *The Servant of YHWH and Cyrus: A Reinterpretation of the Exilic Messianic Programme in Isaiah 40–55* (CBOT 35; Stockholm: Almqvist & Wiksell, 1992).

14. Note the variant reading עליו, however.

Thus says Yhwh, Israel's redeemer and holy one,
To the shamed, the disgraced nation,[15] the servant of rulers,
"Kings will see and rise up, princes bow down,
Because Yhwh has been loyal—Israel's holy one—and he has chosen you."

כה אמר יהוה גאל ישראל קדשו לבזה נפש למתעב גוי לעבד משלים מלכים
יראו וקמו שרים וישתחוו למען יהוה אשר נאמן קדש ישראל ויבחרך

In other words, the political order must experience a series of inversions: the imagined (and real!) hierarchy in which the phrase "foreign king" signaled Israel's subjugation is turned over as the ruler bows to the ruled.[16] As Koole points out, the closest biblical parallel to this imagined turn of events is Ps 72:11, in which foreign kings bow before the king of Israel. The recipient of obeisance in Isa 49 is not the Israelite monarch, for no such character appears (at least explicitly) in Isa 40–55, but rather Israel or the Servant, depending on one's lights (though 49:1–6 equates the two figures).[17] Thus, the typical royal imagery, seen in many ancient texts and pictures, transfers here to a nonroyal figure.

The complexity of the transfer becomes clearer in the much discussed text Isa 52:13–53:12, whose long interpretive history needs no rehearsal at this point.[18] Without trying to address the complex questions of the identity of the servant or the nature of his "resurrection," one can identify several elements of political display that speak to Second Isaiah's political ideas. First, again, Isa 52:15 describes royal astonishment at the servant's state. Part of the reaction derives from the failure of the royal information-gathering system, which has offered wrong intelligence in both oral and written media (לא ספר/לא שמעו).[19] Second, the failure of

---

15. But see the discussion in Baltzer, *Deutero-Isaiah*, 315 and esp. n. 244. LXX's τὸν βδελυσσόμενον ὑπὸ τῶν ἐθνῶν is the *lectio facilior*.

16. On the king of Assyria in the book of Isaiah, see S. Zelig Aster, "The Image of Assyria in Isaiah 2:5–22: The Campaign Motif Reversed," *JAOS* 127 (2007) 249–78; M. Chan, "Rhetorical Reversal and Usurpation: Isaiah 10:5–34 and the Use of Neo-Assyrian Royal Idiom in the Construction of an Anti-Assyrian Theology," *JBL* 128 (2009) 717–33; M. J. de Jong, "A Window on the Isaiah Tradition in the Assyrian Period: Isaiah 10:24–27," in *Isaiah in Context: Studies in Honour of Arie van der Kooij on the Occasion of his Sixty-Fifth Birthday* (ed. M. N. van der Meer et al.; VTSup 138; Leiden: Brill, 2010), 83–107.

17. J. L. Koole, *Isaiah III, vol. 2: Isaiah 49–55* (HCOT; Leuven: Peeters, 1998).

18. See, for example, H. M. Orlinsky, *The So-Called "Suffering Servant" in Isaiah 53* (Cincinnati, OH: Hebrew Union College Press, 1964); J. Alobaidi, *The Messiah in Isaiah 53: The Commentaries of Saadia Gaon, Salomon ben Yerhum and Yefet ben Eli on Is 52:13–53:12* (Berne: Peter Lang, 1998); the essays in W. H. Bellinger and W. R. Farmer, eds., *Jesus and the Suffering Servant: Isaiah 53 and Christian Origins* (Harrisburg, PA: Trinity Press International, 1998); the essays in S. Moyise and M. J. J. Menken, eds., *Isaiah in the New Testament* (London: T. & T. Clark, 2005); J. Blenkinsopp, *Opening the Sealed Book: Interpretations of the Book of Isaiah in Late Antiquity* (Grand Rapids, MI: Eerdmans, 2006), 251–93; R. Heskett, *Messianism within the Scriptural Scroll of Isaiah* (LHBOTS 456; London: T. & T. Clark, 2007); G. Fischer, "Gefährten im Leiden—der Gottesknecht bei Jesaja und der Prophet Jeremia," *BZ* 56 (2012) 1–19.

19. The nature of spy networks in the ancient Near East is imperfectly understood, though major progress in unraveling Assyrian practices has been the contribution of P. Dubovský, *Heze-*

the clandestine services is understandable given the prior state of the servant, who famously appears as lacking physical attractiveness (53:2) and thus in a shamed state. Here Second Isaiah plays off the old royal ideology in which the king is described as having הדר (Ps 21:6; 45:4–5; 110:3; cf. 8:6; Ezek 27:10), an attribute usually ascribed to the deity (Ps 29:4; 11:3; 90:16; 96:6[?]; 104:1; 145:5, 12; 149:9; Job 40:10; 1 Chr 16:27), though occasionally to other high-status human beings. The servant's lack of "aura" or "splendor" marks him as worthy of contempt, which would only be the case if, unlike most human beings, he should have had such a quality in an ideal world. In other words, the reversal of fortune that must be reversed by divine intervention negated an original regal state.

Third, the enigmatic 53:9 (ויתן את רשעים קברו ואת עשיר במתיו על לא חמס עשה ולא מרמה בפיו) speaks of the servant's burial with the wicked and death with the rich, in spite of(?) his lack of violent actions. The collocation of the wealthy and the wicked[20] marks an obvious political gibe, yet whether 9b's על is to be taken as contrastive[21] or causal,[22] the servant experiences a form of postmortem display (burial with the wealthy) that the poet regards as a sample of the shaming that YHWH must reverse, though it is not entirely clear why this should be a bad death. Was the funeral lacking appropriate mourning rituals, or were the rituals excessive displays? Did the burial involve mockery or misplaced honor? The verse is obscure, but since ancient burial of the powerful was itself a political act (2 Sam 3:31–39; Isa 22:15–25), something has gone wrong in the politics of display.[23] Second Isaiah evokes the image of the Servant's funeral in part because tears can, under certain circumstances, reinforce, or even create anew, social relationships and the moral codes valorizing them.[24]

---

kiah and the Assyrian Spies: Reconstruction of the Neo-Assyrian Intelligence Services and Its Significance for 2 Kings 18–19 (BibOr 49; Rome: Pontifical Biblical Institute, 2006). As he notes, moreover, many biblical traditions assume a basic knowledge of surveillance, reconnaissance, information collection, and processes of interpretation and contextualization—that is, of the basics of an intelligence network. To posit such knowledge behind Isa 40–55 seems simple enough.

20. Though a number of commentators have sought other explanations for עשיר; see the discussion in Koole, *Isaiah 49–55*, 315–16.

21. Blenkinsopp, *Isaiah 40–55*, 345, 354; Baltzer, *Deutero-Isaiah*, 393; ESV; JSB/Tanakh; RSV; NRSV; NIV.

22. Koole, *Isaiah 49–55*, 312, 316; KJV.

23. J. A. Wilson, "Funeral Sources of the Egyptian Old Kingdom," *JNES* 3 (1944) 201–18; J. Assmann, *Altägyptische Totenliturgien*, vol. 1: *Totenliturgien in den Sargtexten des Mittleren Reiches* (Heidelberg: Winter, 2002); R. M. Shipp, *Of Dead Kings and Dirges: Myth and Meaning in Isaiah 14:4b–21* (Atlanta: SBL, 2002); S. M. Olyan, "Some Neglected Aspects of Israelite Interment Ideology," *JBL* 124 (2005) 601–16; on the connections between funerary and chronistic/building elements in a single text, see A. Faber, "On the Structural Unity of the Eshmunazor Inscription," *JAOS* 106 (1986) 425–32.

24. A point made in another context by G. L. Ebersole, "The Function of Ritual Weeping Revisited: Affective Expression and Moral Discourse," *History of Religions* 39 (2000) 211–46, esp. 244.

Fourth, however, according to 53:14 the ultimate (postmortem?) reversal of the servant's fortune will lead not only to display before the very "multitude" (רבים) that previously despised him (52:14; 53:11) but also to his sharing in the movement of goods across borders (שלל) and assumption of a place of honor among the powerful (53:12). While the servant is neither a king nor a substitute king,[25] he bears kingly attributes.

To summarize, then, the text's transformation of royal conventions of self-presentation doubtless draws on the development of the Isaiah tradition's earlier shifting of regal imagery to YHWH alone, as seen in ch. 33, which seems to come from the Josianic redaction of the book.[26] At the same time, Isa 40–55 goes in new directions as it reflects on the restoration of Jacob/Israel to a status not merely of survivor but, in the text's imagined world, an equal of Persia. The concentration of royal images of display on Israel, as well as on YHWH, the divine sovereign of the cosmos, marks a further development of the Isaianic tradition in light of new geopolitical realities.

The Gaze

The politics of display informs other parts of Second Isaiah, as well. This can be seen in the prophet's use of the image of the gaze, the practice of looking at objects to give them meaning.[27] Thus "all flesh" sees (40:5) YHWH's acts of redemption, as do kings (49:7; 52:15), islands (41:5), Zion (49:18), the blind (42:18, 20), and unspecified persons (41:20; 52:8, 10). Even if the book of Isaiah constructs its imagined author as deeply ambivalent about what he sees, as Francis Landy has recently argued,[28] the gaze of the outsiders is unambiguous, according to Sec-

---

25. Contra J. H. Walton, "The Imagery of the Substitute King Ritual in Isaiah's Fourth Servant Song," *JBL* 122 (2003) 734–43; differently, though still in a one-sided way, M. C. Lind, "Monotheism, Power, and Justice: A Study in Isaiah 40–55," *CBQ* 46 (1984) 432–46. Lind's sharp contrast between Cyrus and the "servant" rests on an unwarranted distinction, common among biblical scholars, between human and divine kingship. The biblical writers, especially outside some strands of the DH, took a more nuanced view of the interrelationships of the two than is common among modern scholars, influenced as we are by the spread of republicanism since the American and French Revolutions.

26. H. Barth, *Die Jesaja-Worte in der Josiazeit: Israel und Assur als Thema einer produktiven Neuinterpretation der Jesajaüberlieferung* (WMANT 48; Neukirchen-Vluyn: Neukirchener, 1977); M. W. Hamilton, "Isaiah 32 as Literature and Political Meditation," *JBL* 131 (2012) 663–84.

27. The notion is usually attributed to the work of Michel Foucault, particularly his work on imprisonment and sexuality: M. Foucault, *The History of Sexuality* (trans. Robert Hurley; 3 vols.; New York: Vintage, 1978–86); idem, *Discipline and Punish: The Birth of the Prison* (trans. Alan Sheridan; New York: Vintage, 1995). For a thoroughgoing recasting of his work, with ample critique of its conflation of body and sexuality and thus distortion of the nature of the gaze, see the studies in J. I. Porter, ed., *Constructions of the Classical Body* (Ann Arbor, MI: University of Michigan Press, 2002).

28. F. Landy, "I and Eye in Isaiah, or Gazing at the Invisible," *JBL* 131 (2012) 85–97.

ond Isaiah. They "see" a renewed Israel/Jacob. Conversely, the idols cannot reveal (41:23, 28), nor can their votaries see (44:9, 18) or believe themselves seen (47:10). The theme of royal demonstrations of success through the redistribution of goods, destruction or saving of cities, and so on takes many forms in the ancient Near East, and the biblical tradition of foreign nations and their rulers witnessing Yнwн's kingly acts of might goes back to the beginnings of the Israelite tradition (Exod 15:14–16). Yet, Second Isaiah has taken the theme in a new direction: the divinely led parade of peoples does not include captives but only the freed, and kings come making obeisance, not to Israel's ruler but to Israel itself. Hence the transfer of the Davidic promises to the nation as a whole (55:3). What Millard Lind has felicitously called the "kingly characteristics of the servant" applies throughout the work to Israel as a whole.[29] One kingly characteristic is the capacity to see and be seen—that is, the politics of display.

Mental Geography

Display, however, needs a stage, and so Second Isaiah mentions several regions of the world: Qedar (42:11), Egypt (43:3; 52:4), Kush (43:3; 45:14), Babylon (43:14; 47:1; 48:14, 20), and Saba (43:3).[30] Also appearing are the vaguely defined 'isles, littorals' (אִיִּים; 41:1; 42:10, 12, 15; 49:1), presumably the Aegean regions and those further west, part of the region-wide economy of the mid-first millennium.[31] Geographic terms such as 'north' (צָפוֹן; 41:25; 43:6; 49:12) and the even more vague 'far away' (רָחוֹק; 43:6; 46:12; 49:1, 12) signal a move toward comprehensiveness at the cost of precision. Second Isaiah uses these place-names as a synecdoche for the world defined by the Neo-Babylonian empire and its neighbors. Sites in Iran and farther east are noticeably absent. The choice of geographic names does not, however, imply a date to the Neo-Babylonian period but simply that the mental geography of the author has been shaped by the experiences under that empire.

The most elaborate constructions of this mental geography appear in Isa 43:1–7, a *Heilsorakel* often understood to reflect Cambyses's conquest of Egypt,[32]

---

29. M. C. Lind, "Monotheism, Power, and Justice: A Study in Isaiah 40–55," *CBQ* 46 (1984) 432–46, esp. 445.

30. So MT and 1QIsaᵇ, but note the LXX's Σοηνη, apparently an *ad contextum* correction (cf. 49:12). 1QIsaᵃ reads סבאים, thus replacing the land with its inhabitants.

31. In contrast to Isa 60:4–7, which refers to the southeastern and western extensions of the Near Eastern economy, apparently a later reflection on an economic network which, however, dates to Neo-Assyrian times.

32. See J. L. Koole, *Isaiah III*, vol. 1: *Isaiah 40–48* (HCOT; Kampen: Kok Pharos, 1997), 290–92. A possible point of reference here might be the portrayal of Egypt in P as no part of the world, and anti-cosmos, perhaps reflecting the early Persian period, when Egypt lay outside the sphere of Achaemenid control, as argued by K. Schmid, "The Quest for 'God': Monotheistic Arguments in the Priestly Texts of the Hebrew Bible," in *Reconsidering the Concept of Revolutionary Monotheism* (ed. B. Pongratz-Leisten; Winona Lake, IN: Eisenbrauns, 2011), 287.

but in any case concerned with a recapitulation of the exodus in the emigration of Israelites now liberated from their erstwhile lands of sojourning. Yhwh gives Egypt and its neighbors as a ransom (כפר; 43:3b) for Israel, with the Achaemenid Empire apparently the deity's business partner in the exchange. Notably, the text does not press the imagery of exchange, and the oracle to Cyrus in 44:21–45:13 in some respects undercuts the idea of business exchange because Israel's liberation is an act of divine fiat mediated by a chosen viceroy (משיח) rather than a transaction between notional equals. More than one theory of the politics of return (or at least more than one set of metaphors and preunderstandings) is thus in play in Second Isaiah, as one might expect for such an important event. (Moreover, this breadth of thought extents to the potential makeup of the returnees, for at no point does the work envision return from Babylonia alone, nor does it assume that those returning from there hold a special place in the newly unfolding economy of grace, contrary to much literature on the topic.)

In any case, Isa 43:1–7 lays out the triad Egypt, Kush, and Saba (cf. Isa 45:14), hence the regions at the fringe of the Mesopotamian empires (alternatively inside and outside them). Whether or not the word מאשר in v. 4 should be read 'from Assyria', as Maalstad argued with few followers,[33] the widespread Mesopotamian idea of the "four corners" of the world does show up immediately afterward in vv. 5–6 with their reference to the cardinal directions (תימן, צפון, מערב, מזרח).[34] In other words, universal domination includes rule of northeast Africa, and this rule is exercised first by Yhwh (Isa 43) and then by Cyrus (Isa 45). Thus, the Second Isaiah poems both embrace a view inherited from the period's empires—that is, that the ruler of the moment governed the entire earth just as the chief god governed the cosmos itself—and modifies that view to deconstruct the Neo-Babylonian claims to instantiate that imperial ideal.[35] Rather than mere zones for imperial expansion, the various geographic regions in question become the sites of Yhwh's salvation of Israel from its captors.

---

33. So K. Maalstad, "Einige Erwägungen zu Jes. XLIII 4," *VT* 16 (1966) 512–14. But see the dismissive note of Blenkinsopp, *Isaiah 40–55*, 220; and the more careful discussion of Koole, *Isaiah 40–48*, 293. However, Koole's refutation of the comparative "more than Assyria" with the statement "it is not clear why Asshur should be mentioned in this context and even less why it should have been valuable in God's eyes" is itself open to refutation. As Isa 19:18–24 makes clear, at least some tradents of the Isaiah tradition thought of Assyria as a favorite of Yhwh, and even if such an idea takes a different guise in Isa 40–55, then it is conceivable that the weight of the traditional reference to Assyria as a shorthand for Mesopotamian superpowers, a usage that survived at least until the writing of the book of Judith, plays a role in Isa 43 as well.

34. Compare with the MT of Isa 49:12, which gives the directions as מרחוק 'far away', צפון 'north', מים 'seaward, west', and מארץ סינים 'from the land of Syene'. LXX reads ἐκ γῆς Περσων in the last instance, a reading that makes little sense in the context (or, rather, obliterates the concept behind the text), but does illustrate the translators' ideas about distance.

35. P. Machinist, "The Transfer of Kingship: A Divine Turning," in *Fortunate the Eyes That See: Essays in Honor of David Noel Freedman in Celebration of His Seventieth Birthday* (ed. A. B. Beck et al.; Grand Rapids, MI: Eerdmans, 1995), 105–20.

This recasting of ideas takes on two further features, both related to the Persians. First, the oracles naming Cyrus in 44:24–45:13 situate his conquest of the Babylonian Empire within the context of a new creation not anticipated by the oracular knowledge workers (extispicers, astrologers, etc.) of the Mesopotamian priesthoods. At the same time, Cyrus plays the typical role of the king as builder of cities and temples even if the text does not explicitly link his ascendancy with the reconstructions envisaged for Judah. So Isa 44:28 places in parallelism two divine commands:

האמר לכרש רעי וכל חפצי ישלם ולאמר לירושלים תבנה והיכל תוסד

The one saying to Cyrus my shepherd, "and all my desire he will perfect," and to Jerusalem, "Let her be built" and to the temple, "let it be erected."

The ruler and the city are parallel loci of Yʜwʜ's rule.

The second and more striking point is the way in which Second Isaiah conceives of the world. Cyrus's conquests of fortified cities serve the purpose of Jacob/Israel's restoration (למען עבדי יעקב וישראל בחירי [45:4]), thus recasting the relationship of dominator and dominated as one of, to use Fokkelman's happy expression, "an image of splendid reciprocity."[36] The inversion of the ruler-subject relationship appears even further in the expansion of the Cyrus oracle in Isa 45:14, which makes Jerusalem (not Babylon or Pasargadac) the recipient of the obeisance of Egypt, Kush, and Saba—the triad from ch. 43.[37] Again, the regional political structure finds a new center, rebuilt Jerusalem, and a new hierarchy with Israel and Cyrus at the top.

It is instructive, then, to situate this viewpoint in its larger context. To begin, Baruch Levine is probably right to argue that the ascendancy of Yʜwʜ to cosmic rulership, evident in the Isaiah tradition from its earliest layers and taken for granted by Second Isaiah, owes much to the need to respond comprehensively to the claims of Assyria and its god Assur, in the first instance, and then, I would add, to those of the successor empires.[38] As Levine puts it in reference to Isa 9:5–6 and 11:1–10, and thus the 8th-century situation:

---

36. J. P. Fokkelman, "The Cyrus Oracle (Isaiah 44,24–45,7) from the Perspectives of Syntax, Versification and Structure," in *Studies in the Book of Isaiah* (Festschrift W. A. M. Beuken; ed. J. van Ruiten and M. Vervenne; Leuven: Peeters, 1997), 320.

37. On the MT's use of the second-person feminine singular suffix, see Berges, *Jesaja 40–48*, 418; compare with Blenkinsopp, *Isaiah 40–55*, 256–58. The larger issues of the organization of the end of ch. 45 and its relationship to the Cyrus oracle (or rather the boundaries of that oracle and its possible revisions) are thoroughly discussed in the commentaries and need not detain us here.

38. On the mediation (not through Media!) of Mesopotamian repertoires of rule to the Persian Empire, see M. Jursa, "Observations on the Problem of the Median 'Empire' on the Basis of Babylonian Sources," in *Continuity of Empire (?): Assyria, Media, Persia* (ed. G. B. Lanfranchi, M. Roaf, and R. Rollinger; History of the Ancient Near East Monographs 5; Padua: SARGON, 2003), 169–79.

The attributes of the ideal king, his wise counsel and judgment, and his capacity
to resolve conflicts peacefully rather than by use of military force, are said to have
been endowed by the God of Israel. It would be more accurate to invert this statement: Yahweh is the ideal king, by virtue of the fact that kingship serves as the
model for configuring the God-idea.[39]

In other words, the complex interaction of politics and religion—not as unidirec-
tionally as this sentence from Levine would imply—played out in a range of Near
Eastern traditions in the mid-first millennium B.C.E.

It has become widely accepted that the Cyrus oracle presupposes the rise of
that monarch and the later developments of his reign, and thus that the text dates
from later in the 6th century B.C.E. than the fall of Babylon (i.e., that the text is a
vaticinium ex eventu on the model of Mesopotamian "predictive" texts).[40] Thus, a
comparison to Achaemenid practices might, in principle, illuminate Second Isaiah's presuppositions and their articulation. Perhaps most relevant is the way in
which Darius I and his immediate successors constructed a *mappa mundi* of 23 to
31 regions (depending on the text in question) from Afghanistan to Greece, from
the Oxus to the Sahara, making up their empire.[41] This construal of the world as
one of subject peoples in every corner of the world (though lacking interest in listing all subject peoples, since Syria–Palestine usually appears in the lists as part of
"Assyria" or Arabia)[42] led to the creation of not only the famous parade of figures
on the Persepolis terrace but also, perhaps more innovatively, the splendid tomb
reliefs at Naqsh-i-Rustam and Persepolis. The latter repeat the same basic scene,
in which the Persian emperor stands facing an altar atop a platform supported by
two banks of 14 men each (with one additional figure facing the legs of the platform but standing outside it, making 30 in all), with the images representing distinct regions of the empire. Other figures holding their hands before their faces in
the Persian gesture of obeisance flank the main relief. Divinities, the winged disc
of Ahura Mazda and a lunar disc, hover above the scene. Although slight differ-

---

39. B. Levine, "Assyrian Ideology and Israelite Monotheism," *Iraq* 67 (2005) 412.

40. Berges, *Jesaja 40–48*, 375–79; Baltzer, *Deutero-Isaiah*, 223–26 (*mutatis mutandis*); but
H.-J. Hermisson, *Deuterojesaja* (BKAT 11/2; Neukirchen-Vluyn: Neukirchener Verlag, 1987),
60–61. M. Leuenberger ("Kyros-Orakel und Kyros-Zylinder: Ein religionsgeschichtlicher Vergleich ihrer Gottes-konzeptionen," *VT* 59 [2009] 244–56) has shown that a number of royal
themes ("Handergreifung, Namensnennung, Weltherrschaft oder wunderhafter Sieg") appear in
both Isa 44–45 and early Persian propaganda, though the latter clearly borrowed from Neo-
Babylonian (and Neo-Assyrian) practices. On the last point, see also R. Achenbach, "Das Kyros-
Orakel in Jesaja 44,24–45,7 im Lichte altorientalischer Parallelen," *ZAR* 11 (2005) 155–94.

41. For a brief overview, see A. Kuhrt, "The Achaemenid Persian empire (c. 550–330
B.C.E.): Continuities, Adaptations, Transformations," in *Empires* (ed. S. E. Alcock et al.; Cambridge: Cambridge University Press, 2001), 106–9; P. Briant, *From Cyrus to Alexander: A History
of the Persian Empire* (trans. P. T. Daniels; Winona Lake, IN: Eisenbrauns, 2002), 172–73.

42. For Palestine as part of Arabia, see Herodotus *Hist.* 3.91.

ences among the tomb reliefs exist, the basic scene reflects a shared notion of the hierarchy governing the world. As Calmeyer puts it, "Herrscher and Gottheit korrespondieren direkt miteinander—nicht durch das Feuer hindurch . . . aber mit gleichem Gestus, der erhobenen Rechten mit der Handfläche nach innen. . . ."[43] I would add to this that the subjects are an integral part of the scene, according to which the empire existed under a divine aegis but in which the subject peoples were both locked into their supporting role and essential to the preservation of the cosmic structure, the platform on which the emperor stood.[44]

Does Second Isaiah, who almost certainly never saw these tombs, know of the basic idea informing the reliefs at their entrance? The question is difficult to answer because of the uncertainty surrounding both the date of the biblical text and the history of Achaemenid political propaganda. However, although the evidence for the transmission of this propaganda in Jewish settings is circumstantial and later (*inter alia*, the letters in Ezra–Nehemiah and the Aramaic copy of the Bisitun Inscription from Elephantine), mechanisms clearly existed for the dissemination of the political ideas of the elites at the center of the Persian Empire.[45] The question is whether any texts in Second Isaiah reflect the Persian viewpoint, however obliquely. To be sure, several elements of the Persian idea are clearly missing, notably the extended list of place/ethnic-names and the presentation of the king as sacrificing to the deity (indeed, an impossibility given 45:4's acknowledgment that Cyrus did not know Yhwh [ולא ידעתני]). Moreover, the description of the king as warrior and recipient of tribute under the aegis of a divinity (45:1–5), though

---

43. P. Calmeyer, *Die Reliefs der Gräber V und VI in Persepolis* (ed. Svend Hansen; Archäologie in Iran und Turan; Mainz: von Zabern, 2009), 28.

44. Perhaps an instructive comparison would be the artistic program of Augustus, particularly in the second half of his reign, when he sought to portray himself as a model for others in piously protecting the old ways. The Ara Pacis Augustae offers perhaps the most famous example of imperial art portraying an imaginary scene in which all the forces of the world converge pacifically to exhibit the power—and inevitability and therefore rightness—of the imperium. Note broadly the work of P. Zanker, *The Power of Images in the Age of Augustus* (trans. A. Shapiro; Ann Arbor, MI: University of Michigan Press, 1988), 101–66, esp. 159–62; more popularly, J. Elsner, *Art and the Roman Viewer: The Transformation of Art from the Pagan World to Christianity* (Cambridge: Cambridge University Press, 1995), 192–210.

45. See, however, the cautionary notes by L. L. Grabbe, "The 'Persian Documents' in the Book of Ezra: Are They Authentic?" in *Judah and the Judeans in the Persian Period* (ed. O. Lipschits and M. Oeming; Winona Lake, IN: Eisenbrauns, 2006), 531–70. The Bisitun inscription was known in Babylonia as well; see U. Seidl, "Ein Monument Darius' I. aus Babylon," *ZA* 89 (1999) 101–14. Note the discussion in TADAE (3.59), in which the editors opine that the Elephantine copy of the Bisitun inscription served a public ritual, or educational, purpose, perhaps on the centenary of Darius's ascension to the throne. On the spread of Persian political ideas as far east as India, note also the presence of Persian loanwords (mostly political) in the 3rd-century B.C.E. inscription of Aśoka (r. ca. 269–232 B.C.E.) from Kandahar, Afghanistan; G. P. Carratelli and G. Garbini, *A Bilingual Graeco-Aramaic Inscription by Aśoka* (Serie Orientale Roma 29; Rome: Istituto Italiano per il Medio ed Estremo Oriente, 1964).

prominent in Achaemenid reliefs and texts, is far from uniquely Persian, being instead inherited from prior polities and thus ubiquitous in the Near East.[46]

However, the idea of foreign nations as foundation of an empire as it serves a chief deity does appear in Second Isaiah, as well as in a more-developed form in the so-called Third Isaiah (Isa 60:1–22).[47] Within Isa 40–55, the recipient of tribute and thus the center of an imagined empire is a renewed Israel. Hence, the already discussed text 43:1–7, as well as such texts as 49:23

> And kings will be your allies (אמנך) and their princesses your wetnurses;
> They will bow to you palms to the ground, lick your feet's dust. . . .

or 51:4b–5

> For Torah comes from me, and my justice as a light to the nations (אור עמים)
>   I hasten;
> My rightness is near, my deliverance comes, and my arm judges the peoples;
> The isles (לאמים) trust me and to my arm they look. . . .

or the closely related 42:4

> He will not flag or be enervated until he establishes justice on the land,
> And the isles (איים) await his Torah.

The latter two seem to imagine a reality in which distant parts of the world will be subject to Yhwh's (or the Servant's) law. Isa 49:23 (cf. 49:7) is particularly striking because it draws on the widespread ancient Near Eastern theme of subject rulers bowing to an overlord but recasts the theme in light of the exaltation of Israel as a whole (not its leader). Moreover, the juxtaposition of two semiotic planes (surrogate parenting and obeisance before a ruler) implies more than a throne scene in time and space, hence a reality in both the human (political) and divine (religious) realms.[48] The God of Israel, and thus Israel itself, will enjoy some sort of dominion beyond its traditional territory.

Such a notion comes to full flower in chs. 54 and 55, in two ways. The first is the depiction of the rebuilt city of Jerusalem in 54:11b–14aα:

---

46. Briant, *From Cyrus to Alexander*, 204–54. Note also the use of the hunter motif on coinage throughout the Achaemenid empire, again evidence for the transmission of Persian ideas (though with earlier antecedents) to the subject peoples; V. S. Jigoulov, *The Social History of Achaemenid Phoenicia: Being a Phoenician, Negotiating Empires* (London: Equinox, 2010), 91–97.

47. Isaiah 60 itself may have undergone a series of revisions that show continuing reflection on the political situation of the Yehud in imagined perfected state; see J. L. Koole, *Isaiah III*, vol. 3: *Isaiah 56–66* (HCOT; Leuven: Peeters, 2001).

48. Contra Baltzer, *Deutero-Isaiah*, 350–52 (quite apart from the problems of dating posed by Baltzer's reconstruction of the setting of Isa 40–55).

Indeed, I will lay your stones as antimony and make your foundations lapis
lazuli
And I will make your battlements like carnelian (?) and your gates precious
crystal,
And all your perimeter precious stones.
Yes, all your children will be YHWH's pupils, and your builders a
rav-shalom.[49]
In righteousness will you be established.[50]

The reconstruction of the city in such an impossibly grand style points to an awareness on the part of the composer of the intended majesty of imperial capitals (Esth
1:6; Song 5:9–16), which now Jerusalem is to surpass, though the beauty of the city
emphatically does not exist merely to intimidate its foes, as is often the case for
ancient capitals, but to promote שׁלוֹם, even if the peace assumes a new hegemony
with Jerusalem and Persia at its center(s). The vision of the splendid city resumes
the theme articulated in the apostrophe to Jerusalem in 51:17–23, deepening Second Isaiah's interest in the renewed Jerusalem as a political center of some sort.

The second is the almost off-handed allusion to the Davidic dynastic promise
in Isa 55:3b:

And I will cut an age-long covenant with you, the reliable mercies of David
(חסדי דוד הנאמנים).

The line almost certainly does not presume a restoration of the Davidic dynasty
per se, since nothing else in Isa 40–55 points toward such an eventuality, but it
does envision a renewal of the structure of divine benefaction and national success
assumed by the monarchic ideology, perhaps particularly as set forth in Ps 89.[51]
While Conrad's argument that the use of war-oracle imagery in Second Isaiah represents a transference of regal imagery to the people as a whole falls flat because
the formulas he cites are not uniquely royal,[52] his basic idea is correct. Israel as
a whole will stand in the legacy of David, just as it does for Abraham and Sarah
(51:2) and even Noah (54:9). The restoration of the nation, its new exodus, marks
the beginning of a new epoch of human history.

---

49. Reading with 1QIsa[a] בוניכי ('your builders') rather than MT's בניך ('your sons'), though
note LXX τα τεκνα σου. I have rendered v. 13b's רב שׁלוֹם as *rav-shalom* on the model of many
Akkadian locutions equaling "master of/expert in X," thus here 'an expert in peace'.
50. Reading the final ני in תכוננ as an energic form.
51. Koole, *Isaiah 49–55*, 413–14; Baltzer, *Deutero-Isaiah*, 471; see also the possibly contemporaneous texts in Hos 3:5; Amos 9:11.
52. E. W. Conrad, "The Community as King in Second Isaiah," in *Understanding the Word:
Essays in Honor of Bernhard W. Anderson* (ed. J. T. Butler, E. W. Conrad, and B. C. Ollenburger;
JSOTSup 37; Sheffield: JSOT Press, 1985), 99–111.

Conclusions

In this brief essay, I have sought to argue that Second Isaiah draws together a range of ideas, some already adumbrated in earlier stages of the Isaian tradition, and works them out in the context of a larger, region-wide discussion about the proper nature of political power. Like other intellectual creations of the late 6th century, the work drew on older intellectual and representational traditions and conventions to create something new. In doing so, it did not merely copy or, alternatively, reject older forms. The creator of Second Isaiah was not a mere epigone but a true artist for whom politics was a high art and political thought could occur only in the highest possible key. The poetry of Isa 40–55 draws its audience into a world in which politics exists—true!—but politics of a higher order, a transcendental structuring of reality in which the real actors strutting and fretting across the stage are not flesh and blood but types and shadows, idealizations serving to figure a more profound drama, one in which the world is recreated with the heavens and most exotic lands as witnesses. In short, Second Isaiah both does and does not live in a political world, and that very ambiguity or, rather, multivalency gives the work its significance, both for antiquity and for modern readers. The work is thus a gorgeous piece of propaganda, but more than that, it is an invitation to a new way of thinking in which the deepest resources of language do not serve the needs of a given monarch but the purposes of a deity, as humans understand that deity, who renews the world.

Bibliography

Achenbach, R. "Das Kyros-Orakel in Jesaja 44,24–45,7 im Lichte altorientalischer Parallelen." *ZAR* 11 (2005) 155–94.

Albani, M. "Deuterojesajas Monotheismus und der babylonische Religionskonflikt unter Nabonid." Pp. 171–201 in *Der eine Gott und die Götter: Polytheismus und Monotheismus im antiken Israel*. Edited by M. Oeming and K. Schmid. ATANT 82. Zurich: Theologischer Verlag, 2003.

_____. *Der eine Gott und die himmlischen Heerscharen: Zur Begründung des Monotheismus bei Deuterojesaja im Horizont der Astralisierung des Gottesverständnisses im Alten Orient*. ABG 1. Leipzig: Evangelische Verlagsanstalt, 2000.

Albertz, R. *Israel in Exile: The History and Literature of the Sixth Century* B.C.E. Atlanta: SBL, 2003.

Alobaidi, J. *The Messiah in Isaiah 53: The Commentaries of Saadia Gaon, Salomon ben Yerhum and Yefet ben Eli on Is 52:13–53:12*. Berne: Peter Lang, 1998.

Assmann, J. *Altägyptische Totenliturgien*, vol. 1: *Totenliturgien in den Sargtexten des Mittleren Reiches*. Heidelberg: C. Winter, 2002.

_____. "Memory, Narration, Identity: Exodus as a Political Myth." Pp. 3–18 in *Literary Construction of Identity in the Ancient World*. Edited by H. Liss and M. Oeming; Winona Lake, IN: Eisenbrauns, 2010.

Aster, S. Z. "The Image of Assyria in Isaiah 2:5–22: The Campaign Motif Reversed." *JAOS* 127 (2007) 249–78;

Baltzer, K. *Isaiah 40–55.* Hermeneia. Minneapolis: Fortress, 2001.

Bäckersten, O. *Isaiah's Political Message.* FAT 2/29. Tübingen: Mohr Siebeck, 2008.

Bär, J. "Tributdarstellungen in der Kunst des Alten Orients." Pp. 231–61 in *Geschenke und Steuern, Zölle und Tribute: Antike Abgabenformen in Anspruch und Wirklichkeit.* Edited by H. Klinkott, S. Kubisch, and R. Müller-Wollermann. CHANE 29. Leiden: Brill, 2007.

Barth, H. *Die Jesaja-Worte in der Josiazeit: Israel und Assur als Thema einer produktiven Neuinterpretation der Jesajaüberlieferung.* WMANT 48. Neukirchen-Vluyn: Neukirchener, 1977.

Bellinger, W. H. and W. R. Farmer, eds. *Jesus and the Suffering Servant: Isaiah 53 and Christian Origins.* Harrisburg, PA: Trinity Press International, 1998.

Berges, U. *Jesaja 40–48.* HTKAT; Freiburg: Herder, 2008.

Blenkinsopp, J. *Isaiah 40–55.* AB 19A. New York: Doubleday, 2000.

————. *Opening the Sealed Book: Interpretations of the Book of Isaiah in Late Antiquity.* Grand Rapids, MI: Eerdmans, 2006.

Bonacossi, D. M. " 'Landscapes of Power:' The Political Organisation of Space in the Lower Ḫabur Valley in the Neo-Assyrian Period." *SAAB* 10 (1996) 15–49.

Briant, P. *From Cyrus to Alexander: A History of the Persian Empire.* Translated by Peter T. Daniels. Winona Lake, IN: Eisenbrauns, 2002.

Calmeyer, P. *Die Reliefs der Gräber V und VI in Persepolis.* Edited by S. Hansen. Archäologie in Iran und Turan. Mainz: von Zabern, 2009.

Carratelli, G. P., and G. Garbini. *A Bilingual Graeco-Aramaic Inscription by Aśoka.* Serie Orientale Roma 29. Rome: Istituto Italiano per il Medio ed Estremo Oriente, 1964.

Chan, M. "Rhetorical Reversal and Usurpation: Isaiah 10:5–34 and the Use of Neo-Assyrian Royal Idiom in the Construction of an Anti-Assyrian Theology." *JBL* 128 (2009) 717–33.

Cohen, R., and R. Westbrook, eds. *Isaiah's Vision of Peace in Biblical and Modern International Relations.* New York: Macmillan, 2008.

Conrad, E. W. C., "The Community as King in Second Isaiah." Pp. 99–111 in *Understanding the Word: Essays in Honor of Bernhard W. Anderson.* Edited by J. T. Butler, E. W. Conrad, and B. C. Ollenburger. JSOTSup 37. Sheffield: JSOT Press, 1985.

Cooper, F. *Colonialism in Question: Theory, Knowledge, History.* Berkeley: University of California Press, 2005.

Davies, P. R. "God of Cyrus, God of Israel: Some Religio-Historical Reflections on Isaiah 40–55." Pp. 207–25 in *Words Remembered, Texts Renewed: Essays in Honour of John F. A. Sawyer.* Edited by J. Davies, G. Harvey, and W. G. E. Watson. JSOTSup 195. Sheffield: Sheffield Academic, 1995.

Dubovský, P. *Hezekiah and the Assyrian Spies: Reconstruction of the Neo-Assyrian Intelligence Services and its Significance for 2 Kings 18–19.* BibOr 49. Rome: Pontifical Biblical Institute, 2006.

Ebersole, G. L. "The Function of Ritual Weeping Revisited: Affective Expression and Moral Discourse." *History of Religions* 39 (2000) 211–46.

Ellis, M. deJ. "Observations on Mesopotamian Oracles and Prophetic Texts: Literary and Historiographic Considerations." *JCS* 41 (1989) 127–86

Eslner, J. *Art and the Roman Viewer: The Transformation of Art from the Pagan World to Christianity.* Cambridge: Cambridge University Press, 1995.

Faber, A. "On the Structural Unity of the Eshmunazor Inscription." *JAOS* 106 (1986) 425–32.

Fischer, G. "Gefährten im Leiden—der Gottesknecht bei Jesaja und der Prophet Jeremia." *BZ* 56 (2012) 1–19.

Fokkelman, J. P. "The Cyrus Oracle (Isaiah 44,24–45,7) from the Perspectives of Syntax, Versification and Structure." Pp. 303–23 in *Studies in the Book of Isaiah.* Festschrift Willem A. M. Beuken. Edited by J. van Ruiten and M. Vervenne. Leuven: Peeters, 1997.

Foucault, M. *Discipline and Punish: The Birth of the Prison.* Trans. A. Sheridan. New York: Vintage, 1995.

_____. *The History of Sexuality.* Trans. Robert Hurley. 3 vols. New York: Vintage, 1978–86.

Grabbe, L. L. "The 'Persian Documents' in the Book of Ezra: Are They Authentic?" Pp. 531–70 in *Judah and the Judeans in the Persian Period.* Edited by O. Lipschits and M. Oeming. Winona Lake, IN: Eisenbrauns, 2006.

Hamilton, M. W. "Isaiah 32 as Literature and Political Meditation." *JBL* 131 (2012) 663–84.

Hermisson, H.-J. *Deuterojesaja.* BKAT 11/2. Neukirchen-Vluyn: Neukirchener Verlag, 1987.

Heskett, R. *Messianism within the Scriptural Scroll of Isaiah.* LHBOTS 456. London: T. & T. Clark, 2007.

Hilber, J. W. "Psalm CX in the Light of Assyrian Prophecies." *VT* 53 (2003) 353–77.

Hunger, H., and D. Pingree. *Astral Sciences in Mesopotamia.* HdO 1/44. Leiden: Brill, 1999.

Jackson, K. P. "The Language of the Mesha Inscription." Pp. 96–130 in *Studies in the Mesha Inscription and Moab.* Edited by A. Dearman. Atlanta: Scholars, 1989.

Jigoulov, V. S. *The Social History of Achaemenid Phoenicia: Being a Phoenician, Negotiating Empires.* London: Equinox, 2010.

Joannès, F. "L'écriture publique du pouvoir à Babylone sous Nabuchodonosor II." Pp. 113–20 in *Babylon: Wissenskultur in Orient und Okzident.* Edited by E. Cancik-Kirschbaum, M. van Ess, and J. Marzahn. Topoi: Berlin Studies of the Ancient World. Berlin: de Gruyter, 2011.

Jong, M. J. de. "A Window on the Isaiah Tradition in the Assyrian Period: Isaiah 10:24–27." Pp. 83–107 in *Isaiah in Context: Studies in Honour of Arie van der Kooij on the Occasion of his Sixty-Fifth Birthday.* Edited by M. N. van der Meer et al. VTSup 138. Leiden: Brill, 2010.

Jursa, M. "Observations on the Problem of the Median 'Empire' on the Basis of Babylonian Sources." Pp. 169–79 in *Continuity of Empire (?): Assyria, Media, Persia.* Edited by G. B. Lanfranchi, M. Roaf, and R. Rollinger. History of the Ancient Near East Monographs 5. Padua: SARGON, 2003.

Kessler, M. *Battle of the Gods: The God of Israel Versus Marduk of Babylon: A Literary/Theological Interpretation of Jeremiah 50–51.* SSN 42. Assen: Van Gorcum, 2003.

Koole, J. L. *Isaiah III*, vol. 2: *Isaiah 49–55.* HCOT. Leuven: Peeters, 1998.

_____. *Isaiah III*, vol. 3: *Isaiah 56–66.* HCOT; Leuven: Peeters, 2001.

Kuhrt, A. "The Achaemenid Persian empire (c. 550–330 BCE): Continuities, Adaptations, Transformations." Pp. 93–123 in *Empires*. Edited by S. E. Alcock et al. Cambridge: Cambridge University Press, 2001.

Laato, A. *The Servant of YHWH and Cyrus: A Reinterpretation of the Exilic Messianic Programme in Isaiah 40–55.* CBOT 35. Stockholm: Almqvist & Wiksell, 1992.

Lackenbacher, S. *Le Roi Bâtisseur: Les récits de construction assyriens des origines à Teglathphalasar III.* Paris: ERC, 1982.

Landy, F. "I and Eye in Isaiah, or Gazing at the Invisible." *JBL* 131 (2012) 85–97.

Leuenberger, M. "Kyros-Orakel und Kyros-Zylinder: Ein religionsgeschichtlicher Vergleich ihrer Gottes-konzeptionen." *VT* 59 (2009) 244–56.

Levine, B.. "Assyrian Ideology and Israelite Monotheism." *Iraq* 67 (2005) 411–27.

Lind, M. C. "Monotheism, Power, and Justice: A Study in Isaiah 40–55." *CBQ* 46 (1984) 432–46.

Maalstad, K. "Einige Erwägungen zu Jes. XLIII 4." *VT* 16 (1966) 512–14.

Machinist, P. "Assyria and Its Image in the First Isaiah," *JAOS* 103 (1983) 719–37

‾‾‾‾‾‾‾. "Mesopotamian Imperialism and Israelite Religion: A Case Study from the Second Isaiah." Pp. 237–64 in *Symbiosis, Symbolism, and the Power of the Past: Canaan, Ancient Israel, and Their Neighbors from the Late Bronze Age through Roman Palaestina.* Edited by W. G. Dever and S. Gitin. Winona Lake, IN: Eisenbrauns, 2003.

‾‾‾‾‾‾‾. "The Transfer of Kingship: A Divine Turning." Pp. 105–20 in *Fortunate the Eyes That See: Essays in Honor of David Noel Freedman in Celebration of His Seventieth Birthday.* Edited by A. B. Beck et al. Grand Rapids, MI: Eerdmans, 1995.

Marcus, M. "Geography as Visual Ideology: Landscape, Knowledge, and Power in Neo-Assyrian Art." Pp. 193–208 in *Neo-Assyrian Geography*. Edited by M. Liverani. Rome: CNR, 1995.

Maul, S. M. "Die Wissenschaft von der Zukunft: Überlegungen zur Bedeutung der Divination im Alten Orients." Pp. 135–51 in *Babylon: Wissenskultur in Orient und Okzident.* Edited by E. Cancik-Kirschbaum, M. van Ess, and J. Marzahn. Topoi: Berlin Studies of the Ancient World 1. Berlin: de Gruyter, 2011.

Mayer, W. R. "Ein neues Königsritual gegen feindliche Bedröhung," *Or* 57 (1988) 145–65.

Meyer, J.-W. "Tempel und Palastbauten im eisenzeitlichen Palästina und ihre bronzezeitlichen Vorbilder." Pp. 319–28 in *Religionsgeschichtliche Beziehungen zwischen Kleinasien, Nordsyrien und dem Alten Testament.* Edited by B. Janowski, K. Koch, and G. Wilhelm. OBO 129. Göttingen: Vandenhoeck & Ruprecht, 1993.

Moyise, S. and M. J. J. Menken, ed. *Isaiah in the New Testament.* London: T. & T. Clark, 2005.

Nissinen, M. *References to Prophecy in Neo-Assyrian Sources.* SAAS 7. Helsinki: Neo-Assyrian Text Corpus Project, 1998.

Olyan, S. M. "Some Neglected Aspects of Israelite Interment Ideology." *JBL* 124 (2005) 601–16.

Oppenheim, A. L. "Divination and Clestial Observation in the Late Assyrian Empire." *Centaurus* 14 (1969) 97–135.

Orlinsky, H. M. *The So-Called "Suffering Servant" in Isaiah 53.* Cincinnati, OH: Hebrew Union College Press, 1964.

Otto, E. "Psalm 2 in neuassyrischer Zeit: Assyrische Motive in der judäischen Königs-ideologie." Pp. 335–49 in *Textarbeit: Studien zu Texten und ihrer Rezeption aus dem Alten Testament und der Umwelt Israels*. Edited by K. Kiesow and T. Meurer. Münster: Ugarit-Verlag, 2003.

Porter, J. I., ed. *Constructions of the Classical Body*. Ann Arbor, MI: University of Michigan, 2002.

Roberts, J. J. M. "Blindfolding the Prophet: Political Resistance to First Isaiah's Oracles in the Light of Ancient Near Eastern Attitudes Toward Oracles." Pp. 135–46 in *Oracles et Prophéties dans l'Antiquité*. Edited by J.-G. Heintz. Paris: Boccard, 1997.

Schaudig, H. "'Bel Bows, Nabu Stoops!': The Prophecy of Isaiah xlvi 1–2 as a Reflection of Babylonian 'Processional Omens'." *VT* 58 (2008) 557–72.

Schmid, K. "The Quest for 'God': Monotheistic Arguments in the Priestly Texts of the Hebrew Bible." Pp. 271–89 in *Reconsidering the Concept of Revolutionary Monotheism*. Edited by B. Pongratz-Leisten. Winona Lake, IN: Eisenbrauns, 2011.

Seidl, U. "Ein Monument Darius' I. aus Babylon." *ZA* 89 (1999) 101–14.

Shipp, R. M. *Of Dead Kings and Dirges: Myth and Meaning in Isaiah 14:4b–21*. Atlanta: SBL, 2002.

Somers, M. "The Narrative Constitution of Identity: A Relational and Network Approach." *Theory and Society* 23 (1994) 605–49.

Starr, I. *Queries to the Sungod: Divination and Politics in Sargonid Assyria*. SAAS 4. Helsinki: Neo-Assyrian Text Corpus Project, 1990.

Timm, S. "Jes 42,10 ff. und Nabonid." Pp. 237–59 in *"Gott kommt von Teman. . . :" Kleine Schriften zur Geschichte Israels und Syrien-Palästinas*. Edited by C. Bender and M. Pietsch. AOAT 314. Münster: Ugarit-Verlag, 2004.

Walton, John H. Walton, "The Imagery of the Substitute King Ritual in Isaiah's Fourth Servant Song." *JBL* 122 (2003): 734–43.

Wilson, J. A. "Funeral Sources of the Egyptian Old Kingdom." *JNES* 3 (1944) 201–18.

Zanker, P. *The Power of Images in the Age of Augustus*. Trans. A. Shapiro. Ann Arbor, MI: University of Michigan Press, 1988.

Part 5

Prophets and Patriots of the
Second Temple Period
and Early Postbiblical Period

Haggai and Zechariah:
A Maximalist View of the Return
in a Minimalist Social Context

ERIC M. MEYERS

Duke University

Introduction

The ways in which the prophets Haggai and Zechariah interfaced with the Persian state that exercised control over the postexilic province of Yehud are directly related to the changed circumstances and demographics of the people of Judah in the latter part of the 6th century B.C.E. The destruction of the Temple in Jerusalem by the neo-Babylonians and the forced exile of many of the Judean population save for those who resided in Benjamin or went there after the attack on the holy city led to a new reality for the Jewish people: the creation of several Diasporas, one in Egypt and the other in Mesopotamia, each of which was to ultimately produce vibrant and flourishing Jewish communities within a relatively short time. While the homeland was battered and beaten, the neo-Babylonians mainly left Benjamin untouched and allowed an alternative administrative center to be set up in Mizpah;[1] Gedaliah, a non-Davidide governor, was appointed possibly even before the fall of Jerusalem. Archaeological evidence suggests that Mizpah served as the de facto capital of Judea after the destruction and as an arm of the Babylonian bureaucratic structure. The existence of some 40 or more seal inscriptions bearing the letters MṢH/MWṢH, the majority from Mizpah, indicates a certain measure of administrative control by the conquerors, which lasted until around mid-century, when the balance of power in the region shifted once again in favor of the Persians—Cyrus the Great comes to the throne in 559 and conquers Babylon in 539.[2]

Author's note: All quotations from Haggai and Zechariah are taken from Carol and Eric Meyers's Anchor Bible commentaries.

1. O. Lipschits, *The Rise and Fall of Jerusalem* (Winona lake, IN: Eisenbrauns, 2005), 104–5.

2. E. M. Meyers with the assistance of Sean Burt, "Exile and Return: From the Babylonian Destruction to the Beginning of Hellenism," in *Ancient Israel: From Abraham to the Ro-*

The advent of Persian control of the historic territory of Judea and the fact that many exiles stayed in Mesopotamia long-term and even integrated into Babylonian society and the economy meant that the famed Edict of Cyrus allowing Jews to return to the homeland had little or no effect at the outset, when it was decreed in 538 b.c.e. The edict, part of the Cyrus Cylinder, should be understood in the larger context of Persia's response to Babylonian politics. Cyrus even paints himself as a supporter of Marduk, and his policies cannot simply to be viewed as an expression of policies of religious tolerance. On the contrary, Persia was well prepared to respond swiftly and decisively to any perceived threat to its authority or sign of rebellion.[3] The often presumed generosity of spirit reflected in the Cylinder is evident in the Bible's description (Ezra 1:2–4; 2 Chr 36:33), and especially in Second Isaiah Cyrus is recognized as fulfilling the messianic hopes of the people (Isa 44:28 and 45:1). As for the project of rebuilding the Temple, there was apparently widespread support in every corner of society (Ezra 1:5–11), at least from the perspective of a later report. However, the idea of a swift end to the exile followed by a mass return to the Land with the appearance of Cyrus's Edict, as suggested by Ezra 1–3, is not supported by the facts on the ground either in the homeland or in Babylonia. There is absolutely no change in the settlement pattern in Yehud in the beginning of the Persian period from that which characterized the Neo-Babylonian period.[4]

In fact, the evidence for a successful accommodation to life in Babylonia is supported in a number of documents that leave no doubt as to the level of success achieved there, especially the Murashu archive tablets.[5] Though composed in the mid-5th century, the documents indicate that the exiled Judeans were agricultural producers living as semi-free tenants on royal lands, clear signs of a close working relationship with the powers that be. The earlier cuneiform materials also point to a rapid accommodation of the exiles to their new environment, with a significant number of names indicating their Yahwistic leanings, if not more, an attachment to their ethnic past.[6] Whatever the case may be with these two important corpora of evidence, the importance of the Exile and the establishment of the Babylonian Jewish community and their experience in exile cannot be denied. Indeed, numer-

man *Destruction of the Temple* (ed. H. Shanks; Washington, DC: Biblical Archaelogy Society, 2011), 211–12. See also C. E. Carter, "(Re)Defining 'Israel': The Legacy of the Neo-Babylonian and Persian Periods," in *The Wiley Blackwell Companion to Ancient Israel* (ed. Susan Niditch; Malden, MA: Wiley Blackwell, 2016), 215–40.

3. M. Brosius, *The Persians: An Introduction* (Peoples of the Ancient World; London: Taylor & Francis, 2006), 72–76.

4. Lipschits, *The Rise and Fall of Jerusalem*, 267–71.

5. R. Albertz, *Israel in Exile: The History and Literature of the Sixth Century* (Atlanta: SBL, 2003), 101.

6. L. E. Pearce, "New Evidence for Judeans in Babylonia," in *Judah and the Judeans in the Persian Period* (eds. O. Lipschits and M. Oeming; Winona Lake, IN: Eisenbrauns, 2006), 399–412.

ous scholars have argued that it was separation from the Land and the suffering and challenges they endured that enabled Judaism to develop its unique view of monotheism.[7] While to some individuals, turning tragedy into a kind of triumph may seem wrong or inappropriate, the positive aftermath of the destruction and Exile cannot be denied. It now behooves us to examine the situation in Yehud in relation to the prophets of the Return, Haggai and First Zechariah (chs. 1–8), and assess to what degree their views were dependent on the state policies of the Achaemenids who ruled indirectly from Ecbatana far to the east of Jerusalem.

The apparent support or cooperation that the postexilic prophets Haggai and Zechariah gave to the Persian authorities had led previous scholars to question the authenticity of their voices within the prophetic corpus,[8] suggesting that by their tacit support of the governing authority they had compromised the historic position of the prophet as someone who spoke out freely against the local and distant authority. Moreover, by more or less adopting the position of the priestly class, each of them had also sacrificed their independence vis-à-vis the Temple establishment. Hence, the assessment by many scholars of these two prophets was often negative. While the recent past has certainly changed that state of affairs,[9] assessment of the position of Haggai and Zechariah in relation to the power structure of the early Persian period is certainly new and changed. The major historical factors contributing to this situation, as we have noted, are the fact that the monarchy had effectively come to an end after the destruction in 586 and the pro-Temple, pro-priestly point of view adopted by the prophets. Nonetheless, it is hard to deny the true nature of their utterances and the vibrancy of their speech and message. All this is to say that the movement that began more than a generation ago to reclaim the voices of postexilic prophecy, energized in many ways by the work of Peter Ackroyd and his student Rex Mason,[10] has succeeded beyond all expectation.[11] The factors that have most influenced this series of changes in attitude, apart from the anti-Wellhausen reaction of this contemporary cadre of scholars who are not

---

7. A. Lemaire, *The Birth of Monotheism: The Rise and Disappearance of Yahwism* (Washington DC: Biblical Archaeology Society, 2007). Cf. Meyers, "Exile and Return," 215–16; and idem, "The Babylonian Exile Revisited: Demographics and the Canon of Scripture," in *Judaism in Crisis: Crisis as a Catalyst in Jewish Cultural History* (ed. A. Lange, K. F. D. Römheld, and M. Weigold; Göttingen: Vandenhoeck & Ruprecht, 2011), 65–71.

8. P. Hanson, *The Dawn of Apocalyptic* (Philadelphia: Fortress, 1975), passim.

9. T. C. Eskenazi, "From Exile and Restoration to Exile and Reconstruction," in *Exile and Restoration Revisited: Essays on the Babylonian and Persian Periods in Memory of Peter R. Ackroyd* (ed. G. N. Knoppers, L. L. Grabbe, and D. Fulton; Library of Second Temple Studies 73; London: T. & T. Clark, 2009), 78–80.

10. L. L. Grabbe and G. N. Knoppers, "Introduction," in *Exile and Restoration Revisited: Essays on the Babylonian and Persian Periods in Memory of Peter R. Ackroyd* (ed. G. N. Knoppers, L. L. Grabbe, and D. Fulton; Library of Second Temple Studies 73; London: T. & T. Clark, 2009), 1–30.

11. C. L. Meyers and E. M. Meyers, *Haggai, Zechariah 1–8: A New Translation with Introduction and Commentary* (AB 25B; New York: Doubleday, 1987), lxviii–lxxii.

fixated on his axiom that Second Temple Judaism represented a decline from earlier high points of "Old" Testament religion, are these. First and foremost is the fact that, with the near completion of the publication of the Dead Sea Scrolls, there has been a renewed appreciation and understanding of the Second Temple period.[12] In addition, the renewed excavation and survey of both Jerusalem and the territory we associate with Yehud has brought about renewed interest in the postexilic period and new data that has helped to understand it better.

Prophetic Response

Locating Haggai and Zechariah as being enemies or friends of the state does not result in a black-and-white picture. Let us first think of what it might have been like, living in the Exile, to have learned of Persian support for resettlement in the homeland and for rebuilding the historic Temple in Jerusalem that lay in ruins. Even the most assimilated or acculturated Jew living in Mesopotamia must have been touched by this, although I can hardly imagine anyone there reading about this gesture and merely interpreting the imperial motives behind it as benign. Even though most exiles did not heed the call to return, greatly exaggerated in the biblical record, we may regard the prophetic ministries of Haggai and First Zechariah as a positive response to those new circumstances and to the unusual situation of having no monarch and having a new administrative structure that would answer to a foreign power. It has been my view for many years that pragmatic politics took over the mindset of these prophetic figures and that their message(s) were delivered to the people with the higher goals of return to Zion and rebuilding the Temple in mind throughout their careers. The appointment of the Davidic descendant Zerubbabel as governor of Yehud and his priestly counterpart Joshua as high priest[13] and the prophetic endorsement of them, as it were, are the building blocks of this new prophetic posture, whose effectiveness was posited on the success of the new diarchic form of government that was to all intents and purposes answerable to the Persian authorities. The contrast between the two prophets Haggai and First Zechariah illustrates some of the shortcomings of such a policy, since in First Zechariah repeated mention of the two leaders becomes more muted and less explicit as time moved on. So, for example, Zerubbabel is mentioned repeatedly in Haggai and addressed directly in Hag 2:20 and 23, which is a highly eschatological picture of the role of Zerubbbabel as possible restorer of the monarchy:

> I am about to shake the heavens and earth, and I am going to overthrow the throne of kingdoms and destroy the power of foreign kingdoms; and I will over-

---

12. E. M. Meyers and M. A. Chancey, *Alexander to Constantine: Archaeology of the Land of the Bible, Volume III* (The Anchor Bible Reference Library; New Haven, CT: Yale University Press, 2012), 83–112.

13. Meyers and Meyers, *Haggai, Zechariah 1–8*, 14.

> turn the chariotry and its charioteers so that horses and riders will fall, each by the sword and his brother—Oracle of Yahweh of Hosts—"I will take you O Zerubbabel ben-Shealtiel as my servant"—oracle of Yahweh—"and I will set you as my signet. For you have I chosen"—Oracle of Yahweh of hosts. (Hag 2:22–23)

The language of "servant" and "signet" suggests that the heightened eschatology of this oracle either is the result of historical circumstance, possibly even an echo of a revolt or uncertainty regarding Darius I's rise to power, or merely a very strong statement of hope residing on the successful restoration of the monarchy with a Davidic descendant at some time in the not-too-distant future.

In any case, the only mentions of Zerubbabel in First Zechariah occur in ch. 4 and are couched in quietistic language: "This is the word of Yahweh to Zerubbabel: not by might and not by power, but by my spirit, said Yahweh of Hosts" (Zech 4:6). The more subdued character of the messianic language in this passage is carried forward in ch. 6 as well, only without direct mention of the names of the principles in the diarchy—though one can hardly mistake the "Shoot" for any one but Zerubbabel:

> Behold there is a man—Shoot is his name—and from his place he will shoot up and build the Temple of Yahweh. He will build the Temple of Yahweh; and he will bear royal majesty and sit upon his throne and rule. A priest will be on his throne, and there will be peaceful counsel between the two of them. (Zech 6:12–13)

The so-called "disappearance" of Zerubbabel at least in name in First Zechariah, after the passage in ch. 4, has spawned all sorts of conspiracy theories, some suggesting he was done in by Persian authorities who feared that his royal aspirations would be deleterious to their control of the province. Others have suggested that Zerubbabel might have even led an insurrection against them.[14] In any case, the placement of the oracular insert in 4:6b and 10a and Zerubbabel's role in the refoundation of the Temple provides an alternative way of understanding his messianic standing and the author/editor's perspective on relations with Persia in this pivotal moment in Judean history.[15] While we may say that First Zechariah stands at a different place on the continuum of cooperation with the "state" than his predecessor Haggai, both prophets were committed to some sort of cooperative relationship. We should note that each of the references to Zerubbabel in ch. 4 of First Zechariah are without patronymic and without the designation "governor," the latter being the case in Ezra and Nehemiah. This contrasts strikingly with Haggai's use of Zerubbabel seven times, sometimes with patronymic and title (1:1, 14; 2:20, sometimes only with patronymic (1:12; 2:23), once as governor (2:21), and

---

14. A. R. Petterson, *Behold Your King: The Hope for the House of David in the Book of Zechariah* (Library of Hebrew Bible Studies/Old Testament Studies 513; London: T. & T. Clark, 2009), 14–45.

15. Meyers and Meyers, *Haggai, Zechariah 1–8*, 242–49, 255–59.

only once as Zerubbabel alone (2:4). In the case of First Zechariah, who avoids such familiar titles and designations, we may conclude that his expectation of re-establishing the monarchy was relegated to the future, whereas Haggai's hope was rooted more in the present.

We should mention, too, that the back-to-back presentation of the high priest's qualification and purification for service in the Temple in ch. 3, even being given access to the Heavenly Court (Zech 3:7),[16] and Zerubbabel's involvement in the Temple refoundation ceremony in ch. 4 lays the groundwork for the continuing acceptance of the nonmonarchic, diarchic alternative form of rule that undergirds First Zechariah's prophecy. Zerubbabel hence enjoys a special role in the cere-mony normally reserved for kings, the equivalent of a modern ground-breaking or cornerstone-laying ceremony. The oracular insertion (Zech 4:6b–10a) thus pro-claims Zerubbabel's Davidic role in the refounding of the Temple and, though his surrogate action in a sense lacked true legitimacy, it nonetheless enjoyed the legitimacy conveyed by Yahweh's spirit as delivered through the prophetic word.

Demographics and the Restoration

A major new factor in understanding how the prophets Haggai and First Ze-chariah related to the state and the changed circumstances of the postexilic era is the recent surge in estimates of the population of Yehud and Jerusalem, in partic-ular. Given the momentous events described in the Bible regarding the reception of Cyrus's decree and the rebuilding of the Temple one might be inclined to think that Jerusalem at this time at the beginning of the Persians period was a bustling and vibrant city, expanding in population with returnees from Exile. Judging from recent surveys and archaeological work there is nothing further from the truth. On the contrary, we may confidently agree with Haggai on the depressed nature of the economy in 1:6:

> You have sown much but have brought in little; you keep eating but there is never enough to fill up; you keep drinking but there is never enough to be drunk, you keep putting on clothes but there is no warmth for anyone. As for the hired hand he works for a bag full of holes.

It is possible that no work was being done because, simply speaking, there were too few people to undertake it. In the prophet's eyes, the best remedy for rectifying such ills was to get about the business of rebuilding the Temple that was to have begun years ago, after Cyrus's decree in 538. The author of Ezra 1–6 dealt with this delay by concluding that the delay was the result of outside interference by non-Judean enemies.

---

16. Ibid., 196–98.

But it was not only the economy that held back the development of the holy city and province. As we have noted already, many exiles had fully acclimatized to their new environment and enjoyed a degree of success there (for example, the evidence from the Murashu archive). Previous generations of scholars had thought that the population in Jerusalem at the time of Return was ca. 15,000, whereas from the 1990s on many began to drop that estimate to as low as 750 souls but more in the range of 5,000–7,000.[17] Today, however, leading scholars would go even lower, to between 400 and 1,000 souls in all. King and Stager, already in 2001,[18] had suggested that Jerusalem in the early postexilic period was limited to the City of David (4.4 hectares excluding the Temple Mount) and was half that size and had only a few hundred inhabitants. Finkelstein estimates the entire population of Yehud in this period to be 12,000 and growing to 40,000 only later in the early Hellenistic period, in the 160s B.C.E.[19] He says that by the time of Nehemiah the population of Jerusalem was perhaps 400 souls, and only 100 males. I have explored the implications of these figures recently,[20] but since they have tended to go lower and lower, it has become imperative to reassess their significance not only for the larger corpus of biblical literature that is assigned to this period but also to assess the influence this small group of people may have had on the attitude toward the Persian empire and the editing of Scripture. To be sure, we may say that the figures proposed do not constitute in any way a final statement that we may take as gospel truth. However, in view of the fact that for more than 40 years now these figures have been trending downward to a point at which recognized scholars are speaking of hundreds as opposed to thousands in Jerusalem, it is a good time to reassess their implications for Haggai and Zechariah.

A small population would have been called upon to support the Temple bureaucracy, which would have included Aaronide, Zadokite, and Levitical priests (Ezra 8:15–36; Neh 7:1, 39, 43), singers and gatekeepers (Neh 7:1, 23, 45), Temple servants (Neh 3:26, 31; 7:46; 11:19), and a scribal class (Ezra 8:1, 9), not to mention military officials of the province, artisans, and other attendants of the governor, which together would have come to hundreds of individuals, perhaps more.

---

17. Meyers and Chancey, *Alexander to Constantine*, 1–2.

18. P. J. King and L. E. Stager, *Life in Biblical Israel* (Library of Ancient Israel; Louisville: John Knox/Westminster, 2001), 389.

19. I. Finkelstein, "Jerusalem in the Persian (and early Hellenisitc) Period and the Wall of Nehemiah," *JSOT* 32 (2008) 501–20; idem, "The Territorial Extent of Jerusalem and Demography of Yehud/Judea in the Persian and Early Hellenistic Periods," *Revue biblique* 117 (2010) 39–54.

20. E. Meyers, "Exile and Restoration in Light of Recent Archaeology and Demographic Studies," in *Exile and Restoration Revisited: Essays on the Babylonian and Persian Periods in Memory of Peter R. Ackroyd* (ed. G. N. Knoppers, L. L. Grabbe, and D. Fulton; Library of Second Temple Studies 73; London: T. & T. Clark, 2009), 166–73. See also my forthcoming essay, "The Rise of Scripture in a Minimalist Demographic Context," in *Stones, Tablets, and Scrolls: Four Periods of Formation of the Bible* (ed. Peter Dubovsky et al.; Tübingen: Mohr Siebeck).

However, it would have taken only about 5–10% of elites or specialists in an urban preindustrial society to produce works of a high literary character.[21] All of the figures quoted above fall well within this range, and hence we need not doubt that the assembled elites in Jerusalem in the Restoration period and following were sufficient to have accomplished the considerable editing and writing that is attributed to that time and place. That oeuvre would have included the Primary History (Genesis to 2 Kings), the three major prophets, the twelve minor prophets, and other writings as well, all of which together represent a creative response to the crisis of the Exile and a flowering of imagination and hope in the midst of a land that had not yet pulled itself out of the economic doldrums and an array of political and social challenges. To say that this was an astonishing achievement is to state the obvious. In the larger scheme of things, may we not ask if our prophets had any choice but to accept the status quo post-bellum, so to speak, and try to take advantage of the situation on the ground in full knowledge of the power and might of the Persian imperium? Even though we now know that only a handful of returnees would have resided in Jerusalem in the land of Yehud in the early postexilic period, the demographic picture only dramatizes the extent of the literary achievement of the small elite community that doubtless edited and produced so much of what was to become a large segment of the Hebrew Bible, though much of that activity had already begun in Mesopotamia.

In looking at our situation through the eyes of the later books of Ezra and Nehemiah, which stress the difficulties with Jerusalem's enemies and neighbors, casting a glance over to the province of Samaria may also shed light on our question. While to date no recent survey of Samaria has been conducted that can provide up-to-date figures on population and settlement patterns, though its capital in Nablus on Mt. Gerizim has been thoroughly investigated and fairly well though incompletely published, we may say confidently that its capital in the Persian period was much larger, more populous, and wealthier than Jerusalem.[22] If this is the case, the intelligentsia and leaders of Jerusalem at that time could hardly have been ignorant of the situation. Despite the tensions and opposition between the two provinces and their leaders during this period reflected in Ezra and Nehemiah (mid-5th century and later) we should not forget the strong ties of cultural continuity that bind them together except in political and administrative matters. And since there were Yahwists living in both centers and there were many similarities between them, we can imagine that in each community there would be sufficient reason to want to more carefully define themselves over against the other. For the Samaritans, their temple would be an imitation of the Jerusalem one on a smaller

---

21. C. E. Carter, *The Emergence of Yehud in the Persian Period: A Social and Demographic Study* (JSOTSup 294; Sheffield: University of Sheffield, 1999), 288.

22. G. N. Knoppers, "Revisiting the Samarian Question in the Persian Period," in *Judah and the Judeans in the Persian Period* (ed. O. Lipschits and M. Oeming; Winona Lake, IN: Eisenbrauns, 2006), 273.

scale (1:10) and completed by the time of Nehemiah.[23] For the Jerusalem elites, well before the time of Nehemiah and probably in the early Persian period and coterminous with the terms of Haggai and First Zechariah, there would have been "good reason for Jerusalem Temple scribes to authenticate the distinctive positions of their city and shrine."[24] But also, I would want to add that there was also good reason to pull their sacred writings together, not just because the Persian authorities would have encouraged it as they did in Egypt under the priestly leadership of Ujjahoresnet and in other locations, but because it was necessary for the renewed leadership and scribal class to articulate for the homeland audience and Jews in the Diaspora the centrality of Torah and God's word in the form of a written code. This sentiment is exquisitely and metaphorically treated in Zechariah's vision of the Flying Scroll (Zech 5:1–4).[25] The flying scroll represents the authority of sacred literature and law in the community and possibly more specifically a collection of legal materials or divine covenant such as had been encouraged by Darius when he asked the leaders in the new territories to collect and utilize their own legal systems. Even the twenty-by-ten dimensions of the scroll reflects the sacred space of the Temple precincts, not to mention even the measurement of a typical Dead Sea Scroll[26] in the traditional rolled scroll (מגלה) format. But just as the changed demographic situation in Yehud would have influenced how the new leadership expressed itself over against the ruling authority of the Persians and cooperated with it, so too did the existence of the thriving Samaritan community serve as an impetus for them to express their own distinctive identity, which in comparison included much more than the Pentatuech. Yehud's open canon—as it were, its openness to new literary expressions that continued to be composed— was one of its most distinctive features, beginning in the tiny postexilic community of elites in the holy city.

Could there have been any other response? We know that the new emphasis on the office of high priest foreshadows the growing role of the priests in the later Second Temple period, and in the Persian period we know the names of most of them.[27] No other governors in this period except Zerubbabel seems to have descended from the house of David, though Elnathan's wife, Shelomit, was apparently a granddaughter of Zerubbabel and may have enjoyed special power. And so the endorsement of diarchy expressed in Haggai and First Zechariah is entirely fitting and suitable to the time and is an expression of practical politics at its best. However, as the Achaemenids began to lose control over the western provinces, especially as the Greco-Persian wars heated up in the 5th century and the local

---

23. Y. Magen, "Mount Gerizim: A Temple City," *Qadmoniot* 33:2 (2000) 74–118. (Hebrew).

24. Knoppers, "Revisiting the Samarian Question," 279.

25. Meyers and Meyers, *Haggai, Zechariah 1–8*, 287–93.

26. Ibid., 282.

27. J. C. Vanderkam, *From Joshua to Caiaphas: High Priests after the Exile* (Minneapolis: Fortress, 2004), 89–90.

provinces began to get restless, the willingness to accept diarchy for the long term weakened and other attitudes toward the state began to take over, as confidence in diarchy receded. This tendency can be seen in Second Zechariah, in whom we can see the birth of apocalyptic and the reemphasis on the Davidic line and heightened desire for the reestablishment of the monarchy.

Second Zechariah

There can hardly be a more visible way in which the two portions of the "Book of Zechariah" are linked intertextually than by looking at the messianic insert in 9:9–10. Second or Deutero–Zechariah begins at v. 1. The chapter stands apart from the rest of the book in that it is pure poetry, parts of which may have existed in an earlier setting. While most of the chapter may be described as a divine warrior hymn, the tone of the messianic passage in vv. 9–10 provides a strong link with First Zechariah and the passages in which a future righteous king figures so prominently (4:7; 6:12–13, etc.). I use the term "insert" advisedly, since the pacifistic and quietistic tone stands out in marked contrast to the rest of the material in Second Zechariah:

> [9] Exult greatly, O daughter Zion! Shout aloud O Daughter Jerusalem!
> Behold, your king is coming to you, righteous and saved is he;
> Humble, riding on an ass—on a young ass, the foul of a she-ass.
> [10] I will cut off the chariot from Ephraim, and the horse from Jerusalem,
> and the bow of war will be cut off,
> He will promise peace to the nations;
> his rule will be from sea to sea, from the river to the ends of the earth.

The resonances with the earlier passages in First Zechariah at 2:10ff., 4:6, and 6:12–13, as well as with Isa 55:3–5 and Ps 72, suggest that the theme of an ideal king-messiah has been replaced by a more spiritualized center from which Yahweh's rule would spread in a peaceful world. The political setting that lies behind such a shift suggests a time when relations with the Persian authority would not have allowed for a more heightened sense of disappointment or confrontational posture vis-à-vis the prevailing situation. In this regard, the attitude expressed in ch. 9 is consonant with that in First Zechariah—that is, one that is at home with the political situation in the restoration period toward the end of the 6th century. I agree with most scholars that Second Zechariah is normally considered to consist of a collection of three discrete units, chs. 9, 10–11, and 12–14, respectively,[28] we may suggest that ch. 9 has been modified by the insertion of these two verses into an older hymn in an attempt to make it more compatible with the earlier material

---

28. C. L. Meyers and E. M. Meyers, *Zechariah 9–14: A New Translation with Introduction and Commentary* (AB 25C; New York: Doubleday, 1993), 35–50.

in Zechariah. The end of v. 8, "for now I am watching with my own eyes," echoes First Zechariah's familiar expression "to lift up my eyes and see," which occurs 18 times, and it may serve as a linking device employed by the editor or redactor. In any case, the tone of the verses stands out from the rest of the material in Second Zechariah, which, when we take into account the political situation of Yehud over against the ruling power, Persia, could only fit into a time when breaking away from Achaemenid oversight and control was unthinkable because of their strong grip on the provinces. This was a time before the Greco-Persian conflict of the next century and before the onset of the satrapal revolts that began to reverberate in the empire around 460 B.C.E.[29]

The strong references to a resurgent Davidic dynasty, albeit relegated to a time in the future and probably to be dated to a time after which there was no Davidic connection at all to the governorship—the only Davidic descendant after Zerubbabel would have been connected to the governorship of Elnathan (510–490?), who is only mentioned in a bulla and seal—are surely to be related to the time when good relations between the Yehud leadership and Persian authorities were beginning to deteriorate (12:7, 8, 10, 12; 13:1).[30]

In many ways, ch. 12 is a statement about failed leadership in Yehud in a similar vein to the way Malachi comments on it, though Malachi is focused more on priestly leadership and its corrupt ways. Despite such failure, Zech 12:10 includes not only the house of David in God's spirit of favor and supplication but also the "rulers of Jerusalem,"[31] when they will be joined by the community in a spirit of repentance that will effect the changes necessary to return to a more stable form of rule both within and without its borders. God will even protect the weak leadership so that it can be like David "who will be like God, like the angel of Yahweh before them" (v. 8). The use of the term "Angel of Yahweh" is the only occurrence in Second Zechariah and echoes both Hag 1:13 and Zech 1:11, 12; 3:1, 5, 6 and anticipates Mal 2:7; 3:1[2]. Thus, while we may identify the general shape of ch. 12 as apocalyptic we may also infer from it that it is also a creative response to a struggle or power vacuum that is close in time to Malachi when the priesthood was corrupted (1:6–2:9), and a time when the governorship was not in Davidic hands. We know only approximately when this could have happened, after Elnathan and before Nehemiah, who is called into to help repair the situation. This brings us to precisely the period toward the end of the first half of the 5th century when

---

29. E. M. Meyers, "Messianism in First and Second Zechariah and the 'End' of Biblical Prophecy," in *Go to the Land I Will Show You: Studies in Honor of Dwight W. Young* (ed. J. Coleson and V. Matthews; Winona Lake, IN: Eisenbrauns, 1996), 127–35.

30. Meyers and Meyers, *Haggai, Zechariah 1–8*, 14.

31. C. L. Meyers and E. M. Meyers, "The Fortunes of the House of David: The Evidence of Second Zechariah," in *Fortunate the Eyes That See: Essays in Honor of David Noel Freedman in Celebration of His Seventieth Birthday* (ed. A. B. Beck et al. Grand Rapids, MI: Eerdmans, 1995), 207–23.

Persia was having its problems maintaining order in the provinces and when the Yehudite leadership became corrupt in its offices, the governorship and the high priesthood. In the Dirge for the Fallen (12:12–13), however, there is a desire to stay with the old diarchic pattern: v. 12 signifying Davidic leadership (Nathan as David's son), v. 13 signifying priestly leadership (Shimei as descendant of Levi). While the overall context of ch. 12 is elusive and we have no idea who the "stabbed one" (v. 10) was, the metaphor offers a compelling and fitting vehicle for understanding the alienation of the people from the leadership of Yehud at this time. In a real sense, the opening to 13:1 provides a most appropriate ending to ch. 12: "On that day there will be an open fountain for the House of David and the rulers of Jerusalem, for [cleansing] sin and impurity." The cleansing water is especially apposite in the matter of priestly corruption.

The diatribe against prophecy in 13:2–5 carries forward the negative assessment of the leadership at this time and thus attributes to certain prophetic elements their complicity in supporting the events that resulted in the crisis alluded to in ch. 12 and that underlies the elevated Davidic language there. The list of particular abuses is familiar: defilement of the cult and idolatry, brought about by priests (Mal 2:8) and prophets (Zech 13:2) as well as by the failed leadership of 12:2–9. With such a small population in Jerusalem and Yehud even at this time, toward the middle of the 5th century, we are hard pressed to come up with a good explanation for the collapse of a system that had worked for more than two generations and that stayed in place for the entire Persian period.[32] We know very well about the crisis not only because of the prophets' observations but also because of the missions of Ezra and Nehemiah, which date to the beginning of the next half of the 5th century. It is possible that the close relationship of the leaders of Yehud to the Persian authorities led to an all-too-cozy relationship between Yehud and Persia that came to be resented in some quarters, as corruption at the highest levels of Yehud became apparent. In such a small environment, it would be very difficult to hide from such matters. But since the diarchy was able to maintain its administrative controls over Yehud throughout this time, the increasing growth of the region as a whole but especially in Samaria, might well have contributed to the kinds of corruption that crept into the system in the 5th century.

With the issue of intermarriage so important in Ezra and Nehemiah, it is difficult to imagine the crisis as limited solely to the tiny province of Yehud, when so much of the Gentile population was located outside it. Whatever the case may be in Yehud, and despite the backsliding indicated above and alluded to in Second Zechariah and Malachi, those responsible for scribal matters in the Jewish community certainly did their job well, as it was about this time that the Book of the Twelve was put together. The conclusion to the book of Malachi (3:22–23), with its praise of Moses and Elijah, is telling. Moses the archetypal prophet is cast in a

---

32. VanderKam, *From Joshua to Caiaphas*, 110–11.

way similar to Ezra the lawgiver, who in a way is a second Moses. The promise of Elijah to return leaves open the promise of messianic hope and the inspiration of prophecy to continue into the future. And the conclusion to Second Zechariah in 14:16–19 features a call to the "family of Egypt" to come and celebrate the Feast of Booths in Jerusalem, a celebration of the Exodus from Egypt, perhaps an invitation of the exiles there to come back to the land and, for certain, an invitation for Egyptians to come and celebrate and bow down to Yahweh.[33] The Feast of Booths is precisely the occasion on which Ezra read the law in the square before the Water Gate (Neh 8:1–3) and proclaimed the Torah as law. With that event falling approximately 70 years after the rededication of the Second Temple, or midway in the Persian period, we may conclude that the internal situation in Yehud at this time had reached its greatest crisis. Moreover, the disappearance of apostolic prophecy at this very moment signals the shift to a more reformist and practical approach in dealing with religious issues, but the fact of the matter was that the diarchy remained the administrative structure dealing with day-to-day life in Yehud, and the governor was the ranking official to deal with political matters at the highest level. Despite the weakening of the Persian empire due to its continuing struggles with Greece and other provinces such as Babylonia, the Persians managed to stay more or less in control of the Levant until Alexander the Great in the next century.[34]

Conclusion

We may now make a number of observations about the prophets Haggai and Zechariah. Although we have identified two books that constitute the canonical book of Zechariah (chs. 1–8 and 9–14, respectively), we are fully aware of recent approaches in biblical studies that are more open to canonical criticism and hence a more synchronic approach.[35] In separating out the two main segments of the book and calling them First and Second Zechariah, we do not intend to ignore the fact that all of the materials within it came to be folded into the 14 chapters of the canonical book of Zechariah. This we believe happened sometime around the middle of the 5th century B.C.E. and before Ezra and Nehemiah. We have pointed out in our presentation above that while there are strong connections between the two parts of Zechariah, some of which are intentional and crafted to offer a more unified look to the book, there are also significant differences in form and content that cannot fit into a common time-frame or social setting. While Haggai's final prophetic utterance in 2:20–23 is as robust and eschatological as it can get, the entire book is nonetheless grounded in a social context that is clearly pre-Temple re-

33. Meyers and Meyers, *Zechariah 9–14*, 474–77 and 504–7.
34. Meyers and Chancey, *Alexander to Constantine*, 7–10.
35. Petterson, *Behold Your King*, 8–11.

building and close in time to First Zechariah, even with a short overlap. No doubt the presence of the Davidide Zerubbabel on the Restoration ticket, along with his priestly counterpart Joshua, gave special prominence to the diarchy; and perhaps the shaky rise to consolidate power by Darius led some to favor the Davidic side of the ticket. The truth of the matter, however, is that the diarchic structure was endorsed with enthusiasm by Haggai, and the final oracle gives it even more strength. The imminence of the future time in Haggai cannot be truly gauged by the modern reader and though it may seem closer in time than First Zechariah, taken as whole chs. 1–8 constitute a rather strong and similar kind of endorsement of diarchy with the rebuilt Temple, its décor, furnishings, and symbolism at its very core. If Haggai seems to overemphasize the role of the future Davidide then First Zechariah puts the unnamed royal descendant into the more pragmatic context of the Return.

Except for ch. 9, Second Zechariah has a more robust royalist tone than First Zechariah or even Haggai. But as we have pointed out above it is not at the expense of the priestly role that must be assumed from both internal and external sources. To be sure, the social circumstance and setting of those who pulled together the words of earlier Zechariah and later Zechariah, perhaps followers of the original prophet or a redactor, is different from the restoration era. The kind of social malaise alluded to in the text of Second Zechariah gives birth to apocalyptic language and theology, and we find no trace of that in the early period. Rather, we find this sort of social situation on the eve of the missions of Ezra and Nehemiah and in the book of Malachi. This follows upon a period in which some of the provinces in the Persian empire were considering rebellion and breaking away from their authority. We believe that it was such a circumstance that contributed to the kind of exaggerated Davidic consciousness that we find in Second Zechariah, albeit tempered by a strong commitment to priestly concerns. It is those kinds of concerns with which the book ends in ch. 14, especially the last two verses, which obliterate the boundaries between the sacred and mundane. Just as the bells on horses will be inscribed with "Holy to Yahweh," so too will all the pots in Judah and Jerusalem also be holy to God and all who use them.[36] All of the territory surrounding the holy city will one day be transformed into sacred space. This hope is not unlike the hope expressed at the conclusion of 8:20–23, in which many peoples and many nations will ultimately come together and recognize the one God. This is a universalistic hope expressed in particularistic terms.

That is what we mean in our title: despite the reality of such a small population in Jerusalem and Yehud, as attested by archaeological survey and excavation, the children of Israel in the Persian period, though divided by great distance from their main population center in Mesopotamia, hindered perhaps in their limited numbers, nonetheless succeeded in retelling their own story in a variety of literary forms, while at the same time expressing their hopes for the future in

---

36. Meyers and Meyers, *Zechariah 9–14*, 507.

new prophetic language. This language recalled the past and infused it with new and compelling imagery that reflected the changing world about them. The hopes for the reestablishment of the monarchy would have to wait till Hasmonean times, but even then there would be no Davidide to lead them. Let us by all means never again underestimate the achievements of the Restoration and the voices that transmitted them to succeeding generations. The postexilic era was not a period in which there was a narrowing focus on legalism and a lessening of the universal thrust of classical prophecy. It was rather a time more akin to an era when there was a refiner's fire burning in Judah for the remnant of Israel who returned, and that remnant was like Joshua, a "brand plucked from the fire" (Zech 3:20). It was they who came through this crucible and they who enabled the Jewish community in the homeland and abroad to renew itself in the face of a Mediterranean world opening to new ideas and new strategies of understanding the past and addressing the future. That world presented itself when Alexander the Great came to Jerusalem, and the small community that greeted him was ready.

Bibliography

Albertz, R. *Israel in Exile: The History and Literature of the Sixth Century*. Atlanta: SBL, 2003.

Brosius, M. *The Persians: An Introduction*. Peoples of the Ancient World. London: Taylor & Francis, 2006.

Carter, C. E. *The Emergence of Yehud in the Persian Period: A Social and Demographic Study*. JSOTSup 294. Sheffield: University of Sheffield, 1999.

_____. "(Re)Defining 'Israel': The Legacy of the Neo-Babylonian and Persian Periods." Pp. 215–40 in *The Wiley Blackwell Companion to Ancient Israel*. Edited by Susan Niditch. Malden, MA: Wiley Blackwell, 2016.

Eskenazi, T. C. "From Exile and Restoration to Exile and Reconstruction." Pp. 78–93 in *Exile and Restoration Revisited: Essays on the Babylonian and Persian Periods in Memory of Peter R. Ackroyd*. Edited by G. N. Knoppers, L. L. Grabbe, and D. Fulton. Library of Second Temple Studies 73. London: T. & T. Clark, 2009.

Finkelstein, I. "Jerusalem in the Persian (and early Hellenisitc) Period and the Wall of Nehemiah." *JSOT* 32 (2008) 501–20.

_____. "The Territorial Extent of Jerusalem and Demography of Yehud/Judea in the Persian and Early Hellenistic Periods." *Revue biblique* 117 (2010) 39–54.

Grabbe, L. L., and G. N. Knoppers. "Introduction." Pp. 1–30 in *Exile and Restoration Revisited: Essays on the Babylonian and Persian Periods in Memory of Peter R. Ackroyd*. Edited by G. N. Knoppers, L. L. Grabbe, and D. Fulton. Library of Second Temple Studies 73. London: T. & T. Clark, 2009.

Hanson, P. *The Dawn of Apocalyptic*. Philadelphia: Fortress, 1975.

King, P. J., and L. E. Stager. *Life in Biblical Israel*. Library of Ancient Israel. Louisville: John Knox/Westminster, 2001.

Knoppers, G. N. "Revisiting the Samarian Question in the Persian Period." Pp. 265–289 in *Judah and the Judeans in the Persian Period*. Edited by O. Lipschits and M. Oeming. Winona Lake, IN: Eisenbrauns, 2006.

Lemaire, A. *The Birth of Monotheism: The Rise and Disappearance of Yahwism*. Washington, DC: Biblical Archaeology Society, 2007.

Lipschits, O. *The Rise and Fall of Jerusalem*. Winona lake, IN: Eisenbrauns, 2005.

Magen, Y. "Mount Gerizim: A Temple City." *Qadmoniot* 33:2 (2000) 74–118. (Hebrew).

Meyers, C. L. and E. M. Meyers. *Haggai, Zechariah 1–8: A New Translation with Introduction and Commentary*. AB 25B. New York: Doubleday, 1987.

_____. *Zechariah 9–14: A New Translation with Introduction and Commentary*. AB 25C. New York: Doubleday, 1993.

_____. "The Fortunes of the House of David: The Evidence of Second Zechariah." Pp. 512–34 in *Fortunate the Eyes That See: Essays in Honor of David Noel Freedman in Celebration of His Seventieth Birthday*. Edited by A. B. Beck et al. Grand Rapids, MI: Eerdmans, 1995.

Meyers, E. M., and M. A. Chancey. *Alexander to Constantine: Archaeology of the Land of the Bible, Volume III*. The Anchor Bible Reference Library. New Haven, CT: Yale University Press, 2012.

Meyers, E. M., with the assistance of Sean Burt. "Exile and Return: From the Babylonian Destruction to the Beginning of Hellenism." Pp. 209–36 in *Ancient Israel; From Abraham to the Roman Destruction of the Temple*. Edited by H. Shanks. Washington, DC: Biblical Archaeology Society, 2011.

_____. "The Babylonian Exile Revisited: Demographics and the Canon of Scripture." Pp. 61–75 in *Judaism in Crisis: Crisis as a Catalyst in Jewish Cultural History*. Edited by A. Lange, K. F. D. Römheld, and M. Weigold. Göttingen: Vandenhoeck & Ruprecht, 2011.

_____. "The Rise of Scripture in a Minimalist Demographic Context. In *Stones, Tablets, and Scrolls: Four Periods of Formation of the Bible*. Edited by Peter Dubovsky et al. Tübingen: Mohr Siebeck, forthcoming.

Pearce, L. E. "New Evidence for Judeans in Babylonia." Pp. 399–412 in *Judah and the Judeans in the Persian Period*. Edited by O. Lipschits and M. Oeming. Winona Lake, IN: Eisenbrauns, 2006.

Petterson, A. R. *Behold Your King: The Hope for the House of David in the Book of Zechariah*. Library of Hebrew Bible Studies/Old Testament Studies 513. London: T. & T. Clark, 2009.

Vanderkam, J. C. *From Joshua to Caiaphas: High Priests after the Exile*. Minneapolis: Fortress, 2004.

Apocalyptic Resistance in the Visions of Daniel

John J. Collins

Yale University

In his account of the lead-up to the Jewish revolt against Rome, Josephus mentions a series of events that led to the disintegration of the social order. These included the activity of the "brigand" chief Eleazar and the counter-measures of the procurator Felix, and especially the actions of the *sicarii*, or dagger-men, who carried out assassinations in Jerusalem. But he continues:

> Besides these there arose another body of villains, with purer hands but more impious intentions, who no less than the assassins ruined the peace of the city. Deceivers and impostors, under the pretence of divine inspiration fostering revolutionary changes, they persuaded the multitude to act like madmen, and led them out into the desert under the belief that God would give them tokens of deliverance. Against them, Felix, regarding them as but the preliminary insurrection, sent a body of cavalry and heavy-armed infantry, and put a large number to the sword. (*JW* 2.259–60).

There was a succession of such sign prophets in the first century C.E.[1] Josephus admits that the movements they led were not violent but were inspired by the hope of miraculous divine intervention. But he blames them nonetheless for disturbing the peace of the city and creating an atmosphere congenial to rebellion. He also claims that the rebels were inspired by an "ambiguous oracle, which was found in the sacred texts, to the effect that at that time one from their country would become ruler of the world" (*JW* 6.312–15). Josephus claims that the figure prophesied was actually Vespasian, who became emperor of Rome while commanding the Roman forces in Judea.[2] We do not know which oracle this was. Possibilities

---

1. R. A. Horsley and J. S. Hanson, *Bandits, Prophets and Messiahs* (Minneapolis: Winston, 1985); J. J. Collins, *The Scepter and the Star: Messianism in Light of the Dead Sea Scrolls* (Grand Rapids, MI: Eerdmans, 2010) 216–9.

2. The oracle is also reported in Suetonius, *Vespasian*, 4.5, and Tacitus, *History*, 5.13.2. See the classic article by E. Norden, "Josephus und Tacitus über Jesus Christus und eine messianische Prophetie," *Neue Jahrbücher für das klassische Altertum* 16 (1913) 637–66.

include Dan 7 (the "one like a son of man") or Balaam's prophecy of the scepter and the star in Num 24:17.[3] Violent action was not the only means of fomenting resistance and rebellion. No less dangerous to the ruling powers was subversive speech that undermined their authority by swaying the minds and hearts of the subject peoples.

In the Hellenistic and Roman eras, the main literary deposits of subversive speech are found in the apocalyptic literature. The best known expressions of this genre are the canonical books of Daniel and Revelation, but an extensive corpus (1 Enoch, 4 Ezra, 2 Baruch, etc.) was not included in the biblical canon. For our present purposes, we will focus on the book of Daniel, which is one of the fountainheads of apocalyptic tradition in Judaism and has the advantage of addressing state power directly. It is also an advantage that we know precisely when the book was completed—shortly before the death of Antiochus Epiphanes in 164 B.C.E., in the throes of the Maccabean revolt. Its statements about temporal sovereignty do not exist in a vacuum but were formulated to address one of the great upheavals in the history of Judea.

The Pre-Maccabean Tales

Not all of Daniel can be considered apocalyptic literature. The first half of the book consists of tales set in the courts of the Babylonian and Persian kings. Most of these stories are in Aramaic, although the introductory chapter is in Hebrew. These stories serve to establish the identity of the figure called Daniel, who is the recipient of revelation in the second half of the book, but they are traditional stories that took shape before the Maccabean era.

Most scholars in the last forty years or so have followed the lead of W. Lee Humphreys and seen these tales as proposing "a lifestyle for the Diaspora."[4] Daniel and his companions succeed and rise to prominence in the service of foreign rulers, who are benign, with only occasional exceptions. They succeed without compromising their fidelity to their God and their traditional observances. Tensions arise, sometimes through the envy and animosity of rival courtiers, sometimes through the folly or vanity of the king. But there is no question of rebellion. Tensions are overcome, and the kings appreciate both the wisdom of Daniel and the power of his God. Eschatological hope for Judean restoration is maintained, most obviously in ch. 2, but it is deferred. In fact, this positive view of Gentile rule

---

3. A. J. Tomasino, "Oracles of Insurrection: The Prophetic Catalyst of the Great Revolt," *JJS* 59 (2008) 86–111, argues that the oracle in question is Dan 9:24–27.

4. W. L. Humphreys, "A Life-Style for the Diaspora: A Study of the Tales of Esther and Daniel," *JBL* 92 (1973) 211–23. See L. M. Wills, *The Jew in the Court of the Foreign King: Ancient Jewish Court Legends* (Minneapolis: Fortress, 1990); J. J. Collins, *Daniel: A Commentary on the Book of Daniel* (Hermeneia; Minneapolis: Fortress, 1993) 38–52. Much of the following discussion is adapted from my article,"Apocalypse and Empire," *Svensk Exegetisk Årsbok* 76 (2011) 1–19.

as temporarily ordained by God is typical of much of the literature from both the eastern and western Diasporas.

In recent years, there has been a reaction against this way of reading the tales in Daniel. Daniel Smith-Christopher emphasizes their potential "as stories of resistance to cultural and spiritual assimilation of a minority by a dominant foreign power."[5] "The perspective of the book of Daniel toward foreign conquerors," writes Smith-Christopher, "even in the first six chapters, is not nearly so benign as is often thought; in fact, it is openly hostile to their authority."[6] Anathea Portier-Young argues that while the stories in Dan 1 and 3 were probably not composed during the Antiochan persecution, they "demonstrate specific modes of non-violent resistance."[7] The view that the tales resist imperial authority is taken to an extreme by Richard Horsley. For Horsley, the tales portray entirely a situation of conflict and are characterized by "ominous anti-imperial pronouncements."[8] In his view, these tales "would surely have prepared Judean intellectuals for potential resistance to measures and institutions intended to cultivate and enforce loyalty to the empire."[9] He declares that the idea that religious fidelity was compatible with the royal service and could lead to advancement is "a modern Western theological interpretation that assumes the separation of religion and politics."[10] But, in fact, these stories typically end with the promotion or validation of Daniel and his companions (2:48–9; 3:30; 6:28). Horsley also denies that they envision the conversion of the gentile king, despite the declaration of Nebuchadnezzar that Daniel's God is "God of gods and Lord of kings," (2:47) and his confession of the sovereignty of the Most High at the end of Dan 4. In these and other cases he misses the nuance of the stories in his eagerness to depict them as expressions of resistance to empire.

This revisionist reading of the tales has some merit, insofar as Daniel and his companions resist complete assimilation and qualify the claim to sovereignty of the Gentile rulers. But the attitude of the Judean exiles to the king is far from open hostility but rather one of client to patron. God is not the only patron of the Judeans in these stories.[11]

---

5. D. Smith-Christopher, "The Book of Daniel," *The New Interpreter's Bible* (Nashville: Abingdon, 1996) 20. See also D. Valeta, *Lions and Ovens and Visions: A Satirical Reading of Daniel 1–6* (Sheffield: Sheffield Phoenix, 2006); S. Kirkpatrick, *Competing for Honor: A Social-Scientific Reading of Daniel 1–6* (Leiden: Brill, 2005); and from outside the world of academic scholarship, D. Berrigan, *Daniel under the Siege of the Divine* (Farmington, PA: Plough, 1998).

6. Smith-Christopher, "The Book of Daniel," 21.

7. A. Portier-Young, *Apocalypse Against Empire: Theologies of Resistance in Early Judaism* (Grand Rapids, MI: Eerdmans, 2010) 262.

8. R. A. Horsley, *Revolt of the Scribes: Resistance and Apocalyptic Origins* (Minneapolis: Fortress, 2010), 34.

9. Ibid., 40.

10. Ibid., 213 n. 16.

11. *Pace* Kirkpatrick, *Competing for Honor*, 145–46. The ambiguity and irony of these stories is emphasized by D. N. Fewell, *Circle of Sovereignty: Plotting Politics in the Book of Daniel* (Nashville: Abingdon, 1991).

A more nuanced reading of these stories is now made possible by postcolonial theory. James C. Scott has popularized the notion of "hidden transcripts" to characterize the ambivalent and ironic attitudes toward those in power on the part of subordinate people.[12] While Daniel and his companions are outwardly deferential—even obsequious—to the pagan kings, the stories reflect subversive attitudes that mock these kings in various ways and predict the ultimate demise of all gentile kingdoms. So, for example, Daniel prefaces his interpretation of Nebuchadnezzar's dream by saying, "My Lord, may the dream be for your enemies, and its interpretation for your adversaries!" (Dan 4:16), although it is quite clear that it applies to the king himself. Equally, the identification of Nebuchadnezzar as the "head of gold" of the statue in his dream is flattering to the monarch, even though Daniel goes on to predict the destruction of the entire statue. The relevance of Scott's work on "hidden transcripts" is noted by Horsley, who nonetheless concludes that Daniel is "a model of 'speaking truth to power,' even under threat of punishment or death."[13] But the idea of "speaking truth to power" brings to mind rather a prophet like Amos, whose transcripts were not hidden at all, and misses the double-speaking, irony, and ambiguity that characterizes "hidden transcripts" in Scott's work. Only in ch. 5, where Daniel berates Belshazzar for failing to learn from the experience of Nebuchadnezzar, does he "speak truth to power" in the manner of the older prophets, and even then the criticism of Belshazzar is paired with approval of his father. Gentile power is not viewed here as inherently or irredeemably evil. It is not as absolute as Gentile rulers believe, but at least some of them can be brought to recognize their dependence on the God of heaven.

Even more illuminating for the tales in Dan 1–6 is the work of Homi Bhabha.[14] In the words of Stephen Moore:

> For Bhabha, colonial discourse is characterized above all by *ambivalence*. It is riddled with contradictions and incoherences, traversed by anxieties and insecurities, and hollowed out by originary lack and internal heterogeneity. For Bhabha, moreover, the locus of colonial power, far from being unambiguously on the side of the colonizer, inheres instead in a shifting, unstable, potentially subversive, 'in-between' or 'third' space between colonizer and colonized, which is characterized by *mimicry*, on the one hand, in which the colonized heeds the colonizer's peremptory injunction to imitation, but in a manner that constantly threatens to teeter over into mockery; and by *hybridity*, on the other hand, another insidious product of the colonial encounter that further threatens to fracture the colonizer's identity and authority.[15]

---

12. J. C. Scott, *Domination and the Arts of Resistance: Hidden Transcripts* (New Haven, CT: Yale University Press, 1990).

13. Horsley, *Revolt of the Scribes*, 45, 213–4.

14. H. K. Bhabha, *The Location of Culture* (London: Routledge, 1994).

15. S. Moore, *Empire and Apocalypse: Postcolonialism and the New Testament* (Sheffield: Sheffield Phoenix, 2006), 90.

While Bhabha is primarily concerned with the identity of the colonizer, his work also has implications for the hybrid identity of the subject people. Daniel's deference to Nebuchadnezzar is not simply a mocking strategy. He is indeed the king's loyal subject, who does his bidding and accepts his honors, even as he resists the pretensions of Babylonian rule. The hybridity of Daniel and his companions is reflected in their double names, Daniel/Belteshazzar, etc.

The mimicry of colonial subjects is evident in the pride of the Judean author in the honors conferred on Daniel by the pagan kings. The kings are ridiculed by exaggerated depictions of their behavior, but their approval is sought nonetheless (except in the case of Belshazzar). Even the way in which the kingdom of God is conceived is indebted to the universal rule of the Babylonians and Persians. But the stories also insist that the Gentile kings need the services of their Jewish courtiers and depend on them to a degree. This is not simple resistance to Gentile rule but a subtle ambivalence and irony that relativizes the power of the kings even while deferring to it for the present.

The main source of friction between the Judean courtiers and their Gentile overlords is their devotion to the God of Israel. The pagan courtiers who resent Daniel admit that that "we shall not find any ground for complaint against this Daniel unless we find it in connection with the law of his God" (Dan 6:5). Accordingly, they induce the king to establish an ordinance that no one should pray to anyone but him, on pain of being thrown into the lion's den. Similarly, in ch. 3, the charge against the Judean courtiers is that "These pay no heed to you, O King. They do not serve your gods and they do not worship the golden statue that you have set up" (Dan 3:12). In each case, the ground for complaint against the Judeans is their worship of their God.

The manner in which worship is singled out shows that the distinction between religion and politics is not a modern anachronism, as Horsley and many others would have it. Daniel is beyond reproach as a servant of the king, unless a charge can be brought that involves the worship of his God. Therein lies his hybridity, as faithful servant both of the pagan king and of the God of Israel. This stance is typical of Diaspora Judaism in the Hellenistic period. The complaint of Apion against the Judeans of Alexandria was that they did not worship the same gods as the Alexandrians.[16] Even in Jerusalem, the revolt against Antiochus Epiphanes was triggered primarily by the king's offensive against the traditional cult.[17] Daniel and his companions have no problem in adopting the language of the empire or, indeed, in seeking promotion and honor in the imperial system. They are only moved to resistance when the worship of their God is called into question.

---

16. Josephus, *Against Apion*, 2.66.

17. J. J. Collins, "Cult and Culture: The Limits of Hellenization in Judea," in *Jewish Cult and Hellenistic Culture: Essays on the Encounter with Hellenism and Roman Rule* (JSJSup 100; Leiden: Brill, 2005) 21–43.

The Visions in Daniel 7–12

The ambivalence toward Gentile rule in the tales provides a foil for the very different attitude displayed in the visions in Dan 7–12. Even though Dan 7 is still in Aramaic, the language of empire does not here bespeak any deference to empire. Rather, the Gentile kingdoms are portrayed as beasts that rise from the turbulent sea. The fourth beast, representing the Hellenistic kingdoms, is the most terrible of all. In this case, there is no ambivalence. The beast must be put to death and thrown into a fire.

The imagery of the beasts from the sea, who are confronted by a figure riding on clouds, is drawn from the traditional combat myth or *Chaoskampf*.[18] This myth is most fully known from the Ugaritic texts a millennium before Daniel was written but is occasionally reflected in allusions to sea monsters in biblical poetry (for example, Rahab in Isa 51:9; Leviathan in Isa 27:1).[19] Daniel adapts the basic opposition of the Sea with its monsters and the rider of the clouds, although the individual beasts are elaborated in novel ways.[20] In the Ugaritic myth, Baal was the rider of the clouds. In the Hebrew Bible, this role was appropriated by Yahweh.[21] In Dan 7, however, the figure on the clouds is subordinate to the white-headed Ancient of Days (corresponding to El in the Ugaritic myth) and is most plausibly identified as Michael, the leader of the heavenly "holy ones."[22] The mythic language implies that the Gentile kingdoms are manifestations of primordial chaos, which must be subdued if the order of the cosmos is to be restored.

The chaotic force reaches its apex in the actions of an upstart horn, which clearly symbolizes Antiochus IV Epiphanes. The vision hints that these kingdoms embody supernatural power, but they provide explicit assurance that it will be overcome by an even greater force, represented by the angelic "holy ones" and the figure on the clouds. In ch. 8, the kingdom of Greece is represented as a goat, and Epiphanes is again a little horn. This little horn is said to launch an assault on the host of heaven and to cast some of the stars to the ground and trample on them. There is an allusion here to the myth of Helal ben Shachar, Lucifer the son of

---

18. J. J. Collins, *Daniel*, 274–324; idem, "Stirring up the Great Sea: The Religio-Historical Background of Daniel 7," in *Seers, Sibyls, and Sages in Hellenistic-Roman Judaism* (JSJSup 54; Leiden: Brill, 1997) 139–55.

19. See J. Day, *God's Conflict with the Dragon and the Sea: Echoes of a Canaanite Myth in the Old Testament* (University of Cambridge Oriental Publications 35; Cambridge: Cambridge University Press, 1985).

20. See B. H. Reynolds III, *Between Symbolism and Realism: The Use of Symbolic and Non-Symbolic Language in Ancient Jewish Apocalypses 333–63 B.C.E.* (Journal of Ancient Judaism Supplements 8; Göttingen: Vandenhoeck & Ruprecht, 2011) 120–30; U. Staub, "Das Tier mit den Hörnern: Ein Beitrag zu Dan 7,7 f.," in *Hellenismus und Judentum: Vier Studien zur Religionsnot unter Antiochus IV* (ed. O. Keel and U. Staub; OBO 178; Göttingen: Vandenhoeck & Ruprecht, 2000) 37–85.

21. J. A. Emerton, "The Origin of the Son of Man Imagery," *JTS* 9 (1958) 225–42.

22. Collins, *Daniel*, 305–10; Reynolds, *Between Symbolism and Realism*, 130–9.

Dawn, who tried to raise his throne above the stars of El but was cast down to the Netherworld.[23] Again, the Gentile king is an entirely negative figure who cannot be redeemed but only destroyed.

There is no doubt that these visions refer to the actions of Antiochus Epiphanes in Jerusalem in 168–167 B.C.E. Daniel 7 expresses outrage that the king would try to change "the times and the law," referring to the disruption of the cultic calendar and the traditional festivals. Daniel 8 focuses on his actions in the temple, the suspension of the daily sacrifices and the installation of "the abomination that makes desolate," which was probably a Syrian altar.[24] But Daniel does not describe these events in plain prose. The visions of chs. 7 and 8 are presented in symbolic language, often described as "baroque," and often a source of confusion to modern readers unfamiliar with the ancient myths from which the symbols are drawn.[25] These visions are supplemented by a long revelation in the form of an angelic discourse in chs. 10–12. In this case, there is no symbolic vision, and the revelation has even been dubbed a "non-symbolic apocalypse."[26] Yet, even here the historical references are veiled, if only slightly, by an enigmatic discourse that refers to "the king of the north" and "the king of the south," instead of direct mention of the Seleucids and Ptolemies. Also, human history is still set against the background of conflicts on the heavenly level.

The introduction to this revelation by the angel Gabriel, in Dan 10:12–14, 20–21, reveals much about the worldview of the book. Rather than speak directly about human conflicts, between Judeans and Persians or Judeans and Greeks, Gabriel tells how he has been opposed by the (angelic) "prince of Persia," and how "when I am through with him the prince of Greece will come." The empirical conflict in Jerusalem is only a reflection of a struggle going on in heaven between the angelic "princes" or patron deities of the nations. On this level, Israel is represented by the archangel Michael, aided by Gabriel. Here again, the impious king tries to storm heaven: "He shall exalt himself and consider himself greater than any god, and shall speak horrendous things against the God of gods" (Dan 11:36).[27] At the end, Michael arises in victory, corresponding to the advent of the "one like a son of man" on the clouds in Dan 7. The point of the revelation is that it discloses a view of reality different from what is commonly assumed. As Jin Hee Han recently put it, the apocalyptic vision facilitates "an alternative experience of reality."[28] This is

---

23. Collins, *Daniel*, 332; Reynolds, *Between Symbolism and Realism*, 153–55.

24. Collins, *Daniel*, 333–34.

25. Compare A. Santoso, *Die Apokalyptik als jüdische Denkbewegung: Eine literarkritische Untersuchung zum Buch Daniel* (Marburg: Tectum, 2007) 1: "stösst man auf viele Darstellungen, die sehr seltsam oder geheimnisvoll sind."

26. Reynolds, *Between Symbolism and Realism*, 225–62.

27. R. J. Clifford, "History and Myth in Daniel 10–12," *BASOR* 220 (1975) 23–26.

28. J. H. Han, *Daniel's Spiel. Apocalyptic Literacy in the Book of Daniel* (Lanham, MD: University Press of America, 2008) 29. Han emphasizes the importance of apocalyptic language in constructing an alternative view of reality.

equally true of the symbolic visions in chs. 7 and 8, where the alternative reality is evoked by allusions to the ancient myths but also by the vision of the divine court and the angelic host.

In the last section of the book, the heroes in time of persecution are described as "the people who know their God," who stand firm and take action. Despite occasional suggestions to the contrary, there is little reason to find here a reference to military action.[29] The only explicit indication of their activity is that they 'give understanding to the many' (ישׂכילו לרבים); they themselves are characterized as משׂכילים 'wise', a term that recalls the characterization of Daniel and his companions at the beginning of the book as ומשׂכילים בכל חכמה 'versed in all wisdom' (Dan 1:4). The nature of their instruction is not specified, but there can be little doubt that it is typified by the revelations in the book of Daniel itself.

Horsley claims that the משׂכילים were scribes who "had devoted their lives to learning Mosaic covenantal Torah."[30] The fact that they are contrasted with those who betray the covenant (מרשׁיעי ברית) in Dan 11:32 gives some substance to the view that they are teachers of covenantal lore, but this does not necessarily mean that they were expounding Deuteronomy. As Carol Newsom has pointed out:

> In second century Judaism terms such as "torah," "Israel," "covenant," "righteousness," "what is good in his eyes," and many others were precisely the sort of terms that became ideological signs. But as each group used those terms they did so with a different "accentuation." "Torah" has a different flavor in the Maccabean slogan than it does when the Qumran community speaks of "those who do torah." . . . Simply put, every ideological sign is the site of intersecting accents. It is "socially multiaccentual."[31]

In fact, Torah is mentioned in the Book of Daniel only in the prayer in ch. 9, which is most probably secondary, and the book shows little if any interest in halakhic matters.[32]

It is now generally agreed that the authors of Daniel, and of the other apocalypses, were scribes, who were learned in some way.[33] They were not marginal

---

29. See the thorough analysis of the terminology by Portier-Young, *Apocalypse against Empire*, 235–42.

30. So Horsley, *Revolt of the Scribes*, 31.

31. C. A. Newsom, *The Self as Symbolic Space: Constructing Identity and Community at Qumran* (STDJ 52; Leiden: Brill, 2004) 10–11. A. van der Kooij is perhaps too restrictive when he argues that "covenant" in Daniel is only concerned with the cult. See "The Concept of Covenant (*Berît*) in the Book of Daniel," in *The Book of Daniel in the Light of New Findings* (ed. A. S. van der Woude; BETL 106; Leuven: Peeters, 1993) 495–501.

32. Compare Newsom, *The Self as Symbolic Space*, 42, 47; Portier-Young, *Apocalypse against Empire*, 244.

33. See, for example, P. R. Davies, "The Scribal School of Daniel," in *The Book of Daniel: Composition and Reception* (ed. J. J. Collins and P. W. Flint; VTSup 83; Leiden: Brill, 2001) 1.247–65.

in their society; they belonged to the small literate elite. If they adopt a stance of marginality, they do so deliberately, in relation to the regnant empire. In the words of Carol Newsom, they "elect a stance of marginality and seek to use that marginal status to find a place in the cultural conversation."[34] We get some sense of the range of interests of scribes in early 2nd-century B.C.E. Jerusalem from Ben Sira ch. 39, which describes how the scribe "seeks out the wisdom of all the ancients," in all its forms, and even "travels in foreign lands" to learn what is good and what is evil.[35] It would be ridiculous, however, to suppose that all scribes necessarily had the same interests as Ben Sira or indeed that all had the same social location. While we have a good idea how Ben Sira made his living, as a retainer for the ruling priestly class in Jerusalem, we have no reliable evidence of the daily occupation of the משכילים. They were evidently interested in myths and prophecies. While they were certainly familiar with the materials we know as biblical, they were not primarily interpreters of Torah. Rather, they were creative visionaries, who were engaged in constructing a symbolic universe that posed an alternative not only to the Seleucid empire but also to some of the more mundane forms of Judaism, including the practical militancy of the Maccabees.

Perhaps the most striking instance of the contrast between the symbolic universe of Daniel and that of traditional Judaism is the ultimate goal of the משכילים. At the end of the crisis, when the archangel Michael arises in victory, "many of those who sleep in the dust of the earth will awake, some to everlasting life and some to shame and everlasting contempt" (Dan 12:2). The משכילים, however, will shine with the brightness of the sky and will be like the stars forever and ever. This is not mere metaphor. The stars were the heavenly host, and the significance of the imagery is made clear in near-contemporary *Epistle of Enoch*, which promises the righteous that "you will shine like the lights of heaven, and will be seen, and the gate of heaven will be opened to you . . . for you will be associates of the host of heaven."[36] The ultimate goal of life, then was not to live long in the land and see one's children's children, as it had been for traditional Judaism, but fellowship with the angels in eternal life.

Horsley denies that the belief in resurrection constitutes a basic shift in worldview.[37] He dismisses the idea of resurrection as "vague and elusive."[38] But, here again, he shows his failure to grasp the logic of Daniel in his zeal to reduce

---

34. Newsom, *The Self as Symbolic Space*, 48. Newsom adds that her claim is about the rhetoric of the apocalyptic writers, not necessarily their social status.

35. R. A. Horsley describes this as "the full repertoire of Judean culture" in *Scribes, Visionaries, and the Politics of Second Temple Judea* (Louisville: Westminster John Knox, 2007) 12.

36. 1 Enoch 104: 2,6. See G. W. E. Nickelsburg, *Resurrection, Immortality, and Eternal Life in Intertestamental Judaism and Early Christianity* (HTS 56; Cambridge, MA: Harvard University Press, 2006) 152.

37. Horsley, *Scribes, Visionaries*, 199.

38. Ibid., 250 n. 54.

everything to political and economic terms. For it is precisely the hope of resurrection and exaltation that makes it possible for the מַשְׂכִּילִים to lay down their
lives rather than submit to the demands of the king.[39] In the traditional Mosaic
covenant, those who kept the law were supposed to prosper and enjoy life in this
world. The persecution of Antiochus Epiphanes created cognitive dissonance in
this regard, because now those who were faithful to law and tradition were the
ones who lost their lives. This dissonance was relieved by the prospect of reward,
or punishment, after death. The hope of resurrection did not mean a complete
break with the past. Daniel also hoped that "the people of the holy ones of the Most
High" would enjoy "the greatness of the kingdoms under the whole heaven" (Dan
7:27)—a hope that was itself shaped by colonial mimicry. But the hope for fellowship with the angels bespoke a new set of values that did not require long life in the
land and was not concerned only with material reality.

It remains true that Daniel is fundamentally resistance literature—the articulation of a stance of refusal toward the demands of the Seleucid empire. To say
only that much, however, fails to distinguish between the stance of the visions and
that of the tales, which as we have seen was much more nuanced and ambivalent,
and also between the stance of Daniel and that of the Maccabees, who are characterized as at most "a little help" in Dan 11:34. It fails to appreciate the modality
of Daniel's resistance, which is primarily a matter of vision, of seeing the world in
a different way.[40] The prophets of old had mainly relied on direct exhortation to
convey their message. Daniel does not engage in direct exhortation at all. Rather,
the focus is on understanding the vision. Right action will presumably follow from
right understanding.[41] But the overthrow of empires is not to be accomplished by
human means, and Daniel is not a call to militancy. Rather, it is a call to understanding and endurance in expectation of divine deliverance. This is also true,
explicitly, of the New Testament book of Revelation, which is patently dependent
on Daniel for much of its imagery.[42]

---

39. See J. J. Collins, "Apocalyptic Eschatology as the Transcendence of Death," *CBQ* 36
(1974) 21–43; reprinted in idem, *Seers, Sibyls, and Sages in Hellenistic-Roman Judaism* (JSJSup
54; Leiden: Brill, 1997) 75–97.

40. Compare S. Beyerle, "Daniel and Its Social Setting," in *The Book of Daniel: Composition
and Reception* (ed. J. J. Collins and P. W. Flint, VTSup 83; Leiden: Brill, 2001) 1.221: "the transcendent character of Dan 12:1–3 only comes to light in the context of a vision-like reality that
discloses a heavenly salvation."

41. In this sense, Daniel represents a kind of wisdom, as von Rad famously argued
(G. von Rad, *Theologie des Alten Testaments* [Munich: Kaiser, 1965] 2.315–30). Reynolds, *Between Symbolism and Realism*, 157–58, also questions the affinity of Daniel with prophecy but
aligns it instead with dream interpretation and divination.

42. Rev 13:10: "if you are to be taken captive, into captivity you go; if you kill with the
sword, with the sword you must be killed." See A. Y. Collins, "The Political Perspective of the
Revelation to John," in *Cosmology and Eschatology in Jewish and Christian Apocalypticism*
(JSJSup 50; Leiden: Brill, 1996) 198–217.

The contrast between Daniel and the Maccabees calls for some qualification of the revolutionary character of apocalyptic literature. One could very well argue that it is counterrevolutionary in many cases. By enabling people to let off steam by fantasizing divine vengeance, it relieves the pressure toward action and enables people to accommodate themselves to the status quo for the present. Action is deferred, in the hope of divine intervention, which all too often fails to materialize. It was, after all, the militant action of the Maccabees that liberated Jerusalem, not, insofar as we can tell, the intervention of the archangel Michael.

Nonetheless, the subversive power of this literature should not be underestimated, as Josephus recognized in the case of the visionaries and prophets on the eve of the Jewish revolt. If people say that the kingdom of the Seleucids (or Rome, or whatever the reigning power happens to be) is doomed to destruction, this undermines the fear and awe on which such states rely for their authority.[43] Moreover, the vision of an alternative universe enables people to dissent from a culture that they find oppressive or otherwise unacceptable, when they lack the practical means to change it. In this case, it is true, the Maccabees showed that they did have the power to change things by human action, but this was seldom the case in history of Judaism. The Zealots of the first century c.e. followed the example of the Maccabees, as did Bar Kokba some decades later, but the results were catastrophic. The kind of resistance envisioned in Daniel did not lend support to violent revolution, but it shaped minds and preserved values, and its long-term effectiveness should not be underestimated. The potential for resistance is increased in the apocalyptic literature, which imagines an alternative universe more fully than do the late prophetic texts and holds forth the prospect of life in another world after death.

Conclusion

Opposition to imperial rule is certainly a factor in the great majority of apocalypses, but to define the central focus of these works simply as "opposition to empire" is simplistic and misses the nuances of the mode of resistance that is characteristic of the genre. These texts are not generally a call to militant uprising, such as we find in 1 Maccabees. Rather, they are concerned with vision and understanding. In the words of Portier-Young, "apocalyptic faith maintained that what could be seen on the surface told only part of the story."[44] Precisely the part of the story that was not seen on the surface was most important. Moreover, while the apocalyptic writers sought relief and deliverance from state terror and economic

---

43. See J. J. Collins, "Temporality and Politics in Jewish Apocalyptic Literature," in *Apocalyptic in History and Tradition* (ed. C. Rowland and J. Barton; JSPSup 43; Sheffield: Sheffield Academic Press, 2002) 26–43. On the techniques of domination, see Portier-Young, *Apocalypse Against Empire*, 23–24, and on Seleucid domination in Judea, ibid., 49–216.

44. Portier-Young, *Apocalypse against Empire*, 389.

exploitation, they were often even more concerned with defilement and right worship. The solution they sought might include a restored earth but also looked for life beyond this world in the company of angels. Rightly or not, they did not see the world in Marxist terms. In their view of the world, human welfare was inextricably bound up with right worship, and this took precedence over material concerns, although the latter were by no means negligible.

A simplistic reading of these texts as exclusively concerned with "resistance to empire" also obliterates generic distinctions that are essential for nuanced interpretation. The apocalypses differ from earlier prophetic texts in the manifest shift in mode of presentation, from proclamation of the word of the Lord in prophetic oracles to description of veiled realities in the apocalypses. Most fundamentally, they differ from earlier Jewish tradition in the belief in resurrection and the new value placed on individual salvation. This had only exceptional precedents in the biblical world, in figures such as Enoch and Elijah. This belief was the underpinning of a new form of resistance, that of the martyrs, which would henceforth play a prominent role in both Jewish and Christian resistance to imperial demands. In Daniel, and in all the apocalypses, there is an appeal to a further, higher revelation, as the "the spring of understanding, and the river of knowledge," in the words of 4 Ezra. It is the "alternative universe" disclosed in these higher revelations that provides the ultimate grounding for resistance to all earthly empires in the apocalyptic literature. It remains true that the apocalypses are concerned with resistance to imperial oppression, but their resistance was grounded in a view of the world that diverged from the traditional covenantal Judaism and was not shared by all Judeans in the Hellenistic and Roman periods.

Bibliography

Berrigan, D. *Daniel Under the Siege of the Divine*. Farmington, PA: Plough, 1998.

Beyerle, S. "Daniel and Its Social Setting." Pp. 206–28 in *The Book of Daniel: Composition and Reception*. Edited by J. J. Collins and P. W. Flint. VTSup 83. Leiden: Brill, 2001.

Bhabha, H. K. *The Location of Culture*. London: Routledge, 1994.

Clifford, R. J. "History and Myth in Daniel 10–12." *BASOR* 220 (1975) 23–26.

Collins, A. Y. "The Political Perspective of the Revelation to John." Pp. 198–217 in *Cosmology and Eschatology in Jewish and Christian Apocalypticism*. JSJSup 50; Leiden: Brill, 1996.

Collins, J. J. "Apocalyptic Eschatology as the Transcendence of Death." *CBQ* 36 (1974) 21–43, reprinted, pp. 75–97 in *Seers, Sibyls and Sages in Hellenistic-Roman Judaism*. JSJSup 54. Leiden: Brill, 1997.

_____ . *The Scepter and the Star: Messianism in Light of the Dead Sea Scrolls*. Grand Rapids, MI: Eerdmans, 2010.

_____ . *Daniel: A Commentary on the Book of Daniel*. Hermeneia. Minneapolis: Fortress, 1993.

_____. "Stirring up the Great Sea: The Religio-Historical Background of Daniel 7." Pp. 139–55 in *Seers, Sibyls, and Sages in Hellenistic-Roman Judaism*. JSJSup 54. Leiden: Brill, 1997.

_____. "Temporality and Politics in Jewish Apocalyptic Literature." Pp. 26–43 in *Apocalyptic in History and Tradition*. Edited by C. Rowland and J. Barton. JSPSup 43. Sheffield: Sheffield Academic Press, 2002.

_____. "Cult and Culture: The Limits of Hellenization in Judea." Pp. 21–43 in *Jewish Cult and Hellenistic Culture: Essays on the Encounter with Hellenism and Roman Rule*. JSJSup 100. Leiden: Brill, 2005.

_____. "Apocalypse and Empire," *Svensk Exegetisk Årsbok* 76 (2011) 1–19.

Davies, P. R. "The Scribal School of Daniel." Pp. 247–65 in vol. 1 of *The Book of Daniel: Composition and Reception*. Edited by J. J. Collins and P. W. Flint. VTSup 83. Leiden: Brill, 2001.

Day, J. *God's Conflict with the Dragon and the Sea: Echoes of a Canaanite Myth in the Old Testament*. University of Cambridge Oriental Publications 35. Cambridge: Cambridge University Press, 1985.

Emerton, J. A. "The Origin of the Son of Man Imagery." *JTS* 9 (1958) 225–42.

Fewell, D. N. *Circle of Sovereignty: Plotting Politics in the Book of Daniel*. Nashville: Abingdon, 1991.

Han, J. H. *Daniel's Spiel: Apocalyptic Literacy in the Book of Daniel*. Lanham, MD: University Press of America, 2008.

Horsley, R. *Scribes, Visionaries, and the Politics of Second Temple Judea*. Louisville: Westminster John Knox, 2007.

_____. *Revolt of the Scribes: Resistance and Apocalyptic Origins*. Minneapolis: Fortress, 2010.

_____, and J. S. Hanson. *Bandits, Prophets and Messiahs*. Minneapolis: Winston, 1985.

Humphreys, W. L. "A Life-Style for the Diaspora: A Study of the Tales of Esther and Daniel." *JBL* 92 (1973) 211–23.

Kirkpatrick, S. *Competing for Honor: A Social-Scientific Reading of Daniel 1–6*. Leiden: Brill, 2005.

Kooij, A. van der. "The Concept of Covenant (*Berît*) in the Book of Daniel." Pp. 495–501 in *The Book of Daniel in the Light of New Findings*. Edited by A. S. van der Woude. BETL 106. Leuven: Peeters, 1993.

Moore, S. *Empire and Apocalypse: Postcolonialism and the New Testament*. Sheffield: Sheffield Phoenix, 2006.

Newsom, C. A. *The Self as Symbolic Space: Constructing Identity and Community at Qumran*. STDJ 52. Leiden: Brill, 2004.

Nickelsburg, G. W. E. *Resurrection, Immortality, and Eternal Life in Intertestamental Judaism and Early Christianity*. HTS 56. Cambridge, MA: Harvard University Press, 2006.

Norden, E. "Josephus und Tacitus über Jesus Christus und eine messianische Prophetie." *Neue Jahrbücher für das klassische Altertum* 16 (1913) 637–66.

Portier-Young, A. *Apocalypse Against Empire: Theologies of Resistance in Early Judaism*. Grand Rapids, MI: Eerdmans, 2010.

Rad, G. von. *Theologie des Alten Testaments*. Munich: Kaiser, 1965.

Reynolds III, B. H. *Between Symbolism and Realism: The Use of Symbolic and Non-Symbolic Language in Ancient Jewish Apocalypses 333–63 B.C.E.* Journal of Ancient Judaism Supplements 8. Göttingen: Vandenhoeck & Ruprecht, 2011.

Santoso, A. *Die Apokalyptik als jüdische Denkbewegung. Eine literarkritische Untersuchung zum Buch Daniel.* Marburg: Tectum, 2007.

Scott, J. C. *Domination and the Arts of Resistance: Hidden Transcripts.* New Haven, CT: Yale University Press, 1990.

Smith-Christopher, D. "The Book of Daniel." Pp. **17–194** in vol. 7 of *The New Interpreter's Bible.* Nashville, TN: Abingdon, 1996.

Staub, U. "Das Tier mit den Hörnern. Ein Beitrag zu Dan 7,7 f." Pp. 37–85 in *Hellenismus und Judentum: Vier Studien zur Religionsnot unter Antiochus IV.* Edited by O. Keel and U. Staub. OBO 178. Göttingen: Vandenhoeck & Ruprecht, 2000.

Tomasino, A. J. "Oracles of Insurrection: The Prophetic Catalyst of the Great Revolt." *JJS* 59 (2008) 86–111.

Valeta, D. *Lions and Ovens and Visions: A Satirical Reading of Daniel 1–6.* Sheffield: Sheffield Phoenix, 2006.

Wills, L. M. *The Jew in the Court of the Foreign King: Ancient Jewish Court Legends.* Minneapolis: Fortress, 1990.

References to the Prophets in the Old Testament Apocrypha

ROBERT J. OWENS

The General Theological Seminary

The following discussion carries out an assignment to survey references to the Israelite prophets in the group of writings that are considered canonical or of special status by Christian churches but excluded from the rabbinic Hebrew Bible. I have examined the following: Tobit, Judith, Wisdom of Solomon, Wisdom of Jesus Ben Sirach, Baruch, Letter of Jeremiah, 1 Maccabees, 2 Maccabees, Additions to Esther, Additions to Daniel, 1 Esdras, 2 Esdras, Psalm 151, Prayer of Manasseh, 3 Maccabees, and 4 Maccabees. This list includes all the books considered "deuterocanonical" or regularly included in the Bible manuscripts of Roman Catholic and most Eastern Orthodox churches.[1] When any of these writings is missing from the discussion below, it is simply because it contained no references to prophets.

The task has been to look at explicit references to the canonical prophets as persons. The following persons, named as prophets in the Hebrew Bible, were sought: Ahijah, Amos, Azariah, Balaam, Eliezer, Elijah, Elisha, Ezekiel, Gad, Habakkuk, Haggai, Hanani, Hosea, Iddo (Joed), Isaiah, Jeremiah, Joel, Jonah, Malachi, Micah, Micaiah, Nahum, Nathan, Obadiah, Oded, Samuel, Shemaiah, Uriah, Zechariah, Zephaniah. Except where they are explicitly mentioned as prophets, references to Abraham, Moses, Miriam, Joshua, and Daniel are not included.[2] This study makes no attempt to examine all the quotations and allusions in the Apocrypha to passages in the fifteen canonical prophetic books ("Latter Prophets"), which would be an impossibly huge project.

---

1. These are also the works included in the New Revised Standard Version (2001). A reliable introduction to most of these books is available in D. A. DeSilva and J. H. Charlesworth, *Introducing the Apocrypha: Message, Context, and Significance* (Grand Rapids, MI: Baker, 2002). See also M. E. Stone, ed., *Jewish Writings of the Second Temple Period* (CRINT 2.2; Assen: Van Gorcum, 1984).

2. Rabbinic tradition created an expanded category of prophet to include 48 males, 7 females, and 7 Gentiles.

Tobit
(3rd Century B.C.E.)

The Book of Tobit makes only one explicit reference to a canonical prophet, in 2:6. At this point in the story, Tobit interrupts his feasting on the occasion of Pentecost (Weeks) in order to tend to the body of a fellow Jew who has been found murdered. The sorrow he feels at this death and its circumstances prompts him to see his situation as corresponding to that of the prophet Amos: "Then I remembered the prophecy of Amos, how he said against Bethel, 'Your festivals shall be turned into mourning, and all your celebrations into lamentation'" (Amos 8:10). This is a close citation of the LXX text, which, like the MT, has the verb in active mood, with God as the first-person subject: "I will turn your festivals into mourning, and all your celebrations into lamentation." Also, in MS S (probably the older Greek text), the Tobit author changes the noun in the second line from ῳδαι 'songs' (so the LXX and MT) to ευφροσυναι 'celebrations'.[3] This could be a conscious paraphrase to shape the quotation more exactly to the context. Tobit's religious observance so far has been described as a festival, with feasting, but singing has not been mentioned.

Perhaps the Amos text is cited to prevent criticism of Tobit for interrupting his celebration of Weeks or to show the extent of his piety in that even a great festival would not deter him from concern for his fellow.[4] In any case, the author makes it plain that the Amos utterance was a prediction of future punishment for the citizens of ancient Israel.[5] He does not derive any sort of theological warrant from the verse; Tobit simply finds that these ancient words now fit his own current situation. The personal movements of the prophet Amos are of no significance; the prophet is remembered simply as the source of this verse.

Tobit 14:4 possibly refers to the prophet Nahum (MS S) or to the prophet Jonah (MSS A, B, and the Syro-Hexapla): ". . . because I believe the word of God about Nineveh, which He spoke to Nahum/Jonah." This sentence is part of Tobit's warning to his son to leave Nineveh in order to escape the coming destruction in Assyria and Babylonia, which he believes will come about because it was predicted by the prophet. The Old Latin, Vulgate, and Peshitta lack a prophet's name altogether.[6] If a proper name was in the original text, Nahum may be the more likely reading, simply because of that book's lengthy, unconditional predictions of Nineveh's destruction and because the Jonah narrative included the pardon of Nineveh. On the other hand, Jonah 3:4 did also predict Nineveh's imminent de-

---

3. Unlike the NRSV ("your festivals . . . and all your songs"), the RSV translation follows MS S here: "your feasts . . . and all your festivities."

4. J. A. Fitzmyer, *Tobit* (CEJL; Berlin: de Gruyter, 2003) 135.

5. Tobit identifies the addressees as "Bethel," which is the last place-name that occurs in the book of Amos (at 7:13) prior to 8:10.

6. 4Q198, an Aramaic fragment of Tob 14:4, may also lack a proper name.

struction. Jonah, like Tobit, was an Israelite rather than Judahite, and his date in the mid-700s B.C.E. (see 2 Kgs 14:25) would have made him knowable by the Tobit within the fictional setting of the story, whereas the 6th-century Nahum would not have been. Jonah was more popular generally that Nahum, and familiarity with the text of Jonah may be reflected at Tob 3:6, where Tobit's repeated death-wish closely echoes that of Jonah 4:3 and 8 ("For it is better for me to die than to live"). However, death requests by Elijah and Job are also similar (see 1 Kgs 19:4 and Job 7:15).

It actually seems likely that the text originally lacked an individual prophet's name, reading simply, "because I believe the word of God about Nineveh." Scribal desire to add a specific prophet's name would have been only encouraged by the following sentence: "Indeed, everything that was spoken by the prophets of Israel, whom God sent, will occur." Again here, no detail of the prophet's activity is of interest apart from his being an inspired source of this prediction of destruction.

Regardless of the textual history of 14:4, this lengthy verse accurately recalls that some canonical prophets predicted the eventual destruction of Assyria (and Babylonia). In addition to Jonah and Nahum, Tobit could have in mind here such oracles as Isa 10:5–19, 14:24–27, 30:29–33, 31:8–9, Mic 5:5–6, Zeph 2:13–15, and Zech 10:11. Tobit blends his anticipation of the downfall of Assyria with his expectation of further destruction of the covenant people, this time Judah and Jerusalem and its Temple. Speaking in a rather apocalyptic style, he also expects that the exiles will ultimately be restored to the land of Israel, with an imperfect reconstruction of the Temple, a conversion to God of Gentiles around the world, and a mass immigration to Jerusalem. These themes, of course, are found in several canonical prophets, especially Isaiah and Jeremiah, and Tobit's language here does not seem to intend citation of specific passages.

Judith
(1st century B.C.E.?)

The Book of Judith makes no meaningful reference to any prophet. The names of two canonical prophets occur within brief genealogical references, but it is impossible to say whether it is those prophets that are actually intended by the writer or other later persons with the same name. In 8:1, Judith's paternal ancestor eight generations back is Ηλιου υιου Χελκιου , which can be either "Elijah" or "Elihu" son of Hilkiah. If this forebear is the prophet Elijah (whose father is never mentioned in the Kings narratives), the narrative makes nothing of it. In 6:15, one of the Israelite magistrates is "Uzziah son of Micah of the tribe of Simeon." The 8th-century prophet Micah of Moresheth was of course of the tribe of Judah, not Simeon. But the historical confusion that permeates the Book of Judith discourages any identifications based on historical probability.

Wisdom of Solomon
(late 1st century B.C.E.)

This book lacks any reference to a named prophet. In 11:1, within a passage that contrasts the success of ancient Israel, guided by divine wisdom, to the failure of godless Egypt, there is an allusion to Moses as a προφήτης: "[Wisdom] prospered their works by the hand of a holy prophet." No specific prophetic function is in view; the title "prophet" simply connotes Moses' unique closeness to God and his divine inspiration, which produced both extraordinary acts and teachings.[7] There is also one reference to biblical prophets generally (7:27), where the author, extolling the marvelous works of divine wisdom throughout history, observes that "in every generation she passes into holy souls and makes them friends of God and prophets. . . ." Here, too, the emphasis is on wisdom, not prophecy. "Prophets" and "friends of God" seem to denote the same group. The latter phrase derives from references to Abraham as God's friend in 2 Chr 20:7 and Isa 41:8.

Otherwise, canonical prophecy is reflected in Wisdom merely in the form of echoes of passages from a few of the canonical prophetic books. There are no direct quotations, and none of these refers to the personal activities of the biblical prophets. Instead, they are read as source texts for broad religious themes, largely eschatological in nature.

The Wisdom of Jesus Ben Sirach
(ca. 185 B.C.E.)

Ben Sirach clearly was acquainted with a collection of sacred scripture that, at least in the first two sections, the Law and the Prophets, was identical to the rabbinic Hebrew Bible. Notwithstanding his special devotion to the Law, the prophets were quite important to him. He refers by name to Samuel, Nathan, Elijah, Elisha, Isaiah, Jeremiah, Ezekiel, and the Twelve, taking them up in the order they occur within the Hebrew Bible.

For Ben Sirach, the biblical prophets were predictors of the distant future. His extended prayer at 36:1–22 includes the request that the ancient prophecies of salvation for Israel will soon come to pass: "establish the visions spoken in your name.[8] Reward those who wait for you and let your prophets be found trustworthy" (36:20–21).

---

7. The title נביא 'prophet' for Abraham, Moses, Aaron, and Miriam does not occur in the Yahwist, only in the later Elohist and Deuteronomic material (see Deut 34:10). This appellation surely is later, reflecting the prophetism of the monarchical period. The general intimacy with God of these four spiritual heroes, manifesting itself especially in special power to lead, teach, and intercede, was sufficient basis for the label "prophet." J. Blenkinsopp (*A History of Prophecy in Israel* [rev. ed.; Louisville: Westminster John Knox, 1996] 48–55) is doubtless correct that no reliable data about premonarchic Israelite prophetism is to be found in material about these four individuals.

8. The LXX appropriately paraphrases Hebrew חזון 'vision' with προφητειας 'prophecies'.

All other references to prophets occur within the long section, 44:1–50:24, aptly titled in the LXX "Hymn in Honor of Our Ancestors."[9] He reveres Abraham, Moses, and Aaron (Miriam is not mentioned) but does not speak of them directly as prophets. Rather, the language of priesthood predominates in the Moses passage, with emphasis on the priestly succession of Aaron and Phinehas. However, as he begins his praise of Joshua son of Nun in 46:1, Ben Sirach offers the idea of a prophetic succession that started with Moses: "Joshua, son of Nun, was mighty in war, and was the servant of Moses in the prophetic office" (NRSV).[10] This is seen also in his comment that Nathan "arose after" Samuel and, in 48:1 (LXX), that "Then Elijah rose up, the prophet like fire" with Elisha being identified as his successor in 48:12. From 46:1 to at least 49:10, the prophets named are the pivotal persons structuring Ben Sirach's presentation. Even though he discusses four kings (David, Solomon, Hezekiah, and Josiah) as well, the kings are presented as being obedient to the righteousness taught by the prophet or as experiencing historical events predicted by prophets (48:23 and 49:6).

Samuel is the first prophet presented (46:13–20), in a passage surpassed in length only by that of Elijah. Numerous textual uncertainties afflict this passage, with differences between the Hebrew and the LXX. Basically, Ben Sirach catalogs the key positive features of Samuel that emerge in 1 Sam 1–28, with main attention to chs. 1–12. In 46:13 he is beloved by his people (1 Sam 2:26, 3:20) and beloved and approved by God (1 Sam 1:35, 3:2–19). He was one "asked for in his mother's womb" (1 Sam 1:10–13). As a prophet he "established the monarchy" and anointed rulers (1 Sam 8:4–10:1, 10:20–25 [Saul] and 16:1–3 [David]). He was dedicated as a Nazirite to the prophetic ministry (1 Sam 1:11, 22) and functioned as a judge and as a priest (1 Sam 7:6, 15–17, 3:19–4:1, 16:1–5), so that through him the Lord commanded Jacob (46:14). 1 Sam 46:15 describes Samuel's words as a prophet as accurate and trustworthy (1 Sam 3:19–20). With his people surrounded by enemies (46:16–18), Samuel called upon the Lord and sincerely worshiped him by offering a "sucking lamb" (1 Sam 4:1–7:11, especially 7:9); Yahweh answered with thunderous voice and wiped out the attacking Philistines (1 Sam 7:5–13). As he approached his death, Samuel called upon Yahweh and "his anointed one" to confirm his testimony that, unlike the sons of Eli and unlike his own sons, Samuel himself had never used his position to take bribes or confiscate property (46:19; see also 1 Sam 12:3–5). The spiritual power and importance of Samuel was further demonstrated when, after his death, Saul recruited a female medium to summon the spirit of Samuel to give an oracle about Saul's fate in the coming battle with the Philistines (46:20). Samuel's spirit predicted the king's end (1 Sam 28:8–19). The

---

9. Note that the Hebrew text of Sir 46:1–49:13, containing the praise of the prophets discussed here, survives only in a single witness, Cairo Geniza MS B.

10. Hebrew "by/in prophecy"; LXX "in prophecies." The connection of Joshua with the prophetic function of Moses probably derives from Joshua's being named (v. 28) as his assistant at the apportioning of Moses' divine spirit to the seventy elders in Num 11:16–30. It also is based on Joshua's frequent speaking the words of Yahweh during the conquest; see also 1 Kgs 16:34.

LXX of v. 20 adds the explanation that Samuel's prediction of Saul's military defeat and death was because of the wickedness of the people (see 1 Sam 28:17-19).

Immediately following the discussion of Samuel, Ben Sirach introduces his lengthy discussion of David with a single sentence about the prophet Nathan (Sir 47:1):

> Hebrew: "Also after him Nathan arose to station himself before David."
> LXX: "And after this Nathan arose to prophesy in the days of David."
> Syriac: "After him Nathan the prophet arose to speak before David."

The Hebrew verb התיצב here could, theoretically, have an adversative sense, 'to set himself against',[11] and would thus have to allude to Nathan's condemnation of David over the Bathsheba incident. However, Ben Sirach elsewhere (8:8, 38:3, 47:1) uses this verb in the sense of 'position oneself as a servant', and this must be its sense here, especially given the preposition "before." Also, he seems to rely mainly on the Chronicles portrait of David and does not otherwise mention his sins and failures. It is unusual for a prophet to be described as *serving* a king. The LXX and Syriac readings are explanatory of the less specific Hebrew התיצב.

Elijah receives energetic praise in Sir 48:1-11, beginning with his description as a prophet "like fire," whose "word(s) were like a burning oven." The association with fire doubtless comes both from his calling down fire on the prophets of Baal on Mt. Carmel (1 Kgs 18:20-40) and on the messengers from King Ahaziah (2 Kgs 1:9-17), as well as from his departure to heaven in a fiery horse-drawn chariot (2 Kgs 2:11-12). The expression, 'a burning oven' (כתנור בוער) in 48:1, however, comes from Mal 3:19[4:1]. Ben Sirach seems to be reading the entire Malachi passage (3:19-24 [4:1-6]) in terms of Elijah. Elijah's destruction of Israel's "staff of bread" (48:2) refers to the famine he pronounced in 1 Kgs 17:1. The following line, "and in his zeal he made them few," might refer to many deaths from the famine, which are not explicitly mentioned in the narrative, or to Jezebel's extermination of the Yahwistic prophets in retaliation for Elijah's denunciations.[12] It could also have in mind his slaughter of the prophets of Baal after the Mt. Carmel contest (1 Kgs 18:40). Most probably, this reflects Yahweh's instruction to Elijah that he should anoint Jehu and Elisha, who would carry out mass killings of apostates (1 Kgs 19:14-17; compare 2 Kgs 1:9-17).[13]

A second reference to the famine occurs in 48:3 (LXX): Elijah "shut up the sky by the word of the Lord." His bringing down fire three times alludes again to the fiery deaths of the three successive groups of military emissaries from king Ahaziah in 2 Kgs 1:9-17. Sir 48:4 refers to Elijah's being glorified (LXX εδοξασθης; Heb נורא). If this does not refer specifically to the extraordinary manner of his be-

---

11. So in 1 Sam 17:16, Ps 2:2, and Jer 46:4
12. So G. H. Box and W. O. E. Oesterly, "Sirach" in *APOT* 1:500. See 1 Kgs 19:10, 14, 18.
13. R. Smend, *Die Weisheit des Jesus Sirach* (Berlin: Georg Reimer, 1906) 459.

ing taken up to heaven, it must simply be a general verdict on his entire ministry, especially perhaps the actions listed in the following verses:

- In 48:5, he raised a corpse from death, a reference to his resurrecting the son of the Zarepath widow in 1 Kgs 17:17–24.
- In 48:6, he brought kings down to death, referring again perhaps to his anointing of Jehu through Elisha, who would kill Joram and the household of Ahab along with Ahaziah of Judah. The synonymous second line about prominent ones whom he brought down [to death] "from their bed" (LXX) surely has in mind Elijah's pronouncement that Ahaziah, bedfast with injuries from a fall (2 Kgs 1:2) would never recover: "Therefore, you shall not leave the bed to which you have gone, but you shall surely die" (2 Kgs 1:16).
- In 48:7, Elijah's resemblance to Moses is affirmed in the assertion that he "heard rebukes at Sinai and judgments on Horeb" (LXX). This remembers Elijah, in a dejected state after Jezebel's attacks, experiencing a manifestation of Yahweh on Mt. Horeb, in 1 Kgs 1:8–18. Ben Sirach echoes Mal 3:22 [4:4] here, which interposes a reference to Moses amid material that otherwise points to Elijah: "Remember the law of Moses, my servant, to whom I commanded . . . on Horeb, to all Israel, statutes and commandments." Ben Sirach says that Elijah received "rebukes" (because of his apparent hopelessness) and "commandments of vengeance" (LXX); the latter refers to the instruction to anoint Elisha and Jehu to exterminate the apostates in Israel.

The second line of 48:8 (Hebrew) repeats the recollection of "a prophet you made to succeed in place of you" (LXX reads plural "prophets"), who was Elisha; see 2 Kgs 2:9–18. The first line of the verse is uncertain but may also refer somehow to the anointing of Elisha, who would inflict retribution.[14]

The supernatural end of Elijah's earthly life is heralded in 48:9, where he is described as "taken up in a storm wind" (Hebrew)] or "taken up in a storm wind of fire" (LXX). The second line in the LXX— "and in a chariot of fiery horses"[15]— reflects the text of 2 Kgs 2:11–12 more closely than does the broken Hebrew: [. . .]א וּבגדודי ('*troops* of f[ire]').

48:10 draws upon Mal 3:19–24 [4:1–6] rather than 1–2 Kings. "What is written" (Hebrew) or "He who was recorded" (LXX) may be simply Ben Sirach's explicit signal that he is in fact quoting Scripture,[16] but it might indicate that Ben Sirach understands Elijah's righteousness as being included in "a book of remembrance [that] was written of those who revered the LORD and thought on his name" (Mal 3:16). In any case, it is clear that Elijah is the one who will, in the eschaton, stop the

---

14. P. Skehan and A. Di Lella, *The Wisdom of Ben Sira* (AB 39; Garden City, NY: Doubleday, 1987) 531: "Elisha was 'both the *mělě' tašlūmôt* of 8a and the *nābî'* of 8b." Others, such as Smend (*Die Weisheit*, 460), think that Hebrew מלא here is an error for מלכי 'kings'.s Thus, the New American Bible: "You anointed kings who would inflict vengeance."

15. Literally 'chariots of fire and horses of fire' (רכב־אש וסוסי אש).

16. So Skehan and Di Lella, *Wisdom*, 534.

divine wrath, thereby fulfilling Malachi's prediction: "I will send you the prophet Elijah … so that I will not come and strike the land with destruction" (Mal 3:24 [4:6]). "To turn the heart of fathers to sons and to establish [the tribes of Israel]" in Sir 48:10 is a close paraphrase of Mal 3:24a (with an added echo of Isa 49:6b, c), which more fully says: "He will turn the heart of fathers to sons and the heart of sons to their fathers." Verse 11 concludes the Elijah praise with, presumably, a climactic utterance. Unfortunately, the Hebrew is too badly broken for any confident restoration, and the LXX is not clear.[17]

After Elijah, in 48:12–14 Ben Sirach offers a more brief salute to Elisha as his successor. The Hebrew text is almost entirely missing for the first two half-lines in v. 12, but they probably affirm that Elijah was taken up to heaven and that Elisha "was filled with his spirit" (LXX). If the Syriac "treasuries/secret chambers of heaven" indeed directly reflects the original Hebrew, this concept of heavenly chamber will not have come from the biblical narrative about Elijah but from Ben Sirach's own cosmology. He refers to heavenly treasuries also at 39:30 and 43:14. The Hebrew text of the first half of the second line in v. 12 is fragmentary, showing only פי שׁ[. . . . .]בה. This surely read פי שׁנים ('double portion') as in the Elisha narrative in 2 Kgs 2:9. The Syriac reads here, "And Elisha received a double portion of prophecy," but Segal, followed by many, reconstructs: פי שׁנים אתות הרבה and translates it, with the NRSV, "He performed twice as many signs."[18] The original meaning of this numerical phrase in the Kings narrative was that Elisha received the spiritual equivalent of an eldest son's inheritance, which was double what would pass down to any other son (see Deut 21:17). But it is uncertain that Ben Sirach correctly understood the idiom; he may well actually have thought that Elisha performed twice as many signs as Elijah, even though one must force the narrative to find such disproportion numbers of miracles.[19] The last half of this second line clearly offers a general tribute to the many miracle-working utterances

---

17. See the discussion of this verse in E. Puech, "Ben Sira 48:11 et la resurrection," in *Of Scribes and Scrolls: Studies on the Hebrew Bible, Intertestamental Judaism, and Christian Origins* (ed. H. Attridge, J. Collins, and T. Tobin; Lanham, MD: University Press of America, 1990) 81–90; W. T. van Peursen, "Que vive celui qui fait vivre: le texte syriaque de Sirach 48:10–12," in *L'enfance de la Bible hébraïque: Histoire du texte de l'Ancient Testament* (ed. A. Schenker and P. Hugo; MdB 52; Geneva: Labor et Fides, 2005) 286–301; R. Owens, "Christian Features in the Peshitta Text of Ben Sira: The Question of Dependency on the Syriac New Testament," in *The Texts and Versions of the Book of Ben Sira* (ed. J.-S. Rey and J. Joosten; Leiden: Brill, 2011) 193–95.

18. M. Segal, *Sefer Ben Sira ha-Shalem* [Hebrew] (Jerusalem: Bialik Institute, 1958) 330. In his text edition (*The Book of Ben Sira in Hebrew* [VTSup 68; Brill: Leiden, 1997, 86]), P. Beentjes shows a total break between the פ and the שׁ here, but the original facsimile edition shows the bottoms of several letters that could perhaps be readable in autopsy (*Facsimiles of the Fragments Hitherto Recovered of The Book of Ecclesiasticus in Hebrew* [London: Oxford/Cambridge University Press, 1901] ad loc.).

19. This was the view of David Kimchi in his Kings commentary, who found sixteen miracles by Elisha and only eight by Elijah (quoted in *Miqra'oth Gedoloth* [*The Rabbinic Bible*]: *Commentaries of Rashi, Abraham ibn Ezra, David Kimchi, and Mesudoth* [Jerusalem: Eshkol, 1976] at

of Elisha: "and marvels with every utterance of his mouth."[20] The third line of v. 12 speaks of Elisha's courage and strength: "Throughout his days he did not tremble before anyone, and no mortal overpowered his will." This could have been said of Elijah as well. It has in mind here especially Elisha's bold confrontation of hostile kings:[21] Mesha of Moab (2 Kgs 3:4–27); Ben Hadad and another unnamed king of Aram (2 Kgs 6:1–8:15); Joram and Jezebel of Israel and Ahaziah of Judah (2 Kgs 9:1–10:17).

In the general affirmation in 48:13a, the adjectival participle נפלא can mean merely 'difficult', as in the NRSV, "Nothing was too hard for him." But because the root פלא often means 'marvelous, wondrous' (as, for example, the acts of God in Ps 139:14 and Job 37:14), this line may imply the marvelous: "No miraculous act was beyond him." This would nicely anticipate the following summative verse: "In his life he performed wonders (נפלאות), and in his death, marvelous deeds." As Ben Sirach's praise of Elisha's God-given power comes to a climax, he points to its ultimate manifestation: the ability even of his dead corpse to work miracles. In v. 13b, "from its place, his [dead] body prophesied,"[22] "prophesied" has the expanded sense of doing wonder-working actions and refers to the resurrection of the Israelite whose corpse was thrown onto Elisha's dead body in his grave (2 Kgs 13:21).

Ben Sirach thinks of the prophet Isaiah as he extols the great king Hezekiah in 48:17–22. He emphasizes the reliability of Isaiah's instructions and predictions to Hezekiah (48:22), especially his oracle about the divine extension of the king's life, marked by reversing the sun's movement (48:23).[23] Isaiah's power to execute salvation is also remembered in connection with the deliverance of Jerusalem from the besieging Assyrians under Sennacherib: "The Holy One . . . delivered them through Isaiah" (48:20).[24] Isaiah also is praised for his predictions of a blessed final future for the covenant people, which encouraged the Jerusalemites (48:24–25).[25]

As with Isaiah and Hezekiah, the prophet Jeremiah comes to Ben Sirach's mind in connection with the kings he dealt with. He describes the godliness of Jeremiah's contemporary, Josiah, so different from most other Judahite kings (49:1–5) whose sinfulness led to Judah's downfall in 587. The Hebrew and Greek texts of 49:6 make Jeremiah the instrument of Jerusalem's capture and destruction by a foreign state, "who set fire to the chosen city of the sanctuary . . . by the hand

---

"Prophets: 2 Kings 2:14"). In the *Lives of the Prophets*, written in the 1st century B.C.E., the author lists fourteen "signs" by Elisha and only ten by Elijah (§§21–22).

20. Skehan and Di Lella, *Wisdom* 530.

21. The LXX makes this clear by substituting "ruler" for the Hebrew "mortal" (כל בשׂר).

22. Reading with the LXX επροφητευσεν "prophesied," which presupposes Hebrew נבא , instead of נברא in MS B.

23. See Isa 38:1–8.

24. See Isaiah chs. 36–39. Note Ben Sirach's echo here of one of Isaiah's favorite expressions for God, "the Holy One of Israel."

25. Such eschatological visions are found in Isaiah chs. 40–66. Predictably, Ben Sirach considers Isaiah of Jerusalem the author of all that is in the canonical book of Isaiah.

of Jeremiah" (49:6).[26] This apparently refers to the prophet's prediction of Jerusalem's conquest by Babylonia (see Jer 36:2–4, 29–31, 37:6–10, 38:3), a prediction that contained within it also the spiritual power to bring about what it announced. Sirach 49:7 recalls the various persecutions of Jeremiah recorded in his book, as well as his striking call while yet in the womb to prophesy both constructive and destructive events (Jer 1:10).

Moving in canonical order, Ben Sirach next briefly refers to Ezekiel in 49:8, mentioning only his inaugural visions in Ezekiel chs. 1, 9 and 10, which describe the departure of the glory of Yahweh from the Most Holy Place of the Jerusalem Temple. Ezekiel never uses the term chariot, but his visions clearly involve some sort of wheeled vehicle closely connected to the winged creatures, which seem to be Cherubim (Ezek 10:14). The conclusion that this is a divine throne-chariot is explicit already in 1 Chr 28:18 ("gold chariot of the Cherubim") and in a number of Qumran texts,[27] so Ben Sirach's use of "chariot" in this context is not surprising. The expression זני מרכבה—literally 'types/sorts of the chariot'—must refer to the component parts. Thus, thinking especially of the differentiated "living creatures" in Ezek 1:4–14, Box and Oesterly translate it, "the different beings of the chariot."[28] The Syriac 'a type of chariot' (ܡܪܟܒܬܐ ܕܓܢܣ) seems to know a Hebrew text closer to MS B than to the Greek. The singular noun could be due to carelessness, misunderstanding, or to a slightly different Vorlage.

It surely is the reference to Job as a paragon of righteousness in Ezek 14:14, 20 that Ben Sirach has in mind in 49:9: "For he also mentioned Job who held fast to all the ways of justice" (NRSV). Beentjes reconstructs נביא 'prophet' in the break in MS B of v. 9, but any proposal about that very damaged section of the manuscript remains highly conjectural.[29] It seems that Job was grouped with the prophets in some Jewish reckonings.[30] The location of this verse between his reference to Ezekiel in v. 8 and the Twelve Prophets in v. 9 might suggest that Ben Sirach shares this tradition. On the other hand, Job could well come to Ben Sirach's mind at this point simply because he is mentioned in the Book of Ezekiel. In any case, Ben Sirach makes nothing of a distinctly prophetic identity for Job.

---

26. The NRSV paraphrases, "as Jeremiah had foretold."

27. See J. Scott, "Throne-Chariot Mysticism in Qumran and in Paul," in *Eschatology, Messianism and the Dead Sea Scrolls* (ed. C. Evans and P. Flint; Grand Rapids, MI: Eerdmans, 1997) 101–11.

28. Box and Oesterly, *APOT* 1:505; compare Skehan and Di Lella, *Wisdom* 541: "the different creatures of the chariot throne." Oddly, NRSV chooses to follow mainly the Greek, which is almost certainly secondary: "who saw a vision of glory that he showed to him above [ἐπι] the chariot of the cherubim."

29. Beentjes, *Book of Ben Sira* 88. Note Skehan and Di Lella, *Wisdom* 542: "Extra traces after *Job* at the caesura in MS B may be a transfer of ink, adventitious in this place, to be associated with the stain on the paper in this area. They do not yield a word."

30. This may be attested already by Josephus (*Contra Apionem* I,8), but see the cautionary discussion in R. Beckwith, *The Old Testament Canon of the New Testament Church* (Grand Rapids, MI: Eerdmans, 1985), 199, 227.

Otherwise, Ben Sirach seems to know the Hebrew Bible's arrangement of the prophetic books, since after Ezekiel he passes on to the Twelve. In v. 10, the LXX agrees closely with the extant Hebrew and thus permits restoration of two breaks in Hebrew MS B. There can be little doubt about the key ideas in the verse: "And also the Twelve Prophets—may their bones sprout (or, cause to sprout) in their place—who restored health to Jacob and delivered him in hope." Ben Sirach here repeats phraseology he used of the biblical judges in 46:12a: "May their bones sprout from their place . . ." Does he think of the prophet's bones as having restorative power upon contact, similar to the bones of Elisha at 2 Kgs 13:20–21? It seems more likely that he means this expression to function as it does in 46:12, of the judges: "May their bones send forth new life from where they lie, and may the names of those who have been honored live again in their children!" Ben Sirach thinks of the bones of the Twelve Prophets—and the whole covenant people to whom to whom they belong—as living on in future generations of their descendants. This future era of perfect blessedness was of course predicted in various places in the twelve "minor" prophets,[31] but in the light of their many, many denunciations, it is striking that Ben Sirach gives as his terse summary of these prophets that they comforted the people of Jacob "and delivered them with confident hope" (v. 10c, d).

Baruch
(end of 2nd century B.C.E.?)

The fictional author of this book is Baruch, son of Neriah, who is mentioned often in the Book of Jeremiah as the great prophet's companion and secretary.[32] Surprisingly perhaps, while allusion is made to some of Baruch's activities during Jeremiah's ministry, neither Jeremiah nor any other prophet is named here. However, the author knows and esteems the canonical prophetic tradition. Four times he laments the tragic sinfulness of Israel and Judah, which involved their refusal to heed the prophets' admonitions and threats. He terms them "our prophets" (1:1); "the prophets" (1:21); and "your servants the prophets" (2:20, 24). The text of Baruch contains a number of distant echoes, but no explicit citations, of passages from prophetic books, especially Jeremiah.

The Letter of Jeremiah
(2nd century B.C.E.)

This document, sometimes printed as ch. 6 of Baruch, provides another example of interest in the prophet Jeremiah in the traditions of early Second Temple Judaism. The only reference to the person of the prophet occurs in v. 1, where the

---

31. For example, Joel 3:1–21, Amos 9:11–15, Mic 4:1–4, Zech 8:1–8, 9:9–17.
32. Jer 32:12, 13, 16, 36:4, 5, 8, 13–19, 26–27, 32, 43:3, 6, 45:1–2.

entire composition is identified as a letter which Jeremiah sent to Jerusalemites about to be deported to Babylonia. Jer 29:1–15 does describe a letter the prophet wrote to deportees in 597, but the contents of that letter are quite different from the Letter of Jeremiah. This is actually a sermon consisting mainly of ten reflections on the idiocy of worshiping idols (vv. 8–73). It draws on polemical rhetoric against foreign deity-images in the canonical book of Jeremiah, especially 10:1–10, but also in Isa 40:18–20, 41:6–7, 44:9–20, 46:1–7, as well as in some Psalms and Deut 4:27–28. Dependence on the book of Jeremiah is thematic rather than verbal, although the distinctive simile, "like scarecrows in a cucumber field" might be taken from the Hebrew text of Jer 10:5.[33]

Additions to The Book of Daniel:
The Prayer of Azariah and the Three Jews
(late 2nd/early 1st century B.C.E.)

In this hymnic prayer, set on the lips of Azariah (Abednego) when he and Daniel and their two friends were thrown into a furnace by Nebuchadnezzar, confession of Israel's sins predominates, culminating in a cry to God for forgiveness and deliverance so that the world may know Him. As part of the song's description of their tragedy, v. 15 laments the collapse of the nation's institutions: "In our day we have no ruler, or prophet, or leader, no burnt offering, or sacrifice, or oblation, or incense, no place to make an offering before you and to find mercy." Prophets even at this late date are considered as essential as political rulers and the Jerusalem Temple.

Additions to the Book of Daniel:
Bel and the Dragon
(3rd century B.C.E.)

In the story "Bel and the Dragon," the deported Daniel exposes and destroys the idol Bel along with a dragon that the Babylonians revered. When Daniel is punished by being thrown into a den of lions, suddenly the prophet Habakkuk is brought onto the scene as his rescuer.[34] In vv. 33–39, Habakkuk is going about routine affairs in "Judea," taking a bowl of stew and bread out to workers busy with harvest fieldwork. God commands him to take this food instead to Daniel in the

---

33. The meaning "scarecrow" for both Greek προβασκανιον (lit., 'amulet, charm') in v. 70 and for תמר in the MT of Jer 10:5 (the LXX is missing) remains scarcely more than a guess. See the discussion in W. McKane, *A Critical and Exegetical Commentary on Jeremiah* (ICC; Edinburgh: T. & T. Clark, 1986) 1:222, who labels it an "obscure simile."

34. The narrative is oblivious to the chronological problems. Habakkuk's ministry had to have been around the end of the 7th century B.C.E., while the putative setting of this story is well into the sixth century.

lions' den in Babylon. When Habakkuk says that he does not know the location, "Then the angel of the Lord took him by the crown of his head and carried him by his hair; with the speed of the wind, right over the den" (v. 36). Habakkuk drops the food down to Daniel and tells him that it is from the Lord, after which the prophet is taken back home.

This is an odd legend. It contains neither a proclamation nor a miraculous act by Habakkuk that draws upon his particular role as a prophet. Nothing in the canonical book of Habakkuk suggests the prophet's behavior here. The best guess about why Habakkuk figures in this Daniel episode is that the Chaldeans are prominent in both the book of Habakkuk (1:6) and in the book of Daniel (1:4 and nine other times). The Habakkuk section of *The Lives of the Prophets* also knows a tradition of Habakkuk instantaneously going to Babylon to take food to Daniel, but it says nothing about an angel, the wind, or about Daniel's situation in the lions' den. Its source was probably one of the texts of Bel and the Dragon.

The slightly variant Greek texts of the LXX and Theodotion versions are generally thought to be based on different Semitic originals. The Habakkuk episode, which looks like a secondary addition to the story, is "more simple and precise" in the LXX version,[35] but none of the differences between the two Greek editions affects any important feature of the Habakkuk presentation. "The prophet Habakkuk" in Theodotion becomes simply "Habakkuk" in the LXX, but there can be no doubt that the canonical prophet is intended. The "stew and broken bread in a bowl" (v. 33) in Theodotion is "broken bread in a bowl of stew and a jar of mixed wine" in the LXX.

1 Maccabees
(around 100 B.C.E.)

Since this book is given over entirely to a straightforward narrative that traces Jewish history in Israel from about 175–100 B.C.E., it is not surprising that there are almost no references to the canonical prophets. Elijah and Daniel are both briefly mentioned within a list of heroes in 1 Macc 2:51–60, where they are presented as spiritual models.[36] "Elijah was taken up to heaven because of great zeal for the law" (see 2 Kgs 2:11–12). In the Kings narratives, Elijah is never explicitly spoken of in connection with obedience to the law.[37] Apparently, the writer makes a natural equation between the righteousness of the "law" and that of the revealed "word of the Lord," which Elijah faithfully served. This would be suggested also

---

35. C. A. Moore, *Daniel, Esther and Jeremiah: The Additions* (AB44; Garden City, NY: Doubleday, 1977) 47.

36. Abraham, Joseph, Phinehas, Joshua, Caleb, David, Elijah, Hananiah, Azariah, and Mishael, and Daniel are listed.

37. It is interesting that between 1 Kgs 2:3 and 2 Kgs 10:1 there is no reference at all to the law of Moses.

by Elijah's Moses-like experience of God's self-manifestation on Mt. Horeb (1 Kgs 19). Elijah's zeal for Yahweh is evident in the Kings narratives, of course, but the term "law" is not actually used in connection with him in Kings.

The eschatological Elijah of Mal 3:23–24 might be in mind when the stones of the defiled Jerusalem Temple are set aside in 1 Macc 4:46 "until a prophet should come to tell what to do with them." The allusion in 1 Macc 9:27 to "the time that prophets had ceased to appear among them" suggests familiarity with the boundary of the Prophets section of the Hebrew canon, which ends with Malachi and expectation of Elijah's eventual return.

2 Maccabees
(late 2nd century B.C.E.)

This document refers to the prophet Jeremiah twice, each time drawing mainly on postbiblical legends rather than on canonical texts. In 2 Macc 2:1–7, Jeremiah is described as instructing his fellow Judeans who were about to be deported to Babylon to take with them some of the sacred fire from the Temple altar that had been secretly hidden away in a cistern (see 2 Macc 1:19). He also gave the group a farewell discourse in which he urged them to remain faithful to Torah and not to be impressed by the richly ornate deity-images they would see in Mesopotamia. No such oration is preserved in the book of Jeremiah, although of course he had vehemently denounced idols (in ch. 10, for example).[38] It is also said here that when the Babylonians attacked the Jerusalem Temple, Jeremiah removed the tent (sic), the ark of the covenant, and the incense altar, carried them to Mt. Nebo and sealed them up in a cave, the location of which was forgotten until such time as God would disclose it after the exile. None of these events is recorded in the book of Jeremiah, which says quite clearly (43:1–7) that after the fall of Jerusalem Jeremiah remained in the city until forced by a Judahite military contingent to go with them to Tahpanhes in Egypt.[39] The 2 Maccabees writer claims that he found this information "in the records" (2:1), which cannot be any of the canonical books. Variants of this legend are attested also in the Jeremiah section of *The Lives of the Prophets*; in 2 Bar 6:7–10; in 4 Bar 3:3–18; and in Eusebius, *Praeparatio evangelica* 9.39.2–5 (Fragment 4 of Alexander Polyhistor "On the Jews"). While none of these seems likely to be the direct source for 2 Maccabees, they show that similar traditions about Jeremiah were in circulation.

The prophet Jeremiah also comes into 2 Maccabees at 15:14–15, where he appears in a dream to Judas Maccabeus, who is fighting against Nicanor, military governor of Judea appointed by Demetrius I (162–150 B.C.E.). Demetrius had sup-

---

38. The material about idols may also echo The Epistle of Jeremiah.

39. Jer 43:9 does relate that God commanded Jeremiah to carry with him some stones from Judah and bury them before the Pharaonic palace. This could provide a midrashic starting point for this legend.

ported the power-hungry, treacherous Alcimus as high priest. Judas is faced with the compounded disadvantage of being militarily outnumbered, of being reluctant to take up arms on the Sabbath, and of appearing seditious in his action against a legitimate Seleucid king. When Jeremiah appears in the dream, "distinguished by his gray hair and dignity, and of marvelous majesty and authority," he presents to Judas a golden sword. The sword symbolizes God's authorization of Judas as his chosen military leader who will be victorious.[40] It is perhaps important that Jeremiah is the figure conveying this authorization, because Jeremiah would have been remembered for having opposed the plan of his fellow Judahites to rebel against the pagan Babylonians back in the early 6th century (see Jer 27:1–18). His appearance now signals divine authorization for Judas to rebel against Demetrius I, even taking up arms on the Sabbath. Given the role of an ancient prophet in this text, it is curious that only a little later on in the narrative (15:22–24), when Judas encourages his troops by remembering that God delivered Jerusalem from the huge army of the Assyrian king Sennacherib in 701 B.C.E., he makes no mention of the prophet Isaiah.

1 Esdras
(2nd century B.C.E.)

This book makes two general references to the prophets, in addition to a number of specific citations of Samuel, Jeremiah, Haggai, and Zechariah. All these references occur in passages that parallel the canonical books of 2 Chronicles, Ezra, and Nehemiah. Unfortunately, none of them occurs in the original material that is unique to Esdras, in 3:1–4:63.

In 1 Esd 1:51 (= 2 Chr 36:16) and 8:82–85 (= Ezra 9:11), the destruction of the covenant people is attributed to their having scoffed at and forsaken the prophets through whom the Lord spoke. In the latter text, a formal quotation by "your servants the prophets" in fact does not occur as such in the Bible. It is a pastiche of phrases from a number of passages, mostly Deuteronomy (see especially Deut 7:3–4; Lev 18:24–30; Isa 24:5–7), in which Moses commands separation from the native inhabitants of Canaan.

In 1 Esd 1:20, Samuel is mentioned merely as a chronological reference point with regard to Josiah's national Passover: "No Passover like it had been kept in Israel since the times of the prophet Samuel (= 2 Chr 35:18)." Nothing about his actual prophetic activity is in view.[41]

---

40. "The sword of victory handed by a god to his chosen commander or king is an Egyptian motif" (J. Goldstein, *II Maccabees* [AB 41A; Garden City, NY: Doubleday, 1984] 499). See also the coded allusion to this dream in 1 Enoch 90:19.

41. The parallel text in 2 Kgs 23:22 reckons from "the days of the Judges who judged Israel" instead of Samuel.

The prophet Jeremiah is mentioned five times. In 2 Chr 35:22, the Egyptian king Neco tries to dissuade Josiah from joining in the battle, but Josiah "did not listen to the words of Neco from the mouth of God." Rather than have a non-Israelite speaking divine truth, 1 Esdras recasts this so that Josiah "did not listen to the words of the prophet Jeremiah from the mouth of the Lord." There is no such counsel recorded in the Book of Jeremiah; perhaps the writer is encouraged in this revision by 2 Chr 36:12 and 57. After Josiah's death in this battle, Jeremiah wrote lamentations for him (1 Esd 1:32 = 2 Chr 35:25). In 1 Esd 1:47, Zedekiah's eleven-year reign in Jerusalem is characterized as evil, rejecting the preaching of Jeremiah. This verse slightly condenses its Chronicles source, but for no obvious theological reason: "He also did what was evil in the sight of the Lord, and did not heed the words that were spoken by the prophet Jeremiah from the mouth of the Lord."[42]

In 1 Esd 1:57, the narrative describes the deportation of Jerusalemites to Babylon until the Persian dynasty arose, "in fulfillment of the word of the Lord by the mouth of Jeremiah, saying, 'Until the land has enjoyed its sabbaths, it shall keep sabbath all the time of its desolation until the completion of seventy years'." Here 1 Esdras slightly alters the wording of 2 Chr 36:21, changing "it kept sabbath" (εσαββατισεν) to future tense (σαββατιει) and framing it as a formal quotation by Jeremiah. No such pronouncement is preserved in the Book of Jeremiah. In fact, it is a mixture of elements from Jer 25:11–12; 29:10 [LXX 36:10]; and Lev 26:34–35 and 43.

1 Esd 2:1 describes the decree of Cyrus to allow deported Jews to return and rebuild the Jerusalem Temple as the work of the spirit of God "to complete the word of the Lord by the mouth of Jeremiah." This closely paraphrases 2 Chr 36:22, using εις συντελειαν ρηματος κυριου instead of μετα το πληρωθηναι ρημα κυριου. This is another reference to Jeremiah's predictions that the exile would end after seventy years when Babylon fell to another king (Jer 25:11–12, 27:6–7, 29:10).

Psalm 151
(3rd century B.C.E.?)

Variant texts of this psalm exist. The LXX version, occurring at the end of the Book of Psalms, contains no references to prophets. It voices a brief autobiographical retrospective by David, who recalls simply that he was called by God from the life of a musical shepherd to be anointed (king), and that he killed "the Philistine." The Hebrew text, 11QPs[a], which seems to preserve also the beginning of an additional psalm, is generally expansionary by comparison. Scholars are not certain

---

42. 2 Chr 36:12: "He did what was evil in the sight of the Lord his God. He did not humble himself before the prophet Jeremiah who spoke from the mouth of the Lord."

which text is prior.[43] Unlike the LXX, the Hebrew names the prophet in v. 5: "He sent his prophet to anoint me, Samuel to make me great; My brothers went out to meet him handsome of figure and appearance." This is a straightforward reference to 1 Sam 16:1–13 which describes God's command to Samuel to go to Bethlehem and anoint the one he designates as a replacement for Saul. Samuel did so, coming to the family of Jesse, all of whose elder sons were presented first. They were all rejected in favor of the youngest, David, whom Samuel anointed.

Third Maccabees
(1st century B.C.E.?)

This writing refers only one to a prophet. In 6:1–15, an aged rural priest, Eleazar, steps forward to offer a prayer for his fellow Jews in Alexandria who are under threat of death by King Philapator. A large group of Jews has been herded into the hippodrome, where the king plans for them to be trampled by his agitated elephants. Eleazar's prayer recalls five past events in the sacred history when God has saved his people from almost certain destruction: the exodus from Egypt; Jerusalem's miraculous deliverance from Sennacherib's Assyrian army; the rescue of Daniel's three friends from Nebuchanezzar's flaming furnace; and Daniel's preservation in the lion's den. Finally, he mentions Jonah: "And when Jonah was wasting away in the belly of a huge sea-monster [κητους], You, O Father, had regard for him and restored him unharmed to all his family."[44]

It is not surprising that Eleazar recalls the sensational narrative about Jonah's being swallowed and then disgorged by the fish (2:1–10). He echoes the LXX text of Jonah, which renders the Hebrew "giant fish" [דג גדול] with a word for "sea monster," [κητει]. However, it is striking that Eleazar makes no reference to Jonah's mission to Nineveh in chapters three and four, something like, " . . . had regard for him and restored him to deliver his prophecy to the Ninevites." Instead, omitting all reference to the second half of the Book of Jonah, the prayer has Jonah brought out of the fish to be restored unharmed "to all his family." Since there is no reference to his family anywhere in the canonical book, this could be simply an original imaginative reading of Jonah. Later rabbinic writings know nothing of Jonah returning to his homeland, but *The Lives of the Prophets* says that Jonah returned to his own land after his Nineveh mission and then "taking his mother

---

43. See the thorough discussion by J. Sanders, *The Psalms Scroll of Qumran Cave 11 (11QPsᵃ)* (DHDJ 4; Oxford: Clarendon, 1965) 54–64. Against Sanders and the majority view, the originality of the LXX Vorlage is defended by F.-L. Hossfeld and E. Zenger, *Psalms 3: A Commentary on Psalms 101–150* (Hermeneia; Minneapolis: Fortress, 2005) 665–669.

44. The Greek manuscripts vary slightly in one verbal form, but the basic thought of the verse for our purpose is not affected. God either "restored" Jonah or "showed him" again to all his family.

along he sojourned in Sour, a territory inhabited by foreign nations."[45] 3 Maccabees 6:8 might have influenced the author of the *Lives*, or the two documents may
independently reflect an otherwise unattested line of Palestinian folklore about
Jonah's return to his family.

2 Esdras 1–2
(late second century c.e.)[46]

In both the canonical and later rabbinic writings, Ezra is termed a scribe or a
priest, never a prophet. Here in chs. 1–2, Ezra is given a prophetic identity, despite
the priestly genealogy for him in 1:1. The first sentence begins, "The (second) book
of the prophet Ezra son of Seraiah," and repeatedly throughout chs. 1 and 2 Ezra is
described as receiving a prophet-like call to preach revealed material:

> 1:4–5 "The word of the Lord came to me saying, 'Go, declare to my people
> their evil deeds . . .'"
> 1:12 "But speak to them and say, 'Thus says the Lord . . .'"
> 1:15, 28, and 33 "Thus says the Lord (Almighty). . ."
> 2:33 "I, Ezra, received a command from the Lord on Mount Horeb to go to
> Israel."

Clearly, this language is modeled on that of the canonical prophetic books.

The text also makes three general references to prophets. Twice, God tells
Ezra to rebuke his people for having rejected and abused the prophets whom He
sent to them. "I sent you my servants the prophets, but you have taken and killed
them and torn their bodies in pieces" (1:32).[47] "They would not listen to them but
made my counsels void" (2:1). Israel's rejection of the prophets is a theme found
also in 2 Chr 36:15, but no Bible text describes the dismemberment of a prophet.
Legends must underlie this statement, such as the sawing in two of Isaiah in *Lives
of the Prophets* and in chapter five of *The Martyrdom and Ascension of Isaiah* (see
also Heb 11:37).

The theme of the rejection of physical Israel in the first part of ch. 1 shifts
in vv. 33–40 to the prediction of their replacement by a new people—a veiled allusion to Christians. Verse 36 affirms that, even though this new people never
experienced the historical prophets firsthand, they will be able spiritually to access
the insight of the prophets about Israel's righteousness and sin: "They have seen
no prophets, yet will recall their former state" (NRSV). Similarly, the text predicts
that this new nation "from the East" will have as their leaders the spiritual teachers of historical Israel: "To them I will give as leaders Abraham, Isaac, and Jacob,

---

45. D. R. A. Hare, "The Lives of the Prophets," in *OTP* 2:392.

46. Chapters 1–2 constitute a distinct document often termed "5 Ezra"; chs. 3–14 are traditionally called "4 Ezra." To avoid confusion, I have avoided those titles here.

47. This passage is probably influenced by Matt 23:29–39 // Luke 11:49–51, which it echoes
(see also Luke 13:34). 2 Chr 36:15 also speaks of Israel's characteristic rejection of the prophets.

and Hosea and Amos and Micah and Joel and Obadiah and Jonah, and Nahum and Habakkuk, Zephaniah, Haggai, Zechariah and Malachi, who is also called the messenger of the Lord" (NRSV).[48] Although historical Israel did not faithfully follow the teachings and example of these prophetic heroes, the new people will do so. Is the assumption that the teaching of these heroes will be available to them via the written Scriptures?[49] Or is it that the substance of the prophetic teaching will become available mystically, by virtue of their spirituality, perhaps in fulfillment of Jer 31:33–34, so that God will write his law on their hearts without an ordinary teaching process?

The absence of Isaiah, Jeremiah, and Ezekiel from this list is curious, although Isaiah and Jeremiah are added in 2:18. The names of the Twelve here are in the same order as in LXX manuscripts, and it may be because the proper name "Malachi" is rendered as a common noun ("my messenger") in the LXX that the writer feels the need to qualify the name with "also called the messenger of the Lord."

In 2:15, the church is addressed as "Mother," and she is told that after she displaces physical Israel, "I will send you help, my servants Isaiah and Jeremiah" (2:18). "According to their counsel," God will provide twelve trees loaded with various fruits; twelve fountains flowing with milk and honey; and seven large mountains on which roses and lilies are growing (2:19). The connection with Isaiah and Jeremiah is not altogether clear, since those canonical books have no passages that contain or closely parallel these three features. One must assume that their general predictions of a coming era of great fertility and prosperity for Israel underlie the association (for example, Jer 31, Isa 44:1–2, and 55:12). In fact, these specific images are more closely associated with apocalyptic literature than with the canonical prophets. Mountains covered with blooms and twelve trees loaded with fruit evoke 1 Enoch 24:2–6 ("I . . . saw seven dignified mountains . . . all dignified and glorious . . . their heights . . . surrounded by fragrant trees. [One tree] such as I had never smelled . . . its leaves, its flowers, and its wood would never wither . . . with leaves so handsome and blossoms so magnificent . . .").[50] Multiple fountains, albeit of wisdom, are mentioned in 1 Enoch 48:1; a single eschatological fountain is described in 1 Enoch 22:9 and Rev 21:6.

2 Esdras 3–14
(late first century C.E.)

Israel's chronic disobedience of the prophets (including Moses) through the centuries is mentioned also in this document. Here, too, Ezra is given a prophetic

---

48. A variant reading rearranges the list somewhat and adds Jacob, Elijah, Enoch, Mattia, and "twelve angels in flowers."

49. The paraphrase of the *Revised English Bible* seems to reflect this view: "who never saw the prophets, and yet will keep in mind what the prophets taught of old."

50. The translation is by E. Isaac, "1 (Ethiopic Apocalypse of) Enoch" in *OTP* 1:26. Compare Rev 22:2: "On either side of the river is the tree of life with its twelve kinds of fruit . . ."

rather than priestly identity. In 12:42, his exiled fellow Jews in Babylon say to him: "For of all the prophets you alone are left to us." In chs. 3–14, Ezra is the recipient and interpreter of apocalyptic visions, inspired by God, and this would give him, like Daniel, the basic identity of a prophet (compare "the prophet Daniel" in Matt 24:15). Ezra associates himself with the line of Israelite prophets in 7:60 [132], when he says: "But they did not believe him [i.e., Moses] or the prophets after him, or even myself who have spoken to them."

In another section, ch. 7, Ezra converses with God about the fate of people after death. God tells Ezra that, at the time of final judgment, the righteous will not be able to intercede on behalf of ungodly persons, at which point Ezra protests that this contradicts the sacred history, in which godly persons often successfully petitioned God on behalf of others (7:102–41 [111]).[51] He lists eight specific examples of such prayer, including two prophets. "Samuel in the days of Saul" (38 [108]) must refer to 1 Sam 7:3–14, where Samuel prays at Mizpah for Israel and God answered by miraculously destroying the attacking Philistines. "Elijah for those who received the rain, and for the one who was dead, that he might live" (39 [109])" refers to two incidents. After the drought that God had inflicted on Israel during the reign of Ahab, initiated by the pronouncement of Elijah, 1 Sam 18 tells of God's revelation to Elijah that rain will be restored. Just before this, in 17:17–24, God raises from the dead the small son of a widow of Zarephath, who has been providing accommodation for the prophet.

4 Maccabees
(first century C.E.?)

Much of this book relates to the martyrdom of a pious Jewish family, one Eleazar, his six brothers, and his mother, by Antiochus IV (see 2 Macc 7:1–42). Their torture was horrible but their faith was steadfast. 4 Maccabees concludes with the final address of the mother to her sons, prior to her execution. She remembers that her husband had taught their sons "the law and the prophets" (18:10), the latter term clearly being the name of the second section of the Hebrew Bible. She rehearses twelve examples of heroic persons or texts from the Bible that offer encouragement to stand firm in one's faith despite suffering. In 18:14, the eighth reads: "He reminded you of the scripture of Isaiah which says, 'Even though you walk through the fire, the flame shall not burn you.'" This quotes Isa 43:2b, slightly abbreviated. The eleventh item in the mother's list, 18:17 says: "He affirmed the word of Ezekiel, 'Shall these bones live?'"[52] In neither of these cases is the person of the prophet of significance. Their names seem rather to function as scarcely more than book titles.

---

51. The versification here is that of B. Metzger, "The Fourth Book of Ezra," in *OTP* 1:517–559.
52. The translation is that of H. Anderson, "4 Maccabees," in *OTP* 2:564.

Summary[53]

This survey has identified fewer than 40 passages that mention prophetic persons. Of the 35 prophets named in the Hebrew Bible, only 23 occur in our corpus: The 16 identified with canonical books—Isaiah, Jeremiah, Ezekiel, Hosea, Joel, Amos, Obadiah, Jonah, Micah, Nahum, Habakkuk, Zephaniah, Haggai, Zechariah, Malachi, and Daniel (sic)—and, predictably, 4 who are subjects of dramatic narratives in the history books: Samuel, Nathan, Elijah, and Elisha. Moses, Joshua, and Ezra also are occasionally termed prophets. Apart from Ben Sirach, the Apocrypha actually do not show much interest in the prophets. In a number of the passages noted above, the prophet is scarcely more than a name, given merely as the source of an inspired text that is quoted with little or no attention to its canonical or historical context. One must characterize treatment of the prophets in this literature as largely superficial; one finds citation with minimal exposition, and several of the writings mention no prophets at all (for example, Wisdom of Solomon).

References to the prophets in the apocryphal books are widely scattered and usually brief, and they do not have much in common. This is not surprising, inasmuch as these books seem not to have been intentionally collected together on the basis of an identifiable set of criteria. There is considerable variation in their places and dates of composition, their cultural and linguistic settings, and their genres.

Rabinowitz and others have pointed out that in postbiblical Judaism two general ideas emerged in rabbinic views of the biblical prophets. (1) Moses was the ultimate prophet; none of the rest came up to his level of revelatory inspiration, although Isaiah perhaps ran a close second. (2) The prophets did not introduce any new religious doctrines; their preaching was essentially an application and clarification of Torah.[54] It is worth noting that neither of these emphases is reflected yet in references in the Apocrypha. Also, while some of the prophets are adduced as sources of eschatological visions, specifically "messianic" predictions are absent.

The most extensive discussion of the greatest number of prophets (seven plus The Twelve, along with Moses and Joshua) occurs in "In Praise of Ancient Ancestors" in The Wisdom of Ben Sirach 44–51. For Ben Sirach, the prophets faithfully announced the revelatory word of God with courage, even in the face of physical suffering; selected, authorized, and counseled kings; predicted coming disasters (usually near-term) as divine punishment; taught and modeled righteousness; displayed miraculous spiritual power through efficacious prayers and miracles even after their death; effected spiritual renewal among the covenant people; and predicted a future time of restoration and blessedness for them. The other apocryphal books generally display one or two of these same perspectives. Tobit, Baruch, and 2 Esdras all recall the negative judgments and coming punishment on Israel

---

53. I omit here the references in 1 Esdras, since they duplicate material found in the canonical books of Chronicles, Ezra, and Nehemiah.

54. L. I. Rabinowitz, "Prophets and Prophecy—In the Talmud," *EncJud* (2006) 16:580–81.

announced by biblical prophets. Suffering and rejection by prophets such as Elijah and Jeremiah is mentioned also in Tobit and 2 Esdras.

Bel and the Dragon tells of a miraculous rescue by Habakkuk that is not recorded in the canonical writings. 2 Maccabees and the Epistle of Jeremiah narrate three other actions by Jeremiah that are unknown in the Hebrew Bible. Hopeful oracles by the prophets or steadfastness shown by the prophets themselves are cited as a basis for encouragement also in 1 Maccabees, 3 Maccabees, 2 Esdras, and 4 Maccabees. The Prayer of Azariah mourns the absence of prophets as a key symptom of the nation's collapse. Wisdom of Solomon trusts that "in every generation [wisdom] passes into holy souls and makes them friends of God and prophets." 2 Esdras looks forward to a time when the teaching of the canonical prophets will be powerfully effective again, associated with wonderful fertility of the earth and social health. 1 Maccabees may share Ben Sirach's expectation that the return of Elijah will usher in a blessed new era.

Bibliography

Anderson, H. "4 Maccabees." *OTP* 2:564.

Beckwith, R. *The Old Testament Canon of the New Testament Church.* Grand Rapids, MI: Eerdmans, 1985.

Beentjes, P. *Facsimiles of the Fragments Hitherto Recovered of The Book of Ecclesiasticus in Hebrew.* London: Oxford / Cambridge University Press, 1901.

Blenkinsopp, J. *A History of Prophecy in Israel.* Rev. ed. Louisville: Westminster John Knox, 1996.

Box, G. H., and W. O. E. Oesterly. "Sirach." *APOT* 1:500.

DeSilva, D. A., and J. H. Charlesworth. *Introducing the Apocrypha: Message, Context, and Significance.* Grand Rapids, MI: Baker, 2002.

Fitzmyer, J. A. *Tobit.* CEJL. Berlin: de Gruyter, 2003.

Goldstein, J. *II Maccabees.* AB 41A. Garden City, NY: Doubleday, 1984.

Hare, D. R. A. "The Lives of the Prophets." Pp. in *OTP* 2:392.

Hossfeld, F.-L. and E. Zenger. *Psalms 3: A Commentary on Psalms 101–150.* Hermeneia; Minneapolis: Fortress, 2005.

Isaac, E. "1 (Ethiopic Apocalypse of) Enoch." *OTP* 1:26.

McKane, W. *A Critical and Exegetical Commentary on Jeremiah.* ICC. Edinburgh: T. & T. Clark, 1986.

Metzger, B. "The Fourth Book of Ezra." *OTP* 1:517–559.

Moore, C. A. *Daniel, Esther and Jeremiah: The Additions.* AB 44. Garden City, NY: Doubleday, 1977.

Owens, R. "Christian Features in the Peshitta Text of Ben Sira: The Question of Dependency on the Syriac New Testament." Pp. 193–95 in *The Texts and Versions of the Book of Ben Sira.* Edited by J.-S. Rey and J. Joosten. Leiden: Brill, 2011.

Peursen, W. T. van. "Que vive celui qui fait vivre: le texte syriaque de Sirach 48:10–12." Pp. 286–301 in *L'enfance de la Bible hébraïque: Histoire du texte de l'Ancient Testament.* Edited by A. Schenker and P. Hugo. MdB 52. Geneva: Labor et Fides, 2005.

Puech, E. "Ben Sira 48:11 et la resurrection." Pp. 81–90 in *Of Scribes and Scrolls: Studies on the Hebrew Bible, Intertestamental Judaism, and Christian Origins*. Edited by H. Attridge, J. Collins, and T. Tobin. Lanham, MD: University Press of America, 1990.

Rabinowitz, L. I. "Prophets and Prophecy—In the Talmud." *EncJud* (2006) 16:580–581.

Sanders, J. *The Psalms Scroll of Qumran Cave 11 (11QPs^a)*. DJD 4. Oxford: Clarendon, 1965.

Scott, J. "Throne-Chariot Mysticism in Qumran and in Paul." Pp. 101–11 in *Eschatology, Messianism and the Dead Sea Scrolls*. Edited by C. Evans and P. Flint. Grand Rapids, MI: Eerdmans, 1997.

Segal, M. *Sefer Ben Sira ha-Shalem* [Hebrew]. Jerusalem: Bialik Institute, 1958.

————. *The Book of Ben Sira in Hebrew*. VTSup 68. Brill: Leiden, 1997.

Skehan, P. and A. Di Lella. *The Wisdom of Ben Sira*. AB 39. Garden City, NY: Doubleday, 1987.

Smend, R. *Die Weisheit des Jesus Sirach*. Berlin: Georg Reimer, 1906.

Stone, M. E. ed. *Jewish Writings of the Second Temple Period*. CRINT 2.2. Assen: Van Gorcum, 1984.

Prophets, Kittim, and Divine Communication in the Dead Sea Scrolls:

Condemning the Enemy Without, Fighting the Enemy Within

JAMES E. BOWLEY

Millsaps College

Introduction

Just before writing these words, I was driving past the "Iglesia Adventista Séptimo Día" in Mérida, Mexico and wondered what might those people think who scoffed at the American William Miller in 1843, after his failed prediction of the return of Jesus Christ, if they were here? The Seventh Day Adventist Church, a direct descendent of the Millerites, is a world-wide organization, thriving, less that 200 years after Miller predicted the end of the world. Thanks to the influential sociological study, *When Prophecy Fails*, which appeared first in 1956, we have a better understanding of common features of apocalyptic movements and how and why they may fare well after disconfirmation of their predictions.[1] Of course, similar apocalyptic groups have come and gone before and after the Millerites, and this paper is a study of some of the prophetic and apocalyptic ideas of one such ancient group: the Jewish religionists who inhabited the area of Qumran—variously called the Sons of Light or Yaḥad or Qumran covenanters—for about a century and a half beginning in the first half of the second century B.C.E. However, rather than focusing solely on the ancient sect, I have been convinced that taking some comparative glances at other apocalyptic groups can be interesting and insightful. In the fall of 2012, the Association for Jewish Studies dedicated an issue of the magazine, *AJS Perspectives*, to the theme of apocalypse. Albert Baumgarten makes the point that "Qumran was no exception" to a characteristic of people within religious groups who have their own individual hopes for the future, de-

---

1. L. Festinger, H. W. Riecken, and S. Schachter, *When Prophecy Fails* (Minneapolis: University of Minnesota Press, 1956).

spite differing views of communal leaders.[2] Indeed, the people of the community of Qumran share several ideas and behaviors with other religious groups from the past and present, and these similarities are worth exploring. I agree with Lester Grabbe, who writes in his essay comparing the Teacher of Righteousness with David Koresh, the Texas leader of the Branch Davidian group in the 1980–90s, that scholars of ancient religious groups have much to learn from similar groups that "still flourish in our contemporary world."[3] The sociological and ideological studies of apocalyptic groups, such as the Millerites of the 1830s, have proved fruitful and given us opportunity to consider possible parallels with similar ancient groups about which we know so much less. In this study of prophecy, politics, and apocalyptic ideology at Qumran, I will include what I think are some useful comparisons with the modern apocalyptic Christian community known as Family Radio, led by Harold Camping, who predicted that "the rapture," "an enormous earthquake," and the beginning of "God's Judgment" will come on May 21, 2011, and that "we must realize that October 21, 2011 will be the final day of the earth's existence."[4] To aid this comparison, I have included an appendix that consists of a brief, open letter from Camping to his radio and internet audiences that was sent after the disconfirmation of his predictions in March 2012 and has become well-known on the internet as the "March 2012 Letter."

I propose that such comparisons with modern groups are all the more useful when we consider that we lack so much evidence about the Yaḥad community at Qumran. While we certainly have more firsthand knowledge of those who wrote the sectarian scrolls found at Qumran than about many other groups of antiquity, there is much more we do not know. One important aspect of communal life we cannot investigate directly is something we can only guess at for all ancient communities: the oral traditions and conversations. It seems noncontroversial to argue that, for apocalyptic communities who see themselves as living in perilous times and who read the current actions of rulers, enemies, and themselves as actions directed by a God that are personally and fundamentally significant for all of history, oral teachings were/are of primary importance, since the divine narrative was continuously being played out and daily events could be of crucial importance for the community in the final days of earthly existence. In apocalyptic groups today, often it is a weekly sermon or a daily teaching that instructs the faithful and guides them in their thinking and acting. In the case of Family Radio, it was/

---

2. A. Baumgarten, "The Pursuit of the Millennium at Qumran," *AJS Perspectives* (Fall, 2012) 11.

3. L. L. Grabbe, "Prophecy as Inspired Biblical Interpretation: The Teacher of Righteousness and David Koresh" in *Far From Minimal* (ed. D. Burns and J. W. Rogerson; London: T. & T. Clark, 2012), 142.

4. H. Camping, *We Are Almost There!* (Oakland, CA: Family Stations, 2010) 33, 58. I have taken special interest in this group since having interviewed some of their leading members in April of 2011 with my colleague, B. H. Reynolds III. Since then I have maintained a correspondence with one member.

is a radio program, broadcast to thousands.[5] The ancient equivalent materials are now lost, and although some Qumran writings are assumed to comport well with the oral tradition, we can only speculate about the daily teachings that members could hear.

Last, I will note that in my studies of literature from Qumran, I do not assume an ideological harmony among manuscripts, even in those that have been labeled by modern critics as "sectarian." I find compelling what Morton Smith argued long ago and Albert Baumgarten more recently (and differently), that there is "unreconciled diversity" in matters of ideology among the scrolls.[6] This diversity should not just be assumed but neither should it be surprising. For an intellectually and religiously active group with a history, which apparently came to live at the Qumran settlement for approximately 150 years, and which seems to have been related to or part of a larger group known as Essenes, there must have been disagreements and new ideas and arguments and discarded ideas and evolution in ideologies through the decades that are likely still reflected in their literary remains.

The goal of this investigation, then, is to describe ways in which the apocalyptic community of Qumran thought about prophecy and geopolitics, including their external enemies the *Kittim* and, more urgently, I will argue, their internal enemies—those members who may doubt and disbelieve, especially in the face of disconfirmed prophecies.

Prophets:
Divine Communication Continued

Scholarship has shown the historical inaccuracy of the traditional idea that prophecy had ceased in the postexilic period or, to state it in a more appropriate historical fashion, that Jewish religionists of the postexilic and Second Temple period were no longer making or attending to prophetic claims.[7] While some Jewish

---

5. There is, of course, an entire discussion to be had about the sociological construction of "community" and the characteristics, differences, and continuities of the ancient group at Qumran and modern forms of community using such different technologies. See H. Campbell, *When Religion Meets New Media* (London: Routledge, 2010).

6. M. Smith, "What Is Implied by the Variety of Messianic Figures?" *JBL* 78 (1959) 66–72 and A. I. Baumgarten, "Karaites, Qumran, The Calendar, And Beyond: At the Beginning of the Twenty-first Century," in *The Dead Sea Scrolls and Contemporary Culture* (ed. A. D. Roitman, L. H. Schiffman, and S. Tzoref; Leiden: Brill, 2010), 603–19.

7. See J. Barton, *Oracles of God* (Oxford: Oxford University Press, 1992), 102–16; J. Blenkinsopp, *A History of Prophecy in Israel* (Louisville: Westminster John Knox, 1996), 148–245; G. J. Brooke, "Prophecy and Prophets in the Dead Sea Scrolls: Looking Backwards and Forwards," in *Prophets, Prophecy, and Prophetic Texts in Second Temple Judaism* (ed. M. H. Floyd and R. D. Haak; London: T. & T. Clark, 2006), 151–65; L. Grabbe "Poets, Scribes, or Preachers? The Reality of Prophecy in the Second Temple Period," in *Knowing the End from the Beginning: The Prophetic, the Apocalyptic, and Their Relationships* (ed. L. Grabbe and R. Haak; London: T. & T. Clark, 2003), 192–215. The tradition can be found, for example, in Rabbinic literature, such as

religious ideologies contained the idea that their God no longer communicated via prophets, clearly there were other Jews whose ideologies were open to the idea of divine communication to individuals.[8] For example, there is a great deal of evidence of numerous prophetic claims in the first century C.E. The Jewish historian Josephus at the end of the 1st century C.E. writes of a variety of prophetic claimants (and followers), including a certain Theudas, 44–46 C.E. (*Ant.* 20.97–98), an unnamed Egyptian ca. 58 C.E. (*Ant.* 20.169–72, *J.W.* 2.261–63), Jesus son of Ananus in about 62 (*J.W.* 6.300–309), and himself, bringing a divine message to the Roman general Vespasian in 67 (*J.W.* 3.399–408).[9] Similarly, it is clear that communities of the Jewish sect later known as Christians were open to prophetic claims. A certain Anna (Luke 2:36), John the Baptizer (Mark 11:32, Matt 11:9), and Jesus (Mark 6:15, Luke 6:17, Acts 3:17–22) receive the label "prophet" in Christian writings. More significantly for our purposes is the fact that it is not just extraordinary individuals who receive the label but that some early Christians were open to the idea that a "gift of prophecy"—that is, the supernaturally bestowed ability to speak divine messages—could be given to ordinary individuals and used within the community (Acts 2:1–18, 13:1, 1 Cor 12:8–11, 14:1–5, 24, Rom 12:6, Did 11:3–12.[10] The practice of prophesying in regular meetings of groups and communities underscores for us the importance of oral delivery and tradition and the fact that there were many ancient prophecies of which we have no record. We should also point out, as we will discuss below, that claims of receiving knowledge from a deity are often found without the use of a special designation, such as נביא, προφητης, or 'prophet'. Tony Costa's study of Paul's rhetoric clearly demonstrates that the missionary Paul, who never calls himself a prophet, presented and "viewed himself 'among the prophets.'"[11] Obviously, many of the prophetic messages and prophets would not have been accepted by other rival groups—early Christian prophets would have been deemed false prophets and rejected by many other Jews—but this

---

Song Rab. 8.9. I find S. L. Cook's (*On the Question of the "Cessation of Prophecy" in Ancient Judaism* [Tübingen: Mohr Siebeck, 2011]) argument to maintain the view that prophecy did cease unconvincing, due to his narrow definition of prophecy and his extrapolation from some ancient authors to an unwarranted normative or generalized opinion of most Jews.

8. For treatment of some negative Second Temple views of prophecy, see M. Nissinen, "The Dubious Image of Prophecy," in *Prophets, Prophecy, and Prophetic Texts in Second Temple Judaism* (ed. M. H. Floyd and R. D. Haak; London: T. & T. Clark, 2006), 26–41.

9. See the complete treatment of R. Gray, *Prophetic Figures in Late Second Temple Jewish Palestine: The Evidence from Josephus* (Oxford: Oxford University Press, 1993).

10. On the phenomenon of prophetic claims among early Christians, see M. E. Boring, "Prophecy (Early Christian)," in *The Anchor Bible Dictionary* (5 vols.; ed. D. N. Freedman; New York: Doubleday, 1992), 5:495–502; and C. Forbes, *Prophecy and Inspired Speech in Early Christianity and its Hellenistic Environment* (Tübingen: J.C.B. Mohr, 1995).

11. Tony Costa, "'Is Saul of Tarsus Also among the Prophets?' Paul's Calling as Prophetic Divine Commissioning," in *Christian Origins and Hellenistic Judaism* (ed. S. E. Porter and A. W. Pitts; Leiden: Brill, 2013), 235.

is always the case with prophetic claims, no less so during the First Temple than the Second Temple, with Jews or Christians, or today.

In an earlier study on prophecy in the Dead Sea Scrolls, I surveyed the terminology for and overt references to prophets in the Scrolls, concluding that their authors speak of נביאים of the past (obviously), נביאים of the future (most famously in 1QS 9:9–11), and of divinely directed, empowered, and authorized teacher(s) and interpreter(s) of the present, though without employing the term נביאים/נביא, in any extant text in reference for current members. [12] However, there is a good deal of traditional prophetic terminology employed in the scrolls for those community leaders, and the claims of reception of knowledge from the deity are explicit. [13] More recently, Alex Jassen has supported this same idea, arguing that once we "move beyond these terminological limitations ... and examine prophetic phenomena as conceptualized by the community, a rich world of human-divine communication exists at Qumran." [14]

There is one possible exception to this apparent non-use of the term נביא by the community at Qumran for current group members. A text ascribed to Moses and named *Apocryphon of Moses* by John Strugnell (4Q375) [15]—really a pseud-epigraphical *torat-moshe*—gives instructions for deliberations concerning a prophet who has been accused of "turning you from following your God" but who is then defended by his tribe as a "just/true man and faithful prophet."

והנביא אשר יקום ודבר בכה [סרה להש]יבכה מאחרי אלוהיכה יומת וכיא
יקום השבט [אשר] הואה ממנו ואמר לוא יומת כיא צדיק הואה נביא [נ]אמן הואה

And the prophet who stands and speaks among you [a falsehood to tur]n you from following your Elohim must be put to death. And if his tribe arises and says, 'He shall not be put to death because he is true/just, a [t]rustworthy prophet (4Q375 f1i:4–7).

The text goes on to give instructions for a procedure that involves an appearance before elders and judges and a ritual involving an anointed priest, anointing oil, and sin offering in a sacred space. Because very little of the original scroll survives and the second column is especially fragmentary and difficult to read, the majority of the actual instructions are lost, [16] but they certainly went beyond ideas found

---

12. J. E. Bowley, "Prophets and Prophecy at Qumran," in *The Dead Sea Scrolls after Fifty Years* (ed. P. W. Flint and J. C. VanderKam; Leiden: Brill, 1999) 2:354–78.

13. Ibid., 371–76.

14. A. P. Jassen, "Prophecy after 'The Prophets:' The Dead Sea Scrolls and the History of Prophecy in Judaism," in *The Dead Sea Scrolls in Context: Integrating the Dead Sea Scrolls in the Study of Ancient Texts, Languages, and Cultures* (ed. A. Lange et al.; Leiden: Brill, 2011), 592–93.

15. J. Strugnell, "375. 4QApocryphon of Moses^a," in *Qumran Cave 4, XIV: Parabiblical Texts, II* (DJD 19; ed. M. Broshi et al.; Oxford: Clarendon, 1995), 113–15.

16. Strugnell (ibid., 116) argues that it is most likely that the ritual material in column two is a continuation of the case of the prophet from column one.

in Deut 18:20–22; clearly this text is not simply repeating the teachings of another scroll with teachings ascribed to Moses, namely Deuteronomy. But even without knowing the specifics of the instructions, we can see the possibility that at least in this one text, this *torat-moshe*, the author saw the possibility of applying the term נביא to a group member.[17] Obviously this one possible exception stands in clear contrast with the general non-use of the term נביא for current persons in the extant scrolls.

From a sociological and religious ideological standpoint, the ideas and claims of prophetic revelation were present among the scroll authors, if we define prophecy broadly as a claim (explicit or implicit) of divine-human communication. What we witness in the surviving Qumran literature is a shift in terminology from earlier literature of ancient Israel and Judah. The community of Qumran was not producing literature that testifies to contemporary persons they called נביאים. We have no documents that show evidence of claims using some of the earlier popular prophetic formulas, such as כה אמר יהוה ('Thus says YHWH'), which are frequent in older literature (dozens in Isaiah alone) and preserved, read, and studied at Qumran (for example, Isaiah manuscripts from Qumran also preserve the formula כה אמר יהוה more than 50 times). However, there are numerous claims to receiving and possessing communication from the deity among the Dead Sea Scrolls and titles that carry just as much ideological authoritarian weight as the title נביא.

The implicit claim of exclusive authority in the title מורה הצדק 'True Teacher' or 'True Lawgiver'[18] hardly carries less authority than the title נביא, perhaps even more. The seemingly autobiographical psalms of the *Hodayot* scroll are full of explicit claims to divine communication and supernatural inspiration, with echoes of earlier prophetic language, such as this:

ואני משכיל ידעתיכה אלי ברוח אשר נתתה בי. ונאמנה שמעתי לסוד פלאכה
ברוח קודשכה [פ]תחתה לתוכי דעת ברז שכלכה ומעין גבורת[כה

And I, Leader, have known you, my El, by the spirit that you put into me and faithfully I listened to the wonderful secret by your holy spirit. You [e]ntered into me knowledge in the mystery of your wisdom and source of [your] power (1QH^a 20:14–16).

More and similar claims can be found in 1QH^a 4:26, 6:25, 9:21, 12:5–6, 23; 17:32. Jassen has emphasized the fact that the hymn of column twelve presents the writer not only as recipient but also as proclaimer of divine revelation:

ובי האירותה פני רבים ותגבר עד לאין מספר כי הודעתני ברזי פלאכה

---

17. The word נביא is used in lines 4Q375 f1i:4 and f1i:6.

18. For discussion of translation and understanding of this common title for the community's preeminent leader, see J. C. Reeves, "The Meaning of *Moreh Sedeq* in the Light of 11QTorah," *RevQ* 13 (1998) 287–98.

By me you [El] have enlightened the face of Many and strengthened
them beyond counting for you made known to me the mysteries of your
wonders (1QHᵃ 12:28–29).

From this and numerous similar references, Jassen concludes that "the hymnist
deliberately avoids referring to himself with a prophetic designation or more common revelatory language. Yet, there can be little doubt that he viewed his activity
as recounted in this hymn as true revelation and as part of a larger institution of
prophecy."[19]

Far from the notion of prophetic activity diminishing, one could argue that,
in the postexilic period of some Jewish communities, claims of divine communication were actually expanding as ideas evolved among Jewish religionists. John
Reeves has described a process he calls "prophetization," or "bestowal of prophetic
rank upon a number of literary or even historical figures" who did not earlier have
or claim such a status.[20] Taking the example of David, who is never called a prophet
in Israelite literature such as Samuel, Kings, Psalms, or Chronicles, and who in fact,
in ancient narratives about him, employs prophets and looks to others in order to
receive divine instruction (1 Samuel 22; 2 Samuel 7), we find that later traditions
(Jewish, Christian, Muslim) label him a prophet. One of the earliest attestations of
the new "David the prophet" is found in the Qumran Psalms Scroll (11Q5 27:11),
which says that David composed his songs 'through prophecy' (בנבואה). We can
see this trend of prophetization continued and become wider and stronger in a
whole host of later Jewish and Christian texts that read not just David as a prophet
but also read a whole variety of nonprophetic texts, such as Psalms or Genesis narratives, as prophecies speaking of current and/or future events.

The *pešer* or commentary genre that we encounter at Qumran also expands
the ideas and claims of "revelation" by giving us the notion of a divinely inspired
interpreter of ancient texts. Similar to the way the apocalyptic genre may involve
a claim of a supernatural interpreter for dreams or visions, so too the *pešer* form
can include the claim of divinely given interpretations of ancient scrolls.[21] In the
case of the commentary to Habakkuk, this True Teacher is said to be the one "to
whom El made known all the mysteries of the words of his servants the prophets" (מורה הצדק אשר הודיעו אל את כול רזי דברי עבדיו הנבאים, 1QpHab 7:4–5).
Lester Grabbe has pointed out that this kind of inspiration of the interpreter of
sacred texts was also claimed by David Koresh.[22] The idea that the text is full of

19. Jassen, "Prophecy after 'The Prophets,'" 583.

20. J. C. Reeves, "Scriptural Authority in Early Judaism," in *Living Traditions of the Bible*
(ed. J. E. Bowley; St. Louis: Chalice, 1999), 72–74. See also J. Kugel, "David the Prophet," in *Poetry
and Prophecy* (ed. J. Kugel; Ithaca, NY: Cornell University Press, 1990), 45–55.

21. For a lengthy discussion on the move to "inspired interpretation," especially focusing
on Chronicles, see W. M. Schniedewind, *The Word of God in Transition: From Prophet to Exegete
in the Second Temple Period* (Sheffield: Sheffield Academic, 1995).

22. Grabbe, "Prophecy as Inspired Biblical Interpretation," 149.

mysteries underscores the need for divinely given skill and knowledge for understanding what one reads. Similarly, though subtly, Harold Camping of Family Radio also claims divine inspiration (not his term) of his interpretations in these words: "There are three especially important areas of truth that are in view as God, in our day, opens our eyes to much new truth that throughout the church age was not well understood."[23] The three areas have to do with the God's plan for "salvation," "end-times," and "judgment," but our spotlight here is on Camping's claim that God has opened the eyes to new truth.

Returning to our Qumran context, we should also consider other genres of literature, such as the many apocalypses from the postexilic and Second Temple periods that present their audience with a revelation from the God as clear examples of claims to having received divine communications.[24] Thus, the practice of writing works that purport to contain divine messages to honored figures of the past such as Moses (Deuteronomy, Jubilees, 4Q375) and Enoch (Enoch) continued unabated from earlier times.[25]

Finally, we should consider the fact that prophetic activity, broadly defined, has often been especially a practice of oral communication, even in literate societies, and thus it is certainly a possibility that the Qumran community at some time(s) in their long history practiced prophetic speech in their group meetings or outside (regardless of what terminology they might have used), though this remains a matter of speculation. In the text ascribed to Moses considered above, 4Q375, the prophet under review is one 'who stands and speaks among you' (הנביא אשר יקום ודבר בכה), which could suggest a communal meeting, if taken quite literally. Josephus, too, possibly lends support to such an idea when describing the Essenes in his *Jewish War*, for he says that some of them "profess to foretell what will happen, having studied sacred scrolls and sacred purifications and apothegms of prophets and they are seldom wrong" (*J.W.* 2.159). In other parts of both *Jewish War* and the *Antiquities*, he tells of three Essenes, Judas, (*J.W.* 1.78–80; *Ant.*

---

23. Camping, *We are Almost There!*, 5.

24. For an excellent discussion of literary and social categories, such as prophecy, prophet, and apocalypse, see L. L. Grabbe, "Prophetic and Apocalyptic: Time for New definitions—and New Thinking," in *Knowing the End From the Beginning: The Prophetic, the Apocalyptic, and Their Relationships* (ed. L. L. Grabbe and R. D. Haak; London: T. & T. Clark, 2003), 107–33.

25. George Brooke stresses the importance of various written genres at Qumran as prophetic and concludes that "in the wide range of parabiblical compositions there are prophetic continuities both with the literary prophets and with other prophetic figures. Such continuities can also be seen in the inspired explicit interpretations of unfulfilled curses, blessings, oracles, visions and dreams, that are mostly but not exclusively to be found in the writings of the literary prophets. The intellectual transformation of prophetic activity has its setting in a complex matrix of apocalyptic, priestly, scribal and mantological ideas and practices. All this deserves the label "prophecy" as the Qumran Community and the movement from which it came and of which it was a part looked backwards to the prophets of old and their literary legacy and brought that legacy forwards to their present" (Brooke, "Prophecy and Prophets," 165).

13.311–13), Simon (*J. W.* 2.112–13; *Ant.* 17.345–48), Menahem (*Ant.* 15.373–79) who predicted events that indeed happened. Might this linking of study of sacred scrolls and prophetic words to predictions of the future reflect what we find in various *pešarim*? The predictions mentioned by Josephus are certainly evidence for oral prophetic activity by Essenes and, if the Qumranites were a group of Essenes, perhaps they shared the practice.[26]

The continuation of claims among some Jews to possess knowledge from the realm of the divine should not prevent us from noticing evolution and changes in terminology and ideology of various communities.[27] We also should not assume that Jewish communities and individuals all evolved in the same directions. Some may well have denied the legitimacy of or ignored prophetic claims, while others accepted them. Regarding the Qumran community, how was the apparent shift in terminology away from using the title נביא considered by persons of the Qumran community? Unfortunately, no answer is preserved in the scrolls, but it may well have been spoken of or explained in group meetings, study sessions, or conversations. Rebecca Gray, following John Barton, argues that Jews of the time who held that prophecy had declined or ceased were exhibiting a kind of nostalgia for the distant past,[28] a characteristic of many cultures. I would argue that this can also explain the evolution of terminology. The True Teacher and the community looked to the hoary נביאים of old through a common cultural/national historio-mythology of "a golden age" or "good old days," and this is reflected in the tendency not to use the term נביא for themselves, even while their claims of divine communication are just as explicit.

It seems unlikely to me that the evolution in terminology went unnoticed, since the shift reflects issues of ideological authority. The source of one's authority is crucial for any kind of claim to knowing a divine will, and ancient texts often reveal, explicitly and implicitly, conflicts regarding such authority. Israelite stories such as Miriam and Aaron questioning whether YHWH spoke only through Moses (Num 12), instructions for determining a legitimate prophecy of YHWH (Deut 18.15–22), and numerous accounts of conflict among YHWH's prophets (1 Kgs 22, Jer 28) are well-known examples of disputes about authority that doubtlessly reflect real disputes in the authors' social milieu. So also in *Hodayot* 12, the authority of the community leader is pitted against other prophetic claimants who are labeled 'deceitful seers' (רמיה הוזי, 1QH[a]12:10) and 'fraudulent prophets' (כזב נביאי, 12:16). We have already noted that 4Q375 gives directions regarding a prophet who has led others astray but who is defended as a "true and faithful prophet" by some. Clearly, the community was cognizant of and attending to matters of

---

26. Gray, *Prophetic Figures*, 80–111.

27. Already in the ancient Israelite text of Samuel (1 Sam 9:9) we have an editorial comment about a perceived shift from the term ראה 'seer' to נביא 'prophet'. On the function of this antiquarian notice, see P. K. McCarter Jr., *I Samuel* (AB 8; New York: Doubleday, 1980), 177.

28. Gray, *Prophetic Figures*, 8, 34; Barton, *Oracles*, 115–16.

prophetic dispute. Similarly, I can find no place where Harold Camping is called a prophet in materials from Family Radio, yet after his failed prediction of 21 May 2011, it was not uncommon to find him labeled a "false prophet."[29] I would argue that the nostalgia principle applies in many modern religious contexts as well, where some will not classify themselves with "the prophets." But even without the title, claims are being made; who speaks for, or more broadly, who legitimately represents the will of the deity, in this case YHWH, was a question no less important and no easier to answer for the Qumran community than it was for Jeremiah or Howard Camping.

Such conflicts regarding authority are surely inevitable for religious groups at odds with other groups in their social contexts. Furthermore, there would be a heightened sense of need for authorial legitimacy in minority groups, such as the *Yaḥad* community at Qumran, the Millerites in the 1840s, and the modern Family Radio community. Those claiming divine authority in the 7th–6th centuries B.C.E. Judah may well have proclaimed שמעו דבר יהוה 'Hear YHWH's message' (Jer 2:4), but not everyone believed them. In the following centuries, claims of divine communication, explicit and implicit, continued to abound. Apocalypses and other revelatory claims of this period are often found to be, like Jeremiah, "self-authenticating"—that is, as explained by Reeves, "the revelatory event itself supplies the necessary validation for the information that is revealed to the seer or prophet," and I would add that often the formal designation of נביא did not even need to be used.[30] A person (speaker, writer) makes a claim (implicit or explicit) to know the will of the deity and the audience believes them or does not, and no other epistemic evidence is offered. Reeves cites the works of Daniel (chs. 7–12), 1 Enoch, the War Scroll from Qumran, and 4 Ezra as examples. I would also include the statements cited above from the *pešarim* and the *Hodayot* scroll, which state explicitly that the teacher and interpreter(s) have been given supernatural insight to teach and to interpret. We can read the claims of David Koresh and Harold Camping in this same manner. All of these examples may use earlier texts or tropes or traditions, but that usage does not lessen their own claims to divine communication.

However, we also find a disjunction between our ancient and modern apocalyptic movements in this matter. While David Koresh and Harold Camping have claimed divine aid for their interpretations as noted above, they put much greater explicit emphasis on the authority of their sacred text, "The Bible" and its supposed perfections and harmony. This is a characteristic of many modern religionists who consider "the Bible" their ultimate authority and write and speak frequently and

---

29. The headline from May 22, 2011 of the online Religion News Blog reads, "False prophet Harold Camping had no Plan B," no author, n.p. [cited 12 August 2013]. Online: http://www .religionnewsblog.com/25970/harold-camping-false-prophet). That same day, a Facebook page was founded, named "Harold Camping Is A False Prophet."

30. J. C. Reeves, *Trajectories in Near Eastern Apocalyptic* (Atlanta: SBL, 2005), 5–6.

clearly about such conceptions, which they see as foundational to their interpretive enterprise. For example, ch. 1 of Camping's *We Are Almost There!* is entitled "The Glorious Word of God" and expounds at length on the Bible's infallibility and authority.

> The Bible is God's Word. In the original languages of the Bible, mainly Hebrew and Greek, every word, and every letter of every word, is from the mouth of God.... The Bible in its entirety is God's supreme law book.... The Bible is its own dictionary and commentary.[31]

I quote these statements to emphasize that we find no such notions characteristic of authors of the Dead Sea Scrolls and no comparable ideological declarations are made about the texts they interpret. Whatever we might say about the use and authority of older textual traditions among the Qumran community or parallels with later apocalyptic communities, we must carefully distinguish Qumran practices and ideology from later foreign theological traditions and methods of reading. "The Bible," as it is known in the modern world and as many modern traditions understand it theologically, "was invented in the fifteenth and sixteenth centuries," argues Benjamin Braude,[32] and I would argue that proper historical-critical understanding of the Dead Sea Scrolls and all ancient Israelite/Jewish literature must divest itself of ideas about "the Bible," since it did not exist.[33]

Condemning the Enemy Without: Kittim

Looking into some of the sectarian writings, we find that not a few of them are in fact prophecies, declarations of remarkable events that are to occur in the near future in the life of the sect and the geopolitics of their known world, often involving a group known as the "Kittim." In the surviving documents produced by the Qumran community, 46 times the gentilic "Kittim" (כתיאים or כתיים) is employed, mostly within six different compositions—namely, the *War Scroll* (1QM, 4Q491, 4Q492, 4Q496), *Pešer Psalms* (1Q16), *Pešer Isaiah* (4Q161), *Pešer Nahum* (4Q169), *Pešer Apocalypse of Weeks* (4Q247, a small scrap, possibly a nonsectarian composition), and the *Sefer ha-Milḥamah* or *Scroll of the War* (4Q285+11Q14).[34] This is a sizable number of uses in so few compositions when, by comparison, the

---

31. Camping, *We Are Almost There!* 1.

32. B. Braude, "The Sons of Noah and the Construction of Ethic and Geographical Identities in the Early Modern Periods," *The William and Mary Quarterly* 54 (1997) 106.

33. For discussions on this issue, see J. C. VanderKam, *The Dead Sea Scrolls and the Bible* (Grand Rapids, MI: Eerdmans, 2012); J. E. Bowley, "Bible" in *The Oxford Encyclopedia of The Books of the Bible* (ed. M. D. Coogan; Oxford: Oxford University Press, 2011), 1:73–84; J. E. Bowley and J. C. Reeves, "Rethinking the Concept of 'Bible:' Some Theses and Proposals," *Henoch: Studi storicofilologici sull'ebraismo* 25 (2003) 3–18.

34. M. G. Abegg Jr., J. E. Bowley, and E. M. Cook, *The Dead Sea Scrolls Concordance*, Vol. 1 (Leiden: Brill, 2003).

ancient Israelite literature now preserved in Hebrew Bible contains but ten uses of Kittim, most of them somewhat obscure references to peoples dwelling in the West, most likely on Cyprus, based on the name of its city Kition.[35] Hanan Eshel traces the shifting usage of the sobriquet among Qumran and other authors in his useful and compelling essay, "The Changing Notion of the Enemy and Its Impact on the Pesharim."[36]

At least beginning in the 3rd or 2nd century B.C.E., one can find a variety of identifications in other literature as well. Thus, following Eshel, in Jubilees, the author employs the term for Greeks (Jub 24:28–29), 1 Maccabees uses it for Macedonians (1 Macc 1:1, 8:5), the apocalypse in Daniel (11:29–30) relates the term apparently to the Romans, and Josephus says the term applies vaguely to "all the islands and most of the countries near the sea" (*Ant.* 1.128).[37]

We also find a variety of identifications among Qumran compositions. The small fragment 4Q247, apparently related to the Apocalypse of Weeks of Enoch 91 and 93, speaks of the "king of the Kittim" (line 6), and our best guess is that it refers to some Hellenistic ruler. The Kittim in the *War Scroll* (more than 20 times) can be identified more specifically as the Seleucid invaders.[38] In the various *pešarim*, we find that the Isaiah commentary uses the term for Hellenistic armies, and the later-written *pešarim* to Habakkuk and Nahum use it for the Romans. Eshel summarizes these shifts from Greeks/Hellenistic kingdoms to Seleucids to Romans as reflecting "change over time in the views of the Qumran community."[39]

Regardless of which national group the author has in mind, the term is always used with negative connotations; the Kittim are foreign invaders, who are always construed as outsiders, "the other," even if they might be used by the God of Israel for his purposes. In the rhetoric of these scrolls, the Kittim, who are always powerful rulers and players in the geopolitics of the era, are labeled only by a title, a substitute name, almost a generic designation of "Enemy." Certainly the authors knew the national names of such powerful rulers and armies, but to label them with a different name, foreign and negative, a label of their own making, is, within the context of the community, to imagine a kind of rhetorical control over the powerful armies of their day. We find this same kind of rhetorical power practiced in the numerous compositions where Qumran authors give their enemies epithets and titles, such as "The Wicked Priest," "The Liar," or "Spreader of Lies," rather than referring to them by name. Using such titles (negative and positive) functions to label deviants and outsiders and to affirm communal ideals.[40]

---

35. For more on the names and other uses, see D. W. Baker, "Kittim," in *The Anchor Bible Dictionary* (6 vols.; ed. D. N. Freedman; New York: Doubleday, 1992) 4:93.

36. The essay is ch. 9 of Eshel's *The Dead Sea Scrolls and the Hasmonean State* (Grand Rapids, MI: Eerdmans, 2008), 163–79.

37. Ibid., 163–64.

38. Following Eshel's argument and identification, ibid., 166–71.

39. Ibid., 175.

40. On the function of labels, see M. A. Collins, *The Use of Sobriquets in the Qumran Dead Sea Scrolls* (London: T. & T. Clark, 2009).

The author of *Pešer Habakkuk*, in his lengthy description (the longest in any scroll; approximately two columns of text, from 1QpHab 2:12–4:13) of the Kittim, the Romans, puts it starkly: "Kittim, the fear and dread of whom are on all nations. By intention their only thought is to do evil, and in deceit and trickery they conduct themselves with all the peoples" (1QpHab 3:4–6). כתיים becomes a kind of symbol signifying Foreign-Pagan-Enemy.

Use of the sobriquet Kittim as a symbol for an evil foe allowed flexibility, as foreign enemies come and go through history. In this way, "Kittim" can stand for any outsider enemy, no matter how distant or even unrealistic, or however close and threatening. Like many of the prophets of ancient Israelite societies, condemnation of foreign powers was not necessarily a communication delivered to or intended for the ears of the foreigners. Such proclamations were a form of historical-religious claim, meant to convince an insider audience and the speaker/writer. The *Pešer Habakkuk* author concludes his description of the Kittim with this condemnation, beginning with a quotation from Habakkuk 1:12–13:

> "For judgment you have set him; O Rock, and for rebuke you made him. Too pure eyes for seeing evil, and you cannot even watch wrongdoing." The interpretation means that El will not exterminate his people through the Gentiles; and he will give the power to pass judgment on the Gentiles to his chosen (1QpHab 5:1–4).

Thus, the community can look forward to a grand divine reversal of fortunes; they, the faithful and chosen of their God, will be judging the Gentiles, the Kittim, the Romans. Such rhetorical claims may well have encouraged the faithful.

Engaging the Enemy Within:
The Yaḥad

Such apocalyptic encouragement, however, comes with a price, and the flexible symbolic use of the Kittim within the Qumran apocalyptic ideology could create doubts and logical problems for the community. As is well established, Qumran apocalyptic[41] thinking includes the notions that history, in which evil forces on earth and in the heavens do battle with the forces of good led by the God of Israel, is moving toward a predetermined end and that this end involves the conquest of evil powers and the God's final judgment of nations and individuals. Knowledge of this divine plan comes via special revelations (apocalypses)[42] from the divine realm to the faithful community of Israel, apparently especially through their True Teacher (who lived in the second half of the second century B.C.E.). Most importantly for purposes of this essay, the Qumran covenanters saw

---

41. For a full discussion of apocalyptic thought and literature at Qumran, see J. J. Collins, *Apocalypticism in the Dead Sea Scrolls* (London: Routledge, 1997).

42. The use here of "apocalypses" is not limited to the literary genre. I refer to any claim of a revelation, knowledge through divine communication.

themselves as witnesses and participants in the final act of this divine drama, the
'end of days' (אחרית הימים), a popular term in scrolls from Qumran, occurring
more than 30 times.[43] That is to say, many of the scrolls teach or reflect the idea
that the "end of days" events and actions of their God were being observed in their
own lifetime in geopolitical events and in the deeds of people of Israel, including
their own. As Collins observes, "this 'end' was not in the vague and distant future
but was expected at a particular time in the sect's history."[44] Thus, the instructions and beliefs of the speakers and writers obtain urgency, and the community
members must know, plan, and act in accord with this special knowledge that
their God has granted them. One of the most important documents of the sect, a
supplementary guidebook, called the *Community Rule* (1QSa), begins: 'This is the
rule for all the congregation of Israel in the end of days' (וזה הסרך לכול עדת ישראל
באחרית הימים, 1QSa 1:1). Similarly, a letter apparently intended not just for group
members, 4QMMT, informs the readers that 'this is the end of days' (זה הוא אחרית
הימים שישובו בישראל, 4Q398 f11_13:4).

The author of *Pešer Habakkuk,* writing in the mid-1st century B.C.E., also
claims to know that the community is experiencing the "end of days" (1QpHab
2:3–10) and that, while others may not believe, the community's priestly teacher
has been given this knowledge from their God. In column seven of the same commentary, the author seems aware that some have become impatient about the
coming of the final end (הקץ האחרון, 1QpHab 7:7), and he implores the loyal ones
to have patience and to believe what God had made known to the True Teacher
(1QpHab 7:1–14). Apparently, some members were beginning to doubt whether
the predicted end was really upon them. For any apocalyptic community, such
doubts are serious issues that must be confronted and engaged.

What gives rise to such doubts? If one claims that "the end" will come within
100 or 1000 years, or some vague indefinite time, then one's prediction cannot
come true for any contemporary person, and one is merely acknowledging a kind
of agnosticism. Most importantly, such distant or vague predictions lose existen-
tially significant force for the audience. This reduces one's relevance and reveals to
the audience that these revelations for the "end of days" (or the "end times") may
not really be of practical concern to the lives of the living community. The significant urgency has been lost.

We might ask: what is the time limit for an appeal that is still urgent? How
wide can the window of time be open so that one's listeners will be encouraged
and spurred to hope and action? I would suggest that the limit is "us"—that is,
the limit is the lifetime of the audience, and this limit is crucial for creating and

---

43. A. Steudel, "אחרית הימים in the Texts from Qumran," *RevQ* 16 (1993) 225–46.

44. J. J. Collins, "The Expectation of the End in the Dead Sea Scrolls," in *Eschatology, Messianism, and the Dead Sea Scrolls* (ed. C. A. Evans and P. W. Flint; Grand Rapids, MI: Eerdmans,
1997), 82.

maintaining the urgency of any appeal to act, believe, or hope.[45] Only within this timeframe is an existential imminence created. We can hear the urgency in some early Christian writings that also claim that the end is near and reflect this lifetime limit. In 1 Corinthians, for example, Paul writes that "these [stories of divine punishment of Israel] were written down to warn us, upon whom the ends of the ages have come,"[46] or, as the Gospel of Mark puts it, "Indeed I [Jesus] am telling you, that some who are standing right here will not die before they see God's kingdom arrive in power."[47] As we will consider below, the Qumran community at one time seems to have predicted important events to occur in roughly 40 years, which is certainly within a timeframe that allows for the maintenance of the urgency.

Such claims of soon-to-be-experienced events may well enliven, encourage, and activate people, but what happens when the events do not occur? What happens after 40 years of claiming that one's community is living in the "end of days," which apparently are not ending? One of the biggest hurdles to face for an apocalyptic group is disconfirmation of a central tenant of ideology, and face it they will. To date there has been a 100 percent failure rate of groups claiming a "soon" end of the world, so we might call this the Universal Apocalyptic Failure Principle, and it is observable in most every century. It is fascinating to consider the ways the Qumran community may have coped with it's own disconfirmations. We should also be aware of the possibility that much of the coping rhetoric may have been put forward only orally among the Yaḥad and never committed to writing. It is certainly the case with modern apocalyptic movements that times of disconfirmation have resulted in the community banding together to discuss matters and encourage one another.

Although Qumran apocalyptic writings boldly condemn the Kittim, the Foreign-Pagan-Enemy of the day, through authoritative and powerful rhetoric, it is the enemies within—discouragement, doubts, disbelievers, naysayers, and sect dropouts—that must be faced with urgency. These are the actual "enemies" that must be engaged, especially in the face of disconfirmation, in order for the community to survive and prosper in the milieu of Jewish culture of the era.

---

45. It is important to point out, perhaps especially for the sake of frequent claims of modern apocalyptic theologies, that a lack of specificity of date and time does not open the door for correctness/accuracy in one's apocalyptic predictions. Any prediction that is made within a time frame of one generation (those currently alive) or using words such as "soon" has enough specificity to be meaningful and urgent for the current listeners/audience. All such predictions to date have been wrong—proved wrong by history and time.

46. 1 Cor 10:11. See also 1 Cor 7:25–31, 15:51–2; Rom 13:11–12; 1 Thess 4:15–5:11.

47. Mark 9:1. See also Mark 13:24–31 and Luke's revision in Luke 9:27 and 11:20. VanderKam asserts that "both the Qumranites and the first Christians can be called eschatological communities in the sense that both were convinced that the end was near and ordered their beliefs and communal practices accordingly"; see J. Vanderkam, *The Dead Sea Scrolls Today* (Grand Rapids, MI: Eerdmans, 2010), 215.

We should notice that it is the imminence of the "end of days" that creates the urgency for the community and heightens the value of the religious encouragement, but it is also the imminence that carries the seeds of discouragement and doubt. In the *Damascus Document*, the community is told that "from the day of the ingathering of the unique Teacher, until the destruction of all the men of war who turned back with the man of lies there shall be about forty years" (CD 20:14–15). Annette Studel believes that we can be fairly specific about this date, calculating the 'about forty years' (כשנים ארבעים) to be 72 b.c.e.[48] Collins is skeptical that we can calculate so accurately[49] but still sees this text as highly significant for the apocalyptic beliefs of the sect, linking these ideas in CD with *Pešer Habakkuk* 7:4–14, which also speaks of the True Teacher. There, the author weaves words and ideas from Habakkuk with others from Dan 12, which also contains a claim to know that the end was nearly upon his readers. The *Pešer Habakkuk* commentator urges patience, as the community awaits the end. It seems quite clear that expectations of "the end" were high, and the commentator did not discourage such expectations but rather encouraged them to be patiently maintained. Collins concludes that we can reasonably infer "that the 'end' was expected shortly before the *pešer* was written. While we do not know the exact date of the composition of this *pešer*, all indicators point to the middle of the first century BCE."[50] This corresponds with the understanding that the *Damascus Document* predicts that the destruction of all the warriors who went back to the "Man of the Lie" will be in "about forty years," somewhere in the early-to-mid-1st century b.c.e. If this True Teacher and recipient of divine knowledge died around the end of the second century, then the "about forty years" predicted in CD 20 would be approximately the time that *Pešer Habakkuk* was written.[51] It seems likely that in the middle of the 1st century b.c.e., at least some believing Qumranites would have been expecting significant destruction of their enemies and some kind of victory, but instead they would only have experienced the replacement of political overlords, as the Romans under Pompey took the region by force in 63 b.c.e., becoming more and more dominant in the following decades. The disappointment of disconfirmed promises would have weighed heavy on the Qumran covenanters, which explains the admonition to continued patience and loyalty in the *Pešer Habakkuk*:

כיא עוד חזון למועד יפיח לקץ ולוא יכזב פשרו אשר יארוך הקץ האחרון ויתר על
כול אשר דברו הנביאים כיא רזי אל להפלא אם יתמהמה חכה לו כיא בוא יבוא
ולוא יאחר]] [[פשרו על אנשי האמת עושי התורה אשר לוא ירפו ידיהם מעבודת
האמת בהמשך עליהם הקץ האחרון כיא כול קיצי אל יבואו לתכונם כאשר חקק להם
ברזי ערמתו

---

48. Steudel, "אחרית הימים," 236–39.

49. Collins, *Apocalypticism*, 67.

50. Ibid., 83.

51. Ibid., 82–85.

"For the vision is for a specific event; it testifies to that time and does not lie" [Hab 2:3]. The interpretation means that the end time will be longer than the prophets spoke for the mysteries of El are wonderful. "If it delays, be patient for it will certainly come and not delay" [Hab 2:3]. The interpretation refers to people of the truth who do the torah, whose hands do not stop from the work of truth when the end time is stretched on them for all the times of El will come in their order just as he decreed them in the mystery of his arrangement. (1QpHab 7:5–14)

This urge toward patience and loyalty and confidence in the God's plan may well suggest a situation where some sect members were doubting, disagreeing, or even leaving the group.

Eshel has added another argument to the scenario of disconfirmation by focusing on the shift of identification of "Kittim" from Seleucids (*War Scroll*) to Romans (*Pešer Habakkuk* and *Pešer Nahum*). If we bring the ideology of apocalyptic thinking to bear on the meaning of Kittim, the identity of the sobriquet becomes much more complicated for Qumran writers. It is interesting to note that the use of Kittim occurs over and over in writings that are apocalyptic—apocalyptic either in their literary form, such as *The War Scroll* (1QM), or in their worldview, such as the cited *pešarim*.[52] If the deity has revealed that the Kittim are the Seleucids and that "soon" or within a set period of time the forces of the God will defeat the Kittim, then believers of this supposed revelation will be expecting such action, and if it does not occur, they will face the challenge and pain of disconfirmation. Eshel argues that claims of divine revelation, and thus a divine guarantee of accuracy, create a situation in which the community may well be left confused if events do not follow the prophetic script. In the *War Scroll*, likely written in the mid-2nd century B.C.E., the Kittim whom the deity will defeat are the Seleucids, and those who believed this writing, "those who thought the Kittim to be the Seleucids, assumed that salvation was near, and it would have been difficult for them to admit that this identification was wrong." The result was "that this shift in identification must have posed a serious theological problem for the members of the Qumran sect.[53]

Collins asserts that this lack of specificity of a date would have lessened "the trauma of disappointment that the Millerites experienced in nineteenth-century America, when the appointed day passed,"[54] but I would argue that the disappointment for the Qumranites simply came more slowly and with a longer time for questions, disagreements, arguments, and doubts to fester, and also with a longer time for some to attempt to devise coping strategies. The admonition to be

---

52. Collins (*Apocalypticism*, 8) notes that the apocalyptic worldview is pervasive in Qumran texts, far beyond the few compositions that are apocalypses in literary form.

53. Eshel, *The Dead Sea Scrolls*, 177–78.

54. Collins, "Expectation," 85.

patient in *Pešer Habakkuk* 7 is likely a reaction to questioning and doubts and one way to help people cope.

According to Eshel, we can also see some other results of the disconfirmation. Reactions to disconfirmation by Qumran community leaders can be seen as coping mechanisms, and they correspond to those of other apocalyptic groups. First, disappointment produced by any teachings and writings, such as *The War Scroll*, that held the Seleucids to be the soon-to-be-destroyed Kittim caused someone in the community to recalculate and reassign the label "Kittim." Thus, in the mid-1st-century *pešarim* on Habakkuk and Nahum, which were both composed after the 63 B.C.E. take-over by Pompey, the Romans are the Kittim, and obviously "the end of days" has been moved from the time of Seleucid to Roman rule. Second, "the fact that we do not find any references to" the tumultuous political and geologic events of the year 31 B.C.E. "in the *pešarim* found at Qumran, testifies that at some point, before 31 B.C.E., the leaders of the Qumran sect stopped composing new *pešarim*.[55] In other words, Eshel argues that it is not that such interpretations would have ended in the oral practices of the group but that they were no longer committed to writing. Third, Eshel proposes that the legislation found in the 4Q375 text discussed above, which legislates ritual procedures for a prophet who has both led people astray and yet is considered by some a "faithful prophet," "resulted from its authors' awareness that the messianic expectations of the sect had not been fulfilled as had been predicted in the pesharim."[56] This is certainly an intriguing possibility, though certainly not proved, especially because so little of the manuscript is preserved.

What is certain in the *torat-moshe* 4Q375 text, however, is that major dissension and dispute within the community about a prophet is envisioned—a prophet from *within* the community. The scenario involves a prophet who has led others astray and is considered to be deserving of death. Yet, there are others in the community who support him and oppose the punishment. We are in the dark about the social context of this text, but a split in the community is clear. Dissension is common in apocalyptic movements after disconfirmation of predictions, and the offending prophet's word and character are often called into question. It is still easy today to find on the internet evidence of people who were within Family Radio but have left and condemned Harold Camping.

Dissension, if allowed to fester, can completely destroy a community or cause it to splinter into several different organizations. However, groups also find ways to cope, even after serious disconfirmation. Fetsinger, Riecken, and Schachter have observed communal reactions to the dissonance produced by disconfirmation of predictions and describe at least five ways of coping with the intellectual conflict:

---

55. Eshel, *The Dead Sea Scrolls*, 179.
56. Ibid., 178.

1. changing beliefs or behaviors involved in the dissonance,
2. acquiring new information or beliefs that will increase consonance and reduce dissonance,
3. forgetting or reducing the importance of ideas that are in conflict,
4. fortifying themselves to endure the discomfort of dissonance,
5. persuading other people to join the sect since, "*if more and more people can be persuaded that the system of belief is correct, then clearly it must, after all, be correct.*"[57]

Obviously, the logic of the last coping mechanism is fatally flawed (everyone can be wrong!), but it is the psychological and sociological comfort of such thinking that proves effective.

Scholars have identified several such coping mechanisms in ancient Jewish literature.[58] It is now commonly understood that the time predicted in Dan 12:11 must have come and gone, and that a small extension of time was added by another author in what is now Dan 12:12.[59] This would fit well with coping mechanism (2), the attempt to provide new information that will solve the problem of dissonance. The risk, of course, is that if the new information is also proved wrong, then one's credibility will suffer even more. If Eshel is right about the shift in the identity of "Kittim" from Seleucids to Romans, then we have another example of a kind of updating of information in order to lessen disconfirmation. *Pešer Habakkbuk* column 7, with it admonition to hope and wait, can also be read as the presentation of a coping mechanism number (4), a fortification of beliefs to strengthen the resolve of sect members. In addition, encouragements toward loyalty and obedience must have been manifold in the meetings and conversations of the sect.

We find these coping mechanisms illustrated in the modern Family Radio community as well, and I think listening and learning about their reactions to disconfirmation might give possible insights into the behavior of ancient apocalyptic groups, suggesting possibilities for their oral rhetoric and suggesting kinds of rhetoric for scholars to look for in the ancient writings. I have placed in an appendix a short, open letter that was published by Harold Camping and Family Radio in March of 2012, which has become known on the internet as "The March 2012 Letter" and is still available on the Family Radio website (see pp. 511ff. below). It illustrates how one apocalyptic community, which still has strong membership, has reacted to and is coping with the disconfirmation of their predictions.

---

57. Fetsinger, *When Prophecy Fails*, 28. The authors actually list three forms of "attempts to reduce dissonance" (p. 26), but I have separated out two more from their further discussion (pp. 26–28).

58. In Jewish history, perhaps the most famous example of disconfirmation and maintenance of faith by many is the example of Sabbatai Zevi (1626–76), dealt with by Fetsinger, Riecken, and Schachter (*When Prophecy Fails*, 8–12).

59. L. F. Hartman and A. A. Di Lella, *The Book of Daniel* (Garden City, NY: Doubleday, 1977), 313–14.

Just as some Qumran writers may have recalculated their dates and moved the "end of days" from the time of the Seleucids to that of the Romans, so also some members of Family Radio used coping method (2) and acquired "new information" by studying their sacred text more and recognizing an earlier error. This recalculation is actually from a sister organization of Family Radio, eBible Fellowship, which in late 2011 recalculated, admitting a previous calculation error, and arriving at March 9, 2012 as the day of final judgment.[60] In this case, we also witness a schism in the group, with Harold Camping not proclaiming a new date, and a new banner on the Family Radio website stating, "Family Radio is not affiliated with, nor does it endorse any other group, fellowship, or website."[61] In an opposite move, Camping exhibits coping mechanism (1) by denying that he has new information, has explicitly changed his beliefs, and or admitted that he was in error:

> Yes, we humbly acknowledge we were wrong about the timing . . .
> We must also openly acknowledge that we have no new evidence pointing to another date for the end of the world. . . . . . We humbly recognize that God may not tell His people the date when Christ will return, any more than He tells anyone the date they will die physically.
> We realize that many people are hoping they will know the date of Christ's return. In fact for a time Family Radio fell into that kind of thinking. But we now realize that those people who were calling our attention to the Bible's statement that "of that day and hour knoweth no man" (Matthew 24:36 & Mark 13:32), were right in their understanding of those verses and Family Radio was wrong. . . . . . [Our] incorrect and sinful statement allowed God to get the attention of a great many people who otherwise would not have paid attention. . . . However, even so, that does not excuse us. We tremble before God as we humbly ask Him for forgiveness for making that sinful statement. We are so thankful that God is so loving that He will forgive even this sin.[62]

I quote Camping at length to underscore how explicit he is in his admission of error and change. This kind of confession also makes me wonder about the Qumran ritual of 4Q375, which is dictated to be performed with the prophet who led people astray but whose life is spared. In the lost portions of this text is there a stipulation of a confession of error and a reinstatement?

Camping's admission of agnosticism regarding the date of the world's end and his less than subtle reprimanding of those who still claim to know not only distinguishes him from other related groups but also suggests another Qumran parallel. Albert Baumgarten reads literally the lines of the *Pešer Habakkuk*, which declare that the Teacher is the one to whom God reveals all the secrets of the

---

60. Details of the recalculation can be seen online at http://www.ebiblefellowship.com/archives/2012/02/04/fill-the-cup-double/. Accessed 12 August 2012. Obviously, their major presentation was to members of the community (physical and online).

61. http://www.familyradio.com/ Accessed 12 August 2012.

62. Harold Camping, "March 2012 Letter." See Appendix, pp. 511ff..

prophets (1QpHab 7:4–5) "to mean that the Teacher *knew no more than Habak-kuk. As Habakkuk was ignorant of the end, so was the Teacher.*"[63] I do not think this is the best understanding of the passage, but if it is correct, then it stands as an acknowledgment of not knowing, as we saw explicitly in Camping. Baumgarten goes on to argue that other members of the sect did not follow "the Teacher's agnostic lead" and "expected redemption imminently" and are those who apparently did not remain loyal and will be punished by God.[64] Regardless of the correctness of Baumgarten's literally reading, this column of *Pešer Habakkuk* testifies to a community in conflict being urged out of fear of divine punishment and promise of reward to remain loyal, and Baumgarten is right to stress that different members of the community may have had different apocalyptic expectations.

I have not scoured all of the Qumran literature, searching for signs of coping mechanisms from those who may have experienced the disconfirmation of apocalyptic predictions, but it seems a worthwhile task. One of the common reactions to disconfirmation identified in *When Prophecy Fails* and listed as (5) above is proselytism. I have not found clear evidence for this reaction among the Qumran Scrolls, and the "March 2012 Letter" of Camping also does not reveal any new or extraordinary attempts at proselytism, though it certainly maintains and reinforces the missionary traditions of the community. Family Radio, before and after the disconfirmation of their predictions, has been a zealous proselytizing organization, as is clear from their radio broadcasts, website, and literature.

Coping mechanism (3) identified by Festinger, Riecken, and Schachter, the forgetting or reduction of importance of the ideas that caused the intellectual dissonance, seems especially important for ultimate survival of any apocalyptic group. At times, human beings have mercifully short memories, and a prophet's prediction errors can be forgiven, ignored, or, hopefully, forgotten. After all, even the hoary prophets of the "golden age" got it wrong sometimes, as Ezekiel acknowledges regarding his proclamation that Nebuchadnezzar would destroy Tyre (Ezek 26:7–14 and 29:17–20). A beloved or charismatic teacher may well be able to weather a storm of a false prediction and retain her/his position of leadership. Harold Camping seems to have done just that, and his confession can help spur the community to forgiving or at least moving past the error. I would argue that the ritual legislated by the *torat-moshe* of 4Q375 is likely intended to facilitate exactly this kind of rehabilitation for a leader of the community. The partisan defenders of the offending prophet consider him just/true and faithful (צדיק הואה נביא נאמן, 4Q375 f1ii:6). I think it is significant that the ritual procedure involves a 'sin offering' (חטאת, 4 Q375 f1ii:6), which may signify a confession of error by the prophet and for any who followed him. If this interpretation is correct, then it is easy to see this as yet another piece in the ritual intend to help the prophet and community move beyond the prophetic error.

---

63. Baumgarten, "The Pursuit of the Millennium at Qumran," 11.
64. Ibid.

Finally, I would like to add to the list of coping mechanisms for modern apocalyptic movements, one which again shows a distinction from the Qumran literature. In order to overcome the error of their predictions, even predictions that have been presented as divinely inspired interpretation, modern apocalyptic groups will stress the infallibility of their sacred text for their membership. Lester Grabbe noted that David Koresh constantly appealed to "Scripture to interpret Scripture,"[65] and after disconfirmation, a community will focus and emphasize the perfection of the text, thus reducing focus on the apparently errant interpretation. This is not to say that they did not have such beliefs beforehand but, after disconfirmation, the strong emphasis on such beliefs can be an effective coping mechanism. We see in Camping's "March 2012 Letter" that the community is comforted with assertions about the infallibility of their Bible: "In this time of confusion and turmoil, God's Word remains the only truth in which we can trust." In the short nine-paragraph letter, "Bible" is used twelve times, and "God's Word" twice, and an entire paragraph is devoted to how excellent it is that through Camping's error the "world's attention has been called to the Bible." In fact, of course, most of the world's attention had been called to Camping's prediction, claimed to be from divine insight, and now failed. Of course, this too is a psychological comfort, not a logical intellectual solution to the problem of failed prophecy. Statements such as this help the community turn their focus to what they believe is the infallible Bible instead of dwelling on the failed inspired prediction. As I said above, such an explicit stress on "The Bible" or sacred text is not part of the ideology of the Qumran writers, whose use of ancient, honored scrolls is distinctly different.

Conclusion

We do not really know why the community of Jewish religionist who dwelled at Qumran did not ultimately survive to pass on their traditions and scrolls to later generations. I wish they had. Did they weather the storms of apocalyptic disconfirmation, just as other apocalyptic groups, such as early Christians, Millerites, and Family Radio, did, only to become victims of Roman, Kittim, violence? Or did the Yaḥad experience significant losses, schisms, and apostasies from which they could not recover in the middle of the 1st century due to the disappointment of failed hopes and predictions? We will likely never know. What we do know is that members of this apocalyptic community saw themselves as recipients of divine knowledge, which not only instructed them how to live but also revealed to them that they were living in the last days of history. Their ideology gave them hope and the rhetoric to proclaim that they would defeat their enemies, the Kittim and would do so in the not-distant future. They were undoubtedly disappointed when their claimed divine knowledge of soon-to-be events only proved the Universal

---

65. Grabbe, "Prophecy as Inspired," 149.

Apocalyptic Failure Principle. Their reactions to the disconfirmation, as best we can tell from the fragmentary remains, even though we lack a large body of oral testimony that must have contained most of their responses, seem to show the ways in which they and other apocalyptic groups often cope with intellectual dissonance and emotional discouragement, attempting to reduce dissonance and maintain their ideological vision. "Hope springs eternal."[66]

---

66. Alexander Pope, *An Essay on Man* (1734). Harold Camping died 15 December 2013.

Bibliography

Abegg, M., J. Bowley, and E. Cook, *The Dead Sea Scrolls Concordance*, Vol. 1. Leiden: Brill, 2003.

Baker, D. "Kittim." Pp. 93 in vol. 4 of the *The Anchor Bible Dictionary*. Edited by D. N. Freedman. New York: Doubleday, 1992.

Barton, J. *Oracles of God*. Oxford: Oxford University Press, 1992.

Baumgarten, A. "Karaites, Qumran, The Calendar, And Beyond: At the Beginning of the Twenty-first Century." Pp. 603–19 in *The Dead Sea Scrolls and Contemporary Culture*. Edited by A. D. Roitman, L. H. Schiffman, and S. Tzoref. Leiden: Brill, 2010.

Blenkinsopp, J. *A History of Prophecy in Israel*. Louisville: Westminster John Knox, 1996.

Boring, M. E. "Prophecy (Early Christian)." Pp. 495–502 in vol. 5 of *The Anchor Bible Dictionary*. Edited by D. N. Freedman. New York: Doubleday, 1992.

Bowley, J. "Prophets and Prophecy at Qumran." Pp. 354–78 in vol. 2 of *The Dead Sea Scrolls after Fifty Years*. Edited by P. W. Flint and J. C. VanderKam. Leiden: Brill, 1999.

_____. "Bible." Pp. 73–84 in vol. 1 of *The Oxford Encyclopedia of the Books of the Bible*. Edited by M. D. Coogan. Oxford: Oxford University Press, 2011.

_____, and J. Reeves. "Rethinking the Concept of 'Bible:' Some Theses and Proposals." *Henoch: Studi storicofilologici sull'ebraismo* 25 (2003) 3–18.

Braude, B. "The Sons of Noah and the Construction of Ethic and Geographical Identities in the Early Modern Periods." *The William and Mary Quarterly* 54 (1997) 103–42.

Brooke, G. J. "Prophecy and Prophets in the Dead Sea Scrolls: Looking Backwards and Forwards." Pp. 151–65 in *Prophets, Prophecy, and Prophetic Texts in Second Temple Judaism*. Edited by M. H. Floyd and R. D. Haak. London: T. & T. Clark, 2006.

Campbell, H. *When Religion Meets New Media*. London: Routledge, 2010.

_____. "March 2012 Letter." n.p. [cited 12 August 2013] http://www.familyradio.com/announcement2.html.

_____. *We Are Almost There!* Oakland, CA: Family Stations, 2010.

Collins, J. *Apocalypticism in the Dead Sea Scrolls*. London: Routledge, 1997.

_____. "The Expectation of the End in the Dead Sea Scrolls." Pp. 74–90 in *Eschatology, Messianism, and the Dead Sea Scrolls*. Edited by C. A. Evans and P. W. Flint. Grand Rapids, MI: Eerdmans, 1997.

Collins, M. *The Use of Sobriquets in the Qumran Dead Sea Scrolls*. London: T. & T. Clark, 2009.

Cook, L. *On the Question of the "Cessation of Prophecy" in Ancient Judaism*. Tübingen: Mohr Siebeck, 2011.

Costa, T. " 'Is Saul of Tarsus Also among the Prophets?' Paul's Calling as Prophetic Divine Commissioning." Pp. 203–36 in *Christian Origins and Hellenistic Judaism*. Edited by S. E. Porter and A. W. Pitts. Leiden: Brill, 2013.

Eshel, H. *The Dead Sea Scrolls and the Hasmonean State*. Grand Rapids, MI: Eerdmans, 2008.

Forbes, C. *Prophecy and Inspired Speech in Early Christianity and its Hellenistic Environment*. Tübingen: J.C.B. Mohr, 1995.

Grabbe, L. "Poets, Scribes, or Preachers? The Reality of Prophecy in the Second Temple Period." Pp. 192–215 in *Knowing the End from the Beginning: The Prophetic, the Apocalyptic, and Their Relationships*. Edited by L. Grabbe and R. Haak. London: T. & T. Clark, 2003.

_____. "Prophetic and Apocalyptic: Time for New definitions—and New Thinking." Pp. 107–33 in *Knowing the End from the Beginning: The Prophetic, the Apocalyptic, and Their Relationships*. Edited by L. L. Grabbe and R. D. Haak. London: T. & T. Clark, 2003.

_____. "Prophecy as Inspired Biblical Interpretation: The Teacher of Righteousness and David Koresh." Pp. 142–50 in *Far from Minimal: Celebrating the Work and Influence of Philip R. Davies*. Edited by D. Burns and J. W. Rogerson. London: T. & T. Clark, 2012.

_____. "The Pursuit of the Millennium at Qumran." *AJS Perspectives* (Fall, 2012) 10–11.

Gray, R. *Prophetic Figures in Late Second Temple Jewish Palestine: The Evidence from Josephus*. Oxford: Oxford University Press, 1993.

Hartman, L., and A. Di Lella. *The Book of Daniel*. Garden City, NY: Doubleday, 1977.

Jassen, A. "Prophecy after 'The Prophets:' The Dead Sea Scrolls and the History of Prophecy in Judaism." Pp. 592–93 in *The Dead Sea Scrolls in Context: Integrating the Dead Sea Scrolls in the Study of Ancient Texts, Languages, and Cultures*. Edited by A. Lange et al. Leiden: Brill, 2011.

Kugel, J. "David the Prophet." Pp. 45–55 in *Poetry and Prophecy*. Edited by J. Kugel. Ithaca, NY: Cornell University Press, 1990.

McCarter, P. Kyle, Jr. *I Samuel*. AB 8. New York: Doubleday, 1980.

Reeves, J. "Scriptural Authority in Early Judaism." Pp. 63–84 in *Living Traditions of the Bible*. Edited by J. E. Bowley. St. Louis: Chalice, 1999.

_____. "The Meaning of *Moreh Sedeq* in the Light of 11QTorah." *RevQ* 13 (1998) 287–98.

_____. *Trajectories in Near Eastern Apocalyptic*. Atlanta: SBL, 2005.

Schniedewind, W. *The Word of God in Transition: From Prophet to Exegete in the Second Temple Period*. Sheffield: Sheffield Academic, 1995.

Smith, M. "What Is Implied by the Variety of Messianic Figures?" *JBL* 78 (1959) 66–72.

Steudel, A. "אחרית הימים in the Texts from Qumran." *RevQ* 16 (1993) 225–46.

Strugnell, J. "375. 4QApocryphon of Moses^a." Pp. 113–15 in *Qumran Cave 4, XIV: Parabiblical Texts, II*. Edited by M. Broshi et al. DJD 19. Oxford: Clarendon, 1995.

VanderKam, J. *The Dead Sea Scrolls Today*. Grand Rapids, MI: Eerdmans, 2010.

_____. *The Dead Sea Scrolls and the Bible*. Grand Rapids, MI: Eerdmans, 2012.

Appendix

An Important Letter from Mr. Camping—March 2012[67]

THE BOARD OF FAMILY RADIO WISHES TO POST THE FOLLOWING LET-
TER FROM MR. CAMPING. IT WAS OUR WISH, OUT OF RESPECT FOR
OUR LISTENERS, TO MAIL OUT THIS LETTER BEFORE POSTING IT TO
THE WEB SITE. HOWEVER, BECAUSE IT WAS LEAKED TO THE INTER-
NET WITHOUT OUR AUTHORIZATION, WE HAVE MADE THE DECISION
TO POST IT IMMEDIATELY TO AVOID CONFUSION. THIS LETTER WILL
ALSO BE MAILED OUT TO OUR LISTENERS.

"God forbid: yea, let God be true, but every man a liar; as it is written, That
thou mightest be justified in thy sayings, and mightest overcome when thou art
judged." Romans 3:4

Dear Family Radio Family,

In this time of confusion and turmoil, God's Word remains the only truth in
which we can trust. God has shown us again the truth that He alone is true. In
Romans 3:4 God declares: "Let God be true but every man a liar." Events within
the last year have proven that no man can be fully trusted. Even the most sincere
and zealous of us can be mistaken.

The May 21 campaign was an astounding event if you think about its impact
upon this world. There is no question that millions, if not billions of people heard
for the first time the Bible's warning that Jesus Christ will return. Huge portions of
this world that had never read or seen a Bible heard the message the Christ Jesus
is coming to rapture His people and destroy this natural world.

Yes, we humbly acknowledge we were wrong about the timing; yet though
we were wrong God is still using the May 21 warning in a very mighty way. In
the months following May 21 the Bible has, in some ways, come out from under
the shadows and is now being discussed by all kinds of people who never before
paid any attention to the Bible. We learn about this, for example, by the recent
National Geographic articles concerning the King James Bible and the Apostles.
Reading about and even discussing about the Bible can never be a bad thing, even
if the Bible's authenticity is questioned or ridiculed. The world's attention has been
called to the Bible.

We must also openly acknowledge that we have no new evidence pointing to
another date for the end of the world. Though many dates are circulating, Family Radio has no interest in even considering another date. God has humbled us

---

67. H. Camping, "An Important Letter from Mr. Camping—March 2012," n.p. [cited 12
August 2013]. Online: http://www.familyradio.com/announcement2.html.

through the events of May 21, to continue to even more fervently search the Scriptures (the Bible), not to find dates, but to be more faithful in our understanding.

We have learned the very painful lesson that all of creation is in God's hands and He will end time in His time, not ours! We humbly recognize that God may not tell His people the date when Christ will return, any more than He tells anyone the date they will die physically.

We realize that many people are hoping they will know the date of Christ's return. In fact for a time Family Radio fell into that kind of thinking. But we now realize that those people who were calling our attention to the Bible's statement that "of that day and hour knoweth no man" (Matthew 24:36 & Mark 13:32), were right in their understanding of those verses and Family Radio was wrong. Whether God will ever give us any indication of the date of His return is hidden in God's divine plan.

We were even so bold as to insist that the Bible guaranteed that Christ would return on May 21 and that the true believers would be raptured. Yet this incorrect and sinful statement allowed God to get the attention of a great many people who otherwise would not have paid attention. Even as God used sinful Balaam to accomplish His purposes, so He used our sin to accomplish His purpose of making the whole world acquainted with the Bible. However, even so, that does not excuse us. We tremble before God as we humbly ask Him for forgiveness for making that sinful statement. We are so thankful that God is so loving that He will forgive even this sin.

So we must be satisfied to humbly wait upon God, and trust He will guide His people to safety. At Family Radio, we continue to look to God for guidance. If it is His good pleasure for us to continue on with our original mission, the proclamation of the Gospel, God's Word, then we must continue to look to Him.

We consider you to be a real part of this ministry and the tremendous opportunities which God, by His unfathomable mercy and grace, continues to give to us. And, your steadfast involvement and support is so appreciated!

May God bless you,
Harold Camping and the staff of Family Radio.

John the Baptizer:
More Than a Prophet

JAMES D. TABOR

University of North Carolina at Charlotte

The beheading of John the Baptizer[1] by order of Herod Antipas, at the urging of his wife Herodias—who was formerly married to Herod's brother Philip—is surely, next to the crucifixion of Jesus, the most poignant death scene in the New Testament. It has become the stuff of legend, portrayed in countless books, films, dramas, and works of art. John's brutal and untimely death, along with the scene of him baptizing Jesus as a wild desert prophet are embedded in our cultural memories. Yet, as historians we must ask: what do we know about John and how do we know it?

For one to undertake any kind of "quest for the historical John the Baptizer," some of the same challenges confront the historian as those associated with the quest for the historical Jesus—namely, a plethora of theologically based sources that must be critically sifted according to some agreed-upon method. As in the case of Jesus, we have multiple texts dealing with John the Baptizer in all four canonical gospels and the book of Acts, distributed in a complex way throughout all the strata of these sources.[2] Such a systematic quest is far beyond the scope of this present chapter; but, even this more limited query regarding John's relationship to the political and social powers of his day presents similar methodological challenges. This chapter is limited to a focus on John the Baptizer in the NT and in the 1st-century writings of the Jewish historian Josephus, despite the abundance of materials on John in postbiblical traditions.[3] Each NT text has its own tendentious

---

1. John is most often referred to in the New Testament as 'the Baptist' (ὁ βαπτιστής), which appears to be a kind of formal title. However, twice in Mark he is called 'the baptizer' (ὁ βαπτίζων), using the present active participle. The latter form appears to be earlier and is more descriptive of John's activities and is accordingly preferred in this chapter.

2. J. Reumann, "The Quest for the Historical Baptist," *Understanding the Sacred Text: Essays in Honor of Morton S. Enslin on the Hebrew Bible and Christian Beginnings* (ed. J. Reumann; Valley Forge, PA: Judson, 1972), 181–99.

3. See E. Bammel, "John the Baptist in Early Christian Tradition," *NTS* 18 (1971–72) 95–128; S. Gibson, *The Cave of John the Baptist* (New York: Doubleday, 2004), 217–28; and the

perspectives. This is particularly the case in dealing with John the Baptizer, given that emerging forms of Christianity, centrally focused on Jesus, reflect the need to "diminish" John's significance in contrast with that of Jesus as the main redemptive figure.[4] The method here will be to sort through our textual sources in a roughly chronological order, correlating the main elements related to the central query— what was John the Baptizer's relationship to and attitude toward the State?

More Than A Prophet

One of our earliest sources is a series of questions and responses attributed to Jesus regarding the role and mission of John the Baptizer, now embedded in Luke, but drawn from the reconstructed Synoptic source Q. The passage aptly sets the stage for John's identification as a Prophet, as well as his sharp critique of the governing establishment, through his radical message and his countercultural, anti-establishment, lifestyle:[5]

> What did you go out into the wilderness to behold? A reed shaken by the wind? What then did you go out to see? A man clothed in soft raiment? Behold, those who are gorgeously appareled and live in luxury are in kings' courts. What then did you go out to see? A prophet? Yes, I tell you, more than a prophet (Luke 7:24–26).[6]

According to this section of Q, not only is John "more than a Prophet," he is that final 'messenger' (מלאך/ἄγγελος) referred to by Malachi, who prepares the way for the eschatological day of the LORD (Mal 3:1–2).[7] Indeed, the Q text goes on

survey of primary texts by J. Poplin, "Post-Biblical Traditions on John the Baptizer" [cited 20 January 2016] online: https://clas-pages.uncc.edu/james-tabor/christian-origins-and-the-new-testament/post-biblical-traditions-on-john-the-baptizer. The main primary texts are conveniently surveyed by W. Barnes Tatum, *John the Baptist and Jesus: A Report of the Jesus Seminar* (Sonoma, CA: Polebridge, 1994), 84–104.

4. This subordination tendency, ubiquitous in all four gospels and Acts, is outside the scope of this chapter. It is hardly found at all in Q but is then picked up by Mark and increasingly emphasized in Matthew, Luke, and John—more or less finding its culmination in John's own declaration about Jesus: "He must increase but I must decrease" (John 3:30). The book of Acts takes a different but related strategy, not that Jesus is greater than John but that John's time has passed and is now obsolete; see Acts 19:1–7.

5. The literature and debate on the Two Document hypothesis for Synoptic gospel composition that posits Q as a sayings source used by Luke and Matthew is too vast to cite here. For an introductory overview, see J. S. Kloppenborg, *Q, The Earliest Gospel: An Introduction to the Original Stories and Sayings of Jesus* (Louisville: Westminster, 2008).

6. Luke 7:24–26. Quotations from the Bible are from the RSV, *Holy Bible* (New York: Oxford University Press, 2002).

7. The MT reads "and he will prepare the way before me," referring to Yahweh of Hosts, equating this "messenger of the covenant" with the Lord (אדון) who "will suddenly come to his temple," apparently as a single figure. Luke 7:27 reads "who shall prepare your way before you" using the 2nd-person singular pronoun, presumably influenced by Luke's Christology in which

to make the rather startling declaration, "I tell you, among those born of women none is greater than John; yet he who is least in the kingdom of God is greater than he" (Luke 7:28).[8] This extravagant evaluation of John (which seemingly makes him greater than Jesus, who is obviously one "born of a woman") is cast in terms of "salvation history" in Q: "The law and the prophets were until John; since then the good news of the kingdom of God is preached and everyone enters it violently" (Luke 16:16).[9] Based on this Q material, John is a pivotal apocalyptic figure situated in the "middle of time," both culminating an old epoch while initiating a new one. Of all the prophets, he is declared to be the greatest, but his greatness is shadowed by even the "least" in the emerging kingdom that Jesus inaugurates by his own preaching.

John's pivotal role in redemptive history is also emphasized in Mark, our earliest gospel. Following the dramatic scene of Jesus' transfiguration, the inner core of disciples—Peter, James, and John—who had uniquely witnessed this vision of the coming kingdom of God in its glory, ask Jesus "Why do the scribes say that first Elijah must come" (Mark 9:1–11). Jesus' reply is cryptic but altogether momentous in its implications:

> Elijah does come first to restore all things; and how is it written of the Son of man, that he should suffer many things and be treated with contempt? But I tell you that Elijah has come, and they did to him whatever they pleased, as it is written of him (Mark 9:12–13)

John the Baptist as "the messenger," is the forerunner of Jesus the Messiah (see Luke 1:17). 4Q76 2:12 (Mal 3:1) interprets the "messenger" and the "Lord" as two separate figures—"they will suddenly come to [his] te[mple, the Lor]d, whom you seek and the messenger of the co[venant, whom y]ou desire. . . . But] who can endure them; they come?" This notion of "two messiahs," one of Aaron and one of David, is found several places in the Qumran texts and might well have provided the background for understanding John the Baptist and Jesus as dual redemptive figures or "messiahs," see J. J. Collins, ed., *The Scepter and the Star: The Messiahs of the Dead Sea Scrolls and Other Ancient Literature* (Anchor Bible Reference Library; New York: Doubleday, 1995).

8. Ibn Shaprut's version of Hebrew Matthew preserves an alternative Matthean parallel to this Q saying: "among those born of women none has arisen greater than John the Baptizer," without any qualifier (Matt 11:11). Similarly, it has "for all the prophets and the law spoke concerning (על) John" rather than "until (עד) John" (Matt 11:13). See G. Howard, *Hebrew Gospel of Matthew* (Macon, GA: Mercer University Press, 1995), 219–22. Howard argues that this text, independent of our Greek manuscripts, reflects an earlier tradition about John in which his role was more exalted than what later emerged within the Jesus movement.

9. Compare Gos. Thom. 46: "Jesus said: From Adam until John the Baptist there is among those who are born of women none higher than John the Baptist so that his eyes will not be broken. But I have said that whoever among you becomes as a child shall know the Kingdom, and he shall become higher than John." Gos. Thom. 52 "His disciples said to Him: Twenty-four prophets spoke in Israel and they all spoke about you. He said to them: You have dismissed the Living One who is before you and you have spoken about the dead." Translations throughout from *The Gospel According to Thomas* (trans. A. Guillaumont, C. C. Peuch, G. Quispel et al.; Leiden: Brill, 1959).

The disciples have taken the transfiguration of Jesus as Messiah and the appearances of Moses and Elijah as a sure indicator of the imminence of the Kingdom of God—which they had been told would come in their lifetimes (Mark 9:1). Here, Jesus identifies John the Baptizer as Malachi's prophetic messenger—namely, the Elijah who was expected to come before the final judgment:

> Behold, I will send you Elijah the prophet before the great and terrible day of the LORD comes. And he will turn the hearts of fathers to their children and the hearts of children to their fathers, lest I come and smite the land with a curse. (Mal 4:4 [MT 3:23–24])

What is altogether surprising here is that this account in Mark not only makes this identification but also states that John the Baptizer was rejected and killed by the establishment "as it is written of him"—a clear reference to prophetic texts. Jesus, in Mark, is interweaving his own role as a Suffering Servant, rejected and killed—emphasized three times in this section of his gospel—with that of John, who suffers the same kind of fate before Jesus does (Mark 8:31–33; 9:30–32; 10:32–34). Since Malachi says nothing of a suffering/rejected "Elijah," one can assume the Markan tradition, as in the case of Jesus, has a set of texts in mind, whether portions of Isaiah's Servant Songs, or perhaps Zech 12–13, that could be taken to refer to the deaths of a Davidic as well as a Levitical "messiah." It could well be that the writer of Mark has Zech 13:7 in mind as a specific reference to John's beheading by a sword:

> "Awake, O sword, against my shepherd, against the man who stands next to me," says the LORD of hosts. (Zech 13:7; cf. Mark 14:27)

The phrase "they did to him whatever they pleased" (Mark 9:13) is a clear reference to the political and religious establishment rather than the people who apparently flocked to John's preaching.

It is noteworthy that later in Mark, when Jesus sharply confronts the chief priests, scribes, and elders associated with Herod's Temple, he makes the matter of whether one accepted the baptism of John or not the pivotal sign of whether one accepted God's authority:

> And Jesus said to them: "I will ask you a question; answer me, and I will tell you by what authority I do these things. Was the baptism of John from heaven or from men? Answer me." (Mark 11:29–30)

Jesus' enemies refuse to answer because they had rejected John's baptism and "were afraid of the people, for all held that John was a real prophet" (Mark 11:32).

It is rather remarkable that Q 7:24–28 and these references to John the Baptizer in Mark so closely coincide in theme and emphasis. Strikingly, Luke closes this Q pericope with this parenthetical explanation:

When they heard this, all the people and the tax collectors justified God, having been baptized with the baptism of John; but the Pharisees and the lawyers rejected the purpose of God for themselves, not having been baptized by him. (Luke 7:29–30)

It is clear that in our two earliest sources on John the Baptizer that his pivotal role as an eschatological prophet par excellence is affirmed and his acceptance by the crowds and rejection by the establishment is explicitly emphasized.

Returning to the Q source, John's implicit opposition to the political and social establishment is also implied. First, he is in the "wilderness" or desert (ἔρημος), separated from both the Roman and Jewish urban centers of power such as Sepphoris, Tiberius, Caesarea, or Jerusalem, but also from the various towns and villages of Judea, Samaria, and Galilee. One must leave the "civilized" world of human society and "go out" into the desert to encounter him. According to Luke, who is the only source who offers us any background regarding John's family or birth, John was the son of Zechariah, an Aaronic priest of the division of Abijah (Luke 1:5). Luke says that from childhood John was "in the wilderness (ἐρήμοις, lit., 'desert places') till the day of his manifestation to Israel" (Luke 1:80), implying that his deliberate isolation and separation from the religious and civil establishment was lifelong (despite his inherited pedigree as a priest who could have taken his place of service in Jerusalem). Whether or not this was the case we have no way of knowing; however, the possibility underscores the radical stance of John as a countercultural prophet.

As a prophet, John's voice or message was no "reed shaken in the wind" but was firm and unwavering. John's rough clothing—reflecting his entire countercultural lifestyle—is in the sharpest contrast to the luxurious apparel of those who live in "king's houses." This appears to be a clear reference to Herod Antipas and his palace at Sepphoris in the Galilee—and by extension to Pontius Pilate, the newly installed Prefect in Judea with his luxurious quarters in Caesarea and Jerusalem.[10]

A Radical Countercultural Lifestyle

According to Mark's gospel, John the baptizer appeared in the "wilderness" or desert (ἔρημος), immersing those who responded to his preaching in the Jordan River.[11] Mark also portrays John as one who followed a strict ascetic lifestyle reflected most prominently in his austere dress and diet:

---

10. Cf. Gos. Thom. 78 Jesus said: "Why did you come out into the desert? To see a reed shaken by the wind? And to see a man clothed in soft garments? See your kings and your great ones are those who are clothed in soft garments and they shall not be able to know the truth."

11. Mark 1:4. Matt 3:1 specifies that John was preaching in the "wilderness of Judea" whereas Luke 3:3 says he "went about all the region about the Jordan." John offers precise

> Now John was clothed with camel's hair and had a leather girdle around his waist,
> and ate locusts and wild honey (Mark 1·6)[12]

John's clothing appears to be modeled upon that of the prophet Elijah, who was said to have worn a "garment of haircloth, with a girdle of leather about his loins" (2 Kgs 1:8). The Q source specifies further that John, in contrast to Jesus, came "eating no bread and drinking no wine," implying a stricter asceticism than the more common practice of merely abstaining from meat and wine, as the parallel in Matthew has it (Matt 11:18; cf. Rom 14:1, 21). According to Luke, John's father Zechariah is told:

> For he will be great before the Lord, and he shall drink no wine nor strong drink,
> and he will be filled with the Holy Spirit, even from his mother's womb. (Luke
> 1:15)

Such a description reminds one of Hegesippus's description of the lifestyle of James, the brother of Jesus:

> He was holy from his mother's womb. He drank no wine or strong drink, nor
> did he eat flesh; no razor went upon his head. . . . (Eusebius, *Hist. eccl.* 2.23.5–6)

James is clearly presented in this text as a Nazirite from birth—but whether Luke understands John in this way, modeled perhaps after Samuel, is unclear (see Num 6:1–4; 1 Sam 1:11).

Regarding diet, the Q source notes a stricter asceticism that avoided even bread since it has to be processed from grain and does not grow of itself (Luke 7:33–34). Slavonic Josephus also has John shunning bread and only eating the roots and fruits of plants.[13] Such a lifestyle reminds one of the Rechabites men-

---

geographical details—namely, that John was baptizing "at Aenon near Salim," in the Galilee, just south of Beit Shean or Scythopolis when Jesus came to him for baptism.

12. See J. A. Kelhoffer, *The Diet of John the Baptist: "Locusts and Wild Honey" in Synoptic and Patristic Interpretation* (Tübingen: Mohr Siebeck, 2005). It has been suggested, in the interest of arguing that John's diet was strictly vegetarian, that "locusts" refers to the beans of a carob tree, commonly called "St. John's bread," however the Greek word (ἀκρίδες) clearly refers to the *Acrididae* grasshopper. Epiphanius (*Panarion* 30.13. 4–5) quotes the "Gospel of the Ebionites," which has ἔνκρις, a similar word meaning "honey cake," perhaps analogous to the "manna" that the Israelites ate in the desert. See M. R. James, *The Apocryphal New Testament* (Oxford: Clarendon, 1924), 8–10.

13. The Old (Slavonic) Russian version of Josephus's *The Jewish War* offers a similar but even more radical sketch of John's lifestyle: "Now at that time there walked among the Jews a man in wondrous garb, for he had put animals' hair upon his body wherever it was not covered by his (own) hair; and in countenance he was like a savage," living on "roots and fruits of the tree" (inserted at *Jewish War* 2.110). This text insists that he never touched bread, much less the flesh of a lamb, even at Passover; see H. J. Thackeray, trans. "Appendix: The Principle Additional Passages in the Slavonic Version," *Josephus: The Jewish War* (LCL; 9 vols.; Cambridge: Harvard University Press, 1927), 3:644–45.

tioned by Jeremiah, who drink no wine, avoid cultivation of the ground, and live in tents (Jer 35:8–10).[14] We might also recall that Banus, the desert hermit that Josephus followed as a young man for three years, fed only "on such things as grow of themselves" (Josephus, *Vita* 2.11).

The motivations behind such a strict diet seem to go beyond a mere "asceticism" and echo the ideals of the Garden of Eden, where humans before their expulsion are given "every plant yielding seed . . . and every tree with seed in its fruit" (Gen 1:29). But perhaps more relevant are the social implications. Clearly, such a strictly ascetic diet served to both segregate and alienate John from the ruling classes, making any sort of social exchange unlikely. As a result of his radical diet, the charge is made against John that he "has a demon" (Luke 7:33).[15] This is in contrast to the portrait of Jesus in all our sources, where he mixes freely with all classes, whether rich or poor, Jew or non-Jew, and male or female, and seems to move comfortably in urban settings—causing controversy by his practice of "eating with tax collectors and sinners" (Mark 2:15–17).

Mark also alludes to a set practice of fasting by John and his disciples:

> Now John's disciples and the Pharisees were fasting; and the people came and said to him, "Why do John's disciples and the disciples of the Pharisees fast, but your disciples do not fast?" (Mark 2:18)[16]

Along with fasting, John and his disciples apparently practiced special prayers that he had taught them, as well as rites of purification that were either in contrast to, and in conflict with, those of the Pharisees (Luke (Q) 11:1–4; John 3:25). These particular "halakhic" practices and interpretations are consistently presented in our gospels in contrast to the more "libertine" practices of Jesus and his disciples (Mark 2:18; Luke 15:1–2; 19:1–10).

A Message of Imminent Apocalyptic Judgment

John the Baptizer's message, so far as we can recover it, is every bit as radical as his lifestyle—the one echoing and reinforcing the other. The earliest proclamation we have attributed to John is Q 3:7–9 (cf. Matt 3:7–10):

> You brood of vipers! Who warned you to flee from the wrath to come? Bear fruits that befit repentance, and do not begin to say to yourself, "We have Abraham as

---

14. Hegesippus notes that a Rechabite priest tried to stop the stoning of James in the Temple (Eusebius, *Hist. eccl.* 2.23.17).

15. One is reminded here of Jeremiah's isolation and declaration "I did not sit in the company of merrymakers, nor did I rejoice; I sat alone, because thy hand was upon me" (Jer 15:17).

16. Compare Gos. Thom. 104: "They said to Him: Come and let us pray today and let us fast. Jesus said: Which then is the sin that I have committed, or in what have I been vanquished? But when the bridegroom comes out of the bridal chamber, then let them fast and let them pray."

our father": for I tell you, God is able from these stones to raise up children to Abraham. Even now the axe is laid to the root of the trees; every tree therefore that does not bear good fruit is cut down and thrown into the fire.

Luke frames this rather blistering proclamation as directed against the "multitudes that came out to be baptized by him," whereas Matthew aims it at the presumably hypocritical "Pharisees and Sadducees coming for baptism." Neither group fits the content well, so it is best to take this as a generic sample of John's preaching—letting the chips fall as they may. According to Mark, John preached a "baptism of repentance for the forgiveness of sins (Mark 1:4; cf. Luke 3:3; Acts 13:24).

The sharp apocalyptic tone is dominant: "who warned you to flee from the wrath to come," and "even now the axe is laid to the root of the trees." Both reflect John's mission as an Elijah figure who comes preaching repentance before the impending "great and terrible Day of the LORD," with the threat of utter destruction upon those who do not heed (Mal 4:5–6 [MT 4:23–24]). The rejection of any claim of pedigree with Abraham underlines the radical nature of John's sweeping call for repentance: even "stones" could be turned to physical descendants of Abraham. Only good deeds done in response to repentance will rescue one from the imminent wrath of God's judgment. Directly after this opening proclamation of Q 3:7–9, Luke has an intriguing example of John's ethical responses to various groups asking him what they need to do:

[And the multitudes asked him,] "What then shall we do?" And he answered them, "He who has two coats, let him share with him who has none; and he who has food, let him do likewise." Tax collectors also came to be baptized, and said to him, "Teacher, what shall we do?" And he said to them, "Collect no more than is appointed you." Soldiers also asked him, "And we, what shall we do?" And he said to them, "Rob no one by violence or by false accusation, and be content with your wages." (Luke 3:10–14)

This is the only time we have any sample of the social/ethical teachings of the Baptizer, and it was likely part of the Two-Source (Q) tradition but was omitted by Matthew since it echoes too closely the teachings of Jesus—the sharing of clothing and food, the acceptance of tax collectors, and an accommodation even with soldiers—likely Jewish but perhaps even Roman (Luke 7:8; 23:11). There is no good reason to exclude these verses from Q as a valuable glimpse at John's implicit social program based upon his call for repentance.

According to Matthew, both John the Baptizer and Jesus proclaimed an identical message: "Repent, for the Kingdom of Heaven is at hand" (Matt 1:2; 4:17). Mark expands this call in the mouth of Jesus, linking it in language with John's call for repentance:

Now after John was arrested, Jesus came into Galilee preaching the gospel of the Kingdom of God, and saying, "The time is fulfilled, and the kingdom of God is at hand; repent, and believe in the gospel." (Mark 1:14–15)

The clear implication is that following John's arrest, Jesus took up John's mantle as the leader of the Baptizing movement that he had recently joined by being baptized by John.[17]

John's execution by Herod Antipas is our best indicator of the threat he posed to the political establishment. We have two different accounts of the circumstances leading up to John's death: one from the gospel of Mark, the other in Josephus's *Jewish Antiquities*. In Mark, Herod had John arrested at the urging of his wife Herodias as a result of John denouncing the couple for adultery:

> For Herod had sent and seized John, and bound him in prison for the sake of Herodias, his brother Philip's wife; because he had married her. For John said to Herod, "It is not lawful for you to have your brother's wife." And Herodias had a grudge against him, and wanted to kill him. But she could not, for Herod feared John, knowing that he was a righteous and holy man, and kept him safe. When he heard him, he was much perplexed; and yet he heard him gladly. (Mark 6:17–20)

According to Mark, Herod was intrigued by John and superstitiously fearful. It was Herodias who was behind the plot to have him executed. Her opportunity came when Herod celebrated his birthday and rashly promised Herodias's daughter, who had pleased him by dancing, anything she wanted. Prompted by her mother, she asked for the head of John the Baptizer on a platter:

> And the king was exceedingly sorry; but because of his oaths and his guests he did not want to break his word to her. And immediately the king sent a soldier of the guard and gave orders to bring his head. He went and beheaded him in the prison, and brought his head on a platter, and gave it to the girl; and the girl gave it to her mother. When his disciples heard of it, they came and took his body, and laid it in a tomb. (Mark 6:26–29)

Josephus offers an alternative account. He reports that Herod was alarmed by the large crowds John was drawing by his preaching and the influence he was having on the populace. He feared John could easily lead an uprising and decided to strike first—arresting him for sedition. He had him brought in chains to the desert fortress Machaerus, where he was put to death. Josephus notes that some of the Jewish population viewed John with favor and saw the subsequent defeat of Herod's armies by King Aretas of Petra as divine vengeance for his murder of John (*Ant.* 18:116–19).[18]

---

17. The gospel of John has Jesus baptizing in Judea with great success in parallel with John's work in the north along the Jordan River even before John is arrested, apparently putting his own safety in jeopardy (John 3:22–23; 4:1–3). Since Mark (followed by Matthew and Luke) know nothing of Jesus taking on the mantle of John and administering John's baptism either before or after John's arrest, the reference in John is all the more telling. John realizes the implications for viewing Jesus as subordinate to John and thus qualifies his report—namely, that Jesus himself did not do the baptizing, but his disciples.

18. On the question of the authenticity of Josephus's narrative regarding John the Baptist see R. L. Webb, *John the Baptizer and Prophet: A Sociohistorical Study* (Eugene, OR: Wipf & Stock, 1991), 39–41.

The two accounts are difficult to sort out, but they do have some thematic similarities and overlapping differences.[19] That Herod was superstitiously fearful of John as a prophet, and thus was reluctant to have him killed seems unlikely. Herod's fear of a popular uprising, as reported by Josephus, seems much more persuasive, given what we know of the highly ambitious Herod Antipas. Nonetheless, it is entirely possible that part of the grievance the royal family had against John the Baptizer was his denunciation of the couple for adultery. Such a stance is entirely in keeping with what we know about John and his message in our gospel sources.

Taking all our sources together, John the Baptizer fits the typology of an "oracular prophet," as the work of Richard Horsley has shown.[20] Whether he would have ended up fulfilling the role of an "action prophet," such as other such figures mentioned by Josephus (the Samaritan, Theudas, the Egyptian), had he not been arrested and killed remains an open question. Given our sources, with their strong apocalyptic emphasis, it seems more likely that John expected God to intervene and bring about the Day of the LORD, without any need on his part to gather armed followers or overtly make any moves to overthrow the religious or political establishment. Perhaps like Jesus, when threatened with arrest, he no doubt believed he was backed by the proverbial "twelve legions of angels" and needed only to wait upon God's dramatic intervention to usher in the Kingdom of God he was preaching.

---

19. The two accounts are at least circumstantially related since king Aretas went to war with Herod when he divorced Aretas's daughter to marry Herodias.

20. R. Horsley, "Like One of the Prophets of Old: Two Types of Popular Prophets at the Time of Jesus," *CBQ* 47 (1985) 435–63.

Bibliography

Bammel, E. "John the Baptist in Early Christian Tradition." *NTS* 18 (1971–72) 95–128.

Collins, J. J., ed. *The Scepter and the Star: The Messiahs of the Dead Sea Scrolls and Other Ancient Literature.* Anchor Bible Reference Library. New York: Doubleday, 1995.

Gibson, S. *The Cave of John the Baptist.* New York: Doubleday, 2004.

James, M. R. *The Apocryphal New Testament.* Oxford: Clarendon, 1924.

Kelhoffer, J. A. *The Diet of John the Baptist: "Locusts and Wild Honey" in Synoptic and Patristic Interpretation.* Tübingen: Mohr Siebeck, 2005.

Horsley, R. "Like One of the Prophets of Old: Two Types of Popular Prophets at the Time of Jesus." *CBQ* 47 (1985) 435–63.

Howard, G. *Hebrew Gospel of Matthew.* Macon, GA: Mercer University Press, 1995.

Kloppenborg, J. S. *Q, The Earliest Gospel: An Introduction to the Original Stories and Sayings of Jesus.* Louisville: Westminster, 2008.

Poplin, J. "Post-Biblical Traditions on John the Baptizer." [cited 20 January 2016] Online: https://clas-pages.uncc.edu/james-tabor/christian-origins-and-the-new-testament/post-biblical-traditions-on-john-the-baptizer.

Reumann, J. "The Quest for the Historical Baptist." Pp. 181–99 in *Understanding the Sacred Text: Essays in Honor of Morton S. Enslin on the Hebrew Bible and Christian Beginnings*. Edited by John Reumann. Valley Forge, PA: Judson, 1972.

Slavonic Josephus. "The Principle Additional Passages in the Slavonic Version." Pp. 644–45 in *Josephus: The Jewish War*. Trans. H. St. J. Thackeray. Vol. 3. LCL. Cambridge: Harvard University Press, 1927.

Tatum, B. W. *John the Baptist and Jesus: A Report of the Jesus Seminar*. Sonoma, CA: Polebridge, 1994.

Webb, R. L. *John the Baptizer and Prophet: A Sociohistorical Study*. Eugene, OR: Wipf & Stock, 1991.

Jesus of Nazareth:
Prophet of Renewal and Resistance

Richard A. Horsley

University of Massachusetts—Boston

In traditional Christian faith and theology, Jesus was not only the unique revealer and incarnation of the Word of God but also the Messiah (supposedly) long expected in "Judaism." John the Baptist was the prophet identified in the Gospels more particularly as playing the role of the returning Elijah as forerunner to Jesus as the Messiah. Of course, when modern scholars discovered and constructed "eschatology" and came to believe that "late Judaism" (now "early Judaism") was dominated by intense expectation of the "end of the world," they also constructed the role of the "eschatological prophet" who would proclaim that the end was near and call people to repentance. Not surprisingly, Jesus was found to fit this "job description" as well, which had been constructed primarily with his proclamation in mind. As subsequent closer examination of the sources for late Second-Temple Judean culture recognized, however, expectation of an "eschatological prophet" was not attested. The only expectation of a prophet was for the returning Elijah.

One of the principal functions of the biblical studies division of theology 50 years ago was to interpret the principal prophetic and "intertestamental" texts that attested the Jewish expectation of "the Messiah" or of the "eschatological prophet" and to show how Jesus fulfilled that expectation. These were key issues in a general Christian theological scheme of Christian origins in which Jesus was the historically unique individual revealer who inspired the decisive move from the parochial old religion of "Judaism" to the universal and more spiritual new religion of "Christianity."

Biblical scholars then, however, were not aware of two key factors in the history of a people and its culture that have since been recognized, at least by a few. One is that extant written texts (in this case Judean texts that were later included or not included in the Hebrew Bible) from the past are merely the "tip of the iceberg" of a broader and deeper cultural repertoire in which cultural tradition was repeatedly reshaped. The other is that insofar as literacy was severely limited in Judea and the ancient Near East, mainly to the tiny circles of scribes who served the royal or priestly states, extant written texts presented the viewpoint of the political economic religious elite, what anthropologists call the "great tradition." "Underneath" the elite cultural tradition, with its written texts, was "little" or popular cultural tradition/social memory cultivated by the vast majority of the people in their village communities. There was "give and take" between the elite and popular traditions. But extant written texts usually represented only the elite tradition and provide only very indirect evidence for popular tradition. Generally speaking, elite texts mentioned the people only when they were making trouble for the elite in protest or revolt.[1]

The implications of these recognitions are that focusing only on text fragments from the scribal elite produces only a superficial idealist "history of ideas" abstracted from the dynamics of the historical relations. Dominant in those dynamics was the division between the rulers who controlled the state (often in shifting configurations) and the people they ruled and taxed. That dominant conflict was sometimes complicated by lesser conflicts between the rulers who controlled the state and the literate scribes who cultivate the cultural tradition in service of the state. Historically significant figures, moreover, emerge not in splendid isolation from engagement in social forms and political dynamics but in communication and interaction with both followers and opponents.

More adequate investigation of Jesus (as of any other historically significant figure) requires attention to (the crisis of) the historical situation, his interaction with followers and opponents in that situation, and the cultural tradition in which he and his followers interacted in responding to the situation. The cultural tradition, moreover—as is now being recognized by some—included social memory of certain social patterns and roles embodied in previous generations' responses to similar situations.[2] The title of this volume is suggestive for an approach to Jesus' relation to "the state" that begins from the cultural tradition/social memory in which he and his contemporaries were embedded.

Prophets Leading Movements and
Oracular Prophets in Israelite Tradition

The traditions of early Israel, whether they are taken as reshaped social memory or mere legendary ideology of Second-Temple Judea, focus on prophets

---

1. An attempt to coordinate the implications of separate recent research in several interrelated areas is R. A. Horsley, "Oral Communication, Oral Performance, and New Testament Interpretation," in *Method and Meaning: Essays on New Testament Interpretation in Honor of Harold W. Attridge* (ed. A. B. McGowan and K. H. Richards; RBS 67; Atlanta: SBL, 2011), 125–56.

2. See further the provisional sketch of a more comprehensive relational and contextual approach to the historical Jesus in R. Horsley, *The Prophet Jesus and the Renewal of Israel* (Grand Rapids, MI: Eerdmans, 2012); and essays on aspects of such an approach in R. Horsley, *Jesus in Context: People, Power, and Performance* (Minneapolis: Fortress, 2008).

instrumental in the formation of the people (of Israel). Breaking away from the imperial state of Egypt and the satellite city-state monarchies of Palestine/Canaan, the Israelites formed a coalition of upland villages, clans, and tribes free of central state control. In these traditions, the prophet Moses, in the crisis of bondage under the imperial state of Pharaoh, not only led the exodus liberation but mediated the Mosaic covenant on Sinai between YHWH, God of Israel, and the people of Israel and pronounced the covenantal commandments (principles of socioeconomic interaction) and covenantal laws. Moses' successor Joshua led the (peasant) nascent Israelites in liberating themselves from the kings of Canaan by guerrilla warfare and presided over the renewal of the Mosaic covenant (e.g., Josh 8; 11:1–9; 24). In the crisis of resubjugation to the kings of (northern) Canaan, the prophetess (and שׁפטה 'liberator') Deborah both inspired the (northern) villagers of Israel to renew their cooperative alliance (covenant) to fight guerrilla warfare against the rulers' war-chariots and then continued her "liberation/making justice for" the people in adjudicating social conflicts (Judg 4–5). The "liberator" Gideon's blunt rejection of being made "king" illustrates the concern in early Israelite tradition to gain or maintain independence from the centralized power of a state. The prophets, such as Moses and Deborah, were the leaders of the people in movements of independence from state control, denouncing the rulers' oppression and inspiring and/or organizing the resistance and renewal. This was also the role of the "last" liberator and prophet, Samuel, before the narrative shifts his role into mediator of the transition to popularly acclaimed, conditional kingship. And this was the role of Elijah, with the aid of the (other) בני נביאים ('prophetic school'), to lead a movement of resistance and (covenantal) renewal against the centralized state power and its oppression (1 Kgs 17–19). In addition to making pronouncements against the rulers and leading a movement of renewal in opposition to them, Elijah (and Elisha) performed healings and other acts of power as part of the renewal of the people, as in the multiple stories that are clearly derived from popular tradition (judging from the style so different from the Deuteronomistic History in which they are now embedded).

Elijah and his protégé Elisha, like Ahijah and Samuel before them, took on the expanded role of touching off a popular revolt against an oppressive monarchy by anointing a popular king. In the traditions about popular kings, the stories about the prophets' anointing evidently functioned side by side with stories of the people acclaiming or "anointing" ("messiah-ing") the king, especially in the traditions of the young David (2 Sam 2:1–4; 5:1–4).

After Elijah and Elisha, however, the stories of prophets leading movements of resistance and renewal against the state leave off. Different kinds of prophets emerge, both prophets in the service of the state/king, such as Nathan, and prophets who condemn the rulers and their officers, such as Amos and Hosea under the monarchy in Samaria and Micah, Isaiah, and Jeremiah under the monarchy in Jerusalem. For the latter, of course, we have shorter or longer anthologies of oracles. In what appear to be the earliest layer of oracles, perhaps derived from the "historical" prophets themselves, they pronounce God's condemnation/judgment of the kings and/or their officers for their economic oppression and political repression of the people/villagers in violation of Mosaic covenantal commandments. Many of these oracles have distinctive (prophetic) forms, such as laments over the impending judgment of the rulers (Amos 5:2–3, 16–17) or (series of) woes against the rulers or their officers for oppressive practices in violation of covenantal principles, followed by a pronouncement of sentence/punishment (Amos 6:1–3, 4–6, 7; Isa 5:18–19, 20, 21, 22–23, 24; Hab 2:9–11, 12, 15, 16–17). While the oracles of Amos, Micah, and Isaiah, however sharply condemnatory, pronounce judgment on particular regimes for violations of particular covenantal commandments but not on the state itself, Jeremiah's oracle against the Temple (Jer 7, 26) condemns the ruling institution itself for violation of most or all of the covenantal commandments. His oracles against Davidic kings come close to the same level of condemnation, God's condemnation of the monarchy itself for oppressing the people (for example, forced labor), not just particular monarchs.

After the Babylonian destruction of the monarchy and its temple, prophets continued to pronounce oracles, either in support of the establishment of the temple-state (Second Temple) or in criticism of its practices. The "official line" later in the Second Temple elite tradition became that the succession of the prophets had ended with Malachi. The learned scribe Jesus Ben Sira indicates that, by the beginning of the 2nd century B.C.E. at least, the scribes/sages understood themselves as the successors as well as guardians of the prophetic tradition (39:1–11). Since scribal circles controlled the cultural tradition at the elite level, and nonliterate villagers left no written texts as evidence, we have no way of knowing for sure whether prophets continued to rail against the (now temple-) state. The elite polemic against what appear to have been prophets speaking against the temple-state (Zech 13:2–6), however, suggests that they did, among the peasants ("tillers of the soil").

The State and Movements of Resistance and Renewal in Early Roman Palestine

At the time of Jesus, "the state" had become the multiple layers of rulers of the Roman imperial order. The temple-state in Jerusalem had been set up by the Persian regime to maintain imperial control and revenues from the tiny district of Judea. The temple-state headed by high priestly aristocracy was kept in place by the subsequent Ptolemaic, Seleucid, and Roman imperial regimes as the client state in control of the area. In a period of imperial weakness during the 2nd century B.C.E., the Hasmonean high priesthood expanded its rule over Idumea, Samaria, and finally over Galilee, in 104 B.C.E. (after Galilee had been under separate imperial jurisdiction for centuries). The crisis for the people of Israelite heritage at the time of Jesus began with the Roman conquest, imposition of the military

strongman Herod as "King of the Judeans," and repeated reconquests in retaliation for the persistent resistance and revolt by the Judeans and Galileans, which
was unprecedented among subjected peoples. After conquering and reconquering
the country, the Romans imposed client rulers in a succession of different arrangements. After the military strongman Herod ruled all of the districts from 37–4
B.C.E., the Romans set the high priestly aristocracy over Judea under the oversight
of a Roman governor and Herod Antipas as ruler over Galilee and Perea, which
were thus no longer under the temple-state's jurisdiction. "The state" at the time
of Jesus was thus a multilayered imperial rule of Rome through local client rulers,
the temple-state in Judea and Antipas in Galilee.

The Galilean and Judean villagers who comprised the vast majority of the populace in those areas mounted persistent resistance against the rule of the Romans
and their client rulers. The mission of Jesus was framed historically by widespread
revolts after the death of Herod in 4 B.C.E. and even more extensive and prolonged
revolt in 66–70 C.E. According to the accounts by the Judean historian Josephus,
the revolts in all areas in 4 B.C.E. and the organized movement of renewal and
resistance in Judea in 67–70 C.E. were led by figures acclaimed as "kings" by their
followers. These revolts all have the same distinctively Israelite form of popular
"messianic" movements patterned after the social memory (stories) of the young
David "anointed" by first the Judahites and then the elders of all Israel to lead
them in their movement of independence from the Philistine armies (2 Sam 2:1–4;
5:1–4). Although there are precious few scribal texts (that is, in the elite Judean
tradition) from late Second Temple times that mention any sort of "anointed one"
(*messiah*), these movements offer several concrete popular "kings" or "messiahs."
Leaders and followers interacted according to a deeply rooted cultural pattern carried in the popular social memory of the young David and the Israelites of old.

More closely contemporary with Jesus' mission, moreover, were several popular protests and movements of resistance and renewal. In the decades immediately following the mission of Jesus, again according to the accounts of Josephus,
several prophets gathered their followers to experience a new act of deliverance
similar to the great acts of deliverance under Moses and/or Joshua. These have
misleadingly been labeled "sign prophets." In his hostile summary accounts regarding these movements in general (*Ant.* 20.168; *War* 2.259), Josephus has these
"inspired revolutionary impostors" leading their followers "into the wilderness" to
experience "wonders and signs" of "liberation." In Israelite tradition, those metonymic terms were codified references to liberation led by Moses in the exodus
into the wilderness. The main point, the objective, the anticipated goal was the
new act of liberation.

In his accounts of three particular prophets and their movements, Josephus
describes particular (anticipated) acts of deliverance.[3] In Samaria, a new "Moses"

---

3. More extensive analysis and discussion in R. A. Horsley, "'Like One of the Prophets of
Old': Two Types of Popular Prophets at the Time of Jesus," *CBQ* 47 (1985) 435–63.

figure led his followers up to (their sacred) Mount Gerizim, where he would find the holy vessels (of the tabernacle of early Israel) at the spot where Moses had left them (*Ant.* 18.85–87). Anxious about the implications of such a movement, the Roman governor Pontius Pilate had sent out cavalry as well as infantry, killed the followers and executed the leader(s) and fugitives.

About a decade later (45 C.E.?), the prophet Theudas led his followers (with their possessions) out to the Jordan River, where the river would be divided at his command, allowing them to cross—a new Moses (and/or Joshua) anticipating a new exodus (and/or entry into the land, which was closely linked with the exodus in Israelite tradition). Again, the Roman governor, Fadus (44–46 C.E.), sent out the cavalry, which killed many, cut off Theudas' head and carried it back up to (Fadus? in) Jerusalem (*Ant.* 20.97–98). Interestingly, the book of Acts has Gamaliel compare Theudas and his movement (misdated) to Jesus and his movement (5:36).

Another decade later (56 C.E.), under the Roman governor Felix, a (Judean) prophet "from Egypt" led thousands of followers from the countryside up to the Mount of Olives from where, at his command, the walls of Jerusalem would collapse and the people gain entry into the city (*Ant.* 20.169–171; *War* 2.261–263). This prophet is unmistakably a new Joshua leading followers in anticipation of a new "battle of Jericho." Again the Roman governor sent out his troops to kill or capture the people, but this time the prophet escaped.

Judging from these three accounts, as well Josephus' summary sketches, these several prophets and their movements were all of a similar type, all patterned after the great acts of deliverance led by Moses and/or Joshua. The prophets and their followers were interacting according to the deeply ingrained cultural memory of the liberating acts in the origins of the people Israel. While references to some expectation of an "eschatological prophet" are lacking in Judean texts (produced by the literate elite), several prophets emerged from among the people of Judea and Samaria, leading relatively large movements of anticipated liberation and renewal of Israel.

Josephus' history of the great revolt against the Romans and their client rulers in 66–70 includes a lengthier account of another Judean prophet, but of a different kind (*War* 6:300–309). Four years before the outbreak of the great revolt of 66, at the festival of booths, a peasant named Jesus son of Hananiah, standing in the Temple during the festival of booths, began to cry out: "A voice from the east, a voice from the west, a voice from the four winds; a voice against Jerusalem and the Temple, a voice against the bridegrooms and brides, a voice against all the people." He repeated this dirge day and night through the city. Having been seized by the aristocracy and taken to the governor, who had him severely beaten, he continued to cry out, "Woe to Jerusalem." The governor Albinus, deeming him a mere madman, released him, whereupon he continued his daily lament on into the years of the revolt, "Woe to the city, and to the people, and to the Temple." Clearly, Jesus son of Hananiah was an oracular prophet, from among the peasantry, delivering a prophetic lament over the ruling city Jerusalem and its Temple, all of which bears striking resemblance to traditional prophetic laments (such as in Amos) and delivering prophetic woes against the ruling city in the tradition of Amos, Isaiah, and Habakkuk. Since we have only this one account, it is impossible to gauge how common such oracular prophets may have been toward the end of the Second Temple period. It is clear from Josephus's accounts, however, that, in addition to the popular prophets who led movements of renewal, there was also at least one oracular prophet right around the time of Jesus.

In my study of such accounts thirty years ago, it seemed unclear whether John the Baptist was an oracular prophet or a prophet leading a movement of renewal. Keying on the oracles in John's speech with parallels in Luke and Matthew ("Q"/ Luke 3:7–9, 16–17), I opted for the former. I am now convinced by Robert Webb's more extensive subsequent analysis based on Josephus' account (*Ant.* 18.116–119) as well as Gospel references that John was rather the leader of a movement of renewal of the people, his baptism of repentance in the wilderness having been a ritual action of renewal of the Mosaic covenant.[4] Thus, like Moses and Elijah, John both delivered pronouncements against (oppressive) rulers and (re-)formed/ renewed the covenantal people, although there is no indication that he healed as Elijah did.

Jesus of Nazareth, Prophet of Renewal and Resistance

Because of the standard assumptions and approach of study of "the historical Jesus," he has been taken as a prophet of proclamation, if seen as a prophet at all. In the theological scheme of Christian origins heavily influenced by the early chapters of the book of Acts, Jesus stands alone as an individual revealer, unengaged in concrete social-economic-political relations. He did not lead a movement but only attracted followers/disciples, who formed the community in Jerusalem and an expanding movement only after the resurrection appearances evoked their "Easter faith"—after which they proclaimed him as the Messiah/Christ, not as a prophet. Interpretation of Jesus, moreover, focuses on individual sayings of Jesus, isolated from their context in the Gospels, which are dismissed as reliable sources because they are products of that "Easter faith," as well as full of narratives with "miraculous" or "supernatural" elements. The result in recent American interpretation has been a sharp division between liberal interpretation and a revival of the "apocalyptic Jesus" of Albert Schweitzer, a century ago.[5] Based on a sophisticated criticism of individual sayings, liberal interpreters dismiss sayings with judgmental features as well as "apocalyptic" references to "the end of the world" to be secondary and

---

4. R. L. Webb, *John the Baptizer and Prophet: A Sociohistorical Study* (JSNTSup 62; Sheffield: JSOT Press, 1991).

5. Discussed in Horsley, *Prophet Jesus*, 9–66.

find primarily the "sapiential" sayings to be authentic. Limited to this "database," Jesus must have been a "sage," a teacher of an itinerant individual lifestyle. In re-action, others revert to Schweitzer's portrayal of Jesus as having proclaimed an apocalyptic scenario of imminent judgment and the end of the world.

Meanwhile, without attracting much attention from interpreters of Jesus, study of the Gospels has recognized that they are not mere collections or contain-ers of sayings and miracle stories. The Gospels are sustained narratives, whole stories of Jesus' mission in interaction with followers and opponents. Matthew and Luke, moreover, also have large blocks of Jesus' teaching in strikingly parallel form, often verbatim. These blocks of teaching were standardly viewed as a collec-tion of sayings in Matthew's and Luke's common "source" Q (*Quelle*, in German). Closer recent examination, however, recognizes that these blocks of teaching have the form of (a series of) speeches on key issues of concern to the communities of movements of Jesus-loyalists. Working from whole Gospel stories and from the series of speeches in "Q" results in a very different picture of Jesus from those based on the study of individual sayings. To make the presentation manageable, I focus mainly on Mark and Q, by consensus the earliest sources.[6]

The Gospel of Mark was previously assumed to be about Jesus as the Mes-siah. Not only does Mark (in contrast to John) not use "Messiah/Christ" as a title for Jesus, but the Gospel seems to suggest that Jesus was misunderstood as a/the anointed king. In narrative sequence, after Peter acclaims Jesus as "the messiah," Jesus announces that he must suffer and be killed, for which Peter rebukes Jesus, and Jesus in turn rebukes Peter (8:27–33). Then, when James and John ask to be seated is positions of honor and power when he comes to glory, Jesus declares that his mission is not about gaining positions of royal power (10:35–45). Mark is thus indicating that Jesus is not an anointed king, not to be understood as a king leading a revolt, and certainly not an imperial king (in the tradition of 2 Sam 7 or Psalms 2 and 110).

Read as a whole story, the Gospel of Mark presents Jesus engaged in a renewal of the people of Israel in opposition to the rulers of the people. After his baptism by John, Jesus is tested in the wilderness, like Elijah, and then recruits disciples, again like Elijah. In fact, he recruits and then commissions twelve disciples, rep-resentative of the twelve tribes of Israel, as were the twelve stones of the altar constructed by Elijah. In the second major step in the narrative, Mark 4:35–8:22, Jesus performs two series of five "acts of power," the sea crossings and feedings in the wilderness reminiscent of Moses and the healings reminiscent of Elijah, the

---

6. Only brief sketches of the gospel portrayals are possible here. For fuller analysis and discussion, see R. A. Horsley, *Hearing the Whole Story: The Politics of Plot in Mark's Gospel* (Lou-isville: Westminster John Knox, 2001); R. A. Horsley with J. Draper, *"Whoever Hears You Hears Me": Prophets, Performance and Tradition in Q* (Harrisburg, PA: Trinity Press International, 1999); and on the Gospel of John, R. A. Horsley and T. Thatcher, *John, Jesus, and the Renewal of Israel* (Grand Rapids, MI: Eerdmans, 2013).

founding prophet and prophet of renewal, respectively. Among the healings are those of the woman hemorrhaging for 12 years and the almost dead 12-year-old woman, both symbolic of Israel, which, through Jesus, receives renewed life. In the next major narrative step, Jesus appears with Moses and Elijah on the mountain. Just before he marches up to Jerusalem, Jesus holds four dialogues that not only cite the covenantal commandments but focus on commandment-like pronouncements of socioeconomic principles. Later, just before he is arrested, Jesus transforms the Passover meal with the disciples into a covenant renewal meal, as symbolized in the cup (14:24; cf. Exod 24:3–8). The Gospel of Mark is thus presenting Jesus as engaged in the renewal of Israel in the commission and mission of twelve disciples, the healings, the feedings, and the covenant renewal.

The dominant conflict in the story, moreover, is between Jesus and his renewal of the people and the rulers of the people in Jerusalem and their scribal and Pharisaic representatives who "come down from Jerusalem" to challenge Jesus. Shortly after he has performed several healings and an exorcism, the Pharisees and Herodians plot to destroy him (3:1–6). When the scribes and Pharisees accuse him and disciples of not observing their "traditions of the elders," he condemns them for preventing the people from observing the basic commandment(s) of God by siphoning off produce needed for local nourishment to the support of the Temple. He later condemns the scribes for "devouring widows' houses." After he marches up to Jerusalem at Passover, he engages in sustained confrontation with the high priestly rulers in the Temple, beginning with the prophetic demonstration against them in the Temple that alludes explicitly to Jeremiah's earlier pronouncement against the Temple. His prophetic parable pronouncing God's condemnation of the high priestly rulers leads to the attempted entrapment over payment of the tribute to Caesar. In a well-crafted statement usually misconstrued according to the modern Western separation of church and state, Jesus declares in effect that the people do not owe tribute to Caesar. At the end of the sustained confrontation, Jesus declares that the Temple will be destroyed, a pronouncement thrown back at him in his trial and crucifixion. The high priestly rulers finally take action, have him captured surreptitiously, and hand him over to the Roman governor Pilate, who orders him crucified. Finally, in the "open ending" of the story, Jesus meets the disciples back in "Galilee," evidently to continue the movement of renewal of the people. The Gospel of Mark thus portrays Jesus as a new Moses and Elijah engaged in the renewal of Israel in opposition to the rulers, the Romans and their clients in Jerusalem.

The series of speeches in Q is very different material from the narrative sequence of episodes in Mark yet presents a portrayal parallel to that in Mark. John declares that Jesus will bring a baptism of Spirit and fire—that is, of renewal and judgment. The first and longest speech is a renewal of the Mosaic covenant, with Jesus speaking as the new Moses. Another speech commissions the disciples to extend his mission of proclaiming the kingdom and healing. The speech refuting the charge of being himself possessed by Beelzebul concludes with the declaration that "since I am casting out demons 'by the finger of God,' the (direct) rule of God has come upon you," thus indicating that his actions are a new exodus. In other speeches, he pronounces a series of woes against the scribes and Pharisees, concluding with a statement of punishment, and pronounces a prophetic lament anticipating the destruction of the ruling house of Jerusalem. Finally, in what may have been the concluding short speech, Jesus presents the role of twelve disciples as "establishing justice for" or delivering the twelve tribes of Israel. At points in several speeches, Jesus and/or his followers continue to perform the speeches and are represented as the latest in—indeed, the climax of—the long line of prophets whom the rulers persecuted and killed.

The gospels of Matthew and Luke both follow the basic story in Mark, while inserting the Q speeches at key points in the narrative. Thus, while at points they refer to Jesus as a/the messiah, both Matthew and Luke portray Jesus as a prophet leading a movement of renewal. In the "Sermon on the Mount," for example, Matthew heightens Jesus role as the new Moses enacting a renewed covenant on the mountain, and by inserting Jesus' prophetic pronouncements in the Q speeches into Mark's narrative and expanding on them, both Matthew and Luke sharpen Jesus' opposition to the high priestly heads of the Jerusalem temple-state, the face of Roman imperial rule in Judea. The Gospel of John has often been sidelined as a more "spiritual" text of little value as historical representation. It presents Jesus as the fulfilment of every expectation and salvific title in Israelite tradition (as continued into early Jesus tradition). It is worth noting, however, that if we discern that John makes clear regional distinctions among the peoples of Israelite heritage, between the *Galilaioi,* the *Samaritai,* and the *Ioudaioi* (the Judeans, not "the Jews"), then the underlying narrative in John is about Jesus catalyzing a renewal of Israel in all of the Israelite area (Galilee, Samaria, Judea, and the Transjordan) in opposition to "the Judeans" who are the high priests and Pharisees in control of the temple-state in Jerusalem. In having Jesus repeatedly travel up to Jerusalem for various "festivals of the Judeans" in the Temple, where he comes into confrontation with the high priests and Pharisees, John heightens the opposition between the prophet and the state.

It is hardly to be imagined that Mark's (or Matthew' or John's) story is a direct report of what Jesus did or that the speeches in Q are transcripts of what he said. Mark is a composed, plotted story probably developed in repeated performances. Similarly, Q speeches adapted in repeated performances in communities of Jesus-loyalists. The point is that these two earliest "Gospel texts," so different in their form, both portray Jesus as a prophet like Moses or Elijah engaged in the renewal of Israel in opposition to and opposed by the rulers. This portrayal, far from being derived from the "Easter faith" of the disciples, forms the dominant portrayal of Jesus-in-movement that runs consistently and explicitly underneath whatever overlays of "Easter faith" modern scholars detect in the Gospels. Moreover, not only do both portrayals have considerable historical "verisimilitude," insofar as they fit the historical context as known from other sources such as Josephus' histories, but the portrayal of Jesus as a prophet leading a movement of renewal and resistance parallels the popular prophetic movements mentioned by Josephus. Jesus and the movement he catalyzed were evidently rooted in and adapting the same deeply rooted cultural pattern as other popular prophets and their followers.

Jesus' Prophetic Pronouncements against the Jerusalem Rulers and Their Representatives

Although the prophets leading movements and the oracular prophets appear to have been two distinctive types of prophets, the one articulating a vision and agenda of renewal and resistance for the people, the other voicing God's condemnation of the rulers for oppressing the people, they had overlapping agendas. Elijah not only inspired and organized the people in resistance and mounted a great symbolic ceremony of renewal in opposition to Ahab's monarchy (1 Kgs 18) but pronounced oracles against the regime's practices (shift of its loyalty to Lord Storm, symbol of centralized cosmic-political power, 1 Kgs 17:1; seizure of people's ancestral land, 1 Kgs 21). As evident in the Gospels, his prophetic leadership and prophecies continued to be prominent in the popular social memory, and perhaps for that reason also have been taken up into the elite tradition (Mal 3; Sir 48:12). While Jesus and other nonliterate villagers probably had no direct contact with the costly and cumbersome scrolls on which anthologies of prophetic oracles were inscribed, it seems likely that prophetic oracles that voiced popular protest and interest were known among the people. Influenced by the social memory of Elijah, surely, Jesus not only carried out healing and preaching of God's direct rule in village communities but pronounced God's condemnation of high priestly rulers and their scribal and Pharisaic representatives for oppressing the people in violation of covenant commandments and principles. It is striking that some of these pronouncements not only resemble the substance of traditional prophecies but take the distinctive traditional forms of those prophecies. It is possible to focus on only a few examples here.

Woes against the Scribes and Pharisees: Q/Luke 11:39–52

The speech in Q/Luke 11:39–52 is a series of six woes and a declaration of God's judgment against the scribes and Pharisees. Matthew expands these into a more elaborate condemnation of the scribes and Pharisees, along with the whole ruling house of Jerusalem of which they were advisers and representatives (Matt 23). The woes against the scribes and Pharisees, usually taken as separate sayings, have usually been interpreted as disputes about the Law/Torah or, more particularly, about purity laws. Recent interpretations find here a redefinition of purity in ethical terms (by taking 11:39 41 and 44 as the key) or a radicalization of the Law (by taking 11:42 as the key). But only one of the woes even alludes to the Torah/law (the tithes of 11:42) and only two mention purity (11:39–41, 44, and then as a rhetorical device).

Rhetorically, some of the woes mock the Pharisees for their focus on purity or their requiring tithes of every little herb. But what the woes focus on is the effect of the activities or role of the scribes and Pharisees on the people. They not only expect deference and seats of honor (11:43), but they "neglect justice" (11:42) "load the people with burdens too heavy to bear" (11:46), and in their practice of "extortion" have become a "danger" to the people (11:44) and effectively prevent them from knowing or keeping the covenant (11:52; "entering the kingdom," Matt 23:13). In "building the tombs/monuments to the prophets" they share the guilt of their ancestors who killed the prophets. God thus holds them accountable for the blood of the all the martyred prophets (11:29–51, the sentence). The woes against the scribes and Pharisees condemn them for the debilitating effect of their political role on the people, particularly in regard to their advocacy of rigorous tithing, on top of taxes and tribute, and failing to use their scribal office to relax the burden on the people.

The key to understanding this series of woes may be to recognize their prophetic form and to appreciate the prophetic tradition in which they stand. As collected in the books named after them, the prophets Amos, Micah, Isaiah, and Habakkuk pronounced woes consisting of an indictment for violation of a covenantal principle and a statement of sentence or punishment. These they pronounced against the rulers or their officers for having exploited and oppressed the people. Some are single woes with statements of punishment. But many of the woes come in sets of two, three, or four, followed by a statement of sentence (see the references above). Scribes critical of the priestly heads of the Jerusalem temple-state continued the prophetic tradition of woes. Much closer to the time of Jesus, the dissident circle of scribes who produced the "Epistle of Enoch" (*1 Enoch* 94–104) pronounced several sets of woes against the high priestly rulers and their scribes, with sequences of four or five woes (indictments for oppression of the people) concluding with a pronouncement of sentence.

Jesus' woes against the scribes and Pharisees in Q/Luke 11:39–52 thus stand in a long tradition of prophetic woes against the rulers and their officers. In substance they are reminiscent of Jeremiah's charge that "the false pen of the scribes has made [God's law] into a lie" (Jer 8:8) and they continue the same basic form used by Amos, Micah, and Isaiah. As with other prophetic forms, moreover, the woes are performative speech, in which the pronouncement makes it so—regardless of whether the ostensible addressees are standing right there. The woes pronounced by Jesus thus functioned in the same way as those of the earlier prophets. They pronounced indictments of rulers and/or their representatives for oppression of the people in violation of covenantal commandments and pronounced divine punishment.[7]

Lament over the Ruling House of Jerusalem: Q/Luke 13:34–35

Jesus' prophecy against the ruling "house" of Jerusalem in Q/Luke 13:34–35a appears almost verbatim in Matthew's and Luke's parallel texts, suggesting that neither changed it from the tradition they used.[8] The images in the oral poetry are almost palpable, with a mournful repetitive address, parallel lines with parallel sounds, and God as a protective mother hen.

> O Jerusalem, Jerusalem!
> You kill the prophets
> and stone those sent to you.
> How often would I have gathered your children together
> As a hen gathers her brood under her wings,
> And you refused.
> Behold your house is forsaken!
> For I tell you:
> You will not see me until you say:
> "Blessed is he who comes in the name of the Lord." (Q 13:34–35)

In this oracle, Jesus adapts the traditional form of a prophetic lament in which the prophet speaks the words of God. Amos 5:2–3, 16–17 offers a classic example, in which God's lament anticipates the future lamentation of the ruling city when judgment is finally executed. Similarly, in anticipation of God's imminent judgment, Jesus announces that Jerusalem is already desolate (because destroyed) and in mourning. Adding to the likelihood that Jesus of Nazareth continued this tradition of prophetic lament is the similar lament over the imminent destruction of Jerusalem thirty years later by that other Jesus, the rustic son of Hananiah (*War* 6.300–309; discussed above).

Jesus' portrayal of God protecting her children as a mother hen gathers her brood under her wing taps into a traditional image familiar from the "Song of Moses" (Deut 32:1–43), a celebration of the exodus deliverance and covenantal formation of Israel. In this song God is "like an eagle that stirs up its nest and hovers over its young, spreading its wings" (Deut 32:11). In Jesus' lament, God as a mother hen is grieving because, even though she had tried to protect her children, the Jerusalem rulers had exploited them, hence their destruction was already underway.

---

7. Fuller discussion in Horsley with Draper, *Whoever Hears You Hears Me*, 285–91.

8. Fuller discussion in Horsley, *Jesus and the Spiral of Violence*, 300–304; *Jesus and Empire*, 87–91.

Jesus' principal charge in this prophecy—that Jerusalem habitually kills the prophets God has sent—like the same charge in the woes, reverberates with Israelite tradition. Ahab and Jezebel attempted to assassinate Elijah (1 Kgs 19; 18:17). King Jehoiakim even sent agents to Egypt to kill the prophet Uriah son of Shemiah. And after Jeremiah pronounced God's condemnation of the Temple, officials tried to lynch him (Jer 26:7–23). Legends about the prophets in the later *Lives of the Prophets* suggest that Jesus' contemporaries believed that most of the prophets had been martyred for their message. And Herod Antipas had just recently beheaded John the Baptist for his insistence on covenantal justice (Josephus, *Ant.* 18.116–19; cf. Mark 6:17–29).[9]

"House" was a standing term for a monarchy, dynasty, or temple-state with its whole governing apparatus, and the term also resonated within a long prophetic tradition of declarations of judgment against Jerusalem rulers, such as Jeremiah's pronouncement of judgment on the house of David (Jer 22:1–9). The severity of the indictment-and-condemnation that Jesus announces here should not be missed. God has already condemned Jerusalem as the ruling house of Israel.

The last line of the lament (v. 35a), finally, recites a key line of the highly familiar Passover psalm (Ps 118) giving thanks for previous deliverance and appealing for future salvation: "Hosanna! Deliver us!" God, speaking through Jesus, declares to the Jerusalem rulers that they will not see him until they welcome "the one who comes in the name of the LORD," presumably Jesus himself. But of course they were not about to do that. Since they have refused/forsaken God, they are about to be refused/forsaken by God.

Prophecy against Temple: Mark 13:1–2; 14:58; 15:29; John 2:19–21; Gospel of Thomas 71

Three different episodes in Mark cite or refer to Jesus' prophesying against the Temple. Jesus' statement in Mark 13:1–2 that "not one stone will be left here upon another, all will be thrown down" is usually taken as a prophetic reference to the destruction of the Temple. Mark's narrative of Jesus' demonstration in and against the Temple makes clear that it was a prophetic action symbolizing God's destruction of the Temple (Mark 11:12–243). Witnesses at his trial in Mark say they heard him say, "I will destroy this temple that is made with hands and in three days I will build another, not made with hands" (Mark 14:58). Passersby at his crucifixion deride him, saying "Aha! You who would destroy the temple and build it in three days. . . ." (15:29). These reports have parallels in other Gospels. The simplest reference is in the Gospel of Thomas 71: "Jesus said: 'I shall de[stroy this] house, and no one will be able to build it [again]," which is close to the "reports" in Acts 6:13–14 that Stephen had said "that this Jesus of Nazareth with destroy

---

9. In other cases, mentioned above, the Roman governors quickly sent out the military to kill them (Josephus, *Ant.* 20.169–71; *War* 2.261–63).

this place." That Jesus had prophesied destruction (and rebuilding) of the Temple was so deeply embedded in Jesus tradition that (to explain it away) the Gospel of John carefully had Jesus making reference to his body rather than suppressing the prophecy (cf. John 2:19–21).[10]

Several modern attempts have been made to explain (away) this prophecy. Some have argued that at Jesus' trial in Mark the paraphrase of his prophecy is presented as false testimony. Mark's narrative ("But even on this point their testimony did not agree" 15:59) does not really say that. The assumption at the crucifixion scene is that Jesus had indeed spoken about destroying the Temple. And Mark's narrative had earlier represented Jesus as declaring that the stones would all "be thrown down." The witnesses' testimony is that Jesus himself would destroy the Temple. But if he had been uttering prophecy as the mouthpiece of God in the same way that earlier Israelite prophets had, and in the same way as in Q/Luke 13:34–35, then it was God who was about to destroy the Temple.

The form of the prophecy in Mark 14:58 and 15:29 (and in John 2:19–21) is a double saying about the destruction and the rebuilding of the Temple. The temple "not made with hands" was taken as a "spiritual" or "heavenly" temple in earlier Christian interpretation. The appearance of "house" in the Gospel of Thomas version, however, suggests another possibility for understanding the prophecy in its double-saying form. "House (of God)" was used in Second Temple Judean texts not only for the Temple and for the ruling house but also for the people—and often for the restored people of Israel. Terms such "house," "temple," body," and "assembly" could all function as synonyms, usually with reference to a social body (the people). The community at Qumran near the Dead Sea, for example, understood itself as the (true) "temple" (1 QS 5:5–7; 8:4–10; 9:3–6; 4 QFlor 1:1–13).

Jesus' prophecy of destroying and rebuilding the Temple can thus be understood as playing on the double meaning of the term "temple" or (more likely, as in the Gospel of Thomas version) "house." His prophecy declared that God was destroying the/God's "house/temple made with hands" in Jerusalem but rebuilding the/God's "house/temple not made with hands," the people of Israel. This was the agenda of Jesus' mission, as attested in Q as well as Mark, of spearheading a renewal of Israel in opposition to its rulers. If the renewed people itself were understood as the rebuilt "temple" or "house" of God, then of course there would be no need for a temple-state, which was widely resented among the people.

Parables of God's Condemnation of the High Priests: Mark 12:1–9; Q/Luke 14:16–24; Thomas

While Jesus' parables are usually lumped together in discussion of his teaching, it should not be forgotten that parables (and generally rich complex metaphors and analogies) were yet another form of prophetic speech, particularly in

---

10. Fuller exploration in Horsley, *Jesus and the Spiral*, 292–300.

pronouncement against rulers. Best known from earlier Israelite tradition may be the "poor man's lamb" parable that the prophet Nathan told David to induce his own recognition of his dastardly rape of Bathsheba and murder of Uriah, in violation of multiple commandments (adultery, false witness, murder; 2 Sam 11–12). The story of Naboth's vineyard and Elijah's accompanying pronouncement of sentence operates as a parable told against Ahab and Jezebel and any such monarchs' oppressive and violent abuse of power (1 Kgs 19). The "love song" that YHWH sings about his beloved vineyard in Isa 5 functions similarly as a parable (complex metaphor or analogy) that leads to the obvious conclusion, given the covenantal principles of Israel, that YHWH will destroy the vineyard. The parable of the tenants in Mark 12:2–9, in which Jesus alludes to Isaiah's famous prophecy about the vineyard, is just such a prophetic pronouncement of God's condemnation of the rulers for violent oppression of the people.[11] (In contrast to the later anti-Judaism interpretation, the high priests knew that they [not "the Jews" generally] corresponded to the violent tenants and that the "others" were the people [not "the Gentiles"], as indicated clearly in Mark.) The parable of the Great Supper in Q/Luke 14:16–24 and Gospel of Thomas 64 is a parallel prophetic statement of the exclusion of the high priests from the banquet of the restored people in the kingdom of God.

Jesus the Prophet Catalyzing the Renewal of Israel

As evident in the Gospel stories and the Q speeches, however, Jesus was not just a latter-day oracular prophet pronouncing God's judgment on the rulers and their representatives. He was the leader of a renewal of Israel, at least to an extent, on the model of the great prophet of renewal, Elijah. And just as Elijah had both performed healings and revitalized the covenant people as part of the movement of renewal, so Jesus of Nazareth healed and pressed the renewal of cooperative village community life.

Healing

Earlier generations of Jesus-interpreters, well-socialized into the scientific mentality rooted in the modern Enlightenment reduction of reality to nature that can be understood through reason, either avoided dealing with or simply dismissed the healing and exorcism stories of Jesus as "miracles" or "magic," hopelessly tied up with the unbelievable "supernatural." To some form-critics, moreover, stories about Jesus' healings or exorcisms seemed to be nothing more than duplicates of typical stories told of Greco-Roman figures such as Apollonios of Tyana. Recently, standard (re-)translations of the Bible have reduced Jesus' healings of sickness to the modern biomedical concepts of "disease" and "cure," as

---

11. On this and other parables in political context, see W. R. Herzog II, *Parables as Subversive Speech* (Louisville: Westminster John Knox, 1994).

if Jesus were comparable to a modern clinician. Even recent interpreters of Jesus lump the healings and exorcisms into a general category of "miracles" or "magic," modern western concepts for which there is no ancient equivalent. More careful investigation suggests that the stories of Jesus' healing resemble nothing more closely than they do the stories of Elijah and his protégé Elisha. There has been little serious investigation of Jesus' healings and exorcisms. Taking cues from such stories as the exorcism of the demon whose name turns out to be "Legion," that is "Roman troops," however, I am convinced that the healings and exorcisms can be fruitfully investigated as integral aspects of Jesus' more general mission of renewal of Israel in resistance to the rulers—ultimately, the Romans, whose legions had conquered and reconquered the Galileans and Judeans.[12] And an integral part of this investigation would be how Jesus' healing and exorcism can be understood in the tradition of Elijah's and Elisha's healings, as integral to a prophet-led movement of renewal of Israel against oppressive rulers. Fuller discussion must await such an investigation.

Covenant Renewal

The prophet Jesus of Nazareth, like the founding prophet, Moses, and Elijah, the great prophet of renewal, was catalyzing a renewal of the people in their village communities. He commissioned his disciples to extend his own mission of proclaiming the direct rule of God and healing and exorcism in the village communities of Galilee and beyond. The center of this renewal of supportive community in the face of debt and disintegration under the economic pressures of multiple demands for revenues (taxes and tribute on top of tithes and offerings), was renewal of the Mosaic covenant. The prophet Moses had supposedly mediated the formation of the covenant people and the giving of the covenant law. The prophet Deborah had appealed to the covenant bonds and expectation. Elijah had renewed the covenant people. And the subsequent oracular prophets regularly appealed to covenant principles and commandments as the basis of their announcements of indictment and condemnation of rulers and their officers. The fundamental form of the Mosaic covenant was alive and well at the time of Jesus, as we know now from the Community Rule from Qumran, which followed the basic covenant components.

Once the speeches of Jesus parallel in Luke 6:20–49 and Matt 5–7 are no longer read as separate sayings and the overall structure is noted, it is unmistakably clear that these speeches, and the Q speech behind them, are covenant renewal.[13] The core the speech in Q/Luke 6:20–49, the section that begins with "Love your

---

12. I am currently at work on just such an investigation that will be as comprehensive as possible.

13. See further Horsley with Draper, *Whoever Hears You Hears Me*, 195–227; Horsley, *Covenant Economics*, 99–114.

enemies," is full of the terms and phrases reminiscent of traditional Israelite covenantal teaching. Textual notes and commentaries contain numerous lists of the "allusions" or "references" to Mosaic covenantal laws or rulings in the Covenant Code (Exod 21–23), the Holiness Code (esp. Lev 18–19), and Deuteronomy. The speech, moreover, has the same basic structure as the principal texts of the Mosaic covenant in Exod 20 and Josh 24:

Components of Covenant	Exodus 20; Joshua 24; Deuteronomy 28	Q/Luke 6:20–49
declaration of God's deliverance	from bondage in Egypt	blessings of Kingdom
commandments to the people	ten commandments	love enemies, do good, lend
motivating sanctions	blessings and curses	parable: houses on rock/sand

The significant change is that Jesus transforms the blessings and curses, which had originally functioned as sanctions on keeping the commandments, into a new declaration of deliverance in the present-future—similar to what was done in the renewal ceremony outlined in the Community Rule of the Dead Sea community at Qumran (1QS 1–4). In both content and structure, the covenant renewal speech in Q/Luke 6:20–49 is thoroughly rooted in—indeed, is an adaptation of—the continuing practice of Israelite tradition.

Jesus' renewal of the Mosaic covenant was evidently a direct response to the dire economic situation of the people in their village communities. The admonitions in Q/Luke 6:27–38, for example, address circumstances in which hungry people had been borrowing and lending to one another, as admonished in traditional Mosaic covenantal teaching (for example, Exod 22:25–27; Deut 15:7–8), and then coming into social conflict when those in debt were unable to pay back their neighbors, who had meanwhile also become desperate. This situation was the result of the multiple layers of rulers and their demands for revenues, tithes, and offerings for the priesthood and Temple, taxes for the Herodian kings, and tribute to Caesar. As indicated in the Lord's Prayer as well as in the beatitudes, the people were poor and hungry and heavily in debt. As they quarreled among themselves over debts and some families came under the control of creditors (see the "slices of life" in the parables of "the unmerciful servant," Matt 18:23–35, and "the dishonest steward," Luke 16:2–7), the village communities that under less oppressive rulers would have provided a local "safety net" were beginning to disintegrate.

As with most prophetic declarations, Jesus covenant renewal in Q/Luke 6:20–49 is in what linguists call "performative speech": pronouncing it effects what is pronounced. "Jesus," as the performer of the covenant renewal speech in Q/Luke 6:20–49, is enacting a covenant renewal in delivering the speech to a community of a Jesus-movement. Uttered in a situation in which the people assumed that their suffering was due to their own sins and failure to keep the commandments, Jesus' transformation of the blessings and curses into a new declaration of deliverance ("Blessed are you poor, for yours in the kingdom of God," etc.) gave the despairing people a new lease on life.[14] "Your sins are forgiven." Since God is giving the people the kingdom, a new life of justice and sufficiency is now possible, as Jesus' declares in renewed covenantal admonitions to "love your enemies, do good, and lend," in Q/Luke 6:27–36. To poor, hungry, mourning people who are "at each others' throats" in resentment over unrepaid loans, with insults and accusations, Jesus demands that they recommit themselves collectively to the covenantal principles of mutual cooperation and support in the village community. It is surely significant how this commitment to mutual cooperation and sharing parallels the Lord's Prayer (Q/Luke 11:2–4, but with the more concrete "earthy" term "debts" in Matt 6:12), in which the kingdom of God means concretely sufficient bread for subsistence and mutual cancellation of debts.

The Gospel sources for Jesus present an overlay of interpretation, including titles and identifications and early "creeds" that theologians latch onto as sources for Christology. Most prominent among these are "the Messiah/Christ, particularly in John, the identification of Jesus with a heavenly "Son of Man," particularly in Matthew, and the resurrection, particularly in Matthew and John (as well as Paul). Interpreters familiar with the prophetic traditions and anthologies known from the Hebrew Bible have long discerned that some of Jesus' speeches or parables took the form of and stood in the tradition of Israelite prophets of earlier centuries. Now that we are learning to "take the Gospels whole" as sustained narratives, it is becoming evident that Jesus stands in the tradition of prophets leading movements of renewal and resistance, most notably Moses and Elijah, and should be understood as rooted in the same Israelite social memory of prophetic leaders in which those other popular prophets of renewal and resistance emerged under Roman rule in mid-1st-century Palestine.

---

14. See further the analysis in Horsley, *Jesus and the Spiral of Violence*, 181–84.

Bibliography

Herzog II, W. R. *Parables as Subversive Speech*. Louisville: Westminster John Knox, 1994.

Horsley, R. A. "'Like One of the Prophets of Old:' Two Types of Popular Prophets at the Time of Jesus," *CBQ* 47 (1985) 435–63.

———. *Hearing the Whole Story: The Politics of Plot in Mark's Gospel*. Louisville: Westminster John Knox, 2001.

———. *Jesus in Context: People, Power, and Performance*. Minneapolis: Fortress, 2008.

_____. "Oral Communication, Oral Performance, and New Testament Interpretation." Pp. 125–56 in *Method and Meaning: Essays on New Testament Interpretation in Honor of Harold W. Attridge*. Edited by A. B. McGowan and K. H. Richards. RBS 67. Atlanta: SBL, 2011.

_____. *The Prophet Jesus and the Renewal of Israel*. Grand Rapids, MI: Eerdmans, 2012.

_____, with J. Draper. *"Whoever Hears You Hears Me": Prophets, Performance and Tradition in Q*. Harrisburg, PA: Trinity Press International, 1999.

_____. and T. Thatcher. *John, Jesus, and the Renewal of Israel*. Grand Rapids, MI: Eerdmans, 2013.

Webb, R. L. *John the Baptizer and Prophet: A Sociohistorical Study*. JSNTSup 62; Sheffield: JSOT Press, 1991.

Late First-Century Christian Apocalyptic: Revelation

Jennifer Knust

Boston University

It is hardly controversial to claim that John of Patmos, the writer of the Book of Revelation, positioned himself as an "enemy of the state," if by state we mean John's own Roman imperial context. A resident of the Roman province of Asia, John had nothing but disdain for the emperors, their agents, and the city they viewed as sacred: John represents Rome as a vicious sea creature who blasphemes God and makes war on the holy ones (13:1–10), as a monster who marks those tainted by its impure riches with the number 666 (13:1–8, cf. 17:9–13) and as a whore, seated on a seven-headed beast, drunk with the blood of the saints, and carrying a cup filled with the fluids of "her" fornications (17:1–18). Indeed, one would be hard pressed to find a more explicit expression of anti-Roman sentiment among the surviving writings from this period, whether one dates the book early—say, during the reign of Nero (54–68 C.E.)—or late, perhaps during the reign of Domitian (81–96 C.E.) or even Trajan (98–117 C.E.).[1] John, it would seem, hated his "state" (a word I will consider at greater length below) and eagerly antici- pated its violent, dramatic, and divinely sponsored demise.

---

1. Most scholars locate Revelation during the reign of Domitian, an opinion that was also held by Irenaeus of Lyons in the 2nd century and Eusebius of Caesarea in the 4th (it is Eusebius who preserves the appropriate section of Irenaeus's *Against the Heresies* [5.30.3 = Eusebius *Ecclesiastical History* 3.18.1]; cf. *Ecclesiastical History* 3.17–20). See esp. S. J. Friesen, *Imperial Cults and the Apocalypse of John* (Oxford: Oxford University Press, 2001). Also see E. S. Fiorenza, *Invitation to the Book of Revelation* (Garden City, NY: Doubleday, 1981), and idem, *The Book of Revelation: Justice and Judgment* (Philadelphia: Fortress, 1985). Leonard Thompson holds to the Domitianic date, but he also argues that Eusebius's testimony is unreliable (*The Book of Revelation: Apocalypse and Empire* [Oxford: Oxford University Press, 1990], 15–17, 95–115). For an argument for an early date, see J. C. Wilson, "The Problem of the Domitianic Date of Revelation," *NTS* 39 (1993) 586–605, and A. A. Bell, "The Date of John's Apocalypse: The Evidence of Some Roman Historians Reconsidered," *NTS* 25 (1979) 93–102. F. G. Downing argues that Revelation is best placed during the reign of Trajan, though few have been persuaded by his perspective, "Pliny's Persecutions of Christians: Revelation and 1 Peter," *NTS* 34 (1988) 105–23.

Nevertheless, viewing John as an "enemy of the state," as most scholars would today, fails to explain the long history of reception of his book, particularly in a North American context, where John's words have more often been taken as endorsements of privilege by beneficiaries of the current state apparatus.[2] In the United States, Revelation's symbols have inspired leaders like Jerry Falwell, Hal Lindsey, and even the former President Ronald Reagan, each of whom has interpreted contemporary American politics through the lens of John's apocalyptic fervor. Moreover, it is the purveyors of mega-church theologies and evangelical forms of Christianity, loosely defined, whose interpretations have captured the imaginations of the vast majority of the reading public today.[3] According to these readers, Revelation decries not Roman imperialism or "the state" per se but globalization, Satan worship, and a decline in sexual morals, each of which disastrously threatens the chosen status of the American body politic.[4] Whatever may have led John of Patmos to identify Christ the Lamb as Rome's enemy and judge, his book has been as fascinating to privileged "haves" as to various "have-nots," and the "haves" have proven quite capable of viewing themselves as the persecuted minority whom God intends to vindicate.[5]

This chapter takes the surprising dual reception of Revelation as a starting point, asking how it is that a book that seems so obviously positioned "against the state" remains equally inspirational for those who seek to advance what might be considered a statist agenda. Though multiple explanations for this interpretive

---

2. S. D. O'Leary, *Arguing the Apocalypse: A Theory of Millennial Rhetoric* (Oxford: Oxford University Press, 1998). Also see E. Runions, "Biblical Promise and Threat in US Imperialist Rhetoric Before and After September 11, 2001," in *Interventions* (ed. E. A. Castelli and J. R. Jakobsen; New York: Palgrave Macmillan, 2004), 71–88.

3. The stunning success of the *Left Behind* series, a set of popular novels that places the "rapture" (a particularly American version of the end-time salvation of the righteous few) in a fictional here and now offers the most obvious example of this phenomenon, though there are others. Written by Timothy LaHaye and Jerry B. Jenkins, sixteen volumes have now been published, as well as several other books, films, and related merchandise; see http://www.leftbehind .com. Analyses of the politics of *Left Behind* include: M. McAlister, "Prophecy, Politics, and the Popular: The Left Behind Series and Christian Fundamentalism's New World Order," *South Atlantic Quarterly* 102.4 (2003) 773–98, and A. Strombeck, "Invest in Jesus: Neoliberalism and the Left Behind Novels," *Cultural Critique* 64 (2006) 161–95. Amy Johnson Frykholm has written an incisive study of the way the *Left Behind* novels are functioning among their Christian readership; see A. J. Frykholm, *Rapture Culture:* Left Behind *in Evangelical America* (Oxford: Oxford University Press, 2004). Glenn Shuck has considered the rhetorical strategies of the books in G. Shuck, *Marks of the Beast: The Left Behind Novels and the Struggle for Evangelical Identity* (New York: New York University Press, 2004).

4. According to the *Left Behind* series, these threats must be addressed by a "Tribulation Force" dedicated to the sovereignty of the state of Israel, the salvation brought by personal devotion to Christ, the submission of wives to husbands, the brave acts of "manly" Christian men, and a clever use of the vast material resources at their disposal.

5. On this phenomenon, see E. Castelli, *Martyrdom and Memory: Early Christian Culture Making* (New York: Columbia University Press, 2004).

paradox are surely possible, the thesis pursued here focuses less on John's attitude toward Rome—which, I am convinced, was decidedly negative—and more on his attitude toward "the state," or, perhaps better, the sovereign and His purposes. By narrating God's ultimate, irrevocable sovereignty and sorting humanity into various categories of saved and damned, Revelation, I argue, is simultaneously an enemy and friend to states.

Against the State

As David Frankfurter has argued, by describing evil, apocalyptic writings like Revelation offer "organizing devices" that invite individuals and communities to project and then repudiate an Other.[6] In the case of Revelation, this Other is described in decidedly political terms: John's stark vision imagines a world poised for a coming holy war between a conquering lamb and a kingdom ruled by monstrous beasts (5:6; 6:4, 8; 9:4; 13:3, 16–18; 14:9–10; 18:8; 20:4; 30:13). This wicked kingdom will ultimately burn in a divinely instigated conflagration, John warns (9:18; 16:9; 19:3, 20), but those set apart as holy will one day reside forever in an eternal Jerusalem ruled by God and His Son (21:8–22:5). In this way, the book encourages readers to place humanity into two categories: there are citizens of the "New Jerusalem," faithful witnesses obedient to God's law who surround the throne of the Lamb, and extralegal outsiders who either deserve to die or who have never truly lived at all. John's sovereign God constitutes and generates the very order of this universe, which He controls by standing above, beyond, outside, and ultimately against the world He has created and can therefore legitimately destroy. As such, His law and His ordering surpass all human legal systems and orders. Nevertheless, this divine realm is envisioned as a political body with a king (God, the βασιλεύς), an heir to the king (χριστός), and an empire (βασίλεια), complete with nations (ἔθνη), tribes (φυλάι), and priests (ἱερείς) who serve Him. This kingdom also has a territory (all of creation) and a capital city (Jerusalem) from which God rules, even now.

Read through the lens of recent political philosophy, Revelation's message of a divine sovereign with a heavenly kingdom takes on a strikingly statist cast, despite its premodern selection of a divine rather than human guarantee of the "social contract." Adapting what political philosophers have called the "sovereign exception," John privileges the fellow citizens of his own heavenly state while denying full life to others, particularly those destined to suffer what he calls the "second death."[7] In this way, to borrow terms employed by philosopher Georgio Agamben,

---

6. D. Frankfurter, *Evil Incarnate: Rumors of Demonic Conspiracy and Ritual Abuse in History* (Princeton, NJ: Princeton University Press, 2006), 76–85.

7. Georgio Agamben has argued that the states are founded on an "exception," a sovereign who constitutes the law and is simultaneously excluded from that law. Standing both

John's visions identify those who possess merely "bare life" (ζωή) and therefore may be killed but never sacrificed (the Roman *homo sacer*) and those who have a claim to citizen life (βίος) and so can be killed only within some sort of juridical procedure.[8] According to this conception of state sovereignty, violence is the "primordial juridical fact" of political life: founded on violence, sovereignty rests on a "dialectical oscillation" between the violence that both posits and preserves law and the sovereign who guarantees the law by stepping outside of it.[9]

Modern states, committed as they are to "making life" (what scholars since Michel Foucault have called "biopolitics"),[10] employ distancing mechanisms to suggest that deaths are never explicitly caused by the state as such; rather, death is merely permitted, or outsourced to penal colonies, concentration camps, and "primitive" nations who receive the rendered victims of their "modern" allies. Nevertheless, ancient and modern sovereigns alike place control over mortality at the center of their ideological apparatuses, requiring that some die in order that others may live, well and fully. By relegating some lives—discursively, practically and ideologically—to the status of "bare life" while granting certain others a higher, human life, consisting of an acknowledged membership in a discrete body

---

within and without of the state, the sovereign therefore marks the limit of the juridical order; see G. Agamben, *Homo Sacer: Sovereign Power and Bare Life* (trans. D. Heller-Roazen; Stanford, CA: Stanford University Press, 1998), and idem, *State of Exception* (trans. K. Attell; Chicago: University of Chicago Press, 2005). See, further, C. Schmitt, *Politisch Theologie: Vier Kapitel zur Lehre von der Souveränität* (Munich: Duncker and Humboldt, 1922). For a different assessment of Schmitt, see K. Shapiro, "Politics is a Mushroom: Worldly Sources of Rule and Exception in Carl Schmitt and Walter Benjamin," *Diacritics* 37.2–3 (2007) 121–34.

8. *Homo Sacer*, 87–90, 99–103. As Agamben explains, both the sovereign (the emperor, in Roman case) and the non-citizen can be killed, but neither can be sacrificed (in neither instance will the murderer be tried for homicide) because both represent an exclusion upon which the state is in fact theorized.

9. *Homo Sacer*, 31, 63–65. In this instance, Agamben is citing the insights of W. Benjamin, "Zur Kritik der Gewalt," in *Walter Benjamin: Selected Writings* (trans. M. W. Jennings; Cambridge, MA: Harvard University Press, 1996), 1:236–52. Yet Benjamin sought to differentiate this corrupt form of human sovereignty from divine sovereignty, which he viewed as different in kind. (Divine violence employs "pure power over all for the sake of living," whereas human violence "bastardizes" violence through law.) Beatriz Hanssen offers a helpful analysis of Benjamin's turn toward the divine, which aimed to reject Schmitt while nevertheless preserving a ground for revolutionary acts of violence (B. Hanssen, *Critique of Violence: Between Poststructuralism and Critical Theory* [New York: Routledge, 2000], 18–30).

10. Michael Foucault claims that one of the principle transformations from premodern to postmodern theories of sovereignty involves the move from a sovereign who, it was imagined, could "take life or let live" (a fitting description of John's conception of God) to one in which the sovereign state, ostensibly "of and by the people," makes live and lets die. This shift in the theory of sovereignty, Foucault argued, has resulted in a "modern biopolitics" that makes death an extension of living and life subject to an infinite stream of technological, bureaucratic, and institutional interventions (M. Foucault, *"Society Must Be Defended": Lectures at the Collège de France, 1975–1976* [ed. M. Betani and A. Fontana; trans. D. Macey; New York: Picador, 2003]).

politic, a sovereign engages in a "necropolitics" that determines who may live and who may die.[11]

John of Patmos would not have conceived of sovereignty in these terms; even so, assertions of who can and cannot legitimately be killed are central preoccupations of his book. John carefully elevates the status of executed "saints" from what Agamben has called bare life, a status implicitly assigned to them by their ignominious executions, to that of elect citizen-soldiers of heaven who bear "testimony" (μαρτυρία) in anticipation of the coming kingdom of God. Jesus Christ, who, as a crucified provincial could be viewed as a paradigmatic example of the abject Roman *homo sacer* considered by Agamben,[12] becomes instead "the martyr (μάρτυς), the faithful one, the first among the dead" (1:5). Antipas, a deceased member of the assembly of saints at Pergamum, is given this same title; speaking through John, Jesus calls him, "my witness (μάρτυς), my faithful one" (2:13). Other faithful members of John's community are promised similar access to this form of life: death as a μάρτυς elevates the abject bearer of bare life to eternal existence in a bejeweled eternal city, the "New Jerusalem" (21:10–22:7) Moreover, John suggests, Jesus is no *homo sacer*; unlike that specter—the man who is simultaneously cursed and "sacred"—Jesus can and is sacrificed for his country, his people, and his god, a central characteristic of one who achieves βίος in a community of the elect.

As a vindicator who is pierced and yet lives (1:7), John's Christ is an avenging sacrificial Lamb whose blood is so precious that it achieves expiation for his loyal followers, freeing them from sin (1:5) and preparing them for their future role in a heavenly court (7:14). The crucified Jesus is therefore reimagined as both the sacrifice and the one who sets the limit on sacrifice, a role that makes of him the guarantor and enforcer of a legal system designed by his father, God (1:6; 2:28; 3:5, 21; 14:1). This Messiah/Lamb announces doom on insiders and outsiders alike. Those who disappoint the sovereign and his laws with their "fornication," consumption of unclean foods, and cavorting with false prophets will be punished and then killed (2:4–7, 9, 14–16, 20–23; 3:1, 3–5, 9). Those who are already outside of the heavenly company—kings, merchants, persons who buy and sell human lives—

---

11. A. Mbembe, "Necropolitics," trans. Libby Meintjes, *Public Culture* 15.1 (2003) 11–40.

12. Agamben draws the term *homo sacer* from Pompeius Festus, *On the Significance of Words*, a lexicon likely composed in the 2nd century c.e., not directly from Roman law. Still, the ignominy of crucifixion is scarcely in doubt (compare *The Digest of Justinian* 48.19.28, Callistratus, *Judicial Examinations, book 6* [selections]: "The extreme penalty is held to be condemnation to the cross. There is also burning alive; this, however, though deservedly included in the term 'extreme penalty,' is yet regarded as following after the first, because this class of punishment was devised at a later time. Also there is beheading ... 2. It is not the custom for all persons to be beaten with rods, but only freedmen of the poorer classes; men of higher status are not subject to beating with rods, as is specifically laid down in imperial rescripts," English trans. Alan Watson [Philadelphia: University of Pennsylvania Press, 1985], vol. 4, 851). On Festus's lexicon, see *Verrus, Festus & Paul*, ed. Fay Glinister and Clare Woods with J. A. North and M. H. Crawford (BICS Supplement 93; London: Institute of Classical Studies, 2007) 11–108.

will be utterly destroyed. As philosopher Achille Mbembe might put it, Christ, John, and their churches are governed by a "necropolitics" of heavenly design.[13]

Still, one can hardly read Revelation as a "state document," if by these terms we mean to refer to the formal publications and pronouncements of a state entity. John's vision of divine *imperium* plays out on an imaginary, other-worldly stage and, as a narrator, he presents himself as the spokesperson for a heavenly nation, not an earthly one. In fact, while Agamben uses the Greek political language of δῆμος (district, community, people) or βίος (manner of living, a way of life proper to human beings) to describe political arrangements, John prefers terms like nations (ἔθνη), peoples (λαόι), and tribes (φυλάι) when referring to human groups, a vocabulary that better suits his dependence on Hellenistic Jewish precedents and scriptures, and he invokes ζωή (life in general, simple existence) when discussing all life, human or animal. For John, it appears that existence itself is at stake, not human life per se. His sovereign rules a territory that includes all of creation, from the heavens to a lake of fire designed to punish evildoers for eternity. Even so, the politicization of life remains a palpable theme and control over death is offered as a central proof of God's power.[14]

Grievable Lives

John may not have composed a formal work of political philosophy, but, standing in a long line of earlier prophets, he did compose a document designed to reinforce the view that (his) God alone is king. He also envisioned a world where some lives are expendable and others are not, producing vivid images of mourning, death rites, and public laments on the one hand and environmental catastrophe, torture, and holy war on the other. John begins the account of his visions with the following announcement, directed at seven churches in Asia: "Look! He

---

13. John personifies death, presenting him as both God's servant and enemy. In one vision, Death is riding on a pale green horse, followed by Hades. These frightening figures, unleashed by God when the Lamb opens the fourth seal, are "given authority over a fourth of the earth, to kill with sword, famine, and pestilence, and by the wild animals of the earth" (6:8). At the dramatic conclusion to the book, John envisions Death and Hades giving up their dead for judgment prior to being judged themselves (20:14). In these visions, God's sovereignty is so complete that Death itself cannot survive His onslaught.

14. I am influenced here by Jonathan Klawans's understanding of Israelite sacrifice as a form of *imitatio Dei*. Though Klawans is writing of a much earlier period, he views Israelite sacrificial practice as a ritualized performance of God's own actions: God selects, kills, looks inside things, and appears on earth as a consuming fire, activities that are then imitated by Israelite priests. Each of these activities is reserved for God and God's heavenly elect in John's visions as well, even as John extends the performance of *imitatio* to include participation in sacrifice as a "witness." Like Christ, the witness simultaneously offers and becomes the sacrifice. See J. Klawans, "Pure Violence: Sacrifice and Defilement in Ancient Israel," *Harvard Theological Review* 94.2 (2001) 135–57, and idem, *Purity, Sacrifice, and the Temple: Symbolism and Supersessionism in the Study of Ancient Judaism* (Oxford: Oxford University Press, 2006).

is coming with the clouds; every eye will see him, even those who pierced him; and on his account all the tribes of the earth will wail" (Rev 1:7).[15] He then begins his strikingly visual narrative, one in which the audience is repeatedly invited to look, see, and imagine what God sees, a motif that introduces each new vision and frames the entire book: "I saw" (εἶδον) John repeatedly insists (1:12, 17; 4:1; 5:1, 6, 11; 6:1, 2, 5, 8, 9, 12; 7:1, 2, 9; 8:2; 9:1, 17; 10:5; 13:1–2, 11; 14:1, 6, 14; 15:1, 2, 5; 16:13; 17:3, 6, 8, 12, 15, 18; 18:1, 7; 19:11, 19; 20:1, 4, 11; 21:1, 2, 22); "write what you saw" (γράψον οὖν ἃ εἶδες), the Son of Man instructs his seer (1:19); and "they will see" (ὄψονται), promises an angel at the book's climax (22:4). But it is not only John who sees and then writes. God also sees, writing the names of the holy ones in his Book of Life (3:5; 20:15) and judging their performance on the basis of a report given to him by the Son of Man. This Son of Man, John warns, "searches hearts and minds" and gives to each what she deserves (2:23).

John's emphasis on the visual, appropriate to what Christopher Frilingos has described as the spectacular culture of Roman imperialism,[16] also resonates with what Judith Butler has identified as the "selective and differential framing of violence" made possible through cultural and visual modes of affective regulation.[17] Though her interest is in contemporary discourses and not in apocalyptic literature or ancient rhetorical techniques, Butler's insights can be applied to Revelation as well, particularly to John's use of ἔκφρασις, a Greek rhetorical form involving the detailed description of an image, artwork, or other dramatic scene, such as a battle or a funerary monument.[18] In her analysis of contemporary rhetoric and war, Butler has sought to understand how a war-related photographic image frames what can and cannot be seen or, as she puts it, the "field of representability" made possible by operations of power and figuration within both the frame and

---

15. ιδου ερχεται μετα των νεφελων, και οψεται αυτον πας οφθαλμος και οιτινες αυτον εξεκενησαν, και κοψονται επ αυτον πασαι αι φυλαι της γης. Leonard Thompson has offered a helpful close reading of this verse; see L. Thompson, "Lamentation for Christ as a Hero: Revelation 1:7," *JBL* 119 (2000) 683–703. Thompson makes a strong case for the view that John was informed by the Hebrew of Zech 12:9–14 rather than by the LXX. At the same time, however, John exploits the Greco-Roman cult of the hero in his depiction of Christ as a cloud rider who attracts a cult of the dead, complete with funeral rites and lamentations. My own view of John's creative adaptation of multiple cultural framings is similar to Thompson's. For a further example of John's creative repurposing of Greek myth, see A. Y. Collins, *The Combat Myth in the Book of Revelation* (Missoula, MT: Scholars, 1976).

16. C. A. Frilingos, *Spectacles of Empire: Monsters, Martyrs, and the Book of Revelation* (Divinations: Reading Late Ancient Religion; Philadelphia: University of Pennsylvania Press, 2004).

17. J. Butler, *Frames of War: When Is Life Grievable?* (London: Verso, 2009), 1.

18. On ἔκφρασις, S. Goldhill, "What is Ekphrasis for?" *Classical Philology* 102 (2007) 1–19. I do not mean to suggest that John was trained in the formal art of *ekphrasis*. Nevertheless, his use of visual figures and his attention to detail suggest to me that he had some familiarity with the form, which could work well in conjunction with the generic elements of apocalyptic literature.

the viewer.[19] Though a writer rather than a photographer, John was also highly attentive to the framing of the wars and battles he described: he, too, presents startling scenes of public lament, corpse desecration, and torture; he, too, constructs a series of heavenly panoramas designed to focus the viewers' gaze on particular lives and particular deaths; and he, too, works to control the possible meanings of these scenes by carefully arranging the objects and persons who populate the rhetorical pictures he paints.[20] By enlarging his frame to include God's own point of view, he zooms out to offer his readers a heavenly vista, inviting the audience to partake in a divine re-visioning that gazes upon suffering and sees triumph.

John's depiction of the coming destruction of Babylon/Rome and the public laments that will follow offer a vivid example of this procedure. Reinterpreting songs of lament found in earlier Hebrew prophecy, John presents the mourning activities of three sets of devotees to the "Whore" (Babylon/Rome), each drawn from earlier biblical precedents but reinterpreted in light of his own concerns.[21] First, the kings of the earth "weep and wail over her" as they watch her burn, singing, "Alas, alas, the great city, Babylon, the mighty city! For in one hour your judgment has come!" (18:10). Then the merchants add, "Alas, alas, the great city, clothed in fine linen, in purple and scarlet, adorned with gold, with jewels, and with pearls! For in one hour all this wealth has been laid waste!"(18:16). And finally the seafarers and sailors chime in, "Alas, alas, the great city, where all who had ships at sea grew rich by her wealth! For in one hour she has been laid waste!" (18:19).

These lament songs, the singers who sing them, and the funerary gestures they employ are clearly informed by earlier biblical prophecy. In Ezekiel's pronouncement of the doom of Tyre, the prophet depicted seafarers and captains (κωπηλάται, ἐπιβάται, πρωεῖς τῆς θαλάσσης [LXX]) throwing earth on their heads (ἐπιθήσουσιν ἐπὶ τὴν κεφαλὴν αὐτῶν γῆν), wallowing in ashes (σποδὸν ὑποστρώσονται) and offering a lament (θροος; 27:30, 32). Similarly, in Revelation, seafarers and sailors (κυβερνήτης, ὁ ἐπὶ τόπον πλέων, ναῦται ὅσοι τὴν θάλασσαν ἐργάζονται) cast dust on their heads (ἔβαλον χοῦν ἐπὶ τὰς κεφαλὰς αὐτῶν), shed tears (κλαίοντες), and lament (πενθοῦντες) at the loss of their livelihoods (18:17, 19).[22] The prophet Isaiah also announced the coming doom of Tyre and her ships, comparing the city

---

19. Butler, *Frames of War*, 63–100. "Representability" refers to a visual field "structured by state permission," or, rather, to a field that the state seeks to control, "if always with only partial success" (73).

20. In a contemporary setting, the inability to mourn noncombatant "collateral damage" is only the most obvious example that such frames are operative. In Revelation, "collateral damage" is also assumed: readers learn of environmental devastation, poisoned water, torture so severe that those who experience it would prefer death, and an earthquake that kills 7,000 unnamed and unmourned persons (8:7, 11; 9:4–6, 18; 11:11; also see 14:9–10; 16:9, 10).

21. Compare Isa 23:1–18; Jer 51:6–14; Ezek 27:1–36. Also see Zech 12:9–14. Frederick Murphy sees Ezek 27 as the most important precedent, *Fallen is Babylon*, 371–73.

22. John may well be alluding to the Hebrew and not a Greek translation, which may explain some of the discrepencies in vocabulary between the two works. Alternatively, he was

to a prostitute (πόρνη; 23:15–18)—an image redeployed by John in his excoriation of Rome. Finally, Jeremiah described Babylon as a "golden cup" from which the nations have become drunk (51:6–10), a symbol that was repurposed by John as the "golden cup full of abominations and the impurities of her fornication" in his vision of Rome as a Whore (Rev 17:4).[23] By invoking these biblical precedents, John alerted his audience both to the traditions within which he stood and the εθνος to which he belongs. His visions fulfill Hebrew, not Roman, prophecy, though he does employ certain Greek rhetorical forms to make his point.

John's mourning scene also recalls Greek and Roman precedents: the tradition of offering a formal lament at the fall of a city can be found throughout Greek literature in epigrams, tragedies, and longer prose works;[24] John's three songs include a number of rhetorical features found in the Greek tradition of μονῳδια (public lament);[25] and, finally, symbolic acts such as casting dust on one's head and dirtying one's clothes were widely shared mourning gestures, familiar to Greeks, Jews, and Romans alike.[26] The funerary performances depicted by John therefore invoke a number of cultural norms simultaneously. On the one hand, he places his vision of the destruction of Rome within a prophetic trajectory that sets him firmly within Jewish apocalyptic literature as it was emerging in the 1st century. He employs a recognizable series of images and allusions that equated Rome with Israel's former archenemies, recalling a shared memory of Israel, her borders, her place among the nations, and her status as the chief focus of divine concern. On the other hand, he composes μονῳδία that fit equally well within a Greek lament tradition, songs that, in the end, damn the kings, merchants, and seafarers further for their complicity in "her" luxury.[27] As he reveals in a dramatic twist at the end

---

simply offering a rather loose allusion or citing an alterative translation. For further discussion, see Thompson, "Lamentation for Christ," 687–88

23. For further discussion, see Friesen, *Imperial Cults*, 206–8.

24. M. Alexiou, *The Ritual Lament in Greek Tradition* (Cambridge: Cambridge University Press, 1974), 83–85.

25. (Pseudo-) Menander Rhetor, for example, in a 3rd-century rhetorical handbook, offers detailed advice on how to construct a prose monody in response to various tragic deaths. When lamenting the death of a leader of a city, he suggests that one say something like, "the city is splendid, but he who raised it up is he who has fallen," or "Who will take care of it, who will preserve it, as he did?" (οτι λαμπρα μεν η πολις, ο δε εγειρας αυτην ο πεπτωκως εστιν. η ουτω· τις επιμελησεται, τις διασωσει, καθαπερ εκεινος; 434.29–31; D. A. Russell and N. G. Wilson, eds. and trans., *Menander Rhetor* [Oxford: Clarendon, 1981], 202–3).

26. Maud Gleason has written about this shared "body language" in her analysis of Josephus's *Jewish Wars*. As she shows, gestures like ripping and/or dirtying one's clothes, rubbing ashes or dust in one's hair, and holding one's arms behind one's back were recognizable performances that communicated messages quickly and effectively to Roman and Jewish audiences alike; see M. Gleason, "Mutilated Messengers: Body Language in Josephus," in *Being Greek Under Rome: Cultural Identity, the Second Sophistic and the Development of Empire* (ed. S. Goldhill; Cambridge: Cambridge University Press, 2001), 50–85.

27. Like the later Greek orator Aelius Aristides, who recalled the "beautiful and splendid marketplace," the streets "named for gold and sacred rites," "the grace of the temples and the

of this section, the μονῳδίαι of the merchants and kings are misplaced: the proper response to the destruction of Babylon/Rome is not lament but joy.

After the final refrain of the last earthly μονῳδία, "in one hour she has been laid waste" (18:19), John expands the limits of the scene he has just set, enclosing the events transpiring below within a heavenly as opposed to an earthly perspective. From this new point of view, the ruin of Babylon/Rome is not to be seen as a tragedy; it is a fulfillment of a divine promise. Bound by their limited understanding, on earth the kings had watched the city burn and were afraid for her torment (18:9). The merchants also placed themselves far off, thinking of their cargo while they observed her destruction "in fear of her torment" (18:15). Finally, the seafarers, watching her smoke rise, added their voices to the chorus, lamenting the loss of both the city and their trade routes (18:17). But once the constraints of the earthly vision of this scene are shattered, the true meaning of John's picture is revealed.[28] Swept up in a sudden reorientation, the seer and his audience are exhorted to take on the perspective not of kings, merchants, and seafarers but of God's allies—the saints, apostles, and prophets. From this elevated height, they are able to see that the city's purported beauty is actually demonic; it masks "the blood of prophets and saints," which must be avenged (18:24). Responding to this news in heaven, a series of choruses then react with the right sort of singing, offering five hymns of praise, each with a refrain that includes the Hebrew loan word "Hallelujah" (19:1, 3, 4, 5, 6). By the end, the sound is deafening. Unseemly and ultimately weak, Greek μονῳδία are replaced by archaizing Hebrew/Greek songs that expose the true designs of the divine sovereign.

War photography, Butler has argued, depends upon three "hinges" that determine its framings: first, those norms, explicit or implicit, that govern which hu-

---

precincts" utterly lost to Smyrna in a recent earthquake, Revelation's earthly lament songs praise the cargo of "gold, silver, jewels and pearls, fine linen, purple, silk and scarlet, all kinds of scented wood, all articles of ivory, bronze, iron, and marble" that once filled her markets (Rev 18:12). Revelation's singers comment on the riches she once held, the splendor she once boasted, and the greatness of this "queen," a "great city" lost in an hour (Ael. Arist. Oration 18, επι Σμυρνη μονῳδια; Greek text edited by B. Keil, *Aelii Aristidis Smyrnaei Quae Supersunt Omnia*, vol. 2, *Orationes XVII–LIII* [Berlin: Weidmann, 1897], 8–11; English translation C. A. Behr and P. A. Aristides, *The Complete Works*, vol. 2, *Orations XVII–LIII* [Leiden: Brill, 1981], 7–9).

28. "Rejoice over her, O heaven, you saints and apostles and prophets! For God has given judgment for you against her" (18:20). Given the rhetorical structure of the three μονῳδιαι, each of which ends with a refrain about the suddenness of the Whore's destruction, this verse marks the transition point between the earthly response of lament and the heavenly response of joy, which will then be explained to the seer by an angelic interpreter. The lament songs belong to those who view "her" burning from their limited, earthly gaze. The rejoicing, however, belongs to the population of heaven, which also includes three named groupings—saints, apostles, and prophets—who see the burning and are exhorted to respond appropriately. Murphy interprets this statement as an interjection from the narrator (F. J. Murphy, *Fallen is Babylon: The Revelation to John* [New Testament in Context; Harrisburg, PA: Trinity Press International, 1998], 373) while David Aune speculates that it may have been a later interpolation (D. Aune, *Revelation* [Word Biblical Commentary 52; Nashville, TN: Thomas Nelson, 1997], 1006–8).

man lives count and which do not; second, the necessity that "some portion of the visual field" be ruled out of "representability"; and third, the human suffering that is the ostensible subject of the image itself.[29] Though far removed from modern warfare and its visual media, John's vivid description of the destruction of Rome/Babylon is nevertheless dependent upon rhetorical moves that are akin to Butler's "hinges": first, his play on the Greek μονῳδία tradition employs familiar cultural norms to condemn those who benefit from Rome's riches, reversing the expected signification of these songs while painting a graphic and familiar image of public lament; second, his dramatic overturning of the initial, negative framing of Rome's burning makes the "saints, apostles, and prophets" the arbiters of the representability of death itself; finally, human suffering remains the focal point of John's rhetorical lens, even as the seer distances himself from the laments of the kings to reveal the joy of the heavenly multitude. Providing an occasion for God's vindicating destruction and a rationale for the ungrievability of the beautiful, alluring, and yet totally corrupt city, the "blood of the saints and the prophets" justifies the destruction, torture, and natural calamities that must take place. At stake for John, as well as for the war photographer, is the status of the lives and deaths that are placed in view and ruled out of the scene.[30] John shows his audience who is to be mourned, who is not, and why, and it is the sovereignty of God that guarantees the accuracy of his vision.

The Omniscient Gaze of the Sovereign

John's emphasis on the visual, drawn from a combination of biblical precedent, Greek rhetoric, and visionary experience, works to reverse a politics of sight that has made victims of his heroes. His Christ, a pierced Lamb destined to lead God's people to victory, is not simply a crucified provincial hung outside the city as a Roman "public service announcement";[31] this Jesus is the privileged guarantor of God's all consuming fire who arrives on the scene leading the armies of heaven, striking down the nations with the "sword in his mouth," and ruling with a rod of iron (19:14). Similarly, the recently deceased Antipas, however he was killed, serves as an occasion both for commendation of the assembly of Jesus followers at Pergamum and as a warning to them; Christ and his sharp mouth exhort them to behave as they did during Antipas's lifetime, avoiding idol meat (εἰδωλόθυτα) and fornication (πορνεία); otherwise, they will face some undefined but disastrous fate during the coming holy war (2:12–17). Finally, the slaughtered saints, whoever they may be, serve as the ultimate warrant for Rome's destruction: they provoke

---

29. Butler, *Frames of War*, 74–77.

30. As Butler explains, "We can think of the frame as active, as both jettisoning and presenting, and as doing both at once, in silence, without any visible sign of its operation" (ibid., 73).

31. I borrow this striking phrase from P. Fredriksen, *Jesus of Nazareth, King of the Jews: A Jewish Life and the Emergence of Christianity* (2nd ed.;New York: Vintage, 2000), 233. Also see J. Marcus, "Crucifixion as Parodic Exaltation," *JBL* 125 (2006) 73–87.

the final descent of the Lamb and the announcement of the "great supper of God" (το δεῖπνον το μεγα του θεου) in which all the birds of heaven consume the flesh of God's enemies.[32] In this visual/rhetorical framing, those who have been seen by Rome—hanging on crosses on the roads to the provinces, led as prisoners in triumphal marches through the capital city,[33] or forced to participate in spectacular displays[34]—become those who will ultimately both see and judge, penetrating their enemies with eyes, weapons, and the beaks of predatory birds.[35]

In the Roman culture of Asia Minor, looks were seldom innocent. Infused with messages about dominance and submission, masculinity and femininity, and insider and outsider status, who was doing the looking and who was being observed operated within a complex economy of knowledge and power in which, ideally at least, looking was a performance of domination.[36] In this visual economy, ἔκφρασις was a persuasive instrument for those who wanted to provoke the emotions of an audience, stirring them to heights of pathos and therefore also to a commitment to the goals of the speaker.[37] John adds to this broader discursive procedure by employing another, more culturally specific trope—that of the all-

---

32. That is, the kings and military commanders, horses and riders, "[the] flesh of all, both free and slave, both small and great" (19:17–18).

33. The triumph over Judea, celebrated in a march through the city, commemorated on a triumphal arch that stands in the Roman forum to this day, and recalled on coins celebrating "Iudaea Capta" may well have inspired some of John's ire. On the spoils of the war and the Jewish response to the collection and display of them, see R. Boustan, "The Spoils of the Jerusalem Temple in Rome and Constantinople: Jewish Counter-Geography in a Christianizing Empire," in *Antiquity in Antiquity: Jewish and Christian Past in the Greco-Roman World* (ed. G. Gardner and K. L. Osterloh; Texts and Studies in Ancient Judaism 123; Tübingen: Mohr Siebeck, 2008), 327–72.

34. It is unclear whether John of Patmos knew of the execution of fellow Jesus followers in local amphitheaters, but such executions certainly took place, if not during his own time then soon after. On the spectacular character of such performances, see K. M. Coleman, "Fatal Charades: Roman Executions Staged as Mythological Enactments," *JRS* 80 (1990) 44–73; D. Potter, "Martyrdom as Spectacle," in *Theater and Society in the Classical World* (ed. R. Scodel; Ann Arbor, MI: University of Michigan Press, 1993), 53–88; B. Shaw, "Body/Power/Identity: Passions of the Martyrs," *JECS* 4 (1990) 269–312.

35. As Frilingos explains, "Here the penetrated Lamb is an agent of discipline, issuing divine retribution to its former persecutors, 'even those who pierced him' on the cross (Rev 1:7). The structure of power remains stable, the hierarchy of domination and submission intact, but the actors have changed positions . . . the Lamb dominates, controlling and executing the demise of the enemies of God" (*Spectacles of Empire*, 81).

36. For further discussion, see J. Knust, *Abandoned to Lust: Sexual Slander and Ancient Christianity* (New York: Columbia University Press, 2005), 105–7.

37. According to the Roman orator Quintilian, the master of *ekphrasis* "will show the greatest power in the expression of emotions." A veritable *euphantasiotos*, this orator "is exceptionally good at realistically imagining to himself things, words and actions," and the result of his efforts is *enargeia*, "a quality which makes us seem not so much to be talking about something as exhibiting it. Emotions will ensue just as if we were present at the event itself" (*Inst. Orat.* 6.2.29–32; Latin text with English translation by D. A. Russell, *Quintilian: The Orator's Education, Books 6–8* [LCL126; Cambridge: Harvard University Press, 2001], 58–61).

seeing divine sovereign. John's emphasis on God's eye, which sees all and penetrates to the depths of the human heart, was a widespread topos of apocalyptic literature with precedents in biblical prophecy.[38] It was also an especially effective panoptic tool capable of demanding acquiescence to the positions of the writer, as Harry Maier has shown.[39] The revealing of Revelation invites the audience to gaze at itself through the divine eye and to find either objects of contempt or faithful subjects worthy of praise.

When viewed from this angle, John's rhetorical and visual program includes more than an attempted overturning of Rome's optical reasoning. Rival insiders are also targeted by God's penetrating gaze and will suffer dire consequences if they disobey. John's use of the example of Antipas, the μαρτυς of Pergamum who encourages the faithful and shames evildoers, offers only one instance of this rhetorical technique. Members of the "synagogue of Satan" are also promised swift and devastating punishment (3:9), as is the rival prophet "Jezebel," and followers of the so-called teachings of the "Nicolaitans."[40] The disciplinary extent of God's penetrating eye is made especially plain in John's condemnation of Jezebel, who will be "thrown on a bed" (2:22). "I will strike her children dead," John/Christ warns, and all the assemblies "will know that I [Christ] am the one who searches hearts and minds" (2:23). Here John conflates the wicked, idolatrous queen of biblical legend (Jezebel) with a contemporary female prophet, accusing her of seducing Christ's "slaves" into fornication and idolatry and warning all who consort with her that they will suffer greatly.[41] The parallels with the Whore of Babylon could not be more obvious.[42]

---

38. H. O. Maier, "Staging the Gaze: Early Christian Apocalypses and Narrative Self-Representation," *HTR* 90.2 (1997) 131–54. Maier cites passages from 1 and 2 Enoch, the Apocalypse of Zephaniah, 2 Baruch, the Apocalypse of Abraham, the Testament of Benjamin, the Apocalypse of Elijah and the Apocalypse of Paul, among other sources and finds parallels to the concept of the "all seeing eye of God" in 2 Chronicles, Job, Psalms, Proverbs, Jeremiah, Amos and Zechariah (ibid., 141 n. 40)

39. Ibid., 148–51.

40. Indeed, as Paul Duff as recently argued, John's pointed rhetoric is also directed at wealthy insiders, whom he finds to be selfish and corrupt, and "Rome" may simply be a cipher for the enemy within (*Who Rides the Beast? Prophetic Rivalry and the Rhetoric of Crisis in the Churches of the Apocalypse* [Oxford: Oxford University Press, 2001], pp. 14–15, 31–47, 113–25). David Frankfurter has offered another important alternative—John's targets may have been fellow messianists who had become insufficiently "Jewish" in their orientation: by compromising the demands of *halakah* with their "fornications" (that is, they consume of "idol food" [ειδωλοθυτα]), they had threatened the entire community with impurity ("Jews or Not: Reconstructing the 'Other' in Rev 2:9 and 3:9," *HTR* 94 [2001] 403–25). See also D. A. deSilva, "The Revelation to John: A Case Study in Apocalyptic Propaganda and the Maintenance of Sectarian Identity," *Sociological Analysis* 53 (1992) 375–95.

41. On Jezebel, see especially P. Trible, "Exegesis for Storytellers and Other Strangers," *JBL* 114.1 (1995) 3–19.

42. In this account, the female is figured either as a passive victim or as a monstrous enemy to the one true God, and male desire is the subject of the John's urgent appeal. Tina Pippin

By painting a picture of holy war and the public laments that follow, John of Patmos therefore both participates in and reproduces the spectral gaze of Roman imperial power—but to his own rhetorical ends. He envisions a "spectacle of em-pire" that casts his God in the role of an all-seeing eye. [43] He reverses the terms of Roman *imperium* so that the Roman "beast" becomes an Other readily subjected to the divine view. And he subjects both Rome and members of his own commu-nity to a frightening disciplinary apparatus that promises the swift punishment of the wicked. In the process, the rhetoric of Revelation secures everything a "state" could ever want—an all powerful, perfectly just sovereign, a legal system capable of identifying those worthy of life who should be mourned at death, a territory and a city filled with unimaginable riches, and a visual system that guarantees that all will one day be revealed. John may have been an "enemy of the state," but his emnity renounces none of the privileges of statehood. He simply postpones their full realization until the end of time.

Interpreting Revelation

As Adela Yarbro Collins has famously observed, apocalyptic literature works to make conflict more evident, heightening the polarity between an "us" and a "them" in order to provoke a crisis of identity and identification. [44] Contempo-rary, nonscholarly interpretations of Revelation have often pursued a similar path. For example, depicting the United Nations as the center of a demonic plot, the *Left Behind* series, a set of popular novels centered on the trials of a "Tribulation Force" determined to rescue the faithful few from the looming disasters of the end of time, urges readers to choose sides between a future/present characterized by a globalizing totalitarian government, an economic system that requires all par-ticipants to be tattooed with the "Mark of the Beast, and a sexual decadence that corrupts the highest echelons of state power. In the process, readers are urged to ally themselves with a militia-like band that endorses submission to a neoliberal savior God who guarantees their ultimate vindication. [45] Though ostensibly about

---

in particular has called attention to the distressing misogyny that undergirds John's negative portrayal of both Rome and his female rival Jezebel. As she has argued, Revelation produces its critique of imperial rule by offering readers two choices: "desire the Whore [Babylon/Rome] and you die; desire God and the Lamb [Christ] and you will probably die a martyr" (*Death and Desire: The Rhetoric of Gender in the Apocalypse of John* [Louisville: Westminster/John Knox, 1992], 60–65). Also see idem, "The Heroine and the Whore," in *From Every People and Nation* (ed. D. Rhoads; Minneapolis, Fortress, 2005), 127–45; Pippin notes: "The ideological portrayal of the female in the *Apocalypse* remains true to the dominant ideology of its culture. . . . Likewise, women readers of the *Apocalypse* are typed, hunted, adorned, and rejected. The domination of male over female remains intact" (p. 143).

43. Frilingos, *Spectacles of Empire*, 53–55, 81, 104–7.

44. See especially A. Y. Collins, *Crisis and Catharsis: The Power of Apocalypse* (Philadelphia: Westminster, 1984).

45. Basic plot summaries are available at: http://www.leftbehind.com. For discussion, see Strombeck, "Tribulation Force."

the future, the *Left Behind* series employs present images, systems, and symbols to inculcate its own disciplinary reform program and does so, at least in part, by invoking Johannine metaphors such as God's eye, Babylon the whore, and the system of marks that identifies the saved from the damned.

Horrified by these "misuses" of Revelation, biblical scholars have often decried contemporary interpretations of this type.[46] John must be read *in context*, biblical scholars have insisted: one cannot simply read Revelation and apply John's words to today, as many contemporary readers do, as if there were a one-to-one correspondence between John's prophetic visions and present reality. Moreover, as the continuing march of history has proved, the imminent return of Christ is nowhere in sight.[47] Nevertheless, a number of scholars have also employed Revelation in their efforts to move readers to new types of identifications. Elisabeth Schüssler Fiorenza has been an especially prominent proponent of this type of reading. Her "rhetorical-political" interpretation of the document underscores the relations of domination that John denounces, which she identifies as "kyriarchy." John, she argues, offers a vivid condemnation not only of the "murderous power of Rome" but also of an imperialism that oppresses marginalized readers to this day.[48] Thus, when appropriately activated, John, who once opposed the economic

---

46. Thus, as Greg Carey notes, for the last several decades, critical biblical commentaries on Revelation have frequently added a new topos to the genre: in addition to covering the usual subjects like author, date, place, situation, and literary antecedent, commentators have taken it upon themselves to address "misguided popular readings, especially those of dispensational premillennialists," which are singled out for critique. See G. Carey, *Elusive Apocalypse: Reading Authority in the Revelation to John* (Studies in Biblical Hermeneutics 15; Macon, GA: Mercer University Press, 1999), 25. To offer just a few examples: M. Eugene Boring asserts that Revelation is not "propositional," it is metaphorical and pictorial; the book does not teach a doctrine of the second coming upon which certainty about the coming return of Christ can be gained and thus any and all attempts to decode the book and apply it to the current context must be resisted (*Revelation* [Interpretation; Louisville: Westminster John Knox, 1989], 52–53). Loren Johns argues that the ferocious imagery of the book must not be read as a justification of actual violence: the ethics and politics of John's visions are both "radically anti-establishmentarian" and "nonviolent"; readers must therefore pursue quietism and faithful witness, not revenge (*The Lamb Christology of the Apocalypse of John* [Tübingen: Mohr Siebeck, 2003]). David Barr agrees: to interpret Revelation as a justification for aggression is simply wrong; its central message is one of resistance, patience, and persistence; "to read John's story as if it were about divinely sanctioned violence" is to read erroneously ("Doing Violence: Moral Issues in Reading John's Apocalypse," in *Reading the Book of Revelation: A Resource for Students* [ed. D. L. Barr; Resources for Biblical Study 44; Atlanta: SBL, 2003], 97–108).

47. See, for example, Barr, *Reading the Book of Revelation*, 1–9.

48. See E. S. Fiorenza, *Priester für Gott: Studien zum Herrschafts-un Pristermotive in der Apokalypse* (Münster: Aschendorff, 1972); idem, *Revelation: Vision of a Just World* (Minneapolis: Fortress, 1997); and idem, *The Book of Revelation: Justice and Judgment* (2nd ed.; Minneapolis: Fortress, 1998). I am quoting from the epilogue to the second edition of *The Book of Revelation* (p. 226). On Schüssler Fiorenza's method more generally, see idem, *Bread Not Stone: The Challenge of Feminist Biblical Interpretation* (Boston: Beacon, 1984); idem, *Sharing Her Word: Feminist Biblical Interpretation in Context* (Boston: Beacon, 1998); and idem, *The Power of the Word: Scripture and the Rhetoric of Empire* (Minneapolis: Fortress, 2007).

exploitation and hierarchical systems of privilege that troubled his own audience, has been an important ally to those who hope to counter the (post)modern, globalized destruction wrought by neocolonialism, late capitalism, and total war.[49] Once intended for a persecuted minority, John's canonical words continue to offer sustenance to communities struggling for life in the midst of death-dealing and systematic relations of domination, whether in antiquity or today.

My own sense, however, is that any attempt to turn Revelation's all-seeing eye of God against current states and contemporary enemies fails to deal adequately both with the book's ambiguous legacy and John's own rhetorical strategies. To invoke John's divine sovereign in order to overturn an objectionable human one repeats the terms of Revelation's arguments, but without calling John's "necropolitics" into question. When John envisions a divinely sanctioned and ruled state apparatus (a "New Jerusalem") as the answer to the state he derides, his fantasized state retains the privileges of citizenship for his sovereign's son, this man's allies, and all the obedient members of his heavenly community. Rhetorically, John's persistent defense of the sovereignty of his God—God's armies will ultimately triumph, the citizens of God's city will one day receive all the rewards due to them, and God's law rules supreme—pursues a story that repeats familiar terms of sovereign power and reinstitutes relations of domination. Thus, John's theory of sovereignty actually mirrors that of his archenemy, Rome: he too invests his sovereign with the absolute power to kill or let live, his citizens with the privileges due exclusively to them, and God's laws with the status of absolute truth. Perhaps John's double message—adversarial toward one imagined state but ready to demand absolute loyalty to another—can help explain why Revelation's authority has been so effective at serving the needs of both biblical scholars with liberationist sympathies and the inventors of Left Behind's Tribulation Force.

Of course, one should not confuse "the state," especially the "nation state," with the Roman rule familiar to John and his first readers: as has been well docu-

---

49. According to David Rhoads, John's "passionate critique of the oppressive political, economic, social, and religious realities of the Roman Empire" inspires similar passions today, as writers seek a world "free of injustice, racism, patriarchy, destruction of the environment, economic exploitation, and empire" ("Introduction" to From Every People and Nation [ed. D. Rhoads; Minneapolis: Fortress, 2005], 1). A number of scholars would agree. For example, see the essays collected in a special edition of Interpretation 63 (2009): C. R. Koester, "Revelation's Visionary Challenge to Ordinary Empire," 8–19; D. R. Barr, "John's Ironic Empire," 21–31; W. Carter, "Accommodating 'Jezebel' and Withdrawing John: Negotiating Empire in Revelation then and Now," 32–47; and A. D. Callahan, "Babylon Boycott: The Book of Revelation," 48–55. Other proponents of this interpretive position include: B. K. Blount, Can I Get a Witness? Reading Revelation through African American Culture (Louisville: Westminster John Knox, 2005); and idem, "The Witness of Active Resistance: The Ethics of Revelation in African American Perspective," in From Every People and Nation [ed. D. Rhoads; Minneapolis: Fortress, 2005], 28–46; P. Richard, Apocalypse: A People's Commentary on the Book of Revelation (Maryknoll, NY: Orbis Books, 1995); B. Rossing, "Standing at the Door of a New Millenium: Economy, Eschatology, and Hope," Dialog 37 (1998) 263–68.

mented by others, Roman forms of hegemony and ancient political, economic, and juridical strategies do not easily correspond to modern structures, discourses and systems.[50] There clearly are radical disjunctures between ancient and modern institutional systems, political philosophies, and the technologies of rule. Nevertheless, attempts to defend the legitimacy of a chosen sovereign or to identify those worthy of citizen-life are hardly new endeavors. Moreover, foundational changes between ancient and contemporary political arrangements have not necessarily entailed a radical break with everything that has come before, especially when that "before" is included within the important cultural well that is the canonical Christian Bible.[51] Finally, one does not need to posit deep continuity between then and now to notice that, in the case of Revelation, John's image of the divine sovereign is capable of provoking a diverse set of responses even as his basic premise—God alone decides who lives and who dies—goes largely unchallenged by biblical scholars and popular readers both. As a work of literature with a particular interest in holy war and divine sovereignty, Revelation has been especially well suited to public, politically oriented speech of all kinds. In this sense, Revelation remains a friend to the state, no matter how transparent the anti-Roman convictions of the book appear when read within their own historical context.

---

50. Specific studies of the very different ways land and wealth were held include: R. Bagnall, "Landholding in Late Roman Egypt: The Distribution of Wealth," *JRS* 82 (1992) 128–49; W. V. Harris, "A Revisionist View of Roman Money," *JRS* 96 (2006) 1–24; and P. Temin, "A Market Economy in the Early Roman Empire," *JRS* 91 (2001) 169–181. Classic treatments of the Roman economy include M. I. Finley, *The Ancient Economy* (Sather Classical Lectures; Berkeley: University of California Press, 1973) and M. Rostovtzeff, *The Social and Economic History of the Roman Empire* (Oxford: Clarendon, 1926). For the most recent discussion, see W. Scheidel, I. Morris, and R. Saller, eds., *The Cambridge Economic History of the Greco-Roman World* (Cambridge: Cambridge University Press, 2007).

51. As Saskia Sassen suggests in her study of the transformations of medieval and modern states, "critical capabilities," like the theory of the divine sovereign, become "relodged" in new settings such that vocabularies and rhetoricizations remain fundamental to an organizational logic that repositions them. As such, she argues, deep structural shifts underlie surface continuities even as deep structural continuities underlie surface discontinuities (*Territory, Authority, Rights: From Medieval to Global Assemblages* [Princeton, NJ: Princeton University Press, 2006], 11–13).

Bibliography

Agamben, G. *Homo Sacer: Sovereign Power and Bare Life*. Trans. D. Heller-Roazen. Stanford, CA: Stanford University Press, 1998.

———. *State of Exception*. Trans. K. Attell. Chicago: University of Chicago Press, 2005.

Alexiou, M. *The Ritual Lament in Greek Tradition*. Cambridge: Cambridge University Press, 1974.

Aune, D. *Revelation*. Word Biblical Commentary 52. Nashville: Thomas Nelson, 1997.

Bagnall, R. "Landholding in Late Roman Egypt: The Distribution of Wealth." *JRS* 82 (1992) 128–49.

Barr, D. L. "Doing Violence: Moral Issues in Reading John's Apocalypse." Pp. 97–108 in *Reading the Book of Revelation: A Resource for Students*. Edited by D. L. Barr. Resources for Biblical Study 44. Atlanta: SBL, 2003.

_____. *Reading the Book of Revelation: A Resource for Students*. Resources for Biblical Study 44. Atlanta: SBL, 2003.

Barr, D. R. "John's Ironic Empire." *Interpretation* 63.1 (2009) 21–31.

Behr, C. A., and P. A. Aristides, trans. *The Complete Works*, vol. 2, *Orations XVII–LIII*. Leiden: Brill, 1981.

Bell, A. A. "The Date of John's Apocalypse: The Evidence of Some Roman Historians Reconsidered." *NTS* 25 (1979) 93–102.

Benjamin, W. "Zur Kritik der Gewalt." Pp. 236–52 in vol. 1 of *Walter Benjamin: Selected Writings*. Trans. M. W. Jennings. Cambridge, MA: Harvard University Press, 1996.

Blount, B. K. *Can I Get a Witness? Reading Revelation through African American Culture*. Louisville: Westminster John Knox, 2005.

_____. "The Witness of Active Resistance: The Ethics of *Revelation* in African American Perspective." Pp. 28–46 in *From Every People and Nation*. Edited by D. Rhoads. Minneapolis: Fortress, 2005.

Boring, M. E. *Revelation*. Interpretation. Louisville: Westminster John Knox, 1989.

Boustan, R. "The Spoils of the Jerusalem Temple in Rome and Constantinople: Jewish Counter-Geography in a Christianizing Empire." Pp. 327–72 in *Antiquity in Antiquity: Jewish and Christian Past in the Greco-Roman World*. Edited by G. Gardner and K. L. Osterloh. Texts and Studies in Ancient Judaism 123. Tübingen: Mohr Siebeck, 2008.

Butler, J. *Frames of War: When is Life Grievable?* London: Verso, 2009.

Callahan, A. D. "Babylon Boycott: The Book of Revelation." *Interpretation* 63 (2009) 48–55.

Carey, G. *Elusive Apocalypse: Reading Authority in the Revelation to John*. Studies in Biblical Hermeneutics 15. Macon, GA: Mercer University Press, 1999.

Carter, W. "Accommodating 'Jezebel' and Withdrawing John: Negotiating Empire in Revelation then and Now." *Interpretation* 63 (2009) 32–47.

Castelli, E. *Martyrdom and Memory: Early Christian Culture Making*. New York: Columbia University Press, 2004.

Coleman, K. M. "Fatal Charades: Roman Executions Staged as Mythological Enactments." *JRS* 80 (1990) 44–73.

Collins, A. Y. *The Combat Myth in the Book of Revelation*. Missoula, MT: Scholars, 1976.

_____. *Crisis and Catharsis: The Power of Apocalypse*. Philadelphia: Westminster, 1984.

deSilva, D. A. "The Revelation to John: A Case Study in Apocalyptic Propaganda and the Maintenance of Sectarian Identity." *Sociological Analysis* 53 (1992) 375–95.

Downing, F. G. "Pliny's Persecutions of Christians: Revelation and 1 Peter." *NTS* 34 (1988) 105–23.

Duff, P. *Who Rides the Beast? Prophetic Rivalry and the Rhetoric of Crisis in the Churches of the Apocalypse*. Oxford: Oxford University Press, 2001.

Finley, M. I. *The Ancient Economy*. Sather Classical Lectures. Berkeley: University of California Press, 1973.

Fiorenza, E. S. *Priester für Gott: Studien zum Herrschafts-un Pristermotive in der Apokalypse*. Münster: Aschendorff, 1972.

_____. *Invitation to the Book of Revelation*. Garden City, NY: Doubleday, 1981.

_____. *Bread Not Stone: The Challenge of Feminist Biblical Interpretation.* Boston: Beacon, 1984.

_____. *The Book of Revelation: Justice and Judgment.* Philadelphia: Fortress, 1985.

_____. *Revelation: Vision of a Just World.* Minneapolis: Fortress, 1997.

_____. *The Book of Revelation: Justice and Judgment.* 2nd Edition. Minneapolis: Fortress, 1998.

_____. *Sharing Her Word: Feminist Biblical Interpretation in Context.* Boston: Beacon, 1998.

_____. *The Power of the Word: Scripture and the Rhetoric of Empire.* Minneapolis: Fortress, 2007.

Foucault, M. *"Society Must Be Defended:" Lectures at the Collège de France, 1975–1976.* Edited by M. Betani and A. Fontana. Trans. D. Macey. New York: Picador, 2003.

Frankfurter, D. "Jews or Not: Reconstructing the 'Other' in Rev 2:9 and 3:9." *HTR* 94 (2001) 403–25.

_____. *Evil Incarnate: Rumors of Demonic Conspiracy and Ritual Abuse in History.* Princeton, NJ: Princeton University Press, 2006.

Fredriksen, P. *Jesus of Nazareth, King of the Jews: A Jewish Life and the Emergence of Christianity.* 2nd ed. New York: Vintage, 2000.

Frykholm, A. J. *Rapture Culture: Left Behind in Evangelical America.* Oxford: Oxford University Press, 2004.

Friesen, S. J. *Imperial Cults and the Apocalypse of John.* Oxford: Oxford University Press, 2001.

Frilingos, C. A. *Spectacles of Empire: Monsters, Martyrs, and the Book of Revelation.* Divinations: Reading Late Ancient Religion. Philadelphia: University of Pennsylvania Press, 2004.

Gleason, M. "Mutilated Messengers: Body Language in Josephus." Pp. 50–85 in *Being Greek Under Rome: Cultural Identity, the Second Sophistic and the Development of Empire.* Edited by S. Goldhill. Cambridge: Cambridge University Press, 2001.

Glinister, F., et al., eds. *Verrus, Festus & Paul.* BICS Suppleent 93. London: Institute of Classical Studies, 2007.

Goldhill, S. "What is Ekphrasis for?" *Classical Philology* 102.1 (2007) 1–19.

Hanssen, B. *Critique of Violence: Between Poststructuralism and Critical Theory.* New York: Routledge, 2000.

Harris, W. V. "A Revisionist View of Roman Money." *JRS* 96 (2006) 1–24.

Johns, L. *The Lamb Christology of the Apocalypse of John.* Tübingen: Mohr Siebeck, 2003.

Keil, B. *Aelii Aristidis Smyrnaei Quae Supersunt Omnia,* vol. 2, *Orationes XVII–LIII.* Berlin: Weidmann, 1897.

Klawans, J. "Pure Violence: Sacrifice and Defilement in Ancient Israel." *Harvard Theological Review* 94 (2001) 135–57.

_____. *Purity, Sacrifice, and the Temple: Symbolism and Supersessionism in the Study of Ancient Judaism.* Oxford: Oxford University Press, 2006.

Knust, J. *Abandoned to Lust: Sexual Slander and Ancient Christianity.* New York: Columbia University Press, 2005.

Koester, C. R. "Revelation's Visionary Challenge to Ordinary Empire." *Interpretation* 63 (2009) 8–19.

Maier, H. O. "Staging the Gaze: Early Christian Apocalypses and Narrative Self-Representation." *HTR* 90.2 (1997) 131–54.

Marcus, J. "Crucifixion as Parodic Exaltation." *JBL* 125 (2006) 73–87.

Mbembe, A. "Necropolitics." Trans. L. Meintjes, *Public Culture* 15 (2003) 11–40.

McAlister, M. "Prophecy, Politics, and the Popular: The Left Behind Series and Christian
Fundamentalism's New World Order." *South Atlantic Quarterly* 102.4 (2003) 773–98.

Murphy, F. J. *Fallen is Babylon: The Revelation to John.* New Testament in Context. Harrisburg, PA: Trinity Press International, 1998.

O'Leary, S. D. *Arguing the Apocalypse: A Theory of Millennial Rhetoric.* Oxford: Oxford University Press, 1998.

Pippin, T. *Death and Desire: The Rhetoric of Gender in the Apocalypse of John.* Louisville:
Westminster John Knox, 1992.

Potter, D. "Martyrdom as Spectacle." Pp. 53–88 in *Theater and Society in the Classical World.*
Edited by R. Scodel. Ann Arbor, MI: University of Michigan Press, 1993.

Rhoads, D., ed. *From Every People and Nation.* Minneapolis: Fortress, 2005.

Richard, P. *Apocalypse: A People's Commentary on the Book of Revelation.* Maryknoll, NY:
Orbis Books, 1995.

Rossing, B. "Standing at the Door of a New Millenium: Economy, Eschatology, and Hope."
Dialog 37 (1998) 263–68.

Rostovtzeff, M. *The Social and Economic History of the Roman Empire.* Oxford: Clarendon,
1926.

Runions, E. "Biblical Promise and Threat in US Imperialist Rhetoric Before and After September 11, 2001." Pp. 71–88 in *Interventions.* Edited by E. Castelli and J. R. Jakobsen.
New York: Palgrave Macmillan, 2004.

Russell, D. A. *Quintilian. The Orator's Education, Books 6–8.* LCL126. Cambridge, MA:
Harvard University Press, 2001.

_____, and N. G. Wilson, eds. and trans. *Menander Rhetor.* Oxford: Clarendon, 1981.

Sassen, S. *Territory, Authority, Rights: From Medieval to Global Assemblages.* Princeton, NJ:
Princeton University Press, 2006.

Scheidel, W., I. Morris, and R. Saller, eds. *The Cambridge Economic History of the Greco-
Roman World.* Cambridge: Cambridge University Press, 2007.

Schmitt, C. *Politisch Theologie, Vier Kapitel zur Lehre von der Souveränität.* Munich-Leipzig:
Duncker and Humboldt, 1922.

Shapiro, K. "Politics is a Mushroom: Worldly Sources of Rule and Exception in Carl Schmitt
and Walter Benjamin." *Diacritics* 37.2–3 (2007) 121–34.

Shaw, B. "Body/Power/Identity: Passions of the Martyrs." *JECS* 4 (1990) 269–312.

Shuck, G. *Marks of the Beast: The Left Behind Novels and the Struggle for Evangelical Identity.*
New York: New York University Press, 2004.

Strombeck, A. "Invest in Jesus: Neoliberalism and the Left Behind Novels." *Cultural Critique* 64 (2006) 161–95.

Temin, P. "A Market Economy in the Early Roman Empire." *JRS* 91 (2001) 169–181.

Thompson, L. *The Book of Revelation: Apocalypse and Empire.* New York and Oxford: Oxford University Press, 1990.

_____. "Lamentation for Christ as a Hero: Revelation 1:7." *JBL* 119 (2000) 683–703.

Trible, P. "Exegesis for Storytellers and Other Strangers." *JBL* 114.1 (1995) 3–19.

Wilson, J. C. "The Problem of the Domitianic Date of Revelation." *NTS* 39 (1993) 586–605.

Oracles on Accommodation versus Confrontation:

The View from Josephus and the Rabbis

ANDREW D. GROSS

The Catholic University of America

Introduction

Flavius Josephus notoriously became disillusioned with the Great Revolt of 66–70 C.E. Though he had once been one of the leaders in the fight against Rome, by the time he wrote his history of the Revolt years later, he had become a fierce critic of the war's Jewish leadership. In his writings, he sought to assuage the mutual distrust and disdain between the Jews and the Romans and to convince Jews to replace confrontation with accommodation. He often notes that relations between the Jews and the larger political entities to whom they were subject during the Second Temple Period had generally been positive. For example, at several points in his writings, he cites official Greek and Roman proclamations guaranteeing Jewish communities certain rights of religious and social autonomy.[1] Thus, within the broader historical framework Josephus describes, the general pattern was one of Greco-Roman benevolence, with the Great Revolt being an anomaly resulting from the failings and poor decisions of the leadership on both sides.

The present essay illustrates another means by which Josephus expresses this vision of general political comity between the Jews and the larger Greco-Roman world. At two crucial junctures within his writings, Josephus makes use of a similar

Author's note: I would like to thank my colleague Fr. Chris Begg for his encouragement and assistance with this essay, as well as my wife Jill Aizenstein for her support and substantive critiques. All errors and deficiencies remain mine alone.

1. Cf. *Ant.* 12:147–53; 14:185–267. The actual purposes, and even authenticity, of these documents have long come into question. For further discussion, see H. Moehring, "The *Acta Pro Judaeis* in the *Antiquities* of Flavius Josephus: A Study in Hellenistic and Modern Apologetic Historiography," in *Christianity, Judaism and Other Greco-Roman Cults*, Part III: *Judaism before 70* (ed. J. Neusner; Leiden: Brill, 1975), 124–58; and T. Rajak, "Was There a Roman Charter for the Jews?" *The Journal of Roman Studies* 74 (1984) 107–23.

type-scene wherein prophecy, politics, and providence all seem to converge. In these scenes, a Jewish protagonist has a public audience with a foreign conqueror under very tense circumstances. This tension, however, is relieved by dint of an oracle, as divine providence appears to guide the two figures away from an adversarial relationship and toward cooperation. The narrative force of this type-scene was sufficiently powerful that it was later appropriated into rabbinic literature to serve essentially the same rhetorical purpose. All three examples—the two from Josephus and one from Rabbinic tradition—will be discussed below.

Josephus on Prophecy

Before looking at these episodes, it would be worthwhile to briefly discuss Josephus's views on prophecy. Many Jewish writers from the Second Temple and Rabbinic periods believed that true prophecy had ceased with the last of the canonical prophets of the Persian period.[2] Whether Josephus held such beliefs has been a matter of some dispute, especially since—as we will see below—he occasionally describes oracular phenomena that in various ways resemble prophecy. Even so, J. Blenkinsopp and others have noted that Josephus reserves the terms προφήτης and προφητεία almost exclusively for the prophets of the biblical era and thereby maintains a rather strong terminological distinction between them and the divine messengers of subsequent eras.[3] L. Stephen Cook adduces further evidence for Josephus's belief in the cessation of prophecy during the Persian period, including a number of statements scattered throughout his writings such as the enigmatic reference to "the failure of the exact succession of the prophets" in *Ag. Ap.* 1:41.[4]

According to Cook, Josephus characterizes Jewish prophets by roles that "correspond to the past, present, and future. They record history, expound the present will of God, and foretell future events, all for the benefit of the Jewish nation."[5] As will be discussed below, Josephus himself does all of these things as well, and this is

---

2. For a recent survey of this issue, see L. S. Cook, *On the Question of the "Cessation of Prophecy" in Ancient Judaism* (Texts and Studies in Ancient Judaism 145; Tübingen: Mohr Siebeck, 2011). See also R. Gray, *Prophetic Figures in Late Second Temple Jewish Palestine: The Evidence from Josephus* (Oxford: Oxford University Press, 1993), 7–34.

3. On this point, see J. Blenkinsopp, "Prophecy and Priesthood in Josephus," *Journal of Jewish Studies* 25 (1974) 239–62 and S. J. D. Cohen, "Josephus, Jeremiah, and Polybius," *History and Theory* 21 (1982) 369–70. The one notable exception occurs in Josephus's summation of the rule of John Hyrcanus (*Ant.* 12:299–300). According to Josephus, God had privileged Hyrcanus with the rule of the nation, the high priesthood, and the gift of προφητεία. Cook believes, however, that in this exceptional case, Josephus believed there to be limits on Hyrcanus' prophetic abilities (Cook, *On the Question*, 136–38).

4. Cook, *On the Question*, 132–36; see also L. H. Feldman, "Prophets and Prophecy in Josephus," *Journal of Theological Studies* N. S. 41 (1990) 398–407.

5. Cook, *On the Question*, 123. For a similar formulation, see Feldman, "Prophets and Prophecy," 394–97.

certainly no coincidence. In certain ways, Josephus presents himself as a typological successor to the biblical prophets.[6] For example, Jeremiah saw the Babylonian Empire as an agent of God's will to whom Israel should willingly acquiesce and repeatedly delivered this unpopular message to his fellow countrymen at great peril to himself. Similarly, Josephus believed himself to be in the corresponding role with respect to his countrymen and the Romans.[7]

As for his own prophetic abilities, as noted above, Josephus eschewed the term προφήτης for himself and his contemporaries,[8] instead using διάκονος ("minister") or ἄγγελος ("messenger"). While Josephus describes himself as operating under divine inspiration (ἔνθεος), Cook argues that Josephus believed his oracular power to be qualitatively different from that of the earlier biblical prophets.[9] In Cook's view, Josephus believed he possessed a skill that came through extensive study and knowledge of biblical prophecies, along with the assistance of divine inspiration. With these background matters in mind, let us now move to the passages under discussion here.

Alexander the Great and the High Priest Jaddus

The meeting between Alexander and Jaddus occurs toward the end of Book 11 of *Jewish Antiquities*. In 331 B.C.E., Alexander the Great had just pushed the Persians out of Asia Minor and was proceeding down the Mediterranean coast toward Egypt. During his siege of Tyre, Alexander had asked Jaddus, the high priest of Jerusalem, to abandon the Persian realm and to provide him with military assistance. Having previously sworn loyalty to the Persian king Darius III, Jaddus was reluctant to abandon this allegiance while Darius was still alive, and so refused Alexander's request. Furthermore, Sanballat of Samaria, one of Jaddus's regional rivals, sought to exploit these circumstances at Jaddus's expense by quickly allying with Alexander. According to Josephus, once Alexander had taken Tyre and then Gaza, he marched toward Jerusalem, provoking great anxiety in Jaddus as to what would befall both him and his city. Here is Josephus's account of this episode in full:

---

6. On the connections between Jeremiah and Josephus, see Cohen, "Josephus, Jeremiah, and Polybius." For typological similarities with other biblical prophets, including Daniel, see D. Daube "Typology in Josephus," *Journal of Jewish Studies* 31 (1980) 18–36; Gray, *Prophetic Figures*, 70–78; R. K. Gnuse, *Dreams and Dream Reports in the Writings of Josephus: A Traditio-Historical Analysis* (Leiden: Brill, 1996), 21–33; and J. Klawans, *Josephus and the Theologies of Ancient Judaism* (Oxford: Oxford University Press, 2012), 193–94.

7. For examples, where Josephus explicitly makes such comparisons between himself and the biblical prophets, see *J.W.* 5:391, 393; 6:103.

8. Except for false prophets, whom he refers to as ψευδοπροφήτης (cf. *J.W.* 6:285–287). For more on this term, see J. Reiling, "The use of ψευδοπροφήτης in the Septuagint, Philo and Josephus," *Novum Testamentum* 13 (1971) 147–56.

9. Cook, *On the Question*, 140–44.

Alexander, after taking Gaza, was in haste to go up to the city of Jerusalem. When the high priest Jaddus heard this, he was in an agony of fear, not knowing how he could meet the Macedonians, whose king was angered by his former disobedience. He therefore ordered the people to make supplication, and, offering sacrifice to God together with them, besought Him to shield the nation and deliver them from the dangers that were hanging over them. But, when he had gone to sleep after the sacrifice, God spoke oracularly to him in his sleep, telling him to take courage and adorn the city with wreaths and open the gates and go out to meet them, and that the people should be in white garments, and he himself with the priests in the robes prescribed by law, and that they should not look to suffer any harm, for God was watching over them. Thereupon he rose from his sleep, greatly rejoicing to himself, and announced to all the revelation that had been made to him, and, after doing all the things that he had been told to do, awaited the coming of the king.

When he learned that Alexander was not far from the city, he went out with the priests and the body of citizens, and, making the reception sacred in character and different from that of other nations, met him at a certain place called Saphein. This name, translated into the Greek tongue, means "Lookout." For, as it happened, Jerusalem and the temple could be seen from there. Now the Phoenicians and the Chaldaeans who followed along thought to themselves that the king in his anger would naturally permit them to plunder the city and put the high priest to a shameful death, but the reverse of this happened. For when Alexander while still far off saw the multitude in white garments the priests at their head clothed in linen, and the high priest in a robe of hyacinth-blue and gold, wearing on his head the mitre with the golden plate on it on which was inscribed the name of God, he approached alone and prostrated himself before the Name and first greeted the high priest. Then all the Jews together greeted Alexander with one voice and surrounded him, but the kings of Syria and the others were struck with amazement at his action and supposed that the king's mind was deranged. And Parmenion alone went up to him and asked why indeed, when all men prostrated themselves before him, he had prostrated himself before the high priest of the Jews, whereupon he replied, "It was not before him that I prostrated myself but the God of whom he has the honour to be high priest, for it was he whom I saw in my sleep dressed as he is now, when I was at Dium in Macedonia, and, as I was considering with myself how I might become master of Asia, he urged me not to hesitate but to cross over confidently, for he himself would lead my army and give over to me the empire of the Persians. Since, therefore, I have beheld no one else in such robes, and on seeing him now I am reminded of the vision and the exhortation, I believe that I have made this expedition under divine guidance and that I shall defeat Darius and destroy the power of the Persians and succeed in carrying out all the things which I have in mind." After saying these things to Parmenion, he gave his hand to the high priest and, with the Jews running beside him, entered the city. Then he went up to the temple, where he sacrificed to God under the direction of the high priest, and showed due honour to the priests and to the high priest himself. And, when the book of Daniel was shown to him, in which he had declared that one of the Greeks would destroy the empire of the Persians, he believed himself to be the one indicated; and in his joy he dismissed the multitude for the time being, but on the following day he summoned them again and told them to ask for any gifts which they might desire. When the high priest asked that they might observe their country's laws and in the seventh year be exempt from tribute, he granted all this. Then they begged that he would permit the Jews in Babylon and Media also to have their own laws, and he gladly promised to do as they asked. And, when he said to the people that if any wished to join his army while still adhering to the customs of their country, he was ready to take them, many eagerly accepted service with him." (*Ant.* 11:325–339 [Marcus])[10]

Three divine revelations drive this story. In the first, God appears to Jaddus in a dream to assuage his anxiety about Alexander's approach. God assures him that no harm shall befall him at the hand of Alexander and, in addition, instructs Jaddus on how to receive Alexander's party. Unknown to the high priest, these instructions help to fulfill the second revelation within this story. Alexander surprises the members of his entourage by showing great deference to both the high priest and to the God of Israel. Just before having undertaken his campaign, Alexander had received a vision from God foretelling his string of military successes against the Persians. The messenger in his dream was Jaddus himself, whom Alexander recognizes, upon now meeting him, by his distinctive attire. Finally, the third revelation is taken from the book of Daniel, chapter 8, which predicts the conquest of Persia by a Greek champion. When Alexander sees how favorably he is spoken of in Jewish scripture, he is more than willing to establish a privileged role for Jews in his newly founded empire.

In the case of the first two revelations, Josephus employs a literary device known as the "double dream" (or *Doppeltraum*). The double dream is attested elsewhere in contemporaneous Greek and Latin literature, most famously in the New Testament (Acts 9:10–16; 10:1–11:18). A. Wikenhauser collected nineteen examples of this literary device in Late Antique Greek and Latin literature, including the above-cited passage from Josephus.[11] Because Wikenhauser defines the double dream category rather broadly, not all of his examples are particularly apt for our present purposes. M. Frenschkowski offers a useful corrective to Wikenhauser by offering a typology of the visions the latter had collected (along with additional examples).[12] He breaks them down into three categories:

---

10. Translation from *Josephus*, vol. 6: *Jewish Antiquities, Books 9–11*, translated by R. Marcus (LCL; Cambridge, MA: Harvard University Press, 1937), 471–79. This volume also includes a general survey of some critical issues related to this episode (ibid., 512–32, "Appendix C: Alexander the Great and the Jews").

11. A. Wikenhauser, "Doppelträume," *Biblica* 29 (1948) 100–111.

12. M. Frenschkowski, "Traum und Traumdeutung im Matthäusevangelium: Einige Beobachtungen," *Jahrbuch für Antike und Christentum* 41 (1998) 34–38. He also raises the issue of distinguishing between dreams and visions.

1. The double dream in which two or more people either have the same dream or clearly related dreams and thus mutually confirm their supernatural character
2. A dream that is confirmed through some other form of supernatural revelation (oracle, omen, etc.)
3. A dream that a single dreamer has on multiple occasions, thereby indicating its supernatural origins

The Josephus story clearly belongs to the first category, and among the other examples adduced by Wikenhauser and Frenschkowski that belong to this category, the most striking parallel occurs in the *Roman Antiquities* of Dionysius of Halicarnassus.

The story told by Dionysius takes place just after Aeneas and his Trojan warriors have claimed the territory along the Tiber River where, according to an earlier oracle, they will eventually establish the city of Rome. When the local king Latinus hears of this incursion of armed warriors into his territory, he takes this as such a dire act of aggression that he abandons the war in which he had been engaged at the time and leads his army away to face Aeneas's. Upon seeing how well-armed and arrayed they were, however, Latinus decides not to confront them immediately after his army's long march but rather to rest his men and fight the next day. In the course of the subsequent evening, the respective deities of Latinus and Aeneas appear to them in dreams:

> But when he [that is, Latinus] had reached this decision, a certain divinity of the place appeared to him in his sleep and bade him receive the Greeks into his land to dwell with his own subjects, adding that their coming was a great advantage to him and a benefit to all the Aborigines alike. And the same night Aeneas' household gods appeared to him and admonished him to persuade Latinus to grant them of his own accord a settlement in the part of the country they desired and to treat the Greek forces rather as allies than as enemies. Thus the dream hindered both of them from beginning an engagement. And as soon as it was day and the armies were drawn up in order of battle, heralds came to each of the commanders from the other with the same request, that they should meet for a parley; and so it came to pass. (1:57 [Cary])[13]

The two sides eventually negotiate a treaty in which the Trojans receive land in exchange for their military support of Latinus.

In their general outlines, the stories told by Josephus and Dionysius have much in common. They both begin with the anxiety (δέος) of a local leader being aroused upon hearing of a potential conflict with a foreign army. In both cases, however, divine guidance assures that conflict between the two parties is avoided

---

13. Translation from Dionysius of Halicarnassus, *Roman Antiquities*, vol. 1: *Books 1–2*, translated by E. Cary (LCL; Cambridge, MA: Harvard University Press, 1937), 191.

and that they in fact establish mutually beneficial relations. Most importantly, both stories describe the divine guidance as being mediated through the protagonists' sleep (καθ' ὕπνον)—that is, their dreams.

Dionysius' works preceded Josephus's by approximately a century, and some scholars, noting intriguing parallels between the two authors, have suggested that Josephus was familiar with the writings of his Roman predecessor and even that some aspects of *Jewish Antiquities* were modeled on *Roman Antiquities*.[14] Though questions of direct dependence are beyond the scope of the present essay, we can at least note the similarities both in this literary device and in how it is used by these two authors. In both cases, the authors want to show how the parties in their respective tales came to avoid potential hostilities and to establish mutual respect and support for one another. In addition, the role of divine providence in guiding them to this state of affairs could not be any more explicit, since direct revelation shapes the outcomes of both situations.

Alexander and Cyrus

As for the last of the three revelations, the tradition wherein Alexander reads prophecies about himself in the book of Daniel has strong parallels to an earlier episode in Book 11 of *Jewish Antiquities* involving Cyrus the Great:

> In the first year of Cyrus's reign—this was the seventieth year from the time when our people were fated to migrate from their own land to Babylon—God took pity on the captive state and misfortune of those unhappy men and, as He had foretold to them through the prophet Jeremiah before the city was demolished, that, after they should have served Nebuchadnezzar and his descendants and endured this servitude for seventy years, He would again restore them to the land of their fathers and they should build the temple and enjoy their ancient prosperity, so did He grant it them. For he stirred up the spirit of Cyrus and caused him to write throughout all Asia, "Thus says King Cyrus. Since the Most High God has appointed me king of the habitable world, I am persuaded that He is the god whom the Israelite nation worships, for He foretold my name through the prophets and that I should build His temple in Jerusalem in the land of Judaea."
>
> These things Cyrus knew from reading the book of prophecy which Isaiah had left behind two hundred and ten years earlier. For this prophet had said that God told him in secret, "It is my will that Cyrus, whom I shall have appointed king of many great nations, shall send my people to their own land and build my temple." Isaiah prophesied these things one hundred and forty years before the temple was demolished. And so, when Cyrus read them, he wondered at the divine power and was seized by a strong desire and ambition to do what had been written; and,

---

14. On this topic, see L. H. Feldman, *Josephus and Modern Scholarship (1937–1980)* (Berlin: Walter de Gruyter, 1984), 407–8, 935–36.

summoning the most distinguished of the Jews in Babylon, he told them that he gave them leave to journey to their native land and to rebuild both the city of Jerusalem and the temple of God, for God, he said, would be their ally and he himself would write to his own governors and satraps who were in the neighborhood of their country to give them contributions of gold and silver for the building of the temple and, in addition, animals for the sacrifices. (*Ant.* 11:1–7 [Marcus])[15]

Here, as with Alexander, a foreign conqueror reads in Jewish scripture that his victories have already been predicted and, as a result, finds himself predisposed to deal favorably with the Jewish people. In Cyrus's case, his favorable treatment has also been predicted in the prophecies of Isa 44–45, but according to Josephus's description, his embrace of the God of Israel is no less genuine than that of Alexander. Indeed, both Cyrus and Alexander are said to believe that these prophecies of Jewish scripture grant divine legitimacy to their respective reigns, and both are eager to requite this with a show of favor to the Jewish people. There are some differences in the two episodes. While Josephus describes in some detail the vision Alexander receives from God, with Cyrus, he hews relatively close to his biblical source material in Ezra and Chronicles, noting merely that the Persian king's decree fulfills Jeremiah's seventy-year prophecy (Jer 25:11–12) and that God had "stirred"[16] Cyrus to action on behalf of the Jews.

Greco-Roman literature records other divine revelations concerning Alexander's future greatness, such as those he received from the oracles of Apollo at Delphi and of Ammon at the Siwa Oasis.[17] According to S. Cohen, however, Josephus did not model these Cyrus-Isaiah and Alexander-Daniel traditions on any earlier parallels but rather authored them himself in order to show that Jewish scripture had the same predictive power as these Greco-Roman oracles.[18] Furthermore, he also notes that the Cyrus-Isaiah and Alexander-Daniel traditions form what he refers to as a "ring structure" around Book 11 of *Jewish Antiquities*. These two traditions occur at the beginning and end, respectively, of this literary unit and thus bracket off his account of Persian rule over Judea.

---

15. Translation from Marcus, *Josephus*, 315–17.

16. Josephus uses the verb παρορμάω here while the Septuagint to Ezra 1:1 and 2 Chr 36:22 uses εξεγειρειν.

17. On the Delphic oracle, see Plutarch, *Alexander* 14:4. On the Ammon oracle, see E. A. Fredricksmeyer, "Alexander, Zeus Ammon, and the Conquest of Asia," *Transactions of the American Philological Association* 121 (1991) 199–214.

18. S. J. D. Cohen, "Alexander the Great and Jaddus the High Priest According to Josephus," *AJS Review* 7 (1982) 64. Cohen also notes earlier suggestions that Josephus had invented the Alexander-Daniel tradition (ibid., n. 74). Of course, the original visions themselves in both (Deutero-)Isaiah and Daniel are typically understood to be post-factum oracles and therefore would not have been actually available to the historical Cyrus and Alexander (on the dating of Daniel 8, see J. J. Collins, *Daniel: A Commentary on the Book of Daniel* [Hermeneia; Minneapolis: Fortress, 1993], 343).

Vespasian and Josephus

The next example of our type-scene takes place during the Great Revolt and involves Josephus himself as one of the protagonists. In 67 C.E., the Roman general Vespasian had taken the Galilean city of Jotapata after a brief siege. Josephus had led the defense of the city and had managed to escape capture into a nearby cavern, where others from the city had been hiding. After a few days, their position is betrayed to the Romans, who, hoping to capture Josephus alive, send envoys to convince him to surrender. As he weighs an offer from the Roman officer Nicanor, Josephus prays to God and eventually concludes that giving himself up to Rome is not only the most prudent course of action but the providential one as well:

> But as Nicanor was urgently pressing his proposals and Josephus overheard the threats of the hostile crowd, suddenly there came back into his mind those nightly dreams, in which God had foretold to him the impending fate of the Jews and the destinies of the Roman sovereigns. He was an interpreter of dreams and skilled in divining the meaning of ambiguous utterances of the Deity; a priest himself and of priestly descent, he was not ignorant of the prophecies (προφητείας) in the sacred books. At that hour he was inspired to read their meaning, and, recalling the dreadful images of his recent dreams, he offered up a silent prayer to God. "Since it pleases thee," so it ran, "who didst create the Jewish nation, to break thy work, since fortune has wholly passed to the Romans, and since thou hast made choice of my spirit to announce the things that are to come, I willingly surrender to the Romans and consent to live; but I take thee to witness that I go, not as a traitor, but as thy minister (διάκονος)." (*J. W.* 3:351–354 [Thackeray])[19]

Here, Josephus himself is the recipient and interpreter of God's message. Having concluded that Roman victory was not only inevitable but, in fact, in line with God's will,[20] Josephus eventually surrenders to the Romans, though not before having some tense interactions with his companions who attempt to involve him in a suicide pact. Through subterfuge, Josephus manages to avoid this fate and is led into the presence of the Roman general Vespasian. In noting that God had revealed to him the destinies of both the Jews and the Roman leaders, Josephus foreshadows what would happen next:

> ... Josephus expressed a desire for a private interview with him. Vespasian having ordered all to withdraw except his son Titus and two of his friends, the prisoner thus addressed him: "You imagine, Vespasian, that in the person of Josephus you have taken a mere captive; but I come to you as a messenger of greater destinies. Had I not been sent on this errand by God, I knew the law of the Jews and how

---

19. Translation from Josephus, *The Jewish War*, vol. 2: *Books I–III*, translated by H. St. John Thackeray (LCL; Cambridge, MA: Harvard University Press, 1927), 675–76.

20. The key term here is τύχη, translated above in *J. W.* 3:354 as "Fortune." For more discussion on this concept in Josephus, see Cohen, "Josephus, Jeremiah, and Polybius," 372–77; and Klawans, *Josephus*, 46–47, 85–86, and 189–90.

it becomes a general to die. To Nero do you send me? Why then? Think you that [Nero and] those who before your accession succeed him will continue? You will be Caesar, Vespasian, you will be emperor, you and your son here. Bind me then yet more securely in chains and keep me for yourself; for you, Caesar, are master not of me only, but of land and sea and the whole human race. For myself, I ask to be punished by stricter custody, if I have dared to trifle with the words of God." To this speech Vespasian, at the moment, seemed to attach little credit, supposing it to be a trick of Josephus to save his life. Gradually, however, he was led to believe it, for God was already rousing in him thoughts of empire and by other tokens foreshadowing the throne. He found, moreover, that Josephus had proved a veracious prophet in other matters. For one of the two friends in attendance at the private interview remarked: "If these words are not a nonsensical invention of the prisoner to avert the storm which he has raised, I am surprised that Josephus neither predicted the fall of Jotapata to its inhabitants nor his own captivity." To this Josephus replied that he had foretold to the people of Jotapata that their city would be captured after forty-seven days and that he himself would be taken alive by the Romans. Vespasian, having privately questioned the prisoners on these statements and found them true, then began to credit those concerning himself. While he did not release Josephus from his custody or chains, he presented him with raiment and other precious gifts, and continued to treat him with kindness and solicitude, being warmly supported by Titus in these courtesies. (*J.W.* 3:399–408)[21]

Though Vespasian initially suspects Josephus's oracle to be a ruse meant to appeal to his vanity, God begins to "rouse" (διεγείροντος) his imperial ambitions, and the general becomes more receptive to Josephus. It was not uncommon for imperial aspirants to seek *omina imperii* to justify their ambitions or, more accurately, to have such favorable omens recorded in subsequent histories so as to put a divine imprimatur on their reigns.[22] Roman historians, including Suetonius, Tacitus, and Cassius Dio mention a number of portents regarding Vespasian's ascension to the imperial throne.[23] Josephus appears to have been aware of these other *omina imperii* relating to Vespasian, as shown in the reference above to "other tokens (σημείων) foreshadowing the throne."[24] Cohen argues, however, that Josephus downplays these other signs in order to privilege his own oracle.[25] As a result, one is given the impression that Vespasian's divine legitimacy came solely through the divine message delivered by Josephus and that the Roman general's acclama-

---

21. Translation from Thackeray, *Josephus*, 689–91.
22. For this phenomenon in general, see R. S. Lorsch, "*Omina imperii*: The Omens of Power Received by the Roman Emperors from Augustus to Domitian, their Religious Interpretation and Political Influence" (Ph.D. Dissertation, The University of North Carolina at Chapel Hill, 1993), especially pp. 108–32 on Vespasian.
23. Suetonius, *The Life of Vespasian* 4–5; Tacitus, *Histories* 2:78; and Cassius Dio, *Roman History* 76:1. Both Suetonius and Cassius Dio specifically mention Josephus's oracle.
24. Cf. also *J.W.* 1:23 and 4:623.
25. Cohen, "Josephus, Jeremiah, and Polybius," 374.

tion as emperor first occurred in Judea. More significantly, Cohen identifies this oracle as the major turning point in Josephus's account of the war, because divine favor is now clearly with the Roman camp and not with the Jewish rebels.

The overall similarities with the encounter between Jaddus and Alexander are quite intriguing. In both cases, a Jewish leader has an audience before a conquering foreign general, and the encounter redounds positively for the Jewish figure because of an oracle God has provided. Literarily, the supernatural elements are toned down in this latter tale. The narrative in the Alexander story explicitly describes the imparting of the "double dream" as well as the contents of the visions themselves. With regard to his dream about "the destinies of the Roman sovereigns," Josephus merely refers to their contents obliquely. This may partly be because in the context of the Alexander story, Alexander's dream served to immediately confirm both the validity and supernatural nature of Jaddus's vision. With Josephus's encounter with Vespasian, there was no need for such a literary device because the contemporary reader would have been quite aware that the oracle had in fact come true. In both cases, too, Josephus injects a bit of tension into the scene. With Jaddus, despite God's reassurances, the natural reaction would be to expect hostility from Alexander. In the case of Josephus, Vespasian initially shows skepticism, even while resisting calls by his junior officers to have Josephus immediately executed.

One obvious difference between the two episodes is that while the Jewish nation as a whole prospered because of Jaddus's audience with Alexander, it is mainly Josephus himself who prospers from his audience with Vespasian. As a result of this encounter, Josephus's life was spared and he would eventually receive many special favors from the Flavian emperors. Nonetheless, though his oracle seemingly benefits just one person, Josephus was likely trying to deliver a message regarding the fortunes of the Jewish people as a whole through this episode. As will be discussed below, the later Jewish authors who appropriated this story in rabbinic literature certainly received this message. Jaddus's encounter with Alexander resulted in the Jews and the Greeks establishing a *modus vivendi* that benefitted both sides. Josephus hardly had the stature of a high priest, and even if this were true, he would not have been able to create a peaceful resolution at this stage of the Great Revolt. Even so, God let his will be known here by giving Josephus the means to extricate himself from this perilous situation and to make his Roman interlocutor amenable to his message. In other words, Josephus believed divine Providence favored accommodation with Rome, not armed conflict. This was the path God favored, and the only one that would ultimately lead to the Jewish people's survival.[26]

---

26. Josephus, in fact, delivers an excursus on divine Providence at the end of Book X of *Jewish Antiquities* (10:276–281), just before his account of Cyrus and his reading of Isaiah's prophecy.

Yoḥanan ben Zakkai and Vespasian

Josephus's account of his meeting with Vespasian has a well-known parallel in rabbinic literature in a tale involving Vespasian and Rabbi Yoḥanan ben Zakkai.[27] In this rabbinic tradition, the setting shifts from the siege of Jotapata in 67 C.E. to the siege of Jerusalem in 70 C.E., at the end of the Great Revolt. Like Josephus, Rabbi Yoḥanan escapes the besieged city, gains an audience with Vespasian, and during the course of this audience, declares him to be king. The account is clearly ahistorical, as Vespasian was already emperor in 70 C.E. and not present at the siege of Jerusalem.

Rabbinic literature preserves four slightly different versions of this tale; they can be found in the *Babylonian Talmud, Lamentations Rabbah, Avot de-Rabbi Nathan* A, and *Avot de-Rabbi Nathan* B. These versions appear to derive from the same core tradition, though they differ in some significant details.[28] For example, in the *Avot de-Rabbi Nathan* A version, Rabbi Yoḥanan does not predict Vespasian's ascension as emperor until after having been granted Yavneh by him. In *Lamentations Rabbah*, Yoḥanan asks for Jerusalem to be spared rather than for Yavneh. These differences appear to be later editorial alterations of a tradition that was clearly based in some manner on the Josephus episode. An analysis of the complex editorial relationship between these versions is beyond the scope of the present essay. The version that provides us with the closest parallels to Josephus comes from the *Babylonian Talmud*:[29]

> When he reached him [Vespasian], he said to him, "Peace to you, O King. Peace to you, O King." He said to him, "You deserve death on two [counts]. First, I am not a king. Second, if I am a king, why did you not come to me until now?" He said to him, "As for what you said, 'I am not a king,' in truth you are a king. For if you were not a king, Jerusalem would not be delivered into your hands, for it says, *Lebanon shall fall to the mighty one* (Isa 10:34) and 'mighty one' refers to a king, as it says, *His mighty one shall come from his midst* (Jer 30:21), and 'Lebanon' refers to the temple, as it says, *That good hill country and the Lebanon*

---

27. For a more through comparison of these traditions, see A. Schalit, "Die Erhebung Vespasians nach Josephus, Talmud und Midrasch: Zur Geschichte einer messianischen Prophetie," *ANRW*, part 2, Principat 2: *Politische Geschichte (Kaisergeschichte)* (Berlin: de Gruyter, 1975), 208–327.

28. For more specific references and thorough discussions of these variant traditions, see A. J. Saldarini, "Johanan ben Zakkai's Escape from Jerusalem: Origin and Development of a Rabbinic Story," *Journal for the Study of Judaism* 4 (1975) 189–204, and P. Schäfer, "Die Flucht Johanan b. Zakkais aus Jerusalem und die Gründung des 'Lehrhauses' in Jabne," *ANRW*, part 2, Principat 19.2: *Religion (Judentum: Palästinisches Judentum)* (Berlin: de Gruyter, 1979). For a literary analysis of this tradition, see J. L. Rubenstein, *Talmudic Stories: Narrative Art, Composition, and Culture* (Baltimore: Johns Hopkins University Press, 1999), 139–75.

29. Translation from J. L. Rubenstein, *Rabbinic Stories* (Classics of Western Spirituality; Mahwah, NJ: Paulist, 2002), 44–45.

(Deut 3:25). And as for what you said, 'If I am a king, why did you not come to me?'—the thugs among us would not let me." He said to him, "If there is a jar of honey and a snake wound around it, would they not break the jar on account of the snake?" He was silent.

Rav Yosef [and some say R. Akiba] applied to him the verse, "[*God*] *turns sages back and makes nonsense of their knowledge* (Isa 44:25). He should have answered him, 'We take tongs and take away the snake and kill it. And we leave the jar.'"

Just then a messenger came from Rome. He said to them, "Rise, for the emperor has died and the notables of Rome voted to make you the leader." He [Vespasian] had put on one shoe. He tried to put on the other but it would not go on. He tried to take off the first, but it would not come off. He said, "What is this?" He [R. Yoḥanan b. Zakkai] said to him, "Do not worry. You received good news, [as it says], *Good news puts fat on bones* (Prov 15:30)." He said to him, "What is the remedy?" [He said,] "Bring someone who annoys you and have him pass before you, as it says, *Despondency dries up the bones* (Prov 17:22)." He did this. It [the shoe] went on. He said to him, "Since you are so wise, why did you not come to me before now?" He said to him, "Have I not told you?" He said, "I also told you."

He [Vespasian] said to him, "I am going and I will send someone else. Ask something of me and I will give it you." He said, "Give me Yavneh and its sages and the line of Rabban Gamaliel and doctors to heal Rabbi Zadoq."[30]

Rav Yosef, and some say R. Akiba, applied to him the verse, "[*God*] *turns sages back* [*and makes nonsense of their knowledge*] (Isa 44:25). He should have said, 'Let them off this time.'"

But he thought that perhaps he [Vespasian] would not do so much, and he would not even save a little. (*BT Giṭṭin* 56a-b)

The sages have clearly excised oracles and prophecy from this tradition. Rather than using supernatural means to predict Vespasian's status, Rabbi Yoḥanan does so through interpretation of Scripture. One could perhaps see in this use of Scripture a parallel with Josephus's descriptions of Cyrus and Alexander reading about their respective destinies in Isaiah and Daniel. Within the framework of the stories, however, the clearer parallel is between the prophetic visions described in Josephus and Rabbi Yoḥanan's midrashic interpretation. While Rabbi Yoḥanan produces a novel reading of the text through midrash, Cyrus and Alexander merely react to the text's *peshat* or plain meaning. More significantly, the rabbinic sages have substituted midrash here for prophecy. In their view, the era of direct revelation had ended long before the time of Rabbi Yoḥanan,[31] though Scripture and the proper interpretation thereof still afforded the wise reader a means of determining God's will.

---

30. Rabbi Zadoq's health had declined because he had fasted on behalf of Jerusalem.

31. For a survey of Rabbinic attitudes towards prophecy, see Cook, *On the Question*, 149–73.

The rabbinic version also removes the elements of divine intervention in Vespasian's reaction. With both Josephus and Rabbi Yoḥanan, Vespasian initially shows skepticism to their words. In the case of Josephus, God intervenes by "rousing" Vespasian's imperial ambitions, whereas Rabbi Yoḥanan responds to Vespasian's skepticism with scriptural prooftexts, which are quickly confirmed via a Roman messenger. Though the text is once again ahistorical here, as Vespasian had already been emperor for some time when the siege of Jerusalem began, the more significant point is how the rabbis have eliminated these elements of divine action.

In the two Josephus stories, after the foreign general and the Jewish leader have established their relationship, the general responds with a gesture of gratitude. Here, too, Vespasian offers to grant Rabbi Yoḥanan any request. In the Babylonian Talmud's version, Yoḥanan asks for the preservation of the rabbis' leadership infrastructure. Specifically, he asks for the preservation of Yavneh, a site near the Mediterranean coast that served as the seat of a group of sages, as well as the preservation of the line of Rabban Gamliel in the post-70 C.E. period. The line of Rabban Gamliel refers to the dynasty of the Patriarchate, descendants of Hillel, who according to tradition, headed the Rabbinic Sanhedrin.

The above exchange underscores two other important parallels between the traditions reflected in Josephus and in Rabbinic literature. The first concerns the general attitude toward the Great Revolt. After the Jotapata episode, Josephus began to portray the Jewish leadership of the Revolt rather negatively and attempted to distance himself from the revolutionaries. The rabbis express a similar attitude toward the Revolt in the portion of *BT Giṭṭin* 56a that leads up to the above-quoted excerpt. Here, with all of the terrible depredations taking hold of the city during the siege, Rabbi Yoḥanan decides to escape the revolutionaries' tyrannical control of Jerusalem. Because they will not allow anyone to leave under penalty of death, he and his students are compelled to hatch a plan to fake his death and spirit him out of the city in a coffin. Clearly, the rabbis' sympathies are not with the leaders of the revolt.

The second parallel concerns the establishment of a *modus vivendi* between the Jews and the greater Greco-Roman world. Just as Jaddus did with Alexander and the Greeks, so too does Rabbi Yoḥanan establish one with Vespasian and the Romans. Having ingratiated himself with Vespasian, Yoḥanan sees to it that some form of leadership structure will be in place to guide the Jewish people in the aftermath of this devastating revolt. For the purposes of the present study, we can set aside the question as to how historically accurate this picture of the rabbis' role in Jewish society was and whether or not they actually provided such a leadership infrastructure in Judea in the years and decades after 70 C.E.[32] Historical accuracy

---

32. While some historians had taken the rabbinic portrayal of their role in Jewish society after the Great Revolt at face value, there have been challenges to this in recent years. For more

aside, this was the image the rabbis wanted to project regarding their position in Jewish society for that period, and the key fact is that they did so using a tradition adapted from Josephus.

This second parallel is particularly striking because it suggests that the rabbis' use of this tradition goes beyond mere literary structure. When Yohanan ben Zakkai seeks favors from the Romans, he does so on behalf of the rabbinic sages as a whole and, presumably, the interests of the Jewish people in general. Jaddus, in his encounter with Alexander, had likewise requested favors on behalf of the Jewish people as a whole. When Josephus ingratiates himself with Vespasian, however, the only direct beneficiary of this relationship is Josephus himself. This observation is not meant to cast judgment on Josephus's actions, as he was not in the same position to solicit favors on behalf of all Jews as were Jaddus and Yohanan. Rather, the salient point it highlights concerns *how* the rabbis used this story. Though in its basic elements the rabbinic tale clearly resembles Josephus's story about his audience with Vespasian, in its end result, this tale has more in common with the historian's account of Jaddus's audience with Alexander. The Jotapata story lacks the element whereby the relationship between the Jewish leader and the foreign general produces benefits for the Jewish people as a whole. While Josephus believed that accommodation with Rome was the most prudent policy for the Jewish people in general, he does not make this belief an explicit element of this story. The rabbis, on the other hand, do make this an explicit element in their tradition, indicating that they were attuned to Josephus's sentiments or, more likely, to the implicit sentiments underlying this type-scene.

Conclusion

Both Josephus and the rabbinic sages wanted to emphasize the importance of establishing a peaceful *modus vivendi* with the Romans. They expressed the importance of this by representing it not merely as a matter of political prudence but as one of divine providence. In all of these stories, an encounter that begins fraught with tension and hostility resolves itself into a relationship of peaceful collaboration. What defuses the tension and hostility are oracles and prophecy, instruments through which God puts his divine imprimatur on these friendly relations.

The coming of Alexander the Great and the Great Revolt were two key historical points in the ongoing relationship between the Jewish people and the larger Greco-Roman world. At both points, Josephus deploys a similar type-scene to demonstrate where divine providence was leading the Jews. In his view,

---

discussion, see C. Hezser, *The Social Structure of the Rabbinic Movement in Roman Palestine* (Texte und Studien zum antiken Judentum 66; Tübingen: Mohr Siebeck, 1997) and H. Lapin, "The Origins and Development of the Rabbinic Movement in the Land of Israel," in *The Cambridge History of Judaism*, vol. 4: *The Late Roman-Rabbinic Period* (ed. S. T. Katz; Cambridge: Cambridge University Press, 2006), 206–29.

accommodation and not confrontation was the appropriate response, and he sought to express this view both through literary models known in Greco-Roman literature and through others of his own devising. The Rabbinic sages shared Josephus's view and not only adapted his type-scene as a model but used it to express the similar convictions.

Bibliography

Blenkinsopp, J. "Prophecy and Priesthood in Josephus." *Journal of Jewish Studies* 25 (1974) 239–62.

Cohen, S. J. D. "Alexander the Great and Jaddus the High Priest According to Josephus." *AJS Review* 7 (1982) 41–68.

———. "Josephus, Jeremiah, and Polybius." *History and Theory* 21 (1982) 366–81.

Collins, J. J. *Daniel: A Commentary on the Book of Daniel.* Hermeneia. Minneapolis: Fortress, 1993.

Cook, L. S. *On the Question of the "Cessation of Prophecy" in Ancient Judaism.* Texts and Studies in Ancient Judaism 145. Tübingen: Mohr Siebeck, 2011.

Daube, D. "Typology in Josephus." *Journal of Jewish Studies* 31 (1980) 18–36.

Dionysius of Halicarnassus. *Roman Antiquities*, vol. 1: *Books 1–2.* Translated by E. Cary. Loeb Classical Library 319. Cambridge, MA: Harvard University Press, 1937.

Feldman, L. H. *Josephus and Modern Scholarship (1937–1980).* Berlin: de Gruyter, 1984.

———. "Prophets and Prophecy in Josephus." *Journal of Theological Studies* N.S. 41 (1990) 386–422.

Fredricksmeyer, E. A. "Alexander, Zeus Ammon, and the Conquest of Asia." *Transactions of the American Philological Association* 121 (1991) 199–214.

Frenschkowski, M. "Traum und Traumdeutung im Matthäusevangelium: Einige Beobachtungen." *Jahrbuch für Antike und Christentum* 41 (1998) 5–47.

Gnuse, R. K. *Dreams and Dream Reports in the Writings of Josephus: A Traditio-Historical Analysis.* Leiden: Brill, 1996.

Gray, R. *Prophetic Figures in Late Second Temple Jewish Palestine: The Evidence from Josephus.* Oxford: Oxford University Press, 1993.

Hezser, C. *The Social Structure of the Rabbinic Movement in Roman Palestine.* Texte und Studien zum antiken Judentum 66. Tübingen: Mohr Siebeck, 1997.

Josephus. *The Jewish War, Books I–III.* Translated by H. St. John Thackeray. Loeb Classical Library 203. Cambridge, MA: Harvard University Press, 1927.

———. *Jewish Antiquities, Books IX–XI.* **Translated by R. Marcus.** Loeb Classical Library 326. Cambridge, MA: Harvard University Press, 1937.

Klawans, J. *Josephus and the Theologies of Ancient Judaism.* Oxford: Oxford University Press, 2012.

Lapin, H. "The Origins and Development of the Rabbinic Movement in the Land of Israel." Pp. 206–29 in *The Cambridge History of Judaism*, vol. 4: *The Late Roman-Rabbinic Period.* Edited by S. T. Katz. Cambridge: Cambridge University Press, 2006.

Lorsch, R. S. "*Omina imperii*: The Omens of Power Received by the Roman Emperors from Augustus to Domitian, their Religious Interpretation and Political Influence." Ph.D. Dissertation, The University of North Carolina at Chapel Hill, 1993.

Moehring, H. "The *Acta Pro Judaeis* in the *Antiquities* of Flavius Josephus: A Study in Hellenistic and Modern Apologetic Historiography." Pp. 124–58 in *Christianity, Judaism and Other Greco-Roman Cults*. Part III: *Judaism before 70*. Edited by J. Neusner. Leiden: Brill, 1975.

Rajak, T. "Was There a Roman Charter for the Jews?" *The Journal of Roman Studies* 74 (1984) 107–23.

Reiling, J. "The use of ψευδοπροφήτης in the Septuagint, Philo and Josephus." *Novum Testamentum* 13 (1971) 147–56.

Rubenstein, J. L. *Talmudic Stories: Narrative Art, Composition, and Culture*. Baltimore: Johns Hopkins University Press, 1999.

————. *Rabbinic Stories*. Classics of Western Spirituality. Mahwah, NJ: Paulist, 2002.

Saldarini, A. J. "Johanan ben Zakkai's Escape from Jerusalem: Origin and Development of a Rabbinic Story." *Journal for the Study of Judaism* 4 (1975) 189–204.

Schäfer, P. "Die Flucht Joḥanan b. Zakkais aus Jerusalem und die Gründung des 'Lehrhauses' in Jabne." *ANRW* 19.2:43–101. Part 2, Principat 19.2. *Religion (Judentum: Palästinisches Judentum*. Berlin: Walter de Gruyter, 1979.

Schalit, A. "Die Erhebung Vespasians nach Josephus, Talmud und Midrasch: Zur Geschichte einer messianischen Prophetie." *ANRW* 2:208–327. Part 2, Principat 2. *Politische Geschichte (Kaisergeschichte)*. Berlin: Walter de Gruyter, 1975.

Wikenhauser, A. "Doppelträume." *Biblica* 29 (1948) 100–111.

Index of Authors

Index of Scripture

New Testament

Apocrypha and Pseudepigrapha